Law, Business, and Society

Tenth Edition

Tony McAdams
University of Northern Iowa

Nancy Neslund
*University of New Hampshire
School of Law*

Kiren Dosanjh Zucker
*California State University,
Northridge*

McGraw-Hill
Irwin

McGraw-Hill
Irwin

McADAMS: LAW, BUSINESS & SOCIETY, TENTH EDITION

Published by McGraw-Hill, a business unit of The McGraw-Hill Companies, Inc., 1221 Avenue of the Americas, New York, NY 10020. Copyright © 2012 by The McGraw-Hill Companies, Inc. All rights reserved. Previous editions © 2009, 2007 and 2004. Printed in the United States of America. No part of this publication may be reproduced or distributed in any form or by any means, or stored in a database or retrieval system, without the prior written consent of The McGraw-Hill Companies, Inc., including, but not limited to, in any network or other electronic storage or transmission, or broadcast for distance learning.

Some ancillaries, including electronic and print components, may not be available to customers outside the United States.

This book is printed on acid-free paper.

1 2 3 4 5 6 7 8 9 0 DOC/DOC 1 0 9 8 7 6 5 4 3 2 1

ISBN   978-0-07-352500-6
MHID   0-07-352500-6

Vice President & Editor-in-Chief: *Brent Gordon*
Vice President & Director of Specialized Publishing: *Janice M. Roerig-Blong*
Publisher: *Paul Ducham*
Sponsoring Editor: *Daryl Bruflodt*
Marketing Manager: *Jennifer J. Lewis*
Senior Project Manager: *Lisa A. Bruflodt*
Design Coordinator: *Margarite Reynolds*
Cover Designer: *Studio Montage, St. Louis, Missouri*
Cover Image: © *BananaStock/PunchStock*
Buyer: *Kara Kudronowicz*
Media Project Manager: *Balaji Sundararaman*
Compositor: *Aptara®, Inc.*
Typeface: *10/12 Times*
Printer: *R.R. Donnelley*

Library of Congress Cataloging-in-Publication Data

McAdams, Tony.
    Law, business, and society / Tony McAdams, Nancy Neslund, Kiren Dosanjh Zucker.—10th ed.
    p. cm.
    Includes index.
    ISBN-13: 978-0-07-352500-6 (alk. paper)
    ISBN-10: 0-07-352500-6
    1. Business enterprises–Law and legislation—United States. 2. Trade regulation—United States.
    3. Business ethics—United States. 4. Industries–Social aspects—United States. I. Neslund,
    Nancy. II. Zucker, Kiren Dosanjh. III. Title.
    KF1355.M28 2012
    346.73'065—dc23

About the Authors

Tony McAdams

Tony McAdams is a Professor of Management at the University of Northern Iowa. He earned a BA in History from the University of Northern Iowa, a JD from the University of Iowa, and an MBA from Columbia University. Professor McAdams's primary teaching interests include government regulation of business, business and society, and employment law. Professor McAdams's research interests include managerial accountability, business ethics, and employment law. His scholarly articles have appeared in such journals as *The Harvard Business Review*, *The Academy of Management Review*, *The Journal of Business Ethics*, and *The American Business Law Journal*. Professor McAdams has received the Iowa Board of Regents Award for Faculty Excellence, the Distinguished Teacher of the Year Award from the student government at the University of Kentucky, and the University of Northern Iowa College of Business Administration Excellence in Teaching Award.

Nancy Neslund

During the preparation of this edition, Nancy Neslund, author of Chapters 9, 16, 17, and 18, was a visiting professor at the University of New Hampshire School of Law in Concord, New Hampshire. She earned a BA in Economics from Willamette University, a JD from Columbia University, and an LLM from New York University. Prior to entering academia, she was a lawyer in private practice for 14 years. During the academic year 2004 to 2005, she was a visiting professor on the law faculty of Europa Universität Viadrina, in Germany on its border with Poland. She teaches business organizations, business law, and tax law. Her research interests include the World Trade Organization, international and domestic taxation of e-commerce, and international professional regulation.

Kiren Dosanjh Zucker

Kiren Dosanjh Zucker, author of Chapters 12, 13, and 14, is a Professor of Business Law and Management at California State University, Northridge (CSUN) where she also serves as Faculty Development Director. She earned a BA in Political Science from Syracuse University and a JD from the University of Michigan. A member of the State Bar of California, she has served on its Committee of Bar Examiners and Committee on Professional Responsibility and Conduct. Her teaching and research interests focus primarily on employment law. In 2001, she was selected as a Master Teacher by the Academy of Legal Studies in Business, and in 2004 she received the Outstanding Faculty Award from CSUN's Students with Disabilities Resources. In 2004 and 2006, she also received a CSUN University Ambassadors' Polished Apple Award.

Preface

Broadly, our adjustments for this tenth edition were designed to refresh the book and achieve increased reader interest, but more specifically this edition is directed to the nation's ongoing debate about how much government we need in our lives; particularly in our business lives. While the general structure and philosophy of the book are unchanged, we have made significant revisions.

Chapter 1, a survey of the economic continuum from capitalism to collectivism and their various mutations, has been thoroughly rewritten and updated to reflect the striking economic developments of recent years in the United States and around the world.

Several chapters, particularly Chapter 1 as well as those addressing government regulation (Chapter 8) and securities regulation (Chapter 9), give detailed attention to the subprime mortgage crisis, the Dodd-Frank bill, TARP, the new Consumer Financial Protection Bureau, and the broad issue of balancing market power and government intervention.

- Every chapter has been updated to approximately midsummer 2011.
- Material added to this edition includes, in total, 20 edited law cases along with approximately 18 new discussion items per chapter in the form of "boxes," ethics exercises, vignettes, and case/public policy questions.
- Each chapter was carefully edited and rewritten to improve reading ease.
- Learning objectives for each chapter were revised as needed.

OVERVIEW

This text is directed to courses at both the upper-division undergraduate and masters levels in the legal environment of business, government and business, and business and society. Authors of textbooks in these areas often rely on a single discipline (for example, law, economics, or management) as the foundation for their efforts. In this text we take an interdisciplinary approach, using elements of law, political economy, international business, ethics, social responsibility, and management. This large task necessarily requires certain trade-offs, but we hope the product will more accurately capture the fullness of the business environment.

Our primary goal is to produce an interesting, provocative reading experience. Naturally, accuracy and reasonable comprehensiveness cannot be sacrificed. Our feeling, however, is that a law text can be both intellectually and emotionally engaging without sacrificing substantive ends. To meet our objective we have presented the bulk of the book in the form of contemporary legal and ethical conflicts emerging from today's news. We have provided scholarly results, surveys, polls, data, anecdotes, and other specific details that lend credibility, immediacy, and interest to the reading experience.

The book is divided into five units, as follows:

Unit I—Business and Society. We do not begin with the law. Rather, in Chapter 1 (Capitalism and the Role of Government), Chapter 2 (Business Ethics), and Chapter 3 (The Corporation and Public Policy: Expanding Responsibilities), we describe some of the economic and social forces that shape our legal system.

The goals of Unit I are to (a) enhance student awareness of the many societal influences on business, (b) establish the business context from which government regulation arose, and (c) explore the roles of the free market, government intervention, and individual and corporate ethics in shaping business behavior.

The student must understand not merely the law but the law in context. What forces have provoked government intervention in business? What alternatives to our current "mixed economy" might prove healthy? These considerations help the students respond to one of the critical questions of the day: To what extent, if any, should we regulate business?

Unit II—Introduction to Law. Chapter 4 (The American Legal System) and Chapter 5 (Constitutional Law and the Bill of Rights) survey the foundations of our legal system. Here we set out the "nuts and bolts" of law, combining cases and narrative. Then with Chapter 6 (Contracts) and Chapter 7 (Business Torts and Product Liability), we examine the foundations of business law.

Unit III—Trade Regulation and Antitrust. Chapter 8 (Government Regulation of Business) raises the book's central policy inquiry: When should the government intervene in business practice? Chapter 9 (Business Organizations and Securities Regulation), Chapter 10 (Antitrust Law—Restraints of Trade), and Chapter 11 (Antitrust Law— Monopolies and Mergers) survey the core of government oversight of business.

Unit IV—Employer–Employee Relations. Chapter 12 (Employment Law I: Employee Rights), Chapter 13 (Employment Law II: Discrimination), and Chapter 14 (Employment Law III: Labor–Management Relations) are intended not only to survey the law in those areas, but also to introduce some of the sensitive and provocative social issues that have led to today's extensive government intervention in the employment relationship.

Unit V—Selected Topics in Government–Business Relations. Two of the closing chapters of this book—Chapter 15 (Consumer Protection) and Chapter 17 (Environmental Protection)—emphasize the dramatic expansion of the public's demands for socially responsible conduct in business. Chapter 16 (International Ethics and Law) provides an overview of the legal and ethical issues emerging from global business practice, and Chapter 18 (Internet Law and Ethics) surveys some cyberlaw and ethics problems.

ACCREDITATION

Our text conforms to Association to Advance Collegiate Schools of Business (AACSB) International accreditation standards.

Two chapters are devoted exclusively to ethics, and ethics themes emerge throughout the book. The chapter on employment discrimination should be quite helpful in aiding students' understanding of diversity issues.

Furthermore, as required by the rapidly changing nature of commerce and as recommended by the AACSB, the text devotes extensive attention to legal and ethical issues arising from international business. Various topics throughout the text (for example, comparative economic systems, the Foreign Corrupt Practices Act, and global pollution) afford the student a sense of the worldwide implications of American business practice, and Chapter 16 is entirely devoted to international themes.

PHILOSOPHY

As noted, our primary goal is to provoke student thought. To that end, we place heavy emphasis on analysis. We consider the questions we ask more important than the answers to those questions. We introduce the student to existing policy in the various substantive areas, to encourage understanding and retention, as well as careful thought about the desirability of those policies.

Our book takes a strong public policy orientation. Attention in Unit I to political economy and ethics is a necessary foundation on which the student can build a logical understanding of the regulatory process. Thereafter, those business and society themes persist throughout the book. In virtually every chapter, we look beyond the law itself to other social and environmental forces. For example, in the antitrust chapters economic philosophy is of great importance. Antitrust is explored as a matter of national social policy. We argue that antitrust has a good deal to do with the direction of American life generally. Law is at the heart of the fair employment practices section, but we also present material from management, sociology, history, and popular culture to treat fair employment as an issue of public policy rather than as a series of narrower technical legal disputes. These multidimensional approaches characterize most chapters as we attempt to examine the various topics as a whole and in context. At the same time, the law remains the core of the book.

KEY FEATURES/DEPARTURES

Approximately 150 "boxes" and ethics vignettes place the law in a practical context and offer many provocative opportunities for discussion.

Ethics and social responsibility are at the heart of the text rather than an afterthought to meet accreditation standards.

International issues receive extensive attention.

Law cases are long enough to clearly express the essence of the decision while challenging the reader's intellect.

The law is studied in the economic, social, and political context from which it springs.

Critics of business values and the American legal system receive attention.

Approximately 200 selected Web sites, including over two dozen suggested online videos, appear in this edition, and each chapter includes at least one Internet Exercise.

Perhaps the key pedagogical tactic in the book is the emphasis on questions rather than on answers.

INSTRUCTOR'S MANUAL

A package of supplementary materials is included in the instructor's manual. Those materials include (1) chapter outlines, (2) general advice regarding the goals and purposes of the chapters, (3) summaries of the law cases, (4) answers for the questions raised in the text, and (5) a test bank.

TEST BANK

Instructors can test students using a vast bank of test questions divided by chapter. The test bank is found online at **www.mhhe.com/mcadams10e,** in Word format.

POWERPOINTS

This edition's revised PowerPoints contain an easy-to-follow lecture outline summarizing key points for every chapter.

ONLINE LEARNING CENTER

This site, located at **www.mhhhe.com/mcadams10e,** enriches the PowerPoint slides. In addition to offering instructors a downloadable version of the Instructor's Manual and Test Bank, it also contains additional cases, readings, and student quizzes for the benefit of both instructors and students.

ACKNOWLEDGMENTS

Completion of the tenth edition of this book depended, in significant part, on the hard work of others.

The authors are pleased to acknowledge the contributions of these good people: Paul Ducham, publisher; Daryl Bruflodt, sponsoring editor; and Lisa A. Bruflodt, lead project manager.

The authors also thank the reviewers from past editions, and the following professors who reviewed portions of the text and otherwise provided valuable guidance for this edition:

Immouna Ephrem, Sierra Community College; Elizabeth Grimm-Howell, University of Missouri—St. Louis; Dr. G. Howard Doty, Nashville State Community College; Adam Sulkowski, Charlton College of Business, UMass Dartmouth; David L. Torres, University of Arizona South; Cynthia Kramer, William Woods University.

SUGGESTIONS

The authors welcome comments and criticism from all readers.

Tony McAdams

Brief Contents

ix

Contents

Chapter 7
Business Torts and Product
Liability   282

UNIT THREE
TRADE REGULATION AND ANTITRUST 331

Chapter 8
Government Regulation of Business 332

Chapter 10
Antitrust Law—Restraints of Trade   437

Chapter 11
Antitrust Law—Monopolies and Mergers   470

Chapter 13
Employment Law II: Discrimination   555

Chapter 16
International Ethics and Law   685

Links to Brief Videos for Classroom Use

The following video links appear in the body of the text in conjunction with the subject matter of the videos.

Chapter 1

Trailer *Atlas Shrugged* documentary movie [**http://www.youtube.com/watch?v=Tv29SXnd2dk&feature=related**].

Trailer *Inside Job* documentary movie. Oscar winner 2011 [**http://www.youtube.com/watch?v=FzrBurlJUNk**].

Chapter 2

2009 Harvard MBA Ethics Oath, *The Daily Show with John Stewart* [**http://www.thedailyshow.com/watch/wed-august-12-2009/mba-ethics-oath**].

Chapter 3

Vermont Senator Bernie Sanders, "A scandal" (a Senate speech criticizing corporate tax loopholes) [**http://www.youtube.com/watch?v=Sknt-UBRhxo**].

Trailer *Wal-Mart: The High Cost of Low Price* documentary movie [**http://www.walmartmovie.com**].

Chapter 4

"Video: Top Court Blocks Wal-Mart Sex-Bias Suit," *Today* show, 6/21/11 [**http://www.msnbc.msn.com/id/43468398/ns/business-personal_finance/t/wal-mart-ruling-raises-bar-class-actions/**].

"What Is Mediation?" (a brief overview of mediation and arbitration) [**http://www.youtube.com/watch?v=KLdia39awl0**]. (The final two characters in this URL are a lower case l, as in law, and a zero.)

Chapter 5

"1967 ABC News Report on Loving Case" (application of due process and equal protection principles to Virginia anti-miscegenation statute) [**http://abcnews.go.com/video/playerIndex?id=3278653**](upper case I in Index).

Chapter 6

Fox News April 13, 2011 account of Paul Ceglia's contracts-based claim for partial ownership of Facebook [**www.youtube.com/watch?v=CQ9vDJWAeQQ**].

April 28, 2011 humorous, animated overview of the Paul Ceglia—Mark Zuckerberg contracts dispute [**www.wellsvilledaily.com/features/x328920403/VIDEO-Animation-of-Ceglias-Facebook-lawsuit-against-Zuckerberg**].

A video of the Pepsi ad that was the basis of the *Leonard v. Pepsico* lawsuit [**http://www.youtube.com/watch?v=ZdackF2H7Qc**].

Chapter 7

Susan Saladoff, "Hot Coffee" documentary movie trailer [**http://hotcoffeethemovie.com/**].

InjuryBoard, "Mr. Fancy Pants" (a video defense of the tort system) [**http://www.youtube.com/watch?v=h85j1vNxd8A**].

Chapter 8

Cato Institute, "There Are Too Many Bureaucrats and They Are Paid Too Much" [**http://www.youtube.com/watch?v=5xzd3puYmiM**].

Chapter 9

ChinaForbiddenNews, NTDTV.COM, "Insider Trading 'Rats'" [**http://www.youtube.com/watch?v=IT3FArOeIEo**] (capital I as in Iowa, T3FAr, zero, e, capital I as in Iowa, Eo).

"Billionaire Convicted of Insider Trading," *Boston.com,* May 11, 2011 (Raj Rajaratnam) [**http://www.clicker.com/web/bostoncom-featured-necn-video/billionaire-convicted-of-insider-trading-1768946/**].

Chapter 10

The Informant! movie trailer [**http://www.traileraddict.com/trailer/the-informant/trailer**].

Chapter 11

Stephen Colbert, "Mega-Mergers," 2007 [**http://www.businessinsider.com/stephen-colbert-att-2011-3**].

Chapter 12

Inland Valley Daily Bulletin and The San Bernardino Sun, "A Special Report on Immigration" ("Smuggler's Gulch") 2005 [**http://lang.dailybulletin.com/socal/beyondborders/video/121805_smugglers_gulch_video.asp**].

Chapter 13

American Civil Liberties Union, "New Video Shows the Need for a Transgender-Inclusive ENDA"

[**http://www.aclu.org/lgbt-rights_hiv-aids/new-aclu-video-shows-need-transgender-inclusive-enda**]. A federal district judge ruled that the Library of Congress had discriminated against Schroer and awarded her $500,000. See *Schroer v. Billington,* 577 F. Supp. 2d 293 (U.S. Dist. Ct. Dist. of Col. 2008).

Chapter 14

Fox News discussion of NLRB—Boeing Conflict [**http://www.youtube.com/watch?v= j_JvA6yKB_M**].

Chapter 15

A Consumer Financial Protection Bureau video explaining the Bureau's mission [**http://www.consumerfinance.gov/the-bureau/**].

2011 ABC News Visit to Consumer Product Safety Commission Testing Lab [**http:// abcnews.go.com/GMA/video/consumer-product-safety-commission-test-lab-13827984**].

Chapter 16

2004 John Stossel "20/20" overview of sweatshop protests followed by Stossel's defense of low-wage jobs [**http://www.youtube.com/watch?v=0VaHmgoB10E**]. (Both large 0 symbols are zeros.)

Chapter 17

2011 Bill McKibben/Stephen Thompson video editorial about the alleged causal relationship between climate change and recent "extreme weather events" in America and around the world [**http://www.grist.org/climate-change/2011-06-11-the-most-powerful-climate-video-youll-see-all-week**].

Chapter 18

Video Essay: "What Is the 'Digital Divide?'" [**http://www.youtube.com/watch?v= fCIB_vXUptY**]. (In CIB, the middle letter is a capital I, as in Iowa.)

Business and Society

CHAPTER ONE

Capitalism and the Role of Government

At the end of this chapter, students will be able to:

1. Describe capitalism and its relationship to individual rights.

2. Compare and contrast capitalism and collectivism.

3. Differentiate between communism and socialism as collectivist philosophies.

4. Evaluate arguments regarding government's proper role in the global, technology-based economy.

5. Describe the primary characteristics of a "mixed economy."

6. Analyze the impact of capitalism on equality, fairness, and community in American and global society.

7. Discuss the theory and practice of privatization.

8. Discuss the current state of capitalism in China and Russia.

9. Describe the income gap in America.

Part One—Introduction

Are you a capitalist?

Are you a capitalist? If so, what role, if any, should the law play in your business life? How much government does America need? These themes, examining the relationship between government and business in America, are the core of this text. Since the fall of the Soviet Union and the general decline of communist influence, free market reasoning has dominated worldwide economic discourse. Indeed, noted theorist Francis Fukuyama argued that capitalism and Western democracy had so thoroughly proved their worth that the capitalism/collectivism debate was over.[1] Democracy and markets, Fukuyama claimed, were so clearly triumphant that no new forms of civilization are likely to emerge. Thus, he said, we are at the end of history. Events, however, have challenged Fukuyama's bold thesis. The stunning financial plunge of recent years and the turmoil of globalization have raised new questions about capitalism; or at least about America's version of capitalism.

Capitalism Challenged: The Great Recession

In late 2008 America's financial markets seemed near collapse. Lending had essentially frozen. Normal business could not be conducted. A great name in banking, Lehman Brothers, went bankrupt while Wall Street powers Bear Stearns and Merrill Lynch, facing failure, were sold. The remaining banks were burdened with enormous debts and were desperately short of cash. The American and global financial markets were panicked and the market appeared unable to correct its failure. As a result, President George W. Bush (and thereafter, President Obama), Congress, and the Federal Reserve Board stepped in. Fearing a Great Depression as in the 1930s, the government essentially flooded the American economy with cash, took on much of the debt held by endangered banks, and bailed out some of the failing giants with huge loans. One estimate is that the total Federal Reserve aid package, at its peak, reached $3.3 trillion.[2] Through its Troubled Asset Relief Program (TARP) and other initiatives, the government assisted companies considered "too big to fail." Those beneficiaries included, for example, the insurance giant, AIG, Wall Street power, Goldman Sachs, General Motors, and Chrysler along with surprising names such as Harley Davidson and even some giant, privately-owned foreign banks.[3] In rescuing some of those American companies, the government took ownership stakes, most of which have since been bought back from the companies; sometimes at a profit for the government. At this writing, the government believes that most of the money lent through the TARP program (more than $400 billion) has been or will be recovered. The TARP program was particularly controversial because, for a time, the federal government, as primary lender, was dictating policy for those key private sector businesses. That bold extension of federal power amounted, some thought, to a temporary "nationalization" of those businesses—a disquieting direction in a free market economy, but the aggressive intervention may have averted a depression.[4]

> The aggressive intervention may have averted a depression.

Subprime Mortgages

The financial community's near collapse had been most directly ignited by the subprime mortgage crisis; a situation in which the nation's housing bubble burst and millions of Americans were no longer able to pay their home mortgages. Instead of continuing their sometimes meteoric rise in value, those homes had plunged in price and much of the total real estate market had essentially imploded. The resulting mountain of bad debt could not be managed by the American financial institutions that were holding it, fear paralyzed the lending markets, and the government felt obliged to step in to prevent a greater financial tragedy. While greed and inept management were instrumental in the subprime debacle, the role of financial fraud remains unclear. Certainly some big penalties have been imposed: AIG agreed to pay nearly $1 billion to several Ohio pension funds to settle fraud claims,[5] and Countrywide Financial Corporation has paid $600 million to settle shareholder fraud claims stemming from the subprime crisis.[6] Likewise many inquiries are ongoing including, for example, 50 criminal and civil investigations by the Federal Deposit Insurance Corp. of banks that failed in recent years.[7]

[For a critical examination of the 2008 financial meltdown, see the trailer for the 2011 Oscar-winning best documentary, Inside Job, at **http://www.youtube.com/ watch?v=FzrBurlJUNk**]

Stimulus

In addition to bailing out the Wall Street financial community and some industrial firms, the government undertook various stimulative measures including tax breaks, bond sales, and direct injections of federal money to prop up the badly faltering economy. In a centerpiece of the stimulus effort, about $800 billion was spent on such projects as road construction, extension of unemployment benefits, help to states in meeting Medicaid costs, and high-speed rail transportation. National unemployment was in the 10 percent range, and the government decided to use all of its powers to quickly build jobs and otherwise rescue the economy to avert a total crash. As *The Wall Street Journal* reported in 2008:

> Gone is the faith . . . that the best road to prosperity is to unleash the financial markets. . . . Erased is the hope that markets correct themselves. . . . Also scrapped is the notion that government's role is to get out of the way . . . limiting itself to protecting consumers and small investors, setting the rules of the game and stepping in—only rarely—to cushion the economy from shocks. . . .[8]

These immense government interventions and the trillions required to finance them were a dramatic, but arguably necessary, departure from traditional American, capitalist practice. One of the immediate results was that the midterm federal election of 2010 brought a resounding victory for the Republican Party and the Tea Party activists who promised to dramatically shrink the size of the federal government. Meanwhile the economy slowly strengthened but big hazards, including housing, remained. Perhaps the biggest lingering threat was a U.S. budget deficit that was expected to exceed $1.6 trillion for fiscal year 2011, the biggest in the nation's history and the largest as a share of the economy since World War II.[9] (For a detailed accounting of how the government intended to spend nearly $800 billion in one of the stimulus plans, see Farhana Hossain, Amanda Cox, John McGrath, and Stephan Weitberg, "The Stimulus Plan: How to Spend $787 Billion," *The New York Times*. [**http://projects.nytimes.com/44th_president/ stimulus?ref=economicstimulus?ref=economicstimulus**].)

"Stop Picking on Bankers"

Jamie Dimon, CEO of banking giant JP Morgan Chase, in 2011, said he thinks "this constant refrain—bankers, bankers, bankers"[10] is unfair. Dimon was lamenting the world's anger toward bankers who are a chief villain when blame is assigned for the world's financial troubles. Independent U.S. Senator Bernie Sanders of Vermont, on the other hand, leads the critics. He thinks the big banks got off very easily from the damage they did or were a party too. They received, he pointed out, extraordinary government aid but they were not required to lend to small businesses, modify home mortgages, or engage in investments specifically designed to build jobs. As Sanders said: "We bailed these guys out, but the requirements placed upon them had very little positive impact on the needs of ordinary Americans,"[11]

Beyond the price tag for the huge bailouts to save these banks that were considered too big to fail, much of the continuing anger toward the banks is a result of what critics consider insensitive and arrogant pay practices following the bailouts. Nine of the banks receiving government bailouts paid employees nearly $33 billion in bonuses for 2008, the very year of the financial collapse. Those bonuses often were justified as being necessary to retain star talent. Total 2010 Wall Street compensation for 25 large firms reached a record $135 billion, part of which was attributable to new hiring. Of course, the entire investment economy showed very significant growth, but critics argue the outsized pay reflects an unhealthy, even greedy, distribution of resources. The big industrial nations agreed in 2009 to curb pay practices that might encourage risky banking, but the United States has been criticized by European leaders for failing to aggressively act on the agreement.

Economist Paul Krugman says the American economy has become "financialized" with the slicing and dicing of financial packages being rewarded much more generously than the actual production of useful products; a condition that might be desirable if it resulted in more efficient use of capital but the financial mess suggests that has not been the case, he says.

Questions

1. Journalist/lecturer Richard Doak lamenting what he believes to be unfair and excessive pay to executives: "Executive greed has perverted risks, rewards. . . . The American system has been rigged to over-enrich those at the top."[12] What do you think? Is greed the culprit? Has the system been "rigged," or can we continue to count on the market to properly distribute pay? Explain.

2. Should the government limit private sector executive pay? Explain.

3. Federal Reserve Bank of Kansas City president, Thomas M. Hoenig: "[Americans] realize that more must be done to address a threat that remains increasingly a part of our economy: financial institutions that are 'too big to fail.'"[13] Do you agree that our concentrated financial sector is a threat that must be addressed? Explain.

Sources: Paul Krugman, "The Joy of Sachs," *The New York Times*, July 17, 2009 [**http://www.nytimes.com/**]; Aaron Lucchetti and Stephen Grocer, "On Street, Pay Vaults to Record Altitude," *The Wall Street Journal*, February 2, 2011 [**http://online.wsj.com/**]; and "Report Reveals that Even after Financial Free-Fall, U.S. Banks Paid Billions in Bonuses," *Ethics Newsline*, August 3, 2009 [**http://www.globalethics.org/newsline/**].

Capitalism Challenged: Globalization

Globalization represents the international flowering of capitalism in the sense that the power of free markets is being embraced, enthusiastically or reluctantly, almost everywhere on Earth. That power, however, raises new threats as it introduces an unpredictable, unstable new world economic and political order where America's role, thoroughly dominant for more than half a century, is now less clear. Journalist Fareed Zakaria's 2008 book, *The Post-American World,* demonstrates how globalization has reshaped the world with the result, in his view, that the days of American economic dominance are over.[14] He reminds us of the facts: Only two of the world's ten richest people are American. The world's tallest building is in Dubai. The biggest movie industry is

> In Fareed Zakaria's view, the days of American economic dominance are over.

Bollywood, not Hollywood. The biggest factories are in China. America no longer resides serenely at the top of the economic pyramid, but he doesn't envision American decline so much as the ascent of other nations; most prominently of course, China and India. Jonathan Rosenberg summarized Zakaria's explanation for these striking economic shifts:

> Zakaria writes that the global economic explosion is a consequence of political change (the fall of the Soviet state [and its] discredited central planning); the free movement of capital around the world (the daily flow of trillions of dollars lubricates the global economy); and the communication revolution (the Internet and cell phones have transformed business by driving down costs and increasing efficiency).[15]

The global export of capitalist practices has led to "the rise of the rest," Zakaria says, such that the United States is challenged as never before. Still, Zakaria reminds us that America continues to be the world's most competitive economy. We remain dominant in most high tech fields, and we retain perhaps our greatest strength, freedom for all:

> [America] remains the most open, flexible society in the world, able to absorb other people, cultures, ideas, goods, and services. The country thrives on the hunger and energy of poor immigrants. Faced with the new technologies of foreign companies, or growing markets overseas, it adapts and adjusts. When you compare this dynamism with the closed and hierarchical nations that were once superpowers, you sense the United States is different and may not fall into the trap of becoming rich, and fat, and lazy.[16]

For Zakaria, globalization and the resulting "rise of the rest" is one of the great stories in history:

> Billions of people are escaping from abject poverty. The world will be enriched and ennobled as they become consumers, producers, inventors, thinkers, dreamers, and doers. This is all happening because of American ideas and actions.[17]

Thomas Friedman of *The New York Times* illustrated the power of globalization with a report that a Nepali telecommunications firm in late 2010, had begun to provide 3G mobile network service at the summit of Mount Everest, the world's tallest mountain. Friedman explained the change sweeping the world:

> This is just one small node in what is the single most important trend unfolding in the world today: globalization—the distribution of cheap tools of communication and innovation that are wiring together the world's citizens, governments, businesses, terrorists and now mountaintops—is going to a whole new level. In India alone, some 15 million new cell phone users are being added each month.[18]

Globlization Criticized

Clearly, the "rise of the rest" is a great economic blessing for much of the world, but critics see onrushing globalization as a risk in other ways. For some, the near collapse of the interdependent Western financial markets and the continuing ups and downs of international commerce have renewed questions about the effectiveness and wisdom of a global free market. Global polling in 2009 revealed widespread frustration with capitalism. An average of only 11 percent of respondents in 27 countries felt that capitalism works well, but only 23 percent felt capitalism is fatally flawed. The most common view, held by 51 percent of respondents, was that capitalism's problems can be addressed by regulation and reform, but 67 percent support government distributing wealth more evenly.[19]

To some, globalization threatens our commitment to social and ethical agendas, including reduction of child labor and poverty, environmental protection and equality for women.[20] Others fear the steamroller effect of Western culture as it sweeps the globe and challenges ancient values. The cultural distinctions that strengthen diversity of thought and fertilize global discourse are being eroded, the critics say, by the dominant, largely American voice, of popular culture. Cultural imperialism and cultural homogenization may reduce the globe to the intellectual depths of America's "Jersey Shore." *The Omaha World-Herald* explained the concern:

> Baywatch is said (let us hope facetiously) to be the most popular television show on the planet. The McD-ing of the world, the homogenization of fast-food tastes, means that the people of Tokyo and Buenos Aires, Seoul and Bahrain, Canberra and Reykjavik all have the opportunity to chow down on some version of the quintessentially American burger, fries, and a shake.[21]

These cultural concerns may be particularly troubling to the Islamic community that may want to embrace elements of liberal, Western practice while preserving its Muslim identity and religious principles. Based on six years of polling, focus groups and study in Muslim countries, public opinion analyst Steven Kull says anger toward America is common:

> Majorities in most Muslim countries continue to have a negative view of the United States and to perceive the United States as seeking to dominate the Muslim world, to undermine Islam and to impose Western culture.[22]

Nonetheless, a very large 2010 poll provides reason for optimism in that an average of 59 percent of respondents across 49 nations, both Western and Muslim-majority, feel that greater interaction between the two cultures would be beneficial rather than threatening.[23] Similarly, a 2008 poll of six nations with predominantly Muslim populations found generally favorable attitudes toward globalization.[24]

Globalization Encourages a New "Democracy"?

Globalization is a threat to some, but on balance it seems to be accepted in its inevitability and welcomed as a force for bringing economic opportunity to long-suffering peoples. The world's middle class is expected to at least double by 2030. Furthermore, globalization provides the resources to allow all people to establish their own political, cultural and consumer identities. In a sense, globalization brings a new democracy to the globe. Even as we witness increasingly shared commercial values, we also witness increasing division expressed via nationalism and tribalism. At this writing, the democratizing power of globalization is evident in the inspiring struggle for freedom in the Middle East and North Africa. Long-entrenched state control in Egypt, Libya, Yemen, and other countries is being challenged in the streets. Billions of people are now linked by ideas instantly transmitted via the Internet, Facebook, and Twitter, allowing them to more clearly understand the injustices they endure and the attractive possibilities a new life could bring.

> Increasing division expressed via nationalism and tribalism.

Globalization and Kissing in Public

A female student at highly regarded Lahore University of Management Science (LUMS) in Pakistan kissed her boyfriend on the cheek during the Islamic holy month of Ramadan in 2009 and caused a religious/cultural debate. The kiss was witnessed by a fellow student who sent an email to the entire campus documenting that episode and other campus public displays of affection (PDAs). One senior at LUMS then warned campus freshmen about the tempting messages they would receive during their college years:

> At LUMS, you will be bombarded with all sorts of atheistic and secular philosophies and "isms." If you do not have the proper knowledge and conviction about Islam, you may fall prey to the untiring efforts of certain faculty members as well as your fellow students to misguide."

LUMS administrators thereafter promised to institute a code of conduct banning PDAs.

Source: Issam Ahmed, "Top Pakistan University to Ban Kissing," *The Christian Science Monitor*, October 14, 2009. [**http://www.csmonitor.com/2009/1014/p06s05-wosc.html**].

The Decline of America and American Capitalism?

A 2010 nationwide poll found 65 percent of respondents agreeing that America is in decline.[25] Only half of Americans, according to another 2010 poll, continue to believe in the American Dream (Defined as: "If you work hard, you'll get ahead.")[26] Michael Moore's 2009 documentary movie, *Capitalism: A Love Story*, assails capitalism as fundamentally "evil."[27] Moore was questioned about his movie:

> *Wall Street Journal:* Why call the movie "Capitalism: A Love Story?" You don't seem to love very much about capitalism. Mr. Moore: It is a love story about the well-to-do. They happen to love their money very much. Now they love our money and they want all our money and our homes. It's about their love.[28]

Doubts about capitalism reflect the difficult economic times and the rise of China as a challenge to American dominance, but some critics also point to fundamental flaws in capitalism and in the American character. Political scientist Benjamin Barber condemns the radical consumerism of contemporary capitalism; a system, he believes, that reduces our lives to finding satisfaction in brand names and nonstop shopping.[29] Capitalism drags us into decadence, he claims, by encouraging us to buy as many unnecessary products as we can manage thus replacing historical principles of hard work and deferred gratification with infantile hungers for anything that might promise comfort. In America's version of capitalism, as Barber sees it, we find liberty in commerce. We can buy whatever we want; therefore, we are free. But that undemanding vision of liberty means we have no sense of obligation for social and political ideals greater than self-satisfaction.[30] Asking no

> Capitalism drags us into decadence.

more of us than unbridled consumption may undermine democracy itself, as columnist Rod Dreher argues:

> Democracy requires virtue. So does a healthy capitalism. A nation that cannot govern its own appetites will, in time, be unable to govern itself. An economy that divorces economic activity from the restraining virtues that make for good stewardship will implode.[31]

Good News

While America and American capitalism have endured a great shock, shouldn't we find encouragement in the nation's enormous resources? Political scientist Steve Yetiv reminds us that America retains the greatest potential for "cutting-edge" economic growth, that we remain dominant in military and international affairs, that we have the world's best workforce and that our ideals are "slowly but surely" being embraced around the world.[32] Commentator David Brooks says that America is merely in one of its periodic economic pauses, but he is sure that "The gospel of success will recapture the imagination."[33] Brooks summarized our fundamentally commercial nature:

> ... Americans work longer hours than any other people. We switch jobs more frequently, move more often, earn more and consume more.

*   *   *   *   *

> Walt Whitman got America right in his essay, "Democratic Vistas." He acknowledged the vulgarity of the American success drive. He toted up its moral failings. But in the end he accepted his country's "extreme business energy," its "almost maniacal appetite for wealth." He knew that the country's dreams were all built upon that energy and drive, and eventually the spirit of commercial optimism would always prevail.[34]

A "Re-Mix" Needed?

Clearly, we have had at least a free market detour in the United States. Government has stepped in to bail out a failing economy. Does that shift to the left signal the decline of markets? Almost certainly not. According to a 2010 Gallup Poll, 86 percent of Americans have a positive view of "free enterprise,"[35] but perhaps some form of "re-mix" is needed. Journalist Anatole Kaletsky reminds us that capitalism is adaptive, reinventing itself through crises.[36] Scholar Robert Skidelsky, in reviewing Kaletsky's 2010 book, *Capitalism 4.0: The Birth of a New Economy,*[37] summarized Kaletsky's view of the evolution of capitalism:

> Laissez-faire Capitalism 1.0, inspired by Adam Smith, lasted from the Napoleonic wars to the First World War, the Russian Revolution and the mass unemployment of the 1930s. Then came the Capitalism 2.0 of John Maynard Keynes, Franklin D. Roosevelt's New Deal and the welfare state, which eventually provoked Capitalism 3.0 in the 1970s in reaction to rising inflation. Capitalism 3.0, a modified return to laissez-faire, has just self-destructed, leaving the door open to Capitalism 4.0.[38]

Kaletsky thinks his Capitalism 4.0 should involve smaller, smarter governments, less reliance on theory, and greater recognition of the need for pragmatic change.

A New World Consensus?

Notwithstanding Kaletsky's hopes for a more rational market/government balance, other thinkers say the world is already re-shaping itself in two conflicting forms of capitalism.

In his book, *The End of the Free Market*,[39] political scientist Ian Bremmer says that capitalism may have established its claim as the best economic system, but the world is still in conflict over whether Western capitalism is the best political-social-economic system. As *New York Times* columnist David Brooks explained in reviewing Bremmer's work, the world now seems to be divided into a pair of general camps. *Democratic capitalism* in the United States, Japan, Denmark, and other nations favors business to create wealth and government to regulate as needed. *State capitalism* in countries such as Russia, China, and Saudi Arabia employs the market to build wealth, which, in turn, is controlled and distributed by the state for its political purposes. State capitalism varies in its practices across nations, but private enterprise, state-owned corporations, and sovereign wealth funds (huge aggregations of capital controlled by the government for investment purposes) all may play a role. The two systems trade with each other for mutual advantage, but are economic and political rivals.[40]

We do not know what comes next, of course, but Oxford professor Timothy Garton Ash sees the likelihood, in the short term at least, of a fractured, somewhat conflicted world:

> The result? Not a uni-polar world, converging on a single model of liberal democratic capitalism, but a no-polar world, diverging toward many different national versions of often illiberal capitalism. Not a new world order but a new world disorder. . . .[41]

Questions

1. As you see it, is western democratic capitalism or state capitalism more likely to prevail over the long term? Explain.

2. Roger Cohen, writing in *The New York Times,* makes the interesting point that India, as of 2010, had more cell phones than toilets; 563.7 million people connected to modern communication, but only 366 million with access to modern sanitation. He says this imbalance could be seen as "skewed development" favoring private goods over public necessities. In India and in America, he sees a kind of schizophrenia where we are increasingly autonomous, wanting to be left alone; our technology connecting us, allowing us to feel no need for government until a crisis, like the recent meltdown, arrives. Then many desperately plea for the government to save us.[42]

   a. Are we giving too much attention to private needs and too little, via government and taxes, to public goods? Explain.

   b. Can we have an autonomous, free market culture, substantially contemptuous of government, and still maintain a stable, healthy, and fair national and global community? Explain.

3. *a.* Is America deliberately seeking to convert the balance of the globe to American, free market, democratic values?

   b. Would all nations be well served if they adopted American, free market, democratic values? Explain.

4. In what ways might American culture be viewed as offensive and threatening to Muslims and others around the globe?

Our Purpose

Onrushing globalization, the struggle between government intervention and free markets, and the battle between corporations and their critics provide the changing context in which American business operates. Within that context, then, the purpose of this book is to ask two questions:

1. What is the proper role of business in American and global society?
2. How much, if any, government regulation of business is necessary to secure that role?

Markets and Governments   In the United States, we certainly cannot understand our system of laws without a firm appreciation for the principles of capitalism from which those laws spring. We chose a capitalist, democratic approach to life. Other cultures have placed less faith in the market and more in government planning.

In this chapter we will explore the full economic spectrum, moving from a laissez-faire, free market approach on the extreme right to a brief reminder of command economy principles on the far left. The bulk of our attention, however, will rest where the world is at this moment. Most nations are practicing varying combinations of markets and rules that we can label *mixed economies*.

The pure free market approach assumes that we can operate our business structure and our society at large free of all but foundational legal mechanisms such as contract and criminal law. The wisdom of the market—our individual judgments, in combination with our individual consciences—would "regulate" American life. Most forms of government including regulatory agencies, consumer protection, environmental rules, occupational licensure, zoning restrictions, antitrust law, and all but the most basic government services would be eliminated.

As noted, today's debate is no longer about capitalism versus communism but about the mixed economy—that is, about what combination of capitalism and government best serves the world's needs. Substantially open markets have shown themselves to be the stronger vehicle for productivity, efficiency, and personal freedom. But are they also the stronger vehicle for improving living conditions for all citizens, for maximizing democracy, for discouraging crime and corruption, and for building strong communities? In this era of rapid globalization, are America and the world best served by the speed and efficiency of largely unrestrained markets, or do we still need the "civilizing" influence of government rules?

Law   Finally, this chapter should be read as a foundation for the study of law that commences in Chapter 4. Once a society settles on some broad political and economic principles, it employs the law as a primary method of social control. So to understand the law, we need to understand its roots in the economic, political, and social preferences of the world's people.

Questions—Part One

1. The John Templeton Foundation recently asked a number of prominent thinkers the following question: "Does the free market corrode moral character?" Answer that question. [See **www.templeton.org/market**].

2. Iranian President Mahmoud Ahmadinejad in 2009 said a "new era is starting" after the "definite defeat of capitalism."[43] Is capitalism dead (or dying)? Explain.

3. Scholar Robert Skidelsky applauds capitalism for overcoming scarcity, organizing production, and lifting many out of poverty, but he thinks capitalism, at least in rich countries like the United States, has also produced a culture where our main occupation has become the production and consumption of unnecessary goods. He asks whether capitalism can succeed if it continues to produce "more of the same, stimulating jaded appetites with new gadgets, thrills, and excitements? . . . Do we spend the next century wallowing in triviality?"[44] What do you think?

Part Two—Capitalism: Reduce Government?

Capitalism in America was built on the strong philosophical foundation of personal freedom and private property rights. Our great natural resources and personal ambition led to extraordinary prosperity. Monopolistic abuse followed, however, and government grew to curb the power of big business. Thus, America's substantially free market was gradually constrained by government regulation. The proper balance between open markets and government intervention remains perhaps the central public policy debate in American life.

Should we consider a return to a purer form of capitalism; largely free of government oversight? Can we, in large measure, do without government regulation of business? The controversial philosopher and novelist Ayn Rand was an uncompromising advocate of free market principles. She believed the necessary categories of government were only three in number: the police, the armed services, and the law courts. Rand's philosophy of Objectivism contends that the practice of free market principles is necessary for a rational, moral life. Rand's views and the quality of her writing are heavily criticized, but she has been cited as a powerful influence by some of America's leading corporate and political figures. Her books, including *Atlas Shrugged* and *The Fountainhead,* are among the best-selling novels of all time. Indeed, *Atlas Shrugged* is one of the most influential business books in history, and according to a recent survey, has been read by over 8 percent of American adults.[45]

[For the trailer of a 2011 documentary treatment of *Atlas Shrugged,* see **http://www.youtube.com/watch?v=Tv29SXnd2dk&feature=related**]

> Big business leaders are the great heroes of Rand's writing.

Big business leaders, who so often are the villains of contemporary American life, are the great heroes of Rand's writing; in which she championed "the virtue of selfishness" and rejected self-sacrifice. Commentator Stephen Moore explained Rand's core theme in *Atlas Shrugged*:

Politicians invariably respond to crises—that in most cases they themselves created—by spawning new government programs, laws and regulations. These, in turn, generate more havoc and poverty, which inspires the politicians to create more programs . . . and the downward spiral repeats itself until the productive sectors of the economy collapse under the collective weight of taxes and other burdens imposed in the name of fairness, equality and do-goodism.[46]

[See the Center for the Moral Defense of Capitalism at **http://www.moraldefense.com**]
[For a brief look at major league baseball player Orlando Cabrera's devotion to *Atlas Shrugged*
and a journalist's criticism of Rand's admirers, see **http://hardballtalk.nbcsports.com/
2011/06/23/orlando-cabrera-is-john-galt/**]

READING ▶ Man's Rights

Ayn Rand

If one wishes to advocate a free society—that is, capitalism—one must realize that its indispensable foundation is the principle of individual rights. If one wishes to uphold individual rights, one must realize that capitalism is the only system that can uphold and protect them.

* * * * *

Every political system is based on some code of ethics. The dominant ethics of mankind's history were variants of the altruist-collectivist doctrine which subordinated the individual to some higher authority.

* * * * *

Under all such systems, morality was a code applicable to the individual, but not to society. Society was placed *outside* the moral law, and the inculcation of self-sacrificial devotion to social duty was regarded as the main purpose of ethics in man's earthly existence.

Since there is no such entity as "society," since society is only a number of individual men, this meant, in practice, that the rulers of society were exempt from moral law; subject only to traditional rituals, they held total power and exacted blind obedience—on the implicit principle of "The good is that which is good for society . . ."

This was true of all statist systems, under all variants of the altruist-collectivist ethics. . . . As witness: the theocracy of Egypt, with the Pharaoh as an embodied god—the unlimited majority rule or *democracy* of Athens—the welfare state run by the Emperors of Rome—the Inquisition of the late Middle Ages—the absolute monarchy of France—the welfare state of Bismarck's Prussia—the gas chambers of Nazi Germany—the slaughterhouse of the Soviet Union.

All these political systems were expressions of the altruist-collectivist ethics—and their common characteristic is the fact that society stood above the moral law. . . . Thus, politically, all these systems were variants of an *amoral* society.

The most profoundly revolutionary achievement of the United States of America was *the subordination of society to moral law.*

The principle of man's individual rights represented the extension of morality into the social system—as a limitation on the power of the state . . . The United States was the first *moral* society in history.

All previous systems had regarded man as a sacrificial means to the ends of others, and society as an end in itself. The United States regarded man as an end in himself, and society as a means to the peaceful, orderly, *voluntary* coexistence of individuals. All previous systems had held that man's life belongs to society, that society can dispose of him in any way it pleases, and that any freedom he enjoys is his only by favor, by the *permission* of society, which may be revoked at any time. The United States held that man's life is his by *right*, that a right is the property of an individual, that society as such has no rights, and that the only moral purpose of a government is the protection of individual rights.

A "right" is a moral principle defining and sanctioning a man's freedom of action in a social context. There is only *one* fundamental right (all the others are its consequences or corollaries): a man's right to his own life . . .

America's inner contradiction was the altruist-collectivist ethics. Altruism is incompatible with freedom, with capitalism, and with individual rights . . .

It was the concept of individual rights that had given birth to a free society. It was with the destruction of individual rights that the destruction of freedom had to begin.

A collectivist tyranny dare not enslave a country by an outright confiscation of its values, material or moral. It has to be done by a process of internal corruption. . . . The process entails such a growth of newly promulgated "rights" that people do not notice the fact that the meaning of the concept is being reversed . . .

The Democratic Party platform of 1960 summarizes the switch boldly and explicitly. It declares that a democratic administration "will reaffirm the economic bill of rights which Franklin Roosevelt wrote into our national conscience 16 years ago."

Bear clearly in mind the meaning of the concept of *rights* when you read the list which that platform offers:

1. The right to a useful and remunerative job in the industries or shops or farms or mines of the nation.
2. The right to earn enough to provide adequate food and clothing and recreation.
3. The right of every farmer to raise and sell his products at a return which will give him and his family a decent living.
4. The right of every businessman, large and small, to trade in an atmosphere of freedom from unfair competition and domination by monopolies at home and abroad.
5. The right of every family to a decent home.
6. The right to adequate medical care and the opportunity to achieve and enjoy good health.
7. The right to adequate protection from the economic fears of old age, sickness, accidents, and unemployment.
8. The right to a good education.

A single question added to each of the above eight clauses would make the issue clear: *At whose expense?*

Jobs, food, clothing, recreation (!), homes, medical care, education, etc. do not grow in nature. These are man-made values—goods and services produced by men. *Who* is to provide them?

If some men are entitled *by right* to the products of the work of others, it means that those others are deprived of rights and condemned to slave labor.

* * * * *

Observe, in this context, the intellectual precision of the Founding Fathers: they spoke of the right to *the pursuit* of happiness—*not* of the right to happiness. It means that a man has the right to take the actions he deems necessary to achieve his happiness; it does *not* mean that others must make him happy . . .

Property rights and the right of free trade are man's only "economic rights" (they are, in fact, *political* rights)—and there can be no such thing as "an *economic* bill of rights." . . .

And while people are clamoring about "economic rights," the concept of political rights is vanishing . . .

Such is the state of one of today's most crucial issues: *political* rights versus "*economic* rights." It's either-or. One destroys the other. But there are, in fact, no "economic rights," no "collective rights," no "public-interest rights." The term *individual rights* is a redundancy: there is no other kind of rights and no one else to possess them.

Those who advocate laissez-faire capitalism are the only advocates of man's rights.

Source: From *The Virtue of Selfishness* by Ayn Rand. Copyright © 1961, 1964 by Ayn Rand. Copyright, © 1962, 1963, 1964 by the Objectivist Newsletter, Inc. Reprinted by arrangement with New American Library, New York, New York, and with permission of the Estate of Ayn Rand. [For more information about Ayn Rand and objectivism, see **http://www.aynrand.org**]

Questions

1. *a.* As measured by the level of taxation and regulation, protection for property rights, the liberality of trade policy, and the like, would you say the world is increasingly free or increasingly subject to government oversight?
   b. Of all the nations of the world, does the United States enjoy the greatest level of economic freedom? Explain. [See the Index of Economic Freedom at **www.heritage.org**].
2. *a.* Sandy Banks, writing in *The Los Angeles Times:*

   The boys' faces brightened when they got to the front of the line. We're next! They'd been waiting to say it. But their smiles faded when another family was ushered in from the sidelines and slid into "their" Legoland ride. We'd been waylaid by the Premium Play Pass, Legoland's wristband version of the front-of-the-line pass.[47]

   Banks asked her readers what they thought of the fairness of paying to jump to the front of the line. Some said it was not different than flying first class or choosing to drive on a toll road. One thought the kids received a good lesson in the competitiveness of capitalism. Legoland, in Carlsbad, California, said they sell only about 65 of the Premium Play wristbands daily, but those who buy them value the time saved.

What do you think of the fairness of paying to jump to the head of the line at amusement parks?

b. Do you think that drivers who pay more should be entitled to drive in a faster lane? Explain.[48]

c. Addressing his state's budget problems, 2010 candidate for Nevada governor, Eugene DiSimone, proposed allowing people to pay extra to drive up to 90 miles per hour on designated highways.[49] What do you think?

3. Elementary schools often ban tag, dodge ball, touch football, kickball, and other vigorous games from the playgrounds. One school banned touching altogether. Administrators fear physical injuries, reduced self-esteem, and lawsuits. As the *Los Angeles Times* editorialized, "It's hard sometimes to tell whether schools are graduating students or growing orchids."[50] Ayn Rand argued for reduced rules in life, thus relying on the market to address virtually all problems.

a. From Rand's free market point of view, explain why we should reduce playground rules as much as possible, even at the risk of children being hurt.

b. Would you follow the rules approach or Rand's free market approach in managing a playground? Explain.

Free Market Solution to the Baby Shortage?

The following ad appeared in *The Stanford Daily* (Stanford University):

> EGG DONOR WANTED $35,000 (PLUS ALL EXPENSES) Ivy League Professor and High-Tech CEO seek one truly exceptional woman who is attractive, athletic, under the age of 29. GPA 3.5+, SAT: 1400+.

Experts estimate that about 10,000 babies annually are born from "donated" eggs and about $38 million is spent on those eggs. Fees range from a few thousand dollars to $50,000 or more. The fertility industry is lightly regulated by the federal Centers for Disease Control and Prevention. A few states are considering their own rules. Most industrial nations have banned paid "donations."

Questions

1. Harvard Business School professor Debora Spar says, "We are selling children."
   a. Is she correct?
   b. Should we be doing so? Explain.

2. *a.* Does capitalism encourage us to treat people as products?
   b. Are people, in fact, products? Explain.

3. Should we more closely regulate the fertility industry? Explain.

4. Would you favor the increased use of surrogate mothers? Explain. [See Thomas Frank, "Rent-a-Womb Is Where Market Logic Leads," *The Wall Street Journal,* December 10, 2008, p. A17.]

Source: Jim Hopkins, "Egg-Donor Business Booms on Campus," *USA TODAY,* March 16, 2006, p. 1A.

Capitalism in Practice—"Privatization" in America and Abroad

Championed in the 1980s by President Ronald Reagan in the United States and Prime Minister Margaret Thatcher in Great Britain, nations across the globe have increasingly embraced the privatization movement. Those nations have moved toward the free market argument that virtually all services performed by government may be more efficiently and more equitably "managed" by the private sector forces of the market.

Most commonly, privatization follows two patterns: (1) contracting out where government, in effect, turns over a portion of its duties, such as garbage collection, to a private firm; and (2) the sale or lease of public assets, such as an airport, to a private party. Privately operated prisons, now rather common across America, are a primary example of the privatization movement. Of course, privatization also brings worries about job losses, reduced services, reduced responsiveness to consumers, corruption, and so on.

Price-driven, free market solutions range from the mundane to the exotic. Some cities are turning to private companies to run city libraries, auction unclaimed stolen goods, dispose of unwanted equipment, and collect past-due traffic fines.[51] Increasingly cities are supplementing their police service with private guards. Oakland, California, for example, in 2009 could hire four private guards for patrol duty at a cost of about $200,000, reportedly less than the cost of adding a single police officer.[52] Citizens in Oakland were concerned that private guards would not be well trained for their task, but a 2009 study found that violent crime fell 8 percent more in areas of Los Angeles that used supplementary private guards than in the city as a whole.[53] Some doctors and others are arguing for lifting the federal ban on organ sales as a way of addressing the current donor shortage. The resulting increase in supply would save many lives, but others fear the privatized approach would exploit the poor and vulnerable and discourage altruistic donors.[54] Professor Stephanie Coontz pushes the free market argument further by challenging the need for the state's permission to marry. For most of Western history, marriage was a private contract, and Coontz wonders if the time has come to let couples, gay or straight, decide entirely on their own if they want to join together to assume the protections and obligations of a committed relationship.[55] In each of these examples, the underlying idea is that the market can make decisions more efficiently and effectively than government while also maximizing personal freedom. [For a large database supportive of privatization, see **http://reason.org/areas/topic/privatization**]

Space Travel   Trying to save money while emerging from the Great Recession, the U.S. government at this writing in 2011 is retiring its shuttle rockets and will encourage the continuing development of private sector rockets that are expected to carry on space exploration and travel in cooperation with the government. Presumably, space will be "commercialized" with companies hauling space travel customers and exploiting vast mineral resources that may lead to a new "gold rush," but critics think the private sector is unlikely to be able to meet the enormous safety and financial hurdles involved in sustained space travel.[56]

> Private sector rockets are expected to carry on space exploration.

Home Mortgages   The Obama administration, in early 2011, proposed further privatizing the government's role in the mortgage industry by slowly and carefully dissolving government-sponsored mortgage finance corporations, Fannie Mae and Freddie Mac, which currently hold or guarantee about half of all mortgages in the United States.[57] The two mortgage giants collapsed during the subprime mortgage crisis and had to be bailed out by the government.

Toll Roads, Parking Meters, and Congestion Pricing Should users pay fees for access to highways? Private companies are building, maintaining, and operating new toll roads in places such as northern Virginia and suburban San Diego to the Mexican border. Taking the privatization movement a step further, state and local governments are selling or leasing existing roads to private companies. Chicago, for example, leased the Chicago Skyway, an eight-mile elevated road across the city's South Side, to a private Spanish/Australian partnership for $1.8 billion for 99 years.[58]

Critics worry, however, about declining service, excessive tolls, too much profit for the investors, pricing poorer drivers out of access to the roads, and trading secure government jobs with benefits for low-wage private sector jobs without benefits.[59] The record on these transformations is only beginning to emerge. Some toll roads have been successful and others less so. The $843 million, 10-mile south San Diego project, for example, filed for bankruptcy protection in 2010, evidently having been crippled by the Great Recession.[60] Operations continue, but an average of only 22,600 cars per day travel the road that had been projected to serve 60,000 cars daily.[61] [For labor union opposition to privatization, see **http://www.afscme.org/issues/76.cfm**]

The privatization movement is extending beyond toll roads to other infrastructure resources. Chicago sold control of its parking garages to Morgan Stanley for $563 million[62] and entered a 75-year, $1.15 billion lease arrangement with private investors who control and manage its 36,000 parking meters.[63] Chicago also hoped to reach a long-term leasing arrangement for its Midway Airport, but financing could not be arranged for the deal that was projected to involve a $2.52 billion fee in exchange for 99-year lease.[64] Many airports around the world are already controlled, at least in part, by private investors.

While adding to and upgrading infrastructure through privatization, governments and their agents are also turning to pricing/market mechanisms to reduce demand for that infrastructure. One expanding initiative is congestion pricing that involves making a service more expensive at times of peak demand in order to curb that demand. When the new owners took over the Chicago Skyway, they raised tolls for trucks during peak traffic hours. At least 10 metropolitan areas have in place or are contemplating so-called HOT lanes or Lexus Lanes where, for a fee, drivers can move to an express lane with reduced traffic and higher speeds. In some locales, those lanes are also available without charge to motorists in car pools, motorcyclists, buses, and hybrid vehicles.[65]

Pepco, the Washington, D.C., area electric utility, along with others, is experimenting with pricing incentives to curb electrical use at peak times by charging up to 81 cents per kilowatt hour at times of highest demand versus 9 cents at off-peak times, while the average rate is 11 cents.[66] The two-year pilot program, involving several pricing options, reportedly saved customers a 12-month average of $43.83.[67]

Questions

1. Author Joan Didion referred to our highways as America's only communion. Would it be a social/ethical wrong to adopt widespread "congestion fees," privately operated toll roads, and "Lexus Lanes" that would permit those with money to avoid the democracy of the highways? Explain.

2. *Governing Magazine* labeled golf courses "perhaps the most non-essential of the non-essential public services."[68] Studies show that payrolls for city-operated golf courses are about 13 percent higher than for privately operated courses.[69] Why do we subsidize golf, and should we continue doing so? Explain.

3. *a.* The U.S. Postal Service currently loses a few billion dollars annually. Should we privatize the postal service?

   b. Would UPS, for example, want to assume responsibility for delivery to every home in America? Explain.

Schools Is capitalism the answer to poor school performance? The idea was unthinkable a few decades ago, but some increasingly frustrated parents and school boards have adopted a free market "fix." Schools are experimenting with market-based approaches such as open enrollment (students attend the school of their choice regardless of their place of residence), charter schools (funded by taxes but freed of much government oversight), and vouchers (students "spend" their taxpayer-provided dollars on the school of their choice). The hope is that competition will push all schools to higher achievement levels. About half of the states have taken the dramatic step of contracting with private education providers, most notably, New York–based Edison Schools Inc., to manage some of their more troubled schools. Edison hopes to make money running schools and improving student performance. The results to this point, however, indicate that privatization is not the hoped for cure for America's troubled public school system. Some charter schools have had encouraging results, but a 2010 evaluation of Milwaukee, Wisconsin's Parental Choice Program, the biggest and oldest voucher and charter school experiment in America, found that achievement growth rates were about the same as in the public schools, a result that is consistent with a number of other studies.[70] In Dallas, New York City, and other districts, direct payments to students of $100 to $500 per year for improved test performance has produced some success, although experts think the payments may damage students' long-term desire to learn.[71]

> Direct payments to students for improved test performance.

Privatize Higher Education?

Steven Pearlstein, commenting in *The Washington Post*, argues that for-profit universities like Phoenix (400,000 students) and Kaplan (119,000 students) are " . . . the only serious challenge to a hidebound higher education establishment caught up in a self-destructive arms race for students, faculty, athletes, research funding and charitable gifts—a competition that has driven up costs at twice the rate of everything else even as schools lag in meeting the educational needs of students and society."[72]

Enrollment at for-profit colleges and trade schools has tripled in the past decade such that about 10 percent of America's higher education students are enrolled in those schools.[73] Often those are students who could not qualify for nonprofit colleges and universities. Unfortunately, fewer than half of those students graduate. For-profit schools have become a highly profitable industry with a great deal of the schools' revenue coming from federal aid, but 47 percent of all student loan defaults come from for-profit students, according to federal findings.[74] Furthermore, the industry is under assault because of aggressive and deceptive marketing practices discovered by congressional investigators posing as potential students. One investigator received 180 phone calls in one month encouraging enrollment.[75]

Questions

1. *a.* If it is not already, should your college or university become a for-profit institution?
   b. How would your education change?
   c. How would you change?
2. Would our current system of higher education benefit from aggressive private sector competition or is the current competition among schools sufficient? Explain.

International Privatization   Much of the world has joined the privatization movement. Russia, for example, plans to earn about $33 billion through 2013 by selling portions of its top 10 state-owned assets (banking, oil, hydropower, rail, etc.).[76] India's government owns 473 companies valued at about $500 billion.[77] To ease budget pressure, India is committed to privatizing portions of those holdings, although that change likely will be in small steps. With a rapidly expanding population of 1.2 billion, India is also using free market incentives to slow that growth. In parts of India, young married couples who commit to waiting two years before having children are paid about $106 by the government for their forbearance.[78]

Privatization a Success?   Privatization often brings substantially reduced costs and improved expertise, but sometimes the transition does not work well. Fury might be the best word to describe consumer reaction to the higher rates and poor service that accompanied Chicago's parking meter privatization, but Indiana has used the money from its toll road leases to fund a popular, 10-year highway improvement program.[79] Some privatization efforts, such as Florida's plan to lease its "Alligator Alley" toll road, fail because of an absence of private sector bids.[80] Some projects do not generate the anticipated savings. Although more than 30 states contract with private prisons, a 2011 study in Arizona found little or no savings in doing so even though private prisons often "cherry pick" the least expensive prisoners.[81]

Firefighters Watch a House Burn

Obion County, Tennessee, firefighters drew national attention in 2010 when they allowed a rural family home to burn to the ground because the family had not paid their $75 annual subscription fee to the city-operated fire department in nearby South Fulton. Apparently, no one was seriously injured in the fire. The homeowner, Gene Cranick, said that he offered to pay the fee on the spot, but the fire department declined and engaged the fire only to the extent necessary to protect the property of a neighbor who had paid the fee.

Questions

1. *a.* Why did the fire department decline Cranick's money at the time of the fire?
   b. Do you think the fire department should have extinguished the fire even though Cranick had not paid? Explain.
2. Should fire service be privatized across the nation? Explain.

Source: Jason Hibbs, "Firefighters Watch as Home Burns to the Ground," *WPSD Local 6 – News, Sports, Weather,* Paducah, KY, September 30, 2010 [**http://www.wpsdlocal6.com/**].

Questions—Part Two

1. From the capitalist viewpoint, why is the private ownership of property necessary to the preservation of freedom?

2. Ayn Rand argued, "Altruism is incompatible with freedom, with capitalism, and with individual rights."
   a. Define altruism.
   b. Explain why Rand rejected altruism.

3. In describing life in aggressively commercialized Hong Kong, Alvin Rabushka praised the "single-minded pursuit of making money" and the "emphasis on the material things in life." Rabushka admitted to finding "Hong Kong's economic hustle and bustle more interesting, entertaining, and liberating than its lack of high opera, music, and drama." See Alvin Rabushka, *Hong Kong: A Study in Economic Freedom* (Chicago: University of Chicago Press, 1979), pp. 83–86.
   a. Although it is often criticized in America, is materialism the most certain and most interesting path to personal happiness? Explain.
   b. Would "sophisticated" culture (such as opera and drama) substantially disappear in America without government support? Explain.
   c. If so, how may we justify that support? If not, how may we justify that support?

4. Assume the federal government removed itself from the purchase and maintenance of its parks.
   a. Left to the private sector, what sorts of parks would develop under the profit incentive?
   b. Would Yellowstone, for example, survive in substantially its present state? Explain.
   c. Make the argument that the federal parks are an unethical, undemocratic expropriation of private resources.

5. Assume the abolition of the federal Food and Drug Administration. How would the free market protect the citizenry from dangerous food and drug products?

6. Puritan leaders felt concern over the morality of merchants selling goods for "more than their worth." That concern was particularly grave when the goods were scarce or in great demand.
   a. Should our society develop an ethic wherein goods are to be sold only "for what they are worth"? Explain.
   b. Can a seller make an accurate determination of worth? Explain.
   c. Does a product's worth differ from the price that product will bring in the marketplace? Explain.
   d. Personalize the inquiry: Assume you seek to sell your Ford car for $10,000. Assume you know of several identical Fords in a similar state of repair that can be purchased for $9,000. Assume you find a buyer at $10,000. Will you unilaterally lower your price or direct the purchaser to the other cars? Explain.
   e. If not, have you acted justly? Explain.

7. Critics of our capitalist system contend that ability and effort often are less responsible for one's success than "unearned" factors such as family background, social class, luck, and willingness to cheat.

   Do you agree? Explain.

8. Commentator Irving Kristol asked whether it was "just" for Ray Kroc (McDonald's owner, now deceased) to have made so much money by merely figuring out a new way to sell hamburgers. He concluded that capitalism says it is just because he sold a good product; people want it; it is fair.

   Do you agree with Kristol? Explain.

9. Professor Robert E. Lane argued that the person who is motivated by needs for affiliation, rather than by needs for achievement, does less well in the market. Such a person is not rewarded so well as autonomous, achievement-oriented people.
   a. Is Lane correct? Explain.
   b. Is capitalism, in the long run, destructive of societal welfare in that achievement is better rewarded than affiliation? Explain.

10. How would poor people be cared for in a free market society?

11. Kevin Mattson, a researcher at Rutgers University, fears the gated community, where people shut themselves off from public life. "The privatization of everything including garbage service," he said, "disassociates people from contributing to the public good and from their responsibility to other people."

    Do you agree? Explain.

12. Using private money, New York City experimented from 2007 to 2010, with a program that paid poorer residents for practicing good life habits such as holding a job ($150 per month), going to the dentist ($100), regular school attendance ($25 to $50 per month), and passing certain examinations ($600). The average family received about $3,000. Would you expect this program to be an effective encouragement to improved life habits? Explain. See Associated Press, "N.Y.C. Pays Poor for Good Habits . . . ," *The Des Moines Register,* March 31, 2010, p. 10A.

Part Three—Collectivism: Increase Government?

The term collectivism embraces various economic philosophies on the left of the political–economic spectrum—principally, communism and socialism. Capitalism is characterized by economic individualism. Communism and the various styles of socialism feature economic cooperation and varying degrees of centralized control.

Communism

While China, Cuba, North Korea, Vietnam, and a few other nations continue to practice communism, the balance of the world has clearly rejected Marxist-Leninist totalitarianism. China is rapidly and enthusiastically embracing free market practices, with continuing state direction; a strategy that some label state capitalism, as described above. Chinese enthusiasm for elements of free market practice should not be misunderstood; however. The communist state remains firmly in charge.

Fidel Castro's departure from the Cuban presidency in favor of his brother Raul has resulted in initial free market reforms. When he took power, Fidel Castro closed Cuba's golf courses, considering them prime examples of capitalist excess. Now Cuba is welcoming foreign developers who are expected to build more than a dozen golf course resorts.

> Cubans can now own cell phones.

Cubans can now own cell phones and other electronic devices, some state land is being distributed for private farming, and some private cabs are being licensed.[82] *Fox News* reported in early 2011 that 75,000 Cubans had become entrepreneurs in the previous seven months as restaurants, barber shops, scooter repair shops, and other businesses sprang up after the government decided to allow 178 mostly small-scale categories of capitalist activity. The government can no longer afford its complete socialist approach, and it has laid off 500,000 employees (in a nation of 11 million residents where 84 percent of workers hold government jobs).[83] Of course, most Cubans continue to lead a spare, government-supported existence, and political liberty is currently nonexistent.

Communist Vietnam is also embracing elements of capitalism. Canon, Hanesbrands, Intel, and Nokia are among the multinational firms that are building or expanding factories in Vietnam. Manufacturers, attracted by Vietnam's low wages, also are often trying to avoid over-dependence on manufacturing in China.[84] *New York Times* reporter Keith Bradsher says that many Asian executives and some in America, believe that communism encourages the societal stability they value.[85] Perhaps America's investment presence in Vietnam, our enemy in a fierce war of the 1970s, is encouraging evidence of the healing power of international trade? More cynically, perhaps host-country political practices don't trouble foreign investors unless those practices threaten the bottom line?

Communist Principles

Despite the decline of communism, we need to briefly remind ourselves of some Marxist fundamentals, among which the core promise of economic justice for all remains a particularly powerful motivator. Lenin, not Marx, created the communist dictatorship in Russia. Lenin and the other communist totalitarians, most notably Stalin in the Soviet Union and Mao in China, did horrific damage. However, Marx, along with Freud and Einstein, is among the thinkers who most profoundly shaped the 20th century. For our purposes, Marx's central message concerns the severe abuses that can accompany unrestrained capitalism. Marx was particularly concerned about the growing imbalance between rich and poor. Moreover, he felt that the pursuit of wealth and self-interest would erode society's moral core. More broadly, Marx built an economic interpretation of history, arguing that "the mode of production in material life determines the general character of the social, political, and spiritual processes of life."[86] [For an introduction to Marxist thought, see **http://www.cla.purdue.edu/English/theory/marxism**]

Communism to Capitalism: A Bumpy Road

People in former communist nations in Eastern Europe, including Poland, Hungary, The Czech Republic, and Russia, reported mixed feelings in 2009 as they looked back on the 20 years following the fall of the Berlin Wall and the end of the Cold War between the former Soviet Union and the Western European/American allies. When dictatorships were replaced by democracy, the initial reaction was euphoria, but in subsequent years some nostalgia for the certainties of communism has emerged. A Czech professor summarized the current feelings of disappointment: "People here admired the freedom and prosperity of the Western world. Now what they see is materialism, corruption, inflation, lawlessness—and they can't find spiritual or material prosperity."[87] Many in Eastern Europe yearn for the comfort of state-provided healthcare and education and state-subsidized goods and services, but the evidence suggests they tend to forget about the poor quality of those goods and services, state censorship, the absence of freedom, and fear of the state.

Question

1. Do you think capitalism, by its nature, is unfair to ordinary people? Explain.

Source: Michael J. Jordan, "After the Berlin Wall, Nostalgia for Communism Creeps Back," *The Christian Science Monitor*, November 8, 2009 [**http://www.csmonitor.com/2009/1109/p11s01-woeu.html**].

Socialism

Communism appears to have run its course philosophically and pragmatically, but the problems that generated its appeal—poverty, oppression, the rich/poor gap, and so on—remain. Hence government intervention in the market continues to needed. The question is: How much government is appropriate? Socialists provide one answer by rejecting communist totalitarianism and embracing democracy while calling for aggressive government intervention to correct economic and social ills. Historically, socialism has often been associated with democratic governments and peaceful change, whereas communism has been characterized by totalitarianism and violent revolution.

Socialists aim to retain the benefits of industrialism while abolishing the social costs often accompanying the free market. The government is likely to be directly involved in regulating growth, inflation, and unemployment. In the contemporary Western world, Austria, Norway, Denmark, Sweden, South Africa, Finland, and France are among the nations where socialist principles have retained a significant presence. Those nations have now embraced free markets, but socialist welfare concerns remain influential.

Socialist Goals

A critical distinction between socialists and capitalists is that the former believe a society's broad directions should be carefully planned rather than left to what some take to be the whimsy of the market. Furthermore, socialists are convinced that problems of market failure (inadequate information, monopoly, externalities, public goods, and so on—see Chapter 8) mean that the free market is simply incapable of meeting the needs of all segments of society. The socialist agenda includes these elements:[88]

1. **Liberty.** To the capitalist, socialism appears to harshly restrain individual freedom. To the socialist, the freedoms of capitalism are largely an illusion, accessible only to the prosperous and powerful.

2. **Social welfare.** Socialists reserve much of their concern for the condition of the lower class—poverty, exploitation, cultural deprivation, and so on. Socialists feel that the economy must be directed toward the general interest rather than left free to multiply the welfare of

successful capitalists. Hence, socialists advocate income supports, free education, free health care, generous sick pay, family planning, and the like to correct the wrongs of capitalism.

3. **Fulfilling work.** Socialists object to the harshness of working life where a large segment of society is chained to degrading labor.

> Socialists seek a communitarian approach to life.

4. **Community.** Socialists seek a communitarian approach to life where the excessive individualism of capitalism is muted by a concern for the welfare of all.

5. **Equality.** Class distinctions are anathema to the socialist. All humans are equally meritorious, and distinctions among them are inherently unjust.

6. **Rationality.** Socialists fear the "irrationality" of a society based on competition and unrestrained pursuit of industrial growth.

As explained in the account that follows, poverty and claims of corporate exploitation have allowed socialism to regain a tentative foothold in parts of South America.

Socialism in South America

Venezuelan president Hugo Chavez hopes to build a "21st century socialism" in South America that will elevate the poor, forgotten by "savage capitalism," while leading his country and neighbors, including Bolivia, Ecuador, Honduras, and Nicaragua away from American dominance. He wants to destroy what he sees as centuries of plundering, humiliation, and discrimination against indigenous people by monied interests, particularly American multinationals. Chavez says that world power is shifting from America:

> The uni-polar world has collapsed. The power of the U.S. empire has collapsed. Everyday, the new poles of world power are becoming stronger. Beijing, Tokyo, Tehran. . . . It's moving toward the East and toward the South.[89]

Chavez has nationalized many companies, driven out ExxonMobil and ConocoPhillips, and redistributed land from the government and private owners to the poor. While Chavez says he will "bury" Venezuelan capitalism, the private sector continues to control about two-thirds of the Venezuelan economy, and he likely recognizes that complete state control would be unsupportable.

With strong oil prices, Chavez has, for now, a steady and generous revenue stream that has allowed him to dramatically increase state funding of social projects. The government claims to have cut poverty in half, and Chavez has inspired many Venezuelans to engage in civic life and to feel a new concern for the nation's welfare. Critics say he has stifled dissent, taken control of almost every government institution, and subjected the nation to double digit inflation, food and power shortages, a devalued currency, and a murder rate that has doubled in recent years. [At this writing in 2011, Chavez is being treated for cancer, and his future is uncertain.]

Sources: Associated Press, "Chavez Asserts: We'll Bury Capitalism," *The Des Moines Register*, July 19, 2010, p. 10A; Editorial, "The State Department Responds to Repression by Hugo Chavez," *The Washington Post*, January 4, 2011[http://www.washingtonpost.com]; Juan Forero, "Venezuela Tries to Create Its Own Kind of Socialism," *The Washington Post*, August 6, 2007, p. A12; Juan Forero, "Chavez's 'Socialist City' Rises," *The Washington Post*, November 27, 2007, p. A10; Sara Miller Llana, "Where Has Chavez Taken Venezuela?" *The Christian Science Monitor*, February 2, 2009 [http://www.csmonitor.com/2009/0202/p01s03-woam.html]; and *Newsday*, "Indian Rites for President-Elect Symbolize Bolivia's New Direction," *Waterloo/Cedar Falls Courier*, January 22, 2006, p. A3.

Coping with Capitalism—China and Russia

China—Economics

As noted above, scholar Ian Bremmer, in his 2010 book, *The End of the Free Market,* argues that China and some other nations practice "state capitalism" in which the government is the dominant economic force as it intervenes in and shapes the market to further the state's political goals.[90] The result has been something of an economic miracle as China has blended its large but shrinking system of state-owned enterprise with the explosive power of the free market (guided by the government) to sprint ahead of Japan and become in 2010 the globe's second ranking economy as measured by gross national product.[91]

At this writing in 2011, some business leaders and other analysts are seeing signs that China is strengthening and favoring its state-run businesses while gradually diminishing the influence of private capitalism.[92] The 129 giant, state-owned conglomerates that answer directly to the central government (along with thousands of smaller ones run by provinces and cities) seem to be growing in financial and political influence.[93] Similarly, Western business leaders say that China's free market liberalization policies of recent years have slowed; making entry to the Chinese market and competition with Chinese companies increasingly difficult.[94] While China's leaders have publicly affirmed their commitment to "opening up" the Chinese market, *The Wall Street Journal* explained the argument that China is turning inward and relying less on the market and more on its government-controlled businesses:

> Signs of nationalism are evident in the grooming of state-owned companies to dominate their industries as "national champions," often at the expense of private Chinese companies as well as foreign firms. From airlines to coal mining to dairy products, government policies are expanding the state's role.[95]

Whether these signs are precursors of long-term change or mere blips remains to be seen.

Business is exploding in China. The nation of 1.3 billion people is aggressively competing around the globe. After 30 years of increasing capitalism, the signs of material progress are obvious: skyscrapers, cars rapidly replacing bicycles, and McDonalds, KFC, and the like on many urban corners. China's car boom is amazing. Beijing, the capital, was home to perhaps 1,100 private cars in 1985. In 2010 alone, total car sales were projected at 15 million, making China the world's largest car market.[96] China projects a quadrupling of its gross domestic product, boosting its middle class from about 5 percent of today's population to over half by 2020.[97] China estimates that 400 million people have been lifted out of poverty since the shift toward open markets was initiated in the late 1970s.[98] China's per capita gross domestic product, however, was about $7,400 in 2010 while the comparable figure for the United States was $47,400.[99]

> Making China the world's largest car market.

Problems

Of course, China faces many problems as its economy soars. Stunning levels of environmental pollution; stock market manipulation; dangerous foods and drugs; rampant piracy of software, movies and music; and government corruption are among those difficulties. Basic social support structures like affordable access to health care, unemployment insurance, and pensions remain inadequate. More broadly, China's income gap between rich and poor is estimated to be among the world's largest, although China has reduced the disparity in recent years.[100] Furthermore, China has instituted new environmental rules, corruption crackdowns, and social service initiatives.

Cheap Labor

Low wages, often difficult working conditions, and a rapidly shrinking supply of young laborers (the result of strict family planning policies) have caused unrest among workers leading to occasional strikes and some increase in wages, although those wages remain low relative to the economy's overall health. China's reliance on cheap labor to drive its economy is threatened as other nations are able to undercut the Chinese advantage. Li & Fung, for example, a Hong Kong supplier for Walmart, Liz Claiborne, and others, reported that its 2009 production in Bangladesh rose 20 percent while its work in China fell 5 percent.[101]

China—Politics

Freedom   Of course, China remains a dictatorship governed by the Communist Party. Repression is common. The government controls the media as evidenced by Google's ongoing censorship battle with the state spurred by Google's 2010 decision to stop omitting (self-censoring) search results that the Chinese government considered subversive or pornographic. China uses its own "great firewall" of Internet censors to filter Google search results without Google's cooperation. An estimated 30 to 50 thousand regulators monitor the web in China with certain sites such as Facebook, YouTube, and Twitter, blocked from public access.[102] Google's license to operate in China has been renewed until 2012, but Google could be cut off at any time.[103]

> China uses its own "great firewall" of Internet censors to filter Google search results.

Similarly, China has rejected pleas to end forced labor camps and guarantee freedom of speech,[104] and Communist Party leaders have made it clear that democracy should not be expected in the near future.[105] Furthermore, recent reports suggest increasing interest in reviving features of the Maoist movement that led to the harsh repressions of the 1966–76 Cultural Revolution. Led by charismatic Bo Xilai, Communist Party chief in the southwestern city of Chongqing, the "Red" campaign seems to be re-asserting the Communist Party as the primary vehicle for attacking corruption, promoting economic growth, and addressing social problems.

Reforms   Although personal freedom continues to lag in many ways, China has achieved legal reforms in employment, contracts, property, antitrust, and anticorruption that represent very big steps toward a modern, rules-based society. Reform is also reaching farming practices. While Chinese farmers own their crops, they are not allowed to own the land itself. The Communist Party has decided, however, to permit China's 800 million farmers to lease their contracted land to others or to transfer their land-use rights to others; a plan expected to double rural incomes by 2020.[106] In a sign of increasing comfort with Western approaches to dispute resolution, the number of lawyers in China more than doubled from 1997 to 2008 and the number of civil lawsuits has climbed dramatically.[107] [For the latest Chinese news, see **http://thebeijingnews.net**]

> The number of lawyers in China more than doubled.

Russia—Economics

A Western visitor to modern Moscow must be hard-pressed to imagine that this thriving, consuming, competitive place was once the global center of communism, the dour capital of the Union of Soviet Socialist Republics, and the home of America's nuclear enemy. After the fall of the USSR and the ideological defeat of communism, Moscow embraced consumer capitalism, a change described by *The Christian Science Monitor:*

> The heavy, block buildings of Russia's capital are no longer covered in banners of Lenin, Marx, and Engels. Instead, enormous billboards advertise watches, cars, clothing—items unimaginable in Soviet times. Capitalism has taken hold with a vengeance.[108]

Russia remains a relatively poor nation with an average per capita income of about $330 per month, about 10 percent of the U.S. average,[109] and a total economy about half the size of France.[110] Nonetheless, Russia's economic performance from the late 1990s up to the 2008 global financial crash was striking. Since the crash, however, Russia has been kept afloat largely by the export of its enormous natural resources—oil, gas, timber, and so on—and the capital reserves it had amassed during the good years. Following the crash, the state was forced to take shares in big Russian companies in exchange for loans to keep those companies solvent.[111] The power of the oligarchs (billionaire businessmen who have dominated big pieces of the Russian economy) was trimmed by the government. The result is that the Russian state controls as much as half of Russia's GNP[112] but, as mentioned above, the state plans to raise money through an aggressive privatization program. As many as 900 state-owned companies may be partially privatized.[113] Recognizing that a return to the former planned economy would be disastrous, most Russian leaders, for the present at least, see their version of a market economy—state capitalism—as the route to national prosperity and rejuvenated Russian greatness.[114]

Russia—Politics

Russia's future economic success is intimately tied, of course, to its political processes. The state needs to win over foreign multinational investors who fear political tyranny and domestic corruption. Maplecroft, the British political risk consulting firm, in 2011 ranked Russia 186th out of 196 countries in political risk to business (1 being least risky) and according to *Transparency International,* Russia is the world's most corrupt major economy, ranking 154th out of 178 countries (1 being least corrupt).[115]

The Russian government's centralization of economic power has been accompanied by tightened control over politics, courts, activists, and the mass media. Bribery and other forms of corruption in both government and the private sector are standard practice. Former president, now prime minister, Vladimir Putin, holds enormous personal power in Russian political and economic affairs, and space for genuine political opposition is sparse.[116] Russians elected Putin's handpicked successor, Dmitri Medvedev, as president, and Medvedev says he wants Russia to move toward Western entrepreneurship. Doing so, however, will require enormous investments in industrial modernization, education, health care, and infrastructure; reduced bureaucracy and strengthened legal standards; and most of all good governance[117]—a requirement it seems for successful capitalism everywhere.

> Bribery and other forms of corruption are standard practice.

Questions

1. Both China and Russia have population problems, but of quite divergent natures. China believes it has too many babies, and Russia, facing a population decline, has too few. Likewise, they are addressing their problems in quite different ways. China's government allows each couple to have only one child, although exceptions are permitted for those living in rural areas and for minorities. Heavy fines may be imposed on those who violate the rules. In Russia, President Medvedev, in his 2010 State of Russia speech, called for a baby bonus, better health care, and free land for women who will have a third child. China fears it cannot sustain its enormous and growing population while Russia fears its plummeting birthrate threatens the country's future. Can government commands, as in China, or free market incentives, as in Russia, cause people to change their childbearing practices? Explain.

2. Can China maintain its closed, centrally controlled political system while enjoying the benefits of its somewhat open economic markets? Explain.

3. Journalist Dani Rodrik in 2010 asked: "Will China Rule the World?"[118] What do you think? Does it matter? Explain.

Part Four—Middle Ground? A Mixed Economy (The Third Way)

Communism has failed. Socialist principles, to the extent that they require central planning, bloated bureaucracies, and restraints on personal freedom, are discredited. An era has passed, but the shape of the future is unclear. The state capitalism of China, Russia, and other nations has little appeal in America and Western Europe and yet America's brand of free market capitalism has lost a great deal of luster in the recent financial collapse and the ongoing Great Recession. Some middle ground in free market and welfare state principles may be the next step, but the appropriate mixture is proving elusive. For years, the Nordic states of Sweden, Norway, Denmark, and Finland practiced their market socialism or social democracy with such success that it was labeled a "Third Way" between the harsher extremes of capitalism and communism. Their welfare states provided healthy economic growth with cradle-to-grave social care for all in a system emphasizing the collective welfare over individual preferences.

Sweden

Life expectancy in Sweden is 81.07 years, as compared with about 78.37 years in the United States.[119] The government provides education, health care, child care, maternity and paternity leave, unemployment protection, and more. Government incentives promote preferred behaviors. For example, 390 days of paid, state-supported parental work leave was adjusted to encourage couples to split the leave time such that 85 percent of fathers now take some leave. As a result, some evidence suggests that women can expect higher future earnings, perhaps as a consequence of more balanced child care duties. Divorce rates have fallen since the leave policy was implemented, although some males may face a bit of a gender-identity crisis and employers must adjust to more frequent employee absences.[120]

> 390 days of paid state-supported work leave.

Gender Equality

Sweden aggressively encourages gender equality. Believing boys have an unfair edge, eradication of gender stereotypes has become a key ingredient in Swedish education. At Stockholm's "Egalia" (equality) preschool, for example, the staff avoids using the words "him" or "her" and addresses all children as "friends." Children's books often feature homosexual couples, single parents, or adopted children and classics like *Cinderella* are shunned. Egalia's methods are controversial, even in Sweden.

Source: Jenny Soffel, "Swedish School Fosters Gender Neutrality," *Des Moines Register*, June 27, 2011, p. 1A.

Taxes To pay for its cradle-to-grave welfare benefits, Sweden takes about 47 percent of its national income (gross domestic product-GDP) in taxes, while the United States, in contrast, has one of the developed world's lowest total tax burdens at about 27 percent of GDP in recent decades,[121] but down to about 24 percent during the current recession. In order to keep its economy healthy, Sweden has followed a policy of comparatively low corporate taxes (26.3 percent, as compared with 35 percent in the United States).[122] As a result, Sweden's economic performance over the past 20 years has been among the strongest in the world, allowing, for example, all nine million Swedes to have health insurance,[123] whereas 22 to 54 million Americans do not (depending on the final implementation of the Obama-administration health care reform plan).[124] Even so, the pressure of globalization has been felt in Sweden where a more moderate and somewhat right-center government has pushed aside the left-leaning Social Democrats and has significantly lowered taxes, privatized some state-dominated companies, and reduced unemployment by encouraging work over welfare.[125] Business regulations have been dramatically reduced, and tens of thousands of long-term unemployed welfare recipients have been pushed back into the labor market. Sweden hopes to maintain its core welfare commitment in combination with an entrepreneurial spirit more like America's. Economist Anders Aslund explained the new Swedish vision:

> The role of the state is still large and welfare is pretty comprehensive, but public expenditure has shrunk impressively. . . . There is now a sense of proportion of how much a government can do—and more of a reliance on market forces, where suitable, and on efficiency.[126]

Nordic v. Anglo-Saxon Broadly, in the Nordic social democracies, government expenditures for social purposes average about 27 percent of GDP as opposed to about 17 percent in the Anglo-Saxon states (United States, United Kingdom, Canada, Australia, Ireland, and New Zealand), and yet in many ways, the Nordic states perform better economically.[127] One expert attributes the Third Way success to "lavish" spending on research and development and higher education.[128] Sweden, for example, spends nearly 4 percent of its GDP on R&D, the highest ratio in the world.[129] Thus, for Sweden and the other Scandinavian states, wise government spending is a key ingredient in a successful market-based economy. We should remember, of course, that Sweden is a small, homogeneous nation. Replicating its policies in the United States would be difficult.

Speeding Ticket

Ferrari-driving millionaire, "Roland S." was fined $290,000 in 2009 for speeding 60 miles per hour through a small village in Switzerland where the speed limit was 30. In their verdict, which was subject to appeal, judges labeled the driver a "traffic thug." The fine reflected a 2007 Swiss law allowing judges to hand down fines in certain misdemeanor cases based on personal income and wealth. "Roland S." was worth some $20 million, and he was a repeat offender. The maximum Swiss fine is $1 million, while Germany permits as much as a $16 million fine. France, Austria, and the Nordic nations also permit punishments based on personal wealth.

Question

Would you favor penalties in America based on income and wealth? Explain.

Source: Frank Jordans, "Rich Driver Hit with $290,000 Speeding Ticket," *Des Moines Register,* January 11, 2010, p. 1A.

American Capitalism in Europe?

Does the European Union—ranging broadly from the Scandinavian Third Way to Germany's cooperative, but increasingly aggressive capitalism—have a better long-term vision for personal and societal welfare than the United States? Is America's more libertarian "cowboy capitalism" better adapted to the globe's demands than the "coordinated, stakeholder capitalism" characteristic of much of Europe? The evidence is mixed. In building entrepreneurial spirit, personal freedom, and personal wealth and income, the United States is the clear world leader, but the EU's very powerful, 27 nation, over 500 million person bloc generates a gross national product slightly larger than the United States and about three times that of China or Japan.[130] For Europeans, however, quantity seems to be less important than quality. Europeans choose to work less than Americans, and as they see it, enjoy life more. Their economy is less flexible than ours and typically produces fewer jobs, but it is also less harsh.[131] Universal healthcare, job protection, and strong unemployment benefits are part of the European identity. In his 2010 book, *Europe's Promise: Why the European Way Is the Best Hope for an Insecure Age,* Steven Hill points to economic strength, superb health care, family support, "green" policies, and effective politics as evidence of Europe's "bold new vision for human development."[132]

Welfare Reform   Europe's warmer, more communal values and practices are inviting as Hill describes them, but the ongoing recession and the competitive power of globalization have forced political change and austerity measures. Right-of-center parties are now in charge in several traditionally leftist nations, including Britain, France, and Germany. With slow economic growth, low birthrates, and increasing life expectancies, most EU nations cannot afford their traditional generosity. Retirement ages, for example, are rising: from 60 to 62 in France, 65 to 66 in Britain, and 65 to 67 in Spain. Britain will dramatically cut public spending including welfare benefits. The changes are intended both to reduce the country's dangerously large deficit, and to jolt the 1.4 million Britons who have been without work for a decade.[133]

> EU nations cannot afford their traditional generosity.

The European Divide and Young People   These troubled times have led to financial bailouts in Greece, Ireland, and Portugal, with Spain and even Italy struggling for stability. The EU itself is divided economically and culturally. The financially secure northern nations, led particularly by Germany, which is very healthy after tax and labor reforms, are reluctant to aid their southern neighbors whom they take to be undisciplined in their approach to work and life. Young people in southern Europe are deeply frustrated by youth unemployment rates that have risen to 40 percent in Spain and 28 percent in Italy.[134]

> Youth unemployment rates have risen to 40 percent in Spain.

Multicultural Failure?   A troubled economy is only part of the current unease in Europe. With rapidly growing immigrant populations and what many see as a threatening Muslim presence, some European states are torn between seeking a new cultural balance and preserving their ancient heritages. German chancellor Angela Merkel reflected a rising conservative populism in parts of Europe when she explained that Germany welcomes immigrants but is uncertain about how to absorb them:

> This multicultural approach, saying that we simply live side by side and live happily with each other, has failed. Utterly failed.[135]

French President Nicholas Sarkozy and British Prime Minister David Cameron said the same thing, and Sarkozy, while respecting cultural and religious differences, called for a unified, national community:

> If you come to France, you accept to melt into a single community, which is the national community. And if you do not want to accept that, you cannot be welcome in France.[136]

Questions

1. *a.* In your view, do we practice meaningful multiculturalism in America?
   b. If so, is that practice successful?
2. Do you think America should follow Sarkozy's vision by insisting on a unified national community rather than a place where differing cultural communities simply co-exist?

Contrasting Values

Obviously, both Europe and America are struggling in this troubled time, but which vision of life seems most promising over the long term? American commentator and social activist Jeremy Rifkind contrasted the American and European "Dreams":[137]

American Dream	vs.	European Dream
Wealth/Individual success	vs.	Quality of life
Growth	vs.	Sustainable development
Property/Civil rights	vs.	Social/Human rights
Live to work	vs.	Work to live
Religiosity/Piety	vs.	Declining faith
Strong military	vs.	Build peace

Rifkind thinks the European strategy is the better one. What do you think? Which of those two lists of values is more comfortable and inspiring for you? Which is more likely to meet the demands of the ongoing global competition and evolution? [For an overview of "Europe vs. America," including an appraisal of Rifkind's arguments, see **http://www. nybooks.com/articles**]

Is the Welfare State a Key to Personal Happiness?

Denmark turns out to be the happiest place on Earth, according to a large, Gallup Poll-based 2005–2009 study of global happiness in 155 countries. The top of the happiness list includes: 1. Denmark, 2. Finland, 3. Norway, 4. Sweden, 4. Netherlands, 6. Costa Rica, 6. New Zealand, 8. Canada, 8. Israel, 8. Australia, 8. Switzerland. The United States ranks 14th on the list, ahead of the United Kingdom (17), Germany (33), France (44), Cuba (67), Russia (73), Japan (81), India (115), and China (125). Most of the various happiness studies find the Scandinavian countries at or near the top of the list. Why? One theory, according to Gallup researchers, is that basic needs are satisfied in those countries to a higher degree than elsewhere.

   What matters most? Broadly, good health, education, and wealth are associated with happiness, but wealth seems to increase happiness only up to a point. According to a 2010 study, that point is about $75,000 in the United States. Another 2010 study found that getting richer, in and of itself, does not make a nation happier in the long run. Simply "hanging out" with friends and family seems to be critical to the Danes' being first in the world level of happiness. Ninety-two percent of Danes belong to some kind of social club, and the government encourages these get-togethers by helping to pay for them. Likewise, while Danes value nice things, they are said to be a "post-consumerist" society where consumption is not a high priority. Their extraordinarily high taxes (around 50 percent of income) may also play a role in the happiness quotient in that income is substantially leveled, allowing careers to be chosen more on the basis of interest rather than money and also allowing everyone to "hold his/her head high" regardless of occupational status. Finally, experts point particularly to the Danes' very high quotient of trust, which may be a product of the cradle-to-grave security provided by the government. For example, mothers often leave their babies unattended in strollers outside shops and restaurants. Of course, Denmark has the advantage of being a small, homogenous nation largely free of America's worldwide responsibilities.

Purpose? A 2011 *Wall Street Journal* survey of happiness research raised a cautionary note by drawing a distinction between a purposeful life and a happy life. Mounting evidence suggests that people who focus on a meaningful life, while sometimes sacrificing happiness feelings in the moment, may be healthier, live longer, and have a greater sense of well being over time than people who focus on short-term feelings of happiness by eating a good meal, going to a movie, enjoying a big game, etc. Noting that symptoms of depression, paranoia, and psychopathology steadily increased in American college students from 1938 to 2007, San Diego State University researchers have offered as a plausible explanation America's increasing emphasis on pleasure, materialism, and status and decreasing attention to community and meaning in life. [For the " Map of Happiness," see **http://www.jdsurvey.net/jds/jdsurveyMaps.jsp?Idioma=I&Seccion Texto=0404&I**]

Questions

The tiny Himalayan nation of Bhutan has committed to measuring itself, not by Gross Domestic Product (GDP), but by Gross National Happiness(GNH), calculated from the nation's "four pillars" of: sustainable development, environmental protection, cultural preservation, and good governance, each of equal importance. Canada, France, and Great Britain have initiated similar projects.

1. Would the United States be a better nation if we sought GNH rather than GDP?
2. Would pursuit of GNH produce a winner in today's fierce global competition? Explain.

Sources: Brook Larmer, "Bhutan's Enlightened Experiment," *National Geographic Magazine*, March 2008 [**http://ngm.nationalgeographic.com/2008/03/bhutan/larmer-text**]; Associated Press, "Money Can Buy You Happiness Up to a Point, Researchers Find," *Waterloo-Cedar Falls Courier,* August 7, 2010, p. 1A; Alok Jha, "Happiness Doesn't Increase with Growing Wealth of Nations, Study Finds," *guardian.co.uk,* December 13, 2010 [**http://www.guardian.co.uk/science/2010/dec/13/happiness-growing-wealth-nations-study**]; Francesca Levy, "The World's Happiest Countries," *Forbes,* July 14, 2010 [**http://www.forbes.com/2010/07/14/world-happiest-countries-lifestyle-realestate-gallup.html**]; Shirley Wang, "Is Happiness Overrated?" *The Wall Street Journal,* March 15, 2011, p. D1; and Bill Weir and Sylvia Johnson, "Denmark: The Happiest Place on Earth," *ABC News,* January 8, 2007 [**http://abcnews.go.com/2020/story?id=40860928page=1**].

Questions—Parts Three and Four

1. Billionaire investor George Soros, in his book *Open Society,* sees "market fundamentalism as a greater threat to open society today than communism."[138] Soros fears contemporary capitalism's extreme commitment to self-interest, which results, he says, in our greatest challenge today: "to establish a set of fundamental values."[139]
   a. What does Soros mean?
   b. Do you agree with him? Explain.
2. Americans feel a great deal of faith in the free market. Explain some of the weaknesses in the market. That is, where is the free market likely to fail?
3. Writing in *Dissent,* Joanne Barkan says, "[A]lmost all Swedes view poverty, extreme inequalities of wealth, and the degradation that comes with unemployment as unacceptable."[140]
   a. Do you agree with the Swedes? Explain.
   b. Why are Americans more tolerant of those conditions than are the Swedes?
4. Joseph Ackermann, the CEO of Deutsche Bank, Germany's largest bank, said in 2011 that a woman on the bank's board of directors would make the board "more colorful, prettier."[141] Germany is debating a law requiring companies to put women on their boards. (Deutsche Bank has no women on its board as of this writing.) Norway requires public companies to be at least 40 percent male or female, France and Spain are phasing in quotas. About 15 percent of Fortune 500 board members in America are female.
   a. Would you favor a quota of female members on corporate boards in America?
   b. Would those companies with stronger female representation perform better? Explain.
5. a. Should an American citizen's primary duty be to herself or himself or to all other members of society? Explain.
   b. Should all humans be regarded as of equal value and thus equally worthy of our individual support? Explain.
   c. Can social harmony be achieved in a nation whose citizens fail to regard the state as a "superfamily"? Explain.

6. *a.* In your view, is an individual's possession of extravagant wealth a moral wrong?

   b. Would economic justice require that we treat "being rich" as a social wrong? Explain.

   See George Scialabba, "Asking the Right Questions," *Dissent,* Spring 1988, p. 114.

7. In questioning Oakland Athletics general manager Billy Beane, *The Wall Street Journal* described professional football as "socialist" and baseball as "capitalist":

   > The NFL (National Football League) has been successful as a socialist league, equally divvying up the league's revenue among all the teams. Major league baseball, on the other hand, is a capitalist league, with a clear divide between big-market and small-market teams.

   a. Do you think some of major league baseball's financial rules have to be changed to better balance the playing field?[142]

   b. Is "socialism" or "capitalism" the better system for professional sports? Explain.

8. Warren Buffett, one of the richest men in the world, recently called for higher taxes for the wealthy in America:

   > If anything, taxes for the lower and middle class and maybe even the upper middle class should even probably be cut further. But I think that people at the high end—people like myself should be paying a lot more in taxes. We have it better than we've ever had it.[143]

Should rich Americans be paying higher taxes? Explain.

Part Five—America's Economic Future: Where Are We Going?

Greed Is Good

Michael Douglas, as Gordon Gekko in the movie *Wall Street:* "Greed is good! Greed is right! Greed works! Greed will save the USA!"

According to a United Nations report, in 2005 the world's 500 richest people had combined incomes greater than that of the poorest 416 million people.

Source: United Nations Human Development Report, 2005.

How Much Government? Should we expand our faith in free market capitalism, or do we need to move our present mixed economy a bit closer to the welfare state model, which itself is under great pressure? Or must a new model emerge? In sum, how much government do we need? To think further about those questions, let's briefly examine some of the key indicators of America's economic and social health.

Good News   Of course, Americans have a great deal to be proud of. We enjoy extraordinary material comfort along with healthy, generally safe lives. As the *Los Angeles Times* reported, since 1980 the percentage of those earning $100,000 or more, in today's dollars, has doubled, the average size of our homes has doubled in the past 50 years to about 2,200 square feet, and the total hours spent working have declined steadily for over 150 years.[144] We are inventive, adventuresome, free, and zealously democratic. Roughly half of all patents are earned by Americans, minorities now hold high-ranking political office, and more women than men are earning college degrees.[145] Much of the world strives to achieve America's blend of entrepreneurial capitalism along with intellectual and pop culture leadership. And we should not forget that capitalist America is among the most generous of global cultures. In the two months immediately following the devastating 2010 Haiti earthquake, American charities raised nearly one billion dollars in aid.[146]

> Americans have a great deal to be proud of.

The American Dream at Risk?

America is strong but struggling. We went through a period in the middle and late 1990s when crime fell sharply, employment reached new records, gender and racial equality appeared to be improving, children were healthier than ever, and we were making at least some progress with our considerable environmental problems. Then the September 11, 2001, attacks scratched our confidence and undermined our economy. Globalization and new technology, in the short run at least, have chipped away at our job market. Labor unions have lost much of their power. Our multinational giants seem to be more interested in investing abroad than in America. Median household income increased by about $4,000 per decade in the 1980s and 1990s, but in the decade beginning with the year 2000, median household income actually declined slightly.[147] Economic uncertainty abounds. In a broad sense, should we have doubts about the top-to-bottom fairness of our American system? Certainly we approve of America in the abstract, and we are generally comfortable with our overall prosperity and our expansive freedoms, but we also recognize that many tens of millions are not achieving the American Dream. Let's examine a series of concerns that continue to cast a shadow on America's many free market victories.

Overall Quality of Life

The United States enjoys remarkable prosperity with occasional periods of distress. Despite those bumps, most Americans seem to feel we have built the best life has to offer; and according to a United Nations 2010 report on overall quality of life (based on income, life expectancy, etc.), we are doing well, ranking fourth behind Norway (1st), Australia (2nd), and New Zealand (3rd),[148] but when the scores are adjusted for inequality in health, education, and income the United States ranks 12th in the world in overall human development behind Norway(1st), Australia (2nd), and Sweden (3rd), among others.[149] One score of particular note was America's 37th place ranking in gender equality where limited female roles in politics and relatively poor maternal health reduced the American performance.[150]

> America's 37th place ranking in gender equality.

In general, the United States ranks very well on standard economic measures and not so well on standard social measures. Our 2010 estimated GDP per capita of $47,400 ranked 8th in the world behind smaller, more specialized economies such as Qatar (1st at $145,300 and Norway (5th at $59,100) and well ahead of our chief industrial rivals such as Germany (24th at $35,900) and Japan (28th at $34,200).[151] More instructive perhaps is the fact that the average American worker produces $63,885 of wealth per year (GDP divided by number of people employed), exceeding the productivity of all other nations and ranking second only to Norway (boosted by oil dollars) in productivity per hours worked.[152]

> The average American worker produces $63,885 of wealth per year.

In 2011 life expectancy, on the other hand, the United States ranked 50th at an estimated 78.37 years while Japan, for example, ranked 5th at an estimated 82.25 years.[153] Among the most discouraging U.S. performances is in the category of infant mortality (the probability of dying between birth and age one per 1,000 live births) where 46 nations (e.g., Canada, Cuba, Singapore, South Korea, and Sweden) do a better job of keeping babies alive than we do.[154] Similarly, the United States ranks 42nd globally in child mortality rates (keeping children alive until age 5), down from 29th 20 years ago.[155] With 5 percent of the world's population and nearly 25 percent of the world's jail population, the United States leads the world in producing prisoners. [For more details on imprisonment in the United States and around the world, see Adam Liptak, "Inmate Count in U.S. Dwarfs Other Nations'," *The New York Times,* April 23, 2008, **http://www.nytimes.com/2008/04/23/us/ 23prison.html?incamp=article_popular**]

> The United States leads the world in producing prisoners.

Some trends portend a troublesome future. The United States ranks 6th among developed nations, for example, in the percentage of people who have finished an associate's degree or higher and among 25- to 34-year-olds, the United States ranks 12th.[156] Married couples with children now occupy fewer than one in four U.S. households, half the rate of 1960, and the lowest percentage ever recorded by the census.[157] Social scientists fear that the working poor increasingly reject marriage, choosing to live together and have children out of wedlock. The economically and socially productive institution of marriage with children apparently is becoming a sort of luxury item, available largely to the relatively well off.[158] Thus, the United States is clearly the globe's mightiest economic force, but in some important respects, we have not been successful in achieving a high quality of life for all.

Poverty

After significant improvement in the 1990s, the number of Americans living below the poverty line ($22,050 for a family of four in 2009) has since been steadily rising except for a small decline in 2006. About 44 million Americans (14.3 percent of the population) live in poverty, including 20 percent of children under age 18.[159] A 2010 UNICEF study reports the gap in well-being (material goods, education, and health) between average children in a nation and those at the bottom. That gap is largest in the United States, along with Greece and Italy, among 24 of the world's richest countries. Denmark, Finland, The Netherlands, and Switzerland were at the top of the list in limiting child welfare inequality.[160] The result of the welfare gap is that poor people, as commentator Paul Krugman explained, live in a separate America:

> Living in or near poverty has always been a form of exile, of being cut off from the larger society. . . . To be poor in America today, even more than in the past, is to be an outcast in your own country.[161]

As critics point out, even the poor in America often live quite well compared to the balance of the world, but the suffering is real, nonetheless, and it is especially frustrating for the working poor, whose perilous life on the edge was summarized by *BusinessWeek:*

> [M]ost (of the working poor) labor in a netherworld of maximum insecurity, where one missed bus, one stalled engine, one sick kid means the difference between keeping a job and getting fired, between subsistence and setting off the financial tremors of turned-off telephones and $1,000 emergency-room bills. . . .
>
> At any moment, a boss pressured to pump profits can slash hours, shortchanging a family's grocery budget—or conversely, force employees to work off the clock, wreaking havoc on child care plans. Often, as they get close to putting in enough time to qualify for benefits, many see their schedules cut back. The time it takes to don uniforms, go to the bathroom, or take breaks routinely goes unpaid. Complain, and there is always someone younger, cheaper, and newer to the United States willing to do the work for less.[162]

Historically we have accepted difficulties for a significant share of the population in the belief that they would move up, in time, if they worked hard; but as *BusinessWeek* reports, upward mobility is slower and less likely today than in the past:

> Five of the 10 fastest-growing occupations over the next decade will be of the menial, dead-end variety, including retail clerks, janitors and cashiers.[163]

The result of these conditions is an often harsh life in this astonishingly wealthy nation. We are surprisingly unhealthy, for example. One expert recently asked: Why isn't the richest country in the world also the healthiest?[164] Americans spend about 17 percent of the gross domestic product on health, whereas other advanced nations spend about 8 to 12 percent, but our health outcomes are no better than our peers.[165] [For more data on U.S. poverty, see **www.census.gov/hhes/www/poverty.html**].

> Why isn't the richest country in the world also the healthiest?

Pets or People?

We may not take the best care of our disadvantaged fellow Americans, but we seem to be unstinting in generosity toward our pets. Americans in 2010 were projected to spend nearly $48 billion on their pets, a sum that exceeds the gross domestic product of all but about 75 nations. The American Pet Products Manufacturers Association reports that 42 percent of dogs now sleep in the same bed as their owners and about 44 percent of owners expected in 2011 to give their pet a gift on a special occasion such as a birthday.

Question

Would our money for pets be more wisely spent on impoverished children? Explain.

Sources: "American Express Reports Pet-Related Spending Habits," Luxury PAW's Blog, March 9, 2011 [**http://luxurypaw.com/wordpress/?p=652**]; "America's Spending on Pets Continues to Increase, APPA Says," **WaterGardenNews.com**, February 9, 2010 [**www.watergardennews.com**]; "GDP – Official Exchange Rate 2011 Country Ranks," Countries of the World] [**http://www.photius.com/rankings/economy/gdp_official_exchange_rate_2011_0.html**]; and Diane Brady and Christopher Palmeri, "The Pet Economy," *BusinessWeek*, August 6, 2007, p. 45.

The Gaps

Extravagant wealth, side-by-side with punishing poverty, is perhaps the greatest disappointment and injustice, from the critics' point of view, in the global advance of capitalist principles.

The wealthiest 1 percent of Americans now have a greater collective net worth than the bottom 90 percent.[166] The wealth gap is not surprising when we note that annual incomes for the bottom 90 percent of the population rose only 10 percent in real terms from 1973 to 2010.[167] Indeed, the richest 1 percent of Americans earn 24 percent of the nation's income.[168] Income inequality in the United States is now at its highest level since 1967 when the government first started tracking household income, and that disparity is the largest among Western industrialized countries.[169] Furthermore, the odds of moving up from the lower wealth and income levels are now lower in the United States than in almost all developed nations.[170] We should note, however, that the rich-poor gap has been growing in most industrial nations.[171] These enormous gaps are important not just as a matter of fairness and humanity, experts say, but also because they appear to be accompanied by increased social problems such as greater drug use, mental illness, high school dropouts, and homicides.[172]

Average CEO pay has risen from about 40 times the average worker's pay in the 1970s to about 350 times today.[173] Hedge fund manager John Paulson earned an estimated five billion dollars in 2010 thus beating the four billion dollars he earned in 2007.[174] To put his stunning income in perspective, five billion dollars would allow him, for example, to pay the salaries of all of the teachers in the Chicago public school district for a couple of years and still have nearly one billion left over.[175]

The wage gap is beginning to reach the college-educated class in America. Labor expert Lawrence Katz points out that the top half of college graduates, those with high-end analytical capabilities, continue to do very well, but those in the bottom half who engage in more routine engineering, programming, and the like without developing new ideas or generating new revenue streams have not done well and will be under increasing pressure from global competition and immigration.[176] As columnist Thomas Friedman put it, "Just being an average accountant, lawyer, contractor or assembly-line worker is not the ticket it used to be."[177] With more and more ordinary work being outsourced or performed by a computer, big income gains now go to those who can do something "extra" to add to the bottom line.

PRACTICING ETHICS   Are the Gaps Too Big?

Should we care about the vast and growing gaps in income and wealth in the United States and around the world? Commentator Dan Seligman says we should not be troubled because the number of poor is really all that matters, not the gap between the poor and the rich. Furthermore, the Heritage Foundation/*Wall Street Journal* Index of Economic Freedom suggests that the greater the degree of freedom in an economy, the better off the people are at all income levels, and that the income gap is smallest in countries with the most economic freedom. According to the 2011 Index, the United States is 9th among nations in economic freedom (with Hong Kong 1st, Australia 3rd, Canada 6th, and the United Kingdom 16th). Nonetheless, ethicist William Sundstrom argues, among other things, that fairness does matter, that the income we receive should bear some reasonable relationship to what we "deserve," and that democracy may not be able to tolerate too much social stratification.

Questions

1. *a.* Should income bear some reasonable relationship to what we "deserve?"
    b. How would we identify what we deserve?

c. Based on your personal sense of fairness, is a large and growing gap in income and wealth between the rich and poor an ethical wrong? Explain.

Sources: "Index of Economic Freedom World Rankings" [**http://www.heritage.org/Index/ranking**]; Bryan T. Johnson, Kim R. Holmes, and Melanie Kirkpatrick, "Freedom Is the Surest Path to Prosperity," *The Wall Street Journal,* December 1, 1998, p. A22; Dan Seligman, "Gap-osis," *Forbes,* August 25, 1997, p. 74; and William A. Sundstrom, "The Income Gap," *Issues in Ethics,* Fall 1998, p. 13.

Community

Thus we see that American capitalism, despite its extraordinary success, is criticized for problems of poverty, inequality, and unfairness, among others. Perhaps the more interesting concern, however, is mounting evidence that our lives are increasingly solitary, distant, alone, and unshared. The market is driven by and rewards individual achievement. Could that struggle for success be depriving us of the full satisfaction of our humanity? A 2006 study found that even trivial exposure to money changes our goals and behaviors such that our sense of self-sufficiency is elevated and our social interests may decline,[178] whereas a 2008 study showed that how people spend their money may be just as important in happiness as how much money they have. Specifically, the study demonstrated that spending money on others rather than on oneself produced greater levels of happiness.[179]

> Spending money on others rather than on oneself produced greater levels of happiness.

Whether a product of capitalist impulses or not, we do have increasing evidence of declining social connections. Only 30 percent of Americans, according to a 2008 study, report a close confidant at work, down from nearly 50 percent in 1985, and workers in many other nations are much more likely to have close friends at work than are Americans. American workers report inviting 32 percent of their "close" colleagues to their homes, while Polish and Indian workers report inviting more than double that percentage.[180] More worrisome perhaps are findings from a 2006 study where Americans reported an average of only two "core" confidants in their lives, down from a mean of three in 1985.

> Americans reported only two "core" confidants in their lives.

Furthermore, a quarter of Americans reported that they have no one with whom they can discuss matters of importance, a doubling of that demographic since 1985.[181] Are loneliness, social distance, and declining trust somehow products of our aggressive free market?

Declining Social Capital?

In his now famous book, *Bowling Alone,* Robert Putnam meticulously documented the decline of what he labeled social capital, the community and commitment bonds that seem to emerge in a culture where people regularly interact with one another.[182] Putnam's book explains that virtually every measure of social interaction, from voting to picnics to playing cards, to church attendance, to membership in social clubs fell significantly from roughly 1975 to 2000. The most vivid example was a decline of 40 percent in league bowling from 1980 to 2000 while the total number of bowlers increased by about 10 percent; thus the notion of "bowling alone." Even the tradition of inviting others to visit one's home as dinner guests fell by about 40 percent. Criticism of Putnam's thesis was abundant with many saying he focused too much on "older" activities such as social clubs and not enough on emerging interests such as Internet groups.[183]

Expanding his examination of community trust, Putnam's more recent research found that ethnic diversity appears to lower the level of trust in the community, not only among members of different ethnic groups, but within those groups as well. In diverse communities, people minimize the "hits on them from society" by retreating into private space, often in front of a television. So the more diverse the community, he found, the more people tend to withdraw from social engagement, volunteer less, work less on community projects, and so on.[184] Putnam has argued, however, that diversity is highly desirable and that trust can be restored in the longer term.

In 2010, Thomas Sander and Putnam took another look at *Bowling Alone* and found encouraging evidence that young people in the generation following the 9/11/2001 terrorist attacks on America (particularly those born in the 1980s) have displayed a significantly expanded interest in politics and public affairs. Voting rates have risen, and interest in "keeping up to date with political affairs" is climbing among first-year college students.[185]

That good news was somewhat muted, however, by strong evidence that increasing engagement among young people is confined largely to upper-middle-class white people. Those young products of affluent America, Sander and Putnam say, have steadily deepened their community engagement (going to church more, better connecting to their parents, volunteering) while the less affluent young whites have withdrawn or never undertaken that engagement. Indeed, among those less affluent, young whites, trust in other people has plummeted. That disparity in involvement is not present among young blacks, but the overall engagement gap between whites and blacks is wide.[186]

Sander and Putnam found no convincing evidence that community engagement among adult Americans had risen in recent years, but he notes that they are engaging one another in different ways from the past, principally through social media such as Facebook and Twitter.[187]

Questions

1. Is Putnam correct about (a) declining social capital in America and (b) ethnic diversity as a negative force in community trust and involvement? Explain.

2. Putnam pointed to women in the workplace, commuting, and television as primary culprits in the decline of social capital. A 2001 study found that rising income inequality was an important force in weakening community ties. Explain that finding. See Gene Koretz, "Why Americans Grow Apart," *BusinessWeek,* July 23, 2001, p. 30.

3. American Dan Lawton commenting on his first trip to Africa:

   In Ghana, I have danced, eaten, and spoken with more strangers in six weeks than I would have in America in six years, And this paradox—that despite its material wealth and technological might America is so standoffish and lonely—has been burning a hole in my head.[188]

   a. Do you agree that Americans are "standoffish and lonely"?
   b. If so, do you have any explanation for that condition?
   c. Are many of us simply happier alone? Explain.

PRACTICING ETHICS Technology and Loneliness

Since publishing *Bowling Alone*, Robert Putnam has said we need to develop new kinds of connections when old ones die. Electronic links often are considered part of the problem, but he believes they could also be part of the solution. Indeed, a 2008 survey of American adults found 60 percent saying that new technologies had not affected the closeness of their families and 25 percent said family closeness was actually enhanced by cell phones and on-line communications. On the other hand, a 2009 Pew report found that social networking users are 26 percent less likely than others to turn to their neighbors for companionship. Likewise, some researchers speculate that a 40 percent decline in empathy among today's college students as contrasted with those 20 to 30 years ago may be partially attributable to the ease of tuning out online friendships when we do not feel like responding to others' problems, a tendency that might carry over to offline life. The biggest portion of that empathy decline came after 2000, a time

when online communication ascended precipitously. In his book, *Interpersonal Divide: The Search for Community in a Technological Age*,[189] Iowa State University professor Michael Bugeja argued that excessive dependence on media technologies such as e-mail, cell phones, television, radio, and video games is destroying face-to-face relationships, causing each of us to become increasingly isolated.

Questions

1. In your view, is Bugeja correct? Explain.

2. How might our ethical standards and performances be affected by excessive reliance on media technology?

Sources: Charles M. Blow, "Friends, Neighbors and Facebook," *The New York Times*, June 11, 2010 [http://www.nytimes.com]; Ruth Marcus, "Our Gadgets, Ourselves," *The Washington Post*, June 9, 2010, p. A21; and Donna St. George, "Internet, Cell Phones May Strengthen Family Unit, Study Finds," **washingtonpost.com**, October 20, 2008, p. A07.

Too Much Capitalism? Or Too Little?

Has America placed too much faith in the market and too little in government? Is the alleged decline in community in some sense a product of capitalism itself? Are poverty, inequality, crime, and the Wall Street collapse inevitable by-products of a "selfish, greedy" market? Even some conservatives are concerned:

> "What I'm concerned about is the idolatry of the market," says conservative intellectual William Bennett, a former education secretary and author of *The Book of Virtues*. He worries particularly that the market for popular music and movies with sexual or violent content has a corrosive effect. "Unbridled capitalism . . . may not be a problem for production and for expansion of the economic pie, but it's a problem for human beings. It's a problem for . . . the realm of values and human relationships."[190]

> "Capitalism is more efficient . . . But it is not more fair."

The dilemma, in brief, was expressed by a 20-year-old Cuban student and communist organizer: "Capitalism is more efficient . . . But it is not more fair."[191]

Revolution and Capitalism

At this writing, parts of North Africa and the Middle East are exploding in revolution. New ideas and new governments are emerging. In Egypt, where long-time president Hosni Mubarak was forced from office, the revolutionary fervor was, in part, a reaction to Murbarak's free market reforms that encouraged growth but appeared to benefit only the privileged. Corruption and suffering were routine. Now as ordinary Egyptians seek justice, a new balance between the free market's efficiencies and the social needs of the people may emerge.[192]

In India, the business class is enjoying stunning prosperity and hundreds of millions of Indians have better lives. Despite those successes, even many of the wealthy believe something is seriously amiss. Twenty years after abandoning central planning and embracing capitalism, corruption is rampant and hundreds of millions of Indians continue to endure extreme privation. Strikingly, calorie consumption by the bottom 50 percent of the population has been declining since 1987.[193]

Can robust capitalism be sustained if it produces not just efficiency and growth but also extreme income and wealth gaps, corruption, and injustice? As journalist Fareed Zakaria reminds us, capitalism produces growth, but its powerful dynamism also leads to instability and crashes.[194] Can we tolerate capitalism's collapses and injustices? Can we improve the market through judicious regulation? Or must we look for new answers? Consider some interesting possibilities:

- Pope Benedict XVI has called for a strong international institution to manage the global economy and work for the common, moral good.[195]
- Political economist Dani Rodrik envisions a reinvention of capitalism to address the effects of globalization. He argues for rebalancing markets and their regulatory institutions at the global level rather than the national level as is currently the practice.[196]
- In contrast to the concerns noted above, economist Larry Summers thinks the future may lie in what he calls India's "Mumbai Consensus," a "people-centric" economy focusing not on exports but on increasing consumption and a growing middle class. By 2040 he says we may be talking less about the Washington Consensus (free markets and democracy) and the Beijing Consensus (state capitalism) and more about prosperity from the bottom up.[197]
- Microsoft founder Bill Gates advocates a new, "creative capitalism" where businesses, governments, and nonprofits work together to ease the world's inequities. Companies, Gates argues, should begin creating products and services specifically designed for the needs of the poor.[198]

Short Americans

According to a new study, white and black Americans are shrinking in height relative to Europeans. United States citizens through World War II were the tallest in the world, then American growth stagnated while Europeans spurted forward such that the average non-Hispanic white or black male American is about 5'10" tall as compared with, for example, Danes (6') and Dutch (6'1"). Immigrants and people of Asian or Hispanic ancestry were excluded from the study.

Questions

1. Should we be concerned that we have lost our "lead" in height? Explain.
2. Why have we fallen behind?
3. Does our slow physical growth portend a weakened position for America in the world? Explain.

Sources: John Komlos and Benjamin E. Lauderdale, "Underperformance in Affluence: The Remarkable Relative Decline in U.S. Heights in the Second Half of the 20th Century," *Social Science Quarterly* 88, Issue 2 (June 2007), p. 283; and Joshua Holland, "Are You One of the Shrinking Americans?" *AlterNet*, July 9, 2007 [**http://www.alternet.org/story/56303**].

Questions—Part Five

1. *a.* What do you think of Pope Benedict's call for a strong international institution to regulate the global economy?
   b. Why does Dani Rodrik believe we need a shift from a national to an international balance of free markets and government regulation?
   c. Do you think Rodrik is correct? Explain.
2. *a.* What does William Bennett mean by "the idolatry of the market"?
   b. In what sense do we have a market in "values and human relationships"?
   c. What does Bennett mean about the corrosive effect of popular culture?
   d. Can we have a free market in economic affairs without harming our social values and relationships? Explain.
3. Journalist Lauren Soth said, "Let's challenge the sacred goals of economic growth, greater output of goods and services, greater productivity."[199] How could we have a better life if we were to diminish our attention to those seemingly central requirements?

Internet Exercise

The Global Policy Forum provides a broad overview of the globalization movement. Go to the Forum's "Globalization of Law" page [**http://www.globalpolicy.org/globalization/globalization-of-law.html**]. Explain how globalization is changing international legal systems.

Now turn to the Global Policy Forum's "Movement for Global Justice" page [**http://www.globalpolicy.org/globalization/globalization-of-politics/movement-for-global-justice.html**]. Identify and explain some of Forum's concerns about denial of justice around the globe.

Chapter Questions

1. The gravestone of the late baseball great Jackie Robinson is inscribed with this advice: "A life is not important except in the impact it has on other lives." Will your life be meaningful only if you contribute to the well-being of others? Explain.
2. Commenting in *Newsweek,* economist Robert Samuelson said, "The . . . pervasive problem of capitalist economies is that almost no one fully trusts capitalists."[200]
   a. Do you agree? Why?
   b. Do you think free market capitalism is the best economic system? Explain.
   c. Do you think that multinational companies have more power than national governments? Explain.
3. *a.* In your mature years, do you expect to be as wealthy as your parents, or more so? Explain.
   b. Do you think you deserve to be as wealthy as your parents, or more so, or less so? Explain.
4. As compared with today, would you prefer a bigger U.S. government providing more services to the people, or a smaller government providing fewer services? Explain.
5. *a.* Noted economist Lester Thurow argued that the economic demands of the market are destroying the traditional two-parent, nuclear family. Explain his argument.

 b. Child development authority Benjamin Spock likewise blamed capitalism for the "destruction of the American family," but his reasoning differed from Thurow's:

> The overriding problem is excessive competition and our glorification of it. It may contribute to our rapid technological advancement, but it has done so at a great price. We are taught to be rugged individualists, and we are obsessed with getting ahead. The family gets lost in this intense struggle. In a healthy society, family should come first, community second, and our outside jobs third. In this country, it is the other way around.[201]

 Comment.

 c. If Spock was correct, how did we reach this condition?

6. Scholar Donna Wood points to America's poor showing in Gallup's emotional well-being polls of 150 countries that find the United States 68th in sadness, 75th in anger, 89th in worry, and 145th in stress (150th being the lowest ranking). Wood also points to America's poor showing in health and other measures of social well-being and asks why America scores so poorly on these measures.[202] What do you think?

7. We often read that many college professors actively criticize capitalism and support welfare state principles.

 a. Has that been your experience? Explain.

 b. If that assessment is accurate, how do you account for the leftist inclinations among intellectuals?

8. Should we reduce the government's presence throughout our lives? Consider a couple of possibilities.

 a. Facing severe financial problems, the state of Nevada was thinking of expanding legal prostitution from its current rural areas to the gambling centers, Las Vegas and Reno. Do you think legal prostitution managed by the market but subject to reasonable health and safety regulation would be a good policy for your state or any state? Explain.

 b. The bitter, ongoing debate about same-sex marriage raises the question of whether the state's role in marriage should be eliminated. Explain why the state should or should not be involved in regulating marriage. See "Why Do We Need the State's Permission to Get Married Anyway?" *The Wall Street Journal,* January 14, 2010 [**http://blogs.wsj.com/2010/01/14/why-do-we-need-to-ask-the-state-for-permission-to-get-married-anyway/**].

9. If we are fundamentally selfish, must we embrace capitalism as the most accurate and, therefore, most efficient expression of human nature? Explain.

10. According to *The New York Times,* in 2007 for the first time in American history, more than one in 100 American adults (over 2.3 million Americans) were behind bars. One in 36 Hispanic adults, one in 15 black adults, and one in nine black men between the ages of 20 and 34 were behind bars in 2006. According to FBI data, violent crime rates have fallen by about 25 percent in the past 20 years.[203]

 a. In your opinion, does our free market approach to life produce greater levels of crime than would be the case in a more cooperative economic system? Explain.

 b. Does our justice system favor rich, white people over poor people of color? Explain.

11. *New York Times* columnist Nicholas Kristof wrote what he called a "blunt" and "politically incorrect truth" about global poverty:

    > It's that if the poorest families spent as much money educating their children as they do on wine, cigarettes and prostitutes, their children's children's prospects would be transformed.[204]

    He told about one Congolese family that is eight months behind on its $6 per month rent and is unable to pay for mosquito netting ($6 each) or the $2.50 per month school tuition for each of their three school-age children. But the parents do spend $10 per month on cell phone expenses, and the father does drink several times weekly at a cost of about $1 per night.[205]

    a. What solutions would you suggest to protect children from the ill-advised financial choices of their fathers and mothers?

    b. Do you think poor parental choices are a significant feature of child suffering in the United States? Explain.

    c. Do you think reduced government in the United States would likely lead to increased personal responsibility? Explain.

12. Commentator Thomas Friedman reflects on the Islamic terrorists' hatred for America:

    > Their constant refrain is that America is a country with wealth and power but "no values." The Islamic terrorists think our wealth and power is unrelated to anything in the soul of this country. . . . Of course, what this view of America completely misses is that American power and wealth flow directly from a deep spiritual source—a spirit of respect for the individual, a spirit of tolerance for differences of faith or politics, a respect for freedom of thought as the necessary foundation for all creativity, and a spirit of unity that encompasses all kinds of differences. Only a society with a deep spiritual energy, that welcomes immigrants and worships freedom, could constantly renew itself and its sources of power and wealth.[206]

    a. Do you agree that the "spiritual source" Friedman cites is the foundation for American success? Explain.

    b. Is America without a meaningful "soul"? Explain.

13. Socialist Michael Harrington argued for life "freed of the curse of money:"

    > [A]s long as access to goods and pleasures is rationed according to the possession of money, there is a pervasive venality, an invitation to miserliness and hostility to one's neighbor.[207]

    Should we strive to make more goods and services "free?" Raise the competing arguments.

14. The intellectual Adolph Berle once said, "A day may come when national glory and prestige, perhaps even national safety, are best established by a country's being the most beautiful, the best socially organized, or culturally the most advanced in the world."[208]

    a. Is government intervention necessary to achieving Berle's goal? Explain.

    b. If faced with a choice, would most Americans opt for Berle's model or for a nation preeminent in consumer goods, sports, and general comfort? Explain.

15. Marketing research firm GfK Roper and policy advisor Simon Anholt annually rank the 50 most admired nations globally. Their research shows that we can think of

countries as being either primarily useful (competent, efficient, smart) or primarily decorative (stylish, sexy, attractive) or both.[209]

   a. List some nations that you take to be primarily useful and some that you believe to be primarily decorative. Which do you prefer?

   b. Do you regard the United States as primarily useful or primarily decorative or both? Explain.

16. Benjamin Barber, writing in *The Atlantic,* saw two possible political futures, which he labeled the "forces of Jihad" and the "forces of McWorld":

> The first is a retribalization of large swaths of humankind by war and bloodshed . . . culture is pitted against culture, people against people, tribe against tribe—a Jihad in the name of a hundred narrowly conceived faiths against every kind of interdependence. . . . The second is being borne in on us by the onrush of economic and ecological forces that demand integration and uniformity and that mesmerize the world with fast music, fast computers, and fast food—with MTV, Macintosh, and McDonald's pressing nations into one commercially homogeneous global network: One McWorld tied together by technology, ecology, communications, and commerce.[210]

   a. Does either of these scenarios make sense to you? Explain.

   b. Which would you prefer? Explain.

17. Critics argue that socialism requires a uniformity, a "sameness" that would destroy the individuality Americans prize.

   a. Are Americans notably independent and individualistic? Explain.

   b. Explore the argument that socialism would actually enhance meaningful individualism.

18. Hilda Scott wrote a book to which she affixed the provocative title *Does Socialism Liberate Women?*

   a. Answer her question. Explain.

   b. Are minority oppression and oppression of women inevitable by-products of capitalism? Explain.

19. In Wisconsin, members of the Old Order Amish religion declined to formally educate their children beyond the eighth grade. The U.S. Supreme Court held that their First Amendment right to freedom of religion was violated by the Wisconsin compulsory education statute, which required school attendance until the age of 16. Chief Justice Burger explained:

> They object to the high school, and higher education generally, because the values they teach are in marked variance with Amish values and the Amish way of life; they view secondary school education as an impermissible exposure of their children to a "worldly" influence in conflict with their beliefs. The high school tends to emphasize intellectual and scientific accomplishments, self-distinction, competitiveness, worldly success, and social life with other students. Amish society emphasizes informal learning-through-doing; a life of "goodness," rather than a life of intellect; wisdom, rather than technical knowledge; community welfare, rather than competition; and separation from, rather than integration with, contemporary worldly society.[211]

   a. Have the Amish taken the course we should all follow? Explain.

   b. Could we do so? Explain.

20. Distinguished economist Gary Becker argued for a free market approach to America's immigration difficulties:

> In a market economy, the way to deal with excess demand for a product or service is to raise the price. This reduces the demand and stimulates the supply. I suggest that the United States adopt a similar approach to help solve its immigration problems. Under my proposal, anyone willing to pay a specified price could enter the United States immediately.[212]

Comment.

21. Management scholars Rabindra Kanungo and Jay Conger remark that "'Altruism' is a word rarely associated with the world of business," but they ask, "Does altruism have a place in our business lives? And does it make good economic sense?"[213] Answer their questions.

Notes

1. Francis Fukuyama, "Are We at the End of History?" *Fortune,* January 15, 1990, p. 75.
2. Jia Lynn Yang, Neil Irwin and David Hilzenrath, "Fed Aid in Financial Crisis Went Beyond U.S. Banks to Industry, Foreign Firms," *The Washington Post,* December 2, 2010 [**http://www.washingtonpost.com/wp-dyn/content/article/2010/12/01/AR2010120106870.html**].
3. Ibid.
4. Jim Puzzanghera, "Bailouts Are Shaping Up to Be Cheaper than Expected," *latimes.com,* February 28, 2011 [latimes.com/business/la-fi-bailouts-20110228,0,6792583.story].
5. Michael Powell and Mary Williams Walsh, "A.I.G. to Pay $725 Million in Ohio Case," *The New York Times,* July 16, 2010 [**http://www.nytimes.com/**].
6. E. Scott Reckard, "Countrywide Agrees to Pay $600 Million to Settle Shareholder Lawsuits," **latimes.com**, August 2, 2010 [**latimes.com/business/la-fi-countrywide-20100803,0,5383116.story**].
7. Jean Eaglesham, "U.S. Sets 50 Bank Probes," *The Wall Street Journal,* November 17, 2010 [**http://online.wsj.com/**].
8. David Wessel, "In Turmoil, Capitalism in U.S. Sets New Course," *The Wall Street Journal,* September 20–21, 2008, p. A1.
9. Andy Sullivan, "White House to Paint Grim Fiscal Picture: Source," *Reuters,* January 31, 2011 [**http://www.reuters.com/**].
10. Jack Ewing, "Stop Picking on Bankers, JPMorgan Chief Says," DealBook, *The New York Times,* January 27, 2011 [**http://dealbook.nytimes.com/**].
11. Jia Lynn Yang, Neil Irwin, and David S. Hilzenrath, "Fed Aid in Financial Crisis Went Beyond U.S. Banks to Industry, Foreign Firms," *The Washington Post,* December 2, 2010 [**http://www.washingtonpost.com/**].
12. Richard Doak, "Can Capitalism Survive? Sorry, It Already Died," *Des Moines Register,* June 21, 2009, p. 10P.
13. Thomas M. Hoenig, "Too Big to Succeed," *The New York Times,* December 1, 2010 [**http://www.nytimes.com/**].
14. Fareed Zakaria, *The Post-American World* (New York: W.W. Norton, 2008).
15. Jonathan Rosenberg, "A World in which the US Is No Longer No. 1," *Christian Science Monitor,* June 13, 2008 [**http://features.csmonitor.com/books/2008/06/13/a-world-in-which-the-us-is-no-longer-no-1**].

16. Fareed Zakaria, The Rise of the Rest, *Newsweek,* May 12, 2008 [**http://www.newsweek.com/**].

17. Ibid.

18. Thomas L. Friedman, "Do Believe the Hype," *The New York Times,* November 2, 2010 [**http://www.nytimes.com/**].

19. BBC World Service Poll, "Wide Dissatisfaction with Capitalism—Twenty Years after Fall of Berlin Wall," World Public Opinion.org [**http://www.worldpublicopinion.org/pipa/pdf/nov09/BBC_BerlinWall_Nov09_rpt.pdf**].

20. Jagdish Bhagwati, "Does the Free Market Corrode Moral Character? To the Contrary," *The New Republic,* November 5, 2008, p. 24.

21. Editorial, "Cultural Imperialism"? No," *Omaha World-Herald,* November 24, 2001, p. 6B.

22. Steven Kull, "Muslims and America: Internalizing the Clash of Civilizations," World Public Opinion.org, April 28, 2010 [**http://www.worldpublicopinion.org/**].

23. Sara Reef, "Poll Results on Muslim-Western Relations Advocate Action, and Interaction," *The Huffington Post* [**http://www.huffingtonpost.com/sara-reef/poll-results-on-muslimwes_b_804639.html**].

24. "Muslims Positive about Globalization, Trade," World Public Opinion.org, August 27, 2008 [**http://www.worldpublicopinion.org/**].

25. David Brooks, "The Genteel Nation," *The New York Times,* September 9, 2010 [**http://www.nytimes.com/**].

26. Gregory Rodriguez, "The American Dream: Is It Slipping Away?" *latimes.com,* September 27, 2010 [**http://www.latimes.com/**].

27. Michael Corkery, "Capitalism, Love and Mr. Moore," Deal Journal, *The Wall Street Journal,* September 23, 2009, p. C3.

28. Ibid.

29. Benjamin R. Barber, *Consumed: How Markets Corrupt Children, Infantilize Adults, and Swallow Citizens Whole* (New York: W.W. Norton & Company, 2007).

30. Rod Dreher, "Big Business Can Be as Dangerous a Threat as Big Government," *The Waterloo/Cedar Falls Courier,* July 23, 2007, p. A6.

31. Ibid.

32. Steve Yetiv, "Reports of America's Decline Are Greatly Exaggerated," *The Christian Science Monitor,* March 12, 2009 [**http://www.csmonitor.com/2009/0312/p09s02-coop.html**].

33. David Brooks, "The Commercial Republic," *The New York Times,* March 17, 2009 [**http://www.nytimes.com/**].

34. Ibid.

35. Arthur Brooks, "America's New Culture War: Free Enterprise vs. Government Control," *The Washington Post,* May 23, 2010, p. B01.

36. Anatole Kaletsky, "Capitalism 4.0," *OECD Observer,* No. 279, May 2010 [**http://www.oecdobserver.org/**].

37. Anatole Kaletsky, *Capitalism 4.0: The Birth of a New Economy* (New York: Public Affairs/Perseus, 2010).

38. Robert Skidelsky, "For a New World, New Economics," *New Statesman,* August 30, 2010 [**http://www.newstatesman.com/**].

39. Ian Bremmer, *The End of the Free Market* (New York: Portfolio/Penguin, 2010).

40. David Brooks, "The Larger Struggle," *The New York Times,* June 14, 2010 [**http://www.nytimes.com/**].

41. Timothy Garton Ash, "A New World Disorder," *latimes.com,* January 28, 2011 [**latimes.com/news/opinion/**].

42. Roger Cohen, "Toilets and Cellphones," *The New York Times,* May 24, 2010 [**http://www.nytimes.com/**].

43. Scott Peterson, "Iran's Ahmadinejad: Capitalism Is Dead," *The Christian Science Monitor,* November 9, 2009 [**http://www.csmonitor.com/**].

44. Robert Skidelsky, "Life After Capitalism," *Project Syndicate,* January 19, 2011 [**http://www.skidelskyr.com/site/article/life-after-capitalism/**].

45. "Zogby Poll: *Atlas Shrugged* by Ayn Rand Read by 8.1 Percent," *PRWeb,* October 17, 2007 [**http://www.prweb.com/releases/1969/12/prweb561836.htm?tag=poll**].

46. Stephen Moore, "*Atlas Shrugged:* From Fiction to Fact in 52 Years," *The Wall Street Journal,* January 9, 2009, p. W11.

47. Sandy Banks, "When Money Talks to Kids," *latimes.com,* April 17, 2010 [**http://www.latimes.com/**].

48. See "Should Drivers Who Pay More Get a Faster Lane?" *Parade,* October 19, 2008, p. 22.

49. "Nevada Candidate: Let People Pay to Legally Go 90 MPH," *The Des Moines Register,* September 5, 2010, p. 2A.

50. Editorial, "Tag—You're Illegal," *Los Angeles Times,* October 28, 2006 [**http://www.latimes.com/news/opinion/la-ed-tag28oct28,0,59791.story?coll=la=opinion-leftrail**].

51. Raymond Flandez, "Firms Tackle Government Chores," *The Wall Street Journal,* June 17, 2008, p. B7.

52. Bobby White, "Cash-Strapped Cities Try Private Guards Over Police," *The Wall Street Journal,* April 21, 2009, p. A4.

53. Ibid.

54. Laura Meckler, "Kidney Shortage Inspires a Radical Idea: Organ Sales," *The Wall Street Journal,* November 13, 2007, p. A1.

55. Stephanie Coontz, "Taking Marriage Private," *The New York Times,* November 26, 2006 [**http://www.nytimes.com/2007/11/26/opinion/26coontz.html**].

56. Peter Diamandis, "Space: The Final Frontier of Profit?" *The Wall Street Journal,* February 13–14, 2010, p. W3.

57. Associated Press, "Plans Would Cut Federal Role in Mortgages," *The Des Moines Register,* January 12, 2011, p. 16A.

58. Laura Meckler, "Making Public Highways Private," *The Wall Street Journal,* April 18, 2006, p. A4.

59. Emily Thornton, "Roads to Riches," *BusinessWeek,* May 7, 2007, p. 50.

60. Steve Schmidt, "Toll Road Operator Files for Chapter 11," *San Diego Union-Tribune,* March 23, 2010 [**http://www.signonsandiego.com/news/2010/mar/23/south-bay-expressway-builders-file-chapter-11**].

61. Ibid.

62. Thornton, "Roads to Riches," p. 50.

63. Susan Saulny, "Long a Driver's Curse, Chicago Parking Gets Worse," *The New York Times,* May 30, 2009 [**http://www.nytimes.com/**].

64. Daniel Michaels and Amy Merrick, "Debt Threatens Takeover of Midway Airport," *The Wall Street Journal,* April 2, 2009, p. B1.

65. Associated Press, "Toll Lanes Let Drivers Skip Daily Congestion," *Des Moines Register,* December 31, 2008, p. 2A.

66. Lisa Rein, "Off-Peak Laundry? Pricing Power by the Hour," *Washington Post,* December 12, 2007, p. A01.

67. Danielle Douglas, "Pepco Readies New Technology," *The Washington Post,* September 13, 2010, p. A11.

68. Charles Mahtesian, "Revenue in the Rough," *Governing,* October 1997, pp. 42–44.

69. Editorial, "City-Owned Golf Courses Cannot Be Sacred Cows," *Waterloo/Cedar Falls Courier,* July 13, 2003, p. C7.

70. Charles Murray, "Why Charter Schools Fail the Test," *The New York Times,* May 5, 2010 [**http://www.nytimes.com**].

71. Lisa Guernsey, "Rewards for Students Under a Microscope," *The New York Times,* March 2, 2009 [**http://www.nytimes.com/**].

72. Steven Pearlstein, "Despite Scandal, for-Profit Education Offers Valuable Model," *The Washington Post,* August 11, 2010, p. A12.

73. Editorial, "Who Profits? Who Learns?," *The New York Times,* July 28, 2010 [**http://www.nytimes.com**].

74. Editorial, "For-Profit Colleges Need Federal Oversight," *The Des Moines Register,* February 28, 2011, p. 9A.

75. Ibid.

76. Sergei Subbotin, "Government Approves $33 Bln Privatization Plan for 2011-2013," *RIA Novosti,* February 22, 2011 [**http://en.rian.ru/business/20101117/161379825.html**].

77. Vikas Bajaj, "As India Sells Assets, Political Tensions Rise," *The New York Times,* February 25, 2010 [**http://www.nytimes.com/**].

78. Jim Yardley, "India Tries Using Cash Bonuses to Slow Birthrates," *The New York Times,* August 21, 2010 [**http://www.nytimes.com/**].

79. Leslie Wayne, "Politics and the Financial Crisis Slow the Drive to Privatize," *The New York Times,* June 5, 2009 [**http://www.nytimes.com/**].

80. Leslie Williams Hale, "Poll: State Receives No Bids for Alligator Alley Lease," *naplesnews.com,* May 18, 2009 [**http://www.naplesnews.com/**].

81. Richard A. Oppel, Jr., "Private Prisons Found to Offer Little in Savings," *The New York Times,* May 18, 2011 [**http://www.nytimes.com/**].

82. Sara Miller Llana, "Cuba Move to Cut 500,000 Government Jobs Is Biggest Change in Decades," *The Christian Science Monitor,* September 14, 2010 [**http://www.csmonitor.com/**].

83. Phil Keating, "Cuba Capitalism? Baby Steps," *FoxNews.com,* February 11, 2011 [**http://liveshots.blogs.foxnews.com/2011/02/11/cuba-capitalism-baby-steps/**].

84. Keith Bradsher, "Investors Seek Asian Options to Costly China," *The New York Times,* June 18, 2008 [**http://www.nytimes.com**].

85. Ibid.

86. Henry Myers, "His Statues Topple, His Shadow Persists: Marx Can't Be Ignored," *The Wall Street Journal,* November 25, 1991, p. A1.

87. Michael J. Jordan, "After the Berlin Wall, Nostalgia for Communism Creeps Back," *The Christian Science Monitor,* November 8, 2009 [**http://www.csmonitor.com/2009/1109/p11s01-woeu.html**].

88. Elements of this list are drawn from Agnes Heller and Ferenc Feher, "Does Socialism Have a Future?" *Dissent,* Summer 1989, p. 371.

89. Associated Press, "Chavez in China Touts 'New World Order,'" *The Wall Street Journal,* April 8, 2009 [**http://online.wsj.com/article/SB123917904370300585.html**].

90. Bremmer, *The End of the Free Market,* 2010.

91. Hiroko Tabuchi, "China Replaced Japan in 2010 as No. 2 Economy," *The New York Times,* February 13, 2011 [**http://www.nytimes.com**].

92. Michael Wines, "China Fortifies State Businesses to Fuel Growth," *The New York Times,* August 29, 2010 [**http://www.nytimes.com**].

93. Ibid.

94. Andrew Brown and Jason Dean, "Business Sours on China," *The Wall Street Journal,* March 17, 2010 [**http://online.wsj.com/**].

95. Ibid.

96. Staff Writers, "China to Have 200 Million Vehicles by 2020: State Media," *Space Daily,* September 6, 2010 [**http://www.spacedaily.com/reports/China_to_have_200_million_vehicles_by_2020_state_media_999.html**].

97. Associated Press, "China Plans Middle-Class Boom by 2020," *Waterloo/Cedar Falls Courier,* December 26, 2007, p. C4.

98. Ibid.

99. *CIA World Factbook 2011,* reported in "GDP—Per Capita (PPP) 2011 Country Ranks, by Rank," Countries of the World, [**http://www.photius.com/rankings/economy/gdp_per_capita_2011_0.html**].

100. Andrew Batson, "China Narrows Inequity Between the Rich and Poor," *The Wall Street Journal,* February 3, 2010, p. A13.

101. Vikas Bajaj, "Bangladesh, with Low Pay, Moves in on China," *The New York Times,* July 16, 2010 [**http://www.nytimes.com/**].

102. Michael Kan, "Google CEO: China's Internet Censorship Will Fail in Time," *IDG News Service,* November 4, 2010 [**http://www.computerworld.com/**].

103. "Google: Eric Schmidt Hints at China Ambitions," *BBC News Business,* January 27, 2011 [**http://www.bbc.co.uk/news/business-12303735**].

104. Associated Press, "China Rejects Criticism by Human Rights Council," *Des Moines Register,* February 12, 2009, p. 2A.

105. Joseph Kahn, "China's Leader Closes Door to Reform," *The New York Times,* October 16, 2007 [**http://www.nytimes.com/2007/10/16/world/asia/16china.html**].

106. Maureen Fan, "China to Allow Land Leasing, Transfer," *washingtonpost.com,* October 20, 2008, p. A10.

107. Geoffrey A. Fowler, Sky Canaves, and Juliet Ye, "Chinese Seek a Day in Court," *The Wall Street Journal,* July 1, 2008, p. A12.

108. Melanie Stetson Freeman, "In Moscow, Capitalism Now in Full Fashion," *The Christian Science Monitor,* February 21, 2008 [**http://www.csmonitor.com/2008/0221/p13s01-woeu.html**].

109. Jason Bush, "Russia: How Long Can the Fun Last?" *BusinessWeek,* December 18, 2006, p. 50.

110. Stephen Sestanovich, "Russia by the Numbers," *The Wall Street Journal,* December 17, 2007, p. A21.

111. Ben Aris, "Russia Kicks Off Privatization with VTB SPO," *Russia & India Report,* February 17, 2011[**http://indrus.in/articles/2011/02/17/russia_kicks_off_privatization_with_vtb_spo_12178.html**].

112. Philip P. Pan, "Medvedev Calls for Economic Changes," *Washington Post,* November 13, 2009 [**http://www.washingtonpost.com/**].

113. Aris, "Russia Kicks Off Privatization," February 17, 2011.

114. Bremmer, *The End of the Free Market,* 2010.

115. Andrew E. Kramer, "Russia Seeks Foreign Investment to Fill Budget Gap," *The New York Times,* January 24, 2011 [**http://www.nytimes.com/**].

116. Fred Hiatt, "Can Reset Push Russia toward Democracy?" *Washington Post,* July 18, 2010 [**http://www.washingtonpost.com/**].

117. Stephen Kotkin, "Now Comes the Tough Part in Russia," *The New York Times,* March 2, 2008 [**http://www.nytimes.com/2008/03/02/business/worldbusiness/02shelf.html?th&emc=th**].

118. Dani Rodrik, "Will China Rule the World?" *Project Syndicate,* January 12, 2010 [**http://www.project-syndicate.org/commentary/rodrik39/English**].

119. Central Intelligence Agency, "Country Comparison: Life Expectancy at Birth," *The World Factbook 2011* [**https://www.cia.gov/library/publications/the-world-factbook/**].

120. Katrin Bennhold, "In Sweden, the Men Can Have It All," *The New York Times,* June 9, 2010 [**http://www.nytimes.com/**].

121. Ibid.

122. "World Tax Rates 2010-2011," Tax Rates.cc [**http://www.taxrates.cc/**].

123. Roger Cohen "The Nordic Option," *The New York Times,* September 17, 2007 [**http://select.nytimes.com/2007/09/17/opinion/17cohen.html?_r=1&oref=slogin**].

124. Ezra Klein, "Who Is Left Uninsured by the Health-Care Reform Bill?" *Washington Post,* March 22, 2010 [**http://voices.washingtonpost.com/ezra-klein/2010/03/who_is_left_uninsured_by_the_h.html**].

125. Cohen, "The Nordic Option," September 17, 2007.

126. Palash Ghosh, "Sweden Moving Away from Social Welfare Economic Model," *ibtimes.com,* October 27, 2010 [**http://www.ibtimes.com/**].

127. Jeffrey Sachs, "The Social Welfare State, Beyond Ideology," *Scientific American* 295, Issue 5 (November 2006), p. 42.

128. Ibid.

129. Ibid.

130. "GDP—Official Exchange Rate 2011 Country Ranks, by Rank," *CIA World Factbook 2011,* [**http://www.photius.com/rankings/economy/gdp_official_exchange_rate_2011_0.html**].

131. Roger Cohen, "For Europe, A Moment to Ponder," *The New York Times,* March 25, 2007, sec. 4, p. 1.

132. Steven Hill, "Europe Is the New World, Not the Old," *Rorotoko,* March 31, 2010 [**http://www.rorotoko.com/**].

133. Associated Press, "U.K. Toughens Rules for People to Get Welfare," *Des Moines Register,* November 12, 2010, p. 2A.

134. Rachel Donadio, "Europe's Young Grow Agitated over Future Prospects," *The New York Times,* January 1, 2011 [**http://www.nytimes.com/**].

135. Associated Press, "Multicultural Society Has Been Failure, Merkel Says," *Des Moines Register,* October 18, 2010, p. 8A.

136. "France's Sarkozy: Multiculturalism Has Failed," *CBN News,* February 11, 2011 [**http://www.cbn.com/cbnnews/world/2011/February/Frances-Sarkozy-Multiculturalism-Has-Failed/**].

137. Jeremy Rifkin, "Why the European Dream Is Worth Saving," *SpiegelOnline,* July 28, 2005 [**http://www.spiegel.de/international/0,1518,druck-366940,00.html**].

138. Adrian Karatnycky quoting Soros in "The Merits of the Market, the Perils of 'Market Fundamentalism,'" *The Wall Street Journal,* January 9, 2001, p. A20.

139. Ibid.

140. Joanne Barkan, "Not Yet in Paradise, But . . . ," *Dissent,* Spring 1989, pp. 147, 150.

141. NPR Staff, "A Push for More Women on Corporate Boards," *National Public Radio,* February 24, 2011 [**http://www.npr.org/2011/02/24/133875785/a-push-for-more-women-on-corporate-boards**].

142. Jim Chairusmi, "Winning with Smaller Pockets," *Wall Street Journal,* October 18, 2004, p. R2.

143. Juliann Neher, "Warren Buffett Tells ABC Rich People Should Pay Higher Taxes," *Bloomberg,* November 22, 2010 [**http://www.bloomberg.com/**].

144. Michael Shermer, "Life Has Never Been So Good for Our Species," *latimes.com,* April 30, 2010 [**latimes.com/news/opinion/la-oe-shermer-20100430,0,2676540.story**].

145. David Gergen, "Cheer Up, America," *Parade,* April 11, 2010, p. 26.

146. "American Charities Raise Close to $1-Billion for Haiti, Chronicle Tally Finds," *The Chronicle of Philanthropy,* March 16, 2010 [**http://philanthropy.com/article/American-Charities-Raise-Close/64684/**].

147. Harold Meyerson, "Corporate America, Paving a Downward Slide," *Washington Post,* January 5, 2011 [**http://www.washingtonpost.com/**].

148. "United Nations Human Development Index 2010 Rankings," Human Development Reports-United Nations Development Programme [**http://hdr.undp.org/en/statistics/**].

149. United Nations, "The Inequality-Adjusted HDI (2010), Human Development Reports [**http://hdr.undp.org/en/statistics/ihdi/**].

150. Ibid.

151. Central Intelligence Agency, *The World Factbook 2011* [**https://www.cia.gov/library/publications/the-world-factbook/**].

152. Associated Press, "Americans Work Longer, Produce More Than Rest of World," *Waterloo/Cedar Falls Courier,* September 3, 2007, p. C3.

153. Central Intelligence Agency, *The World Factbook 2011* [**https://www.cia.gov/library/publications/the-world-factbook**].

154. Ibid.

155. Noam N. Levey, "Child Mortality Rates Dropping, Study Finds, but U.S. Lags," *latimes.com,* May 24, 2010 [**latimes.com/news/health/la-na-child-mortality-20100524,0,5411983.story**].

156. "Countries with the Most College Graduates," *Huffpost College,* August 21, 2010 [**http://www.huffingtonpost.com/2010/07/22/**].

157. Blaine Harden, "Numbers Drop for the Married with Children," *Washington Post,* March 4, 2007, p. A03.

158. Ibid.

159. Erik Eckholm, "Recession Raises Poverty Rate to a 15-Year High," *The New York Times,* September 16, 2010 [**http://www.nytimes.com**].

160. UNICEF Innocenti Research Centre, Innocenti Report Card 9, November 2010 [**http://www.unicef-irc.org/publications/pdf/rc9_eng.pdf**].

161. Paul Krugman, "Poverty Is Poison," *The New York Times,* February 18, 2008 [**http://www.nytimes.com/2008/02/18/opinion/18krugman.html?em**].

162. Michelle Conlin and Aaron Bernstein, "Working . . . and Poor," *BusinessWeek Online,* May 31, 2004 [**http://www.businessweek.com/print/magazine/content/04_22/b3885 . . .**].

163. Ibid.

164. Carla K. Johnson and Mike Stobbe, "Study Says We Aren't as Healthy as British," *The Des Moines Register,* May 3, 2006, p. 7A.

165. OECD, "How Does the United States Compare?" *OECD Health Data 2011* [**http://www.oecd.org/dataoecd/46/2/38980580.pdf**].

166. Nicholas D. Kristof, "Equality, a True Soul Food," *The New York Times,* January 1, 2011 [**http://www.nytimes.com**].

167. Edward Luce, "The Crisis of Middle-Class America," *FT.com,* July 30, 2010 [**http://www.ft.com/**].

168. Editorial, "The Rich Get Richer," *latimes.com,* September 10, 2010 [**latimes.com/news/opinion/la-ed-taxes-20100910,0,110208.story**].

169. Associated Press, "Income Gap Hits Record High," *Waterloo/Cedar Falls Courier,* September 28, 2010, p. B6.

170. Luce, "The Crisis of Middle-Class America," July 30, 2010.

171. Associated Press, "Rich-Poor Gap Found to Grow Around Globe," *Des Moines Register,* October 22, 2008, p. 4A.

172. Kristof, "Equality, a True Soul Food," January 1, 2011.

173. Robert Reich, "Confessions of a Class Worrier," *Des Moines Register,* August 18, 2010, p. 13A.

174. Svea Herbst-Bayliss, "John Paulson's $5 Billion Payout Shocks, Raise (sic) Questions," *Reuters/,* January 28, 2011 [**http://www.huffingtonpost.com/**].

175. Chicago Public Schools, "Proposed FY2011 Budget FAQs," November 1, 2010 [**http://www.cps.edu/About_CPS/Financial_information/Pages/ProposedFY2011BudgetFAXs.aspx**].

176. Thomas L. Friedman, "The New Untouchables," *The New York Times,* October 20, 2008 [**http://www.nytimes.com/**].

177. Ibid.

178. Kathleen Vohs, Nicole L. Mead, and Miranda R. Goode, "The Psychological Consequences of Money," *Science* 314, no. 5802 (November 17, 2006), p. 1154.

179. Elizabeth W. Dunn, Lara B. Aknin, Michael I. Norton, "Spending Money on Others Promotes Happiness," *Science* 319, no. 5870 (March 21, 2008), p. 1687.

180. "Do Co-Workers Engage or Estrange after Hours," University of Michigan [**http://www. bus. umich.edu/NewsRoom/ArticleDisplay.asp?news_id=11931**].

181. Shankar Vedantam, "Social Isolation Growing in U.S., Study Says," *Washington Post,* June 23, 2006, p. A03.

182. Robert Putnam, *Bowling Alone* (New York: Simon& Schuster, 2000).

183. For a critique of Putnam's declining social capital research, see Garry Wills, "Putnam's America," *The American Prospect,* November 30, 2002 [**http://www.prospect.org/cs/articles?article= putnams_america**].

184. For a commentary on Putnam's diversity research, see Gregory Rodriguez, "Diversity May Not Be the Answer," *Los Angeles Times,* August 13, 2007 [**http://www.latimes.com/news/ opinion/la-oe-rodriguez13aug13,0,3984088.column?coll=la-tot-opinion&track=ntottext**].

185. Thomas H. Sander and Robert D. Putnam, "Still Bowling Alone? The Post-9/11 Split," 21 *Journal of Democracy* 11, no. 1 (January 2010), p. 9.

186. Ibid.

187. Ibid.

188. Dan Lawton, "In Ghana, No One Is a Stranger for Long," *Christian Science Monitor,* November 9, 2009 [**http://www.csmonitor.com/2009/1109/p18s01-hfes.html**].

189. New York: Oxford University Press, 2005.

190. David Wessel and John Harwood, "Capitalism Is Giddy with Triumph; Is It Possible to Overdo It?" *The Wall Street Journal,* May 14, 1998, p. A1.

191. Associated Press, "A Threat to Castro," *Des Moines Register,* August 30, 1994, p. 8A.

192. Yaroslav Trofimov and Matt Bradley, "Cairo Revolution Finds New Target: Free Market," *The Wall Street Journal,* March 31, 2011, p. A10.

193. Paul Beckett, "In India, Doubts Gather over Rising Giant's Course," *The Wall Street Journal,* March 30, 2011, p. A1.

194. Fareed Zakaria, "The Capitalist Manifesto: Greed Is Good," *Newsweek,* June 22, 2009 [**http:// www.newsweek.com/**].

195. Rachel Donadio and Laurie Goodstein, "Pope Urges Forming New World Economic Order to Work for the 'Common Good,'" *The New York Times,* July 8, 2009 [**http://www.nytimes. com/2009/07/08/world/europe/08pope.html**].

196. Dani Rodrik, "Coming Soon: Capitalism 3.0," Project Syndicate, February 11, 2009 [**http:// www.project-syndicate.org/commentary/rodrik28/English**].

197. Ben Schott, "The Mumbai Consensus," *The New York Times,* November 2, 2010 [**http:// schott.blogs.nytimes.com/2010/11/02/the-mumbai-consensus/**].

198. Robert A. Guth, "Bill Gates Issues Call for Kinder Capitalism," *The Wall Street Journal,* January 24, 2008, p. A1.

199. Lauren Soth, "Seek Better Care of People and Earth," *Des Moines Register,* April 24, 1993, p. 5A.

200. Robert Samuelson, "Economics Made Easy," *Newsweek,* November 27, 1989, p. 64.

201. Carla McClain, "Dr. Spock: Restore the Family," *Des Moines Register,* November 7, 1993, p. 3E.

202. Donna Wood, "Don't Give Up on Chance at Happiness," *Waterloo/Cedar Falls Courier,* October 24, 2010, p. F1.

203. Adam Liptak, "1 in 100 U.S. Adults Behind Bars, New Study Says," *The New York Times,* February 28, 2008 [**http://www.nytimes.com/2008/02/28/us/28cnd-prison.html?em&ex= 1204434000&en=f278697addfa4b1**].

204. Nicholas D. Kristof, "Moonshine or the Kids?" *The New York Times,* May 22, 2010 [**http://www.nytimes.com/**].

205. Ibid.

206. Thomas L. Friedman, "Foreign Affairs; Eastern Middle School," *The New York Times,* October 2, 2001. [**http://www.nytimes.com**]

207. Michael Harrington, "Why We Need Socialism in America," *Dissent,* May—June 1970, pp. 240, 286.

208. Adolph Berle, *Power* (New York: Harcourt Brace Jovanovich, 1969), pp. 258–59.

209. John Nylander, "Sweden 10th 'Most Admired Country Globally,'"*swedishwire.com,* October 18, 2010 [**http://www.swedishwisre.com/nordic/6755-sweden-10th-most-admired-country-globally**].

210. Benjamin Barber, "Jihad v. McWorld," *The Atlantic* 269, no. 3 (March 1992), p. 53.

211. *Wisconsin v. Yoder,* 406 U.S. 205, 210–11 (1972).

212. Gary Becker, "Why Not Let Immigrants Pay for Speedy Entry?" *BusinessWeek,* March 2, 1987, p. 20.

213. Rabindra Kanungo and Jay Conger, "Promoting Altruism as a Corporate Goal," *The Academy of Management Executive* 8, no. 3 (August 1993), p. 37.

Business Ethics

At the end of this chapter, students will be able to:

1. Describe some of the ethics issues associated with America's recent banking and finance crisis.

2. Discuss America's current moral climate.

3. Discuss the leading ethical decision-making theories.

4. Distinguish between teleological and deontological ethical systems.

5. Distinguish utilitarianism and formalism.

6. Describe Kohlberg's theory of moral development.

7. Describe some of the forces that encourage unethical behavior in the workplace.

8. Explain the general purpose of ethics codes in the workplace.

9. Explain the general requirements of the Foreign Corrupt Practices Act.

10. Discuss some of the risks and rewards of whistle blowing.

Part One—Introduction to Ethics

Can we count on self-regulation (ethics) as a useful means of controlling managerial/corporate behavior? Put another way, can we count on the free market as discussed in Chapter 1, along with managerial and corporate ethics, to guide business conduct such that government regulation (law) can be significantly reduced?

This chapter will examine the ethical climate of business and the role of ethics in business decision making. Our goal here is not to teach morality but to sensitize the reader to the vital role honor plays in building a sound career and a responsible life.

PRACTICING ETHICS — Baseball Bats Encourage Subprime Loan Approvals

Maggie Hardiman cringed as she heard the salesmen knocking the sides of desks with a baseball bat as they walked through her office. Bang! Bang "'You cut my [expletive] deal!'" she recalls one man yelling at her. "'You can't do that.'" Bang! The bat whacked the top of her desk.[1]

Hardiman was an appraiser for New Century Financial in 2004 and 2005. Her job was to weed out bad mortgage applications. She says most of the applications she reviewed had problems, but if she turned them down, "all hell would break loose" and "her bosses often overruled her and found another appraiser to sign off on it." She says the pressure to approve loans was immense: "The stress in the place was ungodly. It was like selling your soul." Hardiman says she was fired for refusing to approve weak loans.[2]

New Century was the nation's leading specialized subprime mortgage lender in 2006 with $51.6 billion in loans. To achieve that volume, New Century and others often sold subprime mortgages with "teaser" adjustable rates to Americans with poor credit. Then when housing values began to fall and adjustable rates went up, many new homeowners were unable to make their payments. New Century filed for bankruptcy protection in 2007, laid off over 5,000 employees, and admitted it underreported the number of bad loans it had made.[3]

Question

Do you think the pressure to produce—to approve weak loan applications in this instance—that Maggie Hardiman says she faced, is routine in American business practice, or was this episode an exception to the norm? Explain.

The Financial Crisis: A Corporate Scandal? Corporate misconduct has been a staple of the news in this 21st century. The nation's (and the world's) ongoing financial crisis, the most threatening since the Great Depression, appears to have been the product of a variety of forces including inadequate government regulation, dangerously easy credit, overextended borrowers, real estate speculation, greed, and a collapsed housing market (for more, see Chapter 8). The facts may never be fully clear, but the International Monetary Fund has estimated that worldwide losses attributable to the U.S. residential and commercial real estate market collapse at about one trillion dollars or $142 per person in the entire world.[4] The larger financial recession that accompanied the real estate collapse resulted in additional trillions in losses in the United States alone.[5] The portion of those losses attributable to fraudulent and unethical transactions produced, in part, by the kind of pressure that Maggie Hardiman faced will never be known.

Of course, no law is broken when lenders merely show poor judgment or borrowers are unable to pay, but the subprime collapse allegedly involved intentionally fraudulent schemes. Both federal and state authorities have been aggressively pursuing that wrongdoing and some progress has been achieved. Goldman Sachs, while not acknowledging wrongdoing, in 2010 agreed to pay $550 million to settle Securities and Exchange Commission civil charges that it had misled investors by failing to disclose that another investor, hedge fund Paulson & Co., had allegedly played a big role in selecting the mortgages and other loans in an investment portfolio labeled ABACUS2007-AC1, and that Paulson was betting the portfolio would decline in value.[6] J.P. Morgan Chase & Co. has agreed to pay $153.6 million to settle federal civil charges similar to those involving Goldman Sachs. Lee B. Farkas, former chairman of a large Florida private mortgage company, was sentenced in 2011 to 30 years in prison for his alleged role in masterminding a nearly $3 billion mortgage fraud. At this writing the biggest mortgage service companies (Bank of America, Wells Fargo, and others) reportedly are nearing an agreement

> ## "The whole damn industry lost its moral moorings."

with the federal government and the 50 state attorneys general to pay as much as $60 billion to settle claims involving a variety of allegedly fraudulent mortgage practices.

Clearly, Wall Street's reputation has been dangerously undermined. Nearly 70 percent of Americans say "most" of those on Wall Street would be willing to break the law to make "a lot of money" if they felt they could get away with it.[7] Warren Buffet's long-time investments partner, Charlie Munger, was particularly condemnatory in his assessment of Wall Street: "The whole damn industry lost its moral moorings."[8]

"Underwater?" Walk Away

How should homeowners respond to the financial meltdown? University of Arizona Law School professor Brent White has argued that home owners who are "underwater" on their mortgage payments (owe more than the house is worth) should walk away from those payments even if they can afford to pay. He claims that doing so is not an immoral act. About 15 million homeowners are believed to be underwater. Walking away would save thousands of dollars that homeowners have no prospect of recovering in the near future. They can put that money to more productive use elsewhere, he argues, and the penalties for defaulting are modest since the defaulter's credit scores are likely to recover within a couple of years if other payments are maintained. White thinks the imbalance in power between the banks and the borrowers means the system is inherently unfair thus nullifying any immorality claim directed at defaulting borrowers. In any case, mortgage holders who default and lose their property are simply absorbing the penalty they and the lender agreed on in advance: Surrender the property if payment is not completed. Furthermore, businesses quite commonly default on projects if the expected payoff has collapsed.

Critics see these strategic defaults on home mortgages as breaches of promise that will erode trust, produce higher interest rates, and lead to a kind of moral contagion where the stigma attaching to promise breaching will decline throughout society. More specifically, the voluntary failure to pay, the critics say, debases the character of the borrower and the harm spills over on to innocent neighbors since the default likely depreciates the value of their property as well.

Questions

1. Do you think that "underwater" home mortgage holders commit a moral wrong if they decline to make payments when they have the means to do so? Explain.
2. Sometimes those who engage in strategic default are labeled "free riders." Explain that criticism.
3. Some borrowers say they don't feel badly about defaulting because the banking industry brought on the problem by making loans to poor credit risks. Do you agree with that reasoning? Explain.

Sources: Kenneth Harney, "Professor Advises Underwater Homeowners to Walk Away from Mortgages," *Los Angeles Times,* November 29, 2009 [**http://articles.latimes.com/**]; Gail Marksjarvis, "Personal Finance: Vacancies Leading to Ethical Crisis?" *Arizona Daily Sun,* October 10, 2010 [**http://azdailysun.com/**]; and David Streitfeld, "Owners Stop Paying Mortgages, and Stop Fretting," *The New York Times,* May 31, 2010 [**http://www.nytimes.com/**].

A Pattern of Abuse   The extent of criminal and unethical behavior in the mortgage meltdown will be clearer over time, but dubious lending practices are part of a recurring pattern in recent decades of corporations contorting ethical and legal standards. The subprime scandal is reminiscent of the savings and loan crisis of the 1980s when $150 billion evaporated, in part because of criminal behavior. More recently the corporate greed of the Enron era has played out on worldwide televisions as some of the great titans of American commerce have been shuffled off to prison. Tyco Chief Executive Officer Dennis Kozlowski is infamous for his $2 million birthday bash for his wife on Sardinia and his $6,000 shower curtain; a lifestyle allegedly paid for, in good part, with looted corporate money. Adelphia CEO John Rigas allegedly treated the company as his "personal piggy bank to fund dozens of vacation homes, the Buffalo Sabres hockey team" and a private golf course.[9] Most astonishing was Bernard Madoff's colossal Ponzi scheme that stole as much as $65 billion before Madoff was caught and sent to prison in 2009 on a sentence of 150 years. Even Martha Stewart, that paragon of propriety in the home, spent five months in federal prison for lying to the government regarding insider trading allegations. [For a comprehensive archive of the Enron story, see **http://archive.wn.com/2007/12/23/1400/enronfiles**]

His $6,000 shower curtain.

Even Martha Stewart spent five months in federal prison.

Of course, we should not condemn the American business community based on the misconduct of some. The problems are serious, but former General Electric CEO Jack Welch and his wife Suzy remind us that the business community is the source of much of America's greatness:

> Business is a huge source of vitality in the world and a noble enterprise. Thriving, decent companies are everywhere, and they should be celebrated. They create jobs and opportunities, provide revenue for government, and are the foundation of a free and democratic society. . . .[10]

Ethics Survey

We can see that executive wrongdoing has been a significant problem in recent years, but what about questionable employee behavior? Should some commonplace worker practices be considered unethical? The Ethics Officer Association and the Ethical Leadership Group sampled a cross-section of workers at large companies nationwide. How would you respond?

1. "Is it wrong to use company e-mail for personal reasons?"
2. "Is it wrong to play computer games on office equipment during the workday?"
3. "Is it OK to take a $100 holiday food basket?"
4. "Due to on-the-job pressure, have you ever abused or lied about sick days?"

Source: "The Wall Street Journal Workplace-Ethics Quiz," *The Wall Street Journal,* October 21, 1999, p. B1.

America's Moral Climate

Perhaps more than ever, Americans are questioning the nation's moral health. Spectacular corporate corruption as noted above, steroid use by professional athletes, an economy seemingly permanently tilted toward the rich, government officials paying more attention to reelection than to the general welfare, sexual abuse of children by clerics and teachers, and so on cause us to question our decency as a society. For the first time in the history of Gallup's Honesty and Ethics of Professions poll, a majority of Americans, 55 percent in the 2009 poll, say the honesty and ethical standards of members of Congress are low or very low.[11] Fairly or not, the behavior of young people seems to be a particular source of concern. A 2008 survey of nearly 30,000 high school students, reporting on their behavior in the previous year, found that

- 64 percent had cheated on a test
- 42 percent lied to save money
- 30 percent had stolen something from a store.[12]

Fifty-nine percent of high school students in a 2006 survey agreed that, "In the real world, successful people do what they have to do to win, even if others consider it cheating" (65 percent males, 54 percent females), while 42 percent believe that "A person has to lie or cheat sometimes in order to succeed" (50 percent males, 33 percent females).[13]

Sociologist David Callahan's book *The Cheating Culture: Why More Americans Are Doing Wrong to Get Ahead* argues that we are a society in moral decline.[14] The result of this winner-take-all ethos, Callahan thinks, is a nation increasingly falling into two groups: a "winning class" who cheated their way to the top and an "anxious class" who fear falling behind if they too do not cheat.[15]

Do you think Callahan is correct? Is America in moral decline? In fact, the discouraging news is accompanied by important evidence of improving behavior, particularly among young people. Serious violent crime by people under 25 has fallen more than 60 percent since 1994, pregnancy and abortion for girls under age 18 declined by approximately one-third from the mid-1990s, drug use is down among young people, and youth volunteer work is booming.[16] [For the Josephson Institute of Ethics, see **http://www.josephsoninstitute.org**]

Sex or Cell Phone?

Fourteen percent of cell phone users admit to having interrupted sex to answer their cell phones. A 2005 survey of more than 3,000 people, 15 to 35 years of age in 15 nations, found Germans and Spaniards (22 percent) most likely to answer the phone, with Italians least likely at 7 percent and Americans in the middle at 15 percent. Almost half of those responding worldwide thought their cell phones said as much about them as a car, while one-third of the Americans surveyed felt the same way. Advertising giant BBDO commissioned the survey. Christine Hannis, BBDO head of communications, explained, "People can't bear to miss a call. Getting so many calls . . . fulfills a fundamental insecurity."

Sources: Bill Hoffman, "Cell Users Put Sex on Hold," *New York Post* Online Edition; and "BBDO Releases Cell Phones and Sex Acts Reports," [**http://adage.com/news.cms?newsId-44753 or http://www.furl.net/item.jsp?id=2605994**].

College Students

The distinguished Duke University MBA program announced in May 2007 that nearly 10 percent (34 students) of its class of 2008 had been caught cheating on a take-home final examination.[17] The students were punished, some by expulsion or suspension. The scandal should not have been completely surprising since cheating seems to be common among MBA students nationwide. A large, 2006 survey found 56 percent of graduate students in business admitted to cheating at least once in the previous year, the largest percentage of any discipline surveyed.[18] Among nonbusiness graduate students, 47 percent admitted cheating.[19]

Ninety-five percent of 3,000 undergraduate business students polled in 31 universities admit they cheated in high school or college, although only 1 to 2 percent admit having done so "frequently."[20] Professor Joseph Petrick, coauthor of the study, attributes the cheating to "the academic welfare mentality. Business school students feel morally entitled to get what they need to do well in business."[21] Academic ethics expert Donald McCabe's surveys find about 75 percent of college students cheating on either a test or a paper at some point, with business majors, fraternity and sorority members, and male students being among those most likely to cheat.[22] The cheating evidence is discouraging, but in recent years many MBA programs and their students are showing increasing interest in ethics issues. Harvard MBA students, for example, have received a great deal of attention for their voluntary campaign to sign "The MBA Oath," a pledge that Harvard MBA's will act ethically, "serve the greater good," and avoid advancing their own "narrow ambitions" at the expense of others.[23]

[For a video of *The Daily Show's* treatment of the MBA Oath, see **http://www.thedailyshow.com/watch/wed-august-12-2009/mba-ethics-oath**] [For the "Top 10 Cheating Scandals in College History," see **http://collegetimes.us/top-10-cheating-scandals-in-history/**]

Questions

1. If you were to sign an ethics oath as a student, do you think your behavior as a student and thereafter would improve? Explain.

2. Do you think ethics instruction, religious commitment, or higher natural intelligence would reduce academic cheating? Explain. See James M. Bloodgood, William H. Turnley, and Peter Mudrack, "The Influence of Ethics Instruction, Religiosity, and Intelligence on Cheating Behavior," *The Journal of Business Ethics* 82, no. 3 (2008), p. 557.

3. Professor Robert A. Prentice argues: "Those who choose to attend business school on the assumption that an MBA will help them change jobs, make more money, and therefore be happier are very likely misinformed." Do you agree? Explain. See Robert A. Prentice, "What's an MBA Worth in Terms of Happiness?" *The Chronicle of Higher Education,* November 8, 2009 [**http://chronicle.com/article/Whats-an-MBA-Worth-in/49056/**].

Changing Values?

Contemporary cheating behaviors offer a stark and unflattering contrast to the views of a 1928 Princeton University freshman writing home:

> Father, you suggest that the greatest benefit from college is to be found in . . . habits of intellectual diligence and application. I am nonetheless putting my chief emphasis on the study of right and wrong.[24]

UCLA's annual survey of college first-year students provides further evidence of changing values among young people. Responding to the 2009 survey, 78 percent of first-year students valued wealth as a goal, but only 48 percent sought a "meaningful philosophy of life." That result is essentially a reversal of the 1971 survey when 37 percent of freshmen identified being "very well off financially" as an essential or very important objective, and 73 percent felt the same about "developing a meaningful philosophy of life."[25] The college experience, however, seems to strengthen some important ethical values. A 2007 UCLA study found that interest in developing a meaningful philosophy of life rose from 41.2 percent for freshmen in 2004 to 55.4 percent when the same students were surveyed as juniors in 2007.[26] Broadly, as compared with their freshmen attitudes, college juniors are more likely to be engaged in a spiritual quest and more likely to be "caring" persons.[27] On the other hand, a 2007 study based on the Narcissistic Personality Inventory of college students nationwide, responding to such statements as "I think I am a special person," concluded that the average college student today is about 30 percent more self-absorbed than the average student in 1982.[28] One of the study leaders, Jean Twenge of San Diego State University, remarked:

> "We need to stop endlessly repeating, 'you're special.'"

"We need to stop endlessly repeating 'you're special,' . . . Kids are self-centered enough already."[29] Similarly, a 2010 study found today's college students about 40 percent lower in empathy than students of 20 to 30 years ago.[30] [The UCLA freshmen survey Web site: **http://www.heri.ucla.edu/cirpoverview.php**] [Professor Twenge's Web site: **http://www.jeantwenge.com/**]

Questions

1. Do you think you and your college friends are excessively narcissistic and insufficiently empathetic? Explain.

2. Why might empathy be declining among college students? [To measure your own level of empathy and to compare it with the average empathy level of college students, see **http://umichisr.qualtrics.com/SE/?SID=SV_bCvraMmZBCcov52&SVID**].

My Cheating Isn't Really Cheating

An accounting professor at a respected Midwestern university assigned a take-home problem to his 64 undergraduate students, two-thirds of whom were business majors, telling them to work alone and not to make use of computer/online resources in any way. He was unaware that another professor had posted the answer key on the Web. After reviewing the students' papers he knew that many students had violated his rules and the university's honor code by using the online Web site, collaborating with other students, or both. He decided to throw out the test results and examine the cheating episode with the students. He administered a voluntary questionnaire that was completed by all 64 students. By checking the university's records of students who accessed the Web site and by some students' admissions of wrongdoing on the questionnaire, he was able to identify at least 47 students who had cheated. All but two of the 47 "cheaters" wrote answers on the questionnaire indicating that they knew their behavior was wrong or could be considered wrong. The questionnaire then examined the "cheaters'" explanations or rationales for their cheating.

Question

All 47 of the cheating students tried to minimize, justify, or rationalize their behavior. Can you deduce what explanations/rationalizations the students offered for their cheating?

Source: Jeffrey B. Kaufmann, Tim West, Sue Pickard Ravenscroft, and Charles B. Shrader, "Ethical Distancing: Rationalizing Violations of Organizational Norms," *Business & Professional Ethics Journal 24*, no. 3 (Fall 2005), p. 101.

Part Two—Analyzing Ethical Dilemmas

Ethics Theories

We have looked in a preliminary way at some business ethics issues and at America's moral climate. Now we turn to an overview of the primary philosophical theories employed in examining ethics problems. Ethics, of course, involves judgments as to good and bad, right and wrong, and what ought to be. Business ethics refers to the measurement of business behavior based on standards of right and wrong, rather than relying entirely on principles of accounting and management. (In this discussion, the word morals will be used interchangeably with the word ethics. Distinctions certainly are drawn between the two, but those distinctions are not vital for our purposes.)

Finding and following the moral course is not easy for any of us, but the difficulty may be particularly acute for the businessperson. The pressure to produce is intense, and the temptation to cheat may be great. Although the law provides very useful guides for minimum comportment, clear moral answers frequently do not exist. Therefore, when the businessperson faces a difficult decision, a common tactic is simply to do what he or she takes to be correct at any given moment. Indeed, in one survey of ethical views in business, 50 percent of the respondents indicated that the word ethical meant "what my feelings tell me is right."[31]

Philosophers have provided powerful intellectual support for that approach. Existentialists, led by the famed Jean-Paul Sartre, believe standards of conduct cannot be objectively discovered or rationally justified via ethical theory and reasoning. No actions are inherently right or wrong. Thus, each person may reach his or her own choice about ethical principles. Personal freedom is the defining characteristic of every person. Each of us is, therefore, fully and exclusively responsible for our own moral decisions.[32] That view finds its roots in the notion that humans are only what we will ourselves to be. If God does not exist, there can be no human nature, because there is no one to conceive that nature.

Existence precedes essence. In Sartre's famous interpretation, existence precedes essence. First humans exist; then we individually define what we are—our essence. Therefore, each of us is free, with no rules to turn to for guidance. Just as we all choose our own natures, so must we choose our own ethical precepts. Moral responsibility belongs to each of us individually.

Responsibility

Indian spiritual, political, and civil rights leader, Mahatma Gandhi, viewed moral responsibility quite differently from Sartre. Gandhi's view: "All humanity is one undivided and indivisible family, and each one of us is responsible for the misdeeds of all the others."[33] Whose view makes more sense to you?

Universal Truths?

Have we then no rules or universal standards by which to distinguish right from wrong? Have we no absolutes? Philosophers seek to provide guidance beyond the uncertainties of ethical relativism. We will survey two ethical perspectives, teleology and deontology, which form the core of the philosophical approach to ethical analysis. Before proceeding to those theories, we will note the important role of religion in ethics and take a brief look at two additional formulations—libertarianism and virtue ethics—that have been increasingly influential in contemporary moral analysis.

1. **Religion.** Judeo–Christian beliefs, Islam, Confucianism, Buddhism, and other faiths are powerful ethical voices in contemporary life. They often feature efforts such as the Golden Rule to build absolute and universal standards. Scholarly studies indicate that most American managers believe in the Golden Rule and take it to be their most meaningful moral guidepost. From a religious point of view, the deity's laws are absolutes that must shape the whole of one's life, including work. Faith, rather than reason, intuition, or secular knowledge, provides the foundation for a moral life built on religion.

Not surprisingly, Pope Benedict XVI has often advocated a greater role for religious principles in business practice. In a 2009 encyclical, the Pope acknowledged the usefulness of profit "as a means towards an end," but he claimed that the blind pursuit of profit has "wreaked havoc" on the world economy.[34] [For worldwide coverage of ethics issues, see **http://www.bbc. co.uk/ethics**]

Religion at Work

A 2004 Gallup Poll reported that 84 percent of American adults believe religion is either "very" or "fairly" important in their lives. Business scholars and reporters note a renewed interest in religion and spirituality in the workplace. In his book, *Spirituality, Inc.,* Professor Lake Lambert III points to ServiceMaster as an example of an American company built and operating on explicitly Christian principles such that every employee—from exterminator to executive—is regarded in an equal way. The emerging spirituality movement often, however, does not involve religion at all. In many cases, employees and managers view spirituality at work as part of their own broader search for meaning in life to be accomplished in part by embracing the whole person; not merely the intellectual or manual product of the person. They think that business must acknowledge the soul to maximize performance.

2. **Libertarianism.** Contemporary philosopher Robert Nozick (1938–2002) built an ethical theory rooted in personal liberty. For him, morality coincided with the maximization of personal freedom. Justice and fairness, right and wrong are measured not by equality of results (such as wealth) for all, but from ensuring equal opportunity for all to engage in informed choices about their own welfare. Hence Nozick took essentially a free market stance toward ethics.

3. **Virtue ethics.** In recent years, an increasing number of philosophers have argued that the key to good ethics lies not in rules, rights, and responsibilities but in the classic notion of character. As Plato and Aristotle argued, our attention should be given to strategies for encouraging desirable character traits such as honesty, fairness, compassion, and generosity. Aristotle believed that virtue could be taught much as any other skill. Virtue ethics applauds the person who is motivated to do the right thing and who cultivates that motivation in daily conduct. A part of the argument is that such persons are more morally reliable than those who simply follow the rules but fail to inspect, strengthen, and preserve their own personal virtues. [For an overview of virtue ethics, see **http://plato.stanford.edu/entries/ethics-virtue/**]

Teleology or Deontology—An Overview

Religion, libertarianism, and virtue provide crucial ethical lessons. Philosophers have further clarified ethical theory by defining two broad analytical systems, *teleology* and *deontology,* that capture much of our current understanding about how to engage in careful ethical analysis.

Teleological ethical systems (often referred to as *consequentialist ethical systems*) are concerned with the consequences, the results, of an act rather than the act itself. A teleological view of life involves ends, goals, and the ultimate good. Duty and obligation are subordinated to the production of what is good or desirable. For the teleologist/consequentialist, the end is primary and that end or result is the measure of the ethical quality of a decision or act.

To the deontologist, on the other hand, principle is primary and consequence is secondary or even irrelevant. Maximizing right rather than good is the deontological standard. The deontologist might well refuse to lie, as a matter of principle, even if lying would maximize good.

Deontology, derived from the Greek word meaning *duty,* is directed toward what ought to be, toward what is right. Similarly, deontology considers motives. For example, why a crime was committed may be more important than the actual consequences of the crime. Relationships among people are important from a deontological perspective primarily because they create duties. A father may be bound by duty to save his son from a burning building, rather than saving another person who could do more total good for society.

The distinction here is critical. Are we to guide our behavior by rational evaluation of the consequences of our acts, or according to duty and principle—that which ought to be? Let's take a closer look at *utilitarianism,* the principal teleological ethical theory, and *formalism,* the principal deontological ethical theory.

Teleology

Utilitarianism   In reaching an ethical decision, good is to be weighed against evil. A decision that maximizes the ratio of good over evil for all those concerned is the ethical course. Jeremy Bentham (1748–1832) and John Stuart Mill (1806–1873) were the chief intellectual forces in the development of utilitarianism. Their views and those of other utilitarian philosophers were not entirely consistent. As a result, at least two branches of utilitarianism have developed. According to *act-utilitarianism,* our goal is to identify the consequences of a particular act to determine whether it is right or wrong. *Rule-utilitarianism* requires us to follow those rules that generate the greatest value for society. Thus the rule-utilitarian may be forced to shun a particular act that would result in greater immediate good (punishing a guilty person whose constitutional rights have been violated) in favor of upholding a broader rule that results in the greater total good over time (maintaining constitutional principles by freeing the guilty person). In sum, the principle to be followed for the utilitarian is the greatest good for the greatest number. [For an extensive database exploring utilitarianism, see **http://www.hedweb.com/philsoph/utillink.htm**]

Deontology

Formalism   The German philosopher Immanuel Kant (1724–1804) developed perhaps the most persuasive and fully articulated vision of ethics as measured not by consequences (teleology) but by the rightness of rules. In this formalistic view of ethics, the rightness of an act depends little (or, in Kant's view, not at all) on the results of the act. Kant believed in the key moral concept of "the good will." The moral person is a person of goodwill, and that person renders ethical decisions based on what is right, regardless of the consequences of the decision. Moral worth springs from one's decision to discharge one's duty. Thus the student who refuses to cheat on exams is morally worthy if his or her decision springs from duty, but morally unworthy if the decision is merely one born of self-interest, such as fear of being caught.

How does the person of goodwill know what is right? Here Kant propounded the *categorical imperative,* the notion that every person should act on only those principles that he or she, as a rational person, would prescribe as universal laws to be applied to the whole of humankind. A moral rule is "categorical" rather than "hypothetical" in that its prescriptive force is independent of its consequences. The rule guides us independent of the ends we seek. Kant believed that every rational creature can act according to his or her categorical imperative because all such persons have "autonomous, self-legislating wills" that permit them to formulate and act on their own systems of rules. To Kant, what is right for one is right for all, and each of us can discover that "right" by exercising our rational faculties.

Questions

1. Fifty-year-old Wesley Autry, waiting with his two young daughters in January 2007 at a New York City subway station, saw a man collapse and fall off the passenger platform into the space between the train rails. The headlight of a train appeared. Mr. Autry immediately jumped on top of the fallen man holding him down while the train passed over them, inches above Autry's head. Asked later why he jumped to the rescue, Autry said: "I did what I felt was right."[35] What form of ethical reasoning did Autry seem to employ in making his courageous decision?

2. British priest Tim Jones caused a big stir by telling his congregation in 2009 that shoplifting is sometimes morally permissible for desperate people. In a sermon, Jones said that shoplifting can be justified when a person is in real need, is not greedy and takes only what is necessary to get by. Later Jones said: "The point I'm making is that when we shut down every socially acceptable avenue for people in need, then the only avenue left is the socially unacceptable one."[36]

   a. Was Jones arguing from a teleological/consequentialist or a deontological/formalist point of view? Explain.

   b. Do you agree with Jones? Explain.

3. Lance Armstrong, the great cyclist and cancer survivor, has been accused of using doping methods to enhance his performance. Journalist Monte Poole wrote that he hopes Armstrong is never caught, even if he did cheat. Poole took that position because of Armstrong's great contribution as an advocate for cancer research and an inspiration for those with cancer:

   > . . . Armstrong, 38, is the global face of cancer survival. His every appearance, anywhere, gives faith to patients. No matter how much I love sports, this would seem to have a little more lasting value.

   See Monte Poole, "If Armstrong's a Cheat, Here's Hoping He's Never Caught," *The Des Moines Register,* July 31, 2010, p. 9B.

   a. Would you characterize Poole's reasoning as formalist or consequentialist? Explain.

   b. Do you agree with Poole? Explain.

Using Ethical Reasoning: Two Cases

Obviously, ethical theory does not provide magical answers to life's most difficult questions. Those theories are useful, however, in identifying and sorting the issues that lead to better decision making. Apply those theories to the Toyota and Malden Mills cases that follow, as you think about when layoffs are ethical.

Are Layoffs Unethical? Case One—Toyota

Despite its highly publicized product defect problems (see Chapters 3 and 7), Toyota claims to have continued its half-century-old policy of not laying off permanent employees. When Toyota halted production in some of its plants in 2008, the 4,500 idled workers were kept on with full pay and benefits at a cost estimated at more than $50 million.

Toyota executive Norm Bafunno said the retention decision was easy because the company used the economic slowdown as an opportunity to retrain its team members. Bafunno said Toyota used a shared sacrifice approach:

> During these times, we suspended all overtime, we suspended all variable compensation (bonuses), we suspended pay raises, and in addition, for our senior leadership team . . . base pay was reduced . . . everyone needs to sacrifice together.

As Latondra Newton, general manager of Toyota's Team Member Development Center in Erlanger, Kentucky said: "We're not just keeping people on the payroll because we're nice. At the end of all this, our hope is that we'll end up with a more skilled North American workforce."

Despite its protective policies, Toyota has laid off thousands of temporary workers and in 2010, its Fremont, California plant was shut down leaving 4,700 workers without jobs while affecting another 25,000 jobs among suppliers. Soon thereafter, Toyota and Tesla announced plans for a partnership to reopen the plant and build electric cars. Tesla thinks the project may create 1,000 or more jobs.

Questions

1. Do you share Toyota's vision that all workers should sacrifice in order to avoid layoffs for permanent workers?
2. If so, are you a "socialist"?
3. If not, are you selfish?
4. Broadly, is shared sacrifice a moral wrong? Explain.

Sources: Norm Bafunno, "2010 Management Briefing Seminar," August 2, 2010 [**http://pressroom.toyota.com/pr/tms/2010-management-briefing-seminar-165965.aspx**]; Lindsay Chappell, "Toyota Idles Factories but Can't Lay Anybody Off," *Workforce Management*, August 18, 2008 [**http://www.workforce.com/section/00/article/25/71/62.php**]; and KTVU.com, "Tesla Wants NUMMI Operational by 2012," May 20, 2010 [**http://www.ktvu.com/news/23625639/detail.html**].

Are Layoffs Unethical? Case Two (Part I)—Aaron Feuerstein and Malden Mills

Fabric manufacturer Malden Mills of Lowell, Massachusetts, provided 3,100 high-paid manufacturing jobs in the Boston area when a 1995 fire destroyed most of the plant. The next morning Aaron Feuerstein, CEO of the family-controlled mill, announced that the business would be rebuilt and all employees would retain their jobs. Feuerstein said that keeping all of the workers through the rebuilding process was "the right thing to do and there's a moral imperative to do it, irrespective of the consequences." Apparently, Feuerstein was significantly influenced by his Jewish heritage. In his youth, Feuerstein reportedly memorized in Hebrew the Leviticus passage: "You are not permitted to oppress the workingman because he is poor and needy."

The new plant was designed to expand production of the company's patented and very successful Polartec fabric. Following the fire, makeshift production lines were developed in warehouses and about 85 percent of the employees returned to work with the remaining 400 workers or so remaining idle but paid. The new plant, machinery, and business losses cost Feuerstein some $300 million, much of which was covered by insurance. Feuerstein was convinced that the big investment would pay in the long run and since he had a highly successful, patent-protected product and since the company was family-owned and thus under no immediate pressure to perform, he felt he could afford to do what his long-time family investment in the community and workers seemed to require. Professor Michael Useem, commenting on Feuerstein's commitment to his workers, said that the idea had appeal: "The thinking is: employees can be seen as an ultimate competitive advantage. If you treat them well, they'll pay you back in really hard work later on."

Questions

1. Aaron Feuerstein became something of an overnight national hero by protecting his workers. Feuerstein said, "It was the right thing to do and there's a moral imperative to do it, irrespective of the consequences."

    a. Was Feuerstein employing utilitarian or formalist reasoning? Explain.

    b. In your view, was he correct to say that the consequences, in this instance, did not matter? Explain.

2. Commenting on Feuerstein's approach to his employees' needs, Wharton School professor Michael Useem said, "The thinking is: employees can be seen as an ultimate competitive advantage. If you treat them well, they'll pay you back in really hard work later on."

    a. Was Useem expressing formalist or utilitarian reasoning?

    b. In a 1986 pastoral letter, the U.S. Catholic bishops argued that "every economic decision and institution must be judged in light of whether it protects or undermines the dignity of the human person."[37] Does the thinking summarized by Useem undermine that dignity and as such require rejection under either utilitarian or formalist reasoning? Explain.

3. If you were a successful entrepreneur with the flexibility of Aaron Feuerstein, would you operate your business like an extended family? Explain.

Source: Richard Lorant, Associated Press, *The Chicago Tribune,* December 10, 1996, p. 8, and Mary McGrory, "Tale of Two Bankruptcies," *Pittsburgh Post-Gazette,* December 22, 2001, p. A15.

 [For a film treatment of corporate downsizing/layoffs, see "The Company Men" trailer at **http://www.youtube.com/watch?v=xa5qg7cB1ZQ**]

Are Layoffs Unethical? Case Two (Part 2)—Aaron Feuerstein, Malden Mills, and Bankruptcy

In November 2001, Malden Mills was forced to enter Chapter 11 bankruptcy proceedings (see Chapter 15) for the purpose of reorganizing its finances under court protection. At the time, Malden Mills was bearing a $140 million debt load. Lenders demanded the bankruptcy action as a condition for extending an additional $20 million to keep the company afloat. In late 2003, Malden Mills emerged from bankruptcy. Creditors controlled the board of directors with Aaron Feuerstein occupying the family's one seat. Malden's precarious financial position was the product of a variety of forces: Customers were lost during the rebuilding after the fire, cheaper fleece substitutes entered the market, the company took on substantial debt in rebuilding and in keeping on its employees following the fire, and the company probably overbuilt following the fire. As a result, the Malden Mills workforce shrunk to 1,200 employees. Then in 2007, Malden Mills was once again forced into bankruptcy and was purchased by Chrysalis Capital partners, a private-equity firm that renamed the company Polartec LLC. Aaron Feuerstein's association with the company ended with the sale.

Questions

1. *The Wall Street Journal* raised the question, "Are layoffs moral?"[38]
   a. Should we establish a universal, formalist rule forbidding layoffs of all hard-working, competent employees, or should we rely on utilitarian reasoning, libertarian thought, virtue theory, or religious beliefs to answer that question? Explain.
   b. Is morality irrelevant to the question of when layoffs are necessary? Explain.
2. Do you think it would be accurate and fair to say that Feuerstein's ethical choice to protect his employees led to the decline of his business? Explain.
3. Did Feuerstein make an error in judgment in relying on an absolute principle—that is, the protection of his workers at all costs? Explain.
4. How might Feuerstein's workers have benefited by being laid off immediately following the fire?
5. John MacKenzie, in a letter to *The New York Times,* said he had a duty to help Aaron Feuerstein and Malden Mills: "Of course I have an ethical obligation to buy from Malden Mills if I have a choice and if my purchase can make a difference. It would reward Mr. Feuerstein for what he has done and what he is trying to do, and the system needs more of that."[39] Do you have a duty to buy only from the most ethically responsible sellers? Explain.

PRACTICING ETHICS   Career and Family

Parents are often torn between family and career considerations. Sometimes the stress of contemporary life, often including job and child care conflicts, leads to tragic consequences. Each year a small number of mothers and fathers simply forget to remove their babies from their rear-facing car seats. On warm days, the result can be the loss of that child. The following story explains one such tragic moment.

Miles Harrison dressed his 21-month-old son, Chase, put sunscreen on him, and strapped him into his car seat, intending to drop Chase off at day care. On the July 8, 2008, trip, Harrison stopped at the dry cleaner, leaving Chase in the GMC Yukon, and later made 13 cell phone calls while driving. Harrison forgot to stop at Chase's Ashton, Virginia, day care and proceeded to his work site leaving Chase in his car seat where he spent nine hours on a 90-degree day, eventually dying of heat stroke. Harrison was subsequently charged with involuntary manslaughter, but he was found not guilty by the trial judge who concluded that no crime had occurred since Harrison's conduct did not conform to the state's legal standard of "negligence so gross, wanton and culpable as to show a callous disregard for human life." According to trial accounts, Harrison was a good father and a diligent businessperson.

An average of 37 children in the United States die from hyperthermia each year in cars. Janette Fannell, founder of a small nonprofit, Kids and Cars, says these deaths are the result of ordinary memory error, but controversial radio host and psychological counselor, Dr. Laura Schlessinger, attributes the deaths to selfish behavior. Schlessinger says the parents are often "pillars of the community." She goes on to say:

These are the busy, self-involved folks always in a rush, for whom even dropping kids off at a day-care center instead of tending to the little ones themselves was too difficult an assignment. . . . It can happen only when parenting and family are not the highest priorities. It can happen only when parents spend their time focused on maximizing their own personal fulfillment at the expense—and very existence—of their children.

Questions

1. Do you think our two-income, two-career lives and our ambitious pursuit of personal and professional interests are putting our babies at risk? Explain.

2. Are your career and family goals ethically compatible? Explain.

Sources: "Children 'Forgotten' in Overheated Cars," Dr. Laura's Blog, July 29, 2008 [http://www.drlaurablog.com/]; Tom Jackman, "On Stand, Man Tells of Son's Death in Car," *Washington Post,* December 17, 2008 [http://www.washingtonpost.com/]; and Gene

Weingarten, "Fatal Distraction: Forgetting a Child in the Backseat of a Car Is a Horrifying Mistake. Is It a Crime?" *Washington Post,* March 8, 2009, p. W08.

AFTERWORD

According to an Associated Press study of a 10-year period beginning in the mid-1990s, about 340 children died of heat exhaustion while trapped in cars. Charges were filed in about half of the cases, with over 80 percent of those resulting in convictions or guilty pleas. Jail time was imposed in about 50 percent of the cases with a median sentence for parents of about 54 months. Mothers and fathers are charged at about the same rates, but moms are 26 percent more likely to be jailed, and their median sentences, according to the study, are two years longer than those of dads.[40]

Part Three—Managerial Misconduct?

Corporate Ethical Climate

Given the subprime mortgage crisis, Enron and similar scandals, and Wall Street's generous pay and bonuses even as the nation suffers through a recession, we should not be surprised that public attitudes toward big business are significantly unfavorable. A 2009 survey by the Edelman public relations firm found only 30 percent of Americans agreeing that the reputation of large global businesses is good.[41] In Gallup's 2010 poll of confidence in major institutions only 19 percent of Americans expressed a "great deal" or "quite a lot" of confidence in big business. Banks were little better at 23 percent, but confidence in small business registered a more robust 66 percent. For some perspective, we should note that Congress ranked last among the 16 institutions surveyed by Gallup with only 11 percent of Americans expressing a great deal or quite a lot of confidence.[42] And on a more encouraging note, Edelman found that trust in big business and government did rise slightly from 2009 to 2010, although trust in banks in the United States fell significantly during that time period.[43]

Unfortunately, considerable evidence supports Americans' skepticism about big business behavior. For example, KPMG's 2008/2009 survey of 5,000 employees across a number of American industries found 74 percent of those employees having "personally seen" or having had "firsthand knowledge of wrongdoing" in their organizations in the previous 12 months. Nearly half of those episodes of wrongdoing were considered so serious that a "significant loss of public trust" would have resulted if the wrongdoing had been discovered.[44] Similarly, in a 2010 survey, nearly 49 percent of 3,000 American employees surveyed reported having witnessed misconduct on the job, but that number does represent an improvement from the 2007 total of 56 percent.[45]

> Ethical behavior in business is, in many ways, at an historical high.

In assessing America's corporate ethical climate, we should keep in mind ethicist Chris MacDonald's reminder that ethical behavior in business is, in many ways, at an historical high.

Businesses, he argues, are more transparent and more accountable than ever before, and, as he says: "Workplaces, while still far from perfect, are less sexist, less racist, and generally more civilized and humane than at any time in history" (in considerable part as a response to government rules oversight and public pressure).[46] [For "The Business Ethics Blog," see **http://businessethicsblog.com/**]

Questions

British Petroleum (BP) may be the most hated corporation currently doing business in America. BP's Deepwater Horizon oil spill in the Gulf of Mexico threatened the marine life of the Gulf, while also severely damaging the Gulf's economic, recreational, and aesthetic contributions to American life. At this writing, the Gulf appears to be healing itself more quickly than expected and the economic consequences have been mitigated by massive BP payments. Still, the company carries a stigma in the American market. Soon after the 2010 spill, a critic at a locally owned Des Moines, Iowa, BP station berated customers and the station owner by saying: "Do you realize you're buying from a company that's polluting the Earth?"

1. Should we blame local BP station owners for the gulf spill? Explain.
2. Should we boycott those stations? Explain.

See Marc Hansen, "Local BP Retailers Want You to Know They Are Not the Bad Guys," *The Des Moines Register,* June 29, 2010, p. 1A.

Why Do Some Managers Cheat?

Moral Development

Scholars argue that some individuals are better prepared to make ethical judgments than others. Psychologist Lawrence Kohlberg built and empirically tested a comprehensive theory of moral development in which he claimed that moral judgment evolves and improves primarily as a function of age and education.

Kohlberg, via interviews with children as they aged, was able to identify moral development as movement through distinct stages, with the later stages being improvements on the earlier ones. Kohlberg identified six universal stages grouped into three levels:

1. **Preconventional level:**

    Stage 1: Obey rules to avoid punishment.

    Stage 2: Follow rules only if it is in own interest, but let others do the same. Conform to secure rewards.

2. **Conventional level:**

    Stage 3: Conform to meet the expectations of others. Please others. Adhere to stereotypical images.

    Stage 4: Doing right is one's duty. Obey the law. Uphold the social order.

3. **Postconventional or principled level:**

> Stage 5: Current laws and values are relative. Laws and duty are obeyed on rational calculations to serve the greatest number.

> Stage 6: Follow self-chosen universal ethical principles. In the event of conflicts, principles override laws.[47]

At Level 3 the individual is able to reach independent moral judgments that may or may not conform with conventional societal wisdom. Thus the Level 2 manager might refrain from sexual harassment because it constitutes a violation of company policy and the law. A manager at Level 3 might reach the same conclusion, but his or her decision would be based on independently defined universal principles of justice.

Kohlberg found that many adults never pass beyond Level 2. Consequently, if Kohlberg was correct, many managers may behave unethically simply because they have not reached the upper stages of moral maturity.

Kohlberg's model is based on extensive longitudinal and cross-cultural studies over more than three decades. For example, one set of Chicago-area boys was interviewed at 3-year intervals for 20 years. Thus the stages of moral growth exhibit "definite empirical characteristics" such that Kohlberg was able to claim that his model had been scientifically validated.[48] Although many critics remain, the evidence, in sum, supports Kohlberg's general proposition. [For a link to an overview of moral development and moral education, see **http://www.davidsongifted.org/db/Resources_id_11335.aspx**]

Feminine Voice   One of those lines of criticism requires a brief inspection. Kohlberg colleague Carol Gilligan contends that our conceptions of morality are, in substantial part, gender-based.[49] She claims that men typically approach morality as a function of justice, impartiality, and rights (the ethic of justice), whereas women are more likely to build a morality based on care, support, and responsiveness (the ethic of care). Men, she says, tend to take an impersonal, universal view of morality as contrasted with the feminine "voice" that rises more commonly from relationships and concern for the specific needs of others. Gilligan criticizes Kohlberg because his highest stages, 5 and 6, are structured in terms of the male approach to morality while the feminine voice falls at stage 3. Furthermore, Kohlberg's initial experimental subjects were limited to young males. The result, in Gilligan's view, is that women are underscored. Of course, a danger in the ethic of care is that it might be interpreted to restore and legitimize the stereotype of women as care-giving subordinates not deserving of moral autonomy.[50] Subsequent research both challenges[51] and supports[52] Gilligan's view.

Reason or Emotion?

Controlled or automatic? We have seen that Kohlberg and Gilligan (and most moral philosophers) take the position that moral decision making is the controlled product of analysis, deliberation and experience. In recent years, however, new psychological and neuroscience evidence has supported an alternative theory of morality that involves decision making by emotion or intuition. The emotion/intuition approach claims that moral decision making is an automatic, nonreflective process in which our minds, when confronted with a moral question instantaneously generate feelings of approval or disapproval.[53]

Brain-scanning experiments have provided support for the automatic emotion/intuition hypothesis.[54] Some scientists speculate that controlled moral reasoning may be little more than an after-the-fact method of justifying conclusions already reached automatically via emotions/intuitions.[55]

Moral theorist Marc Hauser extends the emotion/intuition thesis in his book *Moral Minds*.[56] He claims that our brains are biologically endowed with a moral faculty that has evolved over eons and is designed to reach very rapid judgments about right and wrong based on unconscious processes that are involuntary and universal. Thus, when we judge an action to be morally right or wrong, Hauser says we are doing so instinctively, using our inborn moral faculty. Even babies seem to make moral judgments. Experiments show that six- and ten-month old infants overwhelmingly prefer helping characters (objects manipulated like puppets in helping/hindering situations) over neutral characters and neutral characters are preferred over those who actively hinder others.[57]

> Even babies seem to make moral judgments.

The emotion/intuition/ biological theory provides a stern challenge to Kohlberg and to our faith in moral reasoning generally. Psychologist Jonathan Haidt compares the intuitive, moral machinery of the brain with an elephant and conscious moral reasoning with a small rider on the elephant's back.[58] Other scholarly evidence, however, continues to support a very robust role for rational moral decision making,[59] and reasoning may at times override intuitions, as Haidt himself acknowledges.[60] Overall, moral decision making may be the product of a dual process system employing both automatic emotions (produced deep in the brain in its older structures) and controlled reasoning (produced in the newer, frontal lobes of the brain).[61]

Moral Identity?

The moral development story does not end with an understanding of moral reasoning and moral emotion. Neither of those forces, according to current research, adequately explains why some among us are moved, after reaching a moral judgment, to take moral action.[62] Early evidence suggests that a critical feature in total moral development, including the will to act, involves what is labeled *moral identity*. In general, moral identity involves the degree to which moral concerns are central to our sense of self. As Professor Sam Hardy explains it, a person might have a stronger sense of moral identity if that identity is centered more on moral virtue than on amoral virtues such as creativity.[63] Some studies find that those with stronger moral identities are more likely to engage in good behaviors such as volunteering or showing respect for members of "out-groups."[64] Remember, however, that the moral identity evidence remains quite tentative.

Organizational Forces

Obviously, individual character is an important determinant of corporate misconduct, but substantial scientific evidence and scholarly opinion support the view that organizational culture is also highly influential.[65] A recent survey of human resource managers and executives shows that 70 percent of those responding blamed ethical lapses on pressure to meet unrealistic goals and deadlines while personal considerations such as furthering one's career had less reported impact.[66] As Jay Jamrog, executive director of the Human

Resource Institute said, "[Y]ou still need people at the top to set the climate."[67] A 2009 Ethics Resource Center survey of nearly 3,000 employees nationwide clearly affirmed the importance of a strong ethical climate. According to the study, in organizations with a strong ethical culture, only 4 percent of employees feel pressure to cheat while 15 percent of those in organizations with weaker cultures reported feeling that pressure.[68] Similarly, the rate of misconduct as observed by coworkers is at 76 percent in companies with weaker cultures while in those with stronger cultures the percentage of observed misconduct was reported at 39 percent.[69] Unfortunately, the Ethics Resource Center, in 2007, found that only 10 percent of American companies report the characteristics that are associated with a "strong ethical culture."[70] Only 38 percent of companies surveyed in 2008 reported established ethics programs (up from 25 percent in 2005), and only 25 percent of employees reported believing that employees in their companies are rewarded for ethical behavior.[71] [For the Business Roundtable Institute for Corporate Ethics, see **http://www. corporate-ethics.org/**]

The pressure to produce is, of course, very great for those at the bottom of the power structure; but often it does not go away with advancement. Thirty graduates of the Harvard MBA program agreed to in-depth interviews about their on-the-job ethics experiences.

One interesting conclusion from the interviews was the degree to which these younger subordinates understood and empathized with the pressure felt by their primarily middle-manager bosses:

> I really feel for people who are middle management, with a wife and four kids, under financial strain. . . . You see it happen all the time, that people are indicted for fraud or larceny. You can empathize with their situation. The world is changing fast. And a lot of people have been blindsided by it—so they've done things that they don't like. I can't say that will never happen to me. It's easy for me as a single person. . . but when you're desperate, you're desperate. [My boss] was not willfully unethical. It was the pressure of the time. . . . I have no idea what pressures were on him to drive the project. It probably wasn't [his] initiative to fudge the numbers. There may have been a good intention at some point in the organization. But as it got filtered through the organization, it changed. Some executive may have said, "This is an interesting project." Unfortunately this got translated as, "The vice president really wants this project." This sort of thing can happen a lot. Things start on high. As they go down they are filtered, modified. What was a positive comment several levels above becomes "do this or die" several levels down.[72] [For a variety of business ethics links, see **http://www.ethics. ubc.ca/resources/business/**]

> "[My boss] was not willfully unethical. It was the pressure of the time."

The Boss

Top corporate bosses have hit a particularly rough patch in American life. Many have been disgraced by various scandals, and a number of them are in jail. Wall Street executives are accused of bringing the economy to near collapse while continuing to collect big bonuses. Despite some recovery in credibility from 2009–2010, CEOs rank last in a list of trusted classes of spokespeople in the United States, according to the 2010 Edelman Trust Barometer.[73]

Notwithstanding the current cynicism, we know that bosses are crucial in setting the ethical climate in an organization. *The Wall Street Journal* reviewed corporate chief Herb Baum's leadership book:

> In *The Transparent Leader,* Herb Baum argues that a climate of integrity is crucial to the success of a public company and that it begins at the top.
>
> Mr. Baum . . . is at the top himself, but he drives a VW Beetle to work, he tells us, and doesn't have a reserved parking space. Not that he minds: He arrives at 5 AM, ahead of the crowd. He espouses straight talk, solid values, and hiring literally good people—as opposed to people who are merely good at their jobs. His catchall term for this ethos is "transparency."
>
> How to create it? Mr. Baum rightly insists that it has to come from the chief executive's office. He emphasizes valuing people by keeping an open door, communicating honestly, listening carefully, and making sure that integrity permeates every aspect of the company. Hypocrisy is anathema: "A lot of CEOs, including me, are overpaid," he says bluntly—and at one point he distributed his annual bonus to Dial's lowest-paid employees.[74]

[For a film treatment of ethical issues in the business community, see the trailer *Wall Street: Money Never Sleeps,* at **http://www.youtube.com/watch?v=HcMFA2SHES4**]

Bill Hawkins: A Tough Decision

CEO decisions and practices are critical in establishing an ethical culture in an organization. Bill Hawkins, CEO at Medtronic ($14.6 billion, Minneapolis-based medical device maker), faced one of those critical ethical decision-making moments in 2007 when he learned that Medtronic's Sprint Fidelis leads might have been malfunctioning at an unacceptably high rate. Leads are very thin wires that connect implanted heart defibrillators to the heart thus allowing a shock to be delivered from the defibrillator to the heart muscle. Sprint (the brand name for Medtronic's leads) Fidelis (the particular model of lead) leads were the company's newest, and thinnest, model. Medtronic began receiving reports of fractures in the Sprint Fidelis leads. Those fractures might prevent a needed shock from reaching the heart, or patients might receive random shocks.

Hawkins had been with Medtronic for about five years and had been serving as president and Chief Operating Officer for about two months when he learned in March 2007 that one hospital was reporting problems with the leads. According to Hawkins, Medtronic's internal experts and an independent physician advisory board investigated and the company concluded that monitoring should continue but the leads should not be removed from the market. In October 2007, when Hawkins had been CEO for two months, he received new data showing that the Fidelis lead's resistance to fracture was 97.7 percent versus 99.1 for the previous model; a statistically insignificant difference, but a gap that would become statistically significant over time if the fracture rates remained constant. After consultation with other company officers and an independent physician advisory board, Hawkins felt that the Fidelis was displaying a negative trend, but he wanted more deliberation. Various Medtronic leaders met for discussion, as did the physicians. The next day they met again by teleconference and after 90 minutes of discussion, the decision was reached to voluntarily recall the Sprint Fidelis.

The leads had been on the market for about 38 months and 268,000 had been implanted. The day the recall was announced, Medtronic had its worst day on the stock market in 23 years with a 12 percent decline and its market share in the category fell from 51 to 47 percent. By March 2009, Medtronic's physician panel had identified 13 deaths that might have been associated with the lead fractures. Within two years, however, Medtronic had largely recovered from the episode, a software package had been developed that would alert patients that a lead might be fracturing, and a favorable U.S. Supreme Court decision was offering Medtronic substantial shelter from lawsuits.

Hawkins described how Medtronic's culture influenced him and his company:

> Our founder wrote in 1960 that the purpose of our company is to "alleviate pain, restore health, and extend life." I am not being coy when I say that I take this very personally and that our company is strongly influenced by this sense of mission. During the course of our Fidelis discussions, not once did we talk about what might happen to the stock price or market share if we suspended distribution. The conversation was about our responsibility to do the right thing.[75]

Questions

1. Beyond market share and stock market prices, what considerations would have influenced Hawkins's decision?
2. Some critics have said that Hawkins's decision could not be considered difficult because lives were at risk. Do you agree that Hawkins's decision was, in fact, easy? Explain.

Sources: Bill Hawkins, as told to Cait Murphy, "Bill Hawkins: How I Made the Toughest Call of My Career," BNET, October 5, 2009 [**http://www.bnet.com/**]; Cait Murphy, "The Price Medtronic Paid," BNET, October 5, 2009 [**http://www.bnet.com/**]; and Chris MacDonald, "Can Life-Saving Decisions Really Be 'Tough Calls'?" *The Business Ethics Blog,* October 15, 2009 [**http://www.businessethics.ca/blog/**].

Bank Robber to Boardroom

Some bosses go wrong but correct their lives—none more dramatically than James Joseph Minder, 74-year-old former chairman of Smith & Wesson Holding Corp. In his twenties, Minder was the notorious "Shotgun Bandit" of Michigan. He committed dozens of armed holdups, some while a student at the University of Michigan. On one occasion he terrorized employees before stealing $53,000 from a branch of Manufacturers National Bank. He served time in prison and was free of trouble, he says, after 1965. After release from prison in 1969, he spent 20 years successfully setting up group homes and programs for troubled children and young adults. After retiring in the 1990s, Minder got involved in the gun industry and eventually became chairman of handgun manufacturer, Smith & Wesson. Then in 2004 a reporter came to his home asking about his past, a life he had not hidden but one he had not advertised either. At first he denied he was the "Bandit," but he reconsidered and decided, "I had better tell the truth." He later told the other members of the Smith & Wesson board, and resigned as chairman.

Source: Vanessa O'Connell, "How Troubled Past Finally Caught Up with James Minder," *The Wall Street Journal,* March 8, 2004, p. A1.

Ethics Teachers?

> Managers are the ethics teachers of their organizations.

Harvard business ethics professor Joseph Badaracco said "managers are the ethics teachers of their organizations."[76] If so, we would be forced to conclude that many corporate leaders have been teaching the wrong ethics lessons. As a 2010 *Wall Street Journal* headline read: "Ethical Lapses Felled Long List of Company Executives."[77] Rather than setting the ethical tone for their organizations, executives sometimes distance themselves as much as possible when wrongdoing is discovered:

> Call it the reverse Nuremberg strategy. Chief executives of scandal-ridden companies such as WorldCom, Sotheby's Holdings Inc., Cendant Corp., and . . . Enron Corp. all have claimed that they didn't know about the alleged fraud at their businesses and blamed it largely on underlings. It is the opposite of the defense used at the Nuremberg trials, when Hitler's minions claimed they were only carrying out orders from above. In the corporate fraud cases, the argument is that the top dog was so above the fray that he didn't know what directives were being issued or carried out by those below him.[78]

On the other hand, many of those corporate leaders have been noble ethical models. Bill Neukom, lead owner of the San Francisco Giants, made a fortune as general counsel of Microsoft. He put a lot of that money in his "guilty pleasure" the Giants, but his other great goal has been to give away much of his money:

> I believe I was overcompensated for my work, said Neukom. . . . I was in a fortunate position, but my worth to the company is not equal to the amount of money I received. I don't see it as money I earned. I see myself as the steward of the money, and that is why I give much of it away.[79]

[For the Business Roundtable Institute for Corporate Ethics, see **http://www.darden. virginia.edu/corporate-ethics**]

Questions—Part Three

1. *a.* Do you think it is important for our character development to have heroes in our lives? Explain.
   b. Do you think we have fewer heroes today than in the past? Explain.
   c. Do you have a hero? Explain.

2. A Business & Media Institute study entitled *Bad Company* looked at the top 12 television dramas from May and November 2005, including shows like *CSI* and *Desperate Housewives*. Thirty-nine episodes featured business-related plots, and among those shows, 77 percent projected unfavorable images of business. The *Law & Order* episodes, for example, had businessmen committing almost 50 percent of the felonies— mostly murders.
   a. Do you think those unfavorable depictions of business are unfair? Explain.
   b. Do you think those depictions significantly harm the image of the business community? Explain. See Editorial, "TV's Killer Capitalists," *The Wall Street Journal,* July 14, 2006, p. W9.

3. Does a corporation have a conscience? Explain. See Kenneth Goodpaster and John B. Matthews, Jr., "Can a Corporation Have a Conscience?" *Harvard Business Review,* January–February 1982, p. 136.

4. "You are being considered for a promotion. Would you flirt with your boss or someone else who can help you get the job?" *Money Magazine* asked this and other ethics questions in a national poll of 1,000 adults. Answer the flirting question, then go online to see how your answer compared with the poll response: "Money and Ethics: How You Stack Up," *CNNMoney.com* [**http://money.cnn.com/galleries/2007/moneymag/0705/ quiz.money_ ethics.moneymag/3.html?score=2**]

5. Kansas City Royals pitcher Gil Meche, 32 years old and troubled by a shoulder injury, decided in 2011 to retire from baseball. The decision would not be considered particularly newsworthy beyond the sports pages except that Meche passed up the $12 million final year of his contract by doing so. Others in similar situations have reported to spring training, gone through the motions and collected their big paychecks. Meche said, "When I signed my contract, my main goal was to earn it. Once I started to realize I wasn't earning my money, I felt bad." Meche thought he had already earned enough from the Royals: "Making that amount of money from a team that's already given me over $40 million for my life and for my kids, it just wasn't the right thing to do."

   a. Would you do the same as Meche if you were similarly situated? Explain.
   b. Have you ever spurned money for reasons of principal?
   c. Why did you do so?
   d. Was Meche employing utilitarian or formalist reasoning? Explain. See Tyler Kepner, "Pitcher Spurns $12 Million, to Keep Self-Respect," *The New York Times,* January 26, 2011 [**http://www.nytimes.com**].

Part Four—Business Ethics in Practice

Introduction: Ethics Codes

Having established a general foundation in ethical climate and theory, we turn now to ethics in practice. Most big companies have voluntarily developed ethics codes, and the 2002 federal Sarbanes-Oxley Act (SOX) encourages all publicly traded companies to do so. Sarbanes was passed after Enron and other corporate scandals as a way to discourage financial and accounting fraud, thus maintaining confidence in America's financial markets. Section 406 of Sarbanes specifically requires publicly traded companies to adopt a code of ethics for senior financial officers or to explain why they have not done so. Section 406 defines a code of ethics as written standards that are reasonably designed to deter wrongdoing and to promote such behaviors as honest conduct, full disclosure in reports, compliance with all applicable laws and rules, prompt reporting of violations, and methods for conforming to the code's expectations.

Responding to SOX and other pressures, many companies now have prepared more detailed and specific codes, displayed them more prominently, required employees to read and sign the codes, and created training methods to more firmly integrate ethical expectations into the company's total decision-making processes. [For the Ethics Officers Association, see **http://www.eoa.org**]

Whether the new attention to codes will prove beneficial remains to be seen. Importantly, the company that can show compliance with its own legitimate code expectations may receive more sympathetic treatment from the justice system if criminal problems do emerge. [For the Ethics Resource Center, see **http://www.ethics.org/**] [For information on global corporate governance and citizenship, see **http://www.conference-board.org/**]

Building an Ethical Culture at General Electric

When adding new employees, sometimes as many as 13,000 in a year, General Electric has struggled to implement effective training methods for achieving the ethical climate worldwide that the company demands. In most cases, GE's new hires undergo compliance training soon after joining the company. Often using online training programs, GE tests employees on problems such as how to deal with unusual requests by a customer for money or to ignore a government rule. GE also requires each business unit to provide a quarterly report to the compliance department detailing what portion of its employees completed the required ethics training and what portion read and signed off on GE's "Spirit and Letter" ethics guide. Rather than burying employees in lists of do's and don'ts, GE and others are building contextual training exercises that attempt to immerse employees in discussions of how to approach actual, on-the-job ethical dilemmas.

Questions

1. Do you think ethics training is likely to have a significant impact on managerial and corporate misconduct? Explain.

2. Do you think companies with reputations for high ethical quality would have an edge in recruiting employees? Explain.

Sources: Kathryn Kranhold, "U.S. Firms Raise Ethics Focus," *The Wall Street Journal*, November 28, 2005, p. B4; and Erin White "What Would You Do? Ethics Courses Get Context," *The Wall Street Journal*, June 12, 2006, p. B3.

Bribery Abroad

Today's closely entwined international markets mean that strategies for curbing corrupt business practices must extend around the world thus raising complex ethical dilemmas for America's multinational businesses. In many cultures, the payment of bribes—baksheesh (Middle East), huilu (China), vzyatku (Russia), mordida (South America), or dash (Africa)—is accepted as a necessary and, in some cases, a lawful way of doing business. American firms and officers wishing to succeed abroad have faced great pressure to engage in practices that are illegal and unethical in the American culture.

The Foreign Corrupt Practices Act (FCPA), the chief federal weapon against bribery abroad, was enacted in 1977 in response to disclosure of widespread bribery by American firms. In brief, the FCPA provides that U.S. nationals and businesses acting anywhere in the world, foreign nationals and companies acting in U.S. territory, and foreign companies listed on a U.S. stock exchange are engaging in criminal conduct if they offer or provide money or anything of value to foreign government officials to obtain or retain business or otherwise secure "any improper advantage." In addition, the FCPA requires rigorous internal accounting controls and careful recordkeeping to ensure that bribes cannot be concealed via "slush funds" and other devices. The act does not forbid "grease" payments to foreign officials or political parties where the purpose of the payments is "to expedite or to secure the performance of a routine governmental action," such as processing papers (like visas), providing police protection, and securing phone service. And those accused may offer the affirmative defense that the alleged payoff was lawful in the host country or was a normal, reasonable business expenditure directed to specific marketing and contract performance activities. Criminal penalties include fines of up to $2 million for companies, while individuals may be fined $250,000 and imprisoned for as long as five years. [For a summary of the FCPA, see **http://fcpaenforcement.com/ explained/explained.asp**]

Controversy

The FCPA has been controversial from the outset. Some businesspeople see it as a blessing both because it is an honorable attempt at a firm moral stance and because it is often useful for an American businessperson abroad to say, "No, our laws forbid me from doing that." On the other hand, some consider the act damaging to our competitiveness. Now other nations are recognizing that corruption is a great risk to the global economy. Once believing that bribery aided the poor, most industrial countries are now moving toward the zero tolerance view held by the United States. In addition to the FCPA, the United States also participates in several other anticorruption initiatives including the U.N. Convention against Corruption, the OECD Anti-Bribery Convention, and the Inter-American Convention. [For details on the OECD Anti-Bribery Convention, see **www.oecd.org**]

United States Corruption   Although the United States has been the clear world leader in pursuing anticorruption efforts, we should not be unduly prideful. Indeed, the United States ranked only 22nd in Transparency International's 2010 Corruption Perceptions Index, which aggregates data provided by experts and business leaders to assess the perceived level of public sector corruption in 178 nations. The countries perceived to be least corrupt were Denmark, New Zealand, and Singapore. Most of northern and Western Europe as well as Canada were perceived to be less corrupt than the United States. France (25), China (78), and Russia (154) were among the nations ranking lower than the United States.[80]

> The United States ranked only 22nd in Transparency International's 2010 Corruption Perceptions Index.

Bribery in Practice

Bribery seems to be a routine cost of daily life in some countries:

> Nikolai can't even count the number of bribes he has paid in his life.

Like many Russians, Nikolai can't even count the number of bribes he has paid in his life. He remembers the big ones, like the $1,000 he paid to avoid mandatory military service or the $1,200 he gave his wife's obstetrician to ensure her a place at one of Moscow's state-run maternity hospitals. But the small ones, like the dozens of $10 to $20 bribes he's handed to traffic police over the years, are instantly forgotten.

Whether it's getting your child into a good school, passing your driving test or even making sure you get medical treatment, there are few areas of life in Russia where a well-placed bribe isn't essential. Experts say corruption in Russia is endemic, especially in the corporate world—where big companies, both domestic and foreign, often have to shell out hundreds of thousands of dollars to get permission for a project or win a government contract.[81]

Russian think tank INDEM estimates that, on average, Russian businesses spend seven percent of their budgets on bribes.[82]

China executed the former head of its food and drug agency in 2007 for accepting $850,000 in bribes from Chinese pharmaceutical companies. Bribery has often been considered a cost of doing business in China, but recent product safety scandals have threatened the reputation of China's enormous export market so the government has indicated that it will crack down on corruption. Skeptics, however, believe that bribery is so deeply rooted in the Chinese system that those who give the bribes, in particular, often "get off easy."[83]

> China executed the former head of its food and drug agency for accepting $850,000 in bribes.

In the United States, we are seeing a remarkable new zeal in attacking bribery. Bribery cases since 2006 have exceeded the total for the previous 30 years combined.[84] Ten years ago about eight investigations were conducted annually while active investigations in 2010 alone exceeded 130.[85] Some spectacular penalties have followed, including a record $800 million settlement in 2009 with Siemens, the German engineering firm. In 2010, German auto manufacturer Daimler agreed to pay $185 million in penalties associated with alleged bribes in 22 countries worldwide.[86] Other countries, including China and Russia, have strengthened their anticorruption laws and prosecutions, and the United Kingdom in 2011 took perhaps the world's toughest stance on bribery by extending the law to bribes between private businesspeople and by enforcing the law even if the person making the payment did not realize the transaction constituted a bribe.[87]

PRACTICING ETHICS Bribe the Terrorists?

Banadex, a subsidiary of Cincinnati-based Chiquita Brands International, paid bribes to Colombian rebels over a period of years, including $1.7 million from 1997 to 2004 to the AUC (Autodefensas Unidas de Colombia), a right-wing Colombian terrorist group. Chiquita, one of the world's leading banana producers with operations in 70 nations, learned of the payments in 2000, but allowed them to continue. Reliable reports indicated that thousands of people had been killed, tortured, raped, or "disappeared" by the AUC (now disbanded). At the time, terrorists in Colombia were holding Americans for ransom or killing some of them, and years earlier four Chiquita employees had been killed by left-wing guerillas. The bribes, then lawful under American and Colombian law, were thought necessary to protect employees and company property at Chiquita's Colombian operations.

In 2003, Chiquita allegedly "stumbled across" news that the AUC had in 2001 been designated a "foreign terrorist organization" by the U.S. government, which meant payments thereafter were unlawful. The payments continued, however, despite warnings from outside counsel to discontinue them or face the risk of felony charges. Chiquita said that stopping the payments would have endangered its employees. By 2003, Chiquita's operations in Colombia were its most profitable. The bribe payments were stopped in 2004 when a new CEO arrived. Chiquita soon sold its Colombian interests. Chiquita had earned about $50 million in profits from the time AUC was designated a terrorist organization until the period when the payments ceased.

In 2007, Chiquita entered a guilty plea to the felony of engaging in transactions with terrorists. A federal judge sentenced Chiquita to $25 million in fines and five years probation. Some evidence suggests Chiquita may have delayed its decision to stop payments by nearly one year as it waited for the U.S. government to review the security implications of a Chiquita withdrawal from Colombia. U.S. Justice Department officials denied that claim, and in 2007 they concluded their investigation by deciding not to bring criminal charges against former Chiquita officials.

Families of Colombians killed or tortured by the terrorists along with human rights groups have filed several civil lawsuits against Chiquita for supporting the terrorists who allegedly used the bribe money to buy weapons. During the period of Chiquita payments to AUC, some 4,000 Colombians were killed in the banana-growing region of Colombia. An Organization of American States investigation concluded that 3,000 Central American rifles and millions of rounds of ammunition reached the terrorists after allegedly being unloaded at a Colombian port by Banadex. Colombian

officials argue that Chiquita was not a victim of extortion and that the company knew AUC was using the bribery proceeds to attack peasants, union workers, and various rival groups.

Questions

1. Chiquita argued that the safety of its employees required payment of the bribes, even after learning of their illegality. What would you have done, had you been in charge? Explain.

2. Should Chiquita's corporate officers have been prosecuted by the U.S. government? Explain.

Sources: Sibylla Brodzinsky, "Chiquita Case Puts Big Firms on Notice," *The Christian Science Monitor*, April 11, 2007 [http://www.csmonitor.com/2007/0411/p01s03-woam.html]; Laurie P. Cohen, "Chiquita Ex-Officials Won't Face Charges," *The Wall Street Journal*, September 12, 2007, p. B2; Carol D. Leonnig, "In Terrorism-Law Case, Chiquita Points to U.S.," *Washington Post*, August 2, 2007, p. A01; David J. Lynch, "Murder and Payoffs Taint Business in Colombia," *USA TODAY*, October 30, 2007, sec. Money, p. 1B; and Sue Reisinger, "Blood Money Paid by Chiquita Shows Company's Hard Choices," *Corporate Counsel*, November 26, 2007 [http://www.law.com/jsp/ihc/PubArticleFriendlyIHC.jsp?id=1195639472310].

Corporate/White Collar Crime

Martha Stewart served five months in prison.

Martha Stewart served five months in prison, the Enron bosses were successfully prosecuted, and dozens of other prominent executives and corporations have been punished in recent years. The subprime mortgage mess, slowly unfolding at this writing, has produced some significant settlements and convictions, as noted earlier in this chapter. While great corporations have collapsed and many good people have lost their life savings, we can find some satisfaction in a system that, at times, brings the mighty to justice. The scandals persist, however. Accounting manipulation, bribery, inside trading, consumer fraud, price fixing, and the like are disappointingly commonplace. In late 2007, *Forbes,* the business magazine, summed up the disturbing situation with the headline: "Corporate Crime Wave Unabated."[88] The 2009 PricewaterhouseCoopers (PwC) Global Economic Crime Survey found that over 30 percent of the 5,400 companies surveyed in more than 40 nations reported having been victims of at least one significant economic crime during the previous year.[89] Accounting fraud was the second most common form of reported economic crime, trailing only "asset misappropriation."[90] Significantly, the PwC report for 2007 concluded that companies cannot rely on internal fraud controls alone to stop this misconduct:

> The answer lies in establishing a corporate culture that supports control efforts and whistle blowing systems with clear ethical guidelines. Companies need to build loyalty to the organization, give employees the confidence to do the right thing, and put in place clear sanctions for those who commit fraud, regardless of their position in the company.[91]

One of the results of the failure to control crime, as *The Wall Street Journal* reported, is that corporations and their bosses may be at greater risk of prosecution than ever before in American history:

> There may never have been a worse time to be a corporate criminal. . . . The reason: After a wave of corporate-fraud cases, prosecutors want to send a signal that executives aren't above the law.[92]

Is Theft Sometimes OK?

A shopper wrote a letter to the editor explaining how he felt after observing what appeared to be a theft:

> [A]t Wal-Mart I saw a person try to put an item in their jacket. At first I thought this person was a jerk. . . . But after I returned home, I became convinced that it was OK to steal. . . . When I compare the theft of a $15 item to the grand larceny by corporate America, which ran Enron into the ground, which reaps record oil profits, . . . which occupies the seats of government and takes bribes, I now see the act of stealing a small gift . . . as heroic.

Questions

1. What do you think the letter writer meant when he applied the label "heroic" to the apparent theft?
2. Should we be more aggressive in pursuing corporate fraud? Explain.

Source: Greg Wilcox, "It's All Relative," *The Des Moines Register*, December 12, 2005, p. 6A.

Punishment   Responding to public outrage as Enron and the other corporate scandals surfaced, Congress felt great pressure to strengthen federal criminal laws dealing with corporate fraud. The result was the aforementioned 2002 Sarbanes-Oxley Act (SOX), which significantly increased penalties and provided other aggressive measures for attacking corporate crime by publicly traded companies. Among its major provisions, the bill:

- Establishes an independent board to oversee the accounting profession.
- Requires corporate executives to personally certify the accuracy of their financial reports.
- Creates new crimes and raises penalties to as much as 25 years of imprisonment along with heavy fines.
- Requires publicly-traded companies to establish internal control systems designed to assure the accuracy of financial information.
- Requires publicly-traded companies to disclose whether they have adopted an ethics code for senior financial management, and if not, why they have not done.

While compliance costs can be quite high, some recent evidence is supportive of the value of SOX. In a 2010 survey of 400 business executives, 87 percent said SOX is good for private enterprise,[93] and a 2009 Securities and Exchange Commission study concluded that the benefits of SOX exceeded its costs.[94] Of course, critics see SOX as a drain on company resources and an impediment to economic growth, but SOX seems to be valuable, not only for ethics assurance, but for encouraging tighter management practice:

> Invitrogen Corp. spent about $2.5 million and 10,000 hours of employees' time last year reviewing its inventory-counting procedures, computer-system access and other "internal controls.". . . Officials at the Carlsbad, California biotechnology company think the costs are excessive. But they say Sarbanes-Oxley helped to spur other changes that made Invitrogen a better-run business. Directors meet more often without executives present. Multiple ombudsmen field employee complaints. Ethics training is more rigorous. And Chief Executive Greg Lucier requires his lieutenants to take more responsibility for their results.[95]

Sentencing   Federal sentencing guidelines, issued by the U.S. Sentencing Commission, provide ranges (e.g., 10–12 months imprisonment) within which judges are advised to impose sentences. Relying on the crime's "offense level" and the defendant's criminal history" the punishment range for each category of both white-collar and "street" crime is established. The guidelines are designed to provide greater predictability and consistency in punishment. Companies must develop programs to prevent and detect crime, provide ethics training and monitor the success of compliance efforts. Responsibility for compliance rests explicitly with the board of directors and top-level executives. Companies, directors, and officers complying with the guidelines may receive leniency while those engaging in aggravating behaviors such as a leadership role in crime may face increased punishment.[96] An important goal of the guidelines is to encourage companies to develop strong compliance systems. Companies involved in crimes may receive reduced penalties if they have effective compliance programs in place; meaning, among other things, that their compliance officers have direct access to the boards of directors, and the offenses were quickly reported to authorities.[97] Think, however, about the challenges of achieving compliance in a big organization. With hundreds of thousands of employees and suppliers, global giants like McDonald's must be very careful both about choosing those employees and suppliers and about monitoring and supervising their behavior.

Recent Supreme Court decisions have reduced the power of the guidelines by restoring federal judges' authority to deviate from them.[98] Judges who follow the guidelines are presumed to have acted reasonably,[99] but departures from the guidelines are now permissible. One of the results of the Supreme Court rulings is that sentences, for at least some classes of crime, are likely to be somewhat more lenient than under strict conformity to the guidelines.[100]

White-Collar Crackdown?

Historically, critics have often argued that white-collar crime was punished more leniently than "street" crime. Recently, however, white-collar penalties have put executives behind bars for many years. Consider this sample:

> Bernard Madoff, 70-year-old investment advisor, admitted to operating a Ponzi scheme involving as much as $65 billion in losses and was sentenced to 150 years in prison.

> Philip Bennett, 59-year-old CEO at Refco, was sentenced to 16 years in prison for his role in a financial cover-up that cost investors about $1.5 billion.

Lance Poulsen, founder of National Century Financial Enterprises, was convicted of leading a $2.9 billion fraud for which he was sentenced to 30 years in prison.

Question

Critics of increased government activism against corporate crime see the open market as the best protection against corporate misconduct. To those critics, the existing laws were adequate, and the new measures and stiff penalties are a politicized overreaction to scandals affecting a relatively small part of the economy. From a free market perspective, the greatest concern is that SOX, the revised sentencing guidelines, and the aggressive prosecutions are government-inflicted drags on the economy. Do you agree with those critics? Explain. [For more on white-collar crime, see **http://www.fbi.gov/about-us/investigate/white-collar/whitecollarcrime**]

Source: Andrew Ross Sorkin, "White-Collar Jail Terms: Who Got What," *The New York Times,* June 29, 2009 [**http://dealbook.blogs.nytimes.com/**].

Whistle Blowing

Doing the right thing sometimes pays in a big, tangible way. Former GlaxoSmithKline quality control manager, Cheryl D. Eckard, will receive at least $96 million as her whistle blower share of the British drug maker's settlement of federal criminal charges involving a contaminated manufacturing plant and the sale of allegedly adulterated drugs.

> Cheryl D. Eckard will receive at least $96 million as her whistle blower share.

GlaxoSmithKline had dispatched Eckard to Puerto Rico in 2002 to lead a 100-person team to fix problems identified by the U.S. Food and Drug Administration. Eckard found widespread deficiencies including pills of differing strengths being mixed in the same bottles, a contaminated water system, and some lots of the antidepressant Paxil that were ineffective because of improper manufacturing. Eckard reportedly complained many times to senior managers, but little was done. She was fired as a "redundancy" after which she blew the whistle by taking her complaint to the FDA. Glaxo was unable to fix the plant and decided to close it in 2009.[101]

Eckard secured her whistle blower recovery under the federal False Claims Act, which forbids fraud in government contracts and rewards those, like Eckard, who help to stop fraud. Many federal statutes include whistle blower provisions and at least 20 states have false claims laws. Whistle blowers typically are entitled to 10 to 30 percent of the award (or settlement) against the wrongdoer. Whistle blowing seems likely to increase with the passage of the 2010 Dodd-Frank Wall Street Reform and Consumer Protection Act (see Chapter 8), which includes a provision that for the first time extends whistle blowing rewards to those revealing financial fraud in private sector contracts. [For an overview of whistle blower activity and protections, see **http://www.whistleblowers.org/** and for a law firm dedicated to representing whistle blowers as well as the stories of some of those whistle blowers, see **http://www.phillipsandcohen.com/**]

Retribution   Despite expanded legal protection, whistle blowers often pay a high price for exercising their consciences. Americans have long deplored "squealing," and we tend to ignore violations, partly out of fear of retribution. A recent survey found that 73 percent of full-time American employees observed wrongdoing on the job, but only about 36 percent of those employees actually reported that wrongdoing to bosses.[102] Jack Liles wrote a letter to *The Wall Street Journal* cautioning readers about the risks of whistle blowing:

> Folks such as whistle blower Sherron Watkins at Enron are rarely given a special status or legal protection merely for uncovering an ugly practice or incident, legal or not.
>
> After only four months in a management position at a large *Fortune* 500 firm, I discovered within my department an unethical practice and culture of soliciting for and accepting lavish gifts from vendors and suppliers in exchange for favorable consideration and favoritism in purchasing decisions and contract negotiations.
>
> When I confronted management on the issue and its clear violation of company rules and basic business ethics standards, I was quickly escorted to the parking lot where the parking decal was scraped from my car and my company I.D. confiscated. I was history.[103]

> Americans have long deplored "squealing."

Questions

1. Why is the role of "squealer" or whistle blower so repugnant to many Americans?
2. *a.* How would you feel about a classmate who blew the whistle on you for cheating on an examination?
   b. Would you report cheating by a classmate if it came to your attention? Explain.

Internet Exercise

Can ethics be taught? Many people say no. Experts at the Markkula Center for Applied Ethics at Santa Clara University explored that question. Look for their answer at [**http://www.scu.edu/ethics/practicing/decision/canethicsbetaught.html**].

a. Explain their conclusion.
b. Do you agree? Explain.

Chapter Questions

1. *Business Ethics* magazine reported the following ethical dilemma submitted by an anonymous reader:

> Mary had only a few days to earn $1,000 in sales that would allow her to reach the $1 million sales plateau where she would receive a $10,000 bonus allowing her to finance the dream home she had found. The sales climate was tough, but she had one remaining prospect, inner-city Lincoln School, which could make especially good use of new educational materials. Lincoln had no budget for discretionary purchases, but Mary considered "donating" $1,000 to the school in return for which they would make the purchases that would put her over the top. She knew her donation would help disadvantaged students and herself, but her conscience was troubled.[104] What should she do? Explain.

2. Resolve this ethical dilemma posed by Carl Kaufmann of Du Pont:[105]

> Assume that federal health investigators are pursuing a report that one of your manufacturing plants has a higher-than-average incidence of cancer among its employees. The plant happens to keep excellent medical records on all its employees, stretching back for decades, which might help identify the source of the problem. The government demands the files. But if the company turns them over, it might be accused of violating the privacy of all those workers who had submitted to private medical exams. The company offers an abstract of the records, but the government insists on the complete files, with employee names. Then the company tries to obtain releases from all the workers, but some of them refuse. If you give the records to the feds, the company has broken its commitment of confidentiality. What would you do?

3. *a.* Would you say that female undergraduate business students are more ethically inclined than their male counterparts? Explain.
   b. Would you say that religious commitment correlates with a stronger ethical inclination among undergraduate business students? Explain.

4. *a.* In her book *Lying,*[106] Sissela Bok argues that lying by professionals is commonplace. For example, she takes the position that prescribing placebos for experimental purposes is a lie and immoral. Do you agree with her position? Explain.
   b. Is the use of an unmarked police car an immoral deception? Explain.
   c. One study estimates that Americans average 200 lies per day if one includes "white lies" and inaccurate excuses. On balance, do you believe Americans approve of lying? Explain.

5. Tonight Show host Jay Leno performed in commercials encouraging his audience to "eat your body weight in Doritos."[107] He says that he turned down alcohol ads at twice the money. "I don't drink . . . And I don't like to sell it. You don't see dead teenagers on the highway with bags of Doritos scattered around them."[108]
   a. Are you in agreement with the moral distinction that Leno drew between encouraging the consumption of alcohol and encouraging the consumption of Doritos? Explain.
   b. Given the influence of television and of "stars," is all television advertising by celebrities inherently unethical? Explain.

6. The following quote and questions are drawn from Leonard Lewin's "Ethical Aptitude Test."

> As with other goods and services, the medical care available to the rich is superior to that available to the poor. The difference is most conspicuous in the application of new and expensive lifesaving techniques.[109]

   a. Is ability to pay an acceptable way to allocate such services? Explain.
   b. If not, how should such services be apportioned?
   c. Many lifesaving drugs can be tested effectively only on human beings. But often subjects are exposed to such dangers that only those who feel they have nothing to lose willingly participate. Are there any circumstances in which it would be right to conduct such tests without ensuring that the persons tested clearly understood the risks they were taking? Explain.
   d. How much in dollars is the average human life worth?

7. Aaron Burr said, "All things are moral to great men." Regardless of your personal point of view, defend Burr's position.

8. A pharmacist in Lexington, Kentucky, refused to stock over-the-counter weight reducers. His reasons were (1) the active ingredient is the same as that in nasal decongestants; (2) he feared their side effects, such as high blood pressure; and (3) he felt weight reduction should be achieved via self-discipline.[110] Assume the pharmacist manages the store for a group of owners who have given him complete authority about the products stocked. Was his decision ethical? Explain.

9. When *Business and Society Review* surveyed the presidents of 500 large U.S. companies, 51 responded with their reactions to hypothetical moral dilemmas. One question was this:

   > Assume that you are president of a firm that provides a substantial portion of the market of one of your suppliers. You find out that this supplier discriminates illegally against minorities, although no legal action has been taken. Assume further that this supplier gives you the best price for the material you require, but that the field is competitive. Do you feel that it is proper to use your economic power over this supplier to make them stop discriminating?[111]

   Respond to this question.

10. *a.* Do you think taking office supplies home from work for personal use is unethical? Explain.
    b. Are employers committing a serious ethics breach when they monitor their employees' e-mail? Explain.

11. Commentator Robert Scheer asked, "What does it mean that a whopping 70 percent of Americans, according to a recent *New York Times–CBS News* poll, believe that mass culture is responsible for debasing our moral values?"[112]
    a. Answer Scheer's question.
    b. Scheer went on to say;

    > Worse, these national moralists—dominated these days by evangelical Christians—politicize the issue by blaming "liberal Hollywood" for what deregulation and the free market have wrought. Never mind that Arnold Schwarzenegger made all those violent movies, it is the Democrats and their ilk who are corrupting youth by promulgating our "relativistic" morality. But that's just bunk.[113]

    Do you agree with Scheer's "that's just bunk" position? If not, why? If so, who is to blame for our arguable moral decay?

12. In general, does the American value system favor "cheaters" who win in life's various competitions over virtuous individuals who "lose" with regularity? Explain.

13. If you were an executive about to hire a new manager, which of the following qualities would you consider most important/least important: verbal skills, honesty/ integrity, enthusiasm, appearance, sense of humor? Explain.

14. Noted University of Sydney psychologist Vince Cakic has warned that students are increasingly using drugs to enhance performance on examinations and papers.

    a. Is the use of drugs to enhance school performance unfair/wrong/immoral in your view? Explain.

    b. Would you advocate urine testing as a means of identifying those using brain-boosting drugs in examination situations? Explain.

15. *a.* Rank the following occupations as to your perception of their ethical quality: businesspeople, lawyers, doctors, teachers, farmers, engineers, carpenters, librarians, scientists, professional athletes, letter carriers, secretaries, journalists.

    b. In general, do you find educated professionals to be more ethical than skilled but generally less educated laborers? Explain.

    c. Can you justify accepting an occupation that is not at or near the top of your ethical ranking? Explain how your ranking affects your career choices.

16. Can businesspeople successfully guide their conduct by the Golden Rule?

17. Comment on the following quotes from Albert Z. Carr:

> [M]ost bluffing in business might be regarded simply as game strategy—much like bluffing in poker, which does not reflect on the morality of the bluffer.
>
>   I quoted Henry Taylor, the British statesman who pointed out that "falsehood ceases to be falsehood when it is understood on all sides that the truth is not expected to be spoken"—an exact description of bluffing in poker, diplomacy, and business.
>
> *   *   *   *   *
>
> [T]he ethics of business are game ethics, different from the ethics of religion.
>
> *   *   *   *   *
>
> An executive's family life can easily be dislocated if he fails to make a sharp distinction between the ethical systems of the home and the office—or if his wife does not grasp that distinction.[114]

18. Is lying a routine ingredient in American sales practice? Explain.

19. Assume you are working as manager of women's clothing in a large department store. You observe the manager of equivalent rank to you in men's clothing performing poorly in that she arrives late for work, she keeps records ineptly, and she is rude to customers. Her work, however, has no direct impact on your department.

    a. Do you have any responsibility either to help her or to report her poor performance? Explain.

    b. If the store as a whole performs poorly, but you have performed well, do you bear any personal responsibility for the store's failure in that you confined your efforts exclusively to your own department even though you witnessed mismanagement in the men's clothing department? Explain.

20. We are often confronted with questions about the boundaries of our personal responsibilities.

    a. How much money, if any, must you give to satisfy your moral responsibility in the event of a famine in a foreign country? Explain.

    b. Would your responsibility be greater if the famine were in America? Explain.

Notes

1. David Cho, "Pressure at Mortgage Firm Led to Mass Approval of Bad Loans," *The Washington Post,* May 7, 2007, p. A01.

2. Ibid.

3. Ibid.

4. Katalina Bianco, "The Subprime Lending Crisis: Causes and Effects of the Mortgage Meltdown," *CCH,* 2008 [**www.business.cch.combanking/finance/focus/. . ./Subprime_WP_rev.pdf**].

5. PEW Economic Policy Group, "The Cost of the Financial Crisis: The Impact of the September 2008 Economic Collapse," *Financial Reform Project,* April 28, 2010 [**http://www.pewfr.org/project_reports_detail?id=0033**].

6. Jean Eaglesham, "Banks in Talks to End Bond Probe," *The Wall Street Journal,* December 2, 2010 [**http://online.wsj.com/**].

7. Carl Hausman, "Most Doubt the Integrity of Wall Street," *Ethics Newsline,* March 15, 2010 [**http://www.globalethics.org/newsline/**].

8. Scott Patterson and Susan Pulliam, "Buffett Is Expected to Fire at Will," *The Wall Street Journal,* April 30, 2010, p. C1.

9. Paul Davies and Kara Scannell, "Guilty Verdicts Provide 'Red Meat' to Prosecutors Chasing Companies," *The Wall Street Journal,* May 26, 2006, p. A1.

10. Jack and Suzy Welch, "The Welch Way," *BusinessWeek,* June 12, 2006, p. 100.

11. "Honesty and Ethics Poll Finds Congress' Image Tarnished," *Ethics Newsline* Research Report, December 14, 2009 [**http://www.globalethics.org/newsline/2009/**].

12. David Crary, "Students Say They Lie, Steal and Cheat," *Des Moines Register,* December 1, 2008, p. 1A.

13. "2006 Josephson Institute Report Card on the Ethics of American Youth: Part One—Integrity (Summary of Data)" [**http://www.josephsoninstitute.org/pdf/ReportCard_press-release?2006-1013.pdf**].

14. David Callahan, *The Cheating Culture: Why More Americans Are Doing Wrong to Get Ahead* (New York: Harcourt, 2004).

15. Eriq Gardner, "Cheat Sheet," *Corporate Counsel,* June 2004, p. 131.

16. Neil Howe and William Strauss, "Will the Real Gen Y Please Stand Up," *latimes.com,* March 2, 2007 [**http://www.latimes.com/news/opinion/la-oe-howe2mar02,0,4956647.story?track=ntottext**].

17. "Duke's B-School Cheating Scandal," *The Christian Science Monitor,* May 4, 2007 [**http://www.csmonitor.com/2007/0504/p08s01-comv.html**].

18. Donald L. McCabe, Kenneth D. Butterfield, and Linda Klebe Trevino, "Academic Dishonesty in Graduate Business Programs: Prevalence, Causes, and Proposed Action," *Academy of Management Learning & Education* 5, no. 3 (2006), p. 294.

19. Ibid.

20. Lee Berton, "Business Students Hope to Cheat and Prosper, New Study Shows," *The Wall Street Journal,* April 25, 1995, p. B1.

21. Ibid.

22. Susan C. Thomson, "Internet Helps Swell E-Cheating on Campuses," *The Washington Post,* March 14, 2004, p. A08.

23. Leslie Wayne, "A Promise to Be Ethical in an Era of Immorality," *The New York Times,* May 30, 2009 [**www.nytimes.com**].

24. Mary Rourke, "What Happened to America's Moral Climate?" *Los Angeles Times,* April 26, 2001, p. E1.

25. Kate Zernike, "Making College 'Relevant,'" *The New York Times,* January 3, 2010 [**www.nytimes.com**].

26. News Release, "Students Experience Spiritual Growth During College," December 18, 2007 [**www.spirituality.ucla.edu**].

27. Ibid.

28. "The Most-Praised Generation Goes to Work," *The Wall Street Journal,* April 20, 2007, p. W1.

29. Jonah Goldberg, "Our Centers of the Universe," *latimes.com,* August 7, 2007 [**http://www.latimes.com/news/opinion/la-oe-goldberg7aug07,0,692285.column?coll=la-tot-opinion&track=ntottext**].

30. Ross Douthat, "The Culture of Narcissism," *The New York Times,* June 2, 2010 [**http://douthat.blogs.nytimes.com**].

31. Raymond Baumhart, *Ethics in Business* (New York: Holt, Rinehart & Winston, 1968), p. 10.

32. For more about existentialism, see Andrew West, "Sartrean Existentialism and Ethical Decision-Making in Business," *Journal of Business Ethics* 81 (2008), p. 15.

33. Carl Hausman, "Responsibility," *Ethics Newsline,* September 28, 2009 [**http://www.globalethics.org/newsline/2009/09/28/responsibility/**].

34. Eric Reguly, "Beware of False Profits: Pope Calls for an Ethical Economy Ahead of G8," *The Globe and Mail* (Canada), July 8, 2009, p. A1.

35. Cara Buckley, "Man Is Rescued by Stranger on Subway Tracks," *The New York Times,* January 3, 2007 [**http://www.nytimes. com/2007/01/03/nyregion/03life.html**].

36. Associated Press, "British Priest: Shoplifting Is Sometimes OK," *Waterloo/Cedar Falls Courier,* December 23, 2009, p. 3A.

37. Timothy Schelhardt, "Are Layoffs Moral? One Firm's Answer: You Ask, We'll Sue," *The Wall Street Journal,* August 1, 1996, p. A1.

38. Ibid.

39. John P. MacKenzie, "Lending a Hand If a Company Asks," *The New York Times,* February 3, 2002, Sec. 3, p. 11.

40. Allen G. Breed, "Sentences Vary When Kids Die in Hot Cars," *Washingtonpost.com,* July 29, 2007 [**http://www.washingtonpost.com/wpdyn/content/article/2007/07/29/AR2007072900213.html**].

41. Geoff Colvin, "Stop Blaming Big Business," *CNNMoney.com,* January 29, 2010 [**http://money.cnn.com/**].

42. Lydia Saad, "Congress Ranks Last in Confidence in Institutions," *Gallup Poll,* July 22, 2010 [**http://www.gallup.com/**].

43. Jaimy Lee, "Trust in Business on Slight Rise in the US," *PR Week* (US), March 16, 2010, p. 6.

44. KPMG, "Integrity Survey 2008-2009," [**http://www.kpmg.com/US/en/IssuesAndInsights/ArticlesPublications/Press-Releases/Documents/IntegritySurvey08_09.pdf**].

45. Jaclyn Jaeger, "Good News: Employee Ethics Improving," *Compliance Week,* February 1, 2010 [**http://www.allbusiness.com/**].

46. Chris MacDonald, "The Golden Age of Ethical Business," *The Business Ethics Blog,* March 15, 2010 [**http://businessethicsblog.com/**].

47. For an elaboration of Kohlberg's stages, see, for example, W.D. Boyce and L.C. Jensen, *Moral Reasoning* (Lincoln, NE: University of Nebraska Press, 1978), pp. 98–109.

48. Lawrence Kohlberg, "The Cognitive–Development Approach to Moral Education," *Phi Delta Kappan* 56 (June 1975), p. 670.

49. Carol Gilligan, "In A Different Voice: Women's Conceptions of Self and Morality," *Harvard Educational Review* 47, no. 4 (November 1977), p. 481.

50. For an overview of the justice versus care debate, see Grace Clement, *Care, Autonomy, and Justice* (Boulder, CO: Westview Press, 1996).

51. James Weber and David Wasieleski, "Investigating Influences on Managers' Moral Reasoning," *Business & Society* 40, no. 1 (March 2001), pp. 79, 83.

52. Diana Robertson et al., "The Neural Processing of Moral Sensitivity to Issues of Justice and Care," *Neuropsychologia* 45 (2007), pp. 755, 763.

53. For a description of the moral intuition argument, see Jonathan Haidt, "The Emotional Dog and Its Rational Tail: A Social Intuitionist Approach to Moral Judgment," *Psychological Review* 108, No. 4 (2001), p. 814.

54. See Joshua Greene & Jonathan Haidt, "How (and Where) Does Moral Judgment Work?" *Trends in Cognitive Science* 6 (2002), p. 517.

55. Joshua Greene et al., "An fMRI Investigation of Emotional Engagement in Moral Judgment," *Science* 293 (2001), p. 2105.

56. Marc Hauser, *Moral Minds* (New York: HarperCollins Publishers, 2006).

57. Paul Bloom, "The Moral Life of Babies," *The New York Times,* May 3, 2010 [**http://www. nytimes.com**].

58. Nicholas Wade, "Is 'Do Unto Others' Written into Our Genes?" *The New York Times,* September 18, 2007 [**http://www.nytimes.com/2007/09/18/science/18mora.html?**].

59. See, e.g., David Pizarro and Paul Bloom, "The Intelligence of the Moral Intuitions Comment on Haidt," *Psychological Review* 110, No. 1 (2003), p. 193.

60. David Brooks, "The End of Philosophy," *The New York Times,* April 7, 2009 [**http://www. nytimes.com/**].

61. Benedict Carey, "Study Finds Brain Injury Changes Moral Judgment," *The New York Times,* March 21, 2007 [**http://www.nytimes.com/**].

62. Sam A. Hardy, "Identity, Reasoning, and Emotion: An Empirical Comparison of Three Sources of Moral Motivation," *Motivation and Emotion* 30 (2006), p. 207.

63. Ibid.

64. Ruodan Shao, Karl Aquino, and Dan Freeman, "Beyond Moral Reasoning: A Review of Moral Identity Research and Its Implications for Business Ethics," *Business Ethics Quarterly* 18, no. 4 (2008), p. 513.

65. Edwin M. Hartman, "Can We Teach Character? An Aristotelian Answer," *Academy of Management Learning & Education* 5, No. 1 (2006), p. 68.

66. Tom Zucco, "Ethics Issues? Check Goals," *St. Petersburg Times,* January 28, 2006, p. 1D.

67. Ibid.

68. "Setting the Right Leadership Values Is Crucial for Ethics in the Workplace," *Ethics World,* December 31, 2010, p. 2 [**http://www.ethicsworld.org/ethicsandemployees/nbes.php**].

69. Ibid.

70. "2007 National Business Ethics Survey," *Ethics World,* December 31, 2010 [**http://www. ethicsworld.org/ethicsandemployees/nbes.php**].

71. Ibid.

72. Joseph L. Badaracco, Jr., and Allen P. Webb, "Business Ethics: A View from the Trenches," *California Management Review 37,* no. 2 (Winter 1995), pp. 8, 12.

73. Len Stein, "Where Has All the Trust Gone?" *Marketing Daily,* February 12, 2010 [**http:// www.mediapost/com/**].

74. Daniel Akst, "Room at the Top, for Improvement," *The Wall Street Journal,* October 26, 2004, p. D8.

75. Bill Hawkins, as told to Cait Murphy, "Bill Hawkins: How I Made the Toughest Call of My Career," BNET, October 5, 2009 [**http://www.bnet.com**].

76. Joseph L. Badaracco, Jr., *Defining Moments: When Managers Must Choose Between Right and Wrong* (Boston: Harvard Business School Press, 1997), p. 65.

77. Ashby Jones and Nathan Koppel, "Ethical Lapses Felled Long List of Company Executives," *The Wall Street Journal,* August 7, 2010 [**http://online.wsj.com/**].

78. Susan Pulliam, "The 'It Wasn't Me' Defense," *The Wall Street Journal,* July 9, 2004, p. B1.

79. Michael S. Schmidt, "With a Bow Tie and a Glove, the No. 1 Giant Relishes His Seat," *The New York Times,* July 15, 2010 [**http://www.nytimes.com**].

80. "Corruption Index 2010 from Transparency International: Find Out How Each Country Compares," DATABLOG, *guardian.co.uk,* October 26, 2010 [**http://www.guardian.co.uk/**].

81. Michael Mainville, "Bribery Thrives as Big Business in Putin's Russia," *SFGate.com,* January 2, 2007 [**http://www.sfgate.com/cgi-bin/article.cgi?file=/c/a/2007/01/02/MNG8QNBCTN1. DTL**].

82. Ibid.

83. Mark Magnier, "In China, Bribers Get Off Easy," *latimes.com,* August 10, 2007 [**http://www. latimes.com/news/la-fg-bribes10aug10,0,2674093.story?coll=la-tot-topstories& track=ntottext**]

84. Christoher W. Madel, Stephen P. Safranski, and E. Casey Beckett, "Enforcement of the Foreign Corrupt Practices Act in the Age of Obama," Robins, Kaplan, Miller & Ciresi, LLP, April 14, 2010 [**http://www.rkmc.com/files/Enforcement-of-the-Foreign-Corrupt-Practices-Act-in-the-Age-of-Obama.pdf**].

85. Mark Brzezinski, "Obama Administration Gets Tough on Business Corruption Overseas," *The Washington Post,* May 28, 2010, p. A23.

86. Matthew S. Queler, Emily Stern, and Benjamin R. Ogletree, "Recent FCPA and Anti-Corruption News Highlights the Ever-Growing Importance of Effective FCPA Compliance Programs," Proskauer Rose LLP, April 22, 2010 [**http://www.lexology.com/**].

87. Dionne Searcey, "U.K. Law on Bribes Has Firms in a Sweat," *The Wall Street Journal,* December 28, 2010 [**http://online.wsj.com/**].

88. Neil Weinberg, "Corporate Crime Wave Unabated," *Forbes.com,* October 16, 2007 [**http:// www.forbes.com/2007/10/16/corporate-crime-report-cx_nw_1016.html**]. 73 Pricewater-houseCoopers, "Global Economic Crime Survey 2007: US Supplement" [**http://www.pwc. com/extweb/pwcpublications.nsf/docid/7380702EC2F7BC248525736F00 5DC595**].

89. PricewaterhouseCoopers, "2009 Global Economic Crime Survey: "Economic Crime in a (Financial) Downturn," November 2009 [**http://www.pwccn.com/home/eng/econ_crime_ survey_nov2009.html**].

90. PricewaterhouseCoopers, "Accounting Fraud Increases," November 2009 [**http://www.pwc. com/gx/en/economic-crime-survey/key-findings/financial-statement-fraud.jhtml**].

91. Ibid.

92. Shawn Young and Peter Grant, "More Pinstripes to Get Prison Stripes," *The Wall Street Journal,* June 20, 2005, p. C1.

93. News Editor, "Sarbanes-Oxley Compliance Benefits Outweigh Costs, Companies Say," *EDGAROnline,* June 28, 2010 [**http://www.edgar-online.com/**].

94. Lora Bentley, "SEC Study: Benefits of Sarbanes-Oxley Compliance Outweigh Cost," *ITBusinessEdge,* October 16, 2009 [**http://www.itbusinessedge.com**].

95. Joann S. Lublin and Kara Scannell, "Critics See Some Good from Sarbanes-Oxley," *The Wall Street Journal,* July 30, 2007, p. B1.

96. Portions of this paragraph relied on Robert G. Morvillo and Robert J. Anello, "White-Collar Crime, Corporate Compliance Programs: No Longer Voluntary," *New York Law Journal,* December 7, 2004, p. 3.

97. "Competition, Antitrust & White-Collar Crime Update: Amendments to Sentencing Guidelines Affect Compliance Programs," *Thompson Hine,* April 16, 2010 [**http://www.thompsonhine.com/**].

98. See *United States v. Booker,* 125 S.Ct. 738 (2005), *Gall v. United States,* 128 S.Ct. 586 (2007), and *Kimbrough v. United States,* 128 S.Ct. 558 (2007).

99. *Rita v. United States,* 127 S.Ct. 2456 (2007).

100. Jeff Eckhoff, "Guidelines Used Less in Sentencing," *Des Moines Register,* March 19, 2006, p. 1B.

101. Gardiner Harris and Duff Wilson, "Glaxo to Pay $750 Million for Sale of Bad Products," *The New York Times,* October 26, 2010 [**http://www.nytimes.com/**].

102. Pallavi Gogoi, "The Trouble with Business Ethics," *BusinessWeek* online, June 25, 2007 [**http:// www.businessweek.com/bwdaily/dnflash/content/jun2007/db20070622_221291.htm**].

103. Jack Liles, "Blow the Whistle . . . Then Watch Out," *The Wall Street Journal,* February 21, 2002, p. A19.

104. Shel Horowitz, "Should Mary Buy Her Own Bonus?" *Business Ethics.* Submitted by Anonymous, August 1, 2007 [**http://www.business-ethics.com/node/65**].

105. Carl Kaufmann, "A Five-Part Quiz on Corporate Ethics," *Washington Post,* July 1, 1979, pp. C-1, C-4.

106. Sissela Bok, *Lying: Moral Choice in Public and Private Life* (New York: Vintage Books, 1999).

107. "Short Takes," *Des Moines Register,* February 5, 1990, p. 2T.

108. Ibid.

109. Leonard C. Lewin, "Ethical Aptitude Test," *Harper's,* October 1976, p. 21.

110. Reported on WKYT TV, Channel 27, Evening News, Lexington, Kentucky, May 12, 1980.

111. "Business Executives and Moral Dilemmas," *Business and Society Review,* no. 13 (Spring 1975), p. 51.

112. Robert Scheer, "The Invisible Hand Holds the Remote," *Los Angeles Times,* November 30, 2004, p. B13.

113. Ibid.

114. Albert Z. Carr, "Is Business Bluffing Ethical?" *Harvard Business Review* 46, no. 1 (January–February 1968), pp. 143–52.

CHAPTER THREE

The Corporation and Public Policy: Expanding Responsibilities

At the end of this chapter, students will be able to:

1. Recognize the interdependent relationship between business and the larger society.

2. Discuss whether business should play a more or less active role in politics, education, and other public-sector activities.

3. Discuss concerns about globalization such as the increasing wealth gap.

4. List some of the critics' primary complaints about the alleged abuse of corporate power in contemporary America.

5. Make a tentative assessment regarding the proper role of business in society.

6. Explain the concept of corporate social responsibility.

7. Discuss whether socially responsible business is "good business."

8. Explain the triple bottom line/sustainability approach to corporate citizenship.

9. Contrast the stakeholder and shareholder approaches to corporate social responsibility.

PRACTICING ETHICS   Yvon Chouinard and Patagonia

Outdoor adventurer Yvon Chouinard and his wife Ellen Pennoyer, in 1972, founded Patagonia, Inc., the sports clothing and outdoor gear retailer. Privately owned, Ventura, California-based Patagonia with annual revenues of more than $300 million is the product of entrepreneurial drive and a corporate culture practicing "green" business and "management by absence."

Chouinard, was an early advocate of doing business in an environmentally friendly way, including for example, placing notes in Patagonia catalogues encouraging customers to buy only what they need. Chouinard's 2005 memoir, *Let My People Go Surfing,* explains his commitment to a workplace where capitalism, ethics, and fun can coexist. Chouinard minimizes workplace monitoring, believing lightly supervised employees will complete their work responsibly. Good surf and fresh snow are embraced at Patagonia where employees are free to take breaks for fun. Patagonia is often recognized as one of the best companies to work for in America.

Chouinard has become famous for his sense of social responsibility and his leadership in the environmental movement. Since 1985, Patagonia has donated 1 percent of its annual sales to environmental groups.

Chouinard threatened to leave Patagonia in 1994 when he learned that the cotton bought by the company often was produced by industrial farming that used toxic chemicals and was having, he felt, a devastating effect on the Earth. That cotton figured in 20 percent of the company's sales, but Patagonia changed over to organic cotton and persuaded others such as Nike and Timberland to begin to do the same. Chouinard said that Patagonia went a year without making a profit while the company found organic suppliers, overcame bankers' resistance, and found new gins and mills. The bigger point is that the switch was profitable and the right thing to do, a concept often missed by corporate America, he said.

Patagonia clothing is made in China, Thailand, Vietnam, and a number of other countries along with limited production in the United States. In establishing ties with a new manufacturing partner, Patagonia's Social and Environmental Responsibility team does a comprehensive analysis and follows up with constant audits, visits, and corrective measures to assure a safe, healthy, environmentally sound operation. Patagonia refuses to contract with companies employing workers under the age of 15, the minimum age acceptable to the International Labor Organization. All workers must be paid "a legal minimum wage," but Patagonia admits to falling short of its goal of a "living wage" for all those who make its products. Having passed age 70, Chouinard continues to consider Patagonia a work in progress, as he tests his view that a company can do the right thing for its workers and the planet, and still prosper. [For more detail about Chouinard and Patagonia, see, e.g., Susan Casey, "Patagonia: Blueprint for Green Business," *Fortune,* May 29, 2007 [http://money.cnn.com/ magazines/fortune/fortune_archive/2007/04/02/8403423/index.htm].

Questions

1. Is Chouinard correct that companies can treat workers well, respect the environment, and still make money? Explain.

2. If he is correct, why aren't all companies following the Patagonia model?

Sources: Keith Garber, "Yvon Chouinard: Patagonia Founder Fights for the Environment," *U.S. News & World Report,* October 22, 2009 [http://www.usnews.com/news/best-leaders/articles/2009/10/22]; Brad Wieners, "The Gospel of Yvon," *Men's Journal,* July 2007, p. 51, "Employees Who March to Their Own Music," *BusinessWeek,* December 19, 2005, p. 81; and "Corporate Social Responsibility—FAQ's" Patagonia.com, [http://www.patagonia.com/us/patagonia.go?assetid=37493#compliance].

Introduction

The Yvon Chouinard/Patagonia story expresses the central mission of this chapter; the examination of the corporation's duties, if any, beyond providing the best products and services at the lowest price. We ask in this chapter whether the corporation must make a broad contribution to the general societal welfare beyond the performance required by the market. Put another way, must the corporation fulfill the role of citizen with all of the responsibilities that corporate wealth and power suggest? Clearly, tomorrow's leaders must understand the increasingly complex and interdependent relationship between business and the larger society. We explore the changing nature of that relationship in four parts: (1) criticism of corporate America, (2) the emergence of the expectation of corporate social responsibility, (3) the management of social responsibility, and (4) the examination of some specific business and society issues.

Part One—Corporate Power and Corporate Critics

Corporate critics have long argued that the public interest has not been well served by America's big corporations. We recognize that colossal size and the economies of scale that accompany it have been critical to American competitiveness in today's tough global market. At the same time, that very size, the critics say, permits continuing abuse of the American public. Of course, we recognize that big companies are a fixture of the American landscape. However, a reminder of the specifics may be useful. (This chapter's examination of corporate America is limited to the critics' objections to corporate conduct. The legal standards governing corporate practice are addressed primarily in Chapter 9.)

Walmart is now the largest company in America (see Table 3.1) and the first service company to hold the top spot. Walmart is, by a wide margin, America's number one employer with some 2.1 million workers globally, 1.4 million of whom work in the United States.[1]

TABLE 3.1   **America's Largest Corporations**

Corporation	Location	Sales Revenue (in billions)
Walmart Stores	Bentonville, AK	$421,849
ExxonMobil	Irving, TX	354,674
Chevron	San Ramon, CA	196,337
ConocoPhillips	Houston, TX	184,966
Fannie Mae	Washington, DC	153,825

Source: *Fortune* 500 2011 Annual Ranking of America's Largest Corporations.

The extraordinary wealth of America's corporate institutions is such that they tower over most countries of the world by some measures of economic might. If we compare corporate revenue with gross national product, (a common approach, but one that somewhat overstates the size of corporations relative to countries) Walmart is the 22nd largest economic entity in the world and 44 of the 100 largest economic entities are corporations.[2]

The critics' concerns seem to be shared by many Americans. According to a 2011 Gallup Poll, 62 percent of Americans want major corporations to have less influence in the United States, and 67 percent expressed dissatisfaction with the size and influence of those corporations. According to the poll, 2002 was the last year in which more Americans were satisfied with corporate size and influence than were dissatisfied. Even among Republicans, who are generally supportive of the business community, 49 percent believe major corporations should have less influence, and among those Americans making $75,000 and over, 73 percent believe those corporations should have less influence.[3]

> Only 19 percent of Americans expressed "a great deal" or "quite a lot" of confidence in big business.

The Corporate State

Clearly, corporate giants are among the most powerful institutions in global life, but as the critics see it, they have failed to fulfill the responsibilities that accompany that dramatic power. Indeed, substantial evidence suggests those corporations have often abused their privileged positions.

Tax Policy

Changing American tax policy graphically reveals the corporate community's extraordinary influence in shaping the nation's priorities. A 2004 study shows that the effective tax rate for America's biggest corporations has declined sharply in recent years, and one-third of those companies paid zero taxes or less in at least one of the three years of the study period.[4] Likewise, revenue from corporate income tax fell from between 5 and 6 percent of U.S. gross domestic product in the early 1950s to 2.1 percent of GDP in 2008.[5] *Forbes* and ABC News explained the critics' view of the corporate tax situation:

> As you work on your taxes this month, here's something to raise your hackles: Some of the world's biggest, most profitable corporations enjoy a far lower tax rate than you do; that is, if they pay taxes at all. The most egregious example is General Electric. Last year (2009) the conglomerate generated $10.3 billion in pretax income, but ended up owing nothing to Uncle Sam.[6]

Successful tax avoidance is the product of a number of strategies, but in very general terms, General Electric and other big companies use lawful accounting maneuvers to allocate income and assets to low-tax countries while attributing expenses to U.S. operations. Thus while the United States' 35 percent corporate tax rate is higher than most industrial nations, much of that burden is escaped. As Warren Buffett, one of the world's richest men put it, "If class warfare is being waged in America, my class is clearly winning."[7]

[See U.S. Senator Bernie Sanders' (Ind.—Vt.) brief speech criticizing corporate tax loopholes at **http://www.youtube.com/watch?v=Sknt-UBRhxo**]

Misconduct/Incompetence?

Of course, the stunning scandals and financial failures of recent years, (the subprime loan collapse, Bernard Madoff's $65 billion Ponzi scheme, Wall Street's meltdown, Enron, WorldCom, and so on) have strengthened doubts about corporate honor and competence. A 2007 national survey shows that Americans are "deeply worried" about America's future and that corporate misconduct is a "major source" of that anxiety.[8] Eighty percent of Americans believe poor management decisions by big businesses and unnecessary risks by banks and other financial institutions bore either "a great deal" or a "good amount" of the blame for the nation's troubled economic condition.[9] (For the U.S. government's official analysis of the causes of the financial crisis, go to Financial Crisis Inquiry Commission Web site [**http://fcic.law.stanford.edu/**].)

The Big Banks

We should not be surprised that giant financial institutions are a particular source of anger and mistrust for Americans. Taxpayer money bailed out these giants during the financial

> **Wall Street appears unreformed and unrepentant.**

collapse of 2007 and thereafter, but Wall Street appears unreformed and unrepentant. Thomas Hoenig, president of the Federal Reserve Bank of Kansas City, notes that the five largest financial institutions are 20 percent larger than they were before the crisis. He calculates their control of financial assets at $8.6 trillion—equivalent to 60 percent of the gross domestic product.[10] And although the Dodd-Frank Wall Street Reform and Consumer Protection Act of 2010 (See Chapter 8) imposes formidable new restraints on the financial industry, enormous risks persist because these banks remain "too big to fail"; that is, we fear that we cannot allow them to fail because our economy would be fatally crippled if we did so.

"Why Isn't Wall Street in Jail?

A 2011 *Rolling Stone* analysis of the big banks' role in the nation's financial crisis claims, "Financial crooks brought down the world's economy—but the feds are doing more to protect them than to prosecute them." Part of the blame, as *Rolling Stone* sees it, is the "Revolving Door" where regulators go to work for banks and bankers sometimes become high-ranking regulators and all maintain a chummy, clubby relationship while "constantly switching sides and trading hats." While researching the article, author Matt Taibbi says he was given the following advice by a former Senate investigator: "Everything's f***ed up, nobody's going to jail. That's your whole story right there. Hell, you don't even have to write the rest of it. Just write that."

The close and cooperative ties between big banks/big business and the government was further illustrated in a recent *New York Times* investigation that claims federal prosecutors, in recent years, have softened their approach to corporate crime. After very aggressive prosecutions that sent senior executives at Enron, WorldCom, Tyco, ImClone, and others to jail, the Justice Department, according to the *Times,* began around 2005 to give companies more credit than in the past for cooperating with authorities while also increasing *deferred prosecutions* which often delayed or canceled criminal action if companies cooperated and promised to improve their conduct. The "gentler" approach can save government money and achieve other efficiencies, but critics think wrongdoers are simply let off too easily.

Sources: Gretchen Morgenson and Louise Story, "As Wall St. Polices Itself, Prosecutors Use Softer Approach," *The New York Times,* July 7, 2011 [**http://www.nytimes.com/**]; and Matt Taibbi, "Why Isn't Wall Street in Jail?" *Rolling Stone,* February 16, 2011 [**http://www.rollingstone.com/politics/news/why-isnt-wall-street-in-jail-200110216**].

Monopoly and More

Corporate monopoly/oligopoly problems are not limited to banking, of course. Barry C. Lynn's 2010 book, *Cornered: The New Monopoly Capitalism and the Economics of Destruction,* makes the claim that much of America's economy is dominated by shared monopolies allowing producers and retailers to charge inflated prices because of a lack of meaningful competition. He points to domination by two or three giants in a wide array of consumer product markets: beer, tooth paste, pet foods, milk, and so on. Walmart and other retail goliaths cooperate so closely with their suppliers in pricing, shelf space assignments, etc., that, Lynn claims, real competition simply doesn't exist in many product lines.[11] (For much more detail about monopoly problems and antitrust law, see Chapters 10 and 11.)

Likewise complaints about the corporate role in pollution, discrimination, white-collar crime, misleading advertising, and so on remain commonplace. But in a democratic, free market society like America's, presumably we all must share some of the blame for our problems. If we are not happy with, for example, Walmart's treatment of its employees, we are free to shop elsewhere. Arguably, then, the role of business in American life merely reflects the values of the American people. Thus, the critics' broader concern is that America has committed its very soul to business values in a way that is progressively undermining our national well-being. We will briefly examine that argument prior to turning to our more detailed study of corporate social responsibility and government regulation of business.

America's Soul?

Critics contend that the power of the business community has become so encompassing that virtually all dimensions of American life have absorbed elements of the business ethic. Values commonly associated with businesspeople (competition, profit-seeking, reliance on technology, faith in growth) have overwhelmed traditional humanist values (cooperation, individual dignity, human rights, meaningful service to society). In the name of wealth, efficiency and productivity, the warmth, decency, and value of life have been debased. We engage in meaningless work. Objects dominate our existence. We operate as replaceable cogs in a vast, bureaucratic machine. Indeed, we lose ourselves, the critics argue. Charles Reich, former Yale University law professor, addressed the loss of self in his influential book of the Vietnam War era, *The Greening of America:*

> Objects dominate our existence.

> Of all of the forms of impoverishment that can be seen or felt in America, loss of self, or death in life, is surely the most devastating. . . . Beginning with school, if not before, an individual is systematically stripped of his imagination, his creativity, his heritage, his dreams, and his personal uniqueness, in order to style him into a productive unit for a mass, technological society. Instinct, feeling, and spontaneity are repressed by overwhelming forces. As the individual is drawn into the meritocracy, his working life is split from his home life, and both suffer from a lack of wholeness. Eventually, people virtually become their professions, roles, or occupations, and are henceforth strangers to themselves.[12]

Some interesting empirical evidence supports Reich's view that we have become hollow men and women dominated by the demands of big institutions. The Harris Alienation Index shows a generally steady rise in Americans' feelings of powerlessness from 1966 when the index stood at 29 to the 1999 poll in which the index stood at 62.[13] Alienation, as defined in the survey, includes feelings of economic inequity (the rich get richer, the poor get poorer), feelings of disdain about the people in power, and feelings of powerlessness (being left out and not counting for much). The results since 1999, however, have improved with the 2010 Index at 52.[14]

> Actor Ben Stein lamented an increasingly divided America.

Actor and conservative commentator Ben Stein, speaking in 2006, lamented an increasingly divided America where the interests of corporations and the wealthy are dominant and the well-being of others is in danger of being forgotten:

> The Saturday before Memorial Day I spoke to a gathering of widows and widowers, parents and children of men and women in uniform who have lost their lives in Iraq and Afghanistan. The

person who spoke before me was a beautiful woman named Joanna Wroblewski, whose husband of less than two years—after four years of dating at Rutgers—had been killed in Iraq. She cried as she spoke. . . . She spoke of her devotion to her country and her husband's pride in the flag. . . .

Are we keeping the faith with Joanna Wroblewski? . . . Are we maintaining an America that is not just a financial neighborhood, but also a brotherhood and a sisterhood worth losing your husband for? Is this still a community of the heart, or a looting opportunity? Will there even be a free America for Mrs. Wroblewski's descendants, or will we be a colony of the people [foreign lenders] to whom we have sold our soul?[15]

Corporations as Psychopaths?

The 2004 movie documentary, *The Corporation,* argues that the corporation has become the dominant institution in American life, exceeding the influence of both religion and government. One result is that corporations often demonstrate the "traits of the prototypical psychopath." The contemporary corporation is depicted as an "exploitative monster" driven not by the greater good but by its first responsibility to stockholders.

Questions

1. In your view are corporations more powerful than government, religion, our educational system, and all other American institutions? Explain.

2. According to some polls, nearly three-quarters of Americans think corporations have too much power. Do you agree that corporations are too powerful? Explain.

Source: Jim Keough, "Film Sees Evil in Corporations," *Worchester Telegram & Gazette,* September 29, 2004, p. C5.

 [For *The Corporation* in 23 chapters, see **http://www.thecorporation.com/index.cfm? page_id=46**]

Politics

Now we turn to a more particularized examination of the corporate critics' concerns. We begin with politics, where critics charge that big money enables the business community to disproportionately influence the electoral and law-making processes.

In recent decades, the corporate community has taken an increasingly direct role in the political process. As a result, corporate critics have been concerned that the financial weight of big business will undermine our pluralist, democratic approach to governance.

Corporate funds cannot lawfully be given directly to candidates for federal office. However, corporations (as well as labor unions, special interest groups, and others) can lawfully establish political action committees (PACs) to solicit and disburse voluntary campaign contributions. That is, corporations can solicit contributions from employees, shareholders, and others. That money is then put in a fund, carefully segregated from general corporate accounts, and disbursed by the PAC in support of a political agenda preferred by officers, managers, or shareholders. Although PAC contributions are voluntary, corporate employees often feel pressured to participate. Unlike the federal rules, about one half of the states allow corporations to lawfully donate corporate funds to parties and candidates for state elections.[16]

The role of PACs in the political process remains important, but a U.S. Supreme Court decision in the 2010 *Citizens United* case[17] opened an additional important avenue for a corporate voice in the political process by striking down federal laws that had restricted some forms of corporate contributions. As a consequence of *Citizens United,* unlimited company funds (money from the corporate treasury) can now lawfully be expended to influence federal elections so long as that money does not go directly to candidates and political parties. In practice, that money goes to independent advocacy groups that favor particular candidates, parties, or issues (such as opposition to gay marriage or support for lower taxes). Unions and other large incorporated organizations also now operate under those same rules. The Supreme Court's highly controversial 5–4 ruling held that federal laws limiting corporate campaign contributions violated corporate free speech rights. Essentially, the decision allows corporations, labor unions and some other aggregations to spend unlimited organizational funds for candidates and causes so long as the money is spent independently of parties and candidates; that is, so long as the corporations, unions and others do not coordinate their spending with the candidates or parties. The *Citizens United* decision did nothing to change rules regulating PAC contributions.

> The Supreme Court's highly controversial 5–4 ruling.

The five "conservative" justices in the *Citizens United* majority, treating dollars as speech, saw political spending limits as a direct denial of liberty guaranteed by the First Amendment. Corporations and labor unions were viewed by the Court as associations of individuals that should possess the same constitutional rights as the individuals themselves. Previous high court rulings had frequently recognized that First Amendment rights extend to corporations and that corporations are persons for some legal purposes. The four dissenters, from the "liberal" wing of the Court, argued that corporations and unions, in many other ways, are not treated as people and doing so in the case of political contributions could allow those organizations to dominate and further corrupt the political process.

A healthy democracy depends on the broad expression of multiple viewpoints; that is, a marketplace of ideas battling for supremacy. Supporters of the *Citizens United* decision see a more robust political process while critics fear the decision has opened the political process to gushers of money from corporate interests thus overwhelming the voice of the people. Eight in 10 Americans oppose the decision, according to a 2010 poll, with Republicans and Democrats holding similar views.[18] The full effect of the decision will not be known for some time, but *The Nation* expressed a broadly shared fear:

> This decision tips the balance against active citizenship and the rule of law by making it possible for the nation's most powerful economic interests to manipulate not just individual politicians and electoral contests but political discourse itself.[19]

Corporate Influence

Corporate donations often seem motivated not so much by ideological goals as by pragmatic efforts to secure influence in Washington, DC During the 2006 election cycle, business PACs gave a total of $234 million, 66 percent of which went to Republicans who were then in control of Congress. After the Democrats regained the congressional majority in that 2006 election, 58 percent of the early, business PAC contributions for the 2008 election went to Democrats.[20] According to *The New York Times,* the business community's primary lobbyist, the U.S. Chamber of Commerce, received $2 million from Prudential Financial in 2009 at the time the Chamber was commencing its campaign to weaken Congress's rewrite of financial regulations, Dow Chemical forwarded $1.7 million to the Chamber in 2009 as the Chamber exerted its leadership against proposed rules to tighten security requirements at chemical facilities, and Goldman Sachs joined others in donating more than $8 million in recent years as the Chamber increased its criticism of federal regulation and spending.[21]

Of course, corporate interests are by no means unified behind one party or one ideology. Furthermore, many powerful voices, including wealthy individuals, issue advocacy groups, and labor unions are also big campaign spenders. Indeed, as the 2010 election approached, the American Federation of State, County and Municipal Employees (a union) had committed $87.5 million to the elections, exceeding the Chamber's expected $75 million total.[22]

Finally, we should acknowledge the strategic importance of political participation by big companies and respect the contribution that voice can make to effective political decision making. On its Web site, U.S. Bancorp, America's 11th largest bank in 2010, explained its "Political Contribution Policy":

> U.S. Bancorp believes that an important part of responsible corporate citizenship is participation in the political and public policy process. The focus of these efforts is on issues that affect the company, our operations and our stakeholders, such as our employees, customers, shareholders and local communities. As a large financial institution, our business is subject to extensive laws and regulations at the federal, state and local levels, and changes to these laws can significantly affect how we operate, our revenues and the costs we incur. It is important for U.S. Bancorp to engage in the political process in order to advance our long-term interests. . . .[23]

Boycott Target?

The *Citizens United* decision seems to have given a legal and psychological boost to corporate political contributions, but the risks can be significant. Minnesota-based Target's $150,000 contribution in 2010 to MN Forward, a group supporting a conservative candidate for Minnesota governor was angrily assailed by some company employees and many Minnesota progressives. The specific objection was that the candidate indirectly supported by Target was an outspoken opponent of gay marriage. Target said it supported the candidate's strong pro-business policies. Nonetheless, protesters rallied against the company and urged a boycott of Target stores. Target, issued an apology, reaffirmed its commitment to diversity and promised a review process for political donations. Many shoppers remained dubious. As one said: "You need to know where your money ends up."[24] (Best Buy, 3M and others likewise made MN Forward contributions, but with much less controversy.)

Questions

1. Would you have boycotted Target under these circumstances? Explain.
2. Had you been Target's CEO, would you have issued an apology? Explain.
3. Should corporations be free under the law to donate corporate treasury funds as they see fit in federal elections? Explain.

Sources: Tom Hamburger and Jennifer Martinez, "Target Stores Negotiate with Gay-Lesbian Group over Political Spending," *latimes.com,* August 13, 2010 [**http://www.latimes.com/**]; and Martiga Lohn, "Target's Gay Employees Are Angered by Political Donation," *The Des Moines Register,* July 28, 2010, p. 1A.

Lobbying

Government decisions have enormous influence on business practice. Consequently, lobbying is an essential ingredient in big business strategy. Lobbying also often serves the very useful role of efficiently educating busy politicians about the vast array of issues they must address but cannot possibly master without assistance. Of course, lobbying is not confined to the business community. Labor unions, consumer and environmental interest groups and myriad others battle to have their voices heard. So lobbying serves a valuable role in government. Unfortunately, that role is often thoroughly corrupt. The clubby, personal nature of the lobbying process with its revolving door of politicians becoming lobbyists and lobbyists taking important government roles often undermines the democratic process. *The Washington Post* provided a discouraging example of these problems:

> It's the kind of story that seems to confirm everything people believe is sleazy about the way Washington works. . . . Sue Ellen Wooldridge, then the head of the Justice Department's environmental division, bought a $1 million vacation home with Don R. Duncan, the top lobbyist for oil company ConocoPhillips. Nine months later, Ms. Wooldridge signed off on a settlement agreement that let ConocoPhillips delay the installation of pollution-control equipment and the payment of fines.[25]

Lobbying by the Numbers

A slightly diminished army of 11,116 lobbyists was registered in 2010 to influence the Washington, DC political process.[26] Big oil and gas interests spent $170 million lobbying in 2009 to reach a total of over $1 billion expended over a 12-year period.[27] With 600 registered lobbyists, the oil and gas contingent is among the biggest and most powerful in Washington, and according to *The Washington Post,* 430 of that group had previously worked in the executive or legislative branches of the federal government.[28] The "revolving door" in the oil lobby is characteristic of the lobbying community generally where, according to the Center for Responsive Politics, more than 340 former members of Congress and nearly 3,700 former government staffers work in lobbying or a related field.[29]

> A slightly diminished army of 11,116 lobbyists was registered in 2010.

Buy Votes?

In the end, does all of the corporate money buy votes? In many cases, apparently not. A recent, highly respected study of lobbying results found that most lobbying simply maintains the status quo; that is, nothing happens. The study concluded that opposing lobbyists and interest groups hold each other in check about 60 percent of the time. Thus, lobbyists, over a four-year period are successful in influencing policy about 40 percent of the time. The study also concluded that money influenced outcomes only when heavily weighted to one side.[30] A veteran nonprofit lobbyist, however, argued that corporations are successful about 20 percent of the time while his nonprofit, Public Citizen, and its modest $3 million budget is successful, he estimates, about five percent of the time.[31] In any case, even if lobbying and corporate money do not buy votes, they certainly buy access and returned phone calls; and contrary to the aforementioned study, a *BusinessWeek* investigation found evidence that lobbying can pay off in very big ways. *BusinessWeek* looked at the nearly 2,000 congressional earmarks (special funding requests outside the regular legislative process) that went to companies in 2005. The study found that companies generated "roughly $28 in earmark revenue for every dollar they spent lobbying."[32] More than 20 of those companies gained $100 or more for each dollar they spent lobbying.[33] [For the Center for Responsive Politics and its extensive database on money in politics, see **http://www.opensecrets.org/**]

Curb Lobbying?

Prompted by recent lobbying scandals, the Honest Leadership and Open Government Act of 2007 is part of the most comprehensive lobbying and ethics reform effort in the federal government in many years. Among its many provisions, the bill toughens penalties, requires much more thorough reporting of lobbying activity, and prohibits members of Congress and their staffs from receiving, with some exceptions, gifts and meals and travel assistance of any value from registered lobbyists, their employers (including corporations and nonprofits), and certain others. The law seems to have had some immediate impact in that the 2010 total of 11,116 registered lobbyists represented a decline of 25 percent in the three years following enactment.[34] Cozy lobbyist/politician moments will not go away soon, however. Critics say that Congress is liberally interpreting the new rules "doing little more than tightening gift rules, replacing full meals with finger food, and barring parties honoring individual lawmakers."[35] (For more details on loopholes in the 2007 lobbying law, see Robert Pear, "Ethics Law Isn't Without Its Loopholes," *The New York Times,* April 20, 2008 [**http://www.nytimes.com/2008/04/20/washington/20lobby.html**].)

The Business Voice Everywhere?

Clearly, the business community's influence in America's political life is enormous, but the critics' concerns only begin there. The corporate message pervades and shapes American life. In an editorial, *The Des Moines Register* commented that commercials have become so interwoven with our total existence that they cannot effectively be "separated out." Commentator Jane Eisner laments the increasing immersion of very young children in America's commercial culture:

> The typical first grader can name 200 brands and acquires an average of 70 new toys a year. American children view an estimated 40,000 commercials annually. Teen purchasing power has risen so rapidly that teenagers spend on average $100 a week.[36]

*   *   *   *   *

The NPD Group reports that the average monthly spending on beauty products for 8 to 12 year-old girls is $9.20,[37] and Professor Gigi Durham in her book, *The Lolita Effect,* laments the constant bombardment of children by sexual messages such as Abercrombie and Fitch's thong underwear for children decorated with phrases "Eye Candy" and "Wink, Wink."[38] Business products, business marketing, and business values saturate and dominate all corners of American life, the critics claim.

Schools

Seeking quality education for their own needs and for the nation, corporations now prepare model curricula and lesson plans while donating money and other resources to improve school performance. Likewise, the corporate community has aggressively encouraged innovative reforms. As former federal Education Secretary Margaret Spellings put it, "business is becoming the voice of reform."[39]

Likewise, as explained in Chapter 1, the profit-making corporation, EdisonLearning, has contracted to consult with and operate schools in about 25 states. The results thus far have not been particularly encouraging, and the free market approach along with the more vigorous corporate role in education reform has intensified critics' concerns that cash-short schools have become vulnerable to corporate marketing strategies that will further indoctrinate students in business values and practices.

Some schools sell ad space on school buses and Web sites, among other places. In late 2010, the financially struggling Los Angeles, California school district, the second largest in the nation, agreed to begin seeking sponsors for school activities including sports, the arts, and academic programs. The district indicated that sponsors might have naming rights for school activities, permission to place their logos in some school locations, or the opportunity to pass out food samples in school cafeterias. Unhealthy food, alcohol, tobacco, and firearms cannot be promoted. The district hopes for millions of dollars in sponsorships.[40] Critics deplore the creeping commercialism:

> "I am enormously sympathetic to the plight of schools today," said Susan Lynn, director of the Campaign for a Commercial-Free Childhood in Boston. But "when schools become businesses, the well-being and education of children is no longer the focus."[41]

Channel One has supplied educational programming and television sets to schools that agree to show the programming and accompanying ads on a regular basis. Nearly 6 million children watch Channel One. The 12-minute telecasts include two minutes of ads. Channel One says that advertisers do not influence the news content, and the programming has won awards for excellence.[42] A 2006 study of middle school students, however, demonstrates the commercial risks of Channel One. The students remembered more of the ads than they did the news programs, and the students reported buying or having their parents buy products advertised on Channel One.[43] (The study made no effort to separate the influence of Channel One ads from other ads that the students might have encountered.) Forty-seven percent of respondents to a 2004 Harris Poll of professionals in youth advertising said that schools should be protected from advertising while 45 percent felt that young people could handle the ads.[44] [For the Channel One news, see **http://www.channelone.com**]

BusRadio would have piped entertainment and ads into school buses.

Many schools have actively resisted growing commercialization. The Louisville, Kentucky, schools responded to parents' outrage by rejecting in 2007 the new BusRadio product that would have piped entertainment programming and ads into school buses in exchange for which the school district would have received a portion of the ad revenue.[45]

Big business is also accused of turning college campuses into marketing and development opportunities. More and more campus buildings and programs, for example, are being named after corporate donors, and students are increasingly being hired as on-campus marketing representatives for companies/products such as EA, Sports Illustrated, Nike, and Red Bull. Pharmacy benefits manager, Express Scripts, became one of the first corporations to put its headquarters directly on a college campus in 2007 when it moved into its $50 million building at the University of Missouri at St. Louis. Students welcome the opportunity to conveniently work at the on-campus company, but critics worry about blending corporate and educational interests.

From kindergarten through graduate school, education is increasingly viewed as a product to be marketed and consumed on the road to prosperity in the corporate state. Are students buying a full life or an empty commercial dream?

Religion

The ideas of management guru Peter Drucker have become the unexpected intellectual foundation of the megachurch movement in America. The giant churches with thousands of parishioners in cavernous halls including former professional basketball arenas have applied Drucker's business principles to their "businesses":

> Bill Hybels, the pastor of the 17,000-strong Willow Creek Community Church in South Barrington, Illinois, has a quotation from Mr. Drucker hanging outside his office: "What is our business? Who is our customer? What does the customer consider the value?"[46]

Religion, in some sense, has become a product.

Churches now routinely employ standard business practices such as advertising, promotional giveaways, and marketing campaigns. Religion, in some sense, has become a product. With the domestic religious market "saturated," some U.S. megachurches are creating international ministries.[47] The Reverend Troy Gramling, pastor of the Flamingo Road Church, based in Broward County, Florida is building a global congregation. He says he has tried to copy the success of Starbucks' branding strategy, and he once attracted new members by giving away $10 Starbucks gift cards.[48]

Megachurch pastor David Platt questions the commercial direction of contemporary religion in his book, *Radical: Taking Back Your Faith from the American Dream*. Platt says the megachurches have taken on corporate characteristics in competing for market

The megachurches have taken on corporate characteristics.

share by serving as social centers while offering day care and comfortable entertainment.[49] Platt asks his followers to put a cap on their consumer lives, believing that our pursuit of the materialist American Dream cannot be reconciled with an authentic spiritual life.[50]

To many Christians, Jesus is a pop-culture icon[51] and thus is the inspiration for a vast array of commercial expressions including T-shirts, license plates, dolls, video games, flip flops, perfume, golf balls, scripture chocolates, and much more. The marriage of religion and commerce has even reached the business of sports where "Faith Nights" have become popular promotional devices at professional ball games. The Atlanta Braves and Arizona Diamondbacks major league baseball teams have sponsored Faith Nights, but that approach has been particularly successful in the minor leagues where Christian entertainers, player testimonies, faith trivia quizzes, and bobbleheads of Samson and other Biblical characters draw big crowds. [For a review of *Christianity Incorporated: How Big Business Is Buying the Church,* see **http://www.directionjournal.org/article/?1301**]

Questions

1. Do you see any risks to religion in treating it as a product to be marketed and sold? Explain.
2. *a.* Why has religion increasingly become a product in the commercial world?
   b. Is everything a product in some sense?

Culture

Does America possess a cultural life? For decades, the concern was that so-called "high" culture—classical music, opera, ballet, and the like—would give way to rock and roll, television, and video games. Now that battle is over; Americans (and the world) have clearly voted for MTV and *American Idol.*

> Americans (and the world) have clearly voted for *American Idol.*

Corporate America has been generous in its financial and organizational support for the traditional intellectual culture. At the same time, corporate bottom-line concerns appear to the critics to be steadily degrading America's cultural life.

For example, a 2007 Los Angeles Museum of Contemporary Art exhibit merged art and commerce by setting up a Louis Vuitton shop in the middle of the museum. The boutique sold limited-edition handbags and small leather goods designed by Japanese artist Takashi Murakami, who has developed a reputation for deliberately blurring the line between art and commerce.[52] Of course, the museum made the decision, and the market will rule on the wisdom of that decision, but the concern of the critics is that corporate financial interests are casting a long shadow of influence across the American cultural scene.[53]

Even popular culture (rock, movies, television, hip hop, and so on), already considered a wasteland, has been further debased the critics say, not merely by a mindless market (that's us), but by limitless corporate greed, indifference to quality, and relentless consolidation.

The *Los Angeles Times* recently asked: "Are the Corporate Suits Ruining TV?"[54] As the *Times* explained, "Your TV may receive 200 channels, but virtually every one of them is owned by one of six big companies—NBC Universal, Disney, Time Warner, Viacom/Paramount, Sony, and News Corp."[55] Similarly, one 1,200 station giant, Clear Channel, dominates and, critics say, debases the radio industry by its "McDonald's approach to programming" that makes one station virtually indistinguishable from another regardless of locale.[56] Syndicated shows and national DJs replace independent programming decisions and local personalities resulting in increasingly standardized playlists and programs.

> Are the Corporate Suits Ruining TV?

Concerns about the corporate threat to the quality of TV and radio have been extended in recent years to the creation of pop music itself. Music artists have turned to the corporate community for the support the recording industry could no longer provide. Red Bull, Nike, Dr. Martens, and Mountain Dew are among the brands that are sponsoring artists, or even creating their own record labels. Converse provides free music studio space (Converse Rubber Tracks) in New York City to selected bands. Converse says it will have no influence on the music, but it does hope that the association with music groups will give it an advantage in the marketplace. Media critic Douglas Rushkoff sounds skeptical about these arrangements: "Artists are finding the only way to achieve any financial safety is to become a lapdog of the great corporations, just like the great painters did in the Renaissance."[57]

Sports

Former National Collegiate Athletic Association (NCAA) president Myles Brand, speaking at an ethics conference, made the argument that: "College sports is not a business. It's about educating young men and women in the field and in the classroom."[58] College men's basketball coaching legend Bob Knight did not agree:

> College sports is not a business.

If it isn't a business then General Motors is a charity. College sports has turned into one of the biggest businesses in the whole sports industry. I use the word industry because that's what sport is. . . .[59]

Agreeing with Knight, sports columnist Michael Rosenberg pointed to the wholesale embrace of business values by America's biggest universities:

I'll give schools this much: They aren't even faking it any more. It's every chancellor for himself out there. Everything is for sale: conference affiliations, rivalries, game times, luxury suites, buildings—you name it.[60]

Of course, profit-seeking in collegiate sports is not without its benefits. Thousands of students complete college every year who might otherwise not have done so, funding is provided for many unprofitable sports including women's programs, and sports revenues often support academic programs. Reportedly, Notre Dame's very lucrative NBC television football contract sustains scholarships, doctoral study, and minority fellowships, and at the University of North Carolina, Chapel Hill, 75 cents of every dollar earned on the sale of trademarked apparel goes to financial aid.[61] Many students share the benefits of the business of college sports, but in the process academic programs become ever more financially intertwined with and dependent on the success of sports teams. Clearly, the market has spoken loudly and clearly for the excitement of college sports, but is the market mistaken?

What Have We Lost?   The conversion of athletics, both professional and collegiate, from sport to business is essentially an accomplished fact, but its significance remains unclear. What have we lost when the innocence and idealism of sports are forfeited in favor of profit? Or are innocence and idealism simply a myth? Perhaps we are better off when corporate and personal profit—the free market—drives sports. Or is the pursuit of profit the route to the slow but sure death of meaningful sports, as one fan lamented?

We would be a healthier society if professional sports did not exist. The love of money, or greed, takes all the fun out of sports, demeans the integrity of the games, corrupts the athletes and belittles the fans. . . . The love of money is slowly, subtly destroying sports and America.[62]

> No sales venue is too tacky for the tastes of sports marketers.

Marketing   Now that major league baseball has authorized the use of team logos on a line of caskets,[63] we know definitively that no sales venue is too tacky for the tastes of sports marketers. What does the future hold for the business of sports? One critic imagines the following:

One day, perhaps the New York Yankees may morph into the IBM Yankees, ballplayers will decorate their uniforms with soft drink brands, and the Exxon Cowboys might win the General Motors Super Bowl.[64]

High School Next?   Business values and practices having spread from professional sports to college athletics, we should not be surprised, although perhaps we should be dismayed, that the same influences are rapidly emerging in high school sports as well. Elite high school teams travel the country to play in special games. Burger King, a sponsor for some of those games, is happy with the potent commercial prospects in high school sports:

"We like the fit with our customer," Burger King chief marketing officer Russ Klein said. "We like what the sport stands for. We like the every-town authenticity and appeal that high school football represents. We think it's an underdeveloped and untapped segment, and we're going to be aggressive about building it on the national stage."[65]

Will high school football emerge as the next great sports marketing opportunity? Some business leaders think so:

"I think high school sports is the next iteration where fans are going," said Ira Stahlberger, senior vice president of strategic partnerships for Intersport . . . "The market follows where the fans are. People are extremely passionate about the NFL. They are extremely passionate about college football. Next is high school football."[66]

PRACTICING ETHICS   The Sports Business and Compromised Values?

I. ESPN.

Great aggregations of money inevitably raise great ethical threats. *The New York Times,* in 2011, reported that ESPN broadcaster, Erin Andrews, had recently signed an endorsement deal with Reebok, and that other personalities at ESPN including Chris Fowler, Kirk Herbstreit, and Lee Corso had deals with Nike. Fowler subsequently decided to end his "minor association" with Nike. An ESPN spokesperson indicated that the network was unaware of the Nike contracts, but that such arrangements were common and were allowed by ESPN on a case-by-case basis. The ESPN personalities apparently had only modest responsibilities, such as speaking engagements, with their Nike sponsors, and Corso indicated that "we wear their product" but the contract had no impact on his work.

Questions

1. The core ethical risk in these contracts for ESPN and its broadcasters is the possibility of conflicts of interest.
   a. Explain those potential conflicts.
   b. As you see it, are those potential conflicts worrisome? Explain.

Source: Richard Sandomir, "Several ESPN Broadcasters Have Had Shoe Contracts," *The New York Times,* February 14, 2011 [http://www.nytimes.com/].

II. Nike.

Timothy Egan in *The New York Times* commented on Nike's relationship with Pittsburg Steelers quarterback Ben Roethlisberger, who was accused in 2010 of sexual assault on a 20-year-old woman:

Is there anything creepier than a big, beer-breathed celebrity athlete exposing himself in a night club and hitting on underage girls, all the while protected by an entourage of off-duty cops? Well, yes. It's the big, corporate sponsor—Nike, in this case—that continues to sell product with the creep as their role model."[67]

No criminal charges were filed in the case, but Roethlisberger was suspended by the National Football League for four games, and the owner of the company that marketed "Big Ben's Beef Jerky" reportedly ended his company's endorsement relationship with the quarterback. Roethlisberger had been accused of similar misconduct in other episodes.

Questions

1. Was Nike wrong to retain its endorsement relationship with Roethlisberger? Explain.

2. Prior to Roethlisberger's appearance with the Steelers in the 2011 Super Bowl, Ward Headley, president of a Cincinnati-based sports marketing company, said the quarterback's endorsement future would be bright, despite past problems, if Pittsburg were to win the game:

To me, winning cures everything. Not just to me, but the reality is to corporate America and to people, winning is the answer.[68]

The Green Bay Packers won that game, but Headley's judgment that winning nullifies past transgressions seems to be accurate. Should we condemn corporate America or the American people for being so willing to forgive winners' past wrongdoing? Explain.

Globalization

The critics' concerns about the domination of American life by big corporations and business values are now being applied to the entire globe. With the triumph of capitalism, in its various permutations (see Chapter 1), the world has come to understand that free markets are simply more efficient than government rules. As a result, national boundaries are receding in importance, technology is shrinking the world, multinational companies are treating the world as one big market, less developed countries are trying to improve living standards by connecting to that market, financial assets flow freely and almost instantaneously from one side of the globe to the other, and the world becomes one highly greased, interconnected mass market. A lot of good news emerges from globalization. In general, less developed countries have the opportunity to raise their standard of living as the benefits of competition and efficiency (better products and services at lower prices) reach added billions of people. Of course, these startling changes also produce enormous new uncertainties.

Fears   From America's viewpoint, globalization has involved the welcome spread of capitalist values to the entire world, but it has also engaged America in an international economic war with China, and emerging powers, including Brazil and India. That commercial war and the enormous power of the corporate community are welcomed as a route to increased prosperity in less-developed parts of the world, but the critics remain concerned about the "Americanization" of the globe and the enormous power of the American state and America's giant, multinational corporations. Capital, technology, goods, and services can be moved rapidly throughout the world aided by free trade arrangements such as the North American Free Trade Agreement (NAFTA), the World Trade Organization (WTO), the European Union (EU), and so on. These free trade mechanisms, in the critics' view, have diminished the regulatory power of national governments and left corporations free to do largely as they wish. [For the World Trade Organization, see **http://www.wto.org**]

The economic meltdown of recent years warned us that economic instability may be the norm in the new global market as the multinational corporations of Western, democratic capitalism compete with the emerging might of state capitalism in China and elsewhere. New regulatory mechanisms to curb volatility in financial markets have been moved into place in America and Western Europe (see Chapter 8), but the power of globalization continues to change the world in ways we cannot fully anticipate. The critics see a world ruled by commercial interests, both corporate- and state-directed, battling for global supremacy, bringing welcome new levels of prosperity but accompanied by enormous risks and inequities:

- The rich get richer and the poor fall farther behind.
- Whole ecosystems, such as the Amazon Basin, are despoiled for profit-seeking purposes.
- Rural cultures are displaced and an urban migration follows.
- Financial instability is inevitable.
- Labor is exploited to satisfy market demands.
- Consumerism swells while traditional values and cultures are submerged.

[See the Corporate Watch Web site for an extensive database of concerns about globalization: **http://www.corpwatch.org**]

Exploitation/Outsourcing

Globalization critics accuse America's giant corporations of exploiting cheap labor abroad under the free trade banner. In Bangladesh, for example, the garment industry consists of about 4,500 factories, 3.5 million jobs, and $12 billion in exports to international clothing companies like JC Penny, Kohl's, and Walmart.[69] Barely surviving on an official, national minimum wage equal to about $25 per month, the Bangladeshi laborers, mostly women, had been paid the lowest wages in the worldwide industry.[70] Then after months of protests in 2010, the minimum wage was nearly doubled to about $43 per month, still considered inadequate for a decent life.[71]

> The minimum wage was nearly doubled to about $43 per month.

To many in the West, however, that so-called exploitation actually represents the wholesale outsourcing of good jobs to underdeveloped nations. Millions of American jobs have moved or will move to India, China, Mexico, and other low-wage nations. So what looks like low-wage exploitation to some represents enormous job losses for others. To corporate managers these dramatic labor shifts reflect a healthy market that will pay off for America and other industrial nations by providing savings that will add investments and new products while putting money in the hands of new customers in the low-wage nations. But to those losing their jobs, outsourcing doesn't work as the market theorizes:

> "The consulting firm I work for is sending jobs to India," said Steve Ward, a computer programmer in Philadelphia. . . . Ward, holding a sign—"Will Code for Food"—dismissed the notion that everyone benefits from the corporate savings generated by offshore outsourcing. "Companies are predatory institutions, and they have to be controlled," he said.[72]

Globalization: A Happy Result?

Clearly, the advance of American corporate interests around the globe and onrushing globalization have produced problems, but enormous gains have also been achieved. One interesting piece of anecdotal evidence about the virtue of globalization comes from France where for years the government and many of its people criticized and resisted the "Americanization" of the French culture via American movies, music, McDonald's, and so on. Today, McDonald's earns more from sales in Europe—particularly Britain and France—than it does in the United States. Similarly, Abercrombie & Fitch and Tommy Hilfiger have made a recent splash in Paris. Older Europeans' concerns about globalization may not have reached the young:

> Young people here don't think badly about America—we're American in our heads, said Mathilde Feuille, 17, who waited for about four and a half hours the day the Abercrombie store first opened. "We watch all the U.S. television series: 'Gossip Girl,' 'Glee,' 'Vampire Diaries.'"[73]

Corporate Duty? Whether the globalization criticisms are fair or not, as the market increasingly "Americanizes" or "Westernizes" the globe, do American corporations bear some responsibility for addressing the resulting conflict? Certainly these problems, to the extent they are addressed at all, have traditionally been the province of government; but as globalization has magnified corporate power, we must wonder whether corporations won't increasingly be expected to fulfill expanded and, doubtless, uncomfortable new roles. Harvard Business School professor Christopher Bartlett explains:

> [T]hose leading today's multinational corporations must become much more attuned to the ways in which their actions can and do impact the fragile social, political, and economic environments in which they operate worldwide. Yet far too often these powerful companies have been so focused on their core economic role that they have ignored the huge social and political impact they have.[74]

Questions

1. *The Wall Street Journal* recently observed that outsourcing will not destroy the American jobs of the future, but that the real problem may be whether outsourcing (and technology) could widen the gap between good "brainpower" jobs and poorly paid physical jobs. Explain how outsourcing may exacerbate the rich–poor income gap.[75]

2. *a.* Do Americans trust the business community? Explain.
   b. Does it matter? Explain.

3. In 1980 Ted Peters, an associate professor of systematic theology at the Pacific Lutheran Seminary and the Graduate Theological Union, asked,

   > How will the advancing postindustrial culture influence the course of religion? It is my forecast that religion will become increasingly treated as a consumer item. Because our economy produces so much wealth, we are free to consume and consume beyond the point of satisfaction. There is a limit to what we can consume in the way of material goods—new homes, new cars, new electronic gadgets, new brands of beer, new restaurants, and so on. So we go beyond material wants to consume new personal experiences—such as broader travel, exotic vacations, continuing education, exciting conventions, psychotherapy, and sky diving.
   >
   >   What will come next and is already on the horizon is the consumption of spiritual experiences—personal growth cults, drug-induced ecstasy, world-traveling gurus, training in mystical meditation to make you feel better, etc. Once aware of this trend, religious entrepreneurs and mainline denominations alike will take to pandering their wares, advertising how much spiritual realities "can do to you." It will be subtle, and it will be cloaked in the noble language of personal growth, but nevertheless the pressure will be on to treat religious experience as a commodity for consumption. . . . [76]

   a. Is Peters's forecast coming true? Explain.
   b. Is marketing necessary to the survival and growth of religion? Explain.
   c. Is marketing a threat to the legitimacy and value of religion? Explain.

4. In your opinion, which of the following will be the biggest threat to America in the future: big government, big labor, or big business?

5. Do you think allegiance to the company will become more important than allegiance to the state? Is that a desirable direction? Raise the arguments on both sides of the latter question.

6. As expressed in *BusinessWeek,* "Increasingly, the corporation will take over the role of the mother, supplying day care facilities where children can be tended around the clock."[77] How do you feel about the corporation as mother? Explain.

Part Two—Corporate Social Responsibility (CSR)

Introduction

We have seen that the business community is intensely criticized. Journalist Daniel Seligman put it this way:

> A standard view of the American corporation . . . is that it is an efficient deliverer of goods and services, yet also a wellspring of social injustice. Driven by a narrow calculus of profits, it is oblivious to the common good. And so, the litany goes, it degrades the environment, promotes unsafe products, skimps on workplace safety and . . . lays off workers who have given it years of service.[78]

That broadly shared perception of business misdeeds or indifference, in conjunction with the growing influence of business values throughout American life, has led in recent decades to the development of the doctrine of *corporate social responsibility* (sometimes also referred to as *corporate citizenship*). We can express the issue this way: Must business decision making include consideration not merely of the welfare of the firm but of society as a whole? For most contemporary readers, the answer is self-evident—of course business bears a social responsibility. Business has enjoyed a central and favored role in American life. As such, it must assume a measure of the burden for the welfare of the total society. Indeed, businesspeople themselves now generally endorse businesses' responsibility to help solve society's problems. Companies continue to put profits first; but responding to a *Wall Street Journal*–Harris poll, 84 percent of corporate recruiters said it is important that MBAs display an awareness and knowledge of corporate social responsibility.[79] And students themselves are increasingly interested in the social responsibility/corporate citizenship approach to business practice. Similar philosophies such as the *triple bottom line* (giving close accounting attention to social and environmental performance as well as financial performance) and the *sustainable* corporation (operating the business with a focus on environmentally sensitive practices that will husband scarce resources and maintain a healthy community now and in the future) have powerful appeal to many students and managers.

Before turning to a more detailed analysis of corporate social responsibility practice, let's think about options you might employ to direct your forthcoming professional life toward socially responsible, ethically sustainable business practice. *Social enterprise or social entrepreneurship* is a movement in which people launch nonprofits and businesses or take jobs using entrepreneurial and managerial skills for the purpose, in part, of addressing social problems.

Social Enterprise/Social Entrepreneurship

Drew Chafetz, in his midtwenties and a huge soccer fan, did not turn directly to the job market following college graduation. Rather, he cofounded love.futbol [see **http://www.lovefutbol.org**], an organization to help build safe soccer fields for children in impoverished nations who otherwise might be forced to play in the streets or other unsafe spaces.

Since founding love.futbol in 2006, Chafetz and his cofounder, Alfredo Axtmayer, have encouraged seven Guatemalan communities to build durable, low-maintenance, concrete soccer pitches, and several other projects are in development. Chafetz says that love. futbol's core competency is not building fields but empowering and mobilizing communities to build their own. Love.futbol provides materials and direction, but communities must provide the land, project planning, and volunteer labor necessary for success.[80]

Jeff Denby shared Chafetz's social welfare goals, but approached them from a profit-seeking direction. Denby started his own underwear business, PACT Organic Underwear (an online-only operation) while studying for his MBA degree at the University of California, Berkeley. With a sustainable and environmentally friendly operational plan, Denby wants to build a profit-seeking business that displays a social conscience and engages in positive social performance.[81]

Others with social concerns, ranging from those just out of college to Gen X managers in their 30s and 40s, are simply looking for socially responsible jobs with organizations that share their zeal. Kate Tierney, for example, was a 42-year-old senior vice president making "big bucks," but she knew her job was not filling the "mission part of my soul." She took a job as national sales director for Alter Eco, a fair trade start-up.[82] Many young graduates are now seeking opportunities to "make a difference" even if doing so may result in a pay cut. Of course, finding jobs that satisfy those social goals is a tough assignment in today's harsh market, but the commitment to social enterprise and social entrepreneurship is increasingly important to young students and managers. [For an introduction to B Corps—benefit corporations—a "new type of corporation that uses the power of business to solve social and environmental problems," see **http://www. bcorporation.net/about**]

> Finding jobs that satisfy social goals is a tough assignment.

Questions

1. *a.* Do you aspire to a social enterprise/social entrepreneurship role in your future professional life?
   b. Should you? Explain.
2. Have your business school courses given sufficient attention to social responsibility issues? Explain.
3. Do consumers care whether companies are socially responsible? Explain.

A New Ideology

The ascendance of the social responsibility doctrine represents a striking ideological shift. Historically, business was expected to concentrate on one goal—the production and distribution of the best products and services at the lowest possible prices. Business was largely exempt from any affirmative duty for the resolution of social problems until the 1950s when business scholars and critics began to encourage a broader conception of corporate duty. Now in the 21st century, expectations for business in society have been radically altered. Profit-seeking remains central and essential, but for most businesspeople, the sometimes awkward ingredient of social responsibility must be a consideration. [For the Business for Social Responsibility home page, see **www.bsr.org**]

What Is Social Responsibility?

The sweeping notion of corporate social responsibility is not readily reduced to a brief definition, but Davis and Blomstrom some years ago captured the core ingredients: "The idea of social responsibility is that decision makers are obligated to take actions which protect and improve the welfare of society as a whole along with their own interests."[83] More systematically, the social role of business can be thought of as an ideological continuum, corresponding roughly to the familiar American political spectrum of conservative/Republican views on the right, moderates in the middle, and liberal/Democrats on the left. Figure 3.1 depicts that continuum and is best understood by reading "backward" from right to left. On the right side of the spectrum lies the free market view holding that *profit maximization* is the best measure of social responsibility. Across the middle (*long-term company interest*) lies a hybrid, blended perspective where profits are the first consideration, but where satisfied workers, customers, and community members are also of importance, within some reasonable limits, in order to secure the firm's long-term survival. On the left side of the spectrum lies the *triple bottom line/sustainability* movement that calls for a revolutionary re-visioning of corporate goals and practices such that profit maximization is only one of three key measures of success. Triple bottom line advocates specifically call for managerial and accounting practices that respect and measure the firm's *social and environmental performance* just as the firm's *financial* performance is respected and measured. The goal is to ensure the long-term viability (sustainability) of the organization and the total society.

Now let's examine the continuum in a bit more detail. [For the "Global Reporting Initiative" on sustainability practices around the world, see **http://www.globalreporting.org**]

FIGURE 3.1
A Social
Responsibility
Continuum

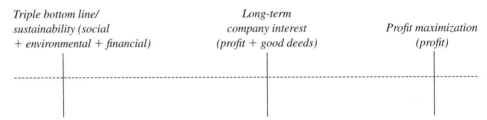

Triple bottom line/ sustainability (social + environmental + financial)

Long-term company interest (profit + good deeds)

Profit maximization (profit)

The only responsible and moral course of behavior is to reap the highest return possible, within the law.

Profit Maximization Here the dominant concern lies in maximizing shareholders' interests. Those shareholders, after all, are the owners of the firm. They are taking the financial risk. Hence, from a profit maximization point of view, the only responsible and moral course of behavior is to reap the highest return possible, within the law. Nobel prize–winning economist Milton Friedman was the most prominent advocate of the profit maximization view:

> [In a free economy] there is one and only one social responsibility of business—to use its resources and engage in activities designed to increase its profits, so long as it stays within the rules of the game, which is to say, engages in open and free competition, without deception or fraud.[84]

Friedman, employing free market reasoning, believed the firm that maximizes its profits is necessarily maximizing its contribution to society. Furthermore, he argued that any dilution of the profit-maximizing mode—such as charitable contributions—is a misuse of the stockholders' resources. The individual stockholder, he contended, should dispose of assets according to her or his own wishes. Finally, he asked how managers could be expected to know what the public interest is.

Herbert Stein, former chair of the President's Council of Economic Advisers, shared Friedman's doubts about the idea of social responsibility, but Stein's concerns were of a more pragmatic nature. He argued that business is simply ill suited for solving social problems:

> Efficiency in maximizing the nation's product . . . is not the only objective of life. But it is the one that private corporations are best qualified to serve. I don't want to be a purist about this. I don't object to corporations contributing to the United Givers Fund. . . . But to rely on corporations' responsibility to solve major social problems—other than the problem of how to put our people and other resources to work most efficiently—would be a wasteful diversion from their most important function. Our other objectives can be better served in other ways, by individuals and other institutions.[85]

Long-Term Company Interest   Across the broad middle ground of our social responsibility continuum lie those firms, doubtless the great majority, who believe that a strong bottom line, in many cases, requires considerations beyond the immediate, short-run, profit-maximizing interests of the firm. In a sense, these managers are merely taking a longer term view of profit maximization. They recognize the imperative of a strong return on the shareholder's investment, but they also believe that achieving that return may require heightened sensitivity to the welfare of employees, consumers, and the community. Furthermore, they often embrace the view that socially responsible behavior, within reasonable bounds, is simply the "right thing" to do. [For the United Nations' initiative to encourage responsible corporate citizenship, see **http://www.unglobalcompact.org**]

Triple Bottom Line/Sustainability   Managers, whether traditional profit maximizers or those embracing the longer-term, more socially conscious attitude, are being pushed by scholars, activists, government, and often the larger community to adopt a bigger, broader conception of social responsibility—one that significantly redefines the corporate role and calls for values and tactics that will produce a sustainable, healthy global community. This redefinition is explained by social responsibility expert, Steve Rochlin:

> The new corporate citizenship challenges executives to find alternatives to zero-sum solutions that often emphasize shareholder value at the cost of social and environmental welfare. Instead, the new corporate citizenship challenges companies to deliver not just financial returns but also environmental and social value—together marking the pillars of what is called a "triple bottom line.". . .
>
> The new corporate citizenship requires business transparency and accountability regarding the ways in which business practices generate benefits and costs for issues ranging from employee diversity, community development, working conditions, clean air and water, human rights, poverty, and corruption.[86]

The triple bottom line/sustainability approach recognizes the necessity for financial success but also argues that social and environmental responsibilities are of equal importance and that corporations giving close attention to those social and economic duties have a powerful competitive advantage that will contribute to both organizational and societal sustainability. As Rochlin notes, the firm committed to triple bottom line principles and sustainability will be concerned about social equity issues such as community philanthropy, employee satisfaction, lawful corporate governance, transparency in business practices, and fair treatment of customers. In the environmental domain, sustainability will require attention to energy efficiency, waste minimization, recycling, and the total ecological agenda. All of this will be achieved via market principles, but the market is expected to work more effectively through a new spirit of cooperation among business, government, nongovernmental organizations (NGOs), and the citizenry. In sum, the idea is that the survival (sustainability) of the corporation and of the global community requires new values and new decision-making tactics that will take a balanced view of the triple bottom line while implementing accounting procedures that measure success not just in profits but in social and environmental goals as well. [For a critique of triple bottom line thinking, see **www.businessethics.ca/3bl**]

"GREEN" JEANS?

Americans spent about $340 billion on clothing and shoes in 2010. That ocean of apparel is the product of globe-spanning supply chains that consume enormous amounts of water, energy, chemicals, cotton, oil, and other resources while casting off equally enormous amounts of waste, carbons, toxic chemicals, dirty water, and much more. Many of the apparel companies have only a faint understanding of the environmental impact of their industry, and we consumers usually know even less. In 2011, a group of apparel companies and others announced the creation of the Sustainable Apparel Coalition to measure the environmental impact of the apparel production process. Walmart, Patagonia, Hanes, Duke University, the nonprofit Environmental Defense Fund, and the Environmental Protection Agency are among the 30 Coalition founders. The Coalition plans to build a database of scores assigned to all elements of every garment's life cycle—among them, cotton producers, dye suppliers, textile mill owners, shippers, retailers, and consumers—based on various social and environmental measures such as land and water use, waste production, greenhouse gases, and so on. The resulting scores could be used by apparel companies to choose materials and suppliers and eventually the Coalition hopes a sustainability score can be calculated for all garments so that consumers can make buying choices with those scores in mind.

Question

Think about shopping. Assume you are considering two pairs of jeans of equal style and quality, one with a favorable sustainability score, one without. Assume the jeans without the favorable score are priced at $50. How much more would you be willing to pay for the jeans with a favorable score?

  a. Nothing more.
  b. $1
  c. $5
  d. $10
  e. $25 Explain.

Source: Tom Zeller, "Clothes Makers Join to Set 'Green Score,'" *The New York Times,* March 1, 2011 [**http://www. nytimes.com/2011/03/01/business/01apparel.html**].

Social Responsibility Pyramid

Professor Archie Carroll proposed another way of visualizing socially responsible business practice as depicted in Figure 3.2. Socially responsible business practice necessarily begins at the foundation of the pyramid with the duty to make a profit in a lawful fashion; but simultaneously the socially responsible firm moves (up the pyramid) beyond the fundamental demands of economics and law to pursue the ethical course of action—the behavior best suited to the demands of virtue and moral principle. In striving for profitable, lawful, ethical conduct, that company may also choose to engage in discretionary philanthropic (charitable) efforts (money, time, facilities, programs) to build a better community. While the social responsibility pyramid has been criticized and revised, it remains a useful way of thinking about corporations' expanding duties.[87]

FIGURE 3.2

The Social Responsibility (CSR) Pyramid

Source: Archie B. Carroll, "The Pyramid of Corporate Social Responsibility: Toward the Moral Management of Organizational Stakeholders." Reprinted from *Business Horizons* 34, no. 4 (July–August 1991), pp. 39, 42. Copyright 1991 by the Foundation for the School of Business at Indiana University. Used with permission.

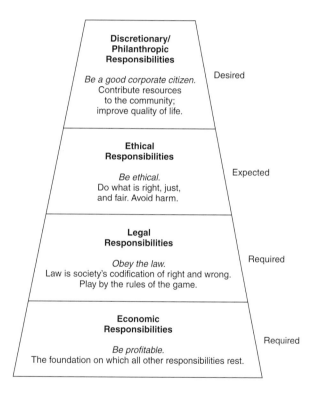

Toyota and the Social Responsibility Pyramid

As perhaps the most respected name in the automobile industry, Toyota's safety struggles of recent years have caused the powerful company to thoroughly review its practices and philosophies to discover where it went so wrong. From fall 2009 to spring 2011, Toyota recalled about 12 million vehicles because of safety and quality concerns, particularly sudden acceleration flaws. Around 90 deaths have been associated with alleged

Toyota problems, but the extent of the company's responsibility/liability is only beginning to be assessed. Toyota paid nearly $50 million in fines for failing to inform regulators promptly when it became aware of confirmed product defects. Numerous individual product liability lawsuits have been filed on behalf of those injured or killed in Toyota mishaps. Among the results of this array of problems was a decline in market share, resale value, and quality ratings.

Thus, in applying Carroll's Social Responsibility Pyramid reasoning, we see that Toyota is struggling to fulfill its economic responsibilities, and it has failed to meet at least some of its legal responsibilities. Furthermore, in its careful and doubtless painful self-examination, Toyota has raised doubts about its own ethical performance. President Akio Toyoda has acknowledged that quality had been sacrificed for faster growth and profits. Toyoda said: ". . . [S]ome people just got too big-headed and focused too excessively on profit." Trying to restore its performance and ethical/reputational posture, Toyota in 2010/2011 announced a series of initiatives to improve performance including reassigning 1,000 engineers to spot check quality and installing a new computer system to gather global repair reports and mine the resulting data to identify trends. Doubtless some of Toyota's legal and ethical luster was restored by the U.S. government's February 2011 conclusion that electronic control systems were not responsible for the sudden acceleration problems. Driver error, floor mat obstruction, and "sticky" pedals have been identified as causes in some instances.

Sources: Ken Bensinger and Ralph Vartabedian, "Toyota to Pay Record Fines for Disclosure Delay," *latimes.com,* December 20, 2010 [latimes.com/business/la-fi-toyota-fine-20101221,0,2995009.story]; Ken Bensinger, "Toyota Recalls 2.17 Million More Vehicles Over Sudden-Acceleration Problems," *latimes.com,* February 24, 2011 [latimes.com/business/la-fi-toyota-recall-20110225,0,6731783.story]; Chester Dawson and Yoshio Takahashi, "Toyota Makes New Push to Avoid Recalls," *The Wall Street Journal,* February 24, 2011, p. B1; Norihiko Shirouzu, "Toyoda Rues Excessive Profit Focus," *The Wall Street Journal,* March 2, 2010, p. B3; and Norihiko Shirouzu, "Inside Toyota, Executives Trade Blame Over Debacle," *The Wall Street Journal,* April 13, 2010 [**http://online.wsj.com/**].

Corporations Practicing Social Responsibility

Obviously we have no shortage of social problems both domestically and globally. In recent years the corporate community seems to have become increasingly convinced that it needs, for various reasons, to take a more active role in addressing those problems. Those efforts can take many forms. American corporations responded quickly to the January 2010 earthquake in Haiti by promising $43 million in aid within 72 hours after the quake struck.[88] Often those social efforts help the company as well as its stakeholders. Target, for example, has a counselor/social worker walking the aisles in its inner-city Compton, California, location listening to employees' problems and thinking with them about solutions. The program is good for employees, but it also serves Target's needs by helping to reduce absenteeism and turnover. Sixty-nine of Target's 1,752 stores now have a social worker and 2009 employee attendance at those stores improved by an average of 17 percent over 2008.[89] Many social responsibility advocates, including Google, believe that an entrepreneurial, profit-seeking, capitalist approach is the best route to correcting social problems.

Google's Multiple CSR Strategies

Google hopes to use capitalism to make life better around the world. Google, through its $2 billion charitable arm, Google.org, makes many generous charitable contributions, but its version of CSR reaches beyond philanthropic efforts to attack some of the world's biggest problems (specifically, the environment, global poverty, and global health) by investing in businesses, lobbying for political causes, and directing portions of its employees' time to developing business and technology solutions for those problems. Google expects to invest in small businesses in the developing world, encourage the commercial development of plug-in cars, and help make renewable energy cheaper than coal. Google is investing $10 million, for example, in eSolar, Inc., a company that is trying to develop very large scale solar power systems.[90]

Google is only one of many companies that have expanded their CSR efforts from giving to building. Many of those companies view social responsibility as workable only if it contributes to the strategic mission of the business and ultimately to the bottom line. Nike, for example, turned aggressively to social responsibility measures as a way of restoring its brand image after criticism for its use of global sweatshop labor. Consumers are willing to pay higher prices at Whole Foods Market, the healthy food grocery chain, in part because of the company's reputation for good works. Vinod Khosla, the billionaire cofounder of Sun Microsystems, invested in SKS Microfinance, a profit-making lender to India's poor women, a venture that earned him $117 million after the company's initial public stock offering. The company, founded in 2006, had 6.8 million customers and a loan portfolio of nearly 1 billion dollars in 2010. Khosla also donates to nonprofit micro-lending organizations, but he has found that the profit-seeking approach grows faster and reaches more needy borrowers.[91] At this writing, however, SKS is reeling. Its shares have lost about 70 percent of their initial value and government officials have labeled it a greedy loan shark. SKS intends to reinvent its approach to lending. Thus we see that entrepreneurial social responsibility practices can both do good and generate big returns, but those honorable motivations alone cannot assure success.[92]

Questions

1. In general, we understand decisions to lay off employees when companies are losing money, but how should we feel about profitable companies that lay off employees? Powerful executive, Barry Diller, in 2009, condemned "preemptive" layoffs:

   The idea of a company that's earning money, not losing money, that's not, let's say, "industrially endangered," to have just cutbacks [sic] so they can earn another $12 million or $20 million or $40 million in a year where no one's counting is really a horrible act when you think about it on every level.[93]

Do you think a socially responsible company that operates at a profit would engage in layoffs? Explain.

2. Some critics argue that Wall Street's financial collapse in 2008–2009 was, at least in part, a product of male "group think." They claim that men take excessive risks and women are more comprehensive thinkers. Hence, they say the financial community needs more women:

   Barnard College president Deborah Spar dubbed our predicament [the Wall Street crash] a "one gender crash," and *The New York Times'* Nicholas Kristof wonders if we might all have been better off had it been "Lehman Brothers and Sisters."[94]

Do finance companies have a social responsibility to hire more women? Explain.

Finding an Employer with a Conscience

Surveys of young people in recent years suggest that employers trying to replace millions of retiring baby boomers may need to demonstrate a social commitment in order to be fully competitive in the hiring market. One of those surveys found that two thirds of respondents 18 to 26 prefer jobs that would permit them to make a contribution to nonprofit groups.

Questions

1. *a.* Will you insist on a job with a "social purpose"?
   b. Do all jobs have a social purpose?
2. Would you expect money to replace social goals in the teen hierarchy as they age?
3. Given today's difficult job market, do you expect social goals to remain important to young people? Explain.

Sources: Lindsey Gerdes, "Get Ready for a Pickier Workforce," *BusinessWeek,* September 18, 2006, p. 82; and Ian Shapira, "For This Generation, Vocations of Service," *Washington Post,* October 14, 2008, p. B01.

But Is Corporate Responsibility Good Business?

The evidence is mixed but substantially supportive of the idea that the market rewards good conduct and punishes bad conduct. A 2004 meta-analysis of 52 studies found a link between corporate social performance and corporate financial performance that is significant and varies from moderately to highly positive.[95] A 2008 meta-analysis of 34 studies found 23 of them showing a significant positive relationship between corporate social performance and corporate financial performance.[96] Looked at from another angle, the number of socially responsible investment funds (those limiting investments to companies displaying favorable social practices) multiplied tenfold from 1995 to 2009,[97] and the performance of those funds has been about equal to the Standard & Poor's 500 over the past 20 years.[98] On the other hand, a 2007 Harris Poll of nearly 2,400 Americans found only 16 percent saying that a company's reputation for social responsibility has a strong impact on their decisions about purchases and with whom to do business.[99]

Question

1. Construct a list of the arguments for and against social responsibility for business.

Part Three—Managing Social Responsibility

Stakeholder Approach

As the principle of social responsibility has become increasingly acceptable to the corporate community, the nature of the debate has shifted to identifying the new duties and assessing whether the corporation is meeting those duties. Many corporations, particularly those of great size, are confronting the practical notion of how best to manage the firm's response to social issues. Corporations are increasingly considering what scholars have labeled the *stakeholder model* of social responsibility. Under that model, the corporation identifies all of the groups (stockholders, customers, employees, communities, governments, unions, schools, and the like) that may significantly affect the firm's performance or be affected by it. These are groups with a "stake" in the activities of the corporation. Of course, we have wide divisions of opinion about how expansive the list of stakeholders should be; and once identified, we have wide divisions of opinion about the extent of the corporation's duties toward those stakeholders. To stakeholder advocates, simply maximizing the interests of the primary stakeholders, that is, the shareholders, would not satisfy the corporation's social duties.

That more expansive view of social responsibility was emphasized in a 2010 discussion among corporate leaders who were thinking about how to restore the public's confidence in business after the financial collapse and scandals of recent years. First among the group's recommendations was "A New Stakeholder Approach:"

> Companies should talk less about benefits to shareholders and short-term profits and instead focus on customer needs, investment in workers and sustainability (from ecology to education). We talk too much about benefits we provide to shareholders. We should be talking about benefits provided to our employees, customers and to the public. This will boost public confidence in business.[100]

Building Stakeholder Relationships   Business consultant Ann Svendsen argues that most business leaders have accepted the claim that companies have multiple stakeholders, but the difficult question lies in the attention given to each stakeholder relationship.[101] Historically, of course, shareholders towered over all other stakeholders in their perceived importance. Now that other stakeholders are asserting claims, how much attention must the firm pay to them? What priorities should be established among stakeholders? Can stakeholder relationships be regarded as opportunities for corporate growth and advantage rather than as burdensome claims on scarce resources? Management consultant Deon Binneman recently suggested the following questions as entry points to the organization's understanding of its stakeholder management process:

Who are our stakeholders?

What are our stakeholders' stakes?

What opportunities and challenges do stakeholders present?

What economic, legal, ethical and social responsibilities does our organization have towards our various stakeholders?

How do you measure results?[102]

Manage or Collaborate?   While many companies now acknowledge the importance of their stakeholder relationships, their dominant goal often amounts to little more than controlling those relationships. An alternative and arguably more "progressive" approach to stakeholders involves a collaborative strategy in which stakeholder relationships are regarded as being mutually defined, cooperative, reciprocal, and thus not subject to "management" by the firm.[103] The firm endeavors to understand and balance the interests and needs of all stakeholders with the view that this collaborative effort results in enhanced firm performance over the long term while building a healthier society.[104]

A.G. Lafley, recently-retired Procter & Gamble CEO, thoroughly and personally embraced stakeholder practice. Making money remained Lafley's first job, but he led P&G on a broader mission, partly to ensure the company's continuing success. Enron and the other scandals of the early 2000s convinced him that he had to engage in a broad dialogue with P&G's stakeholders. He came to think of consumers as citizens who often are concerned about P&G's approach to global warming or its animal-testing methods. Lafley, in fact, dealt directly with groups like Greenpeace and People for the Ethical Treatment of Animals. Lafley also extended his stakeholder engagement to worldwide relief efforts on behalf of P&G. Those are citizenship responsibilities, he said, that go with P&G's big role in the changing global economy and global political environment. "Honest to God, the responsibility is huge," said Lafley.[105]

As Lafley recognized, this expanding complexity in business practice requires the contemporary manager to learn about a much broader range of issues than was the norm historically. Profit now rests not merely in providing the best product or service at the lowest price, but in understanding and dealing with the complex interplay among the corporation, government, and society. Thus today's manager is likely to be increasingly involved in identifying and addressing social issues and stakeholder concerns.

Stakeholder Results   Assessing the success of social responsibility efforts is very difficult, but various measurement systems have emerged including, most prominently, Social Accountability 8000 (SA8000), the first global standard measuring companies' social and environmental records. Social Accountability Accreditation Services in New York City accredits companies that meet the SA8000 standards in the areas of child labor, forced labor, health and safety, freedom of association, discrimination, disciplinary practices, working hours, collective bargaining wages, and management systems. As of 2010, over 2,300 facilities employing over 1.3 million employees in 62 countries had been certified.[106] [For more, see **http://www.saasaccreditation.org**]

Similarly, the Global Reporting Initiative (GRI) was established to develop consistent global guidelines for reporting the economic, environmental, and social performance of corporations. GRI's reporting framework is designed to measure and display corporations' success in achieving "sustainable" development.[107] [For more, see **www.globalreporting.org**]

Bhopal: A Social Responsibility Failure?

One way of measuring the results of stakeholder activism is to review how the business community responds when wrongs occur. The devastating 1984 chemical spill at Bhopal, India, was one of the great tragedies in global industrial history. Water entered a methyl isocyanate storage tank at a Union Carbide plant producing an uncontrollable chemical reaction and a toxic cloud that spread across nearby slums. Up to 3,000 people were killed immediately and more than 15,000 in total have perished. Nearly 600,000 people have qualified for compensation as a result of health problems attributed to the leak. Union

Carbide reached a settlement in 1989 with the Indian government that absolved the company of liability and sent over $500 million to India, including $1,500 for each death and $550 for each contaminated person. Claims totaled $3 billion, and litigation continues over a quarter of a century later. Union Carbide maintained that the gas release resulted from sabotage.

Toxic waste remaining in the heavily populated Bhopal area is estimated at 350 tons and apparently it continues to pollute groundwater, kill crops and cause birth defects, cancer, and more. Both the governmental and corporate responses have been slow and frustrating to local residents. Indeed, Satinath Sarangi, a metallurgist and activist, argues that the fundamental problem is the close relationship between the two. *The New York Times* explained Sarangi's view:

> Union Carbide got off easy in the 1980s because pesticides were a cornerstone of [India's] "green revolution" policy to enhance agricultural productivity, [Sarangi] said. A quarter of a century later, multinationals continue to wield enormous influence over governments that measure progress solely in economic terms. "If you are an ordinary person, you can't depend on your government, judiciary or regulatory bodies to protect you from corporate crime." [Sarangi] said.[108]

Nonetheless, these cataclysmic events can produce a dramatic and positive corporate response as *The Wall Street Journal* reported about Bhopal:

> The chemical leak . . . spurred a revolution in approaches to safety, pollution, and community relations that have made chemical plants in the United States more accessible and more accountable to their neighbors. New laws forced plants to disclose safety and pollution data. And an army of community activists won new powers.[109]

Sources: "Asia: Bhopal's Deadly Legacy; India," *The Economist,* November 27, 2004, p. 76; Manjeet Kripalani, "Dow Chemical: Liable for Bhopal?" *BusinessWeek,* June 9, 2008, p. 061; Mark Magnier, "Anguish Lingers in Bhopal, 25 Years after Chemical Disaster," *latimes.com,* December 3, 2009 [latimes.com/news/nation-and-world/la-fg-india-bhopal3-2009dec03,0,3728767.story]; and Susan Warren, "Chemical Companies Keep Lessons of Bhopal Spill Fresh," *The Wall Street Journal,* February 13, 2001, p. B4.

Shareholder Approach

Stakeholder theory and corporate social performance have gained great credibility with academics and many managers. Others, however, argue that profits and shareholders must remain the consuming concerns of management, and that a skilled focus on the bottom line will, incidentally but inevitably, result in the greatest good for society. That is, the company that maximizes its profits necessarily does not only what is best for its shareholders but also what is best for society generally. The shareholder/stakeholder debate is well illustrated by the heated competition between massive retailers Walmart and Costco. Each week Walmart saves money for millions of Americans by its relentless focus on the bottom line and hence on the interests of its shareholders. Costco, on the other hand, has drawn great praise from management scholars for its close attention

Walmart pays about
$11.75 per hour.

to worker welfare. Costco workers average just under $20 per hour while Walmart pays about $11.75 per hour and the national average for retail workers is $11.84 per hour.[110] Costco is a leader in providing benefits. Costco employees pay 12 percent of the cost of their health care coverage while Walmart employees pay more than 40 percent.[111] Walmart has, however, been improving its coverage in recent years. Costco's employee turnover is a low 20 percent as compared with about 50 percent at Walmart.[112] Costco has performed well in the stock market with an approximate 80 percent gain over the past decade while Walmart's share price is up only about 6 percent during that time.[113] On the other hand, Walmart is more profitable than Costco and has shown stronger earnings growth in many recent years.[114] That bottom line strength is one of the reasons that journalist/financial advisor Malcolm Berko believes Walmart's tough, shareholder-focused approach will prevail in the end:

Walmart is more
profitable than Costco.

> COST (Costco) may be a good neighbor, but WMT (Walmart) is certainly a better managed company. In this business of investing, it's the bottom line that counts while kindness and goodness aren't worth a pickled herring.[115]

Berko made that favorable assessment in 2004, but today Walmart is frustrated with its performance. Same store domestic sales have actually declined in recent years as Walmart pursued wealthier shoppers, moved away from its everyday low prices strategy, and faced increasing competition from dollar stores and others.[116] Because of strong international growth, Walmart continues to be highly profitable, but its performance has been disappointing to investors.

Critics

Walmart, the target of relentless criticism, is accused of widespread sex discrimination and failure to pay legally mandated overtime. (Costco is also facing sex discrimination and wage and hour class action lawsuits.) Entire communities have banished Walmart's big boxes. In response to these public relations shortcomings and needing a boost in the stock market, Walmart has initiated new sustainable, green practices including slashing solid waste and greenhouse-gas emissions and significantly reducing energy consumption. Those efforts are part of a larger "good works" and public relations campaign that includes 2 billion dollars in food donations over five years and support for a universal health care policy in America. Walmart also points to its success in providing economic opportunities for its massive and often modestly educated workforce, 61 percent of whom are women and 32 percent minorities.[117] Walmart's big contribution, however, is in saving money for all Americans: an estimated $30 billion per year, or the equivalent of $270 per American family.[118]

Other lawsuits accuse
Walmart of failing to
pay overtime.

Clearly, Walmart has felt harsh, market-based pressure to respond to social issues, including employee welfare and environmental sustainability. These adjustments should not be misunderstood, however. Walmart's shareholder orientation is intact and remains a clear, strategic contrast to Costco's stakeholder approach.

[For a documentary critique of Walmart, see the trailer for *Wal-Mart: The High Cost of Low Price* at **http://www.walmartmovie.com**]

Questions

1. Costco CEO James Sinegal says high employee pay makes for good business. How can that be so?

2. Professor William Beaver writes: "And what of the stakeholder model? Beyond generating some academic interest, perhaps the best that can be said is that although corporations will not be unmindful of their other stakeholders, the latter's concerns will remain a distant second to those holding the share."[119] Will shareholders or other stakeholders dominate corporate thought in the coming years? Explain.

3. In 1999 Bob Thompson sold his road-building firm for $422 million. Then he divided $128 million among his 550 workers, more than 80 of whom became millionaires. Thompson explained his generosity by saying, "I wanted to go out a winner, and I wanted to go out doing the right thing."[120]

   a. Which management strategy, Walmart's low wages or Thompson's bonuses, is the more socially responsible? Explain.

   b. Can Walmart, a publicly traded company owned by its shareholders, practice the same kind of generosity to employees that Thompson followed in distributing money that was literally his own? Explain.

   c. Stanford professor Jeffrey Pfeffer reflecting on the bonus strategy: "It's how you look at your workforce. . . . When I look at you, do I see a cost or do I see you as the only thing that separates me from my competition?"[121] Comment.

   d. Do you agree with Thompson that he did the "right thing"? Explain.

Part Four—Social Responsibility Cases
Case One: Workplace Diversity

Corporate leaders must produce a profit, but they also must conform to society's expectations for responsible conduct. Will the business community successfully shape its own behavior, or must the government intervene? Workplace discrimination continues to require extensive government oversight (see Chapter 13). But now many corporations have moved beyond mere legal compliance to recognize the power of a diverse workforce combining the strengths of America's various demographic groups. In recent years, that attention to diversity has broadened to embrace lesbian, gay, bisexual, and transgender (LGBT) Americans, as employers strive to "do the right thing" and to compete in a global market that requires all of our available resources.

Since 1999, Nationwide Mutual Insurance Co. of Columbus, Ohio, with 35,000 employees, has offered domestic partner benefits for same-sex partners. " 'As the traditional household has changed, we decided to let our associates define family.' spokesman Eric Hardgrove said." Hardgrove went on to say that the benefits plan

> 286 of the *Fortune*
> 500 companies provide
> equal benefits for same
> sex couples.

"goes along with our commitment to building a workplace that fosters respect, is inclusive and nondiscriminatory."[122] A recent report from the Human Rights Campaign Foundation found that 286 of the *Fortune* 500 companies provide equal benefits for same-sex couples and 85 percent of those companies prohibit sexual orientation discrimination and 35 percent forbid gender identity discrimination. The same study found that the higher the company's revenue the more likely it is to provide benefits for LGBT employees.[123] Overall, about 36 percent of large companies that offer health benefits also provide domestic partner benefits, but most of them do not cover the "extra" taxes that accompany that coverage.[124] (Under federal law, health benefits for domestic partners when provided by an employer are taxable unless the domestic partner is a dependent.) Google, however, decided in 2010 to join a few larger companies that pay the extra tax not required of heterosexual married couples.

The companies offering domestic partner benefits reported that the cost of doing so added only about 1 percent to their total benefits budgets. Even as most states were affirming their opposition to same-sex marriage, these companies took the direction they thought right, both as a matter of principle and for pragmatic reasons. Human Rights Campaign Foundation president Steve Solmonese explained the latter: "Looking at the buying power of the lesbian and gay communities and the need to attract a diverse and talented work force, they've concluded that a fair and inclusive work force serves them best."[125]

A national 2010 survey showed strong support (62 percent of the heterosexual adults questioned) for equal benefits on the job regardless of sexual orientation. Likewise 52 percent of the heterosexual adults surveyed said it was extremely or very important to them that they work for a company offering equal benefits to all employees.[126] The result of these generally favorable opinions is that work life for LGBT employees has improved in recent years, although significant discrimination clearly remains. With the ongoing controversy about same-sex marriage, corporate managers continue to face challenges in addressing equality in the workplace. *BusinessWeek* explained:

> [The legal controversy over gay marriage] will surely make life more complicated for CEOs trying to navigate the contentious issue. While they may not want to alienate cultural conservatives, they will also be loath to drive away the gay community. After all, the GLBT universe in the United States includes some 15 million consumers. Many have high disposable incomes.[127]

Case One Questions

1. What managerial risks and problems accompany gay and lesbian diversity policies in the workplace?
2. In your view, do the gay and lesbian diversity policies constitute socially responsible corporate behavior? Explain.
3. List the issues that you would consider if you were a CEO deciding whether to extend health insurance to the same-sex partners of your employees.
4. Christopher Mossey wrote in a letter to *The Wall Street Journal,*

Your Oct. 11 "In Marketing to Gays, Lesbians Are Often Left Out," raises a provocative question about the direction of the gay advocacy movement: Must gay men and lesbians be "recognized" by the marketing departments of large corporations? The comments in the article by Kate Kendell, executive director of the National Center for Lesbian Rights, suggest that it is a social responsibility of corporations to pitch products to gay people.[128]

In your judgment, do corporations have a social responsibility to "recognize" and practice targeted marketing toward gays and lesbians? Explain.

Social Responsibility Cases Two-Four: Wages

Case Two: Pay More than the Market Requires?

Would the good corporate citizen, the socially responsible company, choose to pay its low-wage employees more than the market requires? The fast-food industry has been dealing with that issue and its very unfavorable publicity in recent years, not for its own employees but for the Florida tomato pickers whose notoriously low wages allow us to eat cheaper tomato-garnished hamburgers. A Florida International University study estimated the state's farm workers' wages at an average of $13,000 annually.[129] Working 10- to 12-hour days, migrant farm workers pick tomatoes by hand, earning about 45 cents for every 32-pound bucket picked. That long day's work typically involves picking, carrying, and unloading about two tons of tomatoes.[130] A farm workers coalition pressed the fast-food companies to raise those wages by paying an extra penny for each pound of tomatoes picked.[131]

A spokesman for the Florida tomato growers disputed the low wage claims saying pickers average $12.46 per hour plus free transportation to the fields. Angel Aguilar, a 36-year-old picker from Mexico, said that claim is a "gigantic lie." Aguilar said he generally earned $40 to $50 per day for five to seven hours of picking. Workers typically begin their day at 5 AM collecting at a parking lot in hopes of being chosen to pick, but paying work usually cannot begin until 10 or 11 AM when the dew has burned off. Workers often rent living space in trailers where they sometimes need to hang their food from wires to prevent rats from eating it.[132]

> Workers sometimes need to hang their food from wires to prevent rats from eating it.

Following a fight of several years, including a boycott, Yum! Brands (Taco Bell, Pizza Hut, and KFC), McDonald's, Burger King, and others agreed to voluntarily raise tomato pickers' pay by one cent per pound, a 71-percent increase, with the result that workers are expected to earn 77 cents, instead of 45 cents, for each 32-pound bucket of tomatoes they pick. Amy Wagner, a senior Burger King vice president, estimated the company's costs would increase by about $300,000 annually, but she said, "If the Florida tomato industry is to be sustainable long term, it must become more socially responsible."[133] Then in 2010, family-owned Pacific Tomato Growers, one of the five largest growers in the United States, also agreed to implement the penny per pound pay raise with the expectation that workers' annual earning would rise from about $10,000 to as much as $17,000.[134] [See; Mark Bittman, "The True Cost of Tomatoes," *The New York Times,* June 14, 2011

(http://opinionator.blogs.nytimes.com/).] [For more information on the pay raise campaign and the Coalition of Immokalee Workers (CIW) that led the campaign, see **http://www.ciw-online.org**]

Case Two Questions

1. *a.* Should the socially responsible company pay very low wage workers more than the market requires? Explain.

   b. Is the free market the best measure of a "fair" wage for all? Explain.

2. Robyn Blumner, writing in the *St. Petersburg Times,* asked: "Would you pay an extra penny per pound of tomatoes if you knew it meant farm workers . . . would nearly double their wages?"[135] Answer her question.

3. Should we, as consumers, blame ourselves for the mistreatment and low wages of Florida tomato workers? Explain.

Case Three: Pay More than the Law Requires?

In 2010, during very difficult economic times, the Hobby Lobby retail chain with 455 stores in 36 states raised its company minimum wage for full-time employees to $11 per hour, nearly $4 more than the $7.25 required under federal law. Why did the company raise its wages well beyond the law's requirements? David Green, the CEO of the privately owned corporation, said, "We have always tried to be a company that serves their employees."[136] Hobby Lobby had raised its minimum wage to $10 per hour in 2009, and the results were so positive that the company decided to provide another raise in 2010. Green explained the company's reasoning:

> Hobby Lobby raised its company minimum wage to $11 per hour.

> We're 100 percent excited about what we've done. We have had single mothers who were able to quit their second jobs. We have had employees come up and cry. The math of it said it would have cost us millions of dollars. But the results from the employees showed us differently; it really didn't cost anything because retention is important.[137]

Case Three Questions

1. How can it make good business sense to pay employees more than the law and the market require?

2. Would you do as Hobby Lobby did? Explain.

Case Four: Making a Profit: Reduce Wages?

Three hundred workers at the Mott's apple juice plant (a Dr Pepper Snapple subsidiary) in Williamson, New York, waged a 16-week strike when the company demanded a $1.50 per hour pay cut even though Snapple had produced a $555 million profit in the previous year (2009)[138] and increased its dividend by 67 percent in May 2010.[139] Snapple claimed the wage cut was justifiable to increase competitiveness, since the workers were averaging $21 per hour while other similar workers were averaging $14.[140] The union, on the other hand, noted that the area suffers from nearly a 50 percent poverty level.[141] The strike ended in September 2010 with a three-year deal freezing rather than reducing wages. Snapple dropped a demand to freeze pensions for current employees, but new hires will join a 401(k) plan instead of receiving a pension. Snapple will save money on retirement plans. Both sides reportedly considered the result a victory.

Case Four Questions

1. Dr Pepper Snapple argued that it had a responsibility as a public company to seek concessions from its workers. Explain that argument.
2. Is it wrong in your judgment for a profitable company to seek wage concessions from its workers? Explain.

Internet Exercise

1. Many critics, activists, international scholars, and others are concerned that corporate/governmental interests threaten global human rights and the global natural environment. Using the Corporate Watch Web site [**http://www.corpwatch.org/**], explain those concerns in more detail.
2. Using the Web site opensecrets.org, find the latest campaign finance data for your congressperson or one of your senators. While there, perhaps you will want to take a look at the personal financial condition of those same politicians. [See **http://www.opensecrets.org/pfds/overview.php**].

Chapter Questions

1. *a.* In general, do you think employers are more concerned with profits or with delivering quality goods and services? Explain.
   b. Which should they be more concerned about? Explain.
   c. Are you most concerned about receiving a quality education or earning a degree? Explain.
2. Scholar Denis Goulet argued that we will find no facile resolution to the conflict between the values of a just society and the sharply opposing values of successful corporations.[142]
   a. Do you agree that the values of a just society oppose those of successful corporations? Explain.
   b. Can a solution be found? Explain.
3. In 2010 the Center for Science in the Public Interest and a concerned parent sued McDonald's for deceptive advertising by using toys in Happy Meals to encourage children to consume unhealthy food.[143] San Francisco approved an ordinance, effective December 1, 2011, banning free toys with food that exceeds certain specified levels of fat, sugar, and calories.[144]
   a. Do you think McDonald's commits an ethical wrong by using toys in Happy Meals to attract children to unhealthy food? Explain.
   b. Should the legal system restrain McDonald's use of toys to encourage the consumption of unhealthy food? Explain.

4. *a.* Given British Petroleum's (BP) catastrophic 2010 Deepwater Horizon oil spill with its 11 deaths and its uncertain toxic threat to the Gulf of Mexico as well as the company's previous history of industrial accidents, should the responsible consumer boycott BP gas stations? Explain.

   b. Did you do so?

   c. Have you ever boycotted a product/producer/retailer?

   d. Can you think of situations where you should have done so? Explain.

5. A Pennsylvania Chick-fil-A franchise, on its own, provided food for a local marriage seminar, "The Art of Marriage: Getting to the Heart of God's Design." A group opposed to gay and lesbian marriage sponsored the seminar. Once news of Chick-fil-A's sponsorship became public, protests and calls for boycotts followed. Chick-fil-A, a privately held company, is always closed on Sundays, has given millions to Christian causes, and includes the glorification of God among its corporate purposes.[145]

   a. In your view, is the operation of a privately held business on Christian principles a moral wrong? Explain.

   b. Would you consider it to be a moral wrong if Chick-fil-A actively opposed gay and lesbian marriage? Explain.

   c. As a business matter, how should Chick-Fil-A handle the objections to its franchise's support of the seminar?

6. Worried about Junior misbehaving? Here's an answer:

   > Call a board meeting. As crazy as it sounds, some Americans are trying to keep tabs on the kids by bringing business strategies into the traditional family meeting. They're hashing out everything from vacations to disputes over toys with techniques that seem right out of a management textbook: mission statements, rotating chairmanships, motivational seminars, even suggestion boxes. The most corporate of clans hire professional meeting facilitators, just to smooth over family squabbles.[146]

   a. List some of the strengths and weaknesses of the business approach to raising children.

   b. Do you regard the business approach in the home as a promising development or another encroachment of business values into life outside of work? Explain.

7. Sam Wong, speaking during his sophomore year at Iowa State University:

   > Materialism, like patience, is a virtue. Ever since my parents bought me my first Transformer, almost everyone has tried to convince me that owning a lot of toys wouldn't make me happy. Oh, how wrong they were. Toys make me very, very happy. That's why today I have more of them than ever. I own every Nintendo. I own two CD-R burners. My drum set cost as much as a semester of school. I drive a Miata. What's more, I'm not ashamed to be a consumer. I consider it part of my American heritage, and I'm proud of it.[147]

   Do you share Wong's values? Explain. Is materialism in America's best interests? Explain.

8. Knights Apparel, a privately held, Spartansburg, South Carolina, clothing company is the leading supplier of college logo apparel to American universities. Knights works closely with the Worker Rights Consortium, a group of 186 universities that lobbies for fair treatment for workers in the plants that produce college-logo goods. Knights contracts with 30 factories worldwide. One of those plants, Alta Gracia in the Dominican Republic, is a Knights experiment in social responsibility. Knights is paying Alta Gracia workers a "living wage" of about $2.83 per hour while the Dominican minimum wage is about 85 cents per hour. The factory was remodeled, including ergonomic chairs for workers and bright lighting. Unionization is permitted, and workers are treated with respect. T-shirts cost about $4.80 to produce, about 20 percent more than if Knights paid the minimum wage. Knights sells the shirts at $8 wholesale, and the normal retail price is about $18. Knights will achieve a lower than usual profit margin on the Alta Gracia apparel.[148] The big question is whether customers will pay as much for the Knights clothing as for premium brands like Nike that are similarly priced. [For the Alta Gracia home page, see **http://altagraciaapparel.com**]

   a. Would you forgo the Nike clothing of similar price and quality in order to support the Alta Gracia brand? Explain.

   b. Do you, as a student, have a responsibility to protest if your college logo appears on sportswear made in low-wage sweatshops? Explain.

   c. Have you ever inquired about the manufacturing source of a product you were considering, or have you declined, as a matter of principle, to buy certain garments or other items because you believe the manufacturer engages in unfair labor practices? Explain.

9. Should American companies refuse to do business in countries that:

   a. Do not practice democracy?

   b. Routinely practice discrimination?

   c. Tolerate or even encourage the abuse of children? Explain.

10. In criticizing General Motors, Ralph Nader is reported to have said,

    > Someday we'll have a legal system that will criminally indict the president of General Motors for these outrageous crimes. But not as long as this country is populated by people who fritter away their citizenship by watching TV, playing bridge and Mah-Jongg, and just generally being slobs.[149]

    a. Is the citizenry generally unconcerned about unethical corporate conduct? Explain.

    b. To the extent that corporations engage in misdeeds, does the fault really lie with the corporate community or with society at large?

11. Journalist Michael Kinsley expresses some serious reservations about corporate social responsibility:

    > In particular, I am not impressed by corporate charity and cultural benefaction, which amount to executives playing Medici with other people's money. You wouldn't know, from the lavish parties corporate officers throw for themselves whenever they fund an art exhibit or a PBS series, that it's not costing them a penny. The shareholders, who aren't invited, pick up the tab.[150]

    Comment on Kinsley's statement.

12. The Pennsylvania garment maker AND1 developed a line of T-shirts directed to young males and adorned with sayings such as "Your game is as ugly as your girl." and "You like that move? So does your girl." A feminist group complained that the shirts "put down" girls and implied that "girls are the property of boys." JC Penney, which was selling the shirts, withdrew them after the complaints.[151] Was JC Penney's decision the socially responsible course of action, or did JC Penney cave in to "politically correct" pressure? Or did JC Penney simply make a wise business move? Explain.

13. Michael Vick, Kobe Bryant, Tiger Woods, and other high-profile athletes have been entangled in very serious legal problems. The great cycling spectacle, the Tour de France, has been plagued by evidence of drug doping by riders and many major league baseball players have been linked to steroid use. Should you refuse to watch these tarnished athletes and refuse to buy products they endorse? Explain.

14. Make the argument that corporations are not well-suited to be stakeholder driven, "do-gooders" looking out for the general welfare of society.

15. You are the sole owner of a neighborhood drugstore that stocks various brands of toothpaste. Assume that scientific testing has established that one brand is clearly superior to all others in preventing tooth decay.
    a. Would you remove from the shelves all brands except the one judged best in decay prevention? Explain.
    b. What alternative measures could you take?
    c. Should the toothpaste manufacturers be required to reveal all available data regarding the effectiveness of their products? Explain.

16. Beyond its economic efficiencies, explain how "globalization/Americanization" is valuable for personal growth in the less developed world.

17. Approximately $10 million is expended annually for alcohol ads in college newspapers. Many millions more are expended in other youth-oriented publications such as *National Lampoon* and *Rolling Stone*. The beer industry sponsors many campus athletic contests. Brewers have established promotional relationships with rock bands. Is beer and liquor advertising directed to the youth market unethical? Explain.

18. U.S. corporations routinely outsource programming, customer support, data entry, and various back-office jobs to lower-paid workers in countries as diverse as India, Romania, and Ghana. Now higher-paying, increasingly sophisticated jobs are also moving abroad. Some countries develop technical specialties, as is the case with Sri Lanka that has an abundance of well-trained accountants who do work for giants such as HSBC and Aviva. That work sometimes involves routine bookkeeping, but it also entails sophisticated derivatives pricing and risk management. In the United States, accounting salaries average just under $60,000 while $5,900 is the norm in Sri Lanka.[152]
    a. Is outsourcing good for America? Explain.
    b. Are you confident that you will be competitive in the American market of the future where outsourcing seems destined to strip away big pieces of the job market? Explain.

19. Former General Motors vice president John Z. DeLorean wrote in his book, *On a Clear Day You Can See General Motors:*

> It seemed to me then, and still does now, that the system of American business often produces wrong, immoral, and irresponsible decisions, even though the personal morality of the people running the business is often above reproach. The system has a different morality as a group than the people do as individuals, which permits it willfully to produce ineffective or dangerous products, deal dictatorially and often unfairly with suppliers, pay bribes for business, abrogate the rights of employment, or tamper with the democratic process of government through illegal political contributions.[153]

  a. How can the corporate "group" possess values at odds with those of the individual managers?

  b. Is DeLorean merely offering a convenient rationalization for corporate misdeeds? Explain.

  c. Realistically, can one expect to preserve individual values when employed in a corporate group? Explain.

20. Do you agree or disagree with the following statements? Explain.

  a. "Social responsibility is good business only if it is also good public relations and/or preempts government interference."

  b. "The social responsibility debate is the result of the attempt of liberal intellectuals to make a moral issue of business behavior."

  c. "'Profit' is really a somewhat ineffective measure of business's social effectiveness."

  d. "The social responsibility of business is to 'stick to business.'"[154]

Notes

1. "Walmart Corporate Fact Sheet," [**www.walmartstores.com/download/2230.pdf**].

2. Tracey Keys and Thomas W. Malnight, "Corporate Clout: The Influence of the World's Largest 100 Economic Entities," *Global Trends* [**http://www.globaltrends.com/features/shapers-and-influencers/66-corporate-clout-the-influence-of-the-world's-largest-100-economic-entities**].

3. Lydia Saad, "In U.S., Majority Still Wants Less Corporate Influence," *Gallup Poll*, February 1, 2011 [**http://www.gallup.com/poll/145871/majority-wants-less-corporate-influence.aspx**].

4. Dan Ackman, "Corporate Taxes Continue to Plummet," *Forbes.com*, September 23, 2004. Reprinted at ReclaimingDemocracy.org [**http://reclaimdemocracy.org/articles_2004/corporate_taxes_lower.html**].

5. Tax Policy Center, "The Numbers: What Are the Federal Government's Sources of Revenue?" *The Tax Policy Briefing Book,* [**http://www.taxpolicycenter.org/briefing-book/background/numbers/revenue.cfm**].

6. Christopher Helman, "GE, Exxon Paid No U.S. Income Taxes in '09," *ABC News,* April 6, 2010 [**http://abcnews.go.com/**].

7. Associated Press, "Buffett in Berkshire's Annual Report: Tax Cuts Favor Corporations, Wealthy," *Waterloo/Cedar Falls Courier,* March 7, 2004, p. A2.

8. Peter D. Hart Research Associates, Inc., "Civil Justice Issues and the 2008 Election" [**http://www.atla.org/pressroom/CJSPollMemo.pdf**].

9. "Americans Blame Businesses, Banks for Crisis," *Angus Reid Global Monitor,* April 10, 2009 [**http://www.angus-reid.com/polls/**].

10. Thomas M. Hoenig, "Too Big to Succeed," *The New York Times,* December 1, 2010 [**http://www.nytimes.com/**].

11. Barry C. Lynn, *Cornered: The New Monopoly Capitalism and the Economics of Destruction* (Hoboken, NJ: Wiley, 2010).

12. Charles Reich, *The Greening of America* (New York: Bantam Books, 1970), pp. 7–8.

13. "Nation's Alienation Index Decreases as Fewer People Feel Powerless," Harris Poll, no. 96, December 1, 2004 [**http://www.harrisinteractive.com/harris_poll/index.asp?PID=525**].

14. "Harris Alienation Index Remains Low . . . But 70% of Adults Believe People in Washington Are Out of Touch with the Rest of the Country," Harris Polls, August 20, 2010 [**http://www.harrisinteractive.com/**].

15. Ben Stein, "A City on a Hill, or a Looting Opportunity," *The New York Times,* July 9, 2006 [**http://www.nytimes.com**].

16. Some portions of this paragraph rely upon Ciara Torres-Spelliscy, "Corporate Political Spending & Shareholders' Rights: Why the U.S. Should Adopt the British Approach," *Social Science Research Network,* September 8, 2009. Available at SSRN: **http://ssrn.cm/abstract=1474421.**

17. *Citizens United v. Federal Election Commission,* 130 S.Ct.876 (2010).

18. Dan Eggen, "Poll: Large Majority Opposes Supreme Court's Decision on Campaign," *The Washington Post,* February 17, 2010 [**http://www.washingtonpost.com/**].

19. The Editors, "Democracy Inc.," *The Nation,* January 28, 2010 [**http://www.thenation.com/article/democracy-inc**].

20. Richard S. Dunham, "As Power Shifts, So Do the Dollars," *BusinessWeek,* April 23, 2007, p. 33.

21. Eric Lipton, Mike McIntire, and Don Van Natta Jr., "Top Corporations Aid U.S. Chamber of Commerce Campaign," *The New York Times,* October 21, 2010 [**http://www.nytimes.com**].

22. Brody Mullins and John D. McKinnon, "Campaign's Big Spender," *The Wall Street Journal,* October 22, 2010, p. A1.

23. "U.S. Bancorp Political Contribution Policy," [**phx.corporate-ir.net/External.File?item=UGFyZW50SUQ9MzkzOXxDaGlsZElEPS0xfFR5cGU9Mw==&t=1**].

24. Associated Press, "Target and Other Companies Spending Money on Political Campaigns," *Cleveland.com,* July 27, 2010 [**http://www.cleveland.com**].

25. "Cozy at the Beach," *The Washington Post,* February 17, 2007, p. A30.

26. Amanda Becker, "Registered Lobbyists Decline in Response to 2007 Rules, Administration Crackdown," *The Washington Post,* July 12, 2010 [**http://www.washingtonpost.com/**].

27. Katrina Vanden Heuvel, "How to Turn Congress Inc. Back to Just Congress," *The Washington Post,* May 12, 2010 [**http://www.washingtonpost.com/**].

28. Dan Eggen and Kimberly Kindy, "Three of Every Four Oil and Gas Lobbyists Worked for Federal Government," *The Washington Post,* July 22, 2010, p. A01.

29. Dana Milbank, "Big Business Is Back in Business," *The Washington Post,* January 12, 2011 [**http://www.washingtonpost.com/**].

30. Melinda Burns, "K Street and the Status Quo," *Miller-McCune,* September-October 2010, p. 62.

31. Ibid.

32. Eamon Javers, "Inside the Hidden World of Earmarks," *BusinessWeek,* September 17, 2007, p. 56.

33. Ibid.

34. Becker, "Registered Lobbyists Decline," [**http://www.washingtonpost.com**].

35. Theo Francis, "Lobbying: What Tougher Rules?" *BusinessWeek,* September 8, 2008, p. 024.

36. Jane Eisner, "Peer Pressure, Ads Aimed at Youth Lead to Culture of Overconsumption," *Waterloo/Cedar Falls Courier,* September 19, 2004, p. C9.

37. Anjali Athavaley, "It's Just Lip Gloss, Mom," *The Wall Street Journal,* February 3, 2011, p. D1.

38. Linzee Kull McCray, "The Pursuit of 'Hotness,'" *The University of Iowa Spectator,* Fall 2008, p. 12.

39. William C. Symonds, "The Reform of School Reform," *BusinessWeek,* June 26, 2006, p. 72.

40. Jennifer Medina, "Los Angeles Schools to Seek Sponsors," *The New York Times,* December 15, 2010 [**http://www.nytimes.com**].

41. Seema Mehta, "Cash-Strapped California Schools Seek Commercial Sponsors to Raise Funds," *latimes.com,* September 7, 2009 [**http://www.latimes.com/**].

42. Carla K. Johnson, "Ads More Memorable than News, Study Says," *The Des Moines Register,* March 6, 2006, p. 8A.

43. Ibid.

44. Robert Weissman, "Resisting the Commercialization of Public Schools." *Counterpunch,* May 25, 2007 [**http://www.counterpunch.org/weissman05252007.html**].

45. Ibid.

46. "Peter Drucker—Toward a More Gentle Marketplace," *Austrian Information* 59, (March/April 2006), p. 9.

47. Alexandra Alter, "Inspired by Starbucks," *The Wall Street Journal,* June 13, 2008, p. W1.

48. Ibid.

49. David Brooks, "The Gospel of Wealth," *The New York Times,* September 6, 2010 [**http://www.nytimes.com/**].

50. Ibid.

51. Stacey Palevsky, "Fashion & Faith," *Waterloo/Cedar Falls Courier,* September 20, 2004, p. B4.

52. Mike Boehm, Louis Vuitton Suit Adds Fraud Allegation," *latimes.com,* April 23, 2009 [**latimes.com/entertainment/news/arts/la-et-vuitton23-2009apr23,0,6238759.story**].

53. Diane Haithman, "MOCA Show Asks: Is It Business or Is It Art?" *latimes.com,* August 9, 2007 [**http://www.latimes.com/news/la-et-moca9aug09,0,5477094.story?coll=la-tot-topstories &track=ntottext**].

54. Marshall Herskovitz, "Are the Corporate Suits Ruining TV?" *latimes.com,* November 7, 2007 [**http://www.latimes.com/news/opinion/la-oe-herskovitz7nov07,0,5402981. story?coll=la-tot-opinion&track=ntothtml**].

55. Ibid.

56. Jacques Steinberg, "Radio Days," *The New York Times,* April 13, 2008 [**http://www.nytimes. com/**].

57. Ben Sisario, "Top Brands Give Voice to New Bands," *China Daily,* October 24, 2010 [**http:// www.chinadaily.com.cn/entertainment/2010-10/24/content_11450495.htm**].

58. "Knight, Big 12 Coaches Agree: College Sports Are Big Business," *USA TODAY,* February 16, 2004 [**http://www.usatoday.com/sports/college/2004-02-16-notes_x.htm**].

59. Ibid.

60. Michael Rosenberg, "Change Is Long Overdue: College Football Players Should Be Paid," *SI.com,* August 26, 2010 [**http://sportsillustrated.cnn.com/2010/writers/Michael_rosenberg/08/26/pay. college/index.html**].

61. Mark Bauerlein, "'The Ivory Tower'—Who Does He Play for?" *The Wall Street Journal,* January 22, 2010, p. W6.

62. Paul Whiteley, Sr., "Fan Fears Greed Is Ruining Sports," *The Des Moines Register,* August 27, 1995, p. 9D.

63. Francis X. Clines, "Pondering the Ultimate Sky Box," *The New York Times,* December 15, 2008 [**http://www.nytimes.com/**].

64. Steve Wilstein, "Let Commercialism Reign," *Waterloo/Cedar Falls Courier,* April 29, 2004, p. C2.

65. Josh Barr, "Business Embraces Prep Football," *The Washington Post,* September 2, 2007, p. D05.

66. Ibid.

67. Timothy Egan, "Nike's Women Problem," *The New York Times,* April 21, 2010 [**http://opinionator.blogs.nytimes.com/**].

68. "Analyst: Endorsements Will Come for Ben Roethlisberger with a Victory," *USA TODAY,* February 6, 2011 [**http://content.usatoday.com/**].

69. Anis Ahmed, "Bangladesh Doubles Minimum Wage for Garment Workers," *Fox Business,* July 29, 2010 [**http://www.foxbusiness.com**].

70. Ibid.

71. Ibid.

72. Associated Press, "Corporations Explore New Ways to Ship Jobs Overseas," *Waterloo/Cedar Falls Courier,* January 22, 2004, p. D6.

73. Stephanie Clifford and Liz Alderman, "American Retailers Try Again in Europe," *The New York Times,* June 15, 2011 [**http://www.nytimes.com**] and Laurie Goering, "Europeans Showing Some Love for Americans," *Chicago Tribune,* February 8, 2009 [**http://articles.chicagotribune.com/**].

74. Christopher A. Bartlett, "Losing in the Court of Public Opinion," *Across the Board,* Jan.–Feb. 2002, p. 27.

75. David Wessel, "The Future of Jobs," *The Wall Street Journal,* March 2, 2004, p. A1.

76. Ted Peters, "The Future of Religion in a Post-Industrial Society," *The Futurist,* October 1980, pp. 20, 22.

77. "More Leisure in an Increasingly Electronic Society," *BusinessWeek,* September 3, 1979, pp. 208, 212.

78. Daniel Seligman, "Helping the Shareholder Helps the Society," *The Wall Street Journal,* June 21, 1996, p. A12.

79. Ronald Alsop, "Recruiters Seek M.B.A.s Trained in Responsibility," *The Wall Street Journal,* December 13, 2005, p. B6.

80. This paragraph relies on materials from Ian Shapira, "For This Generation, Vocations of Service," *washingtonpost.com,* October 14, 2008, p. B01, and Kristie Wang, "love.futbol: Engaging a Global Passion for Soccer and Youth," *Changemakers,* February 17, 2011 [**http://www.changemakers.com/node/101116/**].

81. Diana Middleton, "M.B.A.s Seek Social Change," *The Wall Street Journal,* October 15, 2009, p. B7.

82. Emily Glazer, "'Social Capital' Gains Traction during Upheaval," *Waterloo/Cedar Falls Courier,* September 20, 2009, p. D8.

83. Keith Davis and Robert L. Blomstrom, *Business and Society: Environment and Responsibility,* 3rd ed. (New York: McGraw-Hill, 1975), p. 6.

84. Milton Friedman, *Capitalism and Freedom* (Chicago: University of Chicago Press, 1962), p. 133.

85. Herbert Stein, "Corporate America, Mind Your Own Business," *The Wall Street Journal,* July 15, 1996, p. A10.

86. Steven A. Rochlin, "The New Corporate Citizenship," *BusinessWeek,* December 13, 2003, p. 66.

87. Archie Carroll and others have pointed to some descriptive and theoretical limitations associated with Carroll's social responsibility pyramid; and Carroll has proposed a three-domain approach of economic, legal, and ethical responsibilities arrayed in a Venn framework. The newer model appears to satisfy some of the concerns of Carroll and others about Carroll's pyramid, but for both teaching and research purposes, the pyramid remains a useful construct. For Carroll's newer construct, see Mark S. Schwartz and Archie B. Carroll, "Corporate Social Responsibility: A Three Domain Approach," *Business Ethics Quarterly* 13, no. 4 (October 2003), p. 503. For an example of research employing the Carroll pyramid and a discussion of some of the strengths and weaknesses of the pyramid, see Dane K. Peterson, "The Relationship between Perceptions of Corporate Citizenship and Organizational Commitment," *Business & Society* 43, no. 3 (September 2004), p. 296.

88. Chris Herring and Dana Mattioli, "Companies Send Aid to Haiti," *The Wall Street Journal,* January 19, 2010 [**http://online.wsj.com/**].

89. Andrea Chang, "Target in Compton Helps Store Employees Tackle Their Personal Problems," *latimes.com,* December 12, 2010 [**latimes.com/business/la-fi-compton-target-20101211,0, 7741305.story**].

90. Kevin Delaney, "Google: From 'Don't Be Evil' to How to Do Good," *The Wall Street Journal,* January 18, 2008, p. B1.

91. Vikas Bajaj, "Sun Co-Founder Uses Capitalism to Help Poor," *The New York Times,* October 5, 2010 [**http://www.nytimes.com/**].

92. Portions of the material in this paragraph are drawn from Vikas Bajaj, "Luster Dims for a Public Microlender," *The New York Times,* May 10, 2011 [**http://www.nytimes.com**] and Unmesh Ker, "Getting Smart at Being Good . . . Are Companies Better Off for It?" *Time Inside Business,* January 2006, p. A1.

93. Aaron Task, "Mass Layoffs by Profitable Firms a 'Horrible Act,' Diller Says," *Yahoo! Finance,* December 10, 2008 [**http://finance.yahoo.com/**].

94. Linda Basch, "More Women in Finance, A More Sustainable Economy," *The Christian Science Monitor,* June 24, 2009 [**http://www.csmonitor.com/2009/0624/p09s02-coop. html**].

95. Marc Orlitzky, Frank L. Schmidt, and Sara L. Rynes, "Corporate Social and Financial Performance: A Meta Analysis," Social Investment Forum Foundation, December 2004 [**http://business. auckland.ac.nz/newstaffnet/profile/publications_upload/000000556_orlitzkyschmidtry-nes2003os.pdf**].

96. Peter van Beurden and Tobias Gossling, "The Worth of Values—A Literature Review on the Relation between Corporate Social and Financial Performance," *Journal of Business Ethics* 82, no. 2 (October 2008), p. 407.

97. David J. Craig, "Clean Money," *Columbia Magazine,* Fall 2009, p. 58.

98. Claudia Buck, "'Socially Responsible' Investing Becomes a Growth Industry," *The Des Moines Register,* March 15, 2009, p. 3D.

99. "Social Responsibility: Most People Have Good Intentions but Only a Small Minority Really Practice What They Preach," *The Harris Poll* no. 57, June 18, 2007 [**http://www.harrisinter-active. com/harris_poll/index.asp?PID=774**].

100. John Bussey, "CEO Council (A Special Report)—Restoring Confidence in Business: Not Just about Shareholders," *The Wall Street Journal,* November 22, 2010, p. R3.

101. Ann Svendsen, *The Stakeholder Strategy* (San Francisco: Berrett-Koehler, 1998), p. 49.

102. Deon Binneman, "Crucial Questions to Ask about Stakeholder Management," *Blog: Deon Binneman on Reputation,* January 28, 2011 [**http://deonbinneman.wordpress. com/2011/01/28/crucial-questions-to-ask-about-stakeholder-management/**].

103. Svendsen, *The Stakeholder Strategy,* p. 3.

104. Ibid., p. 4.

105. Alan Murray, "The CEO as Global Corporate Ambassador," *The Wall Street Journal,* March 29, 2006, p. A2.

106. Social Accountability Accreditation Services, "Certified Facilities List," September 30, 2010 [**http://www.saasaccreditation.org/certfacilitieslist.htm**].

107. "A Common Framework for Sustainability Reporting" [**www.globalreporting.org/About GRI/Overview.htm**].

108. Mark Magnier, "Anguish Lingers in Bhopal, 25 Years after Chemical Disaster," *latimes. com,* December 3, 2009 [**latimes,com/news/nation-and-world/la-fg-india-bhopal3-2009dec03,0,3728767.story**].

109. Susan Warren, "Chemical Companies Keep Lessons of Bhopal Spill Fresh," *The Wall Street Journal,* February 13, 2001, p. B4.

110. Leslie Patton and Matthew Boyle, "Wal-Mart Cracks Chicago by Splitting Union, Non-Union Workers," *Bloomberg,* July 22, 2010 [**http://www.bloomberg.com/**].

111. Liza Featherstone, "Wage Against the Machine," *Slate,* June 27, 2008 [**http://www.slate.com/**].

112. Ibid.

113. Miguel Bustillo, "Wal-Mart Tries to Recapture Mr. Sam's Winning Formula," *The Wall Street Journal,* February 22, 2011, p. A6.

114. Featherstone, "Wage Against the Machine," June 27, 2008.

115. Malcolm Berko, "Bottom Line Speaks Louder Than Employees," *Waterloo/Cedar Falls Courier,* May 25, 2004, p. C5.

116. Bustillo, "Wal-Mart Tries to Recapture Mr. Sam's Winning Formula," p. A6.

117. "Wal-Mart Releases Employment Data," *The Des Moines Register,* April 12, 2006, p. 6C.

118. David Vogel, "When Do 'Good' Firms Go 'Bad'?" *latimes.com,* February 13, 2007 [**http:// www.latimes.com/news/opinion/la-oe-vogel13feb13,0,4670297.story?track=tottext**].

119. William Beaver, "Is the Stakeholder Model Dead?" *Business Horizons* 42, no. 2 (March–April 1999), p. 8.

120. Associated Press, "Boss Rewards Workers' Loyalty—Shares $128 Million," *Waterloo/Cedar Falls Courier,* September 12, 1999, p. B1.

121. Greg Miller, "Extreme Generosity Shocks Firm's Employees, Analysts," *The Des Moines Register,* December 18, 1996, p. 1A.

122. Molly Selvin, "Companies Add Same-Sex Benefits to Attract, Keep Workers," *Pittsburgh Post-Gazette.com,* July 3, 2006 [**http://www.post-gazette.com/pg/06184/702548-28.stm**].

123. "286 of *Fortune* 500 Companies Offer Domestic-Partner Benefits," *Business Management Daily,* June 3, 2009 [**http://www.upi.com/Business_News/Business_Daily/**].

124. Tara Siegel Bernard, "Google to Add Pay to Cover a Tax for Same-Sex Benefits," *The New York Times,* June 30, 2010 [**http://www.nytimes.com/2020/0701/your-money/01benefits.html?**

125. Selvin, "Companies Add Same-Sex Benefits . . .," July 3, 2006.

126. "Most Americans Believe Gay, Lesbian Couples Should Receive Equal Workplace Benefits," *San Diego County News,* October 4, 2010 [**http://www.sandiegocountynews.com/2010/10/04/most-americans-believe-gay-lesbian-couples-should-receive-equal-benefits/**].

127. Cliff Edwards, "Coming Out in Corporate America," *BusinessWeek,* December 15, 2003, p. 64.

128. Christopher Mossey, "Marketing to Gays: Why Is It Needed?" *The Wall Street Journal,* October 29, 1999, p. A19.

129. Steven Greenhouse, "Campaign to Raise Tomato Pickers' Wages Faces Obstacles," *The New York Times,* December 24, 2007, Section A, p. 10.

130. Eric Schlosser, "Penny Foolish," *The New York Times,* November 29, 2007 [**www.newyorktimes.com**].

131. Greenhouse, "Campaign to Raise," Section A, p. 10.

132. Ibid.

133. Andrew Martin, "Burger King Grants Raise to Pickers," *The New York Times,* May 24, 2008 [**http://www.nytimes.com/**].

134. Greg Kaufmann, "The Wall Comes Tumbling Down," *The Nation,* October 18, 2010 [**http://www.thenation.com**].

135. Robyn Blumner, "At a Penny Per Pound, A Little Adds Up to a Lot," *St. Petersburg Times,* November 25, 2007, Perspective, p. 5P.

136. Jim Offner, "Hobby Lobby Proactively Hikes Minimum Wage for Full-Timers," *Waterloo/Cedar Falls Courier,* May 30, 2010, p. D1.

137. Ibid.

138. Steven Greenhouse, "Ending Strike, Mott's Plant Union Accepts Deal," *The New York Times,* September 13, 2010 [**http://www.nytimes.com/**].

139. Steven Greenhouse, "In Mott's Strike, More Than Pay at Stake," *The New York Times,* August 17, 2010 [**http://www.nytimes.com/**].

140. Greenhouse, "Ending Strike . . .," September 13, 2010.

141. Dan Margolis, "Mott's Workers OK New Contract," *Peoplesworld,* September 14, 2010 [**http://peoplesworld.org/mott-s-workers-ok-new-contract/**].

142. For an overview of Denis Goulet and his work, see [**http://www.nd.edu/~krocinst/faculty_staff/fellows/goulet.html**]

143. Gael O'Brien, "McDonald's Happy Meal Challenge," *The Week in Ethics,* December 27, 2010 [**http://theweekinethics.wordpress.com/**].

144. Joshua Sabatini, "Happy Meal Toy Ban Official," *San Francisco Examiner,* November 23, 2010 [**http://www.sfexaminer.com/blogs/under-dome/2010/11/happy-meal-toy-ban-official**].

145. Kim Severson, "A Chicken Chain's Corporate Ethos Is Questioned by Gay Rights Advocates," *The New York Times,* January 29, 2011 [**http://www.nytimes.com**].

146. Nancy Jeffrey, "Kids, Come to Order," *The Wall Street Journal,* August 10, 2001, p. W1.

147. Sam Wong, "Materialism Makes Me Feel Happy, Not Guilty," *The Des Moines Register,* September 10, 2000, p. 11A.

148. Steven Greenhouse, "Factory Defies Sweatshop Label, but Can It Thrive?" *The New York Times,* July 16, 2010 [**http://www.nytimes.com**].

149. Charles McCarry, *Citizen Nader* (New York: Saturday Review Press, 1972), p. 301.

150. Michael Kinsley, "Companies as Citizens: Should They Have a Conscience?" *The Wall Street Journal,* February 19, 1987, p. 29.

151. "Penney Hears Protests, Agrees to Trash T-Shirts," *The Des Moines Register,* July 6, 1999, p. 2A.

152. Heather Timmons, "Sri Lankan Accountants Lure Global Outsourcers," *The New York Times,* November 29, 2010 [**http://www.nytimes.com/**].

153. John Z. DeLorean with J. Patrick Wright, "Bottom-Line Fever at General Motors" (excerpted from *On a Clear Day You Can See General Motors*), *The Washington Monthly,* January 1980, pp. 26–27.

154. Steven N. Brenner and Earl A. Molander, "Is the Ethics of Business Changing?" *Harvard Business Review* 55, no. 1 (January–February 1977), p. 68.

Introduction to Law

The American Legal System

After completing this chapter, students will be able to:

1. Describe the importance of law to private enterprise.

2. Compare and contrast the objectives of law in society.

3. Differentiate the elements of a case brief.

4. Distinguish between substantive and procedural law.

5. Differentiate constitutional law, case law, and statutory law.

6. Compare and contrast civil and criminal law.

7. Describe the elements of the basic court system structure.

8. Explain the purposes of subject matter and personal jurisdiction as requirements for a court's power to hear a dispute.

9. Describe the typical steps in the civil trial process.

10. Distinguish trials and appeals.

11. Identify dispute resolution alternatives to trials.

Introduction

Presumably we can agree that some business behavior is bad for America. This text examines what should be done to change that behavior. The fundamental options in the United States have been fourfold: Let the market "regulate" the behavior; leave the problem to the individual decision maker's own ethical dictates; pass a law; or rely on some combination of the market, ethics, and law. Market regulation was discussed in Chapter 1. Self-regulation through ethics was explored in Chapters 2 and 3. This chapter begins the discussion of the legal regulation of business with a brief outline of the

American legal system. We will also look at alternative conflict resolution processes such as negotiation, mediation, and arbitration that do not resort to the legal system. We begin by reminding ourselves of the indispensable role of law in fostering business practice.

Law and the Market   Whatever we may think about lawyers, judges and America's dispute resolution methods, the crucial role of a reliable legal system in fostering and maintaining capitalism is indisputable. The following law review excerpt explains.

READING

The Importance of Law to the Private Enterprise System

Deb Ballam

Nobel economist Frederich von Hayek describes the theoretical importance of law to private enterprise. According to Hayek, law that secures property rights in modern society is a prerequisite to private enterprise. Without the order of law enforcing private property ownership and facilitating the transfer of property rights, business enterprise in a complex, heterogeneous culture is simply infeasible.

The importance of law to the conduct of private enterprise is evident in economic developments in . . . the Republic of China. In moving from state-controlled to private enterprise, [China] faced substantial difficulties arising from the lack of a legal system that would secure property ownership and the contractual transfer of property rights.

. . . China's economy has grown steadily in recent years. Minxin Pei, a political scientist at Princeton University, explains law's contribution to that growth: "Legal reform has become one of the most important institutional changes in China since the late 1970s. . . . Within China, the changing legal institutions have begun to play an increasingly important role in governing economic activities, resolving civil disputes, enforcing law and order, and setting the boundaries between the power of the state and the autonomy of society. . . ."

Of course, the importance of law to private enterprise goes far beyond its initial support as an institutional framework guaranteeing ownership rights. As the market system grows more complex both nationally and internationally, the legal recognition of promise keeping becomes increasingly significant in facilitating business. A condition for emerging economies entering international trade is learning how to keep promises to strangers, and whether enforced through litigation or arbitration, promise keeping in business requires the ordering presence of contract law.

In a democracy, law is important to business for another reason quite separate from its function in establishing ownership rights and facilitating promise keeping necessary to their transfer: It provides the formal expression of democratic social will. That expression implicates private enterprise in a plethora of ways, including regulation of the environment, employment laws, securities regulation, consumer protection statutes, and product liability. As contemporary society becomes increasingly diverse, law grows, not diminishes, in its importance to private enterprise; and in spite of valid concerns about the impact of law on efficiency, future business managers will need to know more, not less, about how law affects business operations. No evidence suggests any other conclusion.

Source: Deb Ballam, quoting from "The Importance of Law to the Private Enterprise System," *The American Legal Studies in Business Task Force Report* by O. Lee Reed. *American Business Law Journal* 36, no. 1 (Fall 1998), p. ix. Reprinted by permission.

Questions

1. *a.* Do you expect to see greater reliance on law as our society becomes increasingly complex?
   b. Can you think of any meaningful substitutes for law as we now practice it? Explain.

Part One—Legal Foundations

Objectives of the Law

Americans differ dramatically in their views of the role the law should play in contemporary life. For some, the courts and the police primarily act as obstructions to personal freedom and to a fully efficient marketplace. Others seek much more law to ensure that everyone is cared for who is in need and everyone is sheltered from wrongdoers. We are in constant conflict about the law's precise path in our lives, but most of us can agree on some foundational expectations for a fair, efficient legal system. Certainly we expect the law to *maintain order* in our diverse, rapidly changing society. Of course, we rely on law to peacefully, fairly, and intelligently *resolve conflict.* Perhaps less obvious, but no less important, the law serves to *preserve dominant values.* Americans differ about core values, but we have reached a workable accord about our most fundamental beliefs. Some of those, such as freedom of speech, press, and religion, are guaranteed by our Bill of Rights, thus setting a steady foundation for an enduring nation. We can see that the law is a vital force in *guaranteeing freedom.* (But freedom can be confusing: Are you free to smoke wherever you wish, or do I have a right to smoke-free air?)

Justice

Broadly, we count on the law to *achieve and preserve justice.* The pursuit of justice often relies on honorable, efficient government. The World Justice Project's 2010 "Rule of Law Index" ranks governmental quality by such measures as access to justice, clear and stable laws, open government, and limited corruption. Among the 35 countries studied, Sweden and The Netherlands ranked particularly well. In most categories, the United States ranked near the bottom of the 11 high-income nations studied.[1] Perhaps the study is correct in the sense that America still has abundant room for improvement. Nonetheless, Americans can properly be proud of a long struggle to build a more just society for all. Efforts, for example, to curb discrimination, guarantee due process, reduce violence, protect those in need, maintain order and security, build fair, efficient regulatory systems and respect the rights of all are central practices in an extraordinarily complex and rapidly evolving American culture. As you read this chapter, ask yourself repeatedly, "Does this rule (this procedure, this case) contribute to the search for justice?" In the end, all legal studies must involve the search for justice. [For a daily update of legal news, see **http://www.law.com**]

> All legal studies must involve the search for justice.

Question

In 2010, a New York City lower court judge ruled that a four-year-old girl can be sued for negligence. According to *The New York Times,* the young girl was riding her bicycle with training wheels on a Manhattan sidewalk. She joined in a race against a five-year-old boy during which the children struck an 87-year-old woman who suffered a hip injury requiring surgery. The woman died three months later of unrelated causes. Both children were under the supervision of their mothers.

The girl's attorney argued that she was too young to be responsible for negligent actions and that she was not engaging in an adult activity at the time of the injury. The judge cited cases dating back to 1928 in concluding that the girl could be sued. The judge noted that children under the age of four are conclusively presumed to be incapable of negligence, but he was unwilling to extend that presumption to the girl who was three months shy of her fifth birthday. (The other child and his mother did not seek dismissal of the negligence action against them.)

As a matter of justice, do you think a four-year-old child should be the subject of a negligence action? Explain. See Alan Feuer, "4-Year-Old Can Be Sued, Judge Rules in Bike Case," *The New York Times,* October 28, 2010 [**http://www.nytimes.com/**].

Too Many Rules in Britain?

All societies struggle to find the proper balance between personal freedom and legal intervention. Great Britain created its antisocial behavior orders (ASBOs) in 1998 to discourage "loutish," conduct involving minor offenses. The government's Antisocial Behavior Action Plan is designed to address everyday headaches from "nuisance neighbors" to begging to graffiti. The orders have been used to ban thousands of people, some as young as 10, from associating with certain people or engaging in activities as varied as shouting, swearing, spray-painting, playing loud music, and walking down certain streets. Breaching an order is a crime, potentially punishable by time in prison. The ASBOs have also reached unusual situations including a woman whose noisy sex disturbed her neighbors, a 60-year-old man who was banned from dressing as a schoolgirl, and a militant atheist who was banned from taking religiously offensive material (e.g., images of religious figures in sexual poses) in a public place. One official summed up the frustration that led to the ASBOs:

> We are not talking about high jinks from a few mischievous youngsters—we are talking about yobs whose persistent criminal activity, intimidation and plain disregard for others are making our city centres a no-go area.

In 2010 after a change in government, British Home Secretary Theresa May said that it was time to review the system: "We need to make anti-social behavior what it once was—abnormal and something to stand up to . . . rather than frequent and tolerated." The opposition Labor Party, however, said that the ASBOs had made a "huge contribution" to curbing crime.

Question

Do we need more rules, perhaps something like ASBOs, to regulate obnoxious, annoying behavior in America? Explain.

Sources: Jill Lawless, Associated Press, "Britain Tries to Rein in Louts with Bans on Misbehavior," *The Des Moines Register,* September 1, 2004, p. 5A; Philip Johnston, "Blair's Asbo Is Failing to Tame a Hard Core of Offenders," *The Daily Telegraph (London),* December 7, 2006, p. 12 (News); and "Time to 'Move Beyond' Asbos, Says Home Secretary May," BBC News, July 28, 2010 [**http://www.bbc.co.uk/news/**].

Primary Sources of Law

United States law is a vast and constantly growing, mutating body of rules and reason. That law is derived from four primary sources: constitutions, statutes, regulations, and cases (called the *common law* or judge-made law).

Constitutions

These are the supreme expressions of law at both the federal and state levels of government. All other law is subordinate to federal constitutional law. Among other things, constitutions prescribe the general structure of governments and provide protection for individual rights. Chapters 5 and 8 give extensive attention to the U.S. Constitution and the Bill of Rights.

Statutes

These are laws that are adopted by legislative bodies, particularly congress and the state legislatures. City councils enact statutes that usually are called *ordinances*. Legislators and the statutes they enact shape the policy direction of American law. Of course, legislators are not free of constraints. Federal legislation cannot conflict with the U.S. Constitution, and state legislation cannot violate either federal law or the constitutions of that state and the nation.

Regulations

Administrative agencies include such bodies as the Federal Trade Commission and the Securities and Exchange Commission at the federal level, and a Public Service Commission (to regulate utilities) and a Human Rights Commission (to address discrimination problems) at the state level. These agencies have the specialized expertise to carry out much of the day-to-day business of government. Among other duties, they produce and oversee regulations that add the details needed to implement the broader mandates provided by federal and state statutes. (For more detail, see Chapter 8.)

Common Law (Also Called Case Law or Judge-Made Law)

Our case law has its roots in the early English king's courts, where rules of law gradually developed out of a series of individual dispute resolutions. That body of law, the common law, was imported to America where it is has grown and evolved as the courts address the constantly changing legal requirements of our complex society.

The development of English common law and American judicial decisions into a just, ordered package is attributable in large measure to reliance on the doctrine of *stare decisis* (let the decision stand). That is, judges endeavor to follow the precedents established by previous decisions. Following precedent, however, is not mandatory. As societal beliefs change, so does the law. For example, a U.S. Supreme Court decision approving racially separate but equal education was eventually overruled by a Supreme Court decision mandating integrated schools. Nonetheless, the principle of stare decisis is generally adhered to because of its beneficial effect. It offers the wisdom of the past and enhances efficiency by eliminating the need for resolving every case as though it were the first of its kind. Stare decisis affords stability and predictability to the law.

The Case Law: Locating and Analyzing

To prepare for the *Nichols* case, which follows, a bit of practical guidance should be useful. The study of law is founded largely on the analysis of judicial opinions. Except for the federal level and a few states, trial court decisions are filed locally for public inspection rather than being published. Appellate (appeals court) opinions, on the other hand, are generally published in volumes called *reports*. State court opinions are found in the reports of that state, and in a regional reporter series published by West Publishing Company that divides the United States into units, such as South Eastern (S.E.) and Pacific (P.).

Within the appropriate reporter, the cases are cited by case name, volume, reporter name, and page number. For example, *Nichols v. Niesen,* 746 N.W.2d 220 (Wisc. S. Ct. 2008) means that the opinion will be found in volume 746 of the North Western Reporter, 2nd series, at page 220 and that the decision was reached in 2008 by the Wisconsin Supreme Court. Federal court decisions are found in several reporters, including the *Federal Reporter* and the *United States Supreme Court Reports.* In practice, of course, those cases can most readily be found via a standard search engine or in online databases such as LexisNexis and Westlaw. [For broad databases of law topics, see **http://www. findlaw.com,http://www.yahoo.com/government/law or www.justia.com**]

Briefing the Case

Most students find the preparation of *case briefs* (outlines or digests) to be helpful in mastering the law. A brief should evolve into the form that best suits the individual student's needs. The following approach should be a useful starting point:

1. Parties   Identify the plaintiff and the defendant at the trial level. At the appeals level, identify the appellant (the party bringing the appeal; Nichols, in this instance) and the appellee (the other party on appeal; Niesen, in this instance).

2. Facts   Summarize only those facts critical to the outcome of the case.

3. Procedure   How did the case reach this court? Who won in the lower court(s)?

4. Issue   Note the central question or questions on which the case turns.

5. Holding   How did the court resolve the issue(s)? Who won?

6. Reasoning   Explain the logic that supported the court's decision.

LEGAL BRIEFCASE

Nichols v. Niesen
746 N.W.2d 220 (Wisc. S. Ct. 2008)

Justice N. Patrick Crooks

The court of appeals allowed the claim of Shannon, Lee, Brooke, and Brittney Nichols (the Nichols) to proceed against the Niesens for common-law negligence. The Nichols claimed that the Niesens were social hosts, who did not provide any alcoholic beverages to underage guests, but allegedly were aware that minors were on their property consuming alcoholic beverages. After leaving the Niesens' premises, one of these guests allegedly caused injuries while driving intoxicated. The circuit court had granted the Niesens' . . . motion to dismiss the Nichols' complaint, after concluding that the complaint failed to state a claim in common-law negligence. The primary issue upon review is whether a claim for common-law negli-

gence should be permitted against social hosts under these circumstances.

I

On June 5, 2004, the Nichols were in a motor vehicle on County Trunk Highway J in Columbia County, Wisconsin, when that vehicle was struck by another motor vehicle, driven by Beth Carr (Carr), which had crossed the highway's center line. The Nichols alleged that the accident was caused by Carr's "failure to properly manage and control the vehicle she was operating, due in part to the voluntary ingestion by her of intoxicating beverages." As a result of the accident, Shannon Nichols "suffered very severe personal injuries," and Brittney, Brooke, and Lee Nichols "suffered injuries requiring medical care and treatment."

On the night of June 4, 2004, and into the early morning of June 5, 2004, the Nichols alleged that "a large gathering of underage high school students" congregated and consumed alcohol at the premises controlled by the Niesens.... [T]he Nichols alleged that "the Niesens were aware that the minors on their property were consuming alcohol." The Nichols did not allege that the Niesens knew, in advance, that the students would be consuming alcohol. The Nichols contended that the Niesens "had a duty to supervise and monitor the activities on their property" and that they were negligent because they failed to do so.

The Nichols contended that the consumption of alcohol by Carr was a substantial factor in causing the accident. Defendant Michael Shumate (Shumate), "or one or more adult residents of his household[,]" not the Niesens, was alleged to have provided the alcohol that was consumed by Carr on the Niesens' property. There was no allegation that Shumate was at the Niesens' property.

II (OMITTED-ED.)

III

On review, the Nichols claim that the Niesens' conduct was negligent, and that it was reasonably foreseeable that someone drinking on the Niesens' property would cause an accident....

[T]he Niesens argue that knowledge of someone drinking on one's premises does not create a foreseeable risk of harm to others, and that public policy issues preclude liability in cases such as this one. The Niesens argue that the court of appeals created a new basis of liability for social hosts in Wisconsin. They argue that social hosts have never been held liable in Wisconsin solely because they were aware that an underage person had been consuming alcohol. To allow the court of appeals' decision to stand would mean that liability would apply to any social hosts who knew of underage drinking, regardless of where the alcohol was possessed or consumed, which would lead to liability with no sensible stopping point. The Niesens argue that they had limited involvement with the party outside of their alleged knowledge of underage drinking at the party, and, as a result, they should not be held liable. To hold social hosts liable in such circumstances would place an unreasonable burden on social hosts. The Niesens argue that a reasonable person would not foresee that knowledge of some unidentified underage person drinking would create an unreasonable risk to others. Rather, a reasonable person would conclude that any such risk was created by the provider of the alcohol and the underage drinker. The Niesens contend that, because they played no role in procuring or furnishing the alcohol, a negligence analysis should not be applied to their actions in this matter. Finally, the Niesens argue that the legislature, not the judiciary, is the branch of Wisconsin's government that should impose any new liability on social hosts who do not provide alcoholic beverages to underage guests.

Whether the Nichols' complaint states a claim for common-law negligence depends on whether they sufficiently pled facts, which if proven true, would establish all four required elements of an actionable negligence claim. First, the plaintiff must establish "'the existence of a duty of care on the part of the defendant....'" Second, the plaintiff must establish that the defendant breached that duty of care. Third, the plaintiff must establish "'a causal connection between the defendant's breach of the duty of care and the plaintiffs injury....'" Fourth, the plaintiff must establish that he or she suffered an actual loss or damage that resulted from the breach.

* * * * *

The court of appeals framed the issue for the first element of the test for common-law negligence as "whether the Niesens owed a duty to refrain from knowingly permitting minors to consume alcohol on their property, thus enabling them, including Carr, to drive away from their property while intoxicated." As a result, the court held that the first factor had been met because "it was reasonably foreseeable that permitting underage high school students to illegally drink alcohol on the Niesens' property would result in harm to some person or something," and because the Nichols had adequately "alleged the Niesens had a duty to refrain from knowingly permitting underage high school students from engaging in illegal alcohol consumption on their property."

[T]he court of appeals also determined that the Nichols had appropriately alleged the second factor of an actionable common-law negligence claim, which is that the Niesens had breached a duty of care that they owed to the Nichols. The court stated, "Because the Nichols' complaint alleges the Niesens knowingly permitted and failed to supervise underage alcohol consumption on their property, it alleges 'a breach of their duty to exercise ordinary care.'" ...

The court also held that the Nichols had established the third factor of a common-law negligence claim by showing "'a causal connection between the defendant's breach of the duty of care and the plaintiff's injury....'" That court stated, "The Nichols have sufficiently alleged that the Niesens' permitting underage alcohol consumption on their property was a substantial factor in causing the automobile accident that resulted in their injuries."

The court of appeals further held that the Nichols had appropriately alleged the fourth factor of a common-law negligence claim, that they had suffered an actual loss or damage that resulted from the Niesens' breach....

For purposes of our public policy analysis, we will assume, without deciding, that the court of appeals was correct in holding that the Nichols had stated a common-law negligence claim. [E]ven if a plaintiff adequately establishes all four elements of a common-law negligence claim, Wisconsin courts have "reserved the right to deny the existence of a negligence claim based on public policy reasons. . . ." As a result, "even if all the elements for a claim of negligence are proved, or liability for negligent conduct is assumed by the court, the court nonetheless may preclude liability based on public policy factors." This is so because '"negligence and liability are distinct concepts.'"

In turning to our analysis of the public policy factors that bear on the Nichols' common-law negligence claim against the Niesens, it is instructive to note what is not alleged by the Nichols. The Nichols do not allege that the Niesens provided alcohol to Carr, that the Niesens were aware that Carr (specifically) was consuming alcoholic beverages, that the Niesens knew or should have known that Carr was intoxicated, or that the Niesens knew or should have known that Carr was not able to drive her motor vehicle safely at the time of the accident We note that there also is no allegation by the Nichols that the Niesens aided, agreed to assist, or attempted to aid Carr or any other person in the procurement or consumption of alcohol on premises under their control. There also are no allegations that the Niesens knew in advance that any underage individuals would be drinking.

* * * * *

If one or more of the public policy "factors so dictates, the court may refuse to impose liability in a case."

The first public policy factor upon which recovery against a negligent tortfeasor may be denied is when "the injury is too remote from the negligence. . . ."

The second public policy factor upon which recovery against a negligent tortfeasor may be denied is when "the injury is too wholly out of proportion to the tortfeasor's culpability. . . ."

The third public policy factor upon which recovery against a negligent tortfeasor may be denied is when "in retrospect it appears too highly extraordinary that the negligence should have brought about the harm. . . ."

The fourth public policy factor upon which recovery against a negligent tortfeasor may be denied is when "allowing recovery would place too unreasonable a burden upon the tortfeasor. . . ."

The fifth public policy factor upon which recovery against a negligent tortfeasor may be denied is when "allowing recovery would be too likely to open the way to fraudulent claims. . . ."

The sixth, and here perhaps the most significant, public policy factor upon which recovery against a negligent tortfeasor may be denied is when "allowing recovery would have no sensible or just stopping point. . . ."

* * * * *

Here, the Niesens and their insurer argue that there would be no sensible or just stopping point if the court of appeals' decision stands. They claim that the decision of the court of appeals would put tort law on the path of strict liability for anyone who owns property in Wisconsin, and who knows even scant details of an underage person consuming alcohol on the property under his or her control. They argue that the next step, beyond such a proposed expansion in common-law negligence liability, may be to include in the framework of liability not just social hosts but anyone who knows that an underage person was drinking on property that is not even under their control, or to include anyone, not just property owners, who knows that any underage individual has had too much to drink.

We note that there is no allegation by the Nichols here that the Niesens knew Carr was intoxicated, impaired, or unable to safely drive a vehicle. The Niesens argue that they could not have foreseen that people coming onto their property, who already had broken the law before they arrived, would break the law again after leaving. The Niesens could not reasonably have foreseen that an underage guest who they were not specifically aware was intoxicated, and who arrived at the premises under their control with alcohol purchased elsewhere, would cause foreseeable harm to others.

We agree with the Niesens . . . that allowing recovery here would have no sensible or just stopping point.

* * * * *

If the Nichols' claim were allowed to proceed, the expansion of liability might also include liability for parents who allegedly should have known that drinking would occur on their property while they were absent, based on the proclivities of teenagers in a given area to consume alcohol. Imposing such liability would be only a short step away from imposing strict liability upon property owners for any underage drinking that occurs on property under their control. As Judge David G. Deininger stated in his dissent in the court of appeals, "if liability is permitted to extend to parents and property owners who fail to 'supervise and monitor the activities on their property,'" as the Nichols contend of the Niesens, "then parents or other owners of property occupied by sixteen- to twenty-year-olds" would "be well-advised to never leave home, or if they must, to ensure that all underage persons go elsewhere as well. . . ." As a result, even assuming that the Nichols had pled a viable claim for common-law negligence against the Niesens using the four-factor test, we are satisfied that the Nichols' claim should be barred on public policy considerations, since allowing recovery here would have no sensible or just stopping point.

* * * * *

Liability has never been applied to conduct like that of the Niesens, and liability has required active, direct and affirmative acts, such as the provision of alcohol. Neither the legislature nor this court has expanded liability to social hosts who have not provided alcohol to minors. The legislature is the appropriate governmental branch to expand liability if it desires to do so. As a result for the reasons stated herein, we reverse the court of appeals, and hold that such an expansion of liability should come from the legislature, if it is to occur at all.

* * * * *

Questions

1. Explain the Nichols' legal claim.
2. *a.* Who won this case and why?
   b. Do you agree with the Court's decision and its reasoning? Explain.
3. Moos consumed alcohol at a party hosted by the Graffs and Hausmons. Allegedly, Moos left the party in an intoxicated condition and was involved in an accident that resulted in an injury to another driver, Beard.
   a. Are the social hosts, the Graffs and Hausmons, liable (along with Moos) for Beard's injuries? Explain.
   b. Should they be liable? Explain. See *Graff, Graff, Hausmon and Hausmon v. Beard and Beard,* 858 S.W.2d 918 (Texas S. Ct. 1993).

4. Nichols, age 26, and Dobler, a minor, were guests at Maldonado's party. Dobler was served alcohol and, while intoxicated, repeatedly hit Nichols with a hammer. Nichols sued Maldanado for negligence in serving alcohol to a minor. The jury found for Nichols. Maldanado appealed. How would you rule on that appeal? Explain. See *Nichols v. Dobler,* 655 N.W.2d 787 (Mich. Ct. App. 2002).

5. Richard Paul Dube suffered serious injuries when the vehicle he was driving was struck head-on by a vehicle being driven in the wrong direction on a Massachusetts highway by Ravindra Bhoge. Bhoge had earlier in the evening consumed a number of drinks with three friends at a bar. Bhoge and his friends met regularly on Fridays after work to drink at local bars. Each person took turns paying the bill, or on some occasions, payment would be equally divided. On the night of the accident Bhoge drank enough that the trial judge inferred that Bhoge's intoxication would have been apparent. Bhoge's three friends said they saw nothing to indicate that Bhoge was impaired, although Bhoge had left his coat behind in the bar on a particularly cold evening, and he was outside the bar for 45 minutes prior to his departure. Bhoge indicated to his friends that he was "okay" as they all prepared to leave in their vehicles. Dube sued Bhoge's three friends claiming they were social hosts and were negligent in permitting Bhoge to continue drinking. How would you rule on Dube's claim? Explain. See *Dube v. Lanphear & Others,* 868 N.E.2d 619 (2007). [For the National Center for State Courts, see **http://www.ncsconline.org/**]

Classifications of Law

We can divide the law into some categories that will help us better understand the many legal domains and processes.

Substantive and Procedural Law

Substantive laws create, define, and regulate legal rights and obligations. Thus, for example, the federal Civil Rights Act of 1964 forbids discrimination in employment and other matters (see Chapter 13).

Procedural law embraces the systems and methods available to enforce the rights specified in the substantive law. So procedural law includes the judicial system and the rules by which it operates. Questions of where to hear a case, what evidence to admit, and which decisions can be appealed fall within the procedural domain. [For a "collaboratively built, freely available legal dictionary and encyclopedia," see **http://topics.law.cornell.edu/wex**]

Law and Equity

Following the Norman conquest of England in 1066, a system of king's courts was established in which the king's representatives settled disputes. Those representatives were empowered to provide remedies of land, money, or personal property. The king's courts became known as *courts of law,* and the remedies were labeled *remedies of law.* Some litigants, however, sought compensation other than the three provided. They took their pleas to the king.

Typically the chancellor, an aide to the king, would hear these petitions and, guided by the standard of fairness, could grant a remedy (such as an injunction or specific performance—see the glossary of legal terms in the back of the book) specifically appropriate to the case. The chancellors' decisions accumulated over time such that a new body of remedies—and with it a new court system, known as *courts of equity*—evolved. Both court systems were adopted in the United States following the American Revolution, but today actions at law and equity are typically heard in the same court.

Public Law and Private Law

Public law deals with the relationship between government and the citizens. Constitutional, criminal, and administrative law (relating to such bodies as the Federal Trade Commission) fall in the public law category. *Private law* regulates the legal relationship among individuals. Contracts, agency, and commercial paper are traditional business law topics in the private category.

Civil Law and Criminal Law

The legislature or other lawmaking body normally specifies that new legislation is either *civil* or *criminal* or both. Broadly, all legislation not specifically labeled criminal law falls in the civil law category. *Civil law* addresses the legal rights and duties arising among individuals, organizations such as corporations, and governments. Thus, for example, a person might sue a company raising a civil law claim of breach of contract. *Criminal law,* on the other hand, involves wrongs against the general welfare as formulated in specific criminal statutes. Murder and theft are, of course, criminal wrongs because society has forbidden those acts in specific legislative enactments. (For a brief discussion of business and white-collar crime and the federal sentencing guidelines, see Chapter 2.)

Crimes   Crimes are of three kinds. In general, *felonies* are more serious crimes, such as murder, rape, and robbery. They are typically punishable by death or by imprisonment in a federal or state penitentiary for more than one year. In general, *misdemeanors* are less serious crimes, such as petty theft, disorderly conduct, and traffic offenses. They are typically punishable by fine or by imprisonment for no more than one year. *Treason* is the special situation in which one levies war against the United States or gives aid and comfort to its enemies.

Elements of a Crime   In a broad sense, crimes consist of two elements: (1) a wrongful act or omission (*actus reus*) and (2) evil intent (*mens rea*). Thus, an individual who pockets a pen and leaves the store without paying for it may be charged with petty theft. The accused may defend, however, by arguing that he or she merely absentmindedly and unintentionally slipped the pen in a pocket after picking it off the shelf to consider its merits. Intent is a state of mind, so the jury or judge must reach a determination from the objective facts as to what the accused's state of mind must have been.

Criminal Procedure In general, criminal procedure following an arrest, and an initial appearance before a magistrate, (and in some cases a preliminary hearing) is structured as follows: For misdemeanor cases, prosecutors typically file what is called an *information,* a formal expression of the charges. The information may be reviewed by a magistrate before issuance. For felony cases, the process begins with the prosecuting officials either filing an information or seeking an *indictment* by bringing their charges before a grand jury of citizens to determine whether the charges have sufficient merit to justify a trial.

After an indictment or information, the individual is brought before the court for *arraignment,* where the charges are read and a plea is entered. If the individual pleads not guilty, he or she will go to trial, where guilt must be established *beyond a reasonable doubt.* In a criminal trial, the burden of proof is on the state. The defendant is, of course, presumed innocent and is entitled to a jury trial, but she or he may choose to have the case decided by the judge alone. If found guilty, the defendant can, among other possibilities, seek a new trial or appeal errors in the prosecution. If found innocent, the defendant may, if necessary, invoke the doctrine of *double jeopardy* under which a person cannot be prosecuted twice in the same tribunal for the same criminal offense. [For an extensive criminal justice database, see **http://www.ncjrs.gov/**]

Miranda **Warnings**

The 1966 *Miranda v. Arizona* U.S. Supreme Court decision provided that a suspect in police custody must be told:

> You have the right to remain silent. Anything you say can and will be used against you in a court of law. You have the right to an attorney. If you cannot afford an attorney, one will be appointed for you.

If warnings are not properly provided, any statements made by the suspect and any evidence derived from those statements cannot subsequently be used in court. The warnings are highly controversial, and the current Supreme Court appears to be inclined to relax the *Miranda* requirements.

Michigan police informed a suspect, Van Thompkins, of his Fifth Amendment rights against self-incrimination including the right to remain silent. Thompkins said he understood, but he did not say he wanted the questioning to stop or that he wanted a lawyer. Rather, he sat through two hours and 45 minutes of questioning without speaking until an officer asked: "Do you pray to God to forgive you for shooting that boy down?" Thompkins said, "Yes." He did not speak further, and he did not sign a confession. He was later convicted of murder, that verdict being based largely on his one-word reply. The U.S. 6th Circuit Court of Appeals overturned the conviction, ruling that the use of the incriminating answer violated Thompkins's Fifth Amendment rights, as defined and required by *Miranda.*

The case, *Berghuis v. Thompkins,* then reached the U.S. Supreme Court in 2010 where the Court chipped away at the *Miranda* requirements in a 5–4 reversal of the

Court of Appeals ruling. The Court said, "A suspect who has received and understood the *Miranda* warnings and has not invoked his *Miranda* rights waives the right to remain silent by making an uncoerced statement to the police." The Court's decision requires a criminal suspect to explicitly and unambiguously tell the police he or she wants to remain silent. Merely remaining silent had previously been treated as an invocation of the right to remain silent, but the Court's *Thompkins* ruling changed that practice and, in the view of critics, ill advisedly diminished rights previously guaranteed to defendants.

The Supreme Court further relaxed the Miranda requirements in two other 2010 decisions (*Florida v. Powell* and *Maryland v. Shatzer*), but in 2011, the Court strengthened *Miranda* protection for young people when it ruled that the police must consider the age of a suspect in deciding whether *Miranda* warnings must be issued. In *J.D.B. v. North Carolina,* a 13-year-old Chapel Hill, North Carolina student confessed to a pair of home break-ins during a half hour of questioning by police officers and school administrators in a middle school conference room. The warnings were not issued and J.D.B. was not permitted to call his grandmother, who was his guardian. The state, however, claimed J.D.B. was not in custody and therefore the warnings were not required. In general, a suspect is considered not to have been in custody if a "reasonable person" under the circumstances would have felt free to leave. The North Carolina courts ruled that J.D.B. was not in custody, but the U.S. Supreme Court held that the police must consider the suspect's age when deciding if custody has been achieved such that the warnings are required. The case was returned to North Carolina to determine whether J.D.B., given his age, was in custody during the questioning.

Questions

1. Do you think Thompkins's response, "Yes." to the police inquiry should have been admissible in court against him? Explain.

2. In general, do you think the *Miranda* warnings offer too much protection for criminal suspects? Explain.

Sources: Berghuis v. Thompkins, 130 S. Ct. 2250 (2010), *Florida v. Powell,* 130 S. Ct. 1195 (2010), *J.D.B. v. North Carolina,* 2011U.S. LEXIS 4557, *Maryland v. Shatzer,* 130 S. Ct. 1213 (2010), *Miranda v. Arizona,* 86 S. Ct. 1602 (1966); Jesse J. Holland, "Miranda Warning Rights Trimmed Bit by Bit by High Court," *Christian Science Monitor,* August 2, 2010 [**http://www.csmonitor.com/**]; and David Savage, "Supreme Court Backs Off Strict Enforcement of Miranda Rights," *latimes.com* [**latimes.com/news/la-na-court-miranda-20100602,0,2431552.story**].

PRACTICING ETHICS   When Sex Becomes Rape

On December 13, 2003, J. L., an 18-year-old female attending community college in Maryland, drove Maouloud Baby, then 16, and his friend, Michael Wilson, 15, to a residential area. Wilson allegedly had sex with J.L. while Baby waited outside of the car. According to court records, Baby then said it was his turn and asked J.L.: "Are you going to let me hit that?" He also said, "I don't want to rape you." J.L. testified in court that she agreed to sex "as long as he stops when I tell him to." When asked if she felt she had a choice about agreeing to sex, J.L. testified: "Not really. I don't know. Something just clicked off and I just did whatever they said." According to J.L.'s testimony, Baby commenced intercourse, but J.L. told him to stop because he was hurting her. Baby, however, continued the sexual intercourse for "five or so" seconds, according to J.L. Baby testified that he believed J.L. had given him permission to have sex with her, and he said that he stopped when she wanted him to do so. After Baby withdrew from J.L., the trio drove to a local McDonald's where J.L. gave her phone number to Baby, at his request, and where Wilson hugged her. J.L. then went shopping for a time and thereafter went to a friend's house where she explained what happened to her friend's mother, who then called the police.[2] Prosecutors attributed J.L.'s delayed disclosure to rape trauma.

Wilson pleaded guilty to second-degree rape and was sentenced to 18 months in prison. Baby was convicted of first-degree rape, among other offenses. He was sentenced to 15 years imprisonment, with all but five years suspended, and five years probation upon his release. Baby appealed, and the conviction was reversed, but upon further appeal, Maryland's highest court ruled that a woman has a right to revoke consent during intercourse, and a man who fails to comply with that altered decision can be charged with rape.[3] Eight state courts have now concluded that consent can be withdrawn after intercourse has commenced, and Illinois passed a statute to that effect. North Carolina law explicitly provides that rape cannot occur once permission is given.

Questions

1. The law aside, was J.L. morally wronged by Baby? Explain.

2. In your view, does rape occur if permission is withdrawn and sexual intercourse continues? Explain.

3. Was Baby morally wronged by J.L.'s rape charge? Explain.

Questions—Part One

1. Jonathan Rauch argued that America is making a mistake in allowing what he calls Hidden Law to be replaced by what he calls Bureaucratic Legalism. Hidden Law refers to unwritten social codes, whereas Bureaucratic Legalism refers to state-provided due process for every problem. Thus, universities formerly expected insults and epithets among students to be resolved via informal modes such as apologies, while today many universities have written codes forbidding offensive or discriminatory verbal conduct. Similarly, four kindergarten students in New Jersey were suspended from school for three days because they were observed "shooting" each other with their fingers serving as guns.

   a. Should we leave campus insults and school-yard finger "shootings" to the Hidden Law? Explain.

   b. Can you think of other examples where we have gradually replaced Hidden Law with Bureaucratic Legalism?

   c. Rauch argued that the breakdown of one Hidden Law, the rule that a man must marry a woman whom he has impregnated, may be "the most far-reaching social change of our era." Do you agree? Explain. See George Will, "Penalizing These Kids Is Zero Tolerance at a Ridiculous Extreme," *The Des Moines Register*, December 27, 2000, p. 11A.

2. A number of nations, including The Netherlands and Germany, have "legalized" and regulated prostitution for safety.

   a. Should the United States do the same? For a discussion of this issue, see Emily Bazelon, "Why Is Prostitution Illegal?" *Slate*, March 10, 2008 [**http://www.slate.com/id/2186243/**].

  b. Should we remove criminal penalties from all of the so-called victimless crimes including vagrancy, pornography, and gambling? Should we regulate those practices in any way? Explain.

3. In 2010, *The Wall Street Journal* reported that Pennsylvania had become the 21st state to consider legislation prohibiting the practice of "sexting" (cell phone transmission of nude photos of themselves and other risqué material) by minors.[4]

  a. What objections would you raise to a criminal law forbidding sexting by minors?

  b. Is this an area where the government should simply refrain from intervention? Explain.

4. A Rhode Island man pleaded guilty to child molestation. As an alternative to imprisonment and as a condition of his probation, the judge ordered him to purchase a newspaper ad displaying his picture, identifying himself as a sex offender, and encouraging others to seek assistance. One Florida judge has sentenced hundreds of shoplifters to carrying in public a sign that reads: "I stole from this store." Constitutional law expert Jonathan Turley says "creative sentencing" is growing, a trend he disapproves of and regards as a strategy for entertaining the public more than deterring crime.[5]

  a. What objections would a defendant's lawyer raise to these public humiliation punishments?

  b. Would you impose a "humiliation sentence" if you were the judge? Explain.

Part Two—The Judicial Process

Most disputes are settled without resort to litigation, but when agreement cannot be reached, we can turn to the courts—a highly technical and sophisticated dispute resolution mechanism.

State Court Systems

While state court systems vary substantially, a general pattern can be summarized. As shown in Figure 4.1, at the base of the court pyramid in most states is a trial court of general jurisdiction, commonly labeled a *district court* or a *superior court.* Most trials—both civil and criminal—arising out of state law are heard here, but certain classes of cases are reserved to courts of limited subject-matter jurisdiction or to various state administrative agencies (such as the state public utilities commission and the workers' compensation board). Family, small claims, juvenile, and traffic courts are examples of trial courts with limited jurisdiction. At the top of the judicial pyramid in all states is a court of appeals, ordinarily labeled the *supreme court.* A number of states also provide for an intermediate court of appeals located in the hierarchy between the trial courts and the highest appeals court.

FIGURE 4.1 **State and Federal Court Systems**

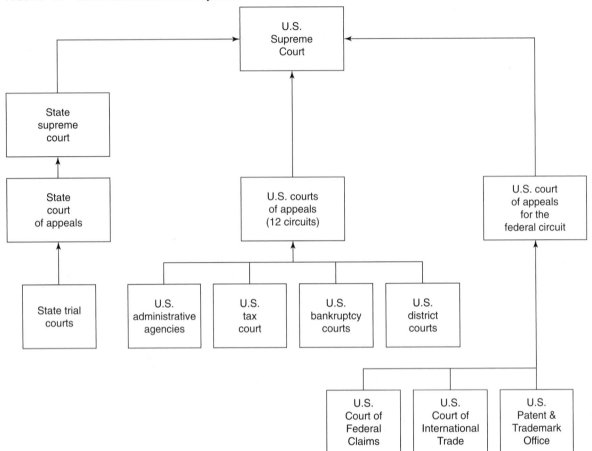

Federal Court System

District Courts

The Constitution provides for a Supreme Court and such inferior courts as Congress shall authorize. Pursuant to that authority, Congress has established at least one district court for each state and territory. The 94 district courts serve as the foundation of the federal judicial system. These are trial courts where witnesses are heard and questions of law and fact are resolved. Most federal cases begin in the district courts or in a federal administrative agency (such as the Federal Communications Commission). Congress has also provided for several courts of limited jurisdiction, including the U.S. Tax Court and the U.S. Court of International Trade.

[For access to all federal court web sites, see the Federal Judicial Center at **http://www.fjc.gov**]

Courts of Appeals

Congress has divided the United States geographically into 11 judicial circuits and the District of Columbia and has established a court of appeals for each. Those courts hear appeals from the district courts within their circuit and review decisions and enforce orders of the various federal administrative agencies. In addition, the U.S. Court of Appeals for the Federal Circuit hears, among others, all patent appeals and all appeals from the U.S. Court of Federal Claims (monetary claims against the United States).

Supreme Court

The Supreme Court consists of nine justices. Those justices (along with the federal district and appeals court judges) are appointed for life by the president and confirmed by the Senate. Almost all of the Supreme Court's work consists of reviewing lower court decisions, principally from the courts of appeal with a small number from state high courts. Virtually all parties seeking Supreme Court review must petition the Court for a *writ of certiorari,* which commands the lower court to forward the trial records to the Court.

Decisions regarding those petitions are entirely discretionary with the Court. Typically it will hear those cases that will assist in resolving conflicting courts of appeal decisions, as well as those that raise questions of special significance about the Constitution or the national welfare. Petitions to the Supreme Court have grown steadily over the years and now total approximately 8,000 cases per year. Formal, written opinions, however, are issued in only about 70 to 90 cases, a decline from, for example, 175 in 1986. Thus, in terms of numbers alone, the Court has backed away from its more activist approach of the 1960s, 1970s, and 1980s.

Critics

Questions of "judicial activism," the liberal/conservative balance on the Supreme Court, the politics of the justices, and the justices' deference to big business interests have made the Court a target for criticism. Citing scholarly studies, *The New York Times* in 2010 said the current Supreme Court under Chief Justice John Roberts is "the most conservative in decades."[6] Journalist E.J. Dionne, Jr. has written about the "Court's Defense of the Powerful:"

> The current Supreme Court is "the most conservative in decades."

> The United States Supreme Court now sees its central task as comforting the already comfortable and afflicting those already afflicted.[7]

More specifically, the current Court is accused of being particularly friendly to business interests and free market values. (Remember the *Citizens United* election law decision we discussed in Chapter 2.) After five full terms, the Roberts Court had ruled for business interests in 61 percent of the relevant decisions, as contrasted with a 42 percent average by all courts since 1953.[8] On the other hand, several decisions in late 2010 and early 2011 supported fired workers, expanded antidiscrimination law, and ruled against the Chamber of Commerce position in four of the five cases the Chamber addressed.[9]

Ideological Rulings?

We want to believe that the Supreme Court reaches its decisions in a rational, objective fashion relying on the commands of the Constitution and precedent to maintain a consistent, fair, orderly judicial system free of political influence. The facts, however, reveal a Supreme Court that is often divided along what appear to be ideological lines. During the Roberts era, decisions have frequently been reached by 5–4 margins with a clear and substantially consistent division between conservative and liberal justices. Analysis of voting patterns shows that four of the six most conservative justices of the 44 justices who have served the Court since 1938 are sitting on the Court now.[10] A recent study by the Brookings Institution provides "striking evidence of a relationship between the political party of the appointing president and judicial voting patterns."[11] Critics say that those conservative ideological inclinations have led the Roberts Court to at times abandon traditional judicial restraint and decide issues that were broader than required by the case before it.[12]

Of course, public respect for the fairness and the rationality of Supreme Court decisions could be undermined if they come to be viewed as the product of liberal or conservative political/ideological views, rather than dispassionate, lawyerly analysis. Perhaps we should be concerned that a decreasing number of high courts around the world are citing U.S. Supreme Court decisions. Declining respect for Supreme Court rulings would undermine the rule of law in America and perhaps threaten democracy itself.[13] One response to these worries is a resurgence of interest in establishing term limits for justices. A prominent current proposal, for example, would fulfill the Constitution's requirement of lifetime appointment for justices by moving justices to some kind of senior role at the Court after 18 years on the bench.[14] [For an overview of the Supreme Court, see **http://www. supremecourtus.gov/**]

Jurisdiction

A plaintiff may not simply proceed to trial at the court of his or her preference. The plaintiff must go to a court with *jurisdiction*—that is, a court with the necessary power and authority to hear the dispute. The court must have jurisdiction over both the subject matter and the persons (or, in some instances, the property) involved in the case.

Subject-Matter Jurisdiction

Subject-matter jurisdiction imposes bounds on the classes of cases a court may hear. The legislation or constitution creating the court will normally specify that court's jurisdictional authority. State courts of general jurisdiction, for example, may hear most types of cases, but a criminal court or probate court is limited in the subject matter it may hear.

The outer bounds of federal jurisdiction are specified in the Constitution, while Congress has further particularized that issue by statute. Essentially, the federal district courts may hear two types of cases: (1) those involving a federal question and (2) those involving diversity of citizenship and more than $75,000.

Federal question jurisdiction exists in any suit where the plaintiff's claim is based on the U.S. Constitution, a U.S. treaty, or a federal statute. Thus litigants can bring cases to the federal courts involving, for example, the federal antitrust statutes, federal criminal laws, constitutional issues such as freedom of the press, and federal tax questions. Federal question jurisdiction does not require an amount in controversy exceeding $75,000. Furthermore, federal and state courts have *concurrent jurisdiction* for some federal questions. Thus, some federal question cases are decided in state courts applying federal law. Federal courts can also hear cases involving state laws. Congress has accorded the federal courts exclusive jurisdiction over certain subjects, including federal criminal laws, bankruptcy, and copyrights.

Under *diversity jurisdiction,* federal district courts may hear cases involving more than $75,000 where the plaintiff(s) and the defendant(s) are citizens of different states. (Corporations are treated as citizens both of their state of incorporation and the state in which their principal place of business is located.) Diversity cases may also be heard in state courts, but plaintiffs frequently prefer to bring their actions in federal courts. The quality of the federal judiciary is generally believed to be superior to that of the states, and the federal courts are considered less likely to be influenced by local bias.

Personal Jurisdiction

Judicial authority over the person is known as *in personam jurisdiction.* In general, a state court's powers are limited to the bounds of the state. Broadly, we can say that state court jurisdiction can be established in three ways: (1) When the defendant is a resident of the state, a summons may be served at that residence. (2) When the defendant is not a resident, a summons may be personally served should he or she be physically present in the state. (3) Most states have legislated "long-arm" statutes that allow a state or federal court to secure jurisdiction against an out-of-state party where the defendant has committed a tort in the state or where the defendant is conducting business in the state. Hence, in an auto accident in Ohio involving both an Ohio resident and a Kentucky resident, the Ohio resident may sue in Ohio and use the long-arm statute to achieve service of process over the defendant living in Kentucky.

A state court may also acquire jurisdiction via an *in rem action.* In that instance the defendant may be a nonresident, but his or her property, which must be the subject of the suit, must be located within the state.

The following case involves a dispute about the commercial use of the name of celebrated actor and former California governor, Arnold Schwarzenegger.

LEGAL BRIEFCASE

Arnold Schwarzenegger v. Fred Martin Motor Company
374 F. 3d 797 (9th Cir. 2004)

Circuit Judge Fletcher

Arnold Schwarzenegger, an internationally known movie star and, currently, the governor of California, appeals the district court's dismissal of his suit against Fred Martin Motor Company ("Fred Martin"), an Ohio car dealership, for lack of personal jurisdiction. Fred Martin had run a series of five full-page color advertisements in the *Akron Beacon Journal,* a locally circulated Ohio newspaper. Each advertisement included a small photograph of Schwarzenegger, portrayed as the "Terminator," without his permission. Schwarzenegger brought suit in California, alleging that these unauthorized uses of his image infringed his right of publicity. We affirm the district court's dismissal for lack of personal jurisdiction.

I. BACKGROUND

Schwarzenegger is a resident of California. When Schwarzenegger brought this suit, he was a private citizen and movie star, best known for his roles as a muscle-bound hero of action films and distinctive Austrian accent. As explained in his complaint, Schwarzenegger was generally cast as the lead character in so-called star-driven films. One of Schwarzenegger's most popular and readily recognizable film roles is that of the title character in "The Terminator" (1984). . . .

Fred Martin is an automobile dealership incorporated under the laws of Ohio and located in Barberton, Ohio, a few miles southwest of Akron. There is no evidence in the record that Fred Martin has any operations or employees in California, has ever advertised in California, or has ever sold a car to anyone in California. Fred Martin maintains an Internet website that is available for viewing in California and, for that matter, from any Internet cafe in Istanbul, Bangkok, or anywhere else in the world.

In early 2002, Fred Martin engaged defendant Zimmerman & Partners Advertising, Inc. ("Zimmerman") to design and place a full-page color advertisement in the *Akron Beacon Journal,* a local Akron-based newspaper. The advertisement ran in the *Akron Beacon Journal* five times in April 2002. Most of the advertisement consists of small photographs and descriptions of various cars available for purchase or lease from Fred Martin. Just below a large-font promise that Fred Martin "WON'T BE BEAT," the advertisement includes a small, but clearly recognizable photograph of Schwarzenegger as the Terminator. A "bubble quotation," like those found in comic strips, is drawn next to Schwarzenegger's mouth, reading, "Arnold says: 'Terminate EARLY at Fred Martin!'" This part of the advertisement refers to a special offer from Fred Martin to customers, inviting them to close out their current leases before the expected termination date, and to buy or lease a new car from Fred Martin.

Neither Fred Martin nor Zimmerman ever sought or received Schwarzenegger's permission to use his photograph in the advertisement. Schwarzenegger states in his complaint that, had such a request been made, it would have been refused. The advertisement, as far as the record reveals, was never circulated outside of Ohio.

Schwarzenegger brought suit against Fred Martin and Zimmerman in Los Angeles County Superior Court alleging six state law causes of action arising out of the unauthorized use of his image in the advertisement. He claims that the defendants caused him financial harm in that the use of his photograph to endorse Fred Martin "diminishes his hard earned reputation as a major motion picture star, and risks the potential for overexposure of his image to the public, thereby potentially diminishing the compensation he would otherwise garner from his career as a major motion picture star." According to Schwarzenegger's complaint, his compensation as the lead actor in star-driven films was based on his ability to draw crowds to the box office, and his ability to do so depended in part on the scarcity of his image. According to his complaint, if Schwarzenegger's image were to become ubiquitous—in advertisements and on television, for example—the movie-going public would be less likely to spend their money to see his films, and his compensation would diminish accordingly. Therefore, Schwarzenegger maintains, it is vital for him to avoid "over-saturation of his image." According to his complaint, he has steadfastly refused to endorse any products in the United States, despite being offered substantial sums to do so.

Defendants removed the action to federal district court in California, and Fred Martin moved to dismiss the complaint for lack of personal jurisdiction. The district court granted Fred Martin's motion, and Schwarzenegger appealed.

II. PERSONAL JURISDICTION

For a court to exercise personal jurisdiction over a nonresident defendant, that defendant must have at least "minimum contacts" with the relevant forum such that the exercise of jurisdiction "does not offend traditional notions of fair play and substantial justice." *International Shoe Co. v. Washington,* 326 U.S. 310, 316. (1945)

A. General Jurisdiction

Schwarzenegger argues, quite implausibly, that California has general personal jurisdiction over Fred Martin. For general jurisdiction to exist over a nonresident defendant such as Fred Martin, the defendant must engage in "continuous and systematic general business contacts," *Helicopteros Nacionales de Colombia, S.A. v. Hall,* 466 U.S. 408 (1984) that "approximate physical presence" in the forum state. *Bancroft & Masters,* 223 F. 3d at 1086. This is an exacting standard, as it should be, because a finding of general jurisdiction permits a defendant to be haled into court in the forum state to answer for any of its activities anywhere in the world.

Schwarzenegger contends that Fred Martin's contacts with California are so extensive that it is subject to general jurisdiction. He points to the following contacts: Fred Martin regularly purchases Asian-made automobiles that are imported by California entities. However, in purchasing these automobiles, Fred Martin dealt directly with representatives in Illinois and New Jersey, but never dealt directly with the California-based importers. Some of Fred Martin's sales contracts with its automobile suppliers include a choice-of-law provision specifying California law. In addition, Fred Martin regularly retains the services of a California-based direct-mail marketing company; has hired a sales training company, incorporated in California, for consulting services; and maintains an Internet website accessible by anyone capable of using the Internet, including people living in California.

These contacts fall well short of the "continuous and systematic" contacts that the Supreme Court and this court have held to constitute sufficient "presence" to warrant general jurisdiction. Schwarzenegger has therefore failed to establish a prima facie case of general jurisdiction.

B. Specific Jurisdiction

Alternatively, Schwarzenegger argues that Fred Martin has sufficient "minimum contacts" with California arising from, or related to, its actions in creating and distributing the advertisement such that the forum may assert specific personal jurisdiction. We have established a three-prong test for analyzing a claim of specific personal jurisdiction:

(1) The nonresident defendant must purposefully direct his activities or consummate some transaction with the forum or resident thereof; or perform some act by which he purposefully avails himself of the privilege of conducting activities in the forum, thereby invoking the benefits and protections of its laws;

(2) the claim must be one which arises out of or relates to the defendant's forum-related activities; and

(3) the exercise of jurisdiction must comport with fair play and substantial justice, i.e., it must be reasonable.

The plaintiff bears the burden of satisfying the first two prongs of the test. If the plaintiff fails to satisfy either of these prongs, personal jurisdiction is not established in the forum state. If the plaintiff succeeds in satisfying both of the first two prongs, the burden then shifts to the defendant to "present a compelling case" that the exercise of jurisdiction would not be reasonable. For the reasons that follow, we hold that Schwarzenegger has failed to satisfy the first prong.

1. Purposeful Availment or Direction Generally

Under the first prong of our three-part specific jurisdiction test, Schwarzenegger must establish that Fred Martin either purposefully availed itself of the privilege of conducting activities in California, or purposefully directed its activities toward California.

* * * * *

A showing that a defendant purposefully availed himself of the privilege of doing business in a forum state typically consists of evidence of the defendant's actions in the forum, such as executing or performing a contract there. By taking such actions, a defendant "purposefully avails itself of the privilege of conducting activities within the forum State, thus invoking the benefits and protections of its laws." *Hanson v. Denckla,* 357 U.S. 235, 253 (1958). In return for these "benefits and protections," a defendant must—as a quid pro quo—"submit to the burdens of litigation in that forum." *Burger King,* 471 U.S. at 476.

A showing that a defendant purposefully directed his conduct toward a forum state, by contrast, usually consists of evidence of the defendant's actions outside the forum state that are directed at the forum, such as the distribution in the forum state of goods originating elsewhere.

2. Purposeful Direction

Schwarzenegger does not point to any conduct by Fred Martin in California related to the advertisement that would be readily susceptible to a purposeful availment analysis. Rather, the conduct of which Schwarzenegger complains—the unauthorized inclusion of the photograph in the advertisement and its distribution in the Akron Beacon Journal—took place in Ohio, not California. Fred Martin received no benefit, privilege, or protection from California in connection with the advertisement, and the traditional quid pro quo justification for finding purposeful availment thus does not apply. Therefore, to the extent that Fred Martin's conduct might justify the exercise of personal jurisdiction in California, that conduct must have been purposefully directed at California.

* * * * *

Here, Fred Martin's intentional act—the creation and publication of the advertisement—was expressly aimed at Ohio rather than California. The purpose of the advertisement was to entice Ohioans to buy or lease cars from Fred Martin and, in particular, to "terminate" their current car leases. The advertisement was never circulated in California, and Fred Martin had no reason to believe that any Californians would see it and pay a visit to the dealership. Fred Martin certainly had no reason to believe that a Californian had a current car lease with Fred Martin that could be "terminated" as recommended in the advertisement. It may be true that Fred Martin's intentional act eventually caused harm to Schwarzenegger in California and Fred Martin may have known that Schwarzenegger lived in California. But this does not confer jurisdiction, for Fred Martin's express aim was local. We therefore conclude that the advertisement was not expressly aimed at California.

CONCLUSION

We hold that Schwarzenegger has established neither general nor specific jurisdiction over Fred Martin in California. Schwarzenegger has not shown that Fred Martin has "continuous and systematic general business contacts," Helicopteros, 466 U.S. at 416, that "approximate physical presence" in California, Bancroft & Masters, 223 F. 3d at 1086, such that it can be sued there for any act it has committed anywhere in the world. Further, while Schwarzenegger has made out a prima facie case that Fred Martin committed intentional acts that may have caused harm to Schwarzenegger in California, he has not made out a prima facie case that Fred Martin expressly aimed its acts at California.

Affirmed.

AFTERWORD

Schwarzenegger's claim was settled out of court in 2004 when the Fred Martin Motor Company issued a written apology and agreed to pay a "substantial" sum to Arnold's All-Stars, an after-school program founded by Schwarzenegger.

Questions

1. Explain Schwarzenegger's complaint.
2. Why was Schwarzenegger unable to sue Fred Martin in California?
3. The Robinsons filed a product liability suit in an Oklahoma state court to recover for injuries sustained in an automobile accident in Oklahoma. The auto had been purchased in New York from the defendant, World-Wide Volkswagen Corp. Oklahoma's long-arm statute was used in an attempt to secure jurisdiction over the defendant. World-Wide conducted no business in Oklahoma. Nor did it solicit business there.
   a. Build an argument to support the claim of jurisdiction for the Oklahoma court.
   b. Decide. See *World-Wide Volkswagen Corp. v. Woodson,* 100 S. Ct. 559 (1980).

4. Burger King conducted a franchise, fast-food operation from its Miami, Florida, headquarters. John Rudzewicz and a partner, both residents of Michigan, secured a Burger King franchise in Michigan. Subsequently, the franchisees allegedly fell behind in payments, and after negotiations failed, Burger King ordered the franchisees to vacate the premises. They declined to do so, and continued to operate the franchise. Burger King brought suit in a federal district court in Florida. The defendant franchisees argued that the Florida court did not have personal jurisdiction over them because they were Michigan residents and because the claim did not arise in Florida. However, the district court found the defendants to be subject to the Florida long-arm statute, which extends jurisdiction to "[a]ny person, whether or not a citizen or resident of this state" who, "[b]reach[es] a contract in this state by failing to perform acts required by the contract to be performed in this state." The franchise contract provided for governance of the relationship by Florida law. Policy was set in Miami, although day-to-day supervision was managed through various district offices. The case ultimately reached the U.S. Supreme Court.
   a. What constitutional argument would you raise on behalf of the defendant franchisees?
   b. Decide. See *Burger King Corp. v. Rudzewicz,* 471 U.S. 462 (1985).

Venue

Once jurisdictional authority—that is, the power to hear the case—is established, the proper *venue* (geographic location within the court system) comes into question. Ordinarily, a case will be heard by the court geographically closest to the incident or property in question or to where the parties reside. Sometimes one of the parties may seek a *change of venue* based on considerations such as unfavorable pretrial publicity or the pursuit of a more favorable legal climate. The importance of venue is evident in a 2010 decision forcing Los Angeles-based Occidental Petroleum to defend itself in an environmental dispute in California rather than in Peru where the conflict emerged. Members of the

> The Achuar tribe, indigenous to the Amazon rain forest, brought a class action in Los Angeles.

Achuar tribe, indigenous to the Amazon rain forest, brought a class action in Los Angeles against Occidental alleging the oil company dumped millions of gallons of waste water into their rivers and contaminated their land with waste.[15] A California federal district court dismissed the Achuar claim, but the 9th Circuit U.S. Court of Appeals reversed the district court. The appeals court ruled, among other things, that Occidental had failed to demonstrate that Peru was the more convenient forum for the lawsuit.[16] The Achuar plaintiffs want the case tried in California, in part, because the Peruvian courts have a history of favoring corporate interests in conflicts with natives. At this writing, the case is expected to go forward in Los Angeles.

Standing to Sue

All who wish to bring a claim before a court will not be permitted to do so. To receive the court's attention, the litigant must demonstrate *standing to sue.* That is, the person must show that her or his interest in the outcome of the controversy is sufficiently direct and substantial as to justify the court's consideration. The litigant must show that she or he is personally suffering, or will be suffering, injury. Mere interest in the problem at hand is insufficient to grant standing to sue. We all suffer injustices. We all have complaints in life. But have we suffered an injury to a legally protected right or interest? That is the question in the *Mayer* case that arose out of "Spygate," an alleged National Football League cheating scandal.[17]

Mayer v. Bill Belichick; The New England Patriots; National Football League
605 F. 3d 223 (3d Cir. 2010); Cert. Den. 2011 U.S. LEXIS 2027

LEGAL BRIEFCASE

FACTS

In an episode popularly known as "Spygate," an employee of the New England Patriots National Football League team was caught videotaping New York Jets' sideline signals, in violation of NFL rules, during a 2007 game with the Jets. The taping was later discovered to have been part of an illicit taping program that reportedly had been ongoing since the 2000 season. The NFL penalized the Patriots and their coach, Bill Belichick.

Mayer sued on behalf of himself and a class of Jets season ticketholders claiming the improper conduct violated the contractual expectations and rights of the ticketholders who had paid to observe an honest football game played in conformance with the rules. Mayer lost at trial where the federal district court ruled that he had failed to demonstrate an actionable injury; that is, he was unable to show the court that the facts he asserted could support a right to relief under the law. Put another way, he did not have standing to sue. Mayer then appealed to the Third Circuit Federal Court of Appeals.

Circuit Judge Cowen

(I-III OMITTED-ED.)

IV

The District Court, while noting that Mayer alleged numerous theories of liability in this case, appropriately turned to the following dispositive question: namely, whether or not he stated an actionable injury (or, in other words, a legally protected right or interest) arising out of the alleged "dishonest" videotaping program undertaken by the Patriots and the NFL team's head coach.

* * * * *

Initially, we consider how tickets to sporting and other entertainment events have been treated in the past. New Jersey has generally followed a so-called "license" approach[1]. . . .

Although it did not use the specific term "license," the ticket stub provided by the Patriots nevertheless appears consistent with this traditional approach. For example, it unambiguously stated that "[t]his ticket only grants entry into the stadium and a spectator seat for the specified NFL game." The stub further made clear that the Jets and the owners of the stadium retain sole discretion to refuse admission or to eject a ticket-holder. . . . Given that Mayer was never barred or expelled from any game at Giants Stadium, much more is needed to establish a cognizable right, interest, or injury. . . .

Mayer possessed either a license or, at best, a contractual right to enter Giants Stadium and to have a seat from which to watch a professional football game. In the clear language of the ticket stub, "[t]his ticket only grants entry into the stadium and a spectator seat for the specified NFL game." Mayer actually was allowed to enter the stadium and witnessed the "specified NFL game[s]" between the Jets and Patriots. He thereby suffered no cognizable injury to a legally protected right or interest.

Accordingly, we need not, and do not decide, whether a ticket-holder possesses nothing more than a license to enter and view whatever event, if any, happens to transpire. Here, Mayer undeniably saw *football* games played by two *NFL* teams. This therefore is not a case where, for example, the game or games were cancelled, strike replacement players were used, or the professional football teams themselves did

[1]A license, for our purposes, is generally defined as "[a] permission . . . to commit some act that would otherwise be unlawful; esp., an agreement that it is lawful for the licensee to enter the licensor's land to do some act that would otherwise be illegal, such as hunting game." *Black's Law Dictionary* 1002 (9th ed. 2009).

something nonsensical or absurd, such as deciding to play basketball.

* * * * *

Furthermore, we do recognize that Mayer alleged that he was the victim, not of mere poor performance by a team or its players, but of a team's ongoing acts of dishonesty or cheating in violation of the express rules of the game. Nevertheless, there are any number of often complicated rules and standards applicable to a variety of sports, including professional football. It appears uncontested that players often commit intentional rule infractions in order to obtain an advantage over the course of the game. . . . Mayer further does not appear to contest the fact that a team is evidently permitted by the rules to engage in a wide variety of arguably "dishonest" conduct to uncover an opponent's signals. For example, a team is apparently free to take advantage of the knowledge that a newly hired player or coach takes with him after leaving his former team, and it may even have personnel on the sidelines who try to pick up the opposing team's signals with the assistance of lip-reading, binoculars, note-taking, and other devices. In addition, even Mayer acknowledged in his amended complaint that "[t]eams are allowed to have a limited number of their own videographers on the sideline during the game."

In fact, the NFL's own commissioner did ultimately take action here. He found that the Patriots and Belichick were guilty of violating the applicable NFL rules, imposed sanctions in the form of fines and the loss of draft picks, and rather harshly characterized the whole episode as a calculated attempt to avoid well-established rules designed to encourage fair play and honest competition. At least in this specific context, it is not the role of judges and juries to be second-guessing the decision taken by a professional sports league purportedly enforcing its *own* rules. . . .

This Court refuses to countenance a course of action that would only further burden already limited judicial resources and force professional sports organizations and related individuals to expend money, time, and resources to defend against such litigation. . . .

In conclusion, this Court will affirm the dismissal of Mayer's amended complaint. Again, it bears repeating that our reasoning here is limited to the unusual and even unique circumstances presented by this appeal. We do not condone the conduct on the part of the Patriots and the team's head coach, and we likewise refrain from assessing whether the NFL's sanctions (and its alleged destruction of the videotapes themselves) were otherwise appropriate. We further recognize that professional football, like other professional sports, is a multi-billion dollar business. In turn, ticket-holders and other fans may have legitimate issues with the manner in which they are treated. . . . Significantly, our ruling also does not leave Mayer and other ticket-holders without any recourse. Instead, fans could speak out against the Patriots, their coach, and the NFL itself. In fact, they could even go so far as to refuse to purchase tickets or NFL-related merchandise. However, the one thing they *cannot* do is bring a legal action in a court of law.

Affirmed.

Questions

1. *a.* Why did Mayer lose this case?
    b. Do you think he should have won?

2. According to the Court, under what circumstances might a plaintiff conceivably have an actionable claim involving a sports event gone wrong?

3. To some extent, the Court's decision was influenced by a decision to protect the judicial system from a flood of litigation. Explain what kinds of legal claims might have been filed if this Court had found that the plaintiff, Mayer, had stated an actionable injury.

Class Actions

In some instances, multiple plaintiffs may join together to represent themselves and all others who are similarly situated to file a single lawsuit alleging similar harm arising from the same, or substantially the same, wrong. The high cost of litigation, the great uncertainty of victory and the likelihood of small individual recoveries have made the class action a very useful tool for plaintiffs. Of course, the class action also enhances judicial efficiency by bringing many claims together in one case.

An important U.S. Supreme Court ruling in the *Wal-Mart Stores v. Dukes* case looks to have sharply reduced the usefulness of the class action in some–perhaps many–business disputes. A small group of current and former Walmart employees sued the company for sex discrimination on behalf of a nationwide class of 1.5 million female employees. Walmart challenged the class action certification, but the plaintiffs prevailed in the lower courts. The U.S. Supreme Court, however, ruled 9-0 in June 2011 that the case did not meet the technical requirements of federal class action procedural rules. Then in a 5-4 portion of the ruling, the Court held that the claims against Walmart did not share enough common elements to tie together the millions of employment decisions affecting women at Walmart. As a matter of company policy, discretion over pay and promotions rested with local managers at the 4,000 or so company stores thus undercutting the plantiffs' claims of a unified national policy or common standard for evaluating workers. The plaintiffs failed to identify a specific employment practice that tied all of their claims together.[18]

Current Walmart female employees and former employees can proceed with the case individually or in store-wide or perhaps regional classes, but that task will be extremely expensive, time-consuming and emotionally wrenching. The 5-4 portion of the decision may discourage other class actions in employment law cases and perhaps in other areas of law as well.

[For a *Today* show account of the *Dukes* ruling, see **http://www.msnbc.msn.com/id/43468398/ns/business-personal_finance/t/wal-mart-ruling-raises-bar-class-actions/**].

The Civil Trial Process

Civil procedure varies by jurisdiction. The following generalizations merely typify the process. (See Figure 4.2.) [For a vast "catalog" of law on the Internet, see **http://www.catalaw.com**]

Pleadings

Pleadings are the documents by which each party sets his or her initial case before the court. A civil action begins when the plaintiff files his or her first pleading, which is labeled a *complaint.* The complaint specifies (1) the parties to the suit, (2) evidence as to the court's jurisdiction in the case, (3) a statement of the facts, and (4) a prayer for relief (a remedy).

The complaint is filed with the clerk of court and a summons is issued, directing the defendant to appear in court to answer the claims alleged against him or her. A sheriff or some other official attempts to personally deliver the summons to the defendant. If personal delivery cannot be achieved, the summons may be left with a responsible party at the defendant's residence. Failing that, other modes of delivery are permissible, including a mailing. Publication of a notice in a newspaper will, in some instances, constitute good service of process. Ordinarily, a copy of the complaint accompanies the summons, so the defendant is apprised of the nature of the claim.

FIGURE 4.2 **Stages of a Lawsuit**

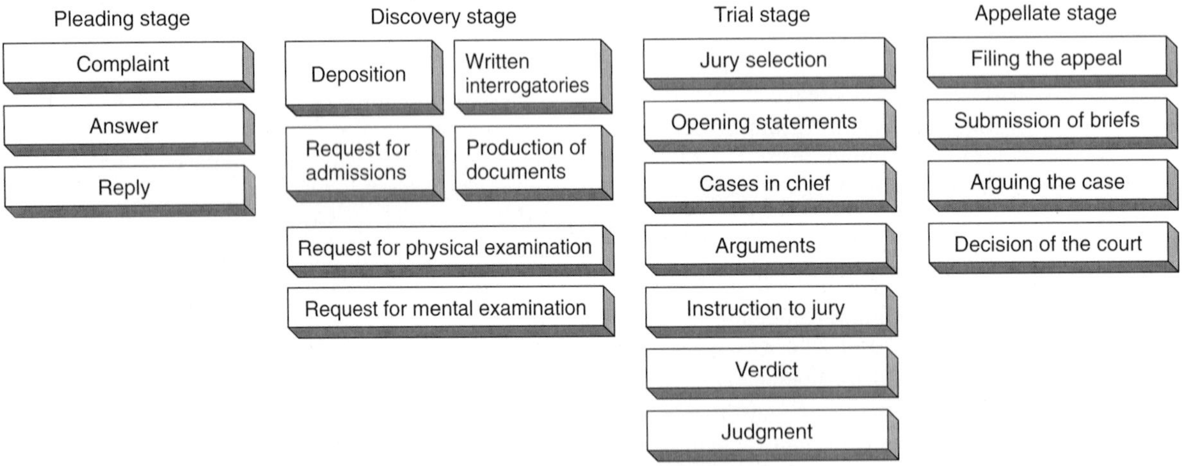

The defendant has several options. He or she may do nothing, but failure to respond may result in a *default judgment* in favor of the plaintiff. The defendant may choose to respond by filing a *demurrer* or a *motion to dismiss,* the essence of which is to argue that even if the plaintiff's recitation of the facts is accurate, a claim on which relief can be granted has not been stated.

Alternatively, the defendant may file with the court an initial pleading, called an *answer,* wherein the defendant enters a denial by setting out his or her version of the facts and law, or in which the defendant simply concedes the validity of the plaintiff's position. The answer may also contain an *affirmative defense,* such as the statute of limitations or the statute of frauds that would bar the plaintiff's claim. The defendant's answer might include a *counterclaim* or *cross-claim.* A counterclaim is the defendant's assertion of a claim of action against the plaintiff. A cross-claim is the defendant's assertion of a claim of action against a codefendant. In some states, these would be labeled *cross-complaints.* In the event of a counterclaim or the assertion of new facts in the answer, the plaintiff will respond with a *reply.* The complaint, answer, reply, and their components are the pleadings that serve to give notice, clarify the issues, and limit the dimensions of the litigation. [For a summary of "Famous Trials" in history, see **http://law2.umkc.edu/faculty/projects/ftrials/ftrials.htm**]

Motions

As necessary during and after the filing of the pleadings, either party may file motions with the court. For example, a party may move to clarify a pleading or to strike a portion deemed unnecessary. Of special importance is a *motion for a judgment on the pleadings* or a *motion for summary judgment.* In a motion for a judgment on the pleadings, either party simply asks the judge to reach a decision based on the information in the pleadings. The judge will do so only if the defendant's answer constitutes an admission of the accuracy of the plaintiff's claim, or if the plaintiff's claim clearly has no foundation in law.

In a motion for a summary judgment, the party filing the motion is claiming that no facts are in dispute. Therefore, the judge may make a ruling about the law without taking the case to trial. In a summary judgment hearing, the court can look beyond the pleadings to hear evidence from affidavits, depositions, and so on. These motions avoid the time and expense of trial.

Discovery

Discovery is the primary information-gathering stage in the pretrial process. That information clarifies the trial issues, promotes pretrial settlements, and helps prevent surprises at the trial, among other things. Discovery may consist of *depositions* (recorded, sworn testimony in preparation for trial), physical and mental examinations, answers to written questions (*interrogatories*), requests for access to documents and property to inspect them prior to trial, and *admissions* (agreement by the parties to stipulated issues of fact or law prior to trial).

The era of electronic communication and storage has added important new expectations and burdens to the discovery process by requiring that litigants exchange all relevant electronically stored information (ESI) during the discovery phase. Individuals and companies must be able to produce ESI from all sources, including e-mail, files, scanned handwritten notes, stored records, voice mail, fax data, instant messages, spreadsheets, videos, PowerPoint presentations, and so on.

Pretrial Conference

Either party may request, and many courts require, a pretrial meeting involving the attorneys, the judge, and occasionally the parties. Usually following discovery, the conference is designed to plan the course of the trial in the interests of efficiency and justice. The participants seek to define the issues and settle the dispute in advance of trial. If no settlement is reached, a trial date is set.

The Judge and Jury

The federal Constitution and most state constitutions provide for the right to a jury trial in a civil case (excepting equity actions). Some states place dollar minimums on that guarantee. At the federal level and in most states, unless one of the parties requests a jury, the judge alone will hear the case and decide all questions of law and fact. If the case is tried before a jury, that body will resolve questions of fact, but all questions of law will be resolved by the judge who will also instruct the jury as to the law governing the case.

Jurors are selected from a jury pool composed of a cross section of the community. A panel is drawn from that pool. The individuals in that panel are questioned by the judge, by the attorneys, or by all to determine if any individual is prejudiced about the case such that he or she could not reach an objective decision on the merits. The questioning process is called *voir dire.*

From an attorney's point of view, jury selection is often not so much a matter of finding jurors without bias as it is a matter of identifying those jurors who are most likely to reach a decision favorable to one's client. To that end, elaborate mechanisms and strategies have been employed—particularly in criminal trials—to identify desirable jurors. For example, sophisticated, computer-assisted surveys of the trial community have been conducted to develop objective evidence by which to identify jurors who would not admit to racial prejudice but whose "profile" suggests the likelihood of such prejudice.

After questioning, the attorneys may *challenge for cause,* arguing to the judge that the individual cannot exercise the necessary objectivity of judgment. Attorneys are also afforded a limited number of *peremptory challenges,* by which the attorney can have a potential juror dismissed without the judge's concurrence and without offering a reason. Peremptory challenges may not be used to reject jurors on the basis of race or gender.

Facebook the Jury Pool

Social media, such as Facebook, MySpace, and Twitter, can be a valuable source of information to attorneys as they try to shape the composition of juries. Information that might not be revealed in voir dire sometimes comes to light online. Jury consultant Amber Yearwood in San Francisco discovered online that a member of a jury pool was highly opinionated and often dispensed medical and sex advice, a personality not well suited to the client's cause. The prospective juror was dismissed.

Source: Ana Campoy and Ashby Jones, "Searching for Details Online, Lawyers Facebook the Jury," *The New York Times,* February 22, 2011, p. A2.

Misleading the Jury?

The case that follows examines allegations of trial misconduct by the plaintiff's attorney in an apparent effort to prejudice the jury.

Minichiello v. Supper Club
296 A.D.2d 350 (S. Ct. N.Y., App. Div., 1st Dept. 2002)

Judges Buckley, Rosenberger, Lerner, Rubin, Marlow

[P]laintiff alleges that he was verbally and physically abused by defendants because of his sexual orientation and then wrongfully discharged when he refused to voluntarily relinquish his position at the Supper Club.

The Supper Club is a dining and dancing establishment operated by defendant, Edison Associates, L.P. (hereinafter Edison), a limited partnership. Defendant Martin Theising is a partner in Edison and defendant Andre Cortez is the general manager of The Supper Club and is responsible for its day-to-day operations. Defendant Oliver Hoffman was an independent consultant to The Supper Club.

In November 1992, plaintiff was hired as The Supper Club's late night manager initially responsible for its disco and later for its cabaret until he was discharged in July 1995. Plaintiff alleges in his complaint, that during the course of his employment, he was repeatedly subjected to humiliation and to discriminatory epithets regarding his sexual orientation and that, two weeks before he was discharged, he was physically held down by Hoffman and another individual while Cortez threatened to cut off his ponytail with a pair of scissors.

After a lengthy trial, the jury found that plaintiff had been subjected to a hostile work environment and had been discharged because of his sexual orientation and that Cortez had committed assault and battery. The jury awarded $160,000 in lost wages, finding that plaintiff could not have mitigated his damages. It further awarded $8,000,000 for past pain, suffering, and emotional distress and $2,000,000 for such future damages. The jury also awarded punitive damages of $1,000,000 against The Supper Club, $54,000 against Cortez and $2,200,000 against Theising with respect to the discrimination claims.

Defendants contend that the damages awarded were so grossly excessive as to be the result of passion and prejudice born of plaintiff's counsel's misconduct and judicial error, that a mere reduction of the awards would not be an adequate remedy.

"When misconduct of counsel in interrogation or summation so violates the rights of the other party to the litigation that extraneous matters beyond the proper scope of the trial may have substantially influenced or been determinative of the outcome, such breaches of the rules will not be condoned." (*Kohlmann v. City of New York*, 8 AD2d 598, 598.) Although evidence of hostility and harassment to other minorities may be relevant to a claim of a hostile work environment based on sexual orientation, the cumulative effect of the many irrelevant and highly prejudicial comments made by plaintiff's counsel in the course of this trial only served to incite the jury's passion and sympathy and effectively prevented a fair and dispassionate consideration of the evidence. Plaintiff's counsel referred to Theising, a German national with an apparent accent, as someone who exhibited an "attitude of hatred" and made forced analogies to Nazi Germany and the Holocaust. While the issue of this case was sexual orientation discrimination, plaintiff's counsel presented to the jury inappropriate matters involving African Americans, Latinos, and Jews that went far beyond any permissible boundaries and served no other purpose than to incite the jury's passions. Similarly, plaintiff's counsel elicited testimony about an alleged physical attack by an assistant to Cortez on an employee dying of AIDS and extensive testimony from several witnesses regarding the consumption of alcoholic beverages by Cortez, Hoffman, and Theising which was highly prejudicial with little or no probative value.

We find that the aggregate effect of such comments and conduct of plaintiff's counsel, which cannot be characterized as inadvertent or harmless, inflamed the jury's passion and sympathy to such an extent as to render the resulting judgment meaningless. . . .

The trial court erred in refusing to allow defendants to introduce evidence that no other employees were treated abusively . . . and in denying defendants' requested jury charge on mitigation. Likewise, . . . the trial court made a number of demeaning comments in the presence of the jury demonstrating a marked antipathy toward defense counsel which, in light of the totality of circumstances at trial, warrant a new trial.

Were this Court not to reverse and remand for a new trial for the reasons stated above, we would have nevertheless reversed on the issue of damages. The jury's grossly excessive compensatory and punitive damages awards totaling approximately $20,000,000 have no rational basis. . . . [Reversed. Remanded to "a different justice."]

Questions

1. *a.* Why did this appeals court reverse the decision of the lower court?
   b. Why was the case remanded to "a different justice"?
2. Did this decision conclude that the plaintiff had not been a victim of sexual harassment, wrongful dismissal, or the like? Explain.
3. According to this appeals court, what errors were made by the judge at trial?

Eminem Inspires Judicial Rap

A Michigan trial judge dismissed a 2003 defamation claim by DeAngelo Bailey against rapper Eminem. Bailey claimed that Eminem falsely depicted him as a bully in a song called "Brain Damage." The song's lyrics recount a childhood attack when Bailey allegedly beat up Marshall Mathers (Eminem). Perhaps inspired by the famous rapper, the judge added a rap footnote to her 13-page opinion. A portion follows:

> Mr. Bailey complains that his rep is trash/so he's seeking compensation in the form of cash/Bailey thinks he's entitled to some monetary gain/Because Eminem used his name in vain.
>
> The lyrics are stories no one would take as fact/they're an exaggeration of a childish act. It is therefore this Court's ultimate position/that Eminem is entitled to summary disposition.

The Michigan Court of Appeals affirmed the trial court decision.

Sources: "Eminem Delivered Favorable Verdict by Rap-Lovin' Judge" [**http://www.chartattack.com/ damn/2003/10/2106.cfm**]; *Bailey v. Mathers,* No. 252123, 2005 WL 857242 (Michigan Ct. App., April 14, 2005).

The Trial

The trial begins with opening statements by the attorneys. Each is expected to outline what he or she intends to prove. The plaintiff, bearing the burden of proof, then presents evidence, which may include both testimony and physical evidence, such as documents and photos. Those are called *exhibits.*

The plaintiff's attorney secures testimony from his or her own witnesses via questioning labeled *direct examination.* After the plaintiff's attorney completes direct examination of a witness, the defense attorney may question that witness in a process labeled *cross-examination. Redirect* and *recross* may then follow. After all of the plaintiff's witnesses have been questioned, the plaintiff rests his or her case.

At this stage, the defense may make a motion for a *directed verdict,* arguing, in essence, that the plaintiff has offered insufficient evidence to justify relief, so time and expense may be saved by terminating the trial. Understandably, the judge considers the motion in the light most favorable to the plaintiff. Such motions ordinarily fail, and the trial goes forward with the defendant's presentation of evidence.

At the completion of the defendant's case, both parties may be permitted to offer *rebuttal* evidence, and either party may move for a directed verdict. Barring a directed verdict, the case goes forward, with each party making a closing argument. When the trial is by jury, the judge must instruct the jurors as to the law to be applied to the case. The attorneys often submit their views of the proper instructions. In most civil cases, a verdict for the plaintiff must be supported by a *preponderance of the evidence* (more likely than not). After deliberation, the verdict of the jury is rendered, and a judgment is entered by the court. [For a company providing a virtual jury in advance of trial, see **http://www.virtualjury.com**]

Experts

In this highly technological and scientific era, one of the biggest dilemmas facing judges and juries is the weight to give to expert testimony. Very often, in cases such as medical malpractice and product liability (see Chapter 7), the testimony of experts is decisive to the outcome; but that testimony varies wildly in its reliability and credibility. The golfing case that follows investigates the theme of experience as a qualification for expert testimony.

LEGAL BRIEFCASE

Nickles v. Schild
617 N.W.2d 659 (S. D. S. Ct. 2000)

Justice Gilbertson

Larry Nickles, the guardian of Mark Nickles, appeals the trial court's admission of expert testimony.

FACTS

On May 5, 1996, Jay Schild (Schild), Mark Nickles and Schild's younger brother drove to the Human Services Golf Course in Yankton, South Dakota, to play golf. All three boys were minors. Both Nickles and Schild had previously received golf instructions and had been taught some golfing rules.

After playing five holes, Schild and Nickles proceeded to the next tee box. Schild's younger brother was still on the fifth hole green retrieving his ball, which Nickles had knocked a short distance from the green. Schild proceeded to tee up his ball at the front center of the tee box and was preparing to hit his next drive. In the meantime, Nickles moved off the tee box approximately 10 feet and was facing the previous green watching Schild's brother. Schild, who had seen Nickles walk off the tee box, stepped back from his ball and took three practice swings. On the third practice swing, Schild hit Nickles in the head, fracturing his skull and permanently injuring his left eye.

Guardian (sic) commenced a personal injury action against Schild for damages sustained as a result of Schild's negligence and failure to exercise reasonable care in swinging his golf club. Schild denied he was negligent and claimed that Nickles was contributory (sic) negligent and assumed the risk of his injuries. During trial, Schild called Robert Boldus as an expert witness. Boldus was a former member of the Professional Golfer's (sic) Association and golf professional at Fox Run Golf Course in Yankton, South Dakota. Boldus had often given golfing lessons to junior golfers while at Fox Run.

Schild asked Boldus whether "as a golf professional," he had "formed any opinions as to what had happened in this case?" Nickles immediately requested permission to briefly interrogate Boldus for purposes of objecting to his opinion. During this interrogation, the following discussion occurred:

Q: (Nickles's attorney): Mr. Boldus, as a professional golfer, a member of PGA or based upon your experience, have you had any training in evaluating liability or standards of care required in golf liability cases?

A: (Boldus): No, I haven't.

Nickles then objected to the opinion by Boldus regarding standards of care or the ultimate issue. The trial judge overruled Nickles's objection and allowed Boldus to give his opinion:

Q: (Schild's attorney): And could you tell the jury what opinions you have come to?

A: (Boldus): In my opinion it was an accident. But one of the players moved, and when you're in your preshot routine if you move, you back away from the ball six inches to a foot or one step, and then you take your practice swings. My opinion, somehow Mark Nickles had moved in the way of the swing and got hit.

Q: (Schild's attorney): In your opinion did [Schild] violate any standards of care?

A: (Boldus): No.

The jury returned a verdict in favor of Schild. Nickles appealed, raising the following issue:

Whether the trial court abused its discretion by permitting expert testimony from Boldus.

* * * * *

DECISION

* * * * *

[A]n expert is not limited to testifying only upon those areas in which he or she has received formal training. Rather, when giving an opinion, an expert is allowed to draw upon all the knowledge, skill, or experience that he or she has accumulated.

[W]hile Boldus may not have had any formal classroom "training" in the applicable liability standards, it is clear Boldus was no novice at the game of golf. He was a former member of the PGA and a golf professional at Fox Run Golf Course in Yankton. While at Fox Run, he had often given golf lessons to junior golfers, which included golf etiquette and safety. He had even previously given golf lessons to Nickles. By any of these methods of acquiring the appropriate expertise or combination thereof, he could have qualified himself as an expert to testify as to "what happened."

It is quite clear from the testimony of Boldus and his vitae that he did have an opinion on the standards of care required in golf and the expertise to give such an opinion. The following testimony regarding the standard of care applicable to the game of golf was elicited from Boldus during direct testimony:

Q: When someone has addressed the ball and stepped back and they're doing their practice swings, what is the person's duty when they're doing those practice swings?

A: Well, basically there's nothing stated that says that you have to look around. You should be, when you begin your preshot routine, prior to taking your practice swings you should look and kind of [get] an idea where people are at so they are out of your way so you can take a swing. Once you begin your practice swings I think it's a duty of the other person to stay out of the way.

Q: So once, right before you start your preshot routine is when you have the duty to check what's going around?

A: Yes.

Q: And then as you start your preshot routine then it's the duty of those around you to become aware that that's what you're going to do, to watch?

A: Yes.

* * * * *

Boldus merely described, in his opinion, "what happened in this case" and that Schild's actions did not violate any standard of care concerning the game of golf. He did not invade the province of the jury as Nickles suggests. Boldus did not testify as to the ultimate issue of negligence. In fact, Boldus did not discuss the issue of liability at all until he was asked upon cross-examination, "but one party is liable, aren't they?" Boldus responded, "I wouldn't—yah—I don't know about liable, but somebody [is responsible for that]."

Nickles' objection as to the qualifications of Boldus goes in part to formal training concerning the issue of ultimate liability. The ultimate liability of one of the parties is not the same as standard of care. One can violate a standard of care and still not be held liable. There could be further potential questions of contributory negligence, assumption of the risk, financial responsibility of a minor and/or his parents, questions of duty to supervise a minor and the like, all of which can have a decisive effect on liability and which clearly are outside the expertise of a golf pro and his knowledge of golf standards of care. Boldus did not testify as to any of these issues; his testimony was limited to describing the standard of care for the game of golf.

Affirmed.

DISSENT

Justice Sabers

I dissent.

I write specially to point out that the majority opinion misses the point—not once, but several times.

Whether Boldus was qualified as an expert witness is immaterial. The point is that under the pretense of being an expert witness, Boldus cannot testify as a fact witness. He was not present at the scene. He does not know what happened. Only fact witnesses can testify "as to what happened?" Therefore, under these circumstances it was totally improper for Boldus to testify to his opinion "as to what happened in this case."

Questions

1. What were Nickles's objections to the expert, Boldus's, testimony?

2. What objection was raised by the dissenting Justice Sabers?

3. Do you agree with the expert, Boldus, that once a golfer has properly started the preshot routine the duty of care shifts to those around the golfer to be aware of what is happening and to keep themselves out of harm's way? Explain.

4. Dodge slipped leaving work and claimed that she suffered knee, ankle, and back injuries. Dodge sued the workplace cleaning service, but she provided no expert testimony to establish that the fall caused the injuries. Rather Dodge provided her own explanation of the fall and resulting injuries. Did the trial court err in admitting Dodge's lay person testimony? Explain, See *Dodge-Farrar v. American Cleaning Services Co.,* 54 P. 3d 954 (Ida. Ct. App. 2002).

Post-Trial Motions

The losing party may seek a *judgment notwithstanding the verdict (judgment n.o.v)* on the grounds that the jury's decision was clearly inconsistent with the law or the evidence. Such motions are rarely granted. The judge is also empowered to enter a judgment n.o.v on his or her own initiative.

Either party may also move for a new trial. The winning party might do so on the grounds that the remedy provided was inferior to that warranted by the evidence. The losing party commonly claims an error of law to support a motion for a new trial. Other possible grounds for a new trial include jury misconduct or new evidence.

Appeals

After the judgment is rendered, either party may appeal the decision to a higher court. The winner may do so if he or she feels the remedy is inadequate. Ordinarily, of course, the losing party brings the appeal. As noted, the appealing party is the *appellant* or the *petitioner,* while the other party is the *appellee* or *respondent.* The appeals court does not try the case again. In theory, at least, its consideration is limited to mistakes of law at the trial level. The appellant will argue, for example, that a jury instruction was erroneous or that the judge erred in failing to grant a motion to strike testimony alleged to have been prejudicial. The appeals court does not hear new evidence. Its decision is based on the trial record, materials filed by the opposing attorneys, and oral arguments.

The appellate court announces its judgment and ordinarily explains that decision in an accompanying document labeled an *opinion.* (Most of the cases in this text are appellate court opinions.) If no error is found, the lower court decision is *affirmed.* In finding prejudicial error, the appellate court may simply *reverse* (overrule) the lower court. Or the judgment may be to *reverse and remand,* wherein the lower court is overruled and the case must be tried again in accordance with the law as articulated in the appeals court opinion. After the decision of the intermediate appellate court, a further appeal may be sought at the highest court of the jurisdiction. Most of those petitions are denied.

Questions—Part Two

1. What are the purposes and uses of the concept of jurisdiction? Why do we limit the courts to which a claim can be taken?

2. Law cases often read like soap operas even as they reveal important truths. A woman and man, each married to others, had engaged in a long-term love affair. The woman's husband died, and she pleaded with her paramour to leave his New York home to visit her in Florida. She affirmed her love for the man. They made arrangements to meet in Miami, but on his arrival at the airport he was served a summons informing him that he was being sued. His Florida "lover" sought $500,000 for money allegedly loaned to him and for seduction inspired by a promise of marriage.

   a. Does the Florida court have proper jurisdiction over him?

   b. What if he had voluntarily come to Florida on vacation? See *Wyman v. Newhouse,* 93 F.2d 313 (2d Cir. 1937).

3. Sea Pines, a privately owned suburban community on Hilton Head Island, South Carolina, was designated a wildlife sanctuary by the state legislature. After study, the

state Department of Natural Resources decided to issue permits to allow limited deer hunting on the land to reduce overpopulation. Various environmental groups challenged the issuance of the permits. What defense would you expect the state to offer in court? Explain. See *Sea Pines Ass'n for Protection of Wildlife v. South Carolina Dept. of Natural Resources,* 550 S.E. 2d 287 (S.C. S. Ct. 2001).

Part Three—Criticism and Alternatives

Criticism

To many Americans, our system of justice is neither systematic nor just. With more than 1.1 million lawyers in a population of over 310 million people, critics argue that excessive, unproductive litigation is inevitable.

Too Many Lawyers and Lawsuits?

Many lawsuits are less a search for justice and more a pursuit of big dollars for attorneys, the critics claim. Former Enron CEO Jeffrey Skilling was found guilty in 2006 of fraud, conspiracy and other crimes in his trial involving the 2001 collapse of Enron, the Texas energy giant. The Enron bankruptcy cost thousands of jobs, more than $60 billion in Enron stock and more than $2 billion in employee pension funds. Skilling was sentenced to 24 years in prison. Skilling's lawyer, Daniel Petrocelli, billed his services at nearly $800 per hour. Petrocelli represented Skilling for a total of five years in various civil suits, testimony before government agencies, and so on. Petrocelli said that Skilling's criminal defense required a team of 12 lawyers, five paralegals, and many temporary staffers. The total legal bill: $70 million.[19] As one attorney later quipped: "What would he have been paid if he had won?"[20] Some five years later at this writing, Skilling is in jail after his latest appeal failed. Presumably the legal bills continue to mount. Are extraordinary legal bills a symptom of a troubled legal system?

> The total legal bill: $70 million. As one attorney later quipped: "What would he have been paid if he had won?"

Legal critic Philip K. Howard argues that we need fewer lawsuits, fewer rules, and greater personal responsibility. He thinks we feel powerless in the face of rules:

> Ordinary choices–by teachers, doctors, officials, managers, even volunteers—are paralyzed by legal self-consciousness. Did you check the rules? Who will be responsible if there is an accident? . . . We have become a culture of rule followers, trained to frame every solution in terms of existing law or possible legal risk. . . . [21]

Even Supreme Court Justice Antonin Scalia has argued that we have too many lawyers:

> Lawyers don't dig ditches or build buildings. When a society requires such a large number of its best minds to conduct the unproductive enterprise of the law, something is wrong with the legal system.[22]

Polling results suggest that Americans have deep reservations about our legal system, but they also recognize its indispensable role in maintaining a just society. U.S. Chamber of Commerce polling, for example, shows that nine of 10 Americans believe we have too many frivolous or unfair lawsuits, that 84 percent of Americans say that meritless lawsuits clog the justice process and that 75 percent of Americans believe our justice system is most beneficial to lawyers themselves.[23] At the same time, a 2007 national poll by the American Association for Justice (formerly the American Trial Lawyers Association) found more concern about corporate abuse than about lawyers and the legal system. In identifying "extremely serious" problems facing the nation, only 34 percent of those polled cited "trial lawyers making too much money when they successfully represent a client in a lawsuit," and 24 percent cited "victims in cases involving personal injury or medical malpractice receiving too much money from juries."[24] "Corporations giving huge salaries and bonuses to CEOs, while cutting the jobs and benefits of employees" topped the list of problems, having been cited by 64 percent of those polled.[25] Broadly, those polled favored careful oversight of corporate conduct:

> They (the poll respondents) tell us that making sure corporations are held accountable when their actions harm consumers, employees, or communities (70 percent) should be a much higher priority for the civil justice system than limiting the amount of compensation that juries can award for pain and suffering "so that lawsuits do not cause as big a burden on our economy" (25 percent). Similarly, they give priority to holding corporations accountable (61 percent) over "reducing the number of frivolous lawsuits" and penalizing those who file them (32 percent).[26]

> Nine of 10 Americans believe we have too many frivolous lawsuits.

The Corporate Perspective

The legal system plays an invaluable role in facilitating and stabilizing commercial practice, but for corporate America the law is also a source of significant expense and abundant frustration. As one expert explained, dealing with legal responsibilities and problems has become a central ingredient in management practice:

> Only a few decades ago, the law was peripheral to the core activities of doing business. When I became a business lawyer in the late 1950s, for example, our involvement was generally limited to forming a corporation or partnership for a client, providing for the investment capital, doing a lease for an office or factory, and maybe handling a key contract with a CEO or a major supplier. . . . Today the law can affect almost every action a manager takes. It has moved closer to the core activities of conducting business and succeeding in a red-hot, competitive environment. More people now have "rights" they can assert against your company, so you face claims from employees, consumers, competitors, and the government. Consequently, today's manager needs to know something about employment law, discrimination claims, sexual harassment rules, product safety issues, the rules of advertising and competition, antitrust rules, environmental law, the value of intellectual property, and more.[27]

[For a site dedicated to laughing at lawyers, see **http://www.power-of-attorneys.com/**] [For a critique of the American legal system, see the U.S. Chamber Institute for Legal Reform (an affiliate of the U.S. Chamber of Commerce) at **http://www.facesoflawsuitabuse.com/**]

Pants: Abusing the Legal System?

Washington, DC administrative law judge, Roy Pearson, attracted the attention of journalists from around the world by suing his neighborhood laundry for $54 million, down from an earlier claim of $67 million, over the alleged loss of the pants belonging to his $1,000 suit. Pearson thought he was entitled to $18,000 per day for each day the pants were missing over a period of nearly four years. Owners Soo and Jin Chung of Custom Cleaners attempted to give Pearson a pair of pants they said were the missing item, but he said the ones offered were not his. Pearson brought claims of mental suffering, inconvenience, discomfort, and fraud (based on the "Satisfaction Guaranteed" sign at Custom Cleaners). Along the way, Pearson had rejected settlement offers that reached $12,000. The Chungs won an easy trial victory with the court concluding that Pearson was unable to prove the pants offered to him were not his and that the "Satisfaction Guaranteed" sign did not require the Chungs to satisfy a customer's unreasonable demands. Pearson was ordered to pay the Chungs' court costs, and the legal fees for the Chungs' defense were covered by contributions. The Chung's dry cleaner went out of business. Pearson subsequently failed in his bid to be reappointed to his judge's position. He sued for wrongful discharge and lost at the federal district court and then appealed to the federal court of appeals where he also lost.

Sources: Henri E. Cauvin, "Court Rules for Cleaners in $54 Million Pants Suit," *The Washington Post*, June 26, 2007, p. A01; and "'Pants Judge' Roy Pearson Strikes Out in Court," *The Wall Street Journal*, May 27, 2010 [**http://blogs.wsj.com/law/**].

Criticized in America; Embraced Abroad

Highly criticized at home, the American legal system, nonetheless, has received a respectful endorsement around the globe. American-style litigation has followed American-style capitalism, and its variants, to all corners of the world. An unexpected consequence of globalization is the remarkable growth in lawyers and lawsuits in many other countries. Consider Japan, a nation that once disdained America's litigation "mania."

Japan   Globalization has changed Japan's traditionally cooperative corporate culture. Historically, the Japanese government maintained quiet order in the cartel-bound, clubby private sector, but the pressure of global competition has provoked increased friction, and lawsuits have soared in a culture that prefers working things out quietly. For most of its post–World War II era, Japan had not felt the need for lawyers, and their numbers today remain among the smallest in the world, but at 29,000 in total, Japanese lawyers have increased by 68 percent since 2000 and from 2004 to 2009 lawsuits increased by 73 percent (totaling 235,509).[28] Regardless of the growth of lawyers, the Japanese legal system remains resistant to legal pressures particularly as applied to manufacturers such as Toyota. *The Wall Street Journal* noted Japan's restrained response to Toyota's many recent vehicle recall problems:

> Over in Japan, meanwhile, pressure on the company is perhaps a bit less intense than it is in the U.S. That's because in Japan, Toyota is largely shielded from lawsuits and regulatory action by rules and customs more deferential to manufacturers.[29]

Furthermore, Japanese courts seldom award punitive damages, and class actions are uncommon, but *BusinessWeek* reports that Japan may need a stronger legal system:

> Despite the changes, it is unlikely Japan will ever fully embrace the kind of legal conflict common in the U.S. . . . But a more sophisticated, and contentious, legal system may be just what the country needs in order to keep its economic overhaul on track.[30]

PRACTICING ETHICS   Private Law for Walmart?

A portion of Walmart's Ethical Standards Program demands employee welfare throughout its vast supply chain:

> We do not own, operate, or manage any factories. Instead, we purchase merchandise from suppliers located in more than 60 countries. Our Ethical Standards team is dedicated to verifying that these supplier factories are in compliance with our Standards for Suppliers. These standards cover compliance with local and national laws and regulations governing compensation, hours of labor, forced/prison labor, underage labor, discrimination, freedom of association and collective bargaining, health and safety, environment, and the right of audit by Walmart Stores, Inc.[31]

Law professor Larry Cata Backer argues that Walmart and other global giants are effectively legislating their own private law in the form of contract and business relationships and ethics standards governing product quality, working conditions and similar matters. Walmart's Standards for Suppliers are the core of its global governance system that, according to Backer, is "an important emerging phenomenon: the development of efficient systems of private law making by nongovernmental organizations that sometimes supplement, and sometimes displace traditional legal systems."[32] Working with the media, nongovernmental organizations (NGOs), consumers, and investors, Walmart and other multinationals, Backer argues, are beginning to build independent mechanisms for efficient regulation of economic behavior on a global scale that may lead to systems of law beyond governments and moderated largely by stakeholders.[33]

Question

1. Should we welcome and encourage the development of a private law system enforced through contractual and ethical standards by giant multinationals, or should we be concerned that strengthened, strictly enforced private law arrangements would place too much authority in the hands of already powerful organizations? Explain.

On the Other Hand—Litigation as a Last Resort

Almost everyone seems to be unhappy about lawyers and lawsuits, but at the same time Americans expect lawyers and the courts to settle disputes, preserve freedom and justice and correct problems not satisfactorily addressed by the market, legislatures and regulators. Feeling threatened by abusive bosses, corporate fraud, dangerous drugs, defective products, environmental decline, and so on, Americans count on the justice system to protect our pecuniary interests as well as the personal freedom and democracy we prize. Lawyers and the courts often are the only available weapons to right what we believe to be a wrong. So the frustration many feel about exploding litigation may be attributable to us as much as to greedy lawyers. Furthermore, laws and lawyers are central to economic efficiency. Lawyers devise the rules, processes, and structures that permit capitalism to operate effectively. As we have read, the balance of the world is coming to recognize that law and lawyers are prerequisites to economic stability and progress.

Fewer Trials Whatever we may feel about lawyers and the justice system, the simple fact, as reported by *BusinessWeek,* is that federal civil trials have declined in recent years:

> Around the country, plenty of lawsuits are getting filed, but fewer and fewer are going to trial. The civil trial is one of the most iconic American institutions, a time-honored forum where disputes over injuries, divorces, and all manner of business disasters are resolved. Yet rising legal costs, decreasing judicial tolerance for weak lawsuits, and the surging use of alternative dispute resolution (ADR) are combining to make courtroom showdowns exceptional occurrences.[34]

According to *BusinessWeek,* civil suits filed in federal district courts in the past 40 years soared from 66,144 to 259,541, but the number of those that eventually went to trial fell to a new low of 3,555 in 2006, down from a peak of 12,018 in 1984.[35] Likewise, in the 21 states with available data, the number of civil jury trials fell 40 percent from 1976 to 2004.[36] Trials often are an inefficient way of resolving disputes so these numbers may be considered very good news. On the other hand, trials are visible affirmations of the indispensability of justice, and they provide the careful reasoning and precedents that identify impermissible behavior.

> Trials often are an inefficient way of resolving disputes.

PRACTICING ETHICS   Declining Access to Lawyers?

One of the reasons for the declining number of trials, despite increasing disputes, may be difficulty in affording a lawyer in civil suits. *The New York Times* and other publications have reported an increasing number of cases going forward with one of the parties serving as a "do-it-yourself" lawyer.[37] Pursuing a claim in a federal district court costs an average of $15,000 with more complicated cases involving scientific evidence often reaching $100,000.[38] Indeed, *The New York Times* reports that expense has become such a hurdle that lawsuits have become investment vehicles: "Large banks, hedge funds and private investors hungry for new and lucrative opportunities are bankrolling other people's lawsuits, pumping hundreds of millions of dollars into medical malpractice claims, divorce battles and class actions against corporations. . . ."[39] Lawsuit investments nationwide are estimated to exceed $1 billion at any given time, and some of those lawsuits are actually initiated and controlled by the investors.[40]

One result is that some litigants appear to be victimized by lawsuit lenders in a lightly regulated industry where interest rates "often exceed 100 percent per year."[41]

Litigants who go it alone may find help on the Internet. Illinois, for example, established Illinois Legal Aid Online to provide introductory education and access to online conversations with volunteer law students.[42] However, with serious matters such as bankruptcy, eviction, and employment rights at stake, experts are concerned that the legal system is failing many Americans.

Question

1. While indigent criminal defendants are assured the right to counsel under American law, the same is not assured in civil disputes. Do you think we must begin to close the "justice gap" by providing taxpayer-funded legal aid for indigents in serious civil cases such as housing, health care, and child custody? Explain.

Reform: Judicial Efficiency

Governments, businesses, lawyers, judges—all are frustrated with the expense and inefficiency of our overburdened judicial system. Some small businesses are now buying legal services insurance or prepaid legal services for a flat monthly fee.

Some cities have taken novel approaches to adjudication such as business courts that hear only commercial claims, thus allowing jurists to become very efficient in handling contract problems, shareholder claims, and the like. Those systems are variations on the small claims courts that have long proven effective in settling minor disputes.

Small Claims Courts

Suppose you move out of your apartment and your landlord refuses to return your $500 damage deposit even though the rooms are spotless. Hiring a lawyer doesn't make good financial sense and is beyond your means anyway, but a small claims court may provide an effective solution.

Small claims courts, for the most part, resolve relatively minor disputes, like your landlord-tenant problem. A wide range of problems, such as divorce or bankruptcy, cannot be litigated in small claims courts. Maximum recoveries vary from place to place but typically range from a few thousand dollars up to $7,500 or so. To prepare for a small claims case, the key is developing and presenting to the judge as much credible evidence as possible. If you can present witnesses on your behalf, do so, but if not, clearly written memos expressing what the witnesses would have said may be acceptable to the judge. You need not hire a lawyer, but in most states you may do so if you wish. Should the small claims litigation not work out well for you, an appeal is permitted in many states.[43]

Alternative Dispute Resolution (ADR)

Businesses, in particular, are increasingly looking outside the judicial system for dispute resolution strategies. Dot-com entrepreneurs are developing interesting new online mechanisms for conveniently addressing Internet-based disputes. Networks of human mediators, dispute resolution software, and PayPal dispute resolution are among the online methods of settling problems outside of court.

Cybersettle is an online system for resolving insurance disputes, often of the fender-bender or slip-and-fall variety. The parties log on to Cybersettle and type in their monetary demands or offers. The system works 24 hours a day, 7 days a week. The computer compares the bids, round by round. When those numbers come within a predetermined range, the two sides are notified that a settlement has been achieved. If necessary, a telephone facilitator may join the process to help reach the final sum to be paid. Cybersettle has patented its system and says it has settled over 200,000 transactions and has facilitated over $1.8 billion in settlements. [See **http://www.cybersettle.com/pub/**] Critics say some Internet legal resources such as **http://www.whocanisue.com/,** a highly-advertised Web site that matches potential clients with lawyers, may degrade the legal profession and serve primarily to generate litigation.[44]

What Is ADR?

Of course, any form of negotiation and settlement would constitute an alternative to litigation, but mediation and arbitration are the most prominent of the substitutes. Given the expense, frustration, and risk of lawsuits, we are seeing increasing imagination in building other ADR options including private trials and minitrials. [For many ADR links, see **www.hg.org/adr.html**]

Mediation

Mediation introduces a neutral third party into the resolution process. Ideally, the parties devise their own solution, with the mediator as a facilitator, not a decision maker. Even if the mediator proposes a solution, it will likely be in the nature of a compromise, not a determination of right and wrong. The bottom line is that only the disputing parties can adopt any particular outcome. The mediator may aid the parties in a number of ways, such as opening up communication between them.

Arbitration

In *arbitration* a neutral third party is given the power to determine a binding resolution of the dispute. Depending on the situation, the resolution may be either a compromise solution or a determination of the rights of the parties and a win–lose solution. Even in the latter case, however, arbitration may be quicker and less costly than a trial, and the arbitrator may be an expert in the subject area of the dispute instead of a generalist, as a judge would be. Arbitration is procedurally more formal than mediation, with the presentation of proofs and arguments by the parties, but less formal than court adjudication.

The arbitrator's decision ordinarily is legally binding and final, although an increasing but still small number of arbitration decisions are reaching court.[45]

[For a brief overview of mediation and arbitration see **http://www.youtube.com/ watch?v=KLdia39awl0**] (The final two characters in this URL are a lowercase l, as in law, and zero.)

Private Trials

"Rent-a-Judge"

A number of states now permit mutually-agreed-on private trials, sometimes labeled "rent-a-judge." Normally a third party such as a mediation firm makes the necessary arrangements, including hiring a retired judge and jurors. The proceedings are conducted much as in a courtroom. Because the parties are paying, however, the process normally moves along more rapidly, and the proceeding may be conducted in private. Appeals to the formal judicial system are provided for in some states. Critics question the fairness of the private system and wonder if it will further erode faith in public trials, but the time and money saved can be quite substantial.

Mini-trials

In recent years, some corporations have agreed to settle their disputes by holding informal hearings that clarify the facts and the issues that would emerge if the dispute were litigated. In the mini-trial, each organization presents its version of the case to a panel of senior executives from each organization. The trial is presided over by a neutral third party who may be expected to issue a nonbinding opinion as to the likely result were the case to be litigated. The executives then meet to attempt to negotiate a settlement. The neutral third party sometimes facilitates that discussion. Mini-trials are voluntary and nonbinding, but if an agreement is reached, the parties can formalize it by entering a settlement contract.

ADR Assessed

ADR mechanisms generally have been sustained in the courts. ADR—particularly arbitration—is often the required dispute-resolution mechanism for employee complaints such as discrimination or harassment. Mandatory arbitration clauses are often included in consumer transactions involving loans, credit cards, cable service, auto warranties, brokerage accounts, insurance and more. Ordinarily, ADR costs less and is resolved more quickly than litigation. ADR is less formal and less adversarial than the judicial process. Furthermore, the parties have more control over the proceedings in that they can choose the facilitator, they can choose when and where the dispute will be heard, and they can keep the dispute private if they wish. Despite those strengths, alternative dispute resolution has some limitations when compared with litigation.

A new study of nearly 4,000 employee arbitration cases found an employee win rate of only 21.4 percent, a lower result than in litigation. In arbitration cases won by employees, the median recovery was $36,500 and the mean was $109,858 both of which are substantially lower than awards reported from litigation. On the other hand, arbitration, on average, was both quicker and less expensive than litigation.[46]

A 2011 U.S. Supreme Court decision makes arbitration less functional for consumers by allowing businesses to continue their commonplace practice of requiring arbitration of disputes but forbidding class action arbitration (and litigation) thus compelling consumers to individually arbitrate alleged wrongdoing. In that case, Vincent and Liza Concepcion

> AT&T Mobility charged them $30.22 for a "free" phone.

complained that AT&T Mobility charged them $30.22 in sales tax and other fees for what was advertised as a "free" phone. They sought class action status for themselves and others, but the 5-4 Supreme Court ruling denied that possibility and left the Concepcions and others similarly aggrieved to file individual claims for very small amounts of money.[47] The case that follows examines whether a mandatory arbitration clause in a travel agency contract to climb Mount Kilimanjaro was unconscionable under California law.

Lhotka v. Geographic Expeditions
181 Cal. App. 4th 816 (2010)
(Petition for review denied *Lhotka v. Geographic Expeditions,* 2010 Cal. LEXIS 3320 [Cal. S. Ct.])[48]

LEGAL BRIEFCASE

Judge Siggins

Geographic Expeditions, Inc. (GeoEx), appeals from an order denying its motion to compel arbitration of a wrongful death action brought by the survivors of one of its clients who died on a Mount Kilimanjaro hiking expedition. . . .

BACKGROUND

Jason Lhotka was 37 years old when he died of an altitude-related illness while on a GeoEx expedition up Mount Kilimanjaro with his mother, plaintiff Sandra Menefee. GeoEx's limitation

of liability and release form, which both Lhotka and Menefee signed as a requirement of participating in the expedition, provided that each of them released GeoEx from all liability in connection with the trek and waived any claims for liability "to the maximum extent permitted by law." The release also required that the parties would submit any disputes between themselves first to mediation and then to binding arbitration. It reads: "I understand that all Trip Applications are subject to acceptance by GeoEx in San Francisco, California, USA. I agree that in the unlikely event a dispute of any kind arises between me and GeoEx, the following conditions will apply: (a) the dispute will be submitted to a neutral third-party mediator in San Francisco, California, with both parties splitting equally the cost of such mediator. If the dispute cannot be resolved through mediation, then (b) the dispute will be submitted for binding arbitration to the American Arbitration Association in San Francisco, California; (c) the dispute will be governed by California law; and (d) the maximum amount of recovery to which I will be entitled under any and all circumstances will be the sum of the land and air cost of my trip with GeoEx. I agree that this is a fair and reasonable limitation on the damages, of any sort whatsoever, that I may suffer. I agree to fully indemnify GeoEx for all of its costs (including attorneys' fees) if I commence an action or claim against GeoEx based upon claims I have previously released or waived by signing this release." Menefee paid $16,831 for herself and Lhotka to go on the trip.

A letter from GeoEx president James Sano that accompanied the limitation of liability and release explained that the form was mandatory and that, on this point, "our lawyers, insurance carriers and medical consultants give us no discretion. A signed, unmodified release form is required before any traveler may join one of our trips. Ultimately, we believe that you should choose your travel company based on its track record, not what you are asked to sign. . . . My review of other travel companies' release forms suggests that our forms are not a whole lot different from theirs."

After her son's death, Menefee sued GeoEx for wrongful death and alleged various theories of liability including fraud, gross negligence and recklessness, and intentional infliction of emotional distress. GeoEx moved to compel arbitration.

The trial court found the arbitration provision was unconscionable and on that basis denied the motion.

* * * * *

This appeal timely followed.

DISCUSSION

The question . . . posed here[is] whether the agreement to arbitrate is unconscionable and, therefore, unenforceable.

* * * * *

II. Unconscionability (I omitted-Ed.)
(1) We turn first to GeoEx's contention that the court erred when it found the arbitration agreement unconscionable. . . .

"[U]nconscionability has generally been recognized to include an absence of meaningful choice on the part of one of the parties together with contract terms which are unreasonably favorable to the other party.' Phrased another way, unconscionability has both a 'procedural' and a 'substantive'

element." The procedural element requires oppression or surprise. Oppression occurs where a contract involves lack of negotiation and meaningful choice, surprise where the allegedly unconscionable provision is hidden within a prolix printed form. The substantive element concerns whether a contractual provision reallocates risks in an objectively unreasonable or unexpected manner.' Under this approach, both the procedural and substantive elements must be met before a contract or term will be deemed unconscionable. Both, however, need not be present to the same degree. A sliding scale is applied so that 'the more substantively oppressive the contract term, the less evidence of procedural unconscionability is required to come to the conclusion that the term is unenforceable, and vice versa.'" . . .

A. Procedural Unconscionability

* * * * *

GeoEx led plaintiffs to understand not only that its terms and conditions were nonnegotiable, but that plaintiffs would encounter the same requirements with any other travel company. This is a sufficient basis for us to conclude plaintiffs lacked bargaining power.

GeoEx also contends its terms were not oppressive . . . because Menefee and Lhotka could have simply decided not to trek up Mount Kilimanjaro. It argues that contracts for recreational activities can *never* be unconscionably oppressive because, unlike agreements for necessities such as medical care or employment, a consumer of recreational activities *always* has the option of foregoing the activity. . . .
(2) While the nonessential nature of recreational activities is a factor to be taken into account in assessing whether a contract is oppressive, it is not necessarily the dispositive factor.

* * * * *

(3) Here, certainly, plaintiffs could have chosen not to sign on with the expedition. That option, like any availability of market alternatives, is relevant to the existence, and degree, of oppression. . . .

But we must also consider the other circumstances surrounding the execution of the agreement. . . .

GeoEx presented its terms as both nonnegotiable and *no different than what plaintiffs would find with any other provider* Under these circumstances, plaintiffs made a sufficient showing to establish at least a minimal level of oppression to justify a finding of procedural unconscionability.

B. Substantive Unconscionability

With the "sliding scale" rule firmly in mind, we address whether the substantive unconscionability of the GeoEx contract warrants the trial court's ruling.

The arbitration provision in GeoEx's release is . . . one-sided. . . . It guaranteed that plaintiffs could not possibly obtain anything approaching full recompense for their harm by limiting any recovery they could obtain to the amount they paid GeoEx for their trip. In addition to a limit on their recovery, plaintiffs, residents of Colorado, were required to mediate and arbitrate in San Francisco—all but guaranteeing both that GeoEx would never be out more than the amount plaintiffs had paid for their trip, and that any recovery plaintiffs might obtain would be devoured by the expense they incur in pursing their remedy. The release also required plaintiffs to indemnify GeoEx for its costs and attorney fees for defending any claims covered by the release of liability form. Notably, there is no reciprocal limitation on damages or indemnification obligations imposed on GeoEx. Rather than providing a neutral forum for dispute resolution, GeoEx's arbitration scheme provides a potent disincentive for an aggrieved client to pursue any claim, in any forum—and may well guarantee that GeoEx wins even if it loses. Absent reasonable justification for this arrangement—and none is apparent—we agree with the trial court that the arbitration clause is so one-sided as to be substantively unconscionable.

Affirmed.

Questions

1. Why was the Lhotka/Geographic Expeditions agreement to arbitrate ruled unconscionable?

2. Differentiate procedural and substantive unconscionability.

3. Kalliope and David Valchine entered court-ordered mediation to try to resolve the problems that had led them to seek a divorce. Lawyers represented both Kalliope and David at mediation. The mediation led to a marital settlement agreement between Kalliope and David. One month later, Kalliope sought to set aside the agreement, arguing that she had been coerced by her husband, her husband's attorney, and the mediator. Kalliope testified that the mediator threatened to report her to the judge for being uncooperative in refusing to sign a reasonable settlement offer. She claimed that the mediator also told her that she could sign the agreement and then object to its provisions at the final hearing. See *Kalliope Vitakis-Valchine v. David L. Valchine*, 793 So.2d 1094 (Fla. App. 4th Dist. 2001); 34 So.3d 17 (Fla. App. 4th Dist. 2010).
Should the settlement be set aside? Explain.

4. Is an arbitration clause as a condition of employment a fair method of alternate dispute resolution, if entered knowingly and voluntarily? Explain.

5. In an effort to reduce legal expenses, some major banks and other businesses follow policies providing that all customer complaints will be subject to arbitration. Is mandatory arbitration fair to consumers? Explain.

Internet Exercise

Go to the "2010 U.S. Chamber of Commerce State Liability Systems Ranking Study," at [**www.instituteforlegalreform.com/lawsuit-climate.html**]. Check your state's ranking according to the study; then click on the Key Issues button to read experts' views about the most important legal problems facing state policy makers. Then for links to some critiques of the Chamber study go to [**http://viztac.com/general/challenge-to-validity-of-annual-u-s-chamber-of-commerce-state-liability-systems-ranking-study**].

Chapter Questions

1. Economist Stephen Magee argues that one way to strengthen the American economy would be to close the law schools:

   > Every time you turn out one law school graduate, you've got a 40-year problem on your hands, he says. These guys run around and generate a lot of spurious conflict. They're like heat-seeking missiles.[49]

   Comment.

2. Professor and criminal justice expert Morgan O. Reynolds argues that sterner punishment has led to reduced crime in the United States:

This reflects a broader pattern: As our crime rates have fallen, serious crime rates in England have risen substantially, as a recent study from the U.S. Bureau of Justice Statistics found. For example, victim surveys show that

- The English robbery rate was about half the U.S. rate in 1981 but was 40 percent higher than America's in 1995.
- The English assault rate was slightly higher than America's in 1981 but more than double by 1995.
- The English burglary rate was half America's in 1981 but nearly double by 1995.

Why these dramatic increases in English crime rates, while Americans' lives and property grew safer? The obvious explanation has been too often downplayed or ignored: The United States has instituted tougher, more predictable punishment for crime. The study's authors attribute the trends they note to the increasing conviction rates and longer sentences meted out in the United States versus the decreasing conviction rates and softer sentences in England and Wales. English conviction rates for rape, burglary, assault, and auto theft have plunged by half or more since 1981, while the likelihood of serving prison time for committing a serious violent crime or a burglary has increased substantially in the United States.[50]

a. Do you agree that harsher and more certain punishment will reduce criminal behavior?

b. Do "root causes" such as being born out of wedlock affect criminal behavior? Explain.

3. Crowley, who became intoxicated at a postrace party on McRoberts's boat, was driving after the party and caused a multicar accident that resulted in serious injuries to Culver, who was driving one of the other vehicles. Culver's passenger was killed, and Crowley was later convicted of reckless homicide. Culver sued McRoberts for negligence. Crowley's drinking took place in the galley of McRoberts's 40-foot boat. McRoberts did not provide the liquor and McRoberts, who was busy with recording race results, was not aware of how much drinking Crowley had done. The Indiana Dram Shop statute provided that "it is unlawful for a person to sell, barter, deliver, or give away an alcoholic beverage to another person who is in a state of intoxication if the person knows that the other person is intoxicated." Expert testimony and a blood alcohol reading suggested that Crowley may have been visibly drunk, but several witnesses on the boat said they did not observe visible signs of intoxication. Did McRoberts violate the Indiana Dram Shop law, and was McRoberts negligent in failing to properly supervise Crowley? Explain. See *Culver v. McRoberts,* 192 F.3d 1095 (7th Cir. 1999).

4. Dubuque, Iowa's City Council and mayor in 2011 enacted a parental responsibility ordinance providing that: "A failure by a parent to exercise reasonable control over the parent's minor which causes the minor to commit an unlawful act is a violation . . ." The ordinance is directed to derelict parents whose negligence or indifference facilitates criminal behavior by children and leads to big investments of police time in simply locating parents. A violation initially results in a warning with increasing fines (or parenting classes) for violations thereafter. The city's plan is to provide resources to aid parents who are in violation of the ordinance.

The city has indicated that "reasonable control" means doing what the average person would do.[51]

   a. What objections would you raise to this ordinance?

   b. Do you think a parent would violate the reasonable control standard if his/her child failed to come home from the movies by the hour agreed on, but the parent then made an effort to find the child? Explain.

   c. Is the ordinance a good idea in your judgment? Explain.

5. After drinking at the Elks Lodge, Dionne was escorted to a taxi where the driver, Grader, was told to take Dionne home because he had too much to drink. Dionne would not give Grader directions to his home and then told Grader to take him to another bar. Dionne paid his fare and went into the second bar, and later that bar summoned the same cab to take Dionne home. On this occasion, Dionne told Grader to take him to a convenience store. Dionne conducted his business there with no overt signs of intoxication. He then returned to the cab and asked to be driven back to the Elks Lodge. Grader deposited Dionne at the Elks Lodge and watched as Dionne passed by his own car in the parking lot. Grader heard other voices in the lot, assumed Dionne would be fine, and resumed his work. Later that evening Dionne died in a single-car accident. His blood-alcohol level was .25. The facts are not clear as to whether Dionne drank more after leaving Grader's cab. The taxi service was sued for negligence for not taking Dionne home. How would you rule on that negligence claim? Explain. See *Mastriano v. Blyer,* 779 A.2d 951 (Sup. Jud. Ct. Maine 2001).

6. A letter to *The Wall Street Journal:*

> The problems with our legal system go much deeper than irresponsible plaintiffs, amoral lawyers, and inept juries. The trouble is, our system of checks and balances has been corrupted; 100 percent of the executive, 100 percent of the judicial, and 43 percent of the legislative branches have been taken over by one group—lawyers.
>
> The Constitution charges Congress to ordain and establish the courts. It is no wonder it has created a system that maximizes the incomes of its own kind. The system is rigged to drag out cases that are billed by the hour, or to find moochers and looters willing to bring huge civil suits against productive citizens and corporations in front of dumbed-down juries.[52]

Do you agree? Explain.

7. In your opinion are attractive criminal defendants likely to receive more favorable treatment in the courts than similarly situated but less attractive defendants? Explain.

8. According to Warren Avis, founder of Avis Rent-a-Car,

> We've reached a point in this country where, in many instances, power has become more important than justice—not a matter of who is right, but of who has the most money, time, and the largest battery of lawyers to drag a case through the courts.[53]

   a. Should the rich be entitled to better legal representation, just as they have access to better food, better medical care, better education, and so on? Explain.

   b. Should we employ a nationwide legal services program sufficient to guarantee competent legal aid to all? Explain.

9. Peremptory challenges may not constitutionally be used to exclude a potential juror from a trial on racial or gender grounds.

   a. Must a criminal jury reflect the ethnic or racial diversity of the community? Explain. See *Powers v. Ohio,* 111 S. Ct. 1364 (1991).

   b. Could potential jurors lawfully be rejected on the basis of their place of residence? Explain. See *U.S. v. Bishop,* 959 F.2d 820 (9th Cir. 1992).

10. French journalist Alain Clement offered a partial explanation for Americans' increasing reliance on lawsuits to resolve conflicts:

    > Diverse causes explain the growth of the contentious mood in America. One could be called the devaluing of the future. In 1911, the Russian political scientist Moise Ostrgorski wrote, "Confident of the future, Americans manifest a remarkable endurance to an unhappy present, a submissive patience that is willing to bargain about not only civic rights, but even the rights of man."[54]

    a. What does Clement mean?

    b. How do you explain our increased reliance on litigation?

11. In 1982, a security guard was murdered during a robbery of a south Chicago McDonald's. Alton Logan was sentenced to life in prison for that murder. At the same time, two Chicago public defenders, Dale Coventry and Jamie Kunz, were representing Andrew Wilson, who was accused of murdering two police officers. Based on a tip, Coventry and Kunz suspected that Wilson was the actual murderer in the McDonald's case. They questioned Wilson who admitted that he, not Logan, was the murderer. Because of their duties under the attorney-client privilege, Coventry and Kunz felt they could not reveal what they knew. Logan, therefore, went to prison an innocent man, they believed. The public defenders decided to write the story in a notarized affidavit and lock it in a box in case something should happen that would allow them to reveal what they knew. When Wilson died in prison of natural causes in 2008, Coventry and Kunz revealed their client's confession. After 26 years, Logan was released from prison. He was granted a certificate of innocence in 2009, and at this writing, he is suing various police officers for framing him.[55]

    a. Why does the legal profession expect lawyers to keep secret their clients' confidential communications?

    b. Had you been Coventry and Kunz, would you have revealed what you knew in order to immediately secure justice for Logan? Explain.

12. On July 5, 1884, four sailors were cast away from their ship in a storm 1,600 miles from the Cape of Good Hope. Their lifeboat contained neither water nor much food. On the 20th day of their ordeal, Dudley and Stevens, without the assistance or agreement of Brooks, cut the throat of the fourth sailor, a 17- or 18-year-old boy. They had not eaten since day 12. Water had been available only occasionally. At the time of the death, the men were probably about 1,000 miles from land. Prior to his death, the boy was lying helplessly in the bottom of the boat. The three surviving sailors ate the boy's remains for four days, at which point they were rescued by a passing boat. They were in a seriously weakened condition.

    a. Were Dudley and Stevens guilty of murder? Explain.

    b. Should Brooks have been charged with a crime for eating the boy's flesh? Explain. See *The Queen v. Dudley and Stephens,* 14 Queen's Bench Division 273 (1884).

13. Tompkins was a citizen of Pennsylvania. While walking on a railroad footpath in that state, he was struck by an object protruding from a passing freight train owned by the Erie Railroad Company, a New York corporation. Tompkins, by virtue of diversity of citizenship, filed a negligence suit against Erie in a New York federal court. Erie argued for the application of Pennsylvania common law, in which case Tompkins would have been treated as a trespasser. Tompkins argued that the absence of a Pennsylvania statute addressing the topic meant that federal common law had to be applied to the case. Should the federal court apply the relevant Pennsylvania state law, or should the court be free to exercise its independent judgment about what the common law of the state is or should be? See *Erie Railroad v. Tompkins,* 304 U.S. 64 (1938).

14. China is rapidly training lawyers and moving toward a more Western approach to judicial systems. The following quote describes China's historic view of dispute resolution:

    > Most Chinese persons engage in a large variety of economic and social activities and resolve disputes involved in those activities without coming in contact with the formal legal system. As in Japan, litigation in a court of law is not considered a normal way to resolve a dispute. Custom and extrajudicial dispute-settling mechanisms are utilized not only by private parties but by public entities. Decisions declaring someone right and someone wrong are not a desirable goal. Settlements and compromises are preferable. Even in court, Chinese litigants generally do not obtain a clear defeat or victory.[56]

    In your view, would China be better off in the contemporary world to retain its traditional means of conflict settlement or should it continue its turn toward Western-style litigation? Explain.

15. Boschetto, a California resident, bought a 1964 Ford Galaxie 500XL advertised on eBay from Hansing, a Wisconsin resident. Hansing said the car was in excellent condition, including an "R code" classification. After delivery to California, Boschetto discovered many problems including the fact that the car was not an "R code." The parties could not reach an out-of-court settlement so Boschetto sued. Hansing moved for dismissal of the claim on the grounds of lack of personal jurisdiction. Does the fact that the transaction was conducted via eBay satisfy the jurisdictional requirement? Explain. See *Boschetto v. Hansing,* 539 F.3d 1011 (9th Cir. 2008); cert. den. *Boschetto v. Hansing,* 129 S. Ct. 1318 (2009).

16. University of Chicago law professor Richard Epstein pointed out how quickly Americans turn to legal remedies rather than relying on informal social customs (negotiation, neighborhood groups, simply accepting small losses and disturbances rather than fighting about them) to resolve conflicts. In your view, why are social customs often ineffective in settling disputes in this country? Explain.

17. Judicial reform advocates often argue that the United States should adopt the English rule providing that the losing party in a lawsuit must pay the reasonable litigation expenses of the winner.

    a. In brief, what are the strengths and weaknesses of the English rule?

    b. Would you favor it? Explain. See "Loser Pays, Everyone Wins," *The Wall Street Journal,* December 15, 2010 [**http://online.wsj.com/**].

18. Plaintiff Jonathan Gold was hired to work at defendant Deutsche Bank after completing his MBA degree at New York University. Before beginning employment, Gold signed

various documents, including Form U-4 that the National Association of Securities Dealers (NASD) required all registered representatives to sign. Form U-4 provided for arbitration for all employment disputes. Gold was fired after working about one year. He then filed suit claiming sexual harassment based on his sexual orientation. Deutsche Bank moved to compel arbitration. Gold resisted arbitration arguing, among other things, that Form U-4 was too difficult to understand and that it raised questions in his mind. Gold also showed that Deutsche Bank had certified that it provided Gold with the relevant NASD rules when it had not. Was Gold required to submit his claim to arbitration? Explain. See *Gold v. Deutsche Aktiengesellschaft*, 365 F.3d 144 (2d Cir. 2004); cert. den. *Gold v. Deutsche Aktiengesellschaft*, 543 U.S. 874 (2004).

Notes

1. AFP, "Sweden Tops Government Ranking—While US Lags," *Swedish Wire,* October 14, 2010 [**http://www.swedishwire.com/**].
2. *Maouloud Baby v. State of Maryland*, 916 A.2d 410 (Md. Ct. Special App. 2007).
3. *State of Maryland v. Maouloud Baby*, 2008 Md. LEXIS 190 (Md. Ct. of Appeals).
4. "Pennsylvania Latest State to Consider Criminalizing Teen 'Sexting'," *The Wall Street Journal,* August 3, 2010 [**http://blogs.wsj.com/**].
5. *Orlando Sentinel*, "More U.S. Judges Impose Creative Punishments," *The Des Moines Register,* October 29, 2010, p. 10A.
6. Adam Liptak, "Court Under Roberts Is Most Conservative in Decades," *The New York Times,* July 24, 2010 [**http://www.nytimes.com**].
7. E.J. Dionne, Jr., "The Supreme Court's Defense of the Powerful," *The Washington Post,* June 29, 2011 [**http://www.washingtonpost.com/**].
8. Adam Liptak, "Justices Offer Receptive Ear to Business Interests," *The New York Times,* December 18, 2010 [**http://www.nytimes.com/**].
9. David G. Savage, "Justices Have Been Siding with Workers, Underdogs," *latimes.com,* March 13, 2011 [**latimes.com/news/nationworld/nation/la-na-court-unanimous-20110313,0,4601488. story**].
10. Liptak, "Court Under Roberts," [**http://www.nytimes.com**].
11. John C. Henry, "Do You Know Who Works Here? They Can Change Your Life," *AARP.org/ Bulletin,* November 2010, p. 26.
12. Editorial, "Our Constitutional Court," *The New York Times,* November 22, 2010 [**http://www. nytimes.com/**].
13. Lincoln Caplan, "A Judge's Warning about the Legitimacy of the Supreme Court," *The New York Times,* September 26, 2010 [**http://www.nytimes.com/**].
14. Robert Barnes, "Legal Experts Propose Limiting Justices' Powers, Terms," *The Washington Post,* February 23, 2009, p. A15.
15. Editorial, "Case Against Oxy Hits Home," *latimes.com,* December 10, 2010 [**latimes.com/ news/opinion/opinionla/la-ed-peru-20101210,0,2576676.story**].
16. *Carijano v. Occidental Petroleum*, 626 F.3d 1137(9th Cir. 2010).
17. For an archive of "Spygate" articles, see "Spygate," *The New York Times,* July 12, 2011 [**http:// topics.nytimes.com/**].
18. *Wal-Mart Stores v. Dukes*, 2011 U.S. LEXIS 4567.
19. Christopher Palmeri, "One of Them Is Still Laughing," *BusinessWeek,* October 30, 2006, p. 13.

20. Ibid.

21. Philip K. Howard, "How Modern Law Makes Us Powerless," *The Wall Street Journal,* January 26, 2009 [**http://online.wsj.com/**].

22. Lyric Wallwork Winik, "Are There Too Many Lawyers?" *Parade,* September 14, 2008, p. 9.

23. John O'Brien, "Poll: Voters Not Worried about Tort Reform," *LegalNewsline.com,* July 12, 2007 [**http://www.legalnewsline.com/news/197868-poll-voters-not-worried-about-tort-reform**].

24. Ibid.

25. Peter Hart Research Associates, Inc., "Civil Justice Issues and the 2008 Election," July 11, 2007 [**http://www.atla.org/pressroom/CJSPollMemo.pdf**].

26. Ibid.

27. Milton Bordwin, "Your Company and the Law," *Management Review,* January 2000, p. 58.

28. "Toyota Lawsuits Not So Big in Japan, but that Might Be Changing," *The Wall Street Journal,* February 23, 2010 [**http://blogs.wsj.com/law/2010/**].

29. Ibid.

30. Ian Rowley and Kenji Hall, "Lawyers Wanted. No, Really," *BusinessWeek,* April 3, 2006, p. 46.

31. "Becoming a Wal-Mart or Sam's Club Supplier" [**http://www.walmartstores.com/Files/Supplier_GettingStarted.pdf**].

32. Larry Cata Backer, "Economic Globalization and the Rise of Efficient Systems of Global Private Lawmaking: Wal-Mart as Global Legislator," 39 *Connecticut Law Review* 1741 (2007).

33. Ibid.

34. Michael Orey, "The Vanishing Trial," *BusinessWeek,* April 30, 2007, p. 38.

35. Ibid.

36. Ibid.

37. John T. Broderick Jr. and Ronald M. George, "A Nation of Do-It-Yourself Lawyers," *The New York Times,* January 2, 2010 [**http://www.nytimes.com/**].

38. Binyamin Appelbaum, "Investors Put Money on Lawsuits to Get Payouts," *The New York Times,* November 14, 2010 [**http://www.nytimes.com**].

39. Ibid.

40. Ibid.

41. Binyamin Appelbaum, "Lawsuit Loans Add New Risk for the Injured," *The New York Times,* January 16, 2011 [**http://www.nytimes.com/**].

42. John Keilman, "Litigants Become Their Own Lawyers," *Los Angeles Times,* August 10, 2009 [**http://www.latimes.com/**].

43. This paragraph is derived from "Small Claims Court FAQ," NOLO [**http://www.nolo.com**].

44. Missy Diaz, "Lawyers Are Divided over WhoCanISue.com," *latimes.com,* October 11, 2009 [**http://www.latimes.com/**].

45. "Arbitration: Increasingly, It's Not Over until the Vacatur Motion Fails," *The Wall Street Journal,* February 14, 2011 [**http://blogs.wsj.com/**].

46. Alexander J.S. Colvin, "An Empirical Study of Employment Arbitration: Case Outcomes and Processes," *Journal of Empirical Legal Studies* 8, Issue 1, (March 2011), p. 1.

47. *AT&T Mobility v. Vincent Concepcion,* 2011 U.S. LEXIS 3367.

48. See related proceedings *Geographic Expeditions, Inc. v. Lhotka,* 2010 U.S. LEXIS 6305.

49. "An Economist Out to Be Sued," *Los Angeles Times,* October 8, 1990, p. D1.

50. Morgan O. Reynolds, "Europe Surpasses America—in Crime," *The Wall Street Journal,* October 16, 1998, p. A14.

51. Dubuque, Iowa Ordinance No. 28-11, March 21, 2011 and Andy Piper, "Police: Ordinance Will ID Derelict Parents," *Dubuque Telegraph Herald,* March 23, 2011 [**http://www.thonline.com/article.cfm?id=315715**].

52. Darrell Dusina, "Lawyers, Everywhere," *The Wall Street Journal,* November 23, 1998, p. A23.

53. Warren Avis, "Court before Justice," *The New York Times,* July 21, 1978, p. 25.

54. Alain Clement, "Judges, Lawyers Are the Ruling Class in U.S. Society," *The Washington Post,* August 22, 1980, p. A25.

55. Associated Press, "Illinois Man Imprisoned for 26 Years Declared Innocent," *Springfield State Journal-Register,* April 17, 2009 [**http://www.sj-r.com/**] and "26-Year Secret Kept Innocent Man in Prison," "60 Minutes," March 8, 2008 [**http://truthinjustice.org/alton-logan.htm**].

56. Percy Luney, "Traditions and Foreign Influences: Systems of Law in China and Japan," *Law and Contemporary Problems* 52 (Spring 1989), pp. 129, 136.

CHAPTER FIVE

Constitutional Law and the Bill of Rights

After completing this chapter, students will be able to:

1. Recognize the purposes of the U.S. Constitution.

2. Describe the separation of powers under the U.S. Constitution.

3. Identify the freedoms protected under the First Amendment.

4. Describe the powerful role the Bill of Rights plays in protecting personal freedoms.

5. Discuss the differences between First Amendment protections of commercial speech versus political speech.

6. Explain the "exclusionary rule."

7. Describe some of the issues arising under the Fourth Amendment "search and seizure" rules.

8. Describe the law of the Fifth Amendment "Takings Clause" and the property rights controversy associated with it.

9. Compare and contrast substantive due process and procedural due process.

10. Identify some examples of the impact of the Equal Protection Clause on business and society.

We the people of the United States, in order to form a more perfect union, establish justice, insure domestic tranquility, provide for the common defense, promote the general welfare, and secure the blessings of liberty to ourselves and our posterity, do ordain and establish this Constitution for the United States of America.

The Preamble to our Constitution summarizes the founders' lofty goals for America. The idealism embodied in the Preamble is both inspiring and touching. In reading it, we should reflect on the dream of America and the Constitution's role in molding and protecting that entirely new image of a nation. That we continue to be guided, more than 220 years later, by those rather few words is testimony to the brilliance and wisdom of its creators and to our determination to build a free, democratic, just society. Our Constitution is a remarkable document, so powerful in its ideas and images that it has helped reshape the world.

Creating a Constitution—The United States

You may recall that the Constitution grew out of the Articles of Confederation as enacted by Congress in 1778. The Articles contemplated a "firm league of friendship," but each state was to maintain its "sovereignty, freedom, and independence." The Articles soon proved faulty. Seven years of war had basically bankrupted the colonies. Currency was largely worthless. The 13 new states fought over economic resources, interstate disputes were routine, and the federal union that emerged under the Articles of Confederation had little real authority. As a result of this distress, and in an effort to strengthen the Articles, the Constitutional Convention was called to order in Philadelphia on May 25, 1787.

The decision to convene the Convention may have been a first in world history in that the state leaders themselves acknowledged that the existing federal government was faulty, the citizenry calmly talked things over, violence was avoided, and the decision was made to go forward with the Convention. In the hot Philadelphia summer, with windows and curtains closed to assure secrecy (as a means of encouraging open debate), the often chubby and usually heavily clothed delegates sweated their way toward a new government. All 55 delegates, our Founding Fathers, were white males, and most of them were wealthy landowners, but they were also immensely talented with a wide range of interests and experiences.

> All 55 delegates, our Founding Fathers, were white males.

The delegates agreed that a stronger central government was needed, but they were split on just how far that notion should go. Virginia, led by the brilliant James Madison, favored a dominant central government with greatly diminished state authority. Alexander Hamilton wanted to go further yet by, among other things, instituting the presidency as a lifetime office. On the other hand, several states, led by New Jersey, wanted to retain strong states' rights. After weeks of debate, a middle ground began to emerge that led toward our current balance of power between big states and small states and between all of the states and the central government. In the end, the delegates reached consensus on a Constitution that guaranteed the revolutionary notion of rule by the people.

On September 17, 1787, the great document, one of the most influential expressions in human history, was formally signed. Following bitter disputes in some states, the Constitution was ratified and the new government haltingly moved forward under the leadership of George Washington and John Adams.[1] [For links to national constitutions around the globe, see **http://confinder.richmond.edu**]

A Right to Bear Arms

Addressing one of the most contentious questions in American constitutional history, the U.S. Supreme Court in 2008 ruled 5–4 that the Second Amendment (see Appendix A) guarantees individual Americans a fundamental right to bear arms. The Supreme Court's four conservative justices, joined by the more moderate Justice Kennedy, ruled that individuals have a constitutional right to keep loaded arms for self-defense, at least in the home. The majority view was based on its reading of the historical record associated with the Second Amendment, while the four dissenting, liberal justices argued that the Second

Amendment guaranteed only a collective right to bear arms in a militia. The decision was the first conclusive interpretation of the Second Amendment since it was ratified in 1791.

The decision struck down a District of Columbia law that effectively banned handgun possession. Security guard Dick Heller applied for and was denied a permit for a handgun in his home located in a dangerous Washington, D.C. neighborhood. He sued the District arguing that the gun ban violated his individual rights under the Second Amendment. The Court did preserve the constitutionality of "reasonable" gun regulations and Justice Scalia, writing for the majority, said nothing in the ruling should "cast doubt on long-standing prohibitions on the possession of firearms by felons or the mentally ill, or laws forbidding the carrying of firearms in sensitive places such as schools and government buildings, or laws imposing conditions and qualifications on the commercial sale of arms." "Dangerous and unusual" weapons also could be banned.

As expected, the Supreme Court in a 2010 decision, *McDonald v. Chicago,*[2] extended the *Heller* Second Amendment ruling (applying only to federal jurisdictions) to all states and cities. The legal battle now shifts to a city-by-city constitutional challenge to gun rules. For example, Washington, DC, responded to the Supreme Court's *Heller* ruling by re-writing its gun rules to promote safety while meeting Second Amendment requirements. Those more focused rules require firearms registration while prohibiting assault weapons and "large capacity ammunition feeding devices." Predictably, those new rules are being challenged in court.[3]

Questions

1. As you interpret the Second Amendment, did the Supreme Court reach a *correct* decision in the *Heller* case? Explain.

2. In Chicago, 32 public school students died of gunshot wounds in 2009.[4] In all of Australia in 2008, by contrast, 30 people died by gun homicide.[5] As a matter of public policy, did the Supreme Court reach a *wise* decision in the *Heller* case? Explain.

Sources: District of Columbia v. Dick Anthony Heller, 2008 U.S. LEXIS 5268; and Dina Temple-Raston, "Supreme Court: Individuals Have Right to Bear Arms," National Public Radio, June 27, 2008 [**http://www.npr.org/ templates/story.php?storyId=91911807**].

Structure and Purpose

The U.S. Constitution is reprinted as Appendix A in the back of this book. Take a moment to review the Constitution's structure and purposes.

The Preamble identifies certain goals for our society, such as unity (among the various states), justice, domestic tranquility (peace), defense from outsiders, increasing general welfare, and liberty. Article I creates Congress and enumerates its powers. Article I, Section 8, Clause 3 is particularly important because it gives Congress the power to regu-late commerce (the Commerce Clause). Article II sets up the executive branch, headed by the president, while Article III establishes the court system. Articles IV and VI, as well as the 14th Amendment, address the relationship between the federal government and the states. Article VI provides in Clause 2 (the Supremacy Clause) for the supremacy of federal law over state law. Article V provides for amendments to the Constitution. The first 10 amendments, known as the Bill of Rights, were ratified by the states and put into effect in 1791. The remaining 17 amendments (11 through 27) were adopted at various times from 1798 through 1992.

From this review we can see that the Constitution serves a number of broad roles:

1. It establishes a national government.
2. It controls the relationship between the national government and the government of the states.
3. It defines and preserves personal liberty.
4. It contains provisions to enable the government to perpetuate itself.[6]

The Founding Fathers—Should We Move On?

Author Mark Kurlansky argues that the Founding Fathers' great accomplishment is losing its luster:

> I am sick and tired of the founding fathers and all their intents. The real American question of our times is how our country in a little over 200 years sank from the great hope to the most backward democracy in the West. The U.S. offers the worst healthcare program, one of the worst public school systems and the worst benefits for workers. The margin between rich and poor has been growing precipitously while it has been decreasing in Europe. Among the great democracies, we use military might less cautiously, show less respect for international law and are the stumbling block in international environmental cooperation. Few informed people look to the United States anymore for progressive ideas. We ought to do something. Instead, we keep worrying about the vision of a bunch of sexist, slave-owning 18th century white men in wigs and breeches.

*   *   *   *   *

> So let us stop worshiping the founding fathers and allow our minds to progress and try to build a nation of great new ideas.

Source: Mark Kurlansky, "WWFFD? Who Cares," *Los Angeles Times*, July 4, 2006 [**http://www.latimes. com/ news/opinion/la-oe-kurlansky4jul04,0,2811373.story?track=totext**].

Government Power and Constitutional Restraints

Among other goals, the Constitution was designed to protect the citizenry from the government. The Constitution does not protect citizens from purely private concentrations of power, such as large corporations. In fact, corporations themselves are often entitled to the protections of the Constitution. The Constitution divides governmental power between the federal and state governments. Congressional authority is formally limited to certain *enumerated powers* (Article I, Section 8), such as the authority to regulate commerce. The 10th Amendment provides that all power not expressly accorded to the federal government in the Constitution resides in the states or the people. Certain constitutional checks or restraints, including the Bill of Rights, limit how far Congress can reach even within its enumerated powers. In practice, however, those enumerated powers have been expansively interpreted giving Congress extensive authority in American life. Furthermore, in the landmark 1819 Supreme Court decision, *McCulloch v. Maryland*,[7] the U.S. Supreme Court interpreted the Necessary and Proper Clause (Article I, Section 8) to afford Congress those implied powers necessary to execute the enumerated powers thus achieving a workable national government. The *McCulloch* court also ruled that the Constitution's Supremacy Clause (Article VI—"This Constitution and the Laws of the United States . . . shall be the Supreme Law of the Land.") nullifies state action that conflicts with federal law. Thus, in one sweeping decision, the Supreme Court dramatically expanded the power of Congress and certified the federal government's superior authority relative to the states.

Too Much Government?

Has that federal power and regulation gone too far? Massive federal intervention in the economy to combat the "Great Recession," to deal with the subprime mortgage crisis, and to reform banking practices (see Chapter 8) generated renewed pleas for restraints on an "overreaching" federal government. The "Tea Party" movement emerged in 2009, and a heated national debate ensued about the appropriate balance between individual rights as expressed in the free market versus an interventionist federal government designed to correct market failures and protect those least able to care for themselves.

> The "Tea Party" movement emerged.

Separation of Powers

As a further means of controlling the power of government, the Constitution sets up the three federal branches and provides mechanisms for them to act as checks and balances on each other. The President, Congress, and the courts each have specialized areas of authority, as provided for by the Constitution. Congress has the sole power to legislate at the federal level, whereas the president, among other things, executes laws, makes treaties, and commands the armed forces; the Supreme Court and the inferior courts have judicial authority at the federal level. The result is a system of separation of powers designed to prevent too much authority from residing in any one branch. Thus, the president has the power to veto acts of Congress, those vetoes can be overridden by a two-thirds vote of each house, and the judiciary can find those acts unconstitutional.

The role of the judiciary has been a matter of particular controversy in recent years. The groundbreaking 1803 *Marbury v. Madison* decision[8] was the first time the Supreme Court had declared an act of Congress unconstitutional, and the decision also established the principle of judicial review; that is, the power of the courts to consider and, if necessary, invalidate congressional and executive branch decisions. Although neither of those powers was expressly provided for in the Constitution, the Court considered them to be implicit in the legal structure created by the Constitution. Critics today argue that the *Marbury* reasoning has been stretched too far and that, in effect, courts have been making law, rather than merely interpreting it. Those critics say that federal and state judicial decisions finding a "constitutional right" to, for example, abortion or same-sex marriage, have reduced the authority of our directly elected legislators and placed too much power in the hands of jurists who are necessarily somewhat removed from the weight of public opinion.[9] On the other hand, an aggressive judiciary has played a crucial role in the advance of justice and the protection of personal freedom. [For the National Constitution Center, see **http://www.constitutioncenter.org**]

Questions

1. *a.* As noted, the Constitution does not expressly authorize judicial review. Should we, therefore, assume that the framers of the Constitution did not intend to afford that power to the courts?

   b. In your view, do the courts have too much power in our lives? Explain.

Federalism

The U.S. government is built on *federalism* principles; that is, the Constitution provides for shared power among national, state, and local governments. A primary role of the Constitution is to balance central federal authority with dispersed state power. The resulting division of power between the federal government and the states is a key battleground in our ongoing liberal–conservative cultural and political war. The American Civil War was provoked in part because of differing conceptions of federalism. Southerners held the view, labeled *states rights,* that each state was entitled to make its own policy decisions about crucial matters such as slavery, while Northerners favored a strong central government. That constitutional divide over federalism persists today. Many "conservative" Americans distrust big government and favor bringing power as close to the people as possible. They think the federal government has often exercised authority beyond its express constitutional powers. "Liberals," on the other hand, tend to fear local biases and favor a more unified national approach to issues such as regulation of business, educational policy, medical care, and civil rights.

The Commerce Clause and the New Federalism

The Constitution's Commerce Clause (Article 1, Section 8, Clause 3) gives the federal government the power to regulate commerce among the states and with other nations. The Supreme Court, beginning with the New Deal era 1930s, had interpreted the Commerce Clause in a flexible, expansive manner that allowed steadily increased power in Washington, D.C. Then in the mid-1990s, the Supreme Court re-visited the federal-state balance with some decisions curbing federal authority. No major federal initiative was struck down, but the Court's attention to limits on federal power signaled legislators and lower courts to look more closely at the balance of power between the federal and state governments.

The intensity of the new federalism debate currently is most evident in the ongoing battle over immigration control in which some states, feeling the federal government has not been aggressive enough, have passed their own laws to curb illegal immigration. Does federal law *preempt* (supersede) state laws regulating immigration? (As noted above, under the Supremacy Clause state law must yield to conflicting federal law.) In a 2011 decision, the U.S. Supreme Court ruled that an Arizona law instructing the courts to suspend or revoke the business licenses (e.g., articles of incorporation) of in-state employers who knowingly or intentionally employ unauthorized immigrants was not preempted by the federal Immigration Reform and Control Act (IRCA—see Chapter12).[10]

On the other hand, at this writing, a three-judge panel of the Ninth Circuit Court of Appeals has struck down a second Arizona immigration law that, among other things, requires police officers to check the immigration status of individuals detained or arrested for some other violation if the officer has a reasonable suspicion that those individuals are in Arizona illegally. Critics are alarmed that the statute will lead to police "profiling" based on ethnic characteristics. While the reasoning differed among the three judges, the core conclusion was that federal immigration law has preempted what Arizona was attempting to do. [See *United States of America v. State of Arizona, 2011 U.S. App. LEXIS 7413.*] That decision is expected to be appealed, and the preemption debate continues on a case-by-case basis.

> The statute will lead
> to "profiling."

The Constitution, the Bill of Rights, and Business

The Constitution and, in particular, the Commerce Clause profoundly shape the practice of American business. Indeed, in some important ways, the Constitution is a commercial document reflecting the economic interests of the framers. We will defer further discussion of the Commerce Clause and the Supremacy Clause until Chapter 8. In this chapter we will devote our attention primarily to the Bill of Rights, which serves to limit the powers of the federal government and the states. When we think of the Bill of Rights, corporations ordinarily do not come to mind. Extensive litigation in recent years, however, serves notice that the relationship between the corporate "person" and the fundamental freedoms is both important and unclear.

The Bill of Rights protects our personal freedoms (speech, religion, and more) from encroachment by the federal government. Furthermore, the Supreme Court has ruled that the Due Process Clause of the 14th Amendment, which is directed at the states, absorbs or incorporates those fundamental freedoms and protects them against intrusion by state governments. [For the "Guide to Law Online," prepared by the U.S. Law Library of Congress, see **http://www.loc.gov/law/help/guide.php**]

The First Amendment

Congress shall make no law respecting an establishment of religion, or prohibiting the free exercise thereof; or abridging the freedom of speech, or the press; or the right of the people peaceably to assemble, and to petition the Government for a redress of grievances.

These few words constitute one of the most powerful and noble utterances in history. Much of the magnificence that we often associate with America is embodied in the protections of the First Amendment. After more than 220 years, we must feel some sense of wonder that our nearly 312 million independent citizens continue to rely on that sentence as a cornerstone of American life. [For the First Amendment Center, see **http://www.firstamendmentcenter.org/**]

1. Freedom of Religion

Christianity in the U.S. Constitution?

A 2007 national survey by the nonpartisan First Amendment Center found that 55 percent of Americans incorrectly believe that the Constitution established the United States as an explicitly Christian nation. In fact, the Constitution clearly established a nation where those of every faith as well as those with no faith are equally protected from government interference. Fifty-eight percent of the respondents said that teachers should be allowed to lead prayers. More than one fourth of the respondents said that constitutional protection of religion does not apply to "extreme" groups. Scholars say that many Americans, especially since 9/11, consider Islam to be an "extreme" religion.

Source: Andrea Stone, "55% in Poll Say Christianity in Constitution," *The Des Moines Register,* September 12, 2007, p. 1A.

The First Amendment forbids (1) the establishment of an official state religion (the Establishment Clause) and (2) undue state interference with religious practice (the Free Exercise Clause). Government may neither encourage nor discourage the practice of religion generally, nor may it give preference to one religion over another. Broadly, the idea of the First Amendment is to maintain a separation between church and state. The precise boundary of that separation, however, has become one of the more contentious social issues in contemporary life. Prayer in the schools and Ten Commandment displays have received extensive publicity, but the debate is widespread. Consider a pair of interesting recent cases. [For the Freedom Forum database on the First Amendment, see **http://www.freedomforum.org**]

God, the Pledge, and Currency

Addressing two longstanding sources of constitutional ferment, three-judge panels of the 9th U.S. Circuit Court of Appeals in 2010 ruled that the use of the words "Under God" in the Pledge of Allegiance and "In God We Trust" on U.S. currency do not violate the separation of church and state principles of the First Amendment.

An atheist, Michael Newdow, said those references amount to an endorsement of religion thus violating the Establishment Clause of the First Amendment. Newdow argued that the phrase, "Under God," was placed in the Pledge for religious purposes. Indeed, the Pledge was amended in 1954 to include the words, "Under God," and some members of Congress, at the time, said it was needed to distinguish the United States from "Godless Communists."[11] The panel, however, saw the Pledge of Allegiance as an expression of American ideals rather than a religious endorsement. Students are not required to recite the pledge.[12] As to currency, a separate panel said that the phrase "In God We Trust" is simply patriotic and ceremonial and has nothing to do with the establishment of religion.[13]

Godless Communists.

God and Student Organizations

The University of California Hastings College of the Law refused to recognize a student organization, the Christian Legal Society (CLS). Hastings said the group's faith-based rules discriminate against gays, lesbians, and others who do not share the group's religious beliefs. The organization's rules require members to pledge they will not engage in a "sexually immoral lifestyle" including "all acts of sexual conduct outside God's design for marriage between one man and one woman." Thus to Hastings officials, the Pledge represented discrimination based on religion and sexual orientation, while CLS members regarded it as an expression of faith. CLS challenged Hastings' policy as a violation of the member students' First Amendment rights to freedom of religion, speech and association. The U.S. Supreme Court, by a 5–4 margin, ruled in 2010 that the students' constitutional rights were not violated in that the University policy was a reasonable, viewpoint-neutral condition on access to student recognition in a public university. The majority reasoned that Hastings was concerned about the group's exclusionary conduct, rather than its religious beliefs. That is, all student groups must be open to all students. Dissenting justices said the decision supported suppression of unpopular and politically incorrect speech.[14]

Burqas, Niqabs, and Crosses in Europe

France, in 2011, began enforcing its new law forbidding, with some exceptions, the wearing of a garment in public that hides the wearer's face. The law was promoted as a matter of security and of cultural assimilation while it was assailed as an affront to the Muslim faith and a political move designed to appeal to voters worried about threats to traditional European values and culture. Only an estimated 2,000 women of the five million French Muslims are believed to wear burqas or niqabs covering the face.

Addressing a similar cultural divide, the European Court of Human Rights in 2011 approved by a 15–2 vote the presence of crucifixes in European public schools. The Court ruled that the crucifix is now an historical and cultural symbol rather than an exclusively religious expression. The crucifix is not a means of indoctrination, the court said, but rather an expression of cultural and religious identity in traditionally Christian countries.

Sources: Robert Marquand, "Face Veil Ban: Will France Take a Hard Line?" *The Christian Science Monitor,* April 11, 2011 [**http://www.csmonitor.com/**]; and Stanley Fish, "Crucifixes and Diversity: The Odd Couple," *The New York Times,* March 28, 2011 [**http://opinionator.blogs.nytimes.com/**].

---

2. Freedom of Speech

Hustler Magazine publisher Larry Flynt: "If the First Amendment will protect a scumbag like me, then it will protect all of you. Because I am the worst."[15]

Freedom of speech is the primary guarantor of the American approach to life. Not only is it indispensable to democracy and personal dignity, but Americans believe that the free expression of ideas is the most likely path to the best ideas. We believe in a marketplace of ideas just as we believe in a marketplace of goods.

> We cannot freely yell "Fire" in a crowded theater.

Freedom of speech is not absolute. Clearly we cannot freely make slanderous statements about others, publicly utter obscenities at will, speak "fighting words" that are likely to produce a clear and present danger of violence, or yell "Fire" in a crowded theater.

At the same time, in general, the state cannot tell us what we can say; that is, the state cannot, for the most part, regulate the *content* of our speech. On the other hand, the state does have greater authority to regulate the *context* of that speech; that is, the state may be able to restrict where, when, and how we say certain things if that regulation is necessary to preserve compelling state interests. We have broad free speech rights in so-called *public forums* such as downtown business districts, parks, college campuses, and public plazas. Even in those places, however, the state may need to impose reasonable time and manner regulations. Thus, although the Ku Klux Klan can express hatred for black people (the content of the message), the state may restrict where and when and how those expressions are made (the context of the message) if necessary for the public safety. [For freedom of speech links, see **http://gjs.net/freetalk.htm**]

Content, Location, and Method of Expression

The message itself, where and when it is uttered, and the form in which it is expressed can all be subjects of dispute in free speech cases.

Content: Vile Words   One of the most controversial Supreme Court cases of recent years involved the Topeka, Kansas, Westboro Baptist Church and its practice of protesting at the funerals of American soldiers killed in service. Pastor Fred W. Phelps and his small congregation, most of whom are family members, contend that battlefield deaths are God's punishment for America's sins, including homosexuality. The funeral protests include signs displaying messages such as "Thank God for dead soldiers," and "God Hates Fags." Pastor Phelps and his family picketed the 2006 funeral of Matthew

God's punishment for America's sins.

Snyder, a Marine who had been killed in Iraq. Snyder's father sued Phelps and Westboro and won a $10.9 million damage award (reduced by the judge to $5 million) based on his claims of invasion of privacy and intentional infliction of emotional distress. That decision was reversed on appeal, and the case reached the U.S. Supreme Court in 2011 where the Church's First Amendment freedom of expression argument prevailed by an 8–1 margin.[16] The majority ruled that the Westboro protests addressed matters of public importance on a public street at a distance from the funeral (approximately 1,000 feet) specified by authorities. The picketing was quiet and without violence. Chief Justice Roberts, who wrote the opinion, said: "Any distress occasioned by Westboro's picketing turned on the content and viewpoint of the message conveyed rather than any interference with the funeral itself."[17]

Thus, the Court's unpopular decision affirmed the longstanding position that the government ordinarily cannot restrict speech based on its content, however tasteless or valueless. As lawyer and commentator Adam Cohen said about the Westboro speech, "We defend it not because these ideas are particularly worthy of being protected, but because all ideas, even the most loathsome, are."[18] In your view, are the Westboro protests so odious and so wanting in value that we should carve out an exception denying First Amendment protection?

The Supreme Court continued its aggressive affirmation of free speech rights in the 2011 *Brown v. Entertainment Merchants Association* case (2011 U.S. LEXIS 4802), when it struck down a California statute restricting the sale or rental of violent video games to minors, ruling that the law was a content-based restriction that violated the First Amendment. (See Chapter 8 for more details.)

Location: Speech at School Joseph Frederick was across the street from his school with many other students watching, with school permission, an Olympic torch parade

> "Bong Hits 4 Jesus."

when Frederick, a Juneau, Alaska, high school senior, and some friends unfurled a large banner reading "Bong Hits 4 Jesus." The banner was a prank designed to attract attention from television cameras. The school principal, Deborah Morse, told Frederick to lower the banner. He refused, and he was suspended from school. Frederick sued, and the case reached the U.S. Supreme Court. Does the First Amendment protect Frederick? [See *Deborah Morse v. Joseph Frederick,* 127 S.Ct. 2618 (2007).]

Method: Speech Without Words Speech is communicated in a variety of ways. First Amendment protection clearly extends to expression in forms other than actual verbiage or writing. In a leading case in this area, the Supreme Court extended First Amendment protection to the wearing of black armbands to high school as a protest against the Vietnam War where no evidence of disruption was presented.[19]

Public Sector Workers Off the Job? On the Job?

Indiana Deputy Attorney General Jeffrey Cox was fired in early 2011 reportedly for comments he made off the job on Twitter. Under the online name JCCentCom, Cox

> "You're damned right I advocate deadly force."

tweeted that "live ammunition" should be used against demonstrators who had gathered in the Wisconsin state capitol building to protest a proposed change in Wisconsin labor law. Reportedly, he called the demonstrators "political enemies" and "thugs," and further said, "You're damned right I advocate deadly force." Does the First Amendment protect Cox in his *off-the-job* remarks? In announcing Cox's dismissal, the Indiana Attorney General's office said:

> . . . We respect individuals' First Amendment right to express their personal views on private online forums, but as public servants we are held by the public to a higher standard, and we should strive for civility.[20]

Generally, the First Amendment shields public sector workers' off-the-job expression when speaking as citizens about matters of public concern, although employer restrictions necessary to effective operation of the enterprise may be permissible. In this case, law professor Jonathan Turley thinks the facts, if proved, would support a strong free speech claim for Cox.[21]

We can much more confidently say that government employees' free speech rights *on the job* can be quite limited. Los Angeles Deputy District Attorney Richard Ceballos lost his job in a whistle-blowing episode. Ceballos sued and the case reached the U.S. Supreme Court in 2006. By a 5–4 vote, the Court ruled that government employees who speak out "pursuant to their official duties" are not protected by the First Amendment. They are speaking as employees, not as citizens, and therefore, the First Amendment does not insulate them from discipline, regardless of the content of their message. The Court also pointed to the importance of the government being able to maintain efficiency and order in the workplace.[22]

Politically Correct Speech

We are largely free of government restraints on what we can say, but should it be so? Is free speech often too hurtful to be tolerated? Radio shock jock Don Imus drew widespread public attention to "politically correct" speech in referring to the 2007 Rutgers women's basketball team, made up largely of black students, as "nappy headed hos," a remark for which Imus was fired. New editions of the Mark Twain novels, *Adventures of Huckleberry Finn* and *Tom Sawyer,* have recently been published with the "N-word" being replaced by the word "slave" in an effort to avoid disturbing readers. Disputes about offensive language often arise in university life where the law requires policies to curb and punish civil rights violations, including racial and sexual harassment (see Chapter 13.) As a result, many universities have

> Many universities have "speech codes."

"speech codes" of one form or another designed to stop hate speech, harassment, bullying, and other offensive conduct. The University of Miami, for example, prohibits "any words or acts . . . which cause or result in physical or emotional harm to others, or which threaten, haze or otherwise interfere with another person's rightful actions or comfort."[23] The codes are designed to maintain safe, civil learning environments that embrace diverse cultures, but critics argue that the restraints are unconstitutionally vague and that they amount to a demand for politically correct speech; that is, speech that avoids hurtful words.

Yale Complaints of a hostile sexual environment and intimidation of female students caused Yale University in 2011 to impose a five-year ban on all campus activities for a prestigious fraternity that counts both Bush presidents among its alumni. One of the complaints involved the fraternity's pledges chanting, "No means yes! Yes means anal!" outside a women's dormitory area. Other, more individualized and more threatening concerns were also raised. The federal government is investigating to determine if civil rights violations have occurred.[24] To what extent should university officials and the government be able to curb student speech, however infantile and offensive, in order to achieve a laudable goal?

> "The right to provoke, offend, and shock lies at the core of the First Amendment."

Maricopa A number of university speech codes have been invalidated as violations of First Amendment rights.[25] Recently, a Maricopa County Community College (Arizona) math instructor won a 9th Circuit U.S. Court of Appeals decision involving his right to send racially charged emails over the school district-maintained server to all employees with an email address. Professor Walter Kehowski sent three messages declaring, for example, that: "It's time to acknowledge and celebrate the superiority of Western Civilization." On his university-maintained Web site, he said, "[t]he only immigration reform imperative is preservation of White majority (sic)." A group of Hispanic employees then sued the school district claiming that it had failed to properly respond to Kehowski's remarks thus allowing the creation of a hostile work environment. The Court of Appeals, however, ruled that the emails addressed matters of public concern and were protected by the First Amendment and thus could not constitute illegal harassment. The Court did note that some workplace harassment, such as racial insults or sexual advances toward particular individuals, may be prohibited because it lacks the expressive quality of speech directed toward a larger audience.[26]

"Be Happy, Not Gay"

Following a day designated to show support for gays and lesbians at her high school in Naperville, Illinois, student Heidi Zamecnik wore a T-shirt to school displaying the expression "Be Happy, Not Gay." The school's dean forbade the expression at the school. Another student, Alexander Nuxoll, unsuccessfully sought to wear a similar shirt. Both students objected to homosexuality on religious grounds. The two students subsequently sued the school for infringing their free speech rights. The 7th Circuit U.S. Circuit Court of Appeals reasoned that the forbidden expression did not constitute "fighting words" or some other recognized First Amendment exception and ruled that the students had a right to wear the shirts and express their opinions.

Judge Richard Posner said:

> [A] school that permits advocacy of the rights of homosexual students cannot be allowed to stifle criticism of homosexuality. The school argued (and still argues) that banning "Be Happy, Not Gay" was just a matter of protecting the "rights" of the students against whom derogatory comments are directed. But people in our society do not have a legal right to prevent criticism of their beliefs or even their way of life.

Source: Zamecnik and Nuxoll v. Indian Prairie School District, 2011 U.S. App. LEXIS 3874.

Ole Miss Universities have sometimes been accorded considerable latitude in dealing with speech issues. The 5th Circuit Court of Appeals, for example, upheld the right of the University of Mississippi to ban flags, including the Confederate flag, at campus events.[27] Specifically banning only the Confederate flag presumably would not have met with the Court's approval.

George Mason Many First Amendment scholars believe the correct antidote to hate speech is simply more speech; that is, they place their faith in the marketplace of ideas rather than in rules, however well intended. The decision that follows demonstrates the First Amendment's role in resolving claims of racism, sexism, and general insensitivity springing from a George Mason University fraternity's "ugly woman contest." [For a vigorous critique of campus "political correctness," see the Foundation for Individual Rights in Education at **http://thefire.org/**]

Senior Circuit Judge Sprouse

George Mason University appeals from a summary judgment granted by the district court to the IOTA XI Chapter of Sigma Chi Fraternity in its action for declaratory judgment and an injunction seeking to nullify sanctions imposed on it by the University because it conducted an "ugly woman contest" with racist and sexist overtones.

I

Sigma Chi has for two years held an annual "Derby Days" event, planned and conducted both as entertainment and as a source of funds for donations to charity. The "ugly woman contest," held on April 4, 1991, was one of the "Derby Days" events. The Fraternity staged the contest in the cafeteria of the student union. As part of the contest, eighteen Fraternity members were assigned to one of six sorority teams cooperating in events. The involved Fraternity members appeared in the contest dressed as caricatures of different types of women, including one member dressed as an offensive caricature of a black woman. He was painted black and wore stringy, black hair decorated with curlers, and his outfit was stuffed with pillows to exaggerate a woman's breasts and buttocks. He spoke in slang to parody African-Americans.

There is no direct evidence in the record concerning the subjective intent of the Fraternity members who conducted the contest. The Fraternity, which later apologized to the University officials for the presentation, conceded during the litigation that the contest was sophomoric and offensive.

Following the contest, a number of students protested to the University that the skit had been objectionably sexist and racist. Two hundred forty-seven students, many of them members of the foreign or minority student body, executed a petition, which stated, "[W]e are condemning the racist and sexist implications of this event in which male members dressed as women. One man in particular wore a black face, portraying a negative stereotype of black women."

Dean for Student Services Kenneth Bumgarner discussed the situation with representatives of the objecting students [and] student representatives of Sigma Chi. [The University decided to impose sanctions on Sigma Chi including] suspension from [most] activities for the rest of the 1991 spring semester and a two-year prohibition....

On June 5, 1991, Sigma Chi brought this action against the University and Dean Bumgarner. It requested declaratory judgment and injunctive relief to nullify the sanctions as violative of the First and Fourteenth Amendments. Sigma Chi moved for summary judgment on its First Amendment claims on June 28, 1991.

... University President George W. Johnson ... presented the "mission statement" of the University:

* * * * *

(3) George Mason University is committed to promoting a culturally and racially diverse student body.... Education here is not limited to the classroom.

(4) We are committed to teaching the values of equal opportunity and equal treatment, respect for diversity, and individual dignity.

(5) Our mission also includes achieving the goals set forth in our affirmative action plan, a plan incorporating affirmative steps designed to attract and retain minorities to this campus.

* * * * *

(7) George Mason University is a state institution of higher education and a recipient of federal funds.

* * * * *

The district court granted summary judgment to Sigma Chi on its First Amendment claim, 773 F.Supp. 792 (E.D. Va. 1991).

II (OMITTED-ED.)

III

We initially face the task of deciding whether Sigma Chi's "ugly woman contest" is sufficiently expressive to entitle it to First Amendment protection.

* * * * *

A

First Amendment principles governing live entertainment are relatively clear: Short of obscenity, it is generally protected. As the Supreme Court announced in *Schad v. Borough of Mount Ephraim*, 452 U.S. 61 (1981), "[e]ntertainment, as well as political and ideological speech, is protected; motion pictures, programs broadcast by radio and television, and live entertainment . . . fall within the First Amendment guarantee." Expression devoid of "ideas" but with entertainment value may also be protected because "[t]he line between the informing and the entertaining is too elusive." *Winters v. New York*, 333 U.S. 507, 510 (1948).

* * * * *

Even crude street skits come within the First Amendment's reach. In . . . *Schacht v. United States*, 398 U.S. 58, 61–62

(1970), . . . Justice Black [declared] that an actor participating in even a crude performance enjoys the constitutional right to freedom of speech.

Bearing on this dichotomy between low- and high-grade entertainment are the Supreme Court's holdings relating to nude dancing. See *Barnes v. Glen Theatre, Inc.,* 111 S.Ct. 2456, 2460 (1991).

[I]n *Barnes,* the Supreme Court conceded that nude dancing is expressive conduct entitled to First Amendment protection.

* * * * *

. . . [I]t appears that the low quality of entertainment does not necessarily weigh in the First Amendment inquiry. It would seem, therefore, that the Fraternity's skit, even as low-grade entertainment, was inherently expressive and thus entitled to First Amendment protection.

B

The University nevertheless contends that discovery will demonstrate that the contest does not merit characterization as a skit but only as mindless fraternity fun, devoid of any artistic expression. It argues further that entitlement to First Amendment protection exists only if the production was intended to convey a message likely to be understood by a particular audience. . . .

As indicated, we feel that the First Amendment protects the Fraternity's skit because it is inherently expressive entertainment. Even if this were not true, however, the skit, in our view, qualifies as expressive conduct under the test articulated in *Texas v. Johnson,* 491 U.S. 397 (1989). It is true that the *Johnson* test for determining the expressiveness of conduct requires "'[a]n intent to convey a particularized message'" and a great likelihood "'that the message would be understood by those who viewed it.'"

* * * * *

[T]he affidavits establish that the punishment was meted out to the Fraternity because its boorish message had interfered with the described University mission. It is manifest from these circumstances that the University officials thought the Fraternity intended to convey a message. The Fraternity members' apology and post-conduct contriteness suggest that they held the same view.

* * * * *

As to the second prong of the *Johnson* test, there was a great likelihood that at least some of the audience viewing the skit would understand the Fraternity's message of satire and humor. Some students paid to attend the performance and were entertained. . . .

* * * * *

. . . [W]e are persuaded that the Fraternity's "ugly woman contest" satisfies the *Johnson* test for expressive conduct.

IV

If this were not a sufficient response to the University's argument, the principles relating to content and viewpoint discrimination recently emphasized in *R.A.V. v. City of St. Paul,* 112 S.Ct. 2538 (1992), provide a definitive answer. Although the Court in St. Paul reviewed the constitutional effect of a city "hate speech" ordinance, and we review the constitutionality of sanctions imposed for violating University policy, St. Paul's rationale applies here with equal force. Noting that St. Paul's city ordinance prohibited displays of symbols that "arouse[d] anger, alarm, or resentment in others on the basis of race, color, creed, religion, or gender," but did not prohibit displays of symbols which would advance ideas of racial or religious equality, Justice Scalia stated, "The First Amendment does not permit St. Paul to impose special prohibitions on those speakers who express views on disfavored subjects."

As evidenced by their affidavits, University officials sanctioned Sigma Chi for the message conveyed by the "ugly woman contest" because it ran counter to the views the University sought to communicate to its students and the community. The mischief was the University's punishment of those who scoffed at its goals of racial integration and gender neutrality, while permitting, even encouraging, conduct that would further the viewpoint expressed in the University's goals and probably be embraced by a majority of society as well. "The First Amendment generally prevents government from proscribing . . . expressive conduct because of disapproval of the ideas expressed."

The University, however, urges us to weigh Sigma Chi's conduct against the substantial interests inherent in educational endeavors. We agree wholeheartedly that it is the University officials' responsibility, even their obligation, to achieve the goals they have set. On the other hand, a public university has many constitutionally permissible means to protect female and minority students. We must emphasize, as have other courts, that "the manner of [its action] cannot consist of selective limitations upon speech." The University should have accomplished its goals in some fashion other than silencing speech on the basis of its viewpoint.

Affirmed.

Questions

1. Is speech that consists merely of entertainment without benefit of meaningful ideas protected by the First Amendment? Explain.

2. Explain the Court's conclusion that the fraternity skit met the *Texas v. Johnson* test of "an intent to convey a particularized message" and a great likelihood "that the message would be understood by those who viewed it."

3. *a.* Should racist/sexist remarks be forbidden in college classrooms?

   b. The Stanford University speech code was ruled unconstitutional in 1995.[28] The Superior Court judge in that case said, among other things, that the code was "overbroad." What did he mean?

   c. Do we give too much attention to freedom of speech at the expense of community civility? Explain.

4. T.W., a minor, was suspended from school for three days after he drew a picture of a Confederate flag on a piece of paper. The Kansas school, Derby Unified, suspended T.W. because it believed he had violated the district's "Racial Harassment or Intimidation" policy, which prohibits students from possessing at school "any written material, either printed or in their own handwriting, that is racially divisive or creates ill will or hatred." Confederate flags were included in a list of prohibited items. The Court found that Derby Unified had a history of racial harassment. Were T.W.'s First Amendment rights violated? Explain. See *West v. Derby Unified School District # 260*, 206 F.3d 1358 (10th Cir. 2000); cert. den. 531 U.S. 825 (2000).

5. The U.S. Supreme Court and lower federal courts have repeatedly ruled that burning the American flag is speech protected by the First Amendment. Congress often considers a flag protection amendment to the Constitution to make flag burning illegal. A 2005 Gallup Poll found 55 percent of Americans favoring that amendment.[29] How would you vote? Explain.

Free Speech in Cyberspace?

A 10-year battle in Congress and the courts may have ended in 2009 when the Supreme Court declined to review a Third Circuit U.S. Court of Appeals decision striking down the federal Child Online Protection Act as a violation of First Amendment freedom of speech protections. The struggle to create a constitutionally permissible piece of legislation to protect children from online smut was commendable in its goal but deficient in its execution. Basically, the Supreme Court, in its several reviews of COPA has been concerned about the content-based nature of the act's restraint on speech, and the Court considered COPA to be overbroad in the sense that its goal of protecting children might have been achieved with less restrictive means, including software filters, that would not threaten speech of interest to adults. Thus, we can conclude that online speech enjoys full First Amendment protections, although computer storage or online sale of sexually explicit material involving children is not protected.

Questions

1. Activist Phyllis Schlafly:

   Do you ever wonder why the Internet is so polluted with pornography? The Supreme Court just reminded us why: It blocks every attempt by Congress to regulate the pornographers. The court props open the floodgates for smut and graphic sex. . . .[30]

   Do you think we should be less concerned about First Amendment rights and more about the welfare of children who may be exposed to online pornography? Explain.

Sources: Editorial, "A Win for Free Speech Online," *The New York Times,* January 27, 2009 [**http://www.nytimes.com**]; and *American Civil Liberties Union v. Michael B. Mukasey,* 534 F.3d 181(3d Cir. 2008) cert. den. *Mukasey v. ACLU,* 2009 U.S. LEXIS 598.

Commercial Speech

Governments often want to regulate commercial expressions ranging from advertisements and billboards to real estate "for sale" signs and circulars placed on car windshields. Does the First Amendment protect those messages from government intervention in the same manner that it protects political speech? In 1942 the U.S. Supreme Court ruled that *commercial speech* was not entitled to First Amendment protection.[31] Subsequently the Court changed its stance and extended First Amendment rights to commercial speech, but those rights were much more limited than for political speech. In more recent years the Court has been gradually expanding protection for commercial speech.

Corporate/Commercial Speech Should corporations enjoy full First Amendment rights? Can we properly think of corporate political expressions as commercial speech? Or is commercial speech limited to those expressions that propose a commercial transaction? Experts differ on these questions, but their importance is evident if we think for a moment about the controversial 2010 *Citizens United* decision allowing corporations to spend more freely on elections (discussed previously in Chapter 3).[32] In the late 1970s Justices William Rehnquist and Byron White had described corporations as "creatures of the law" possessed of wealth-creation powers but not entitled to the rights possessed by voters. By contrast, the *Citizens United* majority described corporations as "associations of citizens" deserving of free speech rights in the manner of individuals.[33] Justice Scalia said: "To exclude or impede corporate speech is to muzzle the principal agents of the modern economy." "We should celebrate rather than condemn the addition of this speech to the public debate."[34] This shift in constitutional interpretation reflects, according to a *Los Angeles Times* analysis, the President Ronald Reagan-era efforts to reduce government regulation of business. All five justices in the *Citizens United* majority were either appointed to the Court by Reagan or worked as young lawyers in the Reagan administration.[35] Hence, the law reflects, to some extent, shifting political views. Do you think a corporation is a "creature of the law" or an "association of citizens?" If we treat corporations as citizens with full First Amendment rights will governments retain their present capacity to regulate corporate conduct?

Car for Sale

Glendale, Ohio, authorities threatened Christopher Pagan with a citation when he put a small "For Sale" sign in the window of his 1970 Mercury Cougar that he parked on the street in front of his house. The sign violated a Glendale ordinance forbidding parking cars for sale on any village streets, public or private, and it forbade parking for the purpose of "any advertising." Pagan had to remove the sign, but he sued Glendale claiming the parking ordinance violated his constitutional rights.

Questions
1. What constitutional challenge was Pagan raising?
2. Defend Glendale.
3. Decide the case. Explain.

Source: Pagan v. Fruchy, 492 F.3d 766 (6th Cir. 2007).

Animal Cruelty Commercial speech disputes raise very difficult legal questions in a wide variety of venues. The Supreme Court in 2010 supported the First Amendment rights of a business selling videos depicting animal cruelty. Robert J. Stevens advertised and sold pit-bull-related videos showing dog fights and dogs attacking wild boar. Stevens was criminally indicted for violating a federal statute forbidding knowingly creating, selling or possessing "a depiction of animal cruelty" to be sold for commercial gain in interstate or foreign commerce. Stevens moved to dismiss the indictment saying that the statute violated his First Amendment right to free speech. The Supreme Court, in an 8–1 ruling, agreed with Stevens by finding the federal statute overbroad in that it could legitimately be applied to legal activities such as hunting or the inhumane treatment of livestock as well as to the dog fights Stevens filmed.[36]

> Selling videos depicting animal cruelty.

In an illustration of the balance of powers concept, Congress and President Obama quickly approved new federal legislation designed to attack certain animal cruelty videos while meeting constitutional requirements. The Animal Crush Video Prohibition Act of 2010 bans the creation and distribution of obscene animal torture videos. Those videos often depict women in high heels slowly crushing small animals, images that appeal to certain sexual fetishists. By limiting the law to obscene crush videos, Congress and the president believe the statute will address the overbreadth problem while fitting the statute into the well-settled obscenity exception to the First Amendment's speech protections.

The *Bad Frog* decision below examines the question of free speech protection for beer advertising.

Bad Frog Brewery v. New York State Liquor Authority

LEGAL BRIEFCASE   134 F.3d 87 (2d Cir. 1998)

Judge Newman

BACKGROUND

Bad Frog is a Michigan corporation that manufactures and markets several different types of alcoholic beverages under its "Bad Frog" trademark. This action concerns labels used by the company in the marketing of Bad Frog Beer, Bad Frog Lemon Lager, and Bad Frog Malt Liquor. Each label prominently features an artist's rendering of a frog holding up its four-"fingered" right "hand," with the back of the "hand" shown, the second "finger" extended, and the other three "fingers" slightly curled.

Bad Frog does not dispute that the frog depicted in the label artwork is making the gesture generally known as "giving the finger" and that the gesture is widely regarded as an offensive insult, conveying a message that the company has characterized as "traditionally . . . negative and nasty." Versions of the label feature slogans such as "He just don't care," "An amphibian with an attitude," "Turning bad into good," and "The beer so good . . . it's bad." Another slogan, originally used but now abandoned, was "He's mean, green and obscene."

Bad Frog's labels have been approved for use by the Federal Bureau of Alcohol, Tobacco, and Firearms, and by authorities in

Reprinted by permission of the trademark holder, Bad Frog Brewery.

at least 15 states and the District of Columbia, but have been rejected by authorities in New Jersey, Ohio, and Pennsylvania.

In May 1996, Bad Frog's authorized New York distributor, Renaissance Beer Co., made an application to the New York State Liquor Authority (NYSLA) for brand label approval and registration. . . .

In September 1996, NYSLA denied Bad Frog's application. . . . Explaining its rationale for the rejection, the Authority found that the label "encourages combative behavior" and that the gesture and the slogan, "He just don't care," placed close to and in larger type than a warning concerning potential health problems,

> foster a defiance to the health warning on the label, entice underage drinkers, and invite the public not to heed conventional wisdom and to disobey standards of decorum.

In addition, the Authority said that it

> considered that approval of this label means that the label could appear in grocery and convenience stores, with obvious exposure on the shelf to children of tender age

and that it

> is sensitive to and has concern as to [the label's] adverse effects on such a youthful audience.

Finally, the Authority said that it

> has considered that within the state of New York, the gesture of "giving the finger" to someone has the insulting meaning of "**k You," or "Up Yours," . . . a

confrontational, obscene gesture, known to lead to fights, shootings, and homicides . . . concludes that the encouraged use of this gesture in licensed premises is akin to yelling "fire" in a crowded theater, . . . [and] finds that to approve this admittedly obscene, provocative confrontational gesture would not be conducive to proper regulation and control and would tend to adversely affect the health, safety, and welfare of the People of the State of New York.

Bad Frog filed the present action in October 1996 and sought a preliminary injunction barring NYSLA from taking any steps to prohibit the sale of beer by Bad Frog under the controversial labels. The District Court denied the motion [and Bad Frog now appeals the District Court decision].

*   *   *   *   *

COMMERCIAL OR NONCOMMERCIAL SPEECH?

In Bad Frog's view, the commercial speech that receives reduced First Amendment protection is expression that conveys commercial information. The frog labels, it contends, do not purport to convey such information, but instead communicate only a "joke." As such, the argument continues, the labels enjoy full First Amendment protection, rather than the somewhat reduced protection accorded commercial speech.

*   *   *   *   *

NYSLA agrees with the District Court that the labels enjoy some First Amendment protection, but are to be assessed by the somewhat reduced standards applicable to commercial speech.

Bad Frog's label attempts to function, like a trademark, to identify the source of the product. The picture on a beer bottle of a frog behaving badly is reasonably to be understood as attempting to identify to consumers a product of the Bad Frog Brewery. In addition, the label serves to propose a commercial transaction. Though the label communicates no information beyond the source of the product, we think that minimal information, conveyed in the context of a proposal of a commercial transaction, suffices to invoke the protections for commercial speech. . . .

Bad Frog contends that its labels deserve full First Amendment protection because their proposal of a commercial transaction is combined with what is claimed to be political, or at least societal, commentary.

*   *   *   *   *

We are unpersuaded by Bad Frog's attempt to separate the purported social commentary in the labels from the hawking of beer. Bad Frog's labels meet the three criteria identified in *Bolger* [463 U.S. 60 (1983)]: the labels are a form of advertising, identify a specific product, and serve the economic interest of the speaker. Moreover, the purported non-commercial message is not so "inextricably intertwined" with the commercial speech as to require a finding that the entire label must be treated as "pure" speech.

* * * * *

We thus assess the prohibition of Bad Frog's labels under the commercial speech standards outlined in *Central Hudson* [447 U.S. 557 (1980)].

THE *CENTRAL HUDSON* TEST

Central Hudson sets forth the analytical framework for assessing governmental restrictions on commercial speech:

At the outset, we must determine whether the expression is protected by the First Amendment. For commercial speech to come within that provision, it at least must concern lawful activity and not be misleading. Next, we ask whether the asserted government interest is substantial. If both inquiries yield positive answers, we must determine whether the regulation directly advances the government interest asserted, and whether it is not more extensive than is necessary to serve that interest.

* * * * *

A. Lawful Activity and Not Deceptive

We agree with the District Court that Bad Frog's labels pass *Central Hudson's* threshold requirement that the speech "must concern lawful activity and not be misleading." The consumption of beer (at least by adults) is legal in New York, and the labels cannot be said to be deceptive, even if they are offensive.

B. Substantial State Interests

NYSLA advances two interests to support its asserted power to ban Bad Frog's labels: (i) the State's interest in "protecting children from vulgar and profane advertising," and (ii) the State's interest "in acting consistently to promote temperance, i.e., the moderate and responsible use of alcohol among those above the legal drinking age and abstention among those below the legal drinking age."

Both of the asserted interests are "substantial" within the meaning of *Central Hudson*. States have "a compelling interest in protecting the physical and psychological well-being of minors," and "[t]his interest extends to shielding minors from the influence of literature that is not obscene by adult standards."

The Supreme Court also has recognized that states have a substantial interest in regulating alcohol consumption. We agree with the District Court that New York's asserted concern for "temperance" is also a substantial state interest.

C. Direct Advancement of the State Interest

To meet the "direct advancement" requirement, a state must demonstrate that "the harms it recites are real and that its restriction will in fact alleviate them *to a material degree*" [*Edenfield v. Fane,* 507 U.S. 761, 771 (1993)].

(1) *Advancing the interest in protecting children from vulgarity.*

* * * * *

NYSLA endeavors to advance the state interest in preventing exposure of children to vulgar displays by taking only the limited step of barring such displays from the labels of alcoholic beverages. In view of the wide currency of vulgar displays throughout contemporary society, including comic books targeted directly at children, barring such displays from labels for alcoholic beverages cannot realistically be expected to reduce children's exposure to such displays to any significant degree.

* * * * *

(2) *Advancing the state interest in temperance.* We agree with the District Court that NYSLA has not established that its rejection of Bad Frog's application directly advances the state's interest in "temperance."

NYSLA maintains that the raised finger gesture and the slogan "He just don't care" urge consumers generally to defy authority and particularly to disregard the Surgeon General's warning, which appears on the label next to the gesturing frog. NYSLA also contends that the frog appeals to youngsters and promotes underage drinking.

The truth of these propositions is not so self-evident as to relieve the state of the burden of marshalling some empirical evidence to support its assumptions. All that is clear is that the gesture of "giving the finger" is offensive. Whether viewing that gesture on a beer label will encourage disregard of health warnings or encourage underage drinking remain matters of speculation.

NYSLA has not shown that its denial of Bad Frog's application directly and materially advances either of its asserted state interests.

D. Narrow Tailoring

Central Hudson's fourth criterion, sometimes referred to as "narrow tailoring," requires consideration of whether the prohibition is more extensive than necessary to serve the asserted state interest. Since NYSLA's prohibition of Bad Frog's labels has not been shown to make even an arguable advancement of the state interest in temperance, we consider here only whether the prohibition is more extensive than necessary to serve the asserted interest in insulating children from vulgarity.

* * * * *

In this case, Bad Frog has suggested numerous less intrusive alternatives to advance the asserted state interest in protecting children from vulgarity, short of a complete statewide ban on its labels. Appellant suggests "the restriction of advertising to point-of-sale locations; limitations on billboard advertising; restrictions on over-the-air advertising; and segregation of the product in the store." Even if we were to assume that the state materially advances its asserted interest by shielding children from viewing the Bad Frog labels, it is plainly excessive to prohibit the labels from all use, including placement on bottles displayed in bars and taverns where parental supervision of children is to be expected. Moreover, to whatever extent NYSLA is concerned that children will be harmfully exposed to the Bad Frog labels when wandering without parental supervision around grocery and convenience stores where beer is sold, that concern could be less intrusively dealt with by placing restrictions on the permissible locations where the appellant's products may be displayed within such stores. Or, with the labels permitted, restrictions might be imposed on placement of the frog illustration on the outside of six-packs or cases sold in such stores.

NYSLA's complete statewide ban on the use of Bad Frog's labels lacks a "reasonable fit" with the state's asserted interest in shielding minors from vulgarity, and NYSLA gave inadequate consideration to alternatives to this blanket suppression of commercial speech.

* * * * *

[W]e conclude that NYSLA has unlawfully rejected Bad Frog's application for approval of its labels.

* * * * *

[Reversed and remanded.] [For an update on Bad Frog, see **http://badfrog.com**]

Questions

1. *a.* Why did the Court of Appeals conclude that the Bad Frog label constituted commercial speech?
   b. What is the significance of that decision?
2. Why did the Court of Appeals rule in Bad Frog's favor?

3. A letter to the *Buffalo News* objecting to the *Bad Frog* decision:

   > . . . The U.S. Court of Appeals' reasoning was that "vulgar materials enjoy wide currency in society today—including comic books for children." Therefore, while offensive it is not illegal. I guess this means the sickies of the world can show us anything they want, even if we don't want to see it. They have the right to offend us, but we have no rights not to be offended.
   >
   > We all know what the extended middle finger means. I personally get offended when this gesture is directed at me, whether by humans or cartoon animals. I would like to show the Court of Appeals my opinion of their decision by extending my middle finger in their direction. I hope they enjoy this gesture. After all, it's not illegal. But maybe it should be.[37]

   a. Do you agree with the letter writer that *Bad Frog* is an unwise decision? Explain.
   b. Should "the finger" be an illegal gesture? Explain.
4. In online fantasy sports leagues, fans "draft" current professional players in baseball, football, etc. to create their own teams that then compete based on the actual performance of those players. A Missouri company, C.B.C. Distribution and Marketing, Inc. operated a for-profit online league. In 2005, Major League Baseball changed its licensing policies and declined to allow C.B.C. a license to continue using the names and statistics of major league baseball players. C.B.C. then sued claiming it had a First Amendment right to use the information while M.L.B. argued that the information was protected by the intellectual property/publicity rights of the players. Decide the case. Explain. See *C.B.C. Distribution and Marketing, inc. v. Major League Baseball Advanced Media*, 505 F.3d 818 (8th Cir. 2007); cert. den. *Major League Baseball v. C.B.C. Distrib. & Mktg*, 2008 U.S. LEXIS 4574.
5. Two Rhode Island statutes prohibited all price advertising on liquor in the state, except for price tags and signs within a store itself which were not visible on the street. The state sought to reduce alcohol consumption. Two licensed liquor dealers challenged the statutes' constitutionality.
   a. How would you rule on that challenge? Explain.
   b. Why would the elimination of price advertising arguably contribute to reduced alcohol consumption? See *44 Liquormart, Inc. v. Rhode Island*, 116 S.Ct. 1495 (1996).

The Fourth Amendment

In an increasingly complex and interdependent society, the right of the individual to be free of unjustified governmental intrusions—that is, to a reasonable degree of privacy—has taken on new significance. The Fourth Amendment provides that

> [T]he right of the people to be secure in their persons, houses, papers, and effects, against unreasonable searches and seizures, shall not be violated, and no Warrants shall issue, but upon probable cause.

Some constitutional limitations on the police powers of government officials are a necessity. The boundaries of freedom from unreasonable search and seizure are, however, the subject of continuing dispute. The police are under great pressure to cope with America's crime problems, but they must do so within the confines of the Constitution, which is designed to protect us all—including criminals—from the power of an unfair, overreaching government.

Certainly, the most controversial dimension of Fourth Amendment interpretation is the *exclusionary rule*, which provides that, as a matter of due process, evidence secured in violation of the Fourth Amendment may not be used against a defendant at trial. As ultimately applied to all courts by the 1961 U.S. Supreme Court decision in *Mapp v. Ohio*,[38] we can see that the exclusionary rule, while a very effective device for discouraging illegal searches, seizures, and arrests, also from time to time has the effect of freeing guilty criminals.

The Supreme Court restricted the exclusionary rule in 2006 holding that the government need not forfeit evidence collected in constitutionally improper "no knock" searches.[39] For many years, police conducting a search have been required to knock and announce themselves then wait a reasonable time to enter. Michigan police, in executing a search warrant, announced themselves but did not wait a reasonable time before entering and finding crack cocaine in Booker T. Hudson's pockets. Hudson was convicted of drug violations, and his appeal eventually reached the U.S. Supreme Court where Justice Antonin Scalia, writing the 5–4 opinion upholding Hudson's conviction, expressed concern about guilty defendants who have been allowed to go free because of the exclusionary rule. He concluded that the social harm accompanying the knock and announce rule was too great as compared with the added privacy offered by the rule. Then in 2009, the Court, in another 5–4 decision, further limited the exclusionary rule by finding that unlawful police conduct does not require the suppression of evidence if the misconduct involved only "isolated negligence."[40]

Guilty defendants allowed to go free.

In general, a *search warrant* issued by a judge is necessary to comply with the Constitution in making a narcotics search. However, a warrantless search is permissible where reasonable, as in association with an arrest or where probable cause exists to believe a drug-related crime has been committed but circumstances make securing a warrant impracticable. Incident to an arrest, a search may lawfully include the person, a car, and the immediate vicinity of the arrest. Further more, a police officer may lawfully secure drugs that have been abandoned or that are in plain view even though a warrant has not been obtained. As the following situations attest, search/privacy problems pervade our lives.

1. **Vehicle Searches.** For nearly 30 years police officers have commonly understood that lawfully arresting an occupant of a vehicle confers the right to search the passenger

compartment of that vehicle. In a 2009 decision, *Gant v. Arizona*,[41] the U.S. Supreme Court significantly diminished that authority by ruling that such searches are permissible in only two circumstances:

a. when the individual being arrested is close enough to the vehicle to reach in for a weapon or evidence and

b. when the officer can reasonably believe that the vehicle contains evidence relevant to the crime of arrest.

Thus, arrests for routine traffic stops ordinarily would not justify vehicle searches while such searches are more likely to be permissible incident to arrests for more serious crimes.[42]

2. **Cell Phones.** An Ohio woman, Wendy Thomas Northern, was hospitalized because of a drug overdose. During police questioning she agreed to call Antwaun Smith whom she identified as the source of the drugs. Police arrested Smith, searched him and his cell phone and discovered call records and numbers confirming that his phone had been used to talk with Northern. That evidence was used at trial against Smith who argued that the cell phone search violated his Fourth Amendment rights. The Ohio Supreme Court agreed with Smith and ruled that the cell phone evidence should have been suppressed.[43] Court decisions supporting cell phone searches have relied on well-settled Supreme Court decisions allowing police to conduct searches incident to lawful arrest. The arrestee's person and immediate area of control including any closed containers in possession of the suspect may be examined by the police in order to insure their safety and to prevent the destruction of evidence. The Ohio Supreme Court declined to treat Smith's cell phone as a container, but others including the California Supreme Court have done so.[44] Privacy advocates point to the vast array of personal information (text messages, photos, emails, etc.) that may be contained on a cell phone. What do you think about the right to privacy in your cell phone?

> Police searched him and his cell phone.

3. **Testing Students.** In 1998 the school board in rural Tecumseh, Oklahoma, instituted a mandatory random urinalysis drug-testing program for all students participating in competitive extracurricular activities. The tests checked for illegal drugs but not for alcohol. Test results were not turned over to the police. An honor student, Lindsay Earls, challenged the program as a violation of her Fourth Amendment rights. A U.S. Court of Appeals agreed with her, ruling that school officials needed to provide evidence of an "identifiable drug abuse problem."[45] The U.S. Supreme Court, however, reversed that decision and held by a 5–4 margin that the school's interest in addressing drug problems outweighed students' privacy rights.[46] The Court reasoned that those participating in extracurricular activities are subjected to many rules and restrictions that diminish their expectation of privacy, and the Court said the program is a health and safety measure rather than an assault on personal privacy. Some state supreme courts, however, have ruled that school drug testing may violate state constitutional law.[47]

> Drug problems outweighed students' privacy.

4. **Voyeurism and the Surveillance Society.** In Washington State, Richard Sorrells and Sean Glas were found guilty of violating a state voyeurism statute for taking pictures up the skirts of some women who were working and shopping in a public mall. Both men appealed their convictions and won a 2002 decision because the voyeurism law did not

apply, the Washington State Supreme Court unanimously ruled, to actions in public places.[48] The women had no "reasonable expectation of privacy" in the shopping mall, so their privacy could not have been invaded. A federal law, the Video Voyeurism Prevention Act, and a number of state laws have expanded protection against photographic voyeurism, but those laws may not meet constitutional requirements.

Technology Meanwhile, threats to privacy are growing exponentially as new technology leads toward a surveillance society. Airport body scanners have outraged many, but outright spying may be the bigger threat to privacy. Hidden cameras, camera phones, and other high-tech probing devices allow voyeurism, identity theft, industrial espionage, keystroke monitoring (to capture account numbers and passwords), personal observations, and much more. Of course, high-tech spying can also document unsafe working conditions and inhumane factory livestock operations, for example, but the risks are enormous. We have long feared government intrusions (Big Brother is watching), but now we have democratized privacy invasions by giving everyone the technological ability to intrude. Will the legal system be able to protect us from one another? Given the omnipresence and influence of social media in our lives, is the ongoing existence of privacy as a concept now at risk of extinction, especially among young people? [For an overview of privacy issues around the world, see **http://epic.org/**]

Questions

1. A local citizen told police that Wilson was growing marijuana in a small, roofless shed at his residence. The police flew over the shed in a small plane at a legal altitude of 500 feet and observed what they believed to be marijuana growing in the shed. They secured a warrant, conducted a search, and seized marijuana plants. Wilson moved to suppress the evidence, claiming the search was illegal. Is he correct? Explain. See *State v. Wilson,* 988 P.2d 463 (Ct. App. Wash. 1999).

2. Police stopped and arrested McFadden for riding a bicycle on a sidewalk in violation of New York City code. A search incident to the stop revealed a firearm. McFadden was later convicted of the crime of being in possession of a firearm as a previously convicted felon. McFadden appealed, claiming the search was unconstitutional. Was he correct? Explain. See *United States v. McFadden,* 238 F.3d 198 (2001); cert. den. 122 S.Ct. 223 (2001).

3. *a.* Can the police lawfully search an individual's garbage once it has been placed at the curb for disposal? A Connecticut resident, Paul DeFusco, was convicted of drug trafficking based on evidence found in his home. The police conducted the home search with a warrant secured on the basis of an informant's information as well as evidence (some short cut straws, glassine baggies, and prescription bottles) turned up in sifting through DeFusco's garbage.

   b. Explain the central issue in this case. See *State of Connecticut v. Paul DeFusco,* 620 A.2d 746 (Conn. S.Ct. 1993).

4. Tucson, Arizona, police, cruising in an area associated with the Crips street gang, stopped a car because its insurance coverage had been suspended. Johnson, a backseat passenger, was wearing the blue colors associated with the Crips and Officer

Trevizo saw that Johnson had a police scanner in his pocket. Trevizo questioned Johnson learning that he was from a town frequented by the Crips gang, that he had recently been in prison and that he had no identification with him. Trevizo asked Johnson to exit the car. He did so. Trevizo conducted a pat-down search, and she felt a gun. Johnson struggled but he was arrested, and a further search revealed marijuana. Johnson was charged with unlawful possession of a gun, possession of marijuana, and resisting arrest. In court, Johnson challenged the legality of the search saying it had nothing to do with the traffic stop. Did the pat-down violate the Fourth Amendment's prohibition on unreasonable searches and seizures? Explain. See *Arizona v. Johnson*, 555 U.S. 323 (2009).

Business Searches

Government tries to protect us from business hazards including pollution, defective products, and unsafe workplaces as well as business crimes such as fraud and bribery. To do so, government agents often want to enter company buildings, observe working conditions, and examine company books. We know our homes are generally protected from searches in the absence of a warrant. Excepting urgent circumstances such as terrorism concerns, can the same be said for a place of business? The Supreme Court has answered that question:

> The Warrant Clause of the Fourth Amendment protects commercial buildings as well as private homes. To hold otherwise would belie the origin of that Amendment, and the American colonial experience. . . . "[T]he Fourth Amendment's commands grew in large measure out of the colonists' experience with the writs of assistance . . . [that] granted sweeping power to customs officials and other agents of the king to search at large for smuggled goods." . . . Against this background, it is untenable that the ban on warrantless searches was not intended to shield places of business as well as of residence.[49]

The Fifth Amendment

Takings—Eminent Domain

The Fifth Amendment prohibits the taking of private property for public use without *just compensation* for the owner. In cases where owners do not want to sell, governments often use the power of *eminent domain* to take private property for public uses such as building highways, bike trails, and parks, while providing just compensation. But what about the situation where the condemned property is to be used for a *private* purpose? Communities across America, hungry for an improved tax base and more jobs, have made the practice routine, but are they violating the Fifth Amendment rights of the property owners? The following 5–4 Supreme Court decision involves a challenge to a New London, Connecticut, plan to clear a portion of the city to make way for a private-sector office/research park along with a waterfront hotel, conference center, residences, a marina, and a river walk. Small businesses and residences were to make room for bigger, more successful private ventures providing a stronger tax base for New London.

Justice Stevens

In 2000 the city of New London approved a development plan that, in the words of the Supreme Court of Connecticut, was "projected to create in excess of 1,000 jobs, to increase tax and other revenues, and to revitalize an economically distressed city, including its downtown and waterfront areas" (843 A.2d 500, 507 [2004]). In assembling the land needed for this project, the city's development agent has purchased property from willing sellers and proposes to use the power of eminent domain to acquire the remainder of the property from unwilling owners in exchange for just compensation. The question presented is whether the city's proposed disposition of this property qualifies as a "public use" within the meaning of the Takings Clause of the Fifth Amendment to the Constitution.

I

The city of New London (hereinafter City) sits at the junction of the Thames River and the Long Island Sound in southeastern Connecticut. Decades of economic decline led a state agency in 1990 to designate the City a "distressed municipality." In 1996 the Federal Government closed the Naval Undersea Warfare Center, which had been located in the Fort Trumbull area of the City and had employed over 1,500 people. In 1998 the City's unemployment rate was nearly double that of the State, and its population of just under 24,000 residents was at its lowest since 1920.

These conditions prompted state and local officials to target New London, and particularly its Fort Trumbull area, for economic revitalization. To this end, respondent New London Development Corporation (NLDC), a private nonprofit entity established some years earlier to assist the City in planning economic development, was reactivated. In January 1998 the State authorized a $5.35 million bond issue to support the NLDC's planning activities and a $10 million bond issue toward the creation of a Fort Trumbull State Park. In February the pharmaceutical company Pfizer Inc. announced that it would build a $300 million research facility on a site immediately adjacent to Fort Trumbull; local planners hoped that Pfizer would draw new business to the area. Upon obtaining state-level approval, the NLDC finalized an integrated development plan focused on 90 acres of the Fort Trumbull area.

The Fort Trumbull area is situated on a peninsula that juts into the Thames River. The area comprises approximately 115 privately owned properties, as well as the 32 acres of land formerly occupied by the naval facility (Trumbull State Park now occupies 18 of those 32 acres). The development plan encompasses seven parcels. Parcel 1 is designated for a waterfront conference hotel at the center of a "small urban village" that will include restaurants and shopping. . . . Parcel 2 will be the site of approximately 80 new residences organized into an urban neighborhood and linked by public walkway to the remainder of the development, including the state park. This parcel also includes space reserved for a new U.S. Coast Guard Museum. Parcel 3, which is located immediately north of the Pfizer facility, will contain at least 90,000 square feet of research and development office space. Parcel 4A is a 2.4-acre site that will be used either to support the adjacent state park, by providing parking or retail services for visitors, or to support the nearby marina. Parcel 4B will include a renovated marina, as well as the final stretch of the riverwalk. Parcels 5, 6, and 7 will provide land for office and retail space, parking, and water-dependent commercial uses.

* * * * *

The city council approved the plan in January 2000 and designated the NLDC as its development agent in charge of implementation. The city council also authorized the NLDC to purchase property or to acquire property by exercising eminent domain in the City's name. The NLDC successfully negotiated the purchase of most of the real estate in the 90-acre area, but its negotiations with petitioners failed. As a consequence, in November 2000 the NLDC initiated the condemnation proceedings that gave rise to this case.

II

Petitioner Susette Kelo has lived in the Fort Trumbull area since 1997. She has made extensive improvements to her house, which she prizes for its water view. Petitioner Wilhelmina Dery was born in her Fort Trumbull house in 1918 and has lived there her entire life. Her husband Charles has lived in the house since they married some 60 years ago. In all, the nine petitioners own 15 properties in Fort Trumbull. . . . There is no allegation that any of these properties is blighted or otherwise in poor condition; rather, they were condemned only because they happen to be located in the development area.

In December 2000 petitioners brought this action in the New London Superior Court. They claimed, among other things, that the taking of their properties would violate the "public use" restriction in the Fifth Amendment. After a seven-day bench trial, the Superior Court granted a permanent restraining order prohibiting the taking of the properties located in parcel 4A (park or marina support). It, however, denied petitioners relief as to the properties located in parcel 3 (office space).

After the Superior Court ruled, both sides took appeals to the Supreme Court of Connecticut. That court held that all of the City's proposed takings were valid.

* * * * *

III

Two polar propositions are perfectly clear. On the one hand, it has long been accepted that the sovereign may not take the property of A for the sole purpose of transferring it to another private party B, even though A is paid just compensation. On the other hand, it is equally clear that a State may transfer property from one private party to another if future "use by the public" is the purpose of the taking; the condemnation of land for a railroad is a familiar example. Neither of these propositions, however, determines the disposition of this case.

As for the first proposition, the City would no doubt be forbidden from taking petitioners' land for the purpose of conferring a private benefit on a particular party. Nor would the City be allowed to take property under the mere pretext of a public purpose, when its actual purpose was to bestow a private benefit. The takings before us, however, would be executed pursuant to a "carefully considered" development plan. The trial judge and all the members of the Supreme Court of Connecticut agreed that there was no evidence of an illegitimate purpose in this case.

* * * * *

On the other hand, this is not a case in which the City is planning to open the condemned land—at least not in its entirety—to use by the general public. Nor will the private lessees of the land in any sense be required to operate like common carriers, making their services available to all comers. But although such a projected use would be sufficient to satisfy the public use requirement, this "Court long ago rejected any literal requirement that condemned property be put into use for the general public." Indeed, while many state courts in the mid-19th century endorsed "use by the public" as the proper definition of public use, that narrow view steadily eroded over time. Not only was the "use by the public" test difficult to administer (e.g., what proportion of the public need have access to the property? at what price?), but it proved to be impractical given the diverse and always evolving needs of society. Accordingly, when this Court began applying the Fifth Amendment to the States at the close of the 19th century, it

embraced the broader and more natural interpretation of public use as "public purpose."

* * * * *

The disposition of this case therefore turns on the question whether the City's development plan serves a "public purpose." Without exception, our cases have defined that concept broadly, reflecting our longstanding policy of deference to legislative judgments in this field.

In *Berman v. Parker,* this Court upheld a redevelopment plan targeting a blighted area of Washington, D.C., in which most of the housing for the area's 5,000 inhabitants was beyond repair. Under the plan, the area would be condemned and part of it utilized for the construction of streets, schools, and other public facilities. The remainder of the land would be leased or sold to private parties for the purpose of redevelopment, including the construction of low-cost housing.

* * * * *

IV

Those who govern the City were not confronted with the need to remove blight in the Fort Trumbull area, but their determination that the area was sufficiently distressed to justify a program of economic rejuvenation is entitled to our deference. The City has carefully formulated an economic development plan that it believes will provide appreciable benefits to the community, including—but by no means limited to—new jobs and increased tax revenue. . . . Given the comprehensive character of the plan, the thorough deliberation that preceded its adoption, and the limited scope of our review, it is appropriate for us to resolve the challenges of the individual owners, not on a piecemeal basis, but rather in light of the entire plan. Because that plan unquestionably serves a public purpose, the takings challenged here satisfy the public use requirement of the Fifth amendment.

To avoid this result, petitioners urge us to adopt a new bright-line rule that economic development does not qualify as a public use. Putting aside the unpersuasive suggestion that the City's plan will provide only purely economic benefits, neither precedent nor logic supports petitioners' proposal. Promoting economic development is a traditional and long accepted function of government.

* * * * *

In affirming the City's authority to take petitioners' properties, we do not minimize the hardship that condemnations may entail, notwithstanding the payment of just compensation. We emphasize that nothing in our opinion precludes any State from placing further restrictions on its exercise of the takings power. Indeed, many States already impose "public use" requirements that are stricter than the federal baseline.

* * * * *

Affirmed.

AFTERWORD—PROPERTY RIGHTS REVOLUTION?

The *Kelo* decision was an angry disappointment for property rights advocates. A government taking of Americans' long-time homes, even for just compensation, is a powerful and frightening image. Susette Kelo eventually settled with New London, vacated her home and received $442,000. Her "little pink house" was disassembled and moved to another lot where it stands as something of a national symbol for property rights.

Clearly, however, governments need, and have long exercised, substantial authority to take property for economic development. Of course, government planning sometimes does not work out as expected, and the Pfizer development appears to be one of those failures. In 2009, Pfizer announced it was abandoning the Fort Trumbull office complex as a cost-saving measure. Fourteen hundred jobs were departing. The hotels, stores, and condominiums planned for the lots taken from Kelo and her neighbors have yet to materialize.

In response to *Kelo,* states and localities are using their legal and democratic systems to achieve an appropriate and difficult balance between important property rights and important public purposes. As one scholar observed, "The backlash against *Kelo* is the largest against any Supreme Court decision in decades, and the legislative response is possibly the most extensive to any Supreme Court decision in history."[50] More than 40 states have passed laws limiting eminent domain, although the effectiveness of those restrictions is unclear.[51] Many of them include exceptions allowing seizure of "blighted" property; a term not yet well defined. A 2011 federal district court decision, however, blocked National City, California's effort to take property belonging to a local boxing

gym for at-risk kids. The city wanted to make the property available to a private developer who hoped to build a condo project. The court ruled that National City had failed to provide the "specific and quantifiable" evidence of blight required by California's post-*Kelo* legislative limitations on government takings.[52] [For property rights analysis and updates and more on the *Kelo* story, see **www.ij.org**]

Questions

1. What reasoning was offered by Justice Stevens to support the majority view that the New London development complied with due process requirements?

2. *a.* What was the issue, the central question, in this case and how did the majority answer that question?

   b. How would you expect the dissent to answer that question?

3. From the dissenting point of view, what harm is likely to emerge from this decision?

4. Marilyn and James Nollan applied for a permit to replace their beachfront home with a larger structure. The California Coastal Commission agreed on the condition that the Nollans grant an easement on their beach that would allow the public to cross that property and thus facilitate movement between the public beaches that lay on both sides of the Nollan beach. The Nollans sued, claiming a violation of the Takings Clause. Decide. Explain. See *Nollan v. California Coastal Commission*, 483 U.S. 825 (1987).

5. Tina Bennis sued when Wayne County (Detroit), Michigan, authorities took the car she jointly owned with her husband after police arrested him for receiving oral sex from a prostitute while parked in the car. A 1925 anti-nuisance law permitted the seizure, but Tina Bennis claimed it amounted to an unconstitutional taking because she was an innocent half owner of the 1977 Pontiac for which the couple had paid $600. Bennis's claim eventually reached the U.S. Supreme Court. Decide the case. Explain. See *Bennis v. Michigan,* 116 S.Ct. 994 (1996).

Takings—Regulatory

We have seen how the law treats situations where the government uses its power of eminent domain to condemn property for either public or private use and pays just compensation. What happens when the government does not take the property but rather *regulates* it in a manner that deprives that property of some or all of its economic usefulness? For example, without providing just compensation, can a state lawfully limit the amount a landlord can charge for rent in an effort to preserve low-income housing? Can the state forbid billboards in order to enhance roadside beauty?

These *regulatory takings,* whether temporary or permanent, normally do not require government compensation because doing so would severely impair the state's ability to govern in an orderly manner. Nonetheless, in recent years the courts have been more aggressive about requiring just compensation for some regulatory takings. Three broad classes of such takings have emerged in court decisions.

1. **Total Takings.** If a governmental body acts in a way that permanently takes all of the economic value of a property or permanently physically invades the property, the taking requires just compensation unless the government is (1) preventing a nuisance or (2) the regulation was permissible under property law at the time of the purchase of the property. When the South Carolina Coastal Commission passed erosion rules having the effect of preventing David Lucas from building any permanent structure on his $975,000 beachfront lots, Lucas sued, claiming a Fifth Amendment violation. The U.S. Supreme Court agreed with Lucas and held that a taking requiring just compensation had occurred because the state had deprived Lucas of *all* economically beneficial use of the property, and the property did not fall in one of the two exceptions.[53]

> The South Carolina Coastal Commission passed erosion rules having the effect of preventing David Lucas from building any permanent structure on his $975,000 beachfront lots.

2. **Exaction/Mitigation.** A second class of regulatory takings involves situations where the government allows land development only if the owner dedicates some property interest (called an *exaction*) or money (called a *mitigation* or *impact fee*) to the government. Thus if you are developing land for housing, the city government might require that you devote a portion of that land to parks. Or you might be required to pay a fee to help the city meet the recreational needs of the citizens your development will be housing. The Supreme Court dealt with just such a case in *Dolan v. Tigard.*[54] Florence Dolan, owner of a plumbing and electrical supply store in Tigard, Oregon, applied for a city permit to nearly double the size of her store and to pave her parking lot. Concerned with increased traffic and water runoff due to the proposed expansion, the city granted the permit, subject to a pair of conditions: (1) Dolan was to dedicate the portion of her property that lay within the 100-year floodplain to the city to improve drainage for the creek that ran along her property, and (2) she was to dedicate an additional 15-foot strip of her land adjacent to the floodplain for use as a bicycle path/walkway to relieve traffic congestion. Dolan sought a variance from the requirements, but her petition was denied. She sued, and her case reached the U.S. Supreme Court, which ruled that government can compel a dedication of private property to public use where it can establish two factors: (1) A nexus or relationship between the government's legitimate purpose (flood and traffic control in *Dolan*) and the condition imposed (the land Dolan was to dedicate to public purposes), and (2) a "rough proportionality" between the burden imposed (the land given over to public use) and the impact of the development (increased water runoff and increased traffic).[55] The Supreme Court, in a firm defense of private property rights, ruled that Tigard had failed to meet those standards, and Dolan won the case.

3. **Partial Takings.** Government may take part of a piece of property in order to expand a road, install a bike path, or establish a buffer zone, for example. These are

neither total takings nor exactions, but rather fall into a case-by-case analysis that depends greatly on the facts in each instance. The primary considerations in these cases are threefold:

1. The importance of the government interest (health, safety, or the like) that generated the regulation.
2. The economic effect on the landowner.
3. The landowner's legitimate, investment-backed expectations at the time of purchase.

In these cases the Court is simply asking whether the regulation goes "too far" in burdening the property owner. That is, should the property owner bear the costs of the regulation or should the public pay compensation to the property owner in exchange for the value (a public beach, a park, an unobstructed view, or whatever) derived from the regulation.[56]

Zoning in the Sixth Century

Government restraints on property development are not merely a modern imposition, as we learn from the following description of a zoning law in the Byzantine Empire:

> Next came the first zoning law for the beach. Coastal vistas were so cherished, and the competition for them so keen, that by the sixth century the Emperor Justinian the Great was compelled to pass an ordinance barring construction within 100 feet of the shore to protect sea views.

Source: Lena Lencek and Gideon Bosker, *The Beach: The History of Paradise on Earth* (New York: Penguin Group, 1998), p. 31.

The 14th Amendment

Due Process

The Due Process Clauses of both the Fifth Amendment (applying to the federal government) and the 14th Amendment (applying to the states) forbid the government to deprive citizens of life, liberty, or property without due process of law.

Substantive Due Process

Laws that arbitrarily and unfairly infringe on fundamental personal rights and liberties such as privacy, voting, and the various freedoms specified in the Bill of Rights may be challenged on due process grounds. Basically, the purpose of the law must be so compelling as to outweigh the intrusion on personal liberty or the law will be struck down. For example, the U.S. Supreme Court ruled that a Connecticut statute forbidding the use of contraceptives violated the constitutional right to privacy (although the word *privacy* itself does not appear in the U.S. Constitution).[57] By judicial interpretation, the 14th Amendment Due Process Clause "absorbs" the fundamental liberties of the *federal*

Constitution and prohibits *state* laws (in this case, the Connecticut contraceptive ban) that abridge those fundamental liberties such as privacy.

Procedural Due Process

Basically, procedural due process means that the government must provide a fair procedure including *notice* and a *fair hearing* before taking an action affecting a citizen's life, liberty, or property. A fair hearing might require, among others, the right to present evidence, the right to a decision maker free of bias, and the right to appeal. However, the precise nature of procedural due process depends on the situation. A murder trial requires meticulous attention to procedural fairness; an administrative hearing to appeal a housing officer's decision to banish a student from a dormitory, while required to meet minimal constitutional standards, can be more forgiving in its procedural niceties.

Due Process: Void for Vagueness

A statute may violate due process rights if it is so vaguely written that the ordinary person cannot understand it. The *Skilling* case that follows involves a void for vagueness claim arising from the infamous Enron fraud scandal that caused the former Houston, Texas energy giant—the seventh largest company in America (according to revenue)—to collapse into bankruptcy in 2001. Enron founder Ken Lay (now deceased), chief executive officer Jeffrey Skilling, and chief accounting officer, Richard Causey, were among those indicted for various crimes in association with Enron's spectacular rise from its founding in 1985 to its collapse fewer than 20 years later. Among other alleged wrongs, Skilling was convicted of depriving the corporation and the public of his "honest services" by deceiving the investors about Enron's finances. Skilling allegedly pumped up Enron's share prices by failing to reveal the company's true financial condition. His appeal reached the Supreme Court in 2010 where he claimed that pre-trial publicity and Enron's financial damage to Houston poisoned the jury pool and denied him his Sixth Amendment right to trial by an impartial jury. That claim was rejected by the Supreme Court, but Skilling also argued that the language of the "honest services" federal statute used to convict him was so vague that he was deprived of his due process rights.

> Skilling allegedly pumped up Enron's share prices.

LEGAL BRIEFCASE

Skilling v. United States
130 S.Ct. 2896 (2010)

Justice Ginsburg

(I AND II OMITTED-ED.)

III

We next consider whether Skilling's conspiracy conviction was premised on an improper theory of honest-services wire fraud. The honest-services statute, Section 1346, Skilling maintains, is unconstitutionally vague....

A

To place Skilling's constitutional challenge in context, we first review the origin and subsequent application of the honest-services doctrine.

1

Enacted in 1872, the original mail-fraud provision, the predecessor of the modern-day mail- and wire-fraud laws, proscribed, without further elaboration, use of the mails to advance "any scheme or artifice to defraud." See *McNally* v. *United States,* 483 U.S. 350, 356, 107 S.Ct. 2875, 97 L.Ed.2d 292 (1987). In 1909, Congress amended the statute to prohibit, as it does today, "any scheme or artifice to defraud, *or for obtaining money or property by means of false or fraudulent pretenses, representations, or promises."* Section 1341 (emphasis added); Emphasizing Congress' disjunctive phrasing, the Courts of Appeals, one after the other, interpreted the term "scheme or artifice to defraud" to include deprivations not only of money or property, but also of intangible rights.

* * * * *

2

In 1987, this Court, in *McNally* v. *United States,* stopped the development of the intangible-rights doctrine in its tracks. *McNally* involved a state officer who, in selecting Kentucky's insurance agent, arranged to procure a share of the agent's commissions via kickbacks paid to companies the official partially controlled. The prosecutor did not charge that, "in the absence of the alleged scheme[,] the Commonwealth would have paid a lower premium or secured better insurance." Instead, the prosecutor maintained that the kickback scheme "defraud[ed] the citizens and government of Kentucky of their right to have the Commonwealth's affairs conducted honestly."

We held that the scheme did not qualify as mail fraud. "Rather than constru[ing] the statute in a manner that leaves its outer boundaries ambiguous and involves the Federal Government in setting standards of disclosure and good government for local and state officials," we read the statute "as limited in scope to the protection of property rights." "If Congress desires to go further," we stated, "it must speak more clearly."

3

Congress responded swiftly. The following year, it enacted a new statute "specifically to cover one of the 'intangible rights' that lower courts had protected . . . prior to *McNally:* 'the intangible right of honest services.'" In full, the honest-services statute stated:

"For the purposes of th[e] chapter [of the United States Code that prohibits, *inter alia,* mail fraud, Section 1341, and wire fraud, Section 1343], the term 'scheme or artifice to defraud' includes a scheme or artifice to deprive another of the intangible right of honest services."

B

Congress, Skilling charges, reacted quickly but not clearly: He asserts that Section 1346 is unconstitutionally vague. To satisfy due process, "a penal statute [must] define the criminal offense [1] with sufficient definiteness that ordinary people can understand what conduct is prohibited and [2] in a manner that does not encourage arbitrary and discriminatory enforcement." *Kolender* v. *Lawson,* 461 U.S. 352, 357, 103 S.Ct. 1855, 75 L.Ed.2d 903 (1983). The void-for-vagueness doctrine embraces these requirements.

According to Skilling, Section 1346 meets neither of the two due process essentials. First, the phrase "the intangible right of honest services," he contends, does not adequately define what behavior it bars. Second, he alleges, Section 1346's "standardless sweep allows policemen, prosecutors, and juries to pursue their personal predilections," thereby "facilitat[ing] opportunistic and arbitrary prosecutions."

In urging invalidation of Section 1346, Skilling swims against our case law's current, which requires us, if we can, to construe, not condemn, Congress' enactments.

* * * * *

There is no doubt that Congress intended Section 1346 to refer to and incorporate the honest-services doctrine recognized in Court of Appeals' decisions before *McNally* derailed the intangible-rights theory of fraud. . . . Congress enacted Section 1346 on the heels *of McNally* and drafted the statute using that decision's terminology.

* * * * *

Satisfied that Congress, by enacting Section 1346, "meant to reinstate the body of *pre-McNally* honest-services law," we have surveyed that case law. In parsing the Courts of Appeals decisions, we acknowledge that Skilling's vagueness challenge has force, for honest-services decisions preceding *McNally* were not models of clarity or consistency.

* * * * *

Although some applications of the *pre-McNally* honest-services doctrine occasioned disagreement among the Courts of Appeals, these cases do not cloud the doctrine's solid core: The "vast majority" of the honest-services cases involved offenders who, in violation of a fiduciary duty, participated in bribery or kickback schemes.

* * * * *

In view of this history, there is no doubt that Congress intended Section 1346 to reach *at least* bribes and kickbacks. Reading the statute to proscribe a wider range of offensive conduct, we acknowledge, would raise the due process concerns underlying the vagueness doctrine. To preserve the statute without transgressing constitutional limitations, we now hold that Section 1346 criminalizes *only* the bribe-and-kickback core of the pre-*McNally* case law.

* * * * *

Interpreted to encompass only bribery and kickback schemes, Section 1346 is not unconstitutionally vague. Recall that the void-for-vagueness doctrine addresses concerns about (1) fair notice and (2) arbitrary and discriminatory prosecutions. . . .

As to fair notice, "whatever the school of thought concerning the scope and meaning of" Section 1346, it has always been "as plain as a pikestaff that" bribes and kickbacks constitute honest-services fraud, *Williams* v. *United States*, 341 U.S. 97, 101, 71 S.Ct. 576, 95 L.Ed. 774 (1951). . . .

As to arbitrary prosecutions, we perceive no significant risk that the honest-services statute, as we interpret it today, will be stretched out of shape. Its prohibition on bribes and kickbacks draws content not only from the *pre-McNally* case law, but also from federal statutes proscribing—and defining—similar crimes.

* * * * *

C

It remains to determine whether Skilling's conduct violated Section 1346. Skilling's honest-services prosecution, the Government concedes, was not "prototypical." The Government charged Skilling with conspiring to defraud Enron's shareholders by misrepresenting the company's fiscal health, thereby artificially inflating its stock price. It was the Government's theory at trial that Skilling "profited from the fraudulent scheme . . . through the receipt of salary and bonuses, . . . and through the sale of approximately $200 million in Enron stock, which netted him $89 million."

The Government did not, at any time, allege that Skilling solicited or accepted side payments from a third party in exchange for making these misrepresentations. ("[T]he indictment does not allege, and the government's evidence did not show, that [Skilling] engaged in bribery.") It is therefore clear that, as we read Section 1346, Skilling did not commit honest-services fraud.

* * * * *

Affirmed in part. Vacated in part. Remanded.

AFTERWORD

The Supreme Court returned Skilling's case to the federal Fifth Circuit Court of Appeals where, in 2011, the Skilling saga appeared to be nearing its conclusion. The Fifth Circuit upheld Skilling's conviction finding the honest services error was "harmless" in that ample evidence unrelated to the honest services charge supported Skilling's conviction on 19 counts of securities fraud, conspiracy, insider trading and making false representations.[58] At this writing, Skilling is serving time in a Colorado federal prison. He was originally sentenced to 24 years imprisonment, but that sentence, the Fifth Circuit concluded, was improperly calculated. A resentencing will follow with what is likely to be a relatively minor downward adjustment in time to be served.

Questions

1. Why did the Court conclude that Skilling did not commit honest-services fraud?

2. Why did the Court conclude that the honest services statute was unconstitutional?

3. How did the Court correct the unconstitutional infirmity in the honest-services statute?

Due Process and Punitive Damages

The Due Process Clause imposes limits on punitive (penalty) damages awards. An Alabama jury awarded Dr. Ira Gore $4,000 in compensatory (make whole) damages and four million dollars in punitive damages in a civil fraud suit springing from his discovery that his new BMW had been repainted due to some minor predelivery damage. The four-million-dollar award was reduced to two million dollars by the Alabama Supreme Court, but BMW took the case to the U.S. Supreme Court, which found the award "grossly excessive" and therefore, violative of BMW's due process rights.[59] The Alabama Supreme Court thereafter reduced Gore's award to $50,000. In a subsequent case involving a $145 million punitive award against State Farm Insurance, the U.S. Supreme Court clarified the outer bounds of punitive awards by suggesting that a 4–1 ratio between punitive and compensatory damages, while not "binding," should be "instructive," while ratios higher than 9–1 would be appropriate only in special circumstances.[60]

> An Alabama jury awarded Gore $4 million in punitive damages.

Exxon Valdez Oil Spill

Corporate America earned a significant victory in 2008 when the U.S. Supreme Court by a 5–3 margin reduced the punitive damages award in the 1989 Exxon Valdez oil spill in Alaska from $2.5 billion to a maximum of $507.5 million, an amount approximately equal to what Exxon had already spent to compensate Alaskans for their losses. Justice Souter, writing for the majority, said that a ratio of no more than one to one between punitive and compensatory damages was appropriate under maritime law.

Exxon was ordered by a lower court to pay the maximum $507.5 million in punitive damages and in 2009 Exxon agreed to pay about $480 million in interest on the punitive damages award. With that interest, the award will provide about $15,000 for each of the 33,000 plaintiffs. Exxon says it has spent more than $3.4 billion in response to the incident that polluted 1,300 miles of coastline and killed hundreds of thousands of seabirds and marine animals. After more than 20 years, the battle seems nearly over, but Exxon continues to argue that its $70 million in legal fees and other expenses should be paid by the plaintiffs. ExxonMobil's 2010 profits totaled $30.4 billion.

The original punitive award was intended to punish Exxon for its role in the accident where its ship, the Exxon Valdez captained by a lapsed alcoholic Joseph Hazlewood, hit a reef and spilled an estimated 11 million gallons of crude oil in the pristine fishing waters of Prince William Sound. Witnesses reportedly indicated that Hazlewood drank five double vodkas on the night of the spill and left the bridge at a crucial moment. [For a comprehensive database of the Exxon Valdez oil spill, see **http://www.arlis.org/docs/vol2/a/EVOS_FAQs.pdf**]

Sources: Exxon Shipping Company v. Baker, 2008 U.S. LEXIS 5363; Adam Liptak, "Damages Cut Against Exxon in Valdez Case," *New York Times,* June 26, 2008 [**www.nytimes.com**]; Erika Bolstad, "Exxon Valdez Damages Cut to $507.5 Million," *Anchorage Daily News,* June 25, 2008 [**http://www.adn.com/exxonvaldez/story/446057.html**]; and Elizabeth Bluemink, "Exxon Agrees to Pay Interest on Oil Spill Penalty," *Anchorage Daily News,* June 29, 2009 [**http://www.adn.com/2009/06/29/847901/Exxon-agrees-to-pay-interest-on.html**].

Equal Protection

The 14th Amendment provides that no state shall "deny to any person within its jurisdiction the equal protection of the laws." The Due Process Clause of the Fifth Amendment has been interpreted to provide that same protection against the power of the federal government. Fundamentally, these laws forbid a government from treating one person (including a corporation) differently from another without a rational basis for doing so. Most notably, the Equal Protection and Due Process Clauses have played an enormous role in attacking discrimination (see Chapter 13), but they can also significantly influence routine business practice in many ways. For example, can we lawfully impose higher taxes on a gambling casino than we impose on the sale of groceries? Or can we require the oil industry to follow more rigorous environmental standards than we expect of coal mines? In general, the answer to these questions is yes, but only if the legislation can pass the rational basis test. If not, such legislation would be unconstitutional and unenforceable.

[The U.S. Supreme Court, in *Loving v. Virginia,* 388 U.S. 1 (1967), employed due process and equal protection principles to declare unconstitutional Virginia's anti-miscegenation statute, thus ending race-based restrictions on marriage in the United States. For a video of the Loving family and its legal battle, see **http://abcnews.go.com/video/playerIndex?id=3278653**]

How Many Renters?

Trying to reduce the flow of university students into certain portions of the community, Ames, Iowa, home of Iowa State University, passed a zoning ordinance that permitted only single-family residences in specified areas. Under the ordinance, "family" was defined as any number of related persons or no more than three unrelated persons. The Ames Rental Property Association challenged the constitutionality of the ordinance.

Questions

1. Describe the constitutional claim raised by the plaintiffs.
2. Criticize the Ames' standards for achieving its housing goals.
3. Decide the case. Explain.

Source: Ames Rental Property Association v. City of Ames, 736 N.W.2d 255 (Ia. S.Ct. 2007).

Gay and Lesbian Marriage

In recent years, perhaps the most interesting and visible equal protection dispute has been the "cultural war" over same-sex marriage and civil unions. The Vermont Supreme Court made headlines across America and around the world in late 1999 when it ruled that gay and lesbian couples in that state had been denied equal protection of the law under the Vermont constitution and were entitled to the same legal benefits and protections as heterosexual couples. That decision led to Vermont legislative approval of *civil unions* allowing same-sex couples to join in a legally recognized relationship that confers all of the legal benefits, protections, and duties of marriage—including, for example, joint property and inheritance rights and child support duties. Since then a national debate, accompanied by a deluge of legislation and court rulings, has educated and agitated the American public but failed to bring anything like consensus to this explosive issue.

In 2009, Vermont's legislature expressly granted the legal right to same-sex marriage. Connecticut, the District of Columbia, Iowa, Massachusetts, New Hampshire, and New York all permit same-sex marriages. A number of other states provide for legal relationships, such as civil unions and domestic partnerships, that do not formally constitute marriage but which provide some of the legal rights of marriage. At this writing in 2011, 44 states do not allow same-sex marriage, and 30 states have approved constitutional amendments expressly forbidding gay marriages.[61] The federal Defense of Marriage Act (DOMA) defines marriage as a union of one man and one woman, forbids federal recognition of same-sex marriages (and the federal benefits that accompany marriage), and allows the states to do the same. All states, therefore, are free to define the relationship as they see fit.

PRACTICING ETHICS   Gay and Lesbian Marriage: How Do You Feel?

Views about same-sex marriage seem to be changing. A 2011 *Washington Post*-ABC News poll found 53 percent of the American public supporting gay marriage.[62] In 2007, 55 percent of Americans were opposed to gay marriage according to a Pew Research Center poll, but a 2006 Pew poll found 54 percent approval of civil unions.[63]

Morally and ethically speaking, which side is "right" about gay marriage? How do we decide? Consider some questions that help us sort through this moral thicket:

1. What issues should one consider in deciding whether gay marriage is morally defensible?

2. Is a civil union arrangement an acceptable "middle ground?"

3. If the American people ultimately favor gay and lesbian marriage, could we then consider it a morally defensible practice?

4. Are children at moral risk if raised by same-sex couples?

5. If scholarly studies ultimately demonstrate that homosexuality and lesbianism are substantially commanded by genetic characteristics, would we be morally required to permit same-sex marriage?

Gay/Lesbian Marriage Abroad

The first same-sex marriages occurred in the Netherlands in 2001. In total, ten nations, on three continents, now allow same-sex marriages, and over 20 permit civil unions.

Sources: "A Decade On, Progress on Same-Sex Marriages," *Human Rights Watch,* March 14, 2011 [**http://www. hrw.org/en/news/2011/03/14/decade-progress-same-sex-marriages**]; and "Civil Union," Wikipedia, May 9, 2011 [**http://en.wikipedia.org/wiki/Civil_union**].

Internet Exercise

At the First Amendment Center, read "About the First Amendment" [**http://www. firstamendmentcenter.org/about.aspx?item=about_firstamd**]. Explain the importance of the First Amendment and why Americans are divided about its application.

Chapter Questions

1. Members of the Jefferson County High School, T varsity football team circulated a petition that said: "I hate Coach Euvard [sic] and I don't want to play for him." Thereafter, all team members were asked if they were involved. Euverard dismissed four players who admitted they signed the petition and refused to apologize for doing so. The players who signed the petition but apologized were retained on the team. The four dismissed players filed suit. (a) Explain their primary legal claim. (b) Decide the case. Explain. See *Lowery v. Euverard,* 497 F.3d 584 (6th Cir. 2007).

2. The American Civil Liberties Union of Ohio challenged the constitutionality of Ohio's state motto, "With God, All Things Are Possible."
   a. Explain the nature of that constitutional challenge.
   b. Decide the case. Explain. See *American Civil Liberties Union of Ohio v. Capitol Square Review and Advisory Board,* 243 F.3d 289 (6th Cir. 2001).

3. Several city ordinances in Arkansas made it illegal for "any person to place a hand-bill or advertisement on any other person's vehicle parked on public property within city limits." Church members contested the constitutionality of the ordinances, which prevented them from lawfully placing religious handbills on parked cars. Decide. Explain. See *Krantz v. City of Fort Smith,* 160 F.3d 1214 (8th Cir. 1998).

4. The Georgia Outdoor Advertising Control Act, in essence, prohibits any off-premises outdoor advertising of commercial establishments where nudity is exhibited. Cafe Erotica lawfully provides food and adult entertainment, including nude dancing, and advertises those services on billboards. Cafe Erotica challenged the constitutionality of the Advertising Control Act. Decide. Explain. See *Georgia v. Cafe Erotica,* 507 S.E.2d 732 (Ga. S.Ct. 1998).

5. Colorado School of Law Professor Pierre Schlag, summarizing the central theme raised by Ronald K.L. Collins and David M. Skover in their book *The Death of Discourse:*

   > Stated most broadly, the predicament is this: with the perfection of communications technology, the refinement of capitalist rationality, and the intensification of market-created desire, the resulting culture is one that renders its own ostensible steering mechanism—namely, reasoned discourse—impossible. This broad scale rendition of the predicament is quite bleak, for there is no exit; everyone is included. We are all living in a culture that is, quite literally, doing itself in, mindlessly devoting itself to frivolous self-amusement: the unbridled pursuit of thrills, chills, titillations, fun, and ultimately, death.[64]

   Do you agree with the argument that reasoned discourse is now impossible in our culture of advanced communications and obsessive, market-induced desire for pleasure? Explain.

6. The Labor Department conducts regular investigations of business records to ensure compliance with the wages and hours provisions (such as higher pay for overtime) of the Fair Labor Standards Act. When a compliance officer sought to inspect certain financial records at the Lone Steer restaurant/motel in Steele, North Dakota, the restaurant declined his admittance until the government detailed the scope of the investigation. Not receiving a satisfactory response, the Lone Steer demanded a search warrant prior to inspection. As provided for under the FLSA, the government secured an administrative subpoena, which, unlike a search warrant, does not require judicial approval. Once again, Lone Steer denied admission. The government then filed suit. Decide. Explain. See *Donovan v. Lone Steer,* 464 U.S. 408 (1984).

7. Would the police violate a suspect's Fourth Amendment rights against unlawful search and seizure by secretly placing a GPS tracking device on the suspect's car for an extended time without first securing a warrant to do so? Explain. See, for example, *United States of America v. Lawrence Maynard,* 615 F.3d 544 (D.C. Cir. 2010); petition for rehearing en banc denied, *United States of America v. Antoine Jones,* 625 F.3d 766 (D.C. Cir. 2010).

8. An Erie, Pennsylvania, public indecency ordinance prohibited knowingly or intentionally appearing in public in a "state of nudity." Pap's, the owners of Kandyland, an Erie

establishment featuring totally nude dancers, challenged the constitutionality of the ordinance.

 a. Explain the nature of that constitutional challenge.

 b. Decide the case. Explain. See *City of Erie v. Pap's A.M.*, 529 U.S. 277 (2000).

9. An individual and a group applied to the Chicago Park District for permits to hold rallies advocating the legalization of marijuana. The Park District, a municipal agency, required a permit to conduct a public assembly, parade, or other event involving more than 50 individuals. Applications for permits had to be processed within 28 days, and denials had to be clearly explained. Denials could be appealed to the general superintendent and then to the courts. The Park District denied some of the permits for pro-marijuana rallies. Those denied filed suit, claiming the Park District permit rules were unconstitutional.

 a. What constitutional challenge was raised by the plaintiffs?

 b. Decide the case. Explain. See *Thomas and Windy City Hemp Development Board v. Chicago Park District*, 534 U.S. 316 (2002).

10. United States Supreme Court Justice Antonin Scalia was asked if the judicial system had "gone off in error" by applying the equal protection requirements of the 14th Amendment to sex discrimination and sexual orientation discrimination. Scalia responded, "Yes, yes. . . . Certainly the Constitution does not require discrimination on the basis of sex. The only issue is whether it prohibits it. It doesn't. . . ."[65]

 a. Explain why Scalia believes the 14th Amendment does not forbid discrimination based on sex and sexual orientation.

 b. Do you agree with Scalia? Explain.

11. Lancaster, California, located about 45 miles from Los Angeles, was trying to build its local economy but was tripped up by the United States Constitution. Costco, a big-box retailer, wanted to expand into next-door space leased to 99 Cents Only Stores. Costco told the city it would move to Palmdale if it could not expand. Lancaster tried to buy 99 Cents' lease, but the company refused. Lancaster then used its power of eminent domain to condemn the 99 Cents property for the purpose of making it available to Costco. The city noted that blight might follow if Costco left, and the city contrasted 99 Cents' under $40,000 per year in sales taxes generated with Costco's more than $400,000. 99 Cents then sued the city seeking an order blocking the effort to take the 99 Cents property.

 a. How would you have ruled on the case when it was tried in 2001? Explain.

 b. Would the result be any different today after the Supreme Court's 2005 decision in the *Kelo* (New London, Connecticut), case? Explain. See *99 Cents Only Stores v. Lancaster Redevelopment Agency*, 237 F.Supp.2d 1123 (C.D. Cal. 2001). Appeal dismissed, 2003 U.S. App. LEXIS 4197.

12. Long Island, New York, resident Stephanie Fuller was secretly videotaped by her landlord, who had installed a video camera in the smoke detector above her bed. Fuller's landlord was found guilty of trespassing and was fined $1,500 and sentenced to 280 hours of community service.

 a. Why was the landlord not charged with a more serious felony offense?

 b. After Fuller's experience, New York enacted a criminal unlawful surveillance statute; the statute includes language forbidding secret surveillance in places where the victim has "a reasonable expectation of privacy." What significance attaches to that language?

13. A California sales and use tax of 6 percent on all personal property sales was applied to the distribution of religious materials by religious organizations. The Jimmy Swaggart Ministries challenged the tax on constitutional grounds.
    a. What constitutional issue was raised by the plaintiff?
    b. Decide. Explain. See *Jimmy Swaggart Ministries v. Board of Equalization of California,* 493 U.S. 378 (1990).

14. Milwaukee prostitutes, who had been arrested on multiple occasions, sued to block the city from enforcing a court-ordered injunction that permanently enjoined them from engaging in certain specified activities in certain specified areas of the city. They were prohibited from "engaging in, beckoning to stop, or engaging male or female passersby in conversation, or stopping or attempting to stop motor vehicle operators by hailing, waving of arms or any other bodily gesture, or yelling in a loud voice" and other such activities. The women challenged the order on constitutional grounds.
    a. Explain the nature of that constitutional challenge.
    b. Decide the case. Explain. See *City of Milwaukee v. Burnette,* 637 N.W.2d 447 (Wis. App. 2001); 638 N.W.2d 590 (Wis. S.Ct. 2001).

15. Milagros Irizarry lived with the same man for more than two decades, during which time they raised two children. Irizarry, an employee of the Chicago public school system, received health benefits, but her male partner did not because the couple had not married. The school system provided health benefits to domestic partners of the same sex, but not to those of the opposite sex. Irizarry raised a constitutional challenge to the denial of benefits to her male partner.
    a. Explain the nature of that constitutional challenge.
    b. Decide the case. Explain. See *Irizarry v. Board of Education of the City of Chicago,* 251 F.3d 604 (7th Cir. 2001).

16. Paul Palmer submitted three shirts to his Waxahachie, Texas school for approval under the school's dress code. Two of the shirts said "John Edwards for President" and one said "Freedom of Speech" on the front and had the text of the First Amendment on the back. The shirts were rejected as violations of the school's dress code that did not allow shirts with printed messages except for those related to the school and those smaller than two inches by two inches. Political messages were permitted on pins, buttons, bumper stickers, and the like. The dress code was designed to curb gang problems, reduce distractions, encourage professional dress, and maintain a safer, more orderly learning environment. Palmer sued the school claiming a violation of his First Amendment freedom of speech rights. Decide that case. Explain. See *Palmer v. Waxahachie Independent School District,* 579 F.3d 502 (5th Cir. 2009); cert. den. *Palmer v. Waxahachie Independent School District,* 130 S.Ct. 1055 (2010).

17. The sons of a murder victim brought a wrongful death/negligence action against a magazine, *Soldier of Fortune,* alleging that it had published an ad creating an unreasonable risk of violent crime. A former police officer had placed the ad offering his services as a bodyguard under the heading "Gun for Hire." The ad resulted in the officer being hired to kill the plaintiffs' father. The ad included the phrases "professional mercenary," "very private," and a statement indicating that "all jobs" would be considered, but it also included a list of legitimate jobs that involved the use of a gun. The plaintiffs

won the negligence action and were awarded a $4.3 million judgment. *Soldier of Fortune* appealed on First Amendment grounds. Decide. See *Braun v. Soldier of Fortune Magazine, Inc.,* 968 F.2d 1110 (11th Cir. 1992); cert. den. 113 S.Ct. 1028 (1993).

18. The Madisonian idea of the First Amendment was to protect serious political discourse. Now the First Amendment often protects hate speech and commercial babble. In a 1996 book review and commentary, lawyer Paul Reidinger raised the concern that we may have "too much" free speech. Reidinger said, "The question these days is not whether government threatens free speech, but whether free speech threatens us. . . . [T]here is a tidal wave of fetid speech washing over the American landscape." Has the marketplace of ideas failed? See Paul Reidinger, "Weighing Cost of Free Speech," *ABA Journal* 82 (January 1996), p. 88.

Notes

1. Portions of this history of the U.S. Constitution rely on Gordon Lloyd, "Introduction to the Constitutional Convention," [**http://teachingamericanhistory.org/convention/intro.html**].
2. *McDonald v. Chicago,* 130 S.Ct. 3020 (2010).
3. See *Heller v. District of Columbia,* 698 F.Supp.2d 179 (2010). (On appeal, at this writing.)
4. Editorial, "The Court: Ignoring the Reality of Guns," *The New York Times,* June 28, 2010 [**http://www.nytimes.com**].
5. Jeffrey Brumer, "Comparing Gun Homicides in U.S. vs. Other Countries," *The Des Moines Register,* January 23, 2011, p. 2A.
6. Jerre Williams, *Constitutional Analysis in a Nutshell* (St. Paul: West, 1979), p. 33.
7. *McCulloch v. Maryland,* 17 U.S. 316 (1819).
8. *Marbury v. Madison,* 5 U.S. (1 Cranch) 137 (1803).
9. For a discussion of judicial activism, see Kevin Baine, "Making Law on the Court," *The Washington Post,* June 9, 2009 [**http://www.washingtonpost.com/**].
10. *Chamber of Commerce of the United States of America v. Whiting,* 2011 U.S. LEXIS 4018.
11. Terence Chea, "'Under God' in Pledge of Allegiance Upheld by Court," *Huffington Post,* March 12, 2010 [**http://www.huffingtonpost.com/**].
12. *Newdow v. Rio Linda Union School District,* 597 F.3d 1007 (9th Cir. 2010).
13. *Newdow v. Lefevre,* 598 F.3d 638 (9th Cir. 2010); cert. den., *Newdow v. Peter Lefevre,* 131 S.Ct. 1612 (2011).
14. *Christian Legal Society v. Leo P. Martinez,* 130 S.Ct. 2971 (2010).
15. Cheryl Lavin, "The Redemption of Larry Flynt," *Chicago Tribune,* December 27, 1996 [**http://articles.chicagotribune.com/**].
16. *Snyder v. Phelps,* 131 S.Ct. 1207 (2011).
17. Ibid.
18. Adam Cohen, "Why Spewing Hate at Funerals Is Still Free Speech," *Time,* September 29, 2010 [**http://www.time.com/**].
19. *Tinker v. Des Moines School District,* 393 U.S. 503 (1969).
20. Debra Cassens Weiss, "Indiana Deputy AG Loses Job after Live Ammo Tweet," *ABA Journal,* February 24, 2011 [**http://www.abajournal.com/**].
21. Ibid.
22. *Garcetti v. Ceballos,* 126 S.Ct. 1951 (2006).

23. "What Are Speech Codes?" *Foundation for Individual Rights in Education—The Torch* [**http://thefire.org/code/whatarespeechcodes/**].

24. Jordi Gasso, "Breaking: DOE's Office for Civil Rights to Investigate Yale for 'Hostile Sexual Environment,'" *Yale Daily News,* March 31, 2011 [**http://www.yaledailynews.com/**].

25. Erica Goldberg, "Universities' Compliance with Speech Code Decisions Leaves Much to Be Desired," September 24, 2009, *Foundation for Individual Rights in Education—The Torch* [**http://thefire.org/article/11121.html**].

26. *Rodriguez v. Maricopa County Community College,* 605 F.3d 703 (9th Cir. 2010).

27. *Barrett v. University of Mississippi,* 232 F.3d 208 (5th Cir. 2000); cert. den. 531 U.S. 1052 (2000).

28. *Corry v. Stanford University,* Superior Court, Santa Clara County (CA), #740309, February 27, 1995.

29. Heather Mason Kiefer, "Support Cooling for Flag-Burning Amendment," Gallup Poll, July 26, 2005 [**http://www.gallup.com/poll/17491/support-cooling-flagburning-amendment.aspx**].

30. Phyllis Schlafly, "High Court Backs Pornographers," *Chattanooga Times Free Press,* July 12, 2004, p. B7.

31. *Valentine v. Chrestensen,* 316 U.S. 52 (1942).

32. *Citizens United v. Federal Election Commission,* 130 S.Ct. 876 (2010).

33. David G. Savage, "Corporate Free-Speech Ruling Speaks of Shift in Supreme Court," *latimes. com,* February 9, 2010 [**http://www.latimes.com/**].

34. *Citizens United,* 2010.

35. David G. Savage, "Corporate Free-Speech," February 9, 2010.

36. *United States v. Stevens,* 130 S.Ct. 1577 (2010).

37. Norman M. Cheektowaga, "And a Rude Gesture to You, Too, Judges," *Buffalo News,* February 5, 1998, p. 3B.

38. 367 U.S. 643.

39. *Hudson v. Michigan,* 126 S.Ct. 2159 (2006).

40. *Herring v. United States,* 555 U.S. 135 (2009).

41. *Arizona v. Gant,* 129 S.Ct. 1710 (2009).

42. This paragraph is derived in part from Adam Liptak, "Supreme Court Cuts Back Officers' Searches of Vehicles," *The New York Times,* April 22, 2009 [**http://www.nytimes.com/**].

43. *Ohio v. Smith,* 920 N.E.2d 949 (Ohio S.Ct. 2009).

44. *The People v. Gregory Diaz,* 244 P.3d 501 (Cal. S.Ct. 2011).

45. *Board of Education of Pottawatomie County v. Earls,* 122 S.Ct. 2559 (2002).

46. *Earls v. Board of Education,* 242 F.3d 1264 (10th Cir. 2001).

47. Floralynn Einesman, "Drug Testing Students in California—Does It Violate the State Constitution?" *San Diego Law Review* 47 (Summer 2010), p. 681.

48. *State of Washington v. Glas,* 2002 Wash. LEXIS 596.

49. *Marshall v. Barlow's,* 436 U.S. 307 (1978).

50. Ilya Somin, "The Limits of Backlash: Assessing the Political Response to *Kelo,*" (March 2007). *George Mason Law & Economics Research Paper No. 07-14.* Available at SSRN: **http://ssrn. com/abstract=976298**.

51. Nathan Koppel, "There Goes the Neighborhood: A Fight Over Defining 'Blight,'" *The Wall Street Journal,* April 30, 2009, p. A11.

52. For an editorial assessment of the Community Youth Athletic Center case, see "Property Rights Knockout," *The Wall Street Journal,* May 2, 2011, p. A14.

53. *Lucas v. So. Carolina Coastal Commission,* 112 S.Ct. 2886 (1992).

54. *Dolan v. City of Tigard,* 114 S.Ct. 2309 (1994).

55. Frank A. Vickory and Barry A. Diskin, "Advances in Private Property Protection Rights: The States in the Vanguard," *American Business Law Journal* 34, no. 4 (Summer 1997), p. 561.

56. See Vickory and Diskin, "Advances in Private Property," p. 561, and David L. Callies, "Regulatory Takings and the Supreme Court," *Stetson Law Review* 28 (Winter 1999), p. 523.

57. *Griswold v. Connecticut,* 381 U.S. 479 (1965).

58. *United States v. Skilling,* 2011 U.S. App. LEXIS 7031.

59. *BMW of N. Am. v. Gore,* 517 U.S. 559 (1996).

60. *State Farm v. Campbell,* 538 U.S. 408 (2003).

61. David Crary, "Gay Marriage Backers: Vote in N.Y. Has National Impact," *The Des Moines Register,* June 26, 2011, p. 1A.

62. "53% in U.S. Support Gay Marriage, says *Washington Post*-ABC News Poll," *Tacoma News Tribune,* March 19, 2011 [**http://www.thenewstribune.com/**].

63. "Same-Sex Marriage: Redefining Marriage around the World," *The Pew Charitable Trusts,* July 11, 2007 [**http://www.pewtrusts.org/our_work_report_detail.aspx?id=37196**].

64. Pierre Schlag, "This Could Be Your Culture—Junk Speech in a Time of Decadence," *Harvard Law Review* 109, no. 7 (1996), p. 1801.

65. "The Originalist," *California Lawyer,* January 2011 [**http://www.callawyer.com/story.cfm?eid= 913358&evid=1**].

Contracts

After completing this chapter, students will be able to:

1. Explain the importance of contracts to a capitalist, free market system.

2. Determine whether the Uniform Commercial Code or common law governs a contract dispute.

3. Identify the elements of a legally enforceable contract.

4. Classify a contract as bilateral or unilateral; express or implied; executory or executed.

5. Distinguish between valid, unenforceable, void, and voidable contracts.

6. Describe the elements of a valid offer.

7. Describe the elements of a valid acceptance.

8. Explain the significance of consideration as an element of a legally enforceable contract.

9. Compare and contrast the rights and duties arising in contractual assignment and delegation.

10. Compare and contrast different types of third-party beneficiaries to a contract.

11. Explain how a contract may be discharged.

12. Describe the remedies available for breach of contract.

Preface: The Role of Contracts in a Complex Society

A capitalist, free market system cannot operate effectively and fairly without a reliable foundation in contract law. At the practical level, all buyers and sellers must have confidence that the deal they are about to make will be completed as specified or that they will have a remedy available if it is not completed. Otherwise, the legal risk in making deals would act as a drag on the commercial process, reducing certainty and depreciating the extraordinary efficiency of the free market. At the philosophical level, the fundamental point of a contract regime is personal freedom. Contract law gives each of us a reliable mechanism for freely expressing our preferences in life. From buying a tube of toothpaste, a car, or a house, to paying tuition, to accepting an employment offer, to franchising a business, to borrowing millions of dollars, to adopting a child, and so on, the direction and value of our lives are shaped and protected to a significant degree by our contractual choices. To a considerable extent, we define ourselves as persons by the contractual choices we make, and contract law protects those choices. The indispensable role of contract law is revealed in the remarkable Facebook story that follows.

Who Owns Facebook?

Mark Zuckerberg, Facebook CEO, developed the fabulously successful social network while still a student at Harvard. At this writing in 2011, however, Zuckerberg's continuing ownership of the company is being challenged on the basis of a document alleged to be a contract signed by Zuckerberg. Paul Ceglia, an entrepreneur and accused felon, has sued Facebook and Zuckerberg claiming that he and Zuckerberg entered into a contract in 2003 that entitles Ceglia to a 50 percent share in the company. A photocopy of the document has been filed with Ceglia's lawsuit. Facebook has said the alleged contract is a forgery, and Zuckerberg has said that he is confident that he never signed any such contract.

Ceglia says the document turned up when he was looking through some old files to find assets to pay customers of his failed wood pellet business, an enterprise that is the subject of fraud charges filed against Ceglia. The document, Ceglia alleges, is a "Work for Hire" contract signed by Zuckerberg when he was an 18-year-old Harvard freshman. The alleged contract shows Ceglia agreeing to pay Zuckerberg $1,000 to write computer code for Street Fax, a company Ceglia was creating. That portion of the deal appears to be unchallenged at this writing. The document also refers to a $1,000 investment by Ceglia in a project repeatedly labeled "The Face Book" or, in one instance, "The Page Book." Ceglia claims a partnership arose from these dealings entitling him to a 50 percent share in Facebook. Ceglia also claims to have e-mail evidence supporting his claim. Facebook has indicated in court that Zuckerberg did sign a contract with Ceglia and did work for Ceglia but did not sign over any interest in Facebook. Indeed, Facebook claims that Zuckerberg could not have transferred a share in Facebook to Ceglia because he did not conceive of the Facebook project until the following year. Facebook presumably will try to establish that the document and the Zuckerberg signature are forgeries and failing that likely will rely on New York's six-year statute of limitations. Of course, if those strategies fail, a settlement could be the eventual resolution of this extraordinary case. [For the alleged Ceglia–Zuckerberg contract, see: "Work for Hire Contract" at **http:// www.businessinsider.com/mark-zuckerbergs-facebook-contract-with-paul-ceglia**]

Zuckerberg received better news on another legal front when a court refused to throw out a 2008 settlement between Zuckerberg and his college business partners, twins Cameron and Tyler Winklevoss. The twins' battle with Zuckerberg over the rights to the Facebook idea was the subject of the 2010 movie, *The Social Network*. The twins claim Zuckerberg stole their social networking idea. Zuckerberg denied that accusation, but the parties reached a settlement of about $65 million in 2008. The twins sued, however, to have the settlement overturned on the grounds that Facebook had not provided accurate valuation information during the settlement process. A court of appeals panel in 2011 rejected the twins' request. They have discontinued the appeals process at this writing.

At the same time, Boston software developer Wayne Chang is suing the Winklevoss twins for breach of contract, among other claims. Chang believes he is entitled to a share of the Winklevoss–Zuckerberg settlement (currently valued at around $160 million) based on a partnership and other understandings he claims to have entered with the twins during their Harvard years to create and operate a social networking site named ConnectU.

[For a Fox News account of Paul Ceglia's contracts-based claim for partial ownership of Facebook, see **www.youtube.com/watch?v=CQ9vDJWAeQQ** or for a humorous, animated overview of the Paul Ceglia–Mark Zuckerberg contracts dispute see **www. wellsvilledaily.com/features/x328920403/VIDEO-Animation-of-Ceglias-Facebook-lawsuit-against-Zuckerberg**]

Sources: Bob Van Voris, "Facebook Claimant Says He Owns 50%, Has E-Mails as Proof," *Bloomberg Businessweek,* April 12, 2011 [**http://www.businessweek.com**]; "Boston Developer Wants Cut of Winklevoss Twins' $65-Million Facebook Settlement," *Los Angeles Times,* May 12, 2011 [**http://latimesblogs.latimes.com/technology/2011/05/ boston-developer-wants-cut-of-winklevoss-twins-65-million-facebook-settlement.html**]; Alice Gomstyn and Ki Mae Heussner, "Paul Ceglia: Facebook Claim Stemmed from Arrest," ABC News, August 2, 2010 [**http://abcnews. go.com**]; and Henry Blodget, "Analyzing the Facebook Contract: Is Mark Zuckerberg Screwed?" *Business Insider,* July 23, 2010 [**http://www.businessinsider.com**].

Part One—Building a Binding Contract

Introduction

We make promises as a matter of routine in our lives. Some of those create binding contracts; some do not. You promise, for example, to meet a friend after class, but you break your promise. Have you breached a contract such that you could be sued in court? Doubtless your answer is "no" and, barring unusual circumstances, you would be correct. But why? Thus, the central question in this chapter is the following: Under what circumstances do promises become enforceable contracts? For the most part, the answer to that question has been provided by court decisions (the common law) accumulating over the many centuries of evolving contract law stretching from the ancient Middle East to England and across the Atlantic to America. Those centuries of decisions provided a substantially fair, consistent, and predictable body of contract law; particularly in a culture where the parties normally dealt with each other face-to-face; often as acquaintances. As business transactions became more complicated, the parties more and more distant from each other and the comparative power between individuals and corporations evermore unbalanced, the need for government intervention increased. State legislatures began to impose new rules on what had been purely private transactions. Look, for example, at state and federal regulation of employment contracts/relationships governing working conditions such as hours of work, safety on the job, break time, etc. (as explained in detail in Chapter 12). State laws and court decisions resulted, to some extent, in a confusing, inefficient patchwork of laws that didn't conform to the reality of complex, contemporary business practice. As a result, the states developed the Uniform Commercial Code, a body of rules to govern commercial law across America.

> **Have you breached a contract?**

The Uniform Commercial Code

The National Conference of Commissioners on Uniform State Laws (NCCUSL) and the American Law Institute (ALI) developed, for state-by-state approval, the Uniform Commercial Code (UCC), a body of rules designed to render commercial law consistent across the 50 states. The UCC has been adopted in 49 states, and Louisiana has adopted portions of it. With a set of uniform, predictable rules, business can be practiced with confidence and minimal legal confusion.

The UCC is divided into a series of articles addressing the multitude of potential problems that arise in complex commercial practice. For our purposes the most important of those articles is Number 2, Sales, which governs all transactions involving the *sale of goods*. Section 2-105 of the UCC defines goods as tangible, movable, things. Hence cars, clothing, appliances, and the like are covered. Real estate, stocks, bonds, money, and so forth are not covered. Nor are contracts for services governed by the UCC. Of course, many transactions involve both goods and services. Characteristically, in determining whether the UCC applies, the courts have asked whether the dominant purpose of the contract is to provide a service or to sell a good. Appendix B, at the back of the text, sets out the complete Article 2.

The first question, then, in contract disputes is whether the UCC or the common law governs the situation. Throughout this chapter, you should remember that the UCC is always controlling (1) if the transaction is addressed by the UCC—that is, it involves a contract for the sale of goods—and (2) if a UCC rule applies to the issue in question. On the other hand, the judge-made, common law of contracts continues to govern transactions (1) not involving the sale of goods or (2) involving the sale of goods but where no specific UCC provision applies. Increasingly, in non-UCC cases, the courts are analogizing to UCC reasoning to render their judgments; that is, the common law is borrowing or absorbing UCC principles. This chapter, while focusing primarily on the common law of contracts, will introduce the role of the sales article in the practice of business. At this writing, NCCUSL/ALI–recommended revisions to the sales article are being considered by the various state legislatures, most of which seem reluctant to make major changes. Article 2A of the UCC governs *leases* of goods. In essence, Article 2A mimics the sales article except that it governs leases of goods rather than sales. Because of space constraints, Article 2A will not receive further attention in this text.

What Is a Contract?

Legally enforceable contracts must exhibit all of the following features:

1. **Agreement**—a meeting of the minds of the parties based on an offer by one and an acceptance by the other. The determination as to whether the parties have actually reached agreement is based on the *objective* evidence (the parties' acts, words, and so on) as a "reasonable person" would interpret it rather than on an effort to ascertain the subjective or personal intent of the parties.

2. **Consideration.** The bargained-for legal value that one party agrees to pay or provide to secure the promise of another.

3. **Capacity.** The parties must have the legal ability to enter the contract; that is, they must be sane, sober, and of legal age.

4. **Genuineness of assent.** The parties must knowingly agree to the same thing. Their minds must meet as evidenced by the objective evidence. If that meeting does not occur

because of mistake, fraud, or the like, a contract does not exist because the parties' assent was not real.

5. **Legality of purpose.** The object of the contract must not violate the law or public policy.

Contracts embracing these five features are enforceable by law and hence are distinguishable from unenforceable promises. As explained later, some contracts must be in writing to be enforceable.

Classification of Contracts

Contracts fall into a series of sometimes overlapping categories. Understanding those categories helps reveal the rather well-ordered logic of our contract system (see Figure 6.1).

Contract Formation

1. **Bilateral and unilateral contracts.** A *bilateral contract* emerges from a situation in which *both* parties make promises. A *unilateral contract* ordinarily involves a situation in which one party makes a promise and the other *acts* in response to that promise. For example, in beginning to establish your new restaurant you promise a college friend that if he completes his degree, you will hire him. He can accept your offer/promise by the act of completing college.

FIGURE 6.1
Classification of Contracts

Contract Formation
1. Bilateral/unilateral
   a. Bilateral contract—a promise for a promise.
   b. Unilateral contract—a promise for an act.
2. Express/implied
   a. Express contract—explicitly stated in writing or orally.
   b. Implied-in-fact contract—inferred from the conduct of the parties.
   c. Quasi-contract—implied contract created by a court to prevent unjust enrichment.

Contract performance
1. Executory contract—not yet fully performed.
2. Executed contract—fully performed by all parties.

Contract enforceability
1. Valid contract—includes all of the necessary ingredients of a binding contract.
2. Unenforceable contract—contract exists, but a legal defense prevents enforcement.
3. Void contract—no contract at all.
4. Voidable contract—one party has the option of either enforcing or voiding the contract.

2. **Express and implied contracts.** When parties overtly and explicitly manifest their intention to enter an agreement, either in writing or orally, the result (if other requirements are fulfilled) is an express contract. For example, in managing your department at an insurance firm, you sign a form contract with a local computer store ordering a new computer. In turn, the supplier's signature on the form creates an express, bilateral agreement.

If, on the other hand, you ask your local computer service to take a look at a machine that is down and one of the service's technicians does so, you have probably entered an *implied-in-fact contract*. A court would infer a promise by you to pay a reasonable price in return for the service's promise to make a commercially reasonable effort to repair the computer. The contract is inferred on the basis of the facts—that is, by the behavior of the parties.

Suppose in managing your insurance department you have received payment for insurance that was, in fact, issued by a rival firm. In these circumstances, it would be unfair for you to be able to keep the unearned money so the courts construct an implied-in-law or quasi-contract permitting the actual insurer to collect the money. This unusual situation in which the court infers the existence of a contract is employed only when necessary to prevent *unjust enrichment* (as would have been the case if you were to collect an insurance premium without having issued a policy).

Contract Performance

1. **Executory contracts.** A contract is labeled *executory* until all parties fully perform.

2. **Executed contracts.** When all parties have completed their performances, the contract is *executed*.

Contract Enforceability

1. **Valid contracts.** A valid contract meets all of the established legal requirements and thus is enforceable in court.

2. **Unenforceable contracts.** An unenforceable contract meets the basic contractual requirements but remains faulty because it fails to fulfill some other legal rule. For example, an oral contract may be unenforceable if it falls in one of those categories of contracts, such as the sale of land, which must be in writing (see the Statute of Frauds later in this chapter).

3. **Void contracts.** A void contract is, in fact, no contract at all because a critical legal requirement is missing; usually it is either an agreement to accomplish an illegal purpose (such as to commit a crime) or an agreement involving an incompetent (such as an individual judged by a court to be insane). In either case what is otherwise an enforceable contract is in fact void.

4. **Voidable contracts.** A voidable contract is enforceable but can be canceled by one or more of the parties. The most common voidable contracts are those entered by minors who have the option, under the law, of either disaffirming or fulfilling most contracts (explained later).

Can I Change My Mind?

Australian Vin Thomas placed his 1946 World War II Wirraway plane for sale on eBay. The plane reportedly is one of only five in the world still flying. Peter Smythe, also of Australia, matched the $128,640 reserve price moments before the online auction ended in 2006. Thomas then declined to convey the airplane to Smythe apparently because Thomas had already agreed to sell the plane to another party for $85,800 more than Smythe's bid. The case involved, among others, a pair of issues frequently arising in contracts law disputes: (1) Did the facts (the eBay auction) create a contract? (2) Can Thomas change his mind about selling the plane to the highest bidder?

Answer those questions according to the U.S. contract law that follows.

The Agreement: Offer

Characteristically, an offer consists of a promise to do something or to refrain from doing something in the future. A valid offer must include all of these elements:

1. Present *intent* to enter a contract.
2. Reasonable *definiteness* in the terms of the offer.
3. *Communication* of the offer to the offeree.

Intent

Assume that you are the purchasing manager for a trucking firm, and you need a small used van to do some local light hauling. Because time is of the essence, you decide to bypass the normal bidding process and go directly to the local dealers to make a quick purchase. At the first lot you find a suitable van. In discussing it, the sales manager says, "Well, we don't usually do this, but since you've been such a good customer, I'll tell you, we paid $10,000 for this one so I guess we are gonna need about $11,000 to deal with you." You say, "Fine. That's reasonable. I'll take it." The manager then says, "Now wait a minute, I was just talking off the top of my head. I'll have to punch up the numbers to be sure."

Do you have a deal at that point? The core question is whether the sales manager made an *offer*. Normally, language of that kind has been treated by the courts as preliminary negotiation lacking the necessary *intent* to constitute an offer. Of course, if no offer exists, you cannot accept, and no contract can emerge absent further negotiation.

Gambling

In 2006, Troy Blackford, a Des Moines, Iowa truck driver, won $9,387 gambling at Prairie Meadows casino. Blackford tried to collect the winnings, but his request was denied by the casino. Officials said that he had been banned from the casino since 1996, and the ban had not been lifted. (In the 1996 episode, Blackford had punched a slot machine and was belligerent with casino security.) Blackford sued the casino.

1. What was the central issue in the case? Explain.
2. Decide the case. Explain.

Source: *Blackford v. Prairie Meadows Racetrack & Casino*, 778 N.W.2d 184 (Ia. S.Ct. 2010).

> Suppose you were responding to an ad that said, "2007 full-size Ford cargo van, $20,000." Is that ad language an offer such that you can accept by promising to pay $20,000?

Advertisements   The question of intent sometimes arises with advertisements. In buying the van for your business, suppose you were responding to an ad that said, "2007 full-size Ford cargo van, $20,000." Is that ad language an offer such that you can accept by promising to pay $20,000? Ordinarily, ads do not constitute offers, but rather are treated by the courts as *invitations to deal*. Were an ad actually treated as an offer, it would put the seller in the commercially impracticable position of being required to provide the advertised product at the advertised price to everyone who sought one, regardless of available supply. Presumably, that open-ended duty was not the seller's intent when issuing the ad. It follows then that the buyer, in responding to an ad, is technically making an offer, with the seller free to accept or decline.

On the other hand, courts have held that some ads do manifest a present intent to make an offer. The critical terms in those ads must be highly specific and complete, leaving nothing open for negotiation.

A Jet Fighter from Pepsi?

A 1995 Pepsico promotion offered merchandise in exchange for points earned by buying Pepsi-Cola. The television ad showed a teenager modeling some of the available merchandise. A Pepsi T-shirt was displayed for 75 points and a leather jacket for 1450 points. At the end of the ad, a U.S. Marine Corps Harrier "jump jet" landed outside a school, and the boy said, "Sure beats the bus." The ad said the jet was redeemable for 7 million points. John D.R. Leonard, at the time a 21-year-old business student in Seattle, Washington, joined five investors in writing a check to Pepsi for $700,008.50 and demanded the 7 million Pepsi points. Pepsi returned the check and said it had no intention of giving Leonard the $24 million jet. Leonard sued. Who wins? Explain.

Source: *John D.R. Leonard v. Pepsico*, 210 F.3d 88 (2d Cir. Ct. App. 2000).

[For a video of the ad, see **http://www.stcl.edu/faculty-dir/ricks/casebook/pepsi1.wmv.** Other versions of the ad can be found at pepsi2 and pepsi3]

Definiteness

Suppose you have completed a management training program for a "big box" retailer. In your first assignment as an assistant manager, your boss asks you to seek bids and make the other arrangements (subject to her approval) to resurface the store's large asphalt parking lot. You secure bids, and the lowest bidder offers to complete the work "later this summer" for $120,000. You briefly explain the offer to your boss, who tells you to take care of all the details. You are busy with other matters and you put off the parking lot project for a couple of weeks. When you get back to the contractor, he says, "Sorry, man, we hadn't heard from you, and we got another deal." Can you hold that contractor to his initial offer?

One of the requirements of a binding offer is that all of its critical terms must be sufficiently clear that a court can determine both the intentions of the parties and their duties. Clearly, in the asphalt case, many critical details—such as precisely when the work would be done, the quality of the surfacing material, its thickness, and the like—had not been established. Consequently, no offer existed. In a contract for the sale of goods, UCC 2-204 relaxes the definiteness standard by providing that "one or more terms" may be missing but the court can find a contract, nonetheless, where (1) "the parties have intended to make a contract" and (2) "there is a reasonably certain basis for giving an appropriate remedy." Under the UCC, the courts can actually fill in missing terms such as specifying a reasonable price where the contract had omitted a stipulation. The following case involving Mariah Carey, the pop music star, demonstrates some of the problems that can arise when an understanding is indefinite.

LEGAL BRIEFCASE

Vian v. Carey   1993 U.S. Dist.
Lexis 5460 (U.S. Dist. Ct. S.D.N.Y. 1993)

Judge Mukasey

Defendant Mariah Carey is a famous, successful and apparently wealthy entertainer. Plaintiff Joseph Vian was her stepfather before she achieved stardom, but at the start of this litigation was in the process of becoming divorced from defendant's mother. He claims defendant agreed orally that he would have a license to market singing dolls in her likeness. . . . Plaintiff claims that he and Carey had an oral contract for him to receive a license to market "Mariah dolls." These dolls would be statuettes of the singer and would play her most popular songs. Plaintiff claims that the contract was in consideration of his financial and emotional support of defendant, including picking her up from late-night recording sessions, providing her with the use of a car, paying for dental care, allowing her to use his boat for business meetings and rehearsals, and giving her various items, including unused wedding gifts from his marriage to her mother, to help furnish her apartment.

The alleged basis of the oral contract is that on at least three occasions, twice in the family car and once on Vian's boat, Vian told Carey, "Don't forget the Mariah dolls," and "I get the Mariah dolls." According to Vian, on one occasion Carey responded "okay" and on other occasions she merely smiled and nodded. Although Carey admits Vian mentioned the dolls two or three times, she testified that she thought it was a joke. For 30 years plaintiff has been in the business of designing, producing, and marketing gift and novelty items. Although it is not clear from the evidence the parties have submitted, it will be assumed that the alleged contract was formed after defendant turned 18. Under New York law, an oral agreement can form a binding contract. . . . In determining whether a contract exists, what matters are the parties' expressed intentions, the words and deeds that constitute objective signs in a given set of circumstances.

Therefore, the issue is whether the objective circumstances indicate that the parties intended to form a contract. Without such an intent, neither a contract nor a preliminary agreement to negotiate in good faith can exist. In making such a determination, a court may look at "whether the terms of the contract have been finally resolved." In addition, a court may consider "the context of the negotiations." Plaintiff has adduced no evidence that defendant ever intended by a nod of her head or the expression "okay" to enter into a complex commercial licensing agreement involving dolls in her likeness playing her copyrighted songs. The context in which this contract between an 18-year-old girl and her stepfather allegedly was made was an informal family setting, either in the car or on plaintiff's boat, while others were present. Vian's own version of events leads to the conclusion that there was no reason for Carey to think Vian was entirely serious, let alone that he intended to bind her to an agreement at that time. He admits he never told her he was serious. The objective circumstances do not indicate that Carey intended to form a contract with plaintiff. Although plaintiff's five-page memorandum of law fails to raise the possibility, plaintiff also has not shown that Carey intended to be bound to negotiate with plaintiff at some later date over the licensing of "Mariah dolls."

There can be no meeting of the minds, required for the formation of a contract, where essential material terms are missing. Thus, even if the parties both believe themselves to be bound, there is no contract when "the terms of the agreement are so vague and indefinite that there is no basis or standard for deciding whether the agreement had been kept or broken, or to fashion a remedy, and no means by which such terms may be made certain."

. . . The word "license" was not even used. As defendant points out, no price or royalty term was mentioned, nor was the duration or geographic scope of the license, nor was Carey's right to approve the dolls. Plaintiff admits he would not have gone ahead without defendant's approval, thus conceding the materiality of that term.

* * * * *

In sum, plaintiff has not raised a triable issue of fact as to the existence of a contract. Defendant's motion for summary judgment is granted.

Questions

1. Why did the court find for Carey?

2. As noted in the text, in UCC cases judges fill in contract terms where the parties clearly intended a deal. Should the court here fill in the missing terms to provide the necessary definiteness? Explain.

3. Pilgrim Village Company had employed Petersen as a construction manager at a specified annual salary and "a share of the profits." Petersen worked at salary for several years and then asked for a 10 percent share of the profits. The company refused, and Petersen sued seeking "some share of the profits." How should the court rule on Petersen's claim? Explain. See *Petersen v. Pilgrim Village*, 42 N.W.2d 273 (Wis. S.Ct., 1950).

Communication

As explained, an effective offer must be the product of a present intent, it must be definite, and it must be communicated to the offeree. Communication of an offer expresses the offeror's intent to make that offer. Suppose a friend tells you that your neighbor has offered to sell his classic jukebox for $10,000. You call your neighbor and say, "I accept. I'll be right over with the $10,000." Do you have a deal? No. The owner did not communicate the offer to you. The fact that it was not communicated to you may suggest that your neighbor does not want to sell or does not want to sell to you.

Duration of an Offer   Communication of an offer affords the offeree the opportunity to create a contract by accepting that offer, but how long does that opportunity last? Here are some general rules:

1. The offeror may revoke the offer anytime prior to acceptance. (Some exceptions are explained later.) Normally, revocation is effective on receipt by the offeree. Under common law the offeror has the right to revoke at any time prior to acceptance, even if he or she expressly promised to keep the offer open for a specified period.
2. The offer may specify that it is open for an express period (such as 10 days).
3. Where a time limit is not specified in the offer it will be presumed to be open for a reasonable period.
4. An offer expires if rejected or on receipt of a counteroffer.

Irrevocable Offers

Some kinds of offers may not be revoked. We will note three of them.

1. **Option contracts.** When an offeror promises to keep an offer open for a specified period and, in return, the offeree pays consideration (usually money), the parties have created an option contract, which is a separate agreement and is enforceable by its terms. For example, a friend has offered to sell to you his customized car that you have long cherished, but you want to think about it for a few days. You might enter an option contract with your friend under which you pay $100 for the seller's promise to keep the offer open for seven days. You are under no obligation to buy the car, but the seller is under a binding obligation not to withdraw the offer or sell to another during the seven days.
2. **Firm offers.** Under the UCC, if the owner of that customized car is a dealer (a merchant) and he made a written, signed offer to sell that car (a good) to you, indicating that his offer would remain open for seven days, he is bound to that promise whether you paid consideration for it or not. That situation is labeled a firm offer as specified in UCC 2-205, which also provides that such offers will be kept open for a reasonable period if the agreement does not mention a time, but that period cannot exceed three months.
3. **Offers for unilateral contracts.** A problem sometimes arises when the offeror attempts to revoke a unilateral offer after the offeree has begun to perform. For example, your neighbor invites you to rake her leaves for $10, and then, when you are virtually done, she yells from the doorway, "Oh, sorry, I changed my mind. You go home now." Historically, the offeror (the neighbor, in this case) was free to revoke at any time; but the modern position holds that the offeror normally cannot revoke if the offeree (you) has commenced performance. If that performance is then completed (you ignore your

neighbor's admonition to go home, and you finish the raking), the offeror (your neighbor) is bound to perform fully is bound to perform fully by paying the $10.

The Agreement: Acceptance

Suppose you are in training with a large real estate firm and your boss has authorized you to enter negotiations to buy a parcel of farmland that your company hopes to develop for housing. After preliminary discussions, you extend a written offer to the owner indicating, among other terms, that your company is willing to pay $10,000 per acre for a 10-acre parcel. Assume the owner responds by writing, "I accept your offer at $10,000 per acre, but I need to keep the two-acre homesite." The offeree has used the word *accept,* but does the response constitute a legally binding *acceptance?*

The general rule is that an effective acceptance must be a mirror image of the offer; that is, ordinarily its terms must be the same as those in the offer. Here the offeree has changed the terms of the offer and in so doing has issued a *counteroffer,* thus extinguishing the original offer.

Communication of Acceptance

An offer may be accepted only by the offeree—that is, the person to whom the offer was directed. Because unilateral offers are accepted by performance, no communication of acceptance beyond that performance ordinarily is necessary. In the case of a bilateral contract (a promise for a promise), acceptance is not effective until communicated.

Broadly, acceptance can be accomplished by a "yes" communicated face-to-face, by a nod of the head or some other appropriate signal, by telephone, or by other unwritten means, unless the law of the state requires writing in that particular kind of transaction.

Mailbox   Confusion sometimes arises when the parties are not dealing face-to-face. In general, acceptance is effective upon dispatch by whatever mode of communication has been explicitly or implicitly authorized by the offeror. This well-settled position is labeled the *mailbox rule* and means, among other things, that an acceptance is effective when sent even if never received. [For one professor's review of the mailbox rule and related rules, see **http://www.tomwbell.com/teaching/KMailbox.pdf**]

Authorization   The offeror controls the acceptance process and may specify an exclusive manner in which an acceptance must be communicated. If so, a contract is not created if the acceptance is communicated in anything other than the stipulated fashion. Traditionally, if the offeror did not give an *express authorization* to a means of communication, an acceptance by the same or faster means than that used by the offeror was implied. *Implied authorization* might also arise from such factors as prior dealings between the parties and custom in their industry.

Modern View   Under the UCC the rules have relaxed a bit. If no specific instructions for acceptance are included in the offer, the offeree is free to accept in any reasonable manner within a reasonable period, and acceptance is effective upon dispatch. Even when the means chosen are "unreasonable," acceptance is effective on dispatch under the UCC 1-201(38) if it is actually received in a timely manner.

Consideration

Earlier we identified the five key ingredients in an enforceable contract: agreement, consideration, capacity, genuineness of assent, and legality of purpose. Having examined the agreement (offer/acceptance) process, we turn now to consideration. As noted earlier, consideration is the bargained-for legal value that one party agrees to pay or provide to secure the promise of another. It is what the promisor demands and receives in exchange for his or her promise. Consideration is used by the courts to distinguish a contract (enforceable) from a gratuitous promise (unenforceable). The *promisee* must suffer a *legal detriment;* that is, the promisee must give up something of value (an act or a promise) or must refrain from doing something that she or he has a legal right to do in order to enforce the promise offered by the *promisor*. Each party, then, must pay a "price" for a contract to be enforceable. In sum, consideration consists of a detriment to the promisee that is bargained for by the promisor.

The classic case that follows explores the idea of consideration and demonstrates that consideration can have legal value without involving monetary loss to the promisee.

LEGAL BRIEFCASE

Hamer v. Sidway
27 N.E. 256 (N.Y. 1891)

FACTS

In 1869 William E. Story Sr. promised his nephew, W.E. Story II, that he would pay the nephew $5,000 upon his 21st birthday if the nephew would refrain from drinking liquor, using tobacco, swearing, and playing cards or billiards for money until he reached that 21st birthday. The nephew agreed and performed his promise, but the uncle died in 1887 without paying the money, and the administrator of the estate, Sidway, declined to pay the $5,000 plus interest. The nephew had assigned (sold) his rights to the money to Louisa Hamer, who sued W.E. Story Sr.'s estate. Hamer, the plaintiff, won at the trial level, lost on appeal, and then appealed to the New York Court of Appeals.

* * * * *

Judge Parker

When the nephew arrived at the age of 21 years and on the 31st day of January 1875, he wrote to his uncle informing him that he had performed his part of the agreement and had thereby become entitled to the sum of $5,000. The uncle received the letter and a few days later and on the sixth of February, he wrote and mailed to his nephew the following letter:

Buffalo, February 6, 1875
W.E. Story, Jr.
Dear Nephew:
Your letter of the 31st came to hand all right, saying that you had lived up to the promise made to me several years ago. I have no doubt but you have, for which you shall have five thousand dollars as I promised you. I had the money in the bank the day you was 21 years old that I intend for you, and you shall have the money certain. Now, Willie I do not intend to interfere with this money in any way till I think you are capable of taking care of it and the sooner that time comes the better it will please me. I would hate very much to have you start out in some adventure that you thought all right and lose this money in one year. The first five thousand dollars that I got together cost me a heap of hard work. You would hardly believe me when I tell you that to obtain this I shoved a jackplane many a day, butchered three or four years, then came to this city, and after three months' perseverance I obtained a situation in a grocery store. I opened this store early, closed late, slept in the fourth story of the building in a room 30 by 40 feet and not a human

being in the building but myself. All this I done to live as cheap as I could to save something. I don't want you to take up with this kind of fare. I was here in the cholera season '49 and '52 and the deaths averaged 80 to 125 daily and plenty of smallpox. I wanted to go home, but Mr. Fisk, the gentleman I was working for, told me if I left then, after it got healthy he probably would not want me. I stayed. All the money I have saved I know just how I got it. It did not come to me in any mysterious way, and the reason I speak of this is that money got in this way stops longer with a fellow that gets it with hard knocks than it does when he finds it. Willie, you are 21 and you have many a thing to learn yet. This money you have earned much easier than I did besides acquiring good habits at the same time and you are quite welcome to the money; hope you will make good use of it. I was 10 long years getting this together after I was your age. Now, hoping this will be satisfactory, I stop . . .
Truly Yours,
W.E. STORY
P.S.—You can consider this money on interest.

The nephew received the letter and thereafter consented that the money should remain with his uncle in accordance with the terms and conditions of the letter. The uncle died on the 29th day of January 1887, without having paid over to his nephew any portion of the said $5,000 and interest.

* * * * *

The defendant contends that the contract was without consideration to support it, and, therefore, invalid. He asserts that the promisee by refraining from the use of liquor and tobacco was not harmed but benefited; that that which he did was best for him to do independently of his uncle's promise, and insists that it follows that unless the promisor was benefited, the contract was without consideration. A contention, which if well founded, would seem to leave open for controversy in many cases whether that which the promisee did or omitted to do was, in fact, of such benefit to him as to leave no consideration to support the enforcement of the promisor's agreement. Such a rule could not be tolerated, and is without foundation in the law.

* * * * *

"In general a waiver of any legal right at the request of another party is a sufficient consideration for a promise" (Parsons on Contracts).

Pollock, in his work on contracts, says, ". . . Consideration means not so much that one party is profiting as that the other abandons some legal right in the present or limits his legal freedom of action in the future as an inducement for the promise of the first."

Now, applying this rule to the facts before us, the promisee used tobacco, occasionally drank liquor, and had a legal right to do so. That right he abandoned for a period of years upon the strength of the promise of the testator that for such forbearance he would give him $5,000. We need not speculate on the effort which may have been required to give up the use of those stimulants. It is sufficient that he restricted his lawful freedom of action within certain prescribed limits upon the faith of his uncle's agreement, and now having fully performed the conditions imposed, it is of no moment whether such performance actually proved a benefit to the promisor, and the court will not inquire into it, but were it a proper subject of inquiry, we see nothing in this record that would permit a determination that the uncle was not benefited in a legal sense.

* * * * *

Reversed.

Questions

1. *a.* What detriment, if any, was sustained by the nephew?
   b. What benefit, if any, was secured by the uncle?
   c. As a matter of law, do we need to inquire into the uncle's benefit? Explain.

2. Lampley began work as an at-will (can be dismissed or can quit at any time) employee of Celebrity Homes in Denver, Colorado, in May 1975. On July 29, 1975, Celebrity announced a profit-sharing plan for all employees if the company reached its goals for the fiscal year, April 1,1975, to March 31, 1976. Lampley was dismissed in January 1976. Celebrity distributed its profits in May 1976. Lampley sued when she did not receive a share of the profits. Celebrity argued that its promise to share its profits was a gratuity, unsupported by consideration. Decide. Explain. See *Lampley v. Celebrity Homes,* 594 P.2d 605 (Col. Ct. App. 1979).

3. An accident in the early 1960s rendered Hoffman paraplegic. At Hoffman's invitation, Thomas lived with and provided extensive physical care for Hoffman until Hoffman's death in 2004. Thomas did not pay rent and Hoffman paid for Thomas' food, provided her with a car and cell phone and made occasional cash payments to Thomas. While never married, the couple exchanged rings in 2002 and Thomas testified that she felt they "lived as man and wife." Thomas filed suit seeking $44,625 for services rendered to Hoffman. According to the trial court, her claim was based on the theories of "express or implied contract of employment" or "unjust enrichment." Thomas lost at the trial level. How would you rule on appeal? Explain. See *In Re Estate of Hoffman,* 2006 Ia. App. LEXIS 473. [For a detailed analysis of *Hamer v. Sidway,* see **http://www.law.smu.edu/firstday/contracts/case.htm**]

Adequacy of Consideration

With certain exceptions, the courts do not, as Judge Parker indicated in the *Hamer* case, inquire into the economic value of the consideration in question. Legal sufficiency depends not on the value of the consideration but on whether the promisee suffered a detriment in some way. To hold otherwise would put the courts in the place of the market in deciding the value of transactions. We are all free to make both good and bad bargains.

On the other hand, the courts will rule that consideration is found wanting in situations of pretense or sham where the parties have clearly agreed on token or nominal consideration in an effort to present the transaction as a contract rather than a gift. Likewise, an extreme inadequacy of consideration will sometimes cause the court to question a contract on the grounds of *fraud, duress, or unconscionability* (all are discussed later in this chapter). In these instances, the agreements would be unenforceable because of a failure of consideration. These cases are uncommon, however, and the courts rarely inquire into the adequacy of consideration.

Appearance of Consideration

Some agreements appear to be accompanied by consideration, but in fact, that appearance turns to be an illusion. Hence, if one agrees to perform a preexisting duty, consideration would be found wanting. For example, if you were to pay your neighbor $50 to keep his dog chained when outdoors and a city ordinance already requires dogs to be chained if outdoors, your promise would be unenforceable because your neighbor already had a preexisting duty under the law to keep his dog chained. So performance of a preexisting legal duty does not constitute consideration because no legal detriment or benefit has arisen.

Similarly, preexisting duties sometimes arise from contracts. Suppose you hire a contractor to resurface the parking lot at your real estate office. You agree on a price of $12,000. With a portion of the work completed, the contractor asks you to amend the agreement to add $2,000 because the project is requiring more time than anticipated. You agree. The work is completed. Could you then legally refuse to pay the additional $2,000? The answer is yes because the contractor failed to provide consideration for the modification of your contract. He was under a preexisting duty to finish the contract; hence he did not sustain a legal detriment in the modified agreement. Note, however, that UCC section 2-209(1) provides that "an agreement modifying a contract within this Article needs no consideration to be binding."

Suppose you learn from your neighbor that your friend Ames wants to sell his house. You, as a realtor, find a buyer for the house and make all of the necessary arrangements for the sale out of regard for your friendship with Ames. Then when the transaction is complete, Ames says, "Well, this has been great of you, but I don't feel right about it. When I get my check for the sale, I'll pay you $2,000 for your hard work. I really appreciate it." What if Ames does not then pay the $2,000? Do you have recourse? No. This is a situation of *past consideration,* where the performance—arranging the sale of your friend's house—was not bargained for and was not given in exchange for the promise and thus cannot constitute consideration. In effect, the performance was a gift. Of course, past consideration is really not consideration at all. In some states, courts enforce promises to pay for benefits already received where doing so amounts to a moral obligation that must be enforced to prevent injustice.

Substitutes for Consideration

When necessary to achieve justice, the courts sometimes conclude that a contract exists even though consideration is clearly lacking. Moral obligation and quasi contract (discussed earlier) are two such instances; but the most prominent of these substitutes for consideration is the doctrine of *promissory estoppel,* in which the promisor is "stopped" from denying the existence of a contract where the promisee has detrimentally relied on that promise. Promissory estoppel requires the following:

1. A promise on which the promisor should expect the promisee to rely.
2. The promisee did justifiably rely on the promise.
3. Injustice can be avoided only by enforcing the promise.

Consider the following. You have been a part-time employee of a small fast-food chain restaurant while attending college. Upon graduation, you tell the manager of the restaurant that you think you could handle your own franchise. He says you need to get more experience and advises you to take a full-time position with the company. You do so. Everything goes well, and when you next approach the manager, he says, "If you can come up with the $50,000 and a good location, we will get you in a franchise right away. But you've gotta move on this. Maybe you better quit your job with us and concentrate on this thing." You take his advice and quit your job. You raise the $50,000 and find a vacant building to rent in a good location for a franchise. You show the building to the manager, and he agrees that it looks like a favorable location and one that can easily be converted to the company's needs. He says, "Looks like you have everything in place. If you can come up with $50,000 more we will make this thing happen." You refuse and decide to bring suit against the fast-food chain for breach of contract. The chain defends by saying that you did not provide consideration for its promise. No formal financing arrangement was ever agreed to, and you had not committed yourself to any franchising obligations. Under these circumstances you may well prevail using a promissory estoppel claim. In brief, you would argue that you had changed your position in reliance on the franchisor's promises and that relief is necessary to prevent injustice. [For a similar case see *Hoffman v. Red Owl Stores,* 133 N.W.2d 267 (Wis. S.Ct. 1965).]

Capacity

Having examined two of the required ingredients in an enforceable contract, agreement and consideration, we turn now to a third, capacity to contract. To enter a binding agreement, one must have the legal ability to do so; that is, one's mental condition and maturity must be such that the agreement was entered with understanding and in recognition of one's own interests. The three primary areas of concern are intoxication, mental impairment, and minority (infancy/youthfulness), with minority being much the more common area of dispute.

> The three primary areas of concern are intoxication, mental impairment, and minority.

Intoxication

Assume you have been drinking to celebrate your 21st birthday. You enter a contract with a friend to sell him your autographed Michael Jordan basketball card for $200. You receive the money and turn over the card. Later, when sober, you regret the deal. Will a court nullify that contract on the grounds of your intoxication? That decision depends on whether you were sufficiently intoxicated that you did not understand the nature and purpose of the contract. If the objective evidence suggests that you did not understand the transaction, the contract would be considered voidable, in which case you could probably disaffirm the contract and demand the return of the card, although courts are often not sympathetic with people who attempt to escape contracts made while intoxicated. In most states, if you recovered the card, you would be required to return the $200 to your friend.

If on recovering your sobriety, your friend argued that the contract was invalid because of your intoxication, and he demanded the return of his $200 in exchange for the card, you could then *ratify* (affirm) the contract and hold him to it. If the contract had been for one of life's *necessaries* (food, shelter, clothing, medical care, tools of one's trade, or the like), you would have been liable for the reasonable value of that necessary.

Mental Incompetence

In most cases an agreement involving a mentally incompetent person is either *void or voidable*. The transaction would be void—that is, no contract would exist—where the impaired party had been *adjudged* insane. If the impaired party was unable to understand the purpose and effect of the contract but had not been legally adjudged insane, the contract would be voidable (void in some states) at the option of the impaired party. The competent party cannot void the contract, and the impaired party would have to pay the reasonable value of any necessaries received under the contract.

Minority

Minors may complete their contracts if they wish, but they also have an absolute right to rescind most of those contracts. They may rescind until they reach adulthood and for a reasonable time thereafter. (Many states have enacted statutes forbidding minors from disaffirming some classes of contracts such as those for marriage, student loans, and life insurance.) The minor has a right of recovery for everything given up in meeting the terms of the contract. Similarly, the minor must return everything that remains in her or his possession that was received from the contract. In many states, if nothing of the bargained-for consideration remains or if its value has been depreciated, the minor has no duty to replace it but can still recover whatever she or he put into the contract. If not disaffirmed in a reasonable time after the minor reaches the age of majority, the contract is considered to be ratified, and the minor is bound to its terms. The minor is also liable for the reasonable value (not necessarily the contract price) of necessaries purchased from an adult. That is, a minor must pay the adult the reasonable value of contracted-for items such as food, clothing, shelter, medical care, basic education, and tools of the minor's trade.

> Minors may complete their contracts if they wish, but they also have an absolute right to rescind most of those contracts.

Despite the flexibility accorded to minors entering contracts, the adults who are parties to those contracts are bound to them and do not have the power to disaffirm. Hence, adults put themselves at risk when they choose to bargain with minors. As noted, in many states a minor need not make restitution if the consideration is lost, destroyed, or depreciated. On the other hand, the case that follows illustrates the growing view that minors do have some monetary obligation after disaffirming a contract.

LEGAL BRIEFCASE

824 S.W.2d 545 (Tenn. S.Ct. 1992)

Justice O'Brien

In early April of 1987, Joseph Eugene Dodson, then 16 years of age, purchased a used 1984 pickup truck from Burns and Mary Shrader. The Shraders owned and operated Shrader's Auto Sales in Columbia, Tennessee. Dodson paid $4,900 in cash for the truck, using money he borrowed from his girlfriend's grandmother. At the time of the purchase there was no inquiry by the Shraders, and no misrepresentation by Dodson, concerning his minority. However, Shrader did testify that at the time he believed Dodson to be 18 or 19 years of age.

In December 1987, nine months after the date of purchase, the truck began to develop mechanical problems. A mechanic diagnosed the problem as a burnt valve, but could not be certain without inspecting the valves inside the engine. Dodson did not want, or did not have the money, to effect these repairs. He continued to drive the truck despite the mechanical problems. One month later, in January, the truck's engine "blew up" and the truck became inoperable.

Dodson parked the vehicle in the front yard at his parents' home, where he lived. He contacted the Shraders to rescind the purchase of the truck and requested a full refund. The Shraders refused to accept the tender of the truck or to give Dodson the refund requested.

Dodson then [sued] to rescind the contract and recover the amount paid for the truck. Before the circuit court could hear the case, the truck, while parked in Dodson's front yard, was struck on the left front fender by a hit-and-run driver. At the time of the circuit court trial, according to Shrader, the truck was worth only $500 due to the damage to the engine and the left front fender.

The case was heard in the circuit court in November 1988. The trial judge, based on previous common-law decisions, and under the doctrine of stare decisis, reluctantly granted the rescission. The Shraders were ordered, upon tender and delivery of the truck, to reimburse the $4,900 purchase price to Dodson. The Shraders appealed.

[T]he rule in Tennessee is in accord with the majority rule on the issue among our sister states. This rule is based on the underlying purpose of the "infancy doctrine," which is to protect minors from their lack of judgment and "from squandering their wealth through improvident contracts with crafty adults who would take advantage of them in the marketplace."

There is, however, a modern trend among the states, either by judicial action or by statute, in the approach to the problem of balancing the rights of minors against those of innocent merchants. As a result, two minority rules have developed that allow the other party to a contract with a minor to refund less than the full consideration paid in the event of rescission.

The first of these minority rules is called the "Benefit Rule." The rule holds that, upon rescission, recovery of the full purchase price is subject to a deduction for the minor's use of the merchandise. This rule recognizes that the traditional rule in regard to necessaries has been extended so far as to hold an infant bound by his contracts, where he failed to restore what he has received under them to the extent of the benefit actually derived by him from what he has received from the other party to the transaction.

The other minority rule holds that the minor's recovery of the full purchase price is subject to a deduction for the minor's "use" of the consideration he or she received under the contract, or for the "depreciation" or "deterioration" of the consideration in his or her possession.

We are impressed by the statement made by the Court of Appeals of Ohio:

> At a time when we see young persons between 18 and 21 years of age demanding and assuming more responsibilities in their daily lives, when we see such persons emancipated, married, and raising families; when we see such persons charged with the responsibility for committing crimes; when we see such persons being sued in tort claims for acts of negligence; when we see such persons subject to military service; when we see such persons engaged in business and acting in almost all other respects as an adult, it seems timely to reexamine the case law pertaining to contractual rights and responsibilities of infants to see if the law as pronounced and applied by the courts should be redefined.

* * * * *

We state the rule to be followed hereafter, in reference to a contract of a minor, to be where the minor has not been overreached in any way, and there has been no undue influence, and the contract is a fair and reasonable one, and the minor has actually paid money on the purchase price, and taken and used the article purchased; that he ought not be permitted to recover the amount actually paid, without allowing the vendor of the goods reasonable compensation for the use of, depreciation, and willful or negligent damage to the article purchased, while in his hands. If there has been any fraud or imposition on the part of the seller or if the contract is unfair, or any unfair advantage has been taken of the minor inducing him to make the purchase, then the rule does not apply. Whether there has been such an overreaching on the part of the seller, and the fair market value of the property returned, would always, in any case, be a question for the trier of fact. . . .

This rule is best adapted to modern conditions under which minors are permitted to, and do in fact, transact a great deal of business for themselves, long before they have reached the age of legal majority. Many young people work and earn money and collect it and spend it oftentimes without any oversight or restriction. The law does not question their right to buy if they have the money to pay for their purchases. It seems intolerably burdensome for everyone concerned if merchants and businesspeople cannot deal with them safely, in a fair and reasonable way.

* * * * *

We note that in this case, some nine months after the date of purchase, the truck purchased by the plaintiff began to develop mechanical problems. Plaintiff was informed of the probable nature of the difficulty, which apparently involved internal problems in the engine. He continued to drive the vehicle until the engine "blew up" and the truck became inoperable. Whether or not this involved gross negligence or intentional conduct on his part is a matter for determination at the trial level. It is not possible to determine from this record whether a counterclaim for tortious damage to the vehicle was asserted. After the first tender of the vehicle was made by plaintiff, and refused by the defendant, the truck was damaged by a hit-and-run driver while parked on plaintiff's property. The amount of that damage and the liability for that amount between the purchaser and the vendor, as well as the fair market value of the vehicle at the time of tender, is also an issue for the jury.

[Reversed and remanded.]

Questions

1. What was the issue in this case?
2. Distinguish the two minority rules that are summarized in this case.
3. To achieve justice in contract cases involving a minor and an adult, what would you want to know about the adult's behavior toward the minor?
4. White, a 17-year-old high school sophomore, operated a trucking business, including hiring drivers, securing jobs, and so forth. He lived with his parents and received his food, clothing, and shelter from them. Valencia operated a garage and repaired White's equipment until they had a disagreement over replacement of a motor. White then disaffirmed his contract with Valencia and refused to pay what he owed. At trial the jury found that White had caused the damage to the motor, but the court held that White could disaffirm the contract and required Valencia to refund any money paid to White under the contract. Valencia appealed.
   a. Is the fact that White was in business for himself in any way relevant to the outcome of this case? Explain.
   b. Decide the case. Explain. See *Valencia v. White*, 654 P.2d 287 (Ariz. Ct. App. 1982).

Genuineness of Assent

Sometimes parties appear to have concluded a binding contract, but the courts will allow them to escape that obligation because they had not, in fact, achieved an agreement. They had achieved the appearance of agreement, but not the reality. That situation arises when the contract is the product of misrepresentation, fraud, duress, undue influence, or mistake. Ordinarily, such agreements are voidable and may be rescinded by the innocent party because of the absence of genuine assent, the fourth of five ingredients in a binding contract.

Misrepresentation and Fraud

An innocent untruth is a misrepresentation. Intentional untruths constitute fraud. In either case, a party to a contract who has been deceived may rescind the deal, and restitution may be secured if benefits were extended to the party issuing the untruth. The test for fraud is as follows:

1. Misrepresentation of a material fact.
2. The misrepresentation was intentional.
3. The injured party justifiably relied on the misrepresentation.
4. Injury resulted.

Note that the test requires a misrepresented fact. In general, misrepresented opinions are not grounds for action; but many courts are now recognizing exceptions to that rule, especially when the innocent party has relied on opinion coming from an expert.

> You are selling a house that allegedly is "haunted."

If you are selling a house that allegedly is "haunted," does your failure to reveal the ghostly presence constitute a misrepresentation? The *Stambovsky* case that follows addresses that unusual question.

LEGAL BRIEFCASE

Stambovsky v. Ackley et al.
169 A.D.2d 254 (S.Ct. N.Y., App. Div., 1st Dept. 1991)

Justice Rubin

Plaintiff, to his horror, discovered that the house he had recently contracted to purchase was widely reputed to be possessed by poltergeists, reportedly seen by defendant seller and members of her family on numerous occasions over the last nine years. Plaintiff promptly commenced this action seeking rescission of the contract of sale.

The unusual facts of this case clearly warrant a grant of equitable relief to the buyer who, as a resident of New York City, cannot be expected to have any familiarity with the folklore of the Village of Nyack. Not being a "local," plaintiff could not readily learn that the home he had contracted to purchase is haunted. Whether the source of the spectral apparitions seen by defendant seller are parapsychic or psychogenic, having reported their presence in both a national publication (*Readers' Digest*) and the local press (in 1977 and 1982, respectively), defendant is estopped to deny their existence and, as a matter of law, the house is haunted. More to the point, however, no divination is required to conclude that it is defendant's promotional efforts in publicizing her close encounters with these spirits which fostered the home's reputation in the community. In 1989, the house was included in five-home walking tour of Nyack and described in a November 27th newspaper article as "a riverfront Victorian (with ghost)." The impact of the reputation thus created goes to the very essence of the bargain between the parties, greatly impairing both the value of the property and its potential for resale. . . .

While I agree that the real estate broker, as agent for the seller, is under no duty to disclose to a potential buyer the phantasmal reputation of the premises and that, in his pursuit of a legal remedy for fraudulent misrepresentation against the seller, plaintiff hasn't a ghost of a chance, I am nevertheless moved by the spirit of equity to allow the buyer to seek rescission of the contract of sale and recovery of his down payment.

New York law fails to recognize any remedy for damages incurred as a result of the seller's mere silence, applying instead the strict rule of caveat emptor. Therefore, the theoretical basis for granting relief, even under the extraordinary facts of this case, is elusive if not ephemeral.

From the perspective of a person in the position of plaintiff herein, a very practical problem arises with respect to the discovery of a paranormal phenomenon: "Who you gonna' call?" as a title song to the movie "Ghostbusters" asks. Applying the strict rule of caveat emptor to a contract involving a house possessed by poltergeists conjures up visions of a psychic or medium routinely accompanying the structural engineer and Terminix man on an inspection of every home subject to a contract of sale. It portends that the prudent attorney will establish an escrow account lest the subject of the transaction come back to haunt him and his client—or pray that his malpractice insurance coverage extends to supernatural disasters. In the interest of avoiding such untenable consequences, the notion that a haunting is a condition which can and should be ascertained upon reasonable inspection of the premises is a hobgoblin which should be exorcised from the body of legal precedent and laid quietly to rest.

It has been suggested by a leading authority that the ancient rule which holds that mere nondisclosure does not constitute actionable misrepresentation "finds proper application in cases where the fact undisclosed is patent, or the plaintiff has equal opportunities for obtaining information which he may be expected to utilize, or the defendant has no reason to think that he is acting under any misapprehension" (Prosser, Torts Section 106, at 696 [4th ed 1971]). However, with respect to transactions in real estate, New York adheres to the doctrine of caveat emptor and imposes no duty upon the vendor to disclose any information concerning the premises unless there is a confidential or fiduciary relationship between the parties or some conduct on the part of the seller which constitutes "active concealment."

Normally, some affirmative misrepresentation or partial disclosure is required to impose upon the seller a duty to communicate undisclosed conditions affecting the premises.

Common law is not moribund. . . . Where fairness and common sense dictate that an exception should be created, the evolution of the law should not be stifled by rigid application of a legal maxim.

The doctrine of caveat emptor requires that a buyer act prudently to assess the fitness and value of his purchase and operates to bar the purchaser who fails to exercise due care from seeking the equitable remedy of rescission. For the purposes of the instant motion to dismiss the action . . . plaintiff is entitled to every favorable inference which may reasonably be drawn from the pleadings, specifically, in this instance, that he met his obligation to conduct an inspection of the premises and a search of available public records with respect to title. It should be apparent, however, that the most meticulous inspection and the search would not reveal the presence of poltergeists at the premises or unearth the property's ghoulish reputation in the community. Therefore, there is no sound policy reason to deny plaintiff relief for failing to discover a state of affairs which the most prudent purchaser would not be expected to even contemplate.

* * * * *

Where a condition which has been created by the seller materially impairs the value of the contract and is peculiarly within the knowledge of the seller or unlikely to be discovered by a prudent purchaser exercising due care with respect to the subject transaction, nondisclosure constitutes a basis for rescission as a matter of equity. Any other outcome places upon the buyer not merely the obligation to exercise care in his purchase but rather to be omniscient with respect to any fact which may affect the bargain. No practical purpose is served by imposing such a burden upon a purchaser. To the contrary, it encourages predatory business practice. . . .

* * * * *

In the case at bar, defendant seller deliberately fostered the public belief that her home was possessed. Having undertaken to inform the public-at-large, to whom she has no legal relationship, about the supernatural occurrences on her property, she may be said to owe no less a duty to her contract vendee. . . . Where, as here, the seller not only takes unfair advantage of the buyer's ignorance but has created and perpetuated a condition about which he is unlikely to even inquire, enforcement of the contract (in whole or in part) is offensive to the court's sense of equity. Application of the remedy of rescission, within the bounds of the narrow exception to the doctrine of caveat emptor set forth herein, is entirely appropriate to relieve the unwitting purchaser from the consequences of a most unnatural bargain.

Accordingly, the judgment of the Supreme Court, New York County (Edward H. Lehner, J.), entered April 9, 1990, which dismissed the complaint should be modified and the first cause of action seeking rescission of the contract reinstated.

DISSENT

Justice Smith (dissenting).
I would affirm the dismissal of the complaint. . . .

* * * * *

"It is settled law in New York State that the seller of real property is under no duty to speak when the parties deal at arm's length. The mere silence of the seller, without some act or conduct which deceived the purchaser, does not amount to a concealment that is actionable as a fraud. . . ."

The parties herein were represented by counsel and dealt at arm's length. . . . There is no allegation that defendants, by some specific act, other than the failure to speak deceived the plaintiff. . . .

Finally, if the doctrine of caveat emptor is to be discarded, it should be for a reason more substantive than a poltergeist. The existence of a poltergeist is no more binding upon the defendants than it is upon this court.

Based upon the foregoing, the [lower] court properly dismissed the complaint.

Questions

1. *a.* According to the court, did the defendant seller engage in a fraudulent misrepresentation in failing to disclose the "ghostly" condition of her house?
   b. The plaintiff won this case on equitable/fairness grounds. Explain the court's reasoning.
   c. Do you agree with the court's equity/fairness reasoning? Explain.
   d. Did the real estate agent engage in fraud for failing to disclose the house's haunted reputation? Explain.

2. *a.* What did the court mean by the phrase "caveat emptor?"
   b. Why did the court find for the plaintiff buyer, even though "caveat emptor" seemed to be the controlling law in this situation?
   c. Would the buyer have been successful in a misrepresentation claim if the seller had said: "This house is so peaceful. We never have any disturbances."?
   d. The defendant seller had fostered the belief that her house was haunted. Did that promotional effort by the defendant influence the court's decision making? Explain.

3. Explain dissenting Justice Smith's objection to the majority's ruling.

Toy Yoda

Former Hooters waitress Jodee Berry sued Gulf Coast Wings for not awarding a new Toyota as a prize for her victory in an April 2001 sales contest. Berry alleged that her manager told the waitresses in their Florida Hooters that the server selling the most beer would be entered in a drawing (involving other Hooters locations) with the winner receiving a new Toyota. At one point during the contest, the manager allegedly said he did not know whether the winner would receive a Toyota car, truck or van, he did know that the winner would be required to pay registration fees. At the close of the contest, the manager told Berry that she had won. He blindfolded her and took her to the restaurant parking lot. He laughed when Berry found, not the car she expected, but a doll based on the character Yoda in the Star Wars movie (a toy Yoda). Berry did not laugh, but she did sue. The case was settled out of court. The terms of that settlement were not disclosed, but Berry's lawyer did say that she would be able to afford whatever Toyota she wanted.

Questions

1. What contract-based causes of action did Berry bring in this case?
2. Defend Hooters.
3. Make the argument that the Hooters manager never actually made an offer to the waitresses.
4. If an offer was made, how did Berry accept that offer?
5. Make the argument that the offer and acceptance, if they existed, were not supported by consideration.

Sources: Berry v. Gulf Coast Wings, Inc., Div. J (Fla. 14th Cir. Ct. July 24, 2001); and Keith A. Rowley, "You Asked for It, You Got It . . . Toy Yoda: Practical Jokes, Prizes, and Contract Law," 3 *Nevada Law Journal* 526 (2003).

Duress

Sometimes genuine assent is not secured and a contract may be rescinded because one of the parties is forced to agree. Fear lies at the heart of a duress claim. The party seeking to escape the contract must establish that a wrongful act was threatened or had occurred, causing the party to enter the contract out of fear of harm such that free will was precluded. Increasingly, courts are also setting aside contracts on the grounds of economic duress. For example, suppose you know that one of your regular customers depends on your timely delivery of steel to his factory and that he cannot expeditiously find an alternative supply. Therefore, you tell your customer that delivery will be delayed until he agrees to pay a higher price for the steel. If he agrees, the resulting contract probably could be rescinded on the grounds of economic duress.

Undue Influence

Under some circumstances, the first party to an apparent contract can escape its terms by demonstrating that the second party so dominated her will that she (the first party) did not act independently. These claims are most common in cases involving those who are old or infirm and who lose their independence of thought and action to the undue influence of a caregiver or adviser.

Mistake

Most of us, on taking a new job, operate at least for a time in fear that we will make a mistake. Assume you are new to your job and are preparing a bid that your company will submit in hopes of securing the general maintenance contract for a large office building. In preparing the bid, you inadvertently submit a final price of $50,000 rather than $500,000. What happens? Do you lose your job?

> You inadvertently submit a final price of $50,000 rather than $500,000. What happens?

In some cases, mistakes involving critical facts can be grounds for rescinding contracts. A *mutual mistake* is one in which both parties to the contract are in error about some critical fact. With exceptions, either party can rescind those contracts because genuine assent was not achieved. Your erroneous bid, however, is a *unilateral mistake;* that is, only one party to the contract made an error. The general rule is that those contracts cannot be rescinded. However, if you are able to show that the other party to the contract knew or should have known about your mistake, many courts would allow you to rescind. Certainly you would make that argument in this instance because the $50,000 bid presumably is dramatically out of line with the other bids and at odds with reasonable business expectations about the value of the contract. In cases where an error is made in drafting a contract, and both parties are unaware of the error (a mutual mistake), the courts will reform the contract rather than void it. That is, the contract will be rewritten to reflect what the parties actually intended.

$4,934 Discount on Alitalia?

The Italian national airline, Alitalia, was charging more than $5,000 for trans-Atlantic, roundtrip, business class airfares in 2006, but by mistake a fare was briefly listed online at $66.00. About the same time, Marriott was offering rooms at a New York City hotel for $24.90 when the intended price was $249.00. Alitalia honored 509 reservations at an expected cost of about $2.6 million. Marriott, however, raised the $24.90 rate to the intended $249.00. Errors of this kind happen with some frequency in the travel industry.

Questions

1. As a matter of business practice, how would you have dealt with your company's error had you been in charge at Alitalia or Marriott?
2. As a matter of law, was Alitalia or Marriott obligated to honor the low prices?

Source: Scott McCartney, "When a Fare Is Too Good to Be True," *The Wall Street Journal,* April 25, 2006, p. D5.

Legality of Purpose

Having examined agreement, consideration, capacity, and genuineness of assent, we turn now to the final requirement for the creation of a binding contract: legality of purpose (see Figure 6.2). *Illegality* refers to bargains to commit a crime or a tort (such as a deal with a coworker to embezzle funds from one's employer); but more broadly, illegality involves bargains that are forbidden by statute or violate public policy. We can identify three general categories of illegal agreements: (1) contracts that violate statutes, (2) contracts that are unconscionable, and (3) contracts that violate public policy. In general, the effect of an illegal contract is that it cannot be enforced, and the courts will not provide a remedy if its terms are unfulfilled. With exceptions, the parties to illegal deals are left where the courts find them.

FIGURE 6.2

Five Requirements of a Binding Contract

1. Agreement
2. Consideration
3. Capacity
4. Genuineness of assent
5. Legality of purpose

1. ***Contracts violating statutes.*** As noted, a contract to commit a crime or a tort is illegal and unenforceable. The states have also specified certain other agreements that are illegal. Those provisions vary from state to state, but they commonly include antigambling laws, laws forbidding the conduct of certain kinds of business on Sundays (*blue laws*), laws forbidding *usury,* and laws forbidding the practice of certain professions (law, real estate, hair care) without a license.

Who Owns the BMW?

Ryno owned Bavarian Motors in Fort Worth, Texas. In 1981 Ryno agreed to sell a 1980 BMW M-l to Tyra for $125,000. Ryno then proposed a double-or-nothing coin flip for the car. Tyra agreed and won the coin flip. Ryno then handed Tyra the keys to the car, saying, "It's yours," while handing the "German title" to the car to Tyra. On several occasions Tyra took the BMW to Ryno for servicing. The car was routinely returned to Tyra until 1982 when Ryno kept the car and sold it. Tyra sued Ryno. Who wins? Explain.

Source: *Ryno v. Tyra,* 752 S.W.2d 148 (Tx. Ct. App. 1988).

2. ***Unconscionable contracts.*** Certain agreements are so thoroughly one-sided that fairness precludes enforcing them. Problems of unconscionability often arise in situations in which the bargaining power of one of the parties is much superior to the other—where one can, in effect, "twist the arm" or otherwise take advantage of the other. Both the common law of contracts and UCC 2-302 give the courts the power to modify or refuse to enforce such deals.

> Certain agreements are so thoroughly one-sided that fairness precludes enforcing them.

3. ***Public policy.*** The courts may decline to enforce certain otherwise binding contracts because to do so would not be in the best interest of the public. For example, an agreement between the local convenience stores to charge $5.00 for a gallon of gasoline would be a restraint of trade (price fixing) and as such would be contrary to public policy and to antitrust laws (see Chapter 10) and thus would be unenforceable. Similarly, suppose as a condition of being hired for a job you must sign an agreement providing that you will not leave your employer to work for one of your employer's competitors. These *noncompete* clauses (see Chapter 12) are common and may be fully

lawful depending largely on whether the time and geographic restrictions imposed are reasonable. If unreasonable, the courts will either not enforce the clause or will alter it to achieve a fair result.

Another commonplace public policy concern is the *exculpatory clause, limited liability clause, or release.* If you participate in any potentially hazardous activity such as attending a professional hockey game, whitewater rafting, joining a school field trip, or entering an amusement park you may be required to agree to release others of any liability for harm that might befall you. If you own or manage a potentially hazardous enterprise such as a water slide, bungee tower, or even a health spa, you may try to protect yourself from litigation should a customer be hurt by including a release in the customer agreement. Often, such agreements are enforceable in the manner of any other contractual provision, but sometimes they are not. Many factors can influence that decision, including how sweeping the exculpation is, whether it was knowingly entered, and the relative bargaining power of the parties. The case that follows examines an airline contract clause limiting liability for lost luggage.

LEGAL BRIEFCASE

Hanson v. America West Airlines 544 F.Supp.2d 1038 (U.S. Dist. Ct. Central Dist. Cal. 2008)

Judge Guilford

BACKGROUND
Plaintiff David Hanson ("Plaintiff") has lost his head. More specifically, Plaintiff has lost an artistically and scientifically valuable robotic head modeled after famous science fiction author Philip K. Dick ("Head"). Dick's well-known body of work has resulted in movies—such as *Total Recall, Blade Runner, Minority Report,* and *A Scanner Darkly,* and a large group of admirers has grown following his death in Orange County, California, in 1982. His stories have questioned whether robots can be human so it seems appropriate that Plaintiff reincarnated Dick as a robot which included the Head, valued at around $750,000.

Plaintiff lost his Head on one of Defendant's planes when flying from Texas to San Francisco with a connection in Las Vegas. Plaintiff brought the Head onto the plane in a carry-on duffel bag and stored it in the overhead bin. Plaintiff fell asleep during the flight from Texas to Las Vegas, and woke up when the plane arrived in Las Vegas. On waking, Plaintiff immediately left the plane to catch his connecting flight to San Francisco. Perhaps because he had just woken up, Plaintiff lacked the total recall to remember to retrieve the Head from the overhead bin.

According to Plaintiff, as soon as he got to San Francisco, he went to the baggage counter, spoke to Defendant's employee, Leanne Miller ("Miller"), and informed her of the problem. Miller told him that the airplane with his Head was in flight, and could not be checked until it landed in Southern California. Plaintiff offered to fly to Southern California to regain his Head, but Miller told him not to do that. According to Plaintiff, he informed Miller of the importance and value of the Head, and she replied that all efforts would be made to recover the Head and that it would receive "special treatment."

Plaintiff asserts that about 45 minutes later, Miller called him with the good news that the Head had been found in Orange County. Plaintiff "remained willing" to go retrieve his Head, but Miller replied that it would be sent to San Francisco. According to Plaintiff, Miller then informed him of the special security procedures that would be taken to protect and deliver the Head. Plaintiff told Miller that Plaintiff's friend Craig Grossman would be at the airport to pick up the Head. Grossman waited for the Head at the San Francisco airport, but it never arrived and has not been found since. While hearts may be left in San Francisco, heads apparently are left in Orange County, or are simply lost or stolen.

Plaintiff sued Defendant in California state court for conversion, negligence, and involuntary bailment. Defendant removed the case to federal court, and here moves for summary judgment.

ANALYSIS

1. Contractual Liability Limitations

Defendant argues that it contractually limited its liability for loss of Plaintiff's goods. . . .

Federal common law allows a carrier to limit its liability for lost or damaged goods if the contract limiting liability offers the shipper (1) reasonable notice of the limited liability, and (2) a fair opportunity to buy higher liability.

* * * * *

If the contract states the limited liability provision and a means to avoid it, the contract is considered prima facie valid. Defendant has satisfied the elements of an enforceable limited liability provision under federal common law. The Contract of Carriage provides that "[liability of loss, delay, or damage to baggage is limited as follows unless a higher value is declared in advance and additional charges are paid." The contract later provides that the monetary limit is "USD 2,800.00 per ticketed passenger for checked baggage." More specifically for this case, the Contract of Carriage provides that Defendant "assumes no responsibility or liability for baggage, or other items, carried in the passenger compartment of the aircraft." Plaintiff admits that he was aware of the limited liability provision. Thus, Defendant provided Plaintiff with reasonable notice of limited liability and a fair opportunity to buy higher liability.

2. Plaintiff's Arguments

Plaintiff argues that Defendant is liable for the lost head because (1) there was a material deviation from the Contract of Carriage and (2) Plaintiff's discussion with Miller altered the terms of the original Contract of Carriage or created a new contract.

2.1 Material Deviation Doctrine

* * * * *

[T]he material deviation doctrine states that where a carrier effects a fundamental breach of a contract by materially deviating from the contract's terms, the carrier is liable for damage to or loss of the shipped goods. Cases have further defined the boundaries of this doctrine. For example, in *Nipponkoa Ins. Co., Ltd., v. Watkins Motor Lines, Inc.,* 431 F.Supp.2d 411 (S.D.N.Y. 2006), a carrier promised to take special measures to protect a shipment of laptop computers, including using high security locks and video surveillance. The court found that the carrier breached that promise by failing to use either high security locks or video surveillance. The court held that the carrier was responsible for the loss of the computers under the material deviation doctrine. The court explained that the doctrine applies when a carrier breaches a "separate, risk-related promise" about the shipment of goods. The court emphasized that the agreement was specific and that the carrier deviated from the expressly agreed-upon security measures.

* * * * *

The Ninth Circuit has limited the material deviation doctrine. In *Vision Air,* for example, a carrier destroyed two trucks by using an inadequate pulley system to transport them. *Vision Air,* 155 F.3d at 1167–68. The Ninth Circuit held that even if that behavior constituted gross negligence or recklessness, it did not constitute a material deviation. "[W]e reject the notion that mere negligence may constitute an unreasonable deviation . . . we reject the notion that gross negligence or recklessness may constitute an unreasonable deviation." The court emphasized that only "more culpable misconduct" could be considered a deviation.

In the cases just discussed, the courts focused on the actual express terms of the agreement, showing that the material deviation doctrine applies only when the shipper makes a "separate, risk-related promise," and then breaches that promise.

With these boundaries, Plaintiff's argument that Defendant materially deviated from the original Contract of Carriage fails. There were no provisions in the original Contract of Carriage directly concerning transporting the Head. Indeed, the original Contract of Carriage declaimed any responsibility for carry-on baggage. Further, nothing in the original Contract of Carriage made provisions for travelers leaving baggage on the airplane. Thus, Defendant did not breach a "separate, risk-related promise" in the original Contract of Carriage, and is not liable under this theory.

2.2 Altered or New Contractual Terms and Agency Law

Plaintiff also argues that Miller either altered the terms of the original Contract of Carriage or created a new contract with Plaintiff, and that Defendant is liable under the new or altered contract.

Agents can bind their principals only if they have actual or apparent authority to do so. Actual authority may be either express or implied. If a principal specifically authorizes an agent to act, the agent has express authority to take that action. If a principle "merely states the general nature of what the agent is to do, the agent is said to have implied authority to do acts consistent with the direction."

Miller did not have express authority to contract with Plaintiff. The original Contract of Carriage provided that:

> No employee of U.S. Airways has the authority to waive, modify, or alter any provisions of these terms of

transportation or any applicable fares/charges unless authorized by a corporate officer of U.S. Airways. U.S. Airways-appointed agents and representatives are only authorized to sell tickets for air transportation on U.S. Airways pursuant to the terms of transportation and applicable fares/charges of U.S. Airways.

There is no evidence that Miller was either a corporate officer of Defendant or that she was authorized by such an officer to modify the terms of transportation. Thus, under the Contract of Carriage, Miller had no express authority either to change the terms of the contract or to create a new contract. Indeed, Miller had express authority only to "sell tickets for air transportation." Likewise, there is no evidence that Miller had implied authority.

The Contract of Carriage also leads to the conclusion that Miller had no apparent authority to change the terms of the contract or to create a new contract. "Apparent authority results when the principal does something or permits the agent to do something which reasonably leads another to believe that the agent had the authority he purported to have." *Hawaiian Paradise Park Corp.*, 414 F.2d at 756 (9th Cir. 1969). Only the acts of the principal, not of the agent, give rise to apparent authority. Plaintiff argues that Miller's station behind a desk near the baggage claim area led Plaintiff to reasonably believe that Miller had the authority to make contracts for the delivery of lost baggage. The Court disagrees.

Plaintiff is a frequent flyer and was aware of the applicable tariffs. Thus, before he lost his Head and spoke with Miller, he was aware of the tariff limiting Miller's authority. Aware of that tariff, he could not reasonably conclude, based on Miller's position behind a desk, that she suddenly had authority to contract with him.

* * * * *

Plaintiff cannot rely on representations altering the contract or creating a new contract when those representations were made by someone whose authority had been expressly limited by contract. The Court must find that Miller had neither actual nor apparent authority to either alter the Contract of Carriage or create a new contract.

2.3 Even Under the New Terms Alleged, Liability Has Not Been Established

Even if Miller had authority to alter the Contract of Carriage or create a new contract, Defendant would still not be liable for the lost Head because there is no evidence that Defendant breached the contract even under the new terms alleged. Plaintiff alleges new terms that provided for tagging and boxing the Head, informing everyone of the value, and scheduling the Head on the next flight. But Plaintiff presents no evidence that such terms were breached. Instead, Plaintiff offers theories of De-

fendant's potential conduct, such as, "[potentially informing the wrong crew of the value of the HEAD" and "[potentially informing the thief of the high value of the HEAD." These theories, while heady, are insufficient.

At best, Plaintiff's theory is that, since the Head did not arrive at its destination, Defendants must have done something wrong. This is not evidence of a breach or material deviation. Defendant may have done everything as promised, only to fall victim to a head hunting thief or other skullduggery. Alternatively, Defendant could have been negligent, and still not have committed a fundamental breach. The possibility of such negligence is "considered an inherent risk of shipping." *Information Control*, 73 Cal. App. 3d at 641. Thus, even if Plaintiff's discussion with Miller altered or created a new contract, there is no evidence establishing Defendant's liability based on breach or material deviation.

3. CONCLUSION

Philip K. Dick and other science fiction luminaries have often explored whether robots might eventually evolve to exercise freedom of choice. But there is no doubt that humans have the freedom of choice to bind themselves in mutually advantageous contractual relationships. When Plaintiff chose to enter the Contract of Carriage with Defendant he agreed, among other things, to limit Defendant's liability for lost baggage. Failing to show that he is entitled to relief from that agreement, Plaintiff is bound by the terms of that contract, which bars his state law claims.

The Court must GRANT Defendant's Motion. But it does so hoping that the android head of Mr. Dick is someday found, perhaps in an Elysian field of Orange County, Dick's homeland, choosing to dream of electric sheep.

Questions

1. As a matter of law, why did America West win this case?

2. Why was this Contract of Carriage not considered unfair and one-sided and thus unenforceable?

3. Why did America West's behavior not constitute a "material deviation" from the Contract of Carriage?

4. Ning Yan went to Gay's fitness center to use a one-week complimentary pass. On each visit he signed in on a sheet that contained a standard exculpatory clause including this language: "I also understand that Vital Power Fitness Center assumes no responsibility for any injuries and/or sicknesses incurred to me. . . ." On February 18, 1999, Yan fell from a treadmill and sustained a severe head injury. He later died from that injury. No one witnessed the fall. Yan's estate claims he struck his head against a window ledge because the treadmill was placed too close to the window. If he did strike the window ledge, who would likely win this case? Explain. See *Xu v. Gay*, 668 N.W.2d 166 (Ct. App. Mich. 2003).

PRACTICING ETHICS — 2010 Gulf Oil Disaster: BP Contracts Unfair/Unconscionable?

In May 2010, British Petroleum (BP) oil company was in the midst of frantic efforts to stop the oil flowing into the Gulf of Mexico from its doomed Macondo 252 well while also trying to clean up the immense quantity that escaped after the explosion of the Deepwater Horizon drilling vessel. "Several hundred" shrimpers, oyster harvesters and others making their living from the Gulf signed contracts with BP to work as paid volunteers in the cleanup process. Among the provisions in those contracts were promises by the volunteers not to file legal claims against the oil company should they sustain damages of any kind in the cleanup process. The provisions, which many of those signing may not have fully understood, included promises not to sue in case of accident or injury and not to talk to anyone about the disaster or cleanup without BP approval. Those provisions also required a 30-day notice before pursuing legal claims against BP, even in the event of an emergency. Reportedly, BP also expected workers to add the oil giant to their personal insurance policies so that worker injuries or damages would fall to each worker's insurance rather than to BP. Commercial fisherman and United Commercial Fisherman's Association president, George Barisich, filed suit to block enforcement of the restrictive promises and U.S. District Judge Helen Berrigan ruled the offending provisions were overbroad and "unconscionable" and declared them null and void. BP and the Fisherman's Association soon reached an agreement removing the waiver language and agreeing not to enforce those provisions in contracts already signed. BP officials said the provisions were a "mistake," and they ordered the provisions removed as soon as they learned about them.

Questions

1. *a.* Were BP's protective provisions "wrong" as a matter of ethical business practice? Explain.
   b. If you were a boss or lawyer at BP, would you have included those protective provisions? Explain.
2. *a.* If you were a boss and you knew you could compel an employee to accept a pay cut in order to enhance an already healthy bottom line, would you do so? Explain.
   b. In your personal life, do you think you have made agreements with friends that were "one-sided" and "unconscionable" because of your possession of superior leverage of some kind?
   c. If so, were you "wrong" to do so. Explain.

Sources: Sabrina Canfield, "Judge Enjoins BP's Unconscionable Contract with Fishermen-Volunteers," *Courthouse News Service,* May 4, 2010, **http://www.courthousenews.com;** and Brendan Kirby, "Full Report: BP Backs Away from Controversial Oil Spill Settlement Language," May 5, 2010, **http://blog.al.com**

Part Two—Interpreting and Enforcing Contracts

We have examined the five ingredients in a binding contract: agreement, consideration, capacity, genuineness of assent, and legality of purpose. Having established those conditions, a contract may have been created, but the door to contract problems has not been closed. Contracts sometimes must fulfill writing formalities to be enforceable. Third parties may have claims against some contracts. And what happens when a party to a contract does not perform as called for by the agreement?

In Writing?

In most cases, oral contracts are fully enforceable.

Certainly a common belief is that agreements must be in writing to be enforceable; but in most cases, oral contracts are fully enforceable. The exceptions, however, are important. Oral contracts are subject to misunderstanding or to being forgotten, and fraudulent claims can readily arise from oral understandings. Consequently, our states have drawn on the English *Statute of Frauds* in specifying that the following kinds of contracts, in most cases, must be in writing to be enforceable:

1. **Collateral contract.** Assume you have just graduated from college, and you want to get started in a small printing business. You secure a bank loan on the condition that you find a creditworthy third party as a guarantor for the loan. Jacobs, a family friend, agrees with the bank to pay the debt if you fail to do so. Jacobs' promise to pay the debt must be in writing to be enforceable.

2. **The sale of land.** Broadly, land is interpreted to include the surface itself, that which is in the soil (minerals) or permanently attached to it (buildings), and growing crops when accompanying the transfer of land. Thus, if a building was permanently attached to a lot you seek for the aforementioned printing business, that building would need to be included in the written contract; but if you contracted to have a building constructed on your lot, you would not need (at least for the purposes of the Statute of Frauds) to execute a written agreement with the building contractor because you would not be contracting for an interest in land. A long-term lease (normally more than one year) for that land and building would, in most states, need to be in writing. All of these principles simply reflect the special role of land in our view of wealth and freedom.

3. **Promises that cannot be performed within one year.** This requirement springs from a concern about faulty memories, deaths, and other impediments to the satisfactory conclusion of long-term contracts. The courts have interpreted this provision narrowly, in effect saying that such a contract need not be in writing if it is *possible,* according to its terms, to perform it within one year from the day of its creation. It follows then that a contract for an indefinite period (such as an employment contract "for the balance of the employee's life") need not be in writing to be enforceable. (It is possible that the employee will die within one year.)

4. **Contracts for the sale of goods at a price of $500 or more.** With exceptions, under both the English-derived Statute of Frauds and UCC 2-201, contracts for the sale of goods (having a value of $500 or more under the UCC) must be in writing to be enforceable. Under the UCC, informal writing will suffice so long as it indicates that a contract was made, it contains a quantity term, and it was signed "by the party against whom enforcement is sought." Section 2-201 provides exceptions for certain transactions of $500 or more in goods in which a contract will be enforceable even though not in writing.

5. **Contracts in consideration of marriage.** The mutual exchange of marriage promises need not be in writing, but any contract that uses marriage as the consideration to support the contract must be in writing to be enforceable. Such contracts would include, for example, prenuptial agreements that are entered prior to marriage and serve the purpose, among others, of specifying how the couple's property will be divided in the event of a divorce. Those contracts must be in writing to be enforceable.

6. **Executor/administrator's promise.** When an individual dies, a representative is appointed to oversee the estate. A promise by that executor/administrator to pay the

estate's debts must be in writing if the payment will be made from the executor/ administrator's personal funds. Thus, where the executor of an estate contracts with an auctioneer to dispose of the decedent's personal property, the executor's promise to pay the auctioneer must be in writing if the funds are to come from the executor's personal resources; the promise need not be in writing if the payment is to come from the estate.

[As we have noted, the state legislatures are considering various changes in the UCC, Article 2, including the Statute of Frauds (UCC 2-201—see the appendix) as recommended by the National Conference of Commissioners on Uniform State Laws (NCCUSL). Among the proposed changes, the $500 sale of goods standard would increase to $5,000, and electronic signatures and writings would satisfy Statute of Frauds requirements.]

Failure to Comply   A fully performed oral contract, even though not in compliance with the Statute of Frauds, will not be rescinded by the courts. However, incomplete oral contracts that fail to comply with the statute are unenforceable. If a party to an unenforceable oral contract has provided partial performance in reliance on the contract, the courts will ordinarily provide compensation under quasi-contract principles for the reasonable value of that performance. [For more on the Statute of Frauds, see **http://www.expertlaw.com/ library/business/statute_of_frauds.html**]

The Parol Evidence Rule

Suppose you are the purchasing manager for a large manufacturer. You entered a written contract for 50 new personal computers. During negotiations, the seller said they would "throw in" 10 new printers if they got the computer order, but you failed to include a provision for the printers in the contract. Is your boss about to have a fit? Perhaps, because you probably will not be able to introduce evidence of that oral understanding to alter the terms of the written contract. In general, whenever a contract has been reduced to writing with the intent that the writing represents a complete and final integration of the parties' intentions, none of the parties can introduce parol evidence (oral or written words outside the "four corners" of the agreement) to add to, change, or contradict that contract when that evidence was expressed/created at the time of or prior to the writing. The written agreement is presumed to be the best evidence of the parties' intentions at the time they entered the contract. (The parol evidence rule under UCC section 2-202 is essentially the same as the common-law provisions discussed here.)

Exceptions   Parol evidence may be admissible under the following exceptional circumstances:

1. To add missing terms to an incomplete written contract.
2. To explain ambiguities in a written contract.
3. To prove circumstances that would invalidate a written contract; that is, to establish one of the grounds of mistake, fraud, illegality, and so forth explained earlier in this chapter.

E-mail a "Signed Writing?"

Stevens' employment agreement with Publicis required that any modification of the agreement was to be signed by the parties. Stevens and Bloom (representing Publicis) exchanged e-mails changing Stevens' employment duties. The parties' names were typed at the end of each e-mail.

Question

1. Does that exchange of e-mails constitute a binding agreement? Explain.

Source: Stevens v. Publicis, 854 N.Y.S.2d 690 (2008).

Third Parties

We turn now to the rights and duties of those who are not parties to a contract but hold legally recognizable interests in that contract. Those interests arise when (1) contract rights are assigned to others, (2) contract duties are delegated to others, or (3) contracts have third-party beneficiary provisions.

Assignment of Rights

Ordinarily, a party to a contract is free to transfer her or his rights under the contract to a third party. Thus, if Ames owes Jones $500 for work performed, Jones can assign that right to Smith, who can now assert her right to collect against Ames. That transfer of rights is labeled an assignment (see Figure 6.3). Jones, the party making the transfer, is the assignor; Smith, the one receiving the right, is the assignee; and Ames, the party who must perform, is the obligor. Ames, the obligor, must now perform the contract for the benefit of the assignee; that is, Ames must pay the $500 to Smith. The completed assignment then extinguishes the assignor's rights under the contract.

Some contracts are not assignable without consent of the obligor. That would be the case where the obligor's duties are materially altered by the assignment. For example, if you have a contract to serve as a personal fitness trainer for a busy chief executive officer, your contract could not be assigned without your consent to another CEO, or movie star, or the like because the highly personal and specific obligations under the contract would necessarily be materially altered with a different client.

FIGURE 6.3

Assignment of Rights

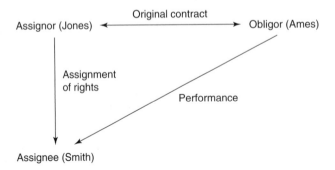

Delegation of Duties

The parties to a contract may also delegate their duties under the contract to one or more third parties. Assume Allen has secured a contract to install windows in Boyd's new office building (see Figure 6.4). Allen could delegate that duty to another contractor, Harms (although Allen would more commonly simply enter a subcontracting arrangement without actually transferring the underlying contract). A delegation of duty leaves Harms, the delegatee (the one to whom the duty is delegated), primarily responsible for performance; but Allen, the obligor/delegator, (the one who made the delegation) remains secondarily liable in case Harms, the delegatee, fails to fulfill the duty to Boyd, the obligee (the one to whom the duty is owed under both the original contract and the delegation). As with the assignment of rights, some contractual duties, particularly those of a personal service nature, cannot be delegated without consent.

FIGURE 6.4
Delegation of Duties

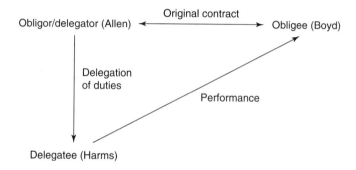

Third-Party Beneficiary Contracts

Normally, those not a party to a contract have no rights under that contract. As we have seen, however, third parties may be assigned rights or delegated duties under a contract. A third party may also enforce a contract where that contract was expressly intended to benefit the third party. An agreement of that nature is a third-party beneficiary contract. Third-party beneficiaries are of three kinds: creditor, donee, and incidental. In general, creditor and donee beneficiaries can enforce contracts made by others for their benefit; incidental beneficiaries cannot do so.

Creditor Beneficiary   Assume you decide to expand your used car business by advertising on television. Your ads appear on TV, and you owe the local station $2,000. Rather than paying the bill directly, you transfer a used car to your friend, Gleason, with the understanding that he will pay off your bill with the television station. Thus the station becomes the creditor beneficiary of the contract between you and Gleason, and the station can sue Gleason for that money if necessary while you remain secondarily responsible for the payment.

Donee Beneficiary   When the promisee's primary purpose in entering a contract is to make a gift to another, that third party is a donee beneficiary of the contract. The most common of these situations involves an ordinary life insurance policy for which the owner (the promisee) pays premiums to the life insurance company (the promisor), which is obliged to pay benefits to the third party upon the death of the promisee/policy owner. If necessary, the third-party beneficiary can sue the insurance company for payment.

Incidental Beneficiary   Often a third party receives benefit from a contract although conferring that benefit was not the contracting parties' primary purpose or intent. For example, assume a General Motors car dealer enters into a contract to buy land adjacent to your used car lot for the purpose of opening a large dealership. You would benefit immensely from the spillover effect of the large, adjacent dealership. In such a situation, you would be an incidental beneficiary of the land sale contract because that contract was not intended for your benefit. If the landowner or the GM dealer failed to perform, you, as an incidental beneficiary, would have no legal rights against either of them.

The case that follows involves a third-party claim by Gill Plumbing against its subcontractor, Jimenez. The dispute arose out of a dormitory construction contract where the general contractor, Gilbane Building, had hired Gill to do the dormitory plumbing and Gill, in turn, had hired Jimenez to install some portion of that plumbing.

Jimenez v. Gilbane Building Company, et al.

LEGAL BRIEFCASE   693 S.E.2d 126 (Ga. Ct. App. 2010)

* * * * *

Judge Adams

The background facts are that Gilbane Building Company was the general contractor for the construction of a new dormitory at Georgia Southern University. Gilbane hired Gill Plumbing as the plumbing contractor, and Gill Plumbing, in turn, hired Jose Alfredo Jimenez to perform plumbing installation work. The building was completed in July 2005, but in October, after the dormitory was occupied by students, a pipe failed causing extensive water damage to the dormitory and to some students' personal belongings. Gilbane was forced to hire Belfor USA Group, Inc. to perform remediation and repair work. Belfor's $990,060.63 bill for the services has not been paid.

Belfor filed this action against Gilbane, Gilbane filed a third-party action against Gill Plumbing, and Gill Plumbing

filed a fourth-party action against Jimenez. The parties have since been realigned. Currently, both Belfor and Gilbane have claims against Gill Plumbing, and Gill Plumbing has a third-party claim against Jimenez for the costs of the remediation and repair.

In its third-party claim, Gill Plumbing asserts that it had a written agreement with Jimenez that included an indemnity agreement, and that the damages to the dormitory resulted from negligent work performed by Jimenez. Jimenez denied that he entered into a valid and enforceable contract or an indemnity agreement with Gill Plumbing and denied the negligence. The trial court granted Gill's motion for partial summary judgment against Jimenez, finding that he was liable "for indemnification to Gill Plumbing" "in the amount, if any, of damages proven to have resulted from Mr. Jimenez's defective work." Jimenez appeals this ruling and contends that "no contract existed between Mr. Jimenez and the

Appellee as a matter of law" or, at least, that there are material issues of fact regarding the contract and the indemnity agreement.

Summary judgment is proper when there is no genuine issue of material fact and the movant is entitled to judgment as a matter of law. . . .

There is no question that the parties had an oral agreement. The issue before us is whether there was an enforceable written agreement and, if so, what were the terms of that agreement. The undisputed facts show that Jimenez was hired by Gill Plumbing to perform plumbing services in the "Eagle Village" construction project at Georgia Southern University, that he performed plumbing services, and that he has been paid for the work in the amount of $167,000.

Jimenez has never worked for any company other than Gill Plumbing and the two have worked together for at least 15 years. On September 15, 2004, Jimenez signed two documents, which, Gill Plumbing contends, constitute the parties' entire written agreement; Jimenez has signed other documents for Gill Plumbing in the past. The first document is contained on one page, it is dated September 15, 2004, and it has Jimenez's typewritten name and his signature. The main body of the document is as follows:

LABOR CONTRACT
Project: Eagle Village.

Item 1	Slab	50,100.00
Item 2	Rough	66,800.00
Item 3	Set Out	50,100.00

- Weekly billing to be submitted in draw format.
  All work must be approved by Larry Pollett.
- Weekly safety meetings must be attended. Sub required to attend all jobsite agenda & safety meetings.
- Subs required to comply with all general contractor regulations & jobsite regulations
- All Subs required to provide certificate of insurance with adequate coverages per limits set by general contractor.
- Subs are required to honor subcontractor Warranty for labor & installation free of all defects for a period of
  (1) year from date of substantial completion.
- *Subs agree & abide by all terms in the attached Exhibit 'A' for insurance & indemnity.*

Total Contract Amount $167,000.00

(Emphasis supplied.) Jimenez's signature appears below the following words, which are written on the side of the above chart:

Sub-Labor
Affidavit

I certify the work for which above payment is requested has been completed according to the plans and specifications and in compliance with the terms of our contract and all labor and material bills applicable to this job have been paid to date and that Federal income, social security, and unemployment taxes have been withheld and will be paid when due on all employees employed by me on this job.

_____/s/_____ CONTRACTOR

Notably, this first document does not name Gill Plumbing anywhere, and the "affidavit" is written in the past tense, as if the project had already been completed; but as of the date on the document, Jimenez's work at Eagle Village had not begun. The second document—"Exhibit A"—is two pages long, and it begins as follows:

INSURANCE AND INDEMNITY SUBCONTRACTOR AGREEMENT

The Work performed by the Subcontractor shall be at the risk of the Subcontractor exclusively. To the fullest extent permitted by law, Subcontractor shall indemnify, defend (at Subcontractor's sole expense) and hold harmless Contractor, the Owner (if different from Contractor), affiliated companies of Contractor, . . . from and against any and all claims for . . . damage to property . . . which arise or are in any way connected with the Work performed, Materials furnished, or Services provided under this Agreement by Subcontractor or its agents. . . .

The exhibit goes on to require the "Subcontractor" to obtain commercial general liability insurance in the amount of $1,000,000, and to meet other related requirements. The exhibit is signed by Jimenez on the second page over the word "Subcontractor," but it is not dated. Also, the document does not include Gill Plumbing's name anywhere. Finally, Jimenez never performed any work at Eagle Village that could be called "Set Out" as stated on page one of the document.

Jimenez contends the three-page document is not an enforceable agreement because it does not state who the other party is or mention Gill Plumbing's name; it does not include a promise by Gill Plumbing, or anyone else, to pay him; it does not specify the location or address where the work is to be performed; it leaves several terms undefined; it does not specify the time for performance; it does not direct Jimenez to perform any work at all; and although it mentions additional documents, none are attached or defined. He argues the "sub-labor affidavit" found on page one of the document is written in the past tense, suggesting that the work was already completed when, in fact, it had not begun as of the only date indicated on the document. He also complains that the indemnification provision fails to identify who should be indemnified and that it fails to define the terms "subcontractor," "contractor," or "owner." Finally, Jimenez contends he cannot read or communicate well in English and he did not know what he signed.

In Georgia,

> The first requirement of the law relative to contracts is that there must be a meeting of the minds of the parties, and mutuality, and in order for the contract to be valid the agreement must ordinarily be expressed plainly and explicitly enough to show what the parties agreed upon. A contract cannot be enforced in any form of action if its terms are incomplete or incomprehensible.
>
> *Bagwell-Hughes, Inc. v. McConnell,* 224 Ga. 659, 661–662 (164 SE2d 229) (1968). But "[a]n objection of indefiniteness may be obviated by performance on the part of one party and the acceptance of the performance by the other." *Aukerman v. Witmer,* 256 Ga. App. 211, 216 (1) (568 SE2d 123) (2002). Nevertheless, performance as a cure has its limits:
>
> > Performance does not cure the deficiencies in an agreement that is so vague, indefinite, and uncertain "as to make it impossible for courts to determine what, if anything, was agreed upon, therefore rendering it impossible to determine whether there had been performance."
>
> *Razavi v. Shackelford,* 260 Ga. App. 603, 605 (1) (580 SE2d 253) (2003).

Here, the attendant and surrounding circumstances show that Jimenez entered into an agreement with Gill Plumbing, that he performed work, and that he was paid by Gill Plumbing. The three-page document shows that the work was to be performed on the "Eagle Village" project; it stated the amount to be paid for each phase of the work; and the total equaled the amount that Jimenez was paid for the work. And Jimenez attended weekly safety meetings. Thus, there is some evidence of performance consistent with the three-page document. But there is also evidence of performance that is inconsistent with the three-page document. Jimenez did not perform some of the work listed in the document, and the document suggests that the work had already been completed when the document was signed.

In addition, the document is ambiguous at best, and the rules of construction do not resolve the ambiguity. Jimenez is identified as the "subcontractor" in the indemnification agreement, which provides that he is to identify the "contractor" and others. Yet, the first page of the three page document identifies Jimenez as the "contractor," suggesting that he should indemnify himself. And there are two contractors who are parties to the lawsuit and other contractors on the entire project.

* * * * *

Here, among other problems, it is impossible to tell from the terms of the written document who Jimenez may have promised to indemnify, and that fact has not been made sufficiently clear by either the rules of construction or any performance under the agreement. The trial court erred by granting partial summary judgment in favor of Gill Plumbing on the purported indemnification agreement. Jury issues remain on the terms of the parties' agreement.

Judgment reversed.

Questions

1. Explain what the trial court meant in finding that Jimenez was liable "for indemnification to Gill Plumbing" "in the amount, if any, of damages proven to have resulted from Mr. Jimenez's defective work."

2. Why did the court conclude that Gill did not have an enforceable agreement with Jiminez?

3. Why did the appeals court overturn the trial court's summary judgment?

Discharge

At some point, obligations under a contract come to an end. When that moment arrives, we say the duties of the contracting parties have been discharged. In this section, we examine some of the methods of contract discharge. Discharge can occur in many ways, but the most important of these are (1) conditions, (2) performance or breach, (3) lawful excuses, (4) agreement, and (5) by operation of law.

Discharge by Conditions

Sometimes a contract is useful to one or more of the contracting parties only if some future event occurs or fails to occur. Under those circumstances, the parties may write into the contract a clause providing that performance is required only if the specified condition occurs or fails to occur. Otherwise, the duty to perform is discharged. Those conditions take three forms: conditions precedent, conditions subsequent, and conditions concurrent.

Conditions Precedent   A conditions precedent clause specifies that an event must occur before the parties to the contract are obliged to perform. Assume you are attempting to establish a business booking rock-and-roll acts for performances. You sign a deal with the rock group Passion Pit, providing for a performance "contingent upon obtaining satisfactory lease arrangements for the university field house within 14 days." If you are unable to achieve an acceptable lease, both parties are discharged from performance requirements under the contract.

> You sign a deal with the rock group Passion Pit.

Conditions Subsequent   A conditions subsequent clause excuses performance if a future event transpires. Thus, in the Passion Pit example, the band might include a clause providing that the agreement will be null and void if any member of the band is ill or otherwise unable to perform on the contracted evening. Hence in a contract with a condition subsequent the parties have bound themselves to perform unless a specified event occurs; whereas in a contract with a condition precedent the parties have no binding duties until the specified event occurs.

Conditions Concurrent   Here the contract simply specifies that the parties are to perform their duties at the same time. Each performance is dependent on the other. So if Passion Pit performs as contracted, you have a simultaneous duty to pay for the band's performance. Your duty to pay is conditioned on Passion Pit's performance and vice versa.

Express or Implied Conditions   Another way of classifying the aforementioned conditions is to treat them either as express or implied. Express conditions are those explicitly agreed to by the parties, as in the situation where you, a concert promoter, expressly conditioned performance on your ability to secure the university field house for the concert. Express conditions are often prefaced by words such as *when, if, provided,* and so forth.

Implied-in-fact conditions are not explicitly stated in the contract but are derived by the court from the conduct of the parties and the circumstances surrounding the bargain. Suppose you contract to remove snow from your neighbor's driveway during the winter. An implied-in-fact condition of your neighbor's duty to pay would be that you would complete the work within a reasonable period.

Implied-in-law conditions (also called *constructive conditions*) are those that, although not expressly provided for in the contract or not able to be reasonably inferred from the facts, the court imposes on the contract to avoid unfairness. Hence, if you contracted to put a new roof on your neighbor's house but your written contract did not include a date for payment, the court might imply a contract clause providing that your neighbor need not pay you until the job is complete.

Whose Ring?

Barry Meyer and Robyn Mitnick became engaged on August 9, 1996, at which time Barry gave Robyn a custom-designed, $19,500 engagement ring. On November 8, 1996, Barry asked Robyn to sign a prenuptial agreement, but Robyn refused. The parties agree the engagement ended at that point, but they each blame the other for the breakup. Robyn did not return the ring, and Barry sued for its return.

Questions

1. Explain each party's argument using contract principles.
2. Does it matter who was "at fault" in the breakup? Explain.
3. Who gets the ring? Explain.

Source: Meyer v. Mitnick, 625 N.W.2d 136 (Ct. App. Mich. 2001).

Discharge by Performance or by Breach of Contract

Complete performance is, of course, the normal way of discharging a contract. Failure to fully perform without a lawful excuse for that failure results in a breach of contract. The consequences of both full performance and breach of contract can be described in four parts.

Complete Performance—No Breach of Contract   Here we find the most common method of discharge—the situation in which the parties simply do precisely what the contract calls for: pay $500, provide a particular product, present the deed for a piece of land, and so on. When fully performed, a contract has been *executed.*

Substantial Performance—Nonmaterial Breach of Contract   In some cases complete performance is not achieved because of minor deviations from the agreed-on performance. Most notably in construction contracts and in many personal or professional service contracts, the courts have recognized the doctrine of substantial performance. For example, assume a contractor painted a house as agreed, except that he replaced the Benjamin Moore paint called for in the contract with a Sherwin-Williams paint of comparable quality. Assuming the variation has not materially altered the end product and assuming that the variation was not the result of bad faith, the court will enforce the contract as written, but require a deduction for any damages sustained as a consequence of the imperfect performance.

Unacceptable Performance—Material Breach of Contract   When a party falls beneath substantial performance and does not have a lawful excuse for that failure, a material breach of contract has occurred. No clear line separates substantial performance (a nonmaterial breach) from unacceptable performance (a material breach). Such decisions must be made case by case. We can say that material breaches are those that fall short of what the nonbreaching party should reasonably expect—that is, full performance in some cases and substantial performance in others. A material breach discharges the nonbreaching party's duties and permits that party to sue for damages or rescind the contract and seek restitution.

Duke University Breached Its Contract with a Student?

Andrew Giuliani (son of former New York mayor, Rudy Giuliani) was recruited by Coach Rod Myers to play golf at Duke University. Coach Myers allegedly said that Giuliani would be given "life-time access" to Duke's "state-of-the-art" training facilities when he became a Duke alum, and that he would be able to compete for the opportunity to play against the best golfers in the NCAA. Giuliani said those promises and others were instrumental in his decision to attend Duke. Giuliani alleged that Duke "promised to provide [Mr. Giuliani] with various educational services, lodging, and a right of access to the Athletic Department's Varsity program and facilities." Coach Myers unexpectedly passed away in the spring of 2007 and Coach O.D. Vincent took over. Vincent decided to cut the squad in half and announced that he was canceling Giuliani's golf eligibility. Vincent pointed to several incidents of alleged bad behavior by Giuliani. Vincent then presented Giuliani with a written agreement setting out the steps that would have allowed Giuliani to rejoin the team. Giuliani refused to sign the agreement. Giuliani then filed a breach of contract suit against Duke University and Vincent.

Questions

1. Giuliani claimed that his contractual right to play golf at Duke was based on (a) Coach Myers's oral statements and (b) Duke's Student-Athlete Handbook, the Duke Student Bulletin, the Duke Athletic Policy Manual, and the NCAA Division I Manual. Giuliani lost the case. Why did the Court reject Giuliani's contract claims?

2. Could you successfully sue your university for breach of contract if you were dismissed from school because of low grades? Explain. See, e.g., *Bissessur v. The Indiana University Board of Trustees,* 581 F.3d 599 (7th Cir. 2009).

Source: Giuliani v. Duke University, 2010 U.S. Dist. LEXIS 32691 (M.D.N.C.).

Advance Refusal to Perform—Anticipatory Breach of Contract   Sometimes one of the parties, before performance is due, indicates by word or deed that she or he will not perform. Normally an anticipatory breach (also called anticipatory repudiation) is the equivalent of a material breach, discharging the nonbreaching party from any further obligations and allowing the nonbreaching party to sue for damages, if any.

When Has a Breach of Contract Occurred? When Should the Law Intervene in a Contract?

The brief case that follows raises many claims, including breach of contract, but it also serves as an interesting test of the role of law. Should sports fans be able to secure a remedy through contract law when an event merely does not meet their expectations? The idea seems preposterous and another instance of abuse of the legal system, but consider the facts.

> Tyson spit out his mouthpiece and bit both of Holyfield's ears.

The case deals with ex-convict and former heavyweight boxing champion Mike Tyson and his famous 1997 bout with then-champion Evander Holyfield, a fight ended by disqualification in the third round when Tyson bit both of Holyfield's ears. Incensed pay-per-view customers joined in a class action seeking their money back

($50–$60 each) claiming they were "ripped off" or "scammed" by Tyson. They sued Tyson, fight promoters, and fight telecasters. A lower court dismissed the complaint for failure to state a cause of action. The plaintiffs appealed.

LEGAL BRIEFCASE

Castillo v. Tyson   701 N.Y.S. 2D 423
(N.Y. S.Ct. App. Div. 2000)

Judge Ramos

Plaintiffs claim that they were entitled to view a "legitimate heavyweight title fight" fought "in accordance with the applicable rules and regulations" of the governing boxing commission—that is, a fight that was to end either in an actual or technical knockout or by decision of the judges after 12 rounds—and that they are entitled to their money back because the fight ended in a disqualification. Many legal theories are invoked in support of this claim—breach of contract, breach of implied covenant of good faith and fair dealing, unjust enrichment, breach of express and implied warranties, tortious interference with contractual relations, "wantonness," fraud, negligent representation—none of which have merit. Plaintiffs are not in contractual privity with any of the defendants, and their claim that they are third-party beneficiaries of one or more of the contracts that defendants entered into among themselves was aptly rejected by the motion court as "contrived." Nothing in these contracts can be understood as promising a fight that did not end in a disqualification. The rules of the governing commission provide for disqualification, and it is a possibility that a fight fan can reasonably expect. Plaintiffs could not reasonably rule out such a possibility by the boxer's and promoters' public statements predicting a "sensational victory" and "the biggest fight of all time," and assuming other representations were made promising or implying a "legitimate fight," there can be no breach of warranty claim absent privity of contract between plaintiffs and defendants and also because defendants provided only a service. Nor is a claim of fraud supported by plaintiffs' allegations that the boxer's former trainer predicted that the boxer would get himself disqualified if he failed to achieve an early knockout and that the boxer came out without his mouthpiece in the beginning of the round that he was disqualified. Plaintiffs' claim for unjust enrichment was properly dismissed by the motion court on the ground that plaintiffs received what they paid for, namely,

"the right to view whatever event transpired." We have considered plaintiffs' other arguments . . . and find them unpersuasive. Affirmed.

Questions

1. Why did the court reject the plaintiffs' breach of contract claim?

2. What is unjust enrichment, and why was that claim denied by the court?

3. Defects discovered in the Michelin tires to be used by 14 of the 20 teams in a Formula One race at the Indianapolis Speedway caused those teams to withdraw prior to the start, leaving only six cars running in the race. The race was completed, but fans sued for breach of contract claiming the race was not what they had purchased tickets to see and that the race advertising had indicated that 20 cars would be racing. Decide the case. Explain. See *Bowers v. Federation Internationale de L'Automobile,* 489 F.3d 316 (7th Cir. 2007).

4. Pelullo promoted boxers and boxing matches through his company, Banner Productions. In 1999 Echols signed an agreement with Banner giving Echols a $30,000 bonus and giving Banner "the sole and exclusive right to secure all professional boxing bouts" for Echols. Banner was to provide no fewer than three bouts per year, and Echols was to be paid not less than a specified minimum amount for each fight, but the payments could be lowered or the whole agreement canceled, at Banner's option, if Echols lost a fight. Echols lost a championship bout, and Banner said it would thereafter negotiate each purse on a bout-by-bout basis. Echols continued to fight for Banner, but various disputes over purses arose, and Echols sued. Among other claims, Echols argued that the agreement was unenforceable for indefiniteness. Decide that claim. Explain. See *Echols v. Pelullo,* 377 F.3d 272 (3d Cir. 2004).

Discharge by Lawful Excuses (for Nonperformance)

Sometimes contracts are discharged lawfully even in the event of nonperformance. This can occur when performance is either impossible or impractical.

Impossibility   After agreement is reached but performance is not yet due, circumstances may be so altered that performance is a *legal impossibility*. In such situations nonperformance is excused. Impossibility here refers not simply to extreme difficulty but to objective impossibility; that is, the contracted-for performance cannot be accomplished by anyone. Notable examples of such situations are a personal service contract where the promisor has died or is incapacitated by illness, a contract where the subject of the agreement was rendered illegal by a change in the law subsequent to the agreement but prior to its performance, or a contract where an ingredient essential to performance has been destroyed and no reasonable substitutes are available. [For more on impossibility of performance, see **http://www.west.net/~smith/imposbl.htm**]

Commercial Impracticability   Akin to the doctrine of impossibility is the situation in which duties are discharged because of unforeseen events that render performance exorbitantly expensive or thoroughly impractical. Commercial impracticability is specifically provided for in UCC 2-615, which reads, "Delay in delivery or nondelivery in whole or in part by a seller . . . is not a breach of his duty under a contract for sale if performance as agreed has been made impracticable by the occurrence of a contingency the nonoccurrence of which was a basic assumption on which the contract was made. . . ."

The UCC's commercial impracticability standard is more easily established than the impossibility doctrine of the common law, but note that only exceptional and unforeseeable events fall within the impracticability excuse for nonperformance. Mere changes in market conditions do not give rise to commercial impracticability. Historically, the commercial impracticability doctrine had been applied only to transactions involving the sale of goods, but now we see courts increasingly willing to apply it to other kinds of contracts as well.

Discharge by Agreement

A contractual discharge is sometimes achieved by a new agreement arrived at after entering the original contract. These agreements take a variety of forms, but one—*accord and satisfaction*—will serve here to illustrate the general category. Parties reach an accord when they agree to a performance different from the one provided for in their contract. Performance of the accord is called satisfaction, at which point the original contract is discharged. A binding accord and satisfaction must spring from a genuine dispute between the parties, and it must include consideration as well as all of the other ingredients in a binding contract.

Discharge by Operation of Law

Under some circumstances, contractual duties are discharged by the legal system itself. Among those possibilities: (1) The contractual responsibilities of a debtor may be discharged by a bankruptcy decree. (2) Each state has a *statute of limitations* that specifies the time within which a performing party can initiate a lawsuit against a nonperforming party. For the UCC statute of limitations, see 2-725.

Remedies

We have looked at the elements of a binding contract and at those circumstances that discharge a party's duties under a contract. Now our concern is with what happens when one of the parties does not fulfill his or her contractual duties—that is, when the contract is breached. Remedies are provided in both law and in equity (see Glossary and Chapter 4).

Remedies in Law

In general, a *breach of contract* allows the nonbreaching party to sue for money damages. The general goal of remedies law is to put the parties in the position they would have occupied had the contract been fulfilled. Normally, the best available substitute for actual performance is monetary damages.

Compensatory Damages In brief, the plaintiff in a breach of contract action is entitled to recover a sum equal to the actual damages suffered. The plaintiff is compensated for her losses by receiving a sum designed to "make her whole," to put her where she would have been had the contract not been breached.

Sale of Goods A breach involving a sale of goods is governed by the UCC. Typically the measure of *compensatory damages* would be the difference between the contract price and the market price of the goods at the time and place the goods were to be delivered (see UCC 2-708 and 2-713). Suppose you are working for a newly established computer manufacturer, and you have contracted with the Internal Revenue Service to deliver 1,000 laptop computers at $1,500 each, although the current market price is $1,600. If you fail to make that delivery, damages could be assessed in the amount of $100,000 ($100 $\times$ 1,000), which is the additional amount the IRS would need to pay to make the substitute purchase.

Consequential Damages The victim of a breach may be able to recover not just the direct losses from the breach but also any indirect losses that were incurred as a consequence of that breach. Such consequential damages are recoverable only if they were foreseen or were reasonably foreseeable by the breaching party. For example, if you contract for a well-known local band to play for the grand opening of your new bar and dance club and the band fails to appear, you may be able to recover damages for any lost profits that you can attribute to the band's absence. Those lost profits are a *consequence* of the breach. Of course, you will have some difficulty in specifying the profits lost and in proving that the loss was attributable to the band's failure to perform.

> The grand opening of your new bar and the band fails to appear.

Incidental Damages The costs incurred by the nonbreaching party in arranging a substitute performance or otherwise reducing the damages sustained because of the breach are recoverable as incidental damages. They would include such items as phone calls and transportation expenses.

Nominal Damages In some cases of breach, the court will award only an insignificant sum, perhaps 1 dollar (plus court costs), because the nonbreaching party has suffered no actual damages. The point of nominal damages is to illustrate the wrongfulness of the breach.

Punitive Damages   Sometimes when the breaching party's conduct is particularly reprehensible, the court will penalize that wrongful behavior by awarding punitive damages to the injured party. The idea is to deter such conduct in the future. Normally punitive damages cannot be awarded in breach of contract cases except when provided for by statute or when the breach is accompanied by a tort such as fraud (as where one buys a defective car having reasonably relied on the falsehoods of a salesperson).

Rescission and Restitution   In some instances, including a material breach, mistake, fraud, undue influence, and duress, the wronged party may rescind (undo) the contract. The effect of a contract rescission is to return the parties to the positions they occupied before they entered the agreement. Generally, both parties must then make restitution to each other by returning whatever goods, property, and so forth were transferred under the contract or an equivalent amount of money.

Mitigation   Obviously the law should penalize a breaching party, as we have discussed; but you may be surprised to learn that the law also imposes expectations on the victim (the nonbreaching party). Specifically, the nonbreaching party is required to take reasonable steps toward mitigation—that is, to minimize her or his damages. What happens, for example, if you are wrongfully dismissed in breach of contract from your first job after college? You are expected to mitigate your damages by seeking another job. You need not take an inferior job, nor must you disturb your life by moving to another state or community; but you must take reasonable measures to minimize your claim against your former employer.

Liquidated Damages   We have reviewed both the legal penalties for breach and the duty to mitigate damages. The law also offers the opportunity to provide some control over the penalty for breach by including in the contract a liquidated damages clause. Here you and the other party to the contract agree in advance about the measure of damages should either of you default on your duties. That clause is fully enforceable so long as it is not designed to be a penalty but rather a good faith effort to assess in advance an accurate measure of damages. A valid liquidated damages clause limits the nonbreaching party to recovery of the amount provided for in that clause.

Remedies in Equity

Where justice cannot be achieved via money damages alone, the courts will sometimes impose equitable remedies. The chief forms of equitable remedy in contract cases are specific performance, injunction, reformation, and quasi-contract.

Specific Performance   In unusual circumstances the court may order the breaching party to remedy its wrong by performing its obligations precisely as provided for in the contract. Normally that specific performance is required only where the subject matter of the contract is unique and thus cannot be adequately compensated with money. Examples of such subject matter might include a particular piece of land, an art work, or a family heirloom. By contrast, specific performance would not be available in contracts involving conventional personal property such as a television or a car unless those items were unique (such as a one-of-a-kind Rolls Royce).

Normally the courts will not grant a specific performance remedy in personal service contracts (like an agreement by a cosmetic surgeon to perform a face-lift). If the surgeon refused to perform, specific performance probably would not be ordered. The quality of the surgery likely would not be equal to what had been bargained for; courts do not want to be in the position of supervising the completion of contracts, and as a matter of public policy, we do not want to put parties, in this case, the surgeon, in a position that amounts to involuntary servitude.

Injunction   An injunction is a court order that may either require or forbid a party to perform a specified act. Injunctions are granted only under exceptional circumstances. Perhaps the most common of those are the noncompetition agreements. For example, you take a computer programming job that will afford you access to company secrets. To protect itself, the company expects you to sign an agreement specifying that you will not take employment with a competing firm for one year after departure from your employer. If you should quit and seek to work for a competitor within one year, your former employer might be able to secure an injunction preventing you from doing so until the year has passed.

Reformation   Reformation is an equitable remedy that permits the court to rewrite the contract where it imperfectly expressed the parties' true intentions. Typically such situations involve a mutual mistake or fraud. Thus, if the parties sign a contract to sell a lot in a housing development, but the contract is written with an incorrect street address for the lot, an equity court could simply correct the error in the contract.

Quasi-Contract   What happens if one party has conferred a benefit on another, but a contract has not been created because of a failure of consideration, the application of the statute of frauds, or something of the sort? To prevent unjust enrichment, the court might then imply a contract as a matter of law. For example, assume a lawn service mistakenly trims your shrubs and you watch them do so, knowing that they are supposed to be caring for your neighbor's lawn. You have not entered a contract with the lawn service, but a court might well require you to pay the reasonable value of trimming your shrubs. To do otherwise would unjustly enrich you.

PRACTICING ETHICS   Bloggers Work for Free?

Liberal journalism blog *The Huffington Post* was sued in a class action in 2011 on the grounds that the blog had failed to pay the more than 9,000 bloggers who had provided content for the blog over a period of years. In submitting copy to *The Huffington Post,* bloggers knew they would not be paid, but presumably they valued the professional/political/personal exposure afforded by publication. The lawsuit, however, claims the agreement to provide content without compensation has resulted in unjust enrichment for Huffington. AOL purchased *The Huffington Post* earlier in 2011 for $315 million. *The Huffington Post* was created in 2005 as a blog aggregator and opinion site.

Questions

1. The law aside, does *The Huffington Post* have a moral duty to compensate the bloggers who knowingly gave away their content when that content subsequently proved to be instrumental in building Huffington into a valuable property? Explain. Do you feel a duty to pay others when you are the beneficiary of "unjust enrichment?" Explain.

Source: Stephanie Francis Ward, "Huffington Post Bloggers Sue, Seeking Payment for Writing," *ABA Journal,* April 12, 2011 [http://www.abajournal.com/news/article/huffpo_bloggers_sue_seeking_payment_for_writing/].

Internet Exercise

Go to the ContractsProf Blog [**http://lawprofessors.typepad.com/contractsprof_blog/**] for August 17, 2010. Read about and explain the breach of contract lawsuit filed against Paris Hilton. Do a broader Internet search to update the status of the Hilton lawsuit.

Chapter Questions

1. Wardle made a standard real estate offer to buy a house owned by Kessler. The offer contained a "time is of the essence" clause specifying that the deal had to be completed on or before 11 AM on September 26, 1997. Owen then submitted a backup purchase offer for the same price as offered by Wardle. Wardle's completed contract was not delivered to Kessler until approximately 11:20 AM on September 26, so Kessler sold to Owen. Wardle then sued Kessler. Decide. Explain. See *Owen v. Kessler,* 778 N.E.2d 953 (App. Ct. Mass. 2002).

2. A Peoples Group representative interviewed Hawley in Missouri. Hawley and Peoples completed a contract (signed by Hawley in Missouri and Peoples' president in Florida) for Hawley to recruit students in Missouri to attend a Peoples college in Florida. Hawley was to be paid a commission for the students he recruited. Hawley was to be able to participate in the Peoples health and life insurance plans, and Peoples was to provide the appropriate payroll taxes for Social Security and so forth. Hawley was to maintain certain licenses and insurance coverage, to exclusively represent Peoples' interests, and to complete Peoples' training program. Hawley was never physically present in Florida. Following training, Hawley was shot and killed while attempting to make one of his first calls in Missouri. Hawley's heirs sought Florida workers' compensation. Peoples said they could not be responsible for workers' compensation payments for Hawley's heirs because Peoples and Hawley had not entered a completed, binding contract.
   a. Explain Peoples' contract argument.
   b. Did the parties achieve a binding contract? Explain. See *Peoples Group v. Hawley,* 804 So. 2d 561 (Fla. Ct. App., 1st Dist. 2002).

3. Allen M. Campbell Co. sought a contract to build houses for the U.S. Navy. Approximately one half hour before the housing bids were due, Virginia Metal Industries quoted Campbell Co. a price of $193,121 to supply the necessary doors and frames. Campbell, using the Virginia Metal quote, entered a bid and won the contract. Virginia Metal refused to supply the necessary doors, and Campbell had to secure an alternative source of supply at a price $45,562 higher than Virginia Metal's quote. Campbell sued. Explain Campbell's claim. Defend Virginia Metal. Decide. See *Allen M. Campbell Co. Inc. v. Virginia Metal Industries,* 708 F.2d 930 (4th Cir. 1983).

4. The Great Minneapolis Surplus Store placed a newspaper ad saying, "Saturday 9:00 AM sharp. 3 Brand New Fur Coats. Worth $100.00. First Come. First Served. $1 each." Lefkowitz was the first customer at the store that Saturday. He demanded a coat and indicated his readiness to pay the dollar, but the store refused saying it was a "house rule" that the coats were intended for women customers only. Lefkowitz sued. Express the issue(s) in this case. Defend Great Minneapolis. Decide. Explain. See *Lefkowitz v. Great Minneapolis Surplus Store,* 86 N.W.2d 689 (Minn. S.Ct. 1957).

5. Blette contracted with ANC in May 2008 for a one-year apartment lease at $605 per month. In February 2009, Blette complained to ANC about substandard maintenance

and other problems. Blette tendered a $752.54 check and wrote an accompanying letter saying that the payment was to settle her forthcoming March, April, and May rent minus her alleged damages. She also wrote that if the check were cashed her terms were being accepted. ANC wrote back saying it would cash the check but that her demands were unacceptable. Was Blette in breach of contract when she failed to make full payment? Explain. See *THG/Apartments Near Campus v. Deeanna Blette,* 2010 Ia. App. LEXIS 571.

6. Sherwood agreed to purchase a cow, Rose 2d of Aberlone, from Walker at a price of 5 1/2 cents per pound (about $80). The parties believed the cow to be barren. Sherwood came to Walker's farm to collect the cow, but at that point it was obvious that Rose was pregnant. Walker refused to give over the cow, which was then worth $750 to $1,000. Sherwood sued. Should he get the cow? Explain. See *Sherwood v. Walker,* 33 N.W. 919 (Mich. S.Ct. 1887).

7. Weaver leased a service station from American Oil. The lease included a clause providing that Weaver would hold American Oil harmless for any negligence by American on the premises. Weaver and an employee were burned when an American Oil employee accidentally sprayed gasoline while at Weaver's station. Weaver had one and one half years of high school education. The trial record provides no evidence that Weaver read the lease, that American's agent asked him to read it, or that Weaver's attention was drawn to the "hold harmless" clause. The clause was in fine print and contained no title heading. Is the contract enforceable against Weaver? Explain. See *Weaver v. American Oil Co.,* 276 N.E.2d 144 (Ind. S.Ct. 1971).

8. Edward Sherman wanted to sell his business, Adgraphics. He retained V.R. Brokers as an agent for the sale. On December 5, 1985, William Lyon offered $75,000 for the business. Later that day, Sherman signed a counteroffer to sell for $80,000. On December 7 at 11:35 AM Lyon signed the counteroffer, and around noon he took it to Brokers. At about 9 AM that same day, Sherman told Brokers' principal, Robert Renault, that he had decided to cancel his counteroffer. Renault told Lyon of that decision immediately before Lyon handed the signed counteroffer to Renault. Lyon then sued for breach of contract. Decide. Explain. See *Lyon v. Adgraphics,* 540 A.2d 398 (Conn. Ct. App. 1988).

9. A building was rented "for use as a saloon" under an eight-year lease. Five years thereafter the state passed a law making the sale of liquor illegal. The renter, a brewery, argued that it no longer had any duties under the contract. Was the brewery correct? Explain. See *Heart v. East Tennessee Brewing Co.,* 113 S.W. 364 (Tenn. S.Ct. 1908).

10. The La Gasse Company contracted with the City of Fort Lauderdale to renovate one of the city's swimming pools. When the job was nearly complete, vandals severely damaged the pool and most of the work had to be redone. La Gasse sought additional compensation, which the city refused. La Gasse sued, claiming that the subject matter of the contract had been destroyed, thus discharging it from responsibility. Therefore, when it repeated the work, additional compensation was warranted. Decide. Explain. See *La Gasse Pool Construction Co. v. City of Fort Lauderdale,* 288 So. 2d 273 (Fla. Ct. App., 4th Dist. 1974).

11. Preference Personnel, a North Dakota corporation, entered a contract with Peterson to help him find employment in the tax law field. The contract provided that the

employer would pay the placement fee, unless Peterson voluntarily quit within 9 days, in which case he would be responsible for the fee, which was 20 percent of one year's salary. Peterson was placed in a job with an annual salary of $60,000, but he quit after one month. Peterson refused to pay the fee, and Preference sued for breach of contract. The lower court found that Peterson breached the contract, but at the time of the contract, Preference Personnel's state-required license to operate had been allowed to lapse. The court, therefore, dismissed the Preference claim ruling that the agreement was unenforceable as a matter of public policy. Preference appealed. Rule on that appeal. Explain. See *Preference Personnel, Inc. v. Peterson,* 710 N.W.2d 383 (N.D.S.Ct. 2006).

12. Panera, the bakery/café chain, had a clause in its lease that prevented the White City Shopping Center in Shrewsbury, Massachusetts, from renting space to another sandwich shop: "Landlord agrees not to enter into a lease, . . . for a bakery or restaurant reasonably expected to have annual sales of *sandwiches* (emphasis added) greater than ten percent (10%) of its total sales . . . " Panera asked a Massachusetts Superior Court to block the Shopping Center from leasing space to a Qdoba Mexican Grill on the grounds that a lease with the Grill would violate the terms of the Panera lease. How should the Court rule? Explain. See *White City Shopping Center, LP v. PR Restaurants, LLC,* 2006 Mass. Super. LEXIS 544.

CHAPTER SEVEN

Business Torts and Product Liability

After completing this chapter, students will be able to:

1. Compare and contrast the three fundamental kinds of torts: intentional, negligent, and strict liability.

2. Describe selected intentional torts against persons including battery, assault, fraud, invasion of privacy, intentional infliction of emotional distress, and defamation.

3. Describe selected intentional torts against property such as trespass and nuisance.

4. Identify selected intentional tort defenses.

5. Discuss the impact of product liability on business practice.

6. Identify the requirements of a successful negligence claim.

7. Differentiate between types of negligence claims emerging from defective products.

8. Analyze whether negligence defenses may be successfully asserted in a negligence claim.

9. Compare and contrast claims based on express warranties and implied warranties.

10. Identify the elements of the strict liability cause of action.

11. Identify the defenses available in strict liability cases.

12. Evaluate arguments for and against tort reform.

PRACTICING ETHICS   Trampled to Death

Despite his 6'5," 270-pound frame, Jdimytai Damour, 34, was no match for the unruly crowd of an estimated 2,000 Black Friday, 2008 shoppers at a Long Island, New York Walmart. The crowd, some of whom had been waiting for many hours, pushed against the double glass doors. Damour, a worker of one week hired through a temporary agency, and six to ten other Walmart employees pushed back from the inside, but at 4:55 A.M., the doors bowed in and the shoppers surged through crushing Damour to his death and injuring others. Damour had no experience with crowd control and reportedly had not been trained for that purpose. Crowd control barriers were not employed and security personnel reportedly were inside the store rather than being outside to monitor and manage the crowd. Police had been on the scene for 30 minutes at 3 AM, but the crowd of 400 at the time was orderly and the police left. Walmart argued that it had taken appropriate and sufficient safety measures, but authorities subsequently questioned those measures and compared them unfavorably with other retailers' approaches.

Without admitting guilt, Walmart avoided criminal charges by agreeing to pay $400,000 into a victims' compensation fund, along with $1.5 million to local social services causes. Walmart also agreed to build improved holiday crowd management plans for all of its New York stores. (Changes also were to be implemented nationwide on a store-by-store basis.) The federal Occupational Safety and Health Administration (OSHA; see Chapter 12) imposed a $7,000 fine for failing to maintain a safe workplace, but Walmart, at this writing, is appealing that fine because of fears it would set a precedent should some similar tragedy occur in the future. Damour's family is suing both Nassau County officials and Walmart for civil damages.

Sources: Associated Press, "Wal-Mart Worker Trampled to Death Lacked Training, Attorney Says," Fox News.com, December 1, 2008; Robert D. McFadden and Angela Macropoulos, "Wal-Mart Employee Trampled to Death," *The New York Times,* November 29, 2008; and Associated Press, "Wal-Mart Fights $7,000 Fine in Black Friday Death," *USA TODAY,* July 8, 2010.

Questions

1. *a.* Who bears the blame for Damour's death? Explain.
    b. How do we decide where blame lies?

2. *a.* Were the shoppers guilty of criminal behavior? Explain.
    b. Immoral behavior? Explain.

3. Did Walmart fail to fulfill its responsibilities to its employees and customers? Explain.

Part One—Torts: An Introduction

We have looked at the Walmart Black Friday story as an ethics dilemma. Now we turn to the law that resolves personal injury claims like those asserted against Walmart. From the Damour family's point of view, Walmart's Black Friday promotion and the subsequent crowd stampede involved both torts and crimes. *Torts* are civil wrongs not arising from contracts. Torts involve breaches of duty to particular persons, whereas *crimes* are regarded as public wrongs breaching duties to all of society (although, of course, they are most commonly directed at a specific person or persons). Crimes are prosecuted by the state; tort actions are initiated by individuals. Criminal law punishes wrongdoers, but the point of tort law is to make whole an injured party. At the same time, many acts can be treated either as a civil wrong (a tort) or as a crime, or both. For example, a physical attack on another can, of course, lead to criminal charges, but it can also produce civil tort claims, most commonly *assault* and *battery*.

The injured party in a tort litigation can seek *compensatory damages* to make up for the harm suffered. Those damages may consist of medical expenses, lost income, and pain and suffering, among other possibilities. In some cases, *punitive damages* may be awarded to punish the wrongdoer and to discourage others from similar behavior. [For a tort law database, see **http://www.mslaw.edu/IR_RG_torts.htm**]

Tort Categories

Fundamentally, torts are of three kinds: (1) intentional, (2) negligent, and (3) strict liability. *Intentional torts* involve voluntary acts that harm a protected interest. Intent is established by showing the defendant meant to do the act that caused the harm. The plaintiff need not show that the harm itself was intended. The defendant would be liable for all reasonably foreseeable injuries from that intentional act.

To explain, if you run an advertisement defaming a fast-food competitor by saying its food processing does not meet government standards, but you cannot prove the truth of your allegations, you will probably be guilty of the intentional tort of *injurious falsehood* (product disparagement).

Negligence involves situations in which harm is caused accidentally. Intent is absent, but because of one party's carelessness, another has suffered injury. Thus, if one of your employees is making a delivery for the printing business you are managing, and carelessly runs a red light, striking another car, the employee appears to be guilty of negligent conduct for which both she and your firm may be subject to civil damages. Furthermore, you and/or your firm might bear responsibility if, for example, you hired her knowing that she had been a careless driver in the past.

A detailed discussion of negligence law follows in Part Two of this chapter, but for the moment we should notice that negligence concerns are ubiquitous in our lives, ranging from traffic accidents, to inadequate snow clearance from our sidewalks, to failure to keep dangerous kitchen utensils away from children, to ill-timed golf shots, and on and on. Negligence ordinarily is the core claim for those suffering a personal injury caused by the carelessness of another. Broadly, negligence litigation involves an analysis of when that alleged carelessness amounts to a breach of the "duty of due care." For example, can an injured party properly bring a negligence claim against homeowners when parts of their dismantled but not yet stowed away trampoline blow into the nearby road causing a passing driver to crash? The Iowa Supreme Court said "yes" because the homeowners had a duty to exercise reasonable care to see that obstructions did not reach the roadway and they breached that duty by creating a foreseeable risk in dismantling the trampoline but failing to secure the parts over the passage of several weeks time. [For the Court's complete negligence analysis, see *Thompson v. Kaczinski*, 774 N.W.2d 829 (Ia. S.Ct. 2009).]

Strict liability is, in essence, a no-fault concept where an individual or organization is responsible for harm without proof of carelessness. Strict liability expands the reach of the law beyond instances where carelessness (negligence) must be established to situations where actual proof of breach of the duty of due care; that is, proof of negligence, is not required because the risks inherent in that situation are so great. Strict liability is limited to "unreasonably dangerous" products and practices about which we have decided, as a matter of social policy, that responsibility for injury will automatically attach without establishing blame. Thus if a product is (1) defective and (2) unreasonably dangerous and someone is hurt, strict (absolute) liability may attach even though fault is not established. Strict liability is explained in the *Gallagher* case below and in greater detail in Part Two of this chapter.

Tort Law

Selected Intentional Torts against Persons

Suppose you are warehouse manager for a plumbing supply business, and a subordinate does a poor job with some work, which in turn brings your boss down on you. In your frustration, you call the subordinate into your office where you chastise him and then light up a cigar and casually but pointedly blow smoke in his face. Could he file a tort claim against you for your insulting behavior? Let's look at the law in this area. (Of course, many states forbid workplace smoking.)

Battery

Intentionally touching another in a harmful or offensive way without legal justification or the consent of that person is a *battery*. Merely touching another's clothing or touching an occupied car may constitute a battery. Our concern here is with civil wrongs, but perhaps the most interesting recent battery allegation involves a criminal claim.

> Krista Bowman was Web surfing in class. Bowman claims Professor Rybicki closed the laptop on her fingers.

Believing his student, Krista Bowman, was Web surfing in class, Professor Frank J. Rybicki of Valdosta State University (Georgia) reportedly asked her to be attentive. Rybicki apparently felt Bowman continued to surf. Bowman claims that Rybicki then closed the laptop on her fingers, injuring one or more of them. Bowman filed a criminal battery charge against Rybicki, who was arrested. The case is pending at this writing. [For more details, see "Laptop and Battery (Arrest)," *Inside Higher Education,* April 4, 2011 at **http://www.insidehighered.com/news/2011/04/04/professor_arrested_for_battery_after_he_shut_laptop_of_a_student_in_class**]

Assault

Intentionally causing another to reasonably believe that he or she is about to be the victim of a battery is an *assault*. The battery need not occur and the victim need not be frightened; but an assault nonetheless transpires if the victim reasonably anticipated a substantially imminent battery. Thus raising one's hand as if to strike another even though the blow never transpires constitutes the tort of assault if the victim reasonably thought herself to be in immediate danger.

False Imprisonment

If you have anticipated a career in retailing, you may have given thought to the problem of shoplifters and strategies for preserving your inventory without yourself violating customers' rights. The statutory and common (judge-made) law of most states now protects store managers and owners from *false imprisonment* claims if they justifiably detain a suspected shoplifter for a reasonable period and in a reasonable manner. Broadly, false imprisonment occurs when someone is intentionally confined against his or her will; that is, his or her freedom of movement is restricted. That restriction might include being shut in a room, being bound, being threatened, and so on. Even a moment could conceivably constitute imprisonment, although simply sending a customer, for example, through a more distant store exit ordinarily would not meet the test.

Nine Hours on Grounded Plane: False Imprisonment?

Catherine Ray and her husband were flying from Oakland, California to Dallas, Texas, in 2006 when their American Airlines plane was rerouted to Austin, Texas because of bad weather in Dallas. Their flight landed in Austin around noon, refueled, and began to depart, but the weather problems had then closed the Dallas airport. After an hour on the ground, a bus took some passengers to the terminal, but Ray and her husband chose not to deplane because, according to Ray's testimony, the pilot said the flight would likely resume in about an hour and anyone who left the plane "would be on their own," a remark Ray interpreted to mean that departing passengers would need to fund their further transportation, something the Rays could not afford. Two to three hours later another bus arrived and, according to Ray, passengers were told that bus offered their last chance for departure. The Rays decided to remain on the plane. Catherine Ray testified that deteriorating conditions on the plane included little food and drink, agitated passengers, and at least some nonfunctioning lavatories. About 6 PM, the pilot said he could no longer fly because he had reached his maximum duty hours. Lightning in Austin delayed ground crew work, but at about 9 PM, the plane was taken to a gate where Ray and all other passengers deplaned. Some time after deplaning, food and lodging vouchers were provided. Ray and her husband decided to spend the night in the terminal. They flew from Austin the following morning. Ray subsequently filed a civil action for false imprisonment, among other claims. How would you rule on that claim? Explain.

Source: Catherine Ray v. American Airlines, 2010 U.S. App. LEXIS 13582.

Fraud

Intentional misrepresentations of facts, sometimes identified by the formal title of *deceit,* can lead to tort claims. We discuss *fraud* in the contracts (Chapter 6) and consumer protection (Chapter 15) chapters. For now, simply note the general test for fraud:

1. A material fact was misrepresented.
2. The misrepresentation was intentional.
3. The injured party justifiably relied on the misrepresentation.
4. Injury resulted.

Defamation

Uttering an untruth about another may constitute a tort. *Slander* is the spoken form of the tort of *defamation. Libel* is defamation in print or some other tangible form such as a picture, movie, or video. Most courts also treat defamatory radio and television statements as forms of libel. The basic test for establishing defamation includes:

1. A false statement.
2. Harm to the victim's reputation.
3. Publication of the statement. (The statement must reach someone other than the one being defamed.)

The law's interest here is in protecting reputations. Any living person or any organization can be the victim of defamation, although *public figures* such as politicians or actors face the additional burden of proving *malice* if they are to be successful in a defamation claim. Malice generally requires a showing of actual knowledge of the falsehood or reckless disregard for the truth. Libel or slander about a company's products or property often is treated as the tort of injurious falsehood, which is discussed below.

A young Chicago woman, Amanda Bonnen, was sued for defamation in 2009 by her landlord, Horizon Group Management, after she tweeted to a friend, "Who said sleeping in a moldy apartment was bad for you? Horizon Realty thinks it's okay." At trial, however, the judge dismissed the case saying the tweet was vague and could be construed to be a statement of opinion. [For more details, see **http://en.wikipedia.org/wiki/Horizon_ Group_v._Bonnen**]

> **A young Chicago woman sleeping in a moldy apartment?**

In general, a claim of slander requires a showing of actual harm, such as job loss. Some statements, however, are so inherently damaging that actual injury need not be shown. Those statements are labeled *slander per se* and include allegations of serious sexual misconduct, commission of a serious crime, professional incompetence, or having a loathsome disease. Similarly, libel, leaving a more permanent stain, generally does not require a showing of actual harm.

Truth acts as a complete defense to a defamation claim. Hence, if we tell the truth about others, we cannot be guilty of the tort of defamation, regardless of our evil intentions. Furthermore, many statements are protected because of the circumstances in which they are made. We label these protections either absolute or qualified privileges. An *absolute privilege* to defame includes, for example, remarks by government officials in the course of their duties or by participants in a trial. A *qualified privilege* to defame protects, most notably, former employers providing references for a job applicant. In that instance, the reference will not be treated as defamatory, even though false, unless it was motivated by malice. [For an overview of online defamation law for bloggers, see **http://www.eff.org/ issues/bloggers/legal/liability/defamation**]

An Angry Dad

On September 24, 2008, Ed Doherty, a franchisee/owner of about 80 Applebee's restaurants in New Jersey, New York, and Pennsylvania said in a newspaper interview that he treats employees "with dignity and respect" and offers "a great opportunity for them to have a good job." Previously, Michael Murray had represented his daughter, Erin Duby, a former Applebee's employee, in an arbitration claim alleging that she was sexually harassed by managers and other employees. In December 2007, Murray rejected a settlement offer arising out of the arbitration process.

Murray then posted an online response to Doherty's interview by saying that "women . . . are routinely sexually harassed and that this behavior is condoned by high-level management at Doherty Enterprises right up to the top." He warned that "any reader who has a daughter, wife, etc. working for Doherty are [sic] more than likely being subjected to similar treatment." Doherty then sued Murray on defamation grounds.

Was Doherty a victim of defamation? Explain.

Source: Mary Pat Gallagher, "Applebee's Restaurateur . . . Over Internet Post Charging Harassment," *Corporate Counsel*, May 20, 2009.

Invasion of Privacy

A key ingredient in personal freedom is the right to be left alone. Our courts recognize a right of recovery in tort law when we are the victims of some kind of unconscionable exposure of our private lives. *Invasion of privacy* takes four forms:

1. **Misappropriation of a person's name or likeness.** When an individual's name or image is wrongfully used without permission for commercial purposes (called a *misappropriation*) that person probably has a cause of action for invasion of privacy. Typically, this problem involves a company's use of a celebrity's name or picture to imply that he or she has endorsed a product even though no such approval was secured. Actress Lindsay Lohan filed a lawsuit in 2010 claiming that E-Trade had misappropriated her "name and characterization" in one of E-Trade's baby commercials involving a "milkaholic" named "Lindsay." This case, if it is litigated, presumably will turn in part on whether Lindsay Lohan can credibly claim single-name recognition in the manner of Oprah or Bono.

> A "milkaholic" named "Lindsay."

2. **Intrusion.** An intentional invasion of a person's solitude is labeled an intrusion if it would be highly offensive to a reasonable person. Physical intrusions such as opening an employee's mail or more subtle strategies such as an electronic probe of an employee's bank account are examples of tortious intrusion.

3. **Public disclosure of private facts.** We believe that certain elements of one's life, such as debt payment practices or sexual preferences, are, with rare exceptions, no one else's business. If the disclosure would be highly offensive to a reasonable person, and the subject of the disclosure is not a matter of public importance, the tort of public disclosure of private facts might be invoked. In these cases, the truth may not constitute a complete defense.

4. **False light.** When claims are published about another that have the effect of casting the victim in a false light in the public mind, a tort claim may emerge. False light claims involve injury to one's mental or emotional well being rather than one's reputation. Again, the claim would need to be highly offensive to the reasonable person. The courts have struggled to differentiate defamation and false light claims, and we will not pursue the distinction further here.

Intentional Infliction of Emotional Distress

Employment terminations (firings), drug tests, and sexual harassment cases have become particularly fertile grounds for emotional distress claims, although it should be understood that the courts have demanded compelling evidence of *outrageous conduct causing severe emotional pain.* Thus, Mahmoud Abdul-Malik, a ramp agent for AirTran at the Atlanta, Georgia, airport was unsuccessful in his intentional infliction of emotional distress claim against his employer after he was fired for allegedly threatening to blow up the house of another employee. Abdul-Malik claimed that his distress from being fired caused him to lose sleep and gain weight, but the Georgia Court of Appeals ruled, among other things, that those problems did not rise to the level of severity needed for a successful claim. [For the full case, see *Abdul-Malik v. Airtran Airways,* 678 S.E.2d 555 (2009); cert den. *Mahmoud Abdul-Malik v. Airtran Airways,* Inc., 2009 Ga. LEXIS 711 (Ga. S.Ct.).]

Selected Intentional Torts Against Property

We will briefly examine four prominent tort claims arising from wrongs to property.

Trespass to real property (land and immovable objects attached to it) occurs with the intentional entry on to the land of another without consent. *Trespass to personal property* (movable property; all property other than real property) involves an intentional interference with a person's right to enjoy his or her personal property—for example, the manager of a parking lot refuses for a day to return a car to its owner in the mistaken belief that the owner has not paid his monthly bill.

More serious and extensive interference with personal property may be labeled a *conversion.* For example, if the parking lot company kept the car for months, and it suffered damage during the impoundment, a conversion probably occurred.

Injurious falsehood, sometimes called *trade libel,* is a form of defamation that is directed against the property of a person. Thus, falsely claiming that a competitor's product is defective or harmful might constitute injurious falsehood. As with defamation, the statement must be false and it must be published. Damages must result. Often malice/intent must also be shown.

Nuisance is the situation in which enjoyment of one's land is impaired because of some tortious interference. That interference often takes the form of light, noise, smell, or vibration. Here, the owner is not deprived of the land and the land has not been physically invaded, but the full enjoyment of the land cannot be achieved because of the interference. The case that follows involves the owner of an historic Baltimore, Maryland, home who raises both strict liability and nuisance claims in a dispute over alleged damage to her home from nearby pile driving. [For the Jurist Torts Guide, see **http://jurist.law.pitt.edu/sg_torts.htm**]

LEGAL BRIEFCASE

Michela Gallagher v. H.V. Pierhomes, LLC et al.
957 A.2d 628 (Md. Ct. of Spec. App., 2008)

Judge Rubin

THE PROCEEDINGS BELOW

On June 14, 2005, Gallagher sued HV Pierhomes LLC and HV Development & Contracting Co. The initial complaint contained claims for negligence, strict liability, and public and private nuisance. On December 21, 2005, Gallagher filed an amended complaint, which abandoned the negligence claim. All of Gallagher's claims for relief arose out of the pile driving operations conducted by the defendants on the site of the former Key Highway Shipyard. Gallagher contended that vibrations from the pile driving damaged her home, located at 423 East Hamburg Street in Baltimore. Key

Highway; a row of mixed use properties; Covington Street; a retaining wall; and a solid earthen wall, on which Gallagher's house rests, separate Gallagher's house from the pile driving site.

The Key Highway Shipyard, formerly owned by the Bethlehem Steel Corporation, was used to repair naval (sic) ships during World War II and through the Vietnam War. A shipyard of some sort has operated at this location from the beginning of the 20th century until 1982, when Bethlehem Steel closed the facility.

The defendants demolished the original shipyard piers, which were built 40 to 50 years ago and constructed new piers in the same location, by driving piles into the Baltimore Inner

Harbor. The defendants built 58 townhomes on these new piers. Pile driving was the only method of constructing the new townhomes in this particular location because the U.S. Army Corps of Engineers would not allow the Inner Harbor to be "back filled." The pile driving of which Gallagher complained occurred periodically between September 2003 and October 2004.

The plaintiff's home was constructed shortly before the War of 1812. She testified that no pile driving was conducted in the area during the years she lived in the house, beginning in 1997, until the defendants' activities commenced in September 2003. Previously, pile driving was used to build the Seagirt Marine Terminal, the Dundalk Marine Terminal, as well as the Pratt and Light Street Pavilions, which are located across from the plaintiff's residence in the Inner Harbor.

Before the defendants began their project, permits were received from the U.S. Army Corps of Engineers, the Maryland Department of the Environment, and the City of Baltimore. The permitting process took approximately two years. Pile driving on the site began only after geotechnical studies were conducted by engineering firms. During the course of actual pile driving, two permanent seismic stations and five mobile geophones were placed in the surrounding neighborhood to ensure that vibrations were monitored and did not exceed the limits established by the engineers. During the course of the defendants' activities, there was only a single recorded vibration that exceeded the limits.

The case proceeded to trial on December 15, 2006. The plaintiff testified that she heard and felt vibrations from the pile driving in her home. She further testified that cracks began to develop in her plaster walls and in other portions of her home soon after the pile driving began and that no cracks occurred once the pile driving was completed. She was not aware of any other residents in the area who made claims or filed lawsuits for damage to their homes as a result of the vibrations caused by the defendants' pile driving. No evidence of any other claims or suits on account of pile driving vibrations was presented at trial.

* * * * *

On December 21, 2006, the jury returned a verdict in Gallagher's favor. The jury found that: (1) pile driving caused damage to Gallagher's home, and HV Pierpont and HV Development were responsible for the pile driving; (2) the pile driving created a public nuisance; (3) the pile driving created a private nuisance; and (4) Gallagher suffered damages in the amount of $ 55,189.14.

After the jury's verdict was announced, the defendants renewed their motions for judgment. . . . By Order entered on August 20, 2007, the circuit court granted the defendants'

motion for judgment notwithstanding the verdict [The judge overruled the jury—Ed.] on all claims. Gallagher [appealed].

* * * * *

STRICT LIABILITY IN MARYLAND

* * * * *

[The Restatement of Torts,] Section 519, sets forth the general principle upon which courts have held defendants to be liable regardless of fault: "One who carries on an abnormally dangerous activity is subject to liability for harm to the person, land or chattels of another resulting from the activity, although he has exercised the utmost care to prevent the harm."

* * * * *

In summary, Maryland recognizes strict liability, [and] adopts the definition of abnormally dangerous activity as set forth in Section 519 of the Restatement (Second) of Torts (1977). In many, but not all cases, the "thrust of the doctrine is that the activity be abnormally dangerous in relation to the area where it occurs."

STRICT LIABILITY IN PILE DRIVING CASES

The circuit court acknowledged that "whether pile driving is an abnormally dangerous activity has yet to be determined by the Maryland Court of Appeals." The circuit court nevertheless concluded, after applying sections 519 and 520 to the facts of the case, that the Court of Appeals would hold that the pile driving activity in this case would not warrant the application of strict liability.

In the 1984 revision of Dean Prosser's landmark treatise, Professor Page Keaton observed that varying formulations of strict liability have been applied by some courts to hold that pile driving is an abnormally or unreasonably dangerous activity warranting liability without fault. The reasoning of these decisions, as well as the results, is far from uniform. Some courts consider pile driving to be no different than blasting, and therefore dangerous enough to warrant strict liability regardless of the place in which it occurs. Others have taken a more fact-based approach, considering the activity in conjunction with the locale and the type of harm that resulted.

For example, in *Caporale v. C.W. Blakeslee & Sons, Inc.*, 149 Conn. 79, 175 A.2d 561 (1961), the Supreme Court of Connecticut held that pile driving activity during the construction of the Connecticut turnpike in 1958 and 1959, in close proximity to the plaintiff's business premises, warranted the application of strict liability. The Connecticut court analogized pile driving to blasting and aligned itself with those courts that imposed strict liability not only for flying debris but also for the vibrations caused by the explosive force of the blast. The

Connecticut court noted, but declined to follow, a line of New York decisions, illustrated by *Fagan v. Pathe Industries, Inc.,* 274 A.D. 703, 86 N.Y.S.2d 859, 863-64 (App. Div., 1st Dept. 1949), that rejected strict liability for pile driving where the damage was caused only by vibrations.

* * * * *

STRICT LIABILITY IN THIS CASE

* * * * *

The appellant argues that pile driving should be considered abnormally dangerous simply because it produces uncontrollable vibrations, similar to blasting. She also asserts that pile driving created an abnormal risk to persons, such as Gallagher, who have historic homes, and that damage resulting from the inevitable emission of vibration cannot be eliminated through the exercise of due care. Although some courts have adopted this view, others have declined to impose strict liability for vibrations resulting from blasting (as opposed to flying debris).

The circuit court, after reviewing the evidence presented at trial, concluded that the defendants' pile driving in the Inner Harbor did not involve a high degree of risk of harm to the person, land or chattels of another, . . . We agree. Comment g to section 520 states: "The harm threatened must be major in degree, and sufficiently serious in its possible consequence to justify holding the defendant strictly liable for subjecting others to an unusual risk." The risk of harm proven in this case, relatively minor damage to a 200 year old home from the vibrations of the pile driving, simply is not a high degree of risk which requires the application of strict liability. . . .

[A] plaintiff must show that the defendants' pile driving was likely to produce significant harm, not simply that she suffered some harm as a result of the pile driving activity.

After considering the factors of section 520 of the Restatement, we agree with the circuit court's conclusion that the pile driving in this case was not an abnormally dangerous activity.

NUISANCE

Gallagher also contends that the defendants' conduct interfered with the use and enjoyment of her land, amounting to a public and private nuisance. The circuit court disagreed, concluding that Gallagher's evidence of a private or public nuisance was insufficient as a matter of law.

Under Maryland law, to sustain a private nuisance claim "there must be a substantial interference with the plaintiff's reasonable use and enjoyment of its property." *Exxon Corp. v. Yarema,* 69 Md. App. 124, 151, 516 A.2d 990 (1986), *cert. denied,* 309 Md. 47, 522 A.2d 392 (1987). In *Yarema,* we held that the

defendants' "contamination of ground water imposed crippling restrictions not only on the contaminated land but on all the property adjacent to the land." A private nuisance requires the interference to be "substantial and unreasonable and such as would be offensive or inconvenient to the normal person."

Nothing of that order occurred in this case. The defendants' activity was reasonable in time, place, manner, and duration and did not substantially interfere with Gallagher's use and enjoyment of her land. . . . Residents of Baltimore City must accept the occasional annoyance and discomforts incidental to city life.

The elements of a public nuisance were discussed by the Court of Appeals in *Tadjer v. Montgomery County.* Quoting Dean Prosser, the Court of Appeals said: "To be considered public, the nuisance must affect an interest common to the general public, rather than peculiar to one individual, or several."

* * * * *

The circuit court concluded that the evidence produced at trial was insufficient to prove a public nuisance under these standards. We agree.

Affirmed.

Questions

1. *a.* The plaintiff, Gallagher, brought three causes of action in her amended complaint. List them.
    b. Why do you think the jury ruled in favor of Gallagher?
    c. Why did Gallagher lose at the trial level even though the jury had ruled in her favor?
    d. Explain why the appeals court upheld the judgment against Gallagher.
    e. Who do you think should have won this case? Explain.

2. Rattigan and Horvitz owned a house and prime ocean front lot in Beverley Farms, Massachusetts. The house was rented during the summer months. Wile owned an adjacent undeveloped ocean front lot. The only land access to Wile's lot was through the Rattigan/Horvitz lot. Rattigan and Horvitz successfully challenged Wile's application for a building permit and thereafter, Wile began a series of retaliatory acts, including putting several portable toilets on his lot immediately adjacent to the Horvitz swimming pool, landing his helicopter on his vacant lot, placing debris such as a rusted crane bucket, broken cement, and the bed of a pickup truck on his property, and holding parties (not attended by Wile) for 150 to 200 guests from the local youth shelter. Some of these tactics by Wile were sporadic rather than persistent. Were Rattigan and Horvitz the victims of a nuisance? Explain. See *Rattigan v. Wile,* 841 N.E.2d 680 (Mass. S. Judicial Ct. 2006).

Selected Intentional Tort Defenses

Let's take a brief look at a few of the more significant defenses to the intentional torts that we have been examining.

Consent

Clearly, if you consent to the use of your picture in an advertising campaign and you subsequently feel that your public image has been harmed, you will have difficulty in pursuing a tort claim. Of course, if you gave permission under mistake, fraud, or duress, your consent was not meaningful.

Mistake

As store security manager, you are radioed by a clerk to "stop the guy in the New York Yankees cap" on suspicion of shoplifting. After stopping someone fitting that description, you later discover that someone else, also wearing a Yankees cap, was the actual suspect. If the store is sued for false imprisonment, can it successfully raise a mistake defense? Unless protected under state law, probably not. Having acted intentionally, you and, by extension, your employer probably will bear responsibility. Of course, false imprisonment does not occur unless the detention was unreasonable.

On the other hand, mistake can be a good defense, particularly in instances in which events happen rapidly. Say, for example, a store's security personnel broke up what looked like an assault and battery in the mall parking lot, only to discover that the incident was merely horsing around by the parties. A mistake defense might be appropriate here.

Necessity

In what we would broadly label emergency situations, one may intentionally commit a tort and yet be excused. A case of public necessity might involve, for example, a person breaking into an unoccupied building late at night because he saw a fire burning inside. An example of a private necessity is when a defendant intrudes on the property of another to save himself only; he might thereafter raise a necessity defense against the tort claim of trespass.

Self-Defense

Suppose your career has taken you into retail management, and you have now decided to buy your own hardware store. You encounter the ups and downs that characterize entrepreneurial life, but you become particularly frustrated by the theft and vandalism that seem so much a part of small business. Finally, in an effort to stop the breaking, entering, and minor theft that has troubled your business, you build a trap in your store. You take up a few floorboards in a rear entryway where vandals have broken in, and you pound nails (points facing up) into those boards. Then you cover the nail points with some soft felt so they are not visible; but when stepped on, the nails will pierce the felt and stab the feet of any intruder. Suppose your trap works, and an intruder is injured. Suppose the intruder then sues you for his injury. Could you cite self-defense of your property as an excuse? What if a police officer stepped on a nail responding to an alarm at your business? The *Katko* case that follows looks at the self-defense theme.

Katko v. Briney, 183 N.W.2d 657 (Ia. S.Ct. 1971)

FACTS

The Brineys, defendants/appellants in this case, owned an unoccupied farmhouse. During the period from 1957 to 1967, trespassers broke into the house, broke windows, and stole some items. The Brineys boarded windows and erected "no trespassing" signs on the land. On June 11, 1967, the Brineys attached a 20-gauge, loaded shotgun to a bed in the house, pointing the barrel toward the bedroom door. They attached a wire to the trigger and the bedroom doorknob so that the gun would fire if the door were opened. At first, Mr. Briney directed the gun so that it would hit an intruder in the stomach, but agreed with Mrs. Briney's suggestion to lower the barrel so that it would strike an intruder's legs. The gun could not be seen from the outside, and no warning about it was posted.

Katko, the plaintiff/appellee, worked in an Eddyville, Iowa, gas station. He and a friend, McDonough, had found antiques—old bottles and fruit jars—on their first trip to the Briney house, which Katko considered to be abandoned. On their second trip, they entered the house through a window. Katko opened the bedroom door and was shot in the right leg. Much of that leg, including part of the tibia, was blown away. Katko was hospitalized for 40 days. His leg was in a cast for approximately one year, and he was required to wear a brace for an additional year. His leg was permanently shortened by the trauma.

Katko sued the Brineys and secured a jury verdict of $30,000. The Brineys appealed to the Iowa Supreme Court.

* * * * *

Chief Justice Moore

The primary issue presented here is whether an owner may protect personal property in an unoccupied, boarded-up farmhouse against trespassers and thieves by a spring gun capable of inflicting death or serious injury.

We are not here concerned with a man's right to protect his home and members of his family. Defendant's home was several miles from the scene of the incident to which we refer.

* * * * *

Plaintiff testified he knew he had no right to break and enter the house with intent to steal bottles and fruit jars therefrom. He further testified he had entered a plea of guilty to larceny in the nighttime of property of less than $20 value from a private building. He stated he had been fined $50 and costs and paroled during good behavior from a 60-day jail sentence. Other than minor traffic charges this was plaintiff's first brush with the law. . . .

The main thrust of the defendants' defense in the trial court and on this appeal is that "the law permits use of a spring gun in a dwelling or warehouse for the purpose of preventing the unlawful entry of a burglar or thief." . . .

In the statement of issues the trial court stated plaintiff and his companion committed a felony when they broke and entered defendant's house. In instruction 2 the court referred to the early case history of the use of spring guns and stated under the law their use was prohibited except to prevent the commission of felonies of violence and where human life is in danger. The instruction included a statement that breaking and entering is not a felony of violence.

Instruction 5 stated, "You are hereby instructed that one may use reasonable force in the protection of his property, but such right is subject to the qualification that one may not use such means of force as will take human life or inflict great bodily injury. Such is the rule even though the injured party is a trespasser and is in violation of the law himself."

Instruction 6 stated, "An owner of premises is prohibited from willfully or intentionally injuring a trespasser by means of force that either takes life or inflicts great bodily injury; and therefore a person owning a premise is prohibited from setting out 'spring guns' and like dangerous devices which will likely take life or inflict great bodily injury, for the purpose of harming trespassers. The fact that the trespasser may be acting in violation of the law does not change the rule. The only time when such conduct of setting a 'spring gun' or a like dangerous device is justified would be when the trespasser was committing a felony of violence or a felony punishable by death, or where the trespasser was endangering human life by his act." . . .

The overwhelming weight of authority, both textbook and case law, supports the trial court's statement of the applicable principles of law.

Prosser on Torts, Third Edition, pages 116–18, states,

> [T]he law has always placed a higher value upon human safety than upon mere rights in property; it is the accepted rule that there is no privilege to use any force calculated to cause death or serious bodily injury to repel the threat to land or chattels, unless there is also such a threat to the defendant's personal safety as to justify a self-defense . . . spring guns and other man-killing devices are not justifiable against a mere trespasser, or even a petty thief. They are privileged only against those upon whom the landowner, if he were present in person, would be free to inflict injury of the same kind.

* * * * *

In *Hooker v. Miller*, 37 Iowa 613, we held defendant vineyard owner liable for damages resulting from a spring gun shot although plaintiff was a trespasser and there to steal grapes. At pages 614, 615, this statement is made: "This court has held that a mere trespass against property other than a dwelling is not a sufficient justification to authorize the use of a deadly weapon by the owner in its defense; and that if death results in such a case it will be murder, though the killing be actually necessary to prevent the trespass. . . ."

In Wisconsin, Oregon, and England the use of spring guns and similar devices is specifically made unlawful by statute.

* * * * *

Affirmed.

Questions

1. Why did the Iowa Supreme Court rule in favor of the criminal intruder, Katko?

2. What classes of people other than intruders are of concern to the courts in cases like *Katko?*

3. Did the Iowa Supreme Court reach a just verdict? Explain.

4. A businessman in Cordele, Georgia, troubled by small thefts from a cigarette machine in front of his store, allegedly booby-trapped the machine after hours with dynamite. A teenager then died when tampering with the machine. What legal action should be taken? Resolve.

Part Two—Product Liability

Introduction

We have examined intentional torts against both persons and property. Now we turn to tort and contract claims arising from products.

How does the law handle the situation where a wheel falls off a car, or a lighter explodes in a consumer's face? Product liability lawsuits deal with cases where buyers, users, and in some cases bystanders are injured or killed by defective products. Those harmed may have causes of action in torts (negligence or strict liability) or contracts (breach of warranty). If so, the manufacturers, distributors, and sellers of that product must then defend themselves against often enormously expensive claims. Part Two of this chapter explains product liability law and raises some of the public policy considerations that have caused critics to call for legal reforms to reduce the burden of product liability lawsuits. [For a product liability overview, see **http://topics.law.cornell.edu/ wex/Products_liability**]

Product Liability and Business Practice "The business of making small airplanes is all but dead in this country, wiped out mainly by product liability lawsuits."[1] That 1991 pronouncement by *The Wall Street Journal* powerfully depicts the influence of product liability laws in the practice of American business. Today, a key ingredient in a successful business is a plan for dealing with litigation costs. Product liability law addresses situations in which injuries result from defective products.

In the early 1990s, as *The Wall Street Journal* observed, the single-engine plane industry in the United States was largely dead. The major American manufacturer, Cessna Aircraft, of Wichita, Kansas, stopped making small planes in 1986. Its chief rival, Piper Aircraft, struggled with bankruptcy. Single-engine aircraft production in the United States fell from a peak of 13,000 units in 1977 to 444 in 1994.[2] The problems were, in part, attributable to poor management, overproduction, high fuel costs, and recession; but the *Journal* argued that a chief cause was the legal system:

> [W]hat is happening now, according to practically every constituency except the lawyers, is a clear case of products-liability law eating a sick industry alive.[3]

Particularly troublesome for the small plane companies was the so-called *liability tail* that accompanied their products. Airplanes must be built to last for many years, but because product liability claims ordinarily have no time limit, a manufacturer could be sued decades after the plane had left its control. The result was that insurance fees skyrocketed, driving up airplane prices and frightening lenders and investors.[4]

Then Congress passed the General Aviation Revitalization Act, which offered protection against serious liability claims while also limiting claims involving planes that are more than 18 years old.[5] The result was a near-miraculous rebirth for the small plane industry. Piper, selling fewer than 50 planes per year, was left in the early 1990s with $1,000 in the bank, 45 employees, and no way to pay its electricity bill.[6] Then, as *USA TODAY* remarked, "salvation arrived" in the form of the General Aviation Act.[7] "Piper's liability risk fell from 64,000 planes to 12,000, cutting insurance costs 90 percent."[8] The results have been good for the company and good for the American economy:

> In a dramatic turnaround sparked by 1994 legislation that limited plane makers' liability from lawsuits, the new Piper Aircraft climbed out of its tailspin and now has more than 1,500 employees.[9]

Furthermore, the number of general aviation planes and pilots is increasing while product and parts innovation is also up, and the number of lawsuits has fallen dramatically.[10] On the other hand, to blame product liability law alone for the decline of the small plane industry would be misleading. Demographic trends, two oil crises, overproduction of planes, inflation and other factors seem to have played a role in industry problems.[11] [For a general database on defective products, see **http://consumerlawpage.com/resource/defect.shtml**]

Justice for Consumers and for Toyota

Product liability law can sometimes be devastating to a company or industry, as apparently was the case with small planes. But the law is often the only recourse for those wronged by defective products, and it is one of the most effective methods of curbing dangerous business practices. Toyota is in the midst of a massive product liability dispute that has blemished the company's quality image while also apparently threatening the safety of many Toyota customers. Hundreds of injuries and deaths are alleged. Several safety problems have been raised, but the core concern is that some Toyota vehicles accelerate suddenly and uncontrollably. The plaintiffs attribute the problem to defects in the electronic throttle control, but a federal study released in 2011, concluded that the likely culprits were mechanical defects in the accelerator system and floor mats that trapped the accelerator pedal. Plaintiffs are also arguing that Toyota failed to disclose what it knew about the acceleration problem, and that Toyota was negligent in failing to install a brake-override system that would automatically release the throttle if the brake is depressed. Toyota reportedly discussed the override system with the federal government in 2007 but did not begin installations until 2010. Toyota acknowledges some problems with floor mats, but argues that many of the incidents are attributable to operator error. In the only case resolved to date, a $10 million settlement was reached following the deaths of four in a California accident after the Lexus they were driving sped out of control in a sudden acceleration episode that apparently stemmed from an oversized floor mat trapping the accelerator. [For more on Toyota, see Chapter 3.]

Question

1. Could the market alone protect us satisfactorily from dangerous products, or do you think the threat of very costly lawsuits is necessary to force American manufacturers to be fully responsible in monitoring the safety of the products they build? Explain.

Sources: Ken Bensinger and Ralph Vartabedian, "Toyota Kept Sudden Acceleration Issue Silent, Lawsuit Says," *latimes.com,* October 29, 2010 [**latimes.com/business/la-fi-toyota-suit-20101029,0,5864831.story**]; Ken Bensinger and Ralph Vartabedian, "Toyota Sudden-Acceleration Lawsuits Focus on Lack of Brake Override," *latimes.com,* January 3, 2011 [**latimes.com/business/la-fi-toyota-legal-20110104,0,867993.story**]; and Mike Ramsey, "U.S. Ends Toyota Probe," *The Wall Street Journal,* February 25, 2011, p. B2.

Negligence

The three major product liability causes of action are negligence, breach of warranty, and strict liability. In dangerously simplified terms, negligence is a breach of the duty of due care. A negligent act is the failure to do what a reasonable person would do or doing what a reasonable person would not do. Thus, a producer or distributor has a duty to exercise reasonable care in the entire stream of events associated with the development and sale of a product. In designing, manufacturing, testing, repairing, and warning of potential dangers, those in the chain of production and distribution must meet the standard of the reasonably prudent person. Failure to do so constitutes negligence. Some decisions also extend potential liability to situations in which a product is being put to an unintended but reasonably foreseeable *misuse.*

Historically, consumers dealt face-to-face with producers and could bring breach of contract claims if injured by a defective product. However, the development in the modern era of multilayered production and distribution systems eliminated that contractual relationship between producer and consumer, making it difficult for consumers to sue producers. Then in a famous 1916 decision (*McPherson v. Buick Motor Co.*),[12] the New York high court ruled that a consumer could bring a negligence claim against the manufacturer of a defective automobile even though the consumer did not purchase the car directly from that manufacturer. That view has since been broadly adopted, thus permitting victims of negligence to bring actions against all careless parties in the chain of production and distribution.

Donald Trump Owes a Duty?

In 1996, Mark Merrill entered a clinic for compulsive gamblers and wrote to Trump Indiana, a casino in Gary, Indiana, asking that he be evicted if he ever entered to gamble. Merrill's name appeared on Trump Indiana's eviction list. Nonetheless, Merrill later gambled at the casino suffering substantial losses. In December 1998 and January 1999, Merrill robbed banks, apparently to cover his gambling losses. He was convicted of bank robbery, but while in prison he filed suit claiming Trump Indiana was negligent in failing to keep him from gambling at the casino. Rule on Merrill's negligence claim. Explain. The four-part negligence test that follows will help you resolve Merrill's claim.

Source: Mark Merrill v. Trump Indiana, Inc., 320 F.3d 729 (7th Cir. 2003).

Negligence Test

To establish a successful negligence claim, the plaintiff must meet each of the following requirements:

1. **Duty.** The plaintiff must establish that the defendant owed a duty of due care to the plaintiff. In general, the standard applied is that of the fictitious reasonable man or woman. That *reasonable person* acts prudently, sensibly, and responsibly. The standard of reasonableness depends, of course, on the circumstances of the situation.

2. **Breach of duty.** The plaintiff must demonstrate that the defendant breached the duty of due care by engaging in conduct that did not conform to the reasonable person standard. Breach of the duty of due care may result from either the commission of a careless act or the omission of a reasonable, prudent act. Would a reasonable man or woman discharge a firearm in a public park? Would a reasonable person foresee that failure to illuminate one's front entry steps might lead to a broken bone? More formally, we might think of reasonable behavior as decision making that weighs the costs and benefits of acting or not acting. The reasonable person "takes precautions against harms when doing so costs less than the discounted value of the harms risked."[13]

3. **Causation**
   a. **Actual cause.** Did the defendant's breach of the duty of due care in fact cause the harm in question? Commonly, the "but for" test is applied to determine cause in fact. For example, but for the defendant's failure to stop at the red light, the plaintiff pedestrian would not have been struck down in the crosswalk.
   b. **Proximate cause.** The plaintiff must establish that the defendant's actions were the proximate cause of the injury. As a matter of policy, is the defendant's conduct sufficiently connected to the plaintiff's injury as to justify imposing liability? Many injuries arise from a series of events—some of them wildly improbable. Did the defendant's negligence lead directly to the plaintiff's harm, or did some intervening act break the causal link between the defendant's negligence and the harm? For example, the community's allegedly negligent maintenance resulted in a blocked road, forcing the plaintiff to detour. While on the detour route, the plaintiff's vehicle was struck by a plane that fell from the sky when attempting to land at a nearby airport. Was the community's negligence the proximate cause of the plaintiff's injury?[14]

4. **Injury.** The plaintiff must have sustained injury, and, due to problems of proof, that injury often must be physical. [For a tort law library, see **http://www.findlaw.com/01topics/22tort**]

The case that follows asks whether a car dealer was negligent in leaving the keys in an unlocked car that was subsequently stolen.

Justice Serna

I. FACTS AND BACKGROUND

Plaintiffs [Herrera et al.] alleged the following facts in their complaint. On May 27, 1996, an individual took his car to Defendant [Quality Pontiac] for repairs. At Defendant's direction, the owner left the keys in the car and the doors unlocked. The lot was fenced, and the gate was unlocked. After 9:00 P.M., Billy Garcia entered the lot, apparently looking inside the cars for something to steal. Garcia stole the vehicle in question. The following day, at approximately 11:00 A.M., a Bernalillo County deputy sheriff observed Garcia driving quickly through a school zone and pursued him, engaging his emergency lights and sirens. Garcia drove at a speed of up to ninety miles per hour and collided head on with Plaintiffs' car, which had pulled over onto the shoulder after hearing the sirens. One occupant was killed and the other seriously injured.

Plaintiffs presented an affidavit of a sociologist to the district court that asserted that "the Albuquerque metropolitan area's motor vehicle theft rate of 1,345.5 per 100,000 residents was the second highest rate in the nation in 1997." The expert estimated that between forty-five and eighty percent of stolen cars had been left unlocked and that between nineteen and forty-seven percent of stolen cars had the ignition keys left inside. The expert claimed that a high proportion of thefts were for the purpose of joy-riding and short term transportation. The expert estimated that there is a high probability that a stolen car will be involved in traffic accidents, relying on a study which "found that nearly [seventeen percent] of all stolen cars are involved in accidents in a matter of hours or days after their theft," and another study which found "the accident rate for stolen cars [to be] approximately 200 times the accident rate for cars that have not been stolen." The expert relied on a study which found that "police pursuit was involved in [thirty-seven] percent of the motor vehicle theft cases examined [in a] national sample."

* * * * *

II. DISCUSSION

Whether Defendant Owed Plaintiffs a Common Law Duty

(a) Stare Decisis

New Mexico precedent resolves this issue in Defendant's favor. See *Bouldin,* 71 N.M. at 333. Plaintiffs ask this Court to overrule *Bouldin.*

* * * * *

(b) *Bouldin*

In *Bouldin,* the plaintiff alleged that the defendant parked his vehicle at a lounge, left it unattended, "and negligently failed to remove the ignition keys" from the vehicle. An unknown individual or group of people "borrowed or stole the truck and later abandoned it in the middle of the highway," and the plaintiff collided with it. In *Bouldin,* this Court addressed the question of whether "the owner of a car who leaves it unattended and without removing the key . . . [is] liable for injuries to persons and property suffered when the car is hit after its having been abandoned on the highway by a thief who stole it."

* * * * *

Our review of *Bouldin* indicates that the Court was hesitant to hold that a defendant who leaves his or her keys in an unattended car owes a duty to a plaintiff injured by the acts of a thief because, as a matter of policy, the theft and subsequent accident are too remote a risk. [W]e believe it is clear that *Bouldin* involved both duty and proximate cause and focused principally on duty. [W]e conclude that we must overrule *Bouldin* on its holding that there is no duty in such a case and that there is no proximate cause as a matter of law between leaving ignition keys in an unattended vehicle and an accident precipitated by a thief.

(c) The Foreseeability Component of Duty

As an initial step in the establishment of a common law duty, . . . "a potential plaintiff must be reasonably foreseeable to the defendant because of defendant's actions." *Kopp v. Wackenhut Corp.,* 113 N.M. 153, 158.

* * * * *

The present case is complicated by the fact that Plaintiffs' injuries were directly caused by Garcia's criminal operation of the stolen vehicle. As Defendant notes, "as a general rule, a person does not have a duty to protect another from harm caused by the criminal acts of third persons unless the person has a special relationship with the other giving rise to a duty." *Ciup v. Chevron U.S.A., Inc.,* 122 N.M. 537. However, "the criminal acts of a third person will not relieve a negligent defendant of liability if the defendant should have recognized that his or her actions were likely to lead to that criminal activity." *Sarracino v. Martinez,* 117 N.M. 193, 195–96 (Ct. App. 1994).

* * * * *

The present case presents a claim whereby Defendant, arguably, knew or should have known that a theft was likely to occur, and Defendant's actions may have enhanced or increased the risk of such criminal conduct. According to Plaintiffs' affidavit, Albuquerque has a high auto theft rate, and thieves are much more likely to steal vehicles to which they have ready access, as when the cars are left unlocked and unattended with the key in the ignition. Stolen cars are much more likely to be involved in automobile accidents. In this context, Defendant's alleged conduct leaving the keys in the ignition of an unlocked and unattended vehicle arguably increased the likelihood that criminal acts would occur, which ultimately led to the accident in which Plaintiffs were injured, so that we impose a duty of ordinary care.

This Court, in *Bouldin,* concluded that it did "not perceive theft of a car as a natural event to be foreseen by a person who is negligent in leaving his [or her] car unattended with the key in the ignition." Plaintiffs presented an affidavit in the district court which alleged a high rate of car thefts and the proposition that stolen vehicles are more likely to be involved in accidents. Thus, Plaintiffs in the present case have persuaded us that the theft of a car left unattended and unlocked with the key in the ignition is a natural event which can be foreseen by the tortfeasor, as is the subsequent accident and resulting injuries.

We cannot conclude that Plaintiffs' injuries were so unforeseeable that we must hold that Defendant did not owe Plaintiffs a duty as a matter of law. We conclude that *Bouldin* is no longer viable in its holding that such ensuing theft and subsequent negligent or criminal operation of the vehicle resulting in injury are not natural, foreseeable events attendant upon leaving one's keys in an unlocked, unattended vehicle. *Bouldin* was based on a set of facts and assumptions that no longer reflects our current situation, and we cannot ignore the connection between stolen vehicles and car accidents. . . .

We hold that Defendant's actions in directing the owner to leave the keys in the vehicle and leaving the vehicle unlocked and unattended created a duty to exercise ordinary care. Without any of these factors, the foreseeability and likelihood of theft and the risk of harm would diminish so substantially that such a claim would fail. We conclude . . . that there is a high rate of vehicle theft and that stolen vehicles are more likely to be involved in accidents, that an owner or one in possession of a vehicle reasonably can foresee that the vehicle might be stolen if he or she leaves it unattended, unlocked, and with keys in its ignition, and that he or she reasonably could anticipate that the thief might drive negligently and injure another, creating a duty to that injured party.

Other Issues
1. Breach of Duty
We recognize a duty in the present case. We do not address whether Defendant breached the duty of ordinary care. . . .

The finder of fact must determine whether Defendant breached the duty of ordinary care by considering what a reasonably prudent individual would foresee, what an unreasonable risk of injury would be, and what would constitute an exercise of ordinary care in light of all surrounding circumstances of the present case, including whether Defendant acted reasonably or negligently by keeping an unlocked, unattended vehicle with the keys in the ignition on a fenced, gated lot.
2. Proximate Cause
Defendant argues that its actions did not proximately cause Plaintiffs' injuries. The issue of proximate cause is also for the jury or factfinder. . . .

While we agree with Defendant that there is not great closeness in the connection between Defendant's wrongful acts and the resulting injuries, especially considering a gap in time of approximately fourteen hours and a distance of many miles, we do not believe that the connection is so tenuous that we must conclude, as a matter of law, that there is no proximate cause. We leave the fact that the accident occurred approximately fourteen hours after Garcia stole the car from Defendant's lot and the fact that the accident took place several miles away from its property for the jury's consideration on the issue of proximate cause. Thus, the finder of fact must determine whether Defendant's acts, which occurred many hours prior to the accident and many miles away, were a proximate cause of Plaintiffs' injuries.

* * * * *

[Reversed.]

Questions
1. In the *Herrera* case, the New Mexico Supreme Court overruled its own precedent (*Bouldin*). Explain the *Bouldin* reasoning, and explain why it was overruled in *Herrera.*
2. Why did the *Herrera* court find that the defendant, Quality Pontiac, had a duty to the plaintiffs?
3. Why did the New Mexico Supreme Court find that the proximate cause element of negligence claims might be present in cases like *Herrera?*
4. Jerry Colaitis, 47, went with his family to a Benihana steakhouse in Munsey Park, New York. The Benihana chain is well-known for hibachi-style cooking with diners gathered around a rectangular wooden table with a hot grill in the

middle from which the chef, as a form of entertainment, often casually tosses pieces of cooked food at the diners. Mrs. Colaitis claimed that the chef struck and burned some family members with pieces of tossed food. Mr. Colaitis asked the chef to stop, but as he was speaking a piece of shrimp was tossed his way causing Mr. Colaitis to jerk away from it resulting in two wrenched vertebrae in his neck. Mr. Colaitis underwent a corrective operation then suffered a post-operative complication that resulted in a blood-borne infection that caused Mr. Colaitis' death. The Colaitis family sued Benihana for negligence causing the death. At trial, the head chef at the Munsey Park restaurant conceded that the food tossing practice could be dangerous. The restaurant discontinued the practice. During the last year of his life, Mr. Colaitis had suffered from fevers that were not associated with his surgery. How would you rule on the Colaitis' negligence claim? Explain. See *Estate of Colaitis v. Benihana, Inc.*, 015439-2002 (Nassau County Supreme Court, 2006) and Andrew Harris, "Jury: Flying Shrimp . . . Kill Diner," **http://www.law.com/ jsp/article. jsp?id51139479516332.**

5. Johnny Burnett, described by his mother, Sheila Watters, as a devoted "Dungeons & Dragons" player, killed himself. (The record did not disclose his age at the time of death.) Watters blamed the death on her son's absorption in the game. She claimed that "he lost control of his own independent will and was driven to self-destruction."

   "Dungeons & Dragons" is an adventure game set in an imaginary ancient world; the players assume the roles of various characters as suggested by illustrated booklets. The play is orchestrated by a player labeled the "Dungeon Master." The outcome of the play is determined by using dice in conjunction with tables provided with the game. The game's materials do not mention suicide or guns. More than 1 million copies of the game have been sold, many to schools where it is used as a learning tool.

   In federal district court, Watters brought a wrongful death claim against TSR, the manufacturer of "Dungeons & Dragons." The plaintiff's complaint alleged that TSR violated its duty of care in two ways: It disseminated "Dungeons & Dragons" literature to "mentally fragile persons," and it failed to warn that the "possible consequences" of playing the game might include "loss of control of the mental processes." Decide. Explain. See *Watters v. TSR, Inc.*, 904 F.2d 378 (6th Cir. 1990).

6. Plaintiff was seven months pregnant and the mother of 17-month-old James. She was standing on the sidewalk, and James was in the street. A truck being negligently driven bore down on the boy, running him over. The shock caused the mother to miscarry and suffer actual physical and emotional injury. She brought suit against the driver for harm to herself and the infant child.

   a. What is the issue in this case?

   b. Decide the case. Explain. See *Amaya v. Home Ice, Fuel & Supply Co.*, 379 P.2d 513 (Cal. S.Ct. 1963). But also see *Dillon v. Legg*, 441 P.2d 912 (Cal. S.Ct. 1968).

7. Is a fireworks manufacturer liable for harm to children who ignited an explosive that had failed to detonate in the town public display the previous day? Explain.

8. The mother of a 12-year-old boy who died in a shooting accident when a gun he was playing with accidentally discharged sued *Boys Life*, a magazine published by the Boy Scouts of America. The mother claimed that the boy was influenced to experiment with a rifle after reading a 16-page firearms advertising section in the magazine.

   a. What product liability claims would the mother raise?

   b. What constitutional defense would the Boy Scouts raise?

   c. Decide. Explain. See *Jan Way v. Boy Scouts of America*, 856 S.W.2d 230 (Tex. 1993).

Classes of Negligence Claims

Negligence claims emerging from defective products fall into three categories of analysis: (1) manufacturing defects, (2) design defects, and (3) inadequate warnings.

Manufacturing Defects

McDonald's sells a billion cups of coffee each year, in part because its coffee is extremely hot—180 to 190 degrees—which is exactly what its customers prefer and which, McDonald's believes, produces tastier coffee than the 140 to 145 degrees normally achieved at home. In

1992, then 79-year-old Stella Liebeck ordered coffee at an Albuquerque, New Mexico, McDonald's drive-thru. Her grandson, who was driving, pulled forward and stopped so that Liebeck could add cream and sugar to her coffee. The dashboard of the car was slanted so that the coffee could not be set on it. Liebeck, therefore, placed the coffee between her legs, and while trying to get the top off the container, she spilled the coffee on her lap, resulting in third-degree burns. She was hospitalized, required skin grafts, and was disabled for two years. She sought a settlement with McDonald's, but according to her family, McDonald's offered only $800.[15] Liebeck sued, accusing McDonald's of gross negligence for selling coffee that was "unreasonably dangerous" and "defectively manufactured."[16]

Liebeck was awarded $200,000 in compensatory and $2.7 million in punitive damages. The jury found Liebeck 20 percent responsible for her own injury, thus reducing her compensatory award to $160,000. The judge subsequently reduced the punitive award to $480,000. The parties then settled out of court for an undisclosed amount. According to news reports, the jury awarded Liebeck $2.7 million in punitive damages because of what it perceived to be McDonald's callous attitude toward the accident and because of the more than 700 previous coffee-burn claims that had been filed against McDonald's. A McDonald's human factors engineer testified that the number of hot coffee burns was "statistically insignificant" when compared with the billions of cups sold by McDonald's annually.[17] [For the "actual facts" on the Liebeck/McDonald's episode, see **http://www.lectlaw.com/files/cur78.htm**]

> **The number of hot coffee burns was "statistically insignificant."**

[For the *Hot Coffee* trailer, see **http://hotcoffeethemovie.com**]

A British High Court justice, however, viewed the hot coffee situation quite differently:

> Persons generally expect tea or coffee purchased to be consumed on the premises to be hot. . . . They accordingly know that care must be taken to avoid such spills.[18]

[For a practical guide to the law of accidents and injuries, see **http://www.nolo.com/legal-encyclopedia/accident-law/**]

McDonald's "Exploding" Chicken Sandwich

Frank Sutton bought a McDonald's fried chicken sandwich at the Daniel Boone Truck Stop in Duffield, Virginia, on August 8, 2005. When he bit into the sandwich, Sutton said, "the grease from the inside of the chicken sandwich spread out all over my bottom lip, my top lip, down onto my chin." Sutton immediately dropped the sandwich. His wife dabbed his face with ice as blisters formed on his lips. Sutton reported the incident to a pair of McDonald's employees, one of whom reportedly said, "This is what happens to the sandwiches when they aren't drained completely." Sutton's lips continued to bother him. He went to a doctor who provided lip balm and told Sutton to avoid excessive exposure to sunlight. Sutton thereafter sued McDonald's and the local franchise owner, Roth, for negligence, among other claims. At trial in a Virginia federal district court, Sutton testified that he thought the sandwich was "negligently prepared" or "defective," but the judge rejected Sutton's negligence claim reasoning that Sutton failed to establish the standard of care that Virginia product liability law requires.

(Using either federal standards, state standards, or reasonable consumer expectations, Sutton was required to demonstrate a standard of care that was breached leading to his injury.) The judge also ruled that Sutton was contributorily negligent (contributed to his own harm) by failing to "exercise reasonable care to see that [he wasn't] eating something too hot." Sutton appealed to the Fourth Circuit Court of Appeals.

   a. In your judgment, was McDonald's negligent in this episode? Explain.
   b. Did Sutton contribute to his own injury? Explain.

Source: Sutton v. Roth, L.L.C.; John Doe; McDonald's Corporation, 361 Fed. Appx. 543 (4th Cir. 2010) (unpublished opinion).

Res Ipsa   As we see with the McDonald's cases, allegedly improper manufacturing of products often generates negligence claims. However, the extremely complex process of producing, distributing, and using a product sometimes so obscures the root of the injury in question that proof of fault is nearly impossible to establish. In those circumstances, many courts have adopted the doctrine of *res ipsa loquitur* (the thing speaks for itself), which in some cases permits the court to infer the defendant's negligence even though that negligence cannot be proved—that is, the facts suggest that the plaintiff's injury must have resulted from the defendant's negligence, but the circumstances are such that the plaintiff is unable to prove negligence. A showing of res ipsa loquitur requires that (1) the injury was caused by an instrumentality under the control of the defendant, (2) the accident ordinarily would not happen absent the defendant's negligence, and (3) there is no evidence of other causes for the accident.[19]

Design Defects

From Cessna's single-engine airplanes to five-gallon buckets (which may hold liquid sufficient to drown a child) to automobile seat belts and on across the spectrum of American products, manufacturers must think about designing products to anticipate and avoid consumer injury. Two principal lines of analysis have emerged in these cases: (1) The *risk–utility test* holds that a product is negligently designed if the benefits of a product's design are outweighed by the risks that accompany that design. (2) The *consumer expectations test* imposes on the manufacturer a duty to design its products so that they are safe not only for their intended use but also for any reasonably foreseeable use.

   In 1997 members of the American Law Institute, a group of legal experts, approved the *Restatement (Third) of Torts,* which does not constitute law but represents those experts' best judgment about what the law should be. They have recommended to the courts a design defect standard that supports the balancing/risk–utility model and gives much less attention to consumer expectations. Furthermore, a product would be considered defective in design only if its foreseeable risks could have been reduced or avoided by a reasonable alternative design and if failure to include that design makes the product not reasonably safe. That is, plaintiffs would need to show that some better design was available and was not incorporated in the product in question. The case that follows involves, according to the California Supreme Court, a risk–benefit argument by the plaintiffs seeking civil damages after a mass murder.[20]

Justice Chin

On July 1, 1993, Gian Luigi Ferri killed eight people and wounded six—and then killed himself—during a shooting rampage at 101 California Street, a high-rise office building in San Francisco. Survivors and representatives of some of Ferri's victims (plaintiffs) sued defendant Navegar, Inc., which made two of the three weapons Ferri used.

We granted review to determine whether plaintiffs may hold Navegar liable on a common law negligence theory.

* * * * *

Navegar advertised the TEC-9/DC9 in a number of gun-related magazines and annuals. . . . A typical advertisement claimed that in light of the TEC-9/DC9's design features—including "32 rounds of firepower," a "'TEC-KOTE' finish," and "two-step disassembly for easy cleaning"—the weapon is "ideal for self-defense or recreation," "stands out among high-capacity 9mm assault-type pistols," and "delivers more gutsy performance and reliability than ANY other gun on the market." Navegar also distributed an advertising brochure or catalog describing its guns and accessories, which it mailed to anyone interested and, on at least one occasion, printed in special issue magazines. In a page describing the TEC-KOTE finish, Navegar claimed the finish provided "natural lubicity [sic] to increase bullet velocities, excellent resistance to fin-gerprints, sweat rust, petroleum distillates of all types, gun solvents, gun cleaners, and all powder residues. Salt spray corrosion resistance, expansion and contraction of the metal will not result in peeling of finish." A different brochure adver-tising to retailers used the slogan, "Intratec: Weapons that are as tough as your toughest customer."

Navegar included a manual with each TEC-9/DC9 it sold. The 1993 manual contained safety warnings, technical infor-mation, and operating instructions. It also claimed the gun was "a radically new type of semi-automatic pistol," which was "designed to deliver a high volume of firepower" and, "thanks to its dimensions and designs," could "be used in modes of fire impossible with most handguns." Regarding the latter claim, the manual described and illustrated several recom-mended shooting positions, including "hipfire at shortest range," a two-handed hold with the nontrigger hand placed on the upper part of the magazine well.

In early 1993 Ferri, a Southern California resident, bought a [used] TEC-9 from the Pawn & Gun Shop in Henderson, Nevada. . . . According to the salesperson, Ferri looked at a wide variety of handguns, but seemed mainly interested in a "high-capacity type" gun, "something relatively compact that holds a lot of rounds." He gave no indication he had previously heard of the TEC-9 or the Intratec brand . . . Later that day, he returned the weapon, stating that he wanted a new gun instead.

On April 25, 1993, Ferri bought a new TEC-DC9 from Super Pawn, a gun store in Las Vegas, Nevada. . . . Ferri questioned [another] customer about the TEC-DC9. . . . The customer said that people at a shooting range would "probably laugh at" Ferri if he used a TEC-DC9 "because it wasn't really an accurate weapon" and that a .22-caliber gun was better for "plinking" than a nine-millimeter gun because ammunition for the former was much cheaper. Ferri nevertheless chose the TEC-DC9.

Ferri purchased another TEC-DC9 on May 8, 1993, at a Las Vegas gun show. . . .

To purchase the new weapons, Ferri showed an appar-ently valid Nevada driver's license and answered required questions about his criminal history and residency. All of the distributors and retailers were licensed by the federal Bureau of Alcohol, Tobacco, and Firearms, and [s]o far as the record shows, all of the transactions were legal . . . other than Ferri's misrepresentations as to his state of residence.

On July 1, 1993, Ferri entered 101 California Street carrying the TEC-9/DC9s and a .45-caliber Norinco Model 1911A1 pistol in a large briefcase and another bag. He had added to the TEC-DC9's Hell-Fire brand trigger systems that made the weapons fire in rapid bursts, and he was equipped with hundreds of rounds of ammunition preloaded into 40- to 50-round magazines. He went to the 34th floor, to the office of a law firm he held a grudge against, and started shooting. During his rampage, he killed eight people and wounded six on three different floors, and then killed himself.

* * * * *

PROCEDURAL BACKGROUND

Plaintiffs' first amended complaint asserted a cause of action against Navegar for "common law negligence." In this claim, plaintiffs alleged that Navegar knew or should have known that (1) the TEC-9/DC9 is a "small, easily con-cealable military, assault weapon; (2) it has "no legitimate sporting . . . or self-defense purpose and is particularly well adapted to a military-style assault on large numbers of people"; (3) it is "disproportionately associated with criminal activity"; (4) it is "more attractive to criminals" because of its "firepower" and "other features"; (5) its "firepower was likely to be enhanced by the addition of products such as high-capacity magazines" and "the Hell-Fire trigger system"; and (6) it "would be used to kill or injure innocent persons in violent criminal acts such as the mass killing committed by Ferri." Plaintiffs also alleged that Navegar "acknowledges that publicity surrounding the [TEC-9/DC9s] reputation as a weapon favored by criminals increases its sales." Thus, plaintiffs alleged, Navegar "acted negligently by manufacturing, marketing, and making available for sale to the general public" the TEC-9/DC9.

*   *   *   *   *

Navegar moved for summary judgment. As to common law negligence, it argued it owed plaintiffs no duty not to advertise the TEC-9/DC9 and that plaintiffs had no evidence Ferri saw or was affected by a Navegar advertisement.

In opposing the motion, plaintiffs argued that Navegar had misconstrued the ordinary negligence claim. They explained that, contrary to Navegar's assertion, their negligence claim did "not depend on whether" Navegar had a "duty . . . not to advertise" or "whether there is a causal link between Navegar's advertising and plaintiffs' injuries." From the start, plaintiffs have made clear their ordinary negligence claim is not based on Navegar's negligent advertising but rather its decision to 'make available for sale to the general public guns . . . which [it] knew or should have known have "no legitimate sporting or self-defense purpose" and which are "particularly well-adapted to a military-style assault on large numbers of people."' Simply put, Navegar breached a duty of care by making the TEC-9 available to the general public, i.e., "by releasing the weapons for sale to the general public even though it knew or should have known that the TEC-9 was particularly attractive to criminals and particularly suited for mass killings." Plaintiffs concluded their argument regarding duty by asserting that "Navegar breached a legal duty to forebear [sic] distributing the TEC-9 to the general public given the likelihood that doing so would lead to the sort of violent criminal act that occurred at the 101 California Street Building."

As to causation, plaintiffs also argued that in light of their negligence theory, "whether Ferri actually saw or was influenced by any particular Navegar advertising is immaterial." They explained, "The ordinary negligence claim is directed to Navegar's conduct in making the TEC-9 available to the public. It is that unreasonable conduct that was a substantial factor in causing plaintiffs' injuries, not Navegar's marketing efforts." "Navegar's advertising is only material to the ordinary negligence claim in that it underscores that the criminal use of the weapon was foreseeable to Navegar. . . . Plaintiffs are not alleging that Ferri was induced to purchase the TEC-DC9s or to commit the 101 massacre by any particular advertisements. The significance of the advertisements is what they say about [Navegar's] knowledge of [its] market."

*   *   *   *   *

DISCUSSION

*   *   *   *   *

[I]n the trial court, Navegar argued in effect that the Legislature, through section 1714.4, established an exception that applies in this case. Section 1714.4 provides; "(a) In a products liability action, no firearm or ammunition shall be deemed defective in design on the basis that the benefits of the product do not outweigh the risk of injury posed by its potential to cause serious injury, damage, or death when discharged. (b) For purposes of this section: (1) The potential of a firearm or ammunition to cause serious injury, damage, or death when discharged does not make the product defective in design. (2) Injuries or damages resulting from the discharge of a firearm or ammunition are not proximately caused by its potential to cause serious injury, damage, or death, but are proximately caused by the actual discharge of the product. (c) This section shall not affect a products liability cause of action based upon the improper selection of design alternatives." . . . Navegar argues that this statute, by establishing a state policy of exempting manufacturers of legal, nondefective firearms "from liability for their criminal use," bars plaintiffs' negligence claim.

Plaintiffs respond that section 1714.4 "has no application to this case because it is not a products liability action." Plaintiffs assert that they "seek to hold Navegar liable for its negligent conduct, not for making a defective product," and that they "make no assertion that Navegar should be liable because the risks posed by the TEC-9 outweigh its benefits." . . . [W]e reject plaintiffs' argument that section 1714.4 is inapplicable because this case "is not a products liability action.". . .

[C]ontrary to the assertion of plaintiffs, the record demonstrates that plaintiffs do, in fact, seek to hold Navegar liable precisely because, as the trial court stated, the TEC-9/DC9's "potential for harm substantially outweighs any possible benefit to be derived from [it]." In their brief, plaintiffs assert that Navegar is liable because it "designed and widely distributed a weapon uniquely suited for mass killing and lacking legitimate civilian uses."

Using the words of the risk–utility test for both products liability theories, plaintiffs essentially allege, argue, and hope to prove that the TEC-9/DC9 is defective in design. Thus this is a products liability action based on negligence, which asserts that the TEC-9/DC9 was defective in design because the risks of making it available to the general public outweighed the benefits of that conduct, and that defendants knew or should have known this fact.

* * * * *

Finally, we also conclude that the evidence in the record regarding Navegar's promotional activities and the literature it distributed with the TEC-9/DC9 does not save plaintiffs' negligence claim. As we have previously explained, in opposing Navegar's summary judgment motion, plaintiffs insisted that "their ordinary negligence claim" was not "directed to" or "based on Navegar's negligent advertising but rather its decision to make [the TEC-9/DC9] available for sale to the general public. . . ." Plaintiffs also insisted that it was Navegar's "unreasonable conduct" in "making the TEC-9 available to the public . . . that was a substantial factor in causing [their] injuries, not Navegar's marketing efforts." Thus, they maintained, "whether Ferri actually saw or was influenced by any particular Navegar advertising is immaterial.". . . . Plaintiffs are not alleging that Ferri was induced to purchase the TEC-DC9s or to commit the 101 massacre by any particular advertisements. The significance of the advertisements is what they say about [Navegar's] knowledge of [its] market."

* * * * *

In any event, the evidence in the record fails to raise a triable factual issue as to whether Navegar's advertising and literature were substantial factors in causing plaintiffs' injuries. Regarding this question, plaintiffs' counsel asserted at oral argument that "Navegar's liability does not depend on its telling the public, here's a great gun to commit a crime," but on its "communicating a message that people who want above all else in their weapons firepower, the capacity to shoot many, many rounds without the need to reload, and to use that gun in a combat fashion, this is the gun for you."

* * * * *

To the extent plaintiffs rely on allegedly more inflammatory aspects of Navegar's advertising, they fail to raise a triable factual issue regarding causation. For example, they offer no evidence, direct or circumstantial, that Ferri ever saw the promotional materials sent to dealers, which used the phrase "tough as your toughest customer," or the early version of the TEC-KOTE product brochure description, which promised "excellent resistance to fingerprints." Moreover, plaintiffs do not dispute that (1) San Francisco police inspectors did "not recall" finding "any TEC-DC9 magazine advertisement in Ferri's apartment" and found "no evidence" that any advertisement

caused Ferri to travel to Nevada to purchase the TEC-DC9s; (2) "there is otherwise no Navegar magazine advertisement in the possession of the City and County of San Francisco as evidence collected in the 101 California Street shootings"; (3) the salesman at the Pawn & Gun Shop in Henderson, Nevada, where Ferri bought the used TEC-9, "never" saw Ferri in possession of any advertisement or literature for the TEC-9 or TEC-DC9, and never heard Ferri mention he had seen any advertisement for the TEC-9 or TEC-DC9; (4) when Ferri bought the first new TEC-9/DC9, he had no firearms advertisement or other type of literature in his possession and did not ask for the TEC-9/DC9 by name; and (5) when Ferri bought the second new TEC-9/DC9, he indicated he already owned another TEC-9/DC9. Plaintiffs have failed to produce, or show that they will be able to produce at trial, substantial evidence "that Navegar's marketing style was 'a factor' in" Ferri's conduct. . . .

In arguing to the contrary, plaintiffs cite evidence that Ferri went to Nevada, where the TEC-9/DC9 was available, to buy guns for his planned attack and that the two stores where he bought TEC-9/DC9s had Las Vegas Yellow Pages advertisements picturing, among other guns, assault weapons. Although this evidence does tend to show Ferri sought to purchase high-firepower guns, it does not tend to show Ferri went to Nevada or the stores in search of a TEC-9/DC9 or other assault pistol in response to Navegar's marketing efforts. The existence of various high-firepower rifles and pistols would have been so widely known from other sources (especially to a reader of gun magazines as, apparently, Ferri was) as to render unjustified any inference that Navegar's marketing efforts were a substantial factor in motivating Ferri's decision to seek such a gun. Thus, we agree with the trial court that "the links plaintiffs seek to establish between advertisements and carnage amount to little more than guesswork." . . .

Accordingly, we conclude the trial court properly granted Navegar summary judgment. . . . In section 1714.4, the Legislature has set California's public policy regarding a gun manufacturer's liability under these circumstances. Given that public policy, plaintiffs may not proceed with their negligence claim.

Reversed.

DISSENTING OPINION BY JUSTICE WERDEGAR

I cannot accept the majority's conclusion that plaintiffs are statutorily barred from suing the maker of the semiautomatic assault weapon used to massacre the victims in this case.

* * * * *

Civil Code section 1714.4 bars product liability actions against gunmakers based on the risk–benefit theory of product defect.

The legislative policy behind the statute might, at most, be deemed also to encompass negligence claims that are substantially identical to risk–benefit product defect claims. Plaintiffs' claim is neither. Plaintiffs' claim of negligence is, at bottom, that defendant Navegar, Inc. acted without due care in distributing the TEC-9/DC9 to the general civilian public rather than restricting its sales to police and military units that might have a legitimate call for such a military-style assault pistol. Plaintiffs do not claim that the TEC-9/DC9 is defective; nor do they even claim that defendant acted negligently simply by making the TEC-9/DC9. Plaintiffs allege negligence, rather, in Navegar's selling that firearm on the general civilian market knowing it would attract purchasers likely to misuse it, rather than restricting sales to buyers with a lawful use for the tools of assaultive violence. . . . This theory of negligence, resting on the allegation that particular marketing choices by Navegar were imprudent, is not substantially identical to a claim of product defect and thus is within neither the letter nor the spirit of Civil Code section 1714.4.

Navegar's conduct was allegedly negligent not because its gun was defective but because, in light of the gun's known attractiveness to violent users and the lack of a compelling need for its availability on the civilian market, a reasonably careful distributor would have restricted sales to groups unlikely to misuse the firearm. Civil Code section 1714.4 simply does not address such a negligent distribution claim.

*   *   *   *   *

AFTERWORD

Subsequent to the *Merrill v. Navegar* decision, Congress and President Bush enacted a 2005 law, the Protection of Lawful Commerce in Arms Act, to substantially shield firearms manufacturers and dealers from civil claims when guns are used in violent crimes.

Questions

1. *a.* Why did the California Supreme Court rule in favor of Navegar in this case?
   b. Explain the plaintiffs' cause of action.
   c. Explain the dissenting opinion.
   d. Argue that the plaintiffs' claim did not involve a risk–benefit analysis of the kind forbidden by the California statute.

2. In your opinion, should gun manufacturers be liable for the criminal use of their products? Explain.

3. Some observers argued that a decision for the plaintiffs in the *Merrill/Navegar* case would have led to a product liability "slippery slope." Explain that argument. Do you agree with it? Explain.

4. Hollister was badly burned when her shirt came into contact with a burner as she leaned over her electric stove. She sued the store where she bought the shirt, claiming that it was defectively designed. What proof will Hollister need to provide to win her defective design claim? See *Hollister v. Dayton-Hudson,* 188 F.3d 414 (6th Cir. 1999).

Warnings

Universal Pictures issued warnings in 2001 that we might be hurt if we tried to mimic the car-racing stunts in its movie, *The Fast and the Furious.* The studio was trying to fend off lawsuits. Warnings seem to be everywhere in our lives. Some of them seem downright silly—so much so that the Foundation for Fair Civil Justice [**www.foundationforfairciviljustice. org/**] hosts a "Wacky Warning Labels" contest. Leading recent entries included these:

> Mimic the car-racing stunts in *The Fast and the Furious.*

> "Remove child before folding"—on a child car safety seat!
> "Harmful if swallowed"—a warning on a brass fishing lure with a three-pronged hook.[21]

So the use of warnings can be abused, but we should remember that they serve the valuable purpose of helping to protect us from foreseeable dangers as, for example, in the situation where the federal Consumer Product Safety Commission (see Chapter 15), recently ordered warnings on all new generators and generator packaging after recording 94 deaths in 2005 from generator-related carbon monoxide poisoning with at least 83 more deaths in 2006 and 43 in 2007.[22]

A product may be considered defective because of inadequate warnings when reasonable warnings would have reduced or avoided the foreseeable risks and the failure to warn resulted in a product that was not reasonably safe. Courts might also consider the feasibility of an effective warning and the probable seriousness of the injury. The case that follows raises a failure to warn product liability claim.

White v. Victor Automotive Products   2010 Mich. App. LEXIS 914 (unpublished)

LEGAL BRIEFCASE

Per Curium (Judges Michael J. Kelly and Douglas B. Shapiro)

1. Summary of Facts and Proceedings

Plaintiff's decedent, Craig White, purchased a muffler repair kit manufactured and marketed by defendants. The kit included a metal patch to be placed over the hole in the muffler, a strip of "bandage" to be wrapped around the patch and the muffler to hold the patch in place, and mechanic's wire to wrap around and secure the bandage. The packaging described the product as a "Muffler and Tail Pipe Repair Kit" and stated, "Just wrap it on for instant repair." The instructions included with the kit, however, directed the user to "start the engine and run at idle for at least 10 minutes" after applying the "bandage." The instructions provided with the kit read in total:

INSTRUCTIONS:

1. Allow exhaust system and muffler to cool to a touch.
2. Clean surface of muffler or pipe to be repaired with sand paper, steel wool or wire brush.
3. Cover holes with included metal heat shield, or by using metal or tin can.
4. Open foil packet containing bandage.
5. Wrap bandage completely around damaged area, overlapping each wrapping at least 3/4 inch. Note: Large repairs may require more than one bandage to adequately cover repair.
6. Secure bandage with mechanic's wire enclosed.
7. Start engine and run at idle for at least 10 minutes.
8. Bandage will cure with heat from exhaust system.

WARNING: Always wear safety classes and cloth or leather gloves when working on exhaust systems. Rust and debris can injure eyes and skin. Flush eyes thoroughly with water if contacted—for skin use soap and water. Never work on vehicle suspended in air NOT supported by adequate jack stands.

IF SWALLOWED, DRINK WATER AND GET IMMEDIATE MEDICAL ATTENTION. [Emphasis in original.]

White attempted to perform the muffler repair on April 29, 2005. According to the testimony of White's wife and son, when they left the house at about 11:00 A.M., White was in the driveway, working on the muffler. When they returned at about 2:15 P.M., they found White dead in the garage with the car up on a floor jack, the motor running and the garage door closed.[1] Tools were under the car and the bandage was found wrapped around the muffler. White was found near the exit to the garage. The police report stated in pertinent part:

> In the garage I observed the Buick to be elevated on a jack stand. Underneath the Buick I observed a small, rolling platform, that is used to enable a subject to crawl underneath a vehicle and assist with mobility while working on the vehicle. I further observed an activated utility light as well as several tools and accessories lying on the floor. On the rear trunk area of the Buick, I observed an empty package that contained a muffler repair kit. By looking at the picture on the muffler repair kit, and observing the muffler underneath the Buick, it was apparent that the victim had in fact used the kit as its contents were on the muffler.
> When Detective Steinaway arrived, I assisted in his investigation. During the investigation, I collected the empty package from the Buick to be placed as evidence at LCSD. While reading instructions listed on the back of the package, *it appeared as though the victim went step by step*

[1] The reason why White moved from the driveway into his garage remains unknown.

with the directions. The final instruction on these directions was to turn on the automobile and allow it to run for approximately ten minutes, which would in turn allow the bonding agent applied to the muffler to heat up and activate properly. This could be a possible explanation for why the vehicle's ignition was activated and running. *While reading the warning label on the package listed directly below the instructions, it did not advise of the dangers of carbon monoxide.* [Emphasis added.]

An autopsy confirmed that White died of asphyxiation from carbon monoxide.

Plaintiff's complaint alleged two violations of the duty to warn. First, plaintiff alleged that "Defendants breached their duty of care . . . in failing to include an instruction with the product that vehicles should not be run in an enclosed space or must be moved outside before starting the engine as directed [in the instructions]." Second, that "Defendant's breached their duty of care . . . in failing to warn of the dangers of carbon monoxide poisoning."

* * * * *

After a hearing, the trial court granted summary disposition to defendants, concluding:

[I]t's clear that the material risk of death due to carbon monoxide poisoning as a result of running a car in an enclosed garage would be obvious to the reasonably prudent user of a muffler repair kit. I don't think you can really argue that much about it. . . . I think it would be obvious and that would be to the general public, and it would be especially obvious to someone who used motors. Granted he may have been an . . . outboard engine mechanic, but nevertheless, it seems to me that he was in a position especially to know this even more than an average citizen. But nevertheless, to a reasonably prudent person it would be obvious this was a highly dangerous thing. I think it is common knowledge that it's a dangerous thing and—especially when you look at so many other options he would have had, like just open the garage door, might have been a lot better.

Plaintiff now appeals.

* * * * *

A. REASONABLY PRUDENT PRODUCT USER

[T]he first issue is whether a reasonable juror could find that the material risk of remaining in a closed garage with a running automobile while the muffler bandage cures is or should be "obvious to a reasonably prudent product user." . . .

* * * * *

Given the lack of an obvious risk of harm contained within the product's appearance or function, defendants argue that

no reasonable person could fail to know that remaining present while running a car in a closed garage while the muffler bandage cured carried with it a risk of material harm. For reasonable minds not to differ on the issue, it would have to be obvious that the exhaust contained carbon monoxide or other injurious chemicals and that exposure for a period long enough for the muffler bandage to cure created a material risk of harm.

A fact-finder may ultimately conclude that defendants are correct that a reasonably prudent person would be aware that automobile exhaust contains carbon monoxide or other injurious chemicals and that exposure for a period long enough for the muffler bandage to cure creates a material risk of harm. However, defendants have not provided any *evidence* from which such a conclusion may be drawn. . . .

At the time of the motion, plaintiff had proffered several articles and data that significant numbers of people, as many as 100 per year die, from accidental carbon monoxide poisoning in Michigan in a manner that supports plaintiff's claim that the danger of exposure to automobile exhaust is not necessarily "obvious to a reasonably prudent user." Plaintiff also presented an expert affidavit in this regard. Finally, plaintiff submitted warnings from devices that create carbon monoxide exhaust.

* * * * *

In contrast to plaintiff's presentation, the defense did not proffer *any* evidence supporting its contention that a reasonable person would know that carbon monoxide is present in automobile exhaust or that an exposure long enough for the muffler bandage to cure presents a material risk of harm.

* * * * *

Defendants provided no evidence in the present case that a reasonable person would know that an exposure to automobile exhaust in a garage for the time needed to cure the muffler repair presented a risk of material harm. Indeed, the only evidence in the record at this time is the data provided by plaintiff that significant numbers of people die from accidental carbon monoxide poisoning and the affidavit from plaintiff's expert supporting plaintiff's claim that the danger was not obvious. Under these circumstances, defendants were not entitled to summary disposition on the question of whether the risk of material harm from carbon monoxide inhalation from running an automobile long enough to cure this muffler product is or should be obvious to a reasonably prudent product user.

* * * * *

We take no position on whether a reasonably prudent user knows that automobile exhaust contains carbon monoxide nor that a exposure long enough to cure the muffler bandage can cause material harm. . . . Rather, we hold that there was insufficient evidence in the record as it presently exists to make that determination as a matter of law. . . .

Reversed and remanded.

Judge Kirsten F. Kelly dissenting

I disagree with my colleagues' conclusion that the trial court's grant of summary disposition in this matter was premature. . . . [R]unning the engine of a car in a small, enclosed space, such as a garage, is an obvious material risk to a reasonably prudent product user and would be especially obvious to a person like decedent whose employment involved servicing and repairing engines. I would affirm the trial court.

* * * * *

Questions

1. Do you agree with the lower court that the risk of carbon monoxide poisoning from running a car in an enclosed garage would be obvious to the reasonably prudent user? Explain.

2. Why did the plaintiff win this case on appeal?

3. Michigan law bars liability in these situations if the risk "is or should be a matter of common knowledge to persons in the same or similar positions." Craig White had some, unspecified experience in servicing and repairing marine engines. He had also served as an "engine dynamo technician" and a "marine technician." Is that background, in and of itself, sufficient to establish that the carbon monoxide risk was a matter of "common knowledge" to White? Explain.

4. Bresnahan, age 50 and 5'8" tall, was driving her Chrysler LeBaron, equipped with a driver's side air bag, at between 25 and 30 miles per hour. She was seated less than one foot from the air bag cover. Bresnahan was distracted by police lights and rear-ended a Jaguar, triggering the LeBaron air bag, which broke Bresnahan's arm and caused various abrasions. The vehicle did not include a warning about the danger of sitting too close to the air bag. Was the vehicle defective because of the absence of a warning? Explain. See *Bresnahan v. Chrysler Corp.,* 65 Cal. App. 4th 1149 (1998).

5. Laaperi installed a smoke detector in his bedroom, properly connecting it to his home's electrical system. Six months later, Laaperi's house burned and three of his children were killed. A short circuit, which caused the fire, also deprived the A.C.-powered smoke detector of electricity. Thus the detector did not sound a warning. Laaperi then claimed that Sears, Roebuck, where he purchased the detector, was guilty of negligence for failing to warn him that a fire might disable his smoke detector such that no warning would issue. How would you rule in this case? See *Laaperi v. Sears, Roebuck & Co.,* 787 F.2d 726 (1st Cir. 1986).

Negligence Defenses: Introduction

Even if the plaintiff has established all of the necessary ingredients in a negligence claim, the defendant may still prevail by asserting a good defense. The two most prominent legal defenses in these cases are (1) comparative or contributory negligence and (2) assumption of the risk.

A trampoline at the Beta Theta Pi fraternity house at the University of Denver led to a broken neck and paralysis when a 20-year-old fraternity member, Oscar Whitlock, unsuccessfully attempted a flip at 10 PM in the dark. Whitlock had extensive experience with trampolines. The day of the accident he had slept until 2 PM after drinking that morning until 2 AM. The trampoline was located in front of the house on university land that was leased by the fraternity. The trampoline had been used over a 10-year period by students and community members. A number of injuries had resulted. The university kept its own trampoline under lock and key because of safety concerns.

> Oscar Whitlock unsuccessfully attempted a flip at 10 PM in the dark.

At trial the jury found the university 72 percent at fault, with the remainder of the blame lying with the plaintiff/student. He recovered 72 percent of $7,300,000 ($5,256,000). On appeal the judgment was upheld; but the dissent argued that the university had no duty to warn against obvious risks, saying that "no reasonable person could conclude that the plaintiff was not at least as negligent as the defendant." Hence the dissent was saying, in effect, that the plaintiff had assumed the risk and, in any case, was himself arguably more negligent than the university.[23]

The Colorado State Supreme Court then reviewed the appeals court decision and reversed on the grounds that the university did not maintain a "special relationship" with the plaintiff that would have justified imposing a duty of due care on the university to ensure safe use of the trampoline.[24]

Questions

Assume you own an amusement park.

1. Would the dissent's reasoning in the *Whitlock* court of appeals decision apply to the trampoline in your amusement park business? Explain.
2. Would a warning and close supervision protect you from liability under the court of appeals decision? Explain.
3. Would you have the duty of due care for your customers that the Supreme Court said the University of Denver did not have for Whitlock? Explain.

Negligence Defenses: Rules

Let's look more closely at the central defenses in negligence cases.

Comparative Negligence

Most states have adopted comparative negligence as a defense; an approach that involves weighing the relative negligence of the parties. Though the formula varies from state to state, typically the plaintiff's recovery is reduced by a percentage equal to the percentage of the plaintiff's fault in the case. Assume a plaintiff sustained $10,000 in injuries in an accident. If the plaintiff's own negligence is found to be 20 percent responsible for the injuries, then the plaintiff's recovery will be reduced to $8,000. In many states, however, when the plaintiff is more than 50 percent at fault, she or he will be barred from recovery.

Contributory Negligence

Rather than employing the comparative negligence doctrine, a few states continue to follow the historic rule that any contribution by the plaintiff to his or her own harm constitutes a complete bar to recovery. This is called contributory negligence. If the plaintiff is found to have contributed in any way to his or her injury, even if that contribution is minuscule, he or she is unable to recover.

Assumption of Risk

A plaintiff who willingly enters a dangerous situation and is injured, in many states, will be barred from recovery. For example, if a driver sees that the road ahead is flooded, he probably will not be compensated for the injuries sustained when he loses control as he attempts to drive through the water. His recovery is barred even though the road was flooded due to operator error in opening a floodgate. The requirements for use of the assumption of risk defense are (1) knowledge of the risk and (2) voluntary assumption of the risk. Assumption of the risk and contributory negligence are distinguishable in that the former is based on consent whereas the latter is rooted in carelessness. Increasingly, states that have adopted the comparative negligence doctrine do not treat assumption of the risk as a complete bar to recovery, but rather as a factor in negligence balancing.

Do Cheerleaders Assume the Risk of Injury?

Underlying the assumption of the risk doctrine is one of the central philosophical themes in this book: To what extent should the law/government shield us from life's risks? Departing for a moment from product liability considerations, how should the law resolve disputes arising from potentially hazardous recreational activities entered freely? Gabriella Ballou, then-9th grader and experienced cheerleader, allegedly improperly performed the "prep cradle twist" causing her head to miss the safety mat and strike the floor. An expert witness testified that the stunt was inadequately supervised, among other problems. Should Ballou be able to recover for injuries she sustained in high school cheerleading tryouts, or should she be deemed to have assumed the risks attendant to that activity?

Source: Ballou v. Ravena-Coeymans-Selkirk School District, 72 A.D.3d 1323 (N.Y. S.Ct. App. Div. 3d Dept. 2010).

Warranties

As explained previously, negligence claims often are difficult to prove. For that reason and others, a wronged consumer may wish to bring a breach of warranty claim in addition to or in place of a negligence action. A warranty is simply a contractually based guarantee. If the product does not conform to the standards of the warranty, the contract is violated (breached), and the wronged party is entitled to recovery. [For the text of the Uniform Commercial Code, Article II, Sales, see Appendix B at the back of this text. For the UCC, in total, see **http://www.law.cornell.edu/ucc**]

Express Warranties

An express warranty exists if a seller of goods states a fact or makes a promise regarding the character or quality of the goods. (Some lease arrangements are also covered by warranty law, but we will limit our discussion to the sale of goods.) Warranties are governed primarily by the Uniform Commercial Code. The UCC is designed to codify and standardize the law of commercial practice.

UCC 2–313. Express Warranties by Affirmation, Promise, Description, Sample

1. Express warranties by the seller are created as follows:
    a. Any affirmation of fact or promise made by the seller to the buyer which relates to the goods and becomes part of the basis of the bargain creates an express warranty that the goods shall conform to the affirmation or promise.

  b. Any description of the goods which is made part of the basis of the bargain creates an express warranty that the goods shall conform to the description.

  c. Any sample or model which is made part of the basis of the bargain creates an express warranty that the whole of the goods shall conform to the sample or model.

The UCC 2–313 standard is straightforward: The seller who seeks to enhance the attractiveness of her product by offering representations as to the nature or quality of the product must fulfill those representations or fall in breach of contract and pay damages. [At this writing, the various state legislatures are considering changes to the UCC.]

Puffing

Perhaps the area of greatest confusion in determining the existence and coverage of an express warranty is distinguishing a seller's promise from a mere expression of opinion. The latter, often referred to as sales talk or puffing, does not create an express warranty. The UCC requires an affirmation of fact or promise. Hence, a statement of opinion is not covered by the code. For example, the sales clerk who says, "This is the best TV around," would not be guaranteeing that the television in question is the best available. The salesperson is expressing a view. We, as consumers, seem to be quite patient with sellers' exaggerations. If, on the other hand, the clerk said, "This TV is rated at 1080 pixels," when in fact it offered only 768 pixels, a breach of warranty action might ultimately be in order. The reasonable expectations test is to be applied in such situations. An expression of opinion coming from an expert may well create an express warranty because the buyer should reasonably be able to rely on the expert's affirmations. That would particularly be the case if the buyer is not knowledgeable about the product.

Implied Warranties

When a seller enters a contract for the sale of goods an implied warranty arises by operation of law. That is, an implied warranty automatically attaches to the sale of goods unless the warranty is disclaimed (disavowed) by the seller.

  Two types of implied warranties are provided:

UCC 2–314. Implied Warranty: Merchantability; Usage of Trade

(1) Unless excluded or modified (Section 2–316), a warranty that the goods shall be merchantable is implied in a contract for their sale if the seller is a merchant with respect to goods of that kind. Under this section the serving for value of food or drink to be consumed either on the premises or elsewhere is a sale.

UCC 2–315. Implied Warranty: Fitness for Particular Purpose

Where the seller at the time of contracting has reason to know any particular purpose for which the goods are required and that the buyer is relying on the seller's skill or judgment to select or furnish suitable goods, there is unless excluded or modified under the next section an implied warranty that the goods shall be fit for such purpose.

The implied warranty of merchantability is a powerful tool for the wronged consumer. If the seller is a merchant regularly selling goods of the kind in question, the warranty of merchantability automatically accompanies the sale unless the warranty is excluded via a disclaimer (explained below). The warranty arises even if the seller made no certification as to the nature or quality of the goods. UCC 2–314 enshrines the consumer's reasonable expectation that only safe goods of at least ordinary quality will appear on the market.

The implied warranty of fitness for a particular purpose likewise arises by operation of law, but only when the seller (merchant or not) knows (or has reason to know) that the goods are to be used for a specific purpose, and the seller further knows that the buyer is relying on the seller's judgment. If those conditions obtain, the warranty exists automatically unless disclaimed. For example, Chris Snapp engages an audio products clerk in a discussion regarding the proper sound system for Chris's classic Austin Healey 3000 sports car. Chris explains the joy he expects to receive in driving his car along the winding Kentucky roads with the convertible top down and his songs booming. Unfortunately, the audio system selected on the clerk's advice proves insufficiently powerful to be heard clearly above the rushing wind. Should Chris recover for breach of the implied warranty of fitness for a particular purpose? Merchantability?

Disclaimers

Express warranties may be disclaimed (excluded) or modified only with great difficulty. In any contract displaying both an express warranty and language disclaiming that warranty (for example, sold "as is" or "with all faults"), the warranty will remain effective unless the warranty and the disclaimer can reasonably be read as consistent.

Implied warranties may be excluded or modified by following either of the two patterns explained in UCC sections 2–316(2) and (3)(a).

2. Subject to subsection (3), to exclude or modify the implied warranty of merchantability or any part of it the language must mention merchantability and in case of a writing must be conspicuous, and to exclude or modify any implied warranty of fitness the exclusion must be by a writing and conspicuous.

3. Notwithstanding subsection (2)

   a. unless the circumstances indicate otherwise, all implied warranties are excluded by expressions like as is, with all faults, or other language which in common understanding calls the buyer's attention to the exclusion of warranties and makes plain that there is no implied warranty.

Finally, when a buyer, before entering a contract, inspects the goods (or a sample thereof) or declines to inspect, no implied warranty exists with regard to defects that should have been apparent on inspection. See UCC 2–316(3)(b).

Magnuson–Moss Warranty Act

The federal Magnuson–Moss Warranty Act extended and clarified UCC warranty rules. Congress found that warranties were often vague, deceptive, or simply incomprehensible to the average purchaser. The act, administered by the FTC, applies only to consumer products and only to written warranties. It does not require offering an express written warranty, but where such a warranty is offered and the cost of the goods is more than $10, the warranty must be labeled full or limited. A full warranty requires free repair of any defect. If repair is not achieved within a reasonable time, the buyer may elect either a refund or replacement without charge. If a limited warranty is offered, the limitation must be conspicuously displayed.

If a warranty is offered on goods costing more than $15, the warrantor must "fully and conspicuously disclose in simple and readily understandable language the terms and conditions of the warranty."

The effect of the Magnuson–Moss Act has not been entirely consistent with Congress's hopes. In practice, many sellers have either offered limited warranties or eliminated them entirely.

In many states, implied warranty law has been incorporated within broader product liability actions reflecting an emerging preference for treating personal injury and property damages as torts rather than contract-based (warranty) claims. The *Hodges* case that follows, however, finds the Kansas Supreme Court examining a breach of warranty claim under conventional contracts reasoning. Notice that the Kansas court struggles, as other courts have, in determining when the warranty of merchantability should apply to used goods.

LEGAL BRIEFCASE

Hodges v. Johnson,
199 P.3d 1251 (Kansas S.Ct. 2009)

Justice Davis

FACTS

Jim Johnson owns a car dealership in Saline County that sells high-end, used vehicles. In January 2005, Johnson sold Dr. Merle Hodges and Melissa Hodges a 1995 Mercedes S320 with 135,945 miles for $17,020 (the sales price of $15,900 plus tax). Johnson had been driving the Mercedes as his personal vehicle for roughly 2 years before the sale. Johnson testified before the district court in this case that he told the Hodgeses when they purchased the Mercedes that it was a nice car in good condition. Dr. Hodges testified that Johnson said the car "was just pretty much a perfect car" and that Johnson "loved driving it."

At the time the Hodgeses bought the Mercedes from Johnson, there was no discussion about the operation of the air conditioning, heating, or other components of the vehicle. Both Dr. Hodges and Johnson testified that they had no reason to believe that the air conditioner did not work when the Mercedes was sold to the Hodgeses.

In February 2005, about a month after he had bought the car from Johnson, Dr. Hodges noticed that the vent in the Mercedes did not circulate cool air and that the car emitted a strange smell. In March of the same year, the Hodgeses noticed that the Mercedes' air conditioning did not work and contacted the Hodgeses' mechanic, Virgil Anderson. Anderson added Freon to the air conditioner. About a month later, the air conditioner again was not working; Anderson added more Freon. The Hodgeses contacted Johnson to notify him of the air conditioning problem, and Johnson told them that some older vehicles may need a yearly boost of Freon to work properly.

In May 2005, the air conditioner failed a third time. After checking the air conditioning system for leaks, Anderson informed the Hodgeses that the Mercedes' evaporator, condenser, and compressor needed to be replaced. Anderson explained that these repairs would cost approximately $3,000 to $4,000.

At some time around May 2005, a mechanic who worked for Anderson told the Hodgeses that Johnson had requested that the mechanic put a product called Super Seal into the Mercedes' air conditioner in May 2003 (when he was using the car as his personal vehicle). The mechanic explained that the use of Super Seal complicated the current repair of the air conditioner and that the mechanic personally would not recommend Super Seal or apply it unless requested.

Johnson testified that he did not recall any problems with the Mercedes' air conditioner after the mechanics added Super Seal in May 2003, though he could not recall whether additional Freon was added during that time. Johnson further testified that the air conditioning problem in 2003 only involved the car's evaporator.

Anderson identified the condenser as the main problem with the Mercedes' air conditioner in 2005. Anderson testified during the pendency of this case that he could not determine whether the problem with the Mercedes' air conditioner existed at the time that the Hodgeses bought the car from Johnson or occurred at some time later.

The Hodgeses asked Johnson to pay to repair the air conditioning unit in the Mercedes. Johnson refused.

Shortly thereafter, the Hodgeses filed an action in small claims court against Johnson, alleging he caused them damages of $3,474—Anderson's estimate of the repair costs. The small claims court found in favor of the Hodgeses and awarded them $3,474 damages, plus $56 in costs and interest.

Johnson appealed to the district court. [T]he district court also found in favor of the Hodgeses, noting that "while [Johnson] may not have known of the failure of the air conditioning unit[,] . . . there is an implied warranty of merchantability," and Johnson "is responsible to the plaintiffs to provide a car that is merchantable." The court therefore entered a judgment in favor of the Hodgeses for $3,474, together with costs of $56 plus interest. The court found that attorney fees were not warranted because Johnson's actions did not rise "to a level of misrepresentation."

[Both parties appealed] to the Court of Appeals. . . . The Court of Appeals reversed . . . and held as a matter of law that the implied warranty of merchantability on a used vehicle extends only to "the operation of major components that are necessary for the vehicle to operate, such as the engine and transmission." The court further held that "it is the responsibility of the buyer to ensure that the components incidental to operation are in working condition."

* * * * *

This court granted the Hodgeses' petition for review.

IMPLIED WARRANTY OF MERCHANTABILITY

Kansas' implied warranty of merchantability is contained in K.S.A. 84-2-314, which states that "a warranty that the goods shall be merchantable is implied in a contract for their sale if the seller is a merchant with respect to goods of that kind." K.S.A. 84-2-314(1). The statute further states that in order for goods to be "merchantable," they must be "at least such as . . . are fit for the ordinary purposes for which such goods are used." K.S.A. 84-2-314(2)(c).

* * * * *

ANALYSIS

The comments to K.S.A. 84-2-314 make clear that this implied warranty of merchantability applies by operation of law to "all sales by merchants" and "arises from the fact of the sale." K.S.A. 84-2-314, Kansas Comment 1. Applying this standard to the facts before us, it is clear that the transaction in this case—the sale of the Mercedes by Johnson to the Hodgeses—fits within the implied warranty. There is no dispute that Johnson is a merchant dealing in the sale of used vehicles or that the Mercedes is a "good" within the meaning of the statute. Thus, when Johnson sold the Mercedes to the Hodgeses, he implicitly warranted that the Mercedes would be "merchantable."

* * * * *

The Court of Appeals majority recognized that the sale of the Mercedes triggered the implied warranty but concluded as a matter of law under K.S.A. 84-2-314(2) that the vehicle's air conditioner was not covered by the warranty because the air conditioner did not affect the vehicle's merchantability. To reach this conclusion, the majority employed a three-part syllogism: First, for goods to be merchantable under the statute, they must be "fit for the ordinary purposes for which such goods are used." K.S.A. 84-2-314(2)(c). Second, the majority concluded that the primary purpose for which used vehicles are used is transportation; thus only the major components of a vehicle that bear upon its ability to effectively transport people from one location to another affect the vehicle's merchantability. Finally, the majority interpreted our past cases involving the warranty of merchantability in the sale of used vehicles to suggest that the warranty may not apply "unless a major component or several components are defective, causing the vehicle to become virtually inoperable." 39 Kan. App. 2d at 225.

Applying this syllogism, the Court of Appeals majority determined that the air conditioner was not a major component of the Mercedes and thus did not impair the primary purpose for which used cars vehicles are employed:

"An air conditioner is not a major component of a car that is 10 years old with over 135,000 miles on it, and does not fall within the implied warranty of merchantability. We find no implied warranty of merchantability, considering the age of the car, the high mileage, and the fact that the Hodges provided no proof that the air conditioner did not work when they purchased the vehicle." *Hodges,* 39 Kan. App. 2d at 225.

This conclusion is not supported by the case law. Although it may be that the implied warranty of merchantability does not extend to some components of a used vehicle in a particular transaction, this is a case-by-case determination in most cases—not a question of law. . . .

The Court of Appeals majority's approach is similarly unsupported by the statutes. K.S.A. 84-2-314(2)(c) defines merchantable goods as goods that are "fit for the ordinary *purposes* for which such goods are used." (Emphasis added.) The Court of Appeals interpreted this provision to mean that a used vehicle must be fit for the *primary* purpose of transportation. This interpretation is inconsistent with the plain language of K.S.A. 84-2-314(2)(c), which clearly contemplates goods that may be put to more than one use. Although there can be little doubt that the *primary* purpose of a vehicle is transportation, the Court of Appeals' opinion ignores the reality that a buyer may purchase a particular vehicle for a number of other purposes—among which may be safety, fuel economy, utility, or *comfort* in traveling to and from various destinations.

Contrary to the Court of Appeals' conclusion, the extent of a merchant's obligation under the implied warranty of merchantability depends on the circumstances of a transaction. . . . The determination as to whether the implied warranty has been breached turns on a number of factors, including "[t]he buyer's knowledge that the goods are used, the extent of their prior use, and whether the goods are significantly discounted." 230 Kan. at 457.

The broad range of used goods that may be covered by the implied warranty of merchantability underscores the wisdom of this court's previous recognition that a "late model, low mileage car, sold at a premium price, is expected to be in far better condition and to last longer than an old, high mileage, 'rough' car that is sold for little above its scrap value." *Dale,* 234 Kan. at 844. In this case, we have a 1995 Mercedes S320 with 135,945 miles selling for $17,020 in 2005. Johnson related to the buyer that it was a nice car in good condition; Dr. Hodges testified that he was told the car "was pretty much a perfect car." In short, this vehicle falls somewhere between the extremes of a "late model, low mileage car, sold at a premium price" and "an old, high mileage, 'rough' car . . . sold for little above its scrap value." 234 Kan. at 844.

The question remaining to be resolved is not the existence of this warranty, but rather the *extent of the seller's obligation* under the warranty. Because this case does not involve either extreme on the spectrum of used vehicles, the resolution of this question is not a question of law, but rather a factual determination. . . .

After hearing the evidence in this case, the district court determined that the Hodgeses were entitled to judgment against Johnson for the sum of $3,474, together with costs of $56 and interest, and thus affirmed the award of the small claims court.

To demonstrate a breach of the implied warranty of merchantability, a plaintiff must show that the purchased goods were defective, that the defect was present when the goods left the seller's control, and that the defect caused the injury sustained by the plaintiff. The circumstantial evidence in this case is sufficient to establish that the defect in the air conditioner existed at the time of sale. In 2003, 2 years before the Hodgeses purchased the vehicle, the Mercedes' air conditioner

failed while Johnson was using it as his personal vehicle. Johnson insisted that his mechanic, against the mechanic's advice, use a product called Super Seal to fix the problem. The Hodgeses discovered that the air conditioner was again defective as soon as the weather became warm enough to require climate control. The use of the Super Seal, the strong odor emanating from the vehicle's ventilation system immediately after the sale, and the complete breakdown of the air conditioner when the buyer first attempted to use it all tend to establish that it was defective at the time of sale. While Johnson may not have known that the Mercedes' air conditioner was defective when he sold the vehicle to the Hodgeses, there is no requirement that a buyer establish that the seller knew of a defective component at the time of sale to trigger the implied warranty.

With regard to damages, there is no question that the complete failure of the air conditioner's operation led to the buyer replacing it. As this court has concluded:

> . . . As concerns used or secondhand goods it is generally understood that the measure of damages is the cost of repair when repair is possible." *International Petroleum Services,* 230 Kan. at 460.

* * * * *

We find that there is substantial competent evidence to support the district court's conclusion that the implied warranty of merchantability in this transaction was not limited to only the Mercedes' major components affecting transportation, but rather extended at a minimum to the vehicle's air conditioning unit. We also find that there was substantial competent evidence to demonstrate that the air conditioning unit was defective at the time of sale and that the required repairs would cost $3,474. Accordingly, we reverse the Court of Appeals' reversal of the district court's judgment in favor of the Hodgeses and affirm the district court's decision.

* * * * *

Questions

1. *a.* Why did the Court of Appeals rule for Johnson, the car dealer?
   b. Why did the Supreme Court reverse the Court of Appeals' judgment that the vehicle's air conditioner was not covered by a warranty?
   c. What test did the Kansas Supreme Court employ to determine whether the implied warranty of merchantability had been breached?
   d. How would the Kansas Supreme Court determine when a used car would be protected by the implied warranty of merchantability?

2. In buying a new motor home, Leavitt told the dealer that he wanted to have plenty of power and braking capacity for driving in the mountains. He was assured by the dealer on both counts. He brought the motor home and found it unsatisfactory for mountain use. After many warranty repairs, he sued for breach of warranty.
   a. What warranty was breached, according to Leavitt?
   b. Decide the case. Explain. See *Leavitt v. Monaco Coach,* 616 N.W.2d 175 (Mich. Ct. App. 2000).

3. Priebe bought a used car without a warranty (sold as is). The seller, Autobarn, told Priebe that the car had not been in any accidents. After driving the car more than 30,000 miles, Priebe crashed the car. Priebe sued Autobarn claiming the car was dangerous to drive because of a previous, undisclosed accident. Priebe did not show that Autobarn had knowledge of the previous accident; nor did Priebe show that the value of the car was reduced by the previous accident. Priebe sued for breach of warranty. Decide. Explain. See *Priebe v. Autobarn,* 240 F.3d 584 (7th Cir. 2001).

4. Douglas Kolarik alleged that he used several imported, pimento-stuffed green olives in a salad. In eating the salad, he bit down on an olive pit and fractured a tooth. The olive jar label included the words "minced pimento stuffed." The defendants are importers and wholesalers of Spanish olives that reach the defendants in barrels and are then inspected for general appearance, pH and acid level and then washed and placed in glass jars suitable for distribution for the purpose of retail sales.
   a. What legal claim would be expected from the plaintiff based on the "minced pimento stuffed" language?
   b. Decide that claim. Explain. See *Kolarik v. Cory International,* 721 N.W.2d 159 (Ia. S.Ct. 2006).

Skoal and Copenhagen and Death?

Bobby Hill of Canton, North Carolina, began chewing tobacco at age 13. He died in 2003 at age 42. U.S. Smokeless Tobacco Co., makers of Skoal and Copenhagen, agreed in 2010 to pay Hill's family $5 million to settle the relatives' wrongful death claim. Apparently, the settlement was the first of its kind involving smokeless tobacco.

Source: Associated Press, "First Lawsuit Won on Chewing Tobacco," *The Des Moines Register,* December 8, 2010, p. 7A.

Strict Liability

Sometimes things happen that businesses can neither prevent nor even explain and yet liability may attach. For example, imagine you are operating a clothing store. A customer enters and decides to try on a pair of slacks. You show her to the dressing room. Soon after, you hear a scream from the room. As it turns out, your customer has been bitten by a spider. Not surprisingly, she thinks the blame lies with your store. She sues, but her negligence and breach of warranty claims are rejected by the court. (Can you explain why she loses?) Finally, she raises a strict liability in tort argument, but the court denies that claim also. Read the overview of strict liability that follows and think about why the court denied her claim. See *Flippo v. Mode O'Day Frock Shops of Hollywood,* 449 S.W.2d 692 (Ark. S.Ct. 1970).

> Your customer has been bitten by a spider.

Strict Liability: Overview

Negligence and warranty claims are helpful to the harmed consumer. However, rapid changes in the nature of commercial practice, as well as an increasing societal concern for consumer protection, led the legal community to gradually embrace yet another cause of action. Strict liability in tort offers the prospect of holding all of those in the chain of distribution liable for damages from a defective product, rather than imposing the entire burden on the injured consumer. Manufacturers and sellers are best positioned to prevent the distribution of defective products, and they are best able to bear the cost of injury by spreading the loss via pricing policies and insurance coverage.

Strict liability as an independent tort emerged in 1963 in the famous California case of *Greenman v. Yuba Power Products, Inc.*[25] In the ensuing 40 years, most states have adopted strict liability in concept. The essence of the strict liability notion is expressed in Section 402A of the Restatement (Second) of Torts. In brief, 402A imposes liability where a product is sold in a defective condition, unreasonably dangerous to the user. Here is the 402A test:

1. One who sells any product in a defective condition, unreasonably dangerous to the user or consumer or to his property, is subject to liability for physical harm thereby caused to the ultimate user or consumer, or to his property, if
   a. the seller is engaged in the business of selling such a product, and,
   b. it is expected to and does reach the user or consumer without substantial change in the condition in which it is sold.
2. The rule stated in Subsection (1) applies although
   a. the seller has exercised all possible care in the preparation and sale of his product, and
   b. the user or consumer has not bought the product from or entered into any contractual relation with the seller.

Thus, we see that strict liability does not require proof of negligence on the part of the defendant. Strict liability law focuses on the condition of the product, rather than the conduct of the parties. Therefore, a seller who is free of actual fault may, nonetheless, be liable for injuries caused by a defective and unreasonably dangerous product. The Aim N Flame lighter case that follows considers the conditions under which a strict liability claim may be raised.

LEGAL BRIEFCASE

Calles v. Scripto-Tokai,
832 N.E.2d 409 (Ill. S.Ct. 2007)

Justice Burke

On March 31, 1998, plaintiff Susan Calles resided with her four daughters, Amanda, age 11, Victoria, age 5, and Jenna and Jillian, age 3. At some point that night, Calles left her home with Victoria to get videos for Amanda. When she left, the twins were in bed and Amanda was watching television. Calles returned to find fire trucks and emergency vehicles around her home. It was subsequently determined by a fire investigator, Robert Finn, that Jenna had started a fire using an Aim N Flame utility lighter Calles had purchased approximately one week earlier. The Aim N Flame was ignited by pulling a trigger after an "ON/OFF" switch was slid to the "on" position. As a result of the fire, Jillian suffered smoke inhalation. She was hospitalized and died on April 21.

Calles filed suit against Tokai, designer and manufacturer of the Aim N Flame, and Scripto-Tokai, distributor (collectively Scripto), alleging that the Aim N Flame was defectively designed and unreasonably dangerous because it did not contain a child-resistant safety device. According to the complaint, a safety device was available, inexpensive, and would have reduced the risk that children could ignite the lighter. Calles' claims sounded in strict liability.

Thereafter, Scripto filed a motion for summary judgment. . . . In her deposition, Calles admitted she was aware of the risks and dangers presented by lighters in the hands of children, and, for this reason, she stored the Aim N Flames on the top shelf of her kitchen cabinet. Calles further admitted that the Aim N Flame operated as intended and expected.

In opposition to Scripto's motion for summary judgment, Calles offered affidavits from several experts. . . . All of [the] experts opined that the Aim N Flame was defective and unreasonably dangerous because it lacked a child-resistant design. They also opined that a technologically and economically feasible alternative design, which included a child-resistant safety device, existed at the time the Aim N Flame was manufactured. Several of the experts averred that Scripto was aware of the desirability of a child-safety device because it knew children could operate the Aim N Flame. Further, according to these experts, Scripto owned the technology to make the Aim N Flame child resistant in 1994 and 1995.

With respect to the cost of an alternative design, . . . the Consumer Product Safety Commission, the regulatory body for lighters, estimated the increased cost of adding a safety device to the lighter would be $ 0.40 per unit. However [one of Calles' experts estimated], the cost would have been negligible.

Calles also offered evidence of the dangerousness of lighters in the hands of children and Scripto's awareness of such dangers. . . . Scripto admitted they had been named as defendants in 25 lawsuits filed between 1996 and 2000 for injuries that occurred between 1992 and 1999 under circumstances similar to this case.

The trial court granted summary judgment in favor of Scripto. . . .

On appeal, the appellate court reversed [the trial court's summary judgment in favor of Scripto. . . .]

STRICT LIABILITY

This court adopted the strict liability doctrine set forth in section 402A of the Second Restatement of Torts. Under this doctrine, strict liability is imposed upon a seller of "any product in a defective condition unreasonably dangerous to the user or consumer or to his property." The test outlined in section 402A for determining whether a product is "unreasonably dangerous" is known as the consumer-expectation test. This test provides that a product is "unreasonably dangerous" when it is "dangerous to an extent beyond that which would be contemplated by the ordinary consumer who purchases it, with the ordinary knowledge common to the community as to its characteristics."

* * * * *

An ordinary consumer would expect that a child could obtain possession of the Aim N Flame and attempt to use it.

Thus, a child is a reasonably foreseeable user. Likewise, an ordinary consumer would appreciate the consequences that would naturally flow when a child obtains possession of a lighter.

Under the facts of this case, the Aim N Flame performed as an ordinary consumer would expect - it produced a flame when used in a reasonably foreseeable manner, i.e., by a child. This leads to the inescapable conclusion that the ordinary consumer's expectations were fulfilled. . . . Thus, as a matter of law, no fact finder could conclude that the Aim N Flame was unreasonably dangerous under the consumer-expectation test. Therefore, Calles cannot prevail under this theory.

This does not end our analysis however. Though the Aim N Flame satisfies the consumer-expectation test, it may, nonetheless, be deemed unreasonably dangerous under the risk-utility test.

RISK–UTILITY TEST

Under the risk-utility test, a plaintiff may prevail in a strict liability design-defect case if he or she demonstrates that the magnitude of the danger outweighs the utility of the product, as designed.

* * * * *

Under the risk-utility test, a court may take into consideration numerous factors. In past decisions, this court has held that a plaintiff may prove a design defect by presenting evidence of "the availability and feasibility of alternate designs at the time of its manufacture, or that the design used did not conform with the design standards of the industry. . . ."

Calles presented specific and detailed evidence as to the likelihood of injury and the seriousness of injury from lighters which do not have child-safety devices.

Factors which would favor Scripto and a finding that the product is not unreasonably dangerous are the utility of the Aim N Flame and the user's awareness of the dangers. As to the utility of the Aim N Flame, it is both useful and desirable to society as a whole - it serves as an inexpensive alternative source of fire. . . . With respect to the user's awareness of the dangers, there is no question, based on Calles' deposition testimony, that it was obvious to her that the lighter could come into the hands of a child and the dangers and risks that situation would pose.

In connection with the remaining relevant factors, we find that these neither weigh for nor against a finding of unreasonably dangerous. Calles claims that a substitute product was available, but the only evidence she relies upon is the fact Bic introduced a child-resistant utility lighter in March 1998, the very same month of the incident here. This is insufficient to demonstrate that a substitute product was available at the time of the manufacture of the Aim N Flame.

Calles offered expert affidavits regarding the availability and feasibility of an alternative design, including product impairment and cost factors, along with industry standards. Each expert opined that a feasible alternative design existed.

* * * * *

There is nothing in our record showing Scripto provided any amount as to the increase in cost of incorporating a safety device. Apparently. . . . an internal Scripto memorandum estimated the cost increase would be $0.03 per unit. In light of the foregoing, we conclude that the question of whether there was a feasible alternative design available cannot be determined on the basis of the record as it currently stands.

Lastly, with respect to the user's ability to avoid the danger, Calles testified she put the Aim N Flames on the top shelf of her kitchen cabinet. However, she also acknowledged she could have left them on the counter.

* * * * *

Based on a review of the foregoing factors, reasonable persons could differ on the weight to be given the relevant factors and thus could differ on whether the risks of the Aim N Flame outweigh its utility. Therefore, reasonable persons could differ as to whether the Aim N Flame is unreasonably dangerous, and we cannot say that Scripto was entitled to judgment as a matter of law. As such, we affirm the appellate court's decision reversing the trial court's decision granting summary judgment in favor of Scripto on the strict liability claims.

* * * * *

Questions

1. *a.* Explain the plaintiff Calles' claim that the Aim N Flame lighter was defective and unreasonably dangerous.
   b. Explain the court's resolution of Calles' claim.
2. What evidence must a plaintiff provide to maintain a successful defective design product liability claim?
3. Is the manufacturer excused from liability if the product's danger is obvious or if the product is used in an unintended but foreseeable fashion?
4. In a case similar to *Calles* [*Griggs v. Bic Corp.,* 981 F.2d 1429 (3rd Cir. 1992)] the court, employing a negligence analysis, found that the central question was whether the foreseeable risk was unreasonable. The court noted that residential fires started by children playing with lighters are estimated to take an average of 120 lives each year, and total damages amount to $300–$375 million or 60–75 cents per lighter sold.
   a. Is the foreseeable risk unreasonable, in your judgment?
   b. How did you reach your conclusion?
   c. In your view, are the parents the responsible parties in these episodes? Explain.
5. Alison Nowak, a 14-year-old girl, tried to spray her hair with Aqua Net. Because the spray valve on the recently purchased aerosol can would not work properly, she punctured the can with an opener. She was standing in her kitchen near a gas stove at the time, and the cloud of spray that gushed from the can ignited. She was severely burned. Nowak sued Faberge, the maker of the spray, on strict liability grounds. Although the back of the can contained the warnings, "Do not puncture," and "Do not use near fire or flame," the jury determined that Faberge had not adequately warned of the fire hazard and awarded her $1.5 million. Faberge appealed. Decide. Explain. See *Nowak v. Faberge USA Inc.,* 32 F.3d 755 (3d Cir. 1994).

Strict Liability: Coverage

All of those engaged in the preparation and distribution of a defective product may be liable for any harm caused by the defect, regardless of proof of actual fault. Furthermore, the courts have extended strict liability coverage to reach injured bystanders. Coverage generally extends to both personal injuries and property damage, but in some states the latter is excluded. Some states limit strict liability recovery to new goods, and some have limited liability to a designated period (for example, 15 years) after the manufacture or sale of the product.

Furthermore, the *Restatement (Third) of Torts* recommends applying strict liability claims to manufacturing defects but not to design and warning defect cases. Thus, in effect, the latest

Restatement recommends applying the reasonableness, fault-based analysis explained earlier in the negligence material to all defective design and failure to warn cases. Of course, the courts may choose to stick with the current expansive use of the strict liability doctrine.

Strict Liability: Defenses

Assumption of risk and *product misuse* are both good defenses and, if factually supported, in many states can act as a complete bar to strict liability recovery. Assumption of the risk involves the plaintiff's decision to proceed to use the product despite obvious dangers associated with that use. Thus, if a pilot decided to fly knowing that the plane's wing flaps were not operating properly, she may well have assumed the risk if she subsequently crashed. When the product is used improperly, or its directions are ignored, or it is used in an unforeseeable way, the defendant would raise the misuse defense. Suppose you find yourself late for class and you decide to save time by drying your tennis shoes in your microwave or ironing your clothes after you have put them on your body. If the microwave blows up or you burn yourself with the iron, not only have you had a very bad day, you probably would not be able to sue successfully for damages because you likely would be found to have misused the products. Some courts, however, hold those in the chain of distribution liable for foreseeable misuses. Because strict liability is a no-fault theory, contributory negligence ordinarily is not a recognized defense. [For the "evolution" of product liability laws, see **http://www.productliabilitylawyer.com/evolutionOfProductLiability.cfm**].

> Drying your tennis shoes in your microwave.

Video Games and *The Basketball Diaries*

Michael Carneal, a 14-year-old high school freshman in Paducah, Kentucky, brought a .22-caliber pistol and five shotguns to Heath High School on December 1, 1997, where he shot and killed three students and wounded a number of others. Carneal regularly played violent video games such as *Doom and Quake,* and viewed violent Internet sites. He also watched violent movies including *The Basketball Diaries,* in which a high school student dreams of killing his teacher and other students. The parents of the dead children sued several video game, movie production, and Internet content providers raising negligence and strict liability claims. Who should win that case? Explain.

Source: James v. Meow Media, 300 F.3d 683 (6th Cir. 2002); cert. den. *James v. Meow Media,* 537 U.S. 1159 (2003).

Part Three—Product Liability and Public Policy

Giant tort awards involving products such as asbestos and breast implants have bankrupted businesses. When we hear about a $28 *billion* punitive damage award in 2002 for a 64-year-old smoker suffering from lung cancer, we may wonder if the justice system has lost its bearings.[26] We may not understand that those giant awards are almost always dramatically reduced.[27] Furthermore, awards in big class action cases often come in the form of product coupons or gifts to charity.[28]*The Wall Street Journal* reported, for example, that exploding tires on Ford Explorers resulted in a 2008 class action settlement for 1,647 eligible claimants of $500 toward the purchase of a new Explorer and $300 toward the purchase of any other Ford vehicle. Only 148 of the eligible claimants redeemed a coupon, while the attorneys who led the litigation received about $19 million in fees.[29] Nonetheless, the threat of tort litigation significantly affects business decision making and, in some instances, actually prevents products from reaching the market.

Because of those problems, many critics, particularly in the business community and among free market advocates, have argued for *tort reform.* They want to change the legal system in ways that would reduce the heavy costs of personal injury claims. The proposed reforms vary widely, but common prescriptions include: limiting class actions, reducing or eliminating punitive damages, curbing attorneys' fees, penalizing frivolous lawsuits, and imposing "loser pays" rules requiring the losing party in a civil lawsuit to pay the other party's legal fees and related costs.

Are big tort judgments harming the American economy and distorting justice, or are lawsuits Americans' only effective protection against callous corporations? Consider some of the evidence.

For Tort Reform Consultants Towers Perrin (now Towers Watson) estimated that 2008 tort costs (not limited to product liability) for the United States totaled $254.7 billion; a sum amounting to a "tort tax" of $838 per year for every American.[30] As a result, critics say, American businesses must struggle with rising costs, innovation is reduced, and new jobs are less plentiful.

> A "tort tax" of $838 per year for every American.

A particular frustration to the critics is that much of the tort money goes to lawyers rather than to the injured plaintiffs. Notably, however, the Towers Perrin report shows the ratio of tort costs to gross domestic product falling substantially since 2003,[31] and a number of states have imposed caps on punitive damages while, as noted in Chapter 5, the U.S. Supreme Court has handed down several decisions curbing punitives. [For further criticism of tort claims and our legal system generally, see **http://over-lawyered.com or www.legalreformnow.com**. For a critique of the Towers Perrin report, see J. Robert Hunter and Joanne Doroshow, "Towers Perrin: 'Grade F' for Fantastically Inflated 'Tort Cost' Report," **www.consumerfed.org/.../Insurance%20Report%20 Towers%20Perrin%202010(1).pdf**]

Against Tort Reform Can we rely on the market and managerial ethics to protect us from dangerous products? Lawyers Mark Robinson and Kevin Calcagnie, writing in *The Wall Street Journal,* point to the long-running battle over Toyota's sudden acceleration problems as evidence that the market alone does not adequately protect consumers from dangerous products.[32] Robinson and Calcagnie argue that nearly a decade passed by before Toyota and the federal government began to aggressively examine the several thousand sudden acceleration claims.[33] Improvements in products such as air bags, seat belts, tires, tobacco products, antidepressants, and many more have been encouraged by product liability litigation, as Robinson and Calcagnie note.[34]

More broadly, those opposing tort reform say that the tort burden simply is not of the magnitude suggested by the critics. Lawsuits, consuming less than 2 percent of spending, constitute a modest part of the cost of doing business; product liability claims are a small fraction of the total legal landscape; and studies show that insurance costs do not decline appreciably when damages are capped.[35] Furthermore, only about 3 percent of tort cases ever make it to trial; those cases that are settled before judgment often involve reasonable sums of money[36] and punitive damages are awarded in only about 3.3 percent of tort cases won by plaintiffs.[37] Even ardent defenders of tort practice often agree, however, that the system needs to be improved so that lawyers do not gobble up so much of the money themselves and so that the system produces a more consistent, predictable form of justice.[38] [For a debate among prominent legal scholars about the value of product liability law, see A. Mitchell Polinsky and Steven Shavell, "The Uneasy Case for Product Liability," *123 Harvard Law Review* 1437 (2010); John C.P. Goldberg and Benjamin C. Zipursky, "The Easy Case for Products Liability Law: A Response to Professors Polinsky and Shavell," *123 Harvard Law Review* 1919 (2010); and A. Mitchell Polinsky and Steven Shavell, "A Skeptical Attitude about Product Liability Is Justified: A Reply to Professors Goldberg and Zipursky," *123 Harvard Law Review* 1949 (2010).]

Kids Need to Swing?

Aggressive public safety programs and the threat of lawsuits have made playground swings, particularly the tall 16-footers, a vanishing delight. Tall swings and slides along with sliding poles are rapidly being replaced by safer but less thrilling playground devices. U.S. playground safety standards, widely adopted in the 1990s, called for new safety surfaces to cushion falls with the result that the swings became very costly. A swing set once costing $800 now costs $4,000. Thus, government rules and the threat of lawsuits have made playgrounds safer while reshaping childhood fun and virtually eliminating the challenge of overcoming the terror of big swings and slides. Are we better off?

Source: Gregg Toppo, "The Great American Swing Set Is Teetering," *USA TODAY,* March 19, 2006 [**http://www.usatoday.com/news/nation/2006-03-19-swing-sets_x.htm**].

Big Case: Lead Paint?

A helpful way to look at tort reform is to consider one of the massive claims that have emerged periodically as plaintiffs attempt to prove themselves wronged by a defective product or wrongful conduct. Tobacco smokers, Ford Explorer drivers, Vioxx users, and victims of gun violence are among those who have made headlines pursuing alleged corporate wrongdoers. Lead paint, banned since 1978, often produces developmental difficulties, including IQ deficiencies, learning disabilities, hyperactivity, and impaired hearing, when ingested or inhaled by children. Ordinarily, lead paint is troublesome only when it is reduced to flakes or dust; commonly in buildings that have not been properly maintained. While the potential for exposure to lead has declined dramatically in recent years, an estimated several hundred thousand young children, often living in old, inner city housing have been victims:

> Crawling across the wooden floor of his mother's Brooklyn (New York) apartment, Jaylin paused to lick his chubby hand, swallowing flecks of toxic paint. The boy's mother had no idea the poison lurked within the cracks of the baseboard.[39]

Should paint manufacturers be responsible for the harm caused by paint applied decades back by willing consumers before anyone fully understood the long-term hazards? What about owners and landlords who failed to properly maintain painted surfaces? Even if we can establish responsibility, how do we apportion damages when we cannot identify the specific producers of the paint in question? Or should we expect the paint manufacturers to share the damages burden according to the percentage each holds in the market (a product liability claim labeled *market share liability*)?

Lead paint lawsuits have been pursued in a number of states. In most cases, the plaintiffs have been states and municipalities that have sued paint manufacturers or landlords/property owners for creating a *public nuisance* (a significant interference with a right common to the general public such as the public health, public safety, or public peace). Market share liability claims have also been raised in some instances, but most claims under both theories of recovery have been rejected in court. For example, a unanimous Rhode Island Supreme Court in 2008 overturned a jury verdict against three paint companies when the Court concluded that "however grave the problem of lead poisoning is in Rhode Island, public nuisance law simply does not provide a remedy for this harm."[40] Lawsuits continue, however, and in 2009, a Mississippi jury ruled that Sherwin-Williams paint company was liable for illnesses suffered by a young boy who had eaten paint chips. The jury awarded $7 million in damages, but the decision is currently on appeal to the Mississippi Supreme Court.[41]

> A young boy who had eaten paint chips.

Fast Food = Fat People = Big Lawsuits?

Fortune magazine's February 2003 issue asked "Is Fat the Next Tobacco?" *Fortune* and many other publications suggested that fast-food companies might soon be buried in lawsuits like those attacking the tobacco industry. The American public shook its collective head at the prospect of blaming McDonald's, Wendy's, and others for obese people's health problems, and those lawsuits, for the most part, have not materialized. Most of the handful of cases filed have been unsuccessful, and those that did gain some traction were based in mislabeling and consumer fraud and thus did not pose a crippling financial threat. Furthermore, at least 23 states have passed "cheeseburger bills" providing some protection for fast-food companies facing obesity lawsuits. Thus, the widely condemned prospect of lawyers launching a new front in the litigation wars is currently unlikely. Of course, some day new information might emerge that could endanger the fast-food companies.

Source: Lianne S. Pinchuk, "Are Fast-Food Lawsuits Likely to Be the Next 'Big Tobacco'?" *The National Law Journal*, February 28, 2007.

Too Much Law?

Perhaps we rely too much on the law. Clearly, legal intervention often is necessary to achieve justice. At the same time, that intervention sometimes can be inefficient and unproductive. As we conclude this chapter, give some thought to the cases you have read. On balance, do you think legal intervention was necessary in those situations, or would our society be stronger if we resolved more of those problems through private arrangements such as arbitration, as we discussed in Chapter 4, or risk assignment provisions included in contracts when we buy a new product?

[For a video defense of the tort system, see *Mr. Fancy Pants* at **www.youtube.com/ watch?v=h85j1vNxd8A**. For the American Tort Reform Association, see **http://www. atra.org**]

Internet Exercise

The Pacific Research Institute's 2010 U.S. Tort Liability Index ranks the 50 states according to their "tort climates."

1. Go to the report's state rankings [**http://special.pacificresearch.org/pub/sab/ entrep/2010/Tort-Index/state.html/**] and determine your state's rank, according to the PRI study. According to the study, is your state's tort system a "Saint," "Sinner," "Salvageable," or "Sucker," and why does it matter?

2. Read the press release for the study [**http://www.pacificresearch.org/press/2010-tort- liability-index-ranks-states-tort-climate**] and explain how United States' tort costs compare with other nations and why high tort costs matter, according to the study.

Chapter Questions

1. Cotillo, a power lifter with 10 years experience, attempted to lift 530 pounds during an American Powerlifting Association–sponsored meet, organized by Duncan, the faculty sponsor of the local high school's weightlifting club and Taylor, the APA president. Lifters were allowed to use spotters of their own choice or those provided by the meet. Cotillo used those provided by the meet, who were high school students with weight-lifting experience. As Cotillo attempted the lift, Duncan was positioned "in the mid-dle," and a student was on each side of the bar. Cotillo dropped the weight shattering his jaw and causing other injuries. The spotters were in the proper positions to provide assistance, but they could not do so quickly enough to prevent injury. Cotillo then sued Duncan, the APA, and the APA Board, claiming, among other things, that the spotters were improperly trained. The spotters had received some instruction prior to the meet, but the record was unclear as to whether the training was improper or inadequate.
   a. What was Cotillo's cause of action?
   b. Defend Duncan et al.
   c. Decide the case. Explain. See *American Powerlifting Association v. Cotillo,* 934 A.2d 27 (Ct. App. Md., 2007).

2. Stopczynski, age 17, had used her neighbor's pool "hundreds of times." Stopczynski and her neighbor's nephew, a 34-year-old male, went to the pool. Stopczynski was

noticed floating face down in the pool. She had broken her neck, apparently from diving into the four-foot deep, above-ground pool. She died a few hours later. The pool originally had stickers around the edge that said "no diving," but that edge had been replaced and the stickers were gone. Stopczynski's mother sued the property owner, Woodcox, for negligence. Decide the case. Explain. See *Stopczynski v. Woodcox,* 258 Mich. App. 226 (2003).

3. Soon after Granny's Rocker Nite Club opened in the mid-1980s, it began having a weekly "fanny" contest, which involved male and female volunteer contestants competing for cash prizes by dancing. The audience judged the contest. While attending the fanny contest on April 4, 1990, plaintiff Jeffrey Loomis got into a fight with another patron. Loomis's right ear was bitten and torn.

    Loomis's claim against Granny's Rocker had two counts, one based on the Illinois Dramshop Act and one based on negligence. The jury found for the defendant on the dramshop count, but it found that Granny's Rocker was negligent in failing to have adequate security to stop a physical altercation on the nights of the fanny contests when it knew or should have known that such contests would result in a large and rowdy group of patrons. Granny's Rocker appealed. Decide the appeal. Explain, See *Loomis v. Granny's Rocker Nite Club,* 620 N.E.2d 664 (Ill. App. 1993).

4. Thomas Woeste died as a result of contracting a bacteria after eating about one dozen raw oysters at the Washington Platform Saloon & Restaurant. The bacteria, vibrio vulnificus, is naturally occurring in oysters harvested in warm waters. Most people are unaffected by the bacteria, but those with weakened immune systems like Woeste can be susceptible to illness or death. Washington Platform's menu contained the following warning:

    > There may be risks associated when consuming shell fish. . . . If you suffer from chronic illness of the liver, stomach or blood. . . or if you have other immune disorders, you should eat these products fully cooked.

    Woeste ordered and ate the oysters without opening the menu and reading the warning. A civil lawsuit was filed against Washington Platform alleging that the restaurant was both negligent and strictly liable for failure to adequately warn. Decide that case. Explain. See *Woeste v. Washington Platform Saloon & Restaurant,* 836 N.E.2d 52 (Ohio Ct. App., First App. Dist. 2005).

5. An 11-month-old child pushed on a window screen that gave way, allowing him to fall from the second story of his aunt's house. The child's parents sued the screen maker.
    a. What product liability claims could they legitimately raise?
    b. Decide. Explain. See *Brower v. Metal Industries, Inc.,* 719 A.2d 941 (Del. S.Ct. 1998).

6. Sandage loaded a car on a transport trailer. The car door could not be fully opened because of a support bar on the trailer. He suffered a back injury when he squeezed out of the car. The trailer had been modified to add several feet to its length, and support poles, including the one in question, had been added. Sandage sued the company that modified the trailer. Sandage sued in strict liability and negligence. Decide the case. Explain. See *Sandage v. Bankhead Enterprises, Inc.,* 177 F.3d 670 (8th Cir. 1999).

7. In 1995 a young Oklahoma couple shot and paralyzed a store clerk, Patsy Byers. The young couple had repeatedly viewed Oliver Stone's 1994 movie *Natural Born Killers,* which is about a young couple who go on a killing spree. The Byers family sued Stone and Warner Brothers movie studio, the film distributor. Should a filmmaker and studio be liable for the alleged copycat behavior of those viewing a movie? Explain.

8. Embs was shopping in a self-serve grocery store. A carton of 7UP was on the floor about one foot from where she was standing. She was unaware of the carton. Several of the bottles exploded, severely injuring Embs's leg. Embs brought a strict liability action against the bottler.

   a. Raise a defense against the strict liability claim.

   b. Decide. Explain. See *Embs v. Pepsi-Cola Bottling Co. of Lexington, Kentucky, Inc.,* 528 S.W.2d 703 (Ky. Ct. App. 1975).

9. Plaintiffs Dr. Arthur Weisz and David and Irene Schwartz bought two paintings at auctions conducted by Parke-Bernet Galleries, Inc. The paintings were listed in the auction catalog as those of Raoul Dufy. It was later discovered that the paintings were forgeries. The plaintiffs took legal action to recover their losses. Parke-Bernet defended itself by, among other arguments, asserting that the conditions of sale included a disclaimer providing that all properties were sold "as is." The conditions of sale were 15 numbered paragraphs embracing several pages in the auction catalog. The bulk of the auction catalog was devoted to descriptions of the works of art to be sold, including artists' names, dates of birth and death, and, in some instances, black-and-white reproductions of the paintings. It was established at trial that plaintiff Weisz had not previously entered bids at Parke-Bernet, and he had no awareness of the conditions of sale. Plaintiffs David and Irene Schwartz, however, were generally aware of the conditions of sale. Is the Parke-Bernet disclaimer legally binding on the plaintiffs? Explain. See *Weisz v. Parke-Bernet,* 325 N.Y.S.2d 576 (Civ. Ct. N.Y.C. 1971), but see *Schwartz v. Parke-Bernet,* 351 N.Y.S.2d 911 (1974).

10. The plaintiff, born and raised in New England, was eating fish chowder at a restaurant when a fish bone lodged in her throat. The bone was removed, and the plaintiff sued the restaurant, claiming a breach of implied warranty under the UCC. Evidence was offered at trial to show that fish chowder recipes commonly did not provide for removal of bones. Decide. Explain. See *Webster v. Blue Ship Tea Room,* 198 N.E.2d 309 (Mass. S. Jud. Ct. 1964).

11. A passenger ran after a train as it was leaving a station. Two railroad employees boosted the passenger aboard, but as they did so a package carried by the passenger fell beneath the wheels of the train and exploded. The package, unbeknownst to the employees, contained fireworks. The force of that explosion caused a scale many feet away to topple over, injuring the plaintiff, Palsgraf. Palsgraf sued the railroad on negligence grounds.

    a. Defend the railroad.

    b. Decide. Explain. See *Palsgraf v. Long Island R.R.,* 162 N.E. 99 (N.Y. 1928).

12. Pat Stalter was injured when a bottle fell through the bottom of a soft drink carton and broke while she was shopping at Food City, a Little Rock, Arkansas, grocery store. A piece of glass went through her slacks, cutting her. A store employee said the carton

was "mushy" and appeared to have been wet for some time. The bottles were in a display maintained by Coca-Cola Bottling Company. Two or three times a week the company cleaned the shelves and rotated the stock. Coca-Cola said that this process ensures that only minimal moisture is on bottles when they are placed in cartons. Most cartons are reused only once. Stalter sued Food City and Coca-Cola Bottling Company for damages.

a. Explain the plaintiff's claims.

b. Decide. See *Pat Stalter v. Coca-Cola Bottling Company of Arkansas and Geyer Springs Food City, Inc.,* 669 S.W.2d 460 (Ark. S.Ct. 1984).

13. Diane Elsroth was visiting her boyfriend, Michael Notarnicola, in the home of his parents. Diane complained of a headache, and Michael provided a Tylenol that his mother had bought earlier that week. Michael noted nothing unusual about the Tylenol packaging. After consuming two Tylenol capsules, Diane went to bed. She died during the night. The medical examiner concluded that the Tylenol had been contaminated with potassium cyanide. The murder was not solved. The evidence established that the tampering with the Tylenol occurred after the product left the manufacturer's control. The packaging included a foil seal glued to the mouth of the container, a "shrink seal" around the neck and cap of the container, and a box with its ends glued shut. The manufacturer, McNeil, a wholly owned subsidiary of Johnson & Johnson, knew through its research that a determined, sophisticated tamperer could breach the packaging and reseal it in a manner that would not be visible to the average consumer. John Elsroth sued McNeil on behalf of Diane's estate. Was the Tylenol packaging defective in design? Explain. See *Elsroth v. Johnson & Johnson,* 700 F. Supp. 151 (S.D.N.Y. 1988).

14. In an attempt to commit suicide, Connie Daniell locked herself in the trunk of her 1973 Ford LTD automobile, where she remained for nine days before being freed. During the nine days, Daniell changed her mind and sought to escape, but she was unable to do so. She sued the Ford Motor Company for the injuries she sustained from her entrapment.

a. What claims would she bring?

b. Decide those claims. Explain. See *Daniell v. Ford Motor Company,* 581 F. Supp. 728 (N.Mex. 1984).

15. Plaintiff James L. Maguire was seriously injured when the motor vehicle in which he was a passenger was struck by another motor vehicle. Plaintiff alleges that Vikki Paulson, the driver of the other vehicle, was intoxicated at the time of the accident. Following the accident, Paulson entered guilty pleas to (1) operating a motor vehicle while under the influence of alcohol, (2) involuntary manslaughter as a consequence of the death of another passenger riding with Maguire, and (3) failure to stop at a stop sign. During the time in question in the case, Pabst Brewing Company had engaged in an advertising campaign promoting the sale of its products. Plaintiff claims the defendant Pabst was liable for his injuries because (among other claims) its advertising promoting the consumption of alcohol by those who drove to taverns constituted a danger to highway safety and because the brewer had failed to warn consumers of the dangers of alcohol consumption. Decide. Explain. See *Maguire v. Pabst Brewing Company,* 387 N.W.2d 565 (Iowa 1986).

16. Twenty-year-old Stephen Pavlik died from inhaling Zeus-brand butane while trying to "get high." His estate sued the Zeus maker, Lane. The fuel came in a small can with a printed warning reading, "DO NOT BREATHE SPRAY." The plaintiff argued that the can was defective because the warning inadequately expressed the hazard. A federal district court ruled that Pavlik was aware of the danger so the warning was adequate, and in any case, a warning would have had no effect so proximate cause could not exist. That decision was appealed. How would you rule on that appeal? Explain. See *Pavlik v. Lane Limited,* 135 F.3d 876 (3d Cir. 1998).

Notes

1. Timothy K. Smith, "Liability Costs Drive Small-Plane Business Back into Pilots' Barns," *The Wall Street Journal,* December 11, 1991, p. A1.

2. Mike Clancy, "Cessna Will Once Again Make Small Aircraft," *The Des Moines Register,* March 15, 1995, p. 8S.

3. Smith, "Liability Costs," p. 8.

4. Smith, "Liability Costs."

5. Barbara Carton, "Cessna Says It Will Make More Small Airplanes," *The Wall Street Journal,* March 14, 1995, p. B1.

6. Thor Valdmanis, "6 Years after Nearly Collapsing, Piper Takes Off Again," *USA TODAY,* July 3, 2001, p. 6B.

7. Valdmanis, "6 Years after Nearly Collapsing."

8. Valdmanis, "6 Years after Nearly Collapsing."

9. Valdmanis, "6 Years after Nearly Collapsing."

10. James F. Rodriguez, "Tort Reform & GARA: Is Repose Incompatible with Safety?" *47 Arizona Law Review* 577 (2005).

11. Scott E. Tarry, "The Rise and Fall of General Aviation: Product Liability, Market Structure, and Technological Innovation," *Transportation Journal* (Summer 1995). Reprinted in AllBusiness [**http://www.allbusiness.com/operations/shipping/526457-1.html**].

12. 111 N.E. 1050 (N.Y. 1916).

13. Heidi Hurd, "The Deontology of Negligence," *Boston University Law Review* 76 (April 1996), p. 249.

14. *Doss v. Town of Big Stone Gap,* 134 S.E. 563 (Va. S.Ct. 1926).

15. Aric Press, Ginny Carrol, and Steven Waldman, "Are Lawyers Burning America?" *Newsweek,* March 20, 1995, p. 30.

16. Press, Carrol, and Waldman, "Are Lawyers Burning America?" p. 34.

17. Kevin Cane, "And Now the Rest of the Story . . . About the McDonald's Coffee Lawsuit," *45 Houston Lawyer* 24 (July/August 2007).

18. Anthony Ramirez, "Hot Coffee Justice," *National Post,* April 11, 2002, p. FP15.

19. *Pat Stalter v. Coca-Cola Bottling Company of Arkansas and Geyer Springs Food City, Inc.,* 669 S.W.2d 460 (Ark. S.Ct. 1984).

20. For another judicial examination of risk-utililty and the Restatement 3d, see *Mikolajczyk v. Ford Motor Co.,* 901 N.E.2d 329 (Ill. S.Ct. 2008).

21. Press Release, "13th Annual Wacky Warning Labels Contest Winners Selected on National Television," July 12, 2010, Foundation for Fair Civil Justice [**http://www.wackywarninglabelstv.com/**].

22. "Generator Danger Warning," The Consumer Product Safety Commission, January, 2007 [**http://www.cpsc.gov/generator.html**].

23. *Whitlock v. University of Denver,* 712 P.2d 1072 (Col. Ct. App. 1985).

24. *University of Denver v. Whitlock,* 744 P.2d 54 (Col. S.Ct. 1987).

25. 27 Cal. Rptr. 697, 377 P.2d 897 (Cal. S.Ct. 1963).

26. Associated Press, "California Jury Awards Former Smoker $28 Billion," *Waterloo/Cedar Falls Courier,* October 6, 2002, p. A10.

27. Associated Press, "Huge Awards Aside, Few Companies Forced to Write Big Checks," *Waterloo/Cedar Falls Courier,* October 12, 1997, p. C5.

28. Dionne Searcey, "Toyota Owners May Reap Little," *The Wall Street Journal,* May 20, 2010, p. B1.

29. Ibid.

30. Towers Perrin, "2009 Update on U.S. Tort Cost Trends," [www.towersperrin.com/.../getweb-cachedoc?.../2009/200912/2009_tort...].

31. Ibid.

32. Mark Robinson and Kevin Calcagnie, "Why We Need Trial Lawyers," *The Wall Street Journal,* February 24, 2010, p. A17.

33. Ibid.

34. Ibid.

35. Dan Zegart, "Tort Reform Advocates Play Fast and Loose with Facts," *The Seattle Post-Intelligencer,* November 21, 2004, p. F1.

36. Lou Dobbs, "Tort Reform Important to U.S. Future," CNN, January 6, 2005 [**http://articles.cnn.com/**].

37. Public Citizen, "Department of Justice Study Disproves Tort 'Reform' Myths," [**http://www.citizen.org**].

38. Zegart, "Tort Reform Advocates Play Fast and Loose with Facts," p. F1.

39. Tina Moore and Benjamin Lesser, "How City Is Poisoning Kids," *New York Daily News,* January 14, 2007, p. 5.

40. Jeremy Singer-Vine and Joseph Pereira, "Court Scraps Key Lead-Paint Verdict," *The Wall Street Journal,* July 2, 2008, p. B1.

41. "Sherwin-Williams States Its Case in Challenge of $7 Million Lead-Paint Verdict in Mississippi," *Durability and Coatings Industry News,* April 26, 2011 [**http://www.durabilityanddesign.com/news/?fuseaction=view&id=5493**].

Trade Regulation and Antitrust

Government Regulation of Business

After completing this chapter, students will be able to:

1. Describe the concept of market failure.

2. Explain some of the considerations involved in deciding to impose government regulations on business practice.

3. Explain the roles of the police power, the Supremacy Clause, the preemption doctrine, and the Commerce Clause in regulating business practice.

4. Explain when the federal government has exceeded its authority in regulating commerce.

5. Describe some of the ways in which state and local regulation affect business practice.

6. List some of the federal agencies that regulate business practice.

7. Identify the three broad categories of federal regulatory agencies' authority.

8. Compare and contrast the federal agencies' executive, legislative, and judicial roles.

9. Describe the executive, congressional and judicial controls placed on agency conduct to maintain appropriate "checks and balances."

10. Analyze the Federal Communications Commission (FCC) role in regulating indecency in broadcasting.

11. Evaluate criticisms of the federal regulatory process, including arguments for and against deregulation.

Part One—An Introduction

PRACTICING ETHICS   Regulate Video Games?

Prior to Christmas 2004, the *Los Angeles Times* reported on growing concerns about violence in video games:

> This holiday season, children searching for the latest video game titles could walk into a store and buy "Grand Theft Auto: San Andreas"—which lets players kill cops, steal cars, solicit prostitutes, and then beat them to get their money back. Or kids could pick up a copy of "The Guy Game" and answer questions to get busty female characters to slip out of their clothes or engage in topless rope jumping and sack races.[1]

Although video games are subject to an industry rating system, California, in 2005, passed legislation providing that "[a] person may not sell or rent a video game that has been labeled as a violent video game to a minor."[2] The act is directed to violence in the form of killing, maiming, dismembering, or sexually assaulting an image of a human being where that violence (a) appeals to a deviant or morbid interest of minors, is patently offensive based on contemporary community standards, and lacks serious literary, artistic, political, or scientific value for minors or where (b) the game enables the player to inflict serious bodily injury on humanlike characters in a manner that is especially heinous, cruel or depraved.

The video industry sued to block the law. That challenge reached the United States Supreme Court in 2011 where the California law was struck down as a violation of free speech rights.[3] The Court ruled that the statute was a content-based restraint on speech requiring California to establish a compelling reason for the law; a standard the state could not satisfy. Studies linking violent video games and harm to children have not established a clear causal relationship between the two. The majority further reasoned that video games are like books, plays and other forms of protected expression. Video games, they said, communicate ideas and even social messages. While the state has the power to protect children, that power does not extend to restricting the ideas children can receive. Some justices pointed specifically to the vagueness of the law that left uncertainty about which games would have been restricted by the law.[4]

Video Game Addiction?

Notwithstanding the Supreme Court's conclusion that California was unable to show a sufficient link between violent video games and damage to children, some of the evidence about video game use generally is disquieting. For example, a 2009 Iowa State University study found that almost one in ten American children, ages 8 to 18 are addicted to video games (the study was not limited to games) in much the way some people are addicted to drugs or gambling.[5] Indeed, South Korea has opened more than 100 clinics to treat video-game addiction. On the other hand, economist Lawrence Katz recently offered the interesting speculation (not yet supported by research) that video game use may serve society by holding down crime. Katz suspects that playing video games may have kept young and idle people, especially young men, busy and less frustrated during the nation's ongoing recession so that they were less likely to be out committing crimes as has happened historically in difficult economic times.[6] [For the Entertainment Software Rating Board, see **http://www.esrb.org/index-js.jsp**]

Questions

1.   *a.* In your judgment, are violent and sexually explicit videos harmful to children?

   b. Would an ethical, socially responsible video store owner decline to sell violent or sexually explicit videos if evidence revealed that those videos often reach children? Explain.

2.   *a.* Will the free market and industry ethics satisfactorily protect society from any harm that may emerge from video game playing or is legal intervention necessary? Explain.

   b. Should the First Amendment protect video games from government oversight? Explain.

3.   A Scottish firm, Traffic Games, released a video game that allows players to simulate the assassination of former U.S. President John F. Kennedy. The game purportedly was

designed to undermine assassination conspiracy theories by showing that one person could have killed the president. The game allows slow-motion tracking of the bullets through the president's image, and blood can be viewed by pressing a blood effects button. Is the production and sale of this game an immoral act? Explain.

4. *a.* Do we need to protect children from video games, whether violent or not? Explain.
   b. If so, would government intervention be the most effective way of offering that protection? Explain.

How Much Government?

In this chapter and all those that follow our central question will be: How much government do we need? In the first three chapters we looked at the role of the free market and ethics as "regulators" of business behavior. In Chapters 4 through 7 we introduced the foundations of the American legal system. Now we turn to the role the law plays in supplementing the market and ethics/self-regulation. The alleged link between video game use and social problems, including violence, is one relatively small example of an enormous array of disputes about the optimal balance between unconstrained business practice and government intervention in the market. America's ongoing financial struggles, healthcare reform, the near-death of giants like General Motors, the Gulf Oil spill, continuing illegal immigration, climate change—these are several of the most visible areas of public policy concern. Do we need more rules to address these problems or does the market in combination with corporate ethics/social responsibility provide the most efficient, effective response? How do we decide when a new rule is needed?

Why Regulation?

Market Failure

In theory, government intervention in a free enterprise economy would be justified only when the market is unable to serve the public interest—that is, in instances of market failure. Market failure is attributed to certain inherent imperfections in the market itself:

Imperfect Information

Can the consumer choose the best pain reliever in the absence of complete information about the characteristics of the competing products? An efficient free market presumes reasoned decisions about production and consumption. Reasoned decisions require adequate information. Because we cannot have perfect information and often will not have adequate information, the government, it is argued, may impose regulations either to improve the available information or to diminish the unfavorable effect of inadequate information. Hence, we have, for example, labeling mandates for consumer goods, licensure requirements for many occupations, and health standards for the processing and sale of goods.

The 2001 Nobel Prize for economics was awarded to three Americans whose research indicates that markets cannot behave as theorized—that is, rationally and efficiently—in part because buyers and sellers often do not have the information they need to make the best decisions. Put another way, their research demonstrates that we often face situations of *asymmetric information* where some parties to a transaction simply know more than the other parties to that transaction, with the result that optimal efficiency cannot be achieved. Furthermore, recent research in behavioral economics suggests that we often pursue social goals and act in other altruistic ways that are contrary to our direct, personal economic interests. More alarmingly, a new line of research suggests that decision making among male financial traders is significantly influenced by testosterone levels thus supporting the revisionist view that financial decisions may prove to be less a product of rational calculus than we have long believed.[7] Thus, while our free market system assumes rational decision making, we might more accurately recognize that we operate with limited or *bounded rationality*. Hence, government intervention might be appropriate.

Monopoly

Of course, the government intervenes to thwart anticompetitive behaviors throughout the marketplace. (That process is addressed in Chapters 10 and 11.) Historically, the primary concern in this area was how to deal with the so-called *natural monopoly* where a single large firm, such as a utility, was more efficient (a natural monopoly) than several small ones. Today, attention in the monopoly area is largely directed to anticompetitive conduct such as price fixing and abuse of market dominance that results in a reduction of open, efficient competition.

Externalities

When all the costs and benefits of a good or service are not fully internalized or absorbed, those costs or benefits fall elsewhere as what economists have labeled *externalities, neighborhood effects, or spillovers*. Pollution is a characteristic example of a *negative externality*. The environment is used without charge as an ingredient in the production process (commonly as a receptacle for waste). Consequently, the product is underpriced. The producer and consumer do not pay the full social cost of the product, so those remaining costs are thrust on parties external to the transaction. Government regulation is sometimes considered necessary to place the full cost on those who generated it, which in turn is expected to result in less wasteful use of resources. *Positive externalities* are those in which a producer confers benefits not required by the market. An example of such a positive externality is a business firm that, through no direct market compulsion, landscapes its grounds and develops a sculpture garden to contribute to the aesthetic quality of its neighborhood. Positive externalities ordinarily are not the subject of regulation.

Public Goods

Some goods and services cannot be provided through the pricing system because we have no method for excluding those who choose not to pay. For such public goods, the added cost of benefiting one person is zero or nearly so, and, in any case, no one can effectively be denied the benefits of the activity. National defense, insect eradication, and pollution control are examples of this phenomenon. Presumably most individuals would refuse to voluntarily pay for what others would receive free. Thus, in the absence of government regulations, public goods would not be produced in adequate quantities.

Regulatory Life Cycle?

These market failures and other forces, to be explained later, sometimes lead to government intervention such as the Clean Air Act (see Chapter 17) or the Occupational Safety and

Health Act (see Chapter 12). Looking at the historical record, law school dean Joseph Tomain argues that a rather predictable pattern or life cycle typically emerges when the government decides to regulate an industry. Stage One in Tomain's life cycle is the free market itself, the period when government regulation is absent from the market in question. In Stage Two, a market failure is identified, suggesting the need for government intervention. In Stage Three, government regulation is imposed in the form of a rule (such as a minimum drinking age). In Stage Four, regulatory failure occurs because, in brief, we believe the benefits of the rule in question no longer exceed its costs. In Stage Five, the government may respond with regulatory reform to correct the failure, or it may move to Stage Six, where the regulation in question is simply eliminated. The market, thus fully deregulated, has returned to Stage One (the free market) and the regulatory life cycle is complete.[8]

Wall Street's financial collapse and our ongoing recession seem to support Tomain's regulatory cycle hypothesis. Ben Bernanke, Federal Reserve chair, attributed our recent housing bubble and the subsequent financial collapse to regulatory failure.[9] Rather than deregulation as a solution, however, Bernanke called for (and, generally, has received) greater financial oversight authority for the Federal Reserve; that is, he called for greater supervision by the government as the best way to prevent a future financial calamity. Of course, Bernanke's many critics believe excessive government intervention was the root cause of the housing collapse and that reduced, rather than increased, regulation is the better remediation. [To read about and submit comments on proposed rules affecting small businesses, see **http://www.sba.gov/advo/laws/law_regalerts.html**]

Steroids

The steroid scandal in baseball allegedly involving Roger Clemens, Barry Bonds, Jason Giambi, and other major league stars led the *The Des Moines Register* to argue for the value of regulation:

> Businesses forever complain about being regulated, but the truth is that reasonable regulation is good for business. It's easier to sell insurance to people who know regulators are helping keep the insurance companies solvent. It's easier to sell stocks to investors who think the SEC is on the job and easier to sell food to shoppers who trust the labels the FDA requires. Name an industry, and a case can be made that regulation helps it.
>
> Unfortunately, the barons of baseball never figured that out. The owners and players in big-league baseball resisted any regulation of performance-enhancing chemicals in their business.

*   *   *   *   *

> Baseball had slipped in the affections of many Americans even before the scandal. Now, it's doubtful the sport can ever reclaim its good name.

Question

1. In your view, should the government regulate performance-enhancing drug use in sports, or will self-regulation by the sports be sufficient?

Source: Editorial, "Baseball Barons Betrayed Game," *The Des Moines Register,* December 14, 2004, p. 8A.

Philosophy and Politics

Correction of market failure arguably explains the full range of government regulation of business, but an alternative or perhaps supplemental explanation lies in the political process. Three general arguments have emerged.

1. One view is that regulation is necessary for the protection and general welfare of the public. We find the government engaging in regulatory efforts designed to achieve a more equitable distribution of income and wealth (such as Social Security and the minimum wage). Many believe government intervention in the market is necessary to stabilize the economy, thus curbing the problems of recession, inflation, and unemployment. Affirmative action programs seek to compensate for racism and sexism. We even find the government protecting us from ourselves, both for our benefit and for the well-being of the larger society (consider seatbelt requirements).

2. Another view is that regulation is developed at the request of industry and is operated primarily for the benefit of industry. Here the various subsidies and tax advantages afforded to business might be cited. In numerous instances, government regulation has been effective in reducing or entirely eliminating the entry of competitors. Government regulation has also permitted legalized price-fixing in some industries. Of course, it may be that regulation is often initiated primarily for the public welfare, but industry eventually "captures" the regulatory process and ensures its continuation for the benefit of the industry. On the other hand, some corporations seek government standards so they can do what is best for society without being undercut by their less socially responsible competitors.

3. Finally, bureaucrats who perform government regulation are themselves a powerful force in maintaining and expanding that regulation.

Bring Back Danger?

We often count on government rules to shelter us from dangers that the market seems ill-suited to deal with. Hence, we created the federal Food and Drug Administration (FDA) to protect us from dangerous food, drugs, and medical devices (see Chapter 15). But sometimes rules do harm. Indeed, safety may not always be in our best interest. Some critics argue that boys, in particular, need a certain amount of danger in their lives. Brothers Conn and Hal Iggulden wrote *The Dangerous Book for Boys* as a manual of activities for boys. Their book describes how to make a bow and arrow, hunt and cook a rabbit, build a tree house, set a trip wire, and so on. They believe our "safety culture" has gone a bit too far. They point to that bygone era when every boy had a jackknife. They believe that taking risks is important to a boy's joy and maturation.

Questions

1. Do you agree with the Iggulden brothers that we should allow boys to experience a certain amount of danger in their lives?

2. How about girls? [See Andrea Buchanan and Miriam Peskowitz, *The Daring Book for Girls*. For an online discussion about giving children greater freedom, see **http:// freerangekids.workpress.com**]

The Constitutional Foundation of Business Regulation

The Commerce Clause of the U.S. Constitution broadly specifies the power accorded to the federal government to regulate business activity. Article I, Section 8 of the Constitution provides that "The Congress shall have the power . . . to regulate Commerce with foreign Nations, and among the several States, and with the Indian Tribes." State authority to regulate commerce resides in the *police power* specified by the Constitution. Police power refers to the right of the state governments to promote the public health, safety, morals, and general welfare by regulating persons and property within each state's jurisdiction. The states have, in turn, delegated portions of the police power to local government units.

Commerce Clause Examined

The Commerce Clause, as interpreted by the judiciary, affords Congress exclusive jurisdiction over foreign commerce. States and localities, nevertheless, sometimes seek in various ways to regulate foreign commerce. For example, a state may seek, directly or indirectly, to impose a tax on foreign goods that compete with those locally grown or manufactured. Such efforts are unconstitutional violations of the Commerce Clause and thus are unenforceable.

Federal authority over "commerce among the several states," that is*, interstate commerce,* affords the federal government very broad power to regulate commercial activities across the United States and was designed to create an open, effectively borderless market throughout the nation, wherein goods would move freely among the states, unimpeded by state and local tariffs and duties. The Constitution does not, however, expressly forbid state regulation of interstate commerce. As with foreign commerce, the states and localities pass laws to influence interstate commerce, often to favor local economic interests. The judiciary has aggressively curbed those efforts, and in the process, the reach of the federal government has been dramatically expanded. Even purely *intrastate* activities can be regulated by the federal government if they have a substantial effect on interstate commerce. In the 1942 case *Wickard v. Filburn,*[10] the U.S. Supreme Court, in interpreting a federal statute regulating the production and sale of wheat, found that one farmer's production of 23 acres of homegrown and largely home-consumed wheat, in combination with other similarly situated farmers growing and consuming wheat locally, could substantially affect interstate commerce and thus was subject to federal regulation. In 2005, the Supreme Court affirmed the Wickard reasoning in an interesting California case, *Gonzalez v. Raich,*[11] involving the federal government's constitutional authority to regulate the use of medical marijuana.

In 1996, California became the first of 10 states to decriminalize the doctor-approved medical use of marijuana. The federal Controlled Substances Act (CSA), on the other hand, forbids the use, cultivation, or possession of marijuana for any purpose. A Californian, Angel Raich, who, under a doctor's prescription, used marijuana for pain control, challenged the application of the CSA against California medical marijuana users. The heart of her claim was that the Commerce Clause does not give the federal government

> Angel Raich used marijuana for pain control.

the authority to regulate the noncommercial cultivation and personal, medical use of marijuana that does not cross state lines. She won at the U.S. Court of Appeals for the Ninth Circuit, but the U.S. Supreme Court, by a 6–3 vote, ruled against Raich. Addressing the central question, the Court reasoned that the wholly *intrastate* use of marijuana had a substantial effect on *interstate* commerce in marijuana and thus was subject to federal regulation, as the Court had ruled decades earlier in *Wickard.* Personal consumption of marijuana, even for medical purposes, has the potential to displace demand for marijuana in the illegal interstate market, thus substantially affecting interstate commerce. To rule otherwise would hinder federal enforcement of the national drug market because authorities would not be able to determine whether marijuana in the possession of a person was grown locally or shipped across state lines.

Too Much Federal Power?

For the long term, the significance of the medical marijuana decision lies in its Commerce Clause reasoning. The decision appears to reaffirm the broad reach of federal power over activities that are economic in some sense. Dissenting in *Raich,* Supreme Court Justice Thomas warned:

> If Congress can regulate this under the Commerce Clause, then it can regulate virtually anything—and the federal government is no longer one of limited and enumerated powers.[12]

Of course, we must remember that the case dealt with the sensitive subject of unlawful drug use, where the courts are more inclined to defer to federal policy. Furthermore, in recent years, the Supreme Court issued two important opinions apparently designed to demonstrate that the Commerce Clause does not accord unlimited power to the federal government. In the 1995 *United States v. Lopez* decision[13] the Supreme Court clearly spoke for states' rights. In 1990 the federal government approved the Gun-Free School Zones Act, which forbade "any individual knowingly to possess a firearm at a place that [he] knows . . . is a school zone."[14] Congress claimed that gun possession in school zones would increase violence, retard learning, and discourage travel, thus affecting commerce.

A 12th-grade San Antonio, Texas, student carried an unloaded, concealed gun into his high school.

Lopez, a 12th-grade San Antonio, Texas, student carried an unloaded, concealed gun into his high school and was charged with violating the act. His case reached the Supreme Court, where he claimed and the Court agreed that Congress did not have the constitutional authority to regulate the matter. By a 5-4 vote, the Court held that the possession of a gun at a school is not an economic activity that could, even if repeated elsewhere, have a substantial effect on interstate commerce.

Strengthening its *Lopez* reasoning, the U.S. Supreme Court in the 2000 *Brzonkala* case[15] ruled by a 5–4 vote that Congress exceeded its Commerce Clause authority in approving some portions of the federal Violence Against Women Act (VAWA). The law allowed women who had been victims of gender-based violence to sue in federal court even though the crimes did not directly involve more than one state. In debating VAWA, Congress held hearings and developed a record on the aggregate economic impact of violence against women, including driving up medical costs and discouraging women from traveling and from holding jobs, but the Supreme Court said Congress did not have the power to regulate noneconomic violent crime because it does not have a substantial effect on interstate commerce. To rule otherwise, the Court said, might "obliterate" the constitutional distinction between federal and state/local authority.

The case involved a woman, Brzonkala, who claimed she was raped by two football players, Morrison and Crawford, when all three were students at Virginia Polytechnic Institute:

> Brzonkala alleges that soon after she met Morrison and Crawford, the two defendants pinned her down on a bed in her dormitory and forcibly raped her. Afterward, Morrison told Brzonkala, "You better not have any f* *ing diseases." And, subsequently, Morrison announced publicly in the dormitory's dining hall, "I like to get girls drunk and f* * * the s* * * out of them."[16]

> Brzonkala claimed she was raped by two football players.

After Brzonkala complained to the university, Morrison was found guilty of abusive conduct by the VPI judicial committee and was suspended for one year, but that punishment was subsequently lifted.[17] Brzonkala then sued for civil damages in federal court under the VAWA. As explained above, Brzonkala eventually lost, however, when the Supreme Court invalidated the portions of the VAWA that she was relying on by ruling that the acts of violence the VAWA was aimed at did not have a substantial effect on interstate commerce. [For the federal Violence Against Women Office, see **http://www.ovw.usdoj.gov/**]

Our Guns: Feds Must Stay Out?

Sixty-five-year-old Gary Marbut of Missoula, Montana, a self-employed shooting-range supplier, manufactures .22-caliber rifles he calls Montana Buckaroos. He produces and sells the guns exclusively in Montana from materials originating in Montana, and the guns are stamped "Made in Montana." He also drafted and promoted the Montana Firearms Freedom Act which has been adopted in Montana and which provides, generally, that Montana guns cannot be subject to federal regulation if made and sold only on an intrastate basis. Other states have approved similar legislation. Marbut (and others) recently brought suit seeking a court order affirming the right in Montana to manufacture and sell guns free of federal regulation. Marbut lost at the federal district court level, and has appealed to the federal Ninth Circuit Court of Appeals. Marbut hopes to reach the Supreme Court to challenge *Wickard v. Filburn* and federal regulatory authority.

Sources: Jess Bravin, "A Gun Activist Takes Aim at U.S. Regulatory Power," *The Wall Street Journal,* July 14, 2011, [**http://online.wsj.com/**]; and *Montana Shooting Sports Association v. Holder,* 2010 U.S. Dist. LEXIS 110891 (D. Montana).

The classic decision that follows illustrates the importance of Commerce Clause reasoning. In this case Congress used its economic authority under the Commerce Clause to open public accommodations (hotels, restaurants, and the like) to all persons, thus reshaping American social and racial practices.

Justice Clark

This is a declaratory judgment action, attacking the constitutionality of Title II of the Civil Rights Act of 1964. [The lower court found for the United States.]

1. THE FACTUAL BACKGROUND AND CONTENTIONS OF THE PARTIES

. . . Appellant owns and operates the Heart of Atlanta Motel, which has 216 rooms available to transient guests. The motel is located on Courtland Street, two blocks from downtown Peachtree Street. It is readily accessible to interstate highways 75 and 85 and state highways 23 and 41. Appellant solicits patronage from outside the State of Georgia through various national advertising media, including magazines of national circulation; it maintains over 50 billboards and highway signs within the state, soliciting patronage for the motel; it accepts convention trade from outside Georgia, and approximately 75 percent of its registered guests are from out of state. Prior to passage of the act the motel had followed a practice of refusing to rent rooms to Negroes, and it alleged that it intended to continue to do so. In an effort to perpetuate that policy this suit was filed.

The appellant contends that Congress in passing this act exceeded its power to regulate commerce under [Article I] of the Constitution of the United States. . . .

The appellees counter that the unavailability to Negroes of adequate accommodations interferes significantly with interstate travel, and that Congress, under the Commerce Clause, has power to remove such obstructions and restraints. . . .

[A]ppellees proved the refusal of the motel to accept Negro transients after the passage of the act. The district court sustained the constitutionality of the sections of the act under attack and issued a permanent injunction. . . . It restrained the appellant from "[r]efusing to accept Negroes as guests in the motel by reason of their race or color" and from "[m]aking any distinction whatever upon the basis of race or color in the availability of the goods, services, facilities, privileges, advantages, or accommodations offered or made available to the guests of the motel, or to the general public, within or upon any of the premises of the Heart of Atlanta Motel, Inc."

2. THE HISTORY OF THE ACT

. . . The act as finally adopted was most comprehensive, undertaking to prevent through peaceful and voluntary settlement discrimination in voting, as well as in places of accommodation and public facilities, federally secured programs, and in employment. Since Title II is the only portion under attack here, we confine our consideration to those public accommodation provisions.

3. TITLE II OF THE ACT

This Title is divided into seven sections beginning with Section 201(a), which provides,

> "All persons shall be entitled to the full and equal enjoyment of the goods, services, facilities, privileges, advantages, and accommodations of any place of public accommodation, as defined in this section, without discrimination or segregation on the ground of race, color, religion, or national origin."

4. APPLICATION OF TITLE II TO HEART OF ATLANTA MOTEL

It is admitted that the operation of the motel brings it within the provisions of Section 201(a) of the act and that appellant refused to provide lodging for transient Negroes because of their race or color and that it intends to continue that policy unless restrained.

The sole question posed is, therefore, the constitutionality of the Civil Rights Act of 1964 as applied to these facts. . . .

[Part 5 omitted.]

6. THE BASIS OF CONGRESSIONAL ACTION

While the act as adopted carried no congressional findings, the record of its passage through each house is replete with evidence of the burdens that discrimination by race or color places upon interstate commerce. . . . This testimony included the fact that our people have become increasingly mobile with millions of people of all races traveling from state to state; that Negroes in particular have been the subject of discrimination in transient accommodations, having to travel great distances to secure the same; that often they have been unable to obtain accommodations and have had to call upon friends to put them up overnight, and that these conditions have become so acute as to require the listing of available lodging for Negroes in a special guidebook which was itself "dramatic testimony to the difficulties" Negroes encounter in travel. These exclusionary practices were found to be nationwide, the Under Secretary of Commerce testifying that there is "no question that this discrimination in the North still exists to a large degree" and in the West and Midwest as well. This testimony indicated a qualitative as well as quantitative effect on interstate travel by Negroes. The former was the obvious impairment of the Negro traveler's pleasure and convenience that resulted when he continually was uncertain of finding lodging. As for the latter, there was evidence that this uncertainty stemming from racial discrimination had the effect of discouraging travel on the part of a substantial portion of the Negro community. This was the conclusion not only of the Under Secretary of Commerce but also of the Administrator of the Federal Aviation Agency, who wrote the Chairman of the Senate Commerce Committee that it was his "belief that air commerce is adversely affected by the denial to a substantial segment of the traveling public of adequate and desegregated public accommodations." We shall not burden this opinion with further details since the voluminous testimony presents overwhelming evidence that discrimination by hotels and motels impedes interstate travel.

7. THE POWER OF CONGRESS OVER INTERSTATE TRAVEL

The power of Congress to deal with these obstructions depends on the meaning of the Commerce Clause.

* * * * *

In short, the determinative test of the exercise of power by the Congress under the Commerce Clause is simply whether the activity sought to be regulated is "commerce which concerns more States than one" and has a real and substantial relation to the national interest. Let us now turn to this facet of the problem.

* * * * *

The same interest in protecting interstate commerce which led Congress to deal with segregation in interstate carriers and the white-slave traffic has prompted it to extend the exercise of its power to gambling, to criminal enterprises, to deceptive practices in the sale of products, to fraudulent security transactions, and to racial discrimination by owners and managers of terminal restaurants. . . .

That Congress was legislating against moral wrongs in many of these areas rendered its enactments no less valid. In framing Title II of this act Congress was also dealing with what it considered a moral problem. But that fact does not detract from the overwhelming evidence of the disruptive effect the racial discrimination has had on commercial intercourse. It was this burden which empowered Congress to enact appropriate legislation, and, given this basis for the exercise of its power, Congress was not restricted by the fact that the particular obstruction to interstate commerce with which it was dealing was also deemed a moral and social wrong.

It is said that the operation of the motel here is of a purely local character. But, assuming this to be true, "[i]f it is interstate commerce that feels the pinch, it does not matter how local the operation which applies the squeeze."

* * * * *

Thus the power of Congress to promote interstate commerce also includes the power to regulate the local incidents thereof, including local activities in both the states of origin and destination, which might have a substantial and harmful effect upon that commerce. One need only examine the evidence which we have discussed above to see that Congress may—as it has—prohibit racial discrimination by motels serving travelers, however "local" their operations may appear.

* * * * *

The only questions are (1) whether Congress had a rational basis for finding that racial discrimination by motels affected commerce, and (2) if it had such a basis, whether the means it selected to eliminate that evil are reasonable and appropriate. If they are, appellant has no "right" to select its guests as it sees fit, free from governmental regulation.

* * * * *

It is doubtful if in the long run appellant will suffer economic loss as a result of the act. Experience is to the contrary where discrimination is completely obliterated as to all public accommodations. But whether this be true or not is of no consequence since this Court has specifically held that the fact that a "member of the class which is regulated may suffer economic losses not shared by others . . . has never been a barrier" to such legislation. . . .

We, therefore, conclude that the action of the Congress in the adoption of the act as applied here to a motel which concededly serves interstate travelers is within the power granted it by the Commerce Clause of the Constitution, as interpreted by this Court for 140 years. . . .

Affirmed.

Questions

1. In your judgment, does the Commerce Clause afford the federal government the authority to regulate a local business like the Heart of Atlanta motel? Explain.

2. Should the federal government regulate local business to further the cause of racial equity? Explain.

3. What arguments were offered by the government to establish that the Heart of Atlanta racial policy affected interstate commerce? Are you persuaded by those arguments? Explain.

4. What test did the Court articulate to determine when Congress has the power to pass legislation based on the Commerce Clause?

5. Ollie's Barbecue, a neighborhood restaurant in Birmingham, Alabama, discriminated against black customers. McClung brought suit to test the application of the public accommodations section of the Civil Rights Act of 1964 to his restaurant. In the suit, the government offered no evidence to show that the restaurant ever had served interstate customers or that it was likely to do so. Decide the case. See *Katzenbach v. McClung*, 379 U.S. 294 (1964).

6. Juan Paul Robertson was charged with various narcotics offenses and with violating the federal Racketeer Influenced and Corrupt Organizations Act (RICO) by investing the proceeds from his unlawful activities in an Alaskan gold mine. He paid for some mining equipment in Los Angeles and had it shipped to Alaska. He hired seven out-of-state employees to work in the Alaskan mine. Most of the resulting gold was sold in Alaska, although Robertson transported $30,000 in gold out of the state. He was convicted on the RICO charge, but appealed claiming that the gold mine was not engaged in or affecting interstate commerce. Was Robertson's gold mine engaged in or affecting interstate commerce? Explain. See *United States v. Juan Paul Robertson*, 115 S.Ct. 1732 (1995).

Supremacy Clause

Sometimes state or local law conflicts with federal law. As we discussed in Chapter 5, such situations are resolved by the Supremacy Clause of the Constitution (Article VI, paragraph 2), which provides that "This Constitution and the Laws of the United States . . . shall be the Supreme Law of the Land." As explained in Chapter 5, ours is a federalist form of government wherein we divide authority among federal, state, and local units of government. Conflicts are inevitable, but each level of government brings strengths to the process. State rules benefit from being enacted by bodies very close to the people themselves. On the other hand, optimal efficiency, especially for the business community, often demands one uniform federal rule rather than a patchwork of 50 state rules.[18]

In the event of an irreconcilable conflict between federal and state law, the Supremacy Clause, as interpreted by the Supreme Court, provides that federal law will preempt (supersede) state or local law rendering it unconstitutional. In general, Supreme Court decisions have affirmed the federal government's regulatory authority even when faced with conflicting state rules. Were it not so, we would have great difficulty in achieving a unified national policy on any issue. Recent Supreme Court preemption decisions have been split; some allowing state law to stand despite conflicts with federal law, others being struck down.[19]

Regardless, the federalism doctrine has become a major source of conflict between states' rights activists and those favoring more unified, federal doctrine. Tea Party supporters and others are making the case for a renewal of attention to the Tenth Amendment command: "The powers not delegated to the United States by the Constitution, nor prohibited by it to the States, are reserved to the States, respectively, or to the people."

> The challengers believe the federal government has reached beyond its constitutional authority.

The challengers believe the federal government has reached beyond its constitutional authority in such highly charged policy disputes as the 2010 health care reform bill (Patient Protection and Affordable Care Act; sometimes called ObamaCare) which will require Americans to carry health insurance and otherwise expands federal control over health care. The bill is currently being challenged in court. [For more on this conflict from the states' rights perspective, see **http://www.tenthamendmentcenter.com/**]

Part Two—State and Local Regulation of Interstate Commerce

As noted, the states via their constitutional police power have the authority to regulate commerce within their jurisdictions for the purpose of maintaining public health, safety, and morals. We have seen, however, that the Commerce Clause accords the federal government broad authority over commerce. As explained, the federal government has exclusive authority over foreign commerce. Purely intrastate commerce, having no significant effect on interstate commerce, is within the exclusive regulatory jurisdiction of the states and localities. Of course, purely intrastate commerce is uncommon. The confusion arises in the middle ground of interstate commerce where regulation by the federal government or state governments or both may be permissible. While federal government regulation of interstate commerce is pervasive, it is not exclusive, especially in matters involving the states' police powers.

Here we are concerned with commerce that is clearly interstate but that is subjected to state and/or local regulation. The issue is whether that regulation is unconstitutional because it (1) *discriminates* against interstate commerce or (2) *unduly burdens* interstate commerce such that the burden imposed clearly exceeds the local benefits.

In the *Granholm* case that follows, we see elements of the continuing conflict between federal and state control of interstate commerce, especially in matters of health and safety (police power). At the commercial level, the case is about another classic conflict: free trade versus protectionism. Can states lawfully protect their local wineries from out-of-state competition? The lower courts were divided on the question of whether the Commerce Clause of the federal constitution is violated when a state permits in-state wineries to ship directly to in-state customers while not permitting out-of-state wineries to do the same. Historically, only a few states had allowed wineries to ship directly to customers; but gradually about half of the states allowed direct shipments, resulting in a confusing situation where some states allowed all shipments, some permitted in-state shipments only, and some forbade all shipments. In the 5–4 decision that follows, the Supreme Court narrowly resolved the split in the lower courts. The central question facing the Court was the conflict between the requirements of the Commerce Clause versus the requirements of the Twenty-First Amendment to the United States Constitution. That Amendment ended Prohibition in 1933 and gave the states broad authority to regulate the sale of alcohol.

> Can states lawfully protect their local wineries from out-of-state competition?

LEGAL BRIEFCASE

Granholm v. Heald   544 U.S. 460 (2005)

Justice Kennedy

These consolidated cases present challenges to state laws regulating the sale of wine from out-of-state wineries to consumers in Michigan and New York. The details and mechanics of the two regulatory schemes differ, but the object and effect of the laws are the same: to allow in-state wineries to sell wine directly to consumers in that state but to prohibit out-of-state wineries from doing so, or, at the least, to make direct sales impractical from an economic standpoint. It is evident that the object and design of the Michigan and New York statutes is to grant in-state wineries a competitive advantage over wineries located beyond the states' borders.

* * * * *

I

Like many other states, Michigan and New York regulate the sale and importation of alcoholic beverages, including wine, through a three-tier distribution system. Separate licenses are required for producers, wholesalers, and retailers. . . . We have held previously that states can mandate a three-tier distribution scheme in the exercise of their authority under the Twenty-First Amendment. As relevant to today's cases, though, the three-tier system is, in broad terms and with refinements to be discussed, mandated by Michigan and New York only for sales from out-of-state wineries. In-state wineries, by contrast, can obtain a license for direct sales to consumers. The differential treatment between in-state and out-of-state wineries constitutes explicit discrimination against interstate commerce.

This discrimination substantially limits the direct sale of wine to consumers. . . . From 1994 to 1999, consumer spending on direct wine shipments doubled, reaching $500 million per year, or 3 percent of all wine sales. . . . [T]he number of small wineries in the United States has significantly increased. At the same time, the wholesale market has consolidated. . . . The increasing winery-to-wholesaler ratio means that many small wineries do not produce enough wine or have sufficient consumer demand for their wine to make it economical for wholesalers to carry their products. This has led many small wineries to rely on direct shipping to reach new markets. Technological improvements, in particular the ability of wineries to sell wine over the Internet, have helped make direct shipments an attractive sales channel.

Approximately 26 states allow some direct shipping of wine, with various restrictions. Thirteen of these states have reciprocity laws, which allow direct shipment from wineries outside the state, provided the state of origin affords similar nondiscriminatory treatment. In many parts of the country, however, state laws that prohibit or severely restrict direct shipments deprive consumers of access to the direct market.

The wine producers in the cases before us are small wineries that rely on direct consumer sales as an important part of their businesses. Domaine Alfred, one of the plaintiffs in the Michigan suit, is a small winery located in San Luis Obispo, California. . . . Domaine Alfred has received requests for its wine from Michigan consumers but cannot fill the orders because of the state's direct shipment ban. . . .

Similarly, Juanita Swedenburg and David Lucas, two of the plaintiffs in the New York suit, operate small wineries in Virginia (the Swedenburg Estate Vineyard) and California (the Lucas Winery). Some of their customers are tourists from other states, who purchase wine while visiting the wineries. If these customers wish to obtain Swedenburg or Lucas wines after they return home, they will be unable to do so if they reside in a state with restrictive direct shipment laws. . . .

A

We first address the background of the suit challenging the Michigan direct shipment law. Most alcoholic beverages in Michigan are distributed through the state's three-tier system. Producers or distillers of alcoholic beverages, whether located in state or out of state, generally may sell only to licensed in-state wholesalers. Wholesalers, in turn, may sell only to in-state retailers. Licensed retailers are the final link in the chain, selling alcoholic beverages to consumers at retail locations and, subject to certain restrictions, through home delivery.

Under Michigan law, wine producers, as a general matter, must distribute their wine through wholesalers. There is, however, an exception for Michigan's approximately 40 in-state wineries, which are eligible for "wine maker" licenses that allow direct shipment to in-state consumers. The cost of the license varies with the size of the winery. For a small winery, the license is $25. Out-of-state wineries can apply for a $300 "outside seller of wine" license, but this license only allows them to sell to in-state wholesalers.

* * * * *

B

New York's licensing scheme is somewhat different. It channels most wine sales through the three-tier system, but it too makes exceptions for in-state wineries. As in Michigan, the result is to allow local wineries to make direct sales to consumers in New York on terms not available to out-of-state wineries. Wineries that produce only from New York grapes can apply for a license that allows direct shipment to in-state consumers. These licensees are authorized to deliver the wines of other wineries as well, but only if the wine is made from grapes "at least seventy-five percent the volume of which were grown in New York state." An out-of-state winery may ship directly to New York consumers only if it becomes a licensed New York winery, which requires the establishment of "a branch factory, office, or storeroom within the state of New York."

* * * * *

C

We consolidated these cases and granted certiorari on the following question: "'Does a state's regulatory scheme that permits in-state wineries directly to ship alcohol to consumers but restricts the ability of out-of-state wineries to do so violate the Commerce Clause in light of Section 2 of the Twenty-First Amendment?'"

II

A

Time and again this Court has held that, in all but the narrowest circumstances, state laws violate the Commerce Clause if they mandate "differential treatment of in-state and out-of-state economic interests that benefits the former and burdens the latter." This rule is essential to the foundations of the Union. The mere fact of nonresidence should not foreclose a producer in one state from access to markets in other States. States may not enact laws that burden out-of-state producers or shippers simply to give a competitive advantage to in-state businesses. This mandate "reflects a central concern of the Framers that was an immediate reason for calling the Constitutional Convention: the conviction that in order to succeed, the new Union would have to avoid the tendencies toward economic Balkanization that had plagued relations among the Colonies and later among the States under the Articles of Confederation."

* * * * *

B

The discriminatory character of the Michigan system is obvious. Michigan allows in-state wineries to ship directly to consumers, subject only to a licensing requirement. Out-of-state wineries, whether licensed or not, face a complete ban on direct shipment. The differential treatment requires all out-of-state wine, but not all in-state wine, to pass through an in-state wholesaler and retailer before reaching consumers. These two extra layers of overhead increase the cost of out-of-state wines to Michigan consumers. The cost differential, and in some cases the inability to secure a wholesaler for small shipments, can effectively bar small wineries from the Michigan market.

* * * * *

The New York scheme grants in-state wineries access to the state's consumers on preferential terms. . . . In-state producers, with the applicable licenses, can ship directly to consumers from their wineries. Out-of-state wineries must open a branch office and warehouse in New York, additional steps that drive up the cost of their wine.

* * * * *

We have no difficulty concluding that New York, like Michigan, discriminates against interstate commerce through its direct shipping laws.

III

State laws that discriminate against interstate commerce face "a virtually per se rule of invalidity." The Michigan and New York laws by their own terms violate this proscription. The two states, however, contend their statutes are saved by Section 2 of the Twenty-First Amendment, which provides,

> The Transportation or importation into any State, Territory, or possession of the United States for delivery or use therein of intoxicating liquors, in violation of the laws thereof, is hereby prohibited.

* * * * *

State policies are protected under the Twenty-First Amendment when they treat liquor produced out of state the same as its domestic equivalent. The instant cases, in contrast, involve straightforward attempts to discriminate in favor of local producers. The discrimination is contrary to the Commerce Clause and is not saved by the Twenty-First Amendment.

IV

We still must consider whether either state regime "advances a legitimate local purpose that cannot be adequately served by reasonable nondiscriminatory alternatives." The states offer two primary justifications for restricting direct shipments from out-of-state wineries: keeping alcohol out of the hands of minors and facilitating tax collection.

The states claim that allowing direct shipment from out-of-state wineries undermines their ability to police underage drinking. Minors, the states argue, have easy access to credit cards and the Internet and are likely to take advantage of direct wine shipments as a means of obtaining alcohol illegally.

The states provide little evidence that the purchase of wine over the Internet by minors is a problem. Indeed, there is some evidence to the contrary. A recent study by the staff of the FTC found that the 26 states currently allowing direct shipments report no problems with minors' increased access to wine.

* * * * *

Even were we to credit the states' largely unsupported claim that direct shipping of wine increases the risk of underage drinking, this would not justify regulations limiting only out-of-state direct shipments. As the wineries point out, minors are just as likely to order wine from in-state producers as from out-of-state ones. Michigan, for example, already allows its licensed retailers (over 7,000 of them) to deliver alcohol directly to consumers . . .

The states' tax collection justification is also insufficient.

* * * * *

Michigan and New York benefit from provisions of federal law that supply incentives for wineries to comply with state regulations. The Tax and Trade Bureau has authority to revoke a winery's federal license if it violates state law. Without a federal license, a winery cannot operate in any state. . . .

These federal remedies, when combined with state licensing regimes, adequately protect states from lost tax revenue.

* * * * *

V

If a state chooses to allow direct shipment of wine, it must do so on evenhanded terms. Without demonstrating the need for discrimination, New York and Michigan have enacted regulations that disadvantage out-of-state wine producers. Under our Commerce Clause jurisprudence, these regulations [are unconstitutional].

* * * * *

Afterword

Thirty-seven states and the District of Columbia now allow wineries to ship directly to residents, although those shipments are often limited to just a few cases or to small wineries, and the *Granholm* decision applied to wineries only so retailers, in most states, still cannot ship directly to consumers. The alcohol industry continues to resist an open market preferring instead the three-tier producer, wholesaler, retailer distribution system that has been in place for decades, in part, to restrict access by minors and to encourage a broader selection of products while affirming states rights, as explained by Paul Pisano, vice president of the National Beer Wholesalers Association: "Our concern is unelected federal judges making alcohol policy instead of state legislatures."[20] At this writing, Congress is considering federal legislation that would make it more difficult to challenge state rules restricting the sale of wine and beer. The result would likely be higher prices and much greater marketing challenges for small wineries and breweries.[21]

Questions

1. *a.* Why did the *Granholm* court strike down the New York and Michigan laws?
   b. What legal and practical justifications were presented by New York and Michigan in defense of their laws?

2. *a.* What choice now faces the states that are affected by this decision?
   b. What practical effect is this decision likely to have on the wine industry?

3. In 1988, Oneida and Herkimer counties in upstate New York created a Solid Waste Management Authority and enacted a "flow control ordinance" requiring that all waste generated within their borders was to be delivered to the Authority's newly created waste processing facilities. In 1995, six waste haulers and a trade association sued the Authority and the counties claiming that the flow control ordinance and associated regulations violated the Commerce Clause by discriminating against interstate commerce. The plaintiffs provided evidence that they could dispose of the waste much less expensively at out-of-state facilities. How would you rule in this case? Explain. See *United Haulers Assn., Inc. v. Oneida-Herkimer Solid Waste Management Authority,* 127 S.Ct 1786 (2007).

4. North Dakota rules require those bringing liquor into the state to file a monthly report, and out-of-state distillers selling to federal enclaves (military bases, in this instance) must label each item indicating that it is for consumption only within the enclave. The United States challenged those rules after sellers said they would discontinue dealing with the military bases or they would raise their prices to meet the cost of dealing with the two rules.
   a. What are the constitutional foundations of the federal government's challenge?
   b. What were the state's reasons for adopting the rules?
   c. Decide. Explain. See *North Dakota v. United States,* 495 U.S. 423 (1990).

5. Premium Standard Farms, a large Missouri hog-raising operation, was pumping manure through a two-mile-long pipe into Iowa to be spread on a farm whose operator sought the manure for fertilizer. Iowa citizens objected and asked Attorney General Tom Miller to act. Can the Iowa attorney general stop the pumping? Explain.

Globalism versus Nationalism

Reliance on rules is more common in most of Europe, for example, than in America. We believe that tendency renders the EU nations less competitive on the world scene, but Europeans often regard rules as necessary for safety and fairness. The EU recently began to phase in its new REACH regulations (Registration, Evaluation, Authorization and Restriction of Chemical substances) which, in brief, require proof of a chemical's safety before it is introduced to the market. American manufacturers must comply or be denied access to the large EU market. Harvard professor Sheila Jasanoff explained her sense of the European view of the free market/regulation balance:

> There's a strong sense in Europe and the world at large that America is letting the market have a free ride. The Europeans believe. . . that being a good global citizen in an era of sustainability means you don't just charge ahead and destroy the planet without concern for what you are doing.[22]

> The Environmental Protection Agency has banned only five chemicals since 1976.

By contrast with the European approach, in America proof of chemical safety prior to market entry is not required by law and following market entry, the Environmental Protection Agency (see Chapter 17) has banned only five chemicals (among 84,000 in use) since 1976.[23] Critics, of course, see REACH as another expensive trade barrier.

While adding new rules like REACH, the EU nations are reducing other rules. For example, a 2007 agreement substantially deregulated air travel between the United States and the European Union allowing generally open access to all cities for all carriers.[24]

Standardization

Consistent global rules achieving seamless international trade would bring dramatic savings, but that goal is far off. In auto safety, for example, a new 10-year pact among 40 nations including the United States seeks to harmonize global rules. At present, when Ford Motor Co. wants to sell its European-market cars in the United States, it must reconcile European and American rules that differ over such standards as the color of turn signals and protections for passengers not wearing seat belts (mandated in America but not in Europe). Addressing those differences, of course, means extra engineering and expense.

Too Many Signs?

Germany is trying to eliminate up to half of its 20 million traffic signs. "Germans like clear rules," said one of the civil servants working on the sign surplus. "There's a sign for toad crossings. There's one that tells drivers when they're on a 'dirty road.' Another warns them not to drive into lakes or rivers. There are 32 different signs regulating how to park at a curb."

Source: Mike Esterl, "Germans Hack at Forest of Signs Distracting Drivers," *The Wall Street Journal*, July 24, 2007, p. 1.

Questions

1. Journalist Max Frankel, writing in *The New York Times,* argued that the 21st century's "Great Revolution" would be the "collapse of nationhood."[25] He said that collapse would be powered largely by technology and the global financial market.
   a. Explain what Frankel meant.
   b. Do you agree? Explain.
   c. Frankel quoted finance experts George Shultz, William Simon, and Walter Wriston, who said, "The gold standard has been replaced by the information standard, an iron discipline that no government can evade." . . . "No country can hide."[26] What did they mean?

2. *a.* Can you envision a time when all of the nations of the world are able to agree on the elimination of regulatory barriers? Explain.

   b. Would you favor that development? Explain.

3. Bohmte, a small community in Germany, decided to remove the traffic lights, curbs, and marked crosswalks from its very busy main street, a state highway, which carries some 13,000 cars and trucks daily. Bohmte was practicing a traffic-management philosophy labeled "shared space," which holds that fewer rules increase traffic safety. Bohmte retained only one rule: Always give way to the person on the right.

   a. European studies thus far show that shared-space policies have reduced accidents. Why?

   b. Which portions of the population might feel particularly at risk from the shared-space policy?

Summary of State and Local Regulation

The federal government receives the greater attention, but state and local rules have an enormous impact on business practice. The states are primarily responsible for regulating the insurance industry and are heavily involved in regulating banking, securities, and liquor sales. Many businesses and professions—from psychology to funeral preparation to barbering to the practice of medicine—require a license from the state. Public utilities (gas, electricity, sewage disposal) are the subject of extensive regulation governing entry, rates, customer service, and virtually all of the companies' activities. All states have some form of public service commission charged with regulating utilities in the public interest. Many states seek to directly enhance competition via antitrust legislation. Many states have passed laws forbidding usury, false advertising, stock fraud, and other practices harmful to the consumer. Furthermore, Congress pushes federal activities such as welfare and highway safety rules back to the states, suggesting that state government growth is unlikely to abate. [For the "largest Internet compilation" of state government materials, see **http://www.hg.org/index.html**]

No Toys in Happy Meals? How Far Should the Rules Go? Who Should Make Them?

In 2008, California became the first state to phase out trans fats in restaurants. New York City and a few other municipalities have similar rules. Then in 2010 San Francisco approved an ordinance disallowing toys in meals that exceed certain guidelines for calories, sodium and fat (e.g., calories must be under 600).

The fast food industry, seeking uniform regulations, has responded with an aggressive lobbying campaign encouraging states to pass laws blocking counties and cities from enacting "Happy Meal" ordinances. As a result, several states have now passed laws limiting local government control over restaurants.

Question

1. Do you support the Happy Meal ordinances or the state laws to block those ordinances? Explain.

Sources: Jennifer Steinhauer, "California Bars Restaurant Use of Trans Fats," *The New York Times,* July 26, 2008 [**http://www.nytimes.com/2008/07/26/us/26fats.html**]; and Dan Levine; and Lisa Baerthlein, "Fast-Food Lobbies U.S. States on 'Happy Meal' Laws," *Thomson Reuters News & Insight,"* May 9, 2011 [**http://newsandinsight. thomsonreuters.com/Legal/News/2011/05_-_May/Fastfood_lobbies_U_S_states_on_Happy_Meals_laws/**].

Licensure Local regulation is much less economically significant than state regulation. Local government intervention in business typically involves various licensure requirements. For example, businesses like bars and theaters are often required to obtain a local permit to operate. Similarly, more than 1,000 of America's occupations (medicine, law, building construction, electrical work, and so on) can be practiced only by those who have secured licensure from state and/or local authorities. Licensure is to protect the public from unsafe, unhealthful, and substandard goods and services, but critics contend that the benefits of licensure are exceeded by its costs in increased prices, decreased services, and administrative overhead. *The Wall Street Journal* explained that argument:

> Overall, the level of licensing regulation in the workplace is rising precipitously, with more than 20 percent of the workforce now required to get a permit to do their jobs—up from 4.5 percent in the 1950s. . . . These requirements are essentially barriers to entry and job creation. . . .[27]

Robin Hood or a Cheat?

New York City's Taxi and Limousine Commission regulates cabs. Ray Kottner, an 80-year-old "hack" drives his unlicensed 1982 vintage Checker cab through the New York City streets picking up passengers for what he says are free rides. In July 2007, Kottner dropped off a passenger who gave him $10, which Kottner said was a tip but which the Commission said was a fare. His cab was impounded, and the passenger said that Kottner had asked for $10. Kottner says the City had been following him and trying to stop his "Robin Hood" practices, but the City says he must abide by the rules:

> "He was observed engaging in an illegal activity, and the vehicle was seized to protect the public, TLC spokesman Allan Fromberg said. The vehicle has not been TLC inspected, isn't properly registered, and does not carry adequate insurance."

Licensed drivers are likewise frustrated with Kottner:

> "This guy is nothing but a crook, and we're all glad he's finally off the streets," said David Pollack, a cabby and editor of *Taxi Insider*. "He flips his finger at our regulatory bodies; he flips his finger at taxi drivers."

The drivers say that Kottner is simply escaping all the overhead they must pay: $425,000 for a medallion (taxi license), $700 per year to renew it, $3,900 per month for insurance. They must also submit to drug testing and training that Kottner avoids.

Questions
1. Is Kottner "Robin Hood" or an unfair "free rider"? Explain.
2. Why do most cities closely regulate the cab industry?

Source: Jeremy Olshan, *The New York Post,* July 21, 2007 [http://www.nypost.com].

Rules and Community Welfare Most of us would say, in the abstract, that we need less government in our lives, but when we are the victims of problems that the market is ill-suited to resolve, those rules become much more attractive. The case that follows shows how Tampa, Florida, tried to apply its rules to the age-old problem of adult entertainment businesses but with a new twist—product distribution by the Internet rather than by face-to-face commerce.

Voyeur Dorm v. City of Tampa
265 F.3d 1232 (11th Cir. 2001); cert. den. 122 S.Ct. 1172 (2002)

LEGAL BRIEFCASE

Circuit Judge Dubina

This appeal arises from Voyeur Dorm L.C.'s alleged violation of Tampa's City Code based on the district court's characterization of Voyeur Dorm as an adult entertainment facility.

BACKGROUND

Voyeur Dorm operates an Internet-based Web site that provides a 24-hour-a-day Internet transmission portraying the lives of the residents of 2312 West Farwell Drive, Tampa, Florida. Throughout its existence, Voyeur Dorm has employed 25 to 30 different women, most of whom entered into a contract that specifies, among other things, that they are "employees," on a "stage and filming location," with "no reasonable expectation of privacy," for "entertainment purposes." Subscribers to "voyeurdorm.com" pay a subscription fee of $34.95 a month to watch the women employed at the premises and pay an added fee of $16.00 per month to "chat" with the women. From August 1998 to June 2000, Voyeur Dorm generated subscriptions and sales totaling $3,166,551.35.

In 1998 Voyeur Dorm learned that local law enforcement agencies had initiated an investigation into its business. In response, counsel for Voyeur Dorm sent a letter to Tampa's zoning coordinator requesting her interpretation of the city code as it applied to the activities occurring at 2312 West Farwell Drive. In February of 1999, Tampa's zoning coordinator, Gloria Moreda, replied to counsel's request and issued her interpretation of the city code:

* * * * *

It is my determination that the use occurring at 2312 W. Farwell Dr., is an adult use. Section 27-523 defines adult entertainment as "Any premises, except those businesses otherwise defined in this chapter, on which is offered to members of the public or any person, for a consideration, entertainment featuring or in any way including specified sexual activities, as defined in this section, or entertainment featuring the displaying or depicting of specified anatomical areas, as defined in this section; 'entertainment' as used in this definition shall include, but not be limited to, books, magazines, films, newspapers, photographs, paintings, drawings, sketches or other publications or graphic media, filmed or live plays, dances or other performances distinguished by their display or depiction of specified anatomical areas or specified anatomical activities, as defined in this section."

Please be aware that the property is zoned RS-60 Residential Single Family, and an adult use business is not permitted use. You should advise your client to cease operation at that location.

Thereafter, in April of 1999, Dan and Sharon Gold Marshlack [owners of the property located at 2312 W. Farwell] appealed the zoning coordinator's decision to Tampa's Variance Review Board. On or about July 13, 1999, the Variance Review Board conducted a hearing. At the hearing, Voyeur Dorm's counsel conceded the following: that five women live in the house; that there are cameras in the corners of all the rooms of the house; that for a fee a person can join a membership to a Web site wherein a member can view the women 24 hours a day, seven days a week; that a member, at times, can see someone disrobed; that the women receive free room and board; that the women are part of a business enterprise; and that the women are paid. At the conclusion of the hearing, the Variance Review Board unanimously upheld the zoning coordinator's determination that the use occurring at 2312 West Farwell Drive was an adult use. Subsequently, Mr. and Mrs. Marshlack filed an appeal from the decision of the

Variance Review Board to the City Council. The Tampa City Council . . . unanimously affirmed the decision of the Variance Review Board.

Voyeur Dorm filed this action in the middle district of Florida. The City of Tampa and Voyeur Dorm then filed cross-motions for summary judgment. The district court granted Tampa's motion for summary judgment, from which Voyeur Dorm now appeals.

ISSUE

1. Whether the district court properly determined that the alleged activities occurring at 2312 West Farwell Drive constitute a public offering of adult entertainment as contemplated by Tampa's zoning restrictions.

[Issues 2. and 3. are omitted.—Ed.]

DISCUSSION

The threshold inquiry is whether section 27-523 of Tampa's city code applies to the alleged activities occurring at 2312 West Farwell Drive. Because of the way we answer that inquiry, it will not be necessary for us to analyze the thorny constitutional issues presented in this case.

* * * * *

Tampa argues that Voyeur Dorm is an adult use business pursuant to the express and unambiguous language of Section 27-523 and, as such, cannot operate in a residential neighborhood. In that regard, Tampa points out that members of the public pay to watch women employed on the premises; that the employment agreement refers to the premises as "a stage and filming location;" that certain anatomical areas and sexual activities are displayed for entertainment; and that the entertainers are paid accordingly. Most importantly, Tampa asserts that nothing in the city code limits its applicability to premises where the adult entertainment is actually consumed.

In accord with Tampa's arguments, the district court specifically determined that the "plain and unambiguous language of the city code . . . does not expressly state a requirement that the members of the public paying consideration be on the premises viewing the adult entertainment." While the public does not congregate to a specific edifice or location in order to enjoy the entertainment provided by Voyeur Dorm, the district court found 2312 West Farwell Drive to be "a premises on which is offered to members of the public for consideration entertainment featuring specified sexual activities within the plain meaning of the city code."

Moreover, the district court relied on Supreme Court and Eleventh Circuit precedent that trumpets a city's entitlement to protect and improve the quality of residential neighborhoods.

Sammy's of Mobile, Ltd. v. City of Mobile (noting that it is well established that the regulation of public health, safety, and morals is a valid and substantial state interest); *Corn v. City of Lauderdale Lakes* (noting that the "Supreme Court has held [that] restrictions may be imposed to protect 'family values, youth values, and the blessings of quiet seclusion'").

In opposition, Voyeur Dorm argues that it is not an adult use business. Specifically, Voyeur Dorm contends that section 27-523 applies to locations or premises wherein adult entertainment is actually offered to the public. Because the public does not, indeed cannot, physically attend 2312 West Farwell Drive to enjoy the adult entertainment, 2312 West Farwell Drive does not fall within the purview of Tampa's zoning ordinance.

The residence of 2312 West Farwell Drive provides no "offering [of adult entertainment] to members of the public." The offering occurs when the videotaped images are dispersed over the Internet and into the public eye for consumption. The city code cannot be applied to a location that does not, itself, offer adult entertainment to the public.

* * * * *

It does not follow, then, that a zoning ordinance designed to restrict facilities that offer adult entertainment can be applied to a particular location that does not, at that location, offer adult entertainment. Moreover, the case law relied upon by Tampa and the district court concerns adult entertainment in which customers physically attend the premises wherein the entertainment is performed. Here, the audience or consumers of the adult entertainment do not go to 2312 West Farwell Drive or congregate anywhere else in Tampa to enjoy the entertainment. Indeed, the public offering occurs over the Internet in "virtual space." While the district court read Section 27-523 in a literal sense, finding no requirement that the paying public be on the premises, we hold that section 27-523 does not apply to a residence at which there is no public offering of adult entertainment.

* * * * *

Reversed.

Questions

1. *a.* Why did the court rule against Tampa?
   b. Make the argument, as the lower court did, that the Tampa statute does apply to Voyeur Dorm.
   c. Why was Tampa concerned about Voyeur Dorm operating in a residential neighborhood?
   d. Does Tampa have any additional legal grounds for challenging Voyeur Dorm? Explain.

2. The city government in Cedar Falls, Iowa, home of the University of Northern Iowa, declined to renew the liquor license of a local bar after 58 of 100 "bar checks" over a period of nearly two years found minors drinking illegally. One hundred and seventy four alcohol-related tickets were issued over that period.[28]
   a. Could the free market satisfactorily protect the public from the various risks associated with excessive drinking by college-age students, or are rules necessary?
   b. Would you vote to renew this bar's liquor license? Explain.

3. Two Dallas, Texas, ordinances were challenged in court. One gave the police very broad authority to deny licenses to "adult" businesses such as bookstores. The other, which was directed at prostitution, barred motel owners from renting rooms for fewer than 10 hours.
   a. What challenges would you raise against these ordinances?
   b. How would you rule? Explain. See *FW/PBS Inc v. City of Dallas,* 493 U.S. 215 (1990).

4. The Los Angeles municipal code prohibits some types of new billboards and restricts the size, placement, and illumination of others. The Los Angeles code seeks to "promote public safety and welfare" by "providing reasonable protection to the visual environment" and by ensuring that billboards do not "interfere with traffic safety or otherwise endanger public safety." One provision of the code specifically forbids new "Freeway Facing Signs" located within 2,000 feet of and "viewed primarily from" a freeway or an on-ramp/off-ramp. Another forbids, with exceptions, new "supergraphics," large format signs projected onto or hung from building walls. The Los Angeles rules allow new signs in some portions of the city while banning them in others.
   a. The billboard rules were challenged on constitutional grounds. Explain those grounds and rule on the constitutionality of the rules. See *World Wide Rush v. City of Los Angeles,* 606 F.3d 676 (9th Cir. 2010).
   b. Should Los Angeles simply allow the market to determine where billboards are placed? Explain.

5. Tattoo and body piercing statutes sometimes require liability insurance, licensing, training, and health inspections, and parents are to accompany minors. Does each of those requirements seem appropriate to you? Explain.

6. a. Can we rely on the market to protect teens from excessive tanning? Explain.
   b. Has the market failed? Explain.

Questions—Parts One and Two

1. Matthew Hale, a law school graduate, was denied a license to practice law in Illinois because Hale was an avowed racist and the leader of a white supremacist group. A state panel assessed the character and general fitness of all those who had passed the bar exam and graduated from law school and decided that Hale's active racism disqualified him. Illinois is one of 32 states with character and fitness standards. Hale appealed on First Amendment grounds, among others. Should Hale be excluded from the practice of law, or should we let the market decide his fitness? Explain.

2. City officials in Machesney Park, Illinois required nine-year-old Gregory Webb to tear down his makeshift tree house on the grounds that it was a nuisance. Webb had built the structure from lawn chairs, leftover carpet, and a pet carrier, among other objects. The city was criticized for its decision.
   a. Why would a city choose to exercise its police power over nuisances in this seemingly trivial case?
   b. What would you do if you were the city planning and zoning director and thus responsible for the situation?

3. Notwithstanding the successful deregulation efforts in recent decades, the larger trend in the United States over the past 50 years, and particularly since the financial crisis of recent years, has been increased government regulation of business. How do you explain that trend?

4. As a safety measure, Arizona enacted a statute that limited the length of passenger trains to 14 cars and freight trains to 70 cars. Trains of those lengths and greater were common throughout the United States. The Southern Pacific Railroad challenged the Arizona statute.

   a. What was the legal foundation of the Southern Pacific claim?

   b. Decide the case. Explain. See *Southern Pacific Railroad v. Arizona,* 325 U.S. 761 (1945).

Part Three—Administrative Agencies and the Regulatory Process

Introduction to Administrative Agencies[29]

Suppose you start a business; a small, relatively simple business, perhaps a restaurant. You quickly come to realize that the government is going to be your partner in that business. Taxes, wages, hours, sanitation, safety, advertising, zoning—at every turn a government rule shapes the conduct of your business. In many cases those rules are created and enforced by administrative agencies, a powerful subset of government little understood by the public but immensely influential in every corner of American life.

The Federal Agencies

Federal law defines an *agency* as any government unit other than the legislature and the courts. Thus, the *administrative law* governing those agencies technically addresses the entire executive branch of government. Our attention, however, will be directed to the prominent regulatory agencies (Federal Trade Commission, Federal Communications Commission, Securities and Exchange Commission, and the like) rather than the various executive departments (Agriculture, Defense, and so on) and nonregulatory welfare agencies (Social Security Administration and Veterans Administration). We will focus on the federal level, but administrative law principles are generally applicable to the conduct of state and local governments. At the state level, public utility commissions and the various state licensure boards for law, medicine, architecture, and the like are examples of administrative agencies. At the local level, one might cite planning and zoning boards and property tax assessment appeals boards. [To search for federal government information on the World Wide Web, see **http://www.gpoaccess.gov/index.html** or **http://www.fedworld.gov**]

History

Congress established the Interstate Commerce Commission (ICC), the first federal regulatory agency, in 1887 for the purpose of regulating railroad routes and rates. The Food and Drug Administration (FDA—1907) and the Federal Trade Commission (FTC—1914) followed, but federal regulation became pervasive only in response to the Great Depression of the 1930s. Congress created the Securities and Exchange Commission (SEC—1934), the Federal

Communications Commission (FCC—1934), the Civil Aeronautics Board (CAB—1940; abolished 1985), and the National Labor Relations Board (NLRB—1935), among others, as a response to the widely shared belief that the stock market crash and the Depression were evidence of the failure of the free market.

The next major burst of regulatory activity arrived in the 1960s and 1970s when Congress created such agencies as the Equal Employment Opportunity Commission (EEOC—1965), the Environmental Protection Agency (EPA—1970), the Occupational Safety and Health Administration (OSHA—1970), and the Consumer Product Safety Commission (CPSC—1972).

Note that the work of most of the early agencies was directed to controlling entire industries such as transportation or communications and that the primary purpose of most of those agencies was to address economic concerns. Then with the arrival of the prosperity and social turbulence of the 1960s and 1970s, Congress built a rather massive array of new agencies directed not to economic issues but to social reform in such areas as discrimination, the environment, job safety, and product safety.

The free market enthusiasm of the 1980s resulted in strenuous efforts to deregulate the economy and reduce the influence of the federal agencies and the government generally. Now, in the early 21st century we have been in a period of great respect for the free market, but current problems in the finance industry, particularly in home mortgages, have resulted in aggressive new rules, as explained below.

Creating the Agencies

Federal agencies are of two kinds: executive and independent. Executive agencies usually are located within the departments of the executive branch of the government. The Federal Aviation Administration, for example, is a part of the Department of Transportation. Our primary interest is in the independent agencies (FTC, FCC, and SEC). Congress created those agencies via statutes labeled *enabling legislation* and accorded them substantial authority to regulate a specified segment of American life. The FTC for example, is empowered by its enabling legislation to pursue unfair trade practices. The president has direct authority over the executive agencies while the independent agencies are intended to operate with less fear of interference. In practice, of course, the president and congress have substantial influence on all the agencies.

In creating an agency, Congress delegates a portion of its authority to that body. Congress acknowledges the existence of a problem and recognizes that it is not the appropriate body to address the specific elements of that problem—hence the agency. The president, ordinarily with the advice and consent of the Senate, appoints the administrator or the several commissioners who direct each agency's affairs. Commissioners are appointed in staggered terms, typically of seven years' duration. The appointment of commissioners for most of the independent agencies must reflect an approximate political balance between the two major parties.

In effect, Congress has created a fourth branch of government. Possessing neither the time nor the expertise to handle issues arising from nuclear power, product safety, racial discrimination, labor unions, and much more, Congress wisely established "mini-governments" supported by the necessary technical resources and day-to-day authority to address those complicated problems.

Agency Duties

The authority of the federal regulatory agencies falls broadly into three categories.

1. **Control of supply.** Some agencies control entry into certain economic activities. The Federal Communications Commission grants radio and television licenses. The Food and Drug Administration (see Chapter 15) decides which drugs may enter the American market. The Securities and Exchange Commission (see Chapter 9) acts as a gatekeeper, preventing the entry of new securities into the marketplace until certain standards are met. The general concern is that the market alone cannot adequately protect the public interest.

2. **Control of rates.** Historically, those federal agencies charged with regulating utilities and carriers (Federal Energy Regulatory Commission, ICC, and CAB) set the prices to be charged for the services offered within their jurisdictions, but the deregulation movement resulted in the elimination of the CAB and the ICC and a general decline in agency rate-setting. The federal government decided to reduce or eliminate its authority in decisions such as the price of airline tickets, cable TV rates, and long-distance telephone rates.

3. **Control of conduct.**

a. Information. Agencies commonly compel companies to disclose consumer information that would otherwise remain private. Warning labels, for example, may be mandated.

b. Standards. Where simply requiring information is deemed inadequate for the public needs, the government may establish minimum standards that the private sector must meet. A ladder might be required to safely hold at least a specified weight, or workers might lawfully be exposed to only a specified maximum level of radiation.

c. Product Banishments. In rare circumstances, products can be banned from the market. The Consumer Product Safety Commission banned the flame retardant Tris (used in children's sleepwear) because of evidence of the product's cancer-causing properties.

Questions

1. The phrase government regulation embraces many functions. Define it.
2. Is the federal regulatory process limited in its goals to the correction of market failures? Should it be so limited? Explain.

Operating the Agencies

As we have noted, the administrative agencies act as mini-governments, performing quasi-executive, quasi-legislative (rule-making), and quasi-judicial (adjudicatory) roles broadly involving control of supply, rates, and conduct in large segments of American life. Agency action is guided generally by the 1946 Administrative Procedure Act (APA), which Congress enacted to provide a framework for agency rule-making and to detail broad standards for judicial review of agency decisions. Let's look at how those agencies practice their business.

Executive Functions

The basic executive duty of the various agencies is to implement the policy provided for in the enabling legislation and in the agencies' own rules and regulations. A large part of agency activity consists of performing mundane, repetitive tasks. Agencies enter into contracts, lease federal lands, register securities offerings, award grants, resolve tax disputes, settle workers' compensation claims, administer government benefits to the citizenry, and so on. Of course, a big part of the agencies' executive duties is the protection of the public by ensuring compliance with laws and regulations. Therefore, most agencies spend a great deal of time conducting inspections and investigations and collecting information.

Most agencies offer informal advice, both in response to requests and on their own initiative, to explain agency policy and positions. Each year the Federal Trade Commission, for example, receives many complaints about alleged fraud in advertising, telemarketing, identity theft, Internet commerce, and so on. Supervisory duties, including most notably the active and close attention given to the banking industry, are a further illustration of agency executive duties.

Legislative Functions

The agencies create *rules* that, in effect, are laws. These rules provide the details necessary to carry out the intentions of the enabling legislation. In day-to-day business practice, the rules are likely to be much more important than the original congressional legislation. The Occupational Safety and Health Act calls for a safe and healthful workplace, but the rules necessary for interpreting and enforcing that general mandate come, not from Congress, but from OSHA.

Rules

Agencies enact three types of rules: (1) procedural, (2) interpretive, and (3) legislative, Procedural rules delineate the agency's internal operating structure and methods. Interpretive rules offer the agency's view of the meaning of those statutes for which the agency has administrative responsibility. Internal Revenue Service regulations are an example of interpretive rules. Legislative rules are policy expressions having the effect of law. The agency is exercising the law-making function delegated to it by the legislature. Federal Trade Commission rules providing for a cooling-off period of three business days within which the buyer may cancel door-to-door sales contracts are an example of agency law-making that significantly affects business behavior.

The Rule-Making Process

The Administrative Procedure Act provides for both *informal* (often called "notice and comment") and *formal* rule-making processes for legislative rules. Under both approaches, the process begins with the publication of a Notice of Proposed Rule Making in the *Federal Register* (a daily publication of all federal rules, regulations, and orders). Thereafter, in the case of informal rule making, the agency must permit written comments on the proposal and may hold open hearings. To enhance participation in the rule-making process, the federal government provides an online portal where the public can comment on proposed rules [**see www.regulations.gov**]. Having received public comments, the agency either discontinues the process or prepares the final rule.

In the case of formal rule-making, after providing notice, the agency must hold a public hearing conducted with most of the procedural safeguards of a trial, where all interested parties may call witnesses, challenge the agency evidence, and so on.

Hybrid Rule-Making   Although not specifically provided for in the APA, agency rule-making now is often achieved by a compromise (hybrid) process that combines elements of formal and informal rule-making. Hybrid rule-making is informal rule making with additions in the form of some trial elements (more oral testimony and hearings) that have the effect of providing a more detailed record without all of the procedural requirements of formal rule-making.

Whether by formal, informal, or hybrid procedures, final agency rules are published in the *Federal Register* and later compiled in the *Code of Federal Regulations.* [To search the Federal Register, see **http://www.gpoaccess.gov/fr/index.html**]

Challenging an Agency Rule

The power and importance of the agencies is evident in the FCC's contentious regulation of media ownership. One FCC rule prohibited any single cable television company from serving more than 30 percent of all pay-television subscribers. The FCC justified the cap as a means of insuring competition and diversity in the cable market, but in 2009 a federal court of appeals tossed out the rule as an "arbitrary and capricious" exercise of federal power.[30] With increased choice via satellite TV and other sources, the court saw no need for the government restraint. Comcast, with about 25 percent of the market, is the only American cable provider that is approaching the old limit.[31]

At this writing the FCC is continuing a long-running dispute with Congress and the courts about the Commission's decision to relax rules limiting a single company's ownership (called cross-ownership) of radio stations, television stations, and newspapers in the same market. The rule was designed to protect communities from media monopolies and to increase diversity in the marketplace of ideas.[32] The FCC, however, points to the Internet and other technological advances that reduce the threat of media monopoly. The critics, including many in Congress, think the industry still needs firm rules limiting cross ownership. They point to the FCC's 1996 decision to lift its limit on how many radio stations one company could own nationally. The result was the development of the 1,200 station Clear Channel network that has been broadly criticized for "homogenizing" radio and sharply reducing local programming.

> Clear Channel has been criticized for "homogenizing" radio.

Broadly, the debate is about economic policy. Will the market on its own provide for the nation's best interests? Or are restraints necessary to prevent too much concentration of power and authority in too few hands?

Judicial Functions

Although informal procedures such as settlements are preferred, agencies commonly must turn to judicial proceedings to enforce agency rules. The National Labor Relations Board may hold a hearing to determine if an employee was wrongfully dismissed for engaging in protected union activities. The Federal Communications Commission may decide whether to remove a radio license because of a failure to serve the public interest. The Federal Trade Commission may judge whether a particular ad is misleading.

Rule-Making or Adjudication?

Many issues facing agencies could properly be resolved either by rule-making or by adjudication. Characteristically, however, an adjudication addresses specific parties involved in a specific present or past dispute. Rule-making ordinarily involves standards to be applied to the future conduct of a class of unspecified parties. The rule-making/adjudication decision is discretionary with the agency (subject to judicial review) and is based on the nature of the issue and fairness to the parties. Regardless, the agencies are, in effect, "making law" either by setting a judicial-like precedent in the case of an adjudication or by passing a rule that has authority much like a law.

Administrative Hearing

Typically, after an investigation, a violation of a statute and/or rule may be alleged. Affected parties are notified. An effort is made to reach a settlement via a *consent order,* in which the party being investigated agrees to steps suitable to the agency but under which the respondent makes no admission of guilt (thus, retarding the likelihood of subsequent civil liability).

ALJ

Failing a settlement, the parties proceed much as in a civil trial. Ordinarily the case is heard by an *administrative law judge (ALJ).* The respondent may be represented by counsel. Parties have the right to present their cases, cross-examine, file motions, raise objections, and so on. They do not have the right to a jury trial, however. The ALJ decides all questions of law and fact and then issues a decision (*order*). In general, that decision is final unless appealed to the agency/commission. After exhausting opportunities for review within the agency, appeal may be taken to the federal court system.

PRACTICING ETHICS

Agency Capture, Iron Triangles, and Revolving Doors?

The Materials Management Service (MMS) is a federal agency charged with collecting oil and gas royalties from companies drilling on federal lands. A 2008 Interior Department internal investigation concluded that several MMS officials "frequently consumed alcohol at industry functions, had used cocaine and marijuana, and had sexual relationships with oil and gas company representatives."[33] Reportedly, MMS staffers took gifts from oil and gas officials with "prodigious frequency."[34] Some MMS decisions, while less vivid than the sex, drugs, and payoffs, were of much more far reaching consequence. The MMS reportedly gave British Petroleum's Gulf of Mexico oil lease a "categorical exclusion" that exempted the lease from a detailed environmental impact analysis in 2009.[35] BP's Deepwater Horizon drilling rig exploded in 2010 leading to the calamitous oil spill that polluted much of the Gulf of Mexico. At this writing, the Interior Department and Congress are taking steps to redesign the MMS, but the agency's misconduct is a particularly lurid and frustrating example of the risk that agencies will be improperly influenced (captured) by the industries they are intended to regulate.

Scholars argue that *agency capture* is a form of government failure that can occur when regulators are too cozy with the industry being regulated or when industry representatives have the interest and resources to offer detailed advice on agency business while the public voice, being much less focused, is seldom or never heard by the agency. Political scientists argue that regulatory capture of both agencies and congressional committees sometimes produces a stable, nearly impregnable, *iron triangle.* Powerful interest groups (often businesses), occupy one corner of the triangle, congressional committees are at another corner, and agency bureaucrats occupy the third. In the resulting alliance, each group cultivates its own welfare by providing political support (from interest groups to members of congress) writing favorable laws (from congress to interest groups) and by agency enforcement of those laws in ways favorable to the interest groups and congress. The likely result is diminished attention to the public good.

Regulatory capture is facilitated by a revolving door wherein agency officials often come from the very industry they are hired to regulate and agency regulators often leave government to work for the industry formerly regulated. ABC News, in investigating Toyota's safety problems, highlighted the revolving door risk when it disclosed

that "federal safety regulators agreed to exclude reports of the most serious cases of alleged 'runaway Toyotas' after the intervention of a former government safety official hired to be a Washington, D.C. representative of Toyota."[36] A later government investigation concluded that the intervention did not violate federal law.[37] Troublesome as these government/industry ties may seem, we should remember that we want and need close associations between government agencies and the industries being regulated. Each benefits from the expertise of the other.

Controlling the Agencies

Although agency influence in business practice and in American life generally is enormous, none of these agencies and their thousands of employees is directly accountable to the people, and all of them operate under necessarily broad grants of power. What is to keep them from abusing their discretion or from being "captured" by special interests? Just as with our constitutional system generally, certain checks and balances constrain agency conduct while allowing the latitude necessary to achieve effectiveness.

Executive Constraints

As noted, the president appoints the top administrators for the various agencies, thus significantly influencing the conservative or liberal slant of the agency. Furthermore, the president obviously has great influence in the budget process.

Recent presidents have strengthened executive oversight of agency action by requiring *cost-benefit analyses* for new rules (President Clinton) and commanding agencies to cite a specific *market failure* before issuing a new rule (President George W. Bush). President Obama has maintained the cost-benefit expectation and he has introduced a new initiative to get rid of what he has labeled "dumb" rules. In 2011, President Obama ordered all federal agencies to systematically review their existing regulations with the goal of eliminating outdated rules that "stifle job creation and make our economy less competitive."[38] [For an OMB "watchdog" see **http://www.ombwatch.org/**]

Congressional Constraints

Congress creates and can dissolve the agencies. Congress controls agency budgets and thus can encourage or discourage particular agency action. Broadly, Congress oversees agency action, and agencies often check with Congress before undertaking major initiatives. Congress can directly intervene by amending the enabling legislation or by passing laws that require agencies to take specific directions. The difficulty in balancing congressional and agency authority is well illustrated by an important 2001 Supreme Court decision involving the federal Clean Air Act (CAA). The case, *Whitman v. American Trucking Associations, Inc.*[39] raised the question of whether Congress had improperly delegated its authority to the Environmental Protection Agency and whether the EPA must take the cost of implementing clean air regulations into consideration when developing new rules. A unanimous Supreme Court ruled that Congress had built into the CAA constitutionally sufficient limitations on agency action, and the Court ruled that Congress clearly did not require the EPA to conduct cost–benefit analyses before establishing new rules. Thus the Court concluded that Congress can constitutionally offer agencies broad authority in carrying out Congress's general intentions.

Judicial Review

Agency rules and orders may be challenged in court. Historically, however, the courts have taken a rather narrow approach to judicial review. The jurists, being generalists in the field of law, have been reluctant to overrule the judgment of specialists, and very crowded judicial calendars act as a natural brake on activist judicial review. For those reasons, judges readily sustain the judgment of the agency where reasonable. Of course, the courts overrule the agencies when appropriate, and review of controversial, high visibility rules such as many of those issued by the Environmental Protection Agency is, according to one expert, "virtually inevitable."[40] When the courts do review agency action, the weight of scholarly evidence concludes that agency decisions are upheld a little more than two thirds of the time.[41]

Not surprisingly, judicial review of agency decisions raises a variety of technical issues of law. Cases turn on questions like these:

1. Does the legislature's delegation of authority meet constitutional requirements?
2. Has the agency exceeded the authority granted by the enabling legislation?
3. Are the agency's findings of fact supported by substantial evidence in the record as a whole?
4. Was the agency's decision "arbitrary and capricious" (a standard provided for in the Administrative Procedure Act and discussed in the *FCC v. Fox* case below)?

While these issues are technically important, their detailed exploration is not necessary for our purposes. The case that follows will be our only consideration of the formalities of judicial review. This 5–4 U.S. Supreme Court ruling examines the question of when the government should regulate distasteful expression over the regulated airways.

LEGAL BRIEFCASE

Federal Communications Commission v. Fox Television Stations 129 S.Ct. 1800 (2009)

Justice Scalia

Federal law prohibits the broadcasting of "any ... indecent ... language," 18 U.S.C. Section 1464, which includes expletives referring to sexual or excretory activity or organs. This case concerns the adequacy of the Federal Communications Commission's explanation of its decision that this sometimes

forbids the broadcasting of indecent expletives even when the offensive words are not repeated.

* * * * *

THE PRESENT CASE

This case concerns utterances in two live broadcasts aired by Fox Television Stations, Inc., and its affiliates. . . . The first occurred during the 2002 Billboard Music Awards, when the singer Cher exclaimed, "I've also had critics for the last 40 years saying that I was on my way out every year. Right. So f*** 'em." The second involved a segment of the 2003 Billboard Music Awards, during the presentation of an award by Nicole Richie and Paris Hilton, principals in a Fox television series called "The Simple Life." Ms. Hilton began their interchange by reminding Ms. Richie to "watch the bad language," but Ms. Richie proceeded to ask the audience, "Why do they even call it 'The Simple Life?' Have you ever tried to get cow s*** out of a Prada purse? It's not so f***ing simple." Following each of these broadcasts, the Commission received numerous complaints from parents whose children were exposed to the language.

On March 15, 2006, the Commission released Notices of Apparent Liability for a number of broadcasts that the Commission deemed actionably indecent, including the two described above. Multiple parties petitioned the Court of Appeals for the Second Circuit for judicial review of the order. Since the order had declined to impose sanctions, the Commission had not previously given the broadcasters an opportunity to respond to the indecency charges. It therefore requested and obtained from the Court of Appeals a voluntary remand so that the parties could air their objections. The Commission's order on remand upheld the indecency findings for the broadcasts described above.

The [Remand] order first explained that both broadcasts fell comfortably within the subject-matter scope of the Commission's indecency test because the 2003 broadcast involved a literal description of excrement and both broadcasts invoked the "F-Word," which inherently has a sexual connotation. The order next determined that the broadcasts were patently offensive under community standards for the medium. Both broadcasts, it noted, involved entirely gratuitous uses of "one of the most vulgar, graphic, and explicit words for sexual activity in the English language." It found Ms. Richie's use of the "F-Word" and her "explicit description of the handling of excrement" to be "vulgar and shocking," as well as to constitute "pandering," after Ms. Hilton had playfully warned her to '"watch the bad language.'" And it found Cher's statement patently offensive in part because she metaphorically suggested a sexual act as a means of expressing hostility to her critics. The order relied upon the "critically important" context of the utterances, noting that they were aired during primetime awards shows "designed to draw a large nationwide audience that could be expected to include many children interested in seeing their favorite music stars." Indeed, approximately 2.5 million minors witnessed each of the broadcasts.

* * * * *

The order explained that the Commission's prior "strict dichotomy between 'expletives' and 'descriptions or depictions of sexual or excretory functions' is artificial and does not make sense in light of the fact that an 'expletive's' power to offend derives from its sexual or excretory meaning." In the Commission's view, "granting an automatic exemption for 'isolated or fleeting' expletives unfairly forces viewers (including children)" to take '"the first blow'" and would allow broadcasters "to air expletives at all hours of a day so long as they did so one at a time." Although the Commission determined that Fox encouraged the offensive language by using suggestive scripting in the 2003 broadcast, and unreasonably failed to take adequate precautions in both broadcasts, the order again declined to impose any forfeiture or other sanction for either of the broadcasts.

Fox returned to the Second Circuit for review of the *Remand Order*. The Court of Appeals reversed the agency's orders, finding the Commission's reasoning inadequate under the Administrative Procedure Act. The majority was "skeptical that the Commission [could] provide a reasoned explanation for its 'fleeting expletive' regime that would pass constitutional muster," but it declined to reach the constitutional question. We granted certiorari.

ANALYSIS

Governing Principles

The Administrative Procedure Act which sets forth the full extent of judicial authority to review executive agency action for procedural correctness permits the setting aside of agency action that is "arbitrary" or "capricious." Under what we have called this "narrow" standard of review, we insist that an agency "examine the relevant data and articulate a satisfactory explanation for its action." We have made clear, however, that "a court is not to substitute its judgment for that of the agency," and should "uphold a decision of less than ideal clarity if the agency's path may reasonably be discerned."

In overturning the Commission's judgment, the Court of Appeals here relied in part on Circuit precedent requiring a more substantial explanation for agency action that changes prior policy.

* * * * *

We find no basis in the Administrative Procedure Act or in our opinions for a requirement that all agency change be subjected to more searching review. The Act mentions no such heightened standard.

* * * * *

APPLICATION TO THIS CASE

Judged under the above described standards, the Commission's new enforcement policy and its order finding the broadcasts actionably indecent were neither arbitrary nor capricious. First, the Commission forthrightly acknowledged that its recent actions have broken new ground, taking account of inconsistent "prior Commission and staff action" and explicitly disavowing them as "no longer good law." There is no doubt that the Commission knew it was making a change. That is why it declined to assess penalties.

Moreover, the agency's reasons for expanding the scope of its enforcement activity were entirely rational. It was certainly reasonable to determine that it made no sense to distinguish between literal and nonliteral uses of offensive words, requiring repetitive use to render only the latter indecent. As the Commission said with regard to expletive use of the F-Word, "the word's power to insult and offend derives from its sexual meaning." And the Commission's decision to look at the patent offensiveness of even isolated uses of sexual and excretory words fits with the context-based approach we sanctioned. Even isolated utterances can be made in "pander[ing,] . . . vulgar and shocking" manners and can constitute harmful '"first blow[s]'" to children. It is surely rational (if not inescapable) to believe that a safe harbor for single words would "likely lead to more widespread use of the offensive language."

* * * * *

The fact that technological advances have made it easier for broadcasters to bleep out offending words further supports the Commission's stepped-up enforcement policy. And the agency's decision not to impose any forfeiture or other sanction precludes any argument that it is arbitrarily punishing parties without notice of the potential consequences of their action.

Reversed and remanded.

Questions

1. *a.* Why did the Second Circuit Court of Appeals overturn the Federal Communications Commission ruling finding the two Fox live broadcasts indecent?

   b. Why did the Supreme Court reverse the Second Circuit ruling?

2. When would an agency ruling be considered "arbitrary or capricious?"

3. Balancing First Amendment considerations (not addressed by the Supreme Court in the *Fox* case) with concerns about the social effects of indecent language and behavior, what policy do you personally think the FCC should follow in regulating "fleeting expletives" like those uttered on television by Cher and Nicole Richie? Explain.

4. In commenting on the ongoing indecency debate, *The New York Times* argued: "The Supreme Court . . . should end all government regulations on the content of broadcasts. Technological change has undermined any justification for limiting the First Amendment rights of broadcast media outlets but not others."[42]

   Explain what the *Times* meant about technology eliminating the need for government oversight of broadcasting content.

The FCC and Indecency Today

We seem to be in the midst of a cultural war over social values, none of which is more hotly contested than the public role of sex in American life. Most famously, perhaps, Janet Jackson's "wardrobe malfunction" (when her right breast was momentarily bared during the halftime show of the 2004 Super Bowl) led to a $550,000 FCC fine levied against CBS television, but a federal court of appeals panel reversed the FCC decision.[43] In 2009, the Supreme Court, following its *FCC v. Fox* decision, ordered the Third Circuit Court of Appeals to consider reinstating the fine against CBS.[44] FCC rules forbid indecent materials on conventional broadcast services between 6 AM and 10 PM—hours when children are likely to be in the audience. The 10 PM to 6 AM slot, on the other hand, offers a "safe harbor" for indecent programming. The rules do not reach subscription services such as programming delivered via satellite and cable services.

At this writing, the FCC's indecency policy is in judicial limbo. Following the *FCC v. Fox* decision set out above, the Supreme Court remanded the case to the Second

Circuit Court of Appeals where a three-judge panel ruled that the FCC indecency policy violates First Amendment free speech rights because it is unconstitutionally vague (an issue not addressed by the Supreme Court in *FCC v. Fox*).[45] The FCC policy, according to the three-judge panel, "chills speech" because broadcasters cannot know what speech is permissible and what might be punished. The judges ruled that the FCC has not provided clear guidelines for its two principal indecency tests: "whether material describes or depicts sexual or excretory organs or activities, and whether a broadcast is 'patently offensive as measured by contemporary community standards.'"[46] At this writing, the Supreme Court has decided to once again review the *Fox* case along with another case involving a display of bare female buttocks on *NYPD Blue*. In the latter case, the FCC levied $27,500 in fines, but a federal court of appeals overturned the FCC ruling.[47]

> **Fines for indecency can reach as high as $325,000.**

Fines for indecency can reach as high as $325,000 per violation. That stiff penalty along with the FCC's broadly drawn indecency standards have caused some stations to refrain from broadcasting shows with profanity, such as the acclaimed movie, *Saving Private Ryan*. Critics worry that FCC rules, designed to protect viewers—particularly children—may have a "chilling effect" on the free flow of ideas that is so vital to the nation's political, cultural, and economic health. [For the FCC overview of obscenity, indecency and profanity, see **http://transition.fcc.gov/eb/oip/**]

Parents' Duty?

Caroline Fredrickson explained the American Civil Liberties Union's objections to close government oversight of broadcasting:

> Congress should reject any proposals that would allow the FCC to regulate what the public sees on television. Members of the American Civil Liberties Union (ACLU) strongly believe that the government should not replace parents as decision makers in America's living rooms. There are some things the government does well, but deciding what is aired on television, and when, is not one of them. Parents already have many tools to protect their children, including blocking programs and channels, changing the channel, or (my personal favorite) turning off the television. . . . Our concern is that imposing standards for television programming would be unconstitutional and damage important values that define America: the right to free speech, and the right of parents to decide the upbringing of their children.

Questions

1. Can we realistically expect parents to be able to fully shield their children from indecent broadcasting?
2. Should parents do so? Explain.

Source: Caroline Fredrickson, "Why Government Should Not Police TV Violence and Indecency," *The Christian Science Monitor,* September 6, 2007 [**http://www.csmonitor.com/2007/0906/p09s01-coop.html**].

Questions—Part Three

1. The Parents Television Council filed 36 indecency complaints with the FCC alleging that popular television shows, including *Friends* and *The Simpsons,* contained indecent scenes that were either sexually explicit or used indecent or profane language. How would you vote on the following scenes?
   a. In the *Gilmore Girls,* one character says to another, "You're a dick."
   b. In *The Simpsons,* students carry picket signs with the phrases "What would Jesus glue?" and "Don't cut off my pianissimo."

2. The Parents Television Council contacted sponsors of the April 6, 2005, episode of the television program *The Shield* to complain about a "graphic" scene in which a police captain was forced to perform fellatio on a gang member at gunpoint. Kia and Castrol were among those sponsors. What would you do if you were in charge of advertising for Kia or Castrol, and you received that complaint?

3. Cable television operators use signal scrambling to ensure that only paying customers have access to some programming. Congress was concerned that some sexually explicit cable programming, even though scrambled, might reach children via signal "bleeding." Section 505 of the Telecommunications Act of 1996 required cable operators to fully block sexually oriented channels or to "time channel"—that is, transmit only in hours when children are unlikely to be viewing. Most cable operators adopted the latter approach, with the result that for two-thirds of the day no viewers in the operators' service areas could receive the sexually explicit programming. Section 504 of the Telecommunications Act required cable operators to block undesired channels at individual households on request. A supplier of sexually oriented programming challenged Section 505 on First Amendment grounds. Decide the case. Explain. See *United States v. Playboy Entertainment Group,* 529 U.S. 803 (2000).

Part Four—The Federal Regulatory Process Evaluated

Free market advocates want to sharply reduce government, while free market skeptics favor an activist government engaged in preventing and correcting market failure. At this writing, President Obama and the Democratic Party have elevated the role of the federal government in American life in an effort to correct problems they believe the market cannot successfully address. Republicans and Tea Party activists, on the other hand, have angrily resisted what they see as an overreaching government intruding in matters such as education and energy policy better left to local communities and the market. They believe the federal government spent so much money stimulating the failing economy and bailing out big banks, car manufacturers and others that the fiscal health of the nation is at risk.

> Republicans and Tea Party activists have angrily resisted what they see as an overreaching government.

The resulting political war has been powerfully projected to the populace through the debate over the aforementioned 2010 national healthcare reform law, the Patient Protection and Affordable Care Act (often labeled ObamaCare). The government expects the bill to reduce America's 57 million uninsured to about 26 million by 2019, and to reduce federal deficits by $132 billion in the first decade and more thereafter,[48] but a 2010 survey of large employers found 94 percent of them believing the bill will actually increase their costs.[49] A January 2011 poll found 48 percent of Americans favoring repeal of the bill and 43 percent preferring retention.[50] Repeal would require approval by the House, Senate, and President and thus is unlikely at present, but opponents have attacked the bill in the courts claiming it is unconstitutional in several respects.

TARP

As explained in Chapter 1, the Bush and Obama administrations injected hundreds of billions into failing banks, car companies and others and actually temporarily took over some failing operations in 2008 and thereafter in order to stimulate an economy that appeared to be on the verge of collapse. At this writing much of that Troubled Asset Relief Program (TARP) money has been repaid, many banks are healthy, General Motors seems to be turning around, and federal financial leaders remain convinced the intervention was necessary to prevent another Great Depression. Of course, many free market advocates are unpersuaded. They believe the government should never take ownership stakes in private companies, and they think TARP subjected the marketplace to a dangerous *moral hazard;* an economics argument claiming that an individual or business that is protected from risk (by government intervention, in this case) will increase its risk-taking behavior in the future in the belief that a bailout will follow, if needed. That is, if these giant firms are *"too big to fail"* as federal decision makers apparently believed, they will in the future be able to operate in less disciplined ways because they can assume, based on the TARP experience, that they will be rescued if necessary for the country's welfare.

> "Too big to fail."

Financial Reform

Concluding that the financial markets needed more effective and thorough oversight in light of the nation's near crash, Congress and President Obama in 2010 approved the Dodd-Frank Wall Street Reform and Consumer Protection Act to improve America's financial regulatory structure and subject more financial companies to federal oversight. As perhaps its chief goal, the new law was designed to prevent "systemic risks," financial collapses that would threaten the entire economy. Toward that objective, a 15-member Financial Stability Oversight Council headed by the Secretary of the Treasury will monitor the health of the entire U.S. financial system. Banks will be required to maintain larger capital holdings in order to reduce risky lending, provide funds for emergencies, and make becoming dangerously large a less attractive direction. The Council will have the power to force a large company to divest some of its holdings if it is considered a threat to the welfare of the total economy, and ultimately the federal government will be able to seize and close down a company that threatens the nation's financial health. Big financial companies will be required to create and update "funeral plans" to provide for their own quick and orderly shutdown in the event of financial failure. Those changes and others seek to prevent a recurrence of the recent collapse that arguably left taxpayers with little choice but to bailout failing financial giants. The act also reforms mortgage lending practices in an effort to ensure that borrowers actually have the wherewithal to repay. The enormous bill (over 2,300 pages) has many more provisions, including the creation of the Consumer Financial Protection Bureau (see Chapter 15), other mortgage reforms, increased oversight of derivatives and hedge funds, new rules for credit rating agencies, a larger shareholder voice in executive pay decisions, and limits (under the so-called Volcker Rule) on the amount of a bank's own assets that can be used for some risky forms of proprietary trading (investing the firm's own money rather than that of its clients).

The finance reforms, while numerous and complex, seem to critics to simply tinker with the existing system rather than providing the restructuring they believe necessary to assure a healthy, safe financial future for the nation. Big financial firms now have somewhat less room to maneuver, but overall the financial landscape looks very much like it did in 2007/08 when the whole structure was approaching a systemic failure.[51] Six giant firms—Bank of America, Citigroup, Goldman Sachs, JPMorgan Chase, Morgan Stanley, and Wells Fargo—have about $9.2 trillion in assets, a sum equal to about 63 percent of America's gross domestic product. Those big banks wield enormous, highly concentrated financial and political influence, a worry left largely unaddressed by Dodd-Frank, and despite Congress's efforts, those big institutions almost certainly remain "too big to fail."[52] At the same time, critics from the free market right see the bill increasing loan costs while discouraging investment and job growth. At this writing in 2011, Republicans in Congress are trying to repeal portions of the bill, block appointment of a director for the agency and deny funding necessary to carry out its mandates. Of course, federal regulators are creating thousands of pages of new rules to implement the broad outlines crafted by Dodd-Frank, and those crucial rules are subject to intense lobbying by the banking industry and consumer groups.

> Big banks wield enormous, highly concentrated financial and political influence.

Regulatory Criticisms

Are our lives excessively regulated, insufficiently regulated, or are government's regulations too often ineffective? Let's consider some evidence.

I. Excessive Regulation

In brief, the excessive regulation argument is that government rules reduce business efficiency, curb freedom, and unjustly redistribute resources while expanding the government bureaucracy and the taxes/borrowing that fund it.

Federal government spending reached nearly 42 percent of the nation's gross national product in 2009 (before falling to just under 40 percent in 2010). Those highly threatening numbers (up from 24 percent in 1950 and 35 percent prior to the current recession[53]) pushed Congress and President Obama to agree in 2011 on a comprehensive budget-cutting package.

According to the federal Small Business Administration, the annual cost (both direct and indirect) of federal regulations (a regulatory "tax," according to critics) exceeded $1.75 trillion in 2008, the equivalent of $15,586 for every person in America.[54]

The Federal Register, the daily journal of federal rules (both final and proposed) along with presidential orders, was expected to total about 80,000 new pages for 2010, a near record amount.[55] The 2010 healthcare law alone is projected to require the creation of 183 new agencies, commissions, panels, and so on while the 2010 financial reform bill directs government to write new rules in 243 separate areas.[56]

Federal government civilian employees total about 2 million, and a new study suggests those people are paid about $8,000 more annually in salary and about $30,000 more annually in benefits than their private sector equivalents.[57] (Critics say the study failed to properly match job categories and that federal employees are generally better educated and older than those in the private sector.)

[For a Cato Institute video, "There Are Too Many Bureaucrats and They Are Paid Too Much," see **http://www.youtube.com/watch?v=5xzd3puYmiM**]

Perhaps the biggest risk from excessive government is slower economic growth and fewer jobs. The U.S. Chamber of Commerce argues that the threat of ever-growing regulations brings such uncertainty to the economy that businesses simply decline to invest out of fear that government might impose costly, new rules at any time. The Chamber pointed to the $1.8 trillion in cash reserves held by American businesses in 2010 and said: "Businesses are reacting by sitting on capital, afraid to invest or hire."[58] [For an array of conservative analyses of tax issues, see **http://www.atr.org.** For more detailed criticisms of the federal regulatory process, see **http://www.heritage.org or http://cei.org or http:// www.cato.org/pubs/regulation**]

Shrink Big Government?

Given the enormous costs involved and the long-term threat of too much government, Americans routinely plead for lower taxes and smaller government, but when it comes to actually cutting specific programs that benefit them, sentiments change dramatically. A 2010 poll found 57 percent of respondents uncomfortable with raising the Social Security retirement age to 69 over the next 60 years. About 70 percent resisted cuts to Medicare, Social Security, and defense. Peter Hart, a codirector of the poll said: "Everybody wants to cut the deficit and cut the spending. But at the end of the day, everybody wants a choice that doesn't affect their well-being."

Source: Peter Wallsten, "Deficit Proposal Draws Mixed Review," *The Wall Street Journal,* November 18, 2010 [**http://online.wsj.com/**].

II. Insufficient Regulation

Constant change in our lives, spurred by technological advances and globalization, along with evolving values, the yearning for personal security and an abiding search for justice have persistently pushed American government at all levels to develop new rules. Responding, for example, to consumer anxiety over food hazards, Congress and President

Obama in late 2010 approved the Food Safety Modernization Act, the first big upgrade in federal food safety requirements in 70 years (for more, see Chapter 15). Advocates of increased regulation point to the many successes of government intervention: legal equality for minorities and women, cleaner air, safer workplaces, greatly diminished child labor, network airways substantially free of pornography and indecency, enhanced auto safety, and so on.

Does government intervention pay off?

Does the government intervention pay off? Free market advocates say "no" in many instances, but some powerful numbers and respected opinions say "yes." The federal Office of Management and Budget's 2010 draft "Report to Congress on the Benefits and Costs of Federal Regulations," found that the estimated annual benefits of major federal rules reviewed by the OMB for which data were available from 1999 to 2009 totaled between $128 billion and $616 billion while the estimated costs were between $43 billion and $55 billion.[59] Legendary investor Warren Buffet weighed in enthusiastically in a 2010 *New York Times* letter to "Uncle Sam" applauding what he viewed as a necessary and highly successful federal government intervention to save the financial markets in 2008 and thereafter. Buffet reminded readers of the economic meltdown the nation faced, the giant banks that were teetering, the major industrial companies that were running out of money and the millions of Americans whose prosperity was at risk. The threat was enormous, as Buffet saw it, and he judged the government to have provided the proper remedy:

> So, again, Uncle Sam, thanks to you and your aides. Often you are wasteful, and sometimes you are bullying. On occasion, you are downright maddening. But in this extraordinary emergency, you came through—and the world would look far different now if you had not.[60]

If we look at one small, relatively insignificant but emotionally powerful example of a recent rule, we achieve some sense of why government intervention may at times be necessary to correct market failures. In late 2009, the federal Department of Transportation announced heavy new fines for airlines that hold passengers in planes on the tarmac too long. Airlines that do not provide food and water after two hours or an opportunity to leave the plane after three hours face fines up to $27,500 per passenger.[61] The airlines said the rules would backfire by forcing the cancellation of many more flights than normal, but early results were very promising. In the month of June 2010, with the new rules in place, only three planes were held on the tarmac for more than three hours; down from 268 such cases one year earlier. Flight cancellations were steady.[62] In this instance, the market did not offer a ready solution, and based on the early results, government rules seem to have proved useful.

III. Ineffective Regulation

Just as the market can fail, so can the regulatory system. The sources of that regulatory failure are multiple, but the *New York Times* recently pointed to one example, the government's willingness, prior to the financial crisis, to allow banks to "shop" for their preferred regulators with the result that "firms switched at will among various overseers, in search of the loosest rules and laxest regulators."[63] Critics further charge that the regulatory process is corrupted by familiar bureaucratic problems including inefficiency, incompetence, low productivity and inconsistent policy enforcement. Of course, the problem of regulatory capture, explained earlier in this chapter, can play a powerful role in ineffectual regulation as Jacob Laksin explains in reviewing Timothy Carney's book, *The Big Ripoff*:

> Another myth—debunked by Mr. Carney—holds that regulations are the scourge of the business world. In fact, as he argues, many top companies welcome these rules. The airline industry sees burdensome federal oversight as a means of discouraging upstart competition. Tobacco giant Philip Morris is only too happy to submit to government curbs on advertising, confident that the effect is to keep smaller, lesser-known manufacturers on the margins, to the benefit of its already famous Marlboro, Merit, and other brands.[64]

Deregulation

Beginning with the Airline Deregulation Act of 1978, America embarked on a 30-year effort to reduce the role of government in the economy. Deregulation spread to energy, trucking, telecommunications, and financial services. Republicans and Democrats alike embraced the idea that greater efficiency, competitiveness, and freedom would accompany reduced government oversight. During that period the U.S. economy doubled in size and yet the executive branch of the federal government, excluding the Defense Department, employed about the same number of people that it did in 1978.[65] Many federal agencies actually shrunk in size.[66]

In cases where a government role continued to be considered necessary, deregulation advocates argued for applying free market incentives and reasoning to achieve regulatory goals. Thus, rather than forbidding undesirable conduct (such as pollution and industrial accidents), the government might impose a tax on behaviors society wants to discourage. In effect, a business would purchase the right to engage in conduct society considers injurious or inefficient. Similarly, rather than rationing portions of the radio spectrum or the right to land at airports at peak times, the government might auction those rights to the highest bidder. In addition, cost–benefit analysis was applied to regulations. [For an argument in support of deregulating marriage, see **http://www.etalkinghead.com/archives/deregulation-of-marriage-2004-03-01.html**]

Your Life: $7 Million?

How much is a life worth? That question is probably the crucial cost–benefit inquiry. When imposing new environmental or car safety rules, for example, we are forced to think about how much money we should spend to save an additional life. Recently, leading scholar Kip Viscusi and colleagues put a $7 to $8 million value on human life based on what we are willing to pay to save an average American life. (In 2010, the FDA valued a life at $7.9 million, while the EPA put the figure at $9.1 million.)

At this writing in 2011, the National Highway Traffic Safety Administration (NHTSA) has proposed a new rule that would essentially phase in rearview, back-up safety cameras in new cars, pickups and SUVs by 2014. The rule was called for by Congress in the 2007 Cameron Gulbransen Kids Transportation Safety Act. The law was named after a two-year-old boy who was killed in the family driveway when his father accidentally backed over him. NHTSA estimates the rule would save 95 to 112 lives per year and prevent 7,000 to 8,000 injuries. The cost would range from $159 to $203 per vehicle or somewhat less if the vehicle were already equipped with a display screen. The total cost for the nearly 17 million vehicles expected to be sold in 2014 would be between $1.9 billion and $2.7 billion. Cheaper but less effective audible warning devices could be required in place of the cameras. NHTSA says that back-over accidents cause an average of 229 deaths and 18,000 injuries per year, with 44 percent of the deaths involving those under age five and 33 percent involving those over age 70.

Questions

1. Would you favor the camera requirement? Explain your reasoning, including the issues and evidence you evaluated in reaching your conclusion.
2. *a.* How much is your life worth?
   b. Should the value of lives be a consideration in federal rules and spending decisions? Explain.

Sources: Binyamin Appelbaum, "As U.S. Agencies Put More Value on a Life, Businesses Fret," *The New York Times,* February 16, 2011 [**http://www.nytimes.com**]; Thomas J. Kniesner, W. Kip Viscusi, and James P. Ziliak, "Policy Relevant Heterogeneity in the Value of Statistical Life: New Evidence from Panel Data Quantile Regression," *Journal of Risk and Uncertainty* 40 (2010), p. 15; and Peter Vales-Dapena, "Autos May Be Required to Have Back-Up Cameras," CNNMoney.com, December 3, 2010 [**http://money.cnn.com/2010/12/03/autos/backup_cameras_nhtsa/index.htm**].

Deregulation Assessed: The Good News

Prior to the current financial crisis, deregulation was a popular, and in many ways, successful strategy. Deregulation often resulted in lower prices, increased innovation, increased consumption, and better lives overall. The power of a competitive, open market is evident in the telecommunications explosion of recent years. As of 2009, 4 billion mobile phone connections had been established worldwide allowing enormous advances in efficiency, idea exchange and enhanced pleasure.[67] A former United States ambassador, David Gross, explained why deregulation has been critical to that growth:

> We didn't reach 4 billion connections by accident. We got there because governments implemented market reforms that allowed new carriers to enter previously protected telecom markets and to compete on price, service, and coverage. By opening up their markets to innovation and competition, developing countries attracted investors. Those investors put their money into infrastructure and training, resulting in millions of new jobs.[68]

Now critics fear that our financial troubles, the Gulf oil spill, widespread food safety problems and other threats are prompting an unwise return to government rules to correct perceived free market failures. United States Chamber of Commerce President Thomas Donohue summarized that fear in 2010:

> Today, a regulatory hurricane threatens our economy and its ability to create the 20 million American jobs that we need by the end of this decade. . . .
>
> We've seen a dramatic acceleration of major regulations and mandates, from the health care and financial reform laws to some of the most activist agendas ever undertaken by federal agencies.[69]

Donohue acknowledged the need for "sensible regulations" to assure workplace safety, guarantee workers' rights and protect the public health, but he argues that the nation is sinking under the weight of the "ever-expanding" regulatory state.[70]

Deregulation Assessed: The Bad News

Journalist Vermont Royster argued that government is vital to civilized life:

> If I hesitate to join the hue for deregulation, even when much of the regulation is misguided, it's because I shudder at the thought of a wholly deregulated society. I prefer knowing my pharmacist has to be licensed and that somebody checks on him; so also with the butcher so that I have some assurance his scale registers a true measure. . . .
>
> So regulation in some form or other is one of the prices we pay for our complex civilization. And the more complicated society becomes, the more need for some watching over its many parts.[71]

Deregulation in practice has produced big benefits, but it has not been a painless process. A Consumers Union study claims that deregulation has created an "increasingly Wild West marketplace" requiring some renewal of regulation in cable, phone, lending, and airline markets.[72] A key doubt lies in fears about monopoly—that deregulated markets are allowing a few firms to control vast pieces of American life. Some specific concerns:

- *Telecommunications.* The federal Telecommunications Act of 1996 substantially deregulated the phone, cable, wireless, and satellite businesses. Wireless and long-distance rates fell dramatically, but local phone and cable rates have been rising. Furthermore, the telecommunications merger wave has allowed a handful of giant companies to control the media[73] with the result that music radio, critics claim, has become "increasingly bland, and formulaic.[74] Similarly, Federal Communications Commissioner Michael Copps warned in 2010 that American media is not producing the news and information content necessary for the citizenry to make intelligent decisions about the nation's democratic future.[75] He says the FCC is partially to blame because its deregulation polices have encouraged a "consolidation mania" that has resulted in fewer and fewer sources of information.He did, however, acknowledge great telecommunications progress.[76]

  > A handful of giant companies control the media.

- *Electricity.* An Associated Press study using 2006 federal data found that electrical rates have climbed significantly more in deregulated states than in those maintaining government oversight.[77]

- *Transportation.* Prior to deregulation in the late 1970s and early 1980s, airlines had been tightly controlled by a federal agency, The Civil Aeronautics Board, which approved routes and set fares such that airlines received a guaranteed 12 percent return on flights if they were at least 55 percent full.[78] Deregulation brought much lower fares, the entry of discounters like Southwest and greatly increased ridership, but many small communities lost airline service or saw it decline in quality, most of the remaining handful of big firms in the market are struggling to remain solvent and airline travel today is often chaotic. Retired American Airlines CEO Bob Crandall favors limited reregulation because of what he sees as the deplorable condition of the industry:

> Our airlines, once world leaders, are now laggards in every category, including fleet age, service quality and international reputation. . . . Airline service, by any standard, has become unacceptable.[79]

Further Deregulation or Reregulation?

Financial Services

The near collapse of America's banking system in 2008 offers a superb "test case" to examine the "What Went Wrong?" question posed by *The Washington Post:*

> How did the world's markets come to the brink of collapse? Some say regulators failed. Other claim deregulation left them handcuffed. Who's right? Both are. . . .[80]

The federal government's Financial Crisis Inquiry Commission's study of the financial collapse pointed to an array of problems including ineffective government oversight; corporate governance failures; reckless borrowing. lending and investment practices; ethical failures, an unregulated financial derivatives market, and failures in the credit rating agencies (e.g., Fitch Ratings, Moody's and Standard & Poor's). [For the Commission's report, see **http://fcic.law.stanford.edu/**]

Doubtless many factors contributed to the meltdown, but our primary concern is the issue of market failure and the resulting need for government intervention. Did the market fail? Unsurprisingly, free market advocates say the market performed well.

> Did the market fail?

They blame the subprime problems on government intervention, especially easy credit policies designed to extend home ownership to as many as possible, with reduced attention to ability to pay.[81] Critics of the free market on the other hand, say that deregulation was a big factor in the collapse. For 30 years prior to the meltdown, the government gradually diminished its oversight of the banking industry in an effort to allow the market a greater voice and to render American banks more competitive in the global market.Most prominently perhaps, the 1933 Glass-Steagall Act was partially repealed in 1999, thus allowing a mingling of commercial and investment banks. In total, the regulatory walls separating commercial banks, investment banks, brokerage firms, insurance and commodities trading came down, giant "financial supermarkets" emerged and risky investing arguably grew.[82]

> Alan Greenspan acknowledged a "breakdown" in self-regulation.

The financial crisis shattered the confidence of some staunch free market advocates including former Federal Reserve chair, Alan Greenspan, who acknowledged, in 2009 a "breakdown" in self-regulation.[83] Testifying before Congress, he said:

> I made a mistake in presuming that the self-interests of organizations, specifically banks and others, were such as that they were best capable of protecting their own shareholders and their equity in the firms.[84]

Whether the market failed or not, we should note general agreement that the government failed in its oversight responsibilities. As former Securities and Exchange Commission chair, Republican Chris Cox, said: "The last six months (of the financial crisis) have made it abundantly clear that voluntary regulation does not work."[85]

Regulatory Virtue

Historian John Steele Gordon argues that capitalism needs regulation and that regulation has made the country more stable and richer:

> Capitalism without regulation and regulators is inherently unstable, Gordon claims, "as people will usually put their short-term interests ahead of the interests of the system as a whole, and either chaos or plutocracy will result. . . . The country since the New Deal has been a far richer, far more economically secure, far more just society."[86]

Government regulation in America normally arises not from ideology but from actual problems.[87] Pollution, industrial accidents, and dangerous food and drugs were clearly the impetus for the creation of agencies such as the EPA, OSHA, and the FDA.

The Public Has Doubts

While applauding government's particularized help in encouraging clean air, safe workplaces, safe food and so on, the American people have repeatedly affirmed their skepticism of big government as an institution. When asked in a 2009 Gallup Poll whether big business, big labor, or big government will be the greatest threat to the country in the future, 55 percent of Americans cited big government (down from 61 percent in 2006) while 32 percent said big business (up from 25 percent in 2006), and 10 percent big labor (slightly up from 9 percent).[88]

> The American people have repeatedly affirmed their skepticism of big government.

The Winner: The Mixed Economy?

Economist and columnist Sebastian Mallaby argues that we should acknowledge a role for both the market and government in our mixed economy and recognize that the American people will continue to demand more and more from the government (security from criminals and terrorists, clean air, safe food, good schools, and so on).[89] Indeed, he argues that those public goods in our prosperous society probably matter more than private pleasures such as DVDs and fancy vacations. As a result, government will likely be under great pressure to spend more.[90] How should we address this ongoing conflict between the market and government? Mallaby offered his advice:

> Conservatives want to deal with this trend toward larger government by pretending we can reverse it, but that is unlikely to happen. Liberals want to celebrate the collapse of "free market ideology," but free markets do a lot of jobs better than government. What we should do is embrace growing government but also be ruthless about making government and markets more efficient.[91]

Global Regulation

We should remember that regulation in the United States remains modest relative to the balance of the globe. While the cost of regulation in the United States is great, government rules are, in fact, less burdensome in America than in most nations. For example, a 2004 study found the United States just behind number one New Zealand among the world's nations in ease of starting and operating businesses.[92] Similarly, a World Bank study finds excess regulation stifling productivity in much of Africa, Latin America, and the former Soviet Union. On the other hand, the United States ranks along with Australia, Canada, New Zealand, and the United Kingdom, among a few others, as the least regulated and most efficient economies. In general, the World Bank study found that the least regulated economies are the strongest economies. Perhaps surprisingly, however, a critical factor in economic growth is the presence of an efficient legal system. A 2006 study found that countries with better regulations grow faster. Improving business regulations from the worst quartile to the best "implies a 2.3 percentage point increase in annual growth."[93] So rules can be helpful if efficient but disastrous if excessive.[94]

We should also understand that regulation, particularly in the banking sector, increasingly involves a cooperative, international effort that recognizes the mutually dependent, closely intertwined nature of the global financial markets. In 2010, the G20 nations (the biggest economic powers) agreed to new measures (labeled Basel III) to promote stability in the global financial system.[95] The core change is an agreement requiring banks to hold in reserve capital equal to 7 percent of their risk-weighted assets with the biggest banks holding 9.5 percent; a figure that could be increased to 10.5 percent for the biggest, most deeply interconnected banks that represent the greatest threat if they experience a crisis. The higher capital requirements provide both a reserve to draw on in the event of future crises and a disincentive to risk taking. Of course, the higher requirements also mean that less money is available for lending and investment thus likely restraining economic growth, but regulators apparently are encouraging banks to become, in some ways, smaller and simpler. [96]

Basel III

Two Concluding Cases

Let's close this chapter about government rules by asking if we should have more of them.

Case I. FDA Ban on Menthol Cigarettes?

At this writing, a special tobacco advisory committee of the federal Food and Drug Administration (see Chapter 15) has recommended that the FDA should banish menthol cigarettes from the market. Antismoking groups say about 80 percent of black smokers prefer the menthol variety. In general, black smokers have the highest rates of smoking-related diseases. Critics also say that menthol cigarettes are particularly appealing to young people because the flavoring hides the harsh cigarette taste. One study found that 45 percent of smokers aged 12 to 17 used menthol brands. Evidence is mixed about whether menthol cigarettes are more difficult to quit than other varieties. Some limited evidence supports the claim that menthol smokers are at a greater risk of disease. A 2010 Morgan Stanley survey found that 40 percent of Newport (the leading menthol brand) smokers likely would try to quit smoking if a menthol ban were imposed. All other flavored cigarettes were previously banned by the FDA.

Lorillard, maker of Newport, is leading the fight against a ban. Lorillard wants to protect the growing popularity of Newport, which has enjoyed a market share increase from 9 percent in 2001 to 13 percent today even as the total market for cigarettes has fallen. Lorillard has pointed to the thousands of jobs that are at stake, and the company argues that a ban would result in a large unregulated black market for the cigarettes. Lorillard also disputes the claim that menthol cigarettes pose greater medical risks than other varieties.

Question

1. The Web site, "Hot Air" thinks the government should not intervene in the menthol cigarette market:

   Once again, we have the federal government acting as nanny rather than allowing adults to make their own decisions. No one forces people to use tobacco products, after all, and we have literally spent decades educating people about the dangers. . . .[97]

   What do you think the government should do? Explain.

   Source: David Kesmodel, "Lorillard Fights to Snuff Menthol Ban," *The Wall Street Journal,* January 5, 2011, p. A1.

Case II. Cell Phones: A Deadly Distraction?

Four in five Americans admit to making phone calls while driving and nearly one in five sends text messages.[98] Forty five percent of Americans say they have been hit or nearly hit by a driver using a cell phone.[99] Texting was considered a "factor" in 200,000 crashes in 2008.[100] A *Houston Chronicle* editorial argued for measures to curb driving while using a cell phone:

> Even a cursory glance at the statistics is evidence enough that swift, comprehensive action must be taken on a national level to curb this reckless, potentially deadly, behavior: Driving while using a cell phone incurs a fourfold greater risk of crashing, equivalent to driving while drunk (with a 0.08 blood-alcohol level). For texters, the risk is eight times greater. A recent study by the Virginia Tech Transportation Institute, which videotaped truck drivers over 18 months, showed that texting made them 23 times more likely to crash or narrowly avoid a crash.[101]

According to the U.S. Department of Transportation, distracted driving was a factor in nearly 6,000 deaths and 500,000 injuries in 2009.[102] Research at the University of Utah indicates that cell phone conversation is much more dangerous as a distraction than is passenger conversation.[103]

No state forbids all cell phone use while driving, but 30 ban text messaging for all drivers, 28 ban cell phone use for novice drivers, and eight states forbid all drivers from using handheld cell phones while driving.[104] Are these restraints effective? The evidence is not particularly encouraging to date. A 2010 national study found no significant reduction in accident claims in states that have forbidden hand-held cell phone use while driving.[105] Of course, the real problem may be distraction rather than merely holding a phone. The Governors Highways Safety Association has advised states to pass texting bans but hold off on cell phone bans until the evidence is more complete.[106]

Questions

1. Mike Hashimoto, assistant editorial page editor at the *Dallas Morning News:*

   I get as mad as the next person at the minivan driver cruising along 5 mph below the speed limit in the left lane, basically causing everyone else with someplace to be to dodge around him/her in a slightly dangerous way. That doesn't mean we need another annoying law in the long-running series of laws intended to remove all risk from our daily lives. . . . A cell phone ban might make us feel better, but at best, it would have the same practical effect as banning

Big Macs while driving, shaving while driving, reading a map while driving or reaching into the back seat for your kid while driving. . . .[107]

    a. Would you favor government rules forbidding cell phone use while driving? Explain.

    b. What about text messaging, grooming, eating, and so on? Explain.

2. *The New York Times* reports that technology companies like Intel and Google are turning their creative attention to car dashboards hoping to bring PC power to the car. Ten-inch screens showing Web pages and the like are being developed for car use. MIT professor Nicholas A. Ashford thinks this technology initiative is reckless:

> This is irresponsible at best and pernicious at worst. . . . Unfortunately, and sadly, it is a continuation of the pursuit of profit over safety—for both drivers and pedestrians.[108]

Do you agree that technology companies are irresponsibly putting profit before safety in developing ever more advanced, and doubtless distracting, technology in cars? Explain.

3. Distinguished economist Herbert Stein, perhaps best known as father of celebrity Ben Stein, said that we are desperate for cell phone conversations to ward off our loneliness:

> It is the way of keeping contact with someone, anyone who will reassure you that you are not alone. You may think you are checking on your portfolio but deep down you are checking on your own existence.[109]

    a. Are you dependent on your cell phone?

    b. If so, should the government discourage that use by, for example, imposing higher taxes on cell phone purchases? Explain.

Guy Davenport: "The telephone is God's gift to the bore."

Source: Interview by John Jeremiah Sullivan. *The Paris Review.* Fall 2002.

Internet Exercise

Should the U.S. government impose new rules requiring all bicyclists to wear helmets? New Zealand has enforced a national mandatory all-age bicycle helmet law since 1994. To help with your recommendation for the United States, consider the evidence from the New Zealand experience at [**http://en.wikipedia.org/wiki/Bicycle_helmets_in_New_Zealand**].

Chapter Questions

1. *a.* Has deregulation affected your life? Explain.
   b. Do you trust the free market? The government? Both? Neither? Explain.
   c. On balance, has business deregulation been a good direction for America? Explain.

2. *The Des Moines Register* advocated a free market approach to cable television, labeling it a "nonessential activity."
   a. Should the government be involved in regulating only those products and services that we cannot do without? Explain.
   b. Has deregulation reduced your cable television rates? Explain.

3. Although the legal landscape is notoriously confusing, the U.S. Justice Department takes the position that federal law, including the 1961 Wire Act (forbidding the use of telecommunication services to place bets) and the 2006 Unlawful Internet Gambling Enforcement Act, render Internet gambling in the United States unlawful. Internet gambling is legal in much of the world and American gamblers can readily access online gambling sites. Federal prosecutors have not pursued individual players and while a number of states forbid Internet gambling, enforcement is not aggressive. Bills have been introduced in Congress in recent years to lift the federal ban and regulate Internet gambling.

   a. List some of the pros and cons of allowing and regulating Internet gambling.

   b. Would you favor that direction? Explain.

4. The Heritage Foundation's 2011 global Index of Economic Freedom generally demonstrates that the nations most successful in increasing their economic freedom (by reducing taxes and so forth) enjoy, according to the editors of the study, higher per capita incomes, and higher overall well being.[110] When the Index was first published in 1995, the United States ranked fifth in the world, but it fell to ninth in the 2011 study. Hong Kong ranked first in 2011, with Canada sixth and the United Kingdom sixteenth.[111]

   a. What is economic freedom?

   b. The Heritage Foundation lists 10 factors including, for example, business freedom, in its list of ingredients in measuring economic freedom. In addition to business freedom, what other factors would you include in a list designed to measure a nation's level of overall economic freedom?

   c. How does economic freedom help an economy grow?

5. Former Secretary of Labor Robert Reich: "The era of big government may be over, but the era of regulation through litigation has just begun.[112] Explain what Reich meant.

6. Sony Ericsson Mobile used actors to pose as tourists to demonstrate its camera phone at attractions in New York City and Seattle.[113] The actors asked passersby to take their photo, thus demonstrating the camera's capabilities, but the actors did not identify themselves as actors representing Sony Ericsson. Advocacy groups have complained to the Federal Trade Commission about this word-of-mouth marketing campaign.

   a. Explain the objections to the Sony Ericsson approach.

   b. Should the FTC intervene in some fashion? Explain.

7. Transportation deregulation resulted in an immediate loss of bus and/or air service to some smaller communities. Some of that loss was compensated for with the entry of smaller, independent firms.

   a. Has deregulation endangered small-town America? Explain.

   b. Should we apply free market principles to the postal service, thus, among other consequences, compelling those in small and remote communities to pay the full cost of service rather than the "subsidized" cost now paid? Explain.

8. The expense of government regulation is not limited to the direct cost of administering the various agencies. Explain and offer examples of the other expenses produced by regulation.

9. To the extent the federal government achieves deregulation, what substitutes will citizens find for protection?

10. Pulitzer Prize–winning author and presidential adviser Arthur Schlesinger:

> The assault on the national government is represented as a disinterested movement to "return" power to the people. But the withdrawal of the national government does not transfer power to the people. It transfers power to the historical rival of the national government and the prime cause of its enlargement—the great corporate interests.[114]

   a. Using 19th- and 20th-century American economic history, explain Schlesinger's claim that corporate interests are the primary cause of big government.

   b. Do you agree with Schlesinger that we continue to need big government to counteract corporate interests and achieve fairness for all in American life? Explain.

11. Make the argument that increasing government rules and jobs leads to decreasing private-sector businesses and jobs.

12. One authority estimates that obesity contributes to the deaths of 100,000 Americans annually.[115] A strategy for reducing the health risks of obesity is to impose a tax on high calorie junk foods such as soda, donuts, and potato chips. Maine, for example, imposed a 5.5 percent snack tax as a means of closing a budget gap, but that state's adult obesity rate doubled during the 10 years the tax was in place.[116] Two-thirds of the states already impose a tax (averaging 5.2 percent) on soft-drinks, but for a 5-foot-10, 279-pound person, the average weight loss associated with the tax has been about three ounces.[117]

   a. What objections would you raise to increased taxes on junk food.

   b. Would you support a significant tax, say, 25 percent, on junk food? Explain.

   c. Would subsidies to lower the price of healthy food be a more effective strategy than taxes on unhealthy food? Explain.

13. The British government spends about $340 per year per Briton on drug costs while the United States spends about $800 per year per American. As *The Wall Street Journal* reported, Great Britain is struggling to find ways to curb rocketing health care costs:

> Millions of patients around the world have taken drugs introduced over the past decade to delay the worsening of Alzheimer's disease. While the drugs offer no cure, studies suggest they work in some patients at least for a while. But this year, an arm of Britain's government health-care system, relying on some economists' number-crunching, said the benefit isn't worth the cost. It issued a preliminary ruling calling on doctors to stop prescribing the drugs. The ruling highlighted one of the most disputed issues in medicine today. If a treatment helps people, should governments and private insurers pay for it without question? Or should they first measure the benefit against the cost, and only pay if the cost-benefit ratio exceeds some preset standard?[118]

   Should the U.S. government and insurers employ cost-benefit calculations in deciding which illnesses and patients receive coverage? Explain.

14. Joseph Stiglitz, the chief White House economist at the time, argued in 1996 that "a huge economic literature" supports his view that "appropriately circumscribed government programs can lead to a higher-growth economy."[119] How can government programs stimulate the economy rather than act as a drag on it?

15. A major issue facing the Federal Aviation Administration is congestion in the airways caused by too many planes seeking to take off or land at peak times at high-demand airports. How might we solve that problem while maintaining reasonable service?

16. In calculating the costs and benefits of a new rule, make the argument that added regulation normally slows the economy and leads to increased deaths.

17. Eighty-three percent of teens had at least one sunburn in 1999, whereas the comparable figure in 1986 was 30 percent.[120] "Right now, we're at the apex of the 'bronze goddess era,'" said Atoosa Rubenstein, editor-in-chief of *CosmoGIRL* magazine.[121] More than a third of the 17-year-old girls in a recent survey reported going to a tanning salon in the previous year.[122] In 2009 the International Agency for Research on Cancer classified tanning beds as Group 1 carcinogens, meaning the evidence is sufficient for experts to conclude that the beds cause cancer.[123] A scientific review of the tanning data found that the risk of melanoma increases by 75 percent if tanning beds and lamps are used prior to age 30.[124] The American Academy of Dermatology Association (AADA) has urged the FDA to ban the sale and use of indoor tanning equipment for non-medical purposes and has called for state or federal laws to, among other things, forbid minors from using tanning devices. Do you support limits on teen tanning? Explain?

18. A bipartisan coalition labeled "Mayors Against Illegal Guns" released a 2010 study finding that 43,000 of the guns confiscated at crimes scenes in 2009 came from out-of-state gun dealers. Georgia, Virginia, West Virginia, Alabama, Mississippi, and Alaska were among the largest gun exporters. States with strong restrictions export guns at only about one seventh the rate of those with lax rules. About 12,000 Americans annually are murdered by guns.[125] Commenting in *The New York Times,* columnist Nicholas Kristof said:

> To protect the public, we regulate cars and toys, medicines and mutual funds. So, simply as a public health matter, shouldn't we take steps to reduce the toll from our domestic arms industry?[126]

Do you think we need firmer gun regulations? Explain.

Notes

1. P.J. Huffstutter, "Illinois Seeks to Curb Explicit Video Games," *Los Angeles Times,* December 16, 2004, p. A1.

2. California Civil Code sections 1746-1746.5.

3. *Brown v. Entertainment Merchants Association,* 2011 U.S. LEXIS 4802.

4. Ibid.

5. Staci Hupp, "Nearly 1 in 10 U.S. Kids Addicted to Video Games, ISU Study Finds," *The Des Moines Register,* April 20, 2009, p. 1A.

6. David Leonhardt, "Do Video Games Equal Less Crime?" *The New York Times,* May 24, 2010 [**http://economix.blogs.nytimes.com/2010/**].

7. Rob Stein, "Born to Be a Trader? Fingers Point to Yes." *The Washington Post,* January 13, 2009, p. A02.

8. Joseph P. Tomain, "American Regulatory Policy: Have We Found the 'Third Way'?" *Kansas Law Review* 48 (May 2000), p. 829.

9. Catherine Rampell, "Lax Oversight Caused Crisis, Bernanke Says," *The New York Times,* January 4, 2010 [**http://www.nytimes.com/2010**].

10. 317 U.S. 111 (1942).

11. 545 U.S. 1 (2005).

12. *Gonzalez v. Raich,* 545 U.S. 1, 57-8 (2005).

13. 115 S.Ct. 1624 (1995).

14. 18 U.S.C. 922 (q) (1) (A).

15. *Brzonkala v. Morrison and United States v. Morrison,* 529 U.S. 598 (2000).

16. *Brzonkala v. Virginia Polytechnic Institute,* 169 F.3d 820, 827 (4th Cir. 1999).

17. Ibid., p. 908.

18. John F. Cooney, "Federalism Spring: Evolution of the Federal-State Balance of Power," 1 *Bloomberg Law Reports-Administrative Law,* No. 4 (2009).

19. See, e.g., *Williamson v. Mazda Motor of Am., Inc.,* 131 S.Ct. 1131 (2011) [state tort suit not preempted] and *Bruesewitz v. Wyeth LLC,* 131 S.Ct. 1068 (2011) [state tort suit preempted].

20. Eric Asimov, "The Comprehensive Alcohol Regulatory Effectiveness Act," *The New York Times Diner's Journal,* May 4, 2010 [**http://dinersjournal.blogs.nytimes.com/**].

21. Kim Geiger, "Bill Uncorks a Brawl over Interstate Sale of Alcohol," *latimes.com,* August 5, 2010 [**http://www.latimes.com/business**].

22. Lyndsey Layton, "Chemical Law Has Global Impact," *The Washington Post,* June 12, 2008, p. A01.

23. Ibid.

24. Daniel Michaels, "Pact Ushers in Competitive Skies," *The Wall Street Journal,* March 23, 2007, p. A3.

25. Max Frankel, "The Next Great Story," *The New York Times,* March 15, 1998, sec. 6, p. 30.

26. Ibid.

27. Editorial, "Licensed to Kill," *The Wall Street Journal,* September 10, 2007, p. A14.

28. Jennifer Jacobs, "Judge Backs City's Refusal to Renew Bar's License," *Waterloo/Cedar Falls Courier,* November 22, 1998, p. C3.

29. The organizational structure of the introductory administrative law materials owes a great deal to the suggestions of Professor Cynthia Srstka, Augustana College (South Dakota).

30. *Comcast v. Federal Communications Commission,* 579 F.3d 1 (D.C. Cir. 2009).

31. Amy Schatz and Fawn Johnson, "Court Lifts FCC Limits on Cable Companies," *The Wall Street Journal,* August 29–30, 2009, p. B1.

32. Matt Schafer, "FCC Defends Discredited Media Ownership Rules," *Free Press,* July 22, 2010 [**http://www.stopbigmedia.com/blog/2010/**].

33. Charlie Savage, "Sex, Drug Use and Graft Cited in Interior Department," *The New York Times,* September 11, 2008 [**http://www.nytimes.com/2008/09/11/**].

34. Ibid.

35. Juliet Eilperin, "U.S. Exempted BP's Gulf of Mexico Drilling from Environmental Impact Study," *The Washington Post,* May 5, 2010, p. A04.

36. Rhonda Schwartz, Joseph Rhee and Brian Ross, "Revolving Door: From US Safety Agency to Toyota Representative," ABC News, February 4, 2010 [**http://abcnews.go.com/**].

37. Ibid.

38. Lori Montgomery, "Obama Orders All Fed Agencies to Review Regulations," *The Washington Post,* January 18, 2011 [**http://www.washingtonpost.com/**].

39. 531 U.S. 457 (2001).

40. Richard G. Stoll, "RCRA Recycling: EPA Issues Long-Awaited 'Definition of Solid Waste' (DSW) Amendments," *Foley & Lardner LLP Publications,* October 10, 2008 [**http://www.foley.com/publications/**].

41. Kathryn Watts, "Grappling with the (In?) Significance of Doctrine in Judicial Review," *Jotwell,* 2010 [**http://adlaw.jotwell.com/grappling-with-the-insignificance-of-doctrine-in-judicial-review/**].

42. Editorial, "Free Speech for Broadcasters," *The New York Times,* July 16, 2010 [**www.nytimes.com**].

43. *CBS v. Federal Communications Commission,* 535 F.3d 167 (3d Cir. 2008).

44. *Federal Communications Commission v. CBS,* 129 S.Ct. 2176 (2009).

45. *Fox Television v. Federal Communications Commission,* 489 F.3d 444 (2d Cir. 2010).

46. Cecilia King, "Court Rules against FCC Policies on Indecency," *The Washington Post,* July 14, 2010, p. 01.

47. *ABC v. Federal Communications Commission,* 2011 U.S. App. LEXIS 72 (2d Cir.).

48. Editorial, "If Reform Fails," *The New York Times,* March 7, 2010, p. 9.

49. John Hollon, "ObamaCare Update: It Won't Cut Costs, but Few Plan to Drop Coverage," TLNT, May 27, 2010 [**http://www.tlnt.com/**].

50. Daniel Strauss, "Poll: Slim Majority Wants Congress to Repeal Healthcare Reform," *The Hill's Blog Briefing Room,* January 18, 2011 [**http://thehill.com/blogs/blog-briefing-room/news/**].

51. John Cassidy, "The Economy: Why They Failed," *The New York Review of Books,* December 9, 2010 [**http://www.nybooks.com/**].

52. Ibid.

53. "US Government Spending as a Percent of GDP," [**http://www.usgovernmentspending.com/us_20th_century_chart.html**].

54. Brad Peck, "The Impact of Regulatory Costs on Small Firms," *The Chamber Post,* September 21, 2010 [**http://www.chamberpost.com/**].

55. Ryan Young, "Federal Register Hits 75,000 Pages," *The American Spectator: AMSPECBLOG,* December 2, 2010 [**http://spectator.org/blog/2010/**].

56. David Brooks, "The Technocracy Boom," *The New York Times,* July 19, 2010 [**www.nytimes.com**].

57. Dennis Cauchon, "Federal Pay Ahead of Private Industry," *USA TODAY,* March 8, 2010 [**www.usatoday.com**].

58. U.S. Chamber of Commerce, "Regulations Pile Up," *Free Enterprise Magazine,* September 2010 [**www.uschambermagazine.com**].

59. Office of Management and Budget, "2010 Report to Congress on the Benefits and Costs of Federal Regulations and Unfunded Mandates on State, Local, and Tribal Entities" [**http://www.whitehouse.gov/sites/default/files/omb/legislative/reports/2010_Benefit_Cost_Report.pdf**].

60. Warren E. Buffett, "Pretty Good for Government Work," *The New York Times,* November 16, 2010 [**http://www.nytimes.com/**].

61. Matthew L. Wald, "Stiff Fines Are Set for Long Wait on the Tarmac," *The New York Times,* December 22, 2009 [**http://www.nytimes.com**].

62. Melanie Trottman, "Excessive Runway Delays Drop after New Rule," *The Wall Street Journal,* August 11, 2010, p. B8.

63. Editorial, "Regulator Shopping," *The New York Times,* May 21, 2009 [**http://www.nytimes.com**].

64. Jacob Laksin, "Why Corporate America Needs Welfare Reform," *The Wall Street Journal,* July 29–30, 2006, p. P9.

65. Michael Mandel, "30-Year Deregulation Era Dies a Sudden Death*,*" *Bloomberg Businessweek,* September 18, 2008 [**http://www.msnbc.msn.com/**].

66. Ibid.

67. David A. Gross, "What Made the Cellphone Revolution Possible," *The Christian Science Monitor,* March 3, 2009 [**http://www.csmonitor.com/2009/0303/p09s02-coop.html**].

68. Ibid.

69. Thomas J. Donohue, "Regulations Devastate Economic Growth," *McClatchy,* October 14, 2010 [**http://www.uschamber.com/press/opeds/regulations-devastate-economic-growth**].

70. Ibid.

71. Vermont Royster, "'Regulation' Isn't a Dirty Word," *The Wall Street Journal,* September 9, 1987, p. 30.

72. Dow Jones Newswires, "Deregulation Is Likened to the 'Wild West,'" *The Wall Street Journal,* June 11, 2002, p. D3.

73. Freepress.net, "Ownership Chart: The Big Six," [**http://www.freepress.nt/ownership/chart/main**].

74. Future of Music Coalition, "Radio, Radio: FMC and the 2010 Media Ownership Review," *Future of Music Blog,* 2010 [**http://futureofmusic.org/blog/2010/07/14/radio-radio-fmc-and-2010**].

75. Joe Flint, "Journalism Is in Hour of 'Grave Peril,' Says Top Government Regulator," Company Town, *Los Angeles Times,* December 1, 2010 [**http://latimesblogs.latimes.com/entertainment-newsbuzz/2010/12/media-is-in-hour-of-grave-peril-says-top-government-regulator-.html**].

76. Ibid.

77. Ryan Keith, "Electric Deregulation Fails to Live Up to Promises as Bills Soar," *USA TODAY,* April 21, 2007 [**http://www.usatoday.com/**].

78. Robert D. Hershey, Jr., "Alfred E. Kahn Dies at 93; Prime Mover of Airline Deregulation," *The New York Times,* December 28, 2010 [**http://www.nytimes.com/**].

79. David Ignatius, "Failing Airlines, Failing Government," *The Washington Post,* June 22, 2008, p. B07.

80. Anthony Faiola, Ellen Nakashima and Jill Drew, "What Went Wrong?" *The Washington Post,* October 15, 2008, p. A01.

81. John H. Makin, "A Government Failure, Not a Market Failure," *Commentary,* July/August 2009 [**http://www.commentarymagazine.com/viewarticle.cfm/a-government-failure-not-a-market-failure-15191**].

82. Jake Ackman,"Economist Richard Parker Discusses Past and Future of Financial Deregulation," *Harvard Kennedy School News & Events,* March 18, 2009 [**http://www.hks.harvard.edu/news-events/news/articles/parker-economy-talk**].

83. Alan Greenspan, "We Need a Better Cushion Against Risk," *Financial Times,* March 26, 2009 [**http://www.ft.com/**].

84. Neil Irwin and Amit R. Paley, "Greenspan Says He Was Wrong on Regulation," *The Washington Post,* October 24, 2008, p. A01.

85. Stephen Labaton, "S.E.C. Concedes Oversight Flaws Fueled Collapse," *The New York Times,* September 27, 2008, Section A, p. 1.

86. John Steele Gordon, *An Empire of Wealth: The Epic History of American Economic Power* (New York: Harper Collins, 2004). Quoted by Wayne E. Yang, "The Wealth of America Is Wealth," *Christian Science Monitor,* December 7, 2004 [**http://www.csmonitor.com/2004/1207/p15s02-bogn.html**].

87. Lester Thurow, *The Zero-Sum Society* (New York: Penguin Books, 1980), p. 136.

88. Jeffrey M. Jones, "Big Gov't Still Viewed as Greater Threat than Big Business," *Gallup Poll,* April 20, 2009 [**http://www.gallup.com/**].

89. Sebastian Mallaby, "Capitalism: The Remix," *Washingtonpost.com,* December 4, 2008, p. A21.

90. Ibid.

91. Ibid.

92. Michael Schroeder, "Regulatory Rules Stifle Business in Poor Countries," *The Wall Street Journal,* September 8, 2004, p. A17.

93. Simeon Djankov, Caralee McLiesh, and Rita Maria Ramalho, "Regulation and Growth," *Social Science Research Network,* March 17, 2006. [**http://ssrn.com/abstract5893321**].

94. Michael Schroeder and Terence Roth, "World Bank Faults Tight Regulation," *The Wall Street Journal,* October 7, 2003, p. A2.

95. Brian Perry, "Understanding the Basel III International Regulations," *Investopedia,* December 17, 2010 [**http://finance.yahoo.com/news/**].

96. David Enrich and Victoria McGrane, "Capital Rules Tighten for Big Banks," *The Wall Street Journal,* June 27, 2011, p. C1.

97. Ed Morrissey, "Should the FDA Ban Menthol Cigarettes?" *Hot Air,* September 10, 2010 [**http://hotair.com/archives/2010/09/10/should-the-fda-ban-menthol-cigarettes/**].

98. Myron Levin, "What the Cellphone Industry Won't Tell You," *The Christian Science Monitor,* February 2, 2009 [**http://www.csmonitor.com/2009/0202/p09s02-coop.html**].

99. William Saletan, "The Mind-Blackberry Problem," *Slate,* October 23, 2008 [**http://www.slate.com/**].

100. Rebecca Webber, "Stop Texting Behind the Wheel," *Parade,* June 6, 2010, p. 14.

101. Editorial, "Deadly Distraction," *Houston Chronicle,* September 22, 2009 [**http://www.chron.com/**].

102. Daniel B. Wood, "Texting-While-Driving Crackdown Coming July 4 Weekend," *CSMonitor.com,* July 1, 2010 [**http://www.csmonitor.com/**].

103. "Chatty Driving: Phones vs. Passengers," Well Blog, *The New York Times,* December 1, 2008 [**http://well.blogs.nytimes.com/2008/**].

104. "State Cell Phone Use and Texting while Driving Laws," Governors Highway Safety Association, January 2011 [**http://www.ghsa.org/html/stateinfo/laws/cellphone_laws.html**].

105. Joseph B. White, "When Cell Phone Bans Don't Curb Crashes," *The Wall Street Journal,* February 3, 2010, p. D2.

106. Ibid.

107. Nicole Stockdale, "Time to Ban Cell Phones while Driving? (Ed Board Sounds Off)," *Dallas Morning Star,* July 22, 2009 [**http://dallasmorningviewblog.dallasnews.com/**].

108. Ashlee Vance and Matt Richtel, "Despite Risks, Internet Creeps onto Car Dashboards," *The New York Times,* January 7, 2010 [**http://www.nytimes.com/2010/**].

109. James Gleick, *The Acceleration of Just about Everything* (New York: Vintage Books, 1999), p. 89.

110. "Government Spending, High Taxes Restrain Growth in North America," Press Release North America, Heritage Foundation, January 12, 2011 [**http://www.heritage.org/**].

111. "Ranking the Countries," Index of Economic Freedom World Rankings," Heritage Foundation, January 2011 [**http://www.heritage.org/**].

112. Robert Reich, "Regulation Is Out, Litigation Is In," *USA TODAY,* February 11, 1999, p. 15A.

113. Annys Shin, "FTC Moves to Unmask Word-of-Mouth Marketing," *The Washington Post,* December 12, 2006, p. D01.

114. Arthur Schlesinger, Jr., "In Defense of Government," *The Wall Street Journal,* June 7, 1995, p. A14.

115. Karen Kaplan, "Calls to Tax Junk Food Gain Ground," *latimes.com,* August 23, 2009 [**http://www.latimes.com/**].

116. Ibid.

117. Ibid.

118. Jeanne Wilson, "Britain Stirs Outcry by Weighing Benefits of Drugs Versus Price," *The Wall Street Journal,* November 22, 2006, p. A1.

119. Bob Davis, "In Presidential Race, the Key Question Is, 'What Causes Growth?'" *The Wall Street Journal,* September 27, 1996, p. A1.

120. Julie Sevrens Lyons, "Doctors See Growing Cancer Risk with Trendy Tans," *Milwaukee Journal,* July 29, 2002, p. 3A.

121. Ibid.

122. Ibid.

123. "Tanning Beds Classified as 'Carcinogenic to Humans,'" *Daily Cancer News,* July 29, 2009 [**http://patient.cancerconsultants.com/**].

124. Steve Reinberg, "Tanning Beds Get Highest Carcinogen Rating," *U.S. News & World Report,* July 28, 2009 [**http://health.usnews.com/health-news/family-health/cancer/articles/2009/07/28/tanning-beds-get-highest-carcinogen-rating**].

125. Editorial, "Lax and Lethal," *The New York Times,* October 3, 2010 [**http://www.nytimes.com/**].

126. Nicholas D. Kristof, "Why Not Regulate Guns as Seriously as Toys?" *The New York Times,* January 12, 2011 [**http://www.nytimes.com**].

CHAPTER NINE

Business Organizations and Securities Regulation

After completing this chapter, students will be able to:

1. Describe the advantages and disadvantages of corporations, partnerships, and limited liability companies.

2. Identify and explain the business judgment rule.

3. Explain the relationship between limited liability and the doctrine of "piercing the corporate veil."

4. Compare and contrast C corporations and S corporations.

5. Define and describe common stock, preferred stock, and debt.

6. Identify the main concerns of corporate governance.

7. Identify some of the goals of the shareholder rights movement.

8. Define the term *initial public offering* (IPO).

9. Describe the securities registration process.

10. Compare and contrast the regulatory roles of the 1933 and 1934 federal securities acts.

11. Explain the due diligence defense.

12. Describe the fraud-on-the-market theory of reliance and explain its importance.

13. Define insider trading.

14. Contrast the classical fiduciary theory of insider trading with the misappropriation theory.

15. Describe the tender offer process and some defenses against it.

Introduction

Against a backdrop of the worst financial crisis since the Great Depression of the 1930s, this chapter provides a brief introduction to some of the fundamental laws governing business—the types and characteristics of available business entities, key corporate governance issues, and business access to capital.

From the outset we need to recognize the overlapping coverage of state and federal regulation of business. Historically, state law governed most issues—such as the creation of business entities, the powers and duties of management, and capital structure. Still today, the laws that regulate a partnership, both among the partners and with outside parties, are state laws; as are the laws that permit the creation of corporations, those under which limited liability companies (LLCs) have been allowed to form and those permitting numerous other business forms. The owners of a corporation are called *stockholders* or *shareholders* because the ownership interests are called shares of stock. The fundamental legal duties that corporations, corporate boards, and officers owe to their shareholders are defined by the state of incorporation. Over 60 percent of the top 500 U.S. corporations ranked by gross revenues are incorporated in Delaware.[1] Thus, when state corporate law issues are discussed, the corporate law of Delaware often drives the discussion. Part One of this chapter will discuss the key characteristics under state law of the most common business entity forms.

The first decade of the 21st century has been scarred by two systemic failures involving corporate actors and the capital markets. The first is commonly referenced by the 2001 collapse of Enron (although that was not the largest of the corporate failures characterizing that event). The second was the financial crisis that hit in the fall of 2008 (which is often referenced by the collapse of Lehman Brothers). Contributing to both events were failures of corporate management. In each case, Congress responded with significant legislation that, in part, imposes additional requirements on the management of *publicly-held corporations* (corporations with publicly traded shares). These federal laws are the Sarbanes-Oxley Act of 2002 (SOX) and the Dodd-Frank Act of 2010 (see Chapter 8 also). Part Two of this chapter will discuss corporate governance issues specific to public corporations, including the relevant provisions of these two federal laws.

Part Three takes a closer look at how businesses are financed—particularly their access to capital beyond the resources of the initial founders. Although state law plays a role here, federal regulation dominates. Triggered by the 1929 stock market crash and the continuing failure of the capital markets and banking system in the Great Depression of the 1930s, the federal government, largely under its powers to regulate interstate commerce, created both the Securities and Exchange Commission (SEC) to regulate the securities markets and the Federal Reserve Bank to oversee and regulate banks. Part Three of this chapter will focus on federal regulation of the securities markets, including relevant changes following the two financial crises of the last decade.

Part One: Business Entities and Their Defining Characteristics

One of the most significant decisions facing the founders of a business is the choice of a legal entity to house the business. Among other things, this decision will affect the legal relationships among the founders, the relationship between them, and the entity and between them and various third parties. It will also affect their access to outside capital and the tax treatment accorded business profits and losses. Thus, Part One outlines each of the principal choices available. It will conclude with a brief discussion of circumstances that might favor the use of one form over another, as well as a look at a few lesser-used forms and newly emerging forms.

The three traditional business forms are *corporations, partnerships,* and *sole proprietorships*. Partnerships and sole proprietorships are default forms. For example, if an individual starts a business and takes no active steps to house that business within an entity structure, the business will, by default, be classed as a sole proprietorship. Strictly speaking, a sole proprietorship is not a business entity at all—the law treats the business and the individual as the same legal person. If, on the other hand, two or more persons join together to start the business and take no active steps to create an entity structure, the law will, again by default, classify the business as a partnership. The only way to establish a business as a corporation, or indeed as any of the other entities discussed in this part, is for its founders to take deliberate steps, specified by state law, to create the entity.

One such other entity is the LLC or *limited liability company*. An LLC is often referred to as a *hybrid* because it was specifically designed to combine various desired characteristics of corporations with others of partnerships. Another hybrid form is known as a *subchapter S corporation,* sub S corporation or, simply, an S corporation. For state corporate law purposes, it is a corporation like any other, but for federal (and most state) income tax purposes the legal entity is largely ignored and all of the business tax consequences instead flow through to the tax returns of the individual shareholders. This is similar, but not identical, to the way the tax consequences of a partnership flow through to the tax returns of individual partners.

If we set aside businesses run as sole proprietorships, today more businesses are housed in these two hybrid entities, LLCs and S corporations, than in the traditional corporate and partnership forms. Based on IRS data for 2007 (the latest data available), a total of 5.8 million tax returns were filed by S corporations and LLCs compared with only 2.6 million returns from traditional corporations (known as C corporations) and general partnerships.[2] Over the prior five years (2002–2007) both hybrid forms grew at a substantial rate—LLCs at 80 percent and S corporations at 25 percent—while the number of C corporations and partnerships have been steadily declining.

Each of these forms will be evaluated below according to the following considerations:

Formation and nontax costs. The method of and costs related to bringing a business form into existence.

Management structure. The degree to which control is centralized in a hierarchical structure or is dispersed among owners.

Limited liability. The extent to which business owners are personally liable for business obligations.

Transferability of ownership interests. Whether the business owners can transfer their interests without state law restrictions.

Duration of existence. The events, including those impacting the business owners, which will end the business entity's existence.

Taxes. The way each business form affects the income tax treatment of the business and its owners.

Capital structure. The impact of the business form on the organization's ability to access additional capital.

[For a table summarizing the key characteristics of each business form, see **http://www.bizfilings.com/learning/comparison.htm**]

Corporations

Although only 21 percent of all business entities are C corporations, they account for 65 percent of all business revenue. Together, C and S corporations represent 66 percent of all business entities and account for 86 percent of all business revenue.[3] There are good reasons for their financial success, which will become evident in the discussion to follow.

Throughout this discussion, we must keep in mind two very different corporate realities: the public corporation and the *closely held corporation* (a corporation with relatively few shareholders, the stock of which has no readily available market).

Corporate Constitutional Rights?

Under state law, corporations are legal persons.[4] This raises the question of whether corporations have constitutionally protected rights. Over the years, the Supreme Court has held that corporations are sometimes entitled to constitutional protections[5] and at other times not so entitled.[6] As discussed in Chapter 1, the issue arose again in *Citizens United v. Federal Election Com'n*, 130 S.Ct. 876 (2010), in which the Court, over a strong dissent, enunciated a wide-reaching principle that "the Government may not suppress political speech on the basis of the speaker's corporate identity." Justice Stevens, with three others, dissented:

> The real issue in this case concerns how, not if, [Citizens United] may finance its electioneering. Citizens United is a wealthy nonprofit corporation that runs a political action committee (PAC) with millions of dollars in assets. Under [the disputed law], it could have used those assets to televise and promote *Hillary: The Movie* wherever and whenever it wanted to. It also could have spent unrestricted sums to broadcast *Hillary* at any time other than the 30 days before the last primary election. Neither Citizens United's nor any other corporation's speech has been "banned." . . . In the context of election to public office, the distinction between corporate and human speakers is significant. Although they make enormous contributions to our society, corporations are not actually members of it. They cannot vote or run for office. . . . The financial resources, legal structure, and instrumental orientation of corporations raise legitimate concerns about their role in the electoral process.

Question

1. When a corporation funds political speech, for whom is it speaking? Consider these possibilities from the *Citizens United* majority and dissenting opinions:

> [W]ealthy individuals and unincorporated associations can spend unlimited amounts on independent expenditures. Yet certain disfavored associations of citizens—those that have taken on the corporate form—are penalized for engaging in the same political speech. *Citizens United*, supra at 908 (majority opinion).

It is an interesting question "who" is even speaking when a business corporation places an advertisement that endorses or attacks a particular candidate.
Presumably it is not the customers or employees, who typically have no say in
such matters. It cannot realistically be said to be the shareholders, who tend to
be far removed from the day-to-day decisions of the firm and whose political
preferences may be opaque to management. Perhaps the officers or directors of
the corporation have the best claim to be the ones speaking, except their fiduciary duties generally prohibit them from using corporate funds for personal
ends. *Citizens United,* supra at 972 (dissent).

Formation and Nontax Costs

To create a corporation, a *promoter* or *incorporator* files *articles of incorporation* with the state
government. A modest fee is typically charged. The articles have mandatory elements, such as
the corporation's name, the person designated to receive certain communications from the state
(legal documents such as subpoenas), and a description of the stock the corporation is permitted
to issue. Discretionary content like voting rules may also appear in the articles.

Once the articles are filed the corporation comes into existence. An *organizational
meeting* will then be held at which the initial members of the *board of directors* will be
appointed by the incorporators (unless they were already designated in the articles). The
board will then meet to undertake the corporation's initial business. Among other things, it
will appoint officers and adopt *bylaws*. Bylaws contain key policies and procedures, such
as how meeting quorums will be determined and the percentage of shareholders that must
approve major corporate actions like mergers. The issuance of stock will be authorized in
exchange for contributions of capital, property or services. [For a large library of business
forms, see **http://www.lectlaw.com/formb.htm**]

At least annually the board of directors and shareholders must hold meetings and the
corporation will have to make brief filings with the state to keep its records up-to-date,
usually accompanied by a small fee. [To see how Delaware computes this fee, see **http://
www.corp.delaware.gov/fee.shtml**]

Corporations are separate accounting entities and need to establish books of account.
The cost of their accounting systems, however, generally reflects their scale of operation,
rather than the decision to operate in corporate form.

Selection and Protection of the Corporate Name

Articles of incorporation are filed in the name of the soon-to-be corporation. States require
corporate names to be distinguishable from names already registered, so it's a good thing
to check the state's database in advance for the desired name and reserve it in advance of
filing the articles. Other steps an entrepreneur should consider include:

Trademark issues—Will someone sue to stop the use of the chosen name? Check with
the U.S. Patent & Trademark Office database to see if the name has been trademarked.
If it has, select a different name. It may be wise to protect the final name selected by
registering it as a trademark [**http://www.uspto.gov/trademarks**].

Domain name—Do an Internet search on the selected corporate name. Is the name still
available as a domain name? If yes, register it. If not, what name is available that will

be effective for customers and others trying to find you? Will customers be confused by the website with your preferred domain name?

Fictitious name—If the domain name differs from the corporate name and will be used separately, it may be prudent to register it with the state as a fictitious name.

Doing business in other states—If business will be conducted in other states, the business name database of those states should also be checked and the corporation registered as a foreign corporation in those states.

Source: Kermit Pattison, "How to Register a Start-Up," *The New York Times,* March 31, 2010.

Management Structure

One strength of the corporate form, an attribute that has allowed it to become a very effective engine of economic growth, is its ability to separate ownership from management. Shareholders contribute the capital that allows the business to be established. In exchange shareholders receive stock, each share of which represents an ownership unit. Annually, the shareholders meet to elect a board of directors. All corporate powers are exercised by or under the authority of the board for and on behalf of the shareholders. Typically, boards do not operate the business on a day-to-day basis. Rather, they are policy and oversight bodies. To actually run the company, boards appoint *officers,* often a CEO (chief executive officer) or president, secretary, CFO (chief financial officer) or treasurer, and several vice presidents. Officers are employees of the corporation and they hire other employees necessary to run the business. This hierarchy is referred to as a centralized management structure. Keep in mind that a small corporation will likely have this same formal structure, but its operational dynamics may be quite different if, as is common, many of the same people who are shareholders are also directors and officers.

Both directors and officers have *fiduciary duties* to the corporation. A *fiduciary* is a person who acts on behalf of another (*beneficiary*) and is required to do so with great integrity. (Another fiduciary relationship is parent-to-minor child.) The *duty of loyalty* requires a fiduciary to act in the best interests of the beneficiary. This prohibits, for example, directors from authorizing the corporation to lease real estate from the board chairman unless the rental terms are consistent with the market. Directors and officers also owe the corporation a *duty of due care,* which requires that they act in good faith toward the corporation and in the manner a reasonably prudent person would employ under the same circumstances. [For an inside look at issues confronting board members today, see **http://boardmember.com**]

Business Judgment Rule

What happens if the board or CEO makes a decision which causes the stock value to decline by 30 percent? Has the duty of due care been violated? The judicial system has developed the *business judgment rule* to help make that determination. A good statement of the rule, which is explored in the *Wrigley* case below, is:

> The rule posits a powerful presumption . . . that a decision made by a loyal and informed board will not be overturned . . . unless it cannot be "attributed to any rational business purpose." [The] shareholder . . . challenging a board decision [must] rebut the . . . presumption [by] providing evidence that directors . . . breached any one of the triads of their fiduciary duty–good faith, loyalty or due care. . . . If a shareholder . . . fails to meet this . . . burden, the . . . rule attaches to protect . . . officers and directors and the decisions they make, and our courts will not second-guess these business judgments.[7]

Shlensky v. Wrigley
237 N.E.2d 776 (Ill. App. Ct. 1968)

FACTS

Shlensky, a minority stockholder in the Chicago Cubs, sued the directors on the grounds of mismanagement and negligence because of their refusal to install lights at Wrigley Field, then the only major league stadium without lights. One of the directors, Wrigley (80 percent owner), objected to lights because of his personal opinion that "baseball is a 'daytime sport' and that the installation of lights and night baseball games would have a deteriorating effect upon the surrounding neighborhood." The other directors deferred to Wrigley.

The Cubs were losing money. Shlensky attributed those losses to poor attendance and argued that without lights the losses would continue. His evidence was that the Chicago White Sox night games drew better than the Cubs' day games. Shlensky sought damages and an order requiring lights and night games. He lost at trial and appealed.

Justice Sullivan

* * * * *

. . . [D]efendants argue that the courts will not step in and interfere with the honest business judgment of the directors unless there is a showing of fraud, illegality, or conflict of interest.

The court in *Wheeler v. The Pullman Iron & Steel Co,.* said:

It is . . . fundamental in the law of corporations that the majority of its stockholders shall control the policy of the corporation. . . . Everyone purchasing [stock] impliedly agrees that he will be bound by the [lawful acts of] a majority of the shareholders, or [of their corporate agents duly chosen,] and courts . . . will not undertake to control the policy or business methods of a corporation, although it may be seen that a wiser policy might be adopted and the business more successful if other methods were pursued.

* * * * *

Plaintiff . . . argues that the directors are acting for reasons unrelated to the . . . welfare of the Cubs. However, we are not satisfied that the motives assigned to . . . Wrigley [and] the other directors . . . are contrary to the best interests of the corporation . . . . For example[,] the effect on the surrounding neighborhood might well be considered by a director who was considering the patrons who would or would not attend the games if the park were in a poor neighborhood. Furthermore, the long-run interest [in the] property value at Wrigley Field might demand all efforts to keep the neighborhood from deteriorating. [W]e do not mean to say . . . that the decision of the directors was a correct one. That is beyond our jurisdiction and ability. We are merely saying that the decision is one properly before the directors and the motives alleged . . . showed no fraud, illegality, or conflict of interest in their making of that decision.

While all . . . courts do not insist that one or more of [these] three elements must be present for a stockholder's derivative action to lie, nevertheless we feel that unless the conduct of the defendants at least borders on one of [them], the courts should not interfere. . . .

* * * * *

Finally, we do not agree . . . that failure to follow . . . the other major league clubs in scheduling night games constituted negligence. [It] cannot be said that directors, even those of corporations that are losing money, must follow the lead of [others] in the field. Directors are elected for their business . . . judgment and the courts cannot require them to forgo their judgment because of the decisions of directors of other companies.

Affirmed.

AFTERWORD—DUTY OF CARE

Some states now require proof of *intentional misconduct* or *recklessness* to establish a breach of the duty of care.

Questions

1. What was the issue in this case?
2. The Cubs added lights in 1988. How could the board be meeting its duty of due care both in the 1960s by not erecting lights and in the 1980s by doing so?

Director, Officer, Employee Liability

Wrigley involved a *shareholder derivative suit.* That action is initiated when the corporation is being harmed or defrauded and neither the board nor the senior executives will take action to protect it. This often involves self-dealing by these parties. The suit is brought by a minority shareholder, but any recovery inures to the corporation.

These cases are extremely difficult to win in light of the business judgment rule, which may apply to the board's decision not to pursue litigation, as well as to the underlying action that, it is argued, harmed the company. Nevertheless, many such suits are filed in the wake of any public corporate disaster. By one count, the Gulf of Mexico oil spill has "triggered more than 70 civil lawsuits."[8] With regard to the Deepwater Horizon rig, shareholders are arguing that the board and executives of British Petroleum "recklessly disregarded accidents and safety warnings for years" in violation of their fiduciary duties. Many such lawsuits have also been filed by shareholders against directors and officers of companies in the mortgage and financial services industry that played key roles in the 2008 financial crisis.

When an employee or director commits a tort or crime while conducting corporate business, both that person and the corporation are liable for the consequences. The legal doctrine that makes the employer liable for an employee's acts is *respondeat superior*. (For more, see Chapter 12.)

Because officers and directors are ultimately responsible for corporate acts and because corporations are frequently sued, these persons face a high risk of becoming involved in costly litigation. Most corporations, therefore, *indemnify* (pay for or reimburse) these individuals for the costs incurred to defend such suits. Many states permit indemnification even in some cases involving the breach of a fiduciary duty. Delaware, for example, permits indemnification for breaches of the duty of care, although not for breaches of the duty of loyalty or for intentional misconduct or knowing violations of the law.[9] When the SEC resolved its civil suit for securities fraud against Angelo Mozilo, CEO of Countrywide Financial, the nation's largest mortgage lender before the housing market collapse, Countrywide and Bank of America (which bought Countrywide in 2008) paid $45 million of Mozilo's $67.5 settlement.[10]

Limited Liability

To a lawyer there are two types of persons: natural and artificial. Natural persons are people. Artificial persons, like corporations, are entities created under the law of a state (or nation), which are considered to have separate legal existence. Corporations can own property, be sued, take on debts, and otherwise act as separate entities. As discussed above, they even have limited constitutional rights. One of the great advantages of this status is that the owners of the corporation are generally not responsible for the corporation's obligations. Should the corporation find that its liabilities overwhelm its assets, its creditors cannot reach the personal assets of the shareholders. That is, the liability of shareholders is limited to the loss of their investment in the corporation, which is the essence of *limited liability* and perhaps the most cherished characteristic of the corporate form. However, for closely held corporations, this feature can be severely restricted because lenders are well aware of limited liability and usually require the principal shareholders to guarantee the corporation's debts. Still, limited liability will exist for other obligations, such as tort claims.

Closely held corporations also face the loss of limited liability through application of the doctrine known as *piercing the corporate veil*. This doctrine, explored in the *Wolfe* case that follows, usually has two elements: (1) misuse of the corporate form and (2) an unjust result if limited liability is allowed to stand.

Judge Battin

* * * * *

Charles E. Wolfe was the sole shareholder and president of [the corporation,] which leased tractor-trailers. [Mr.] Wolfe also operated a business as a proprietorship . . . which was an "over-the-road" trucking business.

[T]he corporation incurred a $114,472.91 federal tax bill. . . . [Mr.] Wolfe paid the taxes . . . after the Internal Revenue Service (Service) [levied against him]. The Service contends . . . the corporation was the alter ego of Mr. Wolfe, thus justifying the piercing of the corporate veil.

* * * * *

As a general rule, a corporation is treated as a legal entity, separate and distinct from its shareholders[, who] enjoy limited liability.

When the corporate entity is abused, however, the protection of limited liability may be lost. In such cases, courts may exercise their equitable powers to pierce the corporate veil. . . .

* * * * *

The facts . . . present the classic case of a shareholder so pervasively dominating corporate affairs that the shareholder and the corporation no longer have separate identities. . . . Mr. Wolfe was the sole shareholder[,] a director and the president of the corporation. Mr. Wolfe made all the corporate decisions without consulting the other directors. The corporation did not even have a bank account. All the corporation's banking transactions were done through the proprietorship's bank account. . . . The corporation and the proprietorship were housed in the same office. The corporation's employee was paid by the proprietorship. Some of the corporation's equipment was purchased on the proprietorship's credit. All of the corporation's purchases were paid for on a proprietorship bank account. When the corporation received payment from third parties, the money was deposited into the proprietorship's bank account. Even Mr. Wolfe could not distinguish between the corporation and the proprietorship. . . .

It is clear that the corporation and the proprietorship were operated as a single instrumentality under the sole control of Mr. Wolfe. Therefore, it was proper for the Service to look to Wolfe's personal assets to satisfy the taxes of his alter ego corporation.

[Held for the Internal Revenue Service.]

Questions

1. Who owed the taxes?
2. How was the corporate form misused?
3. What injustice would have resulted if Wolfe had not been required to pay?

Transferability of Ownership Interests

Federal securities laws impose broad restrictions on the transfer of stock, as we shall see in Part Three of this chapter. Beyond these (and analogous state) laws, no statutory restrictions are generally imposed on stock transfers. It is not uncommon, however, for dispositions to be restricted by contract. For example, an employment contract might require that corporate stock granted to an employee be held until the employee leaves the company.

A common contractual restriction in closely held corporations is a *buy-sell agreement* which, at a minimum, forces a shareholder to offer his or her stock to the corporation or other shareholders before selling it to a third party. [For more on buy-sell agreements, see **http://smallbusiness.findlaw.com/business-structures/corporations/incorporate-shareholders-agreement.html**]

Duration of Existence

In general a corporation has indefinite duration. Nothing that transpires in the lives of the stockholders automatically affects the corporation's existence.

The termination of a corporation, however, can occur—either voluntarily or involuntarily. Voluntary termination requires a vote by the shareholders, who might do so if business prospects are no longer favorable. On termination the corporation is *liquidated,* which involves first satisfying all creditors and then distributing any remaining assets to the shareholders. *Articles of dissolution* are then filed, officially ending the corporation's existence.

Involuntary terminations are caused by the action of a court or of the state corporation regulator. A court might end a closely held corporation's existence if, for example, there is an irreconcilable deadlock among the shareholders. A common reason for the state to terminate a corporation is for failure to pay annual fees or make required annual filings.

Taxes

> "Taxes are what we pay for civilized society."

As Justice Oliver Wendell Holmes said, "Taxes are what we pay for civilized society."[11] But Justice Learned Hand also said, "[T]here is nothing sinister in so arranging one's affairs as to keep taxes as low as possible."[12]

Taxation transfers about one-quarter of the United States' economic output to the government. Virtually everyone wants to minimize tax payments, hopefully by legal *tax avoidance* (careful planning within the law), not by illegal *tax evasion* (committing fraud to lower taxes).

Because the corporation is a separate legal entity, it is subject to taxation in its own right. This leads to what many would say is the corporation's greatest disadvantage, *double taxation.* In the United States, a corporation pays tax on its income. When it later distributes its after-tax income to its shareholders as *dividends,* the shareholders are taxed on that amount as well; hence, "double taxation." Note, however, that dividends are not mandatory. They are paid only after the board declares them, which it is generally not required to do and which it legally cannot do if the corporation's solvency (cash flow and net worth) is insufficient.

To illustrate, assume a corporation is subject to income taxes at the rate of 35 percent[13] and its shareholders all face a marginal rate of 33 percent,[14] but a lower rate on corporate dividends of 15 percent. On an income of $10 million, the corporation would pay $3.5 million in taxes, leaving only $6.5 million for distribution as dividends. If that entire amount were distributed, the shareholders would pay $975,000 in taxes. Thus, of the $10 million corporate income, only $5.525 million can actually be spent by the owners—an effective tax rate of about 45 percent. Had it been possible to own the business in a form that was not subject to taxation in its own right, the total income taxes would have been $3.3 million, leaving $6.7 million available for the owners to spend—21 percent more.

The argument that corporations are necessarily disadvantageous because of double taxation can be misleading, however. There are a variety of circumstances in which employing the corporate form yields clear tax advantages, especially for smaller closely held corporations. For example, if such a corporation wants to inject much of its net income back into the business rather than distributing it as dividends, the corporate form may permit a lower tax rate on those reinvested funds. Another example results from corporations being the only form of business that comprehensively permits tax-deductible fringe benefits. [For more on fringe benefits, see **http://www.irs.ustreas.gov/pub/irs-pdf/p15b.pdf**]

The Hybrid S Corporation: Limited Liability Without Double Taxation

As discussed above, many argue that the principal disadvantage of the corporate form is double taxation. In response in 1958 Congress amended the Internal Revenue Code to establish a separate tax status for some corporations, now known as *S corporations*. An S corporation's income is taxed only once—to the shareholders on their personal returns—much like partnerships, which will be discussed below. Also like partnerships, an S corporation is limited in the deductibility of some fringe benefits. However, unlike partnerships, to the extent the S corporation's income is allocated to its owners as dividends, no self-employment tax is imposed, which is a tax separate from the income tax with an effective tax rate of at least 11.6 percent on the first $106,800 of earned income in 2010. The Internal Revenue Service, however, routinely challenges attempts to distribute an excessive amount as dividends where inadequate wages have been paid to S corporation owners.

Not all corporations can elect to be taxed as an S corporation. It is intended for use by smaller companies. Thus, S corporations may issue only one class of stock and may have no more than 100 shareholders, which in general may be individuals only. Interestingly, an entire family is treated as "one" individual for these purposes. Despite these restrictions, one can find S corporations with multi-billion-dollar revenues.

S corporations are popular and their popularity is growing, as previously noted. They represent about 68 percent of all corporations, but tend to be much smaller, generating only about 25 percent of all corporate revenue.[15]

Keep in mind that "S" status is relevant only for federal (and some state) tax purposes. In all other respects the legal characteristics of S corporations are like all other corporations.

Capital Structure

Businesses often need access to *capital* to finance their activities. Capital is of two types: debt and equity—two ends of the spectrum with a boundary that can be challenging to identify. The providers of both debt and equity capital hold claims against the corporation's assets. However, creditors' (debtholders') claims are always satisfied before equity holders' claims.

Equity capital (stock) has a long-term horizon. Although any given shareholder may intend to hold the stock for only a short period, the stock itself is generally expected to exist for the full life of the corporation. Three *property rights* are associated with stock ownership: the right to participate in earnings (that is, dividends), the right to participate in assets upon liquidation, and the right to participate in control. There are two principal classes of stock: preferred and common. Where only one class exists, it is *common stock*. Common stockholders share all three property rights in proportion to their holdings.

> Institutional investors hold about 60 percent of all stock.

Preferred stock was created, largely for institutional investors (which hold about 60 percent of all stock[16]) like pension funds, to fill the gap on the risk-return spectrum between long-term debt and common stock. Finance professionals find it advantageous to have many different ways to combine risk and return. Preferred stock is associated with "preferences," which relate to distributions. Preferred stockholders are paid their required annual dividend in full before any dividends are distributed to the common stockholders. In addition, preferred stockholders have a preference upon the corporation's liquidation. After the creditors are satisfied, the preferred stockholders receive the next round of distributions up to their stock's *liquidation value* (also called *redemption value*).

The cost of these two preferences is the loss of the right to participate in control. Having no vote, preferred stockholders cannot elect directors to protect their interests. To help ensure that its holders regularly receive dividends, nearly all preferred stock is *cumulative*. This means that if a preferred stock dividend is missed, then before the common stockholders get any dividends, the preferred stock *arrearage* (all dividends not paid in any a prior year) must be made up. Another protection occasionally granted to preferred stockholders is a contingent right to vote if, for example, a dividend is missed twice. This voting power would continue until all arrearages have been satisfied.

Because preferred stockholders never get more than their required dividends and, upon liquidation, little more than the purchase price, all corporate growth inures to the common stockholders. If both you and Bill Gates had invested $1 million in Microsoft at the outset, you taking preferred stock and Gates taking common stock, your stock would still be worth about $1 million, whereas Gates's stock would be worth tens of billions.

Debt capital may be short- or long-term. Companies that provide hard disks to Dell are a source of short-term debt capital. They expect to be paid fairly quickly, although not at the moment of delivery. Therefore, they have extended credit to Dell, a very short-term form of debt. The long-term debt of a closely held corporation is likely to come from a commercial lender who takes a security interest in specified property of the corporation. This is much like an individual who takes out a long-term mortgage from a bank secured by the home the individual purchases with the borrowed funds. Large corporations have another alternative for obtaining long-term debt capital. Just as a public corporation may sell its stock to the public, large corporations may sell units of debt, called *bonds,* to the public. A pension plan that holds Dell's 20-year bonds is providing long-term debt capital to Dell.

Most debt capital specifies an interest rate (or a formula for computing the interest rate) to be paid on the principal borrowed, both of which (principal and interest) are required to be paid in set amounts, usually over a defined term.

Corporations carefully manage their *capital structures* (the balance between debt and equity). If the debt/equity ratio is too high, the corporation may be exposed to severe risk because debt obligations must be timely paid without regard to how profitable the business operations are. Furthermore, the capital structure must be managed to ensure that *debt covenants* are not breached. A debt covenant is a term in the lending contract that makes the debt immediately payable should the condition specified not be satisfied (such as exceeding a specified debt/equity ratio). On the other hand, if the ratio is too low, opportunities for positive *financial leverage* (employing funds at a rate of return that exceeds the interest rate on the borrowed funds) may be forfeited. Executives also recognize that *interest* paid on debt is tax deductible, whereas dividends paid to shareholders are not. This places a strong emphasis on the use of debt capital.

If you compare the characteristics of debt capital with preferred and common stock, you can readily see that preferred stock indeed does bridge the gap between common stock and debt. Increasingly, preferred stock is being issued with more debtlike characteristics. This poses serious classification problems for accountants, tax authorities, and bankruptcy courts.

Questions

1. *a.* What characteristics of the corporate form make it particularly desirable as a business entity?
   b. Particularly undesirable?
   c. Do S corporations share those characteristics?

Partnerships

This section discusses traditional, *general partnerships.* A partnership is two or more persons (*partners*) who carry on a business as co-owners. Recall that this is the default entity form for any business with two or more owners that does not specifically act to create a different entity. About 7.9 percent of all businesses are general partnerships, generating less than 2 percent of all revenue. Whereas corporate ownership interests are called stock or shares, the equity interest of a partner is called a *partnership interest.*

> A general partnership is the default entity form for any business with two or more owners.

Partnerships are *mutual agencies.* Every partner is an agent of the partnership with the capacity to bind the partnership when acting within the scope of the partnership's business. Knowledge held by any partner is deemed held by the partnership. As an agent, each partner is entitled to reimbursement for costs personally incurred in furtherance of the partnership's business. Each partner has the right to examine all partnership records and to demand a formal determination by a court of the value of the partner's interest (an *accounting*).

Although the law of partnerships originated in the common law, all states except Louisiana adopted the Uniform Partnership Act (UPA), originally developed by the National Conference of Commissioners on Uniform State Laws (NCCUSL) in 1914. The UCCUSL adopted a revised form of the UPA in 1994 (RUPA), which to date has been adopted by 35 states and the District of Columbia. Except as noted, the discussion below is based on the provisions of RUPA.

What Is the Law in Your State?

There are significant differences between UPA and RUPA. While 35 have adopted RUPA, 14 have not. (Louisiana has not adopted either.) Which is the law in your state? You can find out at **http://www.nccusl.org**

Formation and Nontax Costs

Under RUPA a partnership is a separate legal entity, distinct from its partners. However, no filing with the state is required to create it. If persons intend to go into business together and take no steps to establish a different form, they will automatically be a partnership. Mere co-ownership of property, however, does not create a partnership. The co-owners must intend to join in the sharing of risks and rewards.

As we shall see below, the partnership relationship carries substantial risks for the individual partners. One might expect the contract that creates and governs the partnership, the *partnership agreement,* to very precisely specify the terms of that relationship. This may be true if the partnership agreement is written. However, the vast majority are oral agreements. If disagreements arise over an oral agreement, the partners may find it very difficult to establish conclusively what the original agreement was. This will not be helped by the fact that when important disagreements arise, the partners often discover that their interests have become adverse and that the hopeful emotions shared at formation have been displaced by anger and a sense of betrayal.

So if the problems associated with a lack of clarity can be substantial, why are partnership agreements often oral and, even if written, often vague? The answer relates in part to the fact that to draft a quality partnership agreement a host of touchy, even unpleasant issues must be concretely addressed. The drafter must ask, "How should the profit-sharing arrangement change if a partner becomes ill or fails to meet expectations?" And, "If the partnership does not work out, how will the relationship be unwound?" Soon-to-be partners often shy away from tough questions like these; there may be a sense that asking them will sour the high spirits in which so many partnerships are born.

Partnership agreements also tend to be expensive to draft because of the many opportunities for customization, because state law provides only a general framework, and because the personal risks of being a partner are so significant. Similarly, partnership accounting systems can be among the most expensive of all the business forms because of the need to track all customized economic arrangements. However, the partnership form generally requires few, if any, annually recurring events such as state filings or statutorily-mandated meetings of owners.

Management Structure

By default, management in a partnership is not centralized. Absent an agreement to the contrary, each partner has an equal right to participate in control on a one-partner, one-vote basis regardless of the size of the partner's ownership interest. As the number of partners grows this can make partnerships unwieldy. In response some partnerships create a central management structure by adding provisions to the partnership agreement in which the partners yield many of their management rights to a subset of partners (perhaps only one— a *managing partner*).

Partners owe each other the fiduciary duties of loyalty, confidentiality, sharing information, and exercising due care. The *Veale* case below explores some of these duties.

LEGAL BRIEFCASE

Veale v. Rose
657 S.W.2d 834 (Texas Ct. of App. 1983)

FACTS

Veal Sr., Beale Jr., Gibson, Parker, and Rose were partners in an accounting firm. The partnership agreement permitted partners to pursue other business interests so long as doing so did not conflict with the partnership practice. Rose performed accounting work for Right Away Foods and Payne, receiving the compensation personally. Rose's partners claimed that he owed them a share in that he had competed with the firm in violation of the partnership agreement. The jury held for Rose. The partners appealed.

Chief Justice Nye

* * * * *

The partnership agreement between Rose and the appellants provided in part:

> Except with the expressed approval of the other partners as to each specific instance, no partner shall perform any public accounting services . . . other than . . . on behalf of this partnership.

Partners . . . occupy a fiduciary relationship towards one another which requires of them the utmost degree of good faith and honesty in dealing with one another. . . .

It is undisputed that while a partner . . . Rose rendered accounting services for Right Away Foods for which he billed and received payment personally. [The] partnership did not share in the proceeds. . . . There was some testimony from which the jury could have inferred that the work which Rose did for Right Away Foods . . . was of the type which did not require the services of a CPA. However, Rose . . . admitted that there was no reason why he could not have rendered

[those services] as a partner in the accounting firm. . . . In fact in regard to services in connection with mergers and acquisitions, [Parker testified] that he was unaware of any [such work that was not] prepared by public accounting firms. The preponderance of all the evidence clearly establishes that Rose . . . performed accounting services for Right Away Foods . . . in competition with the partnership. The [jury] was in error.

. . . Rose also admitted that he performed accounting services for [Payne] for which he billed and received payment personally. There is no question that those services were public accounting services. His later testimony that he performed the services, in effect, after hours, or in addition to his duties to the partnership, is of no value in light of the obligations imposed by the partnership agreement and by the common understanding of the term "competition."

[Reversed and remanded.]

Questions

1. *a.* Why was Rose's work for Right Away Foods considered a violation of the partnership agreement?
   b. Why did Rose's "after-hours" argument fail?
2. Could Rose operate a gas station without violating the partnership agreement?

Limited Liability

> Partners are personally liable for all the partnership's obligations should it default.

A partnership does not offer limited liability to its owners. The partners are personally liable for all of the partnership's obligations should it default. This is clearly the greatest disadvantage of the partnership form.

Under RUPA partners are *jointly and severally liable* for both contract obligations and torts.[17] If a partnership is found liable, the victorious claimant must first exhaust the partnership's assets, but then can proceed to collect the remainder from any or all of the partners.[18] If a wealthy partner pays the debt, that partner is entitled to recoup an appropriate share from the other partners under the *right of contribution*.

Under the doctrine of respondeat superior mentioned previously, the partnership, and therefore the partners, are liable for the torts of the partnership's employees and for the unintentional torts of the partners. For example, an individual injured by the negligent driving of an employee can sue and recover from the partnership and then from individual partners. Once again, this can work to the disadvantage of a wealthier partner.

Under some circumstances, partners may be jointly and severally liable for crimes committed by partnership employees, but they ordinarily will not be liable for crimes committed by partners (unless they themselves participate in or authorize the crime).

Transferability of Ownership Interests

Because partnerships are mutual agencies, involve fiduciary relationships, and do not have limited liability, without an express agreement to the contrary, the law does not allow a partner to transfer a partnership interest to a third person without the unanimous consent of the other partners. A partnership interest can be assigned, but the *assignment* entitles the *assignee* only to the distribution rights of the assigning partner (*assignor*). The assignee has no right to participate in control and does not have the status of partner.

Duration of Existence

Under UPA a partnership is automatically dissolved, or terminated, upon the death, incapacity, bankruptcy, expulsion or withdrawal of any partner. Thus, events in the private lives of the partners could seriously impact the business venture. To minimize the harm from such an automatic dissolution, it became common practice to include a provision in the partnership agreement allowing a partnership to be immediately reformed by the remaining partners. The ex-partner's partnership interest would then be valued and paid out.

Under RUPA the only one of the events listed above that will automatically dissolve a partnership is a partner's express withdrawal. The remaining events will result in the disassociation of the affected partner, but will not dissolve the partnership nor require the formation of a new partnership by the remaining partners. The power of any partner to withdraw cannot be removed by the partnership agreement, but the right to exercise that power can be circumscribed and a wrongfully withdrawing partner can be required to compensate the partnership for any resulting damages. The remaining partners have a statutory right to resume the business as if no dissolution had occurred.[19]

Taxes

The greatest advantage of the partnership form is the extraordinary range of economic relationships that can be crafted. Whereas a 10 percent shareholder is simply entitled to 10 percent of whatever distributions are made by the corporation, a partnership agreement can detach percentage ownership from the stream of distributions and tax consequences. For example, assume L contributes land to a real estate development partnership, K contributes knowledge as the general contractor, and C contributes the cash necessary to undertake the venture. It would be acceptable to allocate the partnership cash flow as follows: C gets all of the net cash flow until C's initial cash contribution is recouped, then L gets all of the net cash flow until the value of L's contributed land has been distributed, then all three share the remaining net cash flow equally.

Double taxation does not apply to partnerships because the Internal Revenue Code does not treat them as separate taxable entities, whether or not the state has adopted RUPA. The partnership's income is taxed only once—on the personal tax returns of the partners as allocated under the terms of the partnership agreement. There is a downside risk, however. Partners must pay tax annually on their share of the partnership income whether or not any cash or property has actually been distributed to them.

There are two important negative tax consequences of a partnership. First, fringe benefits provided to partners are generally not business deductions (although fringes provided to employees are). Second, all of a partner's allocable share of ordinary income is subject to the self-employment tax (at an effective rate of at least 11.6 percent), as was discussed above in the context of S corporations.

Capital Structure

The sole source of equity is the partners themselves, although new partners can be brought into the partnership to infuse new equity capital into the business. Debt capital can be raised based on the creditworthiness of the individual partners, as well as by offering assets to lenders as collateral for loans.

Question

1. What characteristics of the partnership form make it particularly desirable as a business entity? Particularly undesirable?

Limited Liability Companies (LLCs)

Today, a very popular business form is the LLC. After 1958 an S corporation could be elected that combined limited liability for owners with avoidance of double taxation. That form was not attractive to many businesses, however, because of the one class of stock limitation, the ceiling on the number of shareholders, and the requirement that all economic and tax benefits and burdens of the enterprise be shared pro rata according to stock ownership. Wide displeasure with the lack of a limited liability business form that had the flexible tax characteristics of partnerships led the Wyoming legislature to create the *limited liability company* in 1977. By 1997, LLCs were available nationally and are now the fastest-growing business form in the United States, representing over 20 percent of all business entities filing federal tax returns in 2007.

Although a uniform act for LLCs was first established by the NCCUSL in 1994, only nine states ultimately adopted it. In 2006, a revised act was adopted by the NCCUSL, which, as of this writing, has been adopted by six jurisdictions (including the District of Columbia). Thus, there is still considerable variation in governing provisions from state to state. The general outlines of LLCs are discussed below.

To create an LLC, the owners (although some states allow one-member LLCs), called *members,* file *articles of organization* with the state, much as a corporation files articles of incorporation. The equity interests are called *members' interests*. An *operating agreement,* which can be oral or written but is most likely to be written, will be made which sets forth information similar to that often found in partnership agreements. Minor annual filings and fees are generally required, but statutes do not impose annual meetings on the members. The cost of setting up an accounting system for an LLC will be essentially the same as for a partnership because LLCs have the same flexibility over economic and tax matters as does the partnership form.

The management structure of LLCs is extremely flexible: the operating agreement generally specifies whether it will be centrally managed by managers (often one or two of the members) or member-managed (similar to a partnership). Many states require this choice to be set out in the articles of organization. Similarly, a multimember LLC can elect on its creation whether to be taxed like a corporation or like a partnership. (A single-member LLC will elect between treatment as a corporation or as a sole proprietorship.)

LLCs are hybrids because, with regard to limited liability of the owners and the duration of existence, they most closely resemble corporations. With regard to transferability of ownership interests and access to equity capital, however, they most closely resemble partnerships. In many states it is still an open question whether the limited liability of LLC members can be "pierced" as is possible with corporate shareholders. Minnesota's LLC statute expressly provides for piercing the veil of LLCs.[20] In 2002, the Wyoming Supreme Court held, "We can discern no reason, in either law or policy, to treat LLCs differently than we treat corporations. If the members and officers of an LLC fail to treat it as a separate entity, they should not enjoy immunity from individual liability for the LLC's acts that cause damage to third parties."[21]

Sole Proprietorships

Sole proprietorships, business ventures undertaken by a single individual, are not entities—they have no legal existence apart from the owner. However, the same characteristics used to evaluate other business forms can be applied to them. A sole proprietorship comes into existence by the mere decision of the proprietor to pursue a venture. Thus, it is the default business form for single owners. This largely explains why the majority of all business endeavors are sole proprietorships, although they generate only 4.5 percent of all business revenue—averaging less than $60,000. No legal filings or fees are required to establish the operation, but a business license, sales tax license, fictitious name filing, or other permits may be required by the state, county, and/or city where the business is located. Since there is only one owner, centralization of management automatically exists. Like a partnership, the owner is personally liable for all obligations of the business.

A proprietor may dispose of the proprietorship freely, but such a transfer can be accomplished only through the transfer of the assets which underlie the business, not by a transfer of the "business" in its own right. Furthermore, the lack of a separate legal entity generally results in the end of the sole proprietorship if the owner becomes incapacitated or dies. Only a holder of a durable power of attorney, custodian or executor has the legal power to continue operations, but either of the latter two would be forced continually to seek court approval to perform the activities required to operate the business. This impractical arrangement would likely destroy the business' value in short order.

A sole proprietorship is not a taxable entity. All of its revenues and expenses will be incorporated into the personal tax return of the proprietor. Like partnerships, most fringe benefits are not deductible as business expenses and all business income is subject to self-employment tax. The capital structure issues for a sole proprietorship are similar to those of a partnership—without a change in business form, new equity can only come from the sole proprietor. Any debt will be based on the creditworthiness of the proprietor and the property the proprietor can offer as security for any loan.

Other Hybrid Forms

Limited Liability Partnerships (LLPs)

At the same time LLCs were being conceived, the great multinational accounting firms were reeling from an episode in which the quality of their audits proved less than advertised—the savings and loan collapse of the 1980s. Over $1.6 billion in settlements (a staggering sum for that era) was paid out and these firms feared extinction if professional liability damages could not be brought under control. Efforts to obtain tort reform that would limit such liability failed, so a new approach was sought—the *limited liability partnership* (LLP). Some Texas law firms were similarly concerned, with 1,200 becoming LLPs within a year of Texas passing the nation's first LLP enabling statute on August 26, 1991.[22]

Most states now have some form of an LLP. In spite of the similarity of name and its creation in the shadow of LLCs, its closest analogue is a general partnership, not an LLC. For example, its governing law is included as Article 10 of RUPA. To bring an LLP into existence, a document, called a *statement of qualification* in RUPA, is filed with the state. Minor annual filings and fees are required. LLPs (and their partners) are taxed like a general partnership and in all other characteristics most closely resemble partnerships.

As originally conceived and as is still true in some states, an LLP partner's limited liability extended only to the negligence or malpractice of other partners, while retaining full liability for all other partnership obligations. RUPA, and many states, now provide full limited liability "whether arising in contract, tort, or otherwise" to all partners "solely by reason of being" a partner.[23] In those states the only individuals who would continue to use the general partnership form would be those that began business without competent legal advice or who are unable or unwilling to pay the filing fee.

Professional Limited Liability Companies (PLLCs) and Professional Limited Liability Partnerships (PLLPs)

Some states that have established LLPs that confer full limited liability for partners have chosen to prohibit their use by licensed professionals such as accountants, lawyers and doctors. As an alternative, they have created entities (variously named depending on the state) that more closely resemble the original Texas LLP concept and then ensure continued full regulation relating to malpractice by the appropriate state licensing body and/or set malpractice insurance standards for the protection of the public.

Limited Partnerships

Limited partnerships have existed for a considerable time in the United States and were extremely popular until the advent of limited liability companies. They are entities with two classes of owners: general partners and limited partners. *General partners* have the same legal benefits and burdens as the partners of a general partnership. They (often only one) are the sole managers of the entity. *Limited partners* invest in the entity by contributing capital but do not participate in control (except to a limited extent analogous to shareholders). In exchange for limited control, they receive limited liability. The principal disadvantage of status as a general partner is unlimited liability. In practice, however, most general partners are corporations with minimal capital investment, so unlimited liability is little threat unless grounds for piercing the corporate veil exist.

Forty-nine states have adopted the Uniform Limited Partnership Act (ULPA) in one of its three versions. The latest, ULPA (2001), has been adopted in 17 states and the District of Columbia. Limited partnerships come into existence only upon filing a *certificate of limited partnership*. Minor annual filings and fees are required. The law of limited partnerships provides that those events that would terminate a general partnership have minimal impact on a limited partnership's existence. In general, a limited partnership is taxed like a partnership. However, like an S corporation shareholder, the income of the limited partners is not subject to self-employment tax.

Limited Liability Limited Partnerships (LLLPs)

State legislation establishing LLLPs is generally directed at facilitating acquisition of limited liability for the general partners of preexisting limited partnerships. In some cases reorganization of an existing limited partnership would have encountered expensive or impassable hurdles. Under ULPA (2001), an LLLP is created simply by stating the limited partnership is an LLLP in the certificate of limited partnership.[24]

Series Limited Liability Companies (Series LLCs)

A handful of states, including Delaware, have enacted legislation enabling a new species of LLC. The concept is to allow a related set of entities, in this case referred to as "series" or "cells," in which the liability risks of different real estate investments or businesses can be isolated in a separate cell while only one entity, the series LLC, is created under state law. This separation of liability for different activities is somewhat akin to an S corporation and its relationship to its "qualified subchapter S subsidiaries," the tax consequences for all of which are reported on one federal income tax return. To receive that tax treatment the subsidiaries must be wholly owned by the S corporation. State series LLC statutes, however, permit each cell to have different managers and different members. As with the original Wyoming LLC statute, whether this entity form spreads in state enactment and use is likely to depend on whether the IRS takes a favorable position with regard to its tax treatment.

International Hybrids

Dozens of other business forms exist throughout the world. For the most part, these forms are intended to achieve various combinations of the characteristics just discussed. Using these criteria, managers operating in a multinational environment should be prepared to evaluate form of business decisions under a variety of regimes.

Social Businesses on the Horizon?

The concept of a "social business" has been promoted by Dr. Muhammad Yunus, an economist and winner of the 2006 Nobel Peace Prize. The concept occupies a unique place on the continuum that runs from for-profit businesses to not-for-profit organizations. A social business is distinguished from a for-profit business in that it is formed to further a specific positive social objective, rather than primarily seeking profit-maximization for its owners. Profits are applied to the furtherance of its stated social objective; regular reporting would include both financial reporting and identification of concrete progress toward its social goals. A social business is distinct from a nonprofit enterprise in at least two key respects: it is intended to be an economically self-sustaining enterprise, which means it must adhere to commercially reasonable business practices, and its start-up capital is to be returned to its founding investors, although without interest. For such businesses to become a reality, another new form may need to be established. Any enabling legislation would need to address such issues as who would control the enterprise, to whom managers would be accountable, and what tax treatment would be appropriate at both the entity and investor levels.

Circumstances Favoring a Specific Business Form

Before the rise in availability of the various hybrid forms discussed above, some states required certain activities to be carried on in the partnership form, most notably the licensed professions. The primary concern was that these professionals should not be able to escape personal liability for malpractice by incorporating their practices. As can be seen above, all states now offer an alternative to a general partnership for these professions.

Today selection of a particular form is driven by market realities, as well as the desires of the founders for certain characteristics that were discussed above. Some of those market realities will now be addressed.

One consideration in the selection of an appropriate form is the total capital needed by the enterprise. Large businesses need billions of dollars. Only access to global capital markets (like the New York Stock Exchange) can fulfill this need. With very few exceptions, the only form of business that has met with success in these markets is the corporation. In contrast, because partnerships do not offer limited liability, free transferability of interests, or indefinite life, they are (with few exceptions) not appropriate for ventures requiring large amounts of capital accessed via the financial markets.

It is not rare to find someone with a great idea but insufficient resources to take the idea to market. Some investors, like *venture capitalists,* seek out such persons. They will usually insist that the venture have limited liability, as would be true with a corporation or an LLC. [For more on venture capitalists, see **http://www.nvca.org**]

Similarly, *franchisors* normally demand that *franchisees* operate their *franchises* in a business form with limited liability. A franchise is the right to exploit the franchisor's intangible assets (trade name and business systems) and to partake of the franchisor's marketing, purchasing, and other services. The key advantages to the franchisee are a proven product or service, turn-key implementation, and access to support. The franchisor gains by earning fees and by achieving accelerated market penetration using the capital of others (franchisees). Unfortunately, franchisor fraud and oppression are not unusual, so careful investigation is essential. Furthermore, premium franchises can be expensive. [For an extensive listing of franchise opportunities and their minimum cash requirements, see **http://www.franchisedirect.com**]

With the development of such business forms as LLCs, LLPs, and S corporations, under most circumstances the disadvantages of the partnership form are so severe that a person is usually well advised to avoid it.

Questions—Part One

1. Why are corporations the dominant form of business based on revenues in the United States?
2. *a.* Why are sole proprietorships problematic if a proprietor dies or is disabled?
   b. Do partnerships experience similar problems? Explain.
3. *a.* What characteristics of an LLC cause it to be the fastest growing business form in the United States?
   b. What are its advantages over a corporation?

Part Two—Corporate Governance in Public Corporations

Public corporations have thousands of shareholders. The vast majority of these shareholders do not plan to spend their time intimately involved in the company's business. They wish to entrust their resources to the stewardship of the company's management and return to their personal affairs. To ensure the corporation is acting to further their interests, the shareholders elect a board of directors. Public corporation boards generally have both inside and outside directors. *Inside directors* are senior executives. *Outside directors* are not employed by the company. These boards meet at regular intervals to monitor the corporation's activities, establish corporate policies, hire and replace corporate executives, and make major decisions.

> The accounting scandals of the Enron era and the 2008 collapse of the financial markets.

That at least is the textbook description of the management of such corporations. What has become evident, painfully so from both the accounting scandals of the Enron era and the 2008 collapse of the financial markets, is that in practice it can be quite different. Enron called the world's attention to extraordinary failings in corporate governance. Its demise was not an isolated event. It had numerous predecessors that failed to alert the markets and it was quickly followed by many more, at least three of which were actually larger (WorldCom, Parmalat, and Fannie Mae). And while the 2008 crisis primarily involved the financial services industry, for that industry it became clear that corporate governance issues are still a matter of concern. Both the majority and minority reports of the Financial Crisis Inquiry Commission (the body charged by Congress to determine the causes of the financial crisis) point to such failures. As the majority report states, "We conclude dramatic failures of corporate governance and risk management at many systemically important financial institutions were a key cause of this crisis."[25] Or, in the words of Carl Icahn, "The entirely preventable financial catastrophe . . . has many culprits: reckless executives who gambled with their company's futures, feckless regulators and somnambulant boards of directors."[26]

This part of the chapter will look at some of the corporate governance reforms adopted in the wake of both Enron and the recent financial crisis, as well as reforms driven by the shareholder rights movement over the past decade.

The Management Pyramid

Corporations have centralized management. By design, at the apex of the management pyramid is the board of directors. Immediately below is the CEO. In the next layer are the vice presidents and other top officers and executives. This classic management pyramid further expands through layers of middle management, finally coming to the base comprised of rank-and-file employees. The look into the boardroom provided by government investigations and shareholder lawsuits in the Enron era revealed that this pyramid had become inverted at the top. Far too frequently, boards simply abdicated responsibility to their CEOs who often held the ultimate power as a consequence of the authority to nominate board members and to control the information reaching the board. Board memberships can be extremely lucrative—tens or hundreds of thousands of dollars annually for attendance at a modest number of board meetings. Many conflicts of interest were also discovered. At Enron, for example, some directors were personal friends of senior managers, others were academics whose institutions were receiving substantial contributions, and still another was a former senior government official who had exempted Enron from regulation of its principal line of business.

The federal legislation passed in 2002 in the wake of Enron, SOX, attempted to address some of these governance issues. To limit the CEO's control of audit information to the board, it requires that the board's audit committee consist of all independent directors—outside directors without conflicts of interest—one of whom is required to be a financial expert. SOX gives the audit committee direct responsibility for hiring the outside auditing firm and setting its compensation and prohibits that firm from also providing to the corporation most types of consulting services. To remove the CEO's control over board seats, SOX requires that corporate nominating committees also must be composed solely of independent directors.

Even after SOX, there are still issues over who has power at the top of the pyramid. The CEO can still control much of the information that reaches the board. Shortly before the financial crisis hit, *The Wall Street Journal* published a special report on corporate governance. The headline of the lead article was "Why CEOs Need to Be Honest with Their Boards: Too Often Chief Executives Sugarcoat the Truth. That's More Dangerous Than Ever."[27] An important issue for good governance is whether boards are active in setting policies and making major decisions or simply following the lead of the CEO. For example, immediately after the CEO of Lehman Brothers announced a $3.9 billion third quarter loss in 2008, he stated, "I must say the board's been wonderfully supportive."[28]

One reform offered as a partial response is to require that the positions of board chair and CEO be held by different individuals. "No one can reasonably expect a person to oversee himself or herself. . . . The C.E.O. works for the board, not the other way around; the continuation of combined roles inhibits the board in exercising its responsibilities because it creates an insurmountable imbalance of power."[29] At the time the crisis hit in 2008, in *Fortune* 500 companies both positions were more often than not held by a single person.[30] The Dodd-Frank Act, enacted in response to the financial crisis, requires that corporations disclose the reasons for choosing the same person for both positions, but does not prohibit the practice.

Question

1. What should the board's role be? Consider the following two opinions:

> [B]oards [are] supposed to monitor risks, provide judgment and supervise managers on behalf of shareholders.[31]
>
> Most boards meet one or two days a month and are composed of individuals who also hold demanding full-time jobs. Given those circumstances, it's absurd to believe that board members, even the most experienced and best-intentioned of them, will uncover systemic flaws or acts of malfeasance. . . . That's what regulators, outside accountants, and internal controls are for—to help boards ferret out excessive risk and wrongdoing.[32]

The Shareholder Rights Movement

Although shareholders are the owners of the corporation, control and management rests with the board. As we have seen in the discussion of the business judgment rule, state law significantly restricts shareholders' ability to control management, other than through the annual election of the board.

> The notion that shareholders can exercise control is doubtful.

The notion that shareholders can exercise control even through the annual election of the board is itself doubtful. As we saw above, shareholders do not select candidates for board positions, a committee of the existing board does so. Could a dissatisfied shareholder offer a different slate of directors for shareholders to vote on? In theory yes; in practice *proxy fights* are difficult and risky, as well as expensive. Annually, management solicits proxies from its shareholders. A *proxy* is written permission to vote a shareholder's stock, for example, in the election of directors. Management's solicitation is done in conjunction with its required notification to shareholders of the annual meeting and the cost is thus borne by the corporation itself. Shareholders wanting to propose alternative candidates have to be prepared to bear the entire cost themselves. State law gives shareholders the right of access to shareholder lists maintained by the company, but often a shareholder will have to sue, at a substantial cost in time and money, to force the corporation to comply. If successful, the next step is to develop and submit to the SEC for review the materials to be used to solicit shareholders' proxies. Only after receiving SEC approval can a shareholder begin the active solicitation of proxies from fellow shareholders.

Not surprisingly, such proxy fights are rare. Most shareholders who disagree with management's decisions simply sell their shares and invest elsewhere. From society's and shareholders' points of view, management of publicly held corporations proceeds largely unchecked, except for securities law violations which will be discussed in Part Three below. This is what Stephen Davis, executive director of the Center for Corporate Governance at Yale, has referred to as "the myth that boards have been accountable to shareholders."[33]

In recent years various proposals to give shareholders more input have been gaining ground, largely through the efforts of institutional investors and independent activists. Institutional investors, such as pension funds and mutual funds, have significant influence in the capital markets. In 2009 they owned 73 percent of the top 1000 U.S. corporations.[34] When the head of corporate governance for the California Public Employees' Retirement System (CALPERS), the largest U.S. public pension, contacts management at a company in which it holds stock, management is likely to listen.

Majority Rules

One shareholder reform that has gained significant ground addresses the number of votes required to elect a director. Many state laws, including Delaware, allow directors to be elected by just a plurality of the votes cast in person or by proxy. If the only names before the shareholders are management's slate of directors, management nominees will win even if a substantial number of shareholders withhold their votes in protest. In 2006, only 16 percent of firms in the S&P 500 had any form of majority vote requirement. A year and a half later, the number was over 60 percent.[35] Although a positive development, the impact is not as great as it might first appear. In most cases where management has agreed to a majority vote rule, it has not agreed to reject automatically a candidate who has commanded only a plurality, but only to review whether or not to seat such a candidate.

Broker Voting

Another area of movement concerns broker voting. Many individual shareholders do not hold their shares, but leave them on account with their broker. Past practice was that, unless the account owner specifically directed otherwise, the broker could vote the shares, typically in a promanagement fashion. That practice has been reversed by the Dodd-Frank Act, which prohibits broker voting unless specific instructions are received from the beneficial owner. The likely consequence is that fewer shares will be voted, shifting even greater influence to the large institutional shareholders who do vote.

Proxy Access

One of the most controversial issues of recent years has been proxy access. As discussed above, it is possible for dissatisfied shareholders to wage a proxy fight. However, for most shareholders such a course is cost prohibitive. A cost-effective solution for shareholders would be to require management to include shareholder nominees on the company's ballot sent to shareholders in advance of the annual meeting. Although state law does not give shareholders that right, a corporation's bylaws could. To propose such a change would require a shareholder to submit the bylaw proposal to the corporation for inclusion in the annual meeting materials. If management wants to reject the request for inclusion of the proposal, it becomes a matter subject to regulation by the SEC. The SEC under the Bush administration took the position that management was not required to include such proposals in the company's proxy materials, but in 2006 a Federal Circuit Court ruled against the SEC's interpretation of the relevant regulation.[36] In response the SEC opened a rule-making proceeding on proxy access. In August 2010, after a change in both the administration and the composition of the SEC, the commission issued a new rule permitting shareholder groups (owning at least 3 percent of a company's stock for at least three years) to submit nominees for inclusion in the company's ballot, with the caveat that no more than 25 percent of the board can be elected in this fashion. As of the time of this writing, the application of this proxy access rule has been suspended pending the outcome of a suit brought by the U.S. Chamber of Commerce seeking to overturn it.[37]

How to Vote Your Shares

Small investors individually own about 30 percent of publicly traded corporate stock, but few of them vote in annual elections. It may seem like a daunting task to vote responsibly. Here is some straightforward guidance:

- Do the directors own stock in the company and attend more than 75 percent of the board meetings? A chart on the proxy statement will provide this information.
- If a director does business with the company, the director may not be independent. The related-party transactions box in the proxy statement will disclose this.

- If there are too many shareholder proposals, management may not be engaging with shareholders or listening to their concerns.
- Find out how others, such as shareholder activists and active institutional investors, are voting on proposals through such Web sites as **ProxyDemocracy.org**, **Shareowners. org**, and **MoxyVote.com**

Source: Tara Siegel Bernard, "Voting Your Shares May Start to Matter," *The New York Times,* March 5, 2010.

Executive Compensation

Executive compensation has long been an issue for shareholders. The 20th-century American economist John Kenneth Galbraith observed that "[t]he salary of the chief executive of a large corporation is not a market award for achievement. It is frequently in the nature of a warm personal gesture by the individual to himself." It is also an issue that is likely not to go away soon. In the late 1970s CEOs earned 30 to 40 times the income of average workers; by 2007, CEOs of large public corporations earned 344 times the income of average workers.[38] Thanks to the Dodd-Frank Act, that ratio will be disclosed annually. The act also requires disclosure of the relationship between executive compensation and the financial performance of the company giving consideration to both stock price and dividends.

> By 2007, CEOs of large public corporations earned 344 times the income of average workers.

The Act did not stop with mandated disclosures. It also includes a *say on pay* provision requiring companies to put a separate, but nonbinding, resolution before the shareholders to approve the compensation paid to corporate executives. A separate resolution must also be presented to allow shareholders to determine the frequency (but no less often than every three years) of such say on pay resolutions.

PRACTICING ETHICS Excessive Executive Compensation?

An interesting shareholder derivative case alleging a violation of the duty of care arose out of CEO Michael Eisner's hiring, and subsequent firing, of Michael Ovitz from his position as president of Walt Disney Co. The suit alleged that Eisner and the Disney board had violated their duty of care by hiring Ovitz (who had no previous experience as an executive of a public company in the entertainment industry), as well as when Ovitz was granted a no-fault termination. The consequence of invoking the no-fault clause in Ovitz's employment contract was that, after barely one year of employment, Ovitz received over $38 million in cash, as well as three million stock options.

Notably, the maximum salary Ovitz could have earned actually working was $11 million annually. Following a three-month trial, the Delaware judge wrote, "For the future, many lessons of what not to do can be learned from defendants' conduct here. Nevertheless, I conclude that . . . the defendants did not act in bad faith, and were at most ordinarily negligent, in connection with the hiring of Ovitz . . . In accordance with the business judgment rule, . . . ordinary negligence is insufficient to constitute a violation of the fiduciary duty of care." The court also found that Ovitz could not have been fired for cause because he did not commit gross negligence or malfeasance while serving as Disney's president. Thus, Eisner did not breach his duty of care by agreeing to the no-fault termination. In 2006, ten years after Ovitz was terminated, this decision was affirmed on appeal by the Delaware Supreme Court. [*In re Walt Disney Co. Derivative Litigation*, 907 A.2d 693 (Del. Ch. 2005), aff'd 906 A.2d 27 (Del. 2006).]

Since 2007, as a result of a change in SEC disclosure rules, shareholders have been receiving more information on executive compensation packages. According to one source, executive severance packages typically "include a payment of three times salary and bonus, immediate vesting of options and restricted stock awards, and, in many cases, payment of taxes owed. . . .

[D]ozens of executives could have payouts of $100 million or more."

Questions

1. Apart from the legality, is it ethical for a board to agree to an executive severance package when an executive is terminated for poor performance?

2. Such packages are negotiated as part of the hiring process. Would it chill the negotiations for a board to state a corporate policy against severance payments under such circumstances?

Source: Jane Sasseen, "A Better Look at the Boss's Pay," *BusinessWeek*, Feb. 26, 2007, p. 44.

Questions—Part Two

1. Why have corporate governance concerns arisen in the past decade with respect to the relationship between the board and the CEO? Do you believe there are still grounds for continuing concern?

2. Evaluate the opinion that board accountability to shareholders is a myth.

3. Why might it make sense to have only outside directors determine the compensation of senior executives?

4. Select one of the shareholder rights proposals discussed in Part Two and present arguments both for and against its adoption.

Part Three—Regulation of the Securities Markets

Introduction

As the recent financial crisis has shown, the capital markets are much broader than the market for securities, which in turn is far broader than the market for corporate securities. Nevertheless, the focus of this part of the chapter is on business access to capital.

> Vast sums (have been) lost in companies with incompetent or corrupt management.

To amass the capital needed to pursue sizeable business opportunities, particularly global opportunities, a large number of investors must be convinced to entrust their wealth to third parties. History shows that this trust has often been misplaced, with vast sums lost in companies with incompetent or corrupt management. As a result the federal government has undertaken to promote the reliability of the U.S. securities markets through regulation. The backbone of this regulation grew out of the stock market crash of 1929 and the Great Depression that followed. As previously mentioned, significant additional regulation has followed the corporate failures of the Enron era and the financial crisis that hit in 2008. As we turn to our examination of how the securities markets are regulated, we will incorporate discussion of relevant provisions from these later enactments while we keep our primary focus on their impact on the access to capital by business.

Initial Public Offerings

When a corporation wants to sell a new security through the public capital markets (whether debt or equity), if the corporation (*issuer*) and any of the persons to whom the security is offered for sale (*offerees*) are domiciled in different states (*interstate offering*), federal law governs the sale. Should the corporation and all offerees be domiciled in the same state (intrastate offering), state law (considered later) will apply. If a company has not previously offered equity securities to the public, the offering will be referred to as an *initial public offering* or, more colloquially, *going public*. For example, on April 14, 2011, Zipcar, Inc., a membership-based car sharing service with locations in urban centers in the United States, United Kingdom, and Canada, offered its stock at $18 per share to the public for the first time. At the close of its first trading day the shares were trading at over $28.[39] Conversely, if a private investor seeks to purchase all of the publicly held equity securities of a corporation, that company is said to be *going private*.

In this context, the term *security* embraces both the instruments commonly understood to be securities, like stocks and bonds, as well as a much broader class called investment contracts. The *Howey* case that follows defines the term.

LEGAL BRIEFCASE

SEC v. W. J. Howey Co.
328 U.S. 293 (1946)

FACTS

The Howey Company owned large tracts of citrus acreage in Florida. Each prospective customer was offered both a land sales contract and a service contract by which Howey maintained the groves and marketed the produce. Purchases usually were narrow strips that were arranged so that an acre consisted of a row of 48 trees. These tracts were not separately fenced and the purchaser had no right of entry and no right to specific fruit. All the produce was pooled. The purchasers were mostly non-residents of Florida and were predominantly professional people who lacked the knowledge and equipment necessary for the citrus business. They were attracted by the expectation of substantial profits.

Justice Murphy

* * * * *

It is admitted that the mails and instrumentalities of interstate commerce are used in the sale of the land and service contracts and that no registration statement... has ever been filed with the [Securities Exchange Commission.]

[The Securities Act of 1933] defines the term "security" to include the commonly known [instruments like stocks and bonds.] The definition also includes [the term] "investment contract".... The legal issue turns upon the legal determination of whether the land sales contract, the warranty deed and the service contract together constitute an "investment contract" within the meaning of [the Act]. An affirmative answer brings into operation the registration requirements. . . .

By including an investment contract within the scope of . . . the Securities Act, Congress was using a term the meaning of which had been crystallized by this prior judicial interpretation. It is therefore reasonable to attach that meaning to the term as used by Congress, especially since such a definition is consistent with the statutory aims. In other words, an investment contract for purposes of the Securities Act means a contract, transaction or scheme whereby a person invests his money in a common enterprise and is led to expect profits solely from the efforts of the promoter or a third party. . . .

The transactions in this case clearly involve investment contracts as so defined. The respondent [is] offering an opportunity to contribute money and to share in the profits of a large citrus fruit enterprise managed [by respondent. It is] offering this opportunity to persons who reside in distant localities and who lack the equipment and experience requisite to the cultivation, harvesting and marketing of the citrus products. . . .

[Respondent's] failure to abide by the statutory and administrative rules in making such offerings cannot be sanctioned under the Act. . . .

Questions

1. Would an investment in Microsoft stock satisfy the definition of "investment contract"?

2. Why do you think Congress added the term "investment contract" to the definition of "security"?

AFTERWORD

Following the *Howey* case, courts have looked more closely at the final criterion, that the investor "is led to expect profits *solely* from the efforts" of others [emphasis added], and have generally taken a practical view of the requirement. The goal has been to distinguish circumstances in which investors will be primarily passive from those in which there is a reasonable expectation of significant investor control.[40] Thus, membership units in an LLC may or may not qualify as investment contracts, depending on the surrounding facts.[41]

1933 Act

The federal law governing initial securities offerings is the *Securities Act of 1933* (1933 Act), which is administered by the *Securities and Exchange Commission* (SEC). The 1933 Act does not guarantee the economic merits of any investment opportunity. Rather, it seeks (1) to ensure full disclosure of all material facts about the investment opportunity to offerees (potential investors) before they invest and (2) to eliminate fraudulent conduct in the markets. Thus, a securities offering that passes muster under the federal securities law has not been approved by the government as a good investment. [For more on the SEC, see **http://www.sec.gov**]

To promote full disclosure the 1933 Act forbids any interstate offering of a new security until a *registration statement* has been filed with and approved by the SEC. The *registration statement* has two parts: the prospectus and the supplemental information (discussed shortly). The *prospectus* is the major component and is delivered to offerees to satisfy the requirement for preinvestment disclosure. There are three main sections in a prospectus. One contains general information about the company: the industry in which it operates, the quality of its products and services and of its management, its business plan, and so on. Another section contains a risk assessment of the business model, local operating conditions (such as political instability), and the like. For example, although companies have long been required to disclose possible impacts on the business from various environmental factors, in 2010 the SEC began requiring companies to disclose the risks that global climate change might pose to their business, such as whether any new law or treaty limiting carbon dioxide emissions might increase operating costs or a law mandating increased production of renewable electricity might be particularly advantageous to their line of business.[42]

The third portion of the prospectus is the *audited financial statements*. An investor's goal is to make money. Investors want to know how well the corporation under consideration has accomplished this in the past so they can estimate its future economic potential. A corporation's ability to make a profit is shown on its *income statement,* one of the three audited financial statements. The income statement shows the company's revenue and expenses on an annual basis.

Because the income statement seeks to measure economic income, it employs accrual accounting, which recognizes revenue when earned (not when cash is received) and which recognizes expenses in the period in which the related income is reported (regardless of when those expenses are paid). Since the income statement focuses only on economic income, a *statement of cash flows* reconciling the beginning and ending cash balances is also presented.

The third financial statement, the *balance sheet,* presents the company's assets, liabilities and equity. Although balance sheets have numerous deficiencies (such as the use of historical cost rather than current value to measure assets), they attempt to describe the corporation's financial position as of a particular date, such as the end of the year presented in the income statement.

Technically, the financial statements are prepared by the corporation's management. To give comfort to investors that management has prepared these statements properly and honestly, independent *certified public accountants* (CPAs) are engaged to audit them. Audits must be performed in accordance with *generally accepted auditing standards* (GAAS). GAAS are intended to ensure that the procedures used to investigate the financial statements are thorough. The objective of the investigation is to determine whether the financial statements are *not materially misleading,* in accordance with *generally accepted accounting principles* (GAAP). GAAP provides the rules for how revenues, expenses, assets, liabilities, and equity are measured and disclosed. One might paraphrase an audit: independent experts (CPAs) are supposed to "look hard" (GAAS) and decide whether the financial statements accurately measure the income, cash flow and financial position of the corporation (GAAP).

The *supplemental information* portion (the second part) of the registration statement, which is not distributed to offerees, describes such matters as how much it is costing to "float" the offering and what major contracts exist with unions, suppliers, or customers.

The SEC vigorously enforces the 1933 Act's prescribed relationship between solicitation or sales of a security and the registration process. There are three critical stages. During the *prefiling period* (before the registration statement has been filed with the SEC), no solicitation or sales are permitted. During the *waiting period* (after the registration statement has been filed, but before it has been approved by the SEC), no sales are permitted but a limited amount of solicitation is allowed. Specifically, a *tombstone* ad (so called because of its shape) may be published in forums like *The Wall Street Journal* to make the market aware of the upcoming issuance. In addition, a *"red herring"* prospectus (name taken from the prominent red ink cautionary statement required on its first page) may be distributed. This is the draft prospectus included with the filed registration statement. Once the SEC approves the registration statement, the *posteffective period* begins. Solicitations are permitted and sales may be made, but only if the offerees have first received the final prospectus.

Some companies do *shelf registrations* that allow them to issue securities in portions over a two-year period under a single registration statement. This allows issuers to float the securities when market conditions are most favorable, without having to place the entire issue shortly after the registration statement becomes effective.

Typically not wanting to sell the securities themselves, issuers employ one of two kinds of *underwriters*. A best-efforts underwriter acts as the issuer's sales agent, does not take title to the securities and earns its profit from sales commissions. A *firm-commitment under-writer* purchases the securities at a discount, intending to profit by reselling them. Institutional investors and *dealers* typically purchase new offerings—the former for investment, the latter for resale to retail investors.

PRACTICING ETHICS Credit Rating Agencies—Another Cause for Concern?

Corporations may use the securities markets to obtain debt capital by selling corporate bonds, as well as to obtain equity capital through the sale of stock. Bonds are specifically included in the definition of "security" and thus are governed by the federal laws discussed in this part of the chapter. In order to sell a new issuance of bonds, a corporation will usually seek to have the bond rated by a credit rating agency such as Moody's, Standard & Poor's or Fitch. Without such a rating it may be hard for the corporation to sell a sufficient number of, or to obtain the maximum price for, its bonds. Most of the revenues of these agencies come from the fees paid by issuers seeking to have their debt rated. These facts raise potential conflicts of interest for the agencies—on the one hand they are in business to produce credible, independent evaluations of issuers and bonds, but on the other hand they have to compete with other agencies for issuers' business.

It seems clear that such conflicts played a role in the recent financial crisis—not from their rating of corporate bonds, but from their rating of mortgage-backed securities (investment vehicles based on the performance of a pool of mortgages). According to the Financial Crisis Inquiry Report, "Failures in credit rating and securitization transformed bad mortgages into toxic financial assets."[43] Congressional hearings uncovered internal e-mails containing such statements as "sold our soul to the devil for revenue" (Moody's) and "let's hope we are all wealthy and retired by the time this house of cards falters" (Standard & Poor's).[44]

Question

1. A bondholder would be concerned about whether a corporation has purchased a favorable bond rating. Should a shareholder also be worried? Explain.

Exemptions

Exempt securities and *exempt transactions* do not require registration with the SEC. The most common exempt securities are those issued by governments, charities, educational institutions, and financial institutions like banks and insurance companies. Thus, they have little application to most businesses.

Certain transactions, however, are also exempt from at least some of the registration requirements. Depending on the exemption, the presale disclosures and filings with the SEC range from none to something only slightly less than a full registration statement. Most exemptions do not permit general advertising or solicitation.

Five categories of exempt transactions were created at least in part as an accommodation to small issuers, such as private and closely held businesses, to lessen the financial burdens of raising capital. For example, all intrastate offerings are exempt transactions.

There is a statutory exemption for purely private offerings, but it can sometimes be problematic to determine whether a particular offering will be considered private or public. Thus, small issuers are more likely to rely on one of the regulatory exemptions created by SEC. Particularly important are Rule 504 (which exempts transactions with an aggregate offering price of $1 million or less), Rule 505 (which excludes transactions with an aggregate price up to $5 million to no more than 35 investors), and Rule 506 (for which there are no price limitations but which can only be sold to *accredited investors* and up to 35 sophisticated investors). Accredited investors are individuals with a net worth over $1 million or with an income in excess of $200,000 for at least two years with the expectation of similar income in the current year.

Note that even when exemptions apply to registration under the 1933 Act, the Act's sweeping antifraud provisions, discussed later, still apply.

The Secondary Securities Markets

Once a security is issued, it can be sold repeatedly. Such sales may be accomplished on a *physical exchange,* such as the New York Stock Exchange (NYSE), where agents of buyers and sellers deal directly with each other. Others may be made on an *over-the-counter market,* where trades occur electronically over a computer network linking dealers across the nation. An example is NASDAQ, the National Association of Securities Dealers Automatic Quotation system. [To learn more about these exchanges, see **http://www.nyse.com** and **http://www.nasdaq.com**]

The federal law that governs these trades is the *Securities Exchange Act of 1934* (1934 Act), which also created the SEC. Its purposes are the same as those of its 1933 counterpart: (1) to ensure full disclosure of all material information so the market can make informed investment decisions and (2) to prevent fraudulent conduct in the markets. A company is generally subject to the 1934 Act's reporting requirements if it has publicly traded securities and it has both more than $10 million in assets and more than 500 shareholders.[45]

To promote full disclosure, the SEC requires registered corporations to file a variety of reports. Annually, each must file a *Form 10-K,* which includes information very similar to that found in a 1933 Act registration statement, including audited financial statements. Recall, as discussed in Part Two, that the Dodd-Frank Act added some new disclosure requirements, such as the ratio of the CEO's compensation to that of the median compensation for all other employees. To increase the timeliness of information disclosures, the SEC requires additional reports, such as the quarterly *Form 10-Q* and *Form 8-K.* The latter is required whenever a material event occurs, such as a change in control, major asset acquisitions and dispositions, bankruptcy, a change in auditor, and resignations of directors.[46] [To retrieve filings for specific corporations, see **http://www. sec.gov/edgar.shtml**

Not only are certain disclosures mandated, but all corporate communications are subject to certain regulatory standards. This is creating new challenges for corporations that want to make use of blogs, tweets and the growing social media market.[47]

Under the 1934 Act the SEC has the power to *suspend trading* in any security "when it serves the public interest and will protect investors." Thus, the SEC may suspend trading if it suspects price manipulation or has serious questions about a company's assets or operations.[48] Typically, the market price of a security is devastated by a suspension, which provides a strong incentive for corporations to avoid misconduct.

Brokers and Online Trading

When individuals want to buy or sell securities listed on an exchange, they may do so through an intermediary—a broker. In addition to facilitating trades, brokers may provide advisory services and assess the suitability of investments for a particular investor. That is, they make recommendations and trades taking into account the investor's needs, financial situation, investment objectives, and risk tolerance.

> An 80-year-old woman with Alzheimer's disease entrusted $500,000 to a broker.

Occasionally, a broker has faced charges of *churning*—repeatedly and unnecessarily engaging in trades to generate commissions. In one case, an 80-year-old woman with Alzheimer's disease entrusted $500,000 to a broker. Fourteen months later, the account was worth only $15,000. The broker had engaged in over 300 trades and charged the account $94,000 in fees, purchasing only high-tech stocks (versus a balanced, conservative portfolio more appropriate to her situation). In addition, the broker used the account to secure a $422,000 margin loan to buy more such stocks, further decimating the account when the high-tech bubble burst.[49]

One effect of the development of the Internet was the bypassing of full-service securities brokers in many transactions through *online trading*. However, today most major full-service brokers facilitate online trading as well. Online services can be less expensive and provide greater accessibility to the market, but they also tend to leave investors on their own without professional guidance.

Matters get worse when it comes to *day trading*. Day traders rarely hold any security more than a few hours, earning profits by exploiting volatility, not inherent value. It has been reported that only about 10 percent of day traders are successful.[50] The SEC has expressed great concern about advertising that suggests day trading is easy and certain to be profitable. It cautions that tips and analyses are frequently false.[51] Nonetheless, the market has moved inexorably toward global, 24-hour-a-day, electronic trading.

Violating Federal Securities Laws

The consequences for noncompliance with the securities laws are potentially staggering, including damages and civil and criminal penalties. Some of the provisions most commonly violated by corporations and their directors and executives are discussed below.

False or Misleading Statements in Required Filings—1933 Act

Perhaps the greatest deterrent to misconduct in the securities laws is the civil liability that can be imposed on wrongdoers by harmed investors. The 1933 Act's Section 11 establishes this liability with respect to false or misleading registration statements required by the Act.

Virtually anyone with a significant role in preparing the registration statement can be sued (the issuer, its directors, its underwriters, and its accountants and other experts). The liability can be vast—essentially all damages sustained by investors while the misleading registration statements were outstanding. No proof of plaintiff reliance on the content of the registration statement is required. Accounting firms and investment bankers, because of their "deep pockets," are often at the top of the list of defendants. Accounting firms have paid hundreds of millions of dollars to settle securities fraud suits.

The principal defense against a Section 11 claim is *due diligence*. Every defendant, other than the issuer, can raise this defense. The defendant must show that, based on a reasonable investigation, he or she reasonably believed that the registration statement was not misleading. What constitutes "reasonable" is determined by reference to the conduct expected of a prudent person in the management of his or her own property.

The due diligence standard for experts (like accountants and lawyers) is much higher. Their inquiries must rise to the standards expected of professionals, not merely of prudent businesspersons. Thus, at an absolute minimum, an accounting firm that has audited the financial statements included in the registration statement must design its audit process to comport with GAAS and must evaluate the financial statement content in accordance with GAAP. Lawyers, actuaries, appraisers and other experts whose work has a material impact on the registration statement must follow analogous rules established by their professional associations and regulators. The *BarChris* case, below, explores the due diligence defense. Only that part of the court's opinion is presented.

Escott v. BarChris Construction Corporation

LEGAL BRIEFCASE   283 F.Supp. 643 (S.D.N.Y. 1968)

FACTS

Bowling as a leisure activity and sport grew rapidly in the 1950s. BarChris built alleys. Its revenues grew from $800,000 in 1956 to $9,165,000 in 1960. By 1962 overbuilding caused construction to halt. BarChris ran into serious financial problems. It filed a registration statement (effective May 1961) for new bonds to raise cash and the bonds were issued. Circumstances were grave when the registration statement became effective. BarChris filed for bankruptcy in October 1962.

BarChris's financial statements dated December 31, 1960, were included in the prospectus. They were audited by Peat, Marwick (predecessor to KPMG) and contained material errors. Revenues and current assets were overstated and contingent liabilities were understated.

The prospectus overstated the demand for alley construction. It misrepresented how the proceeds would be used (a large portion of which would actually go to pay overdue debts and retire loans from officers). It failed to note that, because of defaults, BarChris was now operating several alleys. Escott and other bondholders sued under Section 11 of the 1933 Act, alleging the prospectus was materially misleading. All defendants but BarChris raised the due diligence defense.

Judge Mclean

I turn now to the question of whether defendants have proved their due diligence defenses. The position of each defendant will be separately considered.

Russo

Russo was, to all intents and purposes, the chief executive officer of BarChris. He was a member of the executive committee. He was familiar with all aspects of the business. . . . [He] knew all the relevant facts. He could not have believed that there were no untrue statements or material omissions in the prospectus. Russo has no due diligence defenses.

Vitolo and Pugliese

They were the founders. . . . Vitolo was president and Pugliese was vice president. Despite their titles, their [control] over BarChris's affairs [was far less] than Russo's. [They are] each men of limited education. It is not hard to believe that for them the prospectus was difficult reading, if indeed they read it at all. But [the] liability of a director who signs a registration statement does not depend upon whether or not he read it or, if he did, whether or not he understood what he was reading.

And in any case, Vitolo and Pugliese were not as naive as they claim to be. They were members of BarChris's executive committee. . . . They must have known what was going on. Certainly they knew of the inadequacy of cash. . . . They knew of their own large advances to the company which remained unpaid. They knew that they had agreed not to deposit their checks until the financing proceeds were received. They knew and intended that part of the proceeds were to be used to pay their own loans.

All in all, [their situation] is not significantly different . . . from Russo's. They could not have believed that the registration statement was wholly true and that no material facts had been omitted. . . . They have not proved their due diligence defenses.

Trilling

[Trilling was . . . a CPA and former member of Peat, Marwick. He was BarChris'] controller. He signed the registration statement in that capacity, although he was not a director. . . .

Trilling may well have been unaware of several of the inaccuracies in the prospectus. But he must have known of some of them. . . . I cannot find that Trilling believed the entire prospectus to be true.

But even if he did, he still did not establish his due diligence defenses. He . . . failed to prove, as to the [nonaudited] parts of the prospectus . . ., that he made a reasonable investigation which afforded him a reasonable ground to believe that it was true. As far as appears, he made no investigation. . . . This would have been well enough but for the fact that he signed the registration statement. As a signer, he could not

avoid responsibility. . . . [He has not proved] his due diligence defenses.

Birnbaum

Birnbaum was a young lawyer [employed as in-house counsel. He was] secretary and a director. . . . He signed the later amendments [to the registration statement], thereby becoming responsible for the accuracy of the prospectus. . . .

. . . He did not participate in the management of the company. As house counsel, he attended to legal matters of a routine nature. . . .

One of Birnbaum's more important duties . . . was to keep the corporate minutes. . . . This necessarily informed him to a considerable extent about the company's affairs. . . .

It seems probable that Birnbaum did not know of many of the inaccuracies in the prospectus. He must, however, have appreciated some of them. In any case, he made no investigation. . . . [He] was entitled to rely upon Peat, Marwick for the 1960 figures. . . . But he was not entitled to rely upon [anyone else] for the other portions of the prospectus. As a lawyer, he should have known his obligations. . . . Having failed to make such an investigation, he did not have reasonable ground to believe that all these statements were true. Birnbaum has not established his due diligence defenses except as to the audited 1960 figures.

Auslander

Auslander was an 'outside' director. . . . He was chairman . . . of Valley Stream National Bank. [He became a director shortly before the sale of the bonds. He signed the registration statement.]

. . . As to the [financial statements], Auslander knew that Peat, Marwick had audited [them, so he] believed them to be correct. . . . He had no reasonable ground to believe otherwise.

As to the [non-audited portions of the prospectus], however, Auslander is in a different position. . . . [He] made no investigation of the accuracy of the prospectus. He relied on the assurance of Vitolo and Russo. . . .

It is true that Auslander became a director on the eve of the financing. He had little opportunity to familiarize himself with the company's affairs. . . .

Section 11 imposes liability . . . upon a director, no matter how new he is. He is presumed to know his responsibility when he becomes a director. He can escape liability only by using that reasonable care to investigate the facts which a prudent man would employ in the management of his own property. In my opinion, a prudent man would not act in an important matter . . . in sole reliance upon representations of persons who are comparative strangers. . . . To say that such minimal conduct measures up to the statutory standard would, to all intents and purposes, absolve new directors from responsibility merely because they are new. This is not a sensible construction of Section 11. . . .

Auslander has not established his due diligence defense [except as to the financial statements].

Grant

. . . [Grant's] law firm was counsel to BarChris in matters pertaining to the registration of securities. Grant drafted the registration statement. . . . As the director most directly concerned with writing [it] and assuring its accuracy, more was required of him in the way of reasonable investigation than could fairly be expected of a director who had no connection with this work. . . .

. . . I find that Grant honestly believed that the registration statement was true and that no material facts had been omitted from it.

In this belief he was mistaken, and the fact is that for all his work, he never discovered any of the errors or omissions which . . . could have been detected without an audit. The question is whether, despite his failure to detect them, Grant made a reasonable effort to that end.

. . . BarChris's affairs had changed for the worse. . . . Grant never discovered this. He accepted the assurances of [others] that any change which might have occurred had been for the better. . . .

It is claimed that a lawyer is entitled to rely on the statements of his client. . . . This is too broad a generalization. It is all a matter of degree. To require an audit would obviously be unreasonable. On the other hand, to require a check of matters easily verifiable is not unreasonable. Even honest clients can make mistakes. The statute imposes liability for untrue statements regardless of whether they are intentionally untrue. . . .

. . . Grant knew that minutes of certain meetings of the BarChris executive committee held in 1961 had not been written up. . . . Grant did not insist that the minutes be written up, nor did he look at Kircher's notes. . . .

. . . He knew that BarChris was short of cash, but he had no idea how short. He did not know that BarChris was withholding delivery of checks already drawn and signed because there was not enough money in the bank to pay them. He did not know that the officers of the company intended to use immediately approximately one-third of the financing proceeds in a manner not disclosed in the prospectus, including approximately $1,000,000 in paying old debts. . . .

Grant was entitled to rely on Peat Marwick for the 1960 figures. [But as to the rest of the prospectus, Grant] was

obliged to make a reasonable investigation. I am forced to find that he did not make one. . . . Grant has not established his due diligence defenses except as to the audited 1960 figures.

Peat, Marwick

. . . The part of the registration statement . . . made upon the authority of Peat, Marwick as an expert was . . . the 1960 [audited financial statements]. But because the statute requires the court to determine Peat, Marwick's belief, and the grounds thereof, "at the time . . . the registration statement became effective," . . . the matter must be viewed as of May 16, 1961. . . .

The 1960 Audit

[The audit] was in general charge of a member of the firm, Cummings. . . . Most of the actual work was performed by a senior accountant, Berardi, [who was about thirty]. He was not yet a C.P.A. He had no previous experience with the bowling industry. This was his first job as a senior accountant. . . .

The S-1 Review

The purpose of reviewing events subsequent to the date of a certified balance sheet, [an S-1 review,] is to ascertain whether any material change has occurred in the company's financial position which should be disclosed in order to prevent the . . . figures from being misleading. The scope of such a review [is not] a complete audit.

Peat, Marwick prepared a written program [which] conformed to generally accepted auditing standards. . . .

Berardi made the S-1 review in May 1961. He devoted a little over two days to it. . . . He did not discover any of the errors or omissions. . . . The question is whether, despite his failure to find out anything, his investigation was reasonable within the meaning of the statute.

What Berardi did was not look at a . . . trial balance as of March 31, 1961[,] compare it with the audited December 31, 1960 figures, discuss with Trilling certain unfavorable developments[,] and read certain minutes. He did not examine any [other] "important financial records." . . .

In substance, what Berardi did is . . . [he] asked questions, he got answers which he considered satisfactory, and he did nothing to verify them. . . .

Berardi had no conception of how tight the cash position was. He did not discover that BarChris was holding up checks in substantial amounts because there was no money in the bank to cover them. He did not know of . . . the officers' loans. Since he never read the prospectus, he was not even aware that there had ever been any problem about loans from officers. . . .

There had been a material change for the worse in BarChris's financial position. That change was sufficiently serious so that the failure to disclose it made the 1960 figures misleading. Berardi did not discover it. As far as results were concerned, his S-1 review was useless.

Accountants should not be held to a standard higher than that recognized in their profession. I do not do so here. Berardi's review did not come up to that standard. He did not take some of the steps which Peat, Marwick's written program prescribed. He did not spend an adequate amount of time on a task of this magnitude. Most important of all, he was too easily satisfied with glib answers to his inquiries.

. . . [T]here were enough danger signals in the materials which he did examine to require some further investigation on his part. Generally accepted accounting standards required such further investigation under these circumstances. It is not always sufficient merely to ask questions.

Here again, the burden of proof is on Peat, Marwick. I find that that burden has not been satisfied. I conclude that Peat, Marwick has not established its due diligence defense.

Questions

1. *a.* Why were so many defendants not held responsible for the misleading audited financial statements?

   b. Which defendants were not successful in claiming the due diligence defense with respect to these financial statements? Why were they denied the defense?

2. Does being "new" make any difference in terms of directorial liability for a signed registration statement?

3. What would you do differently in the future if you were Peat, Marwick?

False or Misleading Statements in Required Filings—1934 Act

Section 18 of the 1934 Act, relating to false or misleading statements in any filing required to maintain the registration of a security, is similar to the 1933 Act's Section 11. However, the only defense offered by Section 18 is that the defendant acted in good faith, without knowledge of the false or misleading nature of the statement. Furthermore, unlike the 1933 Act's Section 11 where reliance by the plaintiff on the false or misleading statements is presumed, under the 1934 Act's Section 18 the plaintiff must prove that he or she relied on the statements.

Fraud

Under the 1933 Act's Section 17(a) and the 1934 Act's Section 10(b) and its related Rule 10b-5, it is illegal, in connection with the sale or purchase of any security, to employ any scheme or to engage in any practice that defrauds another person participating in the financial markets. These provisions intentionally cast a "broad net" and can reach such Ponzi schemes as the one run by Bernard Madoff, the former chairman of NASDAQ, who in 2009 was sentenced to 150 years in prison for perpetrating his $50 billion investment fraud. In essence he promised very lucrative rates of return to investors, which returns were paid out of funds collected from an ever-increasing pool of new investors. When the economy turns down, such schemes collapse, revealing just how widespread the phenomenon is. More than 150 such schemes collapsed in 2009, compared with about 40 in 2008.[52]

> Bernard Madoff was sentenced to 150 years in prison.

Many fraudulent acts covered by these provisions, such as the Ponzi schemes just mentioned, do not involve corporate wrongdoers, but other fraudulent acts do. For example, the making of misleading statements of material facts or failing to state material facts in required disclosure documents or other company communications come under these rules and are a powerful basis for damage suits by harmed investors. Big companies have paid

> In 2009 Merrill Lynch settled a suit for $475 million.

substantial settlements in lawsuits springing from the recent financial collapse. For example, in 2009 Merrill Lynch settled a suit for $475 million with investors who alleged that Merrill had understated its subprime debt exposure. Wells Fargo agreed in 2011 to pay $85 million to settle Federal Reserve claims that the firm pushed borrowers toward unnecessarily costly mortgage loans and falsified data in mortgage applications. J.P. Morgan paid $153.6 million in 2011 to settle SEC charges that the firm misled investors in a complicated deal involving a pool of mortgages and other loans.[53]

Bringing forward direct evidence of reliance on fraudulent statements can be difficult, so the *fraud-on-the-market* theory has evolved. It is the subject of the *Basic, Inc.* case below.

LEGAL BRIEFCASE

Basic Inc. v. Levinson et al.
485 U.S. 224 (1988)

FACTS

Prior to December 20, 1978, Basic Inc. was a publicly traded company primarily engaged in the business of manufacturing chemical refractories for the steel industry. As early as 1965 or 1966, Combustion Engineering, Inc., a company producing mostly alumina-based refractories, expressed some interest in acquiring Basic, but was deterred from pursuing this inclination seriously because of antitrust concerns. Beginning in 1976, Combustion had meetings with Basic concerning the possibility of a merger. During 1977 and 1978, Basic made three public statements denying merger negotiations. On December 19, 1978, Basic's board endorsed the merger.

Respondents were former Basic shareholders who sold their stock after Basic's first public denial but before the December 1978 announcement. They asserted that the defendants issued three false or misleading public statements in violation of Section 10(b) of the 1934 Act and of Rule 10b-5 and, further, that they were injured by selling Basic shares at artificially depressed prices in a market affected by petitioners' misleading statements and in reliance thereon.

Rule 10b-5 provides that it "shall be unlawful [t]o make any untrue statement of a material fact or to omit to state a material fact necessary . . . to make the statements made . . . not misleading . . . in connection with the purchase or sale of any security."

Justice Blackmun

*   *   *   *   *

. . . [T]o fulfill the materiality requirement "there must be a substantial likelihood that the disclosure of the omitted fact would

have been viewed by the reasonable investor as having significantly altered the 'total mix' of information made available." . . .

*   *   *   *   *

We turn to the question of reliance and the fraud-on-the-market theory. Succinctly put:

> The fraud on the market theory is based on the hypothesis that, in an open and developed securities market, the price of a company's stock is determined by the available material information regarding the company and its business. . . . Misleading statements will therefore defraud purchasers . . . even if [they] do not directly rely on the misstatements. . . . The causal connection between the defendants' fraud and the plaintiffs' purchase . . . is no less significant than in a case of direct reliance on misrepresentations.

*   *   *   *   *

. . . Requiring proof of individualized reliance from each member of the proposed plaintiff class . . . would have prevented . . . a class action, since individual issues . . . would have overwhelmed the common ones. The District Court found that the presumption of reliance created by the fraud-on-the-market theory provided "a practical resolution to the problem of balancing the [need for] proof of reliance [against] the procedural [obstacles]." . . .

. . . Reliance provides the requisite causal connection between a defendant's misrepresentation and a plaintiff's injury. There is, however, more than one way to demonstrate the causal connection. . . .

The modern securities markets, literally involving millions of shares changing hands daily, differ from the face-to-face transactions contemplated by early fraud cases, and our understanding of Rule 10b-5's reliance requirement must encompass these differences.

With the presence of a market, the market is interposed between seller and buyer and, ideally, transmits information to the investor in the processed form of a market price. Thus the market is performing a substantial part of the valuation process performed by the investor in a face-to-face transaction. The market is acting as the unpaid agent of the investor, informing him that given all the information available to it, the value of the stock is worth the market price.

* * * * *

Presumptions typically serve to assist courts in managing circumstances in which direct proof, for one reason or another, is rendered difficult. The courts below accepted a presumption, created by the fraud-on-the-market theory and subject to rebuttal by petitioners, that persons who had traded Basic shares had done so in reliance on the integrity of the price set by the market, but because of petitioners' material misrepresentations that price had been fraudulently depressed. Requiring a plaintiff to show . . . how he would have acted if omitted material information had been disclosed . . . or if the misrepresentation had not been made, . . . would place an unnecessarily unrealistic evidentiary burden on the Rule 10b-5 plaintiff who has traded on an impersonal market.

. . . The presumption of reliance employed in this case is consistent with . . . congressional policy embodied in the 1934 Act. In drafting that Act, Congress expressly relied on the premise that securities markets are affected by information, and enacted legislation to facilitate an investor's reliance on the integrity of those markets. . . .

. . . Recent empirical studies . . . confirm Congress' premise that the market price . . . on well-developed markets reflects all publicly available information, and, hence, any material misrepresentations. . . . Because most publicly available information is reflected in market price, an investor's reliance on any public material misrepresentations, therefore, may be presumed for purposes of a Rule 10b-5 action.

* * * * *

Any showing that severs the link between the alleged misrepresentation and [the] decision to trade fair market price will be sufficient to rebut the presumption of reliance. For example, . . . if, despite petitioners' allegedly fraudulent attempt to manipulate market price, news of the merger discussions credibly entered the market and dissipated the effects of the misstatements, those who traded Basic shares after the corrective statements would have no direct or indirect connection with the fraud. . . .

In summary: . . . It is not inappropriate to apply a presumption of reliance supported by the fraud-on-the-market theory. That presumption, however, is rebuttable.

[Remanded for further proceedings consistent with the opinion.]

Questions

1. When is an item of undisclosed information about a company "material" for Rule 10b-5 purposes?
2. Is reliance on a misrepresentation essential in a Rule 10b-5 action?
3. *a.* Why would it be difficult for a plaintiff to demonstrate reliance in fact on a material omission?
   b. What solution did the courts create to deal with this problem?

AFTERWORD

As noted by the Court in *Basic, Inc.* and recently confirmed by the Seventh Circuit, investors who trade with knowledge of the alleged misrepresentations will not be allowed to use the fraud-on-the-market theory. Those investors have not relied on the market price as an accurate reflection of material information.[54] The fraud-on-the-market theory has also been applied against market information providers other than the issuer of the securities in question. In *In re Salomon Analyst Metromedia* litigation, the Second Circuit held that the fraud-on-the-market theory could provide the required reliance element for a plaintiff alleging fraud by a research analyst, Jack Grubman at Salomon Smith Barney. Grubman issued a "Buy" recommendation while withholding adverse information that a reasonable investor would consider important in making an investment decision. The court confirmed, however, that the defendants could seek to rebut the reliance presumption by showing, for example, that the misstatement had not affected the market price.[55]

Insider Trading

Classical illegal insider trading occurs when an "insider" breaches a fiduciary duty to shareholders by buying or selling a security while in possession of material, nonpublic information about the security. An insider is often a director, officer, or an employee of an issuer, but could also be someone who only temporarily has a confidential relationship with an issuer, such as an attorney, accountant or consultant. The prohibition against trading on undisclosed inside information is based on Section 10(b) of the 1934 Act that prohibits the use of any manipulative or deceptive device in connection with the purchase or sale of securities.

In recent years prosecution of insider trading violations has increased substantially and colorful headlines have often followed. Publicized incidents have run from sports to sex and from intricate and clandestine to sad to ridiculous and nearly everything else along the way:

- In the most high profile insider-trading case in many years, billionaire Galleon Group hedge fund manager, Raj Rajaratnam was convicted in 2011 on 14 counts of fraud and conspiracy that allegedly netted some $65 million in profits and losses averted. Rajaratnam allegedly tapped into a web of contacts in top-tier American businesses in order to secure information not publicly known.[56]

- Billionaire Mark Cuban, owner of the Dallas Mavericks basketball team, was charged by the SEC with insider trading after selling his 600,000 shares in Mamma.com, an internet search engine company, within hours of being informed by its CEO that the company intended to do a private stock offering that would dilute the value of his shares.

- A partner at Ernst & Young developed a relationship with a woman he found through a Web site for those in search of extramarital affairs. She testified against him in the trial in which he was convicted of insider trading. She had pled guilty to trading on information he passed to her, and she had agreed to cooperate with the government.[57]

- A lawyer, a trader, and a mortgage broker who jointly pursued one of the longest-running insider trading schemes were caught after the broker, the go-between for 17 years, agreed to record calls with each of the other two men.[58]

- A respected, retired business school professor from St. John's University, who was a popular lecturer at a number of Wall Street firms, was accused by the SEC of passing inside information to another business professor at Pace University.[59]

- An executive secretary at Walt Disney and her boyfriend were charged with insider trading after sending 33 letters to investment firms offering to sell Disney's quarterly earnings reports before they were publicly released. A follow-up e-mail stated, "I was thinking $20,000 is a fair compensation but you are free to make an offer." Multiple hedge funds receiving the offer reported it to the SEC.[60]

The *Texas Gulf Sulphur* case below expresses the rule for those possessing inside information—either disclose the information or refrain from trading until the information is public.

LEGAL BRIEFCASE

SEC v. Texas Gulf Sulphur Co.
401 F.2d 833 (2d Cir. 1968)

FACTS

On November 12, 1963, TGS drilled a "discovery hole," K-55-1, in Canada which revealed possibly one of the largest ore strikes in history. Insiders (geologists at the drill site, certain company officers, and so on) began buying TGS stock at around $18. Lab testing and further test-hole drilling fully confirmed the magnitude of the strike. Rumors began to circulate. On April 12, 1964, when the stock had passed $30 and when the best estimate was 8 million recoverable tons, TGS issued a press release naysaying the rumors. On April 16, a Canadian mining journal story, based on an April 13 site visit and interview, put the tonnage at 10 million. On the same day a Canadian government official, based on information current through April 15, put the tonnage at 25 million in a public announcement. On this day the stock passed $36. By May 15, it exceeded $58. The SEC brought an insider-trading suit.

Judge Waterman

* * * * *

[Rule 10b-5] is based . . . on the justifiable expectation . . . that all investors trading on impersonal exchanges have relatively equal access to material information. . . . The essence of the Rule is that anyone who, trading for his own account [has access] to information intended to be available only for a corporate purpose . . . may not take "advantage of such . . . knowing it is unavailable to those with whom he is dealing," i.e., the investing public. Insiders . . . are, of course[,] precluded from so unfairly dealing, but the Rule is also applicable to one possessing the information who may not be strictly termed an "insider." . . . [A]nyone in possession of material inside information must either disclose it to the investing public [or] abstain from trading in or recommending the securities [while it] remains undisclosed. . . .

. . . An insider's duty to disclose [or] abstain . . . arises only in "those situations . . . which are reasonably certain to have a substantial effect on the market price [if] disclosed." . . .

* * * * *

. . . [W]hether facts are material [will depend] upon a balancing of both the indicated probability that the event will occur and the anticipated magnitude of the event. . . . [Here,] knowledge of the possibility, which surely was more than marginal, of the existence of a mine of the vast magnitude indicated by the remarkably rich drill core . . . would certainly have been an important fact to a reasonable . . . investor in deciding whether he should buy, sell, or hold. . . .

* * * * *

Finally, a major factor in determining whether the K-55-1 discovery was a material fact is the importance attached to the drilling results by those who knew about it. [T]he timing . . . of their stock purchases . . . virtually compels the inference that the insiders were influenced by the drilling results. . . .

* * * * *

We hold, therefore, that all transactions in TGS stock . . . by individuals apprised of the drilling results of K-55-1 were made in violation of Rule 10b-5. . . .

* * * * *

. . . Coates, who placed orders . . . immediately after the official announcement . . . , [contends that his] purchases were not proscribed purchases for the news had already been . . . disclosed. We disagree.

. . . The reading of [the announcement] . . . is merely the first step in the process of dissemination required for compliance with the regulatory objective of providing all investors with an equal opportunity to make informed investment judgments. . . . [A]t the minimum Coates should have waited until the news could reasonably have been expected to appear over the media of widest circulation, the Dow Jones broad tape, rather than hastening to insure an advantage to himself. . . .

Questions

1. If you possess undisclosed inside information, what are your options for trading in the company's stock?
2. How soon after disclosure can an insider trade in the stock?

AFTERWORD

As stated by the *Texas Gulf Sulphur* court, the rule prohibits one who has access to information that was available to them only for a corporate purpose from trading in corporate securities with those who do not have that knowledge. This is the *classical* theory of insider trading. Officers and employees, for example, have a fiduciary duty not to use their principal's—that is, their employer's—information for personal gain.

[For a view of insider trading in China, see *Insider Trading Rats* at **http://www.youtube.com/watch?v=IT3FAr0eIEo**].

Tippees

The insider concept has been extended to include *tippees*. In some cases, the *tipper* (the insider or an "upstream" tippee) intends to improperly convey the inside information to a third party and hopes to derive personal benefit therefrom. In such a case both the tipper and tippee are fully liable. In other cases the tippee is deemed to "misappropriate" the inside information from the inadvertent tipper, knowing that it was confidential. This would occur, for example, if a psychiatrist learned material inside information during a session with a senior corporate executive and traded on that information. Here, the tippee, but not the tipper, would be liable. In the *O'Hagan* case, below, the U.S. Supreme Court approved this second theory, the *misappropriation* theory, that extends insider trading to outsiders.

LEGAL BRIEFCASE — United States v. O'Hagan
521 U.S. 642 (1997)

FACTS

O'Hagan was a partner in the law firm of Dorsey & Whitney. In July 1988, Grand Metropolitan retained the firm to represent it in a tender offer for Pillsbury stock. O'Hagan did no work on this matter. In August, O'Hagan began purchasing Pillsbury stock options. He also purchased Pillsbury stock at $39. When the tender offer was announced, the price rose to $60. O'Hagan sold his options and stock, making a profit of $4.3 million. He used the profits to conceal his previous embezzlement of unrelated client trust funds.

The SEC investigated. O'Hagan was convicted on securities fraud. The Eighth Circuit reversed, rejecting liability under Rule 10b-5 under the "misappropriation theory." The Supreme Court granted certiorari.

Section 10(b) proscribes (1) using any deceptive device (2) in connection with the purchase or sale of securities. It does not confine its coverage to deception of a purchaser or seller; rather, it reaches any deceptive device used "in connection with the purchase or sale of any security."

Justice Ginsburg

* * * * *

Under the "traditional" or "classical theory" of insider trading liability, Section 10(b) and Rule 10b-5 are violated when [an] insider trades in the securities of his corporation on the basis of material, nonpublic information. Trading on such information qualifies as a "deceptive device" . . . because "a relationship of trust [exists] between the shareholders [and the] insiders who have obtained confidential information by reason of their position with [the] corporation." That relationship . . . "gives rise to a duty to disclose [or to abstain from trading]". . . .The classical theory applies not only to officers, directors, and other permanent insiders . . ., but also to attorneys, accountants, consult-

ants, and others who temporarily become fiduciaries of a corporation.

The "misappropriation theory" holds that a person commits fraud "in connection with" a securities transaction . . . when he misappropriates confidential information for securities trading purposes, in breach of a duty owed to the source of the information. Under this theory, a fiduciary's undisclosed, self-serving use of a principal's information to purchase or sell securities, in breach of a duty of loyalty and confidentiality, defrauds the principal of the exclusive use of that information. In lieu of premising liability on a fiduciary relationship between company insider and purchaser or seller of the company's stock, the misappropriation theory premises liability on a fiduciary-turned-trader's deception of those who entrusted him with access to confidential information.

The two theories are complementary, each addressing efforts to capitalize on nonpublic information through the purchase or sale of securities. . . .

In this case, the indictment alleged that O'Hagan, in breach of a duty of trust . . . he owed to his law firm . . . and to its client . . . , traded on the basis of nonpublic information regarding the client's tender offer . . . . This conduct, the Government charged, constituted a fraudulent device in connection with the purchase and sale of securities. . . .

We agree . . . . We observe, first, that misappropriators . . . deal in deception. A fiduciary who "[pretends] loyalty to the principal while secretly converting the principal's information for personal gain" . . . defrauds the principal.

* * * * *

We turn next to the Section 10(b) requirement that the misappropriator's deceptive use of information be "in connection with the purchase or sale of [a] security." This element is satisfied because the fiduciary's fraud is consummated, not when the fiduciary gains the confidential information, but when, without disclosure to his principal, he uses the information to purchase or sell securities. . . .

* * * * *

The misappropriation theory . . . is also well-tuned to an animating purpose of the [1934] Act: to insure honest securities markets and thereby promote investor confidence. Although informational disparity is inevitable in the securities markets, ...[an] investor's informational disadvantage vis-a-vis a misappropriator . . . stems from contrivance, not luck; it is a disadvantage that cannot be overcome with research or skill. . . .

[Reversed and remanded.]

Questions

1. Are both insider trading theories needed to fulfill the 1934 Act's desire to keep the markets "honest"?

2. Both insider trading theories depend heavily on fiduciary relationships. Contrast the parties in the fiduciary relationships under the "classical" and "misappropriation" theories.

3. Would it have made any difference if O'Hagan had established with his broker, long before this trading, a portfolio diversification plan such that, pursuant to the plan, the identical trading would have occurred?

Short-Swing Profits

Closely related to insider trading is liability for short-swing profits. An insider trading case requires proof that the insider had material inside information and traded to exploit it. A short-swing profit case conclusively presumes that the insider had such information and did unlawfully trade on it any time the insider engages in any purchase and sale, or sale and purchase, of an equity security issued by the insider's corporation if both transactions occur within a six-month period. The insider's actual motive is irrelevant. The goal is to prevent insiders from taking advantage of company information to secure short-term profits.

Securities Law Enforcement Actions

Most of the securities laws violations just discussed can be enforced against the violators by harmed private parties seeking damages and by the government seeking civil and/or criminal penalties. The SEC brings civil enforcement actions; the Justice Department brings criminal enforcement actions. In fact, all three types of suits can be brought against the same defendant for the same violation.

Private Enforcement

In civil damage cases harmed plaintiffs typically join together in a class-action lawsuit.(see Chapter 4.) Since the 1990s, actions taken by Congress and, more recently, decisions of the Supreme Court have combined to make the bringing of and prevailing in such suits much more difficult for injured plaintiffs. Some history may be illuminating.

As a consequence of the savings and loan debacle of the 1980s, major accounting firms paid out over $1.6 billion in class-action damages. Responding to these payouts, accounting firms and others began intense lobbying to curtail such suits. Among other things, they argued that law firms specializing in plaintiffs' securities actions selected and groomed "professional plaintiffs" to bring damage suits in which the allegations of wrongdoing were primarily supported by a significant drop in the market price of the securities. Then after filing a complaint, it was argued, plaintiffs could proceed to discovery and undertake "fishing expeditions" until sufficient facts were accumulated to motivate defendants to settle rather than endure litigation.

Some evidence of long-standing systemic abuse by plaintiffs' lawyers was revealed in September 2007 when William Lerach, a former partner of the law firm of Milberg Weiss, pleaded guilty to conspiracy. The allegations were that he and other lawyers in the firm had paid illegal kickbacks to individuals to serve as named plaintiffs in securities actions. This often allowed the firm to be the first to file suit, which in turn resulted in Milberg Weiss more frequently representing the lead plaintiff in many class action cases. The firm's payoff was a larger share of any legal fees.[61] On April 2, 2008, Melvyn Weiss, the senior securities law partner at Milberg Weiss, pleaded guilty to similar charges pursuant to a plea bargain. He was sentenced to 30 months in prison and fined $10 million.

The lobbying against runaway securities class-action suits paid off. In December 1995 Congress enacted the Private Securities Litigation Reform Act (1995 Act). The 1995 Act restricts joint and several liability for accountants and underwriters whose deep pockets have historically attracted plaintiffs' lawyers. It also increased plaintiffs' procedural hurdles in bringing suit. No fraudulent conduct can be presumed from the simple fact that a security's price dropped precipitously. Plaintiffs in their complaints must state with particularity both the facts that constitute the alleged violation, as well as facts evidencing defendant's intention "to deceive, manipulate or defraud."[62]

In early 2008, the Supreme Court reduced the exposure of some noncorporate defendants to claims of *aiding and abetting* securities fraud. In instances in which plaintiffs allege damage based on fraudulent representations by the corporation, third parties who may have aided the fraudulent conduct but whose deceptive acts were not communicated to the public are not liable to private plaintiffs.[63] As discussed below, only the government can bring such lawsuits. [For more on securities class-action lawsuits, see **http://securities.stanford.edu**]

Government Enforcement

The government can bring suits for aiding and abetting securities fraud against third parties. The Dodd-Frank Act expanded the government's reach in such cases to any third party who, knowingly or recklessly, substantially assists the primary wrongdoer.

Whereas private parties sue to recover damages suffered from the violation, the SEC enforces the laws by imposing civil penalties up to $750,000 for individuals and $15 million for corporations, as well as forcing defendants to give up ill-gotten gains, called *disgorgement.* The SEC may impose a penalty of up to 300 percent of the profit gained or loss avoided by insider trading. In addition to imposing monetary penalties, the SEC can issue *cease-and-desist orders,* get injunctions against persons committing securities fraud, and prohibit violators in the future from serving as officers or directors of publicly traded companies.

In contrast, the Department of Justice prosecutes violators seeking criminal sanctions for *willful* (knowing and deliberate) violations of the 1933 and 1934 Acts, including fines of up to $25 million and imprisonment of up to 20 years. As with criminal statutes in general, the principal problem for prosecutors is convincing a jury of the defendants' guilt beyond a reasonable doubt. As a result, civil penalties are often substituted for criminal prosecutions.

Other Regulatory Oversight

Tender Offers

There are several ways to acquire control of a corporation. Where mergers or direct acquisitions fail, a *tender offer* (also called a *takeover*) can be attempted. Alternatively, the person seeking to acquire control can mount a *proxy fight,* as discussed in Part Two, by nominating an alternative slate of directors and then soliciting shareholders for their annual proxies in preference to returning proxies to current management.

In a tender offer, the offeror announces that it wishes to acquire a specific number of shares (often the number needed to gain control). It identifies where stockholders who want to participate must tender (that is, deliver) their shares. (Shares are returned if the tender offer fails.) It also specifies the opening bid price. If less than the desired number of shares is tendered, the tender offeror can either walk away or increase the offering price.

When faced with a tender offer, the target corporation's management realizes that a successful offer will likely result in its dismissal since the offeror will want to put its own management in place. Often the target's management will not be eager to leave. It will resist, which accounts for the term *hostile takeover*. Management has a problem, however, because it is supposed to act exclusively in the best interests of the shareholders and the tender offer may well be in their best interests. To avoid liability, management will generally try to style its resistance as "looking out for the stockholders."

Management can resist in various ways. It could launch its own tender offer (*go private*). Or it could start using corporate cash to buy back shares in the market, driving up the price to discourage the tender offeror. Here management has to worry that it could be sanctioned for violating Section 9 of the 1934 Act, which prohibits price manipulation. However, the SEC provides a safe harbor that allows management each day to purchase up to 25 percent of the security's average daily trading volume.

Another resistance tactic is *greenmail,* in which the target's management uses corporate cash to buy back the tender offeror's current stake, with a significant premium to "go away." Changes in the federal tax law have discouraged this technique.

Management sometimes puts takeover defenses in place by arranging "disasters" if a tender offer is attempted. Two notorious tactics are the *crown jewel* and *poison pill* defenses. In general, the crown jewel defense involves the target company selling off its most attractive assets (its crown jewels). For example, the target company management might arrange for a friendly third party to purchase the target's particularly attractive or critical assets at a reasonable price should a tender offer be launched thus making the target company less appealing to the hostile bidder. At the same time, the target company's management is protected because the third party will continue to make these assets available to the company on "friendly" terms should the tender offer fail and management remains in place. Poison pill tactics take a variety of forms but one notable strategy, called a "flip-in"gives current shareholders in the target company a tender offer-triggered right to buy additional target-company stock at a discount thus diluting the hostile bidder's shares.

If all else fails, the target's officers may find comfort in the *golden parachutes* (severance pay packages) they may have negotiated to protect themselves in the event of a takeover. The Dodd-Frank Act now requires a shareholder vote on such pay packages.

State Securities Regulation

After the enactment of the Securities Act of 1933, the United States operated under a dual regulatory environment for securities. Both the state and federal governments were entitled to regulate issuance of new securities and subsequent purchases and sales. However, the lack of regulatory uniformity among the states led Congress in 1996 to enact the *National Securities Markets Improvement Act,* preempting state registration requirements for securities traded on national markets. Then in 1998, Congress mandated that securities fraud claims related to national market securities be litigated only in federal court under federal law. State securities regulations, known as *blue sky laws*, are now only a shadow of their former significance and are primarily applicable to solely intrastate offerings. [For more on state securities regulation, see **http://www.nasaa.org/About_NASAA/Role_of_State_Securities_Regulators**]

International Securities Regulation

Critics claim the United States is losing its place as the world's leading financial center, citing such evidence as the percentage of large IPOs being listed outside of the United States. Aggressive regulation in America is often blamed for driving those IPOs abroad.

American securities regulation is the world's strongest, but whether that will continue to be true and whether it is responsible for the growth in foreign securities markets is not so certain. Other factors undoubtedly make significant contributions to the shift, such as the natural maturation of international markets, the continuing devaluation of the dollar against foreign currencies, the speed of overall economic growth elsewhere in the world and the concomitant rise in wealth, especially in Europe and Asia.[64] "Because companies want to list in the fastest-rising markets, many are staying in their home countries, which have outperformed the United States in recent years."[65] Furthermore, stringent regulation in the United States is not necessarily a net disincentive for securities registration here. Foreign securities with dual listings in the United States and elsewhere appear to enjoy an advantage in the price they command.[66] Finally, as the securities markets in other countries mature, national regulation seems to be increasing in ways that model U.S. policies.

Nothing equivalent to the SEC exists for Europe. In the wake of the recent financial crisis, however, the European Union may be moving closer to such a body. In 2010 the EU finance ministers endorsed the creation of a supervisory structure for European securities markets, the European Securities and Markets Authority (ESMA). It began its work on January 1, 2011. One role it may eventually be called to take on is the regulation of audit firms.[67] [For more on ESMA, see **http://www.esma.europa.eu**; for more on international securities regulation generally, see **http://www.iosco.org/about**]

Questions—Part Three

1. What is an IPO? What is meant by *going public?* By *going private?*
2. *a.* What information is contained in a registration statement under the 1933 Act?
   b. What role in the registration process is played by the prospectus?
   c. What are audited financial statements? Describe the three components.
3. Explain the general purposes of the Securities Act of 1933 and the Securities Exchange Act of 1934.
4. Assume a midlevel manager learns that his corporation is about to go bankrupt because of about-to-be-disclosed improprieties. He calls his lawyer to ask about his personal exposure. After advising him, the lawyer immediately sells all of her holdings in that stock. Later that day the news breaks and the stock price tumbles 60 percent.
   a. Does anyone have insider trading liability?
   b. If so, in what amount?
5. If a corporate officer knowingly omits material adverse information from a corporate communication, by whom might he be sued?

Internet Exercise

Using the Frequently Asked Questions segment of **http://www.securitieslaw.com** answer the following questions:
1. What duties are owed by stockbrokers and brokerage firms to customers?
2. How does a customer know when he or she has been defrauded?

Chapter Questions

1. From initiating the process through the election of directors, describe the steps generally followed to bring a corporation into existence.
2. Modell owned 80 percent of the Cleveland Stadium Corporation (Stadium) and 53 percent of the Cleveland Browns Football Company (Browns). Gries owned 43 percent of Browns. The Browns' board consisted of Modell, the outside lawyer for both corporations, three individuals employed by both corporations, and Gries. Modell proposed that the Browns buy the Stadium for $6 million. Gries objected, saying that the Stadium appraised for only $2 million. The Browns' board, nonetheless, approved the purchase. (All directors other than Gries voted in favor of the purchase.) Gries commenced a shareholders derivative suit seeking to rescind the purchase. Who should win? See *Gries Sports Enterprises v. Cleveland Browns Football Company,* 496 N.E.2d 959 (Ohio S.Ct. 1986).
3. The Patels owned the CC Motel. They formed a partnership with their son, Raj, to own and operate the motel. Title to the motel was not transferred to the partnership. The partnership agreement required Raj to approve the motel's sale. The Patels sold the motel without telling Raj and without telling the buyers of Raj's right. He learned of the pending sale and refused to agree. The buyers asked the court to compel the sale. Who should win? See *Patel v. Patel,* 260 Cal. Rptr. 255 (Cal. Ct. App. 1989).
4. Each year many shareholder proposals are offered for inclusion in the annual meeting materials so as to be submitted to a vote of the shareholders. Assume you have a

significant investment in Corporation X and the following proposals are included in the proxy materials. Which would you vote for and why?

a. A recommendation that any bonus and performance compensation awarded to executives be paid out evenly over the four years following the grant of the bonus and only if the performance goals continue to be met.

b. A recommendation that the standards for all bonus and performance compensation be benchmarked against the performance of the company's market competitors, requiring superior performance for the award of any bonus.

c. A recommendation that shareholders be permitted to vote on the selection of the state in which to reincorporate the company.

d. A recommendation to the nominating committee that each year it include one "public director" selected in consultation with one or more nonprofit organizations whose missions encompass one or more significant activities of the corporation.

5. Ivan Landreth and his sons owned all of the stock in a lumber business they operated in Tonasket, Washington. The owners offered the stock for sale. During that time a fire severely damaged the business, but the owners made assurances of rebuilding and modernization. The stock was sold to Dennis and Bolten, and a new organization, Landreth Timber Company, was formed with the senior Landreth remaining as a consultant on the side. The new firm was unsuccessful and was sold at a loss. The Landreth Timber Company then filed suit against Ivan Landreth and his sons seeking rescission of the first sale, alleging, among other arguments, that Landreth and sons had widely offered and then sold their stock without registering it as required by the Securities Act of 1933. The district court acknowledged that stocks fit within the definition of a security, and that the stock in question "possessed all of the characteristics of conventional stock." However, it held that the federal securities laws do not apply to the sale of 100 percent of the stock of a closely held corporation. Here the district court found that the purchasers had not entered into the sale with the expectation of earnings secured via the labor of others. Managerial control resided with the purchasers. Thus, the sale was a commercial venture rather than a typical investment. The Court of Appeals affirmed, and the case reached the Supreme Court. Decide. See *Landreth Timber Co. v. Landreth,* 471 U.S. 681 (1985).

6. A *Fortune* 500 CFO admits to having deliberately treated $4 billion in operating expenses as assets, thereby allowing the corporation to show profits instead of losses. The auditor never detects this. The corporation's stock drops 95 percent and bond covenants related to billions in debt are breached. At its peak price last year, the CFO sold stock (acquired through options) for $15 million, generating a $10 million gain.

a. Why might the corporation have to file for bankruptcy protection?

b. What provisions of the securities law could be the basis for a class-action lawsuit by the stockholders?

c. Why will the 1995 Act probably not stop a class-action lawsuit from proceeding to the discovery phase?

d. Why will the CFO be subject to criminal (as well as civil) securities sanctions?

e. Will the SEC likely ever allow the CFO to be an officer or director of a publicly traded corporation in the future?

f. Will the SEC allow the CFO to keep the $10 million gain on the stock?

g. What kind of civil penalties could the SEC impose on the CFO?

Notes

1. Michelle Leder, "Carl Icahn's Move to North Dakota . . . ," April 22, 2009 [**http://www.Morningstar.com**].

2. Data was taken from **http://www.irs.gov/taxstats/bustaxstats**

3. Id. By contrast, LLCs represent 20 percent of all business entities, but account for only 7 percent of business revenues.

4. See, for example, Section 1.40(9) & (16) of the Model Business Corporation Act.

5. *Grosjean v. American Press Co.,* 297 U.S. 233 (1936) (with regard to equal protection and due process).

6. *Western & Southern Life Ins. Co. v. State Bd. of Equalization,* 451 U.S. 648 (1981) (privileges and immunities clause).

7. *Cede & Co. v. Technicolor, Inc.,* 634 A.2d 345 (Del. 1993).

8. Tresa Baldas, "BP Shareholders Head to Court Over Oil Spill's Damage to Company," May 11, 2010 at *law.com.*

9. Del. Gen. Corp. Law Section 102(b)(7).

10. Gretchen Morgenson, "Case on Mortgage Official Is Said to Be Dropped," *The New York Times,* February 19, 2011.

11. *Compania General de Tabacos de Filipinas v. Collector of Internal Revenue,* 275 U.S. 87, 100 (1927) (J. Holmes, dissenting).

12. *Commissioner v. Newman,* 159 F.2d 848, 850 (2d Cir 1947).

13. The largest corporations pay a flat rate federal income tax of 35 percent. Small corporations with a taxable income of less than $75,000 face a marginal tax rate of up to 25 percent, still meaningful.

14. For 2010, an individual taxpayer would reach this marginal tax rate on $171,850 in taxable income; a married couple filing jointly would reach this rate on $209,250 in taxable income. Currently the highest marginal tax rate for individuals is 35 percent.

15. Data was taken from **http://www.irs.gov/taxstats/bustaxstats**

16. [**http://corpgov.net/?page_id=2**].

17. RUPA Section 306(a).

18. RUPA Section 307(d)(1).

19. RUPA Sections 103(b)(6); 601(3), (4), (6), (7); 602(c); 801(1); 802(b).

20. Minn. Stat. Section 322B.303, subd. 2 (1996).

21. *Kaycee Land and Livestock v. Flahive,* 46 P.2d 323 (Wyo. 2002).

22. Robert W. Hamilton, "Registered Limited Liability Partnerships: Present at the Birth (Nearly), 66 *U. of Colorado L. Rev.* 1065 (1995).

23. RUPA Section 306(c).

24. ULPA (2001) Sections 102(9), 201(a)(4).

25. Financial Crisis Inquiry Commission, "The Financial Crisis Inquiry Report" (January 2011) [**http://fcic.law.stanford.edu/report**].

26. Carl C. Icahn, "Corporate Boards that Do Their Job," *The Washington Post,* February 16, 2009.

27. Kaja Whitehouse, "Why CEOs Need to Be Honest with Their Boards," *The Wall Street Journal,* January 14, 2008.

28. Harry Hurt III, "Taking Away Directors' Rubber Stamps," *The New York Times,* January 17, 2010.

29. Id.

30. Carl C. Icahn, "Corporate Boards that Do Their Job."

31. Harry Hurt III, "Taking Away Directors' Rubber Stamps."

32. Jack Welch and Suzy Welch, "How Much Blame Do Boards Deserve?," *BusinessWeek,* January 14, 2009.

33. Tara Siegel Bernard, "Voting Your Shares May Start to Matter," *The New York Times,* March 5, 2010.

34. The Conference Board, "Report: Institutional Investors Owning More of Larger Companies," *Governance Center Blog,* November 23, 2010 [**http://tcbblogs.org/governance/2010/11/23/ report-institutional-investors-owning-more-of-larger-companies**].

35. Judith Burns, "Where the Action Is," *The Wall Street Journal,* January 14, 2008.

36. *American Federation of State, County & Municipal Employees, Employees Pension Plan v. American International Group, Inc.,* 462 F.3d 121 (2d Cir. 2006).

37. Council of Institutional Investors, "Proxy Access," [**http://www.cii.org/resourcesKeyGovern- anceIssuesProxyAccess**].

38. Nicholas D. Kristof, "Need a Job? $17,000 an Hour. No Success Required," *The New York Times,* September 18, 2008.

39. Evelyn M. Rusli, "Zipcar Soars in Market Debut," *The New York Times,* April 14, 2011.

40. *SEC v. Aqua-Sonic Prods. Corp.,* 687 F.2d 577 (2d Cir. 1982).

41. *U.S. v. Leonard,* 529 F.3d 83 (2d Cir. 2008).

42. John M. Broder, "SEC Adds Climate Risk to Disclosure List," *The New York Times,* January 28, 2010.

43. Financial Crisis Inquiry Commission, "The Financial Crisis Inquiry Report," p. 418. This quote is from a minority report, but the majority came to a similar conclusion. Id. p. xxv.

44. Lorraine Woellert and Dawn Kopecki, "Credit-Rating Companies 'Sold Soul,' Employees Said," October 22, 2008 [**http://www.Bloomberg.com**].

45. [**http://www.sec.gov/info/smallbus/qasbsec.htm**].

46. [**http://www.sec.gov/about/forms/form8-k.pdf**].

47. Cari Tuna, "Corporate Blogs and 'Tweets' Must Keep SEC in Mind," *The Wall Street Journal,* April 27, 2009.

48. [**http://www.sec.gov/answers/tradingsuspension.htm**].

49. "Sales-Practice Complaints to SEC Increase," *The Wall Street Journal,* April 26, 2001, p. 1C.

50. "The Return of the Day Trader" [**http://www.cbsnews.com/stories/2002/09/30/eveningnews/ main523766.shtml**].

51. [**http://www.sec.gov/investor/pubs/daytips.htm**].

52. Associated Press, "Meltdown Left Ponzi Schemes in Ashes," *The Des Moines Register,* December 29, 2009.

53. See Ashby Jones, "Banks Winning When Investors Sue," *The Wall Street Journal,* April 8, 2010, Dan Campbell, "Well Fargo to Pay $85M Fine," *StarTribune,* July 20, 2011 [**http://www. startribunecom/business/125906238.html**]**,** and Shira Ovide, "J.P. Morgan to Pay $153.6 Million to Settle SEC Charges," *WSJ Blogs,* June 21, 2011 [**http://blogs.wsj.com/**].

54. *Stark Trading v. Falconbridge Ltd.,* 552 F.3d 358 (7th Cir. 2009).

55. 544 F.3d 474 (2d Cir. 2008).

56. Michael Rothfeld and Chad Bray, "Galleon Founder Convicted on All Counts in Insider-Trading Trial," *The Wall Street Journal,* May 11, 2011 [**http://online.wsj.com/**].

57. "Insider Affair: An SEC Trial of the Heart," *The Wall Street Journal,* July 29, 2009.

58. Chad Bray, Susan Pulliam and Vanessa O'Connell, "Feds: Insider Scheme Spanned 17 Years," *The Wall Street Journal,* April 7, 2011.

59. Louise Story, "Charges of Insider Trading for a Wall Street Luminary," *The New York Times,* May 30, 2008.

60. Ethan Smith, "Disney Drama a Stock Plot Is Foiled," *The Wall Street Journal,* May 27, 2010.

61. Barry Meier, "Lawyer Pleads Guilty in Kickback Case," *The New York Times,* September 19, 2007.

62. *Tellabs, Inc. v. Makor Issues & Rights, Ltd.,* 127 S. Ct. 2499 (2007).

63. *Stoneridge Investment Partners LLC v. Scientific-Atlanta, Inc.,* 128 S. Ct. 761 (2008).

64. Edgar Ortega and Elizabeth Hester, "IPO Fees in Europe Catch Wall Street for First Time Since WWII." May 29, 2007 [**http://www.bloomberg.com**].

65. Walter Hamilton, "Stock Rules Irk NYC as Wall Street Parties on," *The Log Angeles Times,* April 23, 2007.

66. John C. Coffee, "Law and the Market: The Impact of Enforcement," *Columbia Law and Economics Working Paper No. 304,* March 7, 2007 [**http://ssrn.com/abstract=967482**].

67. Stephen Fidler, "Plans Grow for European Audit Cop," *The Wall Street Journal,* October 12, 2010.

CHAPTER TEN

Antitrust Law— Restraints of Trade

After completing this chapter, students will be able to:

1. Recognize the changing goals of antitrust law.

2. Describe the key antitrust statutes.

3. Explain the meaning of "horizontal restraints of trade."

4. Analyze when an unlawful price-fixing arrangement has been created.

5. Identify a group boycott.

6. Define resale price maintenance.

7. Explain the requirements for establishing an unlawful tying arrangement.

8. Describe the commercial advantages and disadvantages of exclusive dealing.

9. Contrast price discrimination and predatory pricing.

10. Explain how predatory pricing may be proved.

Antitrust is a word that is only dimly recognizable to most of us, but antitrust law touches all corners of our lives and significantly shapes our economic and social practices reaching even amateur athletics, as described below.

PRACTICING ETHICS   More "Pay" for College Athletes?

Four former college athletes representing a class of more than 20,000 former college athletes sued the National Collegiate Athletic Association (NCAA) seeking to change NCAA limits on the amount of aid that student-athletes can be granted. Under long-time NCAA rules, so-called "full-ride" scholarships were limited to tuition, books, room, and board. The athletes claimed they were denied approximately $2,500 annually because their universities were not allowed, under NCAA rules, to pay the "full cost of attendance," a package that would include money for insurance, laundry, school supplies, telephone, travel, and so on, in addition to the "full ride."

The class action involved all those playing "major college football" (what was Division I-A and is now the Football Bowl Subdivision) and "major college basketball" (16 top conferences) since 2002. Total damages were estimated at several hundred million dollars. The lawsuit claimed that the NCAA rules constituted a "contract, combination and conspiracy to fix the amount of financial assistance available to student athletes" thus restraining trade in violation of section I of the Sherman Antitrust Act (explained below).

The case was settled in 2008 when the NCAA agreed, among other things, to set aside $10 million over three years to be paid to qualified class members (estimated at 12,000) to reimburse them for bona fide, future educational expenses. Athletes could apply for up to $2,500 per year for three years. The settlement also offers athletes easier access to an existing NCAA pool of $218 million over the years 2008 to 2013 for legitimate educational expenses beyond the "full ride."

As you read this chapter, think about whether the NCAA limit on scholarship funds was, in fact, a violation of antitrust law, but for our immediate purposes, think about the athletes' complaint as a matter of right and wrong; of fairness. [For more on this case, see **www.studentathleteclassaction.com**]

Questions

1. Was it unfair to deny athletes the additional $2,500 or so that they could "earn" in the market for their services (playing "major college" football or basketball)? Detail the fairness argument for both the athletes and the NCAA.

2. Should college athletes be free to "sell" their services to the highest bidder among America's colleges and universities? Explain.

3. *a.* According to *Antitrust Today,* the U.S. Justice Department is concerned that an NCAA rule forbidding NCAA member universities from offering multiyear athletic scholarships might restrain trade. After reading Parts One and Two of this chapter, see if you can explain why the NCAA policy allowing only one-year-at-a-time athletic scholarships rather than multiyear scholarships might violate federal antitrust laws.

   b. Defend the NCAA ban on multiyear scholarships. See "NCAA's One-Year Scholarship Rule Faces Antitrust Exam," *Antitrust Today,* May 20, 2010 [**http://www.antitrusttoday.com/2010/05/**].

Sources: *White, Polak, Harris and Craig v. National Collegiate Athletic Association,* Case No. CV 06-0999 RGK (MANx), (U.S. District Court Central District of California, Western Division). Second Amended Complaint for Violation of Section 1 of the Sherman Act, 15 U.S.C. Section 1, p. 25, lines 3–5; and "Settlement Raises Questions for NCAA, *Inside Higher Ed,* February 4, 2008 [**http://www.insidehighered.com/news/2008/02/04/ncaa**].

Part One—The Foundations of Antitrust Law

Antitrust—Early Goals

Antitrust, perhaps more than any other branch of the law, is a product of changing political and economic tides. Historically, antitrust law sought to allow every American, at least in theory, the opportunity to reach the top. More specifically, antitrust advocates were concerned about the following issues:

1. **The preservation of competition.** Antitrust law was designed to provide free, open markets resulting in enhanced efficiency and increased consumer welfare. The belief was (and generally continues to be) that competition would generate the best products and services at the lowest possible prices.

2. **The preservation of democracy.** Many businesses in competition meant that none of them could corner economic, political, or social power.

3. **The preservation of small businesses, or more generally, the preservation of the American Dream.** Antitrust was designed to preserve the opportunity for ordinary Americans to compete with the giants.

4. **An expression of political radicalism.** At least for a segment of society, antitrust laws were meant to be tools for reshaping America to meet the needs of all people, thus counteracting, to some degree, the power of big business. [For professors' analyses of recent antitrust developments, see **http://lawprofessors.typepad.com/antitrustprof_blog**]

Antitrust Divisions?

At this writing in 2011, the Obama administration has promised to aggressively enforce the antitrust laws. During President George W. Bush's eight years in office, antitrust, with the notable exception of price fixing agreements between competitors, occupied a somewhat passive role in administration policy. While continuing to play a role in ensuring a competitive economy, antitrust certainly was not being used as a lever for social change. Political and sociological concerns took a back seat to efficiency considerations and to pragmatic, case-by-case consideration of the economic facts. Indeed, as *The New York Times* noted: "During the entire [George W.] Bush administration, the Justice Department's antitrust division didn't bring a single case against a big company for anticompetitive behavior to shut out a smaller rival."[1] At this writing, the Obama Administration seems to be taking something of a centrist approach, including a preference for resolving antitrust disputes outside of court.[2] Whether the current Justice Department will prove willing to go to court to challenge corporate giants and big deals remains to be seen.

Antitrust Enforcement and Statutes

Federal government antitrust enforcement is shared by the Antitrust Division of the Department of Justice and the Federal Trade Commission. The government brings relatively few antitrust actions, but a government victory sends powerful messages to the business community about the risks of anticompetitive behavior. The government prefers to avoid litigation, and most cases are settled before going to court. Private parties may also sue under the antitrust laws. Segments of the economy, such as the securities industry, that are already closely regulated by the government can sometimes successfully claim that they are immune from the antitrust laws. [For the Justice Department Antitrust Division, see **http://www.usdoj.gov/atr**]

> A government victory sends powerful messages to the business community.

Sherman Antitrust Act, 1890

Section 1 of the Sherman Antitrust Act forbids restraints of trade, and Section 2 forbids monopolization, attempts to monopolize, and conspiracies to monopolize. Two types of enforcement options are available to the federal government:

1. **Violation of the Sherman Act opens participants to criminal penalties.** The maximum corporate fine is $100 million per violation, whereas individuals may be fined $1 million and/or imprisoned for 10 years.

2. **Injunctive relief is provided under civil law.** The government or a private party may secure a court order preventing continuing violations of the act and affording appropriate relief (such as dissolution or divestiture).

Perhaps the most important remedy is available to private parties. An individual or organization harmed by a violation of the act may bring a civil action seeking three times the actual damages (treble damages) sustained.

Clayton Act, 1914

The Clayton Act forbids price discrimination, exclusive dealing, tying arrangements, requirements contracts, mergers restraining commerce or tending to create a monopoly, and interlocking directorates. Civil enforcement of the Clayton Act is similar to the Sherman Act in that the government may sue for injunctive relief, and private parties may seek treble damages. In general, criminal law remedies are not available under the Clayton Act. [For links to antitrust sites worldwide, see **http://www.justice.gov/atr/contact/otheratr.html**]

Federal Trade Commission Act

The Federal Trade Commission Act created a powerful, independent agency designed to devote its full attention to the elimination of anticompetitive practices in American commerce. The FTC proceeds under the Sherman Act, the Clayton Act, and Section 5 of the FTC Act itself, which declares unlawful "unfair methods of competition" and "unfair or deceptive acts or practices in or affecting commerce." The commission's primary enforcement device is the cease and desist order, but fines may be imposed. [For the FTC Guide to Antitrust Laws, see **http://www.ftc.gov/bc/antitrust/index.shtm**]

Leniency for Cooperating Wrongdoers

Federal pursuit of antitrust conduct is aggressive but pragmatic. The federal Justice Department practices a leniency policy under which antitrust criminal violators that cooperate with the government may avoid prosecution. Those who are first to come forward confessing to antitrust wrongs and otherwise cooperating with the Justice Department can avoid criminal penalties. Likewise, those companies that maintain an "effective" antitrust compliance program designed to prevent and detect criminal conduct within the organization may be treated more leniently in the event of antitrust wrongdoing. Similarly, Congress has passed legislation reducing possible civil penalties for those cooperating with antitrust actions. In 2010, the Justice Department reported that companies had been fined more than $5 billion for antitrust wrongs since 1996 with over 90 percent of that total tied to leniency programs. [For Frequently Asked Questions about the Justice Department's Leniency Program, see **http://www.justice.gov/atr/public/criminal/leniency.htm**]

Sources: John Majoras and Ryan Thomas, "Justice Department Issues Guidance on Antitrust Criminal Leniency Program," *LEXOLOGY,* December 9, 2008 [**http://www.lexology.com/**]; and Gibson, Dunn & Crutcher, LLP, "U.S. Congress Renews Civil Leniency for Companies that Self-Report Sherman Act Criminal Violations," *LEXOLOGY,* June 4, 2010 [**http://www.lexology.com/**].

Federal Antitrust Law and Other Regulatory Systems

State Law

Most states, through legislation and judicial decisions, have developed their own antitrust laws. Some states have recently become more aggressive in antitrust enforcement, as illustrated by their success in conjunction with the federal government in attacking Microsoft's alleged monopoly conduct. (See Chapter 11.)

Patents, Copyrights, and Trademarks

Each of these devices offers limited, government-granted, government-shielded market strength, thus serving to protect and encourage commercial creativity and product development. The resulting antitrust problem essentially amounts to limiting the patent, copyright, or trademark holder to the terms of its government-granted privilege, rather than allowing that privilege to grow into an unlawful monopoly.

Law of Other Nations

Chapter 11 addresses the practical and ideological significance of international antitrust issues in this era of globalization. [For a guide to antitrust resources on the Internet, see **http://www.antitrustinstitute.org/content/antitrust-resources**]

Part Two—Horizontal Restraints

When competitors collude, conspire, or agree among themselves, they are engaging in *horizontal restraints of trade*. Instead of competing to drive prices down and quality up, they may be fixing prices, restricting output, dividing territories, and the like. The various horizontal restraints are governed by Section 1 of the Sherman Act, which forbids contracts, combinations, or conspiracies in *restraint of trade*. What is a restraint of trade? In the *Standard Oil*[3] decision of 1911, the U.S. Supreme Court articulated what has come to be known as the *rule of reason*. In essence, the Court said that the Sherman Act forbids only *unreasonable* restraints of trade. The reasonableness of a restraint of trade is largely determined by a detailed balancing of the pro- and anticompetitive effects of the situation. Thus, the plaintiff must prove the existence of an anticompetitive agreement or conduct and also prove that, on balance, the agreement or conduct harms competition. [For an antitrust overview, see **http://topics.law.cornell.edu/wex/antitrust**]

Some antitrust violations, such as horizontal price fixing, are so injurious to competition that their mere existence ordinarily constitutes unlawful conduct. Plaintiffs must prove that the violation in question occurred, but they need not prove that the violation caused, or is likely to cause, competitive harm. These *per se* violations are simply unlawful on their face.

Antitrust Enforcement Produces Lower Prices?

Antitrust law is often of direct value to consumers as illustrated by a 2008 settlement between the U.S. Justice Department and the National Association of Realtors in which the NAR guaranteed that realtors participating in the NAR-affiliated multiple listing services (MLS—local cooperative arrangements in which realtors list all of their properties for sale in a single database) will allow online real estate agents to have full access to those MLS listings. The newer Internet-based agents claimed they had often been blocked by local MLS associations from access to listings of houses for sale thus restricting their ability to fully compete with the traditional brokers. The online brokers, often achieving productivity efficiencies, are able to charge fees about one percentage point beneath the traditional industry standard of 5 to 6 percent of the purchase price thus generating substantial consumer savings.

Sources: "Justice Department Announces Settlement with the National Association of Realtors," Department of Justice Press Release, May 27, 2008 [**http://www.usdoj.gov/opa/pr/2008/May/08-at-467.html**]; Eric Lichtblau, "Realtors Agree to Stop Blocking Web Listings," *The New York Times,* May 28, 2008 [**nytimes.com**]; and Department of Justice Antitrust Division, "Enforcing Antitrust Laws in the Real Estate Industry," [**http://www.justice.gov/atr/public/real_estate/enforce.htm**].

Horizontal Territorial and Customer Restraints

Principal legislation—Sherman Act, Section 1.

> Every contract, combination in the form of trust or otherwise, or conspiracy, in restraint of trade or commerce, among the several states, or with foreign nations, is declared to be illegal . . .

Assume two big companies dominate the wholesale food market in their small state. Could they lawfully agree between themselves to divide their state geographically with one supplying the eastern half while the other supplies only the western half? Or could they lawfully allocate their customers such that one, for example, supplies all small town grocers while the other restricts itself to grocers in the few major cities? Suppliers might want to eliminate that competition among themselves, but such arrangements ordinarily are *per se* violations of the Sherman Act since they attempt to nullify the powerful benefits of competition.

Horizontal Price Fixing

Principal legislation—Sherman Act, Section 1.

Competitors may not lawfully agree on prices. That principle is simple and fundamental to an efficient, fair marketplace. Establishing the presence of an unlawful price-fixing arrangement, on the other hand, ordinarily is anything but simple.

Proof

The major dilemma in price fixing and all other Sherman Act Section 1 violations is the measure of proof that satisfies the requirement of a contract, combination, or conspiracy. Evidence of collusion arises in a variety of ways. For example, LaQuinta Inns entered an agreement in 2010 with the Connecticut Attorney General to stop its "call around" practice. Reportedly, motel managers identified their primary local competition and called them frequently to give and receive information about occupancy rates and room charges; a practice that is widespread in the motel industry. The fear is that the frequent exchange of information, in effect, constitutes collusion to fix prices among the competitors. LaQuinta agreed to desist from its call around practices throughout the United States.[4] Broadly, a showing of cooperative action amounting to an agreement may be developed by any of the following four methods of proof:

1. **Agreement with direct evidence.** In the easiest case, the government/plaintiff can produce direct evidence such as writings or testimony from participants proving the existence of collusion.

2. **Agreement without direct evidence.** Here the defendants directly but covertly agree, and circumstantial evidence such as company behavior must be employed to draw an inference of collusion.

3. **Agreement based on a tacit understanding.** In this situation no direct exchange of assurances occurs, but the parties employ tactics that act as surrogates for direct assurances and thus "tell" each other that they are, in fact, in agreement.

4. **Agreement based on mutual observation.** These defendants have simply observed each others' pricing behavior over time, and they are able therefore to anticipate each others' future conduct and act accordingly without any direct collusion but with results akin to those that would have resulted from a direct agreement.[5]

Parallel Conduct

An unlawful conspiracy is to be distinguished from independent but parallel business behavior by competitors. So-called *conscious parallelism* is fully lawful because the competitors have not agreed either explicitly or by implication to follow the same course of action. Rather, their business judgment has led each to independently follow parallel paths. On the other hand, a conspiracy can sometimes be established by proof that the parallel behavior in question was not arrived at independently, but rather was the product of a preceding agreement.[6]

Aggressive Enforcement

Both government intervention advocates and free market champions agree that price fixing cripples the market. So government intervention, at the federal and state levels, and damage claims by wronged consumers are sometimes essential to maintain effective competition. Antitrust law, including price-fixing prohibitions, is designed to protect the consumer from a variety of commercial arrangements—some well-intentioned, some overt cheating—that nullify the favorable effects of competition. Consider some prominent examples.

- At this writing, six companies, including LG Display Co., Sharp Corp., and Chunghwa Picture Tubes, Ltd., have pleaded guilty or have agreed to plead guilty to federal criminal charges of conspiring to fix prices for LCD panels and will pay fines totaling over $860 million.[7] The panels were used in computer monitors, notebooks, televisions, and other electronic devices by Apple, Dell, and others. Reportedly, the LCD industry was facing an oversupply problem between October 2000 and August 2001, but despite that market condition, prices began to rise after August 2001, allegedly as a result of the three companies working in concert to fix those prices. The Justice Department described some of the conspiratorial behavior among three of the companies:

  > The three companies . . . allegedly held "crystal" meetings and engaged in communications about setting prices on the TFT-LCD displays. They agreed to charge predetermined prices for the displays, issued price quotes based on those agreements, and exchanged sales information on the display panels, in order to monitor and enforce the agreement, the Justice Department said.[8]

- According to the European Union's Competition Commissioner, Procter & Gamble, Unilever, and Henkel, the leading producers of powder detergents in Europe, met to discuss an environmental plan for shrinking their product packaging and ended up agreeing on a market sharing plan and price floors. As a result, $456 million in fines were levied against Procter & Gamble and Unilever in 2011 with Henkel being excused for blowing the whistle on its coconspirators.[9]

- Ending nine years of litigation over alleged conspiracies to fix corn syrup prices, Archer Daniels Midland, A.E. Staley, and others agreed in 2004 to pay $531 million to settle a class action against them.[10] [For a movie account of former ADM executive Mark Whitacre's decision to blow the whistle on the alleged conspiracy, see *The Informant!* starring Matt Damon. The trailer is available at: **http://www.traileraddict.com/trailer/the-informant/trailer**]

- In May 1999 the U.S. Justice Department secured a criminal fine of more than $750 million from three international vitamin manufacturers. Those three and three other companies later agreed to pay $1.1 billion to settle civil price-fixing claims. The companies' executives allegedly got together to divide the worldwide vitamin market and set prices for the vitamins, and then they allegedly policed themselves to see that all conspirators were adhering to the agreement.[11]

> The companies' executives allegedly got together to divide the worldwide vitamin market.

These are only a few of the many examples in recent years of price-fixing conspiracies in America and around the world. The effect of these unlawful arrangements is to harm competition and raise prices. Price fixing is nothing new, but its aggressive governmental pursuit both domestically and around the world does represent a change in policy, as explained by Phillip Warren, U.S. Department of Justice antitrust chief in San Francisco:

> "I think it's been going on [for a long time], and we have only recently been able to detect and prosecute them," Warren said. "There's a long tradition of cartel activity, not in the United States but around the world. Cartels were accepted." . . .[12]

PRACTICING ETHICS   Antitrust Law and the Price of Beer

We know that college students drink astonishing amounts of alcohol. Each year college students spend about $5.5 billion on alcohol, most of that on beer. That total exceeds what students spend on books, soda, coffee, juice, and milk combined. Could antitrust law affect the consumption, or at least the price, of beer? Perhaps. A group of consumers in Madison, Wisconsin, home of the University of Wisconsin, sued some local bars and the Madison-Dane County Tavern League, Inc., for price fixing. The plaintiffs claimed that the defendant bars had agreed to fix prices by adopting a "voluntary ban on drink specials." The plaintiffs pointed to a September 2002 press release from the "Downtown Tavern Working Group" announcing that drink specials would not be offered after 8 PM on Friday and Saturday nights for "at least a year."

The defendants said the new policy was a self-imposed effort to curb binge drinking, especially by students, and that the policy was a response to pressure from the city and the University of Wisconsin. Further, the defendants said that the press release did not reflect an agreement of any kind and thus could not violate the law because all bar owners remained free to do as they wished. Eventually, the Wisconsin Supreme Court held that the policy was immune from the antitrust laws because the city effectively compelled the arrangement. Given the state legislature's broad grant of regulatory authority over alcohol to municipalities, the Court concluded that the legislature must have intended the defendant taverns' actions to be exempt (immune from scrutiny) from the antitrust laws.

Questions

1. The legality of this arrangement aside, *should* bar owners be free to reach an agreement eliminating drink specials?

2. Is the Madison dispute too trivial and frivolous to justify court time? Explain.

3. Will the market satisfactorily protect youthful drinkers and society? Explain.

4. *a.* How would you expect the Supreme Court decision to affect the consumption of beer in Madison?
   b. Explain how a "voluntary ban on drink specials" might constitute price fixing.

Sources: *Eichenseer v. Madison-Dane County Tavern League,* 748 N.W.2d 154 (Wis. S.Ct. 2008); and "Frequently Asked Questions about College Binge Drinking," AlcoholPolicyMD.com [**http://www.alcoholpolicymd.com/alcohol_and_health/faqs.htm**].

Cigarette Pricing

The case that follows examines alleged horizontal price fixing in the oligopolistic cigarette industry.

Romero and Ferree v. Philip Morris, et al.   2010 N.M. LEXIS 370

LEGAL BRIEFCASE   (N.M. S.Ct.)

Justice Chavez

BACKGROUND

The following facts are undisputed. Plaintiffs are "[p]ersons in the State of New Mexico . . . who purchased cigarettes indirectly from Defendants, or any parent, subsidiary or affiliate thereof, at any time from November 1, 1993 to the date of the filing of this action [April 10, 2000]." The original Defendants were Philip Morris, R.J. Reynolds ("RJR"), Brown & Williamson ("B&W"), Lorillard, and Liggett. The events leading up to this lawsuit were set in motion in response to a Philip Morris strategy beginning with an event known as "Marlboro Friday." Prior to Marlboro Friday, Philip Morris, the market leader, had been steadily losing market share to discount and deep discount cigarettes since 1980, when Liggett pioneered the development of generic cigarettes. In an attempt to regain market share, Philip Morris announced Marlboro Friday on April 2, 1993, "a nationwide promotion on Marlboro that reduced prices at retail by approximately 20 percent, an average of 40[cents] per pack." In response, RJR and B&W instituted similar promotions. As part of its strategy, Philip Morris announced on July 20, 1993, that there would be a similar reduction on all premium brands, discount brands, and deep discount brands starting on August 9, 1993. Defendants RJR and B&W also followed these price reductions. After these decreases, Defendants began to increase their wholesale list prices on premium and discount cigarettes in near lock-step fashion. Some increases were due to settlements with the 50 states, some because of increases in federal excise taxes, and others were simply planned. Even with these increases, wholesale list prices did not exceed pre-Marlboro Friday levels until August 3, 1998, or when adjusted for inflation, ongoing settlement costs, and federal excise taxes, the list prices did not surpass pre-Marlboro Friday amounts until August 1999. During the time period of the alleged agreement to fix prices, 1993 to 2000, Defendants were engaged in competition with one another regarding promotions at the retail level, resulting in a direct reduction of the retail prices of cigarettes.

Plaintiffs filed this class action lawsuit on April 10, 2000, alleging violations of New Mexico antitrust and consumer protection laws. Defendants filed motions for summary judgment. In granting the motion for summary judgment, the district court held that Plaintiffs had met their initial burden of showing a pattern of parallel behavior, but failed to meet their second burden of showing the existence of plus factors that would tend to exclude the possibility that the alleged conspirators acted independently.

* * * * *

On appeal, the Court of Appeals acknowledged that "Marlboro Friday and the industry-wide price reductions that occurred afterward represented the triumph of competition over oligopolistic price coordination." Although the Court affirmed summary judgment in favor of Lorillard and Liggett because the evidence showed that they had merely acted "consistent with conscious parallelism," the Court reversed summary judgment in favor of Philip Morris, RJR, and B&W because "we think that a reasonable factfinder could view conscious parallelism as a relatively implausible explanation for the anticompetitive scenario that played out following Marlboro Friday."

* * * * *

FEDERAL SUBSTANTIVE ANTITRUST LAW: PROVING THE CONSPIRACY

* * * * *

There is no doubt that the tobacco industry, in which five companies manufacture more than 97% of the cigarettes sold in the United States, is a classic oligopoly. Because the cigarette industry is an oligopoly, it is likely that when one tobacco company (*i.e.*, Philip Morris) acts in a certain manner (*i.e.*, Marlboro Friday and subsequent price increases), the other firms (RJR, B&W, Lorillard, and Liggett) will determine whether it is in their best interest to follow the leader's actions. As we will discuss below, when Philip Morris began raising prices after Marlboro Friday, RJR's and B&Ws conduct in following subsequent price increases was just as likely due to their own independent analysis of what was in their best interests as it was the result of an illegal price-fixing agreement. Therefore, Plaintiffs must present evidence that tends to exclude the possibility that Defendants acted independently or they can not meet their burden of establishing a genuine issue of material fact. . . .

The United States Supreme Court has explicitly stated that "when allegations of parallel conduct are set out in order to make a Section 1 claim, they must be placed in a context that raises a suggestion of a preceding agreement, not merely parallel conduct that could just as well be independent action." *Bell Atl. Corp.,* 550 U.S. at 557.

* * * * *

[W]e must determine whether Plaintiffs' proffered evidence of plus factors tends to exclude the possibility that Defendants acted independently. Plaintiffs cite to the following plus factors, in addition to parallel pricing, as tending to exclude the possibility that Defendants acted independently: (1) the economies of the marketplace, such as a highly concentrated market, cigarette fungibility, high barriers to entry in the industry, absence of close substitutes, and a history of collusion; (2) a strong motivation to conspire, resulting from the desperate times facing the cigarette industry, including "a dramatic decline in its sales as a result of . . . increased public awareness of the detrimental health effects of smoking"; (3) the condensation of price tiers to facilitate the conspiracy; (4) actions contrary to self-interest, including Philip Morris's pre-announcing its price reductions and Defendants' failure to attempt to re-widen the price gap by reducing discount prices; (5) conspiratorial meetings in other markets; (6) a smoking and health conspiracy; (7) the manner in which Defendants monitored the conspiracy through Management Science

Associates ("MSA"); (8) opportunities to conspire; and (9) pricing decisions made at high levels.

We reject Plaintiffs' plus factors . . . because Defendants' conduct is just as consistent with lawful, independent action as it is with price fixing, and therefore it does not tend to exclude independent conduct. We briefly discuss Plaintiffs' plus factors to address why they do not tend to exclude the possibility of independent conduct by Defendants. (1) The majority of the economies of the marketplace to which Plaintiffs cite are nothing more than inherent characteristics of an oligopoly and cannot tend to exclude independent action.

* * * * *

(2) The motivation to conspire cited by Plaintiffs cannot serve as tending to exclude independent conduct because "[p]rofit is a legitimate motive in pricing decisions, and something more is required before a court can conclude that competitors conspired to fix pricing in violation of the Sherman Act." *In re Baby Food Antitrust Litig,,* 166 F.3d at 134-35. (3) When Philip Morris took action to condense the price tiers, it is just as likely that they did so to reduce the price gap and maximize profits as to facilitate a price fixing agreement, and thus this does not tend to exclude independent conduct. (4) Plaintiffs argue that Defendants took actions contrary to self-interest by pre-announcing price decisions and failing to re-widen the price gap. Philip Morris argues that the June 20, 1993 pre-announcement of a price decrease to take effect twenty days later was not a signal to the other cigarette manufacturers, but was made to allow wholesalers and retailers to avoid an immediate reduction in the value of their inventory and to accommodate the burden of implementing a price reduction.

* * * * *

(5) The alleged conspiratorial meetings in other markets cannot serve as tending to exclude independent conduct because Plaintiffs offered no support to connect the actions in foreign markets with the actions in the United States. . . . (6) Similarly, concluding that an alleged smoking and health conspiracy facilitated coordination of a conspiracy in this case would require the jury to engage in speculation. . . . (7) The manner in which Defendants monitored the conspiracy through MSA is not evidence tending to exclude independent conduct because there is an equally rational legal explanation for this such as to "devise competitive strategies, gauge the success of their promotions, monitor the impact of new styles or packing on the market, and determine whether increased promotional spending was needed in certain geographic areas to compete with competitors' programs." . . .

Defendants made a prima facie case supporting summary judgment by providing evidence of fierce retail competition that undermined the plausibility of a price-fixing agreement [and by] demonstrating that wholesale prices remained lower than pre-Marlboro Friday levels and did not exceed pre-Marlboro Friday levels until almost five years later. . . . This evidence showed that Defendants '"had no rational economic motive to conspire, and . . . their conduct is consistent with other, equally plausible explanations.'" *Clough,* 108 N.M. at 804, 780 P.2d at 630 (quoting *Matsushita Elec. Indus. Co.,* 475 U.S. at 596-97). In reviewing Plaintiffs' plus factors, we find that the district court properly granted summary judgment.

Reversed.

Questions

1. *a.* Who are the alleged conspirators in this price fixing dispute, and how did they allegedly fix prices?
   b. Who won this case at the New Mexico Court of Appeals, and why did that court rule as it did?
   c. In general, is parallel pricing a lawful behavior? Explain.

2. *a.* Why did the New Mexico Supreme Court require a showing of "plus factors" to demonstrate that the cigarette companies had engaged in price fixing?
   b. Why did the Court reject the plus factors offered by the plaintiffs as evidence of a price fixing conspiracy?

3. Why did the tobacco companies win this case?

4. Assume two drugstores, located across the street from each other and each involved in interstate commerce, agree to exchange a monthly list of prices charged for all nonprescription medications. Is that arrangement lawful in the absence of any further cooperation? Explain.

5. The "Three Tenors," Luciano Pavarotti, Placido Domingo, and Jose Carreras, recorded a 1990 World Cup concert, distributed by Polygram, and a 1994 World Cup concert, distributed by Warner. Polygram and Warner subsequently agreed to jointly distribute and share profits from the 1998 World Cup Three Tenors concert. The 1998 recording apparently was less "new and exciting" than had been hoped. Concerned that sales of the earlier recordings would drain interest from the 1998 recording, Polygram and Warner agreed to cease all discounting and advertising of the two earlier recordings for several weeks surrounding the release of the 1998 album. In 2001, the Federal Trade Commission issued complaints against Polygram and Warner. Those complaints eventually reached the District of Columbia Federal Circuit Court of Appeals where Polygram and Warner defended themselves

by arguing that the agreement was good for competition in that it increased the joint venture's profitability from new recordings, and it eliminated free riding by each company (for the 1990 and 1994 recordings) on the joint venture's 1998 marketing.

a. What antitrust violation was alleged by the Federal Trade Commission?

b. What is free riding, and why is it a problem?

c. Decide the case. Explain. See *Polygram v. Federal Trade Commission,* 416 F.3d 29 (D.C. Cir. 2005).

6. Assume that 10 real estate firms operate in the city of Gotham. Further assume that each charges a 7 percent commission on all residential sales.

a. Does that uniformity of prices in and of itself constitute price fixing? Explain.

b. Assume we have evidence that the firms agreed to set the 7 percent level. What defense would be raised against a price-fixing charge?

c. Would that defense succeed? Explain. See *McLain v. Real Estate Board of New Orleans, Inc.,* 444 U.S. 232 (1980).

Refusal to Deal/Group Boycotts

Principal legislation—Sherman Act, Section 1.

In America we are free to do business with whomever we prefer, correct? Generally, yes; but antitrust problems sometimes emerge. When does a *refusal to deal* with another raise antitrust issues? The clearest problem is a *horizontal group boycott* where competitors agree not to deal with a supplier, customer, or another competitor. Ford and GM, for example, presumably could not jointly refuse to buy tires from Bridgestone/Firestone. Such arrangements so thoroughly subvert the market that they ordinarily are *per se* violations of Sherman I and thus do not require a detailed evaluation of competitive harm and benefits, although a showing of market power by those in the group may be required. A unilateral (individual) refusal to deal by a buyer or a seller sometimes raises antitrust concerns if the firm refusing to deal is a monopolist and harm to competition can be proven,[13] but the Supreme Court has severely restricted the use of the doctrine.[14]

A recent battle among the big bank card companies illustrates refusal to deal reasoning (although for technical reasons the case was not tried under the refusal to deal/boycott label). In 1996, American Express decided to open its own credit card network to compete with Visa and MasterCard. No bank, however, was willing to deal with American Express. Why would the banks turn down the potential to make more money by working with the respected American Express brand? They did so because Visa and MasterCard had rules forbidding their members from issuing American Express and Discover cards. Visa and MasterCard operate as nonprofit joint venture associations owned by the member banks that issue their credit cards. As long as those banks wanted to do business with Visa and MasterCard, the two giants, they could not deal with American Express and Discover. Were the Visa and MasterCard refusal to deal rules lawful? No, as it turns out. The antitrust division of the federal Department of Justice sued the two giants for their alleged exclusionary practices and won in the federal courts.[15] The six-year struggle turned largely on the finding that continued exclusion of Discover, American Express, and others from the market was a horizontal restraint that would likely harm future competition. A key finding was the conclusion that Visa and MasterCard, with their collective market share exceeding 70 percent, had market power. American Express subsequently sued Visa for damages inflicted by the alleged

> MasterCard agreed to pay $1.8 billion to American Express.

exclusionary practices. In 2007, Visa agreed to pay $2.1 billion to settle that lawsuit and in 2008 MasterCard Worldwide agreed to pay $1.8 billion to American Express. [For a trade regulation blog, see **http://traderegulation.blogspot.com/**]

Clarett Boycotted by NFL?

Antitrust shapes all dimensions of our lives, as football running back Maurice Clarett learned when he tried to enter the 2004 National Football League draft. Clarett, as a freshman, led Ohio State University to an undefeated season in 2002. Clarett was ineligible for college football in his sophomore year because of allegations that he accepted improper benefits and lied about doing so. Clarett then tried to enter the NFL draft but was barred by a league rule providing that players must have been out of high school for three seasons. Clarett sued the NFL, claiming its eligibility rules violated federal antitrust laws by, in effect, allowing competing teams to agree among themselves to boycott certain players (including Clarett). Clarett won at the federal district court level, but he lost on appeal when the court ruled that the eligibility rule is exempt from the antitrust laws. The NFL eligibility rule is the product of a collective bargaining agreement between the league and the players' union, the National Football League Players Association. Antitrust promotes competition while unions restrict it in various ways; but in balancing those competing interests, Congress and the courts have long granted unions certain exemptions from antitrust laws. The Supreme Court subsequently declined to review Clarett's case.

In 2010, Clarett was released from prison where he had served a three and one half year sentence for aggravated robbery and carrying a concealed weapon. He played football during the 2010 season with the Omaha Nighthawks of the United Football League.

Questions

1. Should Clarett and future football players be free to sell their services on the open market?
2. Or is the NFL correct to encourage players to stay in college and mature before seeking to become professionals? Explain.
3. Congressman Steve Cohen, Democrat of Tennessee, wrote a letter in 2009 to the National Basketball Association and the NBA players union asking them to repeal the rule requiring players to be 19 years old and one year removed from high school before they are eligible for the NBA. The rule is part of the collective bargaining agreement between the league and the players. Cohen labeled the law "a vestige of slavery."
   a. What did Cohen mean by his "vestige of slavery" remark?
   b. Does the rule constitute an unlawful restraint of trade? Explain.
   c. Do you agree that the rule should be repealed? Explain.

Sources: Clarett v. National Football League, 369 F.3d 124 (2d Cir. 2004); and Pete Thamel, "Congressman Asks N.B.A. and Union to Rescind Age Minimum for Players," *The New York Times,* June 4, 2009 [**http://www.nytimes.com**].

Questions

1. Baptist Eye Institute, a group of nonspecialized ophthalmologists in Jacksonville, Florida, controlling approximately 15 percent of the referral market, sent nearly all of its retina cases to the Florida Retina Institute. Is BEI engaging in an unlawful group boycott against plaintiff Retina Associates, a retina care provider in competition with

the Florida Retina Institute? Explain. See *Retina Associates P.A. v. Southern Baptist Hospital of Florida Inc.,* 105 F.3d 1376 (11th Cir. 1997).

2. Discon, a telephone salvage company, sold services to MECo, a subsidiary of NYNEX, a phone company for the New York/New England area. MECo switched from Discon to AT&T Technologies, a Discon competitor, and paid a higher price to AT&T than it had paid to Discon. Discon claimed that the buyer and NYNEX then received a rebate from AT&T at the end of the year. Discon argued that NYNEX was able to pass on its higher costs to its customers because NYNEX was a part of a regulated phone market. Discon claimed that NYNEX, its subsidiaries, and AT&T were engaging in a group boycott in violation of the Sherman Act in order to drive Discon out of the market. Decide. Explain. See *NYNEX Corp. v. Discon, Inc.,* 119 S.Ct. 493 (1998).

Part Three—Vertical Restraints

We have been studying unfair trade practices by competitors—that is, horizontal restraints of trade. Now we turn to antitrust violations on the vertical axis—that is, restraints involving two or more members of a supply chain (such as a manufacturer and a retailer of that manufacturer's products). *Horizontal restraints* are those arising from an agreement among the *competitors* themselves, while *vertical restraints* ordinarily are those imposed by *suppliers* on their *buyers.* Horizontal restraints, in general, are *per se* unlawful while vertical restraints, in general, are to be resolved under the rule of reason. Horizontal restraints eliminate competition thereby undermining the power of the market while vertical restraints sometimes are harmful and sometimes are beneficial to competition and thus ordinarily should be evaluated on a case-by-case basis.

Resale Price Maintenance

Principal legislation: Sherman Act, Section 1; Federal Trade Commission Act, Section 5.

Manufacturers and distributors often seek to specify the price at which their customers may resell their products, a policy we might think of as vertical price fixing but that is formally called *resale price maintenance*. Having sold its product, why should a manufacturer or distributor seek to influence the price at which the product is resold? The primary reasons are fourfold: (1) establishing a minimum price to enhance the product's reputation, (2) helping retailers make a profit sufficient to provide customer service, (3) preventing discount stores from pricing beneath full-price retail outlets, and (4) preventing *free riders*.

A *unilateral* specification of a resale price, with nothing more involved, has long been permissible. Under the Supreme Court's 1919 *Colgate*[16] decision, sellers can lawfully engage in resale price maintenance if they do nothing more than announce prices at which their products are to be resold and unilaterally refuse to deal with anyone who does not adhere to those prices. On the other hand, an *agreement* between a seller and a buyer dictating the price at which the buyer may resell the product was, for decades, a per se violation of the law. Then in 1997, the Supreme Court ruled that *agreements* specifying *maximum* resale prices would no longer be considered *per se* violations and must be evaluated under the rule of reason.[17] In the 2007 *Leegin* case that follows, the Supreme Court overturned a nearly 100-year-old precedent in the Dr. Miles case[18] to rule that *agreements* specifying *minimum* resale prices must also be analyzed under the rule of reason; that is, those agreements are no longer *per se* violations of the law. Rather, they must be considered on a case-by-case basis weighing their pro- and anticompetitive effects.

LEGAL BRIEFCASE

Leegin Creative Leather Products, Inc. v. PSKS, dba Kay's Kloset   127 S.Ct. 2705 (2007)

Justice Kennedy

I

Petitioner, Leegin Creative Leather Products, Inc. (Leegin), designs, manufactures, and distributes leather goods and accessories. In 1991, Leegin began to sell belts under the brand name "Brighton." The Brighton brand has now expanded into a variety of women's fashion accessories. It is sold across the United States in over 5,000 retail establishments, for the most part independent, small boutiques and specialty stores. . . . Leegin asserts that, at least for its products, small retailers treat customers better, provide customers more services, and make their shopping experience more satisfactory than do larger, often impersonal retailers. [Leegin's president, Jerry] Kohl explained: "[W]e want the consumers to get a different experience than they get in Sam's Club or in Wal-Mart. And you can't get that kind of experience or support or customer service from a store like Wal-Mart."

Respondent PSKS, Inc. operates Kay's Kloset, a women's apparel store in Lewisville, Texas. Kay's Kloset buys from about 75 different manufacturers and at one time sold the Brighton brand. It first started purchasing Brighton goods from Leegin in 1995. Once it began selling the brand, the store promoted Brighton. For example, it ran Brighton advertisements and had Brighton days in the store. Kay's Kloset became the destination retailer in the area to buy Brighton products. Brighton was the store's most important brand and once accounted for 40 to 50 percent of its profits.

In 1997, Leegin instituted the "Brighton retail pricing and Promotion Policy." Following the policy, Leegin refused to sell to retailers that discounted Brighton goods below suggested prices. . . . In the letter to retailers establishing the policy, Leegin stated:

> "In this age of mega stores like Macy's, Bloomingdales, May Co. and others, consumers are perplexed by promises of product quality and support of product which we believe is lacking in these large stores. Consumers are further confused by the ever popular sale, sale, sale, etc.
>
> "We, at Leegin, choose to break away from the pack by selling [at] specialty stores; specialty stores that can offer the customer great quality merchandise, superb service, and support the Brighton product 365 days a year on a consistent basis. . . .

Leegin adopted the policy to give its retailers sufficient margins to provide customers the service central to its distribution strategy. It also expressed concern that discounting harmed Brighton's brand image and reputation.

* * * * *

In December 2002, Leegin discovered Kay's Kloset had been marking down Brighton's entire line by 20 percent. Kay's Kloset contended it placed Brighton products on sale to compete with nearby retailers who also were undercutting Leegin's suggested prices. Leegin, nonetheless, requested that Kay's Kloset cease discounting. Its request refused, Leegin stopped selling to the store. The loss of the Brighton brand had a considerable negative impact on the store's revenue from sales.

PSKS sued Leegin in the United States District Court for the Eastern District of Texas. It alleged, among other claims, that Leegin had violated the antitrust laws by "enter[ing] into agreements with retailers to charge only those prices fixed by Leegin."

* * * * *

The jury agreed with PSKS and awarded it $1.2 million.

* * * * *

The Court of Appeals for the Fifth Circuit affirmed. We granted certiorari to determine whether vertical minimum resale price maintenance agreements should continue to be treated as *per se* unlawful.

* * * * *

II

Resort to *per se* rules is confined to restraints . . . "that would always or almost always tend to restrict competition and decrease output." *Business Electronics,* 485 U.S. at 723 . . .

As a consequence, the *per se* rule is appropriate only after courts have had considerable experience with the type of restraint at issue, and only if courts can predict with confidence that it would be invalidated in all or almost all instances under the rule of reason. . . .

III

The Court has interpreted *Dr. Miles Medical Co. v. John D. Park & Sons Co.,* 220 U.S. 373 (1911), as establishing a *per se* rule against a vertical agreement between a manufacturer and its distributor to set minimum resale prices. . . .

The reasons upon which *Dr. Miles* relied do not justify a *per se* rule. As a consequence, it is necessary to examine . . . the economic effects of vertical agreements to fix minimum resale prices, and to determine whether the *per se* rule is nonetheless appropriate.

A

Though each side of the debate can find sources to support its position, it suffices to say here that economics literature is replete with procompetitive justifications for a manufacturer's use of resale price maintenance.

* * * * *

The justifications for vertical price restraints are similar to those for other vertical restraints. Minimum resale price maintenance can stimulate interbrand competition—the competition among manufacturers selling different brands of the same type of product—by reducing intrabrand competition—the competition among retailers selling the same brand. The promotion of interbrand competition is important because "the primary purpose of the antitrust laws is to protect [this type of] competition." *Khan,* 522 U.S. at 15. . . .

Absent vertical price restraints, the retail services that enhance interbrand competition might be under-provided. This is because discounting retailers can free ride on retailers who furnish services and then capture some of the increased demand those services generate.

Resale price maintenance, in addition, can increase interbrand competition by facilitating market entry for new firms and brands. "[N]ew manufacturers and manufacturers entering new markets can use the restrictions in order to induce competent and aggressive retailers to make the kind of investment of capital and labor that is often required in the distribution of products unknown to the consumer." *GTE Sylvania,* 433 U.S. at 55; . . .

Resale price maintenance can also increase interbrand competition by encouraging retailer services that would not be provided even absent free riding. It may be difficult and inefficient for a manufacturer to make and enforce a contract with a retailer specifying the different services the retailer must perform. Offering the retailer a guaranteed margin and threatening termination if it does not live up to expectations may be the most efficient way to expand the manufacturer's market share by inducing the retailer's performance and allowing it to use its own initiative and experience in providing valuable services.

* * * * *

B

While vertical agreements setting minimum resale prices can have procompetitive justifications, they may have anticompetitive effects in other cases; and unlawful price fixing, designed solely to obtain monopoly profits, is an ever-present temptation. Resale price maintenance may, for example, facilitate a manufacturer cartel. An unlawful cartel will seek to discover if some manufacturers are undercutting the cartel's fixed prices. Resale price maintenance could assist the cartel in identifying price-cutting manufacturers who benefit from the lower prices they offer. Resale price maintenance, furthermore, could discourage a manufacturer from cutting prices to retailers with the concomitant benefit of cheaper prices to consumers.

Vertical price restraints also "might be used to organize cartels at the retailer level." *Business Electronics,* at 725–726. A group of retailers might collude to fix prices to consumers and then compel a manufacturer to aid the unlawful arrangement with resale price maintenance.

A horizontal cartel among competing manufacturers or competing retailers that decreases output or reduces competition in order to increase price is, and ought to be, *per se* unlawful. To the extent a vertical agreement setting minimum resale prices is entered upon to facilitate either type of cartel, it, too, would need to be held unlawful under the rule of reason.

* * * * *

A manufacturer with market power . . . might use resale price maintenance to give retailers an incentive not to sell the products of smaller rivals or new entrants. As should be evident, the potential anticompetitive consequences of vertical price restraints must not be ignored or underestimated.

C

Notwithstanding the risk of unlawful conduct, it cannot be stated with any degree of confidence that resale price maintenance "always or almost always tend[s] to restrict competition and decrease output." Vertical agreements establishing minimum resale prices can have either procompetitive or anticompetitive effects, depending upon the circumstances in which they are formed.

Respondent contends, nonetheless, that . . . the *per se* rule is justified because a vertical price restraint can lead to higher prices for the manufacturer's goods. . . . Respondent is mistaken in relying on pricing effects absent a further showing of anticompetitive conduct. . . . For, as has been indicated already, the antitrust laws are designed primarily to protect interbrand competition, from which lower prices can later result. . . .

Respondent's argument, furthermore, overlooks that, in general, the interests of manufacturers and consumers are aligned with respect to retailer profit margins. . . . A manufacturer has no incentive to overcompensate retailers with unjustified margins. The retailers, not the manufacturer, gain from

higher retail prices. The manufacturer often loses; interbrand competition reduces its competitiveness and market share because consumers will "substitute a different brand of the same product." see *Business Electronics,* at 725. . . .

Resale price maintenance, it is true, does have economic dangers. If the rule of reason were to apply to vertical price restraints, courts would have to be diligent in eliminating their anticompetitive uses from the market. This is a realistic objective. . . .

As a final matter, that a dominant manufacturer or retailer can abuse resale price maintenance for anticompetitive purposes may not be a serious concern unless the relevant entity has market power. If a retailer lacks market power, manufacturers likely can sell their goods through rival retailers.

* * * * *

For all of the foregoing reasons, we think that were the Court considering the issue as an original matter, the rule of reason, not a *per se* rule of unlawfulness, would be the appropriate standard to judge vertical price restraints.

* * * * *

Reversed.

Questions

1. *a.* What potential procompetitive considerations were cited by the court in supporting a rule of reason approach to resale price maintenance?
   b. What potential anticompetitive considerations were cited by the court?
2. Could we fairly conclude from the *Leegin* decision that resale price maintenance agreements are now "*per se* legal"? Explain.
3. Explain why the court said the seller's market power is an important consideration in assessing the legality of a resale price maintenance agreement.

Leegin in Practice (the Law) The *Leegin* ruling seems to affirm the Supreme Court's current preference for free market principles and reduced judicial intervention in business practice. Accordingly, more competition and better service should follow, but critics think the decision simply allows manufacturers to pressure and cut out discounters with the result that consumers will pay higher prices. At this writing, the U.S. Senate Judiciary Committee has passed a bill that would overturn *Leegin.* Most states also oppose *Leegin.* Maryland has passed legislation making resale price maintenance *per se* unlawful while several states, including California and New York, have legislation on the books that arguably forbids resale price maintenance. Furthermore, if anticompetitive behavior emerges, it can still be attacked under the rule of reason standard.

Leegin in Practice (Prices)   Immediately after the *Leegin* decision, women's shoe maker Nine West petitioned to be released from a Federal Trade Commission order dating from 2000 that had barred the company from entering minimum-pricing agreements. The FTC granted that request. Following *Leegin,* the online discounter, BabyAge says one of its suppliers, Stanley Furniture Co., insisted that BabyAge raise the price of one of its baby cribs from $778 to $928. BabyAge refused, and it says that Stanley thereafter stopped shipments.[19] Big discounters like eBay and Costco are pressuring Congress to repeal or adjust the law following *Leegin* because suppliers are monitoring and objecting to their discounted prices. Some manufacturers/ suppliers hire companies such as NetEnforcers to constantly scan online pricing to see if their products are being advertised at prices below their specified minimums. For example, NetEnforcers reportedly found a Panasonic home-theatre projector at an advertised price on Buy.com of $43,208.99 when the Panasonic minimum advertised price (MAP) was $49,000.[20] Buy.com says it quickly boosted the price to $49,000. [For an account of Klipsch Group, Inc.'s (manufacturer of premium audio speakers) use of NetEnforcers to maintain its MAP system, see **http://www.netenforcers.com/pdfs/Net Enforcers Case StudyKlipsch Group Inc.pdf**]

> Stanley insisted that BabyAge raise the price of one of its baby cribs.

Question

1. Is the *Leegin* decision good or bad for consumers? Explain.

Vertical Territorial and Customer Restraints

Principal legislation: Sherman Act, Section 1; Federal Trade Commission Act, Section 5.

In addition to price restraints, manufacturers commonly impose nonprice restraints including where and to whom their product may be resold. Those restrictions typically afford an exclusive sales territory to a distributor. Similarly, manufacturers may prevent distributors from selling to some classes of customers (for example, a distributor might be forbidden to sell to an unfranchised retailer). Of course, such arrangements, necessarily retard or eliminate *intrabrand* competition. Because price and service competition among dealers in the same brand ordinarily benefits the consumer, the courts have frequently struck down such arrangements. Still, those territorial and customer allocations also have merits. The *GTE Sylvania* case[21] enunciated those virtues and established the position that vertical restrictions are to be judged case-by-case, balancing interbrand and intrabrand competitive effects while recognizing that interbrand competition is the primary concern of antitrust law. Thus, the rule of reason is to be applied to vertical territorial and customer restraints.

Tying Arrangements

Principal legislation: Clayton Act, Section 3; Sherman Act, Sections 1 and 2; Federal Trade Commission Act, Section 5.

> Clayton act, section 3. That it shall be unlawful for any person engaged in commerce, in the course of such commerce, to lease or make a sale or contract for sale of goods . . . or other commodities . . . or fix a price charged therefore, or discount from or rebate upon, such price, on the condition, agreement, or understanding that the lessee or purchaser thereof shall not use or deal in the goods . . . or other commodities of a competitor or competitors of the lessor or seller, where the effect of such lease, sale, or contract for sale or such condition, agreement, or understanding may be to substantially lessen competition or tend to create a monopoly in any line of commerce.

Tying arrangements (sometimes called "bundling") are another form of nonprice vertical restraint. Typically, tying arrangements permit a customer to buy or lease a desired product (the tying product) only if the customer also buys or leases another, less desirable product (the tied product). In a battle between commercial titans, a large class of merchants led by Walmart, Sears, and others sued Visa and MasterCard, alleging that the bank card associations engaged in unlawful tying arrangements by requiring the merchants to accept the associations' debit cards (the tied product) if they wanted to retain the right to accept the very popular Visa and MasterCard charge cards (the tying product). The result, the merchant/plaintiffs said, was billions in losses because they were forced to pay higher fees for Visa and MasterCard debit cards rather than the lower fees of the competing debit cards they would have preferred to accept. The parties reached a $3 billion out-of-court settlement in 2003.[22] [See Chapter 11 for a discussion of Microsoft's alleged practice of tying its Internet Explorer browser (the tied product) to its dominant Windows operating system (the tying product).]

The Law   The primary antitrust concerns with trying arrangements are twofold: (1) A party who already enjoys market power over the tying product is able to extend that power into the tied product market; and (2) competitors in the tied product market are foreclosed from equal access to that market.

The basic tying violation test is as follows:

1. The existence of separate products. (That is, two products are present rather than one product consisting of two or more components, or two entirely separate products that happen to be elements in a single transaction.)
2. A requirement that the purchase of one of the products (the tying product) is conditioned on the purchase of another product (the tied product).
3. Market power in the tying product.
4. Substantial impact on commerce in the tied product market. (Some courts require a substantial anticompetitive effect in the tied product market.)

Proof of all four of those ingredients establishes *per se* illegality. When all four ingredients cannot be satisfied, the analysis may proceed on a rule of reason basis, weighing pro- and anticompetitive considerations. Critics argue that tying arrangements often enhance consumer welfare and, as such, the *per se* approach should be overturned, as in the *Leegin* case.

Cable/Satellite TV Bundling

Consumers often are frustrated because their cable and satellite television services ordinarily come in packages of channels rather than in an "a la carte" menu where the subscriber can choose and pay for only the subscriber's preferred individual channels. In a recent California case, a group of consumers sued several television networks and cable and satellite distributors, including NBC, Fox, and Time Warner Cable claiming, among other things, that the defendants engaged in Sherman Act violations. The defendant television networks sold television programming to the defendant cable distribution companies in bundles rather than on a per channel basis. The distributors, in turn, sold to consumers in those prepackaged bundles or on a "tier" basis. The plaintiff consumers claimed the practice of offering subscriptions only in bundles was unlawful under the Sherman Act.

Questions

1. Explain the nature of the alleged Sherman Act violation.
2. Who won the case? Explain.

Source: *Rob Brantley, et al. v. NBC Universal, Inc., et al.,* 2011 U.S. App. LEXIS 11176 (9th Cir.).

Franchise Tying?

The following case examines tying allegations in the context of Shell and Texaco gas station franchises. The case turns in part on market definition, a topic that we address more thoroughly in Chapter 11. In brief, in order to establish market power in the tying product, the market itself must be defined. In doing so we consider the geographic market (where the product is sold in commercially significant quantities) and the product market (those products that are interchangeable and thus compete, one with the other).

Rick-Mik Enterprises, Inc. v. Equilon Enterprises, LLC

LEGAL BRIEFCASE
532 F.3d 963 (9th Cir. 2008)

Judge King

Equilon Enterprises, LLC ("Equilon") does business as Shell Oil Products. Equilon's standard franchise agreement requires its franchisees, Shell and Texaco gasoline stations, to use Equilon to process credit-card transactions. In addition to payment for sales of petroleum products, Equilon allegedly gets (1) transaction fees associated with the processing, or (2) some kind of unspecified "kickback" from unidentified banks that process the transactions, or both. Rick-Mik Enterprises, Inc.,

Mike M. Madani, and Alfred Buczkowski (collectively "Rick-Mik") are Equilon franchisees who—on behalf of themselves and other, similarly-situated Equilon franchisees—allege that Equilon violated antitrust laws by illegally tying two distinct products (the franchises and the credit-card processing services). Rick-Mik contends franchisees could pay lower transaction fees from others for credit-card processing. . . .

The district court dismissed the antitrust and related state-law counts. . . .

DISCUSSION
Tying Claim
a. The market power allegations are flawed.
The alleged tying product here is gasoline franchises. Rick-Mik has a contract for an Equilon franchise to sell Shell branded gasoline and diesel. The alleged tied-product is credit-card processing services. Rick-Mik alleges it cannot get a franchise without the "tied" credit-card processing services.

Rick-Mik's complaint does not allege that Equilon has market power in the relevant market, which is the market for the tying product—gasoline franchises. Indeed, other than stating that "[Equilon] rank[s] number one in the industry in branded gasoline stations," there are no specific allegations at all as to the franchise market. The complaint alleges nothing about, for example, what percentage of gasoline franchises are Equilon's (Shell/Texaco) as compared to other franchises like Chevron, Mobil, Marathon Oil, or Union 76. There are no factual allegations as to the percentage of gasoline retail sales that are made through *non-franchise* outlets. There are no factual allegations regarding the amount of power or control that Equilon has over prospective franchisees. There are no factual allegations regarding the relative difficulty of a franchisee to switch franchise brands.

If Equilon lacks market power in the gasoline-franchise market, there can be no cognizable tying claim. For, in that case, Equilon has no power to force, exploit, or coerce a franchisee to purchase a tied-product such as credit card processing (if the processing is a distinct product for tying purposes) or to affect competition in the tied-product market. Such an arrangement would not raise antitrust concerns.

* * * * *

Rick-Mik argues that it alleged sufficient facts to *infer* that Equilon has sufficient economic power in the gasoline-franchise market, which has significant barriers to entry. It points to statistics indicating Equilon is an important player in the petroleum industry. According to . . . the complaint: (1) Equilon sells petroleum products to approximately 9,000 Shell and

Texaco-branded retail outlets; (2) it ranks first in the industry in branded gasoline stations; (3) at 13 percent of the market, it ranks first in total gallons of gasoline sold in the United States; (4) it has annual gross revenues of approximately $24 billion; (5) it is number one or two in gasoline market share in 17 states; (6) it has four refineries, refining approximately 753,000 barrels of petroleum products per day and owns a 50 percent interest in Motiva's three refineries, refining approximately 865,000 barrels of petroleum products per day; (7) it owns an interest in approximately 10,000 miles of pipeline used to transport its petroleum products throughout the United States; and (8) it serves, on average, more than six million customers per day and sells approximately 19 billion gallons of gasoline per year, most of which is purchased by customers' credit or debit cards issued by thousands of banks, banking associations and financial institutions throughout the United States.

All of those allegations, however, relate to the *retail* gasoline market—a market where Rick-Mik is a seller—not the relevant market for franchises where it is a buyer. Further, the statistics alleged in the complaint do not distinguish between franchise-based sales and other potential types of sales (e.g., sales by directly-owned outlets or sales to other distributors). Thus, the complaint fails to allege market power in the relevant market.

Nor is Rick-Mik's complaint saved by the allegation that "Shell and Texaco-branded gasolines are protected by various trademarks, copyrights and patents providing EQUILON sufficient economic power over Plaintiffs in connection with its tying products to appreciably restrain competition in the tied-product market." . . . Because intellectual property rights are no longer presumed to confer market power, *see Illinois Toolworks Inc.*, 547 U.S. at 42-43, Rick-Mik's conclusory allegation that Equilon's intellectual property rights nonetheless do confer market power, unaccompanied by supporting facts, is insufficient.

Finally, the complaint's allegation of a contractual franchise relationship also fails to plead market power. A tying claim generally requires that the defendant's economic power be derived from the market, not from a contractual relationship that the plaintiff has entered into voluntarily. *See, e.g., Queen City Pizza, Inc.*, 124 F.3d at 443 ("where the defendant's 'power' to 'force' plaintiffs to purchase the alleged tying product stems not from the market, but from plaintiffs' contractual agreement to purchase the tying product, no claim will lie.")

* * * * *

b. Credit-card processing is not a distinct product.
There is another fatal flaw in Rick-Mik's complaint. Equilon's franchises are not a separate and distinct product from the credit-card processing services that are part of the franchise.

Franchises, almost by definition, necessarily consist of "bundled" and related products or services—not separate products.

* * * * *

With franchises, "the proper inquiry is . . . whether [the allegedly tied-products] are integral components of the business method being franchised. Where the challenged aggregation is an essential ingredient of the franchised system's formula for success, there is but a single product and no tie in exists as a matter of law." *Principe v. McDonald's Corp.,* 631 F.2d 303, 309 (4th Cir. 1980).

Here, Equilon's credit card services are an essential part of its franchise. Its agreement authorizes Equilon to use credit card proceeds to pay off a franchisee's account (i.e., money the franchisee owes Equilon for the gasoline Equilon delivers to the franchisee). The agreement also authorizes Equilon to charge or refund unauthorized transactions to the franchisee, helping secure the integrity of point-of-sale transactions.

* * * * *

Equilon points to the many other areas which are part and parcel of a franchise: signs, advertising, marketing, appearance, as well as methods of delivery and payment. Similarly, the method of receiving and processing credit transactions is an integral part of the franchise's operation. The franchise and the method of processing credit transactions are not separate products, but part of a single product (the franchise).

* * * * *

With franchises, the franchisee knows the contractual limitations and duties before entering into the contract. A complaint about such contractual obligations is not an antitrust matter.

* * * * *

Affirmed.

Questions

1. *a.* Identify the tying and tied products in the *Rik-Mik* case.
   b. Explain how Rik-Mik attempted to establish that Equilon had market power in the tying product.

2. How does Rik-Mik claim to have been harmed by the alleged tying arrangement?

3. Why did the Court reason that a franchising contract ordinarily cannot, by itself, be the basis for an antitrust claim?

4. Who won this case and why?

5. Apple has recently been accused of tying violations both in the United States and in Europe. In brief, the plaintiffs are claiming that Apple's software prevents music bought from Apple's iTunes from being played on a player other than Apple's iPod. The plaintiffs argue that Apple has monopoly power in the portable digital player market and the online music market and that it uses that power to force consumers to bundle the iPod and iTunes music. The result, the plaintiffs' claim, is fewer options and higher prices. Do you share these concerns about Apple's iPod/iTunes strategy? Explain. For an overview of several claims arising from the iPod/iTunes strategy, see The Apple iPod iTunes Anti-Trust Litigation; *Stavie Somers v. Apple, Inc.,* 2010 U.S. Dist. LEXIS 64772 (N.D. Cal., San Jose Div.).

6. When *Late Night with David Letterman* was an NBC show, the network, for some time, reportedly required those wanting to advertise on *Late Night* (then generally favored by a younger audience) to also buy spots on another talk show, the *Tonight Show with Johnny Carson* (then generally favored by an older audience).
   a. Does that packaging constitute a tying arrangement?
   b. Was it lawful? Explain.

7. Chrysler included the price of a sound system in the base price of its cars. Chrysler's share of the auto market was 10 to 12 percent. Chrysler did not reveal the "subprice" for the sound systems. Independent audio dealers objected on antitrust grounds. Explain their claim. Decide. See *Town Sound and Custom Tops, Inc. v. Chrysler Motor Corp.* 959 F.2d 468 (3d Cir. 1992); cert. den., 113 S.Ct. 196 (1992).

Exclusive Dealing and Requirements Contracts

Principal Legislation: Clayton Act, Section 3; Sherman Act, Section 1.

An *exclusive dealing contract* is an agreement in which a buyer commits itself to deal only with a specific seller, thereby cutting competing sellers out of that share of the market. A *requirements contract* is one in which a seller agrees to supply all of a buyer's needs, or a buyer agrees to purchase all of a seller's output, or both. Exclusive dealing and requirements contracts typically are lawful, but antitrust problems can arise depending on harm to competition. By its nature an exclusive deal results in *market foreclosure;* that is, competitors are denied a source of supply or a market for sale. Thus antitrust issues can emerge depending ordinarily on the market share controlled by the parties. In general, however, manufacturers, distributors, and retailers have broad latitude in negotiating exclusive deals. We want businesses to produce and distribute their products in the manner they consider most efficient.

Gore-Tex

The top of the line in waterproof, breathable fabric seems to be Gore-Tex, but its rivals, including Columbia Sportswear-owned OutDry, say they have better products but have difficulty marketing them because of Gore-Tex's exclusive dealing arrangements with outdoor clothing and sportswear brands. Gore-Tex allegedly requires those wanting to use its products to agree not to use competing brands. The result is an alleged market foreclosure that allows Gore to control an estimated 70 to 90 percent of the relevant market. Gore is being investigated at this writing by both the FTC and European Commission antitrust authorities. *The Wall Street Journal* reported that the two Italian brothers who invented OutDry have received enthusiastic responses to their product. Nonetheless, brands say "almost universally" they cannot use OutDry without endangering their relationships with Gore. [For more details on the Gore-Tex antitrust story, see Thomas Catan, "Gore-Tex Runs into Antitrust Probes," *The Wall Street Journal,* June 22, 2011, p. B1.]

American Needle

> The National Football League was accused of restraint of trade.

In 2010, exclusive dealing concerns reached the U.S. Supreme Court when the National Football League was accused of restraint of trade for giving Reebok in 2000 an exclusive 10-year right to produce and market nearly all NFL-trademarked headware. The plaintiff, American Needle, a Downer's Grove, Illinois apparel manufacturer, was cut out of the premium cap market by the NFL decision. The NFL won at both the trial and federal court of appeals level with both courts ruling that the NFL is a single entity (one business rather than a collection of competing teams/businesses) and thus could not have conspired as the Sherman Act requires. The U.S. Supreme Court, however, reversed the lower courts in 2010 by a 9–0 margin saying that each of the teams is independently owned and managed and each proceeds as a separate, competing economic enterprise pursuing separate economic interests.[23]

The case has now returned to the lower courts to decide the merits of American Needle's restraint of trade complaint. Had the NFL been successful in its one-entity claim the league arguably would have been free to set prices for everything from tickets, to players' salaries to hot dogs without fear of antitrust intervention. The NFL-Reebok exclusive dealing arrangement in the end may prove lawful and even necessary for the successful operation of the league, but if so, prices—for licensed caps, at least—probably will rise, as American Needle alleges they have since the exclusive deal went into place.[24] The decision is a lesson for other joint ventures by competitors, including the National Hockey League and the National Basketball Association, that cooperative activity may be closely scrutinized for anticompetitive behavior. Antitrust lawyers said the American Needle victory was the first by an antitrust plaintiff at the high court since 1992.[25]

Price Discrimination

Principal Legislation: Clayton Act, Section 2, as amended by the Robinson–Patman Act. [For the statutory language, see **http://assembler.law.cornell.edu/uscode/15/13.html**]

Price discrimination involves selling substantially identical goods (not services) at reasonably contemporaneous times to different purchasers at different prices, where the effect may substantially lessen competition or tend to create a monopoly. A seller may resist a Robinson–Patman charge by establishing one of the following defenses: (1) The price differential is attributable to cost savings. (In practice, the cost savings defense has been difficult to establish.) (2) The price differential is attributable to a good faith effort to meet the equally low price of a competitor. (3) Certain transactions are exempt from the act. Of special note is a price change made in response to a changing market. Thus, prices might lawfully be altered for seasonal goods or perishables.

> A coalition of independent video stores sued Blockbuster.

In recent years, a coalition of independent video stores sued Blockbuster claiming that the rental chain and the movie studios conspired to drive the small stores out of business. That litigation failed, as perhaps it should have since the market itself seems to have resolved the dispute. Blockbuster declared bankruptcy in 2010. Apparently, its business model did not keep pace with current consumer demand which now favors newer, perhaps more technologically astute competitors, Redbox, Netflix, and others. Dish Network then acquired Blockbuster in 2011 for $320 million.

The video store cases are among a number in recent years pitting independent operators (such as neighborhood bookstores and local pharmacies) against chains (such as Barnes & Noble and big hospitals) where the independents claim that suppliers charge their giant rivals lower prices than those charged to the small stores. These complaints reflect the philosophical battle over the role of antitrust law in a rapidly changing global market. Should we use antitrust to protect small businesses, thus protecting small towns and an historic way of life in America? Or should we accept the dictates of the market, where the efficiency of giants like Walmart brings low prices and high quality to all?

Free market advocates condemn price discrimination law as an attack on common, consumer-friendly pricing practices that often result in reduced prices. Why, the critics ask, would we assault those who engage in vigorous price competition? The Antitrust Modernization Commission, appointed by the federal government to study whether the antitrust laws need revision, was generally supportive of the current legislative structure, but it did recommend in 2007 that the Robinson-Patman Act be repealed.[26] In fact, the federal government seldom takes an enforcement action under Robinson–Patman, and in five opinions since 1979, the Supreme Court has progressively increased the requirements for success in a Robinson–Patman litigation.[27] Furthermore, the Modernization Commission argued that the act actually hurts the small businesses it was designed to protect because some suppliers refuse to sell to those small businesses simply because they do not want to create legal problems for themselves. Nonetheless, as the following case illustrates, smaller businesses often do turn to Robinson–Patman in their ongoing struggle against what they believe to be the unfair competition of "giants."

District Judge Pauley

Defendants Barnes & Noble, Borders Group, and Walden move for summary judgment on plaintiff, The Intimate Bookshop, Inc's, price discrimination claims. . . .

BACKGROUND

* * * * *

To summarize, Intimate was an independent bookseller that sold books through retail stores located in the mid-Atlantic United States from 1959 until March 31, 1999. Defendants are retailers that sell books and other goods in large stores across the United States and through Internet Web sites. Defendant Borders Group is a holding company that operates bookstores through its subsidiaries, defendants Borders and Walden. Defendant Barnes & Noble operates bookstores and has an interest in defendant B&N.com, an Internet bookseller. Intimate alleges that defendants violated Sections 2(a) and 2(f) of the act through secondary-line price discrimination because they knowingly induced and/or received illegal lower, discriminatory prices on the publishers' books, and that such discriminatory prices injured competition. . . .

Price discrimination is classified into three categories under the act: (1) primary-line price discrimination, which "occurs when a seller's price discrimination harms competition with the seller's competitors;" (2) secondary-line price discrimination, which "occurs when a seller's discrimination impacts competition among the seller's customers; i.e., the favored purchasers and disfavored purchasers;" and (3) tertiary-line price discrimination, which "occurs when the seller's price discrimination harms competition between customers of the favored and disfavored purchasers, even though the favored and disfavored purchasers do not compete directly against another." *George Haug Co. v. Rolls Royce Motor Cars Inc.,* 148 F.3d 136, 141 n.2 (2d Cir. 1988)

DISCUSSION

Sections 2(a) and 2(f) of the Act

In contrast to other antitrust laws, the Robinson–Patman Act was specifically enacted to protect small businesses from discriminatory pricing by manufacturers in favor of large chain stores. . . .

Section 2(a) of the Robinson–Patman Act makes it unlawful for anyone engaged in commerce

to discriminate in price between different purchasers of commodities of like grade and quality, where . . . the effect of such discrimination may be to substantially lessen competition . . . with any person who either grants or knowingly receives the benefits of such discrimination, or with customers of either of them.

To state a claim for secondary-line price discrimination under Section 2(a), a plaintiff must show that (i) the seller conducted sales in interstate commerce; (ii) the seller discriminated in price between two buyers; (iii) the product sold to competing buyers was of the same grade and quality; and (iv) the price discrimination had an unlawful effect on competition.

Additionally, even if Intimate establishes a prima facie case of unlawful price discrimination, defendants are not liable under Sections 2(f) or 2(a) of the act if the lower, discriminatory prices they received are protected by one of the seller's affirmative defenses to price discrimination. Indeed, Sections 2(a) and 2(b) of the act afford sellers various defenses based on cost justifications and competitive conditions.

Robinson–Patman Act Relief

Proof of a violation itself does not create a compensable private injury under the act. A plaintiff is not entitled to "automatic damages" on a successful Section 2(a) or 2(f) price discrimination claim. Instead, a plaintiff must make some showing of "actual injury attributable to something the antitrust laws were designed to prevent.". . .

In that vein, though a plaintiff need not enumerate all possible sources of its loss, it must make some showing that the injury to its business was not caused by factors unrelated to the defendant's price discrimination. . . .

1. Survey Evidence

Intimate attempts to sustain its burden of showing actual injury and causation through a survey conducted by Dr. Bruce Kardon that purports to show that Intimate lost customers to defendants. . . . In that survey, former members of Intimate's book club were contacted and asked questions about where they purchased books and the reasons for choosing that retailer. Dr. Kardon acknowledged at his deposition, however, that his survey could not be used to show any dollar value of Intimate's lost sales to any defendant. Indeed, the survey does not even question respondents whether they stopped purchasing books from Intimate and switched to another retailer.

Further, the survey did not determine the year, the geographical market, or the extent to which survey respondents shopped at a defendant's store.

Finally, the survey does not provide an adequate basis to discern whether, and the extent to which, the defendants' lawful, as opposed to unlawful, competitive conduct caused injury to Intimate.

Accordingly, this Court finds that Dr. Kardon's survey is insufficient to establish a causal link between Intimate's injuries and the defendants' allegedly unlawful conduct.

2. Expert Reports

Second, Intimate cannot meet the causation requirement through any of its other experts' reports or testimony. As noted, Intimate submitted five expert reports in addition to the Kardon Report that purportedly opine on its damages claim as well as its claim that defendants violated the act. Each of Intimate's experts admitted at their deposition, however, that (i) they could not establish any causal link between Intimate's lost sales and profits and defendants' alleged receipt of unlawful discounts; and (ii) their damages calculations and opinions are based merely on an assumption that the defendants' alleged violations of the act were the sole cause of Intimate's lost sales and profits. . . .

3. Disaggregation

Third, Intimate has provided no evidence, in any form, that defendants' alleged violation of the act, as opposed to other intervening market factors, was a material cause of its [lost] sales and profits. In fact, Wallace Kuralt, one of Intimate's owners, acknowledged at his deposition that some of Intimate's business loss may be attributable to factors other than the defendants' discriminatory activity, including (i) competition with nonparties Books-a-Million and Media Play; (ii) adverse business decisions; (iii) undercapitalization; (iv) a fire at plaintiff's flagship Chapel Hill, North Carolina, location; (v) competition with franchise bookselling chains and other independent bookstores; (vi) competition with nonparty mass merchants, such as Wal-Mart and Kmart and discount warehouses, such as Price Club, Costco, and Sam's Club; and (vii) competition with specialty book retailers such as Williams Sonoma, Office Max, Staples, and Home Depot.

* * * * *

Intimate's survey and damages models are impermissibly fraught with assumptions and speculation, which unquestionably fail to show that the alleged discriminatory prices the defendants received caused Intimate actual injury.

* * * * *

[Summary judgment dismissing the Robinson–Patman claims is granted.]

Questions

1. Why did Intimate Bookshop lose this case?

2. Explain why this case involves secondary-line price discrimination.

3. In what sense does the Robinson–Patman Act arguably reduce efficiency, thus harming consumer welfare?

4. Texaco sold gasoline at its retail tank wagon prices to Hasbrouck, an independent Texaco retailer, but granted discounts to distributors Gull and Dompier. Dompier also sold at the retail level. Gull and Dompier both delivered their gas directly to retailers and did not maintain substantial storage facilities. During the period in question, sales at the stations supplied by the two distributors grew dramatically, while Hasbrouck's sales declined. Hasbrouck filed suit against Texaco, claiming that the distributor discount constituted a Robinson–Patman violation. Texaco defended, saying the discount reflected the services the distributors performed for Texaco, and that the arrangement did not harm competition. Decide. Explain. See *Texaco v. Ricky Hasbrouck,* 496 U.S. 543 (1990).

5. Utah Pie produced frozen pies in its Salt Lake City plant. Utah's competitors, Carnation, Pet, and Continental, sometimes sold pies in Salt Lake City at prices beneath those charged in other markets. Indeed, Continental's prices in Salt Lake City were beneath its direct costs plus overhead. Pet sold to Safeway using Safeway's private label at a price lower than that at which the same pies were sold under the Pet label. Pet employed an industrial spy to infiltrate Utah Pie and gather information. Utah Pie claimed that Carnation, Pet, and Continental were in violation of Robinson–Patman. Decide. Explain. See *Utah Pie Co. v. Continental Baking Co.,* 386 U.S. 685 (1967).

Predatory Pricing

Principal legislation—Sherman Act, Section 2.

Can a giant legally reduce its prices below operating costs until a competing discounter drops out of the market and then raise those prices to supracompetitive levels? In 2009 the

European Commission fined Intel $1.45 billion for *predatory pricing* and other alleged misconduct. Essentially, Intel was accused of reducing chip prices by unlawfully paying rebates/discounts to computer manufacturers and retailers to persuade them not to use rival chips. Among other arguments, Intel claims the rebates had the desirable effect of saving money for consumers, but critics say consumer choice was reduced by discouraging deals with Intel rivals resulting in higher prices and potentially reduced quality, in the long term. Intel also agreed in 2009 to pay Advanced Micro Devices (AMD), a smaller, rival chipmaker, $1.25 billion to settle AMD's allegations of predatory pricing (among other claims).[28]

Predatory pricing charges under European precedents have some reasonable probability of success, but in the United States they are very difficult to win. The U.S. Justice Department claimed that American Airlines engaged in predatory pricing in attempting to monopolize air travel at the Dallas–Fort Worth Airport from 1995 to 1997. Justice argued that American Airlines lowered its prices to drive out seven discount carriers in the expectation that it could then recover its losses by charging monopoly prices. A federal court of appeals, however, ruled for American Airlines, holding that the government was unable to prove that American had priced its flights below cost (as measured by some appropriate formulation, such as average variable cost).[29] Thus, the government had failed to satisfy the standard U.S. two-part test for establishing predatory pricing:

- Pricing below cost.
- A "dangerous probability" of recouping the losses suffered from the below-cost pricing.[30]

The *American Airlines* decision could be seen as a great victory for consumers in that it supports the right to cut prices as low as possible. But consider *BusinessWeek*'s description of American's pricing practices:

> . . . Between Dallas and Kansas City, for instance, American's average one-way ticket was $108 before low-cost start-up Vanguard Airlines Inc. entered the market in early 1995. That prompted American to cut fares to $80 and almost double the number of daily flights to 14. When Vanguard gave up in December 1995, American jacked up prices to $147 and scaled back the number of flights. Justice lawyers even had memos from American execs plotting the upstart's demise.[31]

Antitrust Confronts Intellectual Property

When Google, Pfizer, Monsanto, Adobe, or any other technology innovator, big or small, introduces a new product we probably take for granted the resulting boost in the quality of our lifestyle, the jobs created, and the promise of additional advances in the future. More and more, however, our social and economic welfare is dependent on those technological breakthroughs. In order to encourage and protect *intellectual property* innovations, the law provides *patents* and *copyrights* as shields to preserve the innovator's rights. (For additional patent and copyright materials, refer to the index in the back of this text.) Preserving those rights, however, can lead to antitrust abuse since a patent or copyright often confers market power. In recent years, therefore, the federal government and legal experts have given increasing attention to the quite unsettled line between intellectual property, on the one hand, and antitrust law on the other. Antitrust law, designed for smokestack industries, is struggling to adjust to our contemporary, knowledge-based economy.

We believe patent and copyright protection encourages innovation and protects creators' legitimate interests, but we also believe in free access to knowledge as something of a personal right and as a necessary precondition to continued progress and prosperity. We need the stimulus of antitrust-protected competition to lower prices and maximize consumer welfare, but we also need the shelter of intellectual property rights to encourage innovation and investment. If we do not use patents and copyrights (and sometimes trademarks) to protect intellectual property, will creative efforts be diminished? In providing intellectual property protection, however, do we open the door to monopoly behaviors? As one high-tech blog put it, "Can Antitrust Law Stop Abuses of Intellectual Property and Free Access to Knowledge?"[32] [For more about open global access to knowledge (a2k), see **http://a2knetwork.org**]

The United States Supreme Court has ruled that patents should not automatically be treated as monopolies.[33] Abuse of the market power conferred by a patent, therefore, must be proven rather than presumed. And even if market power is established, an antitrust violation does not occur unless some competitive wrong is established. As the Supreme Court said: "To safeguard the incentive to innovate, the possession of monopoly power will not be found unlawful unless it is accompanied by an element of anticompetitve *conduct*."[34] Generally, intellectual property disputes are analyzed by the same antitrust reasoning—monopoly, exclusive dealing, tying arrangements, etc.—as is applied elsewhere in the economy.

Antitrust versus intellectual property disputes have become rather common. In 2010, for example, the U.S. consumer services company, IDT, filed antitrust charges against Ebay and Skype claiming the two were trying to monopolize the Internet-based telephone market (known as VoIP—Voice over Internet Protocol). IDT had sued both companies in 2006 claiming they had infringed on IDT patents for Internet Protocol-based communications (IP is a method by which data is sent from one computer to another via the Internet). Then later in 2010 the parties abruptly settled all of their disputes out of court.[35]

Intellectual property giant, IBM, is accused in Europe at this writing of abusing its "100 percent monopoly in the market for mainframe [computer] operating systems" by denying customers the opportunity to run that IBM operating system on anything other than IBM's mainframe hardware.[36] The complaint by software developer, Turbo Hercules, alleges that IBM is engaging in an unlawful tying arrangement by requiring customers to use only IBM hardware in order to have access to IBM's dominant operating systems software.

Apple Backs Down

In what *The Wall Street Journal* calls "an uncharacteristic about-face," Apple agreed in September 2010 to relax its rules for developing applications (apps) for its iPhones, iPads, and iPods.[37] In May 2010, Apple had announced that anyone wanting to develop apps for its mobile devices would be required to do so using only Apple software tools. Apple said it did so to maintain quality, but the announcement met stiff resistance from app developers while drawing antitrust inquiries by the federal government. Critics said that Apple might be trying to stop developers from using rival Adobe's Flash software.[38] That is, the concern was that Apple was using its power in one market, mobile device apps, to control another market, apps development software. The Apple about-face, one expert said, "will eventually lead to much more complex and refined apps in the iTunes Store. And everyone should be pleased about that."[39]

Questions

1. *CNET News* asked technology law expert, Jason Schultz, about the antitrust implications of Apple's original plan to restrict the tools used in developing apps: "It's Apple's platform. Why can't it pick what programming languages can be used on its own App Store?"[40] Answer that question.

2. Broadly, how can we decide when antitrust law should intervene to restrict intellectual property rights?

Internet Exercise

Using the "Frequently Asked Questions" on the "Small Business Notes" Web page [**http://www.smallbusinessnote.com/operating/legal/antitrust/faqs.html**], answer these questions:

1. Shopping for a stereo loudspeaker made by Sound Corporation, I couldn't find a dealer who would sell it for less than the manufacturer's suggested retail price. Isn't that price fixing?

2. I own a retail clothing store and the Brand Company refuses to sell me any of its line of clothes. These clothes are very popular in my area, so this policy is hurting my business. Isn't it illegal for Brand to refuse to sell to me?

3. I operate two stores that sell recorded music. My business is being ruined by giant discount store chains that sell their products for less than my wholesale cost. I thought there were laws against price discrimination, but I can't afford the legal fees to fight the big corporations. Can you help?

Chapter Questions

1. After reading this chapter, what is your judgment about the antitrust system?
   a. Does it work? Explain.
   b. How might it be altered?
   c. Could we place more reliance on the market? Explain.
   d. Do the statutes and case law, as a body, seem to form a rational package? Explain.
   e. Should antitrust policy focus exclusively on economic considerations or should social welfare goals (such as maintenance of full employment and the dispersal of political power) assume greater importance? Explain.

2. In recent years, Amazon, Walmart, Target, and others have been dramatically discounting some bestselling books; sometimes selling popular hardcover titles at under $10. In Europe's major publishing markets other than the United Kingdom, most new books, both print and online, must be sold at the price specified by the publisher; that is, discount pricing is forbidden by law.
   a. Why would Europeans accept antidiscounting laws that keep new book prices high?
   b. How would you expect the antidiscounting laws to affect the prices of used books?

    c. Germany, with a population of about 82 million, has about 7,000 bookstores while the United States, with a population of over 300 million, has about 11,000 bookstores. Is America's literary culture threatened by allowing giant retailers to aggressively discount? Explain.

3. Subway sandwich shops required all franchisees to employ a computerized point-of-sale (POS) system. The only approved system was provided by an unrelated company, RBS. Vendors of a competing POS system sued Subway's parent, Doctor's Associates, alleging, among other things, an unlawful tying arrangement.

    a. Describe the alleged tie.

    b. Defend Doctor's Associates (Subway).

    c. Explain what the plaintiffs would need to demonstrate in order to prevail. See *Subsolutions, Inc. v. Doctor's Associates, Inc.,* 62 F.Supp.2d 616 (D. Conn. 1999).

4. In *Continental T.V., Inc. v. GTE Sylvania, Inc.,* 433 U.S. 36 (1977), the U.S. Supreme Court took the position that interbrand, rather than intrabrand, agreements must be the primary concern of antitrust law.

    a. Why did the Court take that view?

    b. In your opinion, is the Court correct? Explain.

    c. Explain the "free-rider" problem that frequently concerns the courts in cases involving vertical territorial restraints, among others.

5. Could Whirlpool, the appliance manufacturer, lawfully refuse to deal with any purchaser that sells the products of a competitor such as General Electric? Explain.

6. The NCAA and the Collegiate Licensing Company (the NCAA's marketing company) license college athletes' likenesses for commercial use in video games, the rebroadcast of games, DVDs, etc. The players receive no compensation either during their college years or thereafter. The NCAA requires athletes to sign a form allowing the use of the athletes' names and pictures to promote the NCAA and its activities. Former UCLA athlete Ed O'Bannon and other plaintiffs claim the form requires athletes to "relinquish all rights in perpetuity to the commercial use of their images, including after they graduate and are no longer subject to NCAA regulations." O'Bannon argues that athletic participation is conditioned on signing the form. Among other claims, the plaintiffs argue that the NCAA rules and marketing arrangements constitute conspiracies among the NCAA, its member schools and others to violate the Sherman Antitrust Act. Explain the plaintiff's antitrust claims. For a preliminary ruling and analysis, see *Edward O'Bannon v. National Collegiate Athletic Association,* 2010 U.S. District LEXIS 19170 (N.D. Cal.)

7. Tanaka played soccer at the University of Southern California, a member of the PAC 10 Conference. She became unhappy, asked if she could transfer, and was told that she could. She decided to go to another PAC 10 school, UCLA. USC, unhappy with that choice, invoked an NCAA rule limiting transfers within a conference. The rule required her to sit out one year and to lose one year of eligibility. She sued USC and the NCAA on restraint of trade grounds.

    a. Explain her claim.

    b. Decide the case. Explain your decision. See *Tanaka v. University of Southern California,* 252 F.3d 1059 (9th Cir. 2001).

8. Assume two fertilizer dealerships, Grow Quick and Fertile Fields, hold 70 percent and 30 percent, respectively, of the fertilizer business in the farm community of What Cheer, Iowa. Assume the owner of Fertile Fields learns via inquiry, hearsay, and the like of Grow Quick's price quotes. Then, each growing season the Fertile Fields owner sets her prices exactly equal to those of her competitor. Is that practice unlawful? Explain.

9. Given functionally identical competing products, why is identical pricing virtually inevitable—at least over the long run?

10. In 1968, Business Electronics Corporation (BEC) became the exclusive retailer in the Houston, Texas, area of electronic calculators manufactured by Sharp Electronics Corporation. In 1972, Sharp appointed Hartwell as a second retailer in the Houston area. Sharp published a list of suggested minimum retail prices, but its written dealership agreements with BEC and Hartwell did not obligate either to observe them, or to charge any other specific price. BEC's retail prices were often below Sharp's suggested retail prices and generally below Hartwell's retail prices, even though Hartwell too sometimes priced below Sharp's suggested retail prices. Hartwell complained to Sharp on a number of occasions about BEC's prices. In 1973, Hartwell gave Sharp the ultimatum that Hartwell would terminate his dealership unless Sharp ended its relationship with BEC within 30 days. Sharp terminated BEC's dealership. BEC filed suit alleging that Sharp and Hartwell had unlawfully conspired to terminate BEC and that the conspiracy was illegal *per se* under the Sherman Act, Section I. Decide the case. Explain. See *Business Electronics Corporation v. Sharp Electronics Corporation,* 485 U.S. 717 (1988).

11. Some antitrust experts argue that a firm possessing market power should be challenged by the government with the goal of eradicating the power as quickly as possible. Others maintain that the government should be patient with short-term market power. Explain those two points of view.

12. Adidas contracts with NCAA schools and their coaches to promote its products. An NCAA rule limits the amount of advertising that may appear on uniforms and equipment. Adidas complained that those restrictions on promotional rights "artificially limit the price and quality options available to apparel manufacturers as consumers of promotional space, force manufacturers to pay additional amounts for billboard space or other advertising, decrease the selection of apparel offered to the end consumer, increase the price of the apparel for end consumers, and financially benefit the NCAA." Adidas sued the NCAA on antitrust grounds.
    a. What antitrust violations were cited by Adidas?
    b. Decide the case. Explain. See *Adidas v. NCAA,* 64 F.Supp.2d 1097 (1999).

13. A board-certified anesthesiologist was denied admission to the Jefferson Parish Hospital staff because the hospital had an exclusive services contract with a firm of anesthesiologists. The contract required all surgery patients at the hospital to use that firm for their anesthesiology work. Seventy percent of the patients in the parish were served by hospitals other than Jefferson. The anesthesiologist who was denied admission sued the hospital, claiming the contract was unlawful.
    a. What antitrust violation was raised by the plaintiff?
    b. Decide. Explain. See *Jefferson Parish Hospital District No. 2 v. Hyde,* 466 U.S. 2 (1984).

14. In 1990 the American Institute of Certified Public Accountants agreed to enforce a change in its ethics rules that allowed its members to accept contingent fees and commissions from nonaudit clients. The agreement was the result of a consent order between the AICPA and the Federal Trade Commission. Likewise, in 1990 the American Institute of Architects signed a consent order with the Justice Department that forbade the Institute from adopting policies that would restrain architects from bidding competitively for jobs, offering discounts, or doing work without compensation.
    a. What antitrust violation was the government seeking to stem in both of these cases?
    b. What defenses were offered by the professions for their policies?

15. Starter Sportswear had a license to manufacture and sell satin professional team jackets marketed as "authentic" because they were styled in the manner of jackets actually worn by the members of the various teams. A Starter policy statement provided that it would sell only to retailers that carry a representative amount of Starter's full line of jackets. Starter also had a minimum order policy specifying that it wouldn't deal with retailers who sought quantities beneath that minimum order. Trans Sport, a retailer, began selling Starter jackets to other retailers who did not meet Starter's requirements. At that point, Starter declined to deal further with Trans Sport. Trans Sport then sued Starter.
    a. List Trans Sport's claims against Starter.
    b. Resolve those claims, raising all the relevant issues. See *Trans Sport, Inc. v. Starter Sportswear, Inc.,* 964 F.2d 186 (2d Cir. 1992).

Notes

1. Editorial, "Return of the Trustbusters," *The New York Times,* May 13, 2009 [**http://www.nytimes. com**].

2. Jia Lynn Yang, "To Consumer Advocates, Obama's Antitrust Enforcement Looks Like More of the Same," *The Washington Post,* September 7, 2010, [**www.washingtonpost.com/**].

3. *Standard Oil Co. of New Jersey v. United States,* 221 U.S. 1 (1911).

4. Alexander McIntyre, Jr., "Halt to 'Call-Arounds' Puts La Quinta in Spotlight," *LEXOLOGY,* May 27, 2010 [**http://www.lexology.com/**].

5. This analysis is drawn from William Kovacic, "The Identification and Proof of Horizontal Agreements under the Antitrust Laws," *Antitrust Bulletin* 38, no. 1 (Spring 1993), p. 5.

6. *Bell Atlantic Corp. v. Twombly,* 127 S.Ct. 1955 (2007).

7. Press Release, "Taiwan LCD Producer Agrees to Plead Guilty and Pay $220 Million Fine for Participating in LCD Price-Fixing Conspiracy," [**http://www.justice.gov/atr/public/press_ releases/2009/252936.htm**].

8. Dawn Kawamoto, "LG, Sharp, Chunghwa Admit to LCD Price Fixing," *Business Tech,* November 12, 2008 [**http://news.cnet.com/8301-1001_3-10095219-92.html**].

9. Associated Press, "Fines Issued in Price-Fixing Scandal," *Waterloo/Cedar Falls Courier,* April 13, 2011, p. B7.

10. Bill Myers, "$100 Million Accord in Price-Fix Lawsuit," *Chicago Daily Law Bulletin,* July 29, 2004.

11. *The Washington Post,* "Vitamin Giants to Settle Antitrust Suit," *Waterloo/Cedar Falls Courier,* September 8, 1999, p. A9.

12. Jeff Chorney, "Amnesty International: S.F. Antitrust Prosecutors Are Breaking Cartels with Immunity," *The Recorder,* September 27, 2004, p. 1.

13. The analysis in this paragraph relies considerably on Donald M. Falk, "Antitrust and Refusals to Deal after *Nynex v. Discon,*" *Practical Lawyer* 46, no. 3 (2000), p. 25.

14. See, e.g., Herbert J. Hovenkamp, "Unilateral Refusals to Deal, Vertical Integration, and the Essential Facility Doctrine," July 1, 2008, *U. of Iowa Legal Studies Research Paper* No. 08-31. Available at SSRN: **http://ssrn.com/abstract=1144675**

15. *United States v. Visa and MasterCard,* 344 F.3d 229 (2d. Cir. 2003); cert. den. *Visa v. United States,* 125 S.Ct. 45 (2004).

16. *United States v. Colgate & Co.,* 250 U.S. 300 (1919).

17. *State Oil Co. v. Khan,* 118 S.Ct. 275 (1997).

18. *Dr. Miles Medical Co. v. John D. Park & Sons Co.,* 220 U.S. 373 (1911).

19. Joseph Pereira, "Price-Fixing Makes Comeback after Supreme Court Ruling," *The Wall Street Journal Online,* August 18, 2008, p. A1.

20. Joseph Pereira, "Discounters, Monitors Face Battle on Minimum Pricing," *The Wall Street Journal,* December 4, 2008, p. A1.

21. *Continental T.V., Inc. v. GTE Sylvania, Inc.,* 433 U.S. 36 (1977).

22. *Wal-Mart v. Visa and MasterCard,* 396 F.3d 96 (2005).

23. *American Needle v. National Football League,* 130 S.Ct. 2201 (2010).

24. Ken Bilson and Alan Schwarz, "Antitrust Case Has Implications Far Beyond N.F.L.," *The New York Times,* January 7, 2010 [**www.nytimes.com**].

25. Editorial, "Throwing the Rule Book at the N.F.L.," *The New York Times,* May 26, 2010 [**www.nytimes.com**].

26. "Panel Urges Repeal of '30s Era Antitrust Law," *Reuters,* April 3, 2007 [**http://www.reuters.com/articleousiv/idUKN0244771620070403**].

27. Elaine Foreman and Robert Skitol, "Volvo v. Reeder: Narrow Holding, Broad Implications," *The Antitrust Source,* March 2006, p. 1.

28. Steve Lohr and James Kanter, "A.M.D.-Intel Settlement Won't End Their Woes," *The New York Times,* November 13, 2009 [**www.nytimes.com**].

29. *United States v. AMR Corp,* 335 F.3d 1109 (10th Cir. 2003).

30. *Brooke Group Ltd. v. Brown & Williamson Tobacco Corp.,* 509 U.S. 209 (1993).

31. Dan Carney, "Predatory Pricing: Cleared for Takeoff," *BusinessWeek,* May 14, 2001, p. 50.

32. Mike Masnick, "Can Antitrust Law Stop Abuses of Intellectual Property and Free Access to Knowledge?" *techdirt,* August 19, 2010. [**http://www.techdirt.com/articles/20100812/03235710603.shtml**].

33. *Illinois Tool Works v. Independent Ink,* 547 U.S. 28 (2006).

34. *Verizon Communications Inc. v. Law Offices of Curtis V. Trinko, LLP,* 540 U.S. 398, 407 (2004).

35. Nancy Gohring, "Skype Avoids Antitrust Suit in Settlement with IDT," *PC World,* August 6, 2010 [**http://www.pcworld.com/**].

36. Catherine Saez, "Open Source Company Alleges IBM Antitrust: IBM Requests Analysis," *Intellectual Property Watch,* April 20, 2010 [**http://www.ip-watch.org/**].

37. Yukari Kane and Thomas Catan, "Apple Blinks in Apps Fight," *The Wall Street Journal,* September 10, 2010 [**http://online.wsj.com/**].

38. "Apple Clamps Down on Code Tools," *BBC News,* April 13, 2010 [**http://newsbbc.co.uk/2/hi/8616274.stm/**].

39. Charlie Sorrel, "Apple Eases App Development Rules, Adobe Surges," *Wired.com,* September 9, 2010 [**http://www.wired.com/gadgetlab/2010/09/**].

40. Erica Ogg, "Apple, the App Store, and Antitrust," *CNET News,* May 5, 2010 [**http://news.cnet.com/**].

Antitrust Law—Monopolies and Mergers

After completing this chapter, students will be able to:

1. Explain how Microsoft violated U.S. antitrust laws.

2. Analyze when a monopoly has been created.

3. Identify the potential benefits and hazards of mergers.

4. Distinguish between horizontal and vertical mergers.

5. Explain premerger notification requirements.

6. Describe remedies for mergers determined to be anticompetitive.

7. Analyze when a horizontal merger is anticompetitive.

8. Analyze when a vertical merger creates anticompetitive "market foreclosure."

9. Contrast antitrust enforcement in the United States and the European Union (EU).

Introduction—Google, Microsoft, and Monopoly

Google Too Big?

Google arguably dominates our Internet era much in the manner that Microsoft stood alone atop the PC era. Google has about two thirds of the U.S. Internet search market and 76 percent of search advertising. Antitrust lawyer Gary Reback has attacked Google's power saying Google is the "arbiter of every single thing on the Web, and it favors its properties over everyone else's. What it wants to do is control Internet traffic. Anything that undermines its ability to do that is threatening." At this writing in 2011, the European Union is investigating allegations that Google is using its online search dominance to harm competitors. Among other things, Google is accused of rigging search-ranking results to favor its interests and harm its competitors. Likewise at this writing, the U.S. Federal Trade Commission and Justice Department have initiated antitrust inquiries into Google's business practices. Should we be worried about market dominance by Google? We have learned a lot about antitrust law in the high-tech era from the long pursuit of Microsoft by the United States, many of the 50 states and the European Union. Read the Microsoft story below and the monopoly analysis that follows. How would you defend Google as a matter of law?

Sources: Associated Press, "Inquiry by FTC Turns Up Heat on Google," *The Des Moines Register,* June 25, 2011, p. 16A; Jim Puzzanghera and David Sarno, "European Inquiry Shows Google's Size Matters," *latimes.com,* December 1, 2010 [**latimes.com/business/la-fi-google-eu-antitrust-20101201,0,5430414.story**]; and Brad Stone, "Sure, It's Big. But Is that Bad?" *The New York Times,* May 21, 2010 [**http://www.nytimes.com/**].

Microsoft a Monopolist?   Is Microsoft an outsized, predatory lawbreaker, an amazing force for technological progress, or both? The U.S. Justice Department, 18 states, and the District of Columbia went to trial against Microsoft in 1998, claiming not that the software giant was too big, but that it had violated various antitrust laws in gaining and maintaining its market dominance. An epic legal struggle followed with major elements of the American justice system challenging one of the world's richest men, Bill Gates.

> An epic legal struggle followed with major elements of the American justice system challenging one of the world's richest men, Bill Gates.

A federal district court in 2000 and later a federal court of appeals ruled that Microsoft had violated federal antitrust laws by maintaining its 95 percent share of the Intel-compatible PC operating systems market through anticompetitive means (basically using its monopoly power to coerce customers to buy other Microsoft products such as its browser, Internet Explorer).[1] The district court judge ordered Microsoft split into two companies as a remedy for its antitrust wrongs, but the court of appeals threw out that order. Thereafter, the case was settled out of court with Microsoft agreeing, among other things, to not retaliate unfairly against other software and computer makers, to disclose some software code, and to be monitored by a federal judge. (That monitoring concluded in 2011.)

The settlement, though somewhat of a victory for Microsoft, might also be regarded as a victory for common sense in allowing Microsoft to go forward with its remarkable work. The decision places considerable faith in the market, as it probably should in America; but the case also represents a powerful affirmation of the government's authority to attack monopoly behavior no matter how prominent the wrongdoer.

Settlements   As it turns out, the federal antitrust charges were only the beginning of Microsoft's battles. Settlements with Novell, Sun Microsystems, AOL, RealNetworks, and others cost Microsoft billions. European Union antitrust enforcers pursued Microsoft for a decade before settling their claims out of court in 2010. The EU argument, much like the concerns in the United States, was that Microsoft's market dominance allowed it to effectively force its Windows operating system users to also use its Internet Explorer browser. The settlement required Microsoft to provide a pop-up screen that would allow European customers to choose a browser other than Explorer thus likely building the market share of rival browsers. The settlement closes Microsoft's European problems that had previously included more than $2 billion in fines. The Microsoft struggles underline the aggressive stance of EU antitrust regulators. Since 25 percent of the global market for many products resides in the European Union, all big companies must now think more carefully about how their practices will be received by EU regulators even if those practices are not of concern to U.S. regulators.

Power   Arguably, antitrust intervention has been healthy for competition. Internet Explorer use is down by 1 percent in Britain and 2.5 percent in France. But perhaps the market has simply corrected itself? In the United States, Microsoft's share of the browser market has fallen from more than 90 percent to about 60 percent, while Firefox (23 percent) and Chrome (9 percent) have grown rapidly.[2] In any case, the pursuit of Microsoft is a powerful testament to our hunger for fairness and justice, but it also offers a less edifying message, as CNBC journalist Alan Murray explained in *The Wall Street Journal:*

> The Microsoft saga serves as a reminder of an important truth: Capitalists, for the most part, don't care much for capitalism. Their goal is to make money. And if they can do it without messy competition, so much the better. As long as it keeps its monopoly, Microsoft can afford to share the wealth with its onetime rivals. For Microsoft, those fines and payments add up to less than a year's profit from the operating system. For the others, it's easier to take Microsoft's money than fight.[3]

> ## Whether a giant bullied its rivals.

The Microsoft battle was about whether a giant bullied its rivals, but it was also about the very nature of capitalism—that is, the role of the market and government in American life. The case obliges us to think about what we want America to be and what role the law should play in securing that ideal. By considering Microsoft and other cases, we can learn the rudiments of the law while thinking about how much faith we want to place in the free market. Most crucially, we should ask ourselves whether the market alone can preserve genuine democracy and social justice, or whether we must employ antitrust law to attack those great concentrations of power that sometimes threaten our core values.

Questions

1. *a.* Do you see increasing concentrations of wealth and power as threats to America's long-term welfare? Explain.
   b. If that concentration is a concern, is antitrust law the best remedy?
2. Does the *Microsoft* case stand simply for the view that bigness is bad? Explain.
3. Critics have argued that technology is eliminating the imperfections of the market, making antitrust law enforcement obsolete in this high-tech era.
   a. Explain that argument.
   b. Now build the argument that high-tech industries may actually be especially susceptible to antitrust problems because of the need to maintain equipment compatibility.

Part One—Monopoly

Both the federal district court and the court of appeals in the *Microsoft* case concluded that the computer giant held monopoly power in the Intel-compatible PC operating systems market. How did those courts reach that conclusion? How do we know when an organization is an unlawful monopolist? An extensive, sophisticated, yet imperfect system of analysis has emerged. [For the American Bar Association Antitrust section, see **http://www.americanbar. org/groups/antitrust_law.html**]

Principal Monopoly Legislation: Sherman Act, Section 2

> Every person who shall monopolize, or attempt to monopolize, or combine or conspire with any other person or persons, to monopolize any part of the trade or commerce among the several States, or with foreign nations, shall be deemed guilty of a felony punishable by a fine.

Section 5 of the Federal Trade Commission Act applies to antitrust cases although the wisdom of that use is disputed.

Monopoly Defined From an economic viewpoint, a monopoly is a situation in which one firm holds the power to control prices and/or exclude competition in a particular market. The general legal test for monopolization is:

1. The possession of monopoly power in the relevant market, and
2. The willful acquisition or maintenance of that power, as distinguished from growth or development as a consequence of a superior product, business acumen, or historic accident.[4]

Thus the critical inquiries are the percentage of the market held by the alleged monopolist and the behavior that produced and maintained that market share. Antitrust law does not punish efficient companies who legitimately earn and maintain large market shares.

Indeed, high market concentration often promotes competition, whereas a fragmented market of many small firms may produce higher prices. (Imagine a retail food market of many corner grocery stores and no supermarkets.) Nonetheless, the federal government continues to rely strongly on market concentration data (structure) in combination with evidence of actual behavior (conduct) to identify anticompetitive situations. Market share alone is highly unlikely to lead to antitrust action, but a high market share acquired and/or maintained via abusive conduct (as alleged in *Microsoft*) is likely to be challenged. In 2009, the Obama antitrust authorities withdrew a Bush-era report that had advocated a monopoly policy that the Obama officials considered too cautious and that showed, they felt, too much faith in self-correcting/self-policing monopoly markets. Nonetheless, the Obama approach to antitrust enforcement at this writing has been measured.

Oligopoly A few firms sharing monopoly power constitute an oligopoly. Oligopolistic markets are common in American life, and they have emerged in some increasingly concentrated global markets as well. A recent *New York Times* headline read: "Rising Beer Prices Hint at Oligopoly."[5] With Belgian brewery giant, InBev's 2008 takeover of Anheuser-Busch and the 2007 MillerCoors joint venture, the two companies control about 80 percent of the U.S. beer market and four megabreweries (Anheuser Busch InBev, SAB Miller, Heineken International, and Molson Coors) account for about half of the world's beer sales.[6] Recently, beer prices in the United States have

> Two companies control about 80 percent of the U.S. beer market.

been rising even as the economy has slowed. The U.S. Justice Department reportedly has been looking into the situation, perhaps not so much because of suspicions of price fixing as because of concerns that the extraordinary concentration in the beer market may give the remaining giants unusual pricing power. On the other hand, oligopoly conditions produce significant economies of scale, and also open the door to small, local, craft brewers. Sales in the U.S. craft segment rose 7 percent in 2009, while overall beer sales in North America declined by 2 percent.[7]

PRACTICING ETHICS   Apple a Monopolist?

The New York Times and Billboard reported in 2010 that the U.S. Justice Department was making preliminary inquiries into Apple's online music marketing practices. Apple controls 69 percent of the online music market with the second-place Amazon MP3 store at 8 percent. Reportedly, the Justice Department is looking into allegations that Apple has pressured music labels to discontinue giving Amazon exclusive access to music about to be released. Billboard reported that Apple urged music labels to stop participating in Amazon's "Daily Deal" where Amazon got one-day exclusive, prerelease sales rights on some new songs in exchange for heavily promoting them. To back up its requests, Apple allegedly withdrew marketing support for some releases featured as Daily Deals.

Questions

1. Is it unethical for Apple to control 69 percent of the online music market? Explain.

2. Would it be unethical of Apple to use its marketing and financial leverage to discourage music labels from giving competitors such as Amazon exclusive dealing opportunities like the "Daily Deal?" Explain.

Sources: Brad Stone, "Apple Is Said to Face Inquiry about Online Music," *The New York Times*, May 25, 2010 [http://www.nytimes.com/2010/05/26/technology/26apple.html?_r=1]; and Ed Christman, "Apple Agonistes," *Billboard.biz*, March 6, 2010 [http://www.billboard.biz/].

AFTERWORD

Apple seems to be receiving some of the antitrust attention that formerly was directed to Microsoft. The online music concern noted above is one of several antitrust inquiries or lawsuits, both private and public, which are now being directed at Apple. As explained in Chapter 10, the federal government in early 2010 commenced an inquiry into Apple's contractual relationships with iPhone and iPad app developers. Apple required those developers to use only Apple software tools to build their programs, thus shutting out competing software tools like those from Adobe. Then later in 2010 Apple announced that it was lifting those restrictions so that competing app conversion tools could be used. Antitrust pressure and the likelihood that developers would soon take their apps to Google's Android platform and other mobile devices may have motivated Apple's change of heart.

Apple has sold over 85 million iPhones and iPad Touches, but purchasers are only able to download apps from Apple itself. This exclusive dealing model and other strategies that take advantage of Apple's technological and market strength have caused critics to complain that Apple is now competing in the manner of Microsoft when it ran into antitrust problems in the 1990s.

Whether Apple is considered to be a monopolist probably would depend primarily on market definition. Is the product market, for example, tablet computers or all digital media? In the former, Apple is a colossus. In the latter, Apple is very strong but probably not a monopolist. [For another allegation of monopoly abuse by Apple, see *Stacie Somers v. Apple, Inc.*, 2011 U.S. Dist. LEXIS 77165 (N.D. Cal., San Francisco Div.).]

Sources: Thomas Catan and Yukari Kane, "Apple Draws Scrutiny from Regulators," *The Wall Street Journal*, May 4, 2010 [http://online.wsj.com/]; and Devindra Hardawar, "Apple Loses Game of Chicken, Allows Flash and other Conversion Tools for iOS Apps," *VentureBeat*, September 9, 2010 [http://venturebeat.com/].

Monopolization Analysis

Although the case law is not a model of clarity, a rather straightforward framework for monopoly analysis has emerged:

1. Define the relevant *product market*.
2. Define the relevant *geographic market*.
3. Compute the defendant's *market power*.
4. Assess the defendant's *intent* (predatory or coercive conduct).
5. Raise any available *defenses*.

1. Product Market

Here the court seeks, effectively, to draw a circle that encompasses categories of goods in which the defendant's products or services compete and that excludes those not in the same competitive arena. The fundamental test is *interchangeability* as determined primarily by the price, use, and quality of the product in question.

An analysis of cross-elasticity of demand is a key ingredient in defining the product market. Assume that two products, X and Y, appear to be competitors. Assume that the price of X doubled and Y's sales volume was unchanged. What does that tell us about whether X and Y are, in fact, in the same product market?

Defining the product market is really the process we all go through in routine purchasing decisions. Let us assume that you feel a rather undefined hunger for salty snack food. You go to the nearby convenience store. Many options confront you, but for simplicity, let's confine them to chips, nuts, and popcorn. Of course, each of those food types is composed of variations. As you sort through the choices—corn chips, cheese curls, peanuts, potato chips, and so on—you employ the criteria of price, use, and quality in focusing your decision. In so doing, you are defining the product market for "salty junk food." Products closely matched in price, use, and quality are interchangeable, and thus are competitors in the same product market. But, for example, an imported salty cheese at $10 per quarter pound presumably is not in the same product market as salted sunflower seeds.

Expressed as a matter of elasticity, the critical question becomes something like the following: If the price of potato chips, for example, falls by 10 percent, does the sales volume of salted nuts likewise fall? If so, we have a strong indication that potato chips and salted nuts lie in the same product market and thus are competitors.

2. Geographic Market

Once the product market has been defined, we still must determine where the product can be purchased. The judicial decisions to date offer no definitive explanation of the geographic market concept. A working definition might be "any section of the country where the product is sold in commercially significant quantities." From an economic perspective, the geographic market is defined by elasticity. If prices rise or supplies are reduced within the geographic area in question (New England, for example) and demand remains steady, will products from other areas enter the market in a quantity sufficient to affect price and/or supply? If so, the geographic market must be broadened to embrace those new sources of supply. If not, the geographic market is not larger than the area in question (New England). Perhaps a better approach is to read the cases and recognize that each geographic market must simply be identified in terms of its unique economic properties.

3. Market Power (Market Share)

Does the market share held by the defendant threaten competition? How large that share must be to raise monopoly concerns depends on a variety of considerations including how fragmented or concentrated the market is. *The Harvard Law Review,* however, notes some approximate boundaries:

> Market share above 70 percent typically suffices to support an inference of monopoly power. Conversely, courts have rarely found monopoly power when a firm's market share is below 50 percent, leaving some uncertainty as to market shares between 50 and 70 percent.[8]

Market share alone, however, does not establish monopoly power. Barriers to entry, economies of scale, the strength of the competition, trends in the market, and pricing patterns all help to determine whether the market remains competitive despite a single firm's large share. (Why are the courts interested in barriers to entry?)

4. Intent (Predatory or Coercive Conduct)

Assuming a threatening market share is established, the next requirement is proof of an intent to monopolize. Remember that a monopoly finding requires a showing of both market power (*structure*) and willful acquisition or maintenance of that power (*conduct*). Antitrust law is not designed to attack legitimately earned market power. Rather, the concern lies with those holding monopoly power that was earned or is maintained wrongfully. Thus, a showing of deliberate, predatory, coercive, or unfair conduct (such as collusion leading to price fixing) will normally suffice to establish the requisite intent.

Intel, the dominant microchip maker with 80 to 90 percent of the microprocessor market, reached a 2011 settlement of Federal Trade Commission charges that it used unfair tactics to earn and maintain that market share. Basically, Intel was accused of providing discriminatory rebates to Dell, IBM, HP, and others in return for those purchasers' agreement not to buy central processing unit chips from Intel's rival, Advanced Micro Devices (AMD). Intel was also accused of designing its chips so that competing processors could not run efficiently with them. Among other terms, the FTC settlement prohibits those practices. In 2009, Intel agreed to pay $1.25 billion to settle claims AMD brought in a patent and antitrust lawsuit, and the European Union fined Intel a record $1.45 billion for antitrust offenses. At this writing, New York State still has antitrust charges pending against Intel. [Explain why giving discounts could constitute an antitrust violation and defend Intel against those charges. See Edward Wyatt and Ashlee Vance, "Intel Settles with F.T.C. on Antitrust," *The New York Times,* August 4, 2010 (**http://www.nytimes.com/**); and Stephen Labaton, "Intel Facing Antitrust Investigation," *The New York Times,* June 7, 2008 (**http://www.nytimes.com**)].

5. Defenses

The defendant may yet prevail if the evidence demonstrates that the monopoly was innocently acquired via "superior skill, foresight, or industry;" that is, the monopoly was earned. Sometimes a monopoly may be "thrust upon" the monopolist because the competition failed or because of "natural monopoly" conditions where the market will support only one firm or where large economies of scale exist (such as for electricity suppliers).

Attempted Monopolization

The Sherman Act forbids attempts to monopolize as well as monopoly itself. In the 1993 *Spectrum Sports* decision[9] the Supreme Court set out a three-part test for attempted monopolization: (1) that the defendant has engaged in predatory or anticompetitive conduct with (2) a specific intent to monopolize and (3) a dangerous probability of achieving monopoly power (by which the court was insisting on evidence of some "realistic" likelihood that monopoly would actually follow).

Is Bob Marley a Product Market?

Music producer Rock River released remixed Bob Marley and the Wailers recordings in 2006. Universal Music Group claimed exclusive rights to those recordings and sent "cease and desist" orders to music distributors (Amazon, iTunes, etc.) who immediately discontinued sale of the Rock River remix. Rock River then sued Universal alleging attempted monopoly of the reggae genre of sound recordings in the United States, among other claims. Rock River alleged that Universal "accounted for 81 percent of the reggae sound recordings sold, and Bob Marley recordings accounted for 76 percent of the total reggae recordings sold."

Questions

1. Is reggae music, in your judgment, an identifiable product market? Explain.
2. Universal claimed there were no significant barriers to entry in the alleged reggae music market. Explain why the absence of barriers to entry would be a significant consideration in resolving the case.
3. Assuming Universal's share of the alleged product market was correctly calculated by Rock River, who will win this lawsuit? Explain.

Source: *Rock River Communications v. Universal Music Group*, 2011 U.S. Dist. LEXIS 46023 (C.D. Cal., Western Div.).

Monopoly Case I

The case that follows is a private antitrust action involving a claim by Christy Sports, a Utah ski rental company, that Deer Valley Resort Company (DVRC), a ski resort developer/operator, had monopoly power over Deer Valley Resort's ski rental business and that DVRC abused that power to harm Christy Sports.

Circuit Judge McConnell

When the Deer Valley Resort Company ("DVRC") was developing its world-renowned ski resort in the Wasatch Mountains, it sold parcels of land within the resort village to third parties, while reserving the right of approval over the conduct of certain ancillary businesses on the property, including ski rentals. For about fifteen years, DVRC granted permission to Cole Sports and plaintiff-appellant Christy Sports to rent skis in competition with its own ski rental outlet. More recently, however, DVRC revoked that permission, presumably in order to gain more business for its own newly-opened mid-mountain ski rental store. The question is whether this revocation violated the antitrust laws.

I. BACKGROUND

Deer Valley is one of three resorts in the vicinity of Park City, Utah. Many—indeed, "the vast majority," according to the Complaint of Deer Valley's patrons are destination skiers who fly into Salt Lake City and then take a forty-five minute bus or shuttle ride to the resort. The resort itself is divided into two areas: the base area, located at the bottom of the mountain, and the ritzier mid-mountain village, located halfway up the slope. DVRC has always been the sole provider of ski rentals at the base area, but at the mid-mountain village, Christy and Cole Sports have operated rental facilities; DVRC itself opened a mid-mountain ski rental facility in 2005.

Originally, DVRC owned all the property at the mid-mountain village, but over the years it has sold parcels to third parties. In 1990, DVRC sold one such parcel to S.Y. and Betty Kimball, subject to a restrictive covenant that prohibited use of the property for either ski rental or real estate sales office purposes without DVRC's express written consent. The Kimballs built a commercial building and leased space in it to Christy's corporate predecessor, Bulrich Corporation. The lease expressly prohibited both the rental of skis and the operation of a real estate office. The next year, though, DVRC gave Bulrich permission to rent skis in return for 15% of the rental revenue. When Bulrich merged with another company in 1994 and formed Christy Sports, LLC, Christy continued to operate the rental business. According to the complaint, Christy stopped paying DVRC 15% of its rental revenue in 1995, though the reason for this change is unknown. Christy rented skis at the Deer Valley mid-mountain village with no objection from DVRC until 2005. During that time, DVRC was the sole purveyor of rental skis at the base area but did not have a ski rental operation at mid-mountain.

DVRC opened a mid-mountain ski rental outlet in 2005. In August of that year, the resort notified Christy that, beginning the following year's ski season, the restrictive covenant would be enforced and Christy would no longer be allowed to rent skis. Christy believes that DVRC issued the same message to Cole's, leaving DVRC as the only rental ski provider at Deer Valley, with the exception of a small operation at the Stein Eriksen Lodge, which serves its own lodgers. This leaves that majority of skiers who fly into Salt Lake City and then shuttle to Deer Valley with few choices: they can carry unwieldy ski equipment onto the plane, take a shuttle into Park City and hunt for cheaper ski rentals in town, or rent from the more conveniently located DVRC location. Christy predicts, not improbably, that most consumers will choose the third option.

Christy argues that DVRC's decision to begin enforcing its restrictive covenant is an attempt to monopolize the market of ski rentals available to destination skiers in Deer Valley, or, alternatively, to the destination skiers in the mid-mountain village itself. It alleges that by eliminating its competitors, DVRC will be able to increase prices and reduce output, thus harming consumers. The complaint states that the number of skis available for rental mid-mountain will decline by 620 pairs, and the price will increase by at least twenty-two to thirty-two percent.

The district court dismissed Christy's antitrust complaints.

II. ANALYSIS

* * * * *

Christy has alleged that DVRC violated Section 2 of the Sherman Act by either actual or attempted monopolization. . . . Under both types of Section 2 claims Christy must plead both power in a relevant market and anticompetitive conduct. The relevant market, according to Christy's complaint, is the market for ski rentals to destination skiers in Deer Valley in general or, even more narrowly, the market for ski rentals in the mid-mountain village. The alleged anticompetitive conduct is the enforcement of the restrictive covenant.

A great many pages in the briefs are devoted to whether the defined market set forth in the complaint—destination skiers at Deer Valley, or alternatively at Deer Valley's mid-mountain village—is too small to constitute a market for antitrust purposes, in light of the proximity of a number of ski rental outlets in Park City, just down the road. For purposes of analyzing the complaint, however, we find it not implausible that destination skiers who arrive at the resort by bus or shuttle will find it sufficiently inconvenient to travel into town to rent skis that a successful monopolist over ski rental at Deer Valley could charge supracompetitive prices. The question, we believe, is not whether DVRC might be able to raise prices and reduce output by becoming the only purveyor of rental skis at the resort, but whether such a market is legally cognizable under the antitrust laws and whether the decision of a resort owner to reserve to itself the right to provide ancillary services counts as anticompetitive conduct.

* * * * *

We begin our analysis with DVRC's original decision to impose the restrictive covenant.

A. IMPOSITION OF THE RESTRICTIVE COVENANT

We agree with the defendant that the creator of a resort has no obligation under the antitrust laws to allow competitive suppliers of ancillary services on its property. A theme park, for example, does not have to permit third parties to open restaurants, hotels, gift shops, or other facilities within the park; it can reserve to itself the right to conduct such businesses and receive revenues from them. Accordingly, if it sells land within the resort to third parties, the antitrust laws do not bar the resort owner from imposing a covenant against use of the property for competitive businesses. This is so even if food, rooms, gifts, or other ancillary goods and services would be cheaper and more plentiful if the resort owner allowed competition in these businesses.

This conclusion can be reached either by reference to the proper definition of a market or by reference to the absence of anticompetitive conduct. Some courts, faced with cases of this sort, have found the market definition implausible. The Seventh Circuit took this approach in *Elliott* v. *United Center,* 126 F.3d 1003 (7th Cir. 1997), when a peanut vendor challenged a sports arena's decision to ban outside food and thereby monopolize the market for food concessions within the arena. The court rejected that market definition as implausible, saying:

> The logic of [the] argument would mean that exclusive restaurants could no longer require customers to purchase their wines only at the establishment, because the restaurant would be "monopolizing" the sale of wine within its interior. Movie theaters, which traditionally (and notoriously) earn a substantial portion of their revenue from the sale of candies, popcorn, and soda, would be required by the antitrust laws to allow patrons to bring their own food.

* * * * *

Although discussion of sports arenas . . . seems to suggest that Christy's shortcomings lie with its alleged geographic market, the actual problem lies with its product market. In these cases the two are difficult to disentangle because the product (rental skis . . .) is intimately related to the location. Consumers do not travel to Deer Valley for rental skis. . . . The true product in these cases is the overall experience. Deer Valley offers a cluster of products that combine to create a destination ski experience; rental skis are only one small component. . . .

The complaint alleges nothing to suggest that destination skiers are choosing their ski resort based on the price of rental skis, separate and apart from the cluster of services associated with the destination-ski experience. To define one small component of the overall product as the relevant product market is simply implausible.

Alternatively, one could say that the monopolization claim would fail because the alleged conduct is not anticompetitive. Even if a firm has monopoly power in a relevant market, a plaintiff must also show "the willful acquisition or maintenance of that power as distinguished from growth or development as a consequence of a superior product, business acumen, or historic accident." *Grinnell Corp.,* 384 U.S. at 570-71. Deer Valley is not required to invite competitors onto its property to rent skis to its patrons, even if a failure to do so would mean it is the sole supplier of rental skis at the ski area.

The Supreme Court has recognized the economic value of allowing businesses to decide with whom they will deal, as it recently re-emphasized: "[A]s a general matter, the Sherman Act 'does not restrict the long recognized right of [a] trader or manufacturer engaged in an entirely private business, freely to exercise his own independent discretion as to parties with whom he will deal.'" *Verizon Commc'ns, Inc.* v. *Law Offices of Curtis V. Trinko, LLP,* 540 U.S. 398, 408 (2004). In *Trinko,* the Court acknowledged that in rare circumstances a refusal to cooperate with competitors might constitute a Section 2 violation, but that "such exceptions, because of the uncertain virtue of forced sharing and the difficulty of identifying and remedying anticompetitive conduct by a single firm," should be few.

Having invested time and money in developing a premier ski resort that attracts skiers from across the nation, DVRC could recoup its investment in a number of ways. It could increase the price of lift tickets, raise room rates, serve only high-priced food, or, as it seems to have chosen, delve more deeply into the rental ski market. . . . This does not mean consumers have no protection. The ski resort industry is competitive (and Christy does not allege otherwise). Families contemplating ski vacations have many options, and they presumably compare quality and price. If they are rational, the price they are concerned about is the sum of all of their prospective vacation costs, including not just lift ticket prices and resort lodging, but air fare, food and drink, apres-ski entertainment, ski rentals, and the like. A resort that facilitates lower ski rental prices by allowing competition is able to price other aspects of the ski vacation experience more aggressively. The competitive discipline comes not from introducing competition with respect to each component of the experience, but from competition with other ski resorts with respect to the entire package. Christy has not alleged, and it would not likely be plausible to allege, that DVRC's decision to foreclose competition in the ski rental business at the mid-mountain village will have any effect on the market for ski resort vacations as a whole.

Indeed, allowing resorts to decide for themselves what blend of vertical integration and third party competition will produce the highest return may well increase competition in the ski resort business as a whole, and thus benefit consumers. This flexibility about business strategies induces entrants into the ski resort business by allowing them to reserve the benefits of their investments to themselves. . . .

Either line of reasoning—whether based on market definition or lack of anticompetitive conduct—leads to the same conclusion. Indeed, they are two sides of the same coin: having created a resort destination, antitrust will not force a resort developer to share its internal profit-making opportunities with competitors. The relevant market requirement reaches this result by finding implausible a market definition that singles out a small component of the cluster of services that constitutes the actual product; the anticompetitive conduct requirement reaches it by saying that it is not anticompetitive to refuse to grant access to competitors.

* * * * *

Although Christy insists that it has shown anticompetitive effects by its allegations of a decline in quantity and increase in price of rental skis at the mid-mountain village, this is just a repackaging of the argument rejected above. A resort operator's ability to reserve to itself the operation of ancillary businesses within the resort is not dependent on the quantity of output being as high or the price being as low as they would be if there were competition from third parties within the resort. It depends, instead, on either the proposition that a market that involves only one component of an interrelated package of services is not a relevant market for purposes of the Sherman Act or that it is not anticompetitive conduct for a resort owner to refuse to invite competitors to supply ancillary services within its resort. The fact . . . that fewer skis will be available for rental and that prices for rental skis will be higher, does not refute either of these legal propositions.

* * * * *

Affirmed.

Questions

1. *a.* Explain why the court concluded that "destination skiers at Deer Valley" or at "Deer Valley's mid-mountain village" constitute a market separate from ski rental outlets in nearby Park City.
   b. How did the Court define the "true product" market?

2. *a.* The plaintiff failed to establish the two core elements of its proof as required by the court. Explain those elements and describe why the court ruled against the plaintiff.
   b. How will consumers be protected from monopoly behavior by the defendant Deer Valley?

3. Why should Deer Valley be allowed to restrict output and raise prices by denying the plaintiff the continuing opportunity to rent skis at Deer Valley?

4. The U.S. government sued DuPont, claiming monopolization of the cellophane market. DuPont produced almost 75 percent of the cellophane sold in the United States. Cellophane constituted less than 20 percent of the "flexible packaging materials" market. The lower court found "[g]reat sensitivity of customers in the flexible packaging markets to price or quality changes."
   a. What is the relevant product market?
   b. Who wins the case? Explain. See *United States v. E.I. DuPont de Nemours & Co.*, 351 U.S. 377 (1956).

Monopoly Case II

The *Syufy* case that follows reflects what is probably the dominant "ideological" view of monopoly among federal court judges. The decision embodies the free market philosophy of the Reagan and Bush administrations and their judicial appointees, and it suggests an increasing judicial acceptance of the position that dominant market shares may be earned and maintained legitimately—particularly where competition can easily enter the market. Remember,

> Judge Kozinski managed to insert nearly 200 movie titles.

however, the Microsoft lesson that a dominant share gained and/or maintained by anticompetitive practices is impermissible.

The *Syufy* case is also notable because Judge Kozinski, in the spirit of the facts, managed to insert nearly 200 movie titles in his 25-page opinion (only a small portion of which is reprinted here).

LEGAL BRIEFCASE

U.S. v. Syufy Enterprises
903 F.2d 659 (9th Cir. 1990)

Circuit Judge Kozinski

Suspect that giant film distributors like Columbia, Paramount, and Twentieth Century Fox had fallen prey to Raymond Syufy, the canny operator of a chain of Las Vegas, Nevada, movie theaters, the U.S. Department of Justice brought this civil anti-trust action to force Syufy to disgorge the theaters he had purchased in 1982–84 from his former competitors. The case is unusual in a number of respects: The Department of Justice concedes that moviegoers in Las Vegas suffered no direct injury as a result of the allegedly illegal transactions; nor does the record reflect complaints from Syufy's bought-out competitors, as the sales were made at fair prices and not precipitated by any monkey business; and the supposedly oppressed movie companies have weighed in on Syufy's side. The Justice Department nevertheless remains intent on rescuing this platoon of Goliaths from a single David.

After extensive discovery and an eight-and-a-half day trial, the learned district judge entered comprehensive findings of fact and conclusions of law, holding for Syufy. He found, inter alia, that Syufy's actions did not injure competition because there are no barriers to entry—others could and did enter the market—and that Syufy therefore did not have the power to control prices or exclude the competition. . . .

FACTS

Gone are the days when a movie ticket cost a dime, popcorn a nickel, and theaters had a single screen: This is the age of the multiplex. With more than 300 new films released every year—each potentially the next Batman or E.T.—many successful theaters today run a different film on each of their 6, 12, or 18 screens. . . .

Raymond Syufy understood the formula well. In 1981 he entered the Las Vegas market with a splash by opening a six-screen theater. Newly constructed and luxuriously furnished, it put existing facilities to shame. Syufy's entry into the Las

Vegas market caused a stir, precipitating a titanic bidding war. Soon theaters in Las Vegas were paying some of the highest license fees in the nation, while distributors sat back and watched the easy money roll in.

It is the nature of free enterprise that fierce, no-holds-barred competition will drive out the least effective participants in the market, providing the most efficient allocation of productive resources. And so it was in the Las Vegas movie market in 1982. After a hard-fought battle among several contenders, Syufy gained the upper hand. Two of his rivals, Mann Theatres and Plitt Theatres, saw their future as rocky and decided to sell out to Syufy. While Mann and Plitt are major exhibitors nationwide, neither had a large presence in Las Vegas. Mann operated two indoor theaters with a total of three screens; Plitt operated a single theater with three screens. Things were relatively quiet until September 1984; in September Syufy entered into earnest negotiations with Cragin Industries, his largest remaining competitor. Cragin sold out to Syufy midway through October, leaving Roberts Company, a small exhibitor of mostly second-run films, as Syufy's only competitor for first-run films in Las Vegas.

It is these three transactions—Syufy's purchases of the Mann, Plitt, and Cragin theaters—that the Justice Department claims amount to antitrust violations. As government counsel explained at oral argument, the thrust of its case is that "you may not get monopoly power by buying out your competitors.". . .

DISCUSSION

*   *   *   *   *

[O]f significance is the government's concession that Syufy was only a monopsonist, not a monopolist. Thus the government argues that Syufy had market power, but that he exercised this power only against suppliers (film distributors), not against consumers (moviegoers). This is consistent with the record, which demonstrates that Syufy always treated moviegoers fairly: The movie tickets, popcorn, nuts, and the Seven-Ups cost about the same in Las Vegas as in other, comparable markets. While it is theoretically possible to have a middleman who is a monopolist upstream but not downstream, this is a somewhat counterintuitive scenario. Why, if he truly had significant market power, would Raymond Syufy have chosen to take advantage of the big movie distributors while giving a fair shake to ordinary people? And why do the distributors, the alleged victims of the monopolization scheme, think that Raymond Syufy is the best thing that ever happened to the Las Vegas movie market?

* * * * *

There is universal agreement that monopoly power is the power to exclude competition or control prices. . . .

1. Power to Exclude Competition
It is true, of course, that when Syufy acquired Mann's, Plitt's, and Cragin's theaters he temporarily diminished the number of competitors in the Las Vegas first-run film market. But this does not necessarily indicate foul play; many legitimate market arrangements diminish the number of competitors. . . . If there are no significant barriers to entry, however, eliminating competitors will not enable the survivors to reap a monopoly profit; any attempt to raise prices above the competitive level will lure into the market new competitors able and willing to offer their commercial goods or personal services for less. . . .

* * * * *

The district court. . . . found that there were no barriers to entry in the Las Vegas movie market. . . . Our review of the record discloses that the district court's finding is amply supported by the record.

* * * * *

Immediately after Syufy bought out the last of his three competitors in October 1984, he was riding high, having captured 100 percent of the first-run film market in Las Vegas. But this utopia proved to be only a mirage. That same month, a major movie distributor, Orion, stopped doing business with Syufy, sending all of its first-run films to Roberts Company, a dark-horse competitor previously relegated to the second-run market. Roberts Company took this as an invitation to step into the major league and, against all odds, began giving Syufy serious competition in the first-run market. Fighting fire with fire, Roberts opened three multiplexes within a 13-month period, each having six or more screens. By December 1986, Roberts was operating 28 screens, trading places with Syufy, who had only 23. At the same time, Roberts was displaying a healthy portion of all first-run films. In fact, Roberts got exclusive exhibition rights to many of its films, meaning that Syufy could not show them at all.

By the end of 1987, Roberts was showing a larger percentage of first-run films than was the Redrock multiplex at the time Syufy bought it. Roberts then sold its theaters to United Artists, the largest theater chain in the country, and Syufy continued losing ground. It all boils down to this: Syufy's acquisitions did not short-circuit the operation of the natural market forces; Las Vegas's first-run film market was more competitive when this case came to trial than before Syufy bought out Mann, Plitt, and Cragin.

The Justice Department correctly points out that Syufy still has a large market share, but attributes far too much importance to this fact. In evaluating monopoly power, it is not market share that counts, but the ability to maintain market share. . . . Syufy seems unable to do this. In 1985 Syufy managed to lock up exclusive exhibition rights to 91 percent of all the first-run films in Las Vegas. By the first quarter of 1988, that percentage had fallen to 39 percent; United Artists had exclusive rights to another 25 percent, with the remaining 36 percent being played on both Syufy and UA screens.

Syufy's share of box office receipts also dropped off, albeit less precipitously. In 1985 Syufy raked in 93 percent of the gross box office from first-run films in Las Vegas. By the first quarter of 1988, that figure had fallen to 75 percent. The government insists that 75 percent is still a large number, and we are hard-pressed to disagree; but that's not the point.

* * * * *

The numbers reveal that Roberts/UA has steadily been eating away at Syufy's market share: In two and a half years, Syufy's percentage of exclusive exhibition rights dropped 52 percent and its percentage of box office receipts dropped 18 percent. During the same period, Roberts/UA's newly opened theaters evolved from absolute beginners, barely staying alive, into a big business.

* * * * *

2. Power to Control Prices
The crux of the Justice Department's case is that Syufy, top gun in the Las Vegas movie market, had the power to push around Hollywood's biggest players, dictating to them what prices they could charge for their movies. The district court found otherwise. This finding too has substantial support in the record.

Perhaps the most telling evidence of Syufy's inability to set prices came from movie distributors, Syufy's supposed victims. At the trial, distributors uniformly proclaimed their satisfaction with the way the Las Vegas first-run film market operates; none complained about the license fees paid by Syufy. . . . Particularly damaging to the government's case was the testimony of the former head of distribution for MGM/UA that his company "never had any difficulty . . . in acquiring the terms that we thought were reasonable,". . . explaining that the license fees Syufy paid "were comparable or better than any place in the United States. And in most cases better.". . .

The documentary evidence bears out this testimony. Syufy has at all times paid license fees far in excess of the national average, even higher than those paid by exhibitors in Los Angeles, the Mecca of Moviedom. In fact, Syufy paid a higher percentage of his gross receipts to distributors in 1987 and 1988 than he did during the intensely competitive period just before he acquired Cragin's Redrock.

While successful, Syufy is in no position to put the squeeze on distributors. . . .

*   *   *   *   *

It is a tribute to the state of competition in America that the Antitrust Division of the Department of Justice has found no worthier target than this paper tiger on which to expend limited taxpayer resources. Yet we cannot help but wonder whether bringing a lawsuit like this, and pursuing it doggedly through 27 months of pretrial proceedings, about two weeks of trial, and now the full distance on appeal, really serves the interests of free competition.

Affirmed.

Questions

1. At one point, Syufy held 100 percent of the first-run market. Why was Syufy not a monopolist?

2. Is this decision rooted more in structural (market share) or conduct (e.g., predatory pricing) considerations? Explain.

3. What role did the issue of Syufy's intent to monopolize play in this case? Explain.

4. Assume we have historical data showing that when the price of rolled steel has increased, the sales volume of rolled aluminum has remained constant. What, if anything, does that fact tell us about the product market for rolled steel?

5. Define the product market for championship boxing matches. See *United States v. International Boxing Club of New York, Inc.*, 358 U.S. 242 (1959).

6. Adidas provides cash, sporting goods, and the like to universities in exchange for various promotional rights, including the team's or coach's agreement to wear Adidas clothing in athletic activities. National Collegiate Athletic Association (NCAA) rules limit the amount of advertising that may appear on a uniform being used in competition. Adidas sued the NCAA claiming, among other things, that the advertising restrictions constitute an attempted monopoly by the NCAA. In pursuing its monopoly claim, Adidas defined the relevant market as "the market for the sale of NCAA Promotional Rights." The NCAA responded by saying that a market consisting solely of the sale of promotional rights by NCAA member institutions (colleges and universities) on athletic apparel used in intercollegiate activity is not a plausible relevant market.

   a. Define the relevant product market from the NCAA point of view.

   b. How would the court decide where the product market actually lies? See *Adidas America, Inc v. NCAA*, 64 F.Supp.2d 1097 (1999).

Too Big to Fail?

Billionaire investor George Soros, in 2010, said that the "oligopoly" shared by America's four biggest banks "does need to be broken up."

What risks accompany so much power concentrated in few hands on Wall Street? Should that power be dispersed?

Source: Gabi Thesing, "Soros Says U.S. Bank 'Oligopoly' Should Be Broken Up," *BusinessWeek*, April 13, 2010 [**http://www.businessweek.com**].

Questions—Part One

1. *a. The Harvard Law Review* argued, "In the New Economy (information technology) . . . there will inevitably be an increasing number of markets with only a few dominant players."[10] Why would that be so?

     b. Are we mistaken in pursuing Microsoft and other "new economy" giants with "old economy" antitrust principles? Explain.

2. Worldwide Basketball Sports Tours promoted early-season, NCAA-certified basketball tournaments. The National Collegiate Athletic Association's Two in Four Rule limited college basketball teams to "not more than one certified basketball event in one academic year, and not more than two certified basketball events every four years." The promoters sued the NCAA on antitrust grounds, claiming the Two in Four rule hampered their ability to make money. The NCAA argued that the limit on games was academically motivated.

     a. Does antitrust law apply to Division I collegiate basketball? Explain.

     b. Define the product market in this case. See *Worldwide Basketball & Sports Tours, Inc. v. NCAA,* 388 F.3d 955 (6th Cir. 2004).

3. *a.* A traditional concern about monopolies is that a lack of competition discourages efficiency and innovation. Argue that monopolies may actually encourage innovation.

     b. Even if monopolies do not discourage invention, we have firm economic grounds for opposing monopolies. Explain.

4. Real estate developer Ernest Coleman built an apartment complex in Stilwell, Oklahoma (population 2,700), and ordered electric service from an out-of-town utility, Ozark Electric. Stilwell officials said they would deny him city water and sewer service if he did not buy his electricity from the city-owned utility service. Because he could not buy water or sewer service elsewhere, Coleman decided to switch to Stilwell's utility. In 1996 the federal Justice Department sued Stilwell. Explain the federal government's complaint and decide the case. See Bryan Gruley, "Little Town Becomes First Municipality Sued by U.S. for Antitrust," *The Wall Street Journal,* June 3, 1996, p. A1.

5. Historically, perhaps the most important interpretation of the Sherman Act's proscription of monopolization was Judge Learned Hand's opinion in the *Alcoa* case. After finding that Alcoa controlled 90 percent of the aluminum ingot market, Hand had to determine whether Alcoa possessed a general intent to monopolize. Hand concluded that Alcoa's market dominance could have resulted only from a "persistent determination" to maintain control:

> It was not inevitable that it should always anticipate increases in the demand for ingots and be prepared to supply them. Nothing compelled it to keep doubling and redoubling its capacity before others entered the field. It insists that it never excluded competitors; but we can think of no more effective exclusion than progressively to embrace each new opportunity as it opened, and to face every newcomer with new capacity already geared into a great organization.[11]

Comment on Judge Hand's remarks.

6. Several smaller airlines sued the two giants, United and American, claiming that the two violated the Sherman Act through their computerized reservation systems (CRSs). The heart of the plaintiffs' position was that United and American were monopolists who violated the law by denying other airlines reasonable access to their CRSs. American and United had the largest CRSs, but other airlines also maintained CRSs. Neither had blocked any other airline's access to its CRS, but they had charged fees (in

American's case, $1.75 per booking to the airline that secured a passenger through American's CRS). United and American each controlled about 12 to 14 percent of the total air transportation market. According to the court, the plaintiffs were "unhappy" about United and American's ability to extract booking fees from them for the use of the CRSs. The U.S. Ninth Circuit Court of Appeals ruled for the defendants, and the Supreme Court declined to review this case.

a. Explain why the plaintiffs felt wronged by American and United.

b. Explain the defendants's argument that they could not successfully charge "excessive" prices for the use of the CRSs. See *Alaska Airlines v. United Airlines,* 948 F.2d 536 (9th Cir. 1991), cert. den. 112 S.Ct. 1603 (1992).

Part Two—Mergers

Mergers are now back in the headlines after a slowdown during the Great Recession. Perhaps the most controversial proposed merger is Frankfurt, Germany-based Deutsche Boerse AG's bid to buy the New York Stock Exchange, the symbolic seat of American capitalism. Microsoft at this writing in 2011 intends to buy Skype for $8.5 billion, and AT&T hopes to buy T-Mobile USA for $39 billion. Both mergers are subject to government approval. Critics are challenging the AT&T deal saying the merger will harm consumers by reducing competition in an already oligopolistic industry. If the merger is permitted, the two top firms in the industry (Verizon and AT&T/T-Mobile) probably will control more than 70 percent of the market, and some experts see little likelihood of improved efficiencies. [For more, see The American Antitrust Institute, "The Acquisition of T-Mobile by AT&T Mobility: Merger Review Issues and Questions," at **http://www.antitrustinstitute. org/sites/default/files/AAI_Brief on ATT-T-Mobile.pdf**]

Merger activity tends to occur in cycles. Reflecting the worldwide economic slowdown, global merger activity for 2009 fell by 24 percent from the 2008 level, reaching a five-year low.[12] Deals began to recover in 2010 and were up sharply in the first quarter of 2011, although the size of those deals was generally smaller than in the boom years before the recession. Regardless of the number of mergers, their strategic significance remains undeniable as was evident in the federal government's decision to facilitate a series of 2008 mergers to stabilize the imperiled banking industry. Government regulators, fearing the

> Too big to fail.

collapse of banks considered "too big to fail," facilitated mergers that put more than 30 percent of America's bank deposits in the hands of three giants, J.P. Morgan Chase, Bank of America, and Wells Fargo. Suffering big losses in the financial crisis, its share prices plummeting, and being pushed toward a deal by worried federal regulators, Wachovia, the nation's fourth largest bank by assets, agreed to be acquired by Wells Fargo, the nation's 5th largest bank.[13] That aggressive consolidation, even when facilitated by the government itself, has intensified fears that the U.S. economy is dangerously consolidated, as *The New York Times* warned in a 2010 editorial:

Banks have gotten so big that they can unleash havoc and bill us for the pleasure. Big Oil is so big that Royal Dutch Shell is the world's 25th-biggest economy, bigger than Norway.

Four-fifths of the chips in the world's PCs come from Intel. In the United States, AT&T and Verizon account for over half of all cellular phone customers. Big companies are likely to become even bigger.[14]

While efficiencies and consumer advantages often are presumed to accompany increased corporate size following mergers, the *Times* cited a study finding higher prices in oil after Pennzoil acquired Quaker State, in tampons after Procter & Gamble bought Tambrands, in cereal after General Mills acquired Chex brands and in scotch whiskey after the merger of Guinness and Grand Metropolitan.[15] Nonetheless, in a global economy where oligopolies increasingly mark the landscape, mergers can make a great deal of economic sense.

Why? Technological change, efficiency enhancement, and piles of available cash are often important motivators for merger activity; but the big drivers in recent years appear to have been growth opportunities and cost cutting. Many companies have extracted maximum value from their own products making growth possible only by purchasing new lines, and cost savings have become essential in fierce global competition.

Merger Virtues

Mergers often have clearly beneficial effects. Some of the potential virtues of mergers include:

1. Mergers permit the replacement of inefficient management, and the threat of replacement disciplines managers to be more productive.
2. Mergers may permit stronger competition with previously larger rivals.
3. Mergers may improve credit access.
4. Mergers may produce efficiencies including economies of scale.
5. Mergers frequently offer a pool of liquid assets for use in expansion and in innovation.
6. Very often, mergers offer tax advantages.
7. Growth by merger is often less expensive than internal growth.
8. Mergers help to satisfy the personal ambitions and needs of management.

PRACTICING ETHICS   Some Media Mergers a Threat to Democracy?

In early 2011 the federal government approved the merger of Comcast, the cable TV giant, with the NBC television network. The deal gave NBC direct access to over a quarter of U.S. homes. The acquisition was delayed by various concerns, including higher prices and reduced choices for consumers. Comcast presumably might choose to keep programming from NBC's rivals off of its expansive cable system. The merged company, with more than two dozen TV stations in the biggest media markets, holds a great deal of power in negotiating ad rates. And as the TV market turns to video delivery over the Internet, one of the fears is that Comcast may be tempted to deny NBC content to rival Internet service providers, or charge them very high fees. The government's approval, however, put safeguards in place designed to prevent those problems.

The resulting company is among the world's largest entertainment conglomerates. Comcast now controls one in five U.S. television hours, according to critics. While fears about high prices and distribution restraints are important in considering this powerhouse merger, perhaps the bigger fear in media consolidation is the resulting risk to democracy. Journalist and blogger Jim Rhyne explained:

> The strength and health of our democracy is completely dependent on a vibrant, independent press. If big companies are allowed to continue their march toward even bigger media companies, the result can only mean fewer reporters, fewer voices and more news sharing than what we have now which is abysmal. In a constant search for profit,

these large media companies will continue to abandon their basic duty to our democracy to hold those in power accountable.[16]

Questions

1. What does Rhyne mean about media companies' duty to "hold those in power accountable?"
2. As you observe America's vast media market, do you see a further consolidation of the TV industry as a threat to democracy? Explain.

Sources: Editorial, "Concerns about Comcast-NBC," *The New York Times,* December 7, 2009 [http://www.nytimes.com/]; Meg James, "Comcast to Buy Control of NBC Universal in $30-Billion Transaction," *latimes.com,* December 4, 2009 [http://www.latimes.com/]; and Todd Shields, "Comcast-NBC Merger Should Be Approved, with Conditions, Rick Boucher Says," *Bloomberg,* August 2, 2010 [http://www.bloomberg.com/].

Merger Problems

Many studies show that mergers often fail in the sense that they do not add value to the merging companies. Experts generally estimate the merger failure rate, measured in various ways, at between 50 and 80 percent. As *CNN.com* described it, "Mergers Fail More Often than Marriages."[17] In addition to those frequent financial failures, other merger hazards should be noted:

> "Mergers Fail More Often than Marriages."

1. Too much power is being concentrated in too few hands.
2. A particular merger, while not threatening in and of itself, may trigger a merger movement among industry competitors.
3. Higher market concentration may lead to higher prices.
4. Innovation may be harmed.
5. Some companies are so large that they can significantly shape political affairs.
6. Some companies may have become so large that we cannot allow them to fail.[18]

When Should the Government Intervene?   The U.S. Justice Department faced that question in reviewing a proposed $3 billion merger between Chicago-based United Airlines, the third largest U.S. carrier and Houston-based Continental Airlines, the fourth-largest U.S. carrier. In looking at the deal, the Justice Department found few overlapping routes. Newark, New Jersey did, however, present concerns in that Continental had 70.9 percent of the annual passenger load. United was only the fifth-largest Newark carrier, but most of its hubs connected directly to Newark.[19] In 2010, the Justice Department and the two airlines agreed on a settlement allowing the merger in exchange for which Dallas-based, low-cost carrier Southwest Airlines, the sixth-largest U.S. carrier, received lease rights to enough of Continental's Newark landing slots to address the Justice Department's Newark concerns. The merged firm will pass Delta to become the world's largest airline with 21 percent of the domestic market and 7 percent globally.[20] Continental and United expect to achieve more than $1 billion in various "synergies" from the deal.[21] A *New York Times* editorial said, "We suspect prices will rise, as the merged company reduces the number of flights on some routes."[22] Some experts, however, think that higher prices are necessary for the health of the industry where making a profit, at least for the old-line, full-price carriers has been difficult to achieve.[23] Airline expert, Steven Morrison, says that prices are likely to rise in the short term on routes where the two airlines previously competed, but in the long run, the price rise may not be sustained in the domestic market because discounters such as Southwest, Allegiant and JetBlue, which control 30 percent of the domestic market, can be expected to force prices down.[24] With little discounter presence in the small-town American market and on international routes, experts believe that prices on those routes may rise as consolidation in the industry continues.[25]

Merger Law: Overview

Mergers are addressed by the Sherman Act, Section 1; but the Clayton Act, Section 7, offers the primary legislative oversight:

> That no person engaged in commerce shall acquire the whole or any part of the stock or the assets of another person engaged also in commerce where the effect of such acquisition may be substantially to lessen competition, or to tend to create a monopoly.

Technically, a merger involves the union of two or more enterprises wherein the property of all is transferred to the one remaining firm. However, antitrust law embraces all those situations in which previously independent business entities are united—whether by acquisition of stock, purchase of physical assets, creation of holding companies, consolidation, or merger.

Mergers fall, somewhat awkwardly, into three categories:

1. A horizontal merger involves firms that are in direct competition and occupy the same product and geographic markets. A merger of two vodka producers in the same geographic market would clearly fall in the horizontal category. Would the merger of a vodka producer and a gin producer constitute a horizontal merger?

2. A vertical merger involves two or more firms at different levels of the same channel of distribution, such as a furniture manufacturer and a fabric supplier.

3. A conglomerate merger involves firms dealing in unrelated products. Thus the conglomerate category embraces all mergers that are neither horizontal nor vertical. An example of such a merger would be the acquisition of a pet food manufacturer by a book publisher. (Conglomerate mergers currently receive little attention from the government, and we will not examine them further.)

Premerger Notification   Under the Hart–Scott–Rodino Antitrust Improvements Act (HSR), mergers and acquisitions must be reported to the Federal Trade Commission and the Justice Department if those deals exceed certain dollar thresholds that change annually in accord with the gross national product. [For more HSR threshold details, see **http://www.ftc.gov/bc/hsr/ index.shtm**] The parties are barred from closing the merger until 30 days after they have made the required HSR filing unless the waiting period is shortened (as it often is) or lengthened by the FTC or the Justice Department. The merging firms are required to provide documentation about the merger's impact on competition. The waiting period gives the government time and information by which to determine whether the merger should be challenged.

Remedies   After the HSR review, the government may decide that the merger is not threatening, and it will be allowed to proceed. The government may, on the other hand,

> Nasdaq sought to outbid Deutsche Boerse AG for the New York Stock Exchange.

conclude that the merger is anticompetitive, as it did in 2011 when Nasdaq sought to outbid Deutsche Boerse AG for the New York Stock Exchange. The federal Justice Department decided that the proposed acquisition would significantly diminish or eliminate competition in some areas, and Nasdaq abandoned its attempt. If the parties persist with a disfavored merger, the government can file suit. The preferred action, however, is to work out an agreeable settlement. A settlement might involve one of the parties selling some of its assets or agreeing to forgo business in some geographic segment of the market for a while, as in the United-Continental deal, noted above.

In cases where negotiation fails and the government decides to sue, it can ask the court for a remedy, such as an order stopping the merger or an order requiring divestiture of certain assets. Government litigation is infrequent, but the resulting message to the business community is powerful. Furthermore, private parties commonly use the antitrust laws to sue for treble damages when they believe a merger has harmed them unlawfully.[26] The threat of those private actions as well as government oversight helps to maintain a marketplace where consumers are offered the benefits of vigorous competition including lower prices, improved quality, and innovation. [To read summaries of recent developments in antitrust law, see *Antitrust Today* at **http://www.antitrusttoday.com/**]

[For a humorous treatment of mergers, see Stephen Colbert's 2007 video segment, "Mega-Mergers," at **http://www.businessinsider.com/stephen-colbert-att-2011-3**]

Horizontal Analysis

Horizontal mergers raise anticompetitive risks because direct competitors seek to join together. Horizontal merger analysis ordinarily follows the FTC/Justice Department merger guidelines, which focus on a pair of concerns:

1. **Coordinated effects/collusion.** Will the merger facilitate cooperation so that the parties might fix prices, reduce output, reduce quality, or otherwise coordinate their activities rather than competing against each other? Broadly, the government takes the position that fewer firms and thus greater market concentration increases the likelihood of collusion—a position the courts often, but not always, embrace.

2. **Unilateral effects.** Will the merger allow a firm to unilaterally raise prices, restrict output, or control innovation? Normally, unilateral effects arise with products that significantly restrain each other prior to the merger. For example, in evaluating the merger of paper products manufacturers Scott and Kimberly-Clark, the Justice Department found that Scott's facial tissue brand, Scotties, and Kimberly-Clark's facial tissue brand, Kleenex, had significantly constrained each other's prices prior to the merger and that the merger would therefore allow unilateral and profitable price increases for both Scotties and Kleenex. In response, Kimberly-Clark agreed to divest itself of Scott's facial tissue brands.[27]

Market Power

Broadly, the guidelines are designed to identify mergers that may result in market power, defined as the ability of a seller "profitably to maintain prices above competitive levels for a significant period of time." The guidelines set out a five-step methodology for analyzing horizontal mergers:

1. Market definition.
2. Measurement of market concentration.
3. Identification of likely anticompetitive effects.
4. Likelihood of future entrants to the market.
5. Appraisal of efficiencies and other possible defenses.

Market The market will be defined as the smallest product and geographic market in which a hypothetical monopolist could raise prices a small but significant and nontransitory amount (usually set at 5 percent above current prices).

Market Concentration The Herfindahl–Hirschman Index (HHI) is employed to measure market concentration. Notwithstanding the formidable title, the index is computed quite easily. The market share of each firm is squared and the results are summed. Thus, if five companies each had 20 percent of a market, the index for that market would be 2,000. The HHI is useful because it measures both concentration and dispersion of market share between big and small firms. If 10 firms each have 10 percent of the market, the resulting HHI is 1,000. The larger the HHI, the more concentrated the market. In general, a post-merger HHI below 1,500 would reflect an unconcentrated market while a postmerger concentration of between 1,500 and 2,500 would be considered mildly concentrated and more than 2,500 a highly concentrated market. The greater the HHI, the more likely the government will be concerned about the merger. The guidelines provide that the potential for competitive concern also depends on the analysis of additional factors, such as a change in the number of competitors along with adverse effects and ease of entry, as explained below. Broadly, the government's guidelines reject the older notion of market size *alone* as a threat to the welfare of the economy.

Adverse Effects The basic point here is the government's worry that the merger may permit monopoly behavior in the merged firm's market.

Ease of Entry If new competitors can readily enter the postmerger market, the existing firms will be forced to charge competitive prices and otherwise conform to the discipline of the market.

Defenses   An otherwise unacceptable merger may be saved by certain defenses. The *failing company doctrine* permits a merger to preserve the assets of a firm that would otherwise be lost to the market. *Efficiencies* include such desirable economic results as economies of scale or reduced transportation costs as a result of the merger.

Guideline Changes

In 2010, the Justice Department and the Federal Trade Commission announced revisions to the Horizontal Merger Guidelines that bring the Guidelines more in line with actual government practice. Much of the analysis will continue as outlined above, but a key revision involves a reduced role for market definition/market share and increased attention to likely adverse competitive effects. The new reasoning is that the analysis will begin in identifying practical, real-world competitive harm (such as customer injury, reduced innovation or reduced product variety) at which point market definition and the balance of the analysis outlined above would be influential. This approach may, therefore, allow the government greater flexibility in proving competition problems even if high market shares cannot be established. Future antitrust decisions will indicate how closely the courts actually follow the new guidance.

"I Am Going to Destroy You."

Whole Foods, the natural foods chain, in 2007 acquired its chief competitor, Wild Oats Market. Whole Foods had about 12 percent of the natural foods market, and Wild Oats held about three percent. Whole Foods had 197 stores and added 110 by purchasing Wild Oats. About 72 percent of Wild Oats' sales were in markets where the two overlapped. Whole Foods argued that the merger was necessary to allow it to compete effectively with big chains such as Safeway and Walmart.

Prior to the purchase, Whole Foods cofounder and CEO John Mackey reportedly shouted, "I am going to destroy you," to Wild Oats CEO, Perry Odak. For nearly eight years until discovered in 2007, Mackey, using an alias, posted more than 1,100 messages on Yahoo Finance's bulletin board bashing his competitors and boosting Whole Foods. According to court records, Mackey allegedly said that the proposed merger would end "forever, or almost forever" the possibility of a big grocery chain buying an existing natural foods chain to compete with Whole Foods. Mackey also allegedly said that buying Wild Oats would prevent "nasty price wars."

The Federal Trade Commission challenged the Whole Foods purchase of Wild Oats concluding that Whole Foods was using the deal as a way to eliminate its major competition in dozens of cities and apparently feeling that Mackey's remarks effectively compelled government action.

Questions

1. What was the primary issue facing the federal courts that reviewed the FTC challenge?
2. Decide the case. Explain.

Sources: Federal Trade Commission v. Whole Foods Market, 502 F.Supp.2d 1 (2007); *Federal Trade Commission v. Whole Foods Market,* 533 F.3d 869 (D.C. Cir. 2008); and David Kesmodel and Jonathan Eig, "A Grocer's Brash Style Takes Unhealthy Turn," *The Wall Street Journal,* July 20, 2007, p. A1.

Vertical Analysis

A vertical merger typically involves an alliance between a supplier and a purchaser. The primary resulting threat to competition is labeled *market foreclosure*. As illustrated in Figure 11.1, a vertical merger may deny a source of supply to a purchaser or an outlet for sale to a seller, thus potentially threatening competition in violation of the Clayton Act. The government would then look closely at that foreclosure to determine whether it actually has an anticompetitive effect. In addition to foreclosing sources of supply or outlets for sale, the government may be concerned about other anticompetitive effects such as raising rivals' costs, facilitating collusion, raising barriers to entry, increasing access to competitively sensitive information, encouraging discrimination in access to products and services, and reducing incentives for innovation.

FIGURE 11.1
Vertical Merger

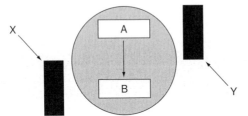

A supplies B. A and B merge. X (A's competitor) had traditionally sold to B, and Y (B's competitor) had traditionally purchased from A. How do we decide the legality of such a merger?

The government has practiced a generally lenient approach to vertical mergers, but under some conditions they will be challenged. That was the case with the Ticketmaster-Live Nation merger that was largely vertical in character although it included some horizontal features. Ticketmaster, the nation's largest ticketing company, also owns a controlling share in Front Line Management whose 200-plus clients include the Eagles and Miley Cyrus.[28] Live Nation, the country's largest concert promoter, was a recent entrant to the ticketing business.[29] Live Nation also owns or manages 135 major concert venues around the world, is the world's largest artist-management company and operates related businesses including online fan clubs and t-shirts.[30] Obama administration antitrust officials made it clear that the government would resist the merger.[31] Litigation was not necessary, however, because the merger partners and the Justice Department in 2010 agreed to a settlement allowing the creation of the new company—to be called Live Nation Entertainment. Ticketmaster agreed to divest itself of one of its ticketing divisions while licensing its ticketing software to a competitor, thus effectively allowing the creation of two new competitors for Ticketmaster. The newly merged firm also agreed to Justice Department monitoring to enforce "tough anti-retaliation provisions" so Live Nation Entertainment will not be able to abuse its power in ticketing, concert venues, artist management and concert touring.[32]

> **Ticketmaster-Live Nation merger.**

Ticketmaster and Live Nation argued that the merger's vertical integration would reduce inefficiencies in the music business, where economic conditions have been very difficult. Critics, however, were unhappy with the settlement that creates a powerhouse that dominates big pieces of the music industry and could put artists at a disadvantage if they do not agree to be represented by Live Nation.

Horizontal Merger Case

The Staples–Office Depot litigation that follows illustrates the standard horizontal merger analysis.

LEGAL BRIEFCASE

Federal Trade Commission v. Staples, Inc. and Office Depot, Inc.   970 F.Supp. 1066 (D.D.C. 1997)

Judge Hogan

BACKGROUND

* * * * *

Staples is the second largest office superstore chain in the United States with approximately 550 retail stores located in 28 states and the District of Columbia, primarily in the Northeast and California. In 1996, Staples' revenues from those stores were approximately $4 billion through all operations. Office Depot, the largest office superstore chain, operates over 500 retail office supply superstores that are located in 38 states and the District of Columbia, primarily in the South and Midwest. Office Depot's 1996 sales were approximately $6.1 billion. OfficeMax, Inc., is the only other office supply superstore firm in the United States.

On September 4, 1996, defendants Staples and Office Depot . . . entered into an "Agreement and Plan of Merger" whereby . . . Office Depot would become a wholly owned subsidiary of Staples. . . . The FTC filed this suit on April 9, 1997, seeking a temporary restraining order and preliminary injunction against the merger. . . .

I. Discussion

Analysis of the likely competitive effects of a merger requires determinations of (1) the "line of commerce" or product market

in which to assess the transaction, (2) the "section of the country" or geographic market in which to assess the transaction, and (3) the transaction's probable effect on competition in the product and geographic markets.

II. The Geographic Market

One of the few issues about which the parties to this case do not disagree is that metropolitan areas are the appropriate geographic markets for analyzing the competitive effects of the proposed merger. In its first amended complaint, the FTC identified 42 such metropolitan areas as well as future areas which could suffer anticompetitive effects from the proposed merger. . . .

III. The Relevant Product Market

* * * * *

The Commission defines the relevant product market as "the sale of consumable office supplies through office superstores," with "consumable" meaning products that consumers buy recurrently, i.e., items which "get used up" or discarded. For example, under the Commission's definition, "consumable office supplies" would not include capital goods such as computers, fax machines, and other business machines or office furniture, but does include such products as paper, pens, file folders, self-stick notes, computer disks, and toner cartridges.

The defendants characterize the FTC's product market definition as "contrived" with no basis in law or fact, and counter that the appropriate product market within which to assess the likely competitive consequences of a Staples–Office Depot combination is simply the overall sale of office products, of which a combined Staples–Office Depot accounted for 5.5 percent of total sales in North America in 1996.

*   *   *   *   *

The general rule when determining a relevant product market is that "[t]he outer boundaries of a product market are determined by the reasonable interchangeability of use [by consumers] or the cross-elasticity of demand between the product itself and substitutes for it." Interchangeability of use and cross-elasticity of demand look to the availability of substitute commodities, i.e., whether there are other products offered to consumers which are similar in character or use to the product or products in question. . . .

[T]he Commission has argued that a slight but significant increase in Staples–Office Depot's prices will not cause a considerable number of Staples–Office Depot's customers to purchase consumable office supplies from other nonsuperstore alternatives such as Wal-Mart, Best Buy, Quill, or Viking. On the other hand, the Commission has argued that an increase in price by Staples would result in consumers turning to another office superstore, especially Office Depot, if the consumers had that option. Therefore, the Commission concludes that the sale of consumable office supplies by office supply superstores is the appropriate relevant product market in this case, and products sold by competitors such as Wal-Mart, Best Buy, Viking, Quill, and others should be excluded. . . .

The Court acknowledges that there is, in fact, a broad market encompassing the sale of consumable office supplies by all sellers of such supplies, and that those sellers must, at some level, compete with one another. However, the mere fact that a firm may be termed a competitor in the overall marketplace does not necessarily require that it be included in the relevant product market for antitrust purposes. The Supreme Court has recognized that within a broad market, "well-defined submarkets may exist which, in themselves, constitute product markets for antitrust purposes."

*   *   *   *   *

[In defining the submarket] the FTC focused on what it termed the "pricing evidence.". . . First, the FTC presented evidence comparing Staples' prices in geographic markets where Staples is the only office superstore, to markets where Staples competes with Office Depot or OfficeMax, or both. Based on the FTC's calculations, in markets where Staples faces no office superstore competition at all, something which was termed a one-firm market during the hearing, prices are 13 percent higher than in three-firm markets where it competes with both Office Depot and OfficeMax.

*   *   *   *   *

This evidence suggests that office superstore prices are affected primarily by other office superstores and not by non-superstore competitors such as mass merchandisers like Wal-Mart, Kmart, or Target, wholesale clubs such as BJ's, Sam's, and Price Costco, computer or electronic stores such as Computer City and Best Buy, independent retail office supply stores, mail-order firms like Quill and Viking, and contract stationers.

*   *   *   *   *

In addition, Staples' own pricing information shows that warehouse clubs have very little effect on Staples' prices.

*   *   *   *   *

There is similar evidence with respect to the defendants' behavior when faced with entry of another competitor. The evidence shows that the defendants change their price zones when faced with entry of another superstore, but do not do so for other retailers.

*   *   *   *   *

Despite the high degree of functional interchangeability between consumable office supplies sold by the office superstores and other retailers of office supplies, the evidence presented by the Commission shows that even where Staples and Office Depot charge higher prices, certain consumers do not go elsewhere for their supplies. This further demonstrates that the sale of office supplies by non-superstore retailers is not responsive to the higher prices charged by Staples and Office Depot in the one-firm markets. This indicates a low cross-elasticity of demand between the consumable office supplies sold by superstores and those sold by other sellers.

*   *   *   *   *

The Court has observed that office supply superstores look far different from other sellers of office supplies. Office supply superstores are high-volume, discount office supply chain stores averaging in excess of 20,000 square feet, with over 11,000 of those square feet devoted to traditional office supplies, and carrying over 5,000 SKUs of consumable office supplies in addition to computers, office furniture, and other nonconsumables. In contrast, stores such as Kmart devote approximately 210 square feet to the sale of approximately

250 SKUs of consumable office supplies. Kinko's devotes approximately 50 square feet to the sale of 150 SKUs. Both Sam's Club and Computer City each sell approximately 200 SKUs.

In addition to the differences in SKU numbers and variety, the superstores are different from many other sellers of office supplies due to the type of customer they target and attract. The superstores' customer base overwhelmingly consists of small businesses with fewer than 20 employees and consumers with home offices. In contrast, mail-order customers are typically midsized companies with more than 20 employees. . . .

*   *   *   *   *

[T]he Court finds that the unique combination of size, selection, depth, and breadth of inventory offered by the superstores distinguishes them from other retailers.

*   *   *   *   *

While it is clear to the Court that Staples and Office Depot do not ignore sellers such as warehouse clubs, Best Buy, or Wal-Mart, the evidence clearly shows that Staples and Office Depot each consider the other superstores as the primary competition.

*   *   *   *   *

[T]he Court finds that the sale of consumable office supplies through office supply superstores is the appropriate relevant product market for purposes of considering the possible anticompetitive effects of the proposed merger between Staples and Office Depot.

*   *   *   *   *

IV. Probable Effect on Competition

[T]he Court next must consider the probable effect of a merger between Staples and Office Depot in the geographic markets previously identified. One way to do this is to examine the concentration statistics and HHIs within the geographic markets. If the relevant product market is defined as the sale of consumable office supplies through office supply superstores, the HHIs in many of the geographic markets are at problematic levels even before the merger. Currently, the least concentrated market is that of Grand Rapids–Muskegon–Holland, Michigan, with an HHI of 3,597, while the most concentrated is Washington, D.C., with an HHI of 6,944. In contrast, after a merger of Staples and Office Depot, the least concentrated area would be Kalamazoo–Battle Creek, Michigan, with an HHI of 5,003, and many areas would have HHIs of 10,000. The average increase in HHI caused by the merger would be 2,715 points. The concentration statistics show that a merged Staples–Office Depot would have a dominant market share in

42 geographic markets across the country. The combined shares of Staples and Office Depot in the office superstore market would be 100 percent in 15 metropolitan areas. It is in these markets the postmerger HHI would be 10,000. In 27 other metropolitan areas, where the number of office superstore competitors would drop from three to two, the postmerger market shares would range from 45 percent to 94 percent, with postmerger HHIs ranging from 5,003 to 9,049. Even the lowest of these HHIs indicates a "highly concentrated" market.

*   *   *   *   *

The HHI calculations and market concentration evidence, however, are not the only indications that a merger between Staples and Office Depot may substantially lessen competition. Much of the evidence already discussed with respect to defining the relevant product market also indicates that the merger would likely have an anticompetitive effect. The evidence of the defendants' own current pricing practices, for example, shows that an office superstore chain facing no competition from other superstores has the ability to profitably raise prices for consumable office supplies above competitive levels. The fact that Staples and Office Depot both charge higher prices where they face no superstore competition demonstrates that an office superstore can raise prices above competitive levels. The evidence also shows that defendants also change their price zones when faced with entry of another office superstore, but do not do so for other retailers.

*   *   *   *   *

V. Entry into the Market

"The existence and significance of barriers to entry are frequently, of course, crucial considerations in a rebuttal analysis. . . ."

*   *   *   *   *

The Commission offered Office 1 as a specific example of the difficulty of entering the office superstore arena. Office 1 opened its first two stores in 1991. By the end of 1994, Office 1 had 17 stores, and grew to 35 stores operating in 11 Midwestern states as of October 11, 1996. As of that date, Office 1 was the fourth largest office supply superstore chain in the United States. Unfortunately, also as of that date, Office 1 filed for Chapter 11 bankruptcy protection. Brad Zenner, president of Office 1, testified through declaration that Office 1 failed because it was severely undercapitalized in comparison with the industry leaders, Staples, Office Depot, and OfficeMax. In addition, Zenner testified that when the three leaders ultimately expanded into the smaller markets where Office 1 stores were located, they seriously undercut Office 1's retail prices and profit margins. Because Office 1 lacked the capitalization of the three leaders and lacked the economies of scale enjoyed by those competitors, Office 1 could not remain profitable.

For the reasons discussed above, the Court finds it extremely unlikely that a new office superstore will enter the market and thereby avert the anticompetitive effects from Staples' acquisition of Office Depot.

* * * * *

VI. Efficiencies

* * * * *

First, the Court notes that the cost savings estimate of $4.947 billion over five years which was submitted to the Court exceeds by almost 500 percent the figures presented to the two Boards of Directors in September 1996, when the Boards approved the transaction. The cost savings claims submitted to the Court are also substantially greater than those represented in the defendants' Joint Proxy Statement/Prospectus "reflecting the best currently available estimate of management," and filed with the Securities and Exchange Commission on January 23, 1997. . . .

* * * * *

[T]he Court cannot find that the defendants have rebutted the presumption that the merger will substantially lessen competition . . .

CONCLUSION

* * * * *

[T]he Court finds that the Commission has shown a likelihood that it will succeed in proving, after a full administrative trial on the merits, that the effect of the proposed merger between Staples and Office Depot "may be substantially to lessen competition" in violation of Section 7 of the Clayton Act. . . . The FTC's motion for a preliminary injunction shall be granted.

AFTERWORD

Citing the time and money involved in battling the federal government, Staples and Office Depot officially called off their proposed merger days after Judge Hogan's decision.

Questions

1. *a.* What "general rule" did the *Staples* court employ in determining the relevant product market?
   b. What evidence supported the use of the "office supply superstore submarket" as the relevant product market?

2. *a.* What evidence supported the FTC's claim that the merger would lead to anticompetitive effects?
   b. In weighing the "public and private equities," why did the court come down on the side of the government?

3. Analysts have argued that in the *Staples* case the government was less worried about market shares than about the price impact of the merger were it to be approved. Explain what those analysts meant.

4. Three firms controlled the $1 billion U.S. baby food market (Gerber—65 percent, Heinz—17.4 percent, and Beech-Nut—15.4 percent). Gerber was sold in over 90 percent of American supermarkets, and it had greater brand loyalty than any other product sold in the United States. Heinz was sold in 40 percent of the supermarkets and Beech-Nut in 45 percent. The baby food HHI was 4775, which would increase by 510 HHI points if Heinz and Beech-Nut were to merge. Heinz and Beech-Nut agreed to merge. The Federal Trade Commission opposed the merger.
   a. What other facts would you want to know to decide the legality of this proposed merger?
   b. Defend the merger.
   c. Decide. Explain. See *Federal Trade Commission v. H. J. Heinz Co.*, 246 F.3d 708 (D.C. Cir. 2001).

5. In 1958, Pabst Brewing Company acquired Blatz Brewing Company. Pabst was America's 10th largest brewer, while Blatz was the 18th largest. After the merger, Pabst had 4.49 percent of the nationwide beer market and was the fifth-largest brewer. In the regional market of Wisconsin, Michigan, and Illinois, the merger gave Pabst 11.32 percent of the sales. After the merger, Pabst led beer sales in Wisconsin with 23.95 percent of that statewide market. The beer market was becoming increasingly concentrated, with the total number of brewers declining from 206 to 162 during the years 1957 to 1961. In *United States v. Pabst Brewing Co.*, 384 U.S. 546 (1966), the Supreme Court found the merger violated the Clayton Act, Section 7. The Court did not choose among the three geographic market configurations, saying that the crucial inquiry is whether a merger may substantially lessen competition anywhere in the United States. Thus the Court held that, under these facts, a 4.49 percent share of the market was too large.

   Respected scholar and jurist Richard Posner labeled the Pabst decision an "atrocity" and the product of a "fit of nonsense" on the part of the Supreme Court.[33] What economic arguments would support Posner's colorful complaint?

CEO Respects Regulators

Staples CEO Thomas Stemberg was interviewed following the *FTC v. Staples* battle:

Q: Should a company expect to be treated fairly by staff members of the antitrust regulators?

A: I do believe that the people in these agencies are well-intentioned and are trying to do the right thing for the consumer. As one who has spent the last decade or more of his business career fighting cartels and trying to induce procompetitive activity in the marketplace, their goals are very much the same as ours, which is to give the consumer the best deal possible. The antitrust regulators are some of the hardest-working people I have ever seen. They are extremely dedicated, and if you aren't prepared to go 15 rounds, you're picking a bad fight. Some of the mergers that are out there today that they are contesting, I'd be contesting if I were them, too.

Source: Del Jones, "Today's Issue: Some Lessons Learned in an Antitrust Fight," *USA TODAY*, March 30, 1998, p. 5B.

Part Three—American Antitrust Laws and the International Market

America's commercial market embraces the entire globe. Antitrust questions can become extremely complex in transactions involving multiple companies in multiple nations, where those transactions are potentially governed by both U.S. and foreign antitrust laws. United States antitrust laws are, of course, applicable to foreign firms doing business here. The Sherman, Clayton, and FTC acts, among others, are all potentially applicable to American business abroad.

Sherman Act

The Sherman Act applies to the conduct of American business abroad when that business has a direct effect on American commerce. That the business was conducted entirely abroad or that the agreement was entered into in another nation does not excuse an American firm from the reach of the Sherman Act (assuming American courts can achieve the necessary jurisdiction).

Clayton Act

Section 7 of the Clayton Act is clearly applicable to acquisitions combining domestic and foreign firms and is potentially applicable to acquisitions not involving American firms if the effect would harm competition in the American market.

Federal Trade Commission Act

As noted earlier, the FTC shares antitrust enforcement authority with the Justice Department, and Section 5 of the act strengthens Clayton 7.

Enforcement

Under its Business Review Procedure, the Justice Department sometimes will prepare a statement of its likely response to a proposed transaction, either foreign or domestic, so that the parties will have advance notice of the government's antitrust stance.

International Antitrust Enforcement

Markets increasingly extend around the globe encouraging antitrust enforcement as an international effort to achieve both consumer welfare and market efficiency. Most antitrust enforcement occurs in the United States and the European Union, but other nations are taking a more aggressive stance, usually by employing laws that largely mimic those of the United States or the European Union.

European Union Antitrust Enforcement   European Union regulators have indicated that they intend to move toward the American antitrust model of concern for consumer welfare rather than attacking dominant companies just because competitors may be harmed. Differences remain, however. In general, the European Union seems to be practicing a more aggressive attitude toward possible market abuse. At the beginning of this chapter, we saw that the European Union arguably took a firmer stance toward Microsoft's allegedly monopolistic conduct than did the United States. Similarly, the European Union blocked the proposed merger of General Electric and Honeywell even though the United States had earlier approved the merger. Given the European Union's powerful economic role, the antitrust decisions of EU regulators necessarily influence business practice worldwide. [For European Union antitrust law, see **http://ec.europa.eu/competition/index_en.html**]

Other Nations   The number of nations with competition laws soared from 40 in 1995 to more than 125 in 2009,[34] and we are seeing the beginning of a worldwide convergence of those laws led by the United States, the European Union, and China.[35] South Korea, Russia, Hong Kong, and Japan are among other countries introducing new antitrust laws or adjusting existing laws, practices and enforcement. The following examples are illustrative of expanding international attention to antitrust enforcement:

- In 2010, China took its first public action under its new antitrust law by fining 21 members of a rice noodle cartel for price fixing.[36]
- Japan's Fair Trade Commission, in 2010, recommended a $92 million fine for fiber-optic cable parts makers who allegedly rigged bids.[37]
- South Korea's Fair Trade Commission, in 2010, fined 19 airlines a record $138 million for unfair practices that included manipulating fuel surcharge rates.[38]

[For an update of China's new Antimonopoly Law, see Hannah Ha, John M. Hickin, and Gerry O'Brien, "China Steps Up Antitrust Capacity Building—Cartels a Focus," *LEXOLOGY*, July 20, 2010 (**http://www.lexology.com/**)].

Extraterritoriality

Since 1992, the U.S. Justice Department has claimed national authority to apply American antitrust law abroad. The general idea is to sue foreign firms that violate U.S. antitrust laws even when the anticompetitive actions take place entirely overseas (extraterritorial application). In practice, the Justice Department files suit in U.S. courts against foreign companies operating in the United States if those foreign companies are taking action abroad that (1) harms competition in the United States or (2) limits American access to markets in other nations. Those lawsuits are permissible under U.S. law only where the conduct abroad has a "direct, substantial, and reasonably foreseeable" effect on the United States' domestic market. Extraterritoriality does not mean, however, that the United States will become the world's antitrust police department. Indeed, the European Union and China likewise have claimed extraterritorial antitrust power. [For a brief assessment of China's Anti-Monopoly law, see **http://www.insidecounsel.com/Exclusive/2010/6/Pages/ Chinas-AntiMonopoly-LawCause-for-Hope-and-Concern.aspx**]

Internet Exercise	"What Do the Antitrust Laws Do for the Consumer?" For an answer, see the U.S. Department of Justice, Antitrust Division, brochure, "Antitrust Enforcement and the Consumer." [**www.justice.gov/atr/public/div_stats/211491.htm**].
Chapter Questions	1. The Chicago Skyway, a toll bridge connecting Chicago and Indiana, was owned and operated by the City of Chicago. Chicago earned $52 million in tolls beyond the amount needed to meet bond payments and to maintain the Skyway. The excess was used to pay for other transportation expenses. Skyway tolls were higher than those of other area highways. Endsley, a bridge user, joined others in a class action against Chicago claiming that the city's control of the Skyway provided monopoly power in high-speed limited access travel between Indiana and Chicago and that the city was abusing that power by collecting excessive fees. Chicago demonstrated that at least two alternative, if less desirable, routes were in competition with the Skyway. Is Chicago a monopolist? Explain. See *Endsley v. City of Chicago,* 230 F.3d 276 (7th Cir. 2000); cert. den. 532 U.S. 972 (2001).

2. Major League Soccer (MLS) was the exclusive Division I professional soccer league in the United States, as recognized by the U.S. Soccer Federation (USSF), the national soccer governing body. MLS owned all of the league's 12 teams, set all schedules, negotiated all stadium leases, controlled all intellectual property rights, and controlled all player contracts. Partial control over some teams was transferred by MLS to certain investors. The investors did not hire their own players. Each employment contract was between the player and the league. MLS assigned the players in a manner designed to maintain competitive balance. MLS had been preceded in U.S. professional soccer by the North American Soccer League, which had failed financially. A group of players sued the MLS on antitrust grounds.

a. What were the players' antitrust claims?

b. Decide those claims. Explain. See *Fraser v. Major League Soccer,* 284 F.3d 47 (1st Cir. 2002).

3. Poplar Bluff is a city of 17,000 people in southeastern Missouri. Sikeston and Cape Girardeau, Missouri, both towns with populations of over 40,000, are 40 and 60 miles away from Poplar Bluff. Tenet Healthcare owns Lucy Lee Hospital in Poplar Bluff and proposed to buy Doctors' Regional Medical Center, also in Poplar Bluff. Both hospitals are profitable, but both are underutilized and have had trouble attracting specialists. The Federal Trade Commission filed suit to block the acquisition. The key

question involved definition of the geographic market. The FTC proposed a relevant geographic market that essentially matched the service area: a 50-mile radius of downtown Poplar Bluff. Ninety percent of the two hospitals' patients come from that area. Four other hospitals are in that area. The merged hospital would have 84 percent of the patients in that geographic market. Tenet argues that the geographic market should encompass a 65-mile radius from downtown Poplar Bluff. That area includes 16 hospitals. How should the Court of Appeals decide where the geographic market lies? See *FTC v. Tenet Health Care Corp.,* 186 F.3d 1045 (8th Cir. 1999).

4. In 2011, the U.S. Justice Department sent a letter to the National Collegiate Athletic Association raising antitrust questions about the Bowl Championship Series (BCS) which is used to determine a national football champion. The letter asked why the BCS schools have not established a playoff system. In your judgment, should the federal government be concerned about the antitrust legality of the Bowl Championship Series? Explain.

5. A major concern with horizontal mergers is the increased potential for collusion. List the structural conditions that would encourage coordinated interaction between competitors.

6. Critics are concerned that increasing mergers, especially those involving media firms, threaten democracy.
   a. Explain that argument.
   b. Do you agree? Explain.

7. In 1986 distinguished economist William Shepherd argued,

> It may not be too late to turn back from this road to serfdom by reviving the case for antitrust, but the odds aren't favorable. More probably, antitrust will continue to sink.[39]

   a. What did Shepherd mean about "this road to serfdom?"
   b. In reading this chapter, do you think antitrust has been revived? Explain.
   c. Is bigness bad, or is it necessary in today's global economy? Explain.

8. Antitrust attorney Joel Davidow said that four policy measures have been critical to the success of formerly socialist nations that moved to a market economy: privatization, restructuring, deregulation, and adoption of competition legislation (antitrust). Now almost all of the industrial nations of the world, including former Soviet states Russia, Poland, and Hungary are practicing all of these measures.
   a. Why is antitrust law important to the success of the new market economies in these formerly collectivist nations?
   b. Is antitrust important to developing nations such as India, Argentina, and Brazil? Explain. See Joel Davidow, "The Relevance of Antimonopoly Policy for Developing Countries," *Antitrust Bulletin* 37, no. 1 (Spring 1992), p. 277.

9. Is the influence of big business so persuasive that it nullifies the effective enforcement of the antitrust laws? Explain.

10. Antitrust authorities must address a critical and empirically difficult policy problem: Does seller concentration in a market ordinarily result in increased prices? That is, in a particular market, are fewer firms with larger shares likely to produce higher prices than would be the case with a more fragmented market? Free market theorists are generally untroubled by concentration. What do you think? Explain.

11. Is a monopolist required to deal with its competitors? That question was the core of a 2004 Supreme Court decision in *Verizon Communications v. Law Offices of Curtis V. Trinko*.[40] The Trinko law firm bought its local phone service from AT&T. Trinko brought a class action claiming Verizon maintained a monopoly by exclusionary practices. Trinko contended that local phone services had difficulty connecting with the giant regional Bell operating companies' (Verizon, Qwest, Bell South, and SBC) local exchange facilities, thus harming competition and consumers. The Telecommunications Act of 1996 specifically requires the regional Bell companies to provide the local phone services with fair, reasonable access. The Supreme Court, however, ruled in favor of Verizon and concluded that antitrust liability in these telephone situations would apply only where a telephone monopolist discontinues a voluntary business relationship with a competitor for the purpose of destroying that competitor. Explain why the Supreme Court decided that Verizon, a telephone monopolist, had no duty to deal with those telephone competitors with whom it had not previously dealt. See Matthew Cantor, "Is Trinko the Last Word on a Telephone Monopolist's Duty to Deal?" *New York Law Journal* 96 (May 19, 2004), p. 4.

12. In the period 1917 to 1919, DuPont acquired 23 percent of the stock in the then-fledgling General Motors Corporation. By 1947, DuPont supplied 68 percent of GM's automotive finish needs and 38 percent of its fabric needs. In 1955, General Motors ranked first in sales and second in assets among all U.S. industrial corporations, while accounting for approximately two-fifths of the nation's annual automobile sales. In 1949 the Justice Department challenged Dupont's 1917–19 acquisitions of GM stock.
    a. Why did the government challenge DuPont's acquisition?
    b. May an acquisition be properly challenged 30 years after the fact, as in DuPont? Explain.
    c. Given your general understanding of finishes and fabrics, how would you defend DuPont?
    d. Decide. Explain. See *United States v.E.I. DuPont de Nemours & Co.,* 353 U.S. 586 (1957).

13. How can a merger benefit society?

14. Which economic considerations support the view that unilateral growth is preferable to growth by merger?

15. Excel, a division of Cargill, was the second largest firm in the beef-packing market. It sought to acquire Spencer Pack, a division of Land-O-Lakes and the third largest beef packer. After the acquisition, Excel would have remained second ranked in the business, but its market share would have been only slightly smaller than that of the leader, IBP. Monfort, the nation's fifth largest beef packer, sought an injunction to block the acquisition, claiming a violation of Clayton Section 7. In effect, Monfort claimed the merger would result in a dangerous concentration of economic power in the beef-packing market, with the result that Excel would pay more for cattle and charge less for its processed beef, thus placing its competitors in a destructive and illegal price–cost squeeze. Monfort claimed Excel's initial losses in this arrangement would be covered by its wealthy parent, Cargill. Then, when the competition was driven from the market, Monfort claimed, Excel would raise its processed beef prices

to supracompetitive levels. Among other defenses, Excel averred that the heavy losses Monfort claimed were merely the product of intense competition, a condition that would not constitute a violation of the antitrust laws. The district court found for Monfort, and the appeals court, considering the cost–price squeeze a form of predatory pricing, affirmed. Excel appealed to the Supreme Court. Decide. Explain. See *Cargill, Inc. v. Monfort of Colorado, Inc.,* 479 U.S. 104 (1986).

Notes

1. See *United States v. Microsoft Corporation,* 87 F.Supp.2d 30 (D.D.C. 2000), and *Microsoft v. United States,* 253 F.3d 34 (D.C. Cir. 2001); cert. den. 122 S.Ct. 350 (2001).
2. "Microsoft Browser Use Down Following Antitrust Settlement," *RedOrbit News,* March 22, 2010 [**http://www.redorbit.com/news/display/?id=1839236**] and Jessica Guynn, "Marc Andreessen Expected to Unveil Social Web Browser, Rock Melt," *latimes.com,* November 8, 2010 [**latimes.com/business/la-fi-web-browser-20101108,0,583984.story**].
3. Alan Murray, "Microsoft Foe Quits Antitrust Crusade—with Check in Hand," *The Wall Street Journal,* December 7, 2004, p. A4.
4. *United States v. Grinnell,* 384 U.S. 563, 570-1 (1966).
5. BreakingViews.COM, "Rising Beer Prices Hint at Oligopoly," *The New York Times,* August 27, 2009 [**http://www.nytimes.com**].
6. David Kesmodel, "Beer Makers Plan More Price Boosts," *The Wall Street Journal,* August 26, 2009, p. B1.
7. "Consolidation Remains on Tap for Brewers," *Value Line,* July 14, 2010 [**http://www.value-line.com/Stocks/Commentary.aspx?id=9044**].
8. Note, "Antitrust and the Information Age: Section 2 Monopolization Analyses in the New Economy," *Harvard Law Review* 114 (March 2001), p. 1623.
9. *Spectrum Sports, Inc. v. Shirley McQuillan,* 506 U.S. 447 (1993).
10. Note, "Antitrust and the Information Age," pp. 1623, 1645.
11. *United States v. Aluminum Co. of America,* 148 F.2d 416 (2d Cir. 1945).
12. "Mergers, Acquisitions at 5-Year Low in 2009: Survey," livemint.com/*The Wall Street Journal,* January 5, 2010 [**http://64.74.118.102/2010/01/05185812/Mergers-acquisitions-at-5yea.html**].
13. Eric Dash, "Wells Fargo in a Deal to Buy All of Wachovia," *The New York Times,* October 3, 2008 [**http://www.nytimes.com**].
14. Editorial, "Big Food," *The New York Times,* January 25, 2010 [**http://nytimes.com**].
15. Ibid.
16. Jim Rhyne, "Comcast Distracts with Corporate 'Goodwill,'" *Stop Big Media,* August 2, 2010 [**http://www.stopbigmedia.com/blog/2010/08/**].
17. "Kevin Voigt, "Mergers Fail More Often than Marriages," *CNN.com/world business,* May 22, 2009 [**http://edition.cnn.com/2009/BUSINESS/05/21/merger.marriage/index.html**].
18. See Michael J. Mandel, "All These Mergers Are Great, But . . ." *BusinessWeek,* October 18, 1999, p. 48; and Jeffrey Garten, "Megamergers Are a Clear and Present Danger," *BusinessWeek,* January 25, 1999, p. 28.
19. Associated Press, "Justice Department Signs Off on United-Continental Deal," *The Des Moines Register,* August 28, 2010, p. 16A.
20. Andrew Ross Sorkin, "United and Continental Announce Merger," DealBook, *The New York Times,* May 3, 2010 [**http://dealbook.blogs.nytimes.com/**].

21. Editorial, "Why Merge?" *The New York Times,* May 9, 2010 [**http://www.nytimes.com/**].

22. Ibid.

23. The Editors, "Who Benefits When Airlines Merge?" Room for Debate, *The New York Times,* May 4, 2010 [**http://roomfordebate.blogs.nytimes.com/**].

24. Dan Reed, "Does This . . . Plus This . . . Equal Higher Airfares," *USA TODAY,* June 22, 2010, p. 1B.

25. Ibid.

26. Private filings have declined in recent years as documented and analyzed in Timothy S. Longman and Joseph Ostoyich, "U.S. Private Enforcement," *The Antitrust Review of the Americas 2011* [**http://www.globalcompetitivenessreview.com/reviews/29/sections/102/chapters/1137/us-private-enforcement/**].

27. Note, "Analyzing Differentiated-Product Mergers: The Relevance of Structural Analysis," *Harvard Law Review* 111 (June 1998), p. 2420.

28. Ben Sisario, "Justice Dept. Clears Ticketmaster Deal," *The New York Times,* January 26, 2010 [**http://www.nytimes.com**].

29. Press Release, "Justice Department Requires Ticketmaster Entertainment Inc. to Make Significant Changes to Its Merger with Live Nation, Inc., United States Department of Justice, January 25, 2010 [**http://www.justice.gov/atr/public/press_releases/2010/254540.htm**].

30. Ethan Smith, "High-Decibel Criticism Greets Completion of Live Nation Merger," *The Wall Street Journal,* January 27, 2010 [**http/online.wsj.com/**].

31. Sisario, "Justice Dept. Clears Ticketmaster Deal."

32. Sisario, "Justice Dept. Clears Ticketmaster Deal."

33. Richard Posner, *Antitrust Law* (Chicago: The University of Chicago Press, 1976), p. 130.

34. Howard W. Fogt, Jr., Alan D. Rutenberg, Max Lin and Wen (Jo) Xu, "Evolving Convergence: Antitrust/Competition Law and Policy/Procedure in the United States, European Union, and China, *LEXOLOGY,* December 9, 2009 [**http://www.lexology.com/**].

35. Ibid.

36. Rajah & Tann, L.L.P., "Competition Review," July 2010 [**http://www.rajahtann.com/eoasis/gn/pdf2010-Jul-Competition-Review.pdf**].

37. Ibid.

38. Ibid.

39. William G. Shepherd, "Bust the Reagan Trustbusters," *Fortune,* August 4, 1986, pp. 225, 227.

40. 540 U.S. 398 (2004).

Employer–Employee Relations

CHAPTER TWELVE

Employment Law I: Employee Rights

After completing this chapter, students will be able to:

1. Distinguish between an employee and independent contractor.

2. Identify potential legal challenges an employer faces in the hiring process.

3. Describe employers' liability under the doctrine of "respondeat superior."

4. Analyze claims of negligent hiring, supervision, and retention.

5. Explain employees' rights under the Fair Labor Standards Act.

6. Describe the role of the Occupational Safety and Health Administration (OSHA) in protecting employees' health and safety at work.

7. Describe the benefits, coverage, and requirements for bringing a successful claim under workers' compensation law.

8. Discuss workplace drug testing and the legal challenges it faces.

9. Describe the Family and Medical Leave Act (FMLA).

10. Distinguish between defined benefit and defined contribution pension plans.

11. Analyze whether a dismissed at-will employee may bring a claim of wrongful discharge.

12. Recognize the purpose and requirements of the employment eligibility verification form (I-9).

Introduction

Scott Rodrigues was fired in 2006 by The Scotts Company, the lawn care giant, because a required drug test revealed nicotine in his urine. Company policy forbade employee smoking both on and off the job. Scotts announced in 2005 that it would no longer hire smokers, and it gave its employees one year to comply with the new policy, a policy designed to improve employee wellness and reduce company healthcare costs. Rodrigues was a pack-a-day smoker when he was hired. He was aware of the no-smoking policy, and he had been warned to quit when a supervisor saw a pack of cigarettes on the dashboard of his car. Rodrigues acknowledged his smoking habit, but said he was trying to quit smoking when he was fired. Rodrigues complained that the company had not offered to help him quit smoking. The Scotts' plan does, however, pay for smoking cessation programs for its employees. Scotts said they were not interested in influencing workers' behavior in their free time, except in the case of smoking.[1] Rodrigues decided to file suit against Scotts because:

> What's to make them stop at just cigarettes? If they're a Republican company, can they try and figure out who you vote for and if you vote the Democrats, they'll fire you? . . ."[2]

According to the American Lung Association's Tobacco Policy Project/State Legislated Actions on Tobacco Issues (SLATI) Web site, 29 states and the District of Columbia have laws protecting smokers from adverse employment action based on smoking tobacco.[3] While Massachusetts law does not provide explicit shelter for smokers, it offers statutory protection from "unreasonable, substantial, or serious interference" with an individual's privacy.[4] Rodrigues brought suit against the Scotts Company claiming, among other things invasion of privacy.

Questions

1. How would you rule on Rodrigues's right to privacy claim?
2. Should employers be able to fire employees who smoke off the job? Explain. See *Rodrigues v. the Scotts Company,* 639 F.Supp.2d 131 (D. Mass 2009).

Managing Lawsuits   Managers traditionally have balanced multiple responsibilities, but in recent years the law has added complex, sometimes daunting expectations. Addressing and mitigating the risk of employment-related lawsuits, like Rodrigues's, has become an important consideration in management decision making. As union strength has declined (see Chapter 14), government regulations and court decisions have arguably broadened employee rights. These increased legal protections, a volatile economy, downsizing, weakened employer–employee loyalty, and other forces have contributed to higher levels of employee litigation.[5]

Part One—The Employment Relationship

Job Classification   Employment-related legal rights and responsibilities depend on the type of relationship the employer decides to build with the worker. The traditional, stable model of long-term direct employer–employee relationships now is often replaced with new, flexible, nontraditional staffing arrangements including outsourcing and employee leasing, along with the use of freelancers and temporary agencies. These *contingent workers,* along with *independent contractors,* who are increasingly relied on to perform specific, shorter-term, nonrecurring jobs, permit employers to rapidly and inexpensively inflate or shrink their workforces as competitive and regulatory conditions change. Employers who choose to provide health and retirement benefits for their traditional employees need not do so for their contingent workers. Nor must they withhold income, Social Security, Medicare, and unemployment taxes. With fringe benefit costs skyrocketing, benefits reduction has become an important consideration for most firms. A firm might contract with professional employer organizations (PEOs) to take responsibility for and administer its payroll and human resources operation. [For an overview of PEOs and their functions, see **http://www.napeo.org/**]

Employee or Independent Contractor?   A key question underlying the legal issues discussed in this chapter is whether the worker in question is an employee or an independent contractor; one who enters a contractual rather than employment relationship with an organization in order to perform a specific task. Degree of control is the dominant test in determining whether a worker is an employee or independent contractor. Where an employer controls or has the right or ability to control the worker's performance, the worker is likely to be considered an employee. In 2008, CBS used the distinction between "independent contractor" and "employee" to successfully defend against an FCC fine after Justin Timberlake and Janet Jackson appeared to cooperatively expose Ms. Jackson's breast at the end of their performance during the 2004 Super Bowl halftime show that CBS broadcast. CBS argued that the performers were independent contractors, not employees, and, therefore, CBS could not be held liable for actions taken outside their control.[6]

What other advantages might a business gain from hiring an independent contractor rather than an employee? A business that hires an independent contractor generally is not required to comply with a wide range of employment and labor law standards that would apply were the worker an employee. Thus a business must provide, for example, unemployment insurance to its employees, but generally would not need to do so for independent contractors. Furthermore, employers generally are not liable for employment discrimination claims by independent contractors or for most torts committed by independent contractors in the course of work. While employers are responsible for payroll taxes such as FICA and federal and state unemployment insurance, as well as for withholding income tax from their employees, these tax obligations of a business do not extend to its independent contractors. [For a sample of independent contractor agreements, see **http://www. uschambersmallbusinessnation.com/toolkits/tool/indcon_m**]

Classification Problems   Employers anxious to reduce financial and legal burdens sometimes improperly classify workers as independent contractors rather than employees. In 2007, a California federal district court ordered a house cleaning service to pay $4.5 million to provide minimum wages and overtime pay for workers who had been misclassified as independent contractors. Employees, unlike independent contractors, are protected by the Fair Labor Standards Act (detailed later in this chapter), which requires, among other things, the payment of the federal minimum wage and overtime pay. The employer claimed that the workers were independent contractors and thus not covered by the FLSA, but the court pointed to a variety of considerations, including control and supervision, that confirmed the workers' correct status as employees.[7] The federal tax implications for misclassification of employees are being addressed by the Internal Revenue Service (IRS). In March 2010, recognizing "that business practices regarding employment tax issues have changed significantly since the 1980s," the (IRS) began the Employment Tax National Research Program, a three-year employment tax audit which will randomly select 2,000 employment tax filers a year to examine whether they are in compliance.[8] [For IRS guidance on determining whether a worker is an employee or independent contractor, see: **http://www.irs.gov/businesses/small/article/0,,id=99921,00.html**]

Selection and Hiring   An array of potential legal problems have arisen from the increasingly complex process of choosing and employing new workers.

- ***Résumé Fraud.*** David J. Edmondson resigned as chief executive of Radio Shack in 2006 a few days after a newspaper reported that Edmondson had not earned either of the two college degrees he had claimed on his résumé when he was hired more than 10 years previously.[9] Misstated qualifications of corporate executives at Herbalife Ltd. and Usana Health Sciences have also been uncovered.[10] A 2008 online poll of 3,000 hiring managers revealed that 49 percent had uncovered a lie on a résumé, including exaggeration of job responsibilities and skills, false claims regarding education, and inflated job titles. One of the more unusual lies involved an applicant who pretended to be related to the Kennedy clan.[11]

- ***Background Checks.*** Résumé fraud, growing concerns regarding workplace violence, and losses due to employee theft may have fueled the booming background screening industry.[12] A 2010 survey conducted by the Society for Human Resource Management (SHRM) showed that 60 percent of employers run credit checks on applicants for at least some positions, and over 90 percent check criminal backgrounds.[13] Using credit checks in hiring arguably helps protect an employer against fraud and employee theft, since applicants who have not handled their personal finances responsibly might be more likely to engage in such misconduct. However, questions about the validity and unintended impact of this practice have been raised in recent years. Not only has the connection between a bad credit report and poor job performance been disputed, but studies showing that African Americans and Latinos tend to have lower credit scores cause concern that credit checks can create a discriminatory impact on these groups' ability to gain employment.[14] Several states have recently passed legislation limiting the use of credit checks. The Illinois Employee Credit Privacy Act, for example, generally prohibits employers from using an employee's or applicant's credit history in making employment decisions such as hiring. However, certain employers, such as banks, insurance companies, and debt collectors are exempt, and all employers may use credit checks in hiring one who will have unsupervised access to more than $2,500.[15]

   Similarly, the practice of conducting criminal background checks in hiring has been challenged under federal antidiscrimination law in recent lawsuits. [For more information on the legal issues surrounding criminal background checks in hiring, see The National Employment Law Project, "65 Million 'Need Not Apply:' The Case for Reforming Criminal Background Checks for Employment" (March 23, 2011) at **http://www.nelp.org/page/-/65_Million_Need_Not_Apply.pdf?nocdn=1**]

   As the use of credit and criminal background checks comes under attack, employers are increasingly searching the online reputation of job applicants. According to a Microsoft

> Posting inappropriate comments online is cited as a top reason for rejecting a job candidate.

study released at Microsoft's 2010 Privacy Day, 79 percent of job recruiters check the Internet to review the online reputations of job candidates, and 70 percent of U.S. employers have rejected applicants based on online reputation. Posting inappropriate comments or unsuitable photos and videos online is cited as a top reason for rejecting a job candidate.[16]

- *Inappropriate Questions.* According to a 2009 survey, 22 percent of job seekers cited interviewers "asking inappropriate questions" as a "top turn-off" in the interview process.[17] Furthermore, such questions as "How old are you?" and "Are you married?" also expose employers to potential liability for discrimination. (see Chapter 13.) But what about the enormous array of awkward, intrusive, but nondiscriminatory interview questions that might leave the candidate feeling uncomfortable if not wronged? For example: "What would you do if I gave you an elephant?" has questionable relevance in a job interview.[18]

- *Restrictive Covenants.* Chris Botticella, a former executive with Bimbo Bakeries, which operates under popular brand names such as Thomas' and Entenmann's, was unable to start work for Hostess, Inc. because of the confidentiality agreement and other restrictive covenants he had signed with Bimbo. Information such as recipes and business strategies to which Botticella had access would likely be shared with Hostess.[19] To address problems like these, employers sometimes require employees to sign agreements providing they will not compete with their employer, solicit its customers or employees, pass trade secrets to others, and so on, for a specified period of time. Shortly after Mark Hurd resigned as Chief Executive Officer of Hewlett-Packard in 2010, he was named co-president of Oracle Corporation. The next day, Hewlett-Packard filed a lawsuit seeking to prevent Hurd from working for Oracle and to enforce the agreements Hurd had entered restricting his ability to enter into competition with his former employer.[20] Such agreements are not limited to upper management,[21] and generally are fully enforceable if reasonable in their requirements. California law, however, prohibits noncompetition agreements in employment, with narrow statutory exceptions.[22]

- *Arbitration.* New employees are sometimes expected to sign agreements specifying that disputes with the employer will be settled by arbitration (see Chapter 4) rather than by litigation. Employers like arbitration because it can be cheaper, faster, and less adversarial than a trial. Employees, on the other hand, argue that arbitration is stacked in favor of corporate interests and amounts to a denial of the fundamental right of access to the legal system. Employment arbitration agreements have been supported by recent U.S. Supreme Court decisions, such as *Circuit City Stores, Inc. v. Adams* upholding the enforceability of legitimate, equitable employment arbitration agreement.[23] While an employee might still challenge an arbitration agreement's validity, in its 2010 decision in *Rent-a-Center West, Inc. v. Jackson,* the U.S. Supreme Court gave the arbitrator in an arbitration proceeding the power to determine whether the agreement is valid, rather than allowing the employee to make that argument in court.[24] However, the U.S. Equal Employment Opportunity Commission (see Chapter 13) still retains authority to file discrimination lawsuits on behalf of employees despite an arbitration agreement.[25]

You decide to fire an employee.

• *References.* As a manager, you decide to fire an employee, Brown, because of what you believe to be convincing evidence that he had sexually harassed a coworker. Brown applies for a new job, and that employer seeks your evaluation of Brown's work. What should you do? If you tell what you know, you and your employer fear Brown might sue you for *defamation* (*slander* when spoken; *libel* when written). If you fail to say what you know, you fear you might be sued for *misrepresentation* or *negligent referral* if Brown is hired and commits further harassment on his new job. Because of those risks, employers often limit their references to purely factual details such as the date of hire, date of departure, and job title.

Broadly, a successful defamation suit requires the following conditions:

1. A false statement.
2. The statement must be "published" to a third party.
3. The employer must be responsible for the publication.
4. The plaintiff's reputation must be harmed.

Truth is a complete defense in defamation cases, and managers who offer factual, honest professional judgments are unlikely to face such claims. Furthermore, many state courts provide the protection of a *qualified privilege*. Under this privilege, legitimate business communications, with some exceptions, are shielded from liability. Similarly, a number of states have enacted legislation providing employers with immunity from liability for good faith employment references.

Part Two—Liability

Once hired, what happens when employees make mistakes or engage in misconduct on the job that hurts others? Must the employer bear the loss in these situations? Job classification is an important first question in determining company liability for workers' job-related injuries, harm to others, and crimes. An enterprise ordinarily will not be liable for the acts of its independent contractors. Employers, on the other hand, often bear legal responsibility for employees' accidents or wrongs. That liability may spring from the doctrine of *respondeat superior* (let the master answer), a form of *vicarious liability* (sometimes called *imputed liability*).

Scope of Employment   Employer liability for employee injuries, accidents, or wrongs is largely dependent on whether the employee was on the job at the time of the incident in question. Employers will be held liable under respondeat superior/vicarious liability reasoning for harm to third parties caused by the intentional or negligent acts of their employees when those acts occur within the *scope of employment* (on the job). A finding of employer liability, of course, does not excuse the employee from her personal liability, but the respondeat superior reasoning does have the potential effect of opening the employer's deeper pockets to the plaintiff. The following questions ordinarily determine whether the harm occurred in the scope of employment:

1. Was the employee subject to the employer's supervision?
2. Was the employee motivated, at least in part, by a desire to serve the employer's business interests?
3. Did the problem arise substantially within normal working hours and in a work location?
4. Was the act in question of the general kind the employee had been hired to perform?

> The City was held liable for a sexual assault committed by a police officer.

In *Mary M. v. City of Los Angeles,*[26] the city was held liable under the doctrine of respondeat superior for a sexual assault committed by a police officer. At 2:30 AM on October 3, 1981, Sergeant Leigh Schroyer was on duty, in uniform, carrying a gun, and patrolling in his marked police car. He stopped Mary M. for erratic driving. She pleaded not to be arrested. He ordered her to enter his patrol car and took her to her home. He entered her home and said that he expected "payment" for not arresting her. He raped her and was subsequently sentenced to a term in state prison.

Mary M. sued the City of Los Angeles. The general inquiry was whether Schroyer was acting within the scope of his employment during the rape episode. The jury found for Mary M. and awarded $150,000 in damages. The Court of Appeals reversed, saying that Schroyer was not acting within the scope of his employment. The case went to the California Supreme Court. The city argued that Schroyer was acting on behalf of his own interests rather than those of the city, and that the city had not authorized his conduct. Therefore, Schroyer could not have been acting within the scope of employment. However, the court said that the correct question was not whether the rape was authorized but whether it happened in the course of a series of acts that were authorized. The court reversed, saying that a jury could find the city vicariously liable (imputed to the principal from the agent) given the unique authority of police officers in our society.

Questions

1. Gonzalez, working for Land Transport, was driving his employer's tractor-trailer behind Nichols, who was driving his pickup. Gonzalez followed at an unsafe distance and twice attempted to pass in no-passing zones. Nichols responded with "predictable obscene gestures." While both drivers were stopped at a red light, Gonzalez left the company truck and attacked Nichols with a rubber-coated metal cable and a knife. Gonzalez was convicted of assault. Nichols sued Land Transport.
   a. What is his claim?
   b. Decide the case. Explain. See *Nichols v. Land Transport,* 233 F.3d 21 (1st Cir. 2000).
2. Ahern, a chef at the Heathwood Nursing and Rehabilitation Center in Chestnut Hill, Massachusetts left work and went to the South Pacific Chinese Restaurant where he met his supervisor, Pacitti, to socialize and discuss work-related matters. Ahern purchased two drinks and consumed at least one drink and one-half of the other before leaving to go home. On his way home, Ahern's vehicle struck Lev as he was crossing a street, causing severe and debilitating injuries. Ahern was arrested and eventually convicted of operating a motor vehicle while under the influence of intoxicating liquor. Lev sued

Heathwood's owner and operator, Beverly Enterprises, alleging that Beverly was vicariously liable for Ahern's negligence based on their employment relationship.

a. What was the central issue in this case?

b. Decide the case. Explain. See *Lev v. Beverly Enterprises,* 457 Mass. 234 (Sup. Jud. Ct. Mass. 2010)

3. What policy justifications support the imposition of liability on an employer for the wrongs of an employee operating within the scope of employment?

Happy Hour?

According to a 2008 survey by Careerbuilder.com, 21 percent of workers attend "happy hours" with their colleagues. Of these, 82 percent go to happy hours to "bond" with their coworkers, 20 percent attend in order to "network," and 15 percent go in hope of hearing the "latest office gossip." Thirteen percent admitted that they show up because they feel they are obligated to attend.

Source: "CareerBuilder.com Happy Hour Survey Reveals How Many Workers Attend, How It Impacts Careers and the Biggest Mishaps" [**http://www.careerbuilder.com/share/aboutus/pressreleasesdetail.aspx?id=pr439&sd=6%2F24%**].

Hiring/Retention/Training/Supervision

Negligence

In addition to vicarious liability for employees' actions, employers may be directly liable for negligence in hiring an employee or retaining an employee who subsequently causes harm to a third party, or for careless training or supervision. Typically, the employer is liable on negligence grounds for hiring or retaining an employee whom the employer knew or should have known to be dangerous, incompetent, dishonest, or the like where that information was directly related to the injury suffered by the plaintiff. Note that under negligence liability an employer may be liable for acts *outside* the scope of employment. The case that follows examines the law of negligent hiring, supervision, and retention.

LEGAL BRIEFCASE

Yunker v. Honeywell, Inc.
496 N.W.2d 419 (Minn.App. 1993)

Judge Lansing

FACTS

Honeywell employed Randy Landin from 1977 to 1979 and from 1984 to 1988. From 1979 to 1984 Landin was imprisoned for the strangulation death of Nancy Miller, a Honeywell coemployee.

On his release from prison, Landin reapplied at Honeywell. Honeywell rehired Landin as a custodian in Honeywell's General Offices facility in South Minneapolis in August 1984. Because of workplace confrontations Landin was twice transferred, first to the Golden Valley facility in August 1986, and then to the St. Louis Park facility in August 1987.

Kathleen Nesser was assigned to Landin's maintenance crew in April 1988. Landin and Nesser became friends and spent time together away from work. When Landin expressed a romantic interest, Nesser stopped spending time with Landin. Landin began to harass and threaten Nesser both at work and at home. At the end of June, Landin's behavior prompted Nesser to seek help from her supervisor and to request a transfer out of the St. Louis Park facility.

On July 1, 1988, Nesser found a death threat scratched on her locker door. Landin did not come to work on or after July 1, and Honeywell accepted his formal resignation on July 11, 1988. On July 19, approximately six hours after her Honeywell shift ended, Landin killed Nesser in her driveway with a close-range shotgun blast. Landin was convicted of first-degree murder and sentenced to life imprisonment.

Jean Yunker, as trustee for the heirs and next-of-kin of Kathleen Nesser, brought this wrongful death action based on theories of negligent hiring, retention, and supervision of a dangerous employee. Honeywell moved for summary judgment and, for purposes of the motion, stipulated that it failed to exercise reasonable care in the hiring and supervision of Landin. The trial court concluded that Honeywell owed no legal duty to Nesser and granted summary judgment for Honeywell.

ISSUE

Did Honeywell have a duty to Kathleen Nesser to exercise reasonable care in hiring, retaining, or supervising Randy Landin?

ANALYSIS

In determining that Honeywell did not have a legal duty to Kathleen Nesser arising from its employment of Randy Landin, the district court analyzed Honeywell's duty as limited by its ability to control and protect its employees while they are involved in the employer's business or at the employer's place of business. Additionally, the court concluded that Honeywell could not have reasonably foreseen Landin's killing Nesser.

Incorporating a "scope of employment" limitation into an employer's duty borrows from the doctrine of *respondeat superior*. However, of the three theories advanced for recovery, only negligent supervision derives from the *respondeat superior* doctrine, which relies on connection to the employer's premises or chattels. We agree that negligent supervision is not a viable theory of recovery because Landin was neither on Honeywell's premises nor using Honeywell's chattels when he shot Nesser.

The remaining theories, negligent hiring and negligent retention, are based on direct, not vicarious, liability. Negligent hiring and negligent retention do not rely on the scope of employment but address risks created by exposing members of the public to a potentially dangerous individual. These theories

of recovery impose liability for an employee's intentional tort, an action almost invariably outside the scope of employment, when the employer knew or should have known that the employee was violent or aggressive and might engage in injurious conduct.

I

Minnesota first explicitly recognized a cause of action based on negligent hiring in *Ponticas* in 1983. *Ponticas* involved the employment of an apartment manager who sexually assaulted a tenant. The Supreme Court upheld a jury verdict finding the apartment operators negligent in failing to make a reasonable investigation into the resident manager's background before providing him with a passkey. The court defined negligent hiring as

> predicated on the negligence of an employer in placing a person with known propensities, or propensities which should have been discovered by reasonable investigation, in an employment position in which, *because of the circumstances of the employment,* it should have been foreseeable that the hired individual posed a threat of injury to others.

Honeywell argues that under *Ponticas* it is not liable for negligent hiring because, unlike providing a dangerous resident manager with a passkey, Landin's employment did not enable him to commit the act of violence against Nesser. This argument has merit, and we note that a number of jurisdictions have expressly defined the scope of an employer's duty of reasonable care in hiring as largely dependent on the type of responsibilities associated with the particular job. See *Connes,* 831 P.2d at 1321 (employer's duty in hiring is dependent on anticipated degree of contact between employee and other persons in performing employment duties).

Ponticas rejected the view that employers are required to investigate a prospective employee's criminal background in every job in which the individual has regular contact with the public. Instead, liability is determined by the totality of the circumstances surrounding the hiring and whether the employer exercised reasonable care. The court instructed that

> [t]he scope of the investigation is directly related to the severity of the risk third parties are subjected to by an incompetent employee. Although only slight care might suffice in the hiring of a yardman, a worker on a production line, or other types of employment where the employee would not constitute a high risk of injury to third persons, when the prospective employee is to be furnished a passkey permitting admittance to living quarters of tenants, the employer has the duty to use reasonable care to investigate his competency and reliability prior to employment.

Applying these principles, we conclude that Honeywell did not owe a duty to Nesser at the time of Landin's hire. Landin was employed as a maintenance worker whose job responsibilities entailed no exposure to the general public and required only limited contact with coemployees. Unlike the caretaker in *Ponticas,* Landin's duties did not involve inherent dangers to others, and unlike the tenant in *Ponticas,* Nesser was not a reasonably foreseeable victim at the time Landin was hired.

To reverse the district court's determination on duty as it relates to hiring would extend *Ponticas* and essentially hold that ex-felons are inherently dangerous and that any harmful acts they commit against persons encountered through employment will automatically be considered foreseeable. Such a rule would deter employers from hiring workers with a criminal record and "offend our civilized concept that society must make a reasonable effort to rehabilitate those who have erred so they can be assimilated into the community."

Honeywell did not breach a legal duty to Nesser by hiring Landin because the specific nature of his employment did not create a foreseeable risk of harm, and public policy supports a limitation on this cause of action. The district court correctly determined that Honeywell is not liable to Nesser under a theory of negligent hiring.

II

In recognizing the tort of negligent hiring, *Ponticas* extended established Minnesota case law permitting recovery under theories of negligent retention.

* * * * *

The difference between negligent hiring and negligent retention focuses on when the employer was on notice that an employee posed a threat and failed to take steps to ensure the safety of third parties. The Florida appellate court has provided a useful definition:

> Negligent hiring occurs when, prior to the time the employee is actually hired, the employer knew or should have known of the employee's unfitness, and the issue of liability primarily focuses upon the adequacy of the employer's pre-employment investigation into the employee's background. Negligent retention, on the other hand, occurs when, during the course of employment, the employer becomes aware or should have become aware of problems with an employee that indicated his unfitness, and the employer fails to take further action such as investigating, discharge, or reassignment.

. . . The record contains evidence of a number of episodes in Landin's postimprisonment employment at Honeywell that demonstrate a propensity for abuse and violence toward coemployees.

While at the Golden Valley facility, Landin sexually harassed female employees and challenged a male coworker to fight. After his transfer to St. Louis Park, Landin threatened to kill a coworker during an angry confrontation following a minor car accident. In another employment incident, Landin was hostile and abusive toward a female coworker after problems developed in their friendship. Landin's specific focus on Nesser was demonstrated by several workplace outbursts occurring at the end of June, and on July 1 the words "one more day and you're dead" were scratched on her locker door.

Landin's troubled work history and the escalation of abusive behavior during the summer of 1988 relate directly to the foreseeability prong of duty. The facts . . . show that it was foreseeable that Landin could act violently against a coemployee and against Nesser in particular.

This foreseeability gives rise to a duty of care to Nesser that is not outweighed by policy considerations of employment opportunity. An ex-felon's "opportunity for gainful employment may spell the difference between recidivism and rehabilitation," but it cannot predominate over the need to maintain a safe workplace when specific actions point to future violence.

Our holding is narrow and limited only to the recognition of a legal duty owed to Nesser arising out of Honeywell's continued employment of Landin. It is important to emphasize that in reversing the summary judgment on negligent retention, we do not reach the remaining significant questions of whether Honeywell breached that duty by failing to terminate or discipline Landin, or whether such a breach was a proximate cause of Nesser's death. These are issues generally decided by a jury after a full presentation of facts . . .

DECISION

We affirm the entry of summary judgment on the theories of negligent hiring and supervision, but reverse the summary judgment on the issue of negligent retention.

AFTERWORD

Published reports indicate the *Yunker* case was settled out of court soon after this decision was handed down.

Questions

1. What did the court mean when it said that "negligent hiring and negligent retention are based on direct, not vicarious, liability?"
2. Why did the court reject the negligent supervision claim?
3. Why did the court reject the negligent hiring claim?
4. Why did the court allow the negligent retention issue to go to trial?

5. Gary Weimerskirch, Assistant Manager at Main Lanes Bowling Alley, walked in on David Coakley, a mechanic at the bowling alley, and Coakley's girlfriend as they were getting dressed, apparently having just engaged in sexual relations. Coakley then told Weimerskirch that he quit and he began to collect his belongings from the work area. Suddenly, Coakley then grabbed a two-by-four plank, ran toward Weimerskirch, and struck him on the head with it. Coakley's criminal record included drug and alcohol-related offenses, along with one misdemeanor assault. However, his employer did not have any knowledge of this criminal record. Furthermore, Coakley had not acted violently at work previously.

a. What causes of action might Weimerskirch bring against the bowling alley?

b. Decide the case. Explain. See *Weimerskirch v. Coakley et al.,* 2008 Ohio 1681 (10th App. Dist. 2008).

Part Three—Fair Labor Standards Act

A note was passed to President Franklin D. Roosevelt in 1936 from a young girl:

> I wish you could do something to help us girls. We have been working in a sewing factory . . . getting our minimum pay of $11 a week. Today, the 200 of us girls have been cut down to $4 and $5 and $6 a week.[27]

Roosevelt reportedly remarked that something needed to be done about child labor. The Depression and its tragic suffering, even of those working hard, shattered many Americans' faith in the free market and led to government intervention including, in 1938, the Fair Labor Standards Act (FLSA), which is directed toward these major objectives:

1. The establishment of a minimum wage that provides at least the foundation for a modest standard of living for employees.
2. A flexible ceiling on hours worked weekly, the purpose of which is to increase the number of employed Americans.
3. Child labor protection.
4. Equal pay for equal work regardless of gender. (See Chapter 13.)

[For the U.S. Department of Labor home page, see **http://www.dol.gov**]

Minimum Wage In 2009, the federal minimum wage was increased to $7.25 per hour, the last of a three-stage increase initiated in 2007. Critics of a federally mandated minimum wage argue that the government should not interfere in the marketplace, and that increases in minimum wages threaten not only job growth but the livelihoods of many small business owners. Supporters of minimum wage increases point to recent studies concluding that raising the minimum wage does not lead to the loss of low-paying jobs.[28] More than 130 municipalities, many where living costs are particularly high, have adopted their own "living wage" requirements.[29] At this writing, Maryland's living wage law requires certain state contractors to pay employees either $12.28 per hour or $9.23 per hour depending on where the services are performed.[30] Despite these legal requirements, more than 25 percent of low-wage workers surveyed in a 2009 study were paid less than the minimum wage.[31] [For state minimum wage laws, see **http://www.dol.gov/whd/minwage/america.htm**]

Overtime   The Fair Labor Standards Act (FLSA) provides rights to minimum wage and overtime pay (generally at the rate of one and a half times the employee's regular rate of pay for time worked over 40 hours per week). However, certain occupational classes, such as managers, outside salespersons, administrators, and some professionals are not protected by FLSA. These workers are referred to as "exempt" employees. *Misclassification* of "nonexempt" workers as "exempt" from minimum wage and overtime protections has resulted in several high-profile wage and hour claims. In 2011, Levi Strauss was ordered to pay over $1 million in overtime back wages to 596 employees after the U.S. Department of Labor found that Levi had misclassified workers as exempt employees.[32] Some employees were labeled assistant store managers, but simply calling them managers did not make them so, they claimed, if their work was not of a managerial character. Walmart paid up to $640 million to settle 63 recent, wage-related lawsuits.[33]

Overtime claims often involve disputes over whether the employee was actually working, rather than being engaged in a noncompensable activity. These *off-the-clock* claims in which employers are accused of not giving employees recorded credit for all of the time they have worked sometimes spring from advancing technology. According to a 2008 report of the Pew Internet & American Life Project, 50 percent of workers with business email accounts check their work-related email while at home, and 34 percent do so while on vacation.[34] An overtime lawsuit filed by current and former T-Mobile employees alleged that they were provided smart phones by their employer and required to check and respond to work-related emails, text messages, and phone calls "off the clock." Frequently they picked up lunch and took it back to the store in order to work through their "lunch break."[35]

To promote enforcement of wage laws, in 2010 the U.S. Department of Labor instituted the "We Can Help" campaign to encourage workers to report employers' violations. [For information on this program, see: **http://www.dol.gov/wecanhelp/**]

Student Interns   In a tough job market, unpaid internships become more attractive to job seekers and employers alike. To address potentially abusive situations in which employers seek "free labor," the U.S. Department of Labor in 2010 issued a test for unpaid internships to determine whether the interns are employees with wage rights or trainees who are receiving an educational opportunity for their sole benefit and are thus excluded from FLSA protection. Generally, the more an internship focuses on an academic or classroom experience rather than the host's operations, the more likely it need not be a paid position. If interns, on the other hand, are assisting with the employer's daily operations such as clerical work, then they have a right to minimum wage and overtime. [For the six criteria of the U.S. Department of Labor's test for unpaid internships, see: **http://www.dol.gov/whd/regs/ compliance/whdfs71.pdf**]

Question

1. Answer this person's complaint: "I work as a pharmacist in a large discount retail store. My employer classifies me as exempt under FLSA. Like other pharmacists, I agree to work a specific number of base hours per week which determines my specific rate of pay. However, the employer has changed my base hours so frequently lately that I am effectively being treated as an hourly employee. There have been weeks I have worked over 40 hours a week. Do I have a right to overtime?"[36]

Part Four—Health and Safety at Work

Gordon Jones   "I am here to describe the profound impact my brother's death, while working on a rig engaged in deepwater drilling, has had on our family," Chris Jones told the U.S. House Committee on Natural Resources in March 2011. He was testifying as the surviving brother of Gordon Jones, one of 11 workers killed in the 2010 oil well explosion in the Gulf of Mexico. "[Gordon] was tragically killed aboard the Deepwater Horizon while earning his living as a mud engineer for MI SWACO, a contractor for BP [British Petroleum]. Gordon had nothing to do with this disaster. He was simply doing his job and making his way through his shift so he could get back home to his family. Instead, he never saw his family again. We can thank poor, and likely grossly negligent, decisions by many people and companies for that."[37] At this writing, federal prosecutors are considering bringing manslaughter charges against BP managers for decisions made before the fatal 2010 explosion that led to the enormous gulf oil spill.[38]

> He was simply doing his job and making his way through his shift so he could get back home to his family.

Fifteen Die in 2005 Refinery Blast   The 2010 Gulf of Mexico oil well explosion echoed the 2005 disaster at the BP oil refinery in Texas City, Texas. Workers were doing their day's work by restarting a unit that had been down for repair when a gasoline overflow exploded injuring 170 and killing 15. BP attributed the 2005 disaster primarily to operator error and six employees were fired, but government investigators concluded that management authorized the restart knowing that three key pieces of equipment were not working properly:

> These things do not have to happen. They are preventable. They are predictable, and people do not have to die because they're earning a living.[39]

In August 2010, BP agreed to pay $50.6 million in fines for failing to fix safety hazards at the Texas City refinery after the 2005 explosion.[40]

Deaths, Illnesses, and Injuries   Some workplaces are unacceptably risky, but America has achieved considerable progress in building safety on the job. Workplace fatalities that totaled 6,632 in 1995 fell to 5,214 in 2008 and 4,340 in 2009, the lowest since data were first collected in 1992.[41]

The rate of fatalities per 100,000 workers fell to 3.3 in 2009 from 3.7 per 100,000 workers in 2008.[42] Nonfatal injuries and illnesses have also declined from 3.9 per 100 workers in 2008 to 3.6 in 2009.[43] The number of workplace deaths among non-Hispanic black or African–American workers declined significantly in 2009. However, the total hours this group worked in 2009 also declined compared with white non-Hispanic and Hispanic workers.[44] Similarly, the overall job safety improvement should be viewed in the context of the U.S. labor shift away from such industries as manufacturing to service roles.

OSHA

A federal agency, the Occupational Safety and Health Administration (OSHA), is responsible for ensuring safe workplaces. The 1970 Occupational Safety and Health Act imposes a *general duty* on most employers to provide a workplace free of "recognized hazards causing or likely to cause death or serious physical harm to employees." Employers have an absolute duty to remove any serious and preventable workplace hazards that are generally recognized in the industry and are known to the employer or should be known to the employer. That general duty is then supplemented with numerous specific *standards*. [For the OSHA home page, see **http://www.osha.gov**]

Standards

OSHA, under the U.S. Department of Labor, promulgates and enforces health and safety standards that identify and seek to correct specific workplace hazards and problems. These can range from exposure to cancer-causing agents (such as the chemical benzene) to the surprisingly commonplace problem of one worker restarting a machine while another is servicing it. For example, under a long-fought-for OSHA standard made effective in 2008, employers must pay for all OSHA-mandated personal protective equipment (safety-specific eyewear, skin creams, clothing, etc.).[45] In 2010, culminating a rule-making process that began in 1998, OSHA issued an "historic new standard" on the use of cranes and derricks in construction that, among other requirements, establishes a procedure for working in the vicinity of power lines and requires that crane operators be qualified or certified.[46]

More New Standards?

The protracted development of OSHA regulations addressing personal protective equipment (PPE) and cranes and derricks typifies the ongoing ideological and practical conflict over imposing additional safety rules in American workplaces. Some of the competing considerations are illustrated by recent disputes over ergonomics and workplace violence.

Ergonomics Repetitive motion and overexertion injuries, such as carpal tunnel syndrome and back strains, account for about one-third of workplace injuries and a big part of the total workplace injury bill, which in 2003 amounted to about $1 billion per week.[47] Employers often try to address these problems with ergonomics, "the science of fitting the job to the worker"[48] (for example, changing the height of a workstation). After years of work, OSHA issued ergonomics standards in 2000, but Congress repealed those rules in 2001 after business complaints about the costs of implementation. OSHA now employs a system of voluntary ergonomics guidelines, but critics consider them weak and vague. OSHA also can apply its general duty authority to address repetitive motion and overexertion. Interestingly, however, such injuries seem to be decreasing. For example, the notorious carpal tunnel syndrome (often wrist or hand pain from repetitive stress, such as keyboard use) fell by one half among professional and business service workers between 2005 and 2006.[49] Experts now believe the carpal tunnel fears about keyboarding may have been exaggerated, although many blue-collar, assembly-line workers certainly are at risk. [For advice on measures to reduce repetitive stress problems for students, see **http://ergo.human.cornell.edu**]

Violence

"Going postal." "Going postal" has become an unfortunate but recognizable shorthand expression for violence in the workplace. The fatal shooting by a professor of three colleagues at a 2010 University of Alabama–Huntsville faculty meeting, however, is a grave reminder that workplace violence is not isolated to certain industries, and no particular job site is immune from such tragedy. Workplace homicides have generally decreased in recent years with the 2009 total at 521,[50] less than half the 1994 high of 1,080.[51] While that trend is quite encouraging, workplace violence remains a concern.

Should OSHA create specific duties for employers regarding workplace violence? Would those rules be effective? Or will the market and naturally evolving workplace conditions provide the most effective and efficient protection?

The answers to these questions might be informed by a 2009 federal appeals court decision upholding an Oklahoma state statute that prohibits employers from banning guns in employees' locked vehicles at the workplace.[52] Several employers challenged the law, arguing successfully at the lower court level that it conflicted with and was preempted by (see Chapters 5 and 8) the Occupational Safety and Health Act. However, the federal appellate court reversed, largely based on OSHA's seeming neutrality on the issue of guns in the workplace.[53] At this writing, similar laws have been passed in 11 other states.[54]

Variances

Employers may seek both permanent and temporary *variances* (exceptions) from OSHA standards. A permanent variance may be granted only if the workplace will be as safe as if the standard were enforced. A temporary variance permits additional time to put in place the necessary compliance measures. Employees have a right to a hearing to contest variances.

Mine Safety

On Monday, April 5, 2010, an explosion at the Upper Big Branch Mine-South in Montcoal, West Virginia, owned by a subsidiary of Massey Energy, Inc., killed 29 miners. In 2009, the Upper Branch Mine suffered a "significant spike in safety violations" leading the U.S. Department of Labor's Mine Safety and Health Administration (MSHA) to issue 515 citations and orders at that mine, and another 124 by April 2010. In November 2010, MSHA took the toughest enforcement measure ever against a mine, seeking a court order to temporarily close a Massey-owned mine in Kentucky which MSHA believed to be engaged in a pattern of failing to inspect and maintain critical areas.

In January 2011, MSHA announced a court order requiring Massey to comply with a plan to ensure the miners' health and safety.

Sources: Briefing by Department of Labor Mine Health and Safety Administration on Disaster at Massey Energy's Upper Big Branch Mine-South [**http://www.msha.gov/performancecoal/DOL-MSHA_president_report.pdf** (April 26, 2010); and **http://www.dol.gov/opa/media/press/MSHA/MSHA20101533.htm**] [**http://www.msha.gov/media/PRESS/2011/NR110105.asp**].

OSHA Information Requirements

Right to Know

OSHA has adopted an employee *hazard communication standard* to protect employees from the dangers associated with chemicals and other toxins in the workplace. Chemical manufacturers and importers must develop *material safety data sheets* (MSDS) for all chemicals. Employers must then label all chemical containers so that employees will know about the chemical and its dangers, and employers must educate employees about chemical hazards and how to deal with them.

Records

Businesses must maintain records listing and summarizing work-related injuries, illnesses, and deaths. A summary of those records must be posted at the job. Notice of any OSHA citations of imminent dangers on the job must also be posted at the job site. OSHA recently reformed and simplified the record-keeping process. Some smaller companies, especially in nonhazardous activities, do not need to meet the record-keeping requirements. In 2009, OSHA announced its National Emphasis Program on Injury and Illness Reporting (NEP) to ensure that record keeping requirements are closely followed.[55]

Does an employee's injury suffered in a go-cart race held as part of an off-site team building event need to be reported? According to a 2009 letter from OSHA responding to this inquiry, an injury in those circumstances is work-related, and therefore reportable, even if the employee had the option to return to work or take a half-day vacation instead of participating in the go-cart race that followed a mandatory off-site meeting.[56]

Enforcement

OSHA's most publicized enforcement mechanism is the unannounced on-site inspection. Inspections arise at the initiative of the agency itself or at the request of employees or their representatives. The inspections must be conducted in a reasonable manner during working hours or other reasonable times, and ordinarily they must not be announced in advance. Employers can demand a warrant prior to inspection. With proper justification, warrants can easily be secured from a federal magistrate. Employer and employee representatives may accompany the inspector.

To enhance efficiency, OSHA practices a targeted, site-specific inspection plan designed to identify and monitor the workplaces most likely to have safety and health problems. In 2009, OSHA's site-specific targeting program focused on nursing homes and manufacturing.[57]

Citations

Citations may be issued if violations are discovered during the inspection process. Immediate, serious threats can be restrained with a court order. Following a citation, the employer may ask to meet with an area OSHA official to discuss the problem. Often a settlement emerges from these meetings. Failing a settlement, the employer can appeal to the independent OSHA Review Commission and thereafter to the federal court of appeals. Violations may lead to fines and/or imprisonment. A 2010 federal appellate court upheld a change made to citation rules at the very end of the Bush Administration, allowing OSHA to assess penalties multiplied by the number of employees. Thus, a $10,000 fine for a violation by a company with 10 employees could be assessed at $100,000.[58]

Firmer Enforcement?

The business community criticizes OSHA for unfairly increasing the cost of production by imposing inflexible and overzealous expectations. Labor organizations and job safety advocates, on the other hand, have criticized OSHA as a timid, faltering safety shield.

As part of the Obama administration's efforts to increase enforcement and become more aggressive in protecting workers' safety, OSHA, in 2010, announced its Severe Violator Enforcement Program (SVEP). SVEP concentrates on employers who have demonstrated indifference to their safety obligations by engaging in willful, repeated, or "failure to abate" violations. SVEP uses mandatory follow-up inspections, press releases, and increased fines, among other tools, to send a clear message that such conduct will be rigorously addressed by OSHA.[59]

But the critics' question remains: Is the market the best vehicle for achieving job safety?

Workers' Compensation

> Korey Stringer, a 27-year-old Pro Bowl tackle, died of heatstroke complications.

Korey Stringer, a 27-year-old Pro Bowl tackle, died of heatstroke complications on August 1, 2001, after going through a preseason Minnesota Vikings workout.[60] Normally, when an employee is injured or dies on the job, the employee or the estate may not sue for damages. Rather, recovery is limited to the fixed sum provided for by the workers' compensation statute, regardless of fault. Stringer's family, however, filed a wrongful death suit seeking to hold the Vikings and various individuals responsible for gross negligence and other wrongs in responding to Stringer's heatstroke. The Vikings argued that the Stringer suit was barred by the state workers' compensation law. Minnesota is one of a number of states, however, that recognize an exception to workers' compensation exclusivity provisions in cases of *gross negligence* by the defendants.[61] The Stringers' case reached the Minnesota Supreme Court in 2005 where the 4–2 majority ruled on technical grounds against the family's gross negligence claim, thus limiting their remedy to workers' compensation, a sum much beneath Stringer's projected commercial worth.[62]

Early in the 20th century, the states began enacting workers' compensation laws to provide an administrative remedy for those, like Stringer, who are injured or killed on the job. Previously, employers' superior financial resources and various technical legal defenses meant that employees often could not successfully sue to recover damages for their on-the-job injuries. All states now provide some form of workers' compensation not requiring a lawsuit. Instead, workers or their families apply for compensation based on illness, injury, or death. Typically, the system is governed by a state board or commission. Most decisions are routine and based on the completed application. Often a claims examiner will verify the nature and severity of the injury. In return for the ease and predictability of the system, however, workers and families are, by law, denied the right to sue for damages resulting from a work-related injury, barring unusual circumstances such as gross negligence, as alleged in the case of Korey Stringer.

In most states, employers are compelled to participate in workers' compensation, depending on state law, either by purchasing insurance privately, by contributing to a state-managed fund, or by being self-insured (paying claims directly from their own funds). Firms with good safety records are rewarded with lower premium payments.

No Joke?

Matthew Simms worked as a server in the Manassas, Virginia, location of a national chain restaurant. During his work shift, Simms walked into the kitchen to enter an order into a computer and to print a check for a customer. Three other employees in the kitchen who were Simms's friends started throwing ice at him, apparently as a joke. As Simms lifted his hand in an attempt to block the ice, he felt his left shoulder disclocate. Simms was taken to a hospital for treatment of his injury. As a result of the injury, Simms alleged he was unable to use his shoulder in daily activities and was unable to work for a period of time. Should Simms receive workers' compensation for his injuries? Explain.

Source: Simms v. Ruby Tuesdays, Inc., 281 Va. 114, 704 S.E.2d 359 (Va. 2011).

Benefits

Medical and rehabilitation expenses along with partial income replacement are provided according to state law. The amount of the income award is normally a percentage of the worker's salary either for a specified period or indefinitely, depending on the severity of the injury. Injury benefits normally amount to one-half to two-thirds of regular wages. Death benefits ordinarily are tied to the wages of the deceased.

Coverage

Certain employment classifications such as agriculture may be excluded from workers' compensation, but about 90 percent of the labor force is covered. Most on-the-job injuries are covered, but those that are self-inflicted (including starting a fight) and others such as those springing from alcohol or drug use may not be.

Legal Requirements

In general, injuries, illnesses, and deaths are compensable where the harm (1) *arose out of the employment,* and (2) *occurred in the course of employment* (explained next in *Wait*). Proof of employer negligence is not required, and the traditional defenses such as contributory negligence are not available to the employer. Thus, workers' compensation provides a form of no-fault protection in the workplace. Workers give up the right to sue, and employers participate in an insurance system that recognizes the inevitability of workplace harm.

Although workers' compensation recovery is the exclusive remedy for workplace injury, illness, or death, some jurisdictions allow litigation in cases of intentional torts and/or gross negligence, as noted earlier. [For the Workers' Compensation Research Institute, see **http://www.wcrinet.org**]

Litigation

Notwithstanding its no-fault character, workers' compensation has generated many lawsuits. Consider the example of David Gross, a 16-year-old employee at KFC, who was injured when he placed water in a pressurized deep fryer to clean it. KFC's employee handbook explicitly instructed against such an action, as did a warning label on the fryer. Furthermore, immediately preceding the incident, Gross's supervisor and two coworkers admonished him to not do it. The employer fired Gross for violating an important workplace safety rule. The Ohio Supreme Court initially terminated his workers' compensation benefits using the "voluntary abandonment" doctrine under which workers' compensation benefits may be terminated because the loss of income is not due to the injury itself. However, the Court then reconsidered and ordered reinstatement of Gross's benefits.[63] The *Wait* case that follows raises some current issues regarding workers' compensation for the telecommuting employee.

LEGAL BRIEFCASE

Wait v. Travelers Indemnity Company of Illinois
240 S.W.3d 220 (Tenn. S.Ct. 2007)

Chief Justice Barker

I. FACTUAL BACKGROUND

From October 1998 until September 3, 2004, the plaintiff, Kristina Wait, worked as Senior Director of Health Initiative and Strategic Planning for the American Cancer Society ("ACS"). Because of the lack of office space at its Nashville, Tennessee facilities, the ACS allowed the plaintiff to work from her East Nashville home. The plaintiff converted a spare bedroom of her home into an office, and the ACS furnished the necessary office equipment, including a printer, a facsimile machine, a dedicated business telephone line, and a budget to purchase office supplies. In all respects, the plaintiff's home office functioned as her work place. Not only did the plaintiff perform her daily work for the ACS at her home office, the plaintiff's supervisor and co-workers attended meetings at the office in her house. There is no evidence in the record with respect to any designated hours or conditions of the plaintiff's employment, nature of her work space, or other work rules. Significantly, the plaintiff's work for the ACS did not require her to open her house to the public. In fact, during working hours the plaintiff locked the outside doors of her home and activated an alarm system for her protection. Unfortunately, however, on September 3, 2004, the plaintiff opened her door to a neighbor, Nathaniel Sawyers ("Sawyers"), who brutally assaulted and severely injured the plaintiff.

The plaintiff met Sawyers in May or early June of 2004 at a neighborhood cookout she attended with her husband. There-

after, Sawyers, who lived approximately one block from the plaintiff's home, came to the plaintiff's home for a short social visit on a *weekend* day in late June. The plaintiff and her husband spoke with Sawyers for approximately five minutes, and then Sawyers left. In August, Sawyers came to the plaintiff's home on a weekday for a social visit; however, the plaintiff was preparing to leave her home office for a job-related television interview. The plaintiff told Sawyers that she was going to a business meeting. When Sawyers replied that he was on his way to a job interview in Nashville, the plaintiff allowed Sawyers to ride with her to his job interview.

On September 3, 2004, the plaintiff was working alone at her home office. Around noon, the plaintiff was in her kitchen preparing her lunch when Sawyers knocked on her door. The plaintiff answered and invited Sawyers into the house, and he stayed for a short time and then left. However, a moment later, Sawyers returned, telling the plaintiff that he had left his keys in her kitchen. When the plaintiff turned away from the door, Sawyers followed her inside and brutally assaulted the plaintiff without provocation or explanation, beating the plaintiff until she lost consciousness. As a result of this assault, the plaintiff suffered severe injuries, including head trauma, a severed ear, several broken bones, stab wounds, strangulation injuries, and permanent nerve damage to the left side of her body.

On December 12, 2005, the plaintiff filed a complaint seeking workers' compensation benefits from Travelers Indemnity Company of Illinois, the insurer of the ACS. (The plaintiff did not name the ACS as a defendant.) The plaintiff alleged that the she was entitled to workers' compensation benefits for the injuries she sustained in the assault because the assault arose out of and occurred in the course of her employment with the ACS. The defendant . . . [denied] that the injuries arose out of or occurred in the course of the plaintiff's employment.

Following discovery, the defendant filed a motion for summary judgment, which the chancery court granted. The chancery court concluded that the plaintiff's injuries did not arise out of or occur in the course of her employment with the ACS. Additionally, the chancery court noted that Sawyers "was not [at the plaintiff's home office] on any kind of business with the [ACS], nor was he really there on any kind of business with the [p]laintiff."

The plaintiff appealed. We accepted review.

* * * * *

(II OMITTED-ED.)

III. ANALYSIS
A. The Workers' Compensation Act and Telecommuting
The Workers' Compensation Act ("Act"), codified at Tennessee Code Annotated sections 50-6-101 to -801 (2005), is a legislatively created quid pro quo system where an injured worker forfeits any potential common law rights for recovery against his or her employer in return for a system that provides compensation completely independent of any fault on the part of the employer. The Act should be liberally construed in favor of compensation and any doubts should be resolved in the employee's favor. However, this liberal construction requirement does not authorize courts to amend, alter, or extend its provisions beyond its obvious meaning.

* * * * *

This case requires us to apply the Act to a new and growing trend in the labor and employment market: telecommuting. An employee telecommutes when he or she takes advantage of electronic mail, internet, facsimile machines and other technological advancements to work from home or a place other than the traditional work site. In 2006, approximately thirty-four million American workers telecommuted to some degree.

* * * * *

Not surprisingly, however, this innovative working arrangement has resulted in an issue of first impression: whether the injuries a telecommuter sustains as a result of an assault at her home arise out of and occur in the course of her employment.

B. Did the plaintiff's injuries occur in the course of her employment?
It is well settled in Tennessee, and in many other jurisdictions, that for an injury to be compensable under the Act, it must both "arise out of" and occur "in the course of" employment. Although both of these statutory requirements seek to ensure a connection between the employment and the injuries for which benefits are being sought, they are not synonymous. As such, the "arising out of" requirement refers to cause or origin; whereas, "in the course of" denotes the time, place, and circumstances of the injury. Furthermore, we have consistently abstained from adopting any particular judicial test, doctrine, formula, or label that purports to "clearly define the line between accidents and injuries which arise out of and in the course of employment [and] those which do not[.]"

* * * * *

In this case, we will consider the second requirement first. An injury occurs in the course of employment "when it takes place within the period of the employment, at a place where the employee reasonably may be, and while the employee is fulfilling work duties or engaged in doing something incidental thereto."

Generally, injuries sustained during personal breaks are compensable.

* * * * *

[T]he defendant here argues that the plaintiff's injuries are not compensable because the' plaintiff was not "fulfilling a work duty" in admitting Sawyers into her kitchen. It is true that the plaintiff suffered her injuries while preparing her lunch in the kitchen of her home; however, the plaintiff's work site was located within her home. Under these circumstances, the plaintiff's kitchen was comparable to the kitchens and break rooms that employers routinely provide at traditional work sites. Moreover, the ACS was aware of and implicitly approved of the plaintiff's work site. Her supervisor and co-workers had attended meetings at the plaintiff's home office. It is reasonable to conclude that the ACS realized that the plaintiff would take personal breaks during the course of her working day. . . .

Thus, after careful review, we conclude that the injuries the plaintiff sustained while on her lunch break, occurred during the course of the plaintiff's employment. The plaintiff was assaulted at a place where her employer could reasonably expect her to be. The ACS permitted the plaintiff to work from home for approximately four years. The plaintiff's supervisor and co-workers regularly came to her home office for meetings. The record does not suggest that the ACS restricted the plaintiff's activities during working hours or prohibited her from taking personal breaks. The facts do not show that the plaintiff was engaging in any prohibited conduct or was violating any company policy by preparing lunch in her kitchen. It is reasonable to conclude that the ACS would have anticipated that the plaintiff would take a lunch break at her home just as employees do at traditional work sites. Importantly, Sawyer's initial visit was very brief and spontaneous. Unless instructed otherwise by the employer, an employee working from a home office who answers a knock at her door and briefly admits an acquaintance into her home does not necessarily depart so far from her work duties so as to remove her from the course of her employment. This is not to say, however, that situations may never arise where more prolonged or planned social visits might well remove the employee from the course of the employment.

In arguing that the plaintiff's injury did not occur "in the course of" her employment, the defendant maintains that the plaintiff's decision to admit Sawyers into her home was not a work duty. However, this argument misses the mark on this requirement because the Act does not explicitly state that the employee's actions must benefit the employer; it only requires that the injuries occur in "the course of" the employment. Because the plaintiff was engaged in a permissible personal break incidental to her employment, we reject the defendant's narrow interpretation of the Act. The question is not whether the plaintiff's injuries occurred while she was performing a duty owed to the ACS, but rather whether the time, place, and circumstances demonstrate that the injuries occurred while the plaintiff was engaged in an activity incidental to her employment. Accordingly, we hold that the plaintiff suffered her injuries during the course of her employment and disagree with the chancery court's conclusion on this important point.

C. Did the plaintiff's injuries arise out of her employment?

Even though the plaintiff's injuries occurred "in the course of" her employment, we nevertheless hold that they did not "arise out of" her job duties with the ACS. The phrase "arising out of" requires that a causal connection exist between the employment conditions and the resulting injury. With respect to whether an assault arises out of employment, we have previously delineated assaults into three general classifications:

(1) assaults with an "inherent connection" to employment such as disputes over performance, pay or termination; (2) assaults stemming from "inherently private" disputes imported into the employment setting from the claimant's domestic or private life and not exacerbated by the employment; and (3) assaults resulting from a "neutral force" such as random assaults on employees by individuals outside the employment relationship.

When an assault has an "inherent connection" to the employment it is compensable. On the other hand, assaults originating from "inherently private" disputes and imported into the work place are not compensable. However, whether "neutral assaults" are compensable turns on the "facts and circumstances of the employment."

The assault in this case is best described as a "neutral assault." In granting the defendant's motion for summary judgment, the chancery court commented: "[T]here's certainly not any evidence that this person who committed the assault was part of the working employment relationship and was not there on any kind of business related to the [ACS] or really any business with the employee." We agree with the chancery court's conclusions. A "neutral force" assault is one that is "neither personal to the claimant nor distinctly associated with the employment."

The categories focus on what catalyst spurred the assault, i.e., was it a dispute arising from a work-related duty, was it a dispute arising from a personal matter, or was it unexplained or irrational? An assault that is spurred by neither a catalyst inherently connected to the employment nor stemming from an inherently private dispute is most aptly labeled as a "neutral force" assault. Here, the undisputed facts clearly show that the assault had neither an inherent connection with the employment, nor did it stem from a personal dispute between Sawyers and the plaintiff. Therefore, we must focus our attention on the facts and circumstances of the plaintiff's employment and its relationship to the injuries sustained by the plaintiff.

Generally, for an injury to "arise out of" employment, it must emanate from a peculiar danger or risk inherent to the nature of the employment. However, in limited circumstances, where the employment involves "indiscriminate exposure to the general public," the "street risk" doctrine may supply the required causal connection between the employment and the injury.

* * * * *

[T]his Court held that the "street risk" doctrine satisfied the causal connection requirement where the employee was assaulted by unknown assailants as he removed paperwork from his employer's van while it was parked at his residence. We carefully limited application of the street risk doctrine to "workers whose employment exposes them to the hazards of the street, or who are assaulted under circumstances that fairly suggest they were singled out for attack because of their association with their employer. . . ."

Unlike our previous cases in which the facts supported application of the "street risk" doctrine to provide the necessary causal connection, the facts here do not establish that the plaintiff's employment exposed her to a street hazard or that she was singled out for her association with her employer. There is nothing to indicate that she was targeted because of her association with her employer or that she was charged with safeguarding her employer's property. Additionally, the plaintiff was not advancing the interests of the ACS when she allowed Sawyers into her kitchen, and her employment with the ACS did not impose any duty upon the plaintiff to admit Sawyers to her home.

The plaintiff argues that had it not been for her employment arrangement, she would not have been at home to suffer these attacks. However, we have never held that any and every assault which occurs at the work site arises out of employment. Additionally, although Sawyers knew from a previous visit that the plaintiff was home during the day, there is nothing in the record which indicates that there was a causal connection between the plaintiff's employment and the assault.

* * * * *

Affirmed.

Questions

1. The Tennessee Supreme Court in *Wait* (and most courts in workers' compensation cases) required a two-part showing that the injury must "arise out of" and "in the course of" employment.
   a. Explain those two standards.
   b. Must an employee be engaged in an activity that benefits the employer in order to be "in the course of employment?" Explain.
   c. Why did the court conclude that Wait's injuries did not arise out of her employment?
2. Why did the court conclude that the "street risk" doctrine did not apply to Wait's injuries?

3. Fernandez, an exotic dancer, left her job drunk and was seriously injured in a crash while riding as a passenger in a car driven by another dancer. The crash came within one hour of leaving work. Her intoxication led to her decision to ride with her intoxicated coworker. Fernandez sought workers' compensation. She claimed that her employer, Bottoms Up Lounge in Council Bluffs, Iowa, required her to socialize with male customers when not dancing and to generate at least two drinks per hour from customers. Dancers were not required to drink, but most dancers consumed six to eight drinks per night or more. Did Fernandez's injury arise out of and in the course of employment so that she can recover workers' compensation? Explain. See *2800 Corp. v. Fernandez,* 528 N.W.2d 124 (Ia. S.Ct. 1995).

4. Joseph Smyth, a college mathematics instructor, was killed while driving his personal auto home from work. At the time, Smyth had student papers with him, which he intended to grade that evening. He often worked at home. Many faculty members took work home in the evenings. However, the college did not require that practice. Indeed, the college neither encouraged nor discouraged working at home.

   The widely adopted "going and coming rule" provides that employees injured while commuting to and from work, in general, are not covered by workers' compensation.
   a. Should Smyth (and other teachers) be exempted from the going and coming rule, thus permitting recovery by Smyth's family? Explain. See *Santa Rosa Junior College v. Workers' Compensation Appeals Board and Joann Smyth,* 708 P.2d 673 (Cal. S.Ct. 1985).
   b. Would you reach a different conclusion had a student been accompanying Smyth? Explain.
5. Casimer Gacioch worked at a Stroh Brewery. The company provided free beer at work. When he began work in 1947 he drank only three to four beers on the weekend. He was fired in 1974, by which time he was drinking 12 bottles of beer daily. After Gacioch's death, his wife sought workers' compensation benefits. The evidence indicated that Gacioch had a predisposition to alcoholism but was not an alcoholic at the time he was hired. How would you rule on the widow's workers' compensation claim? Explain. See *Gacioch v. Stroh Brewery,* 466 N.W.2d 303 (Mich Ct. of Appeals, 1991).

Part Five—Employee Privacy

Privacy on the Job? More than half of Americans between 18 and 25 have done at least one of the following: gotten a tattoo, dyed their hair an untraditional color, or had a body piercing other than on their ear lobe. Fewer than a quarter of those between 40 and 64 have done any of these.[64] Will you have to give up that tongue stud or that butterfly tattoo on your ankle when you move on to the "real world" of professional employment? Typically, employers such as Wells Fargo, for example, have dress codes requiring "a neat, well-groomed appearance . . . "[65] Other employers might have specific requirements, such as covering tattoos during work hours.[66]

> Will you have to give up that tongue stud?

Employer oversight extends well beyond appearance policies. Drug tests, integrity tests, personality tests, surveillance, and as seen earlier in this chapter, searches for applicants' online reputations are routine personnel practices in many firms. Employers have an interest in these strategies not only to hire better employees and improve productivity but to protect coworkers, reduce insurance claims, and shield consumers from poor products and service. On the other hand, job applicants and employees resist parking their personal identity and privacy at the office door.

Privacy off the Job? To encourage state employees to stop smoking and maintain a healthy weight, North Carolina's Comprehensive Wellness Initiative imposes higher health insurance premiums on those state workers who smoke, and as of this writing, will soon include a weight management component.[67] IBM's worksite wellness program offers employees monetary incentives for completing a health program.[68] If you apply for a job with Memorial Health Care System in Tennessee, you may not be hired if you are a smoker.[69] The law offers only limited shelter for employees with these off-duty privacy concerns. About half the states provide some form of "smoking discrimination" protection (as discussed earlier), and the federal Health Insurance Portability and Accountability Act (HIPAA) protects confidentiality in certain medical information. Of course, for employers, controlling cost is a large motivating factor. Obese patients, according to an Emory University study, cost 37 percent more than those of normal weights.[70] Critics, such as Randall Wilson, legal director of the Iowa Civil Liberties Union, worry that employers could extend their demands to, for example, rock climbing or other dimensions of individual choice and build ever more authority over employee lives. As Wilson explained:

> The concern is that with the rise of corporate power, we're beginning to feel at the mercy of a government operating outside a government.[71]

> Robert Barbee was fired for dating Melanie Tomita.

And what about office romance? Robert Barbee, former national sales manager for Household Automotive Finance, sued HAF after he was fired for dating Melanie Tomita, an HAF salesperson. They worked in different locations, and he did not directly supervise her. He claimed that the dismissal violated his right to privacy, but a California appeals court ruled for HAF in part on the grounds that the company needed to prevent conflicts of interest, sexual harassment claims, and the appearance of favoritism.[72] While relatively few office romance cases have reached the courts, most employers appear comfortable in restricting office romance to some degree, such as prohibiting relationships between a supervisor and subordinate or requiring employees who are dating to inform their supervisor.[73]

Search and Seizure in the Office   Do employees have privacy rights in their office computers? The *Ziegler* case that follows examines that important question. (See Chapter 5 for a discussion of privacy rights under the Fourth Amendment prohibition against unreasonable searches and seizures.)

LEGAL BRIEFCASE

United States of America v. Ziegler   474 F.3d 1184 (9th Cir. 2007)

FACTS

Frontline processes online electronic payments in Bozeman, Montana. The FBI received a tip from Frontline's Internet service provider that a Frontline employee, Jeff Ziegler, accessed child pornography from his office computer. Additional evidence confirmed that tip. Frontline employees understood FBI agent James Kennedy to have instructed them to copy Ziegler's hard drive. (Kennedy disputed that understanding.) Those employees got a key to Ziegler's office from Ronald Reavis, Frontline's chief financial officer, entered the office and made two copies of the hard drive. Thereafter, Frontline's corporate counsel told the FBI that the company would voluntarily turn over Ziegler's computer, thus implicitly suggesting, as Kennedy said, that a search warrant was unnecessary. The FBI searched the hard drive and discovered many child pornography images. Ziegler was charged with various child pornography crimes. Ziegler filed a motion to suppress the evidence acquired in the computer search claiming that his Fourth Amendment right to be free of unreasonable searches and seizures had been violated. The district court denied Ziegler's motion, and he was sentenced to two years of probation and a fine of $1,000. Ziegler appealed.

Circuit Judge O'Scannlain

II (I OMITTED.)

A

Ziegler argues that "[t]he district court erred in its finding that Ziegler did not have a legitimate expectation of privacy in his office and computer." He likens the workplace computer to the desk drawer or file cabinet given Fourth Amendment protection in cases such as *O'Connor v. Ortega,* 480 U.S.709 (1987).

* * * * *

[A] criminal defendant may invoke the protections of the Fourth Amendment only if he can show that he had a legitimate expectation of privacy in the place searched or the item seized.

* * * * *

The threshold question then is whether Ziegler had a legitimate expectation of privacy in the area searched or the object seized. If he had no such expectation, we need not consider whether the search was reasonable.

1
The government does not contest Ziegler's claim that he had a subjective expectation of privacy in his office and the computer. The use of a password on his computer and the lock on his private office door are sufficient evidence of such expectation.

* * * * *

[I]n the private employer context, employees retain at least some expectation of privacy in their offices.

Ziegler's expectation of privacy in his office was reasonable on the facts of this case. His office was not shared by co-workers, and kept locked. And while there was a master key, the existence of such will not necessarily defeat a reasonable expectation of privacy in an office given over for personal use.

530 Unit Four *Employer–Employee Relations*

Because Ziegler had a reasonable expectation of privacy in his office, any search of that space and the items located therein must comply with the Fourth Amendment.

III

The next step is to inquire whether there was a search or seizure by the government. While the two Frontline employees may not have scoured the desk drawers and cabinets for evidence, they undoubtedly "searched" Ziegler's office when they entered to make a copy of the hard drive of his computer.

* * * * *

IV
A

The remaining question is whether the search of Ziegler's office and the copying of his hard drive were "unreasonable" within the meaning of the Fourth Amendment. [T]he government does not deny that the search and seizure were without a warrant, and "it is settled for purposes of the Amendment that 'except in certain carefully defined classes of cases, a search of private property without proper consent is 'unreasonable' unless it has been authorized by a valid search warrant.'" . . .

One well-settled exception is where valid consent is obtained by the government. . . .

B

We first consider whether Frontline exercised common authority over the office and the workplace computer such that it could validly consent to a search. . . . [E]ven where a private employee retains an expectation that his private office will not be the subject of an unreasonable government search, such interest may be subject to the possibility of an employer's consent to a search of the premises which it owns.

We are also convinced that Frontline could give valid consent to a search of the contents of the hard drive of Ziegler's workplace computer because the computer is the type of workplace property that remains within the control of the employer "even if the employee has placed personal items in [it]."

* * * * *

Although use of each Frontline computer was subject to an individual log-in, Schneider and other IT-department employees "had complete administrative access to anybody's machine." The company had also installed a firewall, which, according to Schneider, is "a program that monitors Internet traffic . . . from within the organization to make sure nobody is visiting any sites that might be unprofessional." Monitoring was routine, and the IT department reviewed the log created by the firewall "[o]n a regular basis," sometimes daily if Internet traffic was high enough to warrant it. Finally, upon their hiring, Frontline employees were apprised of the company's monitoring efforts through training and an employment manual, and they were told that the computers were company-owned and not to be used for activities of a personal nature.

In this context, Ziegler could not reasonably have expected that the computer was his personal property, free from any type of control by his employer. The contents of his hard drive were work-related items that contained business information and which were provided to, or created by, the employee in the context of the business relationship. Ziegler's downloading of personal items to the computer did not destroy the employer's common authority. Thus, Frontline, as the employer, could consent to a search of the office and the computer that it provided to Ziegler for his work.

C

The remaining question is, given Frontline's ability to consent to a search, did it consent to a search of the office and the computer[?] . . .

[The] testimony makes clear that Ziegler's superiors at Frontline, in particular Reavis, an officer of the company, gave consent to a search of the property that the company owned and which was not of a personal nature.

Although Ziegler retained a legitimate expectation of privacy in his workplace office, Frontline retained the ability to consent to a search of Ziegler's office and his business computer. And because valid third party consent to search the office and computer located therein was given by his employer, the district court's order denying suppression of the evidence of child pornography existing on Ziegler's computer is

Affirmed.

Questions

1. *a.* Why did Ziegler have a reasonable expectation of privacy in his office computer?
   b. Why was a search warrant not required in this situation?
   c. Why was Ziegler's employer, Frontline, able to lawfully consent to the search of Ziegler's office computer?
2. Young was the pastor of Ft. Caroline United Methodist Church in Florida. Young was provided with a private office and a computer in that office. The computer was not networked to any other computers. Young and the church administrator had keys to the office. No one was permitted in the office without Young's permission, and the church administrator was not permitted to log on to the computer unless Young was present.

The church administrator received notice from the church's Internet service provider that spam was linked to the church's Internet address. The administrator ran a "spybot" program on the church computers and found questionable Web addresses. The church's district supervisor and bishop were contacted and permission was given to involve police officials. Officers came to the church, the administrator unlocked Young's office and signed "consent to search" forms for the office and the computer. Officers searched the office and computer and found proscribed images and Web sites.

Young subsequently filed a trial court motion to suppress the evidence gained from the office and computer search. The trial judge granted that motion ruling that the search violated Young's Fourth Amendment right to be free of unreasonable searches and seizures. The state appealed. Rule on that appeal. See *State v. Young*, 974 So.2d 601 (Fla. App. 1 Dist. 2008).

Drug Testing

Mary Wheeler decided that she had to institute an employee drug-testing program for her Chagrin Falls, Ohio, landscaping company. One job applicant at Wheeler's company told the interviewer that he would have no problem with the drug test. Then according to Wheeler: "While filling out his paperwork, the interviewer asked the applicant for a driver's license. The applicant reached into his pocket, and by accident pulled out a small bag of cocaine."[74] That episode certainly confirmed Wheeler's judgment that workplace drug tests were necessary for her company, and the data support Wheeler's fears. According to a federal government study, nearly one out of five workers between the ages of 18 to 25 used illicit drugs in the past month, along with one out of ten between the ages of 26 to 34.[75] One employee high on marijuana dropped his forklift five feet off a loading dock and employees at another job built a meth lab in the back of a truck.[76]

In an effort to address those workplace drug problems, employers provide information about illicit drug abuse, have written policies regarding drug use in the workplace, and offer employee assistance programs (EAPs).[77] Furthermore, as a 2010 Society for Human Resource Management (SHRM) poll revealed, 55 percent of employers use drug testing in hiring employees, while 80 percent of employers conduct "reasonable suspicion" workplace drug testing.[78]

Drug-Free Workplace

The Drug-Free Workplace Act of 1988 applies to employers who have contracts of $100,000 or more with the federal government or who receive aid from the government. Those employers are required to develop an antidrug policy for employees. They must provide drug-free awareness programs for employees, and they must acquaint employees with available assistance for those with drug problems, while also warning them of the penalties that accompany violation of the policy. The act requires employees to adhere to the company policy and to inform the company within five days if they are convicted of or plead no contest to a drug-related offense in the workplace. [For more information on the Federal Drug-Free Workplace Program, see **http://www.workplace.samhsa.gov/**]

Drug Testing in Law and Practice

Drug testing is regulated primarily by state law so generalizations are difficult. Broadly, we can say, however, that private sector drug testing, properly conducted, ordinarily is lawful in the following five situations:

1. *Preemployment testing.* State and local law may impose some restrictions.
2. *In association with periodic physical examinations.* Advance notice is often required.
3. *For cause.* An employer has probable cause or reasonable suspicion.
4. *Postaccident testing* where drug use is suspected.
5. *Follow-up testing* for those returning from drug (or alcohol) rehabilitation.

Random testing, on the other hand, sometimes produces significant legal issues. A number of states forbid random drug testing or limit it to safety-sensitive situations. The U.S. Supreme Court has upheld such testing for public-sector employees where public safety is involved and for those having access to particularly sensitive information.[79] The legality of drug testing often reduces to a balancing test where the employee's right to privacy is balanced against the employer's business needs. Where safety and security are involved and when notice is provided, the courts are more supportive of testing. Particularly intrusive or careless testing often tilts that balance toward employees. Beyond the balancing test, a number of other legal considerations influence employer drug-testing practices, particularly in public sector jobs:

1. **U.S. Constitution.** As explained in Chapter 5, the Fourth Amendment to the U.S. Constitution forbids unreasonable searches and seizures. Thus, government employers ordinarily cannot conduct a search without individualized suspicion—that is, without probable cause. Certain exceptions, however, have been recognized in cases involving such issues as safety, national security, and athletic participation. Remember that the U.S. Constitution protects citizens from the government, not from private-sector employers (with limited exceptions).
2. **State constitutions.** Many state constitutions offer privacy protection, but court decisions, to date, have generally not extended those protections to private-sector employers. On the other hand, certain states, such as California and Massachusetts, explicitly offer constitutional protection to private-sector employees.
3. **Federal statutes.** Drug testing could violate Title VII of the Civil Rights Act of 1964 or the Americans with Disabilities Act (see Chapter 13) if the testing fails to treat all individuals equally. The ADA protects *recovering* drug addicts and those erroneously believed to be drug abusers, but not employees or applicants who are currently abusing drugs.
4. **State and local statutes.** Historically, most state and local drug-testing legislation placed limits on that testing; but in recent years, fears about drug use in the workplace and often intense business community lobbying have, in some cases, relaxed those testing restraints.
5. **Common law claims.** Some of the more prominent judge-made (common law) claims that might provide a challenge to drug testing include invasion of privacy, defamation

(dissemination of erroneous information about an employee), negligence (in testing or in selecting a test provider), intentional infliction of emotional distress, and wrongful discharge (discussed later in this chapter).

Monitoring

The City of Ontario, California, Police Department issued pagers to its police officers for business purposes. The city paid for a text messaging plan, but officers who exceeded the allotted messaging quota were required to pay overage charges. While at work, Sargeant

> Sargeant Jeff Quon sent personal, sometimes sexually explicit, text messages on his police department-issued pager.

Jeff Quon sent personal, sometimes sexually explicit, text messages on his police department-issued pager to both his then-wife and a coworker with whom he was romantically involved. Noticing a frequency in overage charges, the police department audited the content of police officers' texts to determine whether the overage charges were the result of work-related messages that might show the need to upgrade the text-messaging plan. Although a workplace policy stated that employees had no expectation of privacy in using Internet or email provided them at work, it did not address the pagers given to the police officers. As a result of the audit, Quon was disciplined for misusing the pager.

The question facing the Supreme Court in 2010 was whether the police department's review of Sargeant Quon's text messages violated his Fourth Amendment right to privacy. Acknowledging that "workplace norms" regarding technology are evolving, in 2010 the U.S. Supreme Court held in *City of Ontario v. Quon* that even assuming Quon had a reasonable expectation of privacy in his text messages, the police department's review of the text messages did not violate Quon's Fourth Amendment rights. Ontario had a legitimate reason for the search, and the search was not excessive in scope.[80]

The Law

In general, employers can lawfully monitor workers' attendance, performance, e-mail, use of the Internet, and so on, but uncertainty remains. Having a clear, written workplace policy regarding the use and monitoring of workplace technology is a good employment practice. [For a sample policy regarding technology in the workplace, see **http://www.shrm.org/TemplatesTools/Samples/Policies/Pages/CMS_000558.aspx**]

The primary federal legislation, the 1986 Electronic Communications Privacy Act, prohibits private individuals and organizations from intercepting wire, oral, or electronic communications. The act provides for two exceptions, however: (1) prior consent by one of the parties to the communication, and (2) employer monitoring in the "ordinary course of business" by telephone or other device furnished by a provider of wire or electronic communication service. Thus, workplace monitoring of phone calls (except for purely private conversations), workplace computers, voice mail, e-mail, and Internet use are all likely to be considered lawful at this point if approached in a reasonable manner.

Recent state cases have offered employers additional guidance on the intersection of workplace privacy and technology. Marina Stengart, a former executive director of Nursing at Loving Care, Inc., sent emails to her attorney regarding a possible workplace discrimination claim using a company laptop computer and her personal, password-protected email account rather than her business email address. After she resigned and sued, her former employer hired a computer expert who retrieved the emails between Stengart and her attorney, which were then reviewed by the employer's attorney. The New Jersey Supreme Court in 2010 held that Stengart had a reasonable expectation of privacy in those emails.[81] The court also acknowledged that employers could establish rules regarding use of workplace computers and discipline employees accordingly, but this power did not give the right to read privileged communications between the employee and her attorney.[82]

The director of a nonprofit residential facility for neglected and abused children learned that someone was accessing pornographic Web sites late at night from a facility office computer located in an enclosed office. The two employees stationed in that office performed clerical work during normal business hours, and were not suspected. Without telling them, the director installed a hidden camera in the office, trained on the computer in question. The camera did not operate during the day. After discovering the camera, the employees sued for invasion of privacy. While agreeing that the camera was intrusive, the California Supreme Court found that the surveillance did not meet the standards of an invasion of privacy claim. The court did note, however, that offices with doors and blinds on the windows afford employees a higher expectation of privacy than, for example, a workplace with open cubicles.[83]

"Boss in MySpace?"

An employee created an invitation-only group on MySpace.com to "vent" about work, and invited several former and current coworkers to join the group. Posts included sexual references to the employer's managers and customers as well as references to illegal drug use. The employer terminated both the employee who had created the group and one of his invited coworkers.

Question

1. Did the employer violate the employees' right to privacy? Explain.

Source: Pietrylo v. Hillstone Rest. Group, 2008 U.S. Dist. LEXIS 108834 (D.N.J., July 24, 2008): unpublished opinion.

Part Six—Employee Benefits and Income Maintenance

Health care reform and the political battles leading to the 2010 Patient Protection and Affordable Care Act (colloquially labeled ObamaCare) have necessarily included debate over employer-provided health care benefits. For decades employers used benefits to attract and retain the best employees, but the economic downturn in recent years forced employers to shift benefit burdens to employees by raising insurance deductibles and copayments. While 69 percent of firms offered health care benefits in 2010, up from 60 percent in 2009, 30 percent of firms reported that they had reduced the scope of benefits or increased cost-sharing because of the recession.[84]

Nearly 51 million Americans, 16.7 percent of the population, were without health insurance in 2009.[85] The average annual health insurance premium in 2010 for family coverage was $13,770.[86]

These spiraling health care costs threaten family welfare, but they also threaten corporate financial competitiveness. Although those employers providing health insurance may have passed more costs to employees, in 2009 they spent an average of $6,700 per employee, nearly twice the amount spent in 2001.[87]

Under the 2010 Patient Protection and Affordable Care Act, effective in 2014, employers with 50 or more employees that do not provide affordable health insurance coverage for their employees will face penalties. Those with less than 50 employees that do not provide health insurance will not face a penalty, but are eligible for tax credits. Critics argue that this amounts to a mandate for larger employers to provide health insurance for their employees in order to avoid paying penalties, or contrarily, to provide an incentive for employers for whom healthcare costs outweigh the penalties. A November 2010 survey by consulting firm Mercer revealed that a majority of employers are not likely to stop providing health care plans once the penalties take effect.[88] [For more information on health care reform legislation and its impact on employers, see: **http://www.healthcare.gov/foryou/employers/index.html**]

The federal Consolidated Budget Reconciliation Act (COBRA) requires employers with 20 or more employees to permit departing employees to retain group health coverage at their own expense for up to 18 months as long as they are not terminated for gross misconduct.

Unfortunately, COBRA policies are often too expensive for workers who have lost their jobs. The American Recovery and Reinvestment Act of 2009 provides health benefit premium reductions for those who were involuntarily unemployed within a particular time frame.[89]

Along with health care, another pressing social issue affecting the workplace is the care of children and elderly parents: 29 percent of adults in the United States are caregivers to an elderly parent or child with special needs. They provide care an average of 20 hours per week. Approximately three-fourths of these caregivers work outside the home while caregiving, and an increasing number of them report having to make workplace accommodations.[90]

Family Leave

The Family and Medical Leave Act (FMLA) entitles eligible employees of covered employers to take job-protected, *unpaid* leave for certain family-related or medical reasons. Eligible employees are entitled to 12 weeks of FMLA leave in a 12-month period for the birth, adoption, or foster care placement of a child, to care for a child, spouse, or parent who has a serious medical condition, or for the employee's own serious medical condition. Employees taking leave are entitled to reinstatement to the same or equivalent job. Employers with 50 or more employees are covered by FMLA. The 2008 National Defense Authorization Act (NDAA) amended FMLA to provide military family leave to eligible employees to care for their spouse, child, or parent who is undergoing medical treatment for a serious injury or illness incurred in the line of duty, or for "qualifying exigencies" including child care and counseling arising from their spouse's, child's, or parent's call to active duty status from the military reserves.[91]

At this writing, the Department of Labor 2011 FMLA survey is pending, but over 50 million workers have taken FMLA leave. Most of these workers are women, but over 40 percent are male. Over a quarter make under $30,000, and over half make under $75,000 per year.[92] Lost wages often make FMLA leave unattractive, but California, New Jersey, and Washington have begun to address that problem by becoming the first states to require private employers to provide *paid* time off. California's program, for example, is financed by employee payroll deductions and allows up to six weeks of leave.[93] [For more on the FMLA, see **http://www.dol.gov/whd/fmla/**]

Work Abroad?

A 2004 study found that workers in most nations around the world have greater legal rights to time off for family and medical matters than do American workers. Likewise, most of the 168 nations in the study mandate paid leave for pregnancy and illness.

Source: Associated Press, "Harvard Study: U.S. Policies on Time Off Rank at Bottom," *Waterloo/Cedar Falls Courier*, June 17, 2004, p. C10.

Unemployment Compensation

The tragedy of the Great Depression, when up to 25 percent of the workforce was unemployed, led in 1935 to the passage of the Social Security Act, one portion of which provided for an unemployment insurance program. Today, all 50 states and the federal government are engaged in a cooperative system that helps protect the temporarily jobless. The system is financed through a payroll tax paid by employers.

The actual state tax rate for each employer varies, depending on the employer's *experience ratings*—the number of layoffs in its workforce. Thus, employers have an incentive to retain employees.

Rules vary by state, but in general, employees qualify for unemployment benefits by reaching a specified total of annual wages. Those losing their jobs must apply to a state agency for unemployment compensation, which varies by state. Benefits may be collected up to a specified maximum period, usually 26 weeks. During that time, those collecting compensation must be ready to work and must make an effort to find suitable work. Workers who quit or who are fired for *misconduct* are ineligible for unemployment compensation. The episodes that follow illustrate the improbable cases where compensation has been denied:

- The Swiss Valley Farms dairy worker who led her coworkers in an after-hours swim in the cheese vat (filled with water at the time).[94]
- The on-patrol police officer who was charged with having sex with a woman multiple times, sometimes in parking lots.[95]
- The 25-year-old Sheraton hotel worker who used her employer's computer to write a 300-page manuscript describing her successful efforts to avoid doing any work.[96]

On a sobering note, 3.3 million Americans would have fallen below the poverty line in 2009 without unemployment insurance.[97]

WARN

The Worker Adjustment and Retraining Notification Act (WARN) requires firms with 100 or more employees to provide 60 days notice if they lay off one-third or more of their workers at any site employing at least 150 workers, drop 500 employees at any site, or close a plant employing at least 50 workers. A General Accounting Office study concluded, however, that the law had been ineffectual, with half of plant closings not covered by the law. Under the New York State WARN Act, New York employers with 50 or more employees who plan to lay off 25 or more employees must provide those affected with 90 days notice.[98]

Pensions

A 2011 survey revealed that nearly 40 percent of American workers lack confidence about retirement, twice as many as in 2005.[99] Their lack of confidence is supported by the experience of employees at some of America's biggest, most prestigious companies, including Verizon, IBM, Motorola, Sears, and NCR. They have seen their pension benefits shrink or disappear in recent years.[100]

> While a majority of American workers are saving for retirement, more than half report having less than $25,000 in savings and investments.

While a majority of American workers are saving for retirement, more than half report having less than $25,000 in savings and investments. One-fifth of American workers are planning to delay retirement.[101]

Broadly, pensions take two forms: *defined benefit plans* and *defined contribution plans*. Defined benefit pensions are of the traditional form providing specified monthly payments upon retirement. Although many workers have lost those pensions in recent years, some 40 million Americans remain protected by defined benefit plans.[102] Defined contribution plans, such as the popular 401(k), specify in advance the "match" the employer will provide to go with the employee's own contributions. The employee is offered a menu of investment options for that retirement money, but no promises are made about the amount that will be paid upon retirement. Defined contribution plans are now much more common than defined benefit plans. Defined contribution plans can be attractive to employees because the money *vests* (the point at which the employee has a nonforfeitable right to the funds) quickly and follows the employee who changes jobs. From the employer's point of view, the defined contribution plans are less expensive to manage, and they shift the risk from employer to employee.

Various hybrid pension plans have also been developed. A particularly prominent hybrid, a *cash balance plan,* is a defined benefit plan that acts somewhat like a defined contribution plan.The employer makes regular, defined contributions and guarantees a benefit amount to employees based on an established formula, but the benefits are maintained in individual accounts and are expressed in terms of an accumulated lump sum, a cash balance, rather than as a periodic payment during retirement. All of the investment risk in cash balance plans remains with the employer.[103] [See **http://www.401khelpcenter.com** and **http://www.ebri.org** for large databases on 401(k) and other retirement topics.]

Pension Law   The federal Employee Retirement Income Security Act (ERISA) regulates pension funds to help ensure their long-term financial security by reducing fraud and mismanagement. ERISA requires that fund managers keep detailed records, engage in prudent investments, and provide an annual report that has been certified by qualified, impartial third parties. ERISA also establishes strict vesting rights to ensure that employees actually receive the pensions to which they are entitled. Employer contributions typically vest after three years or in a six-year, graduated system. The Pension Benefit Guaranty Corporation (PBGC), funded by company contributions, was created as an element of ERISA to insure defined benefit plans so that vested persons will be paid up to a specified maximum if their plan cannot meet its obligations. Defined contribution arrangements are not covered by the PBGC.

Fears that companies were not sufficiently funding their traditional pension plans led to provisions in the federal Pension Protection Act of 2006 requiring companies to more adequately fund those plans. As some experts worried, a 2007 survey showed that over a third of employers with defined benefit plans anticipated making such changes as closing the plan to new hires or freezing it for all employees.[104]

Now millions of Americans depend on their own investment wisdom and the reliability of their 401(k) plan for their retirement security. In 2008, the U.S. Supreme Court strengthened that security a bit by finding that retirement account holders can sue if the administrator of their plan fails to follow their investment instructions. On the other hand, in 2010 the Court extended the deference given to plan administrators' discretion to include a plan administrator whose first attempt at interpreting the plan had already been ruled unreasonable.[105]

The Future?   Employer-provided pension and health care benefits for retirees increasingly are at risk. As expenses, including pensions and health care, continue to rise, can American companies compete successfully with lower-cost foreign competition? Will the social constructions of "the good life" and the "golden years" be altered, and how? Will you need to work years longer than your parents?

> Will you need to work longer than your parents?

Part Seven—Termination: Protection from Wrongful Discharge

Catherine Wagenseller, an Arizona nurse, her boss, Kay Smith, and some coworkers joined a Colorado River rafting trip where Wagenseller declined to participate in a "Moon River" skit in which the group allegedly "mooned" the audience. Likewise, Wagenseller did not join Smith in the heavy drinking, "grouping up," public urination, and similar behaviors that allegedly marked the trip. Despite favorable job evaluations preceding the trip, Wagenseller's relationship with Smith deteriorated following the trip, and eventually she was terminated. Wagenseller, an at-will employee, sued, claiming that she was wrongfully discharged. An *at-will employee,* by definition, is not under contract for a definite period of time, and as such can be fired at

> Wagenseller declined to participate in a "Moon River" skit.

any time. Wagenseller, however, argued that Arizona should adopt the *public policy exception* to the at-will doctrine. She claimed that she was fired because she refused to engage in behaviors that might have violated the Arizona indecent exposure statute. The state Supreme Court agreed with Wagenseller by finding in the statute a public policy favoring privacy and decency. The case was returned to the trial level, giving Wagenseller the opportunity to prove that her refusal to violate state public policy by engaging in public indecency led to her dismissal.[106]

The *Wagenseller* decision is an exception to the long-standing American rule that at-will employees can be fired for good reasons, bad reasons, or no reason at all. Of course, the employee is likewise free to quit at any time. Furthermore, both employer and employee freely entered the bargain understanding its terms, and thus the court should, in general, enforce those terms. Critics, however, argue that the doctrine ignores the historic inequality of bargaining power between employers and employees. In recent decades the at-will rule has been softened in most states by legislative and judicially imposed limitations. Statutory exceptions to the at-will rule include our labor laws protecting union workers (see Chapter 14) and the equal employment opportunity laws that forbid the dismissal of an employee for discriminatory reasons (see Chapter 13).

Judicial Limitations on At-Will Principles

An increasing number of court decisions provide grounds for dismissed at-will employees to claim that they have been *wrongfully discharged*. Those judicial decisions were often provoked by transparently unjust dismissals including, for example, whistle blowers who exposed their employers' misdeeds and employees who declined to commit perjury on behalf of their employers. Those judicial limitations to the at-will doctrine fall into three categories: (1) express or implied contracts, (2) an implied covenant of good faith and fair dealing, and (3) the tort of violating an established public policy, as in *Wagenseller*. Additional tort claims may substitute for or supplement wrongful discharge claims.

1. **Express or implied employment contracts.** A number of states have adopted a contractual protection for at-will employees arising, typically, either from the employee handbook or from the employer's conduct and oral representations. For example, an employee handbook might contain a policy expecting employees to arrive on time to start their shift, and describing the progressive discipline tardy employees will face— such as an oral warning the first time they are late, a written warning for a second late arrival, and other discipline up to dismissal for continued incidents. This policy creates a contract that employees will not be terminated the first, or even second, time they arrive late to work. Similarly, oral assurances of continued employment, or an employer's practice of providing mentorship to rehabilitate employees' poor performance rather than firing them may create contracts that protect at-will employees from termination.

2. **Implied covenant of good faith and fair dealing.** A few state courts have held that neither party to a contract may act in bad faith to deprive the other of the benefits of

the contract. For example, Bruce Rubenstein gave up his job with Arbor Mortgage to take an at-will position with Huntington Mortgage with the understanding that he would be manager of a new branch office to be opened in central New Jersey. After a few weeks, however, Huntington decided on a downsizing strategy under which the new branch would not be opened. Rubenstein was offered a job as a Huntington loan originator, but he declined. He sued Huntington asserting, among other things, that Huntington had breached the covenant of good faith and fair dealing. Reubenstein believed that Huntington knew of the possibility of downsizing before hiring him. The court agreed that Rubenstein may have had a viable claim for breach of the implied covenant of good faith and fair dealing if the facts, at trial, proved to be as Rubenstein alleged.[107]

3. **Public policy.** Most states have now adopted some form of "public policy" exception to at-will employment, under which a dismissal is wrongful if it results from employee conduct that is consistent with a public good or the public interest as expressed in legislation, constitutional protections, and the like. These exceptions are established case by case, and may differ from state to state. In addition to reporting an employer's illegal activity, commonly known as "whistle blowing," or refusing to commit an illegal act such as perjury, the exception often protects, for example, employees fired for pursuing a lawful claim against their employer (e.g., workers' compensation or wage claims) as well as those fired for fulfilling a civic responsibility such as jury duty.

Additional Torts   Dismissed employees are increasingly turning to a variety of tort actions often labeled "tag-along torts"—seeking compensatory and punitive damages to enhance their potential financial recovery. Potential tort claims arising from termination include, among others, defamation, intentional infliction of emotional distress, interference with contract, and invasion of privacy. The following case raises public policy issues in an employment termination.

LEGAL BRIEFCASE

Lloyd v. Drake University
686 N.W.2d 225 (Iowa S.Ct. 2004)

JUSTICE STREIT

* * * * *

FACTS

Nicholas Lloyd was a Drake University security guard on duty at the annual Drake Relays street-painting event on April 20, 2002. A student told Lloyd about an apparent altercation between Philippe Joseph, a Drake football player, and Erin Kane. Lloyd and Kane were white; Joseph was black. Joseph was holding Kane in the air with her feet kicking. Lloyd and another security guard, Steven Smith, thought Joseph was holding Kane in a headlock. Although Kane later claimed she and Joseph were just friends engaged in horseplay, Lloyd alleges Joseph's girlfriend called Lloyd and said Joseph had admitted to her that he and Kane were fighting. Lloyd ordered Joseph to release Kane. After Lloyd's second command, Joseph did so. Joseph suddenly made a 180-degree turn and lunged toward Lloyd with his fists raised to his chest and "an angry look on his face." Lloyd feared for his own safety and pepper sprayed

Joseph. Smith reached for his pepper spray at the same time and would have sprayed Joseph if Lloyd had not done so first. Another Drake security guard, Sergeant Risvold, attempted to handcuff Joseph, but was unable to do so—Joseph was still writhing from the pepper spray. Lloyd hit Joseph on the thigh with his baton, forcing him to the ground.

Des Moines police officers took Joseph to the police station, where he was charged with disorderly conduct. Meanwhile, witnesses began screaming "racist, racist" at Lloyd. Students immediately discussed the incident with Drake's president, David Maxwell. Maxwell obtained Joseph's release and took him for medical treatment, even though he had not previously complained about any injuries resulting from the arrest. Joseph later pled guilty to disturbing the peace. He also received a settlement from Drake.

As local media reported on the street-painting episode, Lloyd's actions became the subject of a heated controversy. After the NAACP and Black Student Coalition demanded an investigation, Drake organized a panel to study the incident and related topics. The panel concluded Lloyd had overreacted and used unnecessary force. Although the panel determined Lloyd's actions at the street-painting event were not overtly racially motivated, the panel discovered some prior complaints against Lloyd involving minority students. (Lloyd, however, points out he was never reprimanded on any of those occasions.) The panel also criticized Drake for insufficiently training its security guards and its "ambiguous philosophy for security." During the investigation, Drake assigned Lloyd to a desk job. Maxwell assured Lloyd he would not lose his job. One of Lloyd's supervisors told Lloyd he was still in line for a promotion. Nonetheless, Drake fired Lloyd from his security position on June 16, 2002. . . .

WRONGFUL DISCHARGE

Lloyd does not dispute he was an at-will employee. As a consequence, Drake could fire him for any lawful reason, or for no reason at all. A discharge is not lawful, however, when it violates public policy. Lloyd claims Drake violated public policy and thereby committed the tort of wrongful discharge when it fired him simply for upholding the criminal laws, i.e., attempting to arrest Joseph, a man he thought was assaulting a student.

The district court dismissed Lloyd's wrongful-discharge claim. . . . ruling Drake had fired Lloyd for a variety of other lawful reasons, including (1) a desire to capitulate to outside pressures in the hopes of forestalling a lack of public confidence in Drake's security system; and (2) a determination—based upon newly rediscovered prior complaints and the panel's conclusion Lloyd used premature and excessive

force in subduing Joseph—that Lloyd lacked the appropriate demeanor of a security guard. (On appeal, Drake also points out Lloyd's conduct affected its relationships with a variety of constituencies, and his retention could have cost it essential financial support.) . . . We take a different route than the district court, but reach the same conclusion. . . . Even assuming Lloyd was fired simply for upholding the law, we think his claim still fails because the public policy against discharge that Lloyd asserts is neither clearly defined nor well recognized.

. . . [I]n order to prevail on his wrongful-discharge claim Lloyd must first identify a clearly defined and well-recognized public policy that would be undermined by his dismissal. . . . Only such policies are weighty enough "to overcome the employer's interest in operating its business in the manner it sees fit," which we have long and vigorously protected. Over the years we have recognized a number of clearly defined public policies. . . . To date, however, we have not held that a private security guard's actions in "enforcing the criminal laws of the state" to be a well-recognized and clearly defined public policy.

. . . [Lloyd's] argument mostly consists of vague generalizations about the social desirability of upholding the criminal laws of the state. . . . Lloyd also points out that there need not be an express statutory prohibition against discharge to underpin the public policy. In a number of cases, we have "found an implied prohibition against retaliatory discharge based on an employee's exercise of a right conferred by a clearly articulated legislative enactment." The gist of Lloyd's argument is that because upholding the criminal laws is important and socially desirable conduct, this court should find a public-policy exception to the at-will employment doctrine for a private security guard who tried to effectuate an arrest of a suspected criminal.

Lloyd's argument is not well taken. We have little quarrel, however, with one of the basic premises of Lloyd's argument: namely, that the criminal laws of the state reflect a general public policy against crime, and in favor of the protection of the public. That said, the public policy asserted here is far too generalized to support an argument for an exception to the at-will doctrine. In short, the public policy is not clearly defined. Apart from a vague reference to the whole of the criminal law, Lloyd cites no statutory or constitutional provision to buttress his claim. Divorced from any such provision or equivalent expression of public policy, we cannot find a well recognized and clearly defined public policy in such vague generalizations. "Any effort to evaluate the public policy exception with generalized concepts of fairness and justice will result in an elimination of the at-will doctrine itself."

* * * * *

[W]e can find no origin for the well-recognized and clearly defined public policy essential to carve out an exception to the at- will employment doctrine. There is nothing, then, to sustain the tort of wrongful discharge on these facts—however encouraged or frequently beneficial it may be to have private citizens take it upon themselves to enforce the criminal laws. . . . The point is simply this: while we might be persuaded that society would be better off if private security personnel investigated and attempted to stop crimes in progress, we are not convinced it is a clear and well-recognized public policy of this state "that we all become citizen crime fighters."

Affirmed.

Questions

1. *a.* Why did Lloyd lose this lawsuit?
   b. Why did the Iowa Supreme Court decide that Lloyd had failed to establish the public policy exception?
   c. Are you more convinced by the Iowa Supreme Court's reasoning, or the rationale offered by Drake to the District Court and on appeal? Explain.

2. Was Drake's decision to terminate Lloyd an appropriate response to this difficult situation? Explain.

3. Schuster worked, in an at-will relationship, for Derocili for 15 months, during which time she claims he touched her inappropriately and made numerous sexual comments despite her repeated rejections of those behaviors. Schuster received bonuses and good evaluations, but in a meeting between Schuster, Derocili, and Schuster's direct supervisor, Goff, she was fired for poor performance. Schuster's sexual harassment complaint with the Delaware Department of Labor was rejected as unsubstantiated. She sued Derocili for breach of contract, but the trial court dismissed that complaint. She appealed.
   a. Does Schuster have a legitimate wrongful discharge claim? Explain.
   b. Does she have any other plausible causes of action? Explain. See *Schuster v. Derocili*, 775 A.2d 1029 (Del. S.Ct. 2000).

4. Gilmartin took a job as station manager at a Texas television station. He was hired on a year-to-year basis under an oral agreement providing that his employment would continue as long as his work was satisfactory. Gilmartin was subsequently blamed for declining profits, and he was fired. Gilmartin sued. In his pleadings, Gilmartin said that he was informed of his annual salary, vacation time, and possible future raises, that his contract was to be renewed from year to year contingent on satisfactory performance, and that a commitment by KVTV for one to three years was "very doable." He was also told that a written agreement was not necessary. Was Gilmartin wrongfully discharged? Explain. See *Gilmartin v. KVTV-Channel 13*, 985 S.W.2d 553 (Ct. App. Tex. 1998).

5. IBP operated a large hog-processing plant in Storm Lake, Iowa. IBP prohibited possession of "look-alike drugs" on company property. An employee, Michael Huegerich, was randomly and lawfully inspected as he was entering the plant. The inspection revealed an asthma medication, Maxalert, which was identical in appearance to an illegal street drug, "speed." Maxalert contained the stimulant ephedrine. The pills actually belonged to his girlfriend and were in his possession by accident. Huegerich was terminated for possessing a look-alike drug in violation of company policy. Huegerich admitted that he was generally aware of IBP drug policies, but since he was a transfer from another IBP division, he had not gone through the company orientation program where new employees were advised of the policy against look-alike drugs. About six months after his dismissal, two IBP employees told Huegerich that they had heard he was fired for possessing speed. Huegerich then sued IBP for, among other claims, wrongful discharge and defamation.

   At trial, Huegerich provided no evidence as to how, when, and from whom the IBP employees had heard that he was terminated for possession of speed. The district court found for Huegerich in the amount of $24,000 on the wrongful discharge claim and $20,000 on the defamation claim. The court said that IBP was guilty of negligent discharge in failing to inform Huegerich about its drug policy. IBP appealed to the Iowa Supreme Court. Iowa law recognizes the doctrine of at-will employment with "narrow" exceptions for public policy violations and where a contract is created by an employer's handbook. Decide. Explain. See *Huegerich v. IBP*, 547 N.W.2d 216 (Iowa S.Ct. 1996).

6. Freeman, a television anchorperson employed by KSN, gave birth to her second child. On the day she returned from the hospital, she was notified that she had been dismissed. Six weeks later, she became unable to lactate. She sued KSN for wrongful discharge, tortious interference with contract, and negligent infliction of emotional distress. Decide. Explain. See *Freeman v. Medevac Midamerica of Kansas, Inc.*, 719 F.Supp. 995 (D Kan. 1989).

PRACTICING ETHICS Hearing the Whistle Blow?

Kevin Lamson was a sales manager for an Oregon car dealership, Crater Lake Motors. Crater Lake hired Real Performance Marketing Company (RPM), to conduct a five-day sales promotion at the dealership. During the first few days of the sales event, Lamson observed or was informed of a number of activities that he considered to be unethical and possibly unlawful, such as misrepresenting the event as a bank sale, and including various insurance and service agreements in the sales contract without the knowledge of the customer. Lamson complained to the Crater Lake Motors General Manager, Shevlin, who told him to "just go home." The next week, Lamson again expressed his concerns at a Crater Lake Motors meeting.

About a month later, Shevlin criticized Lamson's attitude and recent performance, stating that Lamson "wasn't getting the job done." Shevlin also told Lamson of another planned RPM sales event, and asked if Lamson intended to quit. Lamson replied that he did not intend to quit but that it seemed like Shevlin did not want him to work at Crater Lake Motors anymore. Shevlin replied that he did not want the Lamson he had seen recently.

Lamson later complained to the Crater Lake Motors owner, Coleman, about RPM. Coleman told Lamson that working at the second RPM event was mandatory and that failure to attend could result in dismissal. Lamson told Coleman that he could not participate because doing so would condone unethical behavior. Coleman said the agreement with RPM had been amended to explicitly forbid misrepresentations. Lamson did not attend the second RPM event, and was fired. Lamson then sued Crater Lake Motors for wrongful discharge.

Questions

1. Was Crater Lake Motors wrong to hire RPM?
2. Was Lamson wrong to refuse to work at the second RPM event?
3. Did Lamson have a duty to complain about the conduct he had observed during the first RPM event?
4. Was Crater Lake wrong to terminate Lamson?
5. Who won the wrongful termination lawsuit?

Source: *Lamson v. Crater Lake Motors,* 346 Ore. 628 (Ore. 2009).

Part Eight—Immigration

Immigration is a vital fuel for America's economic and cultural growth, but immigration is also a source of deep political and public policy divisions. In 2010, Arizona became the focus of this debate when it passed an aggressive piece of legislation requiring police officers to make a reasonable attempt to determine the immigration status of anyone lawfully stopped, detained, or arrested whom they suspect might be in the United States illegally.[108] A federal appellate court, however, has agreed with a lower court's ruling that Arizona's 2010 measure unconstitutionally interferes with the federal government's power to regulate immigration.[109]

At this writing, Alabama has enacted a law that encompasses many of the 2010 Arizona provisions but is more broadly restrictive in that it, for example, requires public schools to check the immigration status of their students, and makes it a crime for landlords to knowingly rent to an illegal immigrant or for anyone to transport a known illegal immigrant. The Obama administration has filed suit to block enforcement of portions of the Alabama law on the grounds that those provisions are preempted by federal law and therefore violate the Supremacy Clause of the U.S. Constitution (see Chapters 5 and 8).[110]

Illegal immigrants total about 11.2 million.

One in eight people living in the United States is an immigrant (about 40 million people), and immigration has surged to the highest level in the nation's history with 10.3 million new immigrants arriving from 2000 to 2007, more than half of them without legal status.[111] In 2010, illegal immigrants in the United States totaled about 11.2 million.[112]

[For a 2005 video account of "Smuggler's Gulch" and illegal migrants in Southern California, see "A Special Report on Immigration" at **http://lang.dailybulletin.com/socal/beyondborders/video/121805_smugglers_gulch_video.asp**]

Immigration policy is one of the most divisive issues in American public life. A Pew poll showed that 59 percent of Americans approved of the 2010 Arizona measure.[113] The support for directing police to stop and ask for documentation from those reasonably suspected of being in the United States illegally might reflect resistance to immigration generally, and the perception that illegal immigrants create an economic burden. A study found that in 2002, illegal immigrants living in the United States used $2,700 in government services per person more than they paid in taxes.[114] Furthermore, concerns about the negative impact of large legal and illegal immigrant populations on poor Americans have been raised.[115] But the evidence on the pluses and minuses of immigration is quite mixed. Immigrants to California appear to drive wages up and those immigrants are incarcerated at far lower rates than native-born citizens.[116] A group of 500 economists wrote to Congress in 2006 arguing that immigration is, overall, a "modest" net gain for the American economy.[117] In a more subjective sense, advocates claim that we must benefit from immigration's steady pipeline of new talent and energy including thousands of unaccompanied young children annually, many of whom literally walk to the United States from Central America.[118] The *Los Angeles Times* asked if America's "sheltered and chaperoned children" could manage that feat on their own.[119]

American Immigration Law Businesses in the United States have used the H-1B visa program to bring foreign workers to the United States to fill positions requiring special theoretical or technical expertise in specialized fields such as science, engineering, or computer programming. In seeking an H-1B visa, an employer must affirm to the U.S. Department of Labor that the hiring will not harm wages and working conditions of employees in similar jobs. The number of H-1B visas available annually is limited, and the number of employers' applications significantly decreased in 2009.[120]

In hiring those already in the United States, federal immigration law, including the 1986 Immigration Reform and Control Act, requires employers to verify that each new hire is a U.S. citizen, a permanent resident, or a foreign national with permission to work in this country. To meet this requirement, employers must complete an employment eligibility verification form (I–9) for each new employee. New employees must present documents establishing the employee's identity and eligibility to work in the United States. The employer must examine the documents and complete the I–9 if the documents appear legitimate. Of course, employers cannot knowingly hire illegal immigrants, but neither can they discriminate against legal immigrants because of national origin and similar factors. [For links to the I–9 form and other immigration information, see **http://www.uscis.gov/portal/site/uscis**]

Crackdown?   The Obama administration's increased enforcement of immigration laws focuses on two issues: hiring of illegal immigrants, and employers' illegal discrimination against applicants based on citizenship status or national origin. Critics charge that these policies create a conflict for employers: on the one hand, employers must be sure to verify applicants' ability to work in the United States, but on the other hand, they must take care not to place extra burdens on applicants because they are of a particular national origin, or are U.S. permanent residents as opposed to U.S. citizens.[121] For example, under a settlement reached with the U.S. Department of Justice, a California company, American Education and Travel Services Inc., agreed to pay $10,000 in back pay and compensatory damages to a lawful permanent resident who was denied a residential counselor position because he was not a U.S. citizen or native English speaker.[122] At the same time, the Obama administration's efforts to force employers to dismiss unauthorized workers, rather than use Bush-era workplace raids, has led to illegal immigrants being fired. American Apparel, lauded for paying wages above industry standards and providing health benefits, was a target of a 2009 federal investigation that led to a mass firing of unauthorized workers, a result that was criticized for not focusing enforcement efforts on employers that exploit their workers.[123]

E-Verify is a free online system run by the federal government that determines an employee's eligibility to work in the United States, comparing information reported on an employee's Form I-9 with federal records. For most employers, the use of E-Verify is voluntary and limited to determining the employment eligibility of new hires only.[124] In 2010, over 238,000 employers were enrolled with E-Verify, with over 16 million queries.[125] However, critics note that E-Verify does not address whether the identity provided is authentic, which could lead to a surge in identity theft to help illegal workers clear this employment hurdle.[126] [For overviews of many of the employment law topics in this chapter, see **http://topics.law.cornell.edu/wex/category/employment_law**]

Internet Exercise

Using the Frequently Asked Questions portion of the Occupational Safety and Health Administration (OSHA) Web site [**http://www.osha.gov/as/opa/osha-faq.html**], answer the following:

1. What is OSHA's budget, and how many inspectors does the agency have?
2. How can I get help from OSHA to fix hazards in my workplace?
3. What cooperative programs does OSHA offer?

Chapter Questions

1. In general, employers are forced to bear (or at least share) the legal burden for their employees' negligent conduct on the job.
   a. Why do we force employers to bear that responsibility?
   b. Should we do so? Explain.
2. Abplanalp, a five-year employee of Com-Co Insurance, signed an employment agreement including a restrictive covenant providing that, should he leave Com-Co, he would not use Com-Co customer lists or solicit business from Com-Co clients for three years. Abplanalp moved to Service Insurance, where he sold insurance to some

friends and relatives. He did not sell to any other persons whom he came to know while working for Com-Co. Abplanalp was sued by Com-Co for violating the restrictive covenant. Decide. Explain. See *Com-Co Insurance Agency v. Service Insurance Agency,* 748 N.E.2d 298 (Ill. App. Ct. 2001).

3. Many companies refer to credit reports when investigating job applicants. The Fair Credit Reporting Act requires employers to notify and receive authorization from applicants to use their credit reports in making hiring decisions, and to give them notice if they are rejected because of information in a credit report. (For more information on employers' responsibilities under The Fair Credit Reporting Act, see: **http://business. ftc.gov/documents/bus08-using-consumer-reports-what-employers-need-know**).

   a. In your judgment, does evidence of failure to pay debts constitute useful information in the job selection process? Explain.

   b. Is the use of that information an "invasion of privacy" as you understand it? Explain.

4. A group of Fargo, North Dakota, nurses were paid a subminimum wage for their "on-call" time. When on call, the nurses were required to be able to report to their hospital within 20 minutes, they were required to provide a phone number where they could be reached, and they were not to consume alcohol or drugs. After being called, nurses returned to regular pay. In three years, 36 of the 135 nurses who sued had been called in more than once. The nurses sued the hospital for violating the Fair Labor Standards Act's minimum wage provision. Decide. Explain. See *Reimer v. Champion Healthcare Corp.,* 258 F.3d 720 (8th Cir. 2001).

5. Simons, an engineer at the CIA, downloaded child pornography on his workplace computer. The computer was to be used only for work. The pornography was discovered by a search of employee computers. Simons was then convicted of receiving and possessing child pornography. Simons appealed on Fourth Amendment grounds. Decide. Explain. See *United States v. Simons,* 206 F.3d 392 (4th Cir. 2000); cert. den. 122 S.Ct. 292 (2001).

6. Guz, a longtime Bechtel employee, was dismissed during what Bechtel said was a business slump. Bechtel's personnel policy included a provision saying employees "may be terminated at the option of Bechtel." Guz sued for wrongful dismissal claiming, among other things, that Bechtel breached an implied contract to be terminated only for good cause, and that Bechtel breached the implied covenant of good faith and fair dealing. A lower court concluded that Guz's promotions, raises, favorable performance reviews, together with Bechtel's progressive discipline policy and Bechtel officials' statements of company practices supported Guz's position. Bechtel appealed. Decide. Explain. See *Guz v. Bechtel National Inc.,* 8 P.3d 1089 (Cal. S.Ct. 2000).

7. Hershey Company Retail Sales Representatives (RSRs) were classified as exempt under the Fair Labor Standards Act (FLSA), and Hershey never paid hourly compensation to RSRs for any overtime they worked. While the RSRs received bonuses based on performance, they were not eligible to receive sales commissions. RSRs are part of teams that help sell Hershey products to retail outlets of various sizes from Walmart to independently owned shops. In a wage and hour claim seeking overtime compensation, RSRs contended that they are primarily responsible for merchandising tasks such as delivering and setting up product displays, tagging products, and stocking shelves.

Hershey defended that RSRs' job duties include selling products directly to retailers, meeting with their key decision makers to increase sales, and only occasionally assisting with merchandising at their stores. Are the RSRs nonexempt employees with rights to overtime compensation under FLSA? Decide. Explain. See *Campanelli v. Hershey Co.*, 2011 U.S. Dist. LEXIS 17483 (N.D. Cal. 2011).

8. April 2010 U.S. Department of Labor guidelines require employers to provide educational benefits to interns who participate in unpaid internships. If the interns are completing tasks that further the organization's interests rather than their own, they should be compensated with wages.
   a. What benefit might a college student derive from an unpaid internship, apart from academic credit or an educational experience?
   b. What effect might these guidelines have on the availability of internships?
   c. Why do you think the U.S. Department of Labor addressed unpaid internships in 2010?

9. Safeway in Denver hosted a picnic for its employees. Safeway bought a 40-pound gas tank to use with a grill that was designed for a 20-pound tank. A label on the grill warned against that use. The grill failed to operate properly and a manager asked Lewis to try to fix it. When Lewis did so a "ball of fire" erupted and Lewis was badly burned. The Occupational Safety and Health Administration then issued a citation against Safeway. Safeway appealed to the courts.
   a. Defend Safeway.
   b. Decide the case. Explain. See *Safeway, Inc. v. Occupational Safety & Health Rev. Comm.*, 382 F.3d 1189 (10th Cir. 2004).

10. In most drug-testing cases, courts have balanced the employee's privacy interests against the employer's need for information. What business justifications are likely to be most persuasive to a court reviewing the legality of employee drug testing?

11. Millions of workers can be regarded as telecommuters. As such, they bring new legal problems to the workplace. As a manager, what legal difficulties would you want to anticipate and protect against as more and more of your employees work off-premises and often from their own homes?

12. A reader sent the following story to a newspaper question and answer forum:

    I was fired recently by my employer, an architecture firm, immediately after serving for one month on a federal grand jury. From the moment I informed my boss . . . I was harassed . . . and told I was not putting the company first. I was told to get out of my jury service, "or else." . . . I was fired exactly one week after my service ended.[127]

    Was the dismissal of this at-will employee lawful? Explain.

13. Katherine Born and Rick Gillispie were employed by a Blockbuster Video store in Iowa. Blockbuster maintained a policy that forbade dating between supervisors and their subordinates. Born and Gillispie were dismissed for violating the policy. They denied that they were romantically involved and filed suit for wrongful dismissal. Under Iowa law, an at-will employee can be discharged at any time for any reason, but Iowa law does recognize the public policy exception. To prevail in this lawsuit, what must the plaintiffs show about Iowa law? See *Katherine Born and Rick Gillispie v. Blockbuster Videos, Inc.*, 941 F.Supp. 868 (S.D. Ia. 1996).

14. A pregnant employee at a retail store was operating a buffing machine when propane gas that powered the machine led to a carbon monoxide buildup, causing the worker and others to be taken to a hospital. The worker's fetus sustained oxygen deprivation, resulting in injuries including abnormal motor functions, cerebral palsy, and a seizure disorder. The worker sued on negligence grounds for her child's injuries. The employer defended by arguing that workers' compensation provides the exclusive remedy in such situations. Does workers' compensation bar the child's suit? Explain. See *Snyder v. Michael's Stores, Inc.,* 945 P.2d 781 (Cal. S.Ct. 1997).

15. Diana Vail, who received medical treatment for migraine headaches, worked at Raybestos, a car parts manufacturer. Raybestos had been giving Vail intermittent leave under FMLA for her migrane headaches since April 2004. From May to September 2005, Vail's requests for FMLA leave due to migraine headaches became more frequent, often falling on weekdays when her husband's mowing company was busiest. Growing suspicious that Vail's requests were not genuine, Raybestos monitored Vail's activities by hiring an off-duty police officer to conduct video surveillance. The officer reported that Vail mowed the lawns of a cemetery, her husband's client, on a day when Vail called prior to her shift to request leave. Vail was subsequently terminated based on her performance of physical labor while on FMLA.
    a. Did Vail's termination violate FMLA? Explain.
    b. Did the employer's surveillance of Vail interfere with her rights under FMLA? Explain. See *Vail v. Raybestos,* 533 F.3d 904 (7th Cir. 2008).

16. An employee of Triple B Cleaning in Texas requested personal protective equipment while performing dry cleaning duties. Triple B denied the request. The employee notified the media, and after a reporter contacted the employee's supervisor, the employee was demoted and assigned menial tasks. Following the airing of the employee's complaint by local news, the employee was terminated.

    After being terminated, the employee filed a whistle blower complaint alleging that Triple B acted in retaliation for contacting the media about unsafe working conditions. OSHA investigated the complaint and determined that Triple B Cleaning's decision to terminate the employee was in violation of the whistle blower provisions of the Occupational Safety and Health Act.

    The company entered into a consent judgment under which it paid the employee $30,000 for lost wages, agreed to an injunction prohibiting future discrimination and posted a notice advising its employees of their rights under OSHA's whistle blower protection provision.
    a. What public policy—or policies—are at issue in this situation?
    b. Did Triple B act ethically? Did the employee act ethically? Explain.
    c. In OSHA's press release regarding the settlement, OSHA Regional Administrator Dean McDaniel stated: "Employees should be free to exercise their rights under the law without fear of retaliation by their employers . . ." What consequences might be expected to accompany the fear of retaliation employees often feel when exercising their rights?

See OSHA Regional News Release, "U.S. Department of Labor Settles Whistleblower Case Against Commercial and Industrial Steam Cleaning Company in Houston" April 6, 2009 [**http://www.osha.gov/pls/oshaweb/owadisp.show_document?p_table=NEWS_RELEASES&p_id=17720**].

Notes

1. Sacha Pfeiffer, "Off-the-Job Smoker Sues over Firing," *The Boston Globe,* November 30, 2006 [**http://www.boston.com**].
2. Ibid.
3. American Lung Association's Tobacco Policy Project/State Legislated Actions on Tobacco Issues (SLATI) State "Smoker Protection" Laws [**http://slati.lungusa.org/appendixf.asp** (last updated 9/27/10)].
4. Annotated Laws of Massachusetts, ALM GL ch. 214, Section 1B (2010).
5. Johnathan D. Glater, "Layoffs Herald a Heyday for Employee Lawsuits, *The New York Times,* January 30, 2009 [**http://www.nytimes.com/2009/01/31/business/economy/31employ.html**].
6. *CBS v. FCC,* 535 F.3d 167 (3rd Cir. 2008).
7. *Chao v. Southern California Maid Services & Carpet Cleaning, Inc.,* No. CV-06-3903 (C.D. Cal. 2007).
8. SSA/IRS Reporter (Spring 2010): "IRS Begins Employment Tax Research Study."
9. Floyd Norris, "RadioShack Chief Resigns after Lying," *The New York Times,* February 21, 2006, sec. C, p. 1.
10. Keith J. Winstein, "Inflated Credentials Surface in Executive Suite," *The Wall Street Journal,* November 13, 2008, p. B1.
11. Dan Mascai, "And I Invented Velcro," *BusinessWeek,* June 9, 2008, p. 15.
12. Chad Terhune, "The Trouble with Background Checks," *BusinessWeek,* June 9, 2008, p. 54.
13. "SHRM: Background Checking: Conducting Credit Background Checks," January 22, 2010 [**http://www.shrm.org/Research/SurveyFindings/Articles/Pages/BackgroundChecking.aspx**].
14. Sara Murray, "Credit Checks on Job Seekers by Employers Attract Scrutiny," *The Wall Street Journal,* October 21, 2010, p. A5.
15. Chris Dettro, "New Law Bars Most Credit Checks in Hiring," *The State Journal-Register,* January 1, 2011 [**http://www.sj-r.com/top-stories/x1733657992/New-law-bars-most-credit-checks-in-hiring**].
16. "Online Reputation in a Connected World," presentation by Brendon Lynch at Microsoft 2010 Privacy Day, January 28, 2010 [**http://www.microsoft.com/downloads/en/details.aspx?FamilyID=dfb35812-879a-44b7-8097-a65d3b6b8788**].
17. Scott Erker and Kelli Buczynski, "Are You Failing the Interview?: 2009 Survey of Global Interviewing Practices and Perceptions," p. 14 [**http://www.ddiworld.com/DDIWorld/media/trend-research/are-you-failing-the-interview_tr_ddi.pdf**].
18. Ann Howard, Johanna Johnson, White Paper: "If You Were a Tree, What Kind Would You Be?" Development Dimensions International [**http://www.ddiworld.com/DDIWorld/media/white-papers/interviewing_wp_ddi.pdf?ext=.pdf**].
19. *Bimbo Bakeries v. Botticella,* 613 F.3d 102 (3rd Cir. 2010).
20. David Sarno, "Hewlett-Packard Sues to Keep Former CEO from Going to Oracle," *Los Angeles Times,* Sept, 7, 2010 [**http://www.latimes.com/business/la-fi-hp-hurd-20100908,0,2379734.story**].

21. Kris Maher, "The Jungle," *The Wall Street Journal,* June 8, 2004, p. B4.

22. *Edwards v. Arthur Andersen,* 44 Cal. 4th 937 (Cal. 2008).

23. *Circuit City Stores, Inc. v. Adams,* 532 U.S. 105 (2001).

24. *Rent-a-Center West v. Jackson,* 130 S. Ct. 2772; 177 L. Ed. 2d 403 (2010).

25. *Equal Employment Opportunity Commission v. Waffle House,* 534 U.S. 279 (2002).

26. 54 Cal. 3d 202; 814 P.2d 1341 (Cal. S.Ct. 1991).

27. Jenny B. Davis, "Still Working after All These Years," *ABA Journal,* October 2001, p. 67.

28. Arindrajit Dube, T. William Lester, and Michael Reich, "Minimum Wage Effects Across State Borders: Estimates Using Contiguous Counties," *The Review of Economics and Statistics,* September 25, 2010.

29. National Employment Law Project, "Living Wage and Minimum Wage," [**http://www.nelp. org/index.php/content/content_issues/category/living_wage_and_minimum_wage/**].

30. Maryland Department of Labor, Licensing, and Regulation (DLLR) Division of Labor and Industry: "Maryland's Living Wage Frequently Asked Questions (FAQs)," [**http://www.dllr. state.md.us/labor/prev/livingwagefaqs.shtml#1**].

31. "Down and Out: Low-wage Workers and the Everyday Symptoms of Abuse," *The Washington Post*, September 4, 2009, citing "Broken Laws, Unprotected Workers: Violations of Employment and Labor Laws in America's Cities, September 1, 2009, University of Illinois at Chicago, the National Employment Law Project, and the UCLA Institute for Research on Labor and Employment.

32. U.S. Department of Labor Wage and Hour Division Press Release, "Levi Strauss Agrees to Pay More than $1 Million in Overtime Back Wages to Nearly 600 Employees Following US Labor Department Investigation," March 29, 2011 [**http://www.dol.gov/opa/media/press/ whd/WHD20110379.htm**].

33. Miguel Bustillo, "Wal-Mart to Settle 63 Suits over Wages," *The Wall Street Journal,* December 24, 2008, p. B1.

34. Mary Madden and Sydney Jones, "Networked Workers," Pew Internet & American Life Project, September 24, 2008 [**http://www.pewinternet.org/Reports/2008/Networked- Workers.aspx?r=1**].

35. *Aqui v. T-Mobile USA Inc.,* Case 1:09-cv-02955-RJD-RML(E.D.NY 2009)].

36. *Archuleta v. Wal-Mart Stores,* 543 F. 3d 1226 (10th Cir. 2008).

37. Testimony before the House Committee on Natural Resources, U.S. House of Representatives, March 16, 2011, The Effect Of—A Brother's Statement. Testimony of Christopher K. Jones [**http://naturalresources.house.gov/UploadedFiles/C.JonesTestimony03.16.11.pdf** at p. 2].

38. Justin Blum and Alison Fitzgerald, "BP Is Said to Face U.S. Review for Manslaughter Charges," *Bloomberg.com,* March 29, 2011 [**http://www.bloomberg.com/news/2011-03-29/ bp-managers-said-to-face-u-s-review-for-manslaughter-charges.html**].

39. Associated Press, "Federal Probe of Fatal Texas Plant Explosion Cites Oversight," *Waterloo/ Cedar Falls Courier,* March 21, 2007, p. B4.

40. Melanie Trottman, "BP to Pay $50.6 Million Fine in Texas Refinery Case," *The Wall Street Journal,* August 12, 2010 [**http://www.wsj.com**].

41. U.S. Department of Labor Bureau of Labor Statistics Economic News Release, "Census of Fatal Occupational Injuries Summary, 2009" August 19, 2010 [**http://www.bls.gov/news. release/cfoi.nr0.htm**].

42. Ibid.

43. U.S. Department of Labor Bureau of Labor Statistics News Release, "National Census of Fatal Occupational Injuries in 2009 (Preliminary Results), August 19, 2010 [**http://www.bls.gov/news.release/pdf/cfoi.pdf**].

44. Ibid.

45. Employer Payment for Personal Protective Equipment, Final Rule, 29 CFR Parts 1910, 1915, 1917 et al.

46. "OSHA Cranes and Derricks in Construction–Final Rule," July 28, 2010, [**http://www.osha.gov/as/opa/cranesderricks-factsheet.html**].

47. Morgan O'Rourke, "The Impact of Workplace Injuries," *Risk Management Magazine* 52, Issue 11 (November 1, 2005).

48. Robert J. Grossman, "Making Ergonomics," *HR Magazine,* April 2000, p. 36.

49. Associated Press, "Carpal Tunnel Injuries at Work Decline," *The Des Moines Register,* March 17, 2008, p. 1D.

50. Census of Fatal Occupational Injuries (CFOI) Current and Revised Data [**http://www.bls.gov/iif/oshcfoi1.htm#2008**].

51. U.S. Department of Labor, Bureau of Labor Statistics. Census of Fatal Occupational Injuries: Table 4. "Fatal Occupational Injuries by Worker Characteristics and Event or Exposure," 2003.

52. *Ramsey Winch v. Auto-Crane Co.,* 555 F.3d 1199 (10th Cir. 2009).

53. Ibid.

54. Ogletree Deakins, "Indiana Signs Workplace Gun Bill into Law, March 24, 2010, [**http://www.shrm.org/LegalIssues/StateandLocalResources/Pages/IndianaGovernorSignsWorkplace-Gun.asp**].

55. OSHA Directive 09-08 (CPL 02), Injury and Illness Recordkeeping National Emphasis Program, September 30, 2009 [**http://www.osha.gov/OshDoc/Directive_pdf/CPL_02_09-08.pdf**].

56. OSHA Letter of Interpretation on Standard 1904, 1904.5(b) (1), February 24, 2009 [**http://www.osha.gov/pls/oshaweb/owadisp.show_document?p_table=INTERPRETATIONS&p_id=27415**].

57. OSHA Trade News Release, September 4, 2009 [**http://www.osha.gov/pls/oshaweb/owadisp.show_document?p_table=NEWS_RELEASES&p_id=16338**].

58. *National Association of Home Builders v. OSHA,* 602 F.3d 464 (D.C. Cir. 2010).

59. OSHA Instruction, Severe Violators Enforcement Program (SVEP) [**http://www.osha.gov/dep/svep-directive.pdf**].

60. Associated Press, "Stringer's Widow Settles Lawsuit with NFL," *The New York Times,* January 26, 2009 [**http://www.nytimes.com/2009/01/27/sports/football/27stringerbox.html?ref=koreystringer**]. While Kelci Stringer has settled her claim against the NFL, her lawsuit against football equipment maker Riddell for her husband's death is at this writing still pending, with the federal district court having ruled that Riddell had a duty to warn a football player of the risk of heat exhaustion. *Stringer v. NFL,* 2010 U.S. Dist. LEXIS 98874 (S. Ohio 2010).

61. *Stringer v. Minnesota Vikings,* 705 N.W. 2d 746 (Minn. S.Ct. 2005).

62. Ibid.

63. *State ex. Rel. Gross v. Industrial Commission of Ohio,* 115 Ohio St. 3d 249 (Ohio 2007).

64. The Pew Research Center for The People and The Press, "A Portrait of 'Generation Next'," January 9, 2007, p. 21 [**http://people-press.org/files/legacy-pdf/300.pdf**].

65. "Appearance at Work," January 2011 Wells Fargo Team Member Handbook, p. 26 [**teamworks.wellsfargo.com/handbook/HB_Online.pdf**].

66. See, e.g., Crisis Collection Management's dress code [**http://www.crisiscollections.com/about/eh/cpa/**].
67. North Carolina Comprehensive Wellness Initiative [**http://www.shpnc.org/comp-wellness.html**].
68. Associated Press, "Employees Earn Cash for Exercising More," *The Wall Street Journal,* June 2, 2010, p. D3.
69. Memorial Health Care System, "Careers at Memorial," [**http://www.memorial.org/about_us_careers.html**].
70. S.P. Dinnen, "Employers Slap Fees on Workers Who Smoke," *The Des Moines Register,* November 20, 2005, p. 1A.
71. Ibid.
72. *Robert Barbee v. Household Automotive Finance,* 113 Cal. App. 4th 525 (2003).
73. Sue Shellenbarger, "For Office Romance, the Secret's Out," *The Wall Street Journal,* February 10, 2010, p. D1.
74. Dalia Fahmy, "Aiming for a Drug-Free Workplace," *The New York Times,* May 10, 2007, Sec. C, p. 6.
75. Worker Substance Abuse and Workplace Policies and Programs (2007): Substance Abuse and Mental Health Services Administration (SAMHSA), U.S. Department of Health and Human Services, [**http://oas.samhsa.gov/work2k7/toc**].
76. George Lenard, "Employers Falling Off Drug Testing Bandwagon," February 28, 2005 [**http://www.employmentblawg.com/2005**].
77. Worker Substance Abuse and Workplace Policies and Programs (2007): Substance Abuse and Mental Health Services Administration (SAMHSA), U.S. Department of Health and Human Services [**http://oas.samhsa.gov/work2k7/toc**].
78. "Background Checking: Drug Testing," SHRM Poll, January 22, 2010 [**http://www.shrm.org/Research/SurveyFindings/Articles/Pages/BackgroundCheckDrugTesting.aspx**].
79. *National Treasury Employees Union v. Von Raab,* 109 S.Ct 1384 (1989).
80. *City of Ontario v. Quon,* 130 S. Ct. 2619; 177 L. Ed. 2d 216, 227 (2010).
81. *Stengart v. Loving Care Agency,* Inc., 201 N.J. 300, 308; 990 A.2d 650 (N.J. 2010).
82. Ibid. 201 N.J. at 324–325.
83. *Hernandez v. Hillsides,* 47 Cal. 4th 272, 288-289; 211 P.3d 1063; 97 Cal. Rptr. 3d 274 (Cal. 2010).
84. Claxton, et al, "Heath Benefits in 2010: Premiums Rise Modestly, Workers Pay More Toward Coverage" [**http://content.healthaffairs.org/content/early/2010/09/02/hlthaff.2010.0725.abstract**].
85. Robert Greenstein, Executive Director, Center on Budget Policy and Priorities, on Census 2009 Poverty and Health Insurance Data, September 16, 2010 [**http://www.cbpp.org/cms/index.cfm?fa=view&id=3292**].
86. Claxton, et al, "Heath Benefits in 2010: Premiums Rise Modestly, Workers Pay More Toward Coverage"[**http://content.healthaffairs.org/content/early/2010/09/02/hlthaff.2010.0725.abstract**].
87. Phred Dvorak and Scott Thrum, "Slump Prods Firms to Seek New Compact with Workers," *The Wall Street Journal,* October 19, 2009, p. A1.
88. Mercer, "Few Employers Planning to Drop Health Plans after Reform Is in Place, Survey Finds, November 9, 2010 [**http://www.mercer.com/press-releases/survey-find-few-employers-to-drop-health-plans-after-health-care-reform-in-place**].

89. U.S. Department of Labor Fact Sheet, "COBRA Premium Reduction," April 26, 2010 [**http://www.dol.gov/ebsa/newsroom/fscobrapremiumreduction.html**].

90. National Alliance of Caregiving and AARP, "Caregiving in the U.S. 2009" [**http://www.aarp.org/relationships/caregiving/info-12-2009/caregiving_09.html**].

91. U.S. Department of Labor, "Military Family Leave Provisions of the FMLA: Frequently Asked Questions and Answers,"[**http://www.dol.gov/whd/fmla/finalrule/MilitaryFAQs.pdf**].

92. American Association of University Women, "FMLA Facts and Statistics" [**http://www.aauw.org/act/laf/library/fmlastatistics.cfm**].

93. State of California Employment Development Department, "Paid Family Leave" [**http://www.edd.ca.gov/Disability/Paid_Family_Leave.htm**].

94. Patt Johnson, "Getting the Boot," *The Des Moines Register,* May 4, 2003, p. 1D.

95. W. Zachary Malinowski, "Unemployment Benefits Denied for Fired Cranston Cop," *The Providence Journal* blog, www.projo.com, July 26, 2010 [**http://newsblog.projo.com/2010/07/unemployment-benefits-denied-f.html**].

96. Clark Kauffman, "Diary of a Goof-Off: No Work, No Pay," *The Des Moines Register,* January 19, 2007, p. 1A.

97. Arloc Sherman, Danilo Trisi, Robert Greenstein, and Matt Broaddus, "Census Data Show Large Jump in Poverty and the Ranks of the Uninsured," Center on Budget Policy and Priorities, September 17, 2010 [**http://www.cbpp.org/cms/index.cfm?fa=view&id=3294**].

98. New York State Department of Labor, "New York WARN Act Takes Effect February 1, 2009," [**http://www.labor.state.ny.us/agencyinfo/warnact.shtm**].

99. Employee Benefits Research Institute and Mathew Greenwald & Associates, "2011 RCS Survey Fact Sheet #1: Retirement Confidence," p. 2 [**http://www.ebri.org/pdf/surveys/rcs/2011/FS1_RCS11_Confidence_FINAL1.pdf**].

100. Pension Benefit Guaranty Corporation, "An Analysis of Frozen Defined Benefit Plans," December 21, 2005 [**http://www.pbgc.gov/documents/frozen_plans_1205.pdf**].

101. Employee Benefits Research Institute, "Fast Facts 2011 Retirement Confidence Survey: How Many Workers are Postponing Retirement? Why?" [**http://www.ebri.org/pdf/publications/facts/fastfacts/fastfact07302008.pdf**].

102. Mark Trumbull, "Reform Erodes the Future of US Pensions," *The Christian Science Monitor,* August 18, 2006 [**http://www.csmonitor.com/2006/0818/p02s02-usec.html**].

103. U.S. Department of Labor, "Fact Sheet: Cash Balance Pension Plans," May 2003, [**http://www.dol.gov/ebsa/newsroom/fscashbalanceplans.html**].

104. Jack VanDerhei, Employee Benefits Research Institute Issue Brief No. 307, July 2007, [**http://www.ebri.org/pdf/briefspdf/EBRI_IB_07-20079.pdf**].

105. *LaRue v. DeWolff, Boberg& Associates, Inc.,* 128 S.Ct. 1020 (2008) and *Conkright v. Frommert,* 130 S.Ct. 1640 (2010).

106. *Wagenseller v. Scottsdale Memorial Hospital,* 710 P.2d 1025 (Az. S.Ct. 1985).

107. *Rubenstein v. Huntington Mortgage Company,* N.J. Sup. Ct., App. Div., 1997. For a journalistic account of the case, see Pitney, Hardin, Kipp, and Szuch, "Employers Must Be Cautious about Failing to Disclose Business Plans that Will Affect the Jobs of New Hires," *New Jersey Employment Law Letter,* September 1997.

108. Arizona State Senate Fact Sheet for SB 1070 [**http://www.azleg.gov/legtext/49leg/2r/summary/s.1070pshs.doc.htm**].

109. Nicholas Riccardi, "Judge's Ban on Arizona's Immigration Law Is Upheld," *Los Angeles Times,* April 12, 2011, p. A8.

110. Timothy W. Martin, "Alabama Immigration Law Spurs Wider Fight," *The Wall Street Journal,* August 3, 2011, p. A6.

111. Julia Preston, "Immigration at Record Level, Analysis Finds," *The New York Times,* November 29, 2007 [**http://www.nytimes.com**].

112. Jeffrey S. Passel and D'Vera Cohn, "Unauthorized Immigrant Population: National and State Trends, 2010," February 1, 2011 [**http://pewhispanic.org/reports/report.php? ReportID=133**].

113. Pew Research Center for the People and the Press, "Public Supports Arizona Immigration Law," May 12, 2010 [**http://pewresearch.org/pubs/1591/public-support-arizona-immigration-law-poll**].

114. Patrik Jonsson, "Backlash Emerges against Latino Culture," *The Christian Science Monitor,* July 19, 2006 [**http://www.csmonitor.com/2006/0719/p03s03-ussc.html**].

115. Lawrence Harrison, "The US Should Think Long and Hard about the High numbers of Latino Immigrants," *The Christian Science Monitor.com,* May 28, 2009 [**http://www.csmonitor.com**].

116. Teresa Watanabe, "Immigrants Boost Pay, Not Prison Populations, New Studies Show," *Los Angeles Times,* February 28, 2007 [**http://www.latimes.com/news/local/la-me-immigstudy-28feb28,0,7851813.story?track=ntottext**].

117. David Streitfeld, "Illegal—but Essential," *Los Angeles Times,* October 1, 2006 [**http://www.latimes.com/business/la-fi-immigecon1oct01,0,2945710.story?track=tottext**].

118. Rosa Brooks, "How Immigrants Improve the Curve," *Los Angeles Times,* June 29, 2007 [**http://www.latimes.com/news/opinion/la-oe-brooks29jun29,0,1106152.column?coll=la-tot-opinion&track=ntottext**].

119. Ibid.

120. Miriam Jordan, "Slump Sinks Visa Program," *The Wall Street Journal,* October 29, 2009, p. B12.

121. Miriam Jordan, "Policing Illegal Hires Puts Some Employers in a Bind," *The Wall Street Journal,* July 15, 2010, p. A5.

122. "Justice Department Resolves Citizenship Status Discrimination Charge against California Employer." March 8, 2011 [**http://www.justice.gov/opa/pr/2011/March/11-crt-294.html**].

123. Julia Preston, "Immigration Crackdown with Firings, Not Raids," *The New York Times,* September 30, 2009 [**http://www.nytimes.com**].

124. U.S. Department of Homeland Security, "E-Verify," [**http://www.dhs.gov/files/programs/gc_1185221678150.shtm**].

125. Ibid.

126. Bruce A. Morrison and Paul Donnelly, "A Simple Way to Keep Illegal Immigrants from Getting Jobs," *The Washington Post,* May 1, 2010, A 15.

127. *Washington Post,* "The Boss Can't Fire You for Doing Your Civic Duty," *Waterloo/Cedar Falls Courier,* May 26, 1999, p. C8.

CHAPTER THIRTEEN

Employment Law II: Discrimination

After completing this chapter, students will be able to:

1. Discuss the purpose and history of legal protections against employment discrimination.

2. Compare and contrast the protections offered under the federal statutes prohibiting employment discrimination: Title VII of the Civil Rights Act of 1964; the Equal Pay Act; the Americans with Disabilities Act; and the Age Discrimination in Employment Act.

3. Explain the role of the Equal Employment Opportunity Commission (EEOC) in enforcing federal statutes prohibiting employment discrimination.

4. Identify remedies available to victims of unlawful employment discrimination.

5. Distinguish the primary forms of employment discrimination analysis: disparate treatment, and disparate impact.

6. Identify when unlawful sexual harassment has occurred.

7. Identify when employers are liable for unlawful sexual harassment.

8. Describe protections against retaliation offered under the federal statutes prohibiting employment discrimination.

9. Discuss the purposes and development of affirmative action.

10. Describe the concept of reasonable accommodation as applied to religious- and disability-based discrimination claims.

11. Discuss the current status of protections against sexual orientation discrimination in the workplace.

Introduction

PRACTICING ETHICS   A & F Too White? Too Fashion Forward?

Abercrombie & Fitch, the clothing retailer, was accused in 2003 of maintaining a virtually all-white image by discriminating in recruiting, hiring, and promoting women and minorities. A nationwide class action lawsuit was filed claiming that Abercrombie disproportionately assigned minority employees to stockrooms and other jobs out of the public eye, while white employees were conspicuously on display as a means of projecting the company's "clean-cut, classic" image.

Abercrombie denied the charges, but it decided to settle in 2005 by agreeing to pay $40 million along with $10 million in attorney fees and other expenses. The settlement also required the company to promote diversity in its workforce.[1] In addition, Abercrombie agreed to manifest a more diverse image in its marketing materials, including its catalogs, shopping bags, and store posters.[2]

At this writing in 2011, Abercrombie & Fitch faces two religious discrimination lawsuits filed by the federal government's Equal Employment Opportunity Commission. Both cases involve job applicants who allegedly were denied employment because they were wearing headscarves in keeping with their religious beliefs. The scarves violated A & F's "Look Policy," which prohibits head coverings of any kind. [For more details, see **http://www.eeoc.gov/eeoc/newsroom/release/9-1-10.cfm**]

Questions

1. A & F defenders have argued that the clothier has the right to promote an image of its choice as a means of making a profit.
   a. The law aside, is Abercrombie simply wrong to project a "white image," if, indeed, it did so? Explain.
   b. Would it be wrong for Abercrombie to build its business plan on an ethnic or black or "hip-hop" image in its products?

2. Is discrimination based on appearance an ethical wrong? Explain.

3. Katie Hollenbeck, a Syracuse University junior graphic arts major, was thinking of applying for a job at Abercrombie & Fitch, but she decided that she didn't feel "appropriate" for the job after she observed all of the store's "tall, skinny white girls." Hollenbeck says that, in the long run, hiring only attractive employees will "hurt Abercrombie."[3]
   a. Would the market punish Abercrombie, even if the law had not intervened? Explain.
   b. Should the market punish Abercrombie? Explain. Put another way, should you decline to shop at Abercrombie stores? Explain.

4. a. How would you defend Abercrombie & Fitch against the religious discrimination charges?
   b. In your opinion, should an employer be able to specify a reasonable dress code?
   c. Do you think a "no-head coverings" policy is reasonable and enforceable even if it excludes some religious groups from employment? Explain.
   d. Do you think it would be wrong to put company profits ahead of applicant/employee religious preferences? Explain.

Continuing Discrimination   The ethical issues raised by Abercrombie & Fitch's hiring and staffing practices highlight the challenges of enforcing legal protections against employment discrimination, often referred to as Equal Employment Opportunity (EEO) laws.

Employers compare, distinguish, and choose among applicants and employees based on many factors. However, EEO laws forbid those considerations that would undermine equal employment opportunity. Prohibited factors, also called "protected categories," or "protected classes" include an applicant's or employee's race, color, and gender, among other characteristics. Generally, EEO laws protect all employees and are not restricted to certain groups such as women or racial minorities.

Do we still need EEO laws in the United States? Consider a recent study in which black and white men applied for the same entry-level jobs with nearly identical résumés. Some of the white men were instructed to tell the employer that they had felony drug convictions. Who would receive the employer's call—the white ex-convict or the black with no criminal record? Most likely, the study found, the white applicant with the criminal record would be preferred over the black applicant with no criminal record.[4] As diversity grows in the United States, EEO laws may serve to support and sustain a more inclusive, and, ultimately, more productive workplace.[5]

> **Most likely, the white applicant would be preferred.**

Diversity Grows Throughout the United States

The 2010 U.S. Census revealed that slightly over one-third of Americans reported their race and ethnicity as "minority;" that is, something other than non-Hispanic white. The "minority" group increased by 29 percent from 86.9 million to 111.9 million between 2000 and 2010.

During the decade, Texas joined California, the District of Columbia, Hawaii, and New Mexico in having a "majority-minority" population, that is, more than 50 percent of its population is part of a minority group. Among all states, Nevada's minority population increased at the highest rate, 78 percent.

Source: U.S. Census Bureau, "2010 Census Shows America's Diversity," March 24, 2011 [**http://2010.census.gov/news/releases/operations/cb11-cn125.html**].

Part One—Employment Discrimination: The Foundation in Law

History

In the Reconstruction Era following the Civil War, Congress passed the Civil Rights Act of 1866 to provide the newly freed black slaves with the same right to make and enforce contracts as was enjoyed by white citizens. This law still exists today, with updated language emphasizing its protection against racial discrimination. The Civil Rights Act of 1866 has been interpreted to forbid discrimination on the basis of race in employment, which is essentially a contractual relationship.

However, this legal protection did not prevent discriminatory practices in housing, education, business, and employment. In 1941, A. Philip Randolph, president of the predominantly black Brotherhood of Sleeping Car Porters, organized black leaders who threatened a massive march in Washington, DC, protesting employment discrimination. In response, President Franklin Roosevelt issued Executive Order 8802, which created a Fair Employment Practice Committee. Congress limited the committee's budget, but Roosevelt's action was a striking step for the federal government in addressing racial discrimination.

The next big step toward racial equality was the landmark *Brown v. Board of Education*[6] decision in 1954, in which the Supreme Court forbade "separate but equal" schools. Following

Brown, citizens engaged in sit-ins, freedom rides, boycotts, and the like to press claims for racial equality. It was a turbulent, sometimes violent, era, but those activities were critical ingredients in subsequent advances for the black population. With the passage of the 1964 Civil Rights Act, the campaign against discrimination solidified as one of the most energetic and influential social movements in American history.[7] The Civil Rights Act of 1964 changed American life by forbidding discrimination in education, housing, public accommodation, and, perhaps most importantly, employment. [For the National Civil Rights Museum, see **http://www.civilrightsmuseum.org**]

Civil Rights Act of 1964

Reflecting the increased diversity of the U.S. workforce, in which women had gone beyond traditional roles and where immigrants from around the world could be found, Title VII of the Civil Rights Act of 1964 ("Title VII") marked a new era in employment practices. Title VII forbids discrimination in employment on the basis of race, color, religion, sex, or national origin. Relying on its authority to regulate commerce, Congress applied Title VII to private-sector employers with 15 or more employees, employment agencies, labor unions with 15 or more members as well as those operating a hiring hall, state and local governments, and most of the federal government. Private clubs are exempt from Title VII, and religious organizations may discriminate in employment on the basis of religion. Broadly, Title VII forbids discrimination in hiring, firing, and all aspects of the employment relationship.

Other Legislation and Orders

Title VII is the core of EEO laws in the United States. Other federal statutes, such as the Americans with Disabilities Act of 1990 (ADA) and the Age Discrimination in Employment Act of 1967 (ADEA), have established additional protected categories. The Equal Pay Act of 1963 and the Civil Rights Act of 1991 address particular issues in employment discrimination. For example, the Civil Rights Act of 1991 provides that U.S. citizens working abroad for American-owned or American-controlled companies are protected from discrimination under Title VII and the ADA unless such protection would require the employer to violate the laws of its host nation. These federal laws will be discussed further later in this chapter.

The Constitution

As explained in Chapter 5, the federal constitution, among other purposes, protects us from wrongful government action. The Fourteenth Amendment to the Constitution provides that no state shall deny to any person life, liberty, or property without *due process of law* or deny him or her the *equal protection of the laws.* Thus, citizens are protected from discrimination via state government action. Similarly, the Supreme Court has interpreted the Due Process Clause of the Fifth Amendment ("nor shall any person . . . be deprived of life, liberty, or property, without due process of law") to forbid discrimination by the federal government.

Employment Discrimination Enforcement

EEOC and State Fair Employment Practice Agencies

The Equal Employment Opportunity Commission (EEOC), an independent federal agency, has the authority to issue regulations and guidelines as well as to receive, initiate, and investigate charges of discrimination against employers covered by federal antidiscrimination statutes such as Title VII. [See the Equal Employment Opportunity Commission's Web site at **http://www.eeoc.gov**]

State fair employment practices legislation often mirrors or expands the antidiscrimination protections found in federal statutes such as Title VII. State fair employment practice agencies may serve the same function as the EEOC in enforcing these laws. [For an example, see California Department of Fair Employment and Housing's Web site at **http://www.dfeh.ca.gov**] Municipal ordinances may also address employment discrimination, enforced by a particular branch of the city's government. [For the San Francisco Human Rights Commission, see **http://www.sfgov.org/site/sfhumanrights_index.asp**]

Litigation

The first step in lawsuits claiming employment discrimination is not taken in a courthouse. A victim of employment discrimination, usually referred to as the "charging party," will file a complaint within a limited period of time with either the EEOC or, where applicable, the local or state fair employment practices agency.

What if the allegedly discriminatory act is ongoing rather than an incident occurring on a certain date—at what moment does the clock start ticking on the victim's time to file an EEOC complaint? After 19 years as a Goodyear employee, Lily Ledbetter discovered that her wages were much lower than her male coworkers. She filed an EEOC complaint alleging gender discrimination, and later won a jury verdict for back pay and punitive damages. In 2007, the U.S. Supreme Court held in *Ledbetter v. Goodyear Tire & Rubber Co.* that Ledbetter's claim should have been brought within 180 days of the first pay check at issue.[8] Congress reacted to *Ledbetter* by passing The Lily Ledbetter Fair Pay Act of 2009, signed into law by President Obama in the first days of his administration. Under this statute, each pay check issued by an employer engaged in pay discrimination is a discriminatory act, meaning that the clock resets on potential discrimination claim each time the affected employee is paid, with a two-year cap on back pay damages.[9]

Typically, the EEOC will refer the charging party and employer for mediation. If mediation does not resolve the complaint, then the EEOC will investigate. If the EEOC finds no cause for the complaint, then the EEOC will issue a right-to-sue letter, thus removing itself from the matter and releasing the grievant to file his or her own lawsuit because all administrative remedies have been exhausted. If grounds for complaint are found, the case will first be referred to conciliation. If that fails, the commission may file a civil suit or issue a right-to-sue letter to the grievant.

Many potential employment discrimination lawsuits no longer reach the judicial system because they are resolved in arbitration. Many businesses are now including binding arbitration agreements in job offers, requiring job seekers, as a condition of employment, to waive the right to trial and turn any grievance over to arbitration. A series of U.S. Supreme Court decisions has firmly established the enforceability of those agreements when the arbitration process provided for is legitimate and fair. The Court has also ruled, however, that the EEOC retains its right to sue on behalf of an employee even if the worker has signed away his or her own rights.[10]

Despite headline-grabbing settlements in discrimination cases, a 2010 American Bar Foundation study found that discrimination lawsuits rarely make it to trial and usually end with a modest settlement. If these cases go to court, the plaintiffs have only a one-in-three chance of winning.[11]

Remedies

Recognizing the gravity and nature of injuries caused by intentional discrimination in the workplace, Congress expanded the remedies available for such injury under Title VII and the Americans with Disabilities Act (ADA) to include compensatory damages as well as punitive damages in some cases. Compensatory damages may be sought to redress, for example, emotional pain and suffering, but combined compensatory and punitive damages are capped at $50,000 to $300,000, depending on the size of the employer's workforce. Damages are not capped for front pay (awarded for future earnings) or in cases of intentional discrimination based on race. The EEOC often negotiates consent decrees that may require new procedures to correct wrongful practices. [For the Civil Rights Division of the U.S. Justice Department, see **http://www.justice.gov/crt/**]

Discrimination Claims Up

In 2010, the EEOC received nearly 100,000 workplace discrimination charges, the most in any year since it began its operations in 1965. In 2009, the EEOC reported receiving over 93,000 charges, its second highest level. Then acting-EEOC Chair Stuart Ishimaru stated: "Equal employment opportunity remains elusive for far too many workers and the Commission will continue to fight for their rights. Employers must step up their efforts to foster discrimination-free and inclusive workplaces, or risk enforcement and litigation by the EEOC."

Questions

1. What factors may have contributed to the recent dramatic increase in the number of workplace discrimination charges received by the EEOC? Explain.
2. Evaluate Mr. Ishimaru's statement regarding the 2009 statistics.
   a. What message is being sent to employers?
   b. What impact might this have on the workplace?

Source: U.S. Equal Employment Opportunity Commission, "EEOC Reports Job Bias Charges Hit Record High of Nearly 100,000 in Fiscal Year 2010," EEOC Press Release, January 11, 2011 [**http://www.eeoc.gov/eeoc/newsroom/release/1-11-11.cfm**].

Part Two—"Types of Discrimination"

There are three basic types of illegal employment discrimination: disparate treatment, disparate impact, and harassment. In addition, Title VII and other antiemployment discrimination statutes prohibit *retaliation* for opposing an employment practice reasonably believed to be discriminatory, or for participating in a claim of employment discrimination. Plaintiffs may raise claims of more than one type of employment discrimination, as well as retaliation, against an employer.

Disparate Treatment and Disparate Impact

Title VII of the 1964 Civil Rights Act provides two primary theories of recovery for individuals—disparate treatment and disparate impact (sometimes labeled *adverse impact*). A disparate treatment claim addresses *intentional* discrimination by an employer who has purposefully treated an employee or applicant less favorably because of his/her race, color, religion, national origin, gender, or membership in a group under another protected category. Disparate impact claims arise from "unintentional" discrimination where an employment practice appearing to be neutral has the effect of adversely impacting a particular group under a protected category more than it impacts other groups.

As we turn now to a close look at disparate treatment and disparate impact analysis, keep in mind the various constitutional, statutory, and executive order protections just outlined.

Disparate Treatment

Employees or applicants making claims of disparate treatment must prove their employers' intent to discriminate with either direct or indirect evidence. For example, a company president's remarks that "women were simply 'not tough enough' to supervise collections and that it was a 'man's job,'" (even if tempered by his statement that "I felt that a woman was not competent enough to do this job, but I think maybe you're showing me that you can do it,") may constitute *direct evidence* of intentional sex discrimination, as a federal court of appeals found.[12] A warehouse company seeking truck loaders might send a letter to an employment agency saying that "women would not be welcome as applicants for this physically taxing job." That letter could be used as direct evidence of the employer's intent to treat female applicants adversely compared with male applicants. More often, however, disparate treatment claims must be established by relying on *indirect evidence* in accord with the following test:

1. **Plaintiff's (employee's) *prima facie case*** (sufficient to be presumed true unless proven otherwise) is confirmed by proving each of the following ingredients:

    a. Plaintiff belongs to a protected class.
    b. Plaintiff applied for a job for which the defendant was seeking applicants.
    c. Plaintiff was qualified for the job.
    d. Plaintiff was denied the job.
    e. The position remained open, and the employer continued to seek applicants.

2. **Defendant's (employer's) case.** If the plaintiff builds a successful prima facie case, the defendant must "articulate some *legitimate, nondiscriminatory reason* for the employee's rejection" (for example, greater work experience). However, the defendant need not prove that its decision not to hire the plaintiff was, in fact, based on that legitimate, nondiscriminatory reason. The defendant simply must raise a legitimate issue of fact disputing the plaintiff's discrimination claim.

3. **Plaintiff's response.** Assuming the defendant was successful in presenting a legitimate, nondiscriminatory reason for its action, the plaintiff must show that the reason offered

by the defendant was false and thus was merely a *pretext* to hide discrimination. [For an overview of disparate treatment analysis, see **http://www.hr-guide.com/data/ G701.htm**]

Question

Stalter, an African American, was fired for theft after working at a Walmart loading dock for four months. Stalter ate a handful of taco chips from an open bag on the countertop in the break room. As he was eating, Ellenbecker entered the room, took the bag from Stalter, and placed it in her locker. Stalter later apologized to Ellenbecker and offered to buy a new bag. She said the incident was "no big deal" and told him to "forget about it." Management then investigated, concluded Stalter had stolen the chips, and fired him. Stalter sued, claiming his termination was race based. At court Stalter argued (a) Walmart could not have reasonably believed that he committed theft, especially since the owner told him to forget about it; (b) the punishment was grossly excessive; (c) a similarly situated Caucasian employee who committed a similar offense was treated much more leniently; and (d) Walmart did not investigate his claims of racial harassment. Resolve this case. Explain your reasoning. See *Stalter v. Wal-Mart Stores,* 195 F.3d 285 (7th Cir. 1999).

Disparate Impact

Disparate impact analysis involves situations in which employers use legitimate employment standards that, despite their apparent neutrality, impose a heavier burden on a protected class than on other employees. For example, a preemployment test, offered with the best of intentions and constructed to be a fair measurement device, may disproportionately exclude members of a protected class and thus be unacceptable (barring an effective defense). Alternatively, an employer surreptitiously seeking to discriminate may establish an apparently neutral, superficially valid employment test that has the effect of achieving the employer's discrimination goal. For example, a tavern might require its "bouncer" to be at least 6 feet 2 inches tall and weigh at least 200 pounds. Generally, height and weight are not protected classes. However, the tavern's requirement will disproportionately exclude women, and perhaps members of certain ethnic groups as well. Was this the tavern's intent? Most likely it was not, but remember that while disparate treatment requires proof of intent, disparate impact does not.

The Test

Disparate impact analysis requires the following:

1. The plaintiff/employee must identify the *specific employment practice or policy* (such as test score, skill, or height) that caused the alleged disparate impact on the protected class.
2. The plaintiff must prove (often with statistical evidence) that the protected class is suffering an *adverse or disproportionate impact* caused by the employment practice or policy in question. The statistical analysis to establish a disparate impact (against black job applicants, for example) must be based on a comparison of the racial composition of the group of persons actually holding the jobs in question versus the racial composition of the *job-qualified* population in the relevant labor market.

3. Assuming a prima facie case is established in steps 1 and 2, the plaintiff/employee wins unless the defendant/employer demonstrates that the employment practice/policy is (a) *job related* and (b) *consistent with business necessity*. In the "bouncer" example above, the tavern would have to demonstrate that the height and weight requirements were related to the job in accordance with the needs of taverns.

4. If the defendant/employer succeeds in demonstrating job relatedness and business necessity, the employer wins unless the plaintiff/employee demonstrates that *an alternative, less discriminatory business practice is available and that the employer refuses to adopt it.*

The following classic case examines disparate impact analysis.

LEGAL BRIEFCASE

Griggs v. Duke Power Co.
401 U.S. 424 (1971)

Chief Justice Burger

We granted the writ in this case to resolve the question whether an employer is prohibited by the Civil Rights Act of 1964, Title VII, from requiring a high school education or passing of a standardized general intelligence test as a condition of employment in or transfer to jobs when (a) neither standard is shown to be significantly related to successful job performance, (b) both requirements operate to disqualify Negroes at a substantially higher rate than white applicants, and (c) the jobs in question formerly had been filled only by white employees as part of a longstanding practice of giving preference to whites.

Congress provided, in Title VII of the Civil Rights Act of 1964, for class actions for enforcement of provisions of the Act and this proceeding was brought by a group of incumbent Negro employees against Duke Power Company. . . .

The district court found that prior to July 2, 1965, the effective date of the Civil Rights Act of 1964, the company openly discriminated on the basis of race in the hiring and assigning of employees at its Dan River plant. The plant was organized into five operating departments: (1) Labor, (2) Coal Handling, (3) Operations, (4) Maintenance, and (5) Laboratory and Test. Negroes were employed only in the Labor Department where the highest-paying jobs paid less than the lowest-paying jobs in the other four "operating" departments in which only whites were employed. Promotions were normally made within each department on the basis of job seniority. Transferees into a department usually began in the lowest position.

In 1955 the company instituted a policy of requiring a high school education for initial assignment to any department except Labor, and for transfer from the Coal Handling to any "inside" department (Operations, Maintenance, or Laboratory). When the company abandoned its policy of restricting Negroes to the Labor Department in 1965, completion of high school also was made a prerequisite to transfer from Labor to any other department. From the time the high school requirement was instituted to the time of trial, however, white employees hired before the time of the high school education requirement continued to perform satisfactorily and achieve promotions in the "operating" departments. Findings on this score are not challenged.

The company added a further requirement for new employees on July 2, 1965, the date on which Title VII became effective. To qualify for placement in any but the Labor Department it became necessary to register satisfactory scores on two professionally prepared aptitude tests, as well as to have a high school education. Completion of high school alone continued to render employees eligible for transfer to the four desirable departments from which Negroes had been excluded if the incumbent had been employed prior to the time of the new requirement. In September 1965 the company began to permit incumbent employees who lacked a high school education to qualify for transfer from Labor or Coal Handling to an "inside" job by passing two tests—the Wonderlic Personnel Test, which purports to measure general intelligence, and the Bennett Mechanical Comprehension Test. Neither was directed or intended to measure the ability to learn to perform a particular job or category of jobs. The requisite scores used for both initial hiring and transfer approximated the national median for high school graduates.

The District Court had found that while the company previously followed a policy of overt racial discrimination in a period prior to the Act, such conduct had ceased. The District Court also concluded that Title VII was intended to be prospective only and, consequently, the impact of prior inequities was beyond the reach of corrective action authorized by the Act.

. . . The Court of Appeals concluded there was no violation of the Act.

* * * * *

The objective of Congress in the enactment of Title VII is plain from the language of the statute. It was to achieve equality of employment opportunities and remove barriers that have operated in the past to favor an identifiable group of white employees over other employees. Under the Act, practices, procedures, or tests neutral on their face, and even neutral in terms of intent, cannot be maintained if they operate to "freeze" the status quo of prior discriminatory employment practices.

The Court of Appeals' opinion, and the partial dissent, agreed that, on the record in the present case, "whites register far better on the company's alternative requirements" than Negroes. This consequence would appear to be directly traceable to race. Basic intelligence must have the means of articulation to manifest itself fairly in a testing process. Because they are Negroes, petitioners have long received inferior education in segregated schools.

. . . Congress did not intend by Title VII, however, to guarantee a job to every person regardless of qualifications. In short, the Act does not command that any person be hired simply because he was formerly the subject of discrimination, or because he is a member of a minority group. Discriminatory preference for any group, minority or majority, is precisely and only what Congress has proscribed. . . .

. . . The Act proscribes not only overt discrimination but also practices that are fair in form, but discriminatory in operation. The touchstone is business necessity. If an employment practice which operates to exclude Negroes cannot be shown to be related to job performance, the practice is prohibited.

On the record before us, neither the high school completion requirement nor the general intelligence test is shown to bear a demonstrable relationship to successful performance of the jobs for which it was used. Both were adopted, as the Court of Appeals noted, without meaningful study of their relationship to job-performance ability. Rather, a vice president of

the company testified, the requirements were instituted on the company's judgment that they generally would improve the overall quality of the workforce.

The evidence, however, shows that employees who have not completed high school or taken the tests have continued to perform satisfactorily and make progress in departments for which the high school and test criteria are not used. . . .

The Court of Appeals held that the company had adopted the diploma and test requirements without any "intention to discriminate against Negro employees." We do not suggest that either the District Court or the Court of Appeals erred in examining the employer's intent; but good intent or absence of discriminatory intent does not redeem employment procedures or testing mechanisms that operate as "built-in headwinds" for minority groups and are unrelated to measuring job capability.

* * * * *

The facts of this case demonstrate the inadequacy of broad and general testing devices as well as the infirmity of using diplomas or degrees as fixed measures of capability. . . .

The company contends that its general intelligence tests are specifically permitted by Section 703(h) of the Act. That section authorizes the use of "any professionally developed ability test" that is not "designed, intended *or used* to discriminate because of race. . . ." (Emphasis added.)

The Equal Employment Opportunity Commission, having enforcement responsibility, has issued guidelines interpreting Section 703(h) to permit only the use of job-related tests. The administrative interpretation of the Act by the enforcing agency is entitled to great deference. Since the Act and its legislative history support the commission's construction, this affords good reason to treat the guidelines as expressing the will of Congress.

. . . From the sum of the legislative history relevant in this case, the conclusion is inescapable that the EEOC's construction of Section 703(h) to require that employment tests be job related comports with congressional intent.

Nothing in the Act precludes the use of testing or measuring procedures; obviously they are useful. What Congress has forbidden is giving these devices and mechanisms controlling force unless they are demonstrably a reasonable measure of job performance. Congress has not commanded that the less qualified be preferred over the better qualified simply because of minority origins. Far from disparaging job qualifications as such, Congress has made such qualifications the controlling factor, so that race, religion, nationality, and sex become irrelevant. What Congress has commanded is that any tests used must measure the person for the job and not the person in the abstract.

The judgment of the Court of Appeals is . . . reversed.

Questions

1. According to the Supreme Court, what was Congress's objective in enacting Title VII?

2. Had Duke Power been able to establish that its reasons for adopting the diploma and test standards were entirely without discriminatory intent, would the Supreme Court have ruled differently? Explain.

3. What is the central issue in this case?

4. Why was North Carolina's social and educational history relevant to the outcome of the case?

5. Statistical evidence showed that 35 percent of new hires in grocery and produce at Lucky Stores, a retail grocery chain, were women, while 84 percent of new hires in deli, bakery, and general merchandise were women. Statistical evidence also showed that 31 percent of those promoted into apprentice jobs in grocery and produce were women, while women comprised 75 percent of those promoted into apprentice jobs in deli, bakery, and general merchandise. Grocery and produce jobs generally were higher-paying jobs than those in deli, bakery, and general merchandise. Women received significantly fewer overtime hours than men.

   Do these facts regarding Lucky Stores suggest discrimination? Explain. See *Stender v. Lucky Stores,* Inc., 803 F.Supp. 259 (DC Cal. 1992).

6. Gregory, a black male, was offered employment by Litton Systems as a sheet metal worker. As part of a standard procedure he completed a form listing a total of 14 non-traffic arrests but no convictions. Thereupon the employment offer was withdrawn. Gregory then brought suit, claiming he was a victim of racial discrimination.
   a. Explain the foundation of his argument.
   b. Decide the case. See *Gregory v. Litton,* 412 F.2d 631 (9th Cir. 1972).

7. Eighty-one percent of the hires at Consolidated Service Systems, a small Chicago janitorial company, were of Korean origin. The EEOC brought a disparate treatment claim, saying the firm discriminated in favor of Koreans by relying primarily on word-of-mouth recruiting. Hwang, the owner, is Korean. Seventy-three percent of the job applicants were Korean. One percent of the Chicago-area workforce is Korean, and not more than 3 percent of the janitorial workforce for the area is Korean. The court found no persuasive evidence of intentional discrimination, although the government claimed that 99 applicants were denied jobs because they were not Koreans.
   a. Does restricting hiring to members of one ethnic group constitute discrimination where hiring is accomplished by word of mouth? Explain.
   b. What if a firm, using the word-of-mouth approach, hired only white applicants? Explain.
   c. In this case, the EEOC brought but dropped a disparate impact claim. Analyze the case using the disparate impact test. See *Equal Employment Opportunity Commission v. Consolidated Service Systems,* 989 F.2d 233 (7th Cir. 1993).

Statutory Defenses

In addition to the aforementioned defenses against disparate treatment and disparate impact claims, Title VII also affords specific exemptions or defenses, three of which are of particular note: (1) seniority, (2) employee testing, and (3) bona fide occupational qualification. Bona fide occupational qualifications are addressed in the next section as part of the sex discrimination discussion.

Seniority

Differences in wages and conditions of employment are permissible under the Civil Rights Act of 1964 where those differences are the result of a bona fide (good faith) seniority system, as long as the system was not intended to hide or facilitate discrimination. Seniority is important because it often determines who is laid off first and who gets promotions, vacations, and so forth. Because white people often have greater seniority than blacks, the result is that seniority may perpetuate the effects of historical discrimination. The Supreme Court has made it clear, however, that a bona fide seniority system that perpetuates past wrongs is illegal only if discriminatory intent is proven.[13]

Job-Related Employee Testing

Many employers use testing in making hiring and promotion decisions. The availability of online applications has contributed to an increase in this practice.[14] In order to avoid a disparate impact created by employee testing, an employer must be able to show that the test in question is job-related and consistent with business necessity; that is, the test must evaluate an individual's skills as they relate to the relevant employment opportunity. To prevent unlawful disparate treatment, an employer's test must be uniformly applied regardless of an applicant's or employee's race, sex, or other protected categories. For example, Title VII prohibits an employer from testing the reading ability of African-American applicants or employees while not requiring the same test of their white counterparts.[15]

Spousal Discrimination?

Craig Holcomb, a white male and assistant coach for the Iona College men's basketball team, married an African-American woman. While the team enjoyed a successful record for several years, its lackluster performance and player misconduct between 2001 and 2004 led to changes in the Iona basketball program including the dismissal of Holcomb and an African-American assistant coach. Another white assistant coach, who was not engaged in an interracial relationship, was not fired. Holcomb brought a Title VII claim asserting that he had been discharged because his wife is African American. Holcomb alleged that Iona College's athletic director had made several racist and derogatory remarks about African Americans on the basketball team and had derided Holcomb's decision to marry his wife whom he referred to as "Aunt Jemima." How would you rule on this case? Explain.

Source: Holcomb v. Iona College, 521 F.3d 130 (2nd Cir. 2008).

The Four-Fifths Rule and Disparate Impact

If the selection rate (such as the percentage passing a test, being hired, or being promoted) for any protected class is less than 80 percent of the selection rate for the group with the highest selection rate, then the employment practice in question will be presumed to create a disparate impact. An employer falling below that standard must prove the job relatedness of the employment practice in question and demonstrate that a good-faith effort was made to find a selection procedure that lessened the disparate impact on protected classes. [For an extensive employment discrimination database, see **http://topics.law.cornell.edu/wex/Employment_discrimination**]

Question

David Dunlap, a 52-year-old African-American man, had 20 years' experience as a boilermaker, including 15 years as a foreman. Most of Dunlap's work experience had involved contract or temporary jobs in Tennessee Valley Authority facilities, but he had never been directly employed by the TVA. Dunlap asserted that he had been applying for a position with TVA since the 1970s but had not been successful. When he was one of 21 applicants interviewed for 10 available boilermaker positions, he was rejected. The selection committee, made up of five whites and one African American, individually scored the interviews before engaging in "score balancing" where they discussed their individual opinions to even out the scores, which changed considerably through that process. Dunlap's technical expertise equaled that of five of the selected applicants, but his interview score was lower. Dunlap showed that he received lower scores on attendance than white applicants with similar records, as well as on safety compared with white applicants who had inferior records, as disclosed in the interview process. Dunlap was ranked 14th out of the 21 candidates. One African-American applicant was hired after he filed a discrimination complaint with the EEOC based on his similar failed attempts to secure employment with TVA. What claim or claims under Title VII might Dunlap have against the TVA? How would you rule? Explain. See *Dunlap v. Tennessee Valley Authority,* 519 F.3d 626 (6th Cir. 2008).

National Origin

Employment discrimination often reflects larger social issues that come to influence workplace relations. A dramatic example is found in the aftermath of the September 11, 2001, terrorist attacks on the United States. Between September 11, 2001, and September 11, 2004, the EEOC processed over 900 claims of national origin discrimination associated with the September 11 attacks, resulting in approximately $3.2 million in monetary relief.[16]

In 2005, the EEOC settled a claim it brought against Pesce, an upscale Houston-based restaurant on behalf of Karim El-Raheb, former Pesce general manager. In his August 2001 review, El-Raheb had been told he was doing very well. After business declined following the September 11 terrorist attacks, Pesce's co-owners speculated that customers may be frightened by El-Raheb's appearance and name, suggesting that he could "pass for Hispanic" and should change his name to "something Latin." In November 2001, El-Raheb was fired because "things weren't working out." El-Raheb received $150,000 in monetary relief.[17]

> Customers may be frightened by El-Raheb's appearance and name.

Speak English Only?

Reflecting a national debate over whether English should be the official language of the United States, "Speak English Only" rules in the workplace have generated controversy as well as national origin discrimination claims based on the disparate impact these rules may have on members of ethnic groups whose primary language is not English.

Employers argue that the rules are necessary when dealing with customers, to maintain job safety, and to encourage congenial worker relations. EEOC guidelines prohibit employers from imposing a blanket ban on employees speaking their primary language in the workplace, but an English-only rule at certain times is permissible if justified by business necessity and if adequately explained to the employees.

In *Garcia v. Spun Steak Co.,* the employer, a producer of meat products, instituted an English-only rule for its bilingual employees to enhance safety and product quality and to address allegations that some employees were making rude comments in Spanish to English-speaking employees. The English-only rule applied to work but not to lunch, breaks, or employees' own time. The employer's rule was upheld by a federal appellate court on the grounds that it was narrowly defined and did not create a discriminatory atmosphere.[18]

Question

Rodriguez, a FedEx employee of Hispanic origin, informed FedEx's Regional Human Resources Manager Adkinson that he wanted to obtain a promotion to a supervisory position. After applying and interviewing for an available supervisory position, Rodriguez was rejected. The manager who interviewed Rodriguez found him to be qualified, but did not hire him because of Adkinson's expressed concerns that Rodriguez's "accent and speech pattern" would undermine his ability to rise through the corporate ranks. Another FedEx manager stated that when he asked Adkinson why Rodriguez had not received the promotion, Adkinson made derogatory comments about Rodriguez's "language" and "how he speaks." Is FedEx liable for national origin discrimination based on its failure to promote Rodriguez? Decide. Explain. See *Rodriguez v. FedEx Freight East, Inc.*, 487 F.3d 1001 (6th Cir. 2007).

Racial Harassment

| The hangman's noose. |

The hangman's noose, perhaps the most hurtful and disgraceful expression of racism, sometimes appears in America's increasingly integrated workplaces. On January 24, 2008, the EEOC announced the $465,000 settlement of a racial harassment lawsuit on behalf of African-American employees of Henredon Furniture Industries. The lawsuit alleged that these employees had for years been subjected to a persistent racially hostile work environment that included the display of hangman's nooses. Racial harassment charges filed with the EEOC, some of which similarly involve hangman's nooses as well as verbal threats of lynching, more than doubled between 1991 and 2007.[19]

Legal requirements and the evolving standards for analyzing harassment claims will be explored later in the context of sexual harassment—perhaps the most familiar form of workplace harassment.

In addition to overt forms of harassment such as using racial slurs in the workplace, the use of more subtle "code words" may constitute racial and/or national origin harassment. The manager at an Alabama Tyson Foods chicken plant regularly called African-American male employees "boy" in what witnesses described as a derogatory manner. When one of these employees, a superintendent who had worked over 10 years for Tyson, was rejected for an available promotion to shift manager, he filed a race discrimination complaint. In its 2006 decision in *Ash v. Tyson,* the U.S. Supreme Court unanimously held that "boy" could have racial overtones, even if not modified with a reference to African Americans.[20] However, on remand, the lower appellate court ruled that the use of "boy" alone was not enough to create an inference of racial discrimination.[21] In *Aman v. Cort Furniture Rental Corporation,*[22] two black employees claimed that they were subjected to a racially hostile work environment in part because black employees were labeled by coworkers and managers with racist "code words" such as "all of you," "one of them," and "poor people." The court, in finding for the employees, ruled that certain phrases in the employment setting cannot be excused as mere rudeness and may, in the totality of the circumstances, add up to discrimination so severe that it creates an abusive work environment.

Black History Month

In February 2010, the "Compton Cookout," an off-campus party near the University of California at San Diego, was organized in apparent mockery of Black History Month. The invitation detailed a dress code based on racial stereotypes. The university responded with a teach-in to explore how such incidents arise and the importance of "mutual respect and civility" on its campus. The Office of the Chancellor issued a statement: "We strongly condemn [the party] and the blatant disregard of our campus values. Although the party was not a UC San Diego student-organization sponsored event, participants did include UC San Diego students and that causes us great concern."

Source: UC San Diego Office of the Chancellor, "Condemnation of Off-Campus Party and Affirmation of Principles of Community," *Diversity Matters*, February 16, 2010 [**http://diversity.ucsd.edu/statement.html**].

Part Three—Sex Discrimination

Equality for Women

In 2010, nearly 50 years after the 1963 passage of the Equal Pay Act, American women working full-time earn on average about 81 cents for every dollar earned by men; up dramatically from the 59 cents of the early 1960s, but still far short of equality.[23] Of course, factors beyond discrimination, including decisions to interrupt careers for child rearing, account for some of that disparity; but allegations of sex discrimination remain common.

The power and limits of statutory protections against sex discrimination are evident in recent Title VII class-action lawsuits brought by female employees alleging disparity in pay, work assignments, and promotion. In 2007, a federal judge approved a $46 million settlement of a class-action lawsuit brought against Morgan Stanley representing 3,000 female financial advisers and trainees claiming discrimination in compensation, promotion, and work assignments.[24] But the class action approach to discrimination litigation suffered a significant setback in 2011 when the U.S. Supreme Court denied class action status to a case in which 1.5 million women are suing Walmart for sex discrimination. The plaintiffs argue, among other things, that women have occupied 70 percent of Walmart's hourly jobs but only 33 percent of management positions, but Walmart says females hold a steadily increasing percentage of managerial roles and that the company has instituted developmental programs for women.

The Supreme Court decision did not reach the substantive merits of the discrimination complaint. Rather, the Supreme Court ruled that the case could not go forward as a class action because the plaintiffs did not point to specific, consistent, nationwide employment policies or practices that harmed the class members. The plaintiffs can continue the suit on an individual basis or perhaps in regional groups. (See Chapter 4 for more on the *Walmart* case and class actions.)[25]

Glass Ceiling?   Critics say a "glass ceiling" of prejudice holds women back from roles of power and career advancement. In 2010, female lawyers earned about 77 cents for every dollar earned by men in their profession, and female professional financial advisors earned approximately 58 cents for every dollar earned by their male counterparts, similar to the average earnings of women workers one-half century ago at the time of the Equal Pay Act's passage.[26]

Questions

1. What possible reasons might explain why women generally earn less than men? Should we be concerned? How might this issue be addressed?

2. Why are female lawyers and personal financial advisors earning significantly less than their male counterparts? Should we be concerned? How might this issue be addressed?

3. In 2010, women in food preparing and service occupations earned more than men in these jobs—about $1.12 for every dollar earned by their male counterparts.[27] Why might women make more as food preparers and servers than men? Should we be concerned? How might this issue be addressed?

Analysis of Sex Discrimination: Current Issues

Sex discrimination claims brought under Title VII include disparate treatment and disparate impact, as well as sexual harassment. Employee training and policies targeting sex discrimination have become common in the American workplace. However, after remaining relatively steady from 1997 to 2007, the number of Title VII sex-based discrimination charges filed with the EEOC grew notably in 2008 and increased further in 2009 and 2010.[28] Thus, sex discrimination claims remain a critical area of Title VII analysis.

Sex Discrimination and Disparate Impact

The following case illustrates the analysis of a sex discrimination claim alleging disparate impact.

LEGAL BRIEFCASE

Pietras v. Farmingville Fire District   180 F.3d 468 (2d Cir.1999); cert. den. 528 U.S. 948 (1999)

Circuit Judge Calabresi

The district court found that Farmingville's physical agility test ("PAT"), which all probationary volunteer firefighters were required to pass in order to become full-fledged volunteer firefighters, had a disparate impact on women.

* * * * *

BACKGROUND

Farmingville is the governing body of a volunteer fire department that has approximately 100 members. Pietras was a probationary (i.e., trainee) firefighter in the Farmingville Department. Even as a probationary volunteer, Pietras was entitled to numerous firefighter benefits under state law and the by-laws of the department. These included (1) a retirement pension, (2) life insurance, (3) death benefits, (4) disability insurance, and (5) some medical benefits.

Before Pietras could become a full member of the department, however, she and all other probationary volunteers were required to pass a newly instituted PAT.[1] The PAT consisted of a series of physical tasks that the applicants had to complete within a specified time limit. The most difficult of these nine labors was the "charged hose drag," which involved dragging a water-filled hose—weighing approximately 280 pounds—over a distance of 150 feet.

To determine the appropriate time limit for the PAT, Farm ingville officials asked various members of the department to take the test. Forty-four firefighters participated in these trials. Of the 44 test-takers, 33 were males who served as full firefighters, 6 were male probationary members, 3 were male junior members, one was Jeanine Serpe, a female full firefighter, and one was Pietras. The average times of these subgroups were:

Sample Pool	Average Time
Full males (33)	3:12
Probationary males (6)	2:47
Junior males (3)	2:52
Full female (Serpe)	5:30
Probationary female (Pietras)	5:21

From these results, Farmingville set four minutes as the time within which the labors had to be completed. The four-minute threshold was determined by taking the average of all the (mostly male) test runs (approximately 3:30) and then adding an extra half-minute "to have some leeway." There was some concern expressed at a 1993 Farmingville Board meeting that neither Serpe nor Pietras had been able to finish the PAT in anything close to four minutes, but Farmingville nevertheless instituted the four-minute cutoff.

Following the implementation of the PAT, Pietras tried and failed the test twice. During this same period, six other female probationary firefighters took the test. Four of these women completed the PAT in under four minutes and therefore passed. One woman failed to complete the test for an unknown reason. And one woman did not complete the test despite repeated efforts to drag the water-filled hose over the required distance. All of the 24 male probationary volunteers who took the test at about this time passed.

[1]Pietras passed both a medical exam and a written exam that were also preconditions to becoming a full firefighter.

Following her second failure to pass the PAT, Pietras was fired from her volunteer position at Farmingville.

* * * * *

Pietras filed suit in district court, alleging that Farmingville had violated Title VII of the Civil Rights Act of 1964.

* * * * *

At trial . . . , Pietras presented testimony from Dr. Robert Otto, an expert exercise physiologist. Dr. Otto conducted an extensive review of the physical agility tests administered by various volunteer and paid fire departments and concluded (a) that the four-minute limit in the Farmingville test had a disparate impact on women, and (b) that it was not job related.

After reviewing the evidence, the district court ruled for Pietras.

* * * * *

[T]he court concluded that "the record is bereft of any evidence" that a four-minute time limit to finish the PAT was job related.[2]

In support of its finding of disparate impact, the court noted that the male pass rate on the PAT was 95 percent (63 out of 66) while the female pass rate was only 57 percent (4 out of 7). Relying on the "four-fifths" rule set forth in the EEOC Guidelines, the court reasoned that "a pass rate for women which is less [than] four-fifths (or 80 percent) of the pass rate for men typically signifies disparate impact sufficient to establish a prima facie case. . . . Therefore, the gender imbalance [in this case] more than satisfies the 80 percent standard." This statistical evidence (which was corroborated by Dr. Otto's testimony concerning the effect of the PAT on women) was deemed by the district court to be enough to establish disparate impact.

Farmingville appeals.

DISCUSSION

* * * * *

Disparate Impact

* * * * *

Farmingville asserts that, even if the statistical figures before the district court were correct, a sample of seven female test takers is simply too small to support a disparate impact finding.

[2][T]here is no evidence at all to indicate that the time chosen for the test reflected the needs of the job. In fact, the record makes clear that Farmingville selected the four-minute figure simply by taking the average of all the test scores and then arbitrarily adding some extra time.

* * * * *

In the case before us, however, Pietras presented more than just statistics. After conducting an exhaustive analysis of the practices of other fire departments, Dr. Otto provided expert testimony on the disparate impact of Farmingville's PAT. This expert testimony, combined with the statistics Pietras did present, comfortably tips the scales in favor of the district court's finding of disparate impact.

Affirmed.

Questions

1. *a.* Why did the court conclude that the Farmingville Fire Department had discriminated against Pietras?
   b. Did the court conclude that Farmingville intended to discriminate? Explain.
   c. What, if anything, could Farmingville have done differently to win this case?
2. *a.* Shouldn't we always choose the strongest, fastest firefighters as long as they are otherwise well qualified? Explain.

b. Do the firefighters' rescue efforts at the World Trade Center on September 11, 2001, indicate that only men should serve as firefighters? Explain.

3. *a.* How would you argue that Women's Workout World, a health and exercise club, should be able to lawfully decline to accept men as customers and/or employees?
   b. Decide the case. Explain. See *U.S. EEOC v. Sedita,* 816 F.Supp. 1291 (N.D. Ill. 1993).

4. Dianne Rawlinson sought employment as a prison guard in Alabama. She was a 22-year-old college graduate with a degree in correctional psychology. She was denied employment because she failed to meet the 120-pound weight requirement for the job. The state also required such employees to be at least 5 feet 2 inches tall. Alabama operated four all-male, maximum-security prisons. The district court characterized the Alabama prison system as one of "rampant violence." Rawlinson sued, claiming employment discrimination. Decide. Explain. See *Dothard v. Rawlinson,* 97 S.Ct. 2720 (1977).

Running Upstairs—and Hitting a Ceiling?

The Southeastern Pennsylvania Transportation Authority (SEPTA) was sued on sex discrimination grounds by several female job applicants who had been rejected for employment as police officers. The women were unable to run 1.5 miles in 12 minutes, a job requirement. A disparate impact was established with evidence that 56 percent of the men passed the test, while 93 percent of women could not pass, but the Third Circuit Federal Court of Appeals ruled that the standard was consistent with business necessity and therefore did not violate Title VII. SEPTA was able to satisfy the court that running up and down subway stairs and pursuing wrongdoers required fitness like that measured by the test. Evidence also established that minimal training would allow most women to qualify.

Source: Lanning v. SEPTA, 308 F.3d 286 (3d Cir. 2002).

Bona Fide Occupational Qualification

Often in intentional sex discrimination cases, the key inquiry involves the *bona fide occupational qualification (BFOQ)* defense provided by Title VII. Discrimination is lawful where sex, religion, or national origin is a BFOQ reasonably necessary to the normal operation of that business. The exclusion of race and color from the list suggests Congress thought those categories always unacceptable as bona fide occupational qualifications. The

BFOQ was meant to be a very limited exception applicable to situations where specific inherent characteristics are necessary to the job (for example, wet nurse) or where authenticity (actors), privacy (nurses), or safety(guards) is required. Broadly, the BFOQ defense rests on this question: Is being a female, for example, necessary to perform the *essence* of the job?

Essence

An employer can lawfully insist on a woman to fill a woman's modeling role because being female goes to the essence of the job. Airlines, on the other hand, cannot hire only women as flight attendants even if customers prefer females and even if females perform the supplementary elements of the job (like charming passengers) better than most men. Those duties "are tangential to the essence of the business involved"[29] (the essence being the maintenance of safe, orderly conditions, providing service as needed, etc). Presumably, gender has little to do with the ability to perform those essential ingredients of the job.

Many employers have simply assumed that women could not perform certain tasks. For example, women were thought to be insufficiently aggressive for sales roles, and women were denied employment because they were assumed to have a higher turnover rate because of the desire to marry and have children. Those stereotypes are at the heart of sex discrimination litigation generally and do not support a BFOQ defense.

What about Hooters?

Can the Hooters restaurant chain lawfully decline to hire men to be food servers? Scantily clad "Hooters girls" serve food and beverages to Hooters restaurant customers. In the 1990s, several class action lawsuits were brought against Hooters on behalf of rejected male applicants. Under the 1997 settlement reached in the consolidated class action, Hooters was allowed to maintain its policy of hiring females only as food servers, but it agreed to create other restaurant positions such as bartenders for which men would have equal hiring opportunities. A 2009 gender discrimination claim brought by a Texas man who was allegedly told by a manager at the Corpus Christi Hooters restaurant that he would not be hired as a waiter because of his gender resulted in a confidential settlement with Hooters.

Questions

1. If the lawsuits against Hooters had not settled, do you think Hooters would have been able to raise a successful BFOQ defense? Explain.
2. Is Hooters' hiring policy better left to the market and ethics than to the courts? Explain.

Sources: "Hooters Agrees to Hire Men in Support Roles . . . ," *Baltimore Sun,* October 1, 1997, p. 3C; Matthew Heller, "Texas Man Aims to Bust Open Hooters Girl Hiring," On Point.com (January 13, 2009) [**http://www. onpointnews.com/NEWS/texas-man-aims-to-bust-open-hooters-girl-hiring.html**]; and *Grushevski v. Hooters,* "Plaintiff's Original Complaint," (S.D. Tex. 2009) [**http://www.eeoc.net/CM/Custom/Hooters.pdf**] "Notice of Joint Settlement," April 13, 2009 [**http://www.onpointnews.com/docs/Hooters1.pdf**].

Looks Discrimination

Harrah's Reno, Nevada, casino instituted a "Personal Best" appearance policy requiring its female bartenders to wear makeup while prohibiting their male counterparts from wearing any. After a successful 20-year career as a Harrah's bartender, Darlene Jespersen was fired for refusing to wear makeup under the policy.

Brenna Lewis staffed the front desks of Heartland Inn motels near Des Moines, Iowa, including its Ankeny, Iowa, location. Her performance was excellent, earning her compliments from customers and merit raises. Heartland's new corporate director of operations, Barbara Cullinan, had approved hiring Lewis for a full-time position staffing the Ankeny motel's front desk during the day, but Cullinan became dissatisfied after seeing Lewis in person. Cullinan was heard saying that Heartland staff should be "pretty," especially those working at the front desk. Lewis was self-described as "slightly more masculine." She avoided makeup and often wore her hair short. The front desk job description in Heartland's personnel manual did not mention appearance, stating only that a guest service representative must create "a warm, inviting atmosphere" and perform tasks such as relaying information and receiving reservations. Cullinan instituted a policy requiring videotaping of interviews for front desk hires. Over protests of her direct manager, Lewis was eventually fired.

Both Jespersen and Lewis brought Title VII claims against their former employers.

Questions

1. What do these cases have in common? How do they differ? Explain. Decide each case.
2. Should the law recognize a separate cause of action for "looks discrimination?" Explain.

Sources: Jespersen v. Harrah's, 444 F.3d 1104 (9th Cir. 2006); and *Lewis v. Heartland Inns,* 591 F.3d 1033 (8th Cir. 2010).

Work-Life Balance and Sex Discrimination

Antidiscrimination law has been critical in allowing women to pursue careers and in providing some refuge from the professional disadvantages of pregnancy experienced at some workplaces. The Pregnancy Discrimination Act (PDA) amended Title VII of the Civil Rights Act of 1964 so that discrimination with regard to pregnancy is treated as a form of sex discrimination. Broadly, the PDA requires that pregnant employees be treated the same as all other employees with temporary disabilities. In general, an employer should not ask job applicants about pregnancy, and applicants have no duty to reveal that pregnancy. Nor can a pregnant employee be forced to take time off or be forced to quit due to pregnancy.

FRD

"Family Responsibilities Discrimination" has achieved increased recognition in recent years. While no express antidiscrimination statutory protection is afforded to parents or caregivers, FRD claims may be based on existing statutes such as Title VII. For example, in *Chadwick v. Wellpoint, Inc.,* a federal appeals court allowed the mother of six-year-old triplets and an older child to proceed with a Title VII claim alleging that she was rejected for a promotion in favor of a less-qualified woman as a result of a sex-based stereotype that

> Stereotype that mothers with young children neglect their careers.

mothers with young children neglect their careers because of child care responsibilities.[30] [For the EEOC Enforcement Guidance on FRD, see "EEOC Enforcement Guidance: Unlawful Disparate Treatment of Workers with Caregiving Responsibilities" at **http://www.eeoc.gov/policy/docs/caregiving.html**]

Questions

1. Waitresses at the Rustic Inn were prohibited under a written policy from waiting tables past their fifth month of pregnancy and required either to suspend working or to switch to working as cashiers or hostesses, who are paid less since they do not receive gratuities. The EEOC filed a lawsuit against the employer on behalf of a class of three aggrieved employees, alleging that the policy violated the PDA. Decide. See *EEOC v. W&O Inc.,* 213 F.3d 600 (11th Cir. 2000).

2. Besides avoiding FRD liability, how might an employer benefit from effectively supporting employees' balancing of work and life responsibilities? Should parents and other caregivers be given express statutory protection against employment discrimination? Explain.

Equal Pay

Title VII affords broad protection from discrimination in pay because of sex. The Equal Pay Act of 1963 directly forbids discrimination on the basis of sex by paying wages to employees of one sex at a rate less than the rate paid to employees of the opposite sex for equal work on jobs requiring equal skill, effort, and responsibility and performed under similar working conditions (equal has been interpreted to mean "substantially equal"). The act provides for certain exceptions. Unequal wage payments are lawful if paid pursuant to (1) a seniority system, (2) a merit system, (3) a system that measures earnings by quantity or quality of production, or (4) a differential based on "any . . . factor other than sex." The employer seeking to avoid a violation of the Equal Pay Act can adjust its wage structure by raising the pay of the disfavored sex performing equal work. Lowering the pay of the favored sex violates the act.

If a male employee has a greater skill set—such as computer skills—than his female coworker doing "equal work," the employer may pay the man at a higher rate, as long as the male employee's superior skills are actually considered in making the pay decision.[31]

Women's Basketball Coach

Former University of Southern California head women's basketball coach Marianne Stanley sued the university for violating the Equal Pay Act because she was not as well paid as then head men's basketball coach George Raveling. Both coaches had successful won/lost records. The university defended the pay differential by pointing to Raveling's 14 years of coaching experience beyond Stanley's, his having coached the U.S. Olympic team, his marketing experience outside of coaching, and his books on basketball. Stanley could not point to similar credentials. Did the university violate the Equal Pay Act? See *Stanley v. University of Southern California,* 178 F. 3d 1069 (9th Cir. 1999); cert.den. 528 U.S. 1022 (1999).

Sexual Harassment

If asked, "what is an example of sexual harassment?" a reasonably knowledgeable response might be "a male boss making unwanted sexual advances on a female employee, telling her that such conduct is a job requirement," or "a male employee touching his female coworker in a sexual and unwanted manner." While these examples offer solid bases for sexual harassment claims, they do not provide a complete picture. As a form of sex discrimination actionable under Title VII, sexual harassment protection covers both men and women and strives to maintain equal opportunity in the workplace

According to a recent Society for Human Resource Management (SHRM) poll, nearly two-thirds of organizations received sexual harassment complaints from employees in the previous 24 months, and a quarter of organizations noted an increase in such claims during that time. Nearly one-fifth of organizations reported that the sexual harassment complaints were brought by male and female employees equally.[32]

Women in authority seem to be particularly susceptible to sexual harassment. A 2009 study determined that female supervisors or managers are nearly one and a half times as likely to experience sexual harassment in the workplace as women in non-supervisory positions. Why might women in powerful positions be more likely to experience sexual harassment? How might an employer address this issue? (See Eve Tahmincioglu, "Female Managers Face More Sexual Harassment," *Careers on msnbc.com,* August 24, 2009 [**http://www.msnbc.msn.com/id/32476564/ns/business-careers/**])

Vulgar Language in the Workplace

Ingrid Reeves worked as a transportation sales representative in the Birmingham, Alabama, branch of the shipping company C.H. Robinson. Reeves was the only woman working on the sales floor, an open area structured into a "pod" of cubicles. Six males worked with Reeves. Because there were no large barriers between the cubicles, Reeves could often hear the language of her male coworkers as they spoke over the phone or with each other. Reeves could also hear the central office radio that sat on a bookshelf near the "pod." On a daily basis at work, Reeves heard vulgar language and discussions of sexual topics, including such derogatory phrases as "bitch" and "whore," which her male coworkers used to describe customers. For example, the male branch manager once asked Reeves to speak to "that stupid bitch on line 4." The office radio was used by her coworkers to listen to a crude morning show featuring vulgar discussions of female anatomy. A federal appeals court found that the gender-specific derogatory language was not directed at Reeves, but she was allowed, nonetheless, to bring a Title VII sexual harassment claim based on her exposure to that language at work.

Source: Reeves v. Robinson Worldwide, Inc., 594 F.3d 798 (11th Cir. 2010).

The Law of Sexual Harassment

Sexual harassment, as a form of discrimination, consists of unwelcome sexual advances, requests for sexual favors, and other verbal or physical conduct of a sexual nature that (1) becomes a condition of employment, (2) becomes a basis for employment decisions, or (3) unreasonably interferes with work performance or creates a hostile working environment.

There are two types of sexual harassment: *quid pro quo* ("this for that," such as a sexual favor in exchange for keeping one's job) and *hostile work environment* (a workplace rendered offensive and abusive by such conduct as sexual comments, pictures, jokes, sexual aggression, and the like where no employment benefit is gained or lost). As discussed earlier in this chapter, hostile work environments may be created by offensive or abusive conduct involving protected categories other than sex, including race, religion, national origin, and disability. The law of sexual harassment, particularly in regard to hostile work environments, may apply to these cases.

The Test

Once we have some idea of behavior that constitutes sexual harassment, our concern turns to which remedies are available for the victims. Although the question is not settled, most federal courts to date have ruled that victims of sexual harassment seeking recovery under Title VII cannot sue the person who actually committed the harassment. The victim might be able to sue the wrongdoer under a state statute or by using a tort claim such as assault, but under Title VII, *personal liability* appears not to be available. This result, if the current judicial pattern continues, is not as unfair as might at first appear because well-settled principles of justice hold the employer and not the employer's agents or employees, generally responsible for workplace wrongdoing. The victim, therefore, can seek damages from the employer as the responsible party. A pair of 1998 U.S. Supreme Court decisions in the *Burlington Industries* and *Faragher*[33] cases considerably clarified the circumstances under which an employer is liable for sexual harassment in the workplace. The analysis proceeds as follows:

1. **Proof of sexual harassment**—The plaintiff/employee/victim must prove items a–c:

    a. The harassing conduct is unwelcome.
    b. The harassing conduct is because of sex.
    c. The harassing conduct resulted in a tangible employment action, or was sufficiently severe or pervasive as to unreasonably alter the conditions of employment and create a hostile, abusive work environment.

If the plaintiff is unable to prove items a to c, the claim fails. If the plaintiff proves items a to c, the inquiry then turns to the question of whether the employer bears responsibility for the harassment, as analyzed in Part 2.

2. **Employer liability and the affirmative defense**

    a. If the wrongdoer is a coworker, the plaintiff/employee can bring a negligence claim seeking to prove that the employer unreasonably failed to prevent or remedy the discriminatory harassment of the plaintiff/employee where management knew or should have known about the harassment.

b. If the wrongdoer is a supervisor with authority over the plaintiff/employee, and if the employee suffered a *tangible employment action* (job loss, demotion) because of the harassment, the employer is vicariously liable (indirect liability—see Chapter 12) for the employee's losses. That is, the employer is strictly liable for the employee's wrong and cannot offer a defense regardless of lack of knowledge, absence of negligence, or any other factor.

c. If the wrongdoer is a supervisor with authority over the plaintiff/employee, but the employee suffered no tangible employment action, the employer can avoid liability by proving both elements of the following affirmative defense:

(1) The employer exercised reasonable care to prevent and correct the harassment promptly (by instituting antiharassment training programs, having a policy for reporting harassment, and so on) and (2) the employee unreasonably failed to take advantage of those opportunities.

The case that follows illustrates sexual harassment analysis, and the application of the employer's affirmative defense.

LEGAL BRIEFCASE

Craig v. M & O Agencies, d/b/a Mahoney Group
496 F.3d 1047 (9th Cir. 2007)

Circuit Judge Bybee

Eileen Craig appeals the district court's grant of summary judgment in favor of M&O Agencies (dba The Mahoney Group), Leon Byrd and Patricia Roberts (collectively "Appellees") in her sexual harassment suit.

* * * * *

I. BACKGROUND

Craig worked for The Mahoney Group as the branch manager in Tucson and reported to Byrd who was the interim president. Over the course of several months, Byrd made repeated inappropriate comments to Craig about her legs and how she should wear shorter skirts. Although Craig thought the comments were obnoxious, she was not particularly offended. The situation took a turn for the worse on August 8, 2003, when at Byrd's invitation, Craig met him for drinks after work at an On the Border restaurant. She had previously been to other happy hours and lunches with Byrd to discuss work related matters and thought this would be a similar meeting. Craig and Byrd drank wine and at one point, Byrd asked Craig "if she had

ever thought of making love to him" and told her that he would like to take off the blue dress she was wearing. Later Byrd invited her back to his house to drink more wine in his hot tub and told her that "it's not a matter of if but when" something would happen between them. Craig laughed and shook her head at Byrd's comments but did not leave the restaurant.

Around 8:00 P.M., Craig excused herself to go to the restroom, and moments later Byrd followed her into the women's bathroom. When Craig exited the stall, Byrd approached her, grabbed her arms, "gave her an open-mouthed kiss and stuck his tongue in her mouth." The kiss ended when someone walked into the restroom. Byrd exited and Craig remained in the restroom for five minutes to compose herself, after which she left the restaurant alone while Byrd was paying the check. Byrd called Craig's phone later that night, but hung up when her husband answered. Craig's husband urged her to report the incident, but she refused.

Approximately one week after the happy-hour incident Byrd called Craig from the golf course, told her she was beautiful and asked her out for another drink, which she declined. Undeterred, Byrd later called Craig from a hotel room in Wisconsin and upon his return to Tucson went into Craig's office and repeatedly asked her if she would like to make love to him. Craig's response was consistently and emphatic "no." On August 14, 2003, Byrd told Craig that he "wanted" her and asked her if she remembered telling him that she "wanted to make love to him." Craig denied ever telling him that she "wanted to make love to him."

Shortly thereafter Byrd apologized to Craig and told her that he wanted to remain friends, . . . but two days later asked Craig why she was cold and distant toward him. He again asked her why she didn't remember saying that she wanted to "make love to him," and told her that he still had feelings for her, but said that if she wanted him to leave her alone, he would do so. At some point Byrd told Craig that he didn't think he could work with her anymore, but never explicitly conditioned her continued employment or promotion on entering a sexual relationship with him. On August 27, 2003, Craig finally reported Byrd's conduct to Dawn Zimbleman, one of the individuals (in addition to Byrd) listed on the company's sexual harassment policy to whom complaints should be made. Reporting the claim spurred the company to immediate action. Byrd was instructed to stay away from Craig and to stop making sexual coments to her, and Craig began reporting to John McEvoy, another company executive. Additionally, the company appointed a senior executive to investigate the complaint, but replaced him with the Group's outside corporate counsel, Denis Fitzgibbons, when it was brought to the company's attention that the executive had previously been investigated for sexual harassment. . . .

After investigating, Fitzgibbons recommended that (1) the Group offer Craig and her husband counseling sessions at the company's expense; (2) Byrd receive a severe written reprimand (stating) that if he engaged in this type of behavior again, he would be terminated; (3) Byrd attend sexual harassment sensitivity training; and (4) all of the Group managers and supervisors receive sexual harassment training in the near future.

In late September 2003, Craig was told that the investigation was complete, and she began reporting to Byrd again. The company did conduct sexual harassment training for the executives, but Craig alleges that during one sexual harassment training session, the Company's chairman came in and made an inappropriate joke. . . . Eventually Craig resigned. . . .

Craig filed a complaint, which she later amended, alleging (among other claims) sex discrimination under Title VII . . .

II. DISCUSSION

*   *   *   *   *

1. Liability under a *quid pro quo* theory

To prove actionable harassment under a *quid pro quo* or "tangible employment action" theory, Craig must show that Byrd "explicitly or implicitly condition[ed] a job, a job benefit, or the absence of a job detriment, upon an employee's acceptance of sexual conduct." If a plaintiff is able to make such a showing, the employer is strictly liable for the supervisor's conduct. . . .

Craig does not allege that Byrd explicitly conditioned her continued empoyment with The Mahoney Group on her acquiescing to sexual relations with him. She did testify that she felt she had to consent if she wanted to keep her job, yet she offers little else to support her contention. Byrd's comment "I just don't think I can work with you anymore" is merely a "vague and unsupported allegation," which we have held is insufficient to cause a reasonable woman to believe that retaining her job was conditioned on having sex with her supervisor. Additionally, several other senior executives approached Craig after she reported the harassment and reassured her that her job was not in jeopardy. Because Craig, who did not acquiesce to Byrd's demands, was neither demoted nor fired, nor did she suffer any other "tangible employment action," we agree with the district court that Craig has not made out a prima facie case for liability under Title VII on a theory of *quid pro quo* harassment.

2. Liability under a hostile environment theory

Craig alternatively could sustain her Title VII action under a hostile work environment theory of liability. To make a prima facie case of a hostile work environment, a person must show "that: (1) she was subjected to verbal or physical conduct of a sexual nature, (2) this conduct was unwelcome, and (3) the conduct was sufficiently severe or pervasive to alter the conditions of the victim's employment and create an abusive working environment." Additionally, "[t]he working environment must both subjectively and objectively be perceived as abusive." Objective hostility is determined by examining the totality of the circumstances and whether a reasonable person with the same characteristics as the victim would perceive the workplace as hostile. Finally, to find a violation of Title VII, "conduct must be extreme to amount to a change in the terms and conditions of employment."

An employer may be vicariously liable under a hostile environment theory when the harassment is perpetrated by a supervisor "with immediate (or successively higher) authority over the employee." When no "tangible employment action" (such as firing or demotion) is taken, an employer may avoid liability by asserting a "reasonable care" defense. An employer can sustain the affirmative defense if it shows "(a) that the employer exercised reasonable care to prevent and correct promptly any sexually harassing behavior, and (b) that the plaintiff employee unreasonably failed to take advantage of any preventive or corrective opportunities provided by the employer or to avoid harm otherwise." [W]e conclude that there are sufficient triable issues of fact to overcome summary judgment with respect to Craig's prima facie case, and that The Mahoney Group did not successfully assert the "reasonable care" affirmative defense.

a. Craig's prima facie case

Byrd's behavior was explicitly sexual in nature, and unwelcome, as Craig repeatedly rebuffed his advances and eventually reported his conduct to the company. We also find that Byrd's conduct meets the requirement of being both subjectively and objectively abusive. Craig testified that she felt Byrd's comments and actions—particularly the incident in the bathroom—were abusive and made her feel uncomfortable. The conduct also met the objective standard: A reasonable woman in Craig's position could feel that Byrd's comments and actions were hostile, demeaning and abusive.

Craig's prima facie showing turns on whether or not Byrd's actions were pervasive and serious enough to amount to "a change in the terms and conditions of employment."

* * * * *

Byrd's conduct falls somewhere between mere isolated incidents or offhand comments, which do not amount to a Title VII claim, and serious and pervasive harassment that clearly comes within Title VII . . .

Craig alleges that Byrd's actions resulted in a concrete change in her working environment. Specifically, she alleges she was removed from many of her duties, received budgets late, had some of her duties reassigned, and was forced to interact with Byrd despite his continued propositions. She claims that these additional stresses in the workplace made her nervous, spawned anxiety attacks and affected her health. Each of her complaints standing alone might not satisfy the standard, but in the aggregate, they are sufficiently serious to amount to an alteration in her condition of employment. . . .

b. The Mahoney Group's affirmative defense

The Mahoney Group argues that even if Craig has alleged sufficient facts to support her Title VII claim, because Craig did not suffer "tangible employment action," it is entitled to assert an affirmative defense. See *Pa. State Police v. Suders,* 542 U.S. 129, 148-49 . . .

[W]e hold that The Mahoney Group satisfied the first prong of the affirmative defense—that the company "exercised reasonable care to prevent and correct promptly any sexually harassing behavior." Specifically, the company had a mechanism in place for filing complaints about sexual harassment. When Craig finally did complain, The Mahoney Group addressed the situation promptly: It told Byrd to stay away from Craig, hired outside counsel to investigate and make recommendations, had Craig report to another individual other than Byrd and conducted sexual harassment training.[1] These responsible and prompt actions satisfy the first prong of the test.

The company's affirmative defense fails on the second prong, however, because The Mahoney Group cannot show that Craig "unreasonably failed to take advantage of any preventive or corrective opportunities provided by the employer." The Mahoney Group argues that Craig unreasonably delayed reporting the harassment because she waited until August 27, 2003 to file a complaint with the company, some 19 days after the incident at the restaurant; it suggests that if Craig had reported the behavior earlier, it is quite possible that Byrd would not have made the subsequent phone calls or repeatedly propositioned her at work. However, we do not think that in this situation a 19-day delay is unreasonable; an employee in Craig's position may have hoped the situation would resolve itself without the need of filing a formal complaint, and she justifiably may have delayed reporting in hopes of avoiding what she perceived could be adverse—or at least unpleasant—employment consequences.

We cannot see how a delay of a mere seven days [Byrd's behavior continued until at least August 20-Ed.] rises to the level of being "unreasonable." Craig's delay is markedly different from cases where victims have allowed the harassment to continue for a period of months or years before finally reporting it to the appropriate authority.

We hold that The Mahoney Group's affirmative defense fails, as Craig's minor delay in reporting the behavior did not meet the stringent standard outlined in *Faragher*. Consequently, we reverse the district court's grant of summary judgment for The Mahoney Group and remand for further proceedings.

* * * * *

Questions

1. *a.* According to the court, Craig did not prove quid pro quo harassment based on Byrd's conduct. Do you agree or disagree? Explain. Describe a situation that might meet the court's evidentiary requirements for quid pro quo harassment claims.

---

[1] Craig alleges that the investigation the company undertook was a "sham" and alleges that outside counsel failed to interview several individuals Craig claimed had also been harassed by Byrd. Because The Mahoney Group's affirmative defense fails on the second prong, we need not address this issue, although it may be a relevant inquiry on remand.

b. The court asserted that if taken alone, Craig's individual complaints about the change in her working environment would not meet the standard for a hostile work environment. Do you agree? Should the standard be lowered? Explain.

c. How did the Mahoney Group satisfy the first prong of the affirmative defense? Why did the affirmative defense ultimately fail? What should employers learn from this? What should employees learn?

d. Craig brought individual claims against Byrd, for which the court affirmed the district court's summary judgment citing its prior decisions that Title VII does not provide for separate causes of action against individuals. Do you think that Title VII liability should be extended to supervisors? To coworkers? Why or why not?

2. Truck driver Lesley Parkins claimed she was a victim of hostile environment sexual harassment while employed by Civil Constructors beginning in 1994. Parkins alleged that coworkers subjected her to foul language, sexual stories, and touching. Parkins complained to her dispatcher, Tim Spellman, and to one of her purported harassers, Robert Strong. She saw the job superintendent and the company EEO officer almost daily, but she did not complain to either. In 1996 Parkins filed a grievance with her union—Teamsters Local 325. The union contacted the company EEO officer, who immediately launched an investigation that led to punishment for the employees. Parkins conceded that she was not harassed following the company punishment. Parkins filed suit charging Civil Constructors with sexual harassment. Parkins claimed that two of her harassers, Strong and Charles Boeke, were foremen who supervised her work. Assuming Parkins can prove that she was, in fact, sexually harassed, what must she prove in order to hold Civil Constructors liable? See *Parkins v. Civil Constructors of Illinois,* 163 F.3d 1027 (7th Cir. 1998).

3. Rena Lockard worked for a Pizza Hut franchise in Atoka, Oklahoma, in September 1993. Two male customers made sexually offensive comments to her such as, "I would like to get in your pants." Lockard told her supervisor she did not like waiting on the men, but she did not mention the sexual comments. In November 1993, the men returned to the Pizza Hut, and Lockard was instructed to wait on them. One of them asked what kind of cologne she was wearing, and Lockard replied that it was none of his business. The customer then grabbed her by the hair. Lockard told her supervisor what had happened and said she did not want to wait on the two men. The supervisor ordered her to do so. Lockard returned to the table where one of the men pulled her by the hair, grabbed one of her breasts, and put his mouth on her breast. Lockard then quit her job and later sued the local franchise and Pizza Hut.

   a. What is the central issue(s) in this case?

   b. Is the franchise and/or Pizza Hut responsible for sexual harassment by a customer against an employee? Explain. See *Lockard v. Pizza Hut,* 162 F.3d 1062 (10th Cir. 1998).

4. A female employed as an Installation and Repairs Technician claimed a hostile work environment was created in the garage in which she worked by the routine use of profanity, crude humor, vulgar graffiti depicting sexual acts, and especially by sexually demeaning conversations conveying a profound disrespect for women. While the comments and graffiti demeaned some male employees, the conduct was directed at all the women working in the garage.

   a. In deciding whether the conduct constituted hostile environment sexual harassment, should the court evaluate the facts from the point of view of a "reasonable person" or a "reasonable woman"? Explain.

   b. Why does it matter? See *Petrosino v. Bell Atlantic,* 385 F.3d 210 (2d Cir. 2004); see also *Ellison v. Brady,* 924 F.2d 872 (9th Cir. 1991).

Consider the Source: Sexual Harassment at the Casino

While she was a bartender at Gold Strike Casino Resort in Tunica County, Mississippi, Debra Brockington allegedly was subjected to sexual harassment by her female supervisor, Wanda Haley, as well as her former boyfriend and coworker, Ed Ogden. The alleged harassment included Haley grabbing Brockington's breasts, making sexually suggestive remarks to others about Brockington, and snapping a towel against her buttocks. Brockington admitted to engaging in off-color conversations and conduct with her female coworkers. In her subsequent Title VII claim, a federal trial court, addressing Haley's behavior, held that "within the context of the plaintiff's work environment the alleged harassment in this case was neither severe nor pervasive."

Questions

1. Do you agree with the court's reasoning about the importance of workplace context in determining whether unlawful harassment has occurred? Explain.

2. In its ruling, the court said, "[C]asino bartenders have the same right as other employees to expect that they will not be subjected to unlawful harassment. . . ." What impact might the court's ruling on workplace context have on the sexual harassment protections of casino bartenders and others working in similar environments?

Source: Brockington v. Circus Circus Mississippi, 2008 U.S. Dist. LEXIS 39482 (N.D. Miss 2008).

Same Sex?

Joseph Oncale, a heterosexual who worked on an offshore oil rig, charged a supervisor and two male coworkers with sexually harassing him, including repeated taunts and several sexual assaults, one with a bar of soap while Oncale was showering. Oncale complained to superiors, but to no avail. He then quit his job and sued his employer for sexual harassment. The case went to the U.S. Supreme Court, which unanimously ruled that same-sex harassment is actionable under Title VII.[34] Oncale then settled out of court for an undisclosed amount of money. Justice Scalia, who wrote the Supreme Court opinion, explained that the harassment must be "because of sex" (that is, gender); that harassment can be motivated by hostility as well as by desire; and that common sense and social context count. Thus, smacking a football teammate on the rear end, horseplay, roughhousing, or occasional gender-related jokes, teasing, and abusive language normally would not constitute harassment. Ordinarily, plaintiffs in same-sex harassment cases must show that the behavior was motivated by (a) sexual desire, (b) general hostility to one or other gender, or (c) the victim's failure to conform to sexual stereotypes (such as effeminate behavior by a male). [For an analysis of the significance of the *Oncale* case, see **http://reason.com/archives/2003/01/01/man-trouble**]

> What if the harasser bothers both genders equally?

Oncale settles the big question of protection against same-sex harassment, but it raises other puzzles. For example, what if the harasser bothers both genders equally?

After *Oncale,* a husband and wife, who were also coworkers, brought a Title VII claim against their employer alleging that their supervisor had harassed both of them by soliciting sex from each of them on separate occasions. The federal appeals court affirmed the district court's dismissal, concluding that the "equal opportunity harasser" does not give rise to a Title VII sex discrimination complaint.[35]

Sexual Harassment in Other Nations

American managers working abroad must deal with international differences in attitudes toward sexual behavior in the workplace, although a general shift in harassment law in the direction of the American model is evident. This shift is significant for the American manager working abroad for a U.S.-based company, or a foreign employer controlled by an American company. The Civil Rights Act of 1991 extends Title VII's protection to American employees working abroad for such employers, but offers a "foreign law defense" under which the employer would not be required to comply with Title VII if doing so would violate the host country's law.[36] Now the European Union has adopted laws requiring harassment-free workplaces.[37] In Japan recent rule changes make sexual harassment law very much like the U.S. model.[38] Mexico, Taiwan, Venezuela, and other nations make sexual harassment a crime under some circumstances: Managers can go to jail.[39]

Retaliation

The power in an employment relationship often is unbalanced in favor of the employer. In bringing a discrimination claim, an employee is vulnerable to the employer's retaliatory action. In order to protect against an employer's abuse of power and to encourage exercise of employees' rights, Title VII's antiretaliation provision prohibits an employer from discriminating against an employee for engaging in a protected activity. Protected activities include opposing an employment practice that is reasonably believed to violate Title VII, or participating in any manner in a complaint made under Title VII, such as filing a charge of workplace discrimination. Other civil rights laws, including the Americans with Disabilities Act (ADA), the Age Discrimination in Employment Act (ADEA), and the Civil Rights Act of 1866, offer similar protections against retaliation.

A prima facie case of retaliation requires:

1. Participation in a protected activity.
2. An employment action disadvantaging the plaintiff.
3. A causal connection between the protected activity and the adverse employment action.[40]

In several recent cases, the U.S. Supreme Court has ruled in favor of employees seeking antiretaliation protection under Title VII. In *Crawford v. Metropolitan Gov't of Nashville & Davidson County,*[41] the Court reviewed the case of Vicky Crawford, who agreed to be interviewed during her employer's informal investigation of sexual harassment allegations against a director. Crawford did not make the allegations, but stated in her interview that she had witnessed the director making sexual gestures and comments in the workplace. The investigation resulted in the employer's reprimand of the director. Shortly thereafter, Crawford and the payroll department were investigated. She was fired, along with two coworkers who had also been interviewed and gave accounts of the director's sexual conduct. The Court held that employees who speak about workplace discrimination in answering an employer's questions during informal investigations are engaged in protected activity under Title VII's antiretaliation provision, even if they did not make the complaint being investigated. In *Burlington Northern & Santa Fe Railway v. White,*[42] the U.S. Supreme Court held that assigning a complainant to less desirable duties is an adverse employment action on which a Title VII retaliation claim may be based. The Court recognized that a broad range of employer conduct could dissuade a reasonable employee from making or supporting a discrimination claim.

In 2011, the U.S. Supreme Court held in *Thompson v. North American Stainless*[43] that an employee is protected against retaliation when his fiancée and coworker file a Title VII claim. Eric Thompson and his fiancée Miriam Regalado both worked for North American Stainless when the EEOC notified the employer that Regalado had filed a sex discrimination charge against it. Three weeks later, Thompson was fired. The Court noted that it was "obvious" that a reasonable worker might hesitate to exercise his or her Title VII rights if it would cause a fiancé to be fired. The Court declined to identify a class of relationships that would be protected from retaliation, instead leaving that determination to a case-by-case analysis.

Part Four—Affirmative Action

Some viewed the 2008 election of Barack Obama, the first, African-American president of the United States, as evidence that the racism staining the country's history was no longer an urgent concern. Therefore, it was argued, *affirmative action* efforts on behalf of minorities and women could be reduced or eliminated. However, a 2009 *Washington Post/ABC News* poll revealed that nearly half of African Americans and almost a quarter of white Americans continue to see racism as a significant social problem.[44] Furthermore, a 2009 Pew Research Center Poll found that 60 percent of Americans favor affirmative action programs that would help African Americans get better jobs and education. Less than half, however, favor preferential treatment in hiring and education for qualified African Americans.[45]

In following an affirmative action plan, employers consciously take positive steps to seek out minorities and women for hiring and promotion opportunities, and they often employ goals and timetables to measure progress toward a workforce that is representative of the qualified labor pool. Affirmative action is a means of remedying past and present discriminatory wrongs in a more expeditious and thorough manner than the market might achieve on its own.

Affirmative action efforts arise in four ways: (1) Courts may order the implementation of affirmative action after a finding of wrongful discrimination, (2) employers may voluntarily adopt affirmative action plans, (3) some statutes require affirmative action, and (4) employers may adopt affirmative action in order to do business with government agencies. Federal contractors must meet the affirmative action standards of the Office of Federal Contract Compliance Programs. [For criticisms of affirmative action, see the Center for Equal Opportunity at **http://www.ceousa.org**]

What Are the Odds? Favoring Men in College Admissions

In 2009, the U.S. Civil Rights Commission (USCRC) began an investigation into alleged gender discrimination in admissions at several liberal arts colleges. In recent years, well over half of college students have been women, leaving colleges concerned about gender balance among their students. The USCRC's inquiry aimed to discover if colleges were violating federal protections against gender discrimination in educational programs by favoring men in their admissions processes. As of this writing, the investigation has been suspended because of the apparent refusal of several colleges to disclose their admissions data.

Questions
1. Should men be given special preferences in the college application process? Explain.
2. Besides preferring male applicants, what steps might a college take to create a more gender-balanced campus? Would you agree with those actions? Explain.

Sources: "Civil Rights Panel Suspends Inquiry into Gender Bias in Admissions," *The Chronicle of Higher Education,* March 16, 2011 [**http://chronicle.com/blogs/ticker/civil-rights-panel-suspends-inquiry-into-gender-bias-in-admissions/31368**]; and Nancy Gibbs, "Affirmative Action for Boys," *Time,* April 3, 2008 [**http://www.time.com/time/magazine/article/0,9171,1727693,00.html**].

Early Affirmative Action Law

For nearly 20 years, judicial decisions were firmly supportive of affirmative action. A massive system of remedies emerged at all levels of government and in the private sector. In a 1979 case, *United Steelworkers of America v. Weber*,[46] the U.S. Supreme Court set out perhaps its most detailed "recipe" for those qualities that would allow a voluntary affirmative action plan in the private sector to withstand scrutiny. Weber, a white male, challenged the legality of an affirmative action plan that set aside for black employees 50 percent of the openings in a training program until the percentage of black craft workers in the plant equaled the percentage of blacks in the local labor market. The plan was the product of a collective bargaining agreement between the Steelworkers and Kaiser Aluminum and Chemical. In Kaiser's Grammercy, Louisiana, plant, only 5 of 273 skilled craft workers were black, whereas the local workforce was approximately 39 percent black. In the first year of the affirmative action plan, seven blacks and six whites were admitted to the craft training program. The most junior black employee accepted for the program had less seniority than several white employees who were not accepted. Weber was among the white males denied entry to the training program.

Weber filed suit, claiming Title VII forbade an affirmative action plan that granted a racial preference to blacks where whites dramatically exceeded blacks in skilled craft positions but where there was no proof of discrimination. The federal district court and the federal court of appeals held for Weber, but the U.S. Supreme Court reversed. Several qualities of the Steelworkers' plan were instrumental in the Court's favorable ruling:

1. The affirmative action was part of a plan.
2. The plan was designed to "open employment opportunities for Negroes in occupations which have been traditionally closed to them."
3. The plan was temporary.
4. The plan did not unnecessarily harm the rights of white employees. That is,
   a. The plan did not require the discharge of white employees.
   b. The plan did not create an absolute bar to the advancement of white employees.

Then, in an important 1987 public-sector decision, *Johnson v. Transportation Agency*,[47] the Supreme Court approved the extension of affirmative action to women. The political tides were turning, however. The 1980s were politically conservative years. Appointments to the Supreme Court and to the lower federal courts, by President Reagan in particular, reflected that mood. Affirmative action was under attack.

Rethinking Affirmative Action

From the late 1980s to the present, a series of judicial decisions and increasing public and political skepticism have challenged the legality and the wisdom of affirmative action, at least where the government is involved. The 1989 *City of Richmond v. J.A. Croson Co.*[48] case struck down Richmond, Virginia's, minority "set-aside" program that required prime contractors who were doing business with the city to subcontract at least 30 percent of the work to minority businesses. The Court said such race-conscious remedial plans were constitutional only if (1) the city or state could provide specific evidence of discrimination against a particular protected class in the past (rather than relying on proof of general society-wide discrimination) and (2) its remedy was "narrowly tailored" to the needs of the situation.

Then in *Adarand Constructors v. Pena,* a landmark 1995 decision, the Supreme Court struck down a federal highway program that extended bidding preferences to "disadvantaged" contractors.[49] The suit was brought by Randy Pech, a white contractor whose low bid on a Colorado guardrail project was rejected in favor of the bid of a minority firm. The Supreme Court ruled that the government's preference program denied Pech his right to equal protection under the law as guaranteed by the Fifth Amendment to the federal Constitution. (For a "Timeline of Affirmative Action Milestones," see **http://www.infoplease. com/spot/affirmativetimeline1.html**]

In the 2009 *Ricci v. DeStefano* decision that follows, the U.S. Supreme Court addressed the dilemma employers sometimes face in using hiring and promotion tests that may have a disparate impact on some groups of employees.

LEGAL BRIEFCASE

Ricci v. DeStefano
129 S.Ct. 2658 (2009)

Justice Kennedy

* * * * *

In 2003, 118 New Haven [Connecticut] firefighters took examinations to qualify for promotion to the rank of lieutenant or captain. . . . The results would determine which firefighters would be considered for promotions during the next two years, and the order in which they would be considered. Many firefighters studied for months, at considerable personal and financial cost.

When the examination results showed that white candidates had outperformed minority candidates, the mayor and other local politicians opened a public debate that turned rancorous. Some firefighters argued the tests should be discarded because the results showed the tests to be discriminatory. They threatened a discrimination lawsuit if the City made promotions based on the tests. Other firefighters said the exams were neutral and fair. And they, in turn, threatened a discrimination lawsuit if the City, relying on the statistical racial disparity, ignored the test results and denied promotions to the candidates who had performed well. In the

end the City took the side of those who protested the test results. It threw out the examinations.

Certain white and Hispanic firefighters who likely would have been promoted based on their good test performance sued the City and some of its officials. Theirs is the suit now before us. The suit alleges that, by discarding the test results, the City and the named officials discriminated against the plaintiffs based on their race, in violation of. . . . Title VII of the Civil Rights Act of 1964. . . . The City and the officials defended their actions, arguing that if they had certified the results, they could have faced liability under Title VII for adopting a practice that had a disparate impact on the minority firefighters.

I

* * * * *

A

The [City] charter establishes a merit system. That system requires the City to fill vacancies in the classified civil-service ranks with the most qualified individuals, as determined by job-related examinations. After each examination, the New Haven Civil Service Board (CSB) certifies a ranked list of applicants who passed the test. Under the charter's "rule of three," the relevant hiring authority must fill each vacancy by choosing one candidate from the top three scorers on the list.

* * * * *

Under the [union] contract, applicants for lieutenant and captain positions were to be screened using written and oral examinations, with the written exam accounting for 60 percent and the oral exam 40 percent of an applicant's total score. To sit for the examinations, candidates for lieutenant needed 30 months' experience in the Department, a high-school diploma, and certain vocational training courses. Candidates for captain needed one year's service as a lieutenant in the Department, a high-school diploma, and certain vocational training courses.

* * * * *

The City hired Industrial/Organizational Solutions, Inc. (IOS) to develop and administer the examinations, at a cost to the City of $100,000. IOS is an Illinois company that specializes in designing entry-level and promotional examinations for fire and police departments. In order to fit the examinations to the New Haven Department, IOS began the test-design process by performing job analyses to identify the tasks, knowledge, skills, and abilities that are essential for the lieutenant and captain positions.

* * * * *

At every stage of the job analyses, IOS, by deliberate choice, oversampled minority firefighters to ensure that the results-which IOS would use to develop the examinations-would not unintentionally favor white candidates. With the job-analysis information in hand, IOS developed the written examinations to measure the candidates' job-related knowledge.

* * * * *

After IOS prepared the tests, the City opened a 3-month study period. It gave candidates a list that identified the source material for the questions, including the specific chapters from which the questions were taken. IOS developed the oral examinations as well. These concentrated on job skills and abilities.

* * * * *

Candidates took the examinations in November and December 2003. Seventy-seven candidates completed the lieutenant examination—43 whites, 19 blacks, and 15 Hispanics. Of those, 34 candidates passed—25 whites, 6 blacks, and 3 Hispanics. Eight lieutenant positions were vacant at the time of the examination. Under the rule of three, this meant that the top 10 candidates

were eligible for an immediate promotion to lieutenant. All 10 were white.

* * * * *

Forty-one candidates completed the captain examination—25 whites, 8 blacks, and 8 Hispanics. Of those, 22 candidates passed—16 whites, 3 blacks, and 3 Hispanics. Seven captain positions were vacant at the time of the examination. Under the rule of three, 9 candidates were eligible for an immediate promotion to captain—7 whites and 2 Hispanics.

B

Based on the test results, the City officials expressed concern that the tests had discriminated against minority candidates.

* * * * *

[The City decided] not to certify the results.

C

The [City's] decision not to certify the examination results led to this lawsuit. The plaintiffs—who are the petitioners here—are 17 white firefighters and 1 Hispanic firefighter who passed the examinations but were denied a chance at promotions when the [City] refused to certify the test results. They include the named plaintiff, Frank Ricci. . . .

Petitioners . . . filed timely charges of discrimination with the Equal Employment Opportunity Commission (EEOC); . . . asserting that the City violated the disparate-treatment prohibition contained in Title VII of the Civil Rights Act of 1964. . . . Respondents [the defendants] asserted they had a good-faith belief that they would have violated the disparate impact prohibition in Title VII . . . had they certified the examination results. It follows, they maintained, that they cannot be held liable under Title VII's disparate-treatment provision for attempting to comply with Title VII's disparate-impact bar. Petitioners countered that respondents' good-faith belief was not a valid defense to allegations of disparate treatment. . . .

The District Court granted summary judgment for respondents. . . . The Court of Appeals affirmed. . . .

II

B (A OMITTED-ED.)

Petitioners allege that when the [City] refused to certify the captain and lieutenant exam results based on the race of the successful candidates, it discriminated against them in violation of Title VII's disparate-treatment provision. The City counters that its decision was permissible because the tests "appear[ed] to violate Title VII's disparate-impact provisions."

Our analysis begins with this premise: The City's actions would violate the disparate-treatment prohibition of Title VII absent some valid defense. All the evidence demonstrates that the City chose not to certify the examination results because of the statistical disparity based on race-i.e., how minority candidates had performed when compared to white candidates. . . .

We consider, therefore, whether the purpose to avoid disparate-impact liability excuses what otherwise would be prohibited disparate-treatment discrimination.

* * * * *

If an employer cannot rescore a test based on the candidates' race, then it follows . . . . that it may not take the greater step of discarding the test altogether to achieve a more desirable racial distribution of promotion-eligible candidates-absent a strong basis in evidence that the test was deficient and that discarding the results is necessary to avoid violating the disparate-impact provision. . . .

For the foregoing reasons, we adopt the strong-basis-in-evidence standard as a matter of statutory construction to resolve any conflict between the disparate-treatment and disparate-impact provisions of Title VII.

* * * * *

Title VII does not prohibit an employer from considering, before administering a test or practice, how to design that test or practice in order to provide a fair opportunity for all individuals, regardless of their race. . . . We hold only that, under Title VII, before an employer can engage in intentional discrimination for the asserted purpose of avoiding or remedying an unintentional disparate impact, the employer must have a strong basis in evidence to believe it will be subject to disparate-impact liability if it fails to take the race-conscious, discriminatory action.

* * * * *

C

The City argues that, even under the strong-basis-in-evidence standard, its decision to discard the examination results was permissible under Title VII. That is incorrect.

* * * * *

. . . .[T]here is no evidence—let alone the required strong basis in evidence—the tests were flawed because they were not job-related or because other, equally valid and less discriminatory tests were available to the City. Fear of litigation alone cannot justify an employer's reliance on race to the detriment of individuals who passed the examination and qualified for promotions. The City's discarding the test results was impermissible under Title VII. . . .

Our holding today clarifies how Title VII applies to resolve competing expectations under the disparate-treatment and disparate-impact provisions. If, after it certifies the test results, the City faces a disparate-impact suit, then in light of our holding today it should be clear that the City would avoid disparate-impact liability based on the strong basis in evidence that, had it not certified the results, it would have been subject to disparate-treatment liability.

[Reversed and remanded.]

Questions

1. *a.* Why did the city of New Haven reject the results of the promotion examination?
   b. Why did the court rule that the city had violated Title VII?
   c. Do you agree with the judgment of the court?

2. What could an employer do to avoid the situation New Haven faced in this case?

3. Frederick Claus, a white man with a degree in electrical engineering and 29 years of experience with Duquesne Light Company, was denied a promotion in favor of a black man who had not earned a bachelor's degree and did not have the required seven years of experience. Only 2 of 82 managers in that division of Duquesne Light were black. Claus sued, claiming in effect that he was a victim of "reverse discrimination." At trial, both sides conceded that the black candidate was an outstanding employee and that he was qualified to be a manager. Decide the case. Explain. See *Claus v. Duquesne Light Co.,* 46 F.3d 1115 (1994); cert. den. 115 S.Ct. 1700 (1995).

4. In 1974, Birmingham, Alabama, was accused of unlawfully excluding blacks from management roles in its fire department. After several years of litigation, Birmingham adopted an affirmative action plan that guaranteed black firefighters one of every two available promotions. The city, the Justice Department, and others applauded the arrangement, but a group of 14 white firefighters claimed they were victims of reverse discrimination. After years of wrangling, the white firefighters' claim reached the 11th Circuit Federal Court of Appeals. Was the affirmative action plan lawful? Explain. See *In re Birmingham Reverse Discrimination Employment Litig.,* 20 F.3d 1525 (11th Cir. 1994) cert. den. sub nom.; *Martin v. Wilks,* 115 S.Ct. 1695 (1995).

5. In a 2010 case involving the same promotional examinations at issue in *Ricci,* Michael Briscoe, an African-American firefighter for the city of New Haven who applied to be promoted to lieutenant but was rejected brought a Title VII claim asserting that the city had created a disparate impact against African-Americans by weighing the written test more heavily than the oral examination. The city of New Haven brought a motion to dismiss in federal trial court. Decide. See *Briscoe v. New Haven,* 2010 U.S. Dist. LEXIS 69018 (D. Conn. 2010).

Affirmative Action: Where Are We?

Some confusion remains after *Ricci,* given differences in analysis between cases based on the Constitution and those brought under Title VII,[50] and whether those cases address employers' screening, set-asides, or other practices. What has been made clear is that both quotas and affirmative action justified broadly by "societal discrimination" are unconstitutional.

Quotas are unconstitutional.

A lawful affirmative action remedy in employment cases apparently will be evaluated, in most cases, by the following considerations:

- The plan addresses a compelling interest such as remedying past or present discrimination or correcting the underutilization of women and minorities.
- The plan is temporary.
- The plan is narrowly tailored to minimize layoffs and other burdens.

In *Ricci,* the U.S. Supreme Court noted that employers could still make "affirmative efforts" to encourage equal opportunity in promotions.[51] While ensuring that screening procedures are not discriminatory or irrelevant,[52] employers may undertake diversity initiatives designed to create an inclusive workplace environment that supports fairness, respect, and equal opportunity. [For information on diversity programs at U.S. companies, see Diversity Inc. at **http://diversityinc.com/**]

Part Five—Additional Discrimination Topics

Religious Discrimination

Kimberly Cloutier was employed as a cashier at Costco in West Springfield, Massachusetts. The store revised its dress code in 2001 to prohibit all facial jewelry other than earrings.

A member of the "Church of Body Modification."

Cloutier, a member of the "Church of Body Modification," was advised to remove her facial piercings. She declined to do so saying that her piercings were part of her religion. The church's approximately 1,000 members engaged in such practices as piercing, tattooing, branding, and cutting. Eventually, Cloutier was fired. She sued Costco claiming she was a victim of religious discrimination in violation of Title VII of the Civil Rights Act of 1964. Costco, however, prevailed when the federal First Circuit Court of Appeals ruled in 2004 that excusing Cloutier from the dress code would be an undue hardship for Costco because the company had a legitimate interest in presenting to the public a workforce that was reasonably professional in appearance.[53]

The Law

Title VII's protections against religious discrimination and harassment in the workplace include the employer's duty to reasonably accommodate employees' religious beliefs and practices. As was evident in Cloutier's conflict with Costco, reasonably accommodating religious practices often poses challenges for employers. Consider, for example, the employer who must balance an employee's religious practice of proselytizing or discussing religion in the workplace against other employees' right to be free from religious harassment.

Employers need not accommodate an employee's religious practice or belief if it creates an "undue hardship"—an unreasonable burden—on the workplace. The leading religious discrimination case is *Trans World Airlines, Inc. v. Hardison,* in which the plaintiff, who celebrated his religion on Saturdays, was unable to take that day off from his work in a parts warehouse.[54] Efforts to swap shifts or change jobs were unsuccessful. The company rejected Hardison's request for a four-day week because it would have required the use of another employee at premium pay. The Supreme Court's ruling in the case reduced the employer's duty to a very modest standard: "To require TWA to bear more than a *de minimis* cost in order to give Hardison Saturdays off is an *undue hardship*." Saturdays off for Hardison would have imposed extra costs on TWA and would have constituted religious discrimination against other employees who would have sought Saturday off for reasons not grounded in religion. So any accommodation imposing more than a *de minimis* cost on the employer represents an undue hardship and is not required by Title VII. Of course, the lower courts have differed considerably on what constitutes a *de minimis* cost and an undue hardship. For example, an Ohio court ruled that an employee, a Seventh Day Adventist, was discriminated against when he was fired for refusing to work from sundown Friday to sundown Saturday. The employee could have been moved to an earlier shift at no cost.[55]

An employer might be unsure whether employees who request accommodation are sincere in their religious beliefs or merely seeking an advantage such as a longer break or trying to avoid workplace requirements under attendance or grooming policies. The EEOC defines religion broadly as "moral and ethical beliefs of what is right and wrong which are sincerely held with the strength of religious views."[56] This broad view of religious beliefs arguably indicates that employers should err in favor of moving forward to the central issue: Is an accommodation reasonable or would it create an undue hardship?

Questions

1. Resolving job-related religious conflicts can be among the most emotionally demanding management dilemmas. For example, what challenges would you face as a manager if one of your subordinates, as an expression of her religious beliefs, wore to work an antiabortion button displaying a picture of a fetus? How would you address these challenges? See *Wilson v. U.S. West Communications,* 58 F.3d 1337 (8th Cir. 1995).

2. David Wise, a laboratory worker, became a member of the Living Church of God, which prohibited him from working on the Sabbath, from sundown Friday to sundown Saturday, and on 14 additional religious holidays. After using all his annual, floating, and

unpaid leave for religious holidays, Wise was denied further time off. Wise filed a religious discrimination claim with the EEOC. Decide. Explain. See *EEOC v. Firestone Fibers & Textiles Co.,* 515 F.3d 307 (4th Cir. 2008).

The Americans with Disabilities Act (ADA)

As a child, Edward Carmona was diagnosed with psoriasis, a skin disease causing intermittent but treatable inflammations. As an adult working as a flight attendant for Southwest Airlines, Carmona was diagnosed with psoriatic arthritis, which causes painful joint swelling and stiffness during attacks of psoriasis. Although medication eased some of his discomfort, these attacks left Carmona unable to walk without great pain for one-half to one-third of each month. After his intermittent leave under Family and Medical Leave Act (FMLA— see Chapter 12) expired, he was fired for excessive absenteeism. Carmona brought a disability discrimination claim against Southwest Airlines under the Americans with Disabilities Act (ADA), winning a jury verdict that was vacated by the federal trial court. A federal appeals court overturned the federal trial court's decision to vacate the jury's award, concluding that Southwest Airlines attendance policy was extremely lenient, and the jury could have reasonably found other nondisabled flight attendants with similar absenteeism not being fired, and that Carmona's supervisors were annoyed by his disability-related absences.[57]

This situation illustrates the general purpose of the ADA, which seeks to remove barriers to a full, productive life for individuals with disabilities. The ADA forbids discrimination in employment, public accommodations, public services, transportation, and telecommunications. Small businesses with fewer than 15 employees are exempted from the employment portions of the ADA. The Rehabilitation Act of 1973 protects public sector workers with disabilities from employment discrimination.

Under the ADA, a qualified individual who (1) has a physical or mental impairment that substantially limits one or more *major life activities,* (2) has a record of such an impairment, or (3) is regarded as having such an impairment may not be discriminated against in employment.

In a series of decisions, the U.S. Supreme Court narrowed the scope of the ADA, prompting a leading disabilities rights advocate to call the ADA "the incredible shrinking law."[58] In response, the Americans with Disabilities Amendments Act (ADAAA) was passed by Congress and signed into law by President George W. Bush in 2008 to overturn those decisions and establish broader definitional guidelines under the ADA.

Defining Disabilities

The ADAAA emphasizes that "disability" should be defined broadly in offering protection from employment discrimination. Examples of disabilities under the ADAAA, as offered by the EEOC, include epilepsy, hypertension, asthma, diabetes, major depressive disorder, bipolar disorder, and schizophrenia. A nonexhaustive list of major life activities specified by the ADAAA includes eating, sleeping, standing, lifting, bending, concentrating, thinking, communicating, and all major bodily functions, including reproduction.

Alcoholism, drug addiction, and AIDS are disabilities under the ADA. However, the ADA excludes from its protection job applicants and employees who *currently* use illegal drugs. Employees with past drug or alcohol problems are protected by the ADA, as are employees with current alcohol problems who are able to perform the essential functions of the job. An employer may lawfully take an adverse employment action on the basis of, for example, a drug test showing use of illegal controlled substances or alcohol-induced unprofessional conduct at work. Those who are rehabilitated or are currently in rehabilitation are protected from disabilities discrimination. In sum, the ADA treats alcoholism and drug addiction as medical conditions and protects those who are overcoming these impairments.

The ADAAA makes clear that taking medication or using a prosthetic device to overcome an impairment does not exclude an individual from the ADA's protection. Episodic conditions such as epilepsy, if creating a "substantial limitation" on an individual's major life activities, ordinarily would be covered by the ADA. In addition, an impairment in remission, such as cancer, is covered if it would substantially limit a major life activity when active.[59]

"Regarded as Having" a Disability

An individual who does not have a disability may still be protected under the ADA. If an employer incorrectly assumes that an applicant or employee has a disability, and then takes discriminatory action on that basis, the employer has violated the ADA. For example, an employer who denies an employee a promotion to a managerial position requiring extensive client contact is likely to have violated the ADA if the promotion was denied because of the employer's mistaken belief that the employee is a recovering alcoholic who would not be able to manage client meetings where alcohol is frequently served.

Accommodating Individuals with Disabilities

An employer may not discriminate in hiring or employment against a *qualified person with a disability*. A qualified person is one who can perform the *essential job functions* with or without *reasonable accommodation*. The ADA requires employers to make reasonable accommodations for disabled employees and applicants. Reasonable accommodations might include structural changes in the workplace, job reassignment, job restructuring, or new equipment. Employers are not required to provide an accommodation that would create an *undue hardship*. For example, the employer need not create a new position to reassign an employee who can no longer perform the essential job functions, but rather should place the employee in an appropriate vacant job. The employer should engage in an interactive dialogue with the employee to explore possible reasonable accommodations. [For EEOC advice about small employers and reasonable accommodation, see **http://www.eeoc.gov/facts/accommodation.html**]

"Getting to Work" with Reasonable Accommodation

Jeanette Colwell was hired as a part-time retail clerk at a Rite Aid store in Old Forge, Pennsylvania. She worked various shifts, including 5 PM to 9 PM, and she earned supervisors' recognition for good performance. A few months after being hired, Colwell was diagnosed with "retinal vein occlusion and glaucoma in her left eye," and eventually she became blind in that eye. Colwell informed her supervisor, Susan Chapman, that her partial blindness made it dangerous and difficult for her to drive to work at night. She asked to be assigned to day shifts only so that she would be able to get to work. (Bus service stopped at 6 PM, and there were no taxis serving the area where the store was located.) Chapman refused the request because it "wouldn't be fair" to other workers, and she continued to schedule Colwell for a mix of day and evening shifts. Colwell later sent Chapman a doctor's note recommending that Colwell not drive at night, but Chapman was still unwilling to assign Colwell to day shifts only. Colwell resigned and brought an ADA claim against Rite Aid. The federal trial court ruled that Rite Aid had no duty to accommodate Colwell because she was able to perform all her work duties at the store. The Third Circuit Court of Appeals held that under the ADA, an employer may have a duty to make reasonable changes to shift assignments in order to accommodate a disabled employee's disability-related difficulties in getting to work. The court noted that the ADA mentions modified work schedules as an accommodation, that Colwell had to be at work in order to complete her job, and that changing Colwell's shifts was a workplace condition well within Rite Aid's control.

Questions

1. Is Colwell an "individual with a disability" under the ADA? Explain.
2. How should Chapman have responded to Colwell's request? Explain.
3. A part-time retail clerk who is unable to drive because he is "legally blind" requests a late arrival to his shift due to a long bus commute. The store manager refuses his request, and subsequently terminates him for being late to work on a number of occasions. The clerk brings an ADA claim against his former employer. Decide. Explain.

Source: Colwell v. Rite Aid, 602 F.3d 495 (3rd. Cir. 2010).

The ADA in Practice

Approximately 27 million working-age Americans have a disability.[60] In 2009, the unemployment rate for this group was 14.5 percent compared with 9 percent for those without a disability.[61] A Labor Department leader stated that some employers may hesitate to hire workers with disabilities out of misconceptions and fear of added costs for accommodations.[62] However, in recent years companies have made efforts to increase the presence of individuals with disabilities in the professional workforce. For example, the National Business & Disability Council runs "Emerging Leaders," a summer internship program offering business placements for college and graduate students with disabilities.[63] [For more information see Emerging Leaders at **http://www.emerging-leaders.com/**]

Tax credits to hire and provide access to individuals with disabilities, as well as tax deductions to remove architectural barriers to make its facilities more accessible, also provide incentives for employers to hire and retain employees with disabilities.[64]

Rosa's Law: Changing the Words

Rosa's Law, named after Rosa Marcellino, a nine-year-old with Down Syndrome, changes the language in all federal health, education, and labor laws to remove the phrase "mentally retarded" and replace it with "intellectual disability." President Obama has quoted Rosa's brother Nick as saying: "What you call people is how you treat them. If we change the words, maybe it will be the start of a new attitude towards people with disabilities."

Sources: S. 2781(2010) [**http://www.govtrack.us/congress/bill.xpd?bill=s111-2781**]; and The White House Office of the Press Secretary, "Remarks by the President at the Signing of the 21st Century Communications and Video Accessibility Act of 2010," The White House Press Office, October 8, 2010 [**http://www.whitehouse.gov/the-press-office/2010/10/08/remarks-president-signing-21st-century-communications-and-video-accessib**].

ADA Questions

1. United Parcel Service (UPS) required all its "package-car drivers" to pass a U.S. Department of Transportation (DOT) hearing standard. DOT's standard applies only to those vehicles weighing over 10,001 pounds when loaded with cargo, but UPS's requirement applied to all UPS drivers. A class of UPS employees and applicants unable to pass the DOT hearing standard brought an ADA claim against UPS. Decide the case. Explain. See *Bates v. UPS,* 511 F.3d 974 (9th Cir. 2007).

2. Chenoweth worked for Hillsborough County, Florida, reviewing files of hospital patients. She had to drive to hospitals to examine some of the records. She suffered a seizure, was diagnosed as having epilepsy, and was told not to drive at all until six months had passed without a seizure. She asked her employer to accommodate her by allowing her to work at home two days per week and by eliminating the requirement that she drive to hospitals. Her employer agreed to the former but not the latter. She sued, claiming a violation of the ADA. Decide. Explain. See *Chenoweth v. Hillsborough County,* 250 F.3d 1328 (11th Cir. 2001); cert.den. 534 U.S. 1131 (2002).

Genetic Testing

Genetic testing in the workplace and its discriminatory effects have been addressed by the EEOC. In 2002, the Burlington Northern & Santa Fe Railway Co. agreed to pay 36 workers $2.2 million for the railway's use of a genetic testing program, which, without the workers' knowledge, identified predispositions to carpal tunnel syndrome. In 2008, Congress and the president approved the Genetic Information Nondiscrimination Act (GINA) that prohibits employers from discriminating because of genetic information. With few exceptions, employers are not allowed to gather genetic information regarding an employee or the employee's family members.[65]

Age Discrimination

Can a clothing store featuring styles designed for the college market lawfully prefer youthful salespersons? May a marketing firm reject older applicants in an effort to bring "new blood" into its workforce? While these questions are not definitively resolved, employers taking such actions might face liability for age discrimination.

ADEA Claims The Age Discrimination in Employment Act (ADEA) protects those 40 years and older from employment discrimination based on their age. Disparate treatment and harassment claims may be brought under the ADEA, and a 2005 Supreme Court decision extended ADEA protection to disparate impact claims also.[66] In its 2009 *Gross v. FBL* decision, the U.S. Supreme Court made it more difficult to win an ADEA disparate treatment claim.[67] Jack Gross had worked for FBL for over 30 years when at age 54 he was reassigned from Claims Administration Director to Coordinator, while his former duties were transferred to a younger worker whom he had supervised. Gross filed an ADEA claim against FBL claiming the demotion violated the ADEA, and he won a jury verdict after showing that his age played a role in FBL's decision. FBL appealed. The U.S. Supreme Court held that an ADEA disparate treatment claim requires the plaintiff to show that age was not just one factor, but the deciding or "but-for" factor in the employer's decision.[68] At this writing, Congress is considering the proposed Protecting Older Workers Against Discrimination Act, which would reverse *Gross*.[69]

Defenses The employer may defend against an age discrimination claim by showing that the termination was based on a *legitimate, nondiscriminatory reason* (such as poor performance) or that age is a bona fide occupational qualification (BFOQ). To establish age as a BFOQ, an employer must demonstrate that only employees of a certain age can safely and/or efficiently complete the work in question (such as piloting airplanes). The ADEA also provides that an employer can defeat an age discrimination claim by demonstrating that a "reasonable factor other than age" (like poor attendance) was the actual reason for terminating or otherwise disfavoring an older worker. In 2008 the U.S. Supreme Court held that an employer using this defense in a disparate impact case carries the burden of proving a "reasonable factor other than age."[70]

Reverse Age Discrimination?

Being young is cool, but younger workers may get cold treatment in the workplace. Younger workers often seem to take the brunt of layoffs. Recently, the unemployment rate for those between the ages of 25 and 34 was 9.6 percent as compared with 6.5 percent for those 55 or older. Fear of ADEA lawsuits may be one reason companies use seniority to determine who will be retained in a reduction in force.

Question

1. Should the ADEA protect against age discrimination, regardless of age? Explain.

Source: Dana Mattioli, "With Jobs Scarce, Age Becomes an Issue," *The Wall Street Journal*, May 19, 2009 [**http://www/wsj.com**].

Questions

1. In 2000, when she was 60 years old, Patricia Tomassi was hired as a supervisor of resident services at an apartment complex, but she was fired in 2003. Tomassi filed an ADEA claim alleging that she was fired because of her age. Tomassi alleged that throughout her employment, her supervisor made frequent references to her age, such as saying "in your day and age," suggesting that she could relate well to residents who were senior citizens, and frequently asking if she would be better off retiring to get some rest. Were the supervisor's remarks sufficient evidence to support a claim of age discrimination? Decide. Explain. See *Tomassi v. Insignia Financial Group*, 478 F.3d 111 (2d Cir. 2007).

2. The Insurance Company of North America (ICNA) sought to hire a "loss control representative." The ad called for a B.S. degree, two years of experience, and other qualities. The plaintiff, who had 30 years of loss control experience, applied for the job but was not interviewed. ICNA hired a 28-year-old woman with no loss control experience. The plaintiff sued claiming age discrimination. ICNA said the plaintiff was overqualified.

   a. Explain the plaintiff's argument.

   b. Decide the case. Explain. See *EEOC v. Insurance Co. of N. Am.*, 49 F.3d 1418 (9th Cir. 1995).

Sexual Orientation

A Davenport, Iowa, care center manager allegedly fired six employees because they were homosexual and, in his view, did not exhibit acceptable "moral character."[71] The manager explained,

> When I first came here, there was probably at least three—excuse my French—faggots working here and I had at least three dykes working here.[72]

Are those dismissed employees protected by our expansive network of employment antidiscrimination law? At this writing, neither federal law nor the law of most states offers protection against discrimination on the basis of an employee's sexual orientation. The courts have consistently ruled that Title VII's prohibition of discrimination based on sex refers to gender only, and not sexual orientation. A federal bill, the Employment Non-Discrimination Act (ENDA), which would prohibit employers from discriminating on the basis of an employee's actual or perceived sexual orientation has been proposed in various forms over the years, but has not yet been passed by the U.S. Congress.[73] At this writing, 21 states and the District of Columbia prohibit employment discrimination based on sexual orientation. Most of these state laws also protect those discriminated against based on a perception of their sexual orientation.[74]

Sexual Orientation Discrimination or Sex Stereotyping?

Brian Prowel worked at Wise Business Forms operating a machine called a nale encoder. Prowel, a self-described "effeminate" homosexual man, spoke in a high voice, and came to work neatly dressed and well-groomed. Prowel's coworkers called him "Princess,"

"Rosebud," and on more than one occasion, "fag." In one instance, as Prowel entered the plant he overheard a coworker say: "I hate him. They should shoot all the fags." Prowel was laid off for lack of work, and he brought a Title VII gender discrimination claim against Wise. The federal trial court held that Prowel had raised a sexual orientation claim not covered under Title VII. The Third Circuit Court of Appeals reversed finding that Prowel had asserted a plausible gender stereotyping discrimination claim; that is, a jury could decide Prowel was a victim of sex discrimination because his behavior and appearance did not conform to conventional expectations for a male.

Source: *Prowel v. Wise Business Forms*, 579 F.3d 285 (3d Cir. 2009).

Transgender Discrimination

Twelve states and the District of Columbia prohibit employment discrimination based on gender identity/expression.[75] In 2008, a federal trial court ruled that discrimination against transsexuals based on sex stereotyping is prohibited under Title VII.[76] Diane Schroer is a male-to-female transsexual. In 2004, before she changed her legal name from David to Diane and began presenting as a woman, Schroer was offered a job by the Library of Congress as a specialist on terrorism and international crime. Schroer's military career that included serving as a Special Operations Colonel made her well qualified for the Library job, and she received the highest interview score of all the candidates. The offer was rescinded, however, and given to a less qualified male, when Schroer revealed to the supervisor that she would be transitioning from male to female. The supervisor expressed difficulty in understanding why a man with a military background would undergo gender transition. In viewing photographs of Schroer dressed in female attire, the supervisor said she saw only a man in a woman's clothing. The court held that Schroer had been discriminated against "because of sex" and that she was a victim of sex stereotyping.[77]

> She saw only a man in a woman's clothing.

[For an American Civil Liberties Union video advocating a transgender-inclusive Employment Non-Discrimination Act, see "New Video Shows the Need for a Transgender-Inclusive ENDA" at **http://www.aclu.org/lgbt-rights_hiv-aids/new-aclu-video-shows-need-transgender-inclusive-enda**]

Internet Exercise

At this writing, the Healthy Workplace bill addressing workplace bullying has been introduced in a number of state legislatures. Using the Healthy Workplace Campaign's "frequently asked questions" (FAQ) Web page [**http://www.healthyworkplacebill.org/faq.php**] answer the following questions:

1. How is workplace bullying defined?
2. What is the argument supporting legislation addressing workplace bullying?
3. How is the Healthy Workplace bill different from antidiscrimination protections?
4. What arguments might be raised against the Healthy Workplace bill?

**Chapter
Questions**

1. Blockbuster established a grooming policy forbidding long hair for men but allowing it for women. Four men, who were fired for refusing to cut their long hair, sued Blockbuster for sex discrimination. Has Blockbuster violated Title VII? Explain. See *Kenneth Harper, et al. v. Blockbuster,* 139 F.3d 1385 (11th Cir. 1998; cert. den. 525 U.S. 1000 (1998).

2. In 2006, the EEOC filed a class action against Lawry's Restaurants including Lawry's The Prime Rib, Five Crowns, and The Tam O'Shanter Inn, on behalf of all male applicants for server positions who were systematically rejected because of their gender. Since 1938, Lawry's hired only females as servers, and did not update their policy after the passage of Title VII. Servers' uniforms are antiquated women's costumes. What might Lawry's defense be? Will this defense be successful? Explain. See EEOC Press Release, "Lawry's Restaurants Sued for Sex Bias in Hiring" [**http://www.eeoc. gov/press/4-4-06a.html**].

3. Emma, a Chinese American, applies for an available server position in a Mexican restaurant and is rejected. She suspects it is because of her national origin. What might the Mexican restaurant say in defense of a national origin discrimination complaint made by Emma? Will this defense be successful? Explain. See EEOC Compliance Manual (2002) at 13-II-C [**http://www.eeoc.gov/policy/docs/national-origin.html**].

4. Edwin, a restaurant manager, abused male and female employees alike. However, Edwin singled out female subordinates for especially cruel treatment that included frequent and repeated sexual jokes, crude comments about their bodies, and questions such as whether they "liked to be spanked." One of these female employees, Shelby, asked him to stop making sexual comments, but he persisted despite her visible distress. When Shelby resumed work after quitting due to Edwin's conduct, Edwin continued his behavior toward her. Shelby made several complaints to managers, one of whom advised her that she was overreacting. Though the restaurant conducted an investigation, neither Shelby nor Edwin was interviewed. No disciplinary action was taken. Resolve this case. Explain. See *EEOC v. R&R Ventures, d/b/a Taco Bell,* 244 F.3d 334 (4th Cir. 2001).

5. Breeden, a female employee, met with two male coworkers to review the psychological evaluation reports for four job applicants. Breeden's supervisor read aloud a comment in one of the reports that the applicant had once said to a coworker, "I hear making love to you is like making love to the Grand Canyon." The men chuckled. Breeden complained, and eventually filed a sexual harassment complaint with supervisory personnel. Soon thereafter, she was transferred to another position, a move that had been contemplated for some time. Breeden brought Title VII claims against her employer. What claims might she have asserted? Decide the case. Explain. See *Clark County School District v. Breeden,* 533 U.S. 912 (2001).

6. Rodriguez managed a Walmart store at Fajardo, Puerto Rico. Following an evaluation, his performance was considered unsatisfactory, and he was demoted to assistant manager at another store. Rodriguez filed suit claiming race and national origin discrimination. Rodriguez pointed to two favorable previous performance evaluations, and he argued that he was evaluated in a different manner than non-Puerto Rican managers. Rodriguez was evaluated with the use of an opinion survey given to

all of his subordinates. Rodriguez claimed that non-Puerto Rican managers at other stores were not subject to opinion surveys. Assuming that claim is true, would Rodriguez be able to prevail on a disparate treatment cause of action? Explain. See *Rodriguez-Cuervos v. Wal-Mart Stores,* 181 F.3d 15 (1st Cir. 1999).

7. Assume a company located near your college has asked you to create an outreach program to increase diversity in its workforce. What challenges would you face? What steps would you take? Explain.

8. Diane Piantanida went on maternity leave. While absent, her employer discovered tasks that she had not completed. Before her return, Piantanida was informed that she was being reassigned to a lesser job because of her inability to keep up in her former job. Upon objecting to the change, Piantanida claims she was told that she was being given a position "for a new mom to handle." Piantanida admits that her demotion was not based on her pregnancy or her maternity leave. Piantanida declined the offer and sued, claiming a violation of the Pregnancy Discrimination Act stemming from her status as a new mother. Decide. Explain. See *Piantanida v. Wyman Center,* 116 F.3d 340 (8th Cir. 1997).

9. Thornton worked as a manager at a Connecticut retail store. In accordance with his religious beliefs, Thornton notified his manager that he could no longer work on Sundays as required by company (Caldor, Inc.) policy. A Connecticut statute provided that "No person who states that a particular day of the week is observed as his Sabbath may be required by his employer to work on such day. An employee's refusal to work on his Sabbath shall not constitute grounds for his dismissal." Management offered Thornton the options of transferring to a Massachusetts store where Sunday work was not required or transferring to a lower-paying supervisory job in the Connecticut store. Thornton refused both, and he was transferred to a lower-paying clerical job in the Connecticut store. Thornton claimed a violation of the Connecticut statute. The store argued that the statute violated the Establishment Clause (see Chapter 5) of the First Amendment, which forbids establishing an official state religion and giving preference to one religion over another or over none at all. Ultimately the case reached the U.S. Supreme Court.

   a. Decide. Explain.

   b. Do the religious accommodation provisions of Title VII of the Civil Rights Act violate the Establishment Clause? See *Estate of Thornton v. Caldor, Inc.,* 472 U.S. 703 (1985).

10. Sanchez worked as a host and food server at a pair of Azteca restaurants. Throughout his work experience, male coworkers and a supervisor referred to him as "she" and "her." He was mocked for walking and carrying his serving tray "like a woman." He was called a "faggot" and a "female whore." This abuse occurred repeatedly.

    a. Make the argument that Sanchez was not a victim of sexual harassment.

    b. Decide the case. Explain. See *Nichols v. Azteca Restaurant Enterprises,* 256 F.3d 864 (9th Cir. 2001).

11. Jane Doe was employed by C.A.R.S. Protection Plus for nearly a year when she learned she was pregnant. After amniocentesis revealed severe defects, Doe decided to terminate her pregnancy. Doe then took one week of vacation to recuperate from the

procedure. The following week, she was fired for unexcused absences and job abandonment. Doe filed a claim under the Pregnancy Discrimination Act (PDA), alleging she was fired because of her choice to undergo a surgical abortion. Decide the case. Explain. See *Doe v. C.A.R.S. Protection Plus,* 527 F.3d 358 (3d Cir. 2008).

12. A new Texas airline, flying out of Dallas's Love Field, was in a precarious financial posture. A campaign was mounted to sell itself as "the airline personification of feminine youth and vitality." In commercials, its customers, who were primarily businessmen, were promised "in-flight love," including "love potions" (cocktails), "love bites" (toasted almonds), and a ticketing process (labeled a "quickie machine") that delivered "instant gratification." A male was denied a job with the airline because of his sex. He filed a Title VII action. The airline argued that attractive females were necessary to maintain its public image under the "love campaign," a marketing approach that the company claimed had been responsible for its improved financial condition. Decide. Explain. See *Wilson v. Southwest Airlines Co.,* 517 F.Supp. 292 (ND Tex. 1981).

13. Michael Cooke, an African-American male, worked at Novellus Systems in Silicon Valley where he had to listen on a regular basis to a Vietnamese-American coworker playing and rapping aloud to music lyrics that included racial epithets such as the "N-word." Although Cooke complained several times to his supervisors and made it clear that the language was offensive to him, the coworker continued to sing along to offensive lyrics within Cooke's earshot, and to use slang including racial epithets. The EEOC, on behalf of Cooke, brought a Title VII claim against Novelle Systems for racial harassment. Decide. See U.S. Equal Employment Opportunity Commission, "Silicon Valley Manufacturer Novellus . . . Racial Harassment," *Press Release,* June 24, 2008 [**http://www.eeoc.gov/eeoc/newsroom/release/6-24-08.cfm**].

14. Should employment discrimination based on physical attractiveness be prohibited? Explain.

15. Should American firms abroad adhere to American antidiscrimination policies even if those policies might put the American firms at a competitive disadvantage or offend the values and mores of the host country? Explain.

16. John D. Archbold Memorial Hospital excluded all job applicants whose weight exceeded the maximum desirable weight (based on Metropolitan Life's actuarial survey) for large-framed men and women plus 30 percent of that weight. Sandra Murray claimed she was denied a job as a respiratory therapist because her height-to-weight ratio did not meet the guidelines. Murray did not claim to be morbidly obese.
    a. Explain the plaintiff's argument.
    b. Did the hospital violate the ADA? Explain. See *Murray v. John D. Archbold Memorial Hospital,* 50 F.Supp.2d 1368 (M.D. Ga. 1999).

Notes

1. AFjustice.com. Website of Lieff Cabraser Heimann & Bernstein, LLP [**http://www.afjustice.com**].
2. See Jenny Strasburg, "Abercrombie to Pay $50 Million in Bias Suits," *San Francisco Chronicle,* November 10, 2004, p. C1; and Julie Tamaki, "Judge Accepts Abercrombie Plan to Settle Hiring Lawsuits," *Los Angeles Times,* November 17, 2004, p. C2.
3. Michael Lopardi, "Minority Groups Sue Abercrombie for $40 M," *University Wire,* January 27, 2005.

4. Devah Pager, "The Mark of a Criminal Record," *American Journal of Sociology* 105, no. 5, (March 2003), pp. 937–975 [**www.northwestern.edu/ipr/publications/papers/2003/pagerajs.pdf**].

5. General Accounting Office, Diversity Management: Expert-Identified Leading Practices and Agency Examples, GAO-05-90 (Washington, DC, Jan. 14, 2005) [**http://www.gao.gov/htext/d0590.html**].

6. 347 U.S. 483 (1954).

7. A portion of this paragraph is drawn from William P. Murphy, Julius G. Getman, and James E. Jones Jr., *Discrimination in Employment,* 4th ed. (Washington, DC: Bureau of National Affairs, 1979), pp. 1–4.

8. 127 S.Ct. 2162 (2007).

9. S. 181 (2009–2010).

10. *EEOC v. Waffle House, Inc.,* 534 U.S. 279 (2002).

11. Martha Neil, "Most Job Discrimination Suits Win, at Best, Small Settlements, Study Says," *ABA Journal,* June 9, 2010 [**http://www.abajournal.com/news/article/most_job_discrimination_suits_win_small_settlements_at_best_study_says/**].

12. *Haynes v. W.C. Caye & Co.,* 52 F.3d 926 (11th Cir. 1995).

13. See *International Brotherhood of Teamsters v. United States,* 97 S.Ct. 1843 (1977); *American Tobacco v. Patterson,* 456 U.S. 63 (1982); *Firefighters Local Union No. 1784 v. Stotts,* 467 U.S. 561 (1984).

14. Tresa Baldas, "Employment Tests May Fail Legal Exam," *National Law Journal,* February 18, 2008, p. 4.

15. Equal Employment Opportunity Commission Fact Sheet on Employment Tests and Selection Procedures [**http://www.eeoc.gov/policy/docs/factemployment_procedures.html**].

16. EEOC Receives Award for Post-9/11 Efforts," HR.BLR.com (October 4, 2004) [**http://hr.blr.com/news.aspx?id=10396**].

17. EEOC Litigation Settlements March 2005 [**http://www.eeoc.gov/litigation/settlements/settlement03-05.html**].

18. *Garcia v. Spun Steak Co.,* 998 F.2d 1480, cert. den. 114 S.Ct. 2726 (1994).

19. The U.S. Equal Employment Opportunity Commission, "Henredon Furniture Industries to Pay $465,000 for Racial Harassment, Hangman's Nooses," January 24, 2008 [**http://www.eeoc.gov/press/1-24-08.html**].

20. *Ash v. Tyson,* 546 U.S. 454 (2006).

21. *Ash v. Tyson,* 392 Fed. Appx. 817 (11th Cir. 2010).

22. *Aman v. Cort Furniture Rental Corp.,* 85 F.3d 1074 (3d Cir. 1996).

23. U.S. Bureau of Labor Statistics, "Women at Work," *Spotlight on Statistics,* March 2011 [**http://www.bls.gov/spotlight/2011/women/**].

24. Associated Press, "Judge Approves $46 Million Settlement of Gender Discrimination Claims against Morgan Stanley," *San Jose Mercury News,* October 11, 2007 [**http://www.mercurynews.com/portlet/article/html/fragments**].

25. *Wal-Mart Stores v. Dukes,* 2011 U.S. LEXIS 4567.

26. U.S. Bureau of Labor Statistics, "Women at Work," *Spotlight on Statistics,* March 2011 [**http://www.bls.gov/spotlight/2011/women/**].

27. Ibid.

28. U.S. EEOC, "Sex-Based Charges FY 1997–2010" [**http://www1.eeoc.gov/eeoc/statistics/ enforcement/sex.cfm**].

29. See, generally, *Diaz v. Pan American World Airways, Inc.,* 442 F.2d 385 (5th Cir.), cert. den. 404 U.S. 950 (1971).

30. *Chadwick v. Wellpoint , Inc.,* 561 F.3d 38 (1st Cir. 2009).

31. *Warren v. Solo Cup,* 516 F.3d 627 (7th Cir. 2008).

32. Society for Human Resource Management, "Is Workplace Harassment on the Rise?" SHRM Poll, April 16, 2010 [**http://www.shrm.org/Research/SurveyFindings/Articles/Pages/ SexualHarassmentontheRise.aspx**].

33. *Burlington Industries v. Ellerth,* 524 U.S. 742 (1998); and *Faragher v. Boca Raton,* 524 U.S. 775 (1998).

34. *Oncale v. Sundowner Offshore Services,* 523 U.S. 75 (1998).

35. *Holman v. State of Indiana,* 211 F.3d 299 (7th Cir. 2000).

36. Kiren Dosanjh, "Crossing Boundaries: Sexual Harassment Liability of U.S.-Based Multi-National Corporations in Developing Countries," [**http://www.sba.muohio.edu/abas/2001/brussels/ Dosanjh_Crossing_Boundaries.pdf**].

37. Stephen Miller. "Sexual Jokes No Laughing Matter," *Glasgow Herald,* June 7, 2002, p. 4.

38. Gerald L. Maatman Jr. "A Global View of Sexual Harassment," *HR Magazine,* July 2000. p. 151.

39. Ibid.

40. For a judicial examination of the retaliation prima facie case, see *Brown v. United Parcel Service,* 406 F.Appx. 837 (5th Cir. 2010) (unpublished).

41. 555 U.S. 271 (2009),

42. 548 U.S. 53 (2006).

43. 131 S.Ct. 863 (2011).

44. Michael A. Fletcher and Jon Cohen, "Far Fewer Consider Racism Big Problem," *The Washington Post,* January 19, 2009 [**http://www.washingtonpost.com/wp-dyn/content/article/2009/01/18/ AR2009011802538.html**].

45. Pew Research Center, "Public Backs Affirmative Action, but not Minority Preferences," *Pew Research Center Publications,* June 2, 2009 [**http://pewresearch.org/pubs/1240/sotomayor-supreme-court-affirmative-action-minority-preferences**][**http://www.washingtonpost.com/ wp-dyn/content/article/2009/01/18/AR2009011802538.html**].

46. 443 U.S. 193 (1979).

47. 480 U.S. 616 (1987).

48. 488 U.S. 469 (1989).

49. 115 S.Ct. 2097 (1995).

50. Charles A. Sullivan, "Circling Back to the Obvious: The Convergence of Traditional and Reverse Discrimination in Title VII Proof," *William and Mary Law Review* 46 (December 2004), p. 1031.

51. *Ricci v. DeStefano,* 129 S.Ct 2658 at 2677 (2009).

52. Steven Greenhouse, "Supreme Court Ruling Offers Little Guidance on Hiring," *The New York Times,* June 30, 2009 [**http://www.nytimes.com**].

53. *Cloutier v. Costco,* 390 F.3d 126 (1st Cir. 2004); cert. den., 545 U.S. 1131 (2005).

54. 423 U.S. 63 (1977).

55. *Franks v. National Lime & Stone Co.,* 740 N.E. 2d 694 (Ohio Ct. App. 2000).

56. EEOC Compliance Manual Section 12, Religious Discrimination, July 22, 2008 [**http://www.eeoc.gov/policy/docs/religion.html**].

57. 604 F.3d 848 (5th Cir. 2010).

58. Joan Biskupic, "High Court Raises Bar for ADA," *USA TODAY,* January 9, 2002, p. 3A.

59. *Hoffman v. Carefirst of Fort Wayne, Inc.,* 2010 U.S. Dist. LEXIS 107493 (N.D. Ind. 2010).

60. Sara Murray, "Disabled Face Sharply Higher Jobless Rate," *The Wall Street Journal,* August 26, 2010, p. A5.

61. Ibid.

62. Ibid.

63. Suzanne Robitalle, "Support Grows for Disabled Job Seekers," *The Wall Street Journal,* July 22, 2008, p. D4.

64. Equal Employment Opportunity Commission, "Facts About Disability-Related Tax Provisions" [**http://www.eeoc.gov/facts/fs-disab.html**].

65. Pub. L. 110–233 (2008).

66. *Smith v. City of Jackson,* 2005 U.S. LEXIS 2931.

67. 129 S.Ct. 2343 (2009).

68. Ibid.

69. H.R. 3721 [**http://www.govtrack.us/congress/bill.xpd?bill=h111-3721**].

70. *Meacham v. Knolls Atomic Power Laboratory,* 554 U.S. 84 (2008).

71. John Carlson, "Six Care Center Workers Are Fired," *The Des Moines Register,* June 8, 1997, p. 1B.

72. Ibid.

73. Tyler Lewis, "Employment Non-Discrimination Act Is Re-Introduced in Congress," The Leadership Conference, March 30, 2011[**http://www.civilrights.org/archives/2011/03/1180-enda.html**].

74. U.S. Government Accountability Office, "Sexual Orientation and Gender Identity Employment Discrimination: Overview of State Statutes and Complaint Data" GAP-10-135R, October 7, 2009 [**http://www.gao.gov/htext/d10135r.html**].

75. Ibid.

76. *Schroer v. Billington,* 577 F.Supp.2d 293 (D.D.C. 2008).

77. Ibid.

CHAPTER FOURTEEN

Employment Law III: Labor–Management Relations

After completing this chapter, students will be able to:

1. Describe both the decline of labor unions and their hopes for renewal.

2. Describe the goals of the National Labor Relations Act (NLRA).

3. Identify unfair labor practices by management and unions.

4. Describe the role of the National Labor Relations Board (NLRB) in enforcing the NLRA.

5. Describe the process of union organizing and the related legal issues.

6. Describe "bargaining in good faith."

7. Distinguish between "unfair labor practice strikes" and "economic strikes."

8. Compare and contrast "primary picketing" and "secondary picketing/boycotts."

9. Describe employees' rights within or against unions.

10. Explain the impact of "right to work" laws on union security agreements.

Introduction

Manuel Alvarez is the type of worker that service-sector unions are eager to attract. After 11 years as a houseman at the Hilton Hotel at Los Angeles International Airport, he earns $9.95 an hour, about $20,000 a year.

It's not enough to live on," said Mr. Alvarez, an immigrant from Mexico who vacuums halls and flips mattresses. "I go to two churches each week to pick up donated food." On his days off, he collects bottles and cans for the deposit, adding $200 a month to his income. His hope is to join a union, and soon.[1]

If America's unions have a robust future, it probably lies with people like Manuel Alvarez. Global economic shifts have split America's private sector unions in two pieces; one, the old-line manufacturing organizations represented by the United Auto Workers (UAW), for example; the other, the emerging service sector organized most notably by the Service Employees International Union (SEIU), which represents 2.2 million nurses, security guards, janitors, and others. Traditional union power in manufacturing has been deeply undercut by the outsourcing of jobs abroad to take advantage of cheaper wages. Substantial decreases in private consumption and investment in recent years, leading to declines in manufacturing and construction, have also significantly impacted union membership. In 2010, union membership declined to 11.9 percent of the workforce from 12.3 percent the previous year, and in a reflection of a longer-term descent, union membership has fallen nearly 50 percent since 1983.[2] Job losses in manufacturing and construction accounted for over half of the 2009 decrease in union membership in the private sector.[3] By contrast, low-wage service jobs—for the most part not subject to outsourcing—look ripe for organizing by unions. Currently almost two and one half million such workers belong to unions.[4] However, from 2009 to 2010, union membership among service workers decreased slightly while the number of workers employed in service industries increased a bit.[5]

Union Division   One of the results of the changing manufacturing to service composition of the American workforce is that the union movement itself has split. The AFL-CIO is maintaining its traditional role in manufacturing, construction, transportation, and the like, but the SEIU, Unite Here, and other unions have broken away from the AFL-CIO to form the rival Change to Win federation that, in total, represents some six million workers. However, in 2009, the AFL-CIO, the National Education Association and Change to Win agreed to form the National Labor Coordinating Committee (NLCC) to work together on major initiatives such as the Employee Free Choice Act, a bill addressing issues of union recognition and employers' duty to bargain with unions. [For more information on the NLCC's goals, see **http://www.usw.org/media_center/releases_advisories?id=0191**]

Manufacturing Decline   Union problems in the manufacturing sector were vividly illustrated by the 2007 settlements of new labor agreements between the UAW and the Big Three American automobile manufacturers: General Motors, Ford, and Chrysler. In return for automakers' promises of investments to maintain manufacturing jobs in the United States, UAW members approved dramatic contract changes that are allowing the American Big Three to compete more effectively with their nonunion competitors, Toyota, Honda, and others. Average wages were substantially frozen for a few years at about $28 per hour, and a two-tier wage structure was accepted with all new workers receiving a reduced starting rate averaging $14 to $16 per hour. For the union, the two-tier wage structure and other concessions were designed to preserve auto jobs. A major element of these contracts was the transfer of retiree healthcare liabilities from the auto companies to voluntary employees' beneficiary associations (VEBAs). For the manufacturers, the VEBAs along with other recent changes are expected to reduce the Japanese cost advantage in manufacturing to as little as $250 per car, down from about $2,500 in 2003.[6]

Union Support   Public support for unions, in general, has declined in recent years, according to a 2010 Pew poll. Forty-one percent of those surveyed hold favorable views of unions, down from 58 percent in 2007, while 42 percent had an unfavorable view, up from 31 percent.[7] On the other hand, a 2011 *New York Times* poll registered significant support for public sector unions. Weakening public workers' collective bargaining rights was opposed 60 to 33 percent and cutting pay and benefits was opposed by 56 to 37 percent.[8] The poll was conducted during a period when a number of states were attempting to cut their budgets by curbing union pay, benefits, and collective bargaining rights. Worker productivity jumped a record 20 percent between 2000 and 2006, but real wages increased only 2 percent.[9] Health and pension coverage are falling for many, and the gap between rich and poor is growing. Despite these favorable conditions for unionization, union membership continues to fall. A shift away from traditional unionized industries along with union corruption have certainly played big roles in union struggles, but union supporters say corporate resistance has made organizing very difficult. However, a 2010 deal between Walmart and organized labor regarding Walmart's planned major expansion into Chicago may indicate the future direction of this struggle. Chicago unions opposed the expansion of Walmart, which has resisted unionization. Consequently, Walmart struggled for years to acquire the necessary approvals from the City Council to expand its Chicago presence. Walmart agreed to pay entry-level Chicago workers $8.75 an hour, with raises of 40 cents to 60 cents an hour after one year, and to have future Chicago stores built by union workers.[10] The Chicago City Council subsequently approved a zoning change to allow Walmart's expansion, drawing to a close the stalemate between the discount retailer and the city suffering from high unemployment and low sales and property-tax receipts.[11]

Questions

1. Do we need labor unions to counterbalance the power of big corporations? Explain.

2. The Center for American Progress Action Fund's April 2011 report, "Unions Make the Middle Class," concludes that a decrease in union power contributes to the decline of the middle class:

   > [W]ithout the counterbalance of workers united together in unions, the middle class withers because the economy and politics tend to be dominated by the rich and powerful, which in turn leads to an even greater flow of money in our economy to the top of income scale. . . . Across the globe, the countries with the strongest middle classes all have strong union movements. And in America today, states with higher concentrations of union members have a much stronger middle class.

3. Is the declining power of labor unions a factor in the growing income inequality in America? Explain. See David Madland, Karla Walter, and Nick Bunker, "Unions Make the Middle Class," Center for American Progress, April 4, 2011 [**http://www. americanprogressaction.org/issues/2011/04/unions_middle_class.html**]. [For the federal Bureau of Labor Statistics, see **http://stats.bls.gov/**]

Sweat-Free Manufacturing?

The Yuwei Plastics and Hardware Product Company Ltd. in Dongguan, China, manufactures and exports auto parts to Ford. The Institute for Global Labour and Human Rights reported that Yuwei workers earn 80 cents an hour, work 14-hour shifts seven days a week, and are docked three days' wages if they miss one day's work. Managers' instructions to turn off safety mechanisms to increase workers' speed have resulted in serious injuries:

One employee lost several fingers. Managers and workers stated that Ford accounts for approximately four-fifths of Yuwei's total production. The report urges that "Ford is responsible to clean up the factory and bring the plant into compliance with internationally recognized labor and human rights standards and adherence to occupational health and safety laws."

Question

1. Should American corporations be held responsible for their global suppliers' oppressive working conditions? Explain.

Source: Charles Kernaghan, "Dirty Parts: Where Lost Fingers Come Cheap: Ford in China," International Institute for Global Labour and Human Rights (March 2011), pp. 1 and 11 [**http://www.globallabourrights.org/admin/reports/files/110304-Dirty-Parts.pdf**].

Part One—History

As the United States moved from an agrarian to an industrial society in the late 1880s, business competition was fierce. Costs had to be cut. By paying workers as little as possible and making them work 14- to 18-hour days, employers could prosper. Farmers began moving to the city to be near their jobs and thus left their safety net of gardens, chickens, and cows. Similarly, immigrants streamed into the big cities, and competition for jobs became heated. Wages fell, and deplorable working conditions were the norm.[12] Some of those immigrants brought with them ideas and experiences in labor conflict and class struggle that would soon contribute to dramatic changes in the American workplace.

A Grim Picture

To say that working conditions for many people at this time were unpleasant or even dismal would be a vast understatement. The term *desperate* better describes the problem. Children were impressed into service as soon as they were big enough to do a job and then made to work 12- and 14-hour days.[13] In fact, small children were employed in coal mines for 10 to 12 hours each day, and at a rate of $1 to $3 per week, because they were small enough to fit in the confined spaces.[14] Textile companies sent men called *slavers* to New England and southern farm communities to gather young women to work in the mills.[15]

> Children were employed in coal mines because they were small enough to fit in the confined spaces.

The following firsthand report from the early 20th century reveals the grim picture:

When I moved from the North to the South in my search for work, I entered a mill village to work in a cotton mill as a spinner. There I worked 11 hours a day, five and a half days a week, for $7 a week. In a northern mill I had done the same kind of work for $22 a week, and less hours. I worked terribly hard. . . .

The sanitary conditions were ghastly. When I desired a drink of water, I had to dip my cup into a pail of water that had been brought into the mill from a spring in the fields. It tasted horrible to me. Often I saw lint from the cotton in the room floating on top of the lukewarm water. All of the men chewed tobacco, and most of the women used snuff. Little imagination is needed to judge the condition of the water which I had to drink, for working in that close, hot spinning room made me thirsty. Toilet facilities were provided three stories down in the basement of the mill in a room without any ventilation. Nowhere was there any running water. . . .

Everything in the village is company owned. The houses look like barns on stilts, and appear to have been thrown together. When I would go inside one of them, I could see outside through the cracks in the walls. The workers do all of their trading at the company store and bank, and use the company school and library for they have no means of leaving the village.[16]

Compare those working-class conditions with the lifestyle of John D. Rockefeller, the great tycoon of the same era. Although Rockefeller was notoriously frugal, his estate at Pocantico Hills, New York contained

. . . more than 75 buildings. . . . Within his estate were 75 miles of private roads on which he could take his afternoon drive; private golf links on which he could play his morning game; and anywhere from 1,000 to 1,500 employees, depending on the season.

. . . Rockefeller also owned an estate at Lakewood, [New Jersey] which he occupied in the spring; an estate at Ormond Beach in Florida for his winter use; a townhouse . . . in New York; an estate at Forest Hill, Cleveland which he did not visit; and a house on Euclid Avenue in Cleveland, likewise unused by him.[17]

These circumstances enable us to better understand the sense of injustice felt by many workers and the belief that a redistribution of wealth might provide the only solution to class conflict. [For a history of women in the labor movement, see **http://www.afscme. org/otherlnk/whlinks.htm**]

Organizing Labor

The Knights of Labor, the first major labor organization in the United States, had a large following during the 1870s and 1880s.[18] The order admitted any workers to its ranks, regardless of occupation, gender, or nationality; in fact, the only people excluded from the group were gamblers, bankers, stockbrokers, and liquor dealers.[19] The Knights of Labor dedicated itself to principles of social reform, including the protection of wage and hour laws, improved healthcare systems, and mandatory education.[20] However, the goals of the Knights of Labor were perhaps too broad and far-reaching to bring workers any relief from their immediate problems. Great philosophical divisions within the Knights of Labor brought about its rapid decline.[21]

Skilled Workers

Samuel Gompers, who built and developed the American Federation of Labor (AFL), had more practical, attainable goals in mind for his organization. Gompers, a worker in the cigar industry, saw the need to organize workers along craft lines (such as plumbers, electricians, and machinists) so that each craft group could seek higher wages and better working conditions for its own workers, all of whom had the same type of skills and, presumably, shared the same occupational goals.[22] This approach, a national association of local unions directed to workers' pragmatic needs rather than the more politically motivated activities of the Knights of Labor, proved to be a successful formula for union organization.

Laborers

The Congress of Industrial Organizations (CIO) was organized in response to the needs of ordinary laborers not working in the skilled trades to which the AFL was devoted. The CIO was organized in 1935 and served assembly-line workers and others who often performed repetitive, physically demanding tasks. The AFL and CIO were fierce competitors, but after years of bitter conflict, the two groups united forces in 1955. They function together today as the AFL–CIO. [For the AFL–CIO home page, see **http://www.aflcio.org**]

Unions and the Developing Law

Labor Protection

Responding to mounting public pressure, Congress passed the Norris-LaGuardia Act in 1932 making clear that the terminology "restraint of trade," which was the heart of the 1890 Sherman Antitrust Act (see Chapter 10), was not meant to include labor organizations or activities.

From 1932 to 1935, labor tensions continued to mount. The nation was still caught in the Great Depression. Believing that one element essential to economic recovery was stability in the workforce, Congress addressed the labor question with the Wagner Act of 1935. This legislation gave workers for the first time the unequivocal right to organize and engage in concerted activities for their mutual aid and benefit. To protect this right, Congress identified and made illegal a number of unfair labor practices. Through the Wagner Act, Congress also established the National Labor Relations Board (see below).

Management Protection

Unions grew rapidly with the passage of the Wagner Act, and by 1947 Congress decided management might need a little help in coping with ever-growing labor organizations.[23] Congress enacted the Taft–Hartley Act, identifying as unfair labor practices certain activities unions used to exercise economic leverage over employers as part of the collective bargaining process. The Taft–Hartley Act also ensured employers' right to speak out in opposition to union organizing—in effect, protecting their First Amendment right to freedom of speech. Thus, the Taft–Hartley Act signaled a move by the government away from unconditional support for labor toward a balance of rights between labor and management.[24]

Corrupt Union Leaders

In response to the growing evidence that union leaders were benefiting at the expense of the membership, Congress in 1959 enacted the Landrum–Griffin Act, requiring unions to keep records of their funds. It also prohibits unions from lending money except under specified circumstances and procedures, all of which must be reported annually to the government.

Members' Rights

The Landrum–Griffin Act also contains a set of provisions often referred to as the "Bill of Rights" for individual union members. These provisions are designed to protect union members by requiring that union meetings be held, that members be permitted to speak and vote at these meetings, that every employee covered by a collective bargaining agreement has the right to see a copy of that agreement, and that a union member be informed of the reasons and given a chance for a hearing if the union wishes to suspend or take disciplinary action against that member, unless he or she is being suspended for nonpayment of dues.[25]

The law has also regulated the manner in which unions represent employees in the collective bargaining process. Because a union serves as employees' exclusive bargaining representative, the courts have devised a *duty of fair representation*.[26] To fulfill this duty, a union must represent employees, both in negotiating and enforcing the collective bargaining agreement, "without hostility or discrimination . . . [and] . . . with complete good faith and honesty [so as to] avoid arbitrary conduct."[27]

PRACTICING ETHICS) Fairness in the Workplace?

Workplace Fairness, a nonprofit advocate for "workplace policies and practices that work for everyone," argues that America's workers are "short-changed" by "giving more and getting less":

> Whether you look at job security, career opportunity, income, time spent on the job, health care, retirement security, or the right to organize, it's clear that working people are worse off today than they were several decades ago. . . . Is this because America has fallen on hard times? Hardly. Our economy is stronger than it has

ever been. . . . Today's workplace has winners as well as losers. Executives and investors are winning and winning big. Workers trying to earn their livelihoods are losing.

Question

1. Is America now unfair to its ordinary workers? Explain.

Source: "Short-Changed, America's Workers Are Giving More and Getting Less," Workplace Fairness [**http://www.workplacefairness.org/sc/**].

Part Two—Labor Legislation Today

Today labor–management relations are governed by the National Labor Relations Act (NLRA), as enforced by the NLRB.[28] This act includes within it the Wagner Act, the Taft–Hartley Act, and portions of the Landrum–Griffin Act. The remaining provisions of the Landrum–Griffin Act make up the Labor–Management Reporting and Disclosure Act and the Bill of Rights of Members of Labor Organizations.

Right to Organize

The NLRA gives employees the right to engage in concerted activity, including strikes and collective bargaining. Section 7 of the NLRA states:

> Employees shall have the right to self-organization, to form, join, or assist labor organizations, to bargain collectively through representatives of their own choosing, and to engage in other concerted activities for the purpose of collective bargaining or other mutual aid or protection, and shall also have the right to refrain from any and all of such activities except

to the extent that such right may be affected by an agreement requiring membership in a labor organization as a condition of employment.

When political issues such as immigration become heated, employees' political advocacy efforts may affect the workplace. Political advocacy may in some circumstances be considered a *concerted activity* for "mutual aid or protection" under Section 7. Under 2008 NLRB guidelines, the first question to consider is whether there is a direct connection between the political issue at stake and a "specifically identified employment concern of the participating employees." Even if that direct connection is established, however, the employer may discipline the employees if the political activity, such as attending a rally, violates "neutrally applied" work rules, such as those forbidding stopping or leaving work without permission.[29] [For a vast database of federal and state labor law statutes and regulations, see **http://topics.law.cornell.edu/wex/labor**]

Bleeping Protected Activity?

During ongoing union negotiations, Bill Barker, a company vice president at the *Tampa Tribune,* sent employees a series of letters, which were legal and accurate, describing the negotiation process from his perspective. In talking to supervisors about the letters one night after he arrived for his third shift, an employee, Greg McMillen, said: "I hope that f**king idiot [Barker] doesn't send me another letter. I'm pretty stressed, and if there is another letter you might not see me. I might be out on stress." McMillen was fired for violating a company policy against using threatening and abusive language in the company building. McMillen complained to the NLRB. Did McMillen's firing violate Section 7 of the NLRA? Explain.

Source: Media General Operations v. NLRB, 560 F.3d 181 (4th Cir. 2009).

Unfair Labor Practices by Management

The NLRA describes and outlaws certain activities by employers that would hamper or discourage employees from exercising the rights granted to them in Section 7. Thus Section 8(a) of the act makes it an *unfair labor practice* for an employer to

1. Interfere with, restrain, or coerce employees in the exercise of the rights given to them by Section 7.
2. Dominate, interfere, or assist with the formation of any labor organization, including contributing financial support to it.
3. Encourage or discourage membership in any labor organization by discrimination in regard to hiring, tenure of employment, promotion, salary, or any other term of employment.
4. Discharge or take any other action against an employee because he or she has filed charges or given testimony under the act.
5. Refuse to bargain collectively with a duly certified representative of the employees.

These five provisions are designed to allow employees to organize in an atmosphere free from intimidation by the employer. In addition, if employees have chosen a union as their exclusive collective bargaining representative, Section 8(a) regulates the bargaining between the employer and the union. The provisions also ensure that the employer will not be able to interfere with union activities by either seizing control of the union or rendering it impotent by refusing to bargain collectively.

Unfair Labor Practices by Unions

Section 8(b) lists activities constituting unfair labor practices by a labor organization. Some of these provisions mirror some of the activities prohibited to employers. Moreover, at least since the enactment of the Taft–Hartley Act, the law is not sympathetic to labor organizations that try to use certain coercive tactics, threats of the loss of livelihood, or any other strong-arm methods. Finally, Section 8(b) also regulates the union's collective bargaining practices, including economic action. Thus, a labor organization is not permitted to:

1. Restrain or coerce any employee in the exercise of his or her rights as granted by Section 7.
2. Cause or attempt to cause an employer to discriminate against an employee who has chosen not to join a particular labor organization or has been denied membership in such an organization.
3. Refuse to bargain collectively with an employer on behalf of the bargaining unit it is certified to represent.
4. Induce or attempt to induce an employer to engage in secondary boycott activities.
5. Require employees to become union members and then charge them excessive or discriminatory dues.
6. Try to make an employer compensate workers for services not performed.
7. Picket or threaten to picket an employer in an attempt to force the employer to recognize or bargain with a labor organization that is not the duly certified representative of a bargaining unit.

Representation Procedures

Section 9 of the NLRA specifies the election procedures by which employees may choose whether to be represented by a particular union or no union at all.

Checking Email

The Eugene, Oregon *Register-Guard* newspaper maintained a company policy prohibiting employees from using company communications systems such as email to "solicit or proselytize for commercial ventures, religious or political causes, outside organizations, or other non-job-related solicitations." Employees, however, had not been disciplined for using the email system to invite coworkers to parties, sell sports tickets, etc. Suzi Prozanski, an employee and union president, used the employer's email system to send three union-related messages to other employees at their work addresses. She was disciplined under the company policy.

Question

Did the *Register-Guard* violate the NLRA in disciplining Prozanski? Explain.

Source: Register-Guard v. NLRB, 571 F.3d 53 (D.C. Cir. 2009).

National Labor Relations Board (NLRB)

The NLRB is a federal administrative agency responsible for regulating labor–management relations. Its primary tasks are designating appropriate bargaining units of workers (deciding which workers have a sufficient community of interest so that their needs can best be acknowledged and so that collective bargaining is efficient for the employer and the union); conducting elections for union representation within the chosen bargaining unit; certifying the results of such elections; and investigating, prosecuting, and adjudicating charges of unfair labor practices.[30]

Although the congressional mandate by which the NLRB was formed gives the agency jurisdiction theoretically to the full extent of the interstate commerce powers vested in Congress, the agency has neither the funding nor the staff to administer its duties to all of American industry. Some smaller businesses, government employees, railroad, and airline workers covered by the Railway Labor Act, agricultural workers, domestic workers, independent contractors, and supervisors and other managerial employees are not protected by the board.[31]

Over the years, the five-member NLRB has been criticized for sometimes reaching decisions based on political/philosophical considerations rather than legal reasoning and Board precedent. As successive presidential administrations appoint NLRB members, the Board's decisions often "seesaw" according to the changes in Washington political power.

Extended vacancies on the Board have also created controversy. In 2007, the Board operated with four members, two of whom were "recess appointees" with terms concluding at the end of that year. Beginning on January 1, 2008, the Board operated with just two members. In appealing adverse decisions, employers challenged the two-member Board's authority. In 2010 the U.S. Supreme Court ruled that while the NLRA allows the Board to delegate its powers to three members, the NLRB could not decide cases if fewer than three were sitting.[32] [For the NLRB, see **http://www.nlrb.gov**]

Facebook Update

An employee posted comments on her Facebook page about her employer, Build.com, and possible state labor code violations. Some coworkers who were the employee's "Facebook friends" responded to her comments. The employee, who was not a union member, was fired, and she filed a complaint with the NLRB. As discussed above, under the National Labor Relations Act, employees have the right to engage in "concerted activities" which include discussion of wages and working conditions with coworkers. That right protects employees whether represented by a union or not. The employee and Build.com settled. As part of the settlement, the employer promised to place a notice at the workplace for 60 days stating that employees have the right to post comments about terms and conditions of employment on their social media pages, and that they will not be fired or disciplined for such postings.

Notwithstanding the Build.com settlement and another similar 2011 settlement involving a Facebook posting by an employee [see *American Medical Response of Connecticut, Inc.,* NLRB Case No. 34-CA-12576 (2011)], the NLRB's general position is that employers have substantial rights to regulate employee behavior including speech. Employees' free speech rights remain limited, and as discussed in Chapter 12, *at-will* employees can be fired for virtually any reason.

Source: Office of Public Affairs, National Labor Relations Board Regional News, "Build.com Settles Charge of Unlawful Discharge for Comments Posted on Facebook with NLRB Agreement in San Francisco," April 27, 2011 [**http://www.nlrb.gov/news/regional-news-buildcom-settles-charge-unlawful-discharge-comments-posted-facebook-nlrb-agreemen**].

Part Three—Elections

Choosing a Bargaining Representative

Representation elections are the process by which the NLRB achieves the first of the two statutory goals under the act—employee freedom of choice. That goal, however, is sometimes in conflict with the other statutory goal—stable collective bargaining. The NLRB has devised rules to resolve such conflicts. [For the AFL–CIO view of why workers should join unions, see **http://www.workingamerica.org/issues**]

Election Petition

A union, employee, or employer initiates the formal organizing process by filing an election petition with the NLRB. The petition is sent to the employer, thus providing notice of union activity. Also, the employer must post notices supplied by the NLRB so that employees are aware of the petition. The NLRB then assumes its authority to closely oversee the conduct of employer and union. Of course at that point, the employer is free to simply acknowledge its employees' interest in joining a particular union and to engage in bargaining with that union; a decision normally called *voluntary recognition*.

Sometimes an employer enters an agreement with a union specifying that the employer will voluntarily recognize the union if the union can demonstrate that it has majority support among the employees. Majority support is often established by a *card check* method where employees signify their interest in the union simply by signing authorization cards. The card check approach thus bypasses the secret ballot election and can greatly ease union organizing. One of the controversial NLRB decisions of 2007, however, overturned 40 years of precedent and made the card check method less useful for union organizing. In *Dana Corporation/Metaldyne*,[33] the NLRB ruled that where an employer voluntarily recognizes a union based on a card check majority, antiunion employees now have 45 days to petition the board for a federally supervised, secret ballot election to *decertify* the newly recognized union or to support a petition by a rival union. Under previous rulings, that election ordinarily would not have been permitted until at least 12 months had passed. The NLRB majority believed that elections are more accurate representations of employee preferences than the more open, and easily influenced, card check.

Failing voluntary recognition, the process proceeds according to NLRB rules. The NLRB will accept only those election petitions supported by a substantial showing of interest, which, at a minimum, must include the signatures of at least 30 percent of the employees in the bargaining unit. (In practice today, most unions will not proceed toward an election without 50 to 65 percent of the employees' signatures.) Those signatures accompany the petition, or they may appear on the authorization cards.

Procedure

Prior to an election, the NLRB ordinarily will first attempt to settle certain issues such as whether a union contract already covers the employees or whether the election should be delayed. In determining the timing of the election, the two statutory goals of employee free choice and stable collective bargaining may conflict. For example, if the employees are already covered by a collective bargaining agreement, should they be able to choose again during the term of the agreement? Similarly, if the employees have rejected a union in an election, can they be prohibited from voting again in the name of stable collective bargaining? Alternatively, what if the employees choose to unionize in an election, but reconsider before a collective bargaining agreement is reached? Can they have another election?

The crucial issue to be addressed at this point, however, is normally whether the proposed bargaining unit (the designated employee group—for example, all hourly workers, all welders, or all craftspersons) is appropriate for the election.

Appropriate Bargaining Unit

The key consideration in establishing an appropriate employee bargaining unit is the community of interest among the employees. The NLRB searches for an appropriate bargaining unit because collective bargaining will not be stable and efficient if it involves employees with diverse interests. Therefore, the bargaining unit may range from a portion of a plant to multiple employers in multiple plants. Plants may have more than one appropriate bargaining unit, depending on the composition of the workforce. The NLRB makes the decision regarding the appropriate bargaining unit on the basis of such considerations as physical location of the plants; physical contact among employees; similarity of wages, benefits, and working conditions; differences in skill requirements among job categories; and common supervision.

Certain classes of employees, such as supervisors, are excluded from the bargaining unit. Obviously supervisors are excluded because they act on behalf of the employer and, through their power to direct and assign work and to discipline and discharge employees, exert control over their subordinates who are or may be in the bargaining unit. Often labor and management do not agree about the classification of workers as supervisors. In another decision outraging union activists, the NLRB in 2006 substantially expanded the range of employees who might lawfully be considered supervisors and thus ineligible for union membership.[34] The three-person Republican majority ruled, among other things, that an employee assigned supervisory duties just 10 or 15 percent of the time could be deemed a supervisor. The result, according to some experts, is that more than 8 million workers could be affected by the decision, but others say that number is vastly inflated.[35]

Independent contractors are not protected under the NLRA. In 2009, a federal appeals court set aside the NLRB's decision that FedEx had unlawfully failed to bargain with a union which had been certified to represent drivers at two FedEx home terminals. The appeals court concluded that the drivers were independent contractors who had been *misclassified* as employees by the NLRB.[36]

Solicitation

A 1992 Supreme Court decision in the *Lechmere* case[37] made union organizing much more difficult by ruling that employers do not have to allow on their property union organizers who are not employees. One of the results of that decision has been an increase in *salting*, the practice of union organizers applying for jobs with the intent of unionizing the other employees from the inside. The Supreme Court's 1995 *Town & Country* decision[38] held that salts are employees, thus affording them NLRA protection that forbids discrimination based on union affiliation, but a 2007 NLRB decision limited protection under the NLRA to those salts who are "genuinely interested" in obtaining employment.[39] Many employers saw the *Town & Country* decision as an unfair intrusion on their property rights and on their preference to remain union-free. The case that follows involves a Walmart employee's efforts to interest coworkers in joining a union.

LEGAL BRIEFCASE

Wal-Mart Stores, Inc. v. National Labor Relations Board   400 F.3d 1093 (8th Cir. 2005)

Circuit Judge Melloy

Petitioner appeals the National Labor Relations Board's order finding that it violated the National Labor Relations Act by punishing employee Brian Shieldnight for union solicitation.

I

This case arises from efforts to unionize employees at the Wal-Mart store in Tahlequah, Oklahoma. The store, like all Wal-Mart stores, maintains and enforces a policy that prohibits solicitation during employees' work time, regardless of the cause or organization.

Brian Shieldnight, an employee of the Tahlequah Wal-Mart, contacted the United Food and Commercial Workers Union, Local 1000 ("Union") about possible union representation. He obtained authorization cards from the union to organize employees at the Tahlequah store.

On January 29, 2001, Shieldnight entered the store while off-duty. He wore a T-shirt that read "Union Teamsters" on the front and "Sign a card . . . Ask me how!" on the back. Assistant Store Manager John Lamont and Assistant Night Manager Tammy Flute saw Shieldnight's T-shirt and saw him speak to an associate. Flute told the associate to return to work, and Lamont ordered Shieldnight to leave associates alone. Lamont then consulted a Wal-Mart "union hotline."

The hotline representative told Lamont that Shieldnight's shirt constituted solicitation and that Shieldnight should be removed from the store. Lamont and Flute sought out Shieldnight. They found him in the jewelry department talking to two friends who were not associates. Lamont informed Shieldnight that his shirt constituted a form of solicitation and that he would have to leave the store immediately. Lamont escorted Shieldnight to the front door of the store and instructed him to leave the store and Wal-Mart property.

The next incident occurred on January 30, 2001. While on duty at the store, Shieldnight invited Department Manager Debra Starr and associates Patricia Scott and James Parsons, all of whom were also on duty, to a union meeting. Shieldnight asked Starr to come to the meeting and stated that he would like her to consider signing a union authorization card. Shieldnight separately asked Scott and Parsons to attend the meeting to hear "the other side of the story."

Based on these two incidents, Co-Manager Rick Hawkins and Assistant Manager John Lamont held a written "coaching session" with Shieldnight for violating the no-solicitation rule. A "coaching session" is part of Wal-Mart's progressive discipline process. Verbal coaching and written coaching are the first two steps in a four-step process. Hawkins and Lamont explained to Shieldnight that he had violated the solicitation policy on January 29 by soliciting on the sales floor with his T-shirt and on

January 30 by verbally soliciting employees while on-duty and on the sales floor. Lamont told Shieldnight that it was wrong to have sent Shieldnight off Wal-Mart property completely. Lamont clarified that while Shieldnight could not solicit on the sales floor, he could do so in the parking lot while not on duty. Hawkins, Lamont, and Shieldnight also discussed Shieldnight's questions and concerns regarding Wal-Mart employment policies, such as health insurance for associates. Lamont suggested Shieldnight should raise the matter in "grassroots" meetings that all Wal-Mart stores hold to identify the top three companywide issues. The three men arranged a time to meet in the future. That meeting never occurred.

The union subsequently filed an unfair labor practice charge against Wal-Mart. . . .

[A] divided Board panel found that Shieldnight had not engaged in solicitation when he (1) wore the T-shirt during his shift; (2) asked on-duty employees to attend a union meeting; or (3) asked a coworker to sign a union card. . . . Wal-Mart appeals. . . .

II

* * * * *

A. The T-Shirt

The union contends that Shieldnight's T-shirt did not constitute solicitation, but rather was a "union insignia." Wal-Mart argues that by encouraging people to approach him, Shieldnight's T-shirt was a form of solicitation. In *NLRB v. W.W. Grainger, Inc.*, the board held,

> "Solicitation" for a union usually means asking someone to join the union by signing his name to an authorization card in the same way that solicitation for a charity would mean asking an employee to contribute to a charitable organization . . . or in the commercial context asking an employee to buy a product or exhibiting the product for him. . . .

Ordinarily, employees may wear union insignia while on their employer's premises. . . .

The board stated that the T-shirt should be treated as union insignia because "it did not 'speak' directly to any specific individual . . . and it did not call for an immediate response, as would an oral person-to-person invitation to accept or sign an authorization card." The board found that there was "no claim or evidence that Shieldnight did anything in furtherance of the T-shirt message. . . . He merely walked around and socialized. . . about nonunion matters." Anyone, including any Wal-Mart employee who saw Shieldnight was free to ignore both Shieldnight and the message on the T-shirt. In contrast, a solicitation to sign an authorization card requires more interaction, likely a direct yes or no answer. Absent

further evidence of direct inquiry by Shieldnight, the board's conclusion was supported by substantial evidence.

Wal-Mart alleges that the panel's conclusion is not reasonable because it ignores both Shieldnight's purpose and the long-held rule that an employer may implement rules against solicitation during work time to prevent interference with work productivity.

* * * * *

Wal-Mart failed to demonstrate how the T-shirt interfered in any manner with the operation of the store. Accordingly, substantial evidence supports the board's conclusion that Shieldnight's T-shirt did not constitute solicitation.

B. The Coworker Conversations

* * * * *

Shieldnight invited three coworkers to a union meeting. . . . Shieldnight's statements did not require an immediate response from the three coworkers. Instead of a solicitation that required a response, the record shows that Shieldnight's statements were more akin to a statement of fact that put his coworkers on notice that there was to be a union meeting that night and that they were welcome to attend. Nothing in the record suggests that the environment at Wal-Mart made Shieldnight's actions uniquely disruptive. Accordingly, the panel's conclusion regarding Shieldnight's conversations was supported by substantial evidence. Furthermore, the panel acted reasonably when it concluded that "simply informing another employee of an upcoming meeting or asking a brief, union-related question does not occupy enough time to be treated as a work interruption in most settings."

C. Asking Coworker to Sign a Card

The board concluded that it was not solicitation when Shieldnight asked a coworker to sign a union authorization card. . . .

In light of the totality of the circumstances, Shieldnight's actions constituted solicitation even though he did not actually offer Starr a card at the time he asked her to sign. Shieldnight had contacted the union about obtaining union representation and had obtained cards from the union for the purpose of organizing employees at the Tahlequah store. There is little doubt as to Shieldnight's intent in the words he spoke to Starr. The record indicates that Shieldnight did not have a card in his hand at the time he spoke to Starr. It is silent as to whether he had a card on his person. The fact that he did not place a card directly in front of Starr at the time of his statement makes little difference in regard to the nature of his conversation. Further, Shieldnight's actions in this instance are more analogous to a direct solicitation than when he asked his coworkers to attend the union meeting. Asking someone to sign a union card offers that individual person the choice to be represented by a union. Informing coworkers about a union meeting merely puts fellow employees on notice that a meeting is going to take place.

Accordingly, there is insufficient evidence to support the board's conclusion that Shieldnight's actions were not solicitation, and thus we reverse the board regarding the authorization card issue.

* * * * *

Questions

1. Why was the T-shirt not a form of solicitation?

2. Would statements at work such as "support the union" or "there is a meeting tonight" constitute solicitation? Explain.

3. Why was Shieldnight's invitation to three coworkers to attend a union meeting not a form of solicitation, whereas asking a coworker to sign a card was considered impermissible solicitation?

The Election for Union Representation

If the parties have agreed to conduct an election; alternatively, the NLRB has directed that an election be conducted following a hearing, the board will require that the employer post notices and conduct the election. The union may be selected only by a majority of the votes cast by the employees. The NLRB oversees the election to ensure the process is carried on under "laboratory conditions."[40] In other words, elections must be held under circumstances that, to the extent possible, are free from undue or unfair influence by either the employer or by unions vying for the right to represent the bargaining unit.

For both employers and employees, the circulation of racist propaganda is grounds for setting aside an election. Historically, the board set aside elections tainted by trickery such as falsehoods, allegations, misstatements, and the like but its current position is that misrepresentation alone will not constitute grounds for overturning an election. The burden is on the parties to correct misrepresentations and sort out the truth via the marketplace of ideas. The board will intervene only if the deceptive manner of the misrepresentation (such as a forged document) makes it impossible for the parties themselves to discern the truth. Some courts have endorsed the NLRB view; others have not.

Employers have the right to speak out against unions in the form of ads, speeches, and the like. Section 8(c) of the Taft–Hartley Act is designed to ensure employers' and labor organizations' traditional First Amendment rights as long as they do not overstep certain bounds:

> The expressing of any views, argument, or opinion, or the dissemination thereof, whether in written, printed, graphic, or visual form, shall not constitute or be evidence of an unfair labor practice . . . if such expression contains no threat of reprisal or force or promise of benefit.

Gooseplay?

During a union organizing campaign, a goose wandered from a company pond into the work area where a worker "talked" to the goose and determined that it favored the union. Workers then put a "Vote Yes" card around the goose's neck and drove the goose around the plant on a forklift. The workers were fired for disrupting work and creating a safety hazard. The union claimed the company illegally fired the workers for engaging in union organizing. An administrative law judge agreed with the union, but the NLRB reversed, saying, "Placing a 'Vote Yes' sign on a wild animal does not transform otherwise unprotected 'gooseplay' into activity protected by the National Labor Relations Act."

Source: NACCO Materials Handling Group, Inc., 331 NLRB No. 164 (Aug. 25, 2000).

Threats of Reprisal or Force

As noted above in our discussion of salts, employers cannot discriminate in employment to encourage or discourage union membership. Clearly, an employer who tells employees, for example, that they will all be discharged if they engage in union activity, has interfered with their rights. Similarly, an employer who interrogates employees about their activities or spies on them while they attend union meetings has engaged in unlawful interference. Problems often arise, however, in determining whether antiunion arguments by an employer are legitimate or whether they contain veiled threats. Suppose, for instance, that a company owner warns her employees that if she has to pay higher wages, she will be forced to go out of business and the employees will all lose their jobs. Such statements of economic forecast by employers are more likely to be lawful if based on objective facts not under management's control.

Promise of Benefit

Although threats of force or reprisal are clearly unlawful in union campaigns, the rationale behind the prohibition against promises of benefit is not as intuitively obvious.

In a dispute that reached the U.S. Supreme Court, Exchange Parts sent its employees a letter shortly before a representation election that spoke of "the empty promises of the union" and "the fact that it is the company that puts things in your envelope." After mentioning a number of benefits, the letter said, "The union can't put any of those things in your envelope—only the company can do that." Further on, the letter stated, "It didn't take a union to get any of those things and . . . it won't take a union to get additional improvements in the future." Accompanying the letter was a detailed statement of the benefits granted by the company and an estimate of the monetary value of such benefits to the employees.

> The union can't put any of those things in your envelope.

In the representation election two weeks later, the union lost, but the outcome was challenged in court. Eventually the Supreme Court ruled that the employer's actions constituted an unfair labor practice reasoning that "well-timed increases in benefits" provide a clear message that those who provide advantages are the same people who can withdraw those benefits should their wishes not be followed.[41]

Buying Votes?

An Atlantic City, New Jersey, limousine service held a union election-day raffle for a TV/VCR. The NLRB ruled, 3–2, that the raffle was an unfair labor practice that might reasonably be interpreted to be a reward that would influence voting. A new election was ordered. The NLRB order banned election-day raffles, but minor "gifts" such as food, drinks, and buttons would be considered case-by-case if an objection were lodged.

Source: Atlantic Limousine, 331 NLRB No. 134 (2000).

The case that follows involves allegations that a company illegally interfered with union organizing activity.

Multi-Ad Services v. NLRB
255 F.3d 363 (7th Cir. 2001)

Judge Ripple

This petition asks us to review whether Multi-Ad Services, Incorporated ("Multi-Ad") violated the National Labor Relations Act ("Act") by interfering with its employees' efforts to form a union. The National Labor Relations Board ("Board") concluded that Multi-Ad violated the Act. . . .

BACKGROUND

Multi-Ad employs 450 workers at its full-service advertising art production facility in Peoria, Illinois. Multi-Ad hired Steele in 1989 to work in the bindery department. Fifteen employees work in the department, which manufactures loose-leaf, three-ring binders. The bindery department is a small operation, accounting for a limited percentage of the company's sales and profits. Steele's performance evaluations were above average throughout his tenure at the company.

* * * * *

On July 29, 1996, Multi-Ad held a quarterly meeting for employees of the bindery, press, and finishing departments. After discussing the company's financial performance, plant production manager Jerry Ireland announced the company's plan to implement a new drug-testing policy. Following this announcement, Steele spoke up and openly criticized the policy, contending in a loud and persistent manner that such testing violated employees' right to privacy. Other employees also voiced their displeasure with the policy. Steele and Larry Clore, Multi-Ad's president, then began to argue about the policy's legality. At the end of this exchange, Steele requested a copy of Multi-Ad's laws and bylaws. Clore told Steele that he could have these materials after the meeting.

Later that day, the quarterly meeting split into separate departmental meetings. The bindery department meeting commenced around 3:00 P.M., the normal quitting time for day-shift employees. At this meeting, Clore gave Steele a summary plan description of Multi-Ad's corporate structure. After Steele pointed out that he wanted the complete bylaws and not a summary, Clore responded, "Have your lawyer get them." Clore then told Steele that if he did not like the company's drug policy, "Why don't you think about leaving the company?" Steele responded that he would not give Clore the pleasure of quitting. After Clore departed, Ireland tried to continue with the meeting, but Steele announced that he was leaving because "he was on his own time now." Steele testified that Ireland said, "Okay." Ireland, however, testified that Steele's remark had shocked him and that he had said nothing in

response. Ireland also testified that he had apologized to the group for Steele's behavior. Steele, however, was not ordered to remain for the rest of the meeting, which ended shortly after his exit.

Two days later, Steele and Ireland met at Steele's request. Steele apologized for his conduct at the department meeting and then told Ireland that hourly shop workers were dissatisfied with company policies. Steele told Ireland that "management needed to just sit down with the hourly employees and work some things out." Ireland replied, "That could not be done." Steele then told Ireland that, if they could not sit down and discuss these problems, he would organize a union. Ireland asked Steele to wait until Ireland returned from his vacation to discuss the issue further. Steele agreed and made no effort to contact a union while Ireland was away.

On August 16, 1996, Steele met with Ireland and bindery department manager Marty Heathcoat in Heathcoat's office. During this meeting, the two managers asked Steele why he would want to bring a union into the company. Steele told them that it would be nice to have seniority rights, better working conditions, and raises when possible. Ireland then asked what Steele could do to improve Steele's own situation at the company and pointed out that Multi-Ad posted job openings. After Steele expressed interest in a maintenance position, Ireland told him that he would set up an interview, even though the company did not have an opening for a maintenance position. At the end of the meeting, Ireland asked Steele "what it would take to satisfy him." Steele replied that it would satisfy him if management "would sit down with the hourly employees and work something out." After Ireland responded that he could not do that, Steele informed the two managers that he was leaving the meeting and was going to attempt to organize a union. Ireland asked Steele to come back and talk some more, but Steele responded that there was nothing left to talk about. Steele left at 3:30 P.M., 30 minutes after his shift had ended. No one told Steele to stay, nor was he reprimanded for having left the meeting. The next day, Steele interviewed for a maintenance position, but the interview revealed that he lacked the necessary qualifications. In any event, Steele said that he did not want the job.

Steele twice met with union officials in late August. During this time, employees began to talk about Steele's efforts at organizing a union. At a meeting of bindery department employees in late August, Heathcoat addressed rumors about a union and asked employees why they wanted a union. In response, Steele stated that everyone knew that Heathcoat was referring to Steele's desire to look into unionization. Ted DeRossett, Steele's supervisor, then warned that the bindery department would be the "first to go" if the company unionized. Steele immediately challenged the legality of closing the bindery department in such a fashion. After Steele and DeRossett began to argue heatedly, Heathcoat ended the meeting.

At another bindery department meeting in late August, management informed employees that they would be working mandatory 10-hour shifts. Steele protested that it was unfair to require employees to work overtime when in the past they had been able to decline overtime. Steele also stated that it was decisions like this that caused him to explore bringing in a union.

Shortly after the meeting, Multi-Ad announced that it was adding a second shift in the bindery department and that Steele would be the lead man. On August 29, 1996, Heathcoat and DeRossett asked Steele if he would work the second shift with a positive attitude. The two assured Steele that he could still take his scheduled vacation days from August 30 through September 3. Steele told them that he would go to the second shift, do the job, and represent the company as was expected of him.

The next day, while Steele was on vacation, Multi-Ad received a letter from Steele requesting copies of the company's policies and bylaws. When Steele returned from his vacation on September 4, Heathcoat and DeRossett were waiting for him at the plant's garage door. The two asked Steele if he still wanted to see the materials that he had requested in the letter. Steele said yes, and the two told him that he could pick up the materials in the office of Bruce Taylor, Multi-Ad's vice president of finance. Steele punched the time clock and, as he started to walk toward Taylor's office, noticed DeRossett and Heathcoat accompanying him. Steele told them that he did not need them to pick up the papers. The two replied that they were tagging along in case he had any questions. Steele told them that he could not possibly have any questions because he had not yet read the materials. Nevertheless, both managers followed Steele into Taylor's office. Ireland entered the office shortly thereafter. Steele first asked Taylor for the documents. Taylor replied that Steele already had been given the summary statement at the quarterly meeting. Steele responded that he was not asking for a summary but for complete documents. After again requesting the documents and receiving no response, Steele announced that he would no longer participate in the meeting and walked out. Heathcoat ordered him to remain or be fired. Steele ignored this command and walked back to the plant, pursued by Heathcoat and Ireland. Heathcoat repeated his order that Steele return to the office or be fired. Steele, again, refused.

Ireland then told Steele that "this is the third meeting you have walked out of, you are gone." Steele immediately demanded a termination letter.

Even though Ireland had made the decision to fire Steele, Heathcoat prepared the letter. The letter spells out the purported reasons for Steele's termination:

> He [Steele] said that he didn't come for a meeting, [sic] and then walked out of the room. I told him to get back in Bruce's [Taylor's] office to discuss this with us. He repeated himself again saying that he didn't want a meeting. Jerry Ireland then Fired [sic] him.
>
> Ted Steele has walked out of three meetings within a month because he didn't feel like hearing what was being said to him. He has said that he does not agree with corporate policies set for all the employees of Multi[-]Ad. He has interrupted the work flow of the Bindery Department by persuading it's [sic] employees that this is not a good place to work. Ted will never see eye to eye with Multi[-]Ad's policies and goals for it's [sic] employees and will not even conduct himself in a professional manner when talking to management about his concerns. Ted is terminated on 9-4-96 because of his unwillingness to abide to [sic] corporate policies.

Ireland testified that he fired Steele because he was totally disrespectful to management. Ireland also testified that Steele's exit from the meeting on September 4 was an act of insubordination, particularly after he ignored Heathcoat's order to return.

THE ADMINISTRATIVE PROCEEDINGS

On September 26, 1996, Graphic Communications Union, Local 68C, and Graphic Communications International Union, AFL–CIO, filed an unfair labor charge against Multi-Ad on behalf of its employees, including Steele. Soon thereafter, the Board's General Counsel issued a complaint and a notice of hearing. The complaint alleged that Multi-Ad violated the Act by (1) coercively interrogating Steele about his interest in forming a union during the August 16 meeting with Heathcoat and Ireland; (2) impliedly promising at the August 16 meeting to help Steele improve his employment situation without the need for representation; and (3) threatening to close the bindery department if its employees unionized. The complaint also alleges that Multi-Ad violated the Act by discharging Steele because it believed that he might contact a union to organize employees.

On May 29, 1997, the Administrative Law Judge (ALJ) conducted a hearing on the board's complaint. Based on the evidence presented at the hearing, the ALJ issued his decision on December 2, 1997, and found that Multi-Ad had committed the charged unfair labor practices. On August 25,

2000, the board issued a decision and order affirming the ALJ's conclusions.

On October 10, 2000, Multi-Ad filed this petition for review.

Substantial Evidence

Multi-Ad first challenges the Board's determination that Multi-Ad coercively interrogated Steele on August 16 in violation of the Act.

* * * * *

Substantial evidence supports the Board's conclusion that management coercively interrogated Steele on August 16. The closed-door meeting was conducted in a manager's office by Heathcoat and Ireland, two people who had authority to fire Steele. The two managers questioned Steele regarding why he would want to bring a union into the company. . . . Moreover, Ireland immediately thereafter asked Steele about his own career advancement and arranged an interview for a maintenance position, even though no such opening existed. The managers did not assure Steele that reprisals would not be taken against him for his answers, adding to the potentially coercive nature of the inquiry. Further, this meeting was conducted after company managers had expressed uneasiness over union activity. These circumstances are more than enough evidence to sustain the Board's findings.

Multi-Ad next challenges the Board's finding that it made an implied promise of benefits by asking Steele how he could help his own situation and by arranging the job interview. . . . Here, Ireland asked Steele why he wanted to form a union and then asked Steele how Steele could improve his own situation. Steele expressed an interest in a maintenance position, and Ireland arranged for an interview immediately, even though there were no such openings. The context in which this occurred is significant. Because the managers made this overture during a conversation about the need for a union, the Board reasonably could have concluded that the company was willing to confer a benefit to deter Steele from contacting a union. . . .

Next, Multi-Ad argues that substantial evidence does not support the Board's conclusion that Multi-Ad threatened to close the bindery department. Unlike an interrogation, which is coercive only if reasonable employees would perceive it as such, a threat of plant closure is per se a violation of Section 8(a)(1). In this case, three employees testified unequivocally that DeRossett said that the bindery department would be the "first to go" if they brought in a union, and this evidence is more than sufficient to establish a violation.

Finally, Multi-Ad disputes the Board's conclusion that Steele's discharge violates Sections 8(a)(1) and (3). An employer violates Sections 8(a)(1) or (3) of the Act by firing employees because of their union activities. To prove a violation, the Board must prove that antiunion animus was a substantial or motivating factor in the employer's decision to make the adverse employment decision. If the Board proves such a motivation by a preponderance of the evidence, the employer can avoid a finding of an unfair labor practice by showing that it would have taken the action regardless of the employee's union activities.

[S]ubstantial evidence supports a finding that the company harbored animus, including (1) the timing of Steele's firing, which coincided with his increased efforts to organize a union; (2) the coercive interrogation of Steele regarding his interest in forming a union; (3) management's questioning of other employees about their interest in forming a union; and (4) DeRossett's warning that the bindery department would close if employees unionized. Thus, the Board met its burden of establishing antiunion animus.

Multi-Ad claims as an affirmative defense that it fired Steele for leaving three meetings without permission. The Board concluded, however, that Multi-Ad's proffered reason was pretextual and that the company fired Steele because of his efforts to unionize. That conclusion is supported by substantial evidence, including (1) Multi-Ad's written explanation of termination stating a different reason—that he was discharged because he refused to abide by corporate policies; (2) the September 4 encounter was not a "meeting"—Steele entered the office to pick up materials to which he was legally entitled and twice denied access; and (3) no manager instructed Steele to remain at the previous two meetings, both of which occurred after shift hours. . . .

Order enforced.

Questions

1. *a.* List the four unfair labor practices identified by the court.
   b. What test did the court employ in determining whether the employer coercively interrogated Steele?
   c. What evidence supported the court's conclusion that Steele's firing was motivated by antiunion animus?
   d. Why did the court conclude that the employer's stated reason for dismissing Steele was pretextual?

2. Jose Ybarra was a labor consultant for Met West. A union election was pending at the company. An employee allegedly told Ybarra that his promised raise had not been delivered. Ybarra later allegedly told the employee that management had decided that wages could not be adjusted with an election pending. The union lost the election and filed suit claiming that Ybarra's statement was an

unfair labor practice. Decide. Explain. See *Met West Agri-business, Inc.,* 334 NLRB No. 14 (May 23, 2001).

3. During an election campaign, the general manager's office was used to interview employees in small groups of five or six. The employees had previously visited that office to discuss grievances and obtain loans. That office was the only space available for the conversations. The general manager's remarks were temperate and noncoercive. The union lost the election. Should that result be set aside for unlawful campaigning? Explain. See *NVF Company, Hartwell Division,* 210 NLRB 663 (1974).

Union Persuasion

Unions, like employers, are restricted in the type of preelection persuasion they employ. In cases involving promises of benefits made by the union, the NLRB has been more reluctant to set aside elections than it has when such promises have been made by management. The Board's reasoning is that employees realize that union preelection promises are merely expressions of a union platform, so to speak. Employees recognize that these are benefits for which the union intends to fight. Employers, on the other hand, really do hold the power to confer or withdraw benefits. Nonetheless, a union promise to employees to provide "the biggest party in the history of Texas" if the union won the next day's election was an unfair labor practice.[42]

> "The biggest party in the history of Texas."

Remedies for Election Misconduct

Unfair labor practices during a representation election can result in the imposition of penalties and remedies. If the union loses the election and the employer engaged in wrongful behavior, a new election or other remedies may be ordered.

Decertification

After a union has been certified or recognized, an employee or group of employees may continue to resist the union or may lose confidence in it. If so, they can file a decertification petition with the NLRB. The employees must be able to demonstrate at least 30 percent support for their petition. Once a decertification petition is properly filed with the board the usual election rules are followed to determine whether the union enjoys continuing majority support. If not, the union is decertified, and ordinarily at least one year must pass before a new representation election can be conducted. [For management advice about decertification, see **http://www.nrtw.org/d/decert.htm**]

Withdrawal of Recognition

An employer may unilaterally withdraw recognition of a union that has lost the support of a majority of its members. Objective evidence such as a petition signed by a majority of unit employer is required. The NLRB will review the petition and its specific language, however, to make sure that it shows employees' desire to decline union representation. For example, a petition entitled: "showing of interest for decertification" was found to be insufficient evidence, while a petition's statement of "wish for a vote to remove the Union" is more likely to show whether employees no longer desire the union's representation.[43]

Escape the Union?

If a union clearly is about to win a representation election or already has done so, thus establishing its right to collective bargaining, management sometimes continues to resist. One strategy is to declare bankruptcy. That tactic may be lawful but only after bargaining sincerely with the union and only after convincing the bankruptcy court that fairness requires modification or rejection of the collective bargaining agreement. Similarly, a company may simply choose to shut down its business rather than engage in collective bargaining. Going out of business is fully lawful unless the reason for doing so was to discourage union efforts at plants in other locations. Likewise,

> Companies sometimes employ the *runaway shop* strategy.

companies sometimes employ the *runaway shop* strategy in which the about-to-be-unionized plant is simply shut down and replaced by another in a location less responsive to union interests. If that move was made for the purpose of thwarting union interests, it is an unfair labor practice; but if the move reflected legitimate economic goals such as reduced wages or taxes, the move is probably lawful.

The Union as Exclusive Bargaining Agent

Once a union has been elected and certified as the representative of a bargaining unit, it becomes the exclusive agent for all of the employees within that bargaining unit, whether they voted for the union or not. The exclusivity of the union's authority has a number of implications, but one is particularly relevant in determining whether an employer has failed to demonstrate good faith at the bargaining table. Specifically, the employer must deal with the certified representative who acts on behalf of all employees in the bargaining unit. The employer commits an unfair labor practice if she or he attempts to deal directly with the employees or recognizes someone other than the workers' chosen representative. In both instances, the issue is fairly straightforward. The employer is undermining the position of the representative by ignoring him or her.

Part Four—Collective Bargaining

Section 8(a)(5) of the NLRA requires an employer to engage in *good-faith* collective bargaining with a representative of the employees, and Section 8(b)(3) imposes the same duty on labor organizations. Failure to bargain by either an employer or representative of the employees constitutes an unfair labor practice.

What is collective bargaining? What must one do to discharge the duty imposed? According to Section 8(d) of the NRLA,

> To bargain collectively is the performance of the mutual obligation of the employer and the representatives of the employees to meet at reasonable times and confer in good faith with respect to wages, hours, and other terms and conditions of employment . . . but such obligation does not compel either party to agree to a proposal or require the making of a concession.

Note what is *not* included. The duty to bargain in good faith does not require that the parties reach agreement. The NLRB and the courts recognize that collective bargaining, like any negotiation, is consensual. Thus the act governs only the process, not the result, of collective bargaining.

Bargaining in Good Faith

Good faith is a murky area with no definitive answers. Over the years, various factors (none of which is conclusive in and of itself) have been identified by the board and the courts as being suggestive of good-faith bargaining. Some of these include the following:[44]

1. The employer must make a serious attempt to adjust differences and to reach an acceptable common ground; that is, one must bargain with an open mind and a sincere desire to reach agreement.

2. Counterproposals must be offered when another party's proposal is rejected. This must involve the give and take of an auction system.[45]

3. A position regarding contract terms may not be constantly changed.[46]

Mandatory Bargaining Subjects   Although employers and labor representatives are free to discuss whatever lawful subjects they mutually choose, Section 8(d) of the NLRA clearly sets out some mandatory subjects over which the parties must bargain. These are wages, hours, and "other terms and conditions of employment." Although these topics for mandatory bargaining seem simple enough, questions still arise frequently. For example, suppose the union and employer bargain over wages and agree to institute merit increases for employees. Must the employer also bargain over which employees are entitled to receive these increases or who will make the decision at the time they are to be given? What about a decision to close a plant?

Generally, the board and the courts will balance three factors. First, they look at the effect of a particular decision on the workers—how direct is it and to what extent is the effect felt? Second, they consider the degree to which bargaining would constitute an intrusion into entrepreneurial interest or, from the opposite side, an intrusion into union affairs. Third, they examine the practice historically in the industry or the company itself.[47]

Permissive and Prohibited Bargaining Subjects   Those matters not directly related to wages, hours, and terms and conditions of employment and not falling within the category of prohibited subjects are considered permissive. Either party may raise permissive subjects during the bargaining process, but neither may pursue them to the point of a bargaining impasse. Refusal to bargain over a permissive subject does not constitute an NLRA violation, and permissive subjects must simply be dropped if the parties do not reach agreement.

Permissive subjects ordinarily would include such items as alteration of a defined bargaining unit, internal union affairs, and strike settlement agreements. Prohibited bargaining subjects are those that are illegal under the NLRA or other laws. In the case that follows the NLRB had to decide whether a union has a right to bargain over management's placement of hidden surveillance cameras in the workplace.

> Whether a union has a right to bargain over management's placement of hidden surveillance cameras in the workplace.

FACTS

Colgate–Palmolive's Jeffersonville, Indiana, plant employed approximately 750 workers. Colgate and the employees had a collective bargaining arrangement for over 20 years. In 1994 an employee discovered a surveillance camera in a restroom air vent. The union president later discussed the matter with Colgate's human resources officer, who indicated that the camera had been placed in the vent because of theft concerns and that the camera had been removed after employees objected to it. The Union filed a grievance over the matter, and the parties met for discussion where Colgate argued that it had the absolute right to install internal surveillance cameras. Later, the Union sent a letter to Colgate demanding to bargain over the subject of cameras within the plant. Colgate did not respond, and the Union filed an unfair labor practice charge. The case was heard by an administrative law judge. Evidence indicated that Colgate had installed 11 secret cameras over four years to address problems of theft and misconduct, including sleeping on the job. The cameras were placed in several offices, a fitness center, a restroom, and as a monitor for an overhead door that was not a proper exit from the building. The Union and some employees were aware of various "unhidden" cameras in the workplace and in some instances fortuitously discovered some of the hidden cameras.

The Administrative Law Judge (ALJ) concluded that the use of hidden surveillance cameras is a mandatory subject of bargaining and by failing to do so, Colgate–Palmolive violated the National Labor Relations Act. The ALJ's ruling was then appealed to the National Labor Relations Board. The *NLRB* decision follows.

CHAIRMAN GOULD AND MEMBERS FOX AND HIGGINS

In *Ford Motor Co. v. NLRB,* the Supreme Court described mandatory subjects of bargaining as such matters that are "plainly germane to the 'working environment'" and "not among those 'managerial decisions, which lie at the core of entrepreneurial control.'" As the judge found, the installation of surveillance cameras is both germane to the working environment, and outside the scope of managerial decisions lying at the core of entrepreneurial control.

As to the first factor—germane to the working environment—the installation of surveillance cameras is analogous to physical examinations, drug/alcohol testing requirements, and polygraph testing, all of which the Board has found to be mandatory subjects of bargaining. They are all investigatory tools or methods used by an employer to ascertain whether any of its employees has engaged in misconduct.

The Respondent [Colgate–Palmolive] acknowledges that employees caught involved in theft and/or other misconduct are subject to discipline, including discharge. Accordingly, the installation and use of surveillance cameras has the potential to affect the continued employment of employees whose actions are being monitored.

Further, as the judge finds, the use of surveillance cameras in the restroom and fitness center raises privacy concerns which add to the potential effect upon employees. We agree that these areas are part of the work environment and that the use of hidden cameras in these areas raises privacy concerns which impinged upon the employees' working conditions. The use of cameras in these or similar circumstances is unquestionably germane to the working environment.

With regard to the second criterion, we agree with the judge that the decision is not a managerial decision that lies at the core of entrepreneurial control.

* * * * *

The use of surveillance cameras is not entrepreneurial in character, is not fundamental to the basic direction of the enterprise, and impinges directly upon employment security. It is a change in the Respondent's methods used to reduce workplace theft or detect other suspected employee misconduct with serious implications for its employees' job security, which in no way touches on the discretionary "core of entrepreneurial control."

The Respondent urges that bargaining before a hidden camera is actually installed would defeat the very purpose of the camera. The very existence of secret cameras, however, is a term and condition of employment, and is thus a legitimate concern for the employees' bargaining representative. Thus, the placing of cameras, and the extent to which they will be secret or hidden, if at all, is a proper subject of negotiations between the Respondent and the union. Concededly, the Respondent also has a legitimate concern. However, bargaining about hidden cameras can embrace a host of matters other than mere location. And, even as to location, mutual accommodations can and should be negotiated. The vice in the instant case was the respondent's refusal to bargain.

* * * * *

Accordingly, we affirm the judge's finding that the union has the statutory right to engage in collective bargaining over the installation and continued use of surveillance cameras, including the circumstances under which the cameras will be activated, the general areas in which they may be placed, and how affected employees will be disciplined if improper conduct is observed.

ORDER

The National Labor Relations Board adopts the recommended Order of the administrative law judge as modified and set forth in full below and orders that the Respondent, its officers, agents, successors, and assigns, shall

1. Cease and desist from

   a. Failing and refusing to bargain with Local 15, International Chemical Workers Union, AFL–CIO with respect

to the installation and use of surveillance cameras and other mandatory subjects of bargaining.

2. Take the following affirmative action necessary to effectuate the policies of the Act.

   a. On request, bargain collectively with the Union as the exclusive bargaining representative of the Respondent's employees with respect to the installation and use of surveillance cameras and other mandatory subjects of bargaining.

   b. Within 14 days after the service by the Region, post at its facility in Jeffersonville, Indiana, copies of the attached notice:

**Notice to Employees
Posted by Order of the
National Labor Relations Board
An Agency of the United States Government**

The National Labor Relations Board has found that we violated the National Labor Relations Act and has ordered us to post and abide by this notice. Section 7 of the Act gives employees these rights.

To organize
To form, join, or assist any union
To bargain collectively through representatives of their own choice
To act together for other mutual aid or protection

To choose not to engage in any of these protected concerted activities.

We will not fail and refuse to bargain with Local 15, International Chemical Workers Union, AFL–CIO over the installation and use of surveillance cameras within our facility and other mandatory subjects of bargaining.

We will not in any like or related manner interfere with, restrain, or coerce you in the exercise of the rights guaranteed you by Section 7 of the Act.

We will, on request, bargain collectively with the Union as the exclusive bargaining representative of our employees with respect to the installation and use of surveillance cameras within our facility and other mandatory subjects of bargaining.

Colgate–Palmolive Company.

Questions

1. What test did the ALJ and the NLRB employ to determine whether the placement of hidden surveillance cameras was a mandatory subject of bargaining?

2. Why did the union win this case?

3. If you were managing a workplace where theft, sleeping on the job, and other misconduct were at a worrisome level, would you employ hidden, secret cameras to monitor restrooms, fitness areas, and the like? Explain.

4. At an Anheuser-Busch brewing facility, a supervisor discovered a table, four chairs, a number of foam mattress pads, and cardboard in a room where only authorized personnel were to be, but which was next to a break area. Suspecting illicit activities including illegal drug use, the company installed two surveillance cameras pointed at the entrance and stairs leading to the room. The cameras led to the company identifying 16 employees who engaged in misconduct. The company took down the cameras on June 30, 1998, and then informed the union of their existence. The company fired and otherwise disciplined the employees in question. Did Anheuser-Busch violate the NLRA? Explain. *Brewers & Maltsters v. NLRB,* 414 F.3d (D.C. Circuit 2005).

Administering the Agreement

Union–management bargaining does not end with the negotiation of a labor agreement. Rather, bargaining continues daily as the parties work out the disputes and confusions and conflicting interpretations that are bound to arise and that cannot be entirely provided for in the labor agreement. Often this process of contract maintenance takes the form of resolving *grievances,* as in the *Colgate–Palmolive* case. Those problems are addressed through the grievance procedure that is included in collective bargaining agreements. Often the grievance procedure involves a series of steps beginning with informal discussion mechanisms. Failing there, the dissatisfied employee typically files a written complaint (the grievance). Normally, grievances are presented to management by a union representative, often with the worker also present.

Arbitration

If, after negotiation, the parties cannot resolve their dispute, the collective bargaining agreement ordinarily provides for *final and binding arbitration.* Many court decisions have vigorously supported the arbitration process as the means of settling labor–management contract maintenance disputes and tend to find disputes arbitrable unless the labor agreement explicitly and unambiguously exempts the subject at issue from the arbitration process. Furthermore, but for rare exceptions, neither the company nor the union can turn to the courts to set aside arbitration decisions. However, in 2010 the U.S. Supreme Court held that a dispute between a union and employer over the ratification date of a collective bargaining agreement containing an arbitration clause should be resolved by a court rather than an arbitrator.[48]

Fair Representation

Because grievance processing is part of a union's bargaining responsibility, the union might breach its duty if it declined to represent an employer's grievance. An employee who feels wronged when a union does not process his or her grievance has the option of appealing to the NLRB or to the courts. Nevertheless, as the U.S. Supreme Court ruled in *14 Penn Plaza LLC v. Pyett,* a union may collectively bargain for an agreement providing that individual members' employment discrimination claims must be submitted to arbitration.[49]

Part Five—Labor Conflict

PRACTICING ETHICS   Union Loyalty, Employee Loyalty, or Money?

The Writers Guild of America, the union for show business writers, struck the television and movie industries in 2007 to 2008 pushing for a bigger share of revenues, particularly revenues from movies and television shows distributed over the new media, such as the Internet. The late-night talk shows featuring David Letterman, Jay Leno, Conan O'Brien, Jimmy Kimmel, and others respected the union for weeks by confining their telecasts to reruns. After six weeks, Letterman's production company, Worldwide Pants, was able to reach its own agreement with the striking union, thus allowing Letterman to return to the air with his full staff, including writers. The other talk shows decided to return to the air without their writers, although their network and studio owners had not reached agreements with the Writers' Guild. Many stars, however, declined to appear as talk show guests since they would have been forced to cross the striking writers' picket lines (explained below) to appear on the shows.

Leno and others argued that they needed to return to the air even without a strike settlement because they wanted to avoid laying off their many staff members who would have been without work if the shows stayed off the air. Indeed, some of those shows and hosts had paid their staffs while not working during the rerun period, but that financial burden reportedly could not be sustained. O'Brien, a strong union supporter, said he had to decide whether to "go back to work and keep my staff employed or stay dark and allow 80 people, many of whom have worked for me for 14 years, to lose their jobs."[50]

The 100-day strike was settled in February 2008.

Questions

1. Was it wrong of Leno, Kimmel, and the others to return to the air rather than continuing to honor the writers' strike? Explain.
2. Assume you are a Jimmy Kimmel fan, and you received tickets to the show during the strike. Would you support the writers by refusing to attend the Kimmel show? Explain.

Strikes

For many, the initial image of labor conflict is one of employees on strike, picketing a store or factory. Striking is, however, an extremely drastic measure under which employees must bear an immediate loss of wages and, in many instances, risk job loss. Similarly, employers bear the loss of a disruption to continued operations. As Table 14.1 shows, work stoppages have declined dramatically since World War II. However, the six-day sit-in of 240 workers at Chicago's Republic Windows and Doors in 2008—sparked by management's announcement that the plant would be closing in three days—became a national symbol of workers' frustration at the wave of layoffs around the United States. The sit-in succeeded in gaining bank loans for the company to meet the workers' demands for 60 days' severance pay and earned vacation time under the WARN Act (see Chapter 12).[51]

> The six day sit-in became a national symbol of workers' frustration.

We will examine two kinds of strikes:

1. *Unfair labor practice strikes* are those instituted by workers in response to the employer's commission of an unfair labor practice such as interfering with legitimate union activities or failure to bargain in good faith. These strikers can be temporarily, but not permanently, replaced.
2. *Economic strikes* are those used purely as economic weapons to persuade employers to provide more favorable benefits or better working conditions. All strikes not involving unfair labor practices fall into this category. With some exceptions, economic strikers cannot be fired, but they can be permanently replaced. In what has been labeled "the most significant change in collective bargaining to occur since the passage of the Wagner Act in 1934," employers are now increasingly willing to permanently replace

economic strikers.[52] Employers had enjoyed that right where necessary "in an effort to carry on the business" since a 1938 Supreme Court decision, but for practical reasons they had rarely exercised it.[53] Later decisions imposed some limitations on that right. For example, any striker who is permanently replaced is put on a preferential hiring list and will have priority to be selected to fill subsequent vacancies. However, President Reagan's 1981 dismissal of 11,300 striking air traffic controllers effectively crushed their union (PATCO) and caused private-sector employers to reassess their long-standing reluctance to use replacements during and after strikes.[54] Thus, the use or threat to use permanent replacements has become a powerful tool for employers facing economic strikes.

TABLE 14.1 **U.S. Work Stoppages Involving 1,000 or More Workers**

Year	Number	Workers	Days Idle	Percentage of Estimated Working Time
		(thousands)		
1948	245	1,435	26,127	.22
1958	332	1,587	17,900	.13
1968	392	1,855	35,367	.20
1978	219	1,006	23,774	.11
1988	40	387	4,381	.02
1998	34	387	5,116	.02
2005	22	100	1,736	.01
2010	11	45	302	<.005

Source: [http://www.bls.gov/news.release/wkstp.t01.htm].

The following case examines when employers can legitimately decline to reinstate strikers.

LEGAL BRIEFCASE

Diamond Walnut Growers, Inc. v. NLRB 113 F.3d 1259 (D.C. Cir. 1997); cert. den. 118 S.Ct.1299 (1998)

Circuit Judge Silberman

I

Diamond Walnut processes and packages walnuts for national and international distribution. . . . Diamond's employees have for years been represented by Cannery Workers, Processors, Warehousemen, and Helpers Local 601 of the International Brotherhood of Teamsters, AFL–CIO (the union). In September of 1991, following expiration of the most recent collective bargaining agreement between Diamond and the un-ion, nearly 500 of Diamond's permanent and seasonal employees went on strike. Diamond hired replacement workers to allow it to continue operations.

By all accounts, the strike was, and remains, a bitter affair. The strikers are alleged to have engaged in various acts of violence against the replacement workers. . . . In addition, as part of its effort to exert economic pressure on Diamond, the union undertook an international boycott of its product. The boycott included a well-publicized national bus tour during which union members distributed to the public leaflets which described Diamond's workforce as composed of "scabs" who packaged walnuts contaminated with "mold, dirt, oil, worms, and debris."

Approximately one year into the strike, the Board held a representation election. The union lost the election, but its objections prompted the Board to order a rerun to be held in October of 1993. Just over two weeks prior to the new election, a group of four striking employees, represented by a union official, approached Diamond with an unconditional offer to return to work. According to the letter presented to the company at that time by their representative, the employees were convinced that "a fair election [was] simply impossible." Nonetheless, the employees "fe[lt] that it [was] important that the replacement workers . . . have an opportunity to hear from Union sympathizers." Thus, the group of strikers was "available and willing to return to immediate active employment." The following day, the union notified Diamond that pursuant to the above-quoted letter, two additional strikers were willing to return to work.

It is undisputed that for three of the returning strikers, neither the permanent jobs they held before the strike, nor substantially equivalent ones, were available at the time of their return. Diamond placed these three in various seasonal jobs. Prior to the strike, Willa Miller was a quality control supervisor; she was placed in a seasonal packing position even though a seasonal inspection job was available. Alfonsina Munoz had been employed as a lift truck operator and, despite the availability of a seasonal forklift job, was given a seasonal job cracking and inspecting nuts in the growers' inspection department at the front end of the production process. Mohammed Kussair, formerly an air separator machine operator, was, like Munoz, placed in a seasonal cracking and inspecting position in the growers' inspection department. . . .

The rerun election took place as scheduled, and the union lost. Following that election, the General Counsel filed a complaint alleging that Diamond had violated the National Labor Relations Act by unlawfully discriminating against Miller, Munoz, and Kussair. The General Counsel alleged that because of their protected activity, Diamond declined to put them in certain available seasonal positions for which they were qualified and that were preferable to the positions in which they were actually placed. After a hearing, an administrative law judge recommended that the charges be dismissed. He found that Diamond had "discriminated" insofar as it had placed the employees at least in part because of their protected activity, but he did not think that discrimination "unlawful."

* * * * *

[The NLRB reversed saying] "although [Diamond] was under no legal obligation . . . to reinstate the strikers . . ., once it voluntarily decided to reinstate them, it was required to act in a nondiscriminatory fashion toward the strikers." Diamond had discriminated against Miller, Munoz, and Kussair, in the Board's view, by declining "to place them in the [seasonal] positions of quality control assistant, lift truck operator, and loader, respectively, because of their union status and/or because of certain protected union activity they engaged in while on strike.". . . The Board rejected the contention that the placements were warranted by the employer's concern that the replacement workers might instigate violence against the three and thus justified placement in well-supervised jobs, since "there [was] no evidence that Miller, Munoz, or Kussair were involved" in the strike-related violence allegedly causing Diamond's concern. The Board also dismissed the notion that the placements of Miller and Munoz were justified by their participation in the boycott and the circulation of disparaging leaflets: "[T]he strikers' conduct constituted protected . . . activity and there is no evidence indicating that such protection was lost because of threats made by Miller and Munoz to damage or sabotage [Diamond's] equipment or products." Since Diamond had failed to justify its discrimination, the Board found unfair labor practices.

* * * * *

[Diamond sought judicial review of the NLRB ruling.]

II

Diamond Walnut challenges the Board's determination that it lacked substantial business justification for refusing to place the three employees in the specific jobs they sought—quality control assistant, lift truck operator, and loader. It is undisputed that the *Fleetwood* framework governs this case. The General Counsel under *Fleetwood* must make out a *prima facie* case that the employer discriminated within the meaning of the Act, which means the employer's decision as to how to treat the three returning strikers was attributable to their protected activity. *Rose Printing* establishes that a struck employer faced with an unconditional offer to return to work is obliged to treat the returning employee like any other applicant for work (unless the employee's former job or its substantial equivalent is available, in which case the employee is preferred to any other applicant). But Miller and Munoz were not treated like any other applicant for work. Miller was qualified for a seasonal position in quality control that paid 32 cents per hour more than the packing job to which she was assigned. And Munoz was qualified to fill a forklift operating job, a position that paid between $2.75 and $5.00 per hour more than the walnut cracking and inspecting job she received. Diamond admits that it took into account Miller's and Munoz's protected activity in choosing to place them in jobs that were objectively less desirable than those for which they were qualified. Petitioner [Diamond], although it contended that the discrimination was comparatively slight, does not dispute that its action discriminated against Munoz and Miller within the meaning of the Act.

* * * * *

Under *Fleetwood*, after discrimination is shown, the burden shifts to the employer to establish that its treatment of the employees has a legitimate and substantial business justification. Petitioner declined to give Munoz the forklift driver job because of its concern that driving that piece of equipment throughout the plant would be unduly risky in two respects. First, because of the bad feeling between strikers and replacements, Munoz would be endangered if confronted by hostile replacement workers in an isolated area. Second, since Munoz had participated in the bus tour during which the union had accused the company of producing tainted walnuts, Munoz would be tempted to engage in sabotage by using the 11,000 pound vehicle to cause unspecified damage. As for Miller, who was also on the bus tour, the company declined to put her in the "sensitive position of quality control assistant" where "the final visual inspection of walnuts is made prior to leaving the plant." In that position, she would have "an easy opportunity to let defective nuts go by undetected . . . or to place a foreign object into the final product, thereby legitimizing the Union's claim of tainted walnuts."

* * * * *

A. Munoz

The Board rejected petitioner's proffered justifications for its placement of Munoz on the same ground as did the ALJ. As to Diamond's purported fear for her safety, no evidence had been produced that Munoz was thought to be responsible for any violence, so there was no reason to believe she would have been a special target. The Board said, "[T]here is no specific evidence that any replacements harbored hostility toward these three strikers, and, if such evidence did exist as [Diamond] claims, we fail to see how placing them in the positions to which they were assigned would lessen the perceived danger of retaliatory acts being committed against them." The Board discounted Diamond Walnut's contention that Munoz would be under greater protection if closely supervised, noting that petitioner had admitted that "Munoz freely roamed the plant unsupervised during her breaks."

* * * * *

As for the possibility that Munoz would engage in forklift sabotage, the Board was more terse, stating only that "the strikers' conduct [referring to the bus tour] constituted protected . . . activity," and there was no evidence indicating that such protection was lost because of threats made by Miller and Munoz. If Munoz had uttered specific threats of sabotage, however, she would have lost her protected status. . . . [T]he Board necessarily concluded that the possibility of Munoz engaging in future sabotage by misuse of her forklift was simply not a sufficient risk to constitute a substantial business justification for her treatment.

* * * * *

Similarly, the Board was reasonable in its determination that the risk of Munoz engaging in sabotage while riding around on her 11,000 pound forklift—the petitioner seems to most fear her crashing the forklift into machinery—is not a substantial business justification for her disadvantageous placement in another job. Strikes tend to be hard struggles, and although this one may have been more bitter than most, there is always a potential danger of returning strikers engaging in some form of sabotage. There is therefore undeniably some risk in employing returning strikers during a strike. But it could not be seriously argued that an employer cannot be forced to assume *any* risk of sabotage, because that would be equivalent to holding that an employer need not take back strikers during an ongoing strike at all. . . .

* * * * *

B. Miller

The Miller case is another matter. It will be recalled that petitioner declined to assign her to the post of quality control assistant, the job responsible for the final inspection of walnuts leaving the plant (she received a job paying 32 cents an hour less). The Board rejected the employer's justification, which was based on Miller's participation in the product boycott and bus tour leafleting, saying only "the strikers' conduct constituted protected . . . activity and there is no evidence indicating that such protection was lost because of threats made by Miller and Munoz to damage or sabotage . . . equipment or products." With respect to Miller, we think the Board's determination that petitioner's business justification is insubstantial is flatly unreasonable.

All strikes are a form of economic warfare, but when a union claims that a food product produced by a struck company is actually tainted it can be thought to be using the strike equivalent of a nuclear bomb; the unpleasant effects will long survive the battle. . . . The company's ability to sell the product . . . could well be destroyed.

* * * * *

The Board's counsel argues that it is unfair to assume that an employee would behave in a disloyal and improper fashion. It is unnecessary, however, for us to make that assumption to decide the Board was unreasonable. The Board accepted petitioner's contention that Miller would have been placed "in the sensitive position . . . where final visual inspection of walnuts is made prior to leaving the plant." Miller would therefore have been put in a rather acute and unusual conflict of interest in which her job for her employer could be thought to have as a function the rebutting of her union's claim. A similar conflict would be raised if she wished a bargaining unit job in the company's public relations department. This conflict makes all too likely the possibility that Miller would be *at least* inattentive to her product quality duties. . . . To make matters worse, any "mistake" by Miller on the product quality control line would not be easily attributable to her unless petitioner paid someone to stand all day looking over Miller's shoulder. . . . If Munoz ran her forklift into valuable machinery, she would run a risk of being discovered and would therefore be deterred. But Miller, as a quality control assistant, could simply avert her eye and cause the damage with apparently little risk of discovery. . . .

In short, she would have had a special motive, a unique opportunity, and little risk of detection to cause severe harm. Both the risk Diamond faced in its placement of Miller was qualitatively different than a normal risk of sabotage, and the deterrence to Miller's possible misbehavior was peculiarly inadequate.

* * * * *

[W]e are obliged to ask in the last analysis whether the Board's decision, as to whether the employer's action was substantially justified by business reasons, falls within the broad stretch of reasonableness. In this case, at least with respect to one part of the Board's decision, we conclude the Board exceeded the reasonableness limits.

So ordered.

AFTERWORD

After nearly 14 years of bitter struggle, the Diamond Walnut strike was settled in March 2005. The settlement allowed strikers to return to work with full seniority and benefits, although many of them had already returned to Diamond Walnut or had moved to other jobs. [For a time line of the Diamond Walnut strike, see **http://www.teamster.org/divisions/foodprocessing/diamondwalnut/dwtimeline.htm**]

Questions

1. Set out the two-part test the court employed to determine whether Diamond Walnut violated the National Labor Relations Act by discriminating against its employees because of their participation in protected union activities.

2. Explain why the court found that Munoz had been wronged by Diamond but Miller had not.

3. *a.* How would you vote on federal legislation banning the practice of permanently replacing economic strikers? Explain.
   b. Is there any reason to distinguish between economic strikers and unfair labor practice strikers? Any reason not to do so? Explain.

4. A pilots' union, Airline Professionals Association, had a collective bargaining agreement (CBA) with freight carrier Airborne Express (ABX). The union and ABX had a dispute about time-off provisions in the CBA. The union applied pressure to ABX by asking all pilots not to bid on open flying time not covered in the regular monthly schedule. ABX says it lost jobs due to the lack of pilots and filed a complaint saying the union was engaging in an illegal strike. A district court agreed with ABX, and the union appealed. Decide the case. Explain. See *ABX Air, Inc. v. Airline Professionals Assn.,* 266 F.3d 392 (2001); cert. den. 122 S.Ct. 1459 (2002).

Picketing and Boycotts

Primary Picketing In addition to striking, unions often picket or boycott to publicize their concerns and pressure employers during the negotiating process. Picketing is the familiar process of union members gathering and sometimes marching, placards in hand, at a place of business. Peaceful, informational picketing for a lawful purpose is protected by the NLRA. Some kinds of picketing, however, are forbidden, and all picketing can be regulated by the government to ensure public safety. Primary picketing is expressed directly to the employer with whom the picketers have a dispute. Primary picketing enjoys broad constitutional and statutory protection, but it may be unlawful if violent or coercive.

Secondary Picketing/Boycotts Secondary picketing or boycotting is directed to a business other than the primary employer, and ordinarily it is unlawful. That is, unions are engaging in an unfair labor practice if they threaten or coerce a third party with whom they are not engaged in a dispute in order to cause that third party to put pressure on the firm that is the real target of the union's concern. Consider, however, the mock funeral case summarized below.

Mock Funeral

The Sheet Metal Workers' union staged a mock funeral outside a Florida hospital in 2004. One person dressed in a "Grim Reaper" costume carrying a plastic sickle, and four "pall-bearers" carried a prop coffin and handed out leaflets. Various somber tunes played in the background on a portable audio system. The leaflets detailed several malpractice lawsuits against the hospital with the implication that the malpractice was linked to the hospital's decision to contract with nonunion labor. The demonstration was designed to pressure the hospital, a neutral entity, to stop doing business with the picketers' actual target, the non-union contractors. The "funeral" was conducted about 100 feet from the entrance and was separated from it by a street, a strip of grass, a hedge, and a parking lot. The hospital filed an unfair labor practice charge against the union claiming the funeral constituted illegal secondary picketing in violation of the NLRA. The NLRB issued an order commanding the union to cease and desist. That decision was reviewed by the federal District of Columbia Court of Appeals.

Questions

1. What constitutional law defense would you offer on behalf of the Sheet Metal Workers' union?

2. Decide the case. Explain.

Source: Sheet Metal Workers' International Association, Local 15, AFL-CIO v. National Labor Relations Board, 2007 U.S. App. LEXIS 14361.

Lockouts

Sometimes management takes the initiative in labor disputes by locking its doors to some or all of its employees. Both the NLRB and the courts allow lockouts as defensive acts to protect businesses against sudden strikes and to prevent sabotage or violence. Some court decisions have also expanded lawful lockouts to include those of an offensive nature designed to improve management's bargaining position. Lockouts, however, are clearly not lawful if designed to interfere with bargaining rights and other legitimate union activity.

> Sports fans have learned some labor law.

Sports fans have learned some labor law in recent years. National Hockey League owners locked out players and eventually canceled the entire 2004 to 2005 season. Major league baseball has survived several lockouts and player strikes in the last four decades. At this writing in 2011, the National Basketball Association (NBA) has locked out its players pending a new collective bargaining agreement. Professional football players in 2011 challenged a National Football League owners' lockout, but a 10-year collective bargaining agreement was reached that preserved the 2011 to 2012 season and thereafter and included an interesting provision providing for human growth hormone blood testing of players.[55] (Critics immediately questioned the likely effectiveness of that new testing program.)

Question

George A. Hormel & Co. and the United Food and Commercial Workers Union settled a long labor dispute. Thereafter, an unhappy, long-term employee, Robert Langemeier, drove his car in a parade and attended a rally, both of which were designed to encourage a nationwide boycott of Hormel Products. The employee did nothing to signal his feelings beyond his presence at the two events.

Employees may lawfully be dismissed for disloyalty to their employer. Supporting a boycott of an employer's products ordinarily constitutes disloyalty except where (1) the boycott is related to an ongoing labor dispute and (2) the support does not amount to disparagement of the employer's product.

Was this Hormel employee, Langemeier, engaged in protected activity such that his dismissal was unlawful? Explain. See *George A. Hormel and Company v. National Labor Relations Board*, 962 F.2d 1061 (D.C. Cir. 1992).

Part Six—Employees' Rights within or Against the Union

The Union's Duty of Fair Representation

As you have seen in previous sections of this chapter, the union is given statutory authority to be the exclusive bargaining agent for the employees in the designated bargaining unit. This means that even if an individual employee in the bargaining unit does not agree with union policies or is not a member of the union, he or she cannot bargain individually with the employer. Such an employee is bound by the terms of the collective bargaining agreement, and the union has a duty to fairly represent that employee and all members of the bargaining unit, whether or not they become members of the union.

The Bill of Rights of Labor Organization Members

The Bill of Rights for members of labor organizations is contained in Title 1, Section 101 of the Labor–Management Reporting and Disclosure Act (LMRDA or Landrum–Griffin Act). The Bill of Rights was designed to ensure equal voting rights, the right to sue the union, and the rights of free speech and assembly. These rights of union members are tempered by the union's right to enact and enforce "reasonable rules governing the responsibilities of its members."[56]

Union Security Agreements and Right-to-Work Laws

To maintain their membership, unions typically seek a collective bargaining clause requiring all employees to become union members after they have been employed for some period—generally 30 days (*union shop agreements*)—or, at the least, requiring them to pay union dues and fees (*agency shop agreements*). These union security arrangements are lawful under the NLRA.

Under the 1988 Supreme Court decision in *Communications Workers of America v. Beck*[57] nonunion employees can be compelled to pay union dues and fees only for core collective bargaining activities. Thus nonunion employees' agency shop dues and fees must be reduced by an amount equal to that applied to such noncore purposes as lobbying and political campaigning. In 2009, the Court also held that a local union may charge nonmembers for collective-bargaining litigation expenses in lawsuits brought by the national union, with the expectation that the local union would enjoy the same support from other units if they were to bring a similar lawsuit.[58]

Right to Work   Twenty-two states, primarily in the South and West, have enacted right-to-work laws that prohibit union security arrangements in collective bargaining agreements. In these states, nonmembers do not pay dues or fees, but as members of the bargaining unit, they must be represented by the union. Unions regard those employees as *free riders,* but right-to-work supporters see the matter as one of personal freedom. [For questions and answers on right-to-work laws, see **http://www.nrtw.org/a/a_prime.htm**]

Closed Shop   At one time, powerful unions insisted on *closed-shop* arrangements wherein employers could hire only individuals who already belonged to unions, but those arrangements are now forbidden by the NLRA.

The Labor War Continues

Airplane manufacturer Boeing announced in 2009 its intention to open a second assembly line in a nonunion South Carolina facility to supplement its production of the company's wide-body "787 Dreamliner" at its union-organized Seattle-area plants. The expansion was not viewed by the company as a dilution of work in Washington, since it has been adding jobs in that state. Union officials, however, saw the decision as a transfer of jobs. Boeing's plan would create about 1,000 new jobs in South Carolina, a right-to-work state. Boeing expects to produce seven Dreamliners per month in Washington and three in South Carolina.

In March 2010, the International Association of Machinists and Aerospace Workers filed unfair labor practice charges against Boeing claiming that the decision to open the second production line in South Carolina was made in retaliation for its workers' past strikes in the state of Washington and to discourage them from striking in the future. If the union claims are accurate, that strategy would violate the National Labor Relations Act. In internal documents and statements to media, Boeing officials had cited strike activity and the threat of future such activity as motivations for the South Carolina decision. One Boeing executive, for example, said "we cannot afford to have a work stoppage, you know, every three years."

In April 2011, the NLRB issued a complaint against Boeing alleging a violation of federal labor law for coercing employees and, in effect, discriminating against the union by being motivated to place the new work in a right-to-work state in order to avoid the union presence. Section 8(a) of the NLRA provides that it is an unfair labor practice to "interfere with, restrain, or coerce employees in the exercise of the rights guaranteed" under the act. Similarly, employers may not encourage or discourage union membership "by discrimination in regard to hire or tenure of employment or any term or condition of employment." The NLRB complaint seeks a court order requiring Boeing to operate the second production line in Washington. At this writing in mid-2011, the matter is unresolved.

[For a Fox News discussion of the NLRB—Boeing conflict, see **http://www.youtube.com/watch?v=j_JvA6yKB_M**]

Questions

1. *a.* In your judgment, should the NLRB compel Boeing to keep the second production line in Washington state? Explain.

   b. In your judgment, should the NLRB have the authority to countermand Boeing's business decision?

2. In your judgment, would the nation be healthier, economically and otherwise, if all states enacted right-to-work laws? Explain.

Sources: "Boeing Complaint Fact Sheet," National Labor Relations Board [**http://www.nlrb.gov**]; and Hans A. von Spakovsky and James Sherk, "National Labor Relations Board Overreach against Boeing Imperils Jobs and Investment," *Legal Memorandum* 66, May 11, 2011.

Part Seven—Other Unions

Public-Sector Unions

The public sector is a growth area for union membership. In 2010, 7.6 million public sector employees belonged to a union, compared with 7.1 million union workers in the private sector.[59] The union membership rate for public sector workers is more than five times higher than the rate for private sector workers.[60] In 2011, the states of Wisconsin and Ohio approved legislation dramatically limiting public sector workers' collective bargaining rights (both prohibit bargaining over health coverage and pensions), and many other states are considering similar measures. The cutbacks in union authority are defended as necessary to curb workers' wages and benefits, but critics view the movement as a general assault on unions. As noted at the outset of the chapter, polls have shown diminished support for labor unions generally, but nearly two out of three Americans oppose weakening public sector unions.[61]

Legal regulation of public sector labor–management relations begins with state law. Although the specific provisions of those laws vary, many NLRA concepts have been adopted. Some fundamental policies and doctrines are quite different, however. A particular distinction lies in the ability of public-sector employees to strike.

Some states prohibit those strikes and others permit them only under restricted conditions. In either case, the rationale for treating public employees differently than private-sector employees is the role of public employees as servants of the voters. Public servants arguably have a higher duty than private employees. In addition, certain public employees, including police officers and firefighters, work in positions that clearly involve public safety, and to permit them to strike might endanger the citizenry.

Internet Exercise	Go to National Labor Relations Board's frequently asked questions [**http://www.nlrb. gov/faq/nlrb**].

1. Explain what an employee at a unionized workplace who is "unhappy" with the union can do.
2. Explain how to file an unfair labor practice (ULP) claim.

Chapter Questions	

1. *a.* In your opinion, what are the average blue-collar worker's biggest sources of job dissatisfaction? Can they be eliminated through collective bargaining? Explain.
   b. In your opinion, what are the average white-collar worker's biggest sources of job dissatisfaction? What means do such workers have for eliminating those sources of dissatisfaction? Explain.

2. *a.* Imagine what the world will be like 50 years from now. In what ways do you picture the work life of the average American to have changed? Explain.
   b. Imagine the ideal work world. How close does that picture come to the one you conjured up in response to the previous question? What types, if any, of labor or other legislation would bring society closer to that ideal? Explain.

3. You are the human resources manager for a manufacturing firm that is presently the subject of an organizing campaign by a union that has filed an election petition with the NLRB just 30 days ago. Your plant manager has come to you and said that she wishes to discharge one of her employees. She further explains that the employee in question has worked for the company for three years and throughout that time has had a terrible attendance record. She adds that up to this point the employee has not received any discipline for his attendance. Upon inquiry, the plant manager tells you that the employee has been seen on the plant floor wearing a button that says "Union Yes!" In addition, the plant manager tells you that she knows that the employee is an outspoken union activist. What would you advise the plant manager to do? Why?

4. ACE/CO, a Milwaukee automobile parts manufacturer, was accused of a series of unfair labor practices springing from company conduct both before and after a disputed union representation election. Among the charges were the following:
   - ACE/CO declined to grant its usual across-the-board wage increases and told employees that the union was responsible for the failure to grant a raise.
   - ACE/CO distributed a memorandum asking employees to inform supervisors whenever they felt pressured to sign a union authorization card. One employee testified that union representatives had visited his home 13 times and that he did feel "pressured" to support the union.
   - ACE/CO included in its employee handbook a statement indicating the company's "intention to do everything possible to maintain our company's union-free status for the benefit of both our employees and [the company]."

a. Why might ACE/CO legitimately decline to offer a wage increase during an organizing campaign?

b. Do any of these company behaviors constitute unfair labor practices? See *NLRB v. Aluminum Casting & Engineering Co.,* 230 F.3d 286 (7th Cir. 2000).

5. When assistant manager Diane Gorrell was fired from a Bob Evans restaurant in East Peoria, Illinois, most of the employees walked off the job in protest. They stood outside the restaurant for a time and discouraged customers from entering. The restaurant was left in some disarray and problems persisted for a number of days, clearly harming business. Later all but one of the employees asked to return to their jobs, but were refused. The employees filed an unfair labor practices charge with the NLRB.

a. Justify, as a matter of law, management's decision not to allow the employees to return to work.

b. Explain the employees' unfair labor practices charge.

c. Decide the case. Explain. See Bob Evans Farms, Inc. v. NLRB, 163 F.3d 1012 (7th Cir. 1998).

6. Seawin, an Ohio fittings manufacturer, was forced to lay off 17 employees. The company's net income had declined by 88 percent, it had lost some major customers, and it had excess inventory. At the time of the layoffs, a company vice president said that he "hoped that business . . . would turn around soon." Asked when they would be called back, employees remembered the vice president saying "probably" around two weeks to a month. Others, however, indicated that the layoffs were intended to be permanent, and the company made significant equipment and computer improvements to enhance efficiency. Soon thereafter the NLRB held a representation election at Seawin that resulted in a 31–21 vote in favor of a union. Eleven of the laid-off workers had been allowed to vote in the election. Seawin challenged the election results saying the laid-off employees should not have been allowed to vote. Was Seawin correct? Explain. See *NLRB v. Seawin, Inc.,* 248 F.3d 551 (6th Cir. 2001).

7. Midwestern Personnel Services provided truck drivers to employers in Indiana, Kentucky, and other locations. Midwestern wanted the drivers to join a union so they would be allowed to enter a unionized workplace, AK Steel, where they were to deliver cement. Midwestern management favored Teamsters Local 836 in Middletown, Ohio, for their drivers, but a majority of the drivers voted to join Teamsters Local 215 in Evansville, Indiana. Midwestern refused to recognize Local 215; management and the drivers could not reach agreement about pension rights and contract length; and the drivers went on strike. The drivers later made an unconditional offer to return to work, but Midwestern would not allow them to return because, in its view, the drivers were economic strikers. The NLRB concluded that the drivers were motivated in part by unfair labor practices, and thus should be reinstated to their jobs. Were the drivers entitled to reinstatement? Explain. See *NLRB v. Midwestern Personnel Services,* 322 F.3d 969 (7th Cir. 2003).

8. Local 582 engaged in an economic strike against Broadview Dairy of Spokane, Washington. Local 582 tried to distribute handbills at several Albertson's groceries in the Spokane area. The handbills urged customers to refrain from buying Broadview products, which Albertson's sold. Albertson's formal policy forbade all solicitations,

but some groups, such as Boy Scouts and area schools, were allowed on company property to make solicitations. Albertson's ordered the union members off its property. Later, Albertson's ordered union organizers off its property where they were trying to encourage Albertson's employees to join their union. Local 582 filed an unfair labor practices charge against Albertson's. Does Albertson's have the right to exclude from its property nonemployee union representatives who engage in either nonorganizing or organizing activities? Explain. See *Albertson's Inc. v. National Labor Relations Board*, 301 F.3d 441 (6th Cir. 2002).

9. The Sacred Heart Medical Center, an acute-care hospital, issued a memorandum prohibiting nurses' union members from wearing buttons which read "RNs Demand Safe Staffing" in any areas "on our campus where they may encounter patients or family members." Did the hospital's ban on these buttons constitute an unfair labor practice under the NLRA? Explain. See *Washington State Nurses Ass'n v. NLRB*, 526 F.3d 577 (9th Cir. 2008).

10. An employer, Ashley Furniture of Arcadia, Wisconsin, instructed its employees not to discuss such workplace issues as disciplinary infractions, the expiration of an employee's work permit, or the receipt of a "no-match" letter from the Social Security Administration. Did the employer violate the NLRA? Explain. See *Ashley Furniture Industries*, 353 NLRB 071 (2008).

11. Dick's Sporting Goods used a nonunion contractor to prepare for its opening in a Watertown, New York, shopping mall. The local carpenters' union requested permission of the shopping mall's operator to distribute literature in the mall protesting the use of a nonunion contractor. While the mall had previously allowed such charitable organizations as the American Cancer Society and the Boy Scouts to distribute materials on its property, it rejected the union's request. Did the shopping mall violate the NLRA? Explain. See *Salmon Run Shopping Center v. NLRB*, 534 F.3d 108 (2nd Cir. 2008).

12. Jerry Kirby was discharged from his job at Ford Motor Company, allegedly because of "being under the influence of alcohol, absenteeism, and threatening management." The United Auto Workers union (UAW) immediately filed a grievance on Kirby's behalf. Kirby lost through the first three steps of the grievance process, and the UAW declined to appeal to arbitration on Kirby's behalf. The UAW said that Kirby had no right to appeal because he had allowed his union membership to lapse. Kirby then filed an unfair labor practice charge against the union. Decide. Explain. See *International Union v. NLRB*, 168 F.3d 509 (D.C. Cir. 1999).

13. *a.* Can an employer lawfully discharge a group of employees who walk out in protest of working conditions?
    b. Would it matter if the collective bargaining agreement contains a no-strike clause? Explain.

14. What steps can an employer lawfully take to provide the labor necessary to keep a plant operative during a strike?

15. During a strike resulting from failure to reach a collective bargaining agreement, Pan American Grain laid off 15 striking workers, citing changing labor needs "due to economic reasons and as a result of a substantial decrease in production and sales."

Where labor costs are one of the multiple motives for a layoff, does the employer have a duty to bargain with the union over the decision to impose a layoff? Explain. See *Pan American Grain v. NLRB,* 558 F.3d 22 (1st Cir. 2009).

16. Should a union be able to access Department of Motor Vehicles records to find employees' residential addresses so union organizers can visit employees at home for organizing purposes? Explain. See *Pichler v. UNITE,* 585 F.3d 741 (3rd Cir. 2009).

Notes

1. Steven Greenhouse, "The New Face of Solidarity," *The New York Times,* June 16, 2006 [**http://www.nytimes.com**].

2. "Union Members Summary," Bureau of Labor Statistics *News,* January 21, 2011 [**http://www.bls.gov/news.release/union2.nr0.htm**].

3. Ben Zipperer, "Unions Lost Members in 2009, as Overall Employment Fell," Center for Economic and Policy Research, January 22, 2010 [**http://www.cepr.net/index.php/data-bytes/union-membership-bytes/2010**].

4. "Union Members Summary," Bureau of Labor Statistics *News,* January 21, 2011 [**http://www.bls.gov/news.release/union2.nr0.htm**].

5. Ibid.

6. Joseph Szczesny, "Big Three-UAW Contracts Even the Playing Field—Eventually," *Auto Observer,* November 18, 2007 [**http://www.autoobserver.com/2007/11/big-three-uaw-c.html**].

7. Pew Research Center, "Favorability Ratings of Labor Unions Fall Sharply," February 23, 2010 [**http://pewresearch.org/pubs/1505/labor-unions-support-falls-public-now-evenly-split-on-purpose-power**].

8. Michael Cooper and Megan Thee-Brenan, "Majority in Poll Back Employees in Public Sector Unions," *The New York Times,* February 28, 2011 [**http://www.nytimes.com/**].

9. Harley Shaiken, "Stronger Unions Mean a Strong Middle Class," *Los Angeles Times,* February 17, 2007 [**http://www.latimes.com/news/opinion/la-oe-shaiken17feb17,0,312807.story?track= tottext**].

10. Timothy W. Martin, "Chicago Approves Wal-Mart Store," *Wall Street Journal,* July 1, 2010, p. B3.

11. Ibid.

12. Isaac A. Hourwich, *Immigration and Labor* (New York: Arno Press, 1969), pp. 125–45.

13. John J. Flagler, *The Labor Movement in the United States* (Minneapolis: Lerner Publications, 1972), pp. 26–28.

14. Alan Glassman, Naomi Berger Davidson, and Thomas Cummings, *Labor Relations: Reports from the Firing Line* (New York: Business Publications, Inc., 1988), pp. 5–6.

15. Flagler, *Labor Movement,* pp. 26–28.

16. Eli Ginzberg and Hyman Berman, *The American Worker in the Twentieth Century: A History Through Autobiographies* (New York: Free Press, 1963), pp. 193–95, in *I Am a Woman Worker,* ed. Andria Taylor Hourwich and Gladys L. Palmer, Affiliated Schools for Workers, 1936, pp. 17 ff.

17. Flagler, *Labor Movement,* pp. 33 and 36, quoting Frederick Lewis Allen, *The Big Change: America Transforms Itself, 1900–1950* (New York: Harper, 1952).

18. Flagler, *Labor Movement,* p. 47.

19. J. David Greenstone, *Labor in American Politics* (New York: Alfred A. Knopf, 1969), p. 21.

20. Archibald Cox, with Derek Bok and Robert A. Gorman, *Cases and Materials on Labor Law,* 8th ed. (Mineola, NY: Foundation Press, 1977), pp. 7–8.

21. Greenstone, *Labor in American Politics,* p. 22.

22. Greenstone, *Labor in American Politics,* p. 23.

23. Patrick Hardin, *The Developing Labor Law* (Washington, DC: Bureau of National Affairs, 1992), pp. 31–32.

24. Hardin, *The Developing Labor Law,* p. 94.

25. Hardin, *The Developing Labor Law,* pp. 1, 108.

26. *Steele v. Louisville and Nashville Railroad,* 323 U.S. 192 (1944).

27. *Vaca v. Sipes,* 386 U.S. 171 (1967); *Miranda Fuel Co.,* 140 NLRB 181 (1962).

28. The National Labor Relations Act is found in Title 29 U.S.C. Section 151 et seq.

29. National Labor Relations Board, "Guideline Memorandum Concerning Unfair Labor Practice Charges Involving Political Advocacy," July 22, 2008 [**http://www.nlrb.gov/**].

30. Cox, *Labor Law,* pp. 113–22.

31. Cox, *Labor Law,* pp. 99–101.

32. *New Process Steel v. NLRB,* 130 S.Ct. 2635 (2010).

33. 351 NLRB No. 28 (2007).

34. *Oakwood Healthcare, Inc.,* 348 NLRB No. 37 (2006).

35. Molly Selvin, "U.S. Ruling Could Eliminate Union Eligibility for Millions," *Los Angeles Times,* October 4, 2006 [**http://www.latimes.com/business/la-fi-labor4oct04,0,5076104.story? track=tottext**].

36. *FedEx Home Delivery v. NLRB,* 563 F.3d 492 (D.C. Cir. 2009).

37. *Lechmere, Inc. v. NLRB,* 502 U.S. 527 (1992).

38. *NLRB v. Town & Country Electric, Inc.,* 516 U.S. 85 (1998).

39. *Toering Electric Company,* 351 NLRB No. 18 (2007).

40. See *Sewell Mfg. Co.,* 138 NLRB 66 (1962), which states that the board's goal is to conduct elections "in a laboratory under conditions as nearly ideal as possible to determine the uninhibited desires of employees" and "to provide an atmosphere conducive to the sober and informed exercise of the franchise free from . . . elements which prevent or impede reasonable choice."

41. *NLRB v. Exchange Parts Co.,* 375 U.S. 405 (1964).

42. *Trencor, Inc. v. National Labor Relations Board,* 110 F.3d 268 (5th Cir. 1997).

43. Ronald Meisburg, NLRB Office of the General Counsel, Memorandum GC 09-04, Guideline Memorandum Concerning Withdrawal of Recognition Based on Loss of Majority Support, November 26, 2008, p. 4 citing *Highland Regional Medical Center,* 347 NLRB 1404, 1406 (2006), and *Wurtland Nursing,* 351 NLRB No. 50, slip op. at 2.

44. Benjamin J. Taylor and Fred Whitney, *Labor Relations Law,* 4th ed. (Englewood Cliffs, NJ: Prentice Hall, 1983), p. 406.

45. *Majure Transport Co. v. NLRB,* 198 F.2d 735 (5th Cir. 1952).

46. *NLRB v. Norfolk Shipbuilding & Drydock Corp.,* 172 F.2d 813 (4th Cir. 1949).

47. See *First National Maintenance Corporation v. NLRB,* 101 S.Ct. 2573 (1981).

48. *Granite Rock v. Int'l Brotherhood of Teamsters,* 130 S.Ct. 2847 (2010).

49. *14 Penn Plaza LLC. v. Pyett,* 129 S.Ct. 1456 (2009).

50. Matea Gold, Maria Elena Fernandez, and Richard Verrier, "Jay Leno, Conan O'Brien to Return to the Air Jan. 2," *Los Angeles Times,* December 18, 2007 [**http://www.latimes.com/ news/la-fi-strike18dec18,0,3643358.story?coll=la-tot-topstories&track=ntothtml**].

51. Michael Luo and Karen Ann Cullotta, "Even Workers Surprised by Success of Factory Sit-in," *The New York Times,* December 13, 2008 [**http://www.nytimes.com**].

52. Littler, Mendelson Fastiff and Tichy, *The 1990 Employer* (San Francisco: Littler Mendelson, Fastiff and Tichy, P.C., 1990), p. V6.

53. *NLRB v. Mackay Radio & Tel. Co.,* 304 U.S. 333 (1938).

54. Littler, et al., *The 1990 Employer,* p. V6.

55. ESPN.com News Service, "NFL Players Ratify New CBA," August 5, 2011 [**http://espn.go.com**].

56. *United Steelworkers of America v. Sadlowski,* 457 U.S. 102 (1982).

57. 487 U.S. 735 (1988).

58. *Locke v. Karass,* 555 U.S. 207 (2009).

59. "Union Members Summary," Bureau of Labor Statistics *News,* January 21, 2011. [**http://www.bls.gov/news.release/union2.nr0.htm**].

60. Ibid.

61. Michael Cooper and Megan Thee-Brenan, "Majority in Poll Back Employees," *The New York Times,* February 28, 2011 [**http://www.nytimes.com**].

CHAPTER FIFTEEN

Consumer Protection

After completing this chapter, students will be able to:

1. Identify some consumer protections offered under common law.

2. Describe "lemon laws" as an example of state consumer regulation.

3. Explain the purpose, roles, and power of the federal consumer protection agencies including the Consumer Financial Protection Bureau (CFPB), the Federal Trade Commission (FTC), the Consumer Product Safety Commission (CPSC), and the Food and Drug Administration (FDA).

4. Identify the circumstances in which the Truth in Lending Act (TILA) applies to a consumer loan.

5. Identify protections offered under the Fair Credit Reporting Act (FCRA).

6. Describe the protections offered by the Fair Credit Billing Act (FCBA).

7. Recognize the purpose of the Electronic Fund Transfer Act (EFTA).

8. Explain the purpose of the Equal Credit Opportunity Act (ECOA).

9. Identify debt collection practices forbidden by the Fair Debt Collection Practices Act (FDCPA).

10. Explain the purpose and effect of filing a Chapter 7 liquidation or "straight" bankruptcy.

Introduction

Doubtless the government and lawsuits should not always protect us from our own foolishness, but costly consumer fraud and other forms of consumer abuse (invasion of privacy, dangerous products, identity theft, false advertising, and so on) are not unusual in our consumption-driven lives. Historically we relied on the market to address those problems; but in recent decades legislatures, courts, and administrative agencies have developed laws and rulings to protect us where the market arguably has failed. This chapter surveys some of those legal interventions. For example, at this writing in 2011, the federal government is considering sterner rules to guide the giant for-profit college industry.

For-profit schools like the University of Phoenix and Kaplan enroll about 1.8 million students, but the government is concerned that deceptive marketing practices, fraudulent claims about job placement, and huge student loan burdens are denying many of those students the better future they are seeking.

Chelsi Miller was managing a burger joint when she saw an ad for Everest University promising a better life. The single mother in a small town near Salt Lake City wanted an associate's degree as a first step toward medical school. She said she chose Everest, a for-profit college, after a recruiter guaranteed that she could apply her credits toward a higher degree at the University of Utah.[1]

Once Miller graduated in 2008, she learned that her credits would not transfer. After two years of school and $30,000 in student loans, Miller says she was sold "a lemon." For-profit tuition is about five times that of state schools and 24 percent of government-guaranteed student loans go to for-profit students who account for only 12 percent of all U.S. college students.[2] A 2010 federal government study of 15 for-profit schools found that four of the 15 "encouraged fraudulent practices" while all 15 made deceptive or questionable statements to undercover applicants.[3] Basically, the for-profits are accused of using high-pressure sales tactics and false promises to lure students. Inflated after-college salary projections and misleading tuition information are among the complaints. One undercover agent, for example, was told that barbers could earn $150,000 to $250,000 per year.[4] The schools defend themselves, in part, by saying that the students have more "risk factors" than traditional college students. Do you think higher education admissions practices are best left to the market, or is more aggressive government oversight needed?

Part One—Common Law Consumer Protection

Later in this chapter we will explore government efforts to protect consumers from dangerous products, unfair lending practices, and the like. Before turning to that legislation, we need to appreciate the common law (judge-made law) that preceded and, in some respects, provided the foundation for the many federal, state, and local initiatives of recent years. In addition to the product liability protection (negligence, warranties, and strict liability) discussed in Chapter 7, injured consumers can look to several common law protections, including actions for fraud, misrepresentation, and unconscionability. [For an extensive menu of consumer law sites, see **http://www.lectlaw.com/tcos.html**]

Fraud and Innocent Misrepresentation

If the market is to operate efficiently, the buyer must be able to rely on the truth of the seller's product claims. Regrettably, willful untruths appear to be common in American commerce. A victim of *fraud* is entitled to rescind the contract in question and to seek damages, including, in cases of malice, a punitive recovery. Although fraud arises in countless situations and is difficult to define, the legal community has generally adopted the following elements, each of which must be proved:

1. Misrepresentation of a material fact.
2. The misrepresentation was intentional.
3. The injured party justifiably relied on the misrepresentation.
4. Injury resulted.

In identifying a fraudulent expression, the law distinguishes between statements of objective, verifiable facts and simple expressions of opinion. The latter ordinarily are not fraudulent even if erroneous. Thus normal sales *puffing* ("This baby is the greatest little car you're ever gonna drive") is fully lawful, and consumers are expected to exercise good judgment in responding to such claims. If a misleading expression of opinion comes from an *expert*, however, and the other party does not share that expertise (such as in the sale of a diamond engagement ring), a court probably would offer a remedy.

Of course, fraud can involve false conduct as well as false expression. A familiar example is the car seller who rolls back an odometer with the result that the buyer is misled.

A variation on the general theme of fraud is *innocent misrepresentation,* which differs from fraud only in that the falsehood was *unintentional.* The wrongdoer believed the statement or conduct in question to be true, but he or she was mistaken. In such cases, the wronged party may secure rescission of the contract, but ordinarily damages are not awarded. The following case involves a fraud claim against Harley-Davidson.

LEGAL BRIEFCASE

Tietsworth v. Harley-Davidson
677 N.W.2d 233 (Wis. S.Ct. 2004)

Justice Diane S. Sykes

The circuit court dismissed the entire action for failure to state a claim. [T]he court of appeals reinstated [the claims.]

*   *   *   *   *

FACTS AND PROCEDURAL HISTORY

Plaintiff Steven C. Tietsworth and the members of the proposed class own or lease 1999 or early-2000 model year Harley motorcycles equipped with Twin Cam 88 or Twin Cam 88B engines. Harley's marketing and advertising literature contained the following statement about the TC-88 engines:

> Developing [the TC-88s] was a six-year process. . . . The result is a masterpiece. We studied everything from the way oil moves through the inside, to the way a rocker cover does its job of staying oil-tight. Only 21 functional parts carry over into the new design. What does carry over is the power of a Harley-Davidson™ engine, only more so.

Harley also stated that the motorcycles were "premium" quality, and described the TC-88 engine as "eighty-eight cubic inches filled to the brim with torque and ready to take you thundering down the road."

On January 22, 2001, Harley sent a letter to Tietsworth and other owners of Harley motorcycles informing them that "the rear cam bearing in a small number of Harley-Davidson's Twin Cam 88 engines has failed. While it is unlikely that you will ever have to worry about this situation, you have our assurance that Harley-Davidson is committed to your satisfaction." The letter went on to explain that the company was extending the warranty on the cam bearing from the standard one-year/ unlimited mileage warranty to a five-year/50,000 mile warranty. Separately, Harley developed a $495 "cam bearing repair kit" and made the kit available to its dealers and service departments "to expedite rear cam bearing repair."

*   *   *   *   *

The amended complaint alleges that the cam bearing mechanism in the 1999 and early-2000 model year TC-88 engines is inherently defective, causing an unreasonably dangerous propensity for premature engine failure. [T]he amended complaint alleged that Harley's failure to disclose the cam bearing defect induced the plaintiffs to purchase their motorcycles by causing them to reasonably rely upon Harley's representations regarding the "premium" quality of the motorcycles.

The amended complaint further alleges that if the plaintiffs had known of the engine defect, they either would not have purchased the product or would have paid less for it. The amended complaint does not allege that the plaintiffs' motorcycles have actually suffered engine failure, have malfunctioned in any way, or are reasonably certain to fail or malfunction. Nor does the amended complaint allege any property damage or personal injury arising out of the engine defect. Rather, the amended complaint alleges that the plaintiffs' motorcycles have diminished value, including diminished resale value, because Harley motorcycles equipped with TC-88 engines have demonstrated a "propensity" for premature engine failure and/or fail prematurely.

* * * * *

DISCUSSION
Common-Law Fraud Claim

The plaintiffs' common-law fraud claim is premised on the allegation that Harley failed to disclose or concealed the existence of the cam bearing defect prior to the plaintiffs' purchases of their motorcycles. It is well established that a nondisclosure is not actionable as a misrepresentation tort unless there is a duty to disclose. *Ollerman v. O'Rourke Co., Inc.*, 94 Wis.2d 17, 26, 288 N.W.2d 95 (1980). Our decision in *Ollerman* outlined the three categories of misrepresentation in Wisconsin law—intentional misrepresentation, negligent misrepresentation, and strict responsibility misrepresentation—and described the common and distinct elements of the three torts.

All misrepresentation claims share the following required elements: (1) the defendant must have made a representation of fact to the plaintiff; (2) the representation of fact must be false; and (3) the plaintiff must have believed and relied on the misrepresentation to his detriment or damage. The plaintiffs here allege intentional misrepresentation, which carries the following additional elements: (4) the defendant must have made the misrepresentation with knowledge that it was false or recklessly without caring whether it was true or false; and (5) the defendant must have made the misrepresentation with intent to deceive and to induce the plaintiff to act on it to his detriment or damage.

Ollerman reiterated the general rule that in a sales or business transaction, "silence, a failure to disclose a fact, is not an intentional misrepresentation unless the seller has a duty to disclose." The existence and scope of a duty to disclose are questions of law for the court. *Ollerman* held that "a subdivider–vendor of a residential lot has a duty to a 'noncommercial' purchaser to disclose facts which are known to the vendor, which are material to the transaction, and which are not readily discernible to the purchaser." We specified that this was a "narrow holding," premised on certain policy considerations present in noncommercial real estate transactions.

The transactions at issue here, however, are motorcycle purchases, not residential real estate purchases, and it is an open question whether the duty to disclose recognized in *Ollerman* extends more broadly to sales of consumer goods. . . .

No Legally Cognizable Injury

Ollerman also held that damages in intentional misrepresentation cases are measured according to the "benefit of the bargain" rule, "typically stated as the difference between the value of the property as represented and its actual value as purchased.". . .

[W]e have generally held that a tort claim is not capable of present enforcement (and therefore does not accrue) unless the plaintiff has suffered actual damage. . . . Actual damage is harm that has already occurred or is "reasonably certain" to occur in the future. . . . Actual damage is not the mere possibility of future harm. . . . [T]he amended complaint must adequately plead an actual injury—a loss or damage that has already occurred or is reasonably certain to occur—in order to state an actionable fraud claim. . . .

The injury complained of here is diminution in value only—the plaintiffs allege that their motorcycles are worth less than they paid for them. However, the amended complaint does not allege that the plaintiffs' motorcycles have diminished value because their engines have failed, will fail, or are reasonably certain to fail as a result of the TC-88 cam bearing defect. The amended complaint does not allege that the plaintiffs have sold their motorcycles at a loss because of the alleged engine defect. The amended complaint alleges only that the motorcycles have diminished value—primarily diminished potential resale value—because Harley motorcycles equipped with TC-88 engines have demonstrated a "propensity" for premature engine failure and/or will fail as a result of the cam bearing defect. This is insufficient to state a legally cognizable injury for purposes of a fraud claim.

Diminished value premised upon a mere possibility of future product failure is too speculative and uncertain to support a fraud claim. The plaintiffs do not specifically allege that their particular motorcycles will fail prematurely, only that the Harley product line that consists of motorcycles with TC-88 engines has demonstrated a propensity for premature engine failure. An allegation that a particular product line fails prematurely does not constitute an allegation that the plaintiffs' particular motorcycles will do so, only that there is a possibility that they will do so.

We certainly agree with the court of appeals that the damage allegations in a fraud complaint are not evaluated against a standard of "absolute certainty" for purposes of a motion to dismiss for failure to state a claim. But an allegation that a product is diminished in value because of an event or circumstance that might—or might not—occur in the future is inherently conjectural and does not allege actual benefit-of-the-bargain damages with the "reasonable certainty" required to state a fraud claim.

* * * * *

[Reversed.] [The plaintiffs' additional claims are omitted.—Ed.]

Questions

1. a. According to the Wisconsin Supreme Court, under what circumstances might the nondisclosure by a seller of a defect constitute misrepresentation?
    b. Did the court find that Harley-Davidson had a duty to disclose in this case? Explain.
2. a. What injury, if any, do the plaintiffs claim they suffered in this episode?
    b. According to the Wisconsin Supreme Court, must a plaintiff in a fraud action prove that he or she has suffered actual damages prior to bringing a claim? Explain.
    c. What is the "benefit of the bargain" rule?
3. Why did the Wisconsin Supreme Court rule for the defendant Harley-Davidson in this case?
4. Robert McGlothlin, an employee of Thomson Consumer Electronics in Bloomington, Indiana, was injured while loading televisions into a semitrailer when the trailer's "landing gear" (retractable legs that support the front of the trailer when it is not attached to the semitractor) collapsed. McGlothlin sued the owner of the trailer, among others, claiming that the defendants' repair and inspection procedures for *latent* (hidden) defects were inadequate. Should the court treat latent defects differently than *patent* (observable) defects in determining when a legal duty exists? Explain. See *McGlothlin v. M & U Trucking,* 688 N.E.2d 1243 (Ind. S.Ct. 1997).

Unconscionable Contracts

The doctrine of unconscionability emerged from court decisions where jurists concluded that some contracts are so unfair or oppressive as to demand intervention. (Unconscionability is also included in state statutory laws via the Uniform Commercial Code 2—302.) The legal system intrudes on contracts only with the greatest reluctance. Mere foolishness or want of knowledge does not constitute grounds for unconscionability, nor is a contract unconscionable and hence unenforceable merely because one party is spectacularly clever and the other is not. Unconscionability can take either or both of two forms:

1. *Procedural unconscionability* is a situation where the bargaining power of the parties was so unequal that the agreement, as a practical matter, was not freely entered. Procedural unconscionability usually arises from lack of knowledge (e.g., fine print) or lack of choice (e.g., urgent circumstances).
2. *Substantive unconscionability* is a situation where the clause or contract in question was so manifestly one-sided, oppressive, or unfair as to "shock the conscience of the court." A contract that does not provide a remedy for a breach, or contract terms completely out of line with the relative risks assumed by the parties are among the conditions that might lead to a finding of substantive unconscionability.

PRACTICING ETHICS   Brewers Target Teens?

Lynne and Reed Goodwin's daughter was killed in an accident involving a teenager who was driving under the influence of alcohol. The Goodwins sued Anheuser-Busch and Miller Brewing alleging that the brewers targeted underage teens by placing advertisements in print, radio, and television venues with a high percentage of teen consumers. Among others, the plaintiffs raised public nuisance (in brief, an injury to health affecting a considerable number of persons) and unjust enrichment claims (enriched by illegally selling beer to minors). Under California law, the defendants market their products through a distribution chain, but they cannot lawfully sell directly to consumers.

Questions

1. How would you rule on the public nuisance and unjust enrichment claims? Explain.

2. Do you believe that brewers unethically target underage teens? Explain.

Source: *Goodwin v. Anheuser Busch and Miller Brewing*, 2005 WL 280330 (Cal. Superior Ct.).

Part Two—The Consumer and Government Regulation of Business

State Laws

Having looked at the common law foundation of consumer protection, we turn to some of the many governmental measures that provide shelter in the marketplace. Many states have enacted comprehensive consumer protection statutes. States also have specific statutes addressing such problems as door-to-door sales, debtor protection, and telemarketing fraud. We will look at a pair of high-interest consumer loan situations as well as state "lemon laws," which address the particularly frustrating problem of a hopelessly defective vehicle.

Payday Loans

When Jeffrey Smith of Phoenix needed money quickly to pay a medical bill, he took out a string of payday loans (short-term, high-interest loans to be paid back with the borrower's next pay check) and fell into a downward spiral that found him calling in sick to work to give himself time to drive all over the city taking out new loans to cover those coming due. The result was bankruptcy along with thoughts of suicide by his despondent wife. Annual interest rates on those loans were as high as 459 percent.

Fairness, we could argue, calls for government intervention. Indeed, 17 states have passed laws capping payday loan interest rates or banishing them altogether, and loan volume is down significantly. But will those rules achieve their fairness goal, or will they simply reduce the availability of loans and increase interest rates generally? Perhaps as evidence of the futility of rules or the resourcefulness of the market, those state limits often can simply be avoided entirely. Loans originated by companies owned by American Indian tribes are not subject to the state rules. Those tribes are shielded from the state laws under the sovereign immunity granted the tribes by the U.S. government. Tribes typically link up with established payday lenders who conduct the business operations, sometimes on tribal land, but often elsewhere.

Sources: Associated Press, "States Increasingly Target Payday Lenders," *The Des Moines Register,* April 9, 2010, p. 8A; and Jessica Silver-Greenberg, "Payday Lenders Join with Tribes," *The Wall Street Journal,* February 10, 2011, p. C1.

Lemon Laws   New car purchases are covered by warranty laws (see Chapter 7 for a discussion of UCC warranty provisions and the federal Magnuson—Moss Warranty Act); in

> The quarrel, of course, is about when a car is truly a lemon.

addition, all 50 states have some form of law designed to provide recourse for consumers whose new vehicles turn out to be defective such that they cannot be repaired after a reasonable effort. The quarrel, of course, is about when a car is truly a lemon. Lemon laws differ significantly from state to state, but they often cover new cars for one to two years or up to 24,000 miles after purchase. Typically, state laws provide that the vehicle must have been returned to the manufacturer or dealer three or four times to repair the same defect and that defect must substantially impair the value or safety of the vehicle, or the vehicle must have been unavailable to the consumer for a total of at least 30 days in a 12-month period. A vehicle meeting either or both of those tests often would be a lemon, and the purchaser would be entitled to a replacement vehicle or full refund of the purchase price. In some states, used cars may also be treated as lemons. In almost all states, the determination about whether a car is a lemon is handled by an arbitration panel. If dissatisfied with the ruling, the consumer may then file suit.

The case that follows examines Minnesota's lemon law requirements. [For lemon laws in all 50 states, see **http://www.lemonlawusa.com**]

Paul Sipe v. Workhorse Custom Chassis

LEGAL BRIEFCASE — 572 F.3d 525 (8th Cir. 2009)

Circuit Judge GRUENDER

I. BACKGROUND

On September 18, 2004, Paul Sipe purchased a motor home manufactured by Fleetwood Motor Homes of Pennsylvania, Inc. ("Fleetwood"), from Brambillas, Inc. ("Brambillas"), an authorized Fleetwood motor home dealer and repair facility located in Minnesota. Workhorse manufactured the motor home's chassis, which included the motor home's supporting frame, engine, transmission, and certain electrical components. Sipe purchased the motor home for $105,616.75, and Brambillas delivered it to Sipe on October 21, 2004. Sipe received an owner's manual with the motor home that contained Workhorse's limited warranty for the chassis.

Sipe began experiencing problems with the motor home's engine shortly after he bought it. The engine stalled on three occasions while being driven by Sipe, once in October 2004, once in May 2005, and once in June 2005. Sipe brought the motor home to Brambillas for repairs after each stalling incident. After the first incident, Brambillas conducted diagnostic tests but made no repairs because it

found no defect in the engine. Sipe testified in his deposition that after the second and third incidents, Brambillas claimed it performed diagnostic tests and found no defect but that the work order he received contained no indication that Brambillas performed any such tests. Sipe further testified that the last time the engine stalled was in June 2005 and that the engine problem has not prevented him from taking trips in the motor home.

In February 2006, Sipe listed the motor home for sale for the price of $94,900. After receiving only two offers at lower prices, Sipe reduced the listing price to $84,900, the Kelley Blue Book value of the motor home. Sipe testified that he ultimately decided to reduce the price because of a crack in the kitchen counter and that he did not recall any other defects that contributed to his decision to reduce the asking price. Sipe did not sell the motor home.

In January 2007 and December 2007, Sipe experienced problems with the motor home's transmission when he discovered that transmission fluid had leaked. Sipe testified that Brambillas refused to diagnose or repair the transmission after both incidents of fluid leakage.

Sipe brought this action against Workhorse and Fleetwood in the District Court for Hennepin County, Minnesota, alleging violations of Minnesota's lemon law. . . . The court dismissed Sipe's lemon law claims, finding that Sipe presented no evidence that the alleged engine defect required repair or that the defect substantially impaired the motor home and concluding that Sipe's claim regarding the transmission was time-barred.

*   *   *   *   *

II. DISCUSSION
A. Lemon Law
Sipe contends that the district court erred in granting summary judgment to Workhorse on his lemon law claim because Workhorse failed to repair his motor home's engine and transmission. Minnesota's lemon law provides:

> If the manufacturer, its agents, or its authorized dealers are unable to conform the new motor vehicle to any applicable express warranty by repairing or correcting any defect or condition which substantially impairs the use or market value of the motor vehicle to the consumer after a reasonable number of attempts, the manufacturer shall either replace the new motor vehicle with a comparable motor vehicle or accept return of the vehicle from the consumer and refund to the consumer the full purchase price. . . .

The manufacturer must make the required repairs if "the consumer reports the nonconformity to the manufacturer, its agents, or its authorized dealer during the term of the applicable express warranties or during the period of two years following the date of original delivery of the new motor vehicle to a consumer, whichever is the earlier date."

1. Engine Stalls
After thoroughly reviewing the record, we conclude that Sipe failed to present evidence showing a genuine issue of material fact about whether the engine stalls "substantially impair[ed] the use or market value of the motor [home]," as required by Minnesota's lemon law. In response to being asked if the engine defect "ever prevented [him] from going somewhere [or] taking a trip with [his] motor home," Sipe replied "no." In fact, Sipe traveled over 11,000 miles in the motor home since the first time the engine stalled. As Sipe explained, "I don't know if [the engine problem] affect[s] my use now because I know how to deal with it." Sipe also stated that he had not experienced an engine stall since June 2005. Thus, Sipe's own testimony shows that the engine defect has not impaired his use of the motor home; it follows that the defect has not substantially impaired his use.

With respect to the effect of the engine defect on the market value of the motor home, Sipe argues that the low number of offers he received for the motor home shows that its market value was substantially impaired. However, Sipe cannot avoid summary judgment by merely relying on his conclusory allegation that the engine defect caused the low number of offers. Sipe presented no evidence to suggest that his receipt of only two offers was in any way caused by the engine stalls and not some other factor, such as market conditions for used motor homes. He offered no evidence that potential buyers were even aware of the engine stalls, given that he described the motor home as being in "excellent condition" when he originally listed it for sale in February 2006. Sipe testified that he only reduced the original asking price to the Kelley Blue Book value because of a crack in the kitchen counter and that he did not recall any other defects "that played a role in reducing the price." Further, Sipe submitted no other evidence suggesting that the value of the motor home was impaired, such as expert testimony or an appraisal of the motor home. As with his testimony regarding his use of the motor home, Sipe's own testimony shows that the engine defect has not impaired, substantially or otherwise, the motor home's market value.

*   *   *   *   *

2. Transmission Fluid Leaks
When he received the motor home in October 2004, Sipe received a three-year limited warranty from Workhorse. Thus, to bring an actionable lemon law claim, Sipe must have reported any nonconformities within two years of the date of the original delivery of the motor home. *See* Minn. Stat. Section 325 F. 665, subdiv. 2 (requiring consumers to report a nonconformity "during the term of the applicable express warranties or during the period of two years following the date of original delivery of the new motor vehicle . . ., whichever is the earlier date"). Sipe first reported the transmission fluid leak to Brambillas in January 2007, which was more than two years after the delivery of the motor home. As such, we agree with the district court that Sipe's lemon law claim with respect to the transmission leaks is barred by statute.

*   *   *   *   *

[Affirmed.]

Questions
1. *a.* According to Minnesota's lemon law, what was Sipe required to show in order to win his engine defect claim?
    b. Why did Sipe lose his engine defect claim?
2. Why did Sipe lose his defective transmission claim?
3. Dieter and Hermes agreed to buy a new 1996 Dodge Ram pickup truck from Fascona Chrysler-Plymouth-Dodge Trucks on December 12, 1995. They requested the installation

of some after-market accessories—a tonneau cover, a bug shield, and rust proofing. When Dieter and Hermes returned to take delivery of the truck, they noticed it had been scratched during the installation of the accessories. The salesperson told them the scratches would be repaired. Four months later the dealership sent the truck to a body shop for repairs. After repair, Dieter and Hermes noticed swirl marks in the truck's finish. Dieter then demanded that Frascona repurchase the truck. Eight months later Dieter and Hermes sued Chrysler Corporation under Wisconsin's lemon law.

a. Make the argument that the lemon law does not apply to the facts of this case.

b. Decide the case. Explain. See *Dieter and Hermes v. Chrysler Corporation*, 610 N.W.2d 832 (Wis. S.Ct. 2000).

Federal Laws and Consumer Protection Agencies

Much of the federal government's authority to protect consumers rests with some powerful agencies including a new one approved in 2010 when Congress and President Obama concluded that our financial markets had failed in some important respects.

Consumer Financial Protection Bureau (CFPB)

Placing a bold bet on the capacity of the federal government to protect consumers, Congress and President Obama approved the creation of the CFPB as a direct response to the financial calamity of recent years. The new agency, authorized by the 2010 Dodd-Frank Wall Street Reform and Consumer Protection Act, is charged with writing and enforcing rules covering consumer financial products and services including mortgages, credit cards, payday loans, loan servicing, check cashing, debt collection, and others. Another important element of the Bureau's charge is to provide financial education thereby promoting Americans' financial literacy. [For the Consumer Financial Protection Bureau home page, see **http://www.consumerfinance.gov/**]

[For a CFPB video explaining the Bureau's mission, see: **http://www.consumerfinance.gov/the-bureau/**]

Rather than counting on market forces to insure financial transparency and fair treatment for consumers, new rules will be created in an effort to mandate those results. Broadly, the Bureau will be expected to prohibit and prevent the commission of "an unfair, deceptive, or abusive act or practice" in conjunction with a consumer financial product or service. The expectation is that the Bureau will protect us from a wide array of dishonest practices such as hidden credit card fees and misleading "teaser" rates for mortgages.

The Act generally accords the Bureau authority over financial service firms, including banks, thrifts and credit unions, while it specifically excludes real estate brokerages, accountants, lawyers, and those selling nonfinancial goods and services, among others. The Bureau's new rules must be subjected to cost/benefit reviews, and those rules can be set aside by a two-thirds vote of the new Financial Stability Oversight Council (created as part of the Dodd-Frank bill) if the rule would threaten the nation's financial system.

Having broad authority over federal consumer finance law, the Bureau will consolidate consumer finance programs currently residing in other agencies, and it will be responsible for enforcing the finance laws outlined later in this chapter, including the Electronic Fund Transfer Act, the Equal Credit Opportunity Act, the Fair Credit Billing Act and many more.

The Bureau will be funded, at an initial cost estimated at $500 million per year, by Federal Reserve earnings. The Bureau will have the power to impose penalties including civil fines of up to $1 million per day for knowing violations.[5]

Of course, the Bureau has many doubters and outright enemies. A primary fear is that increased government regulation is likely to reduce the availability of credit or raise the cost of that credit, thereby potentially damaging consumers and the economy. Some of the critics simply want the government to leave the finance market alone while others suggest, for example, that government resources should be limited to consumer education and counseling rather than more rules. The Bureau was launched in July 2011, but fierce congressional battles are expected before all of the necessary rules are written and the Bureau's mission is fully defined.[6] [For a "one-stop shop for the American people to learn how to protect themselves from fraud and to report it wherever—and however—it occurs," see the Federal Financial Fraud Task Force's Web site: **http://www.stopfraud.gov**]

> The Bureau has many doubters and outright enemies.

The Federal Trade Commission (FTC)

The Federal Trade Commission was created in 1914 to prevent "unfair methods of competition and unfair or deceptive acts or practices in and affecting commerce." In conducting its business, the FTC performs as a miniature government with extensive and powerful quasi-legislative and quasi-judicial roles. [For the FTC's Bureau of Consumer Protection home page, see **http://www.ftc.gov/bcp/index.shtml**]

Rule Making

The FTC's primary legislative direction is in issuing trade regulation rules to enforce the intent of broadly drawn congressional legislation. That is, the rules specify particular acts or practices that the commission deems deceptive.

The FTC's quasi-legislative or rule-making power is extensive, as evidenced by the following examples:

- The Federal Trade Commission's Do Not Call Registry forbids telemarketers, with certain exceptions, from placing calls to the more than 200 million Americans who have added their phone numbers to the Federal Trade Commission's list. While some violations continue, the rule has clearly been a success for annoyed consumers. The FTC also issued a 2009 rule banning many types of so-called robocalls (prerecorded telemarketing solicitations). Under the rule, sellers and telemarketers who transmit prerecorded messages to consumers who have not agreed in writing to accept those messages will face penalties of up to $16,000 per call. [Those wanting to be added to the Do Not Call list and those wanting to file complaints can visit **http://www.donotcall.gov**]

- In 2009, the *Los Angeles Times* asked: "Does a moment pass when Kim Kardashian isn't selling? If she's not hyping her workout video, she's touting her online shoe club, her new book or her sisters' 'reality' TV spinoff, a gripping look inside their high-end Miami boutique.[7]"

> "Does a moment pass when Kim Kardashian isn't selling?"

Kardashian and all others hyping products and services on the Internet are now subject to new constraints. The FTC announced rules in 2009 revising its 1980 "Guides Concerning Use of Endorsements and Testimonials in Advertising" to reflect the changes of the Internet era. The rules, among other things, require those offering endorsements on new media sites (blogs, Twitter, Facebook, etc.) to disclose any connection they have (including in most cases, receiving cash or gifts) in exchange for their testimonials. Advertisers, celebrity endorsers like Kardashian, and "ordinary" consumers who offer reviews, endorsements, and testimonials via the Internet must comply or face penalties for false or misleading advertising.

Tobacco Rules

In 2009, four decades after smoking was officially declared a health hazard, Congress and President Obama approved the Family Smoking Prevention and Tobacco Control Act that gave the FDA authority to regulate tobacco products. The law empowers the FDA to set standards that may reduce nicotine and chemicals in tobacco products. Most tobacco flavorings are banned, and the use of the terms "light," "low," and "mild" is restricted. Perhaps the most interesting requirement involves new warnings covering the top half of tobacco packages including one image of a man exhaling smoke through a tracheotomy hole in his throat and another of a mother blowing smoke on her baby. Tobacco marketing to children is forbidden. Thus, tobacco products must be placed behind store counters, and sports and entertainment sponsorships are banned. The new rules are expected to reduce youth smoking by 11 percent and adult smoking by 2 percent, but at this writing the rules are being challenged in court on free speech grounds, among others.

Question

1. Would you expect the new FDA rules to significantly reduce youth smoking? Explain.

Sources: Rob Stein, "New, More Graphic Cigarette Warnings Unveiled," *The Washington Post,* November 10, 2010 [**http://www.washingtonpost.com**]; and Melissa Healy, "U.S. Unveils Grim New Warning Images for Cigarette Packs," *latimes.com,* June 21, 2011 [**http://www.latimes.com/**].

Adjudication

On its own initiative or as a result of a citizen complaint, the FTC may investigate suspect trade practices. At that point the FTC may drop the proceeding, settle the matter, or issue a formal complaint.

Where a formal complaint is issued, the matter proceeds essentially as a trial conducted before an administrative law judge. The FTC has no authority to impose criminal sanctions.

Fraud and Deception

Unfair and deceptive trade practices, including those in advertising, are forbidden under Section 5 of the Federal Trade Commission Act. An unfair trade practice (1) must be likely to cause substantial injury to consumers, (2) must not be reasonably avoidable by consumers themselves, and (3) must not be outweighed by countervailing benefits to consumers or to competition. The FTC test for deception requires that the claim is (1) false or likely to mislead the reasonable consumer and (2) material to the consumer's decision making. Deception can take many forms, including, for example, testimonials by celebrities who do not use the endorsed product or do not have meaningful expertise. Product quality claims are an area of particular dispute.

Quality Claims

"Fewer calories," "faster acting," and "more effective" are the kinds of claims that may lead to allegations of deception unless they are factually supportable. Under the FTC's ad substantiation program, advertisers are engaging in unfair and deceptive practices if they make product claims without some reasonable foundation for those claims. For example, credible survey evidence must be in hand if an advertiser says, "Consumers prefer our brand two to one." Indeed, in recent years the FTC has brought a number of charges and settled many of them. In 2007, the FDA challenged four weight-loss drugs, whose makers were fined a total of $25 million for false advertising claims. Some of the ads promised permanent and fast weight loss or increases in metabolism. Others even claimed effectiveness in reducing Alzheimer's and cancer. The pills, Xenadrine EFX, CortiSlim, One-A-Day WeightSmart, and TrimSpa will remain on the shelves.[8]

The Consumer Product Safety Commission (CPSC)

> Another reason to avoid sleeping with an ex: fear of contracting lead poisoning. Just ask Barbie, who got it from Ken. That's according to "Toxic Toys: A Poisonous Affair," a YouTube attack on the Consumer Product Safety Commission produced by the nonprofit Campaign for America's Future.[9]

The Consumer Product Safety Commission (CPSC) is the federal agency charged with protecting us from "unreasonable risks of injury and death" from consumer products. The YouTube attack was a product of frustration with the CPSC's response to a 2007 wave of toy recalls; largely because of dangerous levels of lead. More than 45 million toys and children's items, most of them made in China, have been recalled in recent years.[10] Congress and President Bush in 2008 responded to widespread outrage over the lead risk by overwhelmingly approving the Consumer Product Safety Improvement Act that lowered permissible levels of lead in children's (up to age 12) products and lowered permissible chemical levels in children's toys and child care products. The law also requires independent testing of children's products to prove their safety before their entry to the market. Critics, however, say the bill is too expensive. *The Wall Street Journal* commented that only one American child was injured in 2008 from lead in toys, but the rules are estimated to cost retailers and manufacturers $2 billion for compliance and for removing children's products from the shelves.[11] The law reaches beyond undeniably dangerous lead paint on the surface of children's products to lead contained within the metal ingredients in products such as zippers, belts, bicycles, and motorcycles.[12]

> More than 30 infant and toddler deaths.

After more than 30 infant and toddler deaths and millions of recalls in the past decade, the CPSC unanimously voted to ban, effective

June 28, 2011, the manufacture, sale, and resale (including yard sales) of the traditional drop-side baby crib that has cradled millions. The new standard requires fixed sides.[13]

The CPSC launched a public database in 2011 that allows all of us to report dangerous products and to search complaints entered by others. Critics, however, fear the database will be misused and misleading. [If you want to report a dangerous product or to search for others' experiences with products, go to **http://saferproducts.gov/**]

The CPSC was created to address product safety problems where for various reasons the market fails to provide the degree of immediate protection demanded by consumers. With responsibility for 15,000 product types but only approximately 400 staffers, the CPSC has struggled to meet its duties,[14] but the new CPS Improvement Act is expected (assuming congressional appropriation) to increase the agency budget from about $80 million prior to the new bill to an anticipated $136 million by 2014.[15] [For the Consumer Product Safety Commission Web site, see **http://www.cpsc.gov**]

 [For an ABC News visit to the Consumer Product Safety Commission Testing Lab, see: **http://abcnews.go.com/GMA/video/consumer-product-safety-commission-test-lab-13827984**]

Reducing Risk　The CPSC, created in 1972, is responsible for reducing the risks in using consumer products such as toys, lawn mowers, washing machines, bicycles, fireworks, pools, portable heaters, and household chemicals. The CPSC pursues product safety, initially, by collecting data and issuing rules. The commission conducts research and collects information as a foundation for regulating product safety. Via its rule-making authority, the CPSC promulgates mandatory consumer product safety, performance, and labeling standards. Public comments and suggestions are encouraged, but industry trade associations often appear to have the bigger voice with the commission.

To enforce its policies and decisions, the CPSC holds both compliance and enforcement powers. In seeking compliance with safety expectations, the commission can exert a number of expectations. Manufacturers must certify before distribution that products meet federal safety standards. Manufacturing sites may be inspected, and specific product safety testing procedures can be mandated. Businesses other than retailers are required to keep product safety records. In cases of severe and imminent hazards, the CPSC has the power to enforce its decisions by seeking a court order to remove a product from the market. In less-urgent circumstances, the commission may proceed with its own administrative remedy. Preferring voluntary compliance, the commission may negotiate with companies to recall dangerous products. In 2009, the CPSC oversaw 456 product recalls involving tens of millions of items.[16] Regulators are concerned that the public is so overloaded with recalls that the system no longer works.[17] [For the federal government recall site, see **http://www.recalls.gov**]

Where voluntary negotiations fail, the commission may proceed with an adjudicative hearing before an administrative law judge or members of the commission. That decision may be appealed to the full commission and thereafter to the federal court of appeals. Civil or criminal penalties may result. Only a few products, such as the drop-side cribs, have actually been banned from the market by the Commission.

The Food and Drug Administration

Drug Safety　The FDA plays a broad, vital role in monitoring much of America's health landscape with responsibility for assuring the safety, effectiveness, and security of food, drugs (prescription and over-the-counter), medical devices, cosmetics, tobacco products, and more. Perhaps the biggest FDA duty is to decide when drugs should be approved for marketing. Companies must subject a new drug to laboratory, animal and eventually human testing before the FDA will consider approval. FDA physicians and scientists review the scientific evidence, and thereafter the FDA approves a drug for marketing only when its benefits exceed its costs. The FDA is empowered to impose fines and remove drugs from the market

> GlaxoSmithKline, agreed to pay a $750 million federal fine.

if their risks exceed their benefits. Thus, in 2010, British pharmaceutical company, GlaxoSmithKline, agreed to pay a $750 million federal fine to settle claims that it had produced and sold adulterated drugs including the antidepressant, Paxil.[18]

> A series of massive food poisoning scares.

Food Safety   In recent years, food safety has climbed the list of FDA worries following a series of massive food poisoning scares. Vegetables, peanut products, eggs, and other foodstuffs have been contaminated by salmonella and *E. coli*. The 2010 salmonella outbreak in eggs (primarily regulated by the FDA, but assisted by the Agriculture Department and other agencies) sickened more than 1,600 people and led to the recall of 550 million eggs.[19] A 2006 *E. coli* outbreak in spinach killed five people.[20] Each year about 5,000 Americans die and 325,000 are hospitalized from food-borne illnesses, and producers bear huge costs such as a $100-million bill for growers and distributors in a 2008 salmonella outbreak in peppers and tomatoes.[21] Consumers are expecting more and more protection from the FDA, but the Centers for Disease Control and Prevention recently concluded that the government's ability to assure food safety has not improved in recent years, following decades of progress.[22] The food industry itself has responded by beginning to develop new technological methods, including high-tech labels, which allow monitoring of food from the fields to the supermarket checkout. Although America's food safety system is considered among the best in the world, 90 percent of Americans in a 2009 survey asked for new food safety measures.[23]

Responding to those food threats and public unease, a bipartisan congress and President Obama approved the 2010 Food Safety and Modernization Act giving the FDA greatly expanded food safety power. The bill allows the FDA to address food dangers before they do harm rather than after problems emerge, as had been the case. More specifically, the FDA will be able to recall dangerous food and increase inspections while putting greater responsibility on farmers and food companies to prevent contamination. Full implementation of the bill will require a substantial congressional budgetary commitment that may or may not come to pass.

Trust the Market or Strengthen the FDA?   The FDA regulates products that account for about one quarter of American consumer spending.[24] With some new crisis every few months, the FDA clearly is struggling, or perhaps as expert Peter Barton Hunt put it: "This is a fundamentally broken agency, and it needs to be repaired."[25] The FDA's growing problems are partially explained by dramatic increases in imported food, drugs and other FDA-regulated products. The FDA relies on its own inspections of foreign plants to help assure imported drug safety, but at the present pace 50 years would be required to visit every drug plant in China alone.[26] The risks in that situation are apparent when we notice that China now produces two-thirds of the world's aspirin and is expected to become the sole global supplier.[27] Magnifying the difficulty, the FDA in 2007 had only 454 inspectors to monitor the more than 18 million annual shipments of food, drugs, and so on, into the 300 American ports.[28]

What Should Be Done?   The FDA budget has been significantly increased in recent years, but more regulators and rules create their own challenges. Historically, the FDA was criticized for being too cautious and slow in allowing potentially helpful, new drugs on the market. Drug industry and free market advocates have long argued for greater faith in the market, but when the agency accelerated its drug approval process, serious safety problems followed. Pharmaceutical companies say the risks of FDA rejection are so high that they are reducing the number of new drugs being prepared for FDA approval. In 2007, the agency approved only 19 new medicines, the fewest in 24 years.[29] While those numbers increased to 24 in 2008, 25 in 2009, and 21 in 2010, they were still less than half the 1996 peak of 53 approvals.[30] For its part, the agency says its processes have not slowed but that the industry's research efforts have faltered.

Consumer Privacy

As *The Wall Street Journal* reported, identity theft has exploded in recent years:

> The biggest known theft of credit card numbers in history began two summers ago outside a Marshalls discount clothing store near St. Paul, Minnesota. There, investigators now believe, hackers pointed a telescope-shaped antenna toward the store and used a laptop computer to decode data streaming through the air between handheld price-checking devices, cash registers, and the store's computers. That helped them hack into the central database of Marshalls' parent, TJX Cos. in Framingham, Mass., to repeatedly purloin information about customers.
>
> The $17.4-billion retailer's wireless network had less security than many people have on their home networks, and for 18 months the company . . . had no idea what was going on.[31]

> More than 40 million card numbers were stolen.

Investigators think more than 40 million card numbers were stolen from TJX and others in 2008 alone.[32] In this case, however, some very good news followed when authorities broke up the ring of Americans, Russians, and others alleged to be responsible for the thefts from TJX and four other big companies. The self-confessed ringleader of the group, Albert Gonzalez, an American, was sentenced in 2010 to 20 years in prison after he apologized for leading the scheme.[33] *The Wall Street Journal* described the thefts this way:

> In computer attacks lasting more than a year, the trio (Gonzalez and two Russians, not named) allegedly scooped up credit-and debit-card numbers and installed so-called back doors in the victim's computer networks to enable them to steal more data in the future, according to the indictment.[34]

Authorities estimate that identity theft annually affects 15 million Americans at a cost of $50 billion.[35] Organizations that had a data breach in 2008 paid an average of $6.6 million to restore their brand and keep their customers.[36] [For Federal Trade Commission advice on fighting ID theft, see **http://www.ftc.gov/bcp/edu/microsites/idtheft/**]

Red Flags   In January 2011, the Federal Trade Commission began enforcing its "Red Flags Rule" that is designed to slow identity theft. Under the Rule, all "financial institutions" and "creditors" must establish a written program to prevent identity theft in their organizations and then mitigate whatever losses may come from identity theft. The FTC identifies "Red Flags" as, for example, suspicious documents, IDs, and account activities. Of course, smoothly flowing information is vital to efficiency in a free market economy. In some sense, we must pay for our privacy because tighter protection, like the Red Flag Rule, probably means higher costs since the flow of information would be restricted. Furthermore, emerging evidence suggests that ID theft may be "more hype than harm," as *BusinessWeek* argued.[37] Losing one's personal information is bound to be traumatic, but one study pointed out that the odds of having stolen data actually misused is about 0.09 percent or one in 1,020 individuals.[38] [For a privacy database and links, see **http://www.privacyrights.org**]

Part Three—Debtor/Creditor Law

Credit Regulations

> Angelique Trammel decided to buy a laptop on a "low weekly payment plan."

According to *The New York Times,* Angelique Trammel, a single mother and telephone operator, decided to buy a laptop for her son on a "low weekly payment plan." She paid $99 down and agreed to have $41 per week withdrawn from her bank account. After six months, a broken computer arrived. Having spent well over $1,000 and after having received two nonworking computers, she demanded a refund from the retailer, Blue-Hippo. Under her agreement, Ms. Trammel allegedly would have paid more than $2,000 for a computer worth much less.[39] Describing sales schemes directed to the poor, Better Business Bureau spokesman Steve Cox said: "The way these companies operate is simply another form of predatory lending."[40] BlueHippo, on the other hand, said that, "before, during and after the sales transaction we fully disclose the total price and all shipping guidelines" to customers.[41]

Situations like Trammel's and broad fears of abuse in credit and lending led Congress and the state legislatures to supplement the market's powerful messages with a substantial array of protective legislation. We will turn now to a look at several particularly important pieces of federal lending practices law. [For a debtor/creditor law database, see **http://www.law.cornell.edu/topics/debtor_creditor.html**]

Dodd-Frank Wall Street Reform and Consumer Protection Act

In addition to creating the Consumer Finance Protection Bureau (CFPB), the 2010 Dodd-Frank bill provides increased legislative oversight of the nation's financial processes. (See Chapter 8 for the bill's provisions designed to stabilize and protect the banking system.) Broadly, the bill's consumer protection provisions move away from the old system that mandated disclosure to consumers of critical financial information (e.g., interest rates) to a more prescriptive regime that requires lenders to affirmatively protect borrowers. Some forms of loans and lending practices are either banned or restricted, and the government will now have much more authority to pursue and punish violators.

Truth in Lending Act (TILA)

As we increasingly turned to credit financing, consumers often did not understand the full cost of buying on credit. The TILA is part of the Consumer Credit Protection Act of 1968. Having been designed for consumer protection, it does not cover all loans. The following standards determine the TILA's applicability:

1. The debtor must be a "natural person" rather than an organization.
2. The creditor must be regularly engaged in extending credit and must be the person to whom the debt is initially payable. Dodd-Frank expressly amends the definition of creditor to include mortgage originators.
3. The purpose of the credit must be "primarily for personal, family, or household purposes" not in excess of $25,000, but "consumer real property transactions" are covered by the act. Hence home purchases fall within TILA provisions.
4. The credit must be subject to a finance charge or payable in more than four installments.

The TILA and Regulation Z interpreting the act were designed both to protect consumers from credit abuse and to assist them in becoming more informed about credit terms and costs so they could engage in comparison shopping. Congress presumed the increased information would stimulate competition in the finance industry. The heart of the act is the required conspicuous disclosure of the amount financed, the finance charge (the actual dollar sum to be paid for credit), the annual percentage rate (APR—the total cost of the credit expressed at an annual rate), and the number of payments. The finance charge includes not just interest but service charges, points, loan fees, carrying charges, and other costs. The TILA covers consumer loans generally, including credit cards and auto purchases. [For consumer information on "abusive lending," see **http://www.ftc.gov/bcp/menu-lending.htm**]

TILA amendments in the Dodd-Frank bill give extensive, new attention to residential mortgages, a recognition of our ongoing subprime mortgage crisis and its destructive impact on the entire American economy. Creditors, for example, are prohibited from making a residential mortgage loan without a good faith determination that the consumer has a reasonable "ability to repay" the loan.

The case that follows examines the application of TILA to a credit card interest rate dispute.

LEGAL BRIEFCASE

Barrer v. Chase Bank USA
566 F.3d 883 (9th Cir. 2009)

Circuit Judge O'Scannlain

We must decide whether a credit card company violates the Truth in Lending Act when it fails to disclose potential risk factors that allow it to raise a cardholder's Annual Percentage Rate.

I

A

Walter and Cheryl Barrer held a credit card account with Chase. The Barrers received and accepted the Cardmember Agreement ("the Agreement") governing their relationship at the relevant time in late 2004. In February 2005, Chase mailed to the Barrers a Change in Terms Notice ("the Notice"), which purported to amend the terms of the Agreement, in particular to increase the Annual Percentage Rate ("APR") significantly. It also allowed the Barrers to reject the amendments in writing by a certain date. They did not do so, and continued to use the credit card. Within two months, the new, higher, APR became effective.

According to the Barrers' First Amended Complaint, they enjoyed a preferred APR of 8.99% under the Agreement. In a section entitled "Finance Charges," the Agreement provided a mathematical formula for calculating preferred and non-preferred APRs and variable rates. In the event of default, the Agreement stated that Chase might increase the APR on the balance up to a stated default rate. The Agreement specified the following events of default: failure to pay at least a minimum payment by the due date; a credit card balance in excess of the credit limit on the account; failure to pay another creditor when required; the return, unpaid, of a payment to Chase by the customer's bank; or, should Chase close the account, the consumer's failure to pay the outstanding balance at the time Chase has appointed.

Another section entirely, entitled "Changes to the Agreement," provided that Chase "can change this agreement at any time, . . . by adding, deleting, or modifying any provision. [The] right to add, delete, or modify provisions includes financial terms, such as APRs and fees." The next section, entitled "Credit Information," stated that Chase "may periodically review your credit history by obtaining information from credit bureaus and others." These sections appeared five and six pages, respectively, after the "Finance Charge" section.

Around April 2005, the Barrers' noticed that their APR had "skyrocketed" from 8.99% to 24.24%, the latter a rate close to a non-preferred or default rate. None of the events of default specified in the Agreement, however, had occurred. When the Barrers contacted Chase to find out why their APR had increased, Chase responded in a letter citing judgments it had made on the basis of information obtained from a consumer credit reporting agency. In particular, Chase wrote that: "outstanding credit loan(s) on revolving accounts . . . [were] too high" and there were "too many recently opened installment/revolving accounts." The Barrers do not dispute the facts underlying Chase's judgments.

Despite the Barrers' surprise, the Notice they had received in February contained some indication of what would be forthcoming. Specifically, it disclosed that Chase would shortly increase the APR to 24.24%, a decision "based in whole or in part on the information obtained in a report from the consumer reporting agency."

The Barrers paid the interest on the credit account at the new rate for three months before they were able to pay off the balance. Then they sued Chase in federal district court.

B

The Barrers filed a class action lawsuit on their own behalf and on behalf of all Chase credit card customers similarly harmed and similarly situated. The complaint asserted one cause of action under the Truth in Lending Act ("the Act"), and Regulation Z. The Barrers claim to have been the victims of a practice they now call "adverse action repricing," which apparently means "raising . . . a preferred rate to an essentially non-preferred rate based upon information in a customer's credit report." Though the Barrers do not claim that the practice itself is illegal, they do claim that it was illegal for Chase not to disclose it fully to them or to the other members of the putative class.

[The federal district court dismissed the Barrers' cause of action. The Barrers appealed.]

II

The Truth in Lending Act is designed "to assure a meaningful disclosure of credit terms so that the consumer will be able to compare more readily the various credit terms available to him and avoid the uninformed use of credit." Rather than substantively regulate the terms creditors can offer or include in their financial products, the Act primarily requires disclosure.

* * * * *

In general, the Act regulates credit card disclosures at numerous points in the commercial arrangement between creditor and consumer: at the point of solicitation and application, at the point the consumer and the creditor consummate the deal, at each billing cycle, and at the point the parties renew their arrangement. Specifically, creditors must disclose "[t]he conditions under which a finance charge may be imposed," "[t]he method of determining the amount of the finance charge," and, "[w]here one or more periodic rates may be used to compute the finance charge, each such rate . . . and the corresponding nominal annual percentage rate."

Regulation Z, 12 C.F.R. Section 226, provides the precise regulations that the Barrers claim Chase violated. In general, these regulations establish two conditions a creditor must meet. "First, it must have disclosed all of the information required by the statute." That is, disclosures must be complete. "And second, [they] must have been true—i.e., . . . accurate representation[s] of the legal obligations of the parties at [the] time [the agreement was made]."

Section 226.6 lists the initial disclosures required of a creditor under a new credit agreement. The list includes "each periodic rate that may be used to compute the finance charge ... and the corresponding annual percentage rate."

* * * * *

Just as section 226.6 states what must be disclosed, so section 226 describes how to disclose it. Among other things, creditors must make the required disclosures "clearly and conspicuously in writing." ...

The Board has also recognized that creditors may reserve the general right to change the credit agreement, as Chase did in this case. Should the creditor make changes in these ways, it may have to disclose anew under Section 226.9(c).

III

The Barrers argue that ... Chase failed to disclose completely under the Act why it would change the APRs of its cardholders, in violation of subsection 226.6(a)(2) of Regulation Z.

The Barrers do not argue that either the Agreement or the Notice failed to disclose the APR, which their complaint puts at 8.99% under the Agreement and 24.24% under the Notice. Rather, ... the gravamen of the Barrers' complaint is that Chase did not disclose that if a cardholder's credit report revealed certain information, what Chase calls "risk factors," the APR might go up.

* * * * *

Regulation Z requires that creditors disclose any APR "that *may* be used to compute the finance charge," and that they do so "clearly and conspicuously."

* * * * *

We are persuaded that Chase adequately disclosed the APRs that the Agreement permitted it to use simply by means of the change-in-terms provision. That provision reserved Chase's right to change APRs, among other terms, without any limitation on why Chase could make such a change. The provision thus disclosed that, by changing the Agreement, Chase could use any APR, a class of APRs that logically includes APRs adjusted on the basis of adverse credit information. Apart from the gloss of Comment 11, neither the Act nor Regulation Z require Chase to disclose the basis on which it would change or use APRs. Therefore the failure to disclose the reason for the change to the Barrers' APR—adverse credit information—and that Chase would look up their credit history to acquire that information does not undermine the adequacy of Chase's disclosure.

Even so, such disclosure must be clear and conspicuous. Neither the Act nor Regulation Z define clarity and conspicuousness in this context. The Staff Commentary explains only

that "[t]he clear and conspicuous standard requires that disclosures be in a reasonably understandable form." ...

Clear and conspicuous disclosures, therefore, are disclosures that a reasonable cardholder would notice and understand. No particular kind of formatting is magical, but, in this case, the document must have made it clear to a reasonable cardholder that Chase was permitted under the agreement to raise the APR not only for the events of default specified in the "Finance Terms" section, but for any reason at all.

... [T]he change-in-terms provision appears on page 10–11 of the Agreement, five dense pages after the disclosure of the APR. It is neither referenced in nor clearly related to the "Finance Terms" section. This provision, as part of the APRs allowed under the contract, is buried too deeply in the fine print for a reasonable cardholder to realize that, in addition to the specific grounds for increasing the APR listed in the "Finance Charges" section, Chase could raise the APR for other reasons.

Therefore, the Barrers have stated a claim because Chase cannot show that, as a matter of law, the Agreement made clear and conspicuous disclosure of the APRs that Chase was permitted to use.

REVERSED and REMANDED.

Questions

1. *a.* How did Chase violate Regulation Z and the TILA?
   b. According to this decision, what is a "clear and conspicuous" disclosure?

2. Green Tree Financial financed Randolph's mobile home purchase. Randolph sued, claiming that Green Tree's financing document contained an arbitration clause that violated TILA because it did not provide the same level of protection as TILA accords. If the arbitration clause provided lesser protection than that provided for by TILA, as Randolph claimed, should the arbitration go forward? Explain. See *Randolph v. Green Tree Financial Corp.,* 531 U.S. 79 (2000).

3. Sarah Hamm sued Ameriquest Mortgage Company claiming a violation of the Truth in Lending Act (TILA). Hamm borrowed money secured by a 30-year mortgage from Ameriquest. She signed a "Disclosure Statement" specifying, among other things, that she was responsible for 359 payments at a specified amount and one payment for the last month of a slightly smaller amount. The Statement did not, however, explicitly specify, as required by the TILA, the total payments due (360). Was the TILA violated? Explain. See *Hamm v. Ameriquest Mortgage,* 506 F.3d 525 (7th Cir. 2007).

Credit and Charge Cards

> College students are burying themselves under a massive pile of debt.

College students are burying themselves under a massive pile of debt. As of mid-2010, student debt ($829.785 billion) exceeded the total amount ($826.5 billion) owed by all Americans in revolving credit—primarily credit card debt.[42] In 2008, the average student left college with over $4,000 in credit card debt.[43] These disturbing, even threatening numbers, caused Congress and President Obama to include in the 2009 Credit Card Accountability, Responsibility and Disclosure Act (CARD Act) a provision forbidding lenders from issuing credit cards to those under age 21 without a parent as cosigner or without proof the applicant can make payments. Many colleges and universities that have allowed credit marketing on campus have profited handsomely from deals with card companies. The University of Michigan alumni association, for example, reportedly is guaranteed $25.5 million for its 11-year credit card agreement with Bank of America.[44] Some banks have reduced on-campus marketing, but others are exploiting loopholes to continue reaching students. For example, the law disallows "any tangible item as a gift," but Citibank reportedly offered a $50 statement credit on its student cards.[45]

Question

1. How would you argue that government intervention in the credit card market is not in the best interest of consumers generally and college students in particular?

TILA Protections

The law offers substantial protections for credit card users. The TILA provides that credit cards cannot be issued to a consumer unless requested. Cardholder liability for unauthorized use (lost or stolen card) cannot exceed $50, and the cardholder bears no liability after notifying the issuer of the missing card. In general, issuers must disclose key cost features, including APR, annual membership fees, minimum finance charges, late payment fees, and so on.

CARD

The aforementioned CARD Act of 2009 provides extensive additional protection for credit card holders. Some of the key provisions:

- Credit card companies are barred from increasing the annual percentage rate on existing account balances except when the cardholder's minimum payment is 60 days overdue.
- Issuers cannot charge interest on bills paid on time.
- Without specific agreement by the consumer, banks cannot accept charges where doing so puts creditors over their limits.
- Interest rates, with some exceptions, cannot be raised in the first year.

Beyond the CARD Act, other recent federal credit card rule changes have provided additional consumer shelter. Those rules cap fees for late payments, banish penalties for inactive accounts (although those accounts can still simply be closed), and allow merchants to set a $10 minimum for credit card purchases. To settle Justice Department antitrust allegations, Visa and MasterCard have both now agreed to allow merchants to offer incentives that encourage customers to use a competing card (e.g., Discover, which typically charges lower fees than Visa and MasterCard).

The CARD Act also imposes restrictions on gift cards such that, among other things, the cards cannot expire in less than five years and issuers cannot charge an inactivity fee unless the card has not been used for at least 12 months.

Success?

Skepticism is often the response to new rules, but the early evidence suggests that the federal government's credit card measures have been good for consumers. A 2011 Pew study found that penalty fees have dropped, overlimit fees (for charges beyond the credit limit) are now rare and annual fees have not proliferated as some critics expected.[46] Furthermore, government officials have praised the industry itself for going even further than the law requires, although some banking officials believe the law has increased credit costs while decreasing credit availability.[47]

Debit Card Fees

At this writing in 2011, Congress, the Federal Reserve, and armies of lobbyists have just concluded a massive battle over new rules capping debit card interchange fees (the charges banks impose for providing the debit processing service). After initially proposing a cap at 12 cents per transaction, the Fed ultimately decided to allow a maximum interchange fee of 21 cents per transaction with additional small fees to cover fraud loss and prevention and with exemptions for smaller banks. Previously, the average fee paid by the merchant to the bank was 44 cents with the median variable cost of each transaction estimated at seven cents. Congress was persuaded by retailers to limit the fees, with the new rule to go into effect in October 2011.

Bankers argue the fee cap will force them to make up for the lost revenue in other ways such as eliminating free checking and rewards programs, and they say the money saved will simply go to retailers rather than to consumers. Under the new rule, banks' debit card revenue is expected to be approximately cut in half to about $10 billion annually. Retailers and consumer advocates say the debit card processing service is effectively a Visa and MasterCard shared monopoly that permits supracompetitive pricing.

Sources: Moe Bedard, "Fed's Rule on 'Swipe Fee' Cap Awaited," *Tulsa World,* April 25, 2011 [**http://www.tulsa-world.com/**], Jim Puzzanghera, "Debit Card Fee Limits Hit a Snag," *latimes.com,* February 17, 2011 [**http://www.latimes.com/business/la-fi-debit-fees-20110218,0,3057034.story**]; and Victoria McGrane and Robin Sidel, "Fed Softens 'Swipe' Fees," *The Wall Street Journal,* June 30, 2011, p. C2.

Credit Cards Good for the World?

By 2020 or so, MasterCard expects Chinese residents to expand their credit card holdings from the current 207 million to 900 million and thereby pass the United States (700 million credit cards as of 2010) as the world's biggest credit card market by number of cards. Credit cards are becoming a commonplace shopping tool in the developing world as consumers in those nations seek a quicker route to material satisfaction. As a result, those consumers are joining Americans and other Westerners in struggling to repay their credit card debt. For example, consumers in both Turkey and Serbia in recent years have embraced credit cards with enthusiasm, but having done so, they increasingly find themselves in a "debt trap" built by high interest rates. The results can be tragic. In one highly publicized episode in Turkey, a

37-year-old policeman shot and killed himself on an Istanbul street. He was despondent over his $40,000 debt load. Turkey has capped banks' permissible monthly interest rates and the worst of the credit excesses have been somewhat curbed, but critics are concerned that consumers around the globe will be caught up in a debt cycle they often do not understand and that they cannot escape.

Question

1. Is the consumer credit path embraced by Americans a wise course for consumers in developing nations around the world? List some of the competing arguments.

Sources: Boris Babic and Yigal Schleifer, "Turkey, Serbia Find Credit Cards Can Soon Mean Huge Debts," *M & C News,* April 20, 2010 [**http://www.monstersandcritics.com/**]; "China to Have Most Credit Cards in Decade: MasterCard," *The Economic Times,* November 24, 2010 [**http://economictimes.indiatimes.com/**]; Mark Landler, "Outside U.S., Credit Cards Tighten Grip," *The New York Times,* August 10, 2008 [**http://www.nytimes.com/**]; and Daniel Ren, "Firm Says 900m Credit Cards Likely," *South China Morning Post,* September 11, 2010, p. 03.

Consumer Credit Reports

Do you want to borrow money for a new car or a house? Want to get a better job? Success in each of those efforts may depend to a considerable extent on your credit score. A favorable credit rating is a vital feature of consumer life, and having reliable credit information is essential to efficient business practice. Thus, the three national credit information giants, Equifax, Experian, and TransUnion, as well as local credit bureaus, provide retailers, employers, insurance companies, and others with consumers' detailed credit histories. From those credit histories, a credit score is computed and sold to lenders. The federal Fair Credit Reporting Act (FCRA) affords consumers the following credit reporting protections, among others:

- Anyone using information from a credit reporting agency (CRA), such as Equifax, to take "adverse action" against you (denying you credit, a job, insurance) must notify you and tell you where it secured the information.

- At your request, a CRA must give you the information in your file and a list of all those who have recently sought information about you.

- If you claim that your credit file contains inaccurate information, the CRA must investigate your complaint and give you a written report. If you remain unsatisfied, you can include a brief statement in your credit file. Notice of the dispute and a summary of your statement normally must accompany future reports.

- All inaccurate information must be corrected or removed from the file, usually within 30 days.

- In most cases, negative information more than seven years old must not be reported.

- You must provide written consent before a CRA can provide information to your employer or prospective employer.

- You can sue for damages if your rights under the act have been violated.

- Lenders are required to provide a consumer's credit score as well as any factors that affected that score if the lender took any adverse action based on that score.[48]

[For an extensive set of practical questions and answers about consumer rights under the Fair Credit Reporting Act, see **http://www.ftc.gov/os/statutes/fcrajump.shtm**]

Fair Credit Billing Act (FCBA)

The FCBA provides a mechanism to deal with the billing errors that accompany credit card and certain other "open-end" credit transactions. A cardholder who receives an erroneous bill must complain in writing to the creditor within 60 days of the time the bill was mailed. The creditor must acknowledge receipt of the complaint within 30 days. Then, within two billing cycles but not more than 90 days, the creditor must issue a response either by correcting the account or by forwarding a written statement to the consumer explaining why the bill is accurate. The creditor cannot threaten the consumer's credit rating or report the consumer as delinquent while the bill is in dispute, although the creditor can report that the bill is being challenged. Where a "reasonable investigation" determines the bill was correct but the consumer continues to contest it, the consumer may refuse to pay, and the creditor will then be free to commence collection procedures after giving the consumer 10 days to pay the disputed amount. If the bill is reported to a credit bureau as delinquent, that report must also indicate the consumer's belief that the money is not owed, and the consumer must be told who received the report. Penalties for a creditor in violation of the act are quite modest. The creditor forfeits the right to collect the amount in question and any accompanying finance charges, but the forfeiture cannot exceed $50 for each charge in dispute.

Electronic Fund Transfers

The Electronic Fund Transfer Act (EFTA) provides remedies for lost or stolen cards, billing errors, and other such problems involving ATMs, point-of-sale machines, electronic deposits, and the like. Under the EFTA, liability for misuse of missing cards is capped at $50 if the consumer provides notice within two business days after learning of the loss. The loss could reach $500 if notice is provided within 60 days and could be unlimited thereafter. The Dodd-Frank bill amended the EFT to provide, among other things, that electronic debit transaction fees charged to merchants by card networks must be "reasonable and proportional to the actual cost incurred." [For consumer information on electronic banking, see **http://www.ftc.gov/bcp/edu/pubs/consumer/credit/cre14.shtm**]

Equal Credit Opportunity

The Equal Credit Opportunity Act is designed to combat bias in lending. ECOA was in large part a response to anger over differing treatment of women and men in the financial marketplace. Credit must be extended to all creditworthy applicants regardless of sex, marital status, age, race, color, religion, national origin, good-faith exercise of rights under the Consumer Credit Protection Act, and receipt of public assistance (like food stamps). ECOA was in large part a response to anger over differing treatment of women and men in the financial marketplace. Creditors often would not lend money to married women in the women's own names, and single, divorced, and widowed women were similarly disadvantaged in securing credit. [For more details about ECOA, see **http://www.ftc.gov/bcp/pubs/consumer/credit/cre15.shtm**] The case that follows applies the ECOA to a "cross-dressing" male.

Judge Lynch

I

[O]n July 21, 1998, [Lucas] Rosa came to the [Park West] Bank to apply for a loan. A biological male, he was dressed in traditionally feminine attire. He requested a loan application from Norma Brunelle, a bank employee. Brunelle asked Rosa for identification. Rosa produced three forms of photo identification: (1) a Massachusetts Department of Public Welfare Card; (2) a Massachusetts Identification Card; and (3) a Money Stop Check Cashing ID Card. Brunelle looked at the identification cards and told Rosa that she would not provide him with a loan application until he "went home and changed." She said that he had to be dressed like one of the identification cards in which he appeared in more traditionally male attire before she would provide him with a loan application and process his loan request.

II

Rosa sued the Bank. Rosa charged that "by requiring [him] to conform to sex stereotypes before proceeding with the credit transaction, [the Bank] unlawfully discriminated against [him] with respect to an aspect of a credit transaction on the basis of sex." He claims to have suffered emotional distress.

   Without filing an answer to the complaint, the Bank moved to dismiss. . . . The district court granted the Bank's motion. The court stated,

> The issue in this case is not [Rosa's] sex, but rather how he chose to dress when applying for a loan. Because the Act does not prohibit discrimination based on the manner in which someone dresses, Park West's requirement that Rosa change his clothes does not give rise to claims of illegal discrimination. Further, even if Park West's statement or action were based upon Rosa's sexual orientation or perceived sexual orientation, the Act does not prohibit such discrimination.

PriceWaterhouse v. Hopkins, which Rosa relied on, was not to the contrary, according to the district court, because that case "neither holds, nor even suggests, that discrimination based merely on a person's attire is impermissible."

   On appeal, Rosa says that the district court "fundamentally misconceived the law as applicable to the Plaintiff's claim by concluding that there may be no relationship, as a matter of law, between telling a bank customer what to wear and sex discrimination."

   The Bank says that Rosa loses for two reasons. First, citing cases pertaining to gays and transsexuals, it says that the ECOA does not apply to cross-dressers. Second, the Bank says that its employee genuinely could not identify Rosa, which is why she asked him to go home and change.

III

The ECOA prohibits discrimination, "with respect to any aspect of a credit transaction[,] on the basis of race, color, religion, national origin, sex or marital status, or age." Thus to prevail, the alleged discrimination against Rosa must have been "on the basis of . . . sex."

   While the district court was correct in saying that the prohibited bases of discrimination under the ECOA do not include style of dress or sexual orientation, that is not the discrimination alleged. It is alleged that the Bank's actions were taken, in whole or in part, "on the basis of . . . [the appellant's] sex." . . . Whatever facts emerge, and they may turn out to have nothing to do with sex-based discrimination, we cannot say at this point that the plaintiff has no viable theory of sex discrimination consistent with the facts alleged.

   The evidence is not yet developed, and thus it is not yet clear why Brunelle told Rosa to go home and change. It may be that this case involves an instance of disparate treatment based on sex in the denial of credit. . . . It is reasonable to infer that Brunelle told Rosa to go home and change because she thought that Rosa's attire did not accord with his male gender: in other words, that Rosa did not receive the loan application because he was a man, whereas a similarly situated woman would have received the loan application. That is, the Bank may treat, for credit purposes, a woman who dresses like a man differently than a man who dresses like a woman. If so, the Bank concedes, Rosa may have a claim. Indeed, under *PriceWaterhouse*, "stereotyped remarks [including statements about dressing more 'femininely'] can certainly be evidence that gender played a part." It is also reasonable to infer, though, that Brunelle refused to give Rosa the loan application because she thought he was gay, confusing sexual orientation with cross-dressing. If so, Rosa concedes, our precedents dictate that he would have no recourse under the federal Act. It is reasonable to infer, as well, that Brunelle simply could not ascertain whether the person shown in the identification card photographs was the same person that appeared before her that day. If this were the case, Rosa again would be out of luck. It is reasonable to infer, finally, that Brunelle may have had mixed motives, some of which fall into the prohibited category.

It is too early to say what the facts will show; it is apparent, however, that, under some set of facts within the bounds of the allegations and nonconclusory facts in the complaint, Rosa may be able to prove a claim under the ECOA.

We reverse and remand.

Questions

1. *a.* Did the court of appeals find that Park West Bank had violated the ECOA? Explain.

 b. If at trial, the facts reveal that the bank employee thought Rosa was gay and demanded that he change clothes for that reason, who will win this case? Explain.

 c. According to the court of appeals, how did the lower court misunderstand this case?

2. *a.* Does federal law protect bank customers based on their style of dress? Explain.

 b. Should it offer that protection? Explain.

PRACTICING ETHICS) Government-Mandated Diversity?

The 2010 Dodd-Frank bill includes a provision creating 20 Offices of Minority and Women Inclusion at various government agencies (Treasury Department, Securities and Exchange Commission, the Consumer Financial Protection Bureau, and so on) charged with regulating the banking industry. Under the bill, the offices will be required to monitor racial and gender diversity at the government agencies themselves as well as private law firms, accounting firms, investment banks, and others contracting and subcontracting with the agencies. If an agency compliance director determines that a contractor has not made a good faith effort to achieve a diverse workforce, the contract may be canceled, among other possible remedies. What will the new law mean? Mark

Calabria of the Cato Institute said the law is so vague it may have little practical effect. Lawrence Zorber, an employment law specialist, said the law largely replicates what is already required by many other antidiscrimination laws. One managing director at a minority-owned investment firm, however, said it may give firms like his "a chance to compete."

Question

Should the government intervene to improve opportunities for women and minorities in the investment banking industry?

Source: Kevin Roose, "Seeking Guidance on Dodd-Frank's Diversity Clause," *The New York Times*, November 11, 2010 [http://dealbook.nytimes.com].

Debtor Protection

The debt collection process continues the nightmare.

Our ongoing financial crisis, one of the most destructive of modern times, has thrown millions of Americans deeply in debt. Wages can be *garnished*. Debts pile up on one another. Then the debt collection process continues the nightmare. *The New York Times* in 2010 recounted the story of Ruth M. Owens, a disabled Cleveland woman who was sued by Discover Bank in 2004 for an unpaid credit card bill. In six years, Ms. Owens had paid nearly $3,500 on her original balance of $1,900, but Discover sued her for $5,564 that had accumulated from late fees, compound interest, penalties, and charges even though she had not used the card to buy anything more. The judge called Discover's behavior "unconscionable" and threw out the case. Discover said that it turned the case over to a lawyer only after repeated unsuccessful efforts to reach Ms. Owens.[49]

Debtors are properly expected to repay what they owe, but debt collection sometimes becomes an abusive process. More than one-third of the states allow borrowers who do not pay to be jailed. From 1999 to 2005, debt collection complaints to the Federal Trade Commission increased sixfold. The FTC received reports of collectors calling at all hours of the night, spewing obscenities, contacting family members or employers and falsely threatening property seizures or imprisonment.[50] As a result, federal and state laws offer considerable protection for wronged debtors.

> The FTC received reports of collectors spewing obscenities.

Debt Collection Law

The federal Fair Debt Collection Practices Act (FDCPA) is designed to shield debtors from unfair debt collection tactics by debt collection agencies and attorneys who routinely operate as debt collectors. The act does not extend to creditors who are themselves trying to recover money owed to them. Several thousand debt collection agencies nationwide pursue those who are delinquent in their debts. The agencies are normally paid on a commission basis and are often exceedingly aggressive and imaginative in their efforts. The FDCPA requires the collector to include a warning in the first communication with the debtor that the communication is an attempt to collect a debt, and any information obtained will be used for that purpose. In any subsequent communication except a court pleading, the collector must always disclose his or her role as a collector.

The FDCPA forbids, among others, the following practices:

- Use of obscene language.
- Contact with third parties other than for the purpose of locating the debtor. (This provision is an attempt to prevent harm to the debtor's reputation.)
- Use of or threats to use physical force.
- Contact with the debtor during "inconvenient" hours. For debtors who are employed during "normal" working hours, the period from 9 PM to 8 AM would probably be considered inconvenient.
- Repeated phone calls with the intent to harass.
- Contacting the debtor in an unfair, abusive, or deceptive manner.

The Federal Trade Commission is responsible for administering the FDCPA. A wronged debtor may also file a civil action to recover all actual damages (for example, payment for job loss occasioned by wrongful debt collection practices as well as damages for associated embarrassment and suffering). [For more details about the FDCPA, see **http://www.ftc.gov/os/statutes/fdcpajump.shtm**]

The case that follows suggests some of the confusion that arises in debt collection.

Circuit Judge Ripple

Sandra Williams . . . sought relief under the Fair Debt Collection Practices Act ("FDCPA"). The district court granted the defendant, OSI Educational Services, Inc., ("OSI"), summary judgment. Ms. Williams then filed a timely appeal to this court.

I. BACKGROUND

A

Ms. Williams is a consumer whose debt was incurred for personal, family or household purposes. OSI is a debt collection agency; it was hired by Great Lakes Higher Education Guaranty Corp. ("Great Lakes") to collect its debts. OSI sent Ms. Williams a letter and a debt validation notice, dated March 28, 2005. The letter sought to collect a sum of $807.89 labeled as "Total Due," which was the outstanding balance owed to Great Lakes. The letter breaks down the amount owed as follows:

Date:	03/28/05
Principal:	$683.56
Interest:	16.46
Fees:	107.87
Total Due:	$807.89

The letter further states:

> The balance may not reflect the exact amount of interest which is accruing daily per your original agreement with your creditor. Contact us to find out your exact payout balance.

B

The district court . . . determined that the letter apprised Ms. Williams of the total amount due, including the amount of the principal, interest and fees due. The district court stated that, . . . the letter clearly advises that additional interest is accruing on a daily basis and that, therefore, additional interest may be added." Comparing this case to *Taylor v. Cavalry Investment, L.L.C.*, the district court took the view that the letter complied with the statute because OSI's "letter states the amount of the debt clearly enough so that an unsophisticated recipient would not misunderstand it."

II. DISCUSSION

Ms. Williams submits that there is an issue of material fact as to whether OSI's letter clearly states the amount of the debt, as required by the FDCPA. In examining that contention, we begin with the wording of the statute. The FDCPA requires that debt collectors state "the amount of the debt" that they are seeking to collect from the consumer. The debt collector's letter must state the amount of the debt "clearly enough that the recipient is likely to understand it." *Chuway v. Nat'/Action Fin.Servs. Inc.* To ensure that this statutory command is implemented properly, we must evaluate the letter to determine whether it causes any "confusion" or "misunderstand[ing]" as to the amount due. In making this determination, we evaluate the letter from the perspective of an "unsophisticated consumer or debtor." The unsophisticated consumer is "uninformed, naive, [and] trusting," but possesses "rudimentary knowledge about the financial world, is wise enough to read collection notices with added care, possesses 'reasonable intelligence,' and is capable of making basic logical deductions and inferences." *Pettit v. Retrieval Masters Creditors Bureau, Inc.* Notably, we have rejected explicitly the notion that we should employ the *least* sophisticated debtor standard, the "very last rung on the sophistication ladder" *Pettit.*

* * * * *

Our past cases indicate that summary judgment may be avoided by showing that the letter, on its face, will "confuse a substantial number of recipients." We also have said that, absent a showing that the face of the letter will precipitate such a level of confusion, the "plaintiff must come forward with evidence beyond the letter and beyond [her] own self-serving assertions that the letter is confusing in order to create a genuine issue of material fact for trial." *Durkin v. Equifax Checking Servs.* (noting that evidence may consist of "carefully designed and conducted consumer survey[s]" or expert witnesses).

Ms. Williams chooses to base her case on the first of these options. She focuses on the following language from OSI's letter:

> The balance may not reflect the exact amount of interest which is accruing daily per your original agreement with your creditor. Contact us to find out your exact payout balance.

In her view, there are three reasons why OSI's letter would confuse a substantial number of recipients. We shall examine each.

First, Ms. Williams argues that the language in OSI's letter is more confusing than that in *Chuway,* which we held could "confuse a substantial number of recipients." *Chuway.* In that case, the letter stated the "balance" and also contained the following language: "Please remit the balance listed above in the return envelope provided. To obtain your most current balance information, please call [phone number]." We held that the letter violated the FDCPA. There, the confusion arose because the letter did not state why the "current balance" would be different than the stated "balance." The plaintiff could have thought that "the reference to the 'current balance' meant that the defendant was trying to collect an additional debt [without] telling her how large an additional debt and thus violating the statute." In contrast, the language in OSI's letter links the difference between the "total due" and the "exact payout balance" to the "interest which is accruing daily per your original agreement with your creditor." OSI's letter thus provides the information that created the confusion in the *Chuway* letter.

Ms. Williams' second and third arguments are best treated together. She submits that the letter's language leaves open the possibility that the actual amount due is less than the amount stated on the letter. She further suggests that the sentence's use of the present tense makes it possible to conclude that the stated amount due was not accurate on the date that the letter was written. In our view, both these contentions are based on a strained reading of the sentence. It would be "unrealistic, peculiar, [and] bizarre" to read OSI's letter in this way. *Durkin.* The common sense reading of the letter is that the balance is accurate as of the date the letter is written, but that the amount due will increase because of interest that is accruing daily. This construction is supported by the letter's itemization of "PRINCIPAL," "INTEREST," "FEES" and "TOTAL DUE" in a box with, and immediately below, the "DATE." Under a natural reading, the language conveys, even to an unsophisticated consumer, that interest will accrue after the letter is sent and therefore that the consumer should call to find out the "*exact* payout balance."

As we said in *Chuway*, "It is impossible to draft a letter that is certain to be understood by every person who receives it; only if it would confuse a significant fraction of the persons to whom it is directed will the defendant be liable."

We believe that the language in this letter is closer to the language in *Taylor* than to the language in *Chuway*. In *Taylor*, the letter similarly set forth the total due and broke down that total into principal and interest. If further stated: "[I]f applicable, your account may have or will accrue interest at a rate specified in your contractual agreement with the original creditor." Three plaintiffs in *Taylor* had submitted affidavits stating that this sentence confused them about the amount of debt that the debt collector was trying

to collect. We held that the language was "entirely clear on its face." . . .

As we noted earlier, in opposing summary judgment, Ms. Williams relied solely on OSI's letter. She submitted no other evidence to support her view that OSI's letter is confusing. Without more, Ms. Williams' unsupported assertion that OSI's letter is confusing is insufficient to create a genuine issue of fact as to confusion.

* * * * *

CONCLUSION

The letter set forth the amount of the debt with sufficient clarity and accuracy to comply with the requirements of the statute.

Affirmed.

Questions

1. *a.* A debt collection letter must be evaluated to determine whether it causes confusion or misunderstanding for the consumer. What level of consumer sophistication was employed by the court to determine whether the debt collection letter to Williams caused confusion or misunderstanding?

   b. Is confusion on the part of an individual consumer conclusive evidence of a violation of the Fair Debt Collection Practices Act? Explain.

   c. Describe the two ways by which a plaintiff/consumer can establish that a debt collection letter caused an impermissible level of confusion or misunderstanding.

2. Miller owed $2,501.61 to the Star Bank of Cincinnati. Payco attempted to collect the debt by sending a one-page collection form to Miller. The front side of the form included, among other words, in very large capital letters a demand for IMMEDIATE FULL PAYMENT, the words PHONE US TODAY, and the word NOW in white letters nearly two inches tall against a red background. At the bottom of the page in the smallest print on the form was the message: NOTICE: SEE REVERSE SIDE FOR IMPORTANT INFORMATION. The reverse side contained the validation notice required under the FDCPA. Does the form conform to FDCPA requirements? Explain. See *Miller v. Payco-General American Credits, Inc.,* 943 F.2d 482 (4th Cir. 1991).

3. Why shouldn't debt collectors be able to use aggressive tactics to encourage payment of legitimate bills?

FORECLOSURE FRAUD?

The mortgage industry, already buried in bad loans and worse publicity, faced another scandal in 2010 when the news emerged that some or perhaps many banks and individuals had not followed proper legal procedures in pursuing foreclosure orders against borrowers (commonly, the situation in which a homeowner fails to make mortgage payments and loses the home). Broadly, the scandal involved allegations that lenders bent rules to speed up the foreclosure process. Sloppy record keeping and outright errors apparently were routine. In a process now called "robo-signing," bank employees sometimes signed thousands of foreclosure affidavits in a single day, clearly never carefully examining them as expected. Critics now believe banks often cannot prove the facts necessary to achieve a lawful foreclosure. In some instances, the sloppy and perhaps negligent record keeping may even prevent banks from proving they are the legal owners of the properties being foreclosed on. Foreclosure proceedings were halted all over the country as bank and government officials reviewed records to see how common these problems were. Hundreds of thousands of homeowners now believe they were foreclosed on unlawfully.

Class actions have been filed, and all 50 state attorneys general are pursuing the banks. Federal regulators settled with a number of banks and others in early 2011 with an agreement to discontinue the wrongful practices, but a July 2011 *Reuters* investigation indicated that some banks and other loan servicers "continue to file questionable foreclosure documents" with some allegedly continuing to practice "robo-signings."

Sources: Associated Press, "Foreclosure Class Actions Pile Up Against Banks," *The Des Moines Register,* November 18, 2010, p. 7B; Associated Press, "Iowa Attorney General: Mortgage Industry Problems Broad," *The Des Moines Register,* November 17, 2010, p. 7B; and Scot J. Paltrow, "Special Report: Banks Continue Robo-Signing," *Reuters,* July 18, 2011 [**http://www.reuters.com/**].

Part Four—Bankruptcy

Fresh Start? Should we lend a hand to those subprime borrowers and others who are down on their luck? Bankruptcy law was specifically designed to provide a fresh start for those whose financial problems were insurmountable. We believed that both the debtor and society benefited from the new beginning. As bankruptcy filings skyrocketed, however, we downsized the fresh start by reforming federal bankruptcy law in 2005 to force more bankrupt parties to repay their creditors. Following the reform, bankruptcies did fall somewhat in 2006, but recently total consumer and business bankruptcies, reflecting the tough times, have been up sharply increasing by 32 percent from 2008 to 2009 and by 8 percent in 2010 over 2009.[51] Of course, those tough times are often of our own making. In 2008, American consumers owed $2.6 trillion in nonmortgage debt, an average of $8,460 for every person in America.[52]

> American consumers owed an average of $8,460 for every person in America.

The Reform Law—An Overview In brief, the 2005 legislation forces some bankruptcy filers to enter their claim under Chapter 13 of the bankruptcy code rather than the more forgiving Chapter 7 (see below). Chapter 13 is directed to those who have the capacity to pay at least some of what they owe, but they will need more time to do so. Those with income above their state's median who can pay $6,000 over five years—$100 per month—ordinarily are forced into Chapter 13, where the court orders a repayment plan. After a few years experience with the new law, one expert estimates that only about one third of Chapter 13 filings are seen through to the end of the process.[53] Those not meeting the Chapter 13 test can file under Chapter 7, thereby achieving a fresh start by escaping most repayment responsibilities while their nonessential property is sold to pay debtors. The law also requires those filing for bankruptcy to pay for credit counseling. [For the American Bankruptcy Institute, see **http://www.abiworld.org**]

The Reform Law—Criticisms   Supporters of the 2005 reforms argue that they reduce the cost of credit for all Americans, but opponents see the changes as a punitive assault on those already down on their luck. For individuals, the 2005 reforms made the process much more complicated, and the average cost of filing more than doubled to over $2,000.[54] Homeowners behind on their house payments now often find mortgage foreclosure more attractive than bankruptcy since the reforms have produced increased expenses and reduced benefits. Thus, the reforms appear to have caused borrowers to simply walk away from their "underwater" homes leaving lenders with mountains of troubled properties on their books.[55]

On the business side, Congress has been considering revisions to the 2005 reform law because the reforms have forced a number of big companies, especially retailers, into liquidation. Under the old rules, debtors had unlimited time to file a restructuring plan, but the reform law limits that time to 18 months.[56] The new rules also require debtor companies to find the cash to pay suppliers and utilities, whereas under the old rules those two groups had to wait until the debtor emerged from bankruptcy in order to be paid. The result has been that most retailers entering Chapter 13 from 2005 to 2009 either sold their assets or liquidated rather than restructuring.[57]

Bankruptcy Rules

Bankruptcy in the United States is governed exclusively by federal law; the states do not have the constitutional authority to enact bankruptcy legislation, but they do set their own rules within the limits provided by Congress. Our attention will be limited to the principal federal statute, the Bankruptcy Reform Act of 1978, as amended.

Bankruptcy is an adjudication relieving a debtor of all or part of his/her/its liabilities. Any person, partnership, or corporation may seek debtor relief. Three forms of bankruptcy action are important to us:

1. **Liquidation** (**Chapter 7** of the Bankruptcy Act), is used by both individuals and businesses. Most debts are forgiven and all assets except exemptions are fairly distributed to creditors.
2. **Reorganization** (**Chapter 11**), used by both individuals and businesses, keeps creditors from the debtor's assets while the debtor, under the supervision of the court, works out a financial reorganization plan and continues to pay creditors.
3. **Adjustment of debts** of an individual with regular income (**Chapter 13**), in which individuals with limited debts are protected from creditors while paying their debts in installments. [For frequently asked bankruptcy questions and links to bankruptcy sites on the Internet, see **http://www.lawtrove.com/bankruptcy**].

Liquidation

A Chapter 7 liquidation petition can be *voluntarily* filed in federal court by the debtor, or creditors can seek an *involuntary* bankruptcy judgment. A Chapter 7 liquidation is commonly called a "straight" bankruptcy.

In a voluntary action, the debtor files a petition with the appropriate federal court. The court then has jurisdiction to proceed with the liquidation, and the petition becomes the *order for relief.* The debtor need not be insolvent to seek bankruptcy.

Creditors often can compel an involuntary bankruptcy. The debtor may challenge that bankruptcy action. The court will enter an order for relief if it finds the debtor has not been paying his or her debts when due or if most of the debtor's property is under the control of a custodian for the purpose of enforcing a lien against that property.

After the order for relief is granted, voluntary and involuntary actions proceed in a similar manner. Creditors are restrained from reaching the debtor's assets. An interim bankruptcy trustee is appointed by the court. The creditors then hold a meeting, and a permanent trustee is elected. The trustee collects the debtor's property and converts it to money, protects the interests of the debtor and creditors, may manage the debtor's business, and ultimately distributes the estate proceeds to the creditors. Debtors are allowed to keep exempt property, which varies from state to state but typically includes a car, a homestead, some household or personal items, life insurance, and other "necessities." Normally a dollar maximum is attached to each.

The debtor's nonexempt property is then divided among the creditors according to the priorities prescribed by statute. Secured creditors are paid first. If funds remain, "priority" claims, such as employees' wages and alimony/child support, are paid. Then, funds permitting, general creditors are paid. Each class must be paid in full before a class of lower priority will be compensated. Any remaining funds will return to the debtor.

When distribution is complete, the bankruptcy judge may issue an order discharging (relieving) the debtor of any remaining debts except for certain statutorily specified claims. Those include, for example, taxes and educational loans. The debtor might fail to receive a discharge if he or she had received one in the previous six years, if property was concealed from the court, or if good faith in the bankruptcy process was lacking in other respects.

Reorganization

Under Chapter 11, the debtor may voluntarily seek reorganization, or the creditors may petition for an involuntary action. When a reorganization petition is filed with the court and relief is ordered, one or more committees of creditors are appointed to participate in bankruptcy procedures. Typically in the case of a business, the debtor continues operations, although the court may appoint a trustee to replace the debtor if required because of dishonesty, fraud, or extreme mismanagement. The company, its bankers, and its suppliers will meet to work out a method for continuing operations. A plan must be developed that will satisfy the creditors that their interests are being served by the reorganization. Perhaps new capital is secured, or perhaps creditors receive some shares in the company. The plan must be approved by the creditors and confirmed by the court. The company is then required to carry out the plan.

GM Bankruptcy/Bailout

General Motors, in 2009, was forced to enter Chapter 11 bankruptcy as part of a federal government-directed, prepackaged bailout of the failing firm. GM had gone from being one of the most prominent corporations in the world to a sprawling, dysfunctional failure. GM reported $82.29 billion in assets and $172.81 billion in debts. The federal government put $49.5 billion into the bailout and took a 60 percent equity stake in the new General Motors, although the company retained control of its day-to-day affairs.

Achieving a remarkable comeback, in 2010, General Motors declared that it was operating profitably and the company began its planned return to the private sector with an initial public offering (IPO) of shares issued at $33 each. At the end of trading on the first day of the IPO, the GM share price had risen to $35. As part of the IPO, the United States sold about half of its interest in GM. The government has since reduced its share to about 27 percent and at this writing in mid-2011, wants to sell the balance—about 500 million shares—but is waiting to achieve the optimal payback for the taxpayers. If the remaining shares are sold at that $35 price, taxpayers will recoup all but about $9 billion of the government's $49.5 billion bailout.

The IPO was cited by some as convincing evidence that the government was correct to rescue General Motors. The government's total automobile industry bailout, including GM, Chrysler, and the auto lender GMAC, saved over 1.1 million jobs and an estimated $23.8 billion in social service costs and lost tax revenue. On the other hand, critics argue the deal was a dangerous abandonment of market principles. Some of those arguments:

- The bailout encouraged future risky behavior by conveying the message that the government will always be there as a backup.
- Private investors would have moved in to cut costs and restore a new, trimmer GM.
- The $50 billion of taxpayer money could have been better spent elsewhere or not spent at all.

Question

Was the federal government wise to bailout General Motors, or should GM have been left to face the force of the market and the decisions of the Chapter 11 bankruptcy judge?

Sources: John Lott, "GM's Bailout Is a Financial Disaster," FoxNews.com, November 18, 2010 [**http://www.foxnews.com**]; Mark Guarino, "With Big GM Stock Offering, Vindication for the Government Bailout?" *Christian Science Monitor,* November 19, 2010 [**http://www.csmonitor.com/2010/**]; Shira Ovide, "GM IPO: Auto Bailout Saved More Than 1 Million Jobs, Study Says," *The Wall Street Journal,* November 17, 2010 [**http://blogs.wsj.com**]; David Welch and Craig Trudell, "GM Bailout Losses Worthwhile for Obama as IPO Shrinks Cost to $9 Billion," *Bloomberg,* November 19, 2010 [**http://www.bloomberg.com/news/**]; and Staff Report, "U.S. Government Wants to Sell Its Share in General Motors for Political Reasons," *International Business Times,* June 28, 2011 [**http://m.ibtimes.com**].

Adjustment of Debts

Under Chapter 13, individuals (not partnerships or corporations) can seek the protection of the court to arrange a debt adjustment plan. Chapter 13 permits only voluntary bankruptcies and is restricted to those with steady incomes and somewhat limited debts. The process can begin only with a voluntary petition from the debtor. Creditors are restrained from reaching the debtor's assets. The debtor develops a repayment plan. If creditors' interests are sufficiently satisfied by the plan, the court may confirm it and appoint a trustee to oversee the plan. The debtor may then have three to five years to make the necessary payments. [For an extensive bankruptcy law database, see **http://www.law.cornell.edu/wex/Bankruptcy**]

PRACTICING ETHICS   Bankruptcy—Who Is to Blame?

Commenting on the 2005 bankruptcy reform law, Todd Zywicki, a George Mason University law professor, said, "This is a matter of morality and personal responsibility." Consumer advocates, on the other hand, say the bankruptcy problem lies with the "enablers"—the credit card companies and mortgage lenders who encourage deeper and deeper indebtedness.

Question

Who bears the moral blame for America's bankruptcy epidemic? Explain.

Source: Michael Schroeder and Suein Hwang, "Sweeping New Bankruptcy Law to Make Life Harder for Debtors," *The Wall Street Journal,* April 6, 2005, p. A1.

Internet Exercise

Go to the Center for Auto Safety Web site [**http://www.autosafety.org/**], click the lemon laws button and find your state's lemon law. Read the brief summary of the law of your state. Read the summary for the states of Texas, Virginia, and West Virginia.

a. Explain the differences among the state laws you reviewed.

b. Which of those three or four states, in your view, provides the "fairest" protection considering the viewpoints of both consumers and dealers?

Chapter Questions

1. A group of parents sued Gerber claiming its "Fruit Juice Snacks" product packaging was misleading. The words "Fruit Juice" appeared on the package beside images of fruits such as peaches and cherries. In fact, the only fruit juice in the "Snacks" was white grape from concentrate. A side panel statement said the product was made "with real fruit juice and other all natural ingredients," but the primary ingredients were corn syrup and sugar. The side panel also displayed the statement, "one of a variety of nutritious Gerber Graduates foods and juices that have been specifically designed to help toddlers grow up strong and healthy." The actual ingredients were correctly listed in "small print" on the side of the box. Is a "reasonable consumer" "likely to be deceived" by the Gerber packaging? Explain. See *Williams v. Gerber Products,* 523 F.3d 934 (9th Cir. 2008).

2. Two-thirds of American adults are either obese or overweight. The rate of overweight children ages 6 to 11 has more than doubled since 1980, and the rate for adolescents has tripled. Timothy Muris, chairman of the Federal Trade Commission, objected to proposals to ban television commercials for "junk food" directed at kids: "Banning junk food ads on kids' programming is impractical, ineffective, and illegal." Explain

what Muris meant. See Timothy J. Muris, "Don't Blame TV," *The Wall Street Journal,* June 25, 2004, p. A10.

3. DeSantis sued a debt collection agency, Computer Credit. DeSantis apparently owed $319.50 to Dr. Jeffrey A. Stahl, who assigned the debt to CC for collection. On April 27, 2000, CC sent the following collection letter to DeSantis:

> This notice will serve to inform you that your overdue balance with Dr. Jeffrey A. Stahl has been referred to Computer Credit, Inc., a debt collector. *[The] doctor insists on payment or a valid reason for your failure to make payment.* The law prohibits us from collecting any amount greater than the obligation stated above. Unless you notify us to the contrary, we will assume the amount due is correct. This communication is sent to you in an attempt to collect this debt. Any information obtained will be used for that purpose. *In the absence of a valid reason for your failure to make payment, pay the above debt or contact the doctor to settle this matter.* Payment can be sent directly to the doctor. [Italics added.]

The Fair Debt Collection Practices Act specifies that the consumer may dispute the alleged debt, in which case the debt collector must desist from collection until the debt collector obtains verification regarding the amount of the debt, if any. Given that statutory requirement, was the FDCPA violated by the italicized sentences in the collection letter? Explain. See *DeSantis v. Computer Credit, Inc.,* 269 F.3d 159 (2d Cir. 2001).

4. A *New York Times* editorial argued that college students are taken advantage of by credit card companies:

> The credit card industry has made a profitable art of corralling consumers into ruinous interest rates and hidden penalties that keep even people who pay their bills permanently mired in debt. The companies are especially eager to target freshly minted college students, who are naïve in money matters and especially vulnerable to credit card offers that are too good to be true.[58]

   a. Do you think beginning college students are often "vulnerable" to manipulation by credit card companies?
   b. Are you vulnerable to that alleged manipulation?
   c. Should the federal government provide more protection against credit card deception? Explain.

5. Snow wrote a $23.12 check to a convenience store, Circle K. The check bounced, and Circle K sent the check to its attorney, Riddle, for collection. Riddle sent Snow a letter demanding payment along with a $15 service fee. Snow paid the $23.12, but refused to pay the $15. Then Snow sued Riddle for violating the Fair Debt Collection Practices Act because the collection letter did not include the required "validation notice" telling him about his legal rights under the FDCPA. Riddle responded by saying that the FDCPA does not apply to dishonored checks. Does a dishonored check constitute a debt such that the FDCPA would apply? Explain. See *Snow v. Riddle,* 143 F.3d 1350 (10th Cir. 1998).

6. Millions of Americans are "underwater" on their home mortgages; that is, they owe more than their homes are worth. Many of those families could simply walk away from their mortgage, rent a similar home and save thousands of dollars per year. Doubtless many decline to abandon their mortgages because they fear the consequences for their credit records and they want to avoid the cost of changing homes, but

surely some continue to make payments simply because they believe defaulting would be immoral. While serving as U.S. Treasury Secretary, Henry Paulson said that anyone who walks away from his or her mortgage is "simply a speculator—and one who is not honoring his obligation."[59]

a. Make the argument that deliberately walking away from an underwater home mortgage situation is immoral.

b. Make the argument that walking away is not immoral.

c. What would you do? Explain. See Richard H. Thaler, "Underwater, but Will They Leave the Pool?" *The New York Times,* January 24, 2010 [**http://www.nytimes. com**] and Brent T. White, "Buyers Have No Moral Duty to Lenders," *Arizona Republic,* April 25, 2010 [**http://www.azcentral.com/arizonarepublic/viewpoints/ articles/2010/04/25/20100425white25.htm**].

7. William Cohan, writing in *The New York Times,* objected to the federal government's consumer protection efforts in the Dodd-Frank Wall Street Reform and Consumer Protection Act, including the creation of the Consumer Financial Protection Bureau. Explain why Cohan and other critics would object to the government's efforts to protect consumers from "devious credit-card companies" and "dishonest mortgage lenders." See William D. Cohan, "The Elizabeth Warren Fallacy," *The New York Times,* September 30, 2010 [**http://opinionator.blogs.nytimes.com/**].

8. Recent studies suggest that consumer bankruptcies are much more common in some states than others. Aside from income levels, what socioeconomic factors would you expect to be closely correlated with high bankruptcy rates?

9. Playtex manufactures the market-leading spill proof cup for children, which a child uses by sucking on a spout to cause a valve to open. Gerber introduced its own version and ran ads showing an unnamed competitor's product and claiming that "Gerber's patented valve makes our cup more than 50 percent easier to drink from than the leading cup." Gerber's claims for the superiority of its cup were backed by tests from an independent laboratory. Playtex said the unnamed cup obviously was its brand and that the superiority claims were false and misleading. Playtex sought an injunction to block the Gerber ads. Would you grant that injunction? Explain. See *Playtex Products v. Gerber Products,* 981 F.Supp. 827 (S.D.N.Y. 1997).

10. Maguire, a credit card holder at Bradlees Department Store, fell behind in her payments. She received a series of dunning letters from Citicorp, which managed Bradlees' accounts, demanding that she pay the overdue amount. Later Maguire received a letter from "Debtor Assistance," which said that "your Bradlees account has recently [been] charged off." Debtor Assistance is a unit of Citicorp, but was not identified as such in the letter, beyond the phrase "a unit of CRS." The back of each Bradlees' account statement includes a notice that Citicorp Retail Services was the creditor that handled Bradlees' accounts. In general, creditors are not subject to the requirements of the Fair Debt Collections Practices Act, but Maguire sued claiming the Debtor Assistance letter violated the FDCPA. Is she correct? Explain. See *Maguire v. Citicorp Retail Services, Inc.,* 147 F.3d 232 (2d Cir. 1998).

11. A door-to-door salesman representing Your Shop at Home Services, Inc., called on Clifton and Cora Jones, who were welfare recipients. The Jones couple decided to buy a freezer from the salesman for $900. Credit charges, insurance, and so on were added

to that $900 base so that the total purchase price was $1,439.69. Mr. and Mrs. Jones signed a sales agreement that accurately stipulated the price and its ingredients. The Joneses sued to reform the contract on unconscionability grounds. They had paid $619.88 toward the total purchase price. At trial, the retail value of the new freezer at the time of purchase was set at approximately $300.

a. What is the issue in this case?

b. Decide. Explain. See *Jones v. Star Credit Corp.,* 298 N.Y.S.2d 264 (1969).

12. Roseman resigned from the John Hancock Insurance Company following allegations of misuse of his expense account. He reimbursed the account. Subsequently he was denied employment by another insurance firm after that firm read a Retail Credit Company credit report on him. The credit report included accurate information regarding Roseman's resignation. Was Retail Credit in violation of the Fair Credit Reporting Act in circulating information regarding the resignation? Explain. See *Roseman v. Retail Credit Co., Inc.,* 428 F.Supp. 643 (Pa. 1977).

13. Once the government decided to intervene in the free market on behalf of consumers, two broad product safety options presented themselves: (a) the government could have limited its effort to generating and distributing information to consumers, or (b) the government could have set safety standards for all products. Assuming the government was forced to choose one or the other but not elements of both, which option should it have chosen? Explain.

14. Consumers sometimes abuse sellers. One familiar technique is shoplifting. Of course, shoplifting is a crime. However, the criminal process is cumbersome and often does not result in monetary recoveries for sellers. As a result, at least 43 states now have laws permitting store owners to impose civil fines, the collection of which is usually turned over to a lawyer or collection agency with a threat to sue in civil court, file criminal charges, or both if payment is not forthcoming. Fines may range from $50 to $5,000 or more, depending on the value of the item stolen.

a. Defense lawyers say this civil fine system is unfair. Why?

b. On balance, is the civil fine approach to shoplifting a good idea? Explain.

c. Cite some other examples of consumers abusing businesspeople.

15. Goswami failed to pay her $900 credit card bill. A collection agency, ACEI, mailed her a collection letter with a blue bar across the envelope saying "Priority Letter." The letter did not, in fact, constitute priority mail. The purpose of the bar was to encourage Goswami to open the envelope. Was the bar a deceptive practice in violation of the Fair Debt Collection Practices Act? Explain. See *Goswami v. American Collections Enterprise, Inc.,* 377 F.3d 488 (5th Cir. 2004); cert. den. 2005 U.S. LEXIS 5511.

Notes

1. Walter Hamilton, "For-Profit Colleges Face Federal Crackdown," *latimes.com,* February 6, 2011 [**http://www.latimes.com/business/la-fi-for-profit-colleges-20110206,0,1109616.story**].

2. Ibid.

3. Herb Greenberg, "GAO Finds For-Profit Schools Encouraged Fraud," CNBC, August 4, 2010 [**http://www.cnbc.com/id/38541939/GAO_Finds_For_Profit_Schools_Encouraged_Fraud**].

4. Walter Hamilton, "For-Profit Colleges," February 6, 2011.

5. For a detailed overview of the CFPB, see **http://www.aba.com/RegReform/RR10_overview.htm**.

6. The materials in this section relied in significant part on Martin J. Bishop, "Meet the New Boss: The Bureau of Consumer Financial Protection," *The CFSL Bulletin,* July 23, 2010 [**http://www.cfslbulletin.com/**].

7. James Rainey, "Truth in Advertising Meets the Blogosphere," *latimes.com,* October 7, 2009 [**http://www.latimes.com/**].

8. Donna De La Cruz, "Diet-Pill Companies Fined $25 Million," *The Des Moines Register,* January 5, 2007, p. 5A.

9. Monica Hesse, "Barbie Tells CPSC to Get the Lead Out in Viral Video," *Washington Post,* November 24, 2007, p. C01.

10. Leslie Wayne, "Burden of Safety Law Imperils Small Toymakers," *The New York Times,* October 31, 2009 [**http://www.nytimes.com**].

11. Anne M. Northup, "There Is No Joy in Toyland," *The Wall Street Journal,* December 24, 2009, p. A10.

12. Ibid.

13. Associated Press, "New Crib Rules Toughest in World," *The Des Moines Register,* June 30, 2011, p. 7B.

14. David Lazarus, "Gaping Holes in Product Safety Net," *Los Angeles Times,* August 19, 2007 [**http://www.latimes.com**].

15. "Consumer Product Safety Improvement Act of 2008: New Regulatory Landscape for Product Safety," Consumer Product Regulation Lawflash, August 5, 2008 [**http://www.morganlewis.com**].

16. Lyndsey Layton, "Officials Worry about Consumers Lost among the Recalls," *Washington Post,* July 2, 2010, p. A01.

17. Ibid.

18. "Drug Manufacturer Agrees to Pay $750 Million Fine," *The Des Moines Register,* October 27, 2010, p. 2A.

19. P.J. Huffstutter, "Amid Mounting Safety Concerns, Technology Helps Track Food from Farm to Table," *latimes.com,* October 3, 2010 [**http://www.latimes.com**].

20. Ibid.

21. Andrew Zajac, "Bill Giving FDA New Powers to Oversee Food Supply Has Wide Support," *latimes.com,* October 22, 2009 [**http://www.latimes.com**].

22. Gardiner Harris, "U.S. Food Safety No Longer Improving," *The New York Times,* April 10, 2009 [**http://www.nytimes.com**].

23. Zajac, "Bill Giving FDA New Powers" [**http://www.latimes.com**].

24. Gardner Harris, "The Safety Gap," *The New York Times,* November 2, 2008 [**http://www.nytimes.com**].

25. Ibid.

26. Ibid.

27. Ibid.

28. Ibid.

29. Avery Johnson and Ron Winslow, "Drug Makers Say FDA Safety Focus Is Slowing New-Medicine Pipeline," *The Wall Street Journal,* June 30, 2008, p. A1.

30. Catherine Larkin, "New Drug Approvals Fall in 2010 as Safety Concerns Slow U.S. FDA Decisions," *Bloomberg,* December 30, 2010 [**http://www.bloomberg.com/**], and Associated

Press, "FDA's Approvals Flat in 2009, Safety Up," *msnbc.com,* January 5, 2010 [**http://www. msnbc.com**].

31. Joseph Pereira, "How Credit-Card Data Went Out Wireless Door," *The Wall Street Journal,* May 4, 2007, p. A1.

32. Joseph Menn and Andrea Chang, "11 Charged in Largest ID Theft in U.S. History," *Los Angeles Times,* August 6, 2008 [**http://www.latimes.com**].

33. "Hacker Sentenced to 20 Years for Stealing Credit Card Data," *The Des Moines Register,* March 26, 2010, p. 2A.

34. Siobhan Gorman, "Arrest in Epic Cyber Swindle," *The Wall Street Journal,* August 18, 2009, p. A1.

35. Menn and Chang, "11 Charged in Largest ID Theft in U.S. History."

36. Brian Krebs, "Data Breaches Are more Costly than Ever," *WashingtonPost.com,* February 3, 2009, p. D03.

37. Dean Foust, "ID Theft: More Hype than Harm," *BusinessWeek,* July 3, 2006, p. 34.

38. Ibid.

39. Erik Eckholm, "Enticing Ad, Little Cash and Then a Lot of Regret," *The New York Times,* July 14, 2007 [**http://www.nytimes.com**].

40. Ibid.

41. Ibid.

42. "Student-Loan Debt Surpasses Credit Cards," *The Wall Street Journal,* August 9, 2010 [**http:// blogs.wsj.com/economics/2010/08/09/**].

43. Sandra Block, "Reform Swipes Easy Plastic from Students," *The Des Moines Register,* May 31, 2009, p. 3D.

44. Jonathan Glater, "Colleges Profit as Banks Market Credit Cards to Students," *The New York Times,* January 1, 2009 [**http://www.nytimes.com/**].

45. Jessica Silver-Greenberg and Mary Pilon, "Cards Return to School," *The Wall Street Journal,* May 7, 2011 [**http://online.wsj.com/**].

46. Associated Press, "Positive Results Seen from Credit Card Law," *Waterloo/Cedar Falls Courier,* May 10, 2011, p. B7.

47. Jennifer Liberto, "Bank Critic Praises Credit Card Companies," *CNNMoney.com,* February 22, 2011 [**http://money.cnn.com/fdcp?1298396190777**].

48. This summary of FCRA requirements was drawn largely from the FTC document, "A Summary of Your Rights under the Fair Credit Reporting Act" [**http://www.ftc.gov/bcp/conline/edcams/ fcra/summary.htm**].

49. John Collins Rudolf, "Pay Garnishments Rise as Debtors Fall Behind," *The New York Times,* April 1, 2010 [**http://www.nytimes.com**] and *Washington Post,* "Punitive Charges Dog Credit Card Users," *Waterloo/Cedar Falls Courier,* March 7, 2005, p. A1.

50. Editorial, "When a Stranger Calls," *The New York Times,* July 9, 2006 [**http://www.nytimes.com**].

51. American Bankruptcy Institute, "Total Bankruptcy Filings Increase 32 Percent in 2009; Approach Pre-BAPCPA Levels," *Press Release* [**http://www.abiworld.org/**] and "ABI: Annual Bankruptcy Levels Finally Slow Down Growth Rate," *Subprime Auto Finance News,* February 17, 2011 [**http://www.subprimenews.com/**].

52. David Lazarus, "Public Likely to Pay for Rising Personal Bankruptcies," *Los Angeles Times,* October 22, 2008 [**http://www.latimes.com/business/la-fi-lazarus22-2008oct22,0,6123538. column?track=ntothtml**].

53. David Colker, "Consumer Bankruptcy: A Guide," *Los Angeles Times,* April 26, 2009 [**http://www.latimes.com/business/la-fi-cover26-2009apr26,0,2241881.story**].

54. John Collins Rudolf, "Pay Garnishments Rise as Debtors Fall Behind," *The New York Times,* April 1, 2010 [**http://www.nytimes.com/2010/04/02/**].

55. Jessica Silver-Greenberg, "Bankruptcy Blowback," *BusinessWeek,* September 22, 2008, p. 036.

56. Kristina Doss, "A Kinder Bankruptcy Law Is Sought as Filings Soar," *The Wall Street Journal,* January 21, 2009 [**http://online.wsj.com/**].

57. Ibid.

58. Editorial, "The College Credit Scam," *The New York Times,* August 27, 2007 [**http://www.nytimes.com**].

59. Richard H. Thaler, "Underwater, but Will They Leave the Pool?" *The New York Times,* January 24, 2010 [**http://www.nytimes.com**].

International Ethics and Law

After completing this chapter, students will be able to:

1. Discuss the role of the World Trade Organization (WTO) in reducing global trade barriers.

2. Compare and contrast an American firm's social responsibility to its host country with its social responsibility to its home country.

3. Discuss the interrelationship of religion, culture, and legal rules with comparisons to American and Islamic viewpoints.

4. Evaluate arguments in favor of global social responsibility standards.

5. Describe the basic forms of global business expansion.

6. Compare and contrast treaties, custom, and comity and give illustrations of each.

7. Describe examples of the law governing international business in sales of goods, trade in-services, and employment.

8. Identify and describe the three main forms of intellectual property covered in the text and the international agreements that address them.

9. Discuss how and why nations regulate imports and exports.

10. Describe the purposes and effects of the General Agreement on Tariffs and Trade (GATT) and the General Agreement on Trade in Services (GATS).

11. Identify and evaluate the means for resolving international disputes.

12. Explain the act of state doctrine.

13. Describe the doctrine of sovereign immunity and its exceptions as codified under the Foreign Sovereign Immunities Act (FSIA).

14. Discuss the recent use of the Foreign Tort Claims Act against corporate defendants.

15. Identify some challenges to the enforcement of foreign judgments.

Introduction

The preceding chapters have addressed law and ethics primarily in an American context. However, ours is undeniably a global economy, as painfully evidenced by the global economic recession triggered in 2008. Many factors contributing to the recession were international in source: worldwide capital surpluses (particularly generated in China and oil-producing countries) made borrowing relatively inexpensive and allowed credit bubbles to develop in both the United States and Europe. Capital naturally seeks investment opportunities. One booming opportunity was the market for derivatives. A derivative is a financial contract the price of which is determined (derived) from the value of an underlying asset, such as a pool of real estate mortgages. In the United States, the market took off for derivatives such as collateralized debt obligations (CDOs) based on mortgage-backed securities and credit default swaps (CDS) that transferred the risk of a default from the CDS purchaser to the CDS seller. Worldwide banks and other financial institutions bought these CDOs and the insurance industry traded in CDS contracts with little investigation or understanding of their inherent risks—the rewards seemingly too great to pass up. Many of these institutions turned out to be inadequately capitalized relative to the risks. Some collapsed or nearly so when the credit bubble burst, thereby contributing to the global recession that has followed.

> Globalization is the breaking down of national boundaries to allow free interchange of people, communications, services, goods, businesses, investments, and ideas.

The process of globalization is the breaking down of national boundaries and rules to allow free interchange around the world—the free interchange of people, communications, services, goods, businesses, investments (as just illustrated), and ideas. Evidence of our global economy is everywhere. Travel the world and you can readily access automated teller machines (ATMs) for local currency that will be instantaneously debited from your domestic bank account. You will see such American logos as Starbucks, McDonalds, and KPMG adorning shops and buildings. Back at home, on streets and in malls, you can see branches and outlets for HSBC (formerly the Hongkong and Shanghai Banking Corporation, now the world's sixth-largest banking group and headquartered in London), Godiva Chocolatier (founded in Brussels), Hyundai cars (Korean), and H&M clothing stores (Swedish).

But how is business practice affected by this networked global economy? Which laws govern company behavior? The laws of the "home" country? The laws of the "host" country? The laws where the company's suppliers or customers reside? What happens if the laws of the host country and the home country conflict? And what happens when a corporation changes its home country? When the German corporation, Daimler Benz, merged with Chrysler, becoming Daimler Chrysler, did the laws to which it was subject change? Did those changes have to be unwound when Daimler later sold Chrysler to Cerberus Capital Management, an American private equity fund, in 2007? In 2009 the U.S. government financed a deal to get Chrysler out of bankruptcy. The Italian automaker Fiat then bought a 30 percent stake in the company. What law will govern the company if the new Chrysler pays back the U.S. government and Fiat gains control? As firms become companies of the world, rather than of one nation, difficult issues of ethics and law arise.

The International Environment

Ever since Adam Smith wrote *The Wealth of Nations* in 1776, many have argued that it is axiomatic that a decrease in trade barriers between any number of countries will stimulate the total world economy, not simply the economies of the countries involved in the specific trade agreement. Belief in this principle is affirmed each time a new nation joins the World Trade Organization (WTO). As of this writing, 153 countries are members. A fundamental principle set forth in the preamble to the 1994 Marrakesh Agreement, which established the WTO effective January 1, 1995, is that "substantial reduction of tariffs and other barriers to trade" will contribute to the objectives of "raising standards of living, ensuring full employment and a large and steadily growing volume of real income."[1] Member countries in the WTO represent a diverse array of the world's governments: from communist to socialist to capitalist, from Buddhist to Jewish to Christian to Muslim, and from all points around the globe. Thus belief in the benefits of decreasing trade barriers is widely shared in the international community.

Trade Negotiations

The commitment to decreased trade barriers has been tested, however, by the struggle of member states during the long-running round of WTO multilateral trade negotiations, known as the Doha Round (after the city in Qatar where the round was initiated). The Doha negotiations have collapsed several times since their start in 2001. One sticking point has been the extensive domestic farm subsidy programs maintained by both the United States and the European Union. These are strenuously objected to by developing nations, led by Brazil and India, who argue that "massive subsidies allow rich nations to flood global markets with farm products, depressing prices and impeding the economic development of poor countries that rely on agriculture as their primary source of exports.

> African nations complain that American cotton subsidies contribute to the impoverishment of thousands of African growers.

For example, African nations complain that American cotton subsidies contribute to the impoverishment of thousands of African growers."[2] Another issue is the push, particularly by the United States, for certain developing nations, notably China, to lower their own tariffs on manufactured goods. Because the WTO talks are based on consensus, not on votes, even less powerful nations, particularly when they act in concert, can make their concerns felt. The fear is that, in the absence of viable multilateral trade negotiations under the auspices of the WTO, there will be a return to bilateral trade talks in which the imbalance of power between rich and poor nations is more pronounced. [The WTO maintains an extensive online presence, including full text documents, through its Web site at **http://www.wto.org**]

Trade Agreements

The desire to reach a common legal ground in international business is not a recent development. As early as 1778 U.S. commercial treaties (largely bilateral) have regulated shipping and trading rights and rules between individuals of different countries. The 20th century saw an unprecedented expansion of world trade facilitated by the development of many regional trade agreements, such as the General Agreement on Tariffs and

Trade (GATT—now a foundation agreement of the WTO) and the North American Free Trade Agreement (NAFTA). A number of regional common markets also developed, including the MERCOSUR Common Market (created by Argentina, Brazil, Paraguay, and Uruguay) and the East African Community (created by Kenya, Tanzania, and Uganda). New international trade agreements continue to be reached. For example, China and New Zealand now have a free trade agreement and Libya made an agreement allowing it to grow wheat in the Ukraine in exchange for including the latter in construction and gas deals.

European Union

The European Union is a particularly noteworthy example for our purposes, and despite debt problems in some nations, it continues to grow as an economic powerhouse. The EU is made up of 27 member countries and it has four candidate countries: Croatia, Macedonia, Turkey, and Iceland. The EU population far surpasses the United States (495 million compared with 311 million, as of this writing) and its gross domestic product is larger than the United States GDP ($15.2 trillion compared with $14.6 trillion). Like the United States, the European Union has a robust domestic regulatory regime that impacts foreign companies seeking to do business there. For example, U.S. chicken growers lost a $63 million market in Romania when Romania joined the European Union in 2007 and then imposed certain EU food safety standards, which differ from those approved by the U.S. Food and Drug Administration. [EUROPA is the portal site of the European Union, found at **europa.eu/index_en.htm**]

In coming years it may prove useful to watch the international economic roles and relationships among the United States, the European Union, and China. In 2008, a foreign-policy scholar, Parag Khanna, published a book, *The Second World,* which forecasts "a multipolar and multicivilizational world of three distinct superpowers competing on a planet of shrinking resources." By population, China is first, the European Union is third, and the United States fourth in size. (India is second.) By current size of its domestic economy, the European Union is first, the United States second, and China third. In this context remember that the European Union is not, and does not always act like, a single country with a single voice. It is more unified as to economics and trade and less so as to foreign policy. For example, all 27 EU member countries are individually members of the WTO (and, thus, collectively, have 27 votes). If and when the European Union becomes more politically united, its position as a superpower may similarly strengthen.

Globalization and Countervailing Forces

> Globalization has not been uniformly beneficial.

A broad consensus shares the view that globalization has not been uniformly beneficial. Recognition is growing that promotion of free trade divorced from social concerns is problematic. Those concerns include protection of historical, social, and cultural identities along with various economic and political issues. WTO's own Web site acknowledges countervailing considerations: "But the WTO is not just about liberalizing trade, and in some circumstances its rules support maintaining trade barriers—for example, to protect consumers or prevent the spread of disease. . . . The system's overriding purpose is to help trade flow as freely as possible—so long as there are no undesirable side-effects."[3]

As one commentator has observed, "The real question isn't whether free markets are good or bad. It is why they are producing such wildly different results in different countries."[4] One reason for disparate results may be whether the local government develops in tandem with the economy and is able to and does capture an appropriate portion of the wealth created to put to use on behalf of its population. Where that is not occurring, it has been argued that "multinationals—which account for the bulk of direct cross-border investment and one third of trade—have social responsibilities in nations where the rule of law is weak. And this view dispenses with the erroneous notion that open markets will magically produce prosperity in all conditions."[5]

Questions

1. Consider the critics from the United States and elsewhere who have expressed concern about continued globalization. What do you think they are most concerned about—the free interchange of people, businesses, goods, services, investments, communications, or ideas? Explain.

2. If multinational corporations have affirmative social responsibilities in "nations where the rule of law is weak," who should select and impose those responsibilities? If you believe that it is a matter for corporate management, what forces might cause management to act more responsibly? What forces exist that might impede more corporate social responsibility on the part of multinationals? On the other hand, if you believe that social responsibilities should be imposed on multinationals, what body should do so? How will that body obtain the power to legislate and enforce such responsibilities?

The Intercultural Environment: Ethics Across International Borders

The September 11, 2001, World Trade Center attack foregrounded difficult ethical and legal tensions between the American and Islamic cultures. America's continued presence in Iraq and Afghanistan has kept these cultural divisions in the public eye. Bridging cultural differences is an essential first step in creating an effective working relationship. Language is an obvious cultural difference. Chinese diplomats in Arab-speaking countries "show deference to local culture by learning Arabic and even taking Arabic names."[6]

Religion often provides the foundation for a culture's ethical structure. Thus, two countries with different religious heritages are likely to have divergent ethical and legal norms. For example, separation of church and state is a basic legal precept in the United States. By contrast, in Islamic countries, religion is the basis for many legal, as well as ethical, standards. In reading the following article, consider what human rights you believe to be "fundamental." Keep in mind that cultures differ in their judgments about which rights are so important that they should be protected.

> In Islamic countries, religion is the basis for many legal, as well as ethical, standards.

Islamic Law: Myths and Realities

Dennis J. Wiechman, Jerry D. Kendall, and Mohammad K. Azarian

... Mohammed Salam Madkoar explains the theoretical assumptions of Islamic Law:

> In order to protect the five important indispensables in Islam (religion, life, intellect, offspring, and property), Islamic Law has provided a worldly punishment in addition to that in the hereafter. Islam has, in fact, adopted two courses for the preservation of these five indispensables: the first is through cultivating religious consciousness in the human soul and the awakening of human awareness through moral education; the second is by inflicting deterrent punishment, which is the basis of the Islamic criminal system. Therefore "Hudoud," Retaliation (Qesas), and Discretionary (Tazir) punishments have been prescribed according to the type of the crime committed.

Islamic Law and Jurisprudence are not always understood by the Western press. Although it is the responsibility of the mass media to bring to the world's attention violations of human rights and acts of terror, many believe that media stereotyping of all Muslims is a major problem. The [1993] bombing at the World Trade Center in New York City is a prime example. The media often used the term "Islamic Fundamentalists" when referring to the accused in the case. They also referred to the Egyptian connections in that case as "Islamic Fundamentalists." The media have used the label of "Islamic Fundamentalist" to imply all kinds of possible negative connotations: terrorists, kidnappers, and hostage takers. Since the media do not use the term "Fundamentalist Christian" each time a Christian does something wrong, the use of such labels is wrong for any group, Christians, Muslims, or Orthodox Jews.

A Muslim who is trying to live his religion is indeed a true believer in God. This person tries to live all of the tenets of his religion in a fundamental way. Thus, a true Muslim is a fundamentalist in the practice of that religion, but a true Muslim is not radical, because the Quran teaches tolerance and moderation in all things. When the popular media generalize from the fundamentalist believer to the "radical fundamentalist" label they do a disservice to all Muslims and others.

NO SEPARATION OF CHURCH AND STATE

To understand Islamic Law one must first understand the assumptions of Islam and the basic tenets of the religion. The meaning of the word *Islam* is "submission or surrender to Allah's (God's) will." Therefore, Muslims must first and foremost obey and submit to Allah's will. Mohammed the Prophet was called by God to translate verses from the Angel Gabriel to form the most important book in Islam, the Quran, Muslims believe.

* * * * *

The most difficult part of Islamic Law for most Westerners to grasp is that there is no separation of church and state. The religion of Islam and the government are one. Islamic Law is controlled, ruled, and regulated by the Islamic religion. The theocracy controls all public and private matters. Government, law, and religion are one. There are varying degrees of this concept in many nations, but all law, government, and civil authority rest upon it and it is a part of Islamic religion. There are civil laws in Muslim nations for Muslim and non-Muslim people. Sharia [Islamic law] is only applicable to Muslims. ... The U.S. Constitution (Bill of Rights) prohibits the government from "establishing a religion." The U.S. Supreme Court has concluded in numerous cases that the U.S. Government can't favor one religion over another. That concept is implicit, for most U.S. legal scholars and many U.S. academicians believe that any mixture of "church and state" is inherently evil and filled with many problems.

* * * * *

CRIMES IN ISLAM

Crimes under Islamic Law can be broken down into three major categories.

1. Had crimes (most serious).
2. Tazir crimes (least serious).
3. Qesas crimes (revenge crimes restitution).

Had crimes are the most serious under Islamic Law, and Tazir crimes are the least serious. Some Western writers use the felony analogy for Had crimes and misdemeanor label for Tazir crimes. The analogy is partially accurate, but not entirely true. Common law has no comparable form of Qesas crimes. ...

Had Crimes

Had crimes are those which are punishable by a pre-established punishment found in the Quran. These most serious of all crimes are found by an exact reference in the Quran to a specific act and a specific punishment for that act. There is no plea-bargaining or reducing the punishment for a Had crime. ...

The Had crimes are

1. Murder.
2. Apostasy from Islam (making war upon Allah and his messengers).
3. Theft.
4. Adultery.
5. Defamation (false accusation of adultery or fornication).
6. Robbery.
7. Alcohol drinking.

* * * * *

Had crimes have fixed punishments because they are set by God and are found in the Quran. Had crimes are crimes against God's law and Tazir crimes are crimes against society. . . .

Tazir Crimes

Tazir crimes are less serious than the Had crimes found in the Quran. . . .

* * * * *

Tazir crimes . . . can be punished if they harm the societal interest. [Islamic] Law places emphasis on the societal or public interest.

* * * * *

In some Islamic nations, Tazir crimes are set by legislative parliament. Each nation is free to establish its own criminal code and there is a great disparity in punishment of some of these crimes. Some of the more common Tazir crimes are bribery, selling tainted or defective products, treason, usury, and selling obscene pictures. The consumption of alcohol in Egypt is punished much differently than in Iran or Saudi Arabia because they have far different civil laws. Islamic law has much greater flexibility than the Western media portray.

Qesas Crimes and Diya

Islamic Law has an additional category of crimes that common law nations do not have. A Qesas crime is one of retaliation. If you commit a Qesas crime, the victim has a right to seek retribution and retaliation. The exact punishment for each Qesas crime is set forth in the Quran. If you are killed, then your family has a right to seek Qesas punishment from the murderer. Punishment can come in several forms and also may include "Diya." Diya is paid to the victim's family as part of the punishment. Diya is an ancient form of restitution for the victim or his family. The family also may seek to have a public execution of the offender or the family may seek to pardon the offender. Traditional Qesas crimes include

1. Murder (premeditated and non-premeditated).
2. Premeditated offenses against human life, short of murder.
3. Murder by error.
4. Offenses by error against humanity, short of murder.

. . . Qesas crimes are based upon the criminological assumption of retribution. The concept of retribution was found in the first statutory "Code of Hammurabi" and in the Law of Moses in the form of "an eye for an eye." Muslims add to that saying "but it is better to forgive." Contemporary common law today still is filled with the assumptions of retribution. . . . The idea of retribution is fixed in the U.S. system of justice. Qesas crime is simple retribution: if one commits a crime he knows what the punishment will be.

Diya has its roots in Islamic Law and dates to the time of the Prophet Mohammed. . . . Today, the Diya is paid by the offender to the victim if he is alive. If the victim is dead, the money is paid to the victim's family or to the victim's tribe or clan.

* * * * *

CONCLUSIONS

Islamic Law is very different from English Common Law or the European Civil Law traditions. Muslims are bound to the teachings of the Prophet Mohammed whose translation of Allah or God's will is found in the Quran. Muslims are held accountable to the Sharia Law, but non-Muslims are not bound by the same standard (apostasy from Allah). Muslims and non-Muslims are both required to live by laws enacted by the various forms of government such as tax laws, traffic laws, white-collar crimes of business, and theft. These and many other crimes similar to Common Law crimes are tried in modern "Mazalim Courts." The Mazalim Courts can also hear civil law, family law, and all other cases. Islamic Law does have separate courts for Muslims for "religious crimes" and contemporary nonreligious courts for other criminal and civil matters.

Source: Office of International Criminal Justice, Criminal Justice International Online, 12, no. 3 (May 1996) [**http://www.iol.ie/~afifi/ Articles/law.htm**]; reprinted by permission of Criminal Justice International Online.

Laws and Social Norms for Dress

Standards for appropriate dress are regulated both by norms and, in many cases, by local law. In the United States, for example, some restaurants require men to wear jackets and state law generally prohibits even partial public nudity. Public schools often have enforceable dress codes. In the sixties, those codes often prohibited female students from wearing pants. Consider the following:

> In 2010, the French Parliament passed a law forbidding people from concealing their faces in public, punishable by fines. Higher fines and prison sentences up to one year could be imposed on individuals who encouraged others to ignore the ban. Although freedom of religion is constitutionally protected in France, the generally acknowledged purpose of the law is to prohibit Muslim women from wearing traditional head coverings and full-body robes. According to estimates, fewer than 2,000 women in France, most of whom are French nationals, wear those garments. Some supporters of the ban have said that the rules are a means of forcing women to be submissive and are a sign of enslavement or debasement. Some of the wearers say that the dress is a method of concentrating on their religious faith.[7]

One province in Indonesia, the world's most populous Muslim-majority nation, in 2010 banned Muslim women from wearing revealing clothes such as tight skirts and pants. After their third violation, women may be subject to two weeks' detention. Shopkeepers violating restrictions on selling inappropriate clothing can lose their business licenses.[8]

Questions

1. Do the laws discussed in the sections above seem logical to you? On what basis should you judge them?
2. Would conflicts with cultural issues, such as those addressed by the local laws discussed in this section, impact your decision as a manager about where to conduct your business? Should they impact your decisions? Explain.
3. If your job required you to live in a country with laws you disapproved of on moral grounds, would you follow those laws? Explain.
4. Consider the difference between fundamental rights and culturally based rights. Conduct a Web search of responses to and/or criticisms of the implementation of Islamic laws, and identify those that seem culturally based and those that seem based on some concept of fundamental, universally recognized rights.

Social Responsibility to Host Country

When doing business abroad, does a firm have social responsibilities to the host country beyond those required by the market and the law of that country? This issue has arisen in many contexts, including child labor. For instance, many of the world's soccer balls have been made in the Pakistani city of Sialkot. Nearly all of those balls are hand-stitched and sold to companies such as Adidas, Nike, and Puma. In 1996, in advance of the European soccer championships, the press widely reported that child labor was common in Sialkot and working conditions were poor. The end result, following a public outcry, was implementation of an agreement among the United Nations (U.N.) Children's Fund (UNICEF), the International Labour Organization, and all Sialkot manufacturers that banned all child labor.

Some in Sialkot, however, were not so approving of the agreement. Prior to the agreement, many balls were made locally in villages. In order to ensure compliance with the agreement, manufacturing became increasingly centralized in large halls. Workers then had to commute, but the piecework rate was not increased. Some women, as well as the children, lost their livelihood because Pakistan's Islamic culture discourages women from working in the same environment as men. Global competition is also taking its toll: Sialkot's hand-stitched balls now have to compete with cheap, mechanically stitched balls from China and high-tech, glued balls from Thailand.[9]

Substandard Working Conditions

Some corporations have been chastised for allowing working conditions in their foreign operations or in their suppliers' plants that Western cultures consider substandard. Such *sweatshops* pose a host of commercial, economic, ethical, political, and social questions.

Traditionally, free market economists have believed that sweatshops are necessary and beneficial. Sweatshops allow the economies of developing countries to improve because their export sectors expand and consumers in global markets are better off because they pay less for the products they buy. This faith in the market is based on the concept of comparative advantage: that developing countries typically have a comparative competitive advantage in cheap labor while developed countries have comparative advantages in such things as an educated workforce, manufacturing infrastructure and expertise, certain particularly well-developed industries, and so on. These economists argue that sweatshops have been an element of every developed country's transformation from an agrarian society to an urban-based, highly industrialized economy. If poor countries want to develop, a sweatshop stage is necessary, they say.

Other economists disagree that all developing countries must necessarily endure a sweatshop phase. Neither industrialized countries nor the developing world actually have true free market, or hands-off, economies. Governments often play a role in creating comparative advantages. Recall the discussion of the stalled Doha round of WTO talks in which developing countries object to the domestic agricultural subsidy programs maintained by the United States and the European Union. Dani Rodrik, a Harvard professor and an expert in helping developing countries organize export industries, offers the example of Costa Rica, which "is not a natural place to manufacture semiconductors," but it "got Intel to come in and do just that."[10] China is another example. "It nurtured the manufacture of electronic products and auto parts. It forced foreign investors into joint ventures with domestic producers. Beijing lowered trade barriers . . . 'only after it developed a relatively sophisticated manufacturing capacity.'"[11]

[For journalist John Stossel's 2004 overview of sweatshop protests followed by his defense of low-wage jobs, see: **http://www.youtube.com/watch?v=0VaHmgoB10E**]

Question

If you were the vice president for supply chain management for a large manufacturer or retailer, what type of labor standards would you impose on suppliers from other countries, if any?

Social Responsibility to Home Country?

We have noted a potential responsibility to a host country, but does a firm have any special obligation to its home country? Social responsibility to a home country might necessitate operating in accord with the values of one's home country even when doing business abroad. Microsoft and other U.S. companies, for example, have had difficulties with software piracy in foreign countries. Russia, supported by Microsoft lawyers, has taken some action to crackdown on such piracy. However, Russian human rights and environmental organizations have alleged that the government selectively investigates the use of illegal software in order to muzzle opposition voices while government allies are rarely if ever investigated. In late 2010, Microsoft initiated a new policy of providing blanket software licenses to advocacy groups in Russia so as to limit the government's ability to use software piracy as a pretext for government censorship or harassment.[12]

The United States exports its values structure in a variety of ways, including through the *extraterritorial* application of its laws. When the U.S. Supreme Court declared that antidiscrimination provisions of U.S. statutes such as Title VII of the Civil Rights Act of 1964 did not apply extraterritorially,[13] Congress reversed the decision with its 1991 Amendments to Title VII. Extraterritorial application is considered essential because over five million Americans work abroad. Accordingly, American firms that do not maintain certain Title VII standards abroad may be subject to liability in the United States. For instance, if a firm conducts operations in Saudi Arabia, where women are not expected to hold certain management positions, that firm is still held to Title VII's prohibition against gender discrimination. Compliance with American civil rights laws is not required, however, where doing so would violate the host country's laws.

The Foreign Corrupt Practices Act (FCPA)

Consider the problem of bribery and other forms of corruption. Some nations argue that bribery is acceptable behavior, whereas others criticize it severely. How would you define bribery? What problems are created by a culture of bribery? For years, U.S. firms have dealt with bribery issues in America and abroad. Congress has attempted to respond harshly to corruption in other governments and to support U.S. firms that do not participate in foreign corruption.

As we saw in Chapter 2, the FCPA prohibits U.S. business from making certain payments or gifts to government officials for the purpose of influencing business decisions. In recent years the United States has stepped up its enforcement of the FCPA, both through criminal suits brought by the Department of Justice and through civil cases brought by the Securities Exchange Commission.[14] Discovery and enforcement may increase further in light of new legislation allowing whistleblowers to receive 10 to 30 percent of any fine collected by the government.[15]

Although well intentioned, some critics argue that the FCPA unduly restricts American companies operating abroad and prevents them from competing effectively. Others argue the United States should not use foreign trade to unilaterally impose its sense of morality around the globe. Many other countries, however, are enforcing similar antibribery measures.

Question

Is it ethical for the U.S. Congress to impose federal laws on the operations of U.S. corporations abroad? Why or why not?

Social Responsibility to Humanity?

Are we evolving toward a set of common international ethical standards that can be supported and implemented globally? Would international ethical standards simply represent a natural progression from national standards? At one time, agreements were achieved only at a city level, but state-level agreements followed, and those, in turn, evolved to agreements among federated states. Is a similar progression to global standards inevitable? [Does a framework that divides ethical issues between those of the "host" country and those of the "home" country remain a useful analytical tool?]

> If we are moving toward global social responsibility, can we do so without sacrificing the existence of wonderfully diverse and unique cultures?

If we are moving toward global social responsibility, can we do so without sacrificing the existence of wonderfully diverse and unique cultures? Do we have to become ever more uniform in our beliefs and practices? Can we agree on fundamentals, but still appreciate diversity?

Consider the evidence. Not only are businesses interacting with stakeholders of ever more diverse nationalities (investors/owners/shareholders, customers/clients, suppliers, general citizenry impacted by business decisions), but the cultural identity of businesses themselves may be unclear. Consider the "Big Four" accounting firms: Deloitte Touche Tohmatsu (United States), Ernst & Young (United Kingdom), KPMG (The Netherlands), and PricewaterhouseCoopers (United Kingdom). Although each of these firms has roots in the United States, they are each now a global network with partners from a wide variety of nationalities.

We have growing evidence of voluntary international cooperation to establish acceptable business practices, as suggested by this brief list:

- As far back as 1948, the U.N. General Assembly adopted its Universal Declaration of Human Rights. Inherent in the structure of the declaration is a recognition of the connection between work (and business, by extension) and the protection of fundamental human values. Article 23 declares that everyone has a right "to just and favourable conditions of work" and "to just and favourable remuneration ensuring for himself and his family an existence worthy of human dignity."[16]

- In 2000 the United Nations launched a voluntary initiative to promote corporate social responsibility globally. The 10 principles of the *Global Compact* address human rights, labor standards, the environment, and corruption. Over 5,300 businesses from 130 countries have joined the Compact. [For more on the Global Compact, see **http://www.unglobalcompact.org**]

- Social Accountability International has developed SA8000, a social accountability standard based on international norms (such as the Universal Declaration of Human Rights previously mentioned) that companies can adopt to develop and assure an equitable and safe workplace for their employees and those of their suppliers. A verification system was simultaneously developed so results are auditable. Currently over 2300 facilities with 1.3 million employees in 62 countries are certified. [For more on SAI and SA8000, see **http://www.sa-intl.org**]

- In an effort to raise awareness among lawyers about corporate social responsibility and to provide resources for their use in advising clients, the Council of the Bars and Law Societies of the European Union has published "Corporate Social Responsibility and the Role of the Legal Profession."[17]

- In 1994 a group of business leaders from Europe, Japan, and the United States developed a code of ethical conduct for global firms, known as the *Caux Round Table Principles*. After a decade of experience, the principles were expanded to address obligations not only of business, but of government, in the Round Table's revised Principles for Responsible Globalization.[18]

PRACTICING ETHICS   Individual Social Responsibility to Humanity?

Consider the following excerpt from a speech delivered September 28, 2001, by Jose Ramos-Horta, Nobel Peace Prize Laureate (1996), and Minister for Foreign Affairs and Cooperation for the East Timor Transition Government:

> There is no dispute that abject poverty, child labor, and prostitution are a moral indictment of all humanity.
>
> However, poverty should not only touch our conscience: It is also a matter of peace and security because it destabilizes entire countries and regions. In turn it threatens the integration of the global economy that is vital if the rich are to stay rich or if the poor are to move up, if only an inch.

> Peace will be illusory as long as the rich ignore the clamor of the poor for a better life, as long as hundreds of millions of people live below the poverty line, cannot afford a meal a day, do not have access to clean water and a roof.[19]

Questions

Should most of us, not just active international businesses, accept a social responsibility to humanity? If we answer yes to this question how might our actions as students, employees, employers, and investors change?

Laws Governing Cross-Border Business

All businesses must, of course, follow the laws of the countries in which they are physically present and operating. (Whether a business with no physical presence but which solicits or performs business in a foreign country electronically must follow the laws of the foreign country will be examined in Chapter 18.) Foreign firms often wish to establish operations in the United States, in part because Americans are more inclined to buy goods made in this country. Doing business in the United States brings with it the requirement that these foreign businesses comply with U.S. laws and regulations.

Conversely, when U.S. businesses operate abroad, they are required to follow the law of the host country. In 2006 when Google began operating its search engine in China it accepted the government's requirement that it filter results to remove material the government deemed unsuitable for its citizens. In March 2010, Microsoft ceased that practice and automatically redirected search requests coming from China to its uncensored site in Hong Kong. China then threatened Google with the loss of its license (to provide other online services such as its music, mapping, and translation). The license was renewed when Google proposed to stop automatically redirecting search requests and instead simply present would-be searchers with a clickable link to **google.com.hk**.[20]

Businesses may also be required, even in their foreign operations, to continue to follow certain laws of their home country, as previously discussed. Interestingly, although there is a presumption against the extraterritorial application of U.S. criminal law, where Congress has clearly indicated an intent to cover actions outside of the United States, U.S. citizens can be held accountable in America for their criminal actions abroad.[21]

Finally, businesses operating across national borders will also be subject to international law. The foundation and some examples of international business law will be discussed soon, but first it will be useful to explore some of the different forms of business available to companies wishing to expand their operations into foreign countries.

Forms of Global Business Expansion

Multinational Enterprise (MNE)

The term *multinational enterprise* traditionally refers to a company that conducts business in more than one country. Any of the following operations, except for a direct contract with a foreign purchaser, may qualify a company as an MNE.

Direct Contract

A firm may expand its business across territorial borders using a variety of methods. The simplest, from a contractual perspective, occurs where a firm in one country enters an agreement with a firm or individual in another country. For example, a firm might decide to sell its product to a purchaser in another country through a basic contractual agreement. This is called a *direct sale* to a foreign purchaser. In this situation, the parties agree on the terms of the sale and record them in the contract.

Where the contract is silent as to a term of the sale, the law that will apply to the missing term will be the law specified in the contract; where none is specified, the applicable law will depend on the country in which the court is located. Some courts will employ the *vesting of rights doctrine,* thus applying the law of the jurisdiction in which the rights in the contract vested. Other courts may apply the *most significant relationship doctrine* where the applicable law is that of the jurisdiction that has the most significant relationship to the contract and the parties. Finally, some courts will apply the *governmental interest doctrine* where the court will apply the law either of its own jurisdiction or of the jurisdiction that has the greatest interest in the outcome of the issue.

> Payment is one of the most complicated issues pertaining to direct sales.

Payment is one of the most complicated issues pertaining to direct sales. The seller should and usually does require an *irrevocable letter of credit,* which the buyer obtains from a bank after paying that amount to the bank (or securing that amount of credit). The bank then promises to pay the seller the amount of the contract after conforming goods have been shipped. The "irrevocable" component is that the bank may not revoke the letter of credit without the consent of both the buyer and the seller. In this way the seller is protected because the buyer has already provided adequate funds for the purchase, confirmed by a bank. The buyer is protected because the funds are not turned over to the seller until it has been determined that the goods conform to the contract. It is important to the buyer, however, that the letter of credit be specific as to the conformance of the goods because the bank will only ensure that the goods conform to the letter of credit and not to the contract itself.

Foreign Representation   A second type of foreign expansion is a sale through a distributor, agent, or other type of representative in the foreign country. A firm may decide to sell through an *agent*—that is, the firm hires an individual who will remain permanently in the foreign country, negotiate contracts, and assist in the performance of the contracts. Agents are generally compensated on a commission basis. On the other hand, the firm may act through a *representative,* who may solicit and take orders but, unlike an agent, may not enter into contracts on behalf of the firm. In some countries laws may substantially restrict the actions a representative may take. For example, in China a representative may generally only gather information and market research, but no direct business activities may be undertaken.[22]

Distributors purchase the goods from the seller, then negotiate sales to foreign purchasers on their own behalf. In so doing, a distributor may be more likely to invest resources to develop the foreign market for the good. *Exclusive dealing agreements* with distributors, where a distributor agrees to sell only the goods of one manufacturer and the manufacturer agrees to sell only to that distributor in that area, are generally not allowed abroad, although they often are legal in the United States.

Export trading companies specialize in acting as the intermediary between business and purchasers in foreign countries. The trading company will take title to the goods being sold and then complete the sale in the foreign country. *Export management companies,* on the other hand, merely manage the sale but do not take title to the goods; consequently, they do not share in any of the risk associated with the sale.

Joint Venture   Foreign expansion may also occur through a *joint venture* agreement between two or more parties. This type of agreement is usually for one or several specific projects and is in effect for a specified period. For instance, Toyota and General Motors operated a joint venture at a plant in Fremont, California from 1984 to 2009. Toyota currently has a joint venture with Subaru in Lafayette, Indiana.

Branch Office or Subsidiary   A *branch office* is simply an extension of a foreign corporation into the host country. A *subsidiary* is a legally separate entity formed under the laws of the host country and substantially owned by the foreign parent company. For example, an Indian paper company may open a branch office in London to market and sell its products. That office would be a mere extension of the offices already established in India. On the other hand, the Indian firm could create a British subsidiary to handle its British business from its London offices. Either a subsidiary or branch office relationship could also come about through acquisition of an existing firm in the host country.

The distinction between a subsidiary as a legal entity separate from its foreign parent and a branch office that is not legally distinct from the home office has a number of ramifications. For example, many countries may require a local subsidiary to have in-country directors and/or shareholders. On the other hand, setting up a branch office will likely subject the parent company to taxation in the host country. Indeed, the parent company is legally liable for all obligations of a branch office.

In contrast, when a subsidiary is sued, the parent company is not generally liable. For example, in *U.S. v. Philip Morris, Inc.,*[23] the U.S. district court dismissed British American Tobacco (BAT) from the federal government's suit against various cigarette manufacturers for recovery of health care expenses. BAT was the British parent of the U.S. company, Brown & Williamson. The subsidiary, B&W, remained a part of the suit.

Licensing   Where a company has no interest in commencing operations in a foreign country but instead merely wants to have its product or name in that market, the company may decide to license the rights to the name or to manufacturing the product to a company in the target market. The benefit to this type of relationship is that the licensor (holder of the right) has the opportunity to enter the foreign market, but the licensee assumes all of the obligations of running the business.

Franchising   In a franchise agreement the franchisee pays the franchisor for a license to use trademarks, formulas, and other trade secrets. The difference between a franchising agreement and a licensing contract is that a franchise agreement is usually made up of a number of licensing arrangements, as well as other obligations. For instance, in a typical fast-food franchise agreement the franchisor will license to the franchisee the right to use its trademark, name, logo, recipes, menus, and other recognized resources. Ben & Jerry's offers franchise opportunities in Europe, Asia, Australia, and New Zealand.

Question

Assume that you are interested in importing silk blouses from Bangkok, Thailand, to France. What facts might persuade you to enter into an agency agreement with a Thai blouse manufacturer rather than a distributorship or vice versa?

Foundations of International Law

A firm with manufacturing plants in Argentina and Thailand, and corporate headquarters in Bangkok, enters into a contract with a French firm to distribute its products produced in the Argentinean plant. The French firm is not satisfied with the quality of the products being sent. What law would apply to this situation? Argentinean? Thai? French? Or are there, perhaps, specific provisions of international law that will govern? The answer to this question is not simple, even for seasoned lawyers; yet the firms involved will be greatly affected by the result.

> What law would apply to this situation? Argentinean? Thai? French?

The source of law applicable to an international dispute depends in part on the issue involved. In general, private parties are free to form agreements in whatever manner they wish. The parties to the agreement can determine, for instance, which nation's law will govern the contract, where disagreements in connection with the contract will be settled, and even in which language the transactions will be made. This is referred to as the *private law* of contracts. Whenever the parties to a transaction are from different jurisdictions and are involved in a lawsuit, the court will start by looking at the agreement of the parties themselves to resolve these issues. Where the contract is silent as to the choice of law, jurisdiction, and other questions, the court must decide. Generally, the law of the jurisdiction in which the transaction occurred is applied. If the transaction is consummated through some form of cross-border communication, as are many international trade negotiations, most often the law of the jurisdiction of the seller's place of business will apply. Recall, however, that the parties may always reach a contrary agreement.

Public law, on the other hand, includes those rules of each nation that regulate the contractual agreement between the parties—for instance, import and export taxes, packaging requirements, and safety standards. In addition, public law regulates the relationships among nations.

Public law derives from a number of sources. The most familiar source of international public law is a *treaty* or *convention* (essentially a contract between nations). For example, the United States, Canada, and Mexico have entered into the North American Free Trade Agreement (NAFTA), a convention regarding free trade among those countries. Some treaties and conventions are self-executing, which means that once a country has ratified them, a business can rely on and directly enforce their terms in court. The United Nations Convention on Contracts for the International Sale of Goods (CISG), which will be discussed soon, is an example of a self-executing convention. On the other hand, some treaties and conventions apply only to government signatories and not directly to private parties. Such a convention may, for example, require an adopting country such as the United States to amend its domestic law to accomplish the purposes of the convention.

Public law is also found in *international custom* or *generally accepted principles of law*. These terms refer to practices that are commonly accepted as appropriate business or commercial practices among nations. For instance, sovereign immunity, discussed later in this chapter, is an accepted principle of international law. A *custom* is derived from consistent behavior over time that is accepted as binding by the countries that engage in that behavior.

The Development of Customs

Historically, merchants followed certain accepted *customs* or principles in connection with the sale of goods. These customs or manners of dealing between merchants were often recognized and applied in court decisions and later in the United States became codified in the Uniform Commercial Code (UCC) Article 2 that regulates the sale of goods generally as well as sales between merchants. In this way, customs or practices traditionally followed by merchants have become accepted principles of law throughout the United States (except Louisiana).

In the international legal arena customary practices are still evolving. For instance, the practice had been that personal information moved freely between countries to encourage efficient information exchange in the business world. However, the European Union in 1998 established minimum standards for the protection of personal data. Any country receiving information from an EU country must comply with those standards. (See Chapter 18 for more on the European Union's Directive on Data Protection.)

Two factors are used to determine whether an international custom exists: (1) consistency and repetition of the action or decision and (2) recognition by nations that this custom is binding. The first merely holds that the action or decision must be accepted by a number of nations for a time long enough to establish uniformity of application. The second dictates that the custom be accepted as binding by nations observing it. If the custom is accepted as merely persuasive, it does not rise to the level of a generally accepted principle of law. Through persistent objections, any nation may ensure that such custom is not applied to cases in which it is involved.

Piracy on the High Seas

In recent years events off the coast of Somalia have raised public awareness of modern-day piracy. One might think that the international law against piracy would be clear given that piracy has existed as a threat to security since well before Britain's Royal Navy returned to port in 1718 with the severed head of Blackbeard. A recent federal case in Virginia, as well as attempts to prosecute raiders in other countries, suggest otherwise. What does seem clear is that generally accepted principles of international law give any country the right to capture pirates on the high seas. What process a government may use to prosecute pirates or even what a pirate is, however, remains a puzzle. United States law states that "whoever on the high seas, commits the crime of piracy as defined by the law of nations . . . shall be imprisoned for life."

A federal court in Virginia recently had before it several Somali men who by skiff had approached a U.S. amphibious dock landing ship in the Gulf of Aden in the early morning hours of July 7, 2010. One man shot an AK-47 rifle at the USS Ashland, which returned fire, sank the skiff and then took the assailants into custody. The U.S. government brought piracy charges arguing that piracy under the law of nations does not require the active taking of property. Any unauthorized armed assault or direct violent act on the high seas is enough. The defense argued the charge could not stand because the defendants "did not board, take control, or otherwise rob the USS Ashland." Relying on an 1820 U.S. Supreme Court decision defining piracy as robbery on the high seas and holding that contemporary international law is unsettled on the definition of piracy, the court dismissed the piracy charge.

Adding further uncertainty to the piracy issue, two months later a second Virginia federal district court judge upheld piracy charges against five other Somali men who allegedly attacked the USS Nicholas also off the coast of Somalia. Those men were subsequently sentenced to life in prison plus 80 years. The government has appealed the dismissal of the piracy charge in the USS Ashland case and the defendants are expected to appeal in the later case, thereby perhaps bringing some clarity to U.S. piracy law.[24]

Comity

The unique aspect of public international law is that countries are generally not subject to law in the international arena unless they consent to such jurisdiction. For instance, a country is not bound by a treaty unless that country has signed the treaty. A country is not bound by international custom unless it has traditionally participated in that custom. Prior judicial decisions are only persuasive if a country is convinced by and accepts these decisions as precedent. Perhaps the most critical element in understanding international law is recognizing that it is not "law" in the way we generally think of that term. Countries are not bound to abide by it except through *comity*. Comity is the concept that countries should abide by international custom, treaties, and other sources of international direction because that is the civil way to engage in relationships. Nations must respect one another and respect some basic principles of dealing in order to have effective relationships. Although some believe that the origins of law are in religion and its commandments, others argue that law derives from a natural tendency to prevent chaos. International law is an attempt to prevent chaos in the international arena through the application of universal or widely held principles. Comity is the means by which those principles are encouraged.

The concept of comity also includes the respect one country gives to the actions another country takes in its own territory. Specifically, as stated by the Second Circuit in *Finanz AG Zurich v. Banco Economico S.A.,*[25] comity includes "the recognition which one nation allows within its territory to the legislative, executive, or judicial acts of another nation." Under this principle U.S. courts "ordinarily refuse to review acts of foreign governments and defer to proceedings taking place in foreign countries." Thus, the *Finanz* court held that a creditor could not sue in the United States to collect a debt that was subject to the jurisdiction of a bankruptcy proceeding in Brazil.

Regulation of International Trade

As we have just seen, there is no such thing as one body of international law per se that regulates international contracts and trade. Instead, a contract between firms in different countries may be subject to the laws of one country or the other, depending on (1) whether it is a sales contract subject to the U.N. CISG, discussed below, (2) whether the contract itself stipulates the applicable law and forum in which a dispute will be heard, and (3) the rules regarding conflict of laws in each jurisdiction.

In addition, every country has domestic laws that regulate business conducted within its borders and that sometimes regulate its domestic firms outside of its borders. These laws govern the areas of employment-related activities and discrimination, product liability, intellectual property, antitrust and trade practices, and import taxes, to name a few. Consequently, a business owner may actually decide to market a good in one country over another simply because of that country's laws relating to the particular good or to commercial contracts in general. What follows is a brief look at several specific examples of the law governing international business. [For an extensive international trade law database, see **http://www.jus.uio.no/lm**]

U.N. Convention on Contracts for the International Sale of Goods (CISG)

In 1988, 10 nations signed and became bound by the U.N. Convention on Contracts for the International Sale of Goods. At this writing the CISG is enforceable in 76 nations. The CISG applies to contracts between parties of countries that have signed the convention and provides uniform rules for the sale of goods.

The CISG contains rules regarding the interpretation of contracts and negotiations and the form of contracts. Many obligations of the parties are enunciated by the CISG. For instance, the seller is required to deliver the goods and any documents relating to the goods, as well as to make sure that the goods conform to the contract terms. The buyer, on the other hand, is required to pay the contract price and to accept delivery of the goods. [For the Pace University CISG database, see **cisgw3.law.pace.edu**]

The Convention, however, does not answer all questions that may arise in a transaction. For instance, questions of a contract's validity are left to national law. As we saw in Chapter 6, under American law, an enforceable contract requires five elements:

- *Capacity* to enter the contract.
- *Offer and acceptance* of the terms of the contract.
- *Consideration* for the promises in the contract.
- *Genuineness of assent.*
- *Legality of purpose* of the contract.

Countries with civil law systems do not, however, require consideration for a valid contract.

Generally, once a contract has been created it is enforceable according to its terms by all parties to the contract. In the following case, read carefully to see what law the judge applied. He considered first the *private* law of the parties (that is, the express terms of the contract); then he looked to *custom;* and finally he applied the concept of *commercial impracticability.*

Transatlantic Financing Corporation v. United States

LEGAL BRIEFCASE

363 F.2d 312 (D.C. Cir. 1966)

Judge J. Skelly Wright

[In 1956, Transatlantic Financing, a steamship operator, contracted with the United States to ship wheat from Texas to Iran. Six days after the ship left port for Iran, the Egyptian government was at war with Israel and blocked the Suez Canal to shipping. The steamer therefore was forced to sail around the Cape of Good Hope. Transatlantic accordingly sued the United States for its added expenses as a result of this change of circumstances. Transatlantic contended that it had contracted only to travel the "usual and customary" route to Iran and that the United States had received a greater benefit than that for which it contracted. The district court held for the United States; Transatlantic appealed.]

Transatlantic's claim is based on the following train of argument. The charter was a contract for a voyage from a Gulf port to Iran. Admiralty principles and practices, especially stemming from the doctrine of deviation, require us to [infer] into the contract the term that the voyage was to be performed by the "usual and customary" route. The usual and customary route from Texas to Iran was, at the time of contract, via Suez, so the contract was for a voyage from Texas to Iran via Suez. When Suez was closed this contract became impossible to perform. Consequently, appellant's argument continues, when Transatlantic delivered the cargo by going around the Cape of Good Hope, in compliance with the Government's demand under claim of right, it conferred a benefit upon the United States for which it should be paid on quantum meruit.

The contract in this case does not expressly condition performance upon availability of the Suez route. Nor does it specify "via Suez" or, on the other hand, "via Suez or Cape of Good Hope." Nor are there provisions in the contract from which we may properly [infer] that the continued availability of Suez was a condition of performance. Nor is there anything in custom or trade usage, or in the surrounding circumstances generally, which would support our constructing a condition of performance. The numerous cases requiring performance around the Cape when Suez was closed indicate that the Cape route is generally regarded as an alternative means of performance. So the implied expectation that the route would be via Suez is hardly adequate proof of an allocation to the promisee of the risk of closure. In some cases, even an express expectation may not amount to a condition of performance. The doctrine of deviation supports our assumption that parties normally expect performance by the usual and customary route, but it adds nothing beyond this that is probative of an allocation of the risk.

If anything, the circumstances surrounding this contract indicate that the risk of the Canal's closure may be deemed to have been allocated to Transatlantic. We know or may safely assume that the parties were aware, as were most commercial men with interest affected by the Suez situation, that the Canal might become a dangerous area. No doubt the tension affected freight rates, and it is arguable that the risk of closure became part of the dickered terms. We do not deem the risk of closure so allocated, however. Foreseeability or even recognition of a risk does not necessarily prove its allocation. Parties to a contract are not always able to provide for all the possibilities of which they are aware, sometimes because they cannot agree, often simply because they are too busy. Moreover, that some abnormal risk was contemplated is probative but does not necessarily establish an allocation of the risk of the contingency which actually occurs. In this case, for example, nationalization by Egypt of the Canal Corporation and formation of the Suez Users Group did not necessarily indicate that the Canal would be blocked even if a confrontation resulted.

The surrounding circumstances do indicate, however, a willingness by Transatlantic to assume abnormal risks, and this fact should legitimately cause us to judge the impracticability of performance by an alternative route in stricter terms than we would were the contingency unforeseen.

We turn then to the question whether occurrence of the contingency rendered performance commercially impracticable under the circumstances of this case. The goods shipped were not subject to harm from the longer, less temperate Southern route. The vessel and crew were fit to proceed around the Cape. Transatlantic was no less able than the United States to purchase insurance to cover the contingency's occurrence. If anything, it is more reasonable to expect owner–operators of vessels to insure against the hazards of war. They are in the best position to calculate the cost of performance by alternative routes (and therefore to estimate the amount of insurance required), and are undoubtedly sensitive to international troubles that uniquely affect the demand for and cost of their services. The only factor operating here in appellant's favor is the added expense, allegedly $43,972.00 above and beyond the contract price of $305,842.92, of extending a 10,000-mile voyage by approximately 3,000 miles. While it may be an overstatement to say that increased cost and difficulty of performance never constitute impracticability, to justify relief there must be more of a variation between expected cost and the cost of performing by an available alternative than is present in this case, where the promisor

can legitimately be presumed to have accepted some degree of abnormal risk, and where impracticability is urged on the basis of added expense alone.

We conclude, therefore, as have most other courts considering related issues arising out of the Suez closure, that performance of this contract was not rendered legally impossible. Affirmed.

Questions

1. *a.* What did the court find with respect to the private law of the parties?
    b. What did it find with respect to the application of custom?
2. Would the result in this case be different if the shipment had been tomatoes as opposed to wheat? Explain.
3. Would the result in this case be different if the United States and Transatlantic agreed by contract that shipment was to arrive in Iran within a period of time that was only possible if the shipper used the canal route? Explain.
4. What do you think it would take for a court to render a contract commercially impracticable? In this case, the shipper was forced to spend almost $44,000 more than it had expected to spend in performing the $306,000 contract. What if the added cost had amounted to $100,000? Would you be persuaded that the contract was then commercially impracticable? What if the closing of the canal doubled the price of the contract? Explain.

International Trade in Services

Services, as opposed to goods, are a large component of the world's gross domestic product, accounting for 64 percent in 2010.[26] In the United States this percentage is even higher—services were 76.7 percent of gross national product (GNP) in 2010.[27] Furthermore, trade in services represents about 30 percent of the total dollar value of U.S. exports.[28] The United States isn't the only country exporting services. The popular press continues to report on the "outsourcing" and "offshoring" of U.S. service sector jobs. Outsourcing generally refers to the contracting by U.S. companies of such services as call centers, accounting, and customer services to foreign companies located in low-wage markets. Offshoring refers to U.S. companies setting up their own offices in foreign low-wage markets to perform services previously done by U.S. employees. Economists argue about whether the net effect on jobs in the United States is negative (through the direct loss of jobs) or positive (through corporate and consumer cost savings that permit job growth in the United States).[29]

What international agreements exist to regulate trade in services? Although international trade in goods has been the subject of international agreement since shortly after WWII, until 1994 no similar agreement existed covering international trade in services.

This was remedied with the creation of the General Agreement on Trade in Services (GATS), which is now one of the foundation agreements along with the General Agreement on Tariffs and Trade (GATT) to which all member countries of the World Trade Organization (WTO) must subscribe. [The foundation agreements can be found at the WTO Web site, in the document area, at **http://www.wto.org**]

The GATS agreement, still in its infancy, sets forth the general principles for the future of trade in services across borders, but at this time requires very little of member countries in moving toward the realization of those principles. Rather, it sets the stage for future negotiations to reduce barriers to trade in services. The services covered by GATS, and therefore by such negotiations, are broad: "any service in any sector except services supplied in the exercise of governmental authority."[30]

Two important general principles that govern international services negotiations are:

- *Most favored nation (MFN) status.* WTO members get treatment by the host country no less favorable than that given to suppliers from any other country, whether or not the other country is a member of the WTO.

- *National treatment.* The national treatment standard calls for a comparison of the treatment accorded to suppliers from WTO member countries with the treatment accorded to domestic suppliers. As a general rule, the treatment is to be "no less favorable" than that received by domestic suppliers.

Question

The WTO member nations have only recently turned their consideration to the barriers between nations that impede the flow of services across boundaries. In the professions, such as medicine, law, and accounting, substantial barriers currently exist. Some barriers are in the form of domestic licensure requirements, which in turn often require a particular educational background for the applicant. Would establishing a clearinghouse for educational equivalencies around the world and requiring WTO members to honor the educational achievements received by applicants in other member countries be a good idea? Why or why not?

Employment-Related Regulations

Social responsibility principles such as those in the U.N. Universal Declaration of Human Rights set aspirational goals for countries and business managers, but they are not enforceable laws. In the absence of enforceable global labor standards, MNEs are left with the obligation to apply substantially varying laws to their employees in different jurisdictions, as well as perhaps having to adhere to their home country laws that have extraterritorial application, such as Title VII for U.S. companies. That said, globalization has transformed workplace governance worldwide, both for good and for ill. A government seeking to improve domestic labor conditions can look to policies and practices that have been successful in other countries, but a government more focused on developing a competitive advantage may specifically exploit its lower labor standards, such as low wages, to attract direct investment by foreign businesses.[31]

Even within countries with protective labor regimes, responsible MNEs may be challenged by legal compliance requirements. Not only do substantive laws differ (for example, Germany requires a company either to hire the disabled or pay for an exclusion), but required procedures governing employer-employee relationships vary tremendously. For example, as a result of the recent global recession an MNE might reasonably determine that a reduction in force across its operations is prudent. Managing such a decision equitably and effectively could be a daunting task. In many countries nearly all employees may be covered by a works council or trade union with whom the MNE might be required to negotiate a reduction, whereas in the United States less than 10 percent of employees outside the public sector are covered by collective bargaining agreements.[32] In the Netherlands the government must approve most layoffs; in Venezuela, Japan, and China a successful reduction in force might require either agency or court approval. In Europe an employer even considering such a reduction must consult in good faith with employees about avoiding or mitigating such an action, even if the reduction policy was set by the board of directors at its foreign headquarters.[33] Similar issues can face MNEs involved in international mergers or acquisitions.

Compulsory Retirement

In late 2007 the European Court of Justice ruled that the European Framework Directive on Equal Treatment, which prohibits unjustified age discrimination in the workplace, applied to national laws requiring age-based compulsory retirement. The case challenged a Spanish law permitting employers to impose a compulsory retirement age. Although the Court held the Directive applied to the Spanish law, it nevertheless ruled that the Spanish legislation was a lawful, appropriate means of achieving a legitimate government aim. In this case the law had been passed during a period of high unemployment in Spain and was intended to further a national policy for a better distribution of work between generations.

In the United States, the Age Discrimination in Employment Act (ADEA) prohibits discrimination on the basis of age against individuals who are 40 or older. It applies to decisions to hire or fire, as well as to discriminatory compensation or other terms or conditions of employment. Interestingly, a narrow exception allows universities to require retirement of tenured faculty who reach the age of 70. The ADEA specifically applies to American citizens employed overseas by American companies.

Questions

1. A U.S. corporation operates a branch in Spain. Consistent with Spanish law, it adopts a compulsory retirement age of 62. Is this a violation of the ADEA?
2. Which policy do you favor—the Spanish or the American approach to compulsory retirement? Why? Is this an issue over which countries should be allowed to differ?

Intellectual Property Regulations

Intellectual property generally refers to copyrights, patents, and trademarks. Intellectual property is a form of personal property or *personalty,* which is the legal term used to denote all forms of property, both tangible and intangible, other than real property or realty. *Realty* is comprised only of land or real estate and items permanently affixed to the land, such as buildings.

Trademarks

A *trademark* distinguishes the source of a particular good or service, whether that is accomplished by a trade name, packaging, logo, or other distinguishing mark. When the law protects a trademark it grants to the holder of the mark a limited monopoly: No one else may use that mark without the holder's permission. Under the Tariff Act of 1930 it is unlawful to import goods bearing a trademark registered with the Patent and Trademark Office that is "owned by a citizen of, or by a corporation or association . . . organized within the United States" without the permission of the mark holder.

This provision safeguards a U.S. trademark holder's rights in the United States from infringement by foreign actors. But what about an American company that wants to obtain trademark protection in other countries? Each country has distinct trademark regulations and offers different levels of protection to marks registered in other countries. For example, McDonald's sued McCurry, a Kuala Lumpur restaurant that specializes in Malaysian chicken curry, claiming that the McCurry name infringed on McDonald's trademark. In 2009, McDonald's lost that suit when Malaysia's highest court ruled that McDonald's did not have a monopoly on the "Mc" prefix as long as other restaurants using the "Mc" prefix distinguished their food from McDonald's.[34]

Paris Convention   In 1883 several countries entered an agreement called the International Convention for the Protection of Industrial Property. As of this writing, 173 countries including the United States are parties to the agreement, now called the *Paris Convention*. According to the Paris Convention member countries ensure trademark protection to marks registered in other member countries. The convention also provides for *national treatment*, which requires that any individual claiming infringement must have the same protection as would a national of that country. A member country may not favor its own nationals over foreigners. The Madrid Agreement Concerning the International Registration of Marks, established after the Paris Convention, attempts to create an international trademark system. If a holder registers a trademark with the World Intellectual Property Organization (WIPO) in Switzerland, that mark is protected in all member countries requested by the holder. A Protocol relating to the agreement was concluded in 1989 with the "aim of rendering the Madrid system more flexible and more compatible with the domestic legislations of certain countries which had not been able to accede to the Agreement."[35] The United States is a party to the Protocol but has not acceded to the Agreement. [For extensive information on WIPO, see **http://www.wipo.int**]

That said, trademark issues still arise between countries, both of which are parties to the Paris Convention and the Madrid Protocol, as is evident by the difficulties faced by many international corporations in having their trademarks effectively protected in China. A walk in Beijing's famous Silk Street Market would quickly reveal a booming business in counterfeit goods bearing designs and tags from such companies as Coach, Dolce & Gabbana, Chloe and others.[36]

In the case below, the European Court of Justice considered whether under EU trademark law Google's AdWords service violated the Louis Vuitton trademark when Google sold ad space to a Vuitton competitor next to the search results returned any time Louis Vuitton was entered as a search phrase.

The Court (Grand Chamber)

Google operates an internet search engine. When an internet user performs a search on the basis of one or more words, the search engine will display the sites which appear best to correspond to those words, in decreasing order of relevance. These are referred to as the 'natural' results of the search.

In addition, Google offers a paid referencing service called 'AdWords'. That service enables any economic operator, by means of the reservation of one or more keywords, to obtain the placing, in the event of a correspondence between one or more of those words and that/those entered as a request in the search engine by an internet user, of an advertising link to its site. That advertising link appears under the heading 'sponsored links', which is displayed either . . . to the right [or] above the natural results.

That advertising link is accompanied by a short commercial message. . . .

A fee for the referencing service is payable by the advertiser for each click on the advertising link. That fee is calculated on the basis . . . of the 'maximum price per click' which the advertiser agreed to pay . . . and on the basis of the number of times that link is clicked on by internet users.

A number of advertisers can reserve the same keyword. The order in which their advertising links are then displayed is determined according to . . . the maximum price per click, the number of previous clicks on those links and the quality of the ad as assessed by Google. . . .

Google has set up an automated process for the selection of keywords and the creation of ads. Advertisers select the keywords, draft the commercial message, and input the link to their site.

Vuitton, which markets, in particular, luxury bags and other leather goods, is the proprietor of the Community trade mark 'Vuitton' and of the French national trade marks 'Louis Vuitton' and 'LV'. It is common ground that those marks enjoy a certain reputation.

At the beginning of 2003, Vuitton became aware that the entry, by internet users, of terms constituting its trade marks into Google's search engine triggered the display, under the heading 'sponsored links', of links to sites offering imitation versions of Vuitton's products. It was also established that Google offered advertisers the possibility of selecting not only keywords which correspond to Vuitton's trade marks, but also those keywords in combination with expressions indicating imitation, such as 'imitation' and 'copy'.

Vuitton brought proceedings against Google with a view, inter alia, to obtaining a declaration that Google had infringed its trade marks.

[Google was found guilty of infringing Vuitton's trademarks by two lower French courts. It appealed to the highest French court, which in turn submitted particular questions of EU law to this court, the European Court of Justice, for a ruling on the application of two EU directives (89/104 and 2000/31) and an EU regulation. Reference to the regulation has been omitted throughout the opinion.]

[The French court] asks . . . whether Article 5(1)(a) and (b) of Directive 89/104 [is] to be interpreted as meaning that the proprietor of a trade mark is entitled to prohibit a third party from displaying, . . . on the basis of a keyword identical with, or similar to, that trade mark which that third party has, without the consent of that proprietor, selected or stored in connection with an internet referencing service, an ad for goods or services identical with, or similar to, those for which that mark is registered.

* * * * *

THE INTERPRETATION OF ARTICLE 5(1)(a) OF DIRECTIVE 89/104

With regard, firstly, to the advertiser purchasing the referencing service and choosing as a keyword a sign identical with another's trade mark, it must be held that that advertiser is using that sign within the meaning of [the Directive following prior case law of this court].

* * * * *

With regard, next, to the referencing service provider [e.g., Google], it is common ground that it is carrying out a commercial activity with a view to economic advantage when it stores as keywords, for certain of its clients, signs which are identical with trade marks and arranges for the display of ads on the basis of those keywords.

It is also common ground that that service . . . is provided without the consent of the proprietors and is supplied to their competitors or to imitators.

Although . . . the referencing service provider operates 'in the course of trade' when it permits advertisers to select, as keywords, signs identical with trade marks, stores those signs and displays its clients' ads on the basis thereof, it does not follow . . . that that service provider itself 'uses' those signs within the terms of Article 5. . . .

In that regard, [a] referencing service provider allows its clients to use signs . . . without itself using those signs.

That conclusion is not called into question by the fact that that service provider is paid by its clients for the use of those signs. The fact of creating the technical conditions necessary for the use of a sign and being paid for that service does not mean that the party offering the service itself uses the sign. . . .

It follows from the foregoing that a referencing service provider is not involved in use in the course of trade within the meaning of Directive 89/104.

* * * * *

[THE INTERPRETATION OF ARTICLE 14 OF DIRECTIVE 2000/31]

[The French court] asks . . . whether Article 14 of Directive 2000/31 is to be interpreted as meaning that an internet referencing service constitutes an information society service [on these facts and] therefore cannot be held liable prior to its being informed of the unlawful conduct of that advertiser.

* * * * *

The restriction on liability set out in Article 14(1) of Directive 2000/31 applies to cases '[w]here an information society service is provided .' . . . [If the restriction applies, it] means that the provider of such a service cannot be held liable for the data which it has stored at the request of a recipient of that service unless that service provider, after having become aware, because of information supplied by an injured party or otherwise, of the unlawful nature of those data or of activities of that recipient, fails to act expeditiously to remove or to disable access to those data.

* * * * *

[The] exemptions from liability . . . cover only cases in which the activity of the information society service provider is 'of a mere technical, automatic and passive nature', which implies that that service provider 'has neither knowledge of nor control over the information which is transmitted or stored'.

Accordingly, . . . it is necessary to examine whether the role played by that service provider is neutral, in the sense that its conduct is merely technical, automatic and passive, pointing to a lack of knowledge or control of the data which it stores.

[In the instant case] with the help of software which it has developed, Google processes the data entered by advertisers and the resulting display of the ads is made under conditions which Google controls. Thus, Google determines the order of display according to, inter alia, the remuneration paid by the advertisers.

[The] mere facts that the referencing service is subject to payment, that Google sets the payment terms or that it provides general information to its clients cannot have the effect of depriving Google of the exemptions from liability provided for in Directive 2000/31.

Likewise, concordance between the keyword selected and the search term entered by an internet user is not sufficient of itself to justify the view that Google has knowledge of, or control over, the data entered into its system by advertisers and stored in memory on its server.

By contrast, . . . the role played by Google in the drafting of the commercial message which accompanies the advertising link or in the establishment or selection of keywords is relevant.

* * * * *

. . . Article 14 of Directive 2000/31 . . . applies to an internet referencing service provider in the case where that service provider has not played an active role of such a kind as to give it knowledge of, or control over, the data stored. [Such] service provider cannot be held liable for the data which it has stored at the request of an advertiser, unless, having obtained knowledge of the unlawful nature of those data or of that advertiser's activities, it failed to act expeditiously to remove or to disable access to the data concerned.

[The court concluded that Google had not impermissibly "used" the Louis Vuitton trademark simply by allowing a competitor to place an ad next to search results for Louis Vuitton. The case was returned to the French court for a determination of the degree to which Google was active in "drafting the commercial message" displayed by the competitor next to the search results. No liability would attach to Google if its role proved to be "merely technical, automatic and passive."–Ed.]

Questions

1. The court determined that Google did not infringe on the Louis Vuitton trademark solely by selling ad space to competitors displayed next to the natural results of internet searches for "Louis Vuitton." However, the decision leaves open the possibility that Google might be liable on a different basis. What facts might still subject to Google to liability?

2. Does this decision by the European Court of Justice have precedential value in U.S. courts for suits brought by U.S. trademark holders against Google for its AdWords service? Consider this question again after reading the materials later in this chapter under "International Dispute Resolution."

AFTERWORD

Louis Vuitton has registered trademarks, but even among countries with reciprocal recognition agreements, the cost of protecting a trademark can be significant in both time and money. Multinational enterprises want to protect their marks worldwide, which often means prosecuting suits in foreign courts. Such courts will recognize the existence of a valid trademark, but will still determine whether infringement has occurred under their own laws. Similar challenges exist for holders of patents and copyrights, discussed below.

Patents

A *patent* is a monopoly on a product, process, or device where the item or process claimed is an innovation, unique and inventive, and useful. The Paris Convention covers patents as well as trademarks; however, it does not establish a worldwide network of protection. Instead, it requires that member countries follow simplified procedures for registration. The most important provision provides the *right of priority,* which grants the first person to obtain a patent in any member country priority over other individuals seeking to register the same patent. In addition, because a patent must be original to be registered in any country, many countries hold that patents previously awarded in other countries automatically preclude additional patent registration.

The European Patent Convention was established in 1978 to create an international registration procedure for patents. Since then there has been cross-border protection among member nations, but those nations have thus far fallen short of the goal of establishing a single European patent and a single patent court for all patent disputes.

PRACTICING ETHICS   A Patent for the Isolation of Human Genes?

Should human genes be patentable to those who do the work of isolating particular genes? Isolating the gene associated with a specific condition can be the first step in creating an effective diagnosis procedure and may allow the development of individually tailored treatments in the future. Today, the cost of such research is substantial. Granting patents may increase the amount of basic research on genes because, if successful, those research costs could be recoverable through the marketing of diagnostic tests and treatments. On the other hand, genes themselves are naturally occurring and granting patents to those who first isolate them may ultimately keep the costs of diagnosis and treatment prohibitively high during the period of patent protection for individuals seeking medical treatment. About 20 percent of human genes have already been patented, but in 2010 a U.S. district court judge struck down patents on genes linked to breast and ovarian cancer.[37] The case is on appeal to the Second Circuit.

Questions

Should human genes be considered patentable? If you were a legislator in a country whose laws were not clear on the patentability of human genes, would you be in favor of proposed legislation permitting such protection? Why or why not?

Copyrights

A *copyright* is a government grant giving the copyright holder exclusive control over the reproduction of a literary, musical, or artistic work. Most developed nations provide copyright protection within their borders, but many also belong to international copyright protection pacts. The Berne Convention of 1886 and the Universal Copyright Convention (UCC) of 1952 both provide a measure of international protection against the unauthorized reproduction of books, photos, drawings, movies, and the like. Copyright protection extends for a period provided by national law. For example, in the United States a copyright currently spans the author's life plus 70 years. The United States is a party to the UCC and the Berne Convention. Thus the Second Circuit Court of Appeals upheld the application of Russian copyright law when a Russian news agency sued a Russian-language newspaper located in New York for copyright violation of an article that had originally been published in Russia.[38]

As should now be readily apparent, a solid international system of protection for intellectual property does not yet exist. Consider a recent illustration to add to those previously cited—in Spain in 2009 as many as 3 billion illegal downloads of music and videos occurred, far in excess of the 21 million legal downloads that same year.[39] That said, the foundation for future progress was made with the adoption in the mid-1990s by WTO member countries of the Agreement on Trade-Related Aspects of Intellectual Property Rights (the TRIPS agreement). The agreement establishes certain minimum levels of protection for copyrights, trademarks, and patents, and also requires WTO members to adopt effective enforcement measures. In furtherance of its obligations under the TRIPS agreement, the United States passed federal legislation, which was upheld by the Eleventh Circuit in *U.S. v. Moghadam*,[40] when it affirmed a criminal conviction for selling bootleg CDs featuring live performances of such groups as the Beastie Boys. Effective enforcement by other member countries remains an issue regularly raised in WTO settings.

Libel Tourists: American Authors Beware

Libelous statements are false statements that may damage the reputation of the subject of the statements and that are communicated to a third person, in writing or another medium. (Such statements when spoken are classified as slander.) Many countries permit the harmed party to seek damages from the maker of the statements. What law should apply to, and what court should be able to hear, libel cases brought by persons referenced by writers and publishers of books and newspapers that are widely available through the Internet? Consider the following two scenarios:

- In a book published in the United States in 2003, an American author identified a billionaire Saudi businessman as having financed Osama bin Laden. Twenty-three copies of the book were purchased in England over the Internet. The Saudi sued the American in a British court, which court asserted jurisdiction over the American author based on the availability of the book to British citizens through the Internet. British libel law is considerably more plaintiff-friendly than U.S. libel law, in part because of the free speech protections in the U.S. Constitution. Britain requires defendants to prove the truth of their statements, while restricting what can be provided as evidence. In the United States, the plaintiff first has to convince a jury the statements were false before the defendant has to present evidence of truth. The American author did not appear before the British court and in 2004 the Saudi won a default judgment of about $230,000 against the author.[41] Some Britons have expressed dissatisfaction with their reputation as a destination for "libel tourists," a phrase coined by a member of the House of Lords in 2003 when a Russian tycoon successfully sued *Forbes*, an American magazine. In 2006, Britain's highest court recognized a new defense against libel for statements made in the "public interest."

- In the United States celebrities have difficulty winning libel suits against gossip and rumors appearing in U.S. publications. Public figures, such as celebrities, have to prove "actual malice" on the part of the defendant to win. Because EU courts may assert jurisdiction over a defendant based on distribution of the libel through publication or the Internet, many U.S. celebrities (including Cameron Diaz, Kate Hudson, Jennifer Lopez, and Britney Spears) have gone abroad to sue U.S.-based publications, particularly to Britain where, as noted above, the libel law is more plaintiff-friendly.

Afterword In 2010, Congress passed the Securing the Protection of our Enduring and Established Constitutional Heritage (SPEECH) Act that makes foreign libel judgments unenforceable in the United States if enforcement would violate free speech rights. As of this writing the British government has published a bill, which, if enacted, would limit the jurisdiction of British courts in libel cases unless Great Britain is clearly the most appropriate place to bring the suit.

Questions

1. Should an American author be required to defend a libel lawsuit in Great Britain? Is it appropriate for British libel law to apply to the American author? What facts might make you feel such a suit would be appropriate? What facts do you believe should be insufficient to permit suit in Britain or the application of British law?

2. Should an American be permitted to sue an American author or publisher in Great Britain? Is it appropriate for British libel law to apply to such a case? What facts might make you feel that such a suit would be appropriate? What facts do you believe should be insufficient to permit suit in Britain or the application of British law?

3. Based on your answers in Questions 1 and 2, can you create a single rule that would satisfy your sense of justice about both of these situations?

Regulation of Multinational Enterprises (MNEs)

With globalization, the number of MNEs has vastly expanded. Precisely because MNE operations span the globe, regulating their activities has become quite difficult. In the absence of effective international regulatory regimes, which do not currently exist, MNEs are subject to many different overlapping, often contradictory, national regulatory schemes. Countries that impose regulatory requirements on MNEs may, in any given circumstance, be viewed with approval or be accused of "regulatory imperialism"[42] or be charged with domestic protectionism.[43]

Although our primary focus is on regulation of MNEs generally, in light of the global financial crisis a brief look at international regulation of required capital reserves for financial institutions is warranted. There is broad consensus that stability of the global financial system requires international agreement on the amount and type of capital reserves to be required of the world's banks. There is also substantial agreement that the pre-2008 requirements under an agreement known as Basel II were too low. Reserves set too high restrict the amount of lendable capital; reserves set too low leave banks at risk when unexpected losses occur. In turn, the global economy may be at risk if a systemic event triggers widespread losses. Individual national standards are ineffective in a world in which capital can quickly move to friendlier jurisdictions. Since 1988 an international agreement (Basel I) has established standards for required capital reserves, although implementation of the standard is left to each individual nation. The standard-setting institution, the Basel Committee on Banking Supervision, has 27 member nations from all over the globe including Brazil, China, India, Russia, Saudi Arabia, and Turkey. Some elements of an updated agreement (Basel III), such as an increased capital reserve requirement were agreed on in the fall of 2010. Additional provisions, such as the type of assets that should count toward meeting that requirement, are still under negotiation.[44]

We now consider four additional areas of governmental oversight: securities regulation, imposition of financial accounting and auditing standards, anticompetitive restraints of trade, and mergers. The U.S. law covering these areas was presented in Chapters 9 through 11. Here we will look at their international dimensions, particularly with regard to overseeing the behavior of MNEs.

Securities Regulation

Anyone following the business news over the past decade is well aware of numerous corporate financial scandals that have rocked the world: Enron and WorldCom in the United States, Barings Bank in the United Kingdom, HIH Insurance in Australia, and Parmalat in Italy, to name a few. In the United States, the Securities and Exchange Commission (SEC) has played a major role in uncovering and pursuing financial corporate wrongdoing. But it also has a reputation outside the United States, as one commentator put it, "as the cop on the beat for the world's securities markets."[45] The SEC has a broad reach because of its jurisdiction to regulate all companies that choose to list their equity or debt securities on any U.S. securities market, such as the New York Stock Exchange. However, in recent years the quality of SEC investigation and enforcement functions have been questioned, as illustrated by its failure to act on information it received related to Bernard Madoff's massive and fraudulent Ponzi scheme. In 2009, the U.S. Government Accountability Office concluded that SEC penalty policies in prior years "led to less vigorous pursuit of corporate penalties, may have made penalties less punitive in nature and could have compromised the quality of settlements."[46] Penalties imposed on companies by the SEC fell from $1.59 billion in 2005 to $256 million in 2008. Many of the policies set by the SEC in those years have now been reversed by the new chair, Mary L. Shapiro.[47]

> The SEC has been "the cop on the beat for the world's securities markets."

Accounting Standards

An important component of securities regulation is the establishment of the financial accounting standards that underlie financial statements provided to the public. In the United States accounting standards are under the authority of the SEC. Internationally, however, the growth in the number of MNEs and the integration of the world's capital markets have propelled the development of financial accounting standards that could be applied transnationally. In 2001, one set of such standards, International Financial Reporting Standards (IFRS), was offered for adoption by the International Accounting Standards Board (IASB) based in London. Well over 100 countries, including the entire European Union, have implemented these standards, although many have adopted local variations. In February 2006 the IASB and the SEC initiated a harmonization project, generally referred to as convergence, between U.S. Generally Accepted Accounting Principles (GAAP) and IFRS. The process is intended to eliminate major differences so that investors can more readily make comparative evaluations among companies regardless of their home country. The convergence project is ongoing. Whether or when there may be universal adoption of either system is highly uncertain. However, as of this writing the European Union permits U.S. companies to file GAAP financial statements without requiring reconciliation to IFRS and the SEC permits foreign corporations to file IFRS financial statements (so long as there are no local variations), without reconciliation to GAAP. The SEC has before it a proposed rule that would permit U.S. companies to select IFRS reporting for their SEC filings, but it is unclear when or if that rule will be adopted. [For more information on the IASB, see **http://www.iasb.org**]

Anticompetitive Restraints

Many countries regulate anticompetitive behaviors such as collusion among competitors and abuse of monopoly power. Perhaps the most notorious modern example of anticompetitive behavior involved Microsoft, which was repeatedly charged with abusing its monopoly market power in computer operating systems (Windows) to advantage its browser (Internet Explorer), media player, and servers. In the United States alone Microsoft faced three successive bouts of litigation brought by the U.S. Department of Justice, as well as numerous suits by private plaintiffs, resulting in payment of substantial settlement sums and long-term government oversight. All of these suits applied U.S. antitrust law. However, Microsoft also found itself scrutinized by the European Commission for violations of the European Union's Competition Law. While increasingly convergent in practice, the policies behind the U.S. and EU laws remain distinct, and Microsoft discovered that an activity not violative of one law may nevertheless be actionable under the other.[48] After an adverse decision by the European Commission in 2004, which it unsuccessfully appealed in 2007, Microsoft announced it would not seek further appeal. Since the beginning of the dispute in 1998, the Commission has levied fines against Microsoft totaling about $2.5 billion (measured at 2008 exchange rates). The ceasefire didn't last long, however. In January 2008 the European Commission opened another investigation, this time questioning whether Microsoft unfairly bundled Internet Explorer with Windows to the detriment of other Web browsers, such as Opera, produced by a Norwegian company.[49] Instead of litigating, the commission and Microsoft settled the dispute with the company agreeing to load a ballot box on all new Windows 7 computers sold in Europe that would allow purchasers to select any one of 12 competing browsers.

Mergers

The approximately 70 countries with merger review systems as yet do not have an agreement coordinating their processes—not even at the level of coordinating review thresholds, timetables, and required filings.[50] Some bilateral agreements are in place, but they are entirely inadequate to address the issues faced by proposed mergers among MNEs. China has now entered the fray, having enacted an antimonopoly law that took effect in 2008.[51]

Imports

The General Agreement on Tariffs and Trade (GATT), now governed by the WTO, regulates import duties among signatory countries to reduce barriers to trade and to ensure fair treatment. Without GATT, it is argued, countries with stronger markets would be able to secure better deals on imports than would other countries. In addition, countries with strong market economies could use the threat of higher import taxes as a bargaining chip in other negotiations. To limit such discriminatory practices, the concepts of MFN status and national treatment are integral to GATT, just as they are to GATS as discussed earlier in the context of international trade in services. Thus, under GATT, a reduced tariff offered to one WTO member country must be offered to all WTO members and, once a good has been imported, it must be treated just as domestic goods are treated. That, at any rate, is the ideal. In practice GATT has not actually done away with nonconforming tariffs. Rather, it prohibits countries from moving further away from the ideal, while providing successive rounds of multilateral trade negotiations to encourage countries to collectively move forward on achieving these goals. The decade-long stall on the Doha Round talks previously discussed is a serious impediment to the realization of such trade benefits.

A Closer Look at U.S. Tariffs

In addition to the fact that the imposition of any tariffs runs counter to the avowed goal of free trade, little logic or defense seems to exist for the disparities in the U.S. system of tariffs. For example, an 8.5 percent duty is imposed on imported women's wool suits, but no duties are imposed on men's suits. Furthermore, when a broader view is taken that incorporates whether U.S.-imposed tariffs hit imports from all countries fairly or evenly, it is readily discovered that they do not. In 2006, both France and Cambodia paid $367 million in duties to the United States; but for its payment, France was able to import $36.8 billion in goods, whereas Cambodia paid the same duties for the importation of only $2.2 billion in goods.[52]

Questions

1. Who in the United States is hurt by the tariffs described above? Who in the United States is advantaged by them?
2. Why might U.S. tariffs be friendlier to French products than Cambodian goods?

Fair Trade

To promote fair trade the WTO prohibits the practice of *dumping*. Dumping occurs when a manufacturer sells its goods in a foreign country for less than their normal value. If this practice causes or threatens material injury to a domestic or established foreign manufacturer in the foreign country, the act is prohibited. The price is considered less than normal value if it is less than the price charged in the producer's home country. A firm may want to dump its goods in a foreign market for two reasons. First, its home market may be saturated and cannot support any further supply. Second, a firm might sell its goods in a foreign market at a price below other competitors and support that price with higher prices in its home country in an effort to establish itself and perhaps drive other firms out of the market. After its competitors are forced from the market, the producer may raise prices to the normal level or above. GATT permits retaliatory duties to be imposed on countries that have dumped goods in other member countries.

The WTO also prohibits the payment of *unfair subsidies* by governments. This occurs when a government, perhaps in an effort to encourage growth in a certain industry, offers subsidies to producers in that industry. The producers are therefore able to sell their goods at a price lower than the prices of their worldwide competitors. Subsidies are considered unfair when governments use them to promote export trade that harms another country. When unfair subsidization is found, the WTO permits the harmed country to impose countervailing duties on those products in an amount sufficient to counteract the effect of the offending subsidy. If a country feels such *countervailing duties* have been illegally imposed, it must either sue in the courts of the country imposing the duties based on that country's law or take the dispute through the adjudication process provided by the WTO, discussed later in this chapter.

Question

Why do developed countries like the United States impose import duties? Why might a less developed country do so?

Exports

Whereas imports are regulated to protect American businesses, exports by these businesses may be regulated for several purposes. The U.S. Export Administration Act of 1979 permits restrictions on goods and technology where exportation would harm national security, significantly advance U.S. foreign policy, prevent an excessive drain of scarce materials, or reduce serious inflationary impacts from foreign demand. [To learn more about U.S. import and export practices, see **http://www.customs.gov/sp/cgov/trade**]

Rare Earth Elements

China controls 93 percent of the production of rare earth elements—metals less scarce than precious metals but still relatively rare. Many of these metals have turned out to be important to a wide range of green technologies, such as those used in wind turbines and in the electric motors for the Toyota Prius and Chevrolet Volt. They are also used in the electric motors in some U.S. missile guidance systems. China has been reducing production and exports of such metals to ensure it has an adequate supply for its own needs and to reduce environmental damage from the mines, although it seems willing to allow global manufacturers to move factories to China to get access to the metals. China's domination in this market may in part have been due to its willingness to allow high-pollution, but low-cost mining operations. Some of these metals are also found in Australia, Canada, and California.[53]

Question

If these actions were being taken by the United States instead of China, do you think they would be defensible under the Export Administration Act? Why or why not?

Trade Restrictions—A Tangled Web

Even if all could agree that as a whole the world would be better off if all national trade restrictions were ended, it does not follow that all countries or that all persons would be better off, certainly not in the short run. International trade has never been free of national barriers in modern times. WTO negotiations start with existing historical protections and member countries agree not to increase barriers and commit to participating in multilateral trade negotiations with the goal of lessening restrictions over time. New countries are admitted to the WTO only after sometimes prolonged negotiations with existing members over modifications of their existing trade barriers deemed necessary before they can be admitted. Every country has companies and industries that benefit directly from existing barriers, businesses whose profits rely on, and sometimes depend on, protection. Each of these businesses in turn have employees, suppliers, and communities that indirectly benefit from those protections. Thus any change in a nation's trade policies will have a negative effect on some segment of the economy, even if it can be demonstrated that a change would produce a positive effect on the total economy.

Take a specific example: The United States has had an ongoing dispute with China over its protection of and trade in intellectual property. Recently a WTO dispute resolution panel ruled that China must permit foreign companies to sell music online in China. The panel said China's prohibition on downloaded music violates a promise China made on joining the WTO to open access to foreign mass-produced art. China responded that it never promised to open markets in the electronic distribution of sound recordings in a non-physical form and that the restriction was necessary to protect China's "public morals."[54] Interestingly, only once has the public morals defense previously been used before the WTO—by the United States when it argued in support of its ban on Internet gambling over the objections of Antigua. The United States lost. To succeed, a proponent has to be able to show that the restriction is "necessary" to defend public morals.

Now consider more broadly the trade relationship between the United States and China. What other forces influence the resolution of a particular dispute? Consider, for example, that China exports to the United States $4.46 of goods for every $1 of goods that the United States exports to China, which would suggest that China is more dependent on trade with the United States than the reverse.[55] Conversely, in significant part because of China's large positive trade balance with the United States, China invests its abundance of U.S. dollars in U.S. Treasury bonds. China's demand for treasuries keeps the interest rates the United States pays on those bonds significantly lower than they would otherwise be, thus reducing the cost of borrowing by the United States.

The United States also has an ongoing trading dispute with Brazil. Brazil forced the United States into the WTO dispute resolution process arguing that the $3 billion per year the United States has been paying to cotton growers (mostly large agribusinesses in the South) constitutes an unfair subsidy. United States companies account for about 40 percent of cotton exports globally. The WTO ruled in favor of Brazil and ultimately authorized the imposition of countervailing duties. In order to avoid the imposition of those duties, the United States negotiated a settlement that permits the United States to keep paying the $3 billion in subsidies, at least until Congress passes a new farm bill, so long as the United States also pays Brazil $147.3 million per year in the interim.[56]

Questions

1. How would you challenge China's assertion that prohibiting music downloads is necessary to protect public morals in China? What facts might you look for to support your argument?

2. Is it ethical for the United States to dispute China's protectionist policies while itself spending years defending subsidies for a well-developed U.S. industry? Explain.

International Dispute Resolution

As we have seen to this point, international business relationships are highly complex. Disputes are inevitable. Resolution of international disputes often faces roadblocks. Three significant international dispute resolution bodies presently exist: the International Court of Justice, the European Court of Justice, and the WTO Dispute Settlement Body.

International Court of Justice

The only court devoted entirely to hearing cases of international public law is the International Court of Justice (ICJ) in the United Nations. The ICJ is made up of 15 judges from 15 different member countries. It may issue two types of decisions. It has advisory jurisdiction where the United Nations asks the court for an opinion on a matter of international law. These opinions do not bind any party. It has contentious jurisdiction where two or more nations (not individual parties) have consented to its jurisdiction and have requested a binding opinion. Such opinions are not, however, precedent for the ICJ in later cases. [For more information about the ICJ, see **http://www.icj-cij.org**]

How Binding Are ICJ Decisions?

Just how binding an ICJ contentious case decision actually is on U.S. state and federal courts has been called into question by the 2008 U.S. Supreme Court decision in *Medellin v. Texas.*[57] The Court, in a 6–3 decision, held that a Texas court did not have to give effect to an ICJ ruling in spite of the fact that the case was submitted to the ICJ pursuant to a treaty obligation specifying that the ICJ has "compulsory jurisdiction" for all "disputes arising out of the interpretation or application" of the treaty. In the view of the majority, the "most natural reading" of the "compulsory jurisdiction" language is "as a bare grant of jurisdiction. . . . The [treaty] says nothing about the effect of an ICJ decision and does not itself commit signatories to comply with an ICJ judgment." In his dissent, Justice Breyer observed:

> In the majority's view, the [treaty] simply sends the dispute to the ICJ . . . and the U.N. Charter contains no more than a promise to "undertak[e] to comply" with that judgment. Such a promise, the majority says, does not as a domestic law matter . . . "operat[e] of itself without the aid of any legislative provision." Rather, here (and presumably in any other ICJ judgment rendered pursuant to any of the approximately 70 U.S. treaties in force that contain similar provisions for submitting treaty-based disputes to the ICJ for decisions that bind the parties) Congress must enact specific legislation before ICJ judgments entered pursuant to our consent to compulsory ICJ jurisdiction can become domestic law. . . . In my view . . . we must look instead to our own domestic law, in particular, to the many treaty-related cases interpreting the Supremacy Clause. Those cases . . . lead to the conclusion that the ICJ judgment before us is enforceable as a matter of domestic law without further legislation.[58]

European Court of Justice

The European Court of Justice (ECJ) hears cases involving European Community law. Although not required, one judge from each member nation traditionally sits on the ECJ. At first glance the ECJ may not seem a particularly important court for American business. But in an age of MNEs, its decisions can be very important, as we saw earlier in *Google Inc. v. Louis Vuitton Malletier SA*. There a question of EU law was submitted to the ECJ by France's high court. [For information on the ECJ, see **curia.europa.eu/jcms/jcms/Jo2_6999/**]

WTO Dispute Settlement Body

While the WTO Dispute Settlement Body (DSB) is not a true court, it is a significant forum for the resolution of international trade disputes between WTO members. The DSB is made up of all member governments, usually represented by ambassadors or the equivalent. The DSB establishes a panel to hear a particular dispute brought by a member state. The panel then reports back to the DSB, which can either accept or reject the panel's findings. Either side can then appeal to the WTO Appellate Body. Again, the DSB can either accept or reject the appeals report. If a WTO member fails to comply with the final decision of the DSB, the opposing party may seek compensation. If compensation is not agreed on between the parties within 20 days, the complaining party can seek authorization for retaliation—that is, the suspension of favorable trade concessions to the noncompliant party. The reality of this power was demonstrated by the DSB's authorization of import duties against U.S. goods by Brazil as previously discussed. [For more information on the WTO dispute resolution function and dispute documents, see **http://www.wto.org/english/tratop_e/dispu_e/dispu_e.htm**]

In addition to these three institutions, particular treaties may implement specific dispute resolution processes for disputes arising under the treaty between its signatories. For example, NAFTA provides for special tribunals before which corporations can, and have, brought complaints against governments for actions perceived to be unfair or inequitable to them as foreign investors. Of concern to some commentators is that a tribunal under NAFTA can, as a practical matter, operate as a further review of the decision of a domestic court. Thus, after the U.S. Supreme Court declined to review a Massachusetts case brought by a Canadian real estate company, the company took its dispute to a NAFTA tribunal (which decided that Massachusetts had not violated international law).[59] [For information on proceedings before NAFTA tribunals against the governments of Canada, Mexico, and the United States, see the U.S. State Department site at **http://www.state.gov/s/l/c3439.htm**, as well as a private site, **http://www.NaftaClaims.com**]

Of course, national courts also rule on matters of international law and on matters involving business in international settings. In fact, because of the absence of any international courts of general jurisdiction, national courts are where most international business disputes are heard. When the underlying dispute seems to have little association with the forum state, but that state's national court agrees to rule on the substantive claim, legal commentators may lay charges of "judicial imperialism."[60] The principle of comity previously discussed also applies to the exercise of a national court's jurisdiction.

The Long Road through Court

In the summer of 2007 12 banana plantation workers from Nicaragua got their day or, rather, their four months in a California federal district court.

The workers were employed by Dole Food Co. on banana plantations in Nicaragua, where a pesticide known as DBCP, manufactured by Dow Chemical Co., was used to increase the weight of the banana harvest and help with rodent and pest control. In 1977 the U.S. government suspended the use of the chemical after complaints arose of sterility in California workers. When Dow informed Dole that it would no longer be producing the chemical, the two companies agreed that Dow would sell to Dole, for use in Central America, the more than 500,000 gallons that had been returned to it by other purchasers.

The plaintiffs were some of the workers who were exposed to DBCP while working for Dole in Nicaragua, workers who then became sterile.

After a successful suit was brought in the United States in the early 1980s on behalf of affected California workers, U.S. law firms began suing in U.S. courts on behalf of workers from other countries. Nearly every case ended when American courts ruled that the principle of forum non conveniens required the lawsuits to be maintained in the countries where the workers had suffered their injuries. Their view was that Nicaragua was a more appropriate forum for the dispute. So the workers tried again at home. After lengthy delays and, ultimately, a change in Nicaraguan law to facilitate the DBPC lawsuits, in 2002 a Nicaraguan court awarded nearly $490 million in damages and other judgments followed. But so far Dole and Dow have successfully blocked all enforcement of the judgments in U.S. courts. The new laws in Nicaragua have meant, however, that Dole and Dow have ceased invoking the forum non conveniens argument against new suits in the United States.

After a month of deliberations in the 2007 case in California, the jury awarded six of the Nicaraguan workers a total of $3.3 million. Following a number of posttrial motions, the companies successfully reduced the award to $1.58 million to be shared among four of the plaintiffs. The jury decision as to one plaintiff was overturned and Dole was granted a new trial as to another.[61] In the years following, Dole filed posttrial motions to have the jury verdict thrown out and in 2011, the judgment was vacated. At the same time, each side accused the other of fraud, including fraud instigated by the opposing attorneys, but the California State Bar is no longer pursuing investigations of those attorneys.[62]

Questions

1. Why do you think Dole and Dow did not object to the new suits brought in the United States after the plaintiffs' successful suit in Nicaragua?

2. Do you think the Nicaraguan judgments should be enforceable in the United States? Why or why not?

3. Apart from whether Dole or Dow Chemical or both are liable for health issues associated with exposure to DBCP, was it ethical for Dole to use and Dow to supply DBCP for use in Nicaragua and elsewhere after the chemical was banned in the United States? Explain.

Arbitration

In light of the difficulty of litigation between parties of diverse nationalities and the desire for more certainty and expediency in business transactions, parties to an international contract may prefer to insert a clause that calls for the international arbitration of any dispute. As discussed in Chapter 4, arbitration is a nonjudicial means to settle a conflict where the parties agree to a hearing in front of a neutral third party who will issue a binding award decision. [For more information on international arbitration, see **http://www. arbitration-adr.org and www.i-a-a.ch**]

Government Defenses

"Some evil acts don't violate international law unless they are performed by someone acting with government authority."[63] Even where government action is the source of the wrong, two additional doctrines, accepted as general principles of international law, may pose barriers to the judicial enforcement of a party's rights: the *act of state doctrine* and the *doctrine of sovereign immunity*.

Act of State Doctrine

It is generally accepted that a country has absolute rule over what occurs within its borders. Consequently, the act of state doctrine holds that a judge in one country does not have the authority to examine or challenge the acts of another country within that country's borders. For instance, an American court may not declare invalid the acts of the British government taken within its own jurisdiction because it is presumed that the foreign country (Britain) acted legally within its own territory.

One government action that has caused a great deal of dispute in connection with the act of state doctrine is *expropriation*. Expropriation is the taking by a national government, without adequate compensation, of property and/or rights of a foreign person within that government's borders. The United States contends that international law requires compensation for the taking. Not all governments agree with the United States' position.

Doctrine of Sovereign Immunity

The doctrine of sovereign immunity is based on the concept that "the king can do no wrong." In other words, if the king makes the rules, how could the king ever be wrong? As Chief Justice Marshall explained in *The Schooner Exchange v. McFaddon*,[64] "The jurisdiction of the nation within its own territory is necessarily exclusive and absolute. It is susceptible of no limitation not imposed by itself; deriving validity from an external source would imply a diminution of its sovereignty to the extent of the restriction, and an investment of that sovereignty to the same extent in that power which could impose such restriction."

The doctrine has been codified in the United States by the Foreign Sovereign Immunities Act of 1976 (FSIA), which provides that foreign countries may not be sued in American courts, subject to several exceptions. Accordingly, U.S. citizens usually would not be allowed to sue Britain in the U.S. courts. A foreign country may be sued in American courts, however, if the claim falls into one of the following FSIA exceptions:

- The foreign country has waived its immunity (that is, it has consented to be sued in another country's courts).

- The legal action is based on a commercial activity by the foreign country in the United States or outside the United States but having a direct effect in the United States.
- The legal action is based on personal injuries "caused by an act of torture, extrajudicial killing, aircraft sabotage, hostage taking, or the provision of material support or resources" for such acts.[65]

Therefore, a country that conducts a commercial activity in a foreign country may not hide behind sovereign immunity if sued, while a country acting on its own behalf and not for a commercial purpose would be able to avail itself of the protection. In 2010 the Supreme Court further clarified the FSIA, holding that it provides immunity only to a foreign state and not to a foreign official, even if that official is acting on behalf of the state.[66]

The "restrictive theory of immunity" recognized and applied by the United States is to be contrasted with the policies of some countries that contend that immunity is absolute—no exceptions exist. The following case examines sovereign immunity.

Butters v. Vance International, Inc.

LEGAL BRIEFCASE   225 F.3d 462 (4th Cir. 2000)

Chief Judge Wilkinson

Appellant Nyla Butters brought suit against her employer, Vance International, claiming that Vance discriminated against her on the basis of gender. The district court held that Vance was entitled to immunity from Butters' suit under the Foreign Sovereign Immunities Act because Vance's client, the Kingdom of Saudi Arabia, was responsible for Butters not being promoted.

I

Vance International, headquartered in Oakton, Virginia, provides security services to corporations and foreign sovereigns. In October 1994, Saudi Arabia hired Vance to augment the security provided to Princess Anud, a wife of Saudi King Fhad, while the Princess was undergoing medical treatments in California. The Saudi military was responsible for protecting Princess Anud. The Princess' residence in Bel Air, California, was referred to as "Gold." Saudi Arabian Colonel Mohammed Al-Ajiji supervised all security at the site—three Saudi military officers and the Vance agents. . . . The Saudi government paid Vance for its services.

In August 1995, Vance hired Nyla Butters as a part-time, at-will security agent. From 1995 until April 14, 1998 . . . [on] several occasions, Butters temporarily worked in Gold's command post.

In early April 1998, Vance supervisors at Gold recommended that Butters serve a full rotation in the command post. . . . Gregg Hall, the Vance detail leader, spoke with Mohammed. Colonel Mohammed denied Hall's request for Butters to serve a rotation in the command post. Colonel Mohammed told Hall that such an assignment was unacceptable under Islamic law, and Saudis would consider it inappropriate for their officers to spend long periods of time in a command post with a woman present. This in turn could have political ramifications at home for the Saudi royal family. Mohammed also informed Hall that the Princess and her contingent wanted to speak only to male officers when they called the command post. In total, three Vance supervisors recommended Butters for the assignment. Saudi military officers denied every request.

* * * * *

On May 28, 1998, Butters filed a charge of gender discrimination with the California Department of Fair Employment and Housing. On October 15, 1998, Butters filed suit . . . for discriminatory constructive termination, retaliatory constructive termination, and wrongful constructive termination in violation of public policy under California's Fair Employment and Housing Act. Vance filed a motion for summary judgment with respect to these counts.

On July 30, 1999, the district court granted Vance's motion, finding Vance immune from Butters' suit under the Foreign Sovereign Immunities Act (FSIA). . . . The district court held that derivative FSIA immunity attached to Vance because it was "acting under the direct military orders of Colonel Mohammed when [it] did not allow the plaintiff to work a full rotation in the command center." Butters appeals.

II

Butters first contends that FSIA immunity does not attach to Vance because the action here was a "commercial activity." . . .

The FSIA defines "commercial activity" as "a regular course of commercial conduct or a particular commercial transaction or act. The commercial character of an activity shall be determined by reference to the nature of the course of conduct or particular transaction or act, rather than by reference to its purpose." . . . The Court elaborated on the distinction: "[A] state engages in commercial activity . . . where it exercises 'only those powers that can also be exercised by private citizens,' as distinct from those 'powers peculiar to sovereigns.'"

The relevant act here—a foreign sovereign's decision as to how best to secure the safety of its leaders—is quintessentially an act "peculiar to sovereigns." . . . Indeed, it is difficult to imagine an act closer to the core of a nation's sovereignty. Providing security for the royal family in this country is not a commercial act in which the state is acting "in the manner of a private player within the market." . . .

* * * * *

III

Butters next argues that Vance is not entitled to immunity since Vance, as opposed to the Saudi officials, was responsible for the decision not to promote Butters.

A

If Vance was following Saudi Arabia's orders not to promote Butters, Vance would be entitled to derivative immunity under the FSIA. . . .

. . . To abrogate immunity would discourage American companies from entering lawful agreements with foreign governments and from respecting their wishes even as to sovereign acts. Under the circumstances here, imposing civil liability on the private agents of Saudi Arabia would significantly impede the Saudi government's sovereign interest in protecting its leaders while they are in the United States.

* * * * *

IV

Any type of governmental immunity reflects a trade-off between the possibility that an official's wrongdoing will remain unpunished and the risk that government functions will be impaired. FSIA immunity presupposes a tolerance for the sovereign decisions of other countries that may reflect legal norms and cultural values quite different from our own. Here Saudi Arabia made a decision to protect a member of its royal family in a manner consistent with Islamic law and custom. The Act requires not that we approve of the diverse cultural or political motivations that may underlie another sovereign's acts, but that we respect them. We thus affirm the judgment.

Questions

1. Why did the court hold that Vance, a U.S. corporation, could avoid Butters's claim of discrimination based on a claim of sovereign immunity? Why did Butters argue that sovereign immunity should not apply?

2. How do you feel about the end result of this decision? Did Butters suffer discrimination? Explain.

Subjecting MNEs to Compliance with the Law of Nations

The largest MNEs have economic strength equaling or exceeding that of some countries. In this chapter we have seen how challenging it can be to effectively regulate their activities. That makes it worth asking whether MNEs should be held liable if, in furtherance of their economic objectives, they either (1) take advantage of foreign government actors willing to subdue a local population or (2) are complicit in a foreign government's perpetuation of its own dominance where the action of the foreign government violates the law of nations.

Some foreign plaintiffs are attempting to hold MNEs liable under such circumstances in suits brought in U.S. federal courts under the Alien Tort Statute. In one sentence this statute authorizes foreign nationals to file civil suits in the United States against those who violate "the law of nations or a treaty of the United States." Enacted in 1789, it was rediscovered in the 1980s and successfully used by Paraguayan citizens residing in the United States against a Paraguayan police official for kidnapping and torturing plaintiffs' family members in Paraguay. In the 1990s the statute began to be used to sue major corporations for alleged complicity in crimes violating human rights by foreign governments, including torture, extrajudicial killings, and war crimes.

To date, many such suits have withstood motions to dismiss by corporate defendants and are continuing through the judicial process. In two cases, juries found against the plaintiffs, and a number of suits have been settled, subject to a restriction that the settlement terms not be publicly disclosed. An exception to such nondisclosure was the 2009 settlement for $15.5 million of claims against Royal Dutch Shell for its role in the Nigerian government's execution of local activists who protested the environmental damage caused by oil drilling in the Niger delta. Claims in other suits have alleged such abuses as the use of forced labor to construct a pipeline in Burma (settled with Unocal) and experimental involuntary drug testing on 200 Nigerian children (allowed to proceed against Pfizer after the Second Circuit ruled in 2009 that such testing, if proven, would violate a universally accepted norm of international law).[67]

Enforcement of Decisions

As we have just seen, even if a harmed party in an international dispute successfully initiates a judicial proceeding, many procedural hurdles are likely to be encountered. Recall the *forum non conveniens* principle that initially kept the Nicaraguan workers from obtaining substantive hearings in U.S. courts, as well as the more stringent evidentiary rules faced by defendants in libel suits in Britain, as compared with the United States. And what happens after the successful conclusion of such a suit? Do challenges arise in the enforcement of the court's decision?

The answer is yes, particularly in those cases where the losing defendant has insufficient or no assets located in the same jurisdiction as the court awarding the plaintiff monetary relief. In those cases the plaintiff may need to present the judgment to a court in a country where assets of the defendant are located and seek local enforcement of that decision. This is an added expense, in time and money, for successful plaintiffs. Furthermore, enforcement may be difficult or impossible to obtain.

Enforcing Foreign Judgments   When a plaintiff is successful in a California court, but the defendant's assets are in New York, the plaintiff may have to seek enforcement from a New York court. In that situation, the U.S. Constitution requires the New York court to give "full faith and credit" to the decision of the California court. No such broad policy exists in U.S. law with respect to decisions of foreign courts; nor does such a broad policy exist in international law. Instead, the court from which enforcement is being requested is likely to consider whether the original foreign judgment violates local notions of justice and morality, or is otherwise contrary to public policy, so as not to be entitled to enforcement. This is also true of foreign arbitration awards if the losing party has refused to satisfy the award—even if both countries are among the 142 current signatories of the United Nations Convention on the Recognition and Enforcement of Foreign Arbitral Awards (also known as the New York Convention).[68]

To illustrate, consider the previously discussed Nicaraguan banana plantation workers. After U.S. courts largely refused to allow substantive hearings in the 1980s based on *forum non conveniens,* the workers took their claims back to Nicaragua, which was exactly what U.S. courts had told them to do. Although resolution of claims in Nicaragua took a long time, some plaintiffs obtained substantial judgments there. In response to plaintiffs' applications to U.S. courts for recognition and enforcement of these Nicaraguan judgments, however, the defendant U.S. corporations have thus far been successful in avoiding the requested enforcement.

Now consider the American author with the outstanding $230,000 British libel judgment against her in favor of the Saudi businessman. The British ruling was a *default judgment;* that is, the Saudi won because the American author did not appear in court to defend the suit. The American author did not offer a defense because of: (1) the cost of doing so, (2) an expectation that the British court would not assert personal jurisdiction over the author (who was not a British citizen and who had no contacts to Britain other than the 23 copies of her book that had been ordered over the Internet), and (3) the substantial risk under British libel law that she would lose even with a substantive hearing.

Since the author's assets were in the United States, the Saudi needed to request recognition of the British award from a U.S. court. Believing that the British libel decision would not be enforced by a U.S. court, in part because it offended the fundamental value of free speech, the author filed a *declaratory judgment* action in a federal district court in New York, requesting a ruling on her constitutional claim and seeking to have the issue finally resolved. The Saudi businessman argued that the district court did not have personal jurisdiction over him and, thus, could not hear the author's substantive claim. The district court agreed. The author appealed to the federal Second Circuit, which said the issue was a matter of *first impression* under New York law; that is, the highest court of New York had never ruled on similar facts. Therefore, the Second Circuit certified (sent) the question to the New York Court of Appeals for a determination. On December 20, 2007, that court agreed with the federal district court.[69] Thus, the American author was left in limbo until Congress passed the SPEECH Act in 2010, as previously discussed.

Enforcing U.S. Judgments   Similar problems can arise when a U.S. citizen obtains a judgment from a U.S. court against a foreign national, which judgment is then sent for enforcement to the home courts of the foreign national. Consider the case of an Alabama 15-year-old, who died in an accident when the buckle of his motorcycle helmet failed. The helmet was made by an Italian company. His mother sued in an Alabama court and won a $1 million judgment. The Italian company refused to pay and the mother presented the judgment to an Italian court for enforcement. The Italian Supreme Court found the award of punitive damages so offensive to its notion of justice that it refused to enforce any of the award. Many countries share the Italian court's distaste for punitive damages in such situations.[70]

Question

On balance, do you think it would be better for countries to agree mutually to simply enforce judgments in favor of private citizens (nationals or nonnationals) obtained from foreign courts, respecting the effort and delay the plaintiff has already undergone in obtaining the judgment and without applying culturally based notions of justice? Why or why not? If not, try generating a list of principles you think should permit a court to refuse enforcement of a foreign judgment.

Internet Exercise

Identify a multinational firm that conducts business with suppliers in developing countries. Find its code of vendor conduct on its Web site and evaluate the areas of enforcement that might prove to be the most difficult.

Chapter Questions

1. America has embraced fast food. This may be part of the reason that obesity, in the United States, has risen at an epidemic rate during the past 30 years. According to the Centers for Disease Control and Prevention, currently one-third of the adults in the United States are considered obese. Seventeen percent of those between 2 and 19 are obese.
    a. Should other countries be concerned about the influx of American fast-food chains? Why or why not?
    b. What about countries that provide universal health care?
    c. If a country is concerned about its citizens' dietary changes, what actions should it take in response? Explain. [For more on obesity in the United States, see the Web site for the Centers for Disease Control and Prevention, **http://www.cdc.gov/nc-cdphp/dnpa/obesity/index.htm**]

2. A nation's cultural values can sometimes conflict with "outside" values spread through the process of globalization. Consider the following:

    > A group called the Hindu Jagran Manch, or the Hindu Awakening Platform, said Valentine's Day was an affront to Indian traditional culture and warned against Feb. 14 celebrations in the city. Many conservative segments of Indian society view the day—a celebration of romantic love—as indecent.
    >
    > "Valentine's Day, Mother's Day, and Father's Day . . . these are all the gimmicks of multinational companies to market their products. Valentine's Day is against the culture and ethics of Indian society," said Vinay Tewari, a Manch leader.[71] As a result of threatened attacks by Manch, many shopkeepers in India's largest state closed for Valentine's Day.

    a. Should the shopkeepers have closed their doors?
    b. Do you understand how a celebration of "romantic love" might be offensive to some?
    c. Do you think that Valentine's Day and other U.S. holidays are promoted more for their commercial value than to further the stated purpose for the day? Explain. Consider the dates when Halloween, Thanksgiving, and Christmas decorations go up in U.S. stores.

3. Thomas Friedman in his 2005 book, *The World Is Flat: A Brief History of the Twenty-First Century,* argues that countries with connected manufacturing supply chains won't go to war with one another. He offers an example of Dell's multicountry supply chain for the manufacture of its laptops. On balance, do you think globalization is a catalyst for bringing world peace or a tinderbox that may set international disputes on fire through the collision of differing ideals? Explain.

4. a. Why do you think China, one of the most communist of nations, wanted to join the WTO?
    b. Would it surprise you to learn that Afghanistan, Iraq, Russia, and Uzbekistan, while not currently WTO members, are all formally enrolled as observer countries? This means they are (or are considering) pursuing accession negotiations to become WTO member states. Why might they be interested in joining the WTO?

5. Judge Leo Strine, the Vice Chancellor of the Delaware Court of Chancery (the Delaware Court with original jurisdiction over state corporate law cases), has suggested that effective regulation of corporate behavior will require nations to give up some of their sovereignty to international institutions in exchange for regulation of the global product and financial markets in which multinational corporations conduct their business.[72]
   a. Do you agree?
   b. Will some form of corporate global regulation be necessary to protect all of the stakeholders of such corporations?

6. a. What are the relative advantages and disadvantages of each form of doing business in a foreign country?
   b. Why would a firm choose one form over another?

7. What may look to one observer like the application of objective standards may appear to another observer as improper protectionism. Originally signed in the mid-1990s, NAFTA calls for an open border for commercial truck traffic among Canada, the United States, and Mexico. But in early 2005 Mexican trucks were still not allowed into the United States, due in part to litigation brought by environmental and labor groups. Their claim was that the United States hadn't appropriately considered the environmental impact of letting Mexican trucks roll on American roads because there are no standardized emissions rules for commercial vehicles. On balance, does this argument sound to you more like a principled objection or like protection for U.S. jobs? Why? See *Dept. of Transportation v. Public Citizen*, 541 U.S. 752 (2004).

8. Original Appalachian Artworks (OAA) was the manufacturer and license holder of Cabbage Patch Kids dolls. Granada Electronics imported and distributed Cabbage Patch Kids dolls to the United States that were made in Spain by Jesmar under a license from OAA. Jesmar's license permitted manufacture and distribution of the dolls in Spain, the Canary Islands, Andorra, and Ceuta Melilla. Under the license, Jesmar agreed not to make, sell, or authorize any sale of the dolls outside its licensed territory and to sell only to those purchasers who agreed not to use or resell the licensed products outside the territory as well. Jesmar's argument that Granada's sales did not constitute "gray market" sales was that OAA's dolls sold in the United States had English-language adoption papers, birth certificates, and instructions while Granada's dolls came equipped with Spanish-language adoption papers, birth certificates, and instructions. In addition, Granada argued that the role of trademark law was to prevent an infringer from passing off its goods as being those of another. Such was not the case here. Are these sales prohibited? Explain. See *Orig. Appalachian Artworks v. Granada Electronics*, 816 F.2d 68 (2d Cir. 1987); cert. den. 484 U.S. 847 (1987).

9. Camel Manufacturing imported nylon tents to the United States. The tents held nine people and weighed over 30 pounds. The tents' floors ranged from 8 feet by 10 feet to 10 feet by 14 feet. The tents were to be used as shelter during camping. The importer categorized the goods as "sports equipment," which carried a 10 percent import duty, whereas the U.S. Customs Service considered the tents "textile articles not specifically provided for," with a duty of $.25 per pound plus 15 percent import

duty. The importer appealed the decision. What should be the result? Explain. See *Camel Manufacturing Co. v. United States,* 686 F.Supp. 912 (C.I.T. 1988); aff'd 861 F.2d 1266 (Fed. Cir. 1988).

10. Should a Mexican citizen who bought a Chrysler vehicle in Mexico be allowed to sue the manufacturer in a U.S. court under U.S. product liability laws when the plaintiff's three-year-old son was killed when the passenger-side air bag deployed during an accident in Mexico? See *Gonzalez v. Chrysler Corp.,* 301 F.3d 377 (5th Cir. 2002); cert. den. 538 U.S. 1012 (2003).

11. Prior to 1941, Kalmich owned a business in Yugoslavia. In 1941 the Nazis confiscated his property as a result of Kalmich's Jewish heritage and faith. Bruno purchased the business from the Nazis in 1942 without knowledge of the potential unlawful conversion. Kalmich contended that because the confiscation was in violation of well-defined principles of international law prior to the German occupation, the transfer to Bruno was ineffective. Kalmich sought to apply a 1946 Yugoslavian law called "Law Concerning the Treatment of Property Taken Away from the Owner." That law provided that where property is taken from its owners, the owner may bring an action against "responsible persons" for recovery.

    a. Did the act of state doctrine apply in this case?

    b. If not, what should be the result in an American court? Explain. See *Kalmich v. Bruno,* 450 F.Supp. 227 (N.D. IL 1978).

12. Zedan received a telephone call from a Saudi Arabian organization offering him an engineering position at a construction project in Saudi Arabia. The Ministry of Communications, an agency of the government, guaranteed payment to Zedan for any work he performed there, whether for the government or for a nonsovereign third party. After three years, Zedan left the country without being fully paid. After he returned to the United States, he filed an action in federal court seeking to enforce the ministry's guarantee. The ministry argued that it was protected under the Foreign Sovereign Immunities Act.

    a. Was Zedan's recruitment in the United States a commercial activity as required by the act?

    b. Did this action have a direct effect in the United States as required by the act? Explain. See *Zedan v. Kingdom of Saudi Arabia,* 849 F.2d 1511 (1988).

13. From time to time courts are called on to determine the enforceability of an arbitration clause contained in a contract. One such case was *DiMercurio v. Sphere Drake Insurance,* 202 F.3d 71 (1st Cir. 2000). DiMercurio was injured in 1994 when the commercial fishing vessel in which he was working sank. The vessel was owned by R&M, which was found by a court to be liable to DiMercurio for his injuries and ordered to pay $350,000 in compensation. However, because R&M had no other assets, it assigned to DiMercurio all the rights it had against Sphere Drake, the London-based insurer of the fishing vessel. When DiMercurio looked to Sphere Drake for payment, it denied the claim and invoked the arbitration clause in its insurance policy with R&M, which required the arbitration to take place in England. Should DiMercurio be required to pursue his claim through arbitration in England? Explain.

Notes

1. "Agreement Establishing the World Trade Organization" [**http://www.wto.org/english/docs_e/legal_e/legal_e.htm**].

2. Bill Sing, "Deal to Loosen Trade Reached," *Los Angeles Times,* August 1, 2004, p. A1.

3. [**http://www.wto.org/english/thewto_e/whatis_e/tif_e/fact1_e.htm**].

4. Pete Engardio, "Global Capitalism: Can It Be Made to Work Better," *BusinessWeek,* November 6, 2000, p. 72.

5. Id.

6. Parag Khanna, *The Second World* (New York: Random House, 2008), as quoted by Raymond Bonner, "Guess Who's Coming to Power," *The New York Times,* March 30, 2008 [**http://www.nytimes.com**].

7. David Gauthier-Villars and Charles Forelle, "Burqa Is Banned in France," *The Wall Street Journal,* September 15, 2010 [**http://online.wsj.com**].

8. Fakhrurradzie Gade, "Indonesia's Aceh Province Enacted a Strict Muslim Law Thursday: A Tight Pants Ban," *Christian Science Monitor,* May 27, 2010 [**http://www.csmonitor.com**].

9. Much of this discussion was based on Jess Smee, "Rights: Workers Score with Fair-Trade Soccer Balls," *Inter Press Service,* April 3, 2006; and Uwe Buse, "Balls and Chains," *Spiegel Online,* May 26, 2006 [**http://www.spiegel.de/international/**].

10. Louis Uchitelle, "Economist Wants Business and Social Aims to Be in Sync," *The New York Times,* January 30, 2007 [**http://www.nytimes.com**].

11. Id.

12. Clifford J. Levy, "Microsoft Changes Policy over Russian Crackdown," *The New York Times,* September 13, 2010 [**http://www.nytimes.com/**].

13. *EEOC v. Arabian American Oil Co.,* 499 U.S. 244 (1991).

14. Dionne Searcey, "Watergate-Era Law Revitalized in Pursuit of Corporate Corruption," *The Wall Street Journal,* October 15, 2010 [**http://online.wsj.com/**].

15. Kara Scannell and Tomas Catan, "Settlements Near in Bribery Case," *The Wall Street Journal,* October 15, 2010 [**http://online.wsj.com/**].

16. A copy of the Declaration can be found in the University of Minnesota's Human Rights Library [**http://www1.umn.edu/humanrts/instree/b1udhr.htm**].

17. A copy of the report can be downloaded from [**http://www.ccbe.eu/fileadmin/user_upload/NTCdocument/csr_guidelines_0405_1_1182254964.pdf**].

18. The principles can be found at [**http://cauxroundtable.org/index.cfm?&menuid=103**].

19. Jose Ramos-Horta, "Speech to the Northern Medical Foundation Tribute to Military Medicine and Lt-Gen. P. Cosgrove," Sydney, Australia, September 28, 2001. Copy with author's work papers.

20. Amir Efrati and Andrew Batson, "Google to Alter Access to Its China Site," *The Wall Street Journal,* June 30, 2010, p. B3 and "China Renews Google's license," *The Waterloo/Cedar Falls Courier,* July 9, 2010, p. A11.

21. See, for example, *U.S. v. Kim,* 246 F.3d 186 (2d Cir. 2001), where a New York resident was convicted of wire fraud while working for the United Nations in Croatia.

22. Mayer Brown JSM, *Guide to Doing Business in the PRC* (2010), p. 9.

23. 116 F.Supp.2d 116 (D.D.C. 2000).

24. *U.S. v. Said,* 2010 Am. Maritime Cases 2034 (E.D. Va. 2010) and Brock Vergakis, "Judge Refuses to Overturn Piracy Convictions," *Navy Times,* March 11, 2011 [**http://www.navytimes.com/news/2011/03/ap-navy-nicholas-judge-wont-overturn-piracy-convictions-031111**].

25. 192 F.3d 240 (2d Cir. 1999).

26. From the CIA's *World Factbook* [**https://www.cia.gov/library/publications/the-world-factbook/geos/xx.html**].

27. From the CIA's *World Factbook* [**https://www.cia.gov/library/publications/the-world-factbook/geos/us.html**].

28. From the U.S. Census Bureau, Foreign Trade Division [**http://www.census.gov/foreign-trade/statistics/historical/gands.pdf**].

29. Michael Schroeder, "Outsourcing May Create U.S. Jobs," *The Wall Street Journal,* March 30, 2004, p. A2.

30. GATS, Art. I, para. 3(b).

31. Harry W. Arthurs, "Extraterritoriality by Other Means: How Labor Law Sneaks Across Borders, Conquers Minds, and Controls Workplaces Abroad," Osgoode CLPE Research Paper No. 25/2010 [**http://ssrn.com/abstract=1645248**].

32. Donald C. Dowling, Jr. and Oliver Brettle, "Globally Aligning Collective Bargaining Strategy," White & Case LLP, June 1, 2010 [**http://www.lexology.com/library/detail.aspx?g=3f66a46b-d041-4d66-82d6-ac611b8bbfd6**].

33. Donald C. Dowling, Jr., "Reductions-in-Force Outside the US," White & Case LLP, December 1, 2008 [**http://www.lexology.com/library/detail.aspx?g=36c0b923-0d90-4e11-8eac-e524a21314cc**].

34. Associated Press, "McDonald's Loses Trademark Suit," *The Waterloo/Cedar Falls Courier,* September 8, 2009, p. A10.

35. [**http://www.wipo.int/treaties/en/**].

36. Sharon LaFraniere, "Facing Counterfeiting Crackdown, Beijing Vendors Fight Back," *The New York Times,* March 2, 2009 [**http://www.nytimes.com/**].

37. *Association for Molecular Pathology v. U.S. Patent and Trademark Office,* 702 F.Supp.2d 181 (S.D.N.Y. 2010).

38. *Itar-Tass Russian News Agency v. Russian Kurier, Inc.,* 153 F.3d 82 (2d Cir. 1998).

39. Raphael Minder, "Pressure Grows on Spain to Curb Digital Piracy," *The New York Times,* May 16, 2010 [**http://www.nytimes.com/**].

40. 175 F.3d 1269 (11th Cir. 1999); cert. den., 529 U.S. 1036 (2000).

41. See *Ehrenfeld v. Mahfouz,* 881 N.E.2d 830 (NY 2007), and Michael J. Broyde and Deborah E. Lipstadt, "Home Court Advantage," *The New York Times,* October 11, 2007 [**http://www.nytimes.com/**].

42. Michael Schroeder and Silvia Ascarelli, "New Role for SEC: Policing Companies beyond U.S. Borders," *The Wall Street Journal,* July 30, 2004, p. A1 [**http://online.wsj.com/**].

43. "European Imperialism," *The Wall Street Journal,* October 31, 2007, p. A20.

44. Damian Paletta and David Wessel, "Bank Rules Win Muted Praise," *The Wall Street Journal,* September 14, 2010, p. C1 [**http://online.wsj.com/**]; and Binyamin Appelbaum, "Regulators Seek Global Capital Rule," *The New York Times,* May 25, 2010 [**http://www.nytimes.com/**].

45. Schroeder and Ascarelli, "New Role for SEC." p. A1.

46. Zachary A. Goldfarb, "In Cox Years at the SEC, Policies Undercut Action," *The Washington Post,* June 1, 2009 [**http://www.washingtonpost.com/**].

47. Stephen Labaton, "S.E.C. Chief Pursues Tougher Enforcement," *The New York Times,* February 23, 2009 [**http://www.nytimes.com/**].

48. Amanda Cohen, "Surveying the Microsoft Antitrust Universe," *Berkeley Technology Law Journal* 19 (2004), p. 333.

49. Charles Forelle, "EU Regulators Begin New Microsoft Probes," *The Wall Street Journal,* January 15, 2008, p. A3.

50. For a good comparison of U.S. and EU merger analysis and Enforcement, see Cento Veljanovski, "EC Merger Policy after GE/Honeywell and Airtours," *Antitrust Bulletin* 49 (Spring 2004), p. 153.

51. John Markoff, "China Law Could Impede Microsoft Deal for Yahoo," *The New York Times,* March 28, 2008 [**http://www.nytimes.com/**].

52. Editorial, "The Other Boot," *The New York Times,* May 4, 2007 [**http://www.nytimes.com/**].

53. Keith Bradsher, "China Tightens Grip on Rare Minerals," *The New York Times,* September 1, 2009 [**http://www.nytimes.com/**].

54. "Hollywood Upstages Beijing," *The Wall Street Journal,* August 13, 2009, p. A1.

55. Keith Bradsher, "China Moves to Retaliate against U.S. Tire Tariff," *The New York Times,* September 14, 2009 [**http://www.nytimes.com/**].

56. "Brazil's Victory in Cotton Trade Case Exposes America's Wasteful Subsidies," *The Washington Post,* June 3, 2010, p. A16.

57. 128 S.Ct. 1346 (2008).

58. Id. at 1377.

59. Adam Liptak, "NAFTA Tribunals Stir U.S. Worries," *The New York Times,* April 18, 2004 [**http://www.nytimes.com/**].

60. Klaus-Heiner Lehne, "Hands Off Our Torts," *The Wall Street Journal,* November 18, 2003, p. A20.

61. Based on information from T. Christian Miller, "Plantation Workers Look for Justice in the North," *Los Angeles Times,* May 27, 2007 [**http://www.latimes.com/**]; Justin Rebello, "U.S. District Court in Calif. Rules against Dow Chemical in Pesticide Exposure Case," *Lawyers USA,* December 2007; and "Dole Food Co. Inc. Wins Court Rulings," *Business Wire,* March 10, 2008.

62. Based on information from Victoria Kim, "Judge Throws Out Verdict Awarding Millions to Dole Workers," *Los Angeles Times,* July 16, 2010 [**http://www.latimes.com/**]; *Business Wire,* "Dole Food Company Announces that Court Enters Final Order Vacating Judgment, Dismissing Fraudulent Lawsuit Brought by Nicaraguans Claiming to Have Been Banana Workers," Press Release, March 15, 2011 [**http://www.thestreet.com/story/11046743/1/dole-food-company-announces-that-court-enters-final-order-vacating-judgment-dismissing-fraudulent-law-suit-brought-by-nicaraguans-claiming-to-have-been-banana-workers.html**]; Amanda Bronstad, "California Bar Drops Complaint Against Dole's Lawyers," *The National Bar Journal,* February 28, 2011 [**http://www.law.com**]; and "Juan Dominguez Cleared of any Wrongdoing by State Bar," March 17, 2011 [**http://www.bananasthemovie.com**].

63. Steve Garmisa, "U.S. Courts Handle International Law," *Chicago Sun-Times,* September 24, 1997.

64. 11 U.S. (7 Cranch) 116 (1812).

65. *Sutherland v. Islamic Republic of Iran,* 151 F.Supp.2d 27 (D.D.C. 2001).

66. *Samantar v. Yousuf,* 130 S.Ct. 2278 (2010).

67. Based on information from Brent Kendal, "High Court Rejects Pfizer Appeal in Nigeria Drug-Trial Case," *The Wall Street Journal,* June 29, 2010 [**http://online.wsj.com/**]; Nathan Koppel, "Arcane Law Brings Conflicts from Overseas to U.S. Courts," *The Wall Street Journal,* August 27, 2009 [**http://online.wsj.com/**]; Jad Mouawad, "Shell to Pay $15.5 Million to Settle Nigerian Case," *The New York Times,* June 9, 2009 [**http://www.nytimes.com/**]; Jad Mouawad, "Oil

Industry Braces for Trial on Rights Abuses," *The New York Times,* May 22, 2009 [**http://www.nytimes.com/**]; Russell Gold, "Chevron Case Weighs Extent of Overseas Liability," *The Wall Street Journal,* December 1, 2008 [**http://online.wsj.com/**]; and Warren Richey, "U.S. High Court Allows Apartheid Claims Against Multinationals," *Christian Science Monitor,* May 13, 2008 [**http://www.csmonitor.com/**].

68. Current information on the status of the convention, as well as additional information, can be found at [**http://www.uncitral.org/uncitral/en/uncitral_texts/arbitration/NYConvention.html**].

69. See *Ehrenfeld v. Mahfouz,* 881 N.E.2d 830 (NY 2007).

70. Adam Liptak, "Foreign Courts Wary of U.S. Punitive Damages," *The New York Times,* March 26, 2008 [**http://www.nytimes.com/**].

71. Rupan Bhattacharya, "Valentine's Day Menace Causes Shop Closings," *The Des Moines Register,* February 14, 2001, p. 2A.

72. Leo E. Strine, "Human Freedom and Two Friedmen: Musings on the Implications of Globalization for the Effective Regulation of Corporate Behavior," University of Pennsylvania Law School Law and Economics Research Paper Series, November 1, 2007.

CHAPTER SEVENTEEN

Environmental Protection

After completing this chapter, students will be able to:

1. Identify some of the ways market incentives can be used to prevent and correct environmental problems.

2. Evaluate particular environmental problems using the concepts of causation and correlation, cost-benefit analysis, future impacts, and identification of costs imposed.

3. Describe the National Environmental Policy Act (NEPA).

4. Identify duties of the Environmental Protection Agency (EPA).

5. Describe the uses of the Clean Air Act (CAA) including its application to greenhouse gas emissions.

6. Describe the uses of the Clean Water Act (CWA).

7. Describe the legal issue involving the reach of the CWA.

8. Identify some of the major federal laws that address land pollution.

9. Discuss the purpose and effect of the Comprehensive Environmental Response, Compensation, and Liability Act of 1980 (CERCLA), commonly known as "the Superfund."

10. Identify penalties and other enforcement mechanisms under federal and state regulations.

11. Describe some of the challenges to protecting a species under the Endangered Species Act.

12. Describe the primary common law remedies for environmental damage.

13. Evaluate both the strengths and weaknesses of a global process for addressing climate change.

14. Give concrete examples of environmental degradation in the United States and globally.

Introduction

From local decisions—such as routing a new highway around a wetland or allowing the use of wood stoves—to colossal fears such as global climate change, environmental issues mark our lives in a manner that was unimaginable a few decades ago. From the moment a firm begins to produce, service, manufacture, or create, its operations affect the environment. Imagine all the small decisions made by a company: Does it pack its glassware in plastic bubbles or corrugated wrapping? Does it publish a catalog in paper or only through the Internet? Does it meet with the community before choosing a disposal system? Each decision will have an impact on our physical world, so it is critical to understand the legal and ethical dimensions of each such decision.

Pollution has often been analyzed by economists as a *market failure,* a perspective that will be explored in Part One. Part Two will survey the primary U.S. laws and regulations designed to address these market failures and the resulting degradation of our air, water, and land. In the discussion of air quality we will begin our consideration of greenhouse gases, climate change, and the responses of our state and federal governments. Part Three identifies the consequences that can be imposed on those who violate our environmental laws, including injunctions against future violations, remediation of damage, fines and penalties, and criminal convictions. Part Four discusses judicially created common law remedies long used to redress pollution damage and their possible application to greenhouse gas emitters. We end the chapter in Part Five by looking at climate change as a global problem, subject to remediation only on a global basis.

A Global Snapshot

As we begin, it is important to achieve a sense of the magnitude of the environmental problems we face, even apart from climate change. The scope of these problems often extends beyond political boundaries, and all countries are affected. Consider the following:

- "New glimpses of Earth from space show air pollution wrapping around the planet, spreading haze and hazardous gases across oceans and continents and posing new challenges for cleanup. . . . Increasingly, researchers are discovering air pollution is not a transient phenomenon. Emissions climb high into the atmosphere, borne on trade winds that circumnavigate the globe."[1]

> For 86 days oil spewed out of British Petroleum's Macondo well.

- For 86 days in 2010, oil spewed out of British Petroleum's (BP) Macondo well in the Gulf of Mexico. The long-term impacts on sea life, shorelines, and coastal communities from the still suspended, submerged, and buried portion of the nearly 5 million barrels spilled, as well as the effects of the chemical dispersants used to combat the spill, are unknown.[2] By volume it was far larger than the 1989 Exxon Valdez spill in Prince William Sound, Alaska. Globally, these are not isolated events. For example, in the Niger delta where Royal Dutch Shell, Chevron, and ExxonMobil have significant drilling operations, over the last 50 years as many as 546 million gallons of oil have leaked into the waters,[3] averaging annually the rough equivalent of the Exxon Valdez spill.

- "Villagers [in a community in Thailand] avoid walking in the rain because they say it burns their skin and causes their hair to fall out. They have trouble breathing at night

> The rain burns their skin.

when, they say, factories release toxic fumes. And they are terrified by what studies show are unusually high cancer rates." Twenty-seven of those villagers sued in 2007, an action that ultimately led to injunctions halting $9 billion of new industrial projects, including both German chemical plants and Japanese steel factories. But preexisting plants have been allowed to continue operating.[4]

- According to the World Health Organization, about 1.2 billion people or almost one fifth of the world's population live in areas where water is physically scarce.[5] In an area in northern China about the size of New Mexico the underground water table is sinking about four feet each year and most natural streams in the area have disappeared.[6]

- In 2010, a report for the academic journal *Science* analyzed the danger level for 25,000 species, classifying 13 percent of birds as threatened with extinction, 25 percent of mammals, and 41 percent of amphibians.[7]

PRACTICING ETHICS   Global Environmental Justice

The concept of *environmental justice* includes the expectation that environmental risks and hazards should be equally distributed when measured against wealth or race. Studies in the United States have shown that at least some risks, such as proximity to hazardous waste disposal sites, are not equally distributed.[8] Is the concept of equally distributed environmental risks a useful tool in assessing global environmental hazards? Consider the following:

- The Niger delta provides 10 percent of U.S. oil imports and routinely suffers substantial oil spills, as noted above.

- Eighty percent of Nigeria's government revenue comes from the Niger delta, but life expectancy in the delta is the lowest in Nigeria.[9]

Question

Are oil companies guilty of unethical behavior if their drilling procedures off the coast of Africa do not take environmental precautions equivalent to those they take when drilling in U.S. or European waters? Explain.

Part One—A Return to Fundamentals: The Market, Government Regulation, and Self-Regulation

The first three chapters of this text set up a framework for analyzing the substantive law topics that have followed: (1) consideration of how well market forces achieve the goals we have for our society; (2) a brief investigation of whether very aggressive government intervention, particularly in the manner of the Scandinavian welfare states, can bring us closer to those societal goals; and (3) reflection on the role that self-regulation, through ethical decision making and corporate social responsibility, can and does play in realizing our goals. Now we will apply market forces and ethics/social responsibility reasoning to our consideration of the relationship between business and our natural environment.

Market Failure?

Without regulation, a firm may consider that dumping its garbage into a nearby canal is no big deal. In fact, perhaps the slight amount of garbage the firm dumps is no big deal. However, if every firm were allowed to dump that amount, the canal might become thoroughly polluted. Or consider the possibility that we may all prefer less costly cars that pollute more. Would future generations concur?

As discussed in Chapter 8, these examples of water and air pollution would be categorized by economists as *negative externalities*. Wilfred Beckerman, a British economist, described the analysis as follows:

> [T]he costs of pollution are not always borne fully, if at all, by the polluter. . . . Naturally, he has no incentive to economize in the use [of the environment] in the same way that he has for other factors of production that carry a cost, such as labor or capital. . . . This defect of the price mechanism needs to be corrected by governmental action in order to eliminate excessive pollution.[10]

Thus environmentalists claim the market has failed to protect us from pollution so rules are necessary. The public and Congress have apparently agreed: A substantial number of environmental laws have been enacted since the early 1970s—laws that address pollution of our air and waterways, that regulate use, disposal, and cleanup of hazardous and toxic wastes, and that protect rare plant and animal species. Many of these laws will be discussed in Part Two.

Market Incentives

As we will see, one approach federal regulation has taken is to dictate standards with which businesses must comply. Such legislation has led to steady, and at times even spectacular, strides forward in environmental protection in the United States. But this progress has not dispelled the view, particularly among economists and businesspeople, that standard-setting regulation may not be the best approach to remedy environmental problems. They believe that pollution control is not so much a matter of law as of economics. It follows that, with proper incentives, the market will in some instances prove superior to traditional regulation in preventing and correcting environmental problems. Some examples of market incentives follow.

Pollution Credits

Perhaps the most prominent example in the United States of free market tactics employed to address an environmental issue was the government-created market in pollution credits established by the 1990 Clean Air Act. The Acid Rain Program set a cap on the number of tons of certain pollutants to be permitted in the air, a cap lower than the actual amount then being emitted. Pollution credits were issued to several hundred of the largest power plants and factories. Credit recipients could either reduce their discharges to within their credit limit or they could buy credits from other companies who had reduced their emissions below their own credit amounts. Companies with a relatively low cost to reduce their emissions made plant improvements and then paid for some of their own improvements by selling their excess credits. Companies with a relatively high cost to reduce emissions found it more economical to help pay to reduce another company's emissions (by purchasing that plant's excess credits) than incur their own higher-cost pollution reduction.[11] By 1999, electric utilities produced about 41 percent more electricity than they had in 1980 while emitting 25 percent fewer tons of sulfur dioxide, a major factor in the creation of acid rain.[12] In 2007, total sulfur dioxide emissions dropped below the long-term goal, ahead of the 2010 statutory deadline.[13]

Taxes and Government Rebates

Tax provisions can also affect behavior, either by encouraging particular behavior through tax incentives or government rebates or by discouraging other behavior through additional taxes. For example, between 2006 and 2010 anyone purchasing a new fuel-efficient car, including certain hybrids, received a credit that reduced their federal income taxes in the year of purchase. Another tax incentive program allows employers to offer employees a tax-free fringe benefit to cover the cost of mass transit passes or reimburse bicycle commuting costs. On the rebate side, for two months in 2009 the government ran the so-called Cash for Clunkers program.

Cash for Clunkers program.   Nearly 678,000 clunkers with a mean miles per gallon (MPG) of 15.7 were traded in for new vehicles with a mean MPG of 24.9. The estimated annual reduction in oil consumption is about 800,000 barrels and in greenhouse gas (GHG) emissions is approximately 360,000 metric tons.[14]

Global Examples

Australia, Greenland, Iceland, New Zealand, and the Netherlands have each been quite successful using market incentives to address overfishing. "Government authorities cap the total allowable catch and then allocate quotas among fishermen, usually based on the historical catch. The quotas become a 'property right' that can be bought and sold among fishermen—helping to reduce fleet capacity. And because fishermen have access to a guaranteed share of the catch, they don't race to compete, . . . prices rise and fish stocks grow."[15]

Ireland has successfully addressed a different urban pollutant—plastic and paper shopping bags. Induced by a 2002 tax on shopping bags, which is now about 63 cents per bag, nearly everyone brings their own, reusable cloth bags for shopping. In the beginning merchants were skeptical of the new tax, but it was illegal for them to pay for customers' bags themselves, forcing individual consumers to choose between bringing reusable bags or paying the tax. The taxes collected pay for environmental enforcement and cleanup programs.[16] [For more on the environmental impact of paper and plastic bags, see **http://www.reusablebags.com**]

A tax on shopping bags.

Question

Other suggested free market incentives for pollution control include government taxes or fees on pollution and government rules mandating refundable deposits on hazardous materials. Explain how those incentives might work.

Valuing Ecosystem Services

As discussed, traditional economics ignores the external, "spillover" environmental costs of doing business. One practical reason for that approach is the difficulty in determining those costs. Some ecologists and economists are working to change that by systematically inventorying and valuing the services nature performs, such as carbon absorption, flood control, water filtration, and provision of habitats. Such an analytical framework would allow land use decisions that could "keep the essential ecological process of larger ecosystem webs intact" and permit targeted conservation investments that would yield the highest ecological returns. In the longer run, it might support the creation of markets in ecosystem services. For example, in 1997, Costa Rica began paying landowners under five-year contracts to "sequester carbon, maintain water quality and protect biodiversity . . . primarily by practicing sustainable forestry on their land."

One critic, however, says, "One might argue that farmers should not be paid to reduce their water pollution any more than I should be paid to stop mugging people." A former deputy director in the U.S. Department of Agriculture sees the possibility of a hybrid "stoplight" approach. "The red part is: Here's some things you can do to your land that are so bad that we're gonna take you to prison. The yellow light is: Here's . . . some minimal stuff that you really ought to do. Then the green light is: Here's some stuff that's above and beyond the stewardship obligation, and we're going to pay you for doing it, because it's to the benefit of society."

Source: Matt Jenkins, "Mother Nature's Sum," *Miller-McCune* (October 2008) [**http://www.miller-mccune.com**].

Question

If burning fossil fuels is a major catalyst of global climate change, then the developed world is the major cause. But citizens of the least developed countries will suffer the most severe consequences. If you already suffer food and water insecurity, any further disruption is catastrophic. "Because hunger and misery cannot afford to make the distinctions of the well-fed—to choose between cutting a tree or saving it—poverty is among the greatest environmental threats in the world."[17] Does this reasoning provide a response to the critic who argues that farmers should not be paid to reduce their water pollution? Explain.

Ethical Business Decision Making

On a particularly busy corner in a suburb of Auckland, New Zealand, the proprietors of a small café, Triniti of Silver, do a brisk breakfast, lunch, and coffee trade. Their menu declares their philosophy: "Only organic eggs of free-range chickens are used here; only paddock-reared pigs; only certified organic beef—we do not feel happy to encourage the inhumane treatment of animals." Just one example of grassroots, intentional, ethical business decision making.

But what level of environmental concern can we expect from managers of publicly held corporations? Can we identify examples of environmental corporate social responsibility? The answer is a resounding yes—all one has to do is review a sampling of corporate Web sites. Why are corporate giants voluntarily doing now what they haven't done in the past? In part, the answer may be that the market has changed and market forces are operating to reward corporate responsibility. For example, managers may believe that being "green," or being seen as being green by consumers and investors, will improve the corporate bottom line. Or a manager may believe that a proactive approach may lessen the likelihood of future regulation on an issue that is becoming increasingly visible.[18] This is one example of a pay-now-or-pay-later analysis. Managers may take a more environmentally responsible approach now because they think the future cost of not doing so could be enormously larger—in negative publicity or in the cost of more stringent future regulation—than the present actual cost of the action.

Does the market actually reward sound environmental practices? We cannot yet be sure, but an interesting 1997 study found a strong relationship between environmental high performance and high profitability.[19] Some companies simply comply with environmental laws, whereas others take affirmative steps to improve their environmental performance.

The study's authors theorize that the latter companies build more skillful workers by expecting them to cope with the complexities of "clean technologies." Prevention and improvement are more complicated than mere compliance, so perhaps the environmentally active firms are actually building their performance "muscles" by their activist approach, whereas the compliance firms are expending their energies on the external world in an effort to fend off new rules. [For many examples of environmentally responsible actions of business, see **http://www.bsr.org/en/about/in-the-news**]

Question

"The single most important and pervasive moral obligation facing mankind is to ensure survival of a healthy planet for our grandchildren and theirs."[20] Do you agree? Why or why not?

Part Two—Laws and Regulations

Having reviewed both market forces and ethical business decision making, we turn now to government regulation as an approach for meeting our environmental goals. The United States has developed a wide variety of environmental protection laws and remedies, some of which are covered in this section. In evaluating a particular regulation, it will be helpful to keep in mind the following concepts:

- **Cost–Benefit Analysis.** Environmental protection can be expensive. How much as a society are we willing to pay? Do we want clean air at any cost? We may (or may not) be able to estimate the cost of a particular pro-environment action, but how do we measure its benefit? How do we value human life, represented by a statistical decrease in deaths or illness from exposure to environmental pollutants? Does environmental protection cause the sacrifice of short-term economic development? If so, can this cost be measured? These are not easy questions. The answers will necessarily be inexact and require subjective judgments and the use of estimates. A 2003 study by the federal Office of Management and Budget concluded that a prior toughening of clean air regulations was well worth the cost to industry and consumers. The "value of reductions in hospitalization and emergency room visits, premature deaths, and lost work-days resulting from improved air quality" was estimated between $120 and $193 billion over a 10-year period, where the cost to comply was only $23 to $26 billion.[21] Industry critics, however, argued that the costs of compliance were greatly understated. [For more information on cost–benefit analysis and environmental protection, see the Georgetown Environmental Law and Policy Project at **http://www.law.georgetown.edu/gelpi/research_archive/cost_benefit_analysis/cba_pub.cfm**]

> How do we value human life?

- **Impact on Future Generations.** When performing a cost–benefit analysis, how do we evaluate the cost to future generations of our not taking action? How can we measure the value to those generations if we do take action? In some cases, future generations will bear the brunt of the decision, whatever choice we make. For example, if greenhouse gases cause global climate change, how do we measure that impact on future generations? This is a complex question about which there is no scientific or economic consensus.

- **Proving Causation.** If event A occurs and event B follows, is it necessarily true that event A *caused* event B? It could simply be a coincidence that first A was observed and then B. Or there could, in fact, be a *correlation* between events A and B, but no actual causation. For example, event Z might cause both A and B, but no causal link may exist between A and B. In the environmental area, issues of coincidence, correlation, and causation may be extremely difficult to determine. For example, does exposure to secondhand smoke cause lung cancer in some nonsmokers? Is the observed increase in greenhouse gases a contributor to global warming, such that sea levels rose and increased the intensity of Hurricane Katrina, which in turn caused property damage to a degree that would not otherwise have occurred?[22] If, in the example of Z, A, and B, we spend a lot of effort trying to stop A to prevent B from occurring, we will be wasting our money. On the other hand, how long can we wait to determine definitively whether a causal link exists between A and B? Our answer may depend on the severity of the harm we believe is associated with B.

- **Who Pays?** If we decide to correct an environmental problem, who should pay for the correction? If we require corporate America to invest in pollution control devices, the cost may be shared between consumers (through increased prices) and investors (through a reduced corporate profit). If habitats of endangered species are to be preserved, current landowners may simply lose all or a portion of their investment and workers employed on the land may lose their jobs. Who should pay? Sometimes the issue is where a particular facility, such as a hazardous waste disposal site, should be located. Not surprisingly, a common response of citizens near a proposed location is, "yes, it's necessary, but *not in my backyard!*" This response is so common, that it is now referred to as NIMBY.

> "Not in my backyard!"

- **Politics.** Environmental protection in the United States is not just a matter of science, cost assessment, and social policy; it is also a matter of politics. California, for example, has historically received permission from the Environmental Protection Agency (EPA) to impose stricter vehicle emission standards than federal law requires. California sought similar permission in 2005, in part to add greenhouse gases to the emissions regulated. After delaying the decision for two years, California's request was denied. California responded by taking the EPA to court. A year later, in his first month in the White House, President Obama directed the EPA to reconsider California's application, signaling a sharp break with the Bush administration's less aggressive stance on climate change.[23]

Question

What environmental issue do you care about most? Greenhouse gases? Deforestation? Clean up of the Gulf oil spill? Select an issue you care about. (If it's climate change, select a particular possible response to it, such as sharing environmental technologies with developing countries, increasing mileage requirements, requiring the use of energy-efficient light bulbs, etc.) Do some online research for related data and then explore your issue in light of the five concepts discussed above.

The Federal Role

The federal government has long maintained a role in the protection of the environment—some argue too great a role. As early as 1899, Congress enacted a law that required a permit to discharge refuse into navigable waters. When it became apparent that private, state, and local environmental efforts were not adequate to address the burgeoning problems, Congress began taking more aggressive legislative initiatives in the early 1970s.

National Environmental Policy Act (NEPA)

The 1970 National Environmental Policy Act established a strong federal presence in the promotion of a clean and healthy environment. NEPA represents a general commitment by the federal government to "use all practicable means" to conduct federal affairs in a fashion that both promotes "the general welfare" and operates in "harmony" with the environment.

> The CEQ is a watchdog of sorts.

NEPA established the Council on Environmental Quality (CEQ), which serves as an adviser to the president. The CEQ is a watchdog of sorts. It is required to conduct studies and collect information regarding the state of the environment. The council then develops policy and legislative proposals for the president and Congress. [For more on the CEQ, see **http://www.whitehouse.gov/ceq**]

NEPA's primary influence, however, results from its *environmental impact statement* (EIS) requirements. With few exceptions, "proposals for legislation and other major federal action significantly affecting the quality of the human environment" must be accompanied by an EIS explaining the impact on the environment and detailing reasonable alternatives. Completing an EIS requires undertaking a cost–benefit analysis. It also requires consideration of cause and effect links. Major federal construction projects (highways, dams, nuclear reactors) would normally require an EIS, but less visible federal programs (ongoing timber management or the abandonment of a lengthy railway) may also require EIS treatment. Although the focus here is on federal actions, thus exempting solely private acts from this scrutiny, a major private-sector action supported by federal funding or by one of several varieties of federal permission may also require an EIS. Hence private companies receiving federal contracts, funding, licenses, and the like may be parties to the completion of an EIS.

Questions

Should a state be required to prepare an EIS if it wants to use federal funds to promote statewide tourism? Does it matter which state it is? Consider Iowa and then consider Hawaii.[24]

Environmental Protection Agency

The private sector was not left without regulation or constraint. The EPA was created in 1970 to mount a coordinated attack on environmental problems. EPA duties include, among other things, (1) gathering information, particularly by surveying pollution problems, (2) conducting research on pollution problems, (3) assisting state and local pollution control efforts, and (4) administering many of the federal laws directed to environmental concerns. [For the EPA home page, see **http://www.epa.gov**]

Regulation of Air Pollution

In the United States we depend on (indeed, we emotionally embrace) the automobile. In doing so, we have opened vistas of opportunity not previously imagined. However, motor vehicles also discharge carbon monoxide, nitrogen oxide, and hydrocarbons as by-products of the combustion of fuel, thus fouling our air. Today we know those vehicles also are significant emitters of greenhouse gases. Industrial production, manufacturing, generation of electricity, and the combustion of fossil fuels in homes and workplaces are also significant contributors to the dilemma of dirty air and greenhouse gases.

Clean Air Act of 1990 (CAA)

Early clean air legislation in 1963 and 1965 afforded the government limited authority. The Clean Air Act amendments of 1970 and 1977 gave the EPA the power to set air quality standards and to ensure that those standards are achieved according to a timetable prescribed by the agency. Politics brought clean air to the fore in 1990 and a new Clean Air Act followed. The Clean Air Act of 1990, which phased in new standards over a period of years, generally required tougher auto emission controls, cleaner-burning gasoline, and new equipment to capture industrial and business pollution, all of which worked toward the general goal of reducing airborne pollutants by about 50 percent. Under the CAA, air quality standards are set federally, but the states are required to establish implementation plans to achieve and maintain those standards.

In recent years, there has been considerable high-profile litigation over clean air standards. The Supreme Court's decision in *Massachusetts v. EPA,* presented below, has had the most profound effect. In this case a number of states, cities, and private organizations joined as petitioner to argue that the EPA had abdicated its responsibility under Section 202(a)(1) of the CAA to "prescribe . . . standards applicable to the emission of any air pollutant" when it refused to regulate greenhouse gas emissions from new motor vehicles.

L E G A L   B R I E F C A S E

Massachusetts v. Environmental Protection Agency   127 S.Ct. 1438 (2007)

Justice Stevens

A well-documented rise in global temperatures has coincided with a significant increase in the concentration of carbon dioxide in the atmosphere. Respected scientists believe the two trends are related. For when carbon dioxide is released into the atmosphere, it acts like the ceiling of a greenhouse, trapping solar energy and retarding the escape of reflected heat. It is therefore a species—the most important species—of a "greenhouse gas."

Calling global warming "the most pressing environmental challenge of our time," a group of states, local governments, and private organizations, alleged . . . [that the] EPA has abdicated its responsibility under the Clean Air Act to regulate the emissions of four greenhouse gases, including carbon dioxide. Specifically, petitioners asked us to answer two questions concerning . . . the Act: whether EPA has the statutory authority to regulate greenhouse gas emissions from new motor vehicles; and if so, whether its stated reasons for refusing to do so are consistent with the statute.

I

Section 202(a)(1) of the Clean Air Act . . . provides:

> The [EPA] Administrator shall by regulation prescribe (and from time to time revise) . . . standards applicable to the emission of any air pollutant from any class or classes of new motor vehicles or new motor vehicle engines, which in his judgment cause, or contribute to, air pollution which may reasonably be anticipated to endanger public health or welfare. . . .

The Act defines "air pollutant" to include "any air pollution agent or combination of such agents, including any physical, chemical, biological, radioactive . . . substance or matter which is emitted into or otherwise enters the ambient air." "Welfare" is also defined broadly: among other things, it includes "effects on . . . weather . . . and climate."

* * * * *

II

On October 20, 1999, a group of 19 private organizations filed a rulemaking petition asking EPA to regulate "greenhouse gas emissions from new motor vehicles under Section 202 of the Clean Air Act." . . . As to EPA's statutory authority, the petition observed that the agency itself had already confirmed that it had the power to regulate carbon dioxide. In 1998, Jonathan Z. Cannon, then EPA's General Counsel, prepared a legal opinion concluding that "CO[2] emissions are within the scope of EPA's authority to regulate," even as he recognized that EPA had so far declined to exercise that authority. Cannon's successor, Gary S. Guzy, reiterated that opinion before a congressional committee just two weeks before the rulemaking petition was filed.

* * * * *

On September 8, 2003, EPA entered an order denying the rulemaking petition. The agency gave two reasons for its decision: (1) that contrary to the opinions of its former general counsels, the Clean Air Act does not authorize EPA to issue mandatory regulations to address global climate change; and (2) that even if the agency had the authority to set greenhouse gas emission standards, it would be unwise to do so at this time.

* * * * *

Having reached that conclusion, EPA believed it followed that greenhouse gases cannot be "air pollutants" within the

meaning of the Act. . . . The agency bolstered this conclusion by explaining that if carbon dioxide were an air pollutant, the only feasible method of reducing tailpipe emissions would be to improve fuel economy. But because Congress has already created detailed mandatory fuel economy standards subject to Department of Transportation (DOT) administration, the agency concluded that EPA regulation would either conflict with those standards or be superfluous.

Even assuming that it had authority over greenhouse gases, EPA explained in detail why it would refuse to exercise that authority. The agency began by recognizing that the concentration of greenhouse gases has dramatically increased as a result of human activities, and acknowledged the attendant increase in global surface air temperatures. EPA nevertheless gave controlling importance to the [National Resource Council] Report's statement that a causal link between the two cannot be unequivocally established. Given that residual uncertainty, EPA concluded that regulating greenhouse gas emissions would be unwise.

The agency furthermore characterized any EPA regulation of motor-vehicle emissions as a "piecemeal approach" to climate change and stated that such regulation would conflict with the president's "comprehensive approach" to the problem. That approach involves additional support for technological innovation, the creation of nonregulatory programs to encourage voluntary private-sector reductions in greenhouse gas emissions, and further research on climate change—not actual regulation. According to EPA, unilateral EPA regulation of motor-vehicle greenhouse gas emissions might also hamper the president's ability to persuade key developing countries to reduce greenhouse gas emissions.

V (III-IV OMITTED-ED.)

* * * * *

[We] "may reverse any such action found to be . . . arbitrary, capricious, an abuse of discretion, or otherwise not in accordance with law."

VI

On the merits, the first question is whether Section 202(a)(1) of the Clean Air Act authorizes EPA to regulate greenhouse gas emissions from new motor vehicles in the event that it forms a "judgment" that such emissions contribute to climate change. We have little trouble concluding that it does. . . .

The statutory text forecloses EPA's reading. The Clean Air Act's sweeping definition of "air pollutant" includes "*any* air pollution agent or combination of such agents, including *any* physical, chemical . . . substance or matter which is emitted into or otherwise enters the ambient air. . . . " On its face, the definition embraces all airborne compounds of whatever stripe, and underscores that intent through the repeated use of the word "any." Carbon dioxide, methane, nitrous oxide, and hydrofluorocarbons are without a doubt "physical [and] chemical . . . substance[s] which [are] emitted into . . . the ambient air." The statute is unambiguous.

* * * * *

EPA finally argues that it cannot regulate carbon dioxide emissions from motor vehicles because doing so would require it to tighten mileage standards, a job (according to EPA) that Congress has assigned to DOT. But that DOT sets mileage standards in no way licenses EPA to shirk its environmental responsibilities. EPA has been charged with protecting the public's "health" and "welfare," a statutory obligation wholly independent of DOT's mandate to promote energy efficiency. The two obligations may overlap, but there is no reason to think the two agencies cannot both administer their obligations and yet avoid inconsistency.

* * * * *

VII

The alternative basis for EPA's decision—that even if it does have statutory authority to regulate greenhouse gases, it would be unwise to do so at this time—rests on reasoning divorced from the statutory text. While the statute does condition the exercise of EPA's authority on its formation of a "judgment," that judgment must relate to whether an air pollutant "cause[s], or contribute[s] to, air pollution which may reasonably be anticipated to endanger public health or welfare." Put another way, the use of the word "judgment" is not a roving license to ignore the statutory text. It is but a direction to exercise discretion within defined statutory limits.

If EPA makes a finding of endangerment, the Clean Air Act requires the agency to regulate emissions of the deleterious pollutant from new motor vehicles. . . . EPA no doubt has significant latitude as to the manner, timing, content, and coordination of its regulations with those of other agencies. But once EPA has responded to a petition for rulemaking, its reasons for action or inaction must conform to the authorizing statute. Under the clear terms of the Clean Air Act, EPA can avoid taking further action only if it determines that greenhouse gases do not contribute to climate change or if it provides some reasonable explanation as to why it cannot or will not exercise its discretion to determine whether they do. To the extent that this constrains agency discretion to pursue other priorities of the administrator or the president, this is the congressional design.

EPA has refused to comply with this clear statutory command. Instead, it has offered a laundry list of reasons not to regulate. For example, EPA said that a number of voluntary executive branch programs already provide an effective response to the threat of global warming, that regulating greenhouse gases might impair the president's ability to negotiate with "key developing nations" to reduce emissions, and that curtailing motor-vehicle emissions would reflect "an inefficient, piecemeal approach to address the climate change issue."

Although we have neither the expertise nor the authority to evaluate these policy judgments, it is evident they have nothing to do with whether greenhouse gas emissions contribute to climate change. Still less do they amount to a reasoned justification for declining to form a scientific judgment. . . .

Nor can EPA avoid its statutory obligation by noting the uncertainty surrounding various features of climate change and concluding that it would therefore be better not to regulate at this time. If the scientific uncertainty is so profound that it precludes EPA from making a reasoned judgment as to whether greenhouse gases contribute to global warming, EPA must say so. That EPA would prefer not to regulate greenhouse gases because of some residual uncertainty . . . is irrelevant. The statutory question is whether sufficient information exists to make an endangerment finding.

In short, EPA has offered no reasoned explanation for its refusal to decide whether greenhouse gases cause or contribute to climate change. Its action was therefore "arbitrary, capricious, . . . or otherwise not in accordance with law." . . .

[Reversed and remanded.]

Questions

1. Under what conditions did the Supreme Court say it had the power to reverse the EPA's decision not to regulate the carbon dioxide emissions of new vehicles?

2. What did the petitioners, including the State of Massachusetts, want the EPA to do?

3. The EPA said that, even if it had the authority to regulate greenhouse gas emissions from motor vehicles, it would not do so. What reasons did the EPA give for this refusal? What did the Supreme Court say about those reasons?

4. Following this decision of the Supreme Court, what was the EPA required to do? Was the EPA required to set a standard for greenhouse gas emissions from new vehicles?

5. Look back at the discussion about proving causation at the start of Part Two of this chapter. Did the Supreme Court say that greenhouse gas emissions from vehicles caused global warming? What did the Court observe about causation?

AFTERWORD

Despite the Court's ruling in *Massachusetts v. EPA*, the progress in the United States toward controlling greenhouse gas (GHG) emissions in the intervening four years has been modest at best. Much of what has occurred has been driven by state action, not federal action. Not until President Obama took office did the EPA rule that GHG emissions are pollutants that threaten public health. The EPA has now also issued final rules mandating that major stationary sources such as electric generators and oil refineries annually report their GHG emissions, requiring that major sources of non-GHG pollutants be reviewed for GHG emissions under a prevention of significant deterioration standard, and subjecting new GHG sources and major modifications of existing sources to a GHG emission permitting process.

Many have argued that regulation of GHG by the EPA under the Clean Air Act cannot and will not be as effective or as timely as could be accomplished by a federal climate bill such as the cap and trade proposal that died in the Senate in July 2010.[25] Since Congress has not acted, in this too the states have taken the lead. In 2006, California passed a law requiring state GHG emissions to be cut to 1990 levels by 2020. Its goal is to reduce emissions 80 percent by 2050.[26] At least 22 states have set standards for utility companies regarding the percentage of energy that must come from renewable sources by 2020. In October 2007, Kansas became the first government in the United States to refuse a permit for a proposed coal-fired electricity generating plant on the basis of carbon dioxide emissions.[27] Furthermore, several regional GHG initiatives have been started. Each involves a cap-and-trade program intended to stabilize and reduce regional emissions to meet specified goals. The Regional Greenhouse Gas Initiative covering 10 northeastern and mid-Atlantic states auctioned off its first pollution allowances in the fall of 2008.[28]

Motor Vehicle Emission Standards

Some thought the financial crisis and gas prices approaching or exceeding $4 per gallon might finally reduce our use of automobiles, but that seems not to be the case. After a drop in 2008, and then again in 2009, our total gallons of gas consumed rose again in 2010—to a level even higher than in 2008.[29]

In December 2007, Congress set a new fuel efficiency target requiring auto manufacturers to reach a fleet average of 35 miles per gallon (MPG) by 2020. The legislation did not contain any explicit requirements regarding GHG emissions, although any increase in average MPG would naturally reduce GHG emissions. California had a long and uninterrupted history of receiving EPA permission to set its own higher standards, and California's rule also set specific standards for carbon dioxide emissions. California applied to the EPA in 2005 for a waiver from the national EPA standards in order to enforce its own tough, new standards, but on the day in 2007 when President Bush signed into law the federal 35 MPG standard, the EPA denied California's waiver request. California sued, along with several other states that had already announced an intention to piggyback on California's waiver (also a routine practice). When President Obama took office he directed the EPA to reconsider California's request, and it approved the waiver in June 2009. By mid-2010, with the agreement of the auto industry, the California standard essentially became the federal standard. Fleet averages in Europe and Japan already exceed 35 MPG and Europe is aiming for a 60 MPG standard by 2020.[30]

> Fleet averages in Europe and Japan already exceed 35 MPG.

Non-GHG Air Quality

Greenhouse gases are, of course, not the only air pollutant hazardous to health. In controlling smog, primarily a result of ozone, the United States has been falling behind other industrialized countries. A study of environmental performance ranked the United States near the bottom of the Group of 8 industrialized nations, higher only than Russia. The primary reasons identified were our greenhouse gas emissions and a persistent problem with smog.[31] In early 2010, the EPA proposed stricter standards on ozone,[32] which could result in the closing of as many as 20 percent of U.S. coal-burning power plants. By and large these facilities are over 40 years old, and they lack any emissions controls because they were "grandfathered" in under the CAA. The market may diminish this problem, in any case. Even if the government intervenes, retirement of the plants will be accelerated by only four to five years because they are becoming less economical to operate since natural gas has become cheaper than coal for power generation.[33]

Regulation of Water Pollution

As with the air, we often treat our water resources as free goods. Rather than paying the full cost of producing goods and services, we have simply dumped a portion of that cost into the nearest body of water. The results range from smelly to dangerous to tragic. The evidence can be found in our local rivers and lakes, but also in our global gulfs, seas, and oceans.

BP's oil spill in the Gulf of Mexico has done and will do untold damage, but the waters of the Gulf before the spill were hardly pristine. Ninety percent of America's offshore drilling occurs there, drilling that has gone on for over 60 years and that provides tens of thousands of jobs. Since 1964 over 300 spills releasing over a half million barrels of oil have occurred, not to mention the thousands of tons of "produced water"—a by-product of drilling that includes oil, grease, and heavy metals—that are dumped annually. After World War II, the Gulf was even used by the government to dispose of surplus mines, bombs, and ammunition.[34]

The debris of our modern lives—including light bulbs, bottle caps, toothbrushes, and all manner of plastics—also shows up in our oceans. In the Pacific, a garbage patch of detritus has been estimated at roughly twice the size of Texas.[35] We have ample evidence of the consequences for fish and other aquatic life. As one observer who has worked on the Gulf his whole life noted, "You can fool people, but you can't fool the fish."[36]

"You can fool people, but you can't fool the fish."

Federal Policy

The 1972 Clean Water Act (CWA), designed to "restore and maintain the chemical, physical, and biological integrity of the nation's waters," established two national goals: (1) achieving water quality sufficient for the protection and propagation of fish, shellfish, and wildlife and for recreation in and on the water; and (2) eliminating the discharge of pollutants into navigable waters. The states have primary responsibility for enforcing the CWA, but the EPA is empowered to assume enforcement authority if necessary.

There is no doubt the CWA has resulted in enormous improvements, but there are problems as well. The goals of the Act are implemented primarily by imposing limits on the amount of pollutants that may lawfully enter the waters of the United States from any "point source" (typically a pipe). The National Pollutant Discharge Elimination System (NPDES) requires all dischargers to secure a permit, most often from the EPA but at times from some other government agency, before pouring effluent into a navigable stream. The permit specifies maximum permissible levels of effluent and typically also mandates the use of a particular pollution control process or device to ensure that level is not exceeded. It also requires the permit holder to monitor its own performance and report the results to the state or the EPA.

But regulation of point sources leaves many pollutants unmonitored. Surface water runoff is polluted with our lawn fertilizer, pet waste, and grease and oil from vehicles. In spite of rules put in place in 1999, surface water is also polluted by runoff from large row crop, hog, cattle, and poultry farms. Nitrogen from fertilizers finds its way into the Mississippi River from sources hundreds of miles from the Gulf—1.5 million tons of it yearly. As a result, in the Gulf there is a dead zone, comparable in size with Lake Ontario, in which little life can exist.[37]

> In the Gulf there is a dead zone.

Discouragingly, even sources covered by the NPDES nevertheless violate the terms of their permits, often with impunity. *The New York Times* published a series of articles over the fall of 2009 based on records received in response to Freedom of Information Act requests made to every state and the EPA. In them journalist Charles Duhigg presented an alarming picture of CWA violations rising steadily across the nation. Many violations were relatively minor but about 60 percent were deemed to be in "significant noncompliance." Fewer than 3 percent resulted in fines or other substantial punishment. Some, but not all, of the rise is attributable to insufficient enforcement resources. The number of regulated facilities more than doubled in a 10-year span, but state enforcement budgets remained essentially flat. The EPA made promises to regulate the discharge of such toxic substances as arsenic, lead, and cadmium, but has never done so. [To read the articles in this series, go to **http://www.nytimes.com/toxicwaters**]

How Did Your State Respond?

The New York Times Web site provides the data it received from responding states regarding CWA permits, violations, and enforcement actions. The *Times* also provides information from each state on staffing and budgets related to oversight of water pollution. What information was provided from your state? See **http://www.nytimes.com/toxic-waters/polluters/state-data**

Covered Waters

Decades after CWA enactment, it remains unclear exactly what waters are actually covered by the act and therefore subject to EPA regulation. In the 2001 *Northern Cook County* case that follows, the Supreme Court looked at what qualifies as "navigable waters" for purposes of the CWA. Only a bare majority (five) of the justices agreed with this decision; the remaining four dissented. In 2006, the Supreme Court again looked at the issue. That decision will be discussed following *Northern Cook County*.

Solid Waste Agency of Northern Cook County v. U.S. Army Corps of Engineers   531 U.S. 159 (2001)

Chief Justice Rehnquist

Section 404(a) of the Clean Water Act (CWA or Act) regulates the discharge of dredged or fill material into "navigable waters." The United States Army Corps of Engineers (Corps) has interpreted Section 404(a) to confer federal authority over an abandoned sand and gravel pit in northern Illinois that provides habitat for migratory birds. We are asked to decide whether the provisions of Section 404(a) may be fairly extended to these waters, and, if so, whether Congress could exercise such authority consistent with the Commerce Clause. We answer the first question in the negative and therefore do not reach the second.

Petitioner, the Solid Waste Agency of Northern Cook County (SWANCC), is a consortium of 23 suburban Chicago cities and villages that united in an effort to locate and develop a disposal site for baled nonhazardous solid waste. The Chicago Gravel Company informed the municipalities of the availability of a 533-acre parcel, . . . which had been the site of a sand and gravel pit mining operation for three decades up until about 1960. Long since abandoned, the old mining site eventually gave way to a successional stage forest, with its remnant excavation trenches evolving into a scattering of permanent and seasonal ponds of varying size (from under one-tenth of an acre to several acres) and depth (from several inches to several feet).

The municipalities decided to purchase the site. . . .

Section 404(a) grants the Corps authority to issue permits "for the discharge of dredged or fill material into the navigable waters at specified disposal sites." The term "navigable waters" is defined under the Act as "the waters of the United States, including the territorial seas." The Corps has issued regulations defining the term "waters of the United States" to include.

> waters such as intrastate lakes, rivers, streams (including intermittent streams), mudflats, sandflats, wetlands, sloughs, prairie potholes, wet meadows, playa lakes, or natural ponds, the use, degradation or destruction of which could affect interstate or foreign commerce.

In 1986, in an attempt to "clarify" the reach of its jurisdiction, the Corps stated that Section 404(a) extends to intrastate waters

a. Which are or would be used as habitat by birds protected by Migratory Bird Treaties; or

b. Which are or would be used as habitat by other migratory birds which cross state lines; or

c. Which are or would be used as habitat for endangered species; or

d. Used to irrigate crops sold in interstate commerce.

This last promulgation has been dubbed the "Migratory Bird Rule."

The Corps initially concluded that it had no jurisdiction over the site. . . . However, after the Illinois Nature Preserves Commission informed the Corps that a number of migratory bird species had been observed at the site, the Corps reconsidered and ultimately asserted jurisdiction over the balefill site pursuant to subpart (b) of the "Migratory Bird Rule." The Corps found that approximately 121 bird species had been observed at the site, including several known to depend upon aquatic environments for a significant portion of their life requirements. . . .

* * * * *

[The] Corps refused to issue a Section 404(a) permit. The Corps found that SWANCC had not established that its proposal was the "least environmentally damaging, most practicable alternative" for disposal of nonhazardous solid waste; that SWANCC's failure to set aside sufficient funds to remediate leaks posed an "unacceptable risk to the public's drinkingwater supply"; and that the impact of the project upon area-sensitive species was "unmitigatable since a landfill surface cannot be redeveloped into a forested habitat."

Petitioner filed suit. . . . Petitioner argued that respondents had exceeded their statutory authority in interpreting the CWA to cover nonnavigable, isolated, intrastate waters based upon the presence of migratory birds. . . .

The Court of Appeals [held] that respondents' "Migratory Bird Rule" was a reasonable interpretation of the Act.

We granted certiorari. . . .

Congress passed the CWA for the stated purpose of "restoring and maintaining the chemical, physical, and biological integrity of the Nation's waters." In so doing, Congress chose to "recognize, preserve, and protect the primary responsibilities and rights of States to prevent, reduce, and eliminate pollution, to plan the development and use (including restoration, preservation, and enhancement) of land and water resources, and to consult with the Administrator in the exercise of his authority under this chapter." Relevant here, Section 404(a) authorizes respondents to regulate the discharge of fill material into "navigable waters," which the statute defines as "the waters of the United States, including the territorial seas." Respondents have interpreted these words to cover the abandoned gravel pit at issue here because it is used as habitat for migratory birds. We conclude that the "Migratory Bird Rule" is not fairly supported by the CWA.

This is not the first time we have been called upon to evaluate the meaning of Section 404(a). In *United States v. Riverside Bayview Homes, Inc.,* 474 U.S. 121 (1985), we held that the Corps had Section 404(a) jurisdiction over wetlands that actually abutted on a navigable waterway. In so doing, we noted that the term "navigable" is of "limited import" and that Congress evidenced its intent to "regulate at least some waters that would not be deemed 'navigable' under the classical understanding of that term." But our holding was based in large measure upon Congress' unequivocal acquiescence to, and approval of, the Corps' regulations interpreting the CWA to cover wetlands adjacent to navigable waters. We found that Congress' concern for the protection of water quality and aquatic ecosystems indicated its intent to regulate wetlands "inseparably bound up with the 'waters' of the United States."

It was the significant nexus between the wetlands and "navigable waters" that informed our reading of the CWA in *Riverside Bayview Homes.* . . . In order to rule for respondents here, we would have to hold that the jurisdiction of the Corps extends to ponds that are *not* adjacent to open water. But we conclude that the text of the statute will not allow this.

Indeed, the Corps' *original* interpretation of the CWA, promulgated two years after its enactment, is inconsistent with that which it espouses here. Its 1974 regulations defined Section 404(a)'s "navigable waters" to mean "those waters of the United States which are subject to the ebb and flow of the tide, and/or are presently, or have been in the past, or may be in the future susceptible for use for purposes of interstate or foreign commerce." The Corps emphasized that "it is the water body's capability of use by the public for purposes of transportation or commerce which is the determinative factor." Respondents put forward no persuasive evidence that the Corps mistook Congress' intent in 1974.

* * * * *

We hold that [the regulations], as clarified and applied to petitioner's balefill site pursuant to the "Migratory Bird Rule," [exceed] the authority granted to respondents under Section 404(a) of the CWA. The judgment of the Court of Appeals for the Seventh Circuit is therefore Reversed.

Questions

1. Summarize the arguments made by the Army Corps of Engineers for finding that the government had the power to regulate this site under the CWA.

2. Explain the Supreme Court's response to each of the Army Corps of Engineers' arguments previously identified.

3. Did the Supreme Court hold that the government could not regulate this type of site or only that Congress had not in fact sought to extend its regulation to this type of site?

4. In your view, should the federal government be able to regulate bodies of water that are of significant use by migratory birds? Explain.

AFTERWORD

In the *Northern Cook County* case the Supreme Court evaluated a regulation of the Army Corps of Engineers and determined that the Corps exceeded its scope of authority under the CWA. All nine justices agreed that the term "navigable waters" should be interpreted more broadly than its literal meaning, but only four of the justices would have approved the Corps' expansive reading of the statute.

In the 2006 case *Repanos v. United States,* the Supreme Court once again reviewed the term "navigable waters."[38] The same four justices dissented, arguing that the revised, but still broad authority asserted by the Corps was permissible under the statute. This time, however, the remaining five justices did not agree on the reach of the CWA, but only agreed that the Corps was still asserting an authority broader than allowable. The result was that the case was remanded for "further proceedings" but without a standard on which to base those proceedings. The bottom line was that the government was required once again to define the scope of its regulatory authority.

In the meantime, enforcement under the Act has been substantially hampered. "In drier states, some polluters say the act no longer applies to them and are therefore refusing to renew or apply for permits, making it impossible to monitor what they are dumping." A case in point—Cannon Air Force Base in New Mexico has informed the EPA that it "no longer considers itself subject to the act." According to *The New York Times,* it "dumps wastewater—containing bacteria and human sewage—into a lake on the base."[39] In April 2011 the EPA announced new guidelines,[40] which will no doubt be challenged in court.

> In drier states, some polluters say the act no longer applies to them.

Regulation of Land Pollution

Pollution does not fit tidily into the three compartments (air, water, land) used for convenience in this text. Acid rain debases air and water as well as the fruits of water and land such as fish and trees. Similarly, the problems of land pollution addressed in this section can seep into the soil, polluting groundwater, and harming plants and animals directly and indirectly. What we look at in this section is how we dispose of waste—solid, hazardous, and toxic.

Toxic Substances Control Act (TSCA)

Because our disposal laws vary based on the classification of the materials to be disposed of, the primary law governing classification is a good place to start. In 1976, Congress approved the Toxic Substances Control Act to identify toxic chemicals, assess their risks, and control dangerous chemicals. Under the terms of TSCA, the EPA requires the chemical industry to report any information it may have that suggests any new chemical it intends to market poses a "substantial risk." The EPA is empowered to review and limit or stop the introduction of new chemicals.

That, at least, is the theory. The reality is not as comforting. Only a small fraction of the over 80,000 chemicals in use in the United States have been tested for safety according to an Annual Report of the President's Cancer Panel.[41] The names and physical properties of nearly 20 percent of that 80,000 are secret from all but a handful of EPA employees who are required by law to protect the trade secrets of the manufacturers.[42] That protection prohibits disclosure to other federal officials, state health and environmental regulators, and physicians, as well as the public. Although many of these unknown chemicals are likely harmless, in just one month "more than half of the 65 'substantial risk' reports filed" with the EPA by manufacturers "involved secret chemicals." Only Congress can change the law and until it does we are all trading knowledge in exchange for "ensuring the long-term competitiveness of the U.S. [chemical] industry."[43] [For more on programs under TSCA, see **http://www.epa.gov/opptintr/index.html**]

Pollution in the Movies

Perhaps surprisingly, toxic pollution has provided the central theme in two major Hollywood movies: *Erin Brockovich* and *A Civil Action*. The 2000 movie *Erin Brockovich* tells the story of a California community's battle against Pacific Gas & Electric for allegedly causing groundwater pollution resulting in extensive illness. [For more information on the pollutant at issue in the movie, hexavalent chromium, see **http://www.atsdr.cdc.gov/csem/chromium/cr_clinical-evaluation.html**]

In the 1998 Disney movie *A Civil Action,* John Travolta played a plaintiff's lawyer based on a true story about some middle-class families who sued two corporate giants, Beatrice Food and W. R. Grace & Co., for allegedly polluting the groundwater in East Woburn, Massachusetts where eight children died of leukemia. [For more information on this pollutant, Trichloroethylene, see **http://www.atsdr.cdc.gov/phs/phs.asp?id=171&tid=30**]

Question

Look back at the discussion of proving causation at the start of Part Two. Using that terminology, describe the causation issues that had to be addressed in the real-life counterparts
to these movies.

Resource Conservation and Recovery Act (RCRA)

By 1976 the dangers of hazardous substances were becoming apparent to all and Congress
complemented the TSCA with the Resource Conservation and Recovery Act. The act addresses both nonhazardous and hazardous solid wastes. Its provisions for nonhazardous
wastes are more supportive than punitive in tone and approach. The federal government is
authorized, among other strategies, to provide technical and financial assistance to states
and localities; to prohibit future open dumping; and to establish cooperative federal, state,
local, and private-enterprise programs to recover energy and valuable materials from
solid waste.

Subtitle C of the RCRA is designed to ensure the safe movement and disposal of hazardous solid wastes. The generator of the waste must determine if that waste is hazardous
under EPA guidelines. If so, the waste generator must then create a manifest to be used in
tracking the waste from its creation to its disposal. Along the cradle-to-grave path, all those
with responsibility for it must sign the manifest and safely store and transport the waste.
Once the waste reaches a licensed disposal facility, the owner or manager of that site signs
the manifest and returns a copy of it to the generator. Disposal sites must be operated
according to EPA standards, and remedial action must be taken should hazardous wastes
escape from the sites. [For more information, see the EPA Web site at **http://www.epa.gov/
epawaste/hazard/tsd/index.htm**]

A preliminary issue to this cradle-to-grave tracking, however, is the statutory requirement that to be a solid waste, the material must be "discarded." The U.S. Court of Appeals
for the District of Columbia has ruled that "discarded" means "disposed of," "abandoned,"
or "thrown away" and has repeatedly held that various versions of the EPA's rules have
been too broad because they improperly covered recycling practices when the materials
were not discarded within the meaning of the statute.[44] Thus, *recycled* hazardous materials
are not covered by RCRA, although they may be subject to other EPA regulations.[45]

Household Recycling

Our lifestyles result in mountains of waste that grow higher every year. Indeed, New
York City's Fresh Kills Landfill is one of the world's largest man-made structures and one
of the highest points of land on the East Coast. In 2009, on average each of us produced
4.3 pounds of garbage daily.[46] Of course, we pay an immediate price to dispose of all the
leftovers of our lives, but the long-term concern is that the waste will
come back to haunt us. Even state-of-the-art landfills can leak, with
the result that toxic elements can enter our groundwater. We had
long assumed that much of the waste would simply decompose, but
studies show that does not happen. A leading "garbologist," Professor
William Rathje, explains, "The thought that after 30 or so years
newspapers and food would disintegrate is off-track. Things become

> We had long assumed that much of the waste would simply decompose, but studies show that does not happen.

mummified. We found hot dogs that could be recooked and perfectly legible newspapers."[47] The suggested solution, of course, is to "reduce, reuse, recycle."

Recycling turns materials that would otherwise become waste into usable resources, which can reduce dependence on new materials (reducing deforestation, for example). Recycling can also reduce the amount of waste that is burned in incinerators, reducing particulate matter and other pollutants that would otherwise be released into the air. The EPA reports that 83 million tons of material was recycled in 2008.[48] One man in Huntsville, Texas, has built a unique recycling business—building low-income housing out of recycled materials. He started in 1997 and by 2009 had built 14 homes using materials salvaged from other construction projects, as well as "mismatched bricks, shards of ceramic tiles, shattered mirrors, bottle butts, wine corks, old DVDs and even bones from nearby cattle yards." He worked with city officials to set up a nonprofit warehouse for the donation of recycled building materials. There are no dumping fees for the builders, demolition crews and manufacturers donating materials and donations are tax deductible because the materials are used exclusively by charitable groups or for low-income housing. At least four other cities have consulted with him to set up similar operations in their locales.[49]

> **Freegans attempt to live totally on free goods found in dumpsters and at "freemeets."**

The ultimate recycling approach, however, may be that taken by a group of anticonsumerists who call themselves freegans (as compared with vegans)—who attempt to live totally on free goods found in dumpsters and at "freemeets."[50] [For sites identifying the availability of free goods, see **http://www.craigslist.org** (select "free" from the for sale menu), and **http://www.freecycle.org**]

Of course, the most cost-effective, environmentally friendly practice of all is to simply *reduce* consumption.

Superfund—Comprehensive Environmental Response, Compensation, and Liability Act of 1980 (CERCLA)

December 2010 marked the 30th anniversary of CERCLA, more commonly known as the Superfund, which is designed to help clean up hazardous dumps and spills. "Under CERCLA, the EPA may take actions to clean up a site from which hazardous substances have been released or where there is the threat of such a release. CERCLA also authorizes the federal government to order private parties to undertake the cleanup activities. The government and private parties who incur response costs cleaning up a site may seek recovery of those costs from liable parties."[51] Potentially responsible parties include present owners of the site as well as past owners who operated the site when the hazardous wastes were deposited; parent firms can be liable for actions of subsidiaries; and transferors (successive owners of businesses discharging hazardous wastes) are also liable. Any parties found to be responsible are strictly liable—that is, liability attaches without proof of either intent or negligence.

> **Any parties found to be responsible are strictly liable.**

Cleanup tends to be very expensive and generally requires considerable time to accomplish. The first listed Superfund site, Love Canal in Niagara Falls, New York, was finally clean enough to be delisted in 2004.[52] Originally cleanup costs were paid from a trust fund created by taxes on chemicals and petroleum; but that taxing authority lapsed in 1995. The

Superfund program has since been running on annual appropriations and reserve funds. According to a recent Government Accountability Office report, that funding is likely to be inadequate for the foreseeable future. The annual estimated remediation costs for the five years ending in 2014 run from $335 to $681 million, but from 2000 to 2009 the highest funding received was only $267 million.[53] As of April 1, 2011, there are 66 proposed new Superfund sites, 1290 sites currently on the national priorities list, and only 347 sites that have been delisted.[54]

How Does Your Community Compare?

Treece, Kansas, and Picher, Oklahoma, are adjacent communities, both part of a lead, zinc, and iron ore mining district until the last of the mines closed in the 1970s. Picher, the larger community, once had a population of 20,000 as well as most of the services used by both communities, such as stores and gas stations. Treece is entirely residential, with a remaining population of about 140. The town centers were no more than two miles apart and the legal boundary between them only a gravel road, albeit also a state line. Both communities have been on the Superfund list since the 1980s. In an almost unprecedented move, the government bought out and relocated nearly the entire population of Picher. Not so for the citizens of Treece. As to them, the EPA has said that soil cleansing can be accomplished in 10 years and people there are safe in the meantime. "You can turn and see one block away is Oklahoma, unsafe. They got bought out, and we didn't? It's incredibly unfair. The people here, if they wanted to leave, they can't. They can't sell their property. . . . They're just stuck."[55]

What do you know about the pollution in your community? Find out by logging onto **http://www.scorecard.org** and inserting your zip code. Then visit the EPA's site and discover any Superfund sites near you on its maps at **http://www.epa.gov/superfund/sites/npl/where.htm**

Questions

1. Are there any Superfund sites in or near your community?
2. How does your home town rate with regard to the industrial release of toxic chemicals?
3. How does your air quality stack up with other communities in the United States?
4. How clean are your rivers and lakes?

Small Business Liability Relief and Brownfields Revitalization Act

There has been considerable dissatisfaction over CERCLA for a number of reasons, including the percentage of Superfund dollars that have gone to administration expenses and litigation, as well as the slow remediation process at most sites. Worried about liability risks, developers were often reluctant to buy and improve brownfield sites, but that problem was alleviated with the passage of the 2002 Small Business Liability Relief and Brownfields Revitalization Act (Brownfields Act). This law provides liability protection for prospective purchasers and contiguous property owners and authorizes increased funding for state and local programs that assess and clean up brownfields. [For more on brownfields, see **http://www.epa.gov/swerosps/bf/about.htm**]

PRACTICING ETHICS) Environmentally Aware Decision Making

Imagine you have just been hired as the business manager for a chain of restaurants in your state. During the interview process you were told that part of your responsibilities would be to develop more environmentally friendly practices to be implemented at all 10 locations, while making sure that the changes overall either have a neutral or a positive impact on the business's bottom line. A local business school professor is interested in having her students do semester projects on the feasibility of various green projects for local businesses. Develop a list of possible practices your restaurants could implement to share with the professor for further development by her students.

Part Three—Penalties and Enforcement under Federal Law

Many environmental statutes require companies to monitor their own environmental performance and report that information, including violations, to the government. As noted above in discussing the Clean Water Act, such disclosure does not necessarily lead to any form of corrective or enforcement action. Government agencies also have broad authority to conduct environmental inspections of both plants and records as necessary, although they must obtain search warrants if criminal prosecutions are anticipated.

A broad array of enforcement actions are available to both state and federal agencies. Often violators initially are simply warned and a compliance schedule may be prescribed. If corrective action is not forthcoming, sterner measures may follow, including an administrative order to comply. Where problems persist or the difficulties are more serious, the government may resort to litigation. The government may seek an injunction to prevent continued or future violations or to require the polluter to remediate the environmental damage that has occurred. Monetary civil penalties and fines may be imposed under most environmental statutes. Governments that have incurred cleanup costs responding to the violation may also seek recovery of those costs. Although many suits are litigated, most are settled. Settlement opens the possibility of somewhat more creative solutions, often referred to as Supplemental Environmental Projects or SEPs. Such projects involve the violator undertaking some environmental "good work" or community service project. [To find actual examples of SEPs, explore the database maintained by the EPA at **http://www. epa-echo.gov/echo/index.html**]

Many environmental laws also provide for the imposition of criminal penalties, as well as imprisonment. Individual corporate officers can be held criminally liable if they either had actual knowledge of the criminal action or they are held to be a "responsible person" under the appropriate law.

Of course, the importance and effectiveness of any enforcement measure depends to a significant degree on the extent to which it is both sought and imposed. According to one report based on Justice Department and EPA data, "criminal cases against polluters . . . dropped off sharply during the Bush administration, with the number of prosecutions, new investigations and total convictions all down by more than a third" in comparison with such cases during the Clinton administration.[56] According to another study of sentences imposed after convictions were obtained, the "bark" of federal sentencing guidelines for environmental crimes "remains considerably worse than their bite."[57]

BP Gulf Oil Spill: A Case Study of Costs

The cost to BP as a result of the Gulf oil spill may well exceed the $40 billion that BP has publicly expected. Here is an estimate of what BP may pay:

- As of the end of 2010, BP had already spent $10.7 billion to plug the Macondo well and clean up the spilled oil.

- Under the Clean Water Act, any fine will be based in part on the volume of oil spilled as well as the level of BP's culpability. Based on a 4.9 million barrel spill, the fines could run from $5.4 to $21.1 billion.

- State and local governments around the Gulf are likely to pursue compensation for both environmental damage suffered and for lost tax revenues. BP has already agreed to provide an initial $1 billion for some restoration projects.

- BP set up a $20 billion compensation fund in August 2010, which in its first phase paid out $2.2 billion in emergency funds to those most immediately affected by the spill. The second phase will pay negotiated lump sum settlements. Individuals and businesses that accept a final settlement from this fund will lose their right to sue for additional damages, including damages as yet unknown.

- Individuals and businesses not accepting settlements are likely to sue. These suits can cover damages from lost wages or profits, as well as personal injury claims from oil rig workers, their families, and cleanup crews.

- BP will also have legal fees, estimated by one account at $2 billion, including fees of experts necessary to pursue and defend the various legal actions.

- As of April 2011 the Department of Justice was still considering potential criminal charges.

BP may, however, recoup some of these costs if it is successful in any of its suits against its minority partners or the rig owner, Transocean Ltd.

Sources: "Gulf of Mexico Oil Spill (2010)," as of April 25, 2011 [**http://www.nytimes.com**]; and Associated Press, "Tallying the Spill's Cost," *The Des Moines Register,* December 30, 2010, p. 8B.

Additional Enforcement Mechanisms

In addition to the mechanisms mentioned above, many environmental statutes allow citizen suits, in which individuals may challenge government environmental decisions, such as the granting of a permit, and generally demand both governmental and private-sector compliance with the law. *Massachusetts v. EPA,* the Clean Air Act case above, was brought by a group of states, local governments, and private organizations as a citizen suit.

Citizens suits have often been brought under the Endangered Species Act (ESA), which provides a federal program for the protection of threatened and endangered species and their habitats. Such suits may either seek greater protection for a species or argue that proposed protections exceed that which is necessary. The two cases that follow illustrate both types of concerns. In the first, more protection for the Cook Inlet beluga whale was sought; in the second, plaintiffs argued that too large an area had been designated for the protection of the Mexican spotted owl in the southeastern United States. In both cases petitioners lost. When reading the cases, pay attention to the process required of the government in listing a species as threatened or endangered and in defining its protected habitat.

LEGAL BRIEFCASE

Cook Inlet Beluga Whale v. Daley 156 F.Supp.2d 16 (D.C.D.C. 2001)

Judge James Robertson

The Cook Inlet Beluga Whale . . . is a genetically distinct, geographically isolated marine mammal with a remnant population that inhabits Cook Inlet from late April or early May until October or November. NMFS [National Marine Fisheries Service] estimates that in the mid-1980s, between 1,000 and 1,300 whales inhabited the inlet. Today, the population is estimated at between 300 and 400 whales. It is not disputed that the single most significant factor in the population decline has been Native American hunting. . . . That is why, in March 1999, the plaintiffs filed a petition to list the Cook Inlet Beluga Whale under the Endangered Species Act (ESA).

The Endangered Species Act delegates to the Secretary of Commerce the authority to determine whether fish, wildlife, or plant species should be listed as endangered or threatened. A species is "endangered" when it is in "danger of extinction throughout all or a significant part of its range," and it is "threatened" when it is "likely to become an endangered species within the foreseeable future." The Secretary's ESA determination is made on the basis of five statutorily prescribed factors, any one of which is sufficient to support a listing determination.

Within 30 days of plaintiffs' request for an ESA listing, the NMFS published formal notice that action under the ESA "may be warranted." That notice triggered a one-year status review period. On October 19, 1999, the NMFS published a proposed rule, not under the ESA, but under the Marine Mammal Protection Act (MMPA), to list the whale as "depleted." . . . Under the MMPA, the Secretary can designate a species as "depleted" . . . if the Secretary determines that the stock is below its Optimum Sustainable Population. Once a marine mammal has been

listed as "depleted," the Secretary is authorized to promulgate regulations limiting takings by Native Americans, but a listing under the MMPA does not have the regulatory, economic, and environmental fallout of a listing as "threatened" or "endangered" under the ESA.

On June 22, 2000, the NMFS determined that an ESA listing was "not warranted." It is that determination which, in plaintiffs' submission, was "arbitrary, capricious, an abuse of discretion, or otherwise not in accordance with law."

ARGUMENT

"In exercising its narrowly defined duty . . . , the Court must consider whether the agency acted within the scope of its legal authority, adequately explained its decision, based its decision on facts in the record, and considered the relevant factors." Plaintiffs argue that the agency decision in this case improperly applied the law and facts to the five-factor determination; failed to apply the best scientific and commercial data available; and improperly considered political and economic factors.

I. Statutory Factors

A decision whether or not to list a species shall be made "solely on the basis of the best scientific and commercial data available . . . after conducting a review of the status of the species and after taking into account those efforts, if any, being made by any State or foreign nation." Applying this standard, the Secretary must list a species as endangered or threatened if "any of Section 1533(a)(1)'s five factors are sufficiently implicated." Each of the five factors is considered below.

(A) The Present or Threatened Destruction, Modification, or Curtailment of the Species' Habitat or Range   The agency's

conclusion that "no indication exists that the range has been, or is threatened with being modified or curtailed to an extent that appreciably diminishes the value of the habitat for both survival and recovery of the species," was not arbitrary or capricious. There is no dispute that the Cook Inlet, the whale's habitat, has changed over time in response to the increasing demand of municipal, industrial, and recreational activities, but there is no record basis for concluding that these changes have had a deleterious effect on the whale. Plaintiffs can point only to the fact that the whales have increasingly inhabited the upper inlet in recent decades. The agency concedes that this change in whale behavior might be in response to human activities, but no data suggest that the change threatens extinction. The agency is not required to conduct further testing to determine the effect of various environmental factors, such as oil drilling, on the whale population. "The 'best available data' requirement makes it clear that the Secretary has no obligation to conduct independent studies."

(B) Overutilization   All agree that Native American harvesting has been the most significant factor in the declining whale population. The agency has found "that a failure to restrict the subsistence harvest would likely cause CI beluga whales to become in danger of extinction in the foreseeable future." But the agency has also concluded that "overutilization" does not support ESA listing because it has been stopped—by designating the whale as "depleted" under the MMPA. Plaintiffs attack that conclusion as unreasonable.

If the moratorium fails to control Native American harvesting in the future, ESA listing will be warranted. That much is agreed. But plaintiffs have been unable to point to anything in the record indicating that the current whale population is unsustainable if the harvest is indeed restricted successfully. . . .

[There] is no reason to believe that the MMPA's enforcement mechanisms, which are identical to those of the ESA, will be less effective in controlling illegal takings. Plaintiffs' concerns are reasonable, and enforcement should be carefully monitored, but the record contains support for the agency's conclusion that future takings will be minimal and that the current population is sustainable.

(C) Disease or Predation   The agency concedes that both disease or predation "occur in the CI beluga population and may affect reproduction and survival," but it has concluded

that these factors are not causing the stock to be threatened or endangered. Plaintiff has not shown that conclusion to be arbitrary or capricious. . . .

(D) Inadequacy of Existing Regulatory Mechanisms   We have found nothing in the record, and plaintiff has identified nothing, showing that there are inadequacies in existing regulatory mechanisms or, if there were, what the effects of such inadequacies would be. Plaintiffs argue that the MMPA is inadequate to ensure that illegal hunting does not occur . . . , but that argument simply asserts plaintiffs' policy preference for a remedy under the ESA and begs the question of whether ESA listing is required.

(E) Other Natural or Manmade Factors Affecting Its Continued Existence   Plaintiffs argue that there are many other factors—strandings, oil spills, takings through commercial fishing, effects of pollutants, ship strikes, noise, urban runoff, etc.—that put the species at risk and that it was arbitrary and capricious for the agency to determine that "the best available information . . . indicates that these activities, alone or cumulatively, have not caused the stock to be in danger of extinction and are not likely to do so in the foreseeable future." . . .

It is true that the absence of "conclusive evidence" of a real threat to a species does not justify an agency's finding that ESA listing is not warranted. But neither is listing required simply because the agency is unable to rule out factors that could contribute to a population decline. It was not arbitrary or capricious for the agency to place its principal reliance on the cessation of Native American hunts and the [study that concluded] that the Cook Inlet Beluga Whale population could sustain itself, even accounting for stochastic events.

[Plaintiffs' remaining arguments have been omitted.]

Ordered that defendant's motion for summary judgment is granted.

Questions

1. Why did the plaintiffs want the Cook Inlet Beluga Whale listed as endangered under the ESA?
2. What was the standard of review that the court applied to the agency's decision?
3. What five factors are to be considered in the listing of a species as endangered under the Endangered Species Act?

Judge Betty B. Fletcher

Litigation History

In 1993 the Mexican Spotted Owl was listed as a threatened species under the Endangered Species Act ("ESA"). The listing decision prompted a series of lawsuits alternately seeking to compel the FWS [U.S. Fish and Wildlife Service] to designate critical habitat for the owl and, following the FWS's designation of habitat, attacking that designation.

The first such lawsuit was in 1995 to compel the FWS to designate critical habitat and resulted in the FWS's issuing a final rule designating 4.6 million acres of critical owl habitat, a designation that was quickly challenged in court and then revoked in 1998. After another lawsuit was filed to compel the FWS to designate habitat, the FWS proposed a rule in 2000 to designate 13.5 million acres of critical habitat and in 2001 the agency promulgated a final rule that again designated 4.6 million acres. That rule was later struck down and . . . the FWS reopened the comment period on the rule it proposed in 2000. In 2004 the FWS designated approximately 8.6 million acres of critical habitat. It is this designation, the 2004 Final Rule, that Arizona Cattle challenges in the current action.

Arizona Cattle moved for summary judgment to set aside the 2004 Final Rule. . . . The District Court rejected Arizona Cattle's arguments. . . .

THE 2004 FINAL RULE

The FWS relied on three types of habitat management areas . . . as a starting point for the 2004 Final Rule: protected areas, restricted areas, and other forest and woodland types. Protected areas are those areas containing known owl sites, termed Protected Activity Centers ("PACs"); "steep slope" areas meeting certain forest conditions; and legally and administratively reserved lands. "PACs include a minimum of 600 acres . . . that includes the best nesting and roosting (i.e., resting) habitat in the area . . . and the most proximal and highly used foraging areas." However, PACs contain only 75% of necessary foraging areas for the owl. Restricted areas include non-steep slope areas with appropriate forest conditions that are "adjacent to or outside of protected areas." "Areas outside of PACs, including restricted areas, provide additional habitat appropriate for foraging." . . .

* * * * *

THE ESA AND THE DEFINITION OF "OCCUPIED"

The ESA defines a species' critical habitat as . . . "the specific areas within the geographical area occupied by the species, at the time it is listed. . . ."

The statute thus differentiates between "occupied" and "unoccupied" areas. . . . [We] face the preliminary issue of what it means for an area to be "occupied" under the ESA.

It is useful to unpack this inquiry into two components: uncertainty and frequency. Uncertainty is a factor when the FWS has reason to believe that owls are present in a given area, but lacks conclusive proof of their presence. Frequency is a factor when owls are shown to have only an intermittent presence in a given area. Occasionally, both factors will play a part in determining whether an area is "occupied." Because the ESA permits only one of two possible outcomes for this inquiry-occupied or unoccupied- . . . we must determine the scope of the FWS's authority to categorize as "occupied" those areas that may not fit neatly into either pigeonhole.

We have ample guidance on the "uncertainty" issue. The ESA provides that the agency must determine critical habitat using the "best scientific data available." This standard does not require that the FWS act only when it can justify its decision with absolute confidence. . . .

Turning to the "frequency" component, Arizona Cattle asserts that the word "occupied" is unambiguous and must be interpreted narrowly to mean areas that the species "resides in." In the context of the owl, they argue that such areas consist only of the 600-acre PACs. The FWS argues . . . that where a geographic area is used with such frequency that the owl is likely to be present, the agency may permissibly designate it as occupied. FWS contends that, at a minimum, this includes the owl's "home range" and may include other areas used for intermittent activities.

We cannot agree that "occupied" has an unambiguous, plain meaning as Arizona Cattle suggests. The word "occupied," standing alone, does not provide a clear standard for how frequently a species must use an area before the agency can designate it as critical habitat. Merely replacing the word "occupied" with the word "resides" does not resolve this ambiguity. . . . Viewed narrowly, an owl resides only in its nest; viewed more broadly, an owl resides in a PAC; and viewed more broadly still, an owl resides in its territory or home range. Determining whether a species uses an area with sufficient regularity that it is "occupied" is a highly contextual and fact-dependent inquiry. . . . Such factual questions are within the purview of the agency's unique expertise and are entitled to the standard deference afforded such agency determinations.

* * * * *

The FWS has authority to designate as "occupied" areas that the owl uses with sufficient regularity that it is likely to

be present during any reasonable span of time. This interpretation is sensible. . . . Arizona Cattle's "reside in" interpretation would make little sense as applied to nonterritorial,
mobile, or migratory animals-including the owl-for which it
may be impossible to fix a determinate area in which the
animal "resides." Such a narrow interpretation also would
mesh poorly with the FWS's authority to act in the face of
uncertainty.

* * * * *

It is possible for the FWS to go too far. Most obvious is that
the agency may not determine that areas unused by owls are
occupied merely because those areas are suitable for future
occupancy. Such a position would ignore the ESA's distinction
between occupied and unoccupied areas. . . . The fact that a
member of the species is not present in an area at a given instant does not mean the area is suitable only for future occupancy if the species regularly uses the area.

Having thus framed the inquiry, we turn to the primary issue before the court: whether the FWS included unoccupied
areas in its critical habitat designation.

THE FWS DID NOT DESIGNATE UNOCCUPIED AREAS AS CRITICAL HABITAT

* * * * *

. . . PACs are explicitly defined with reference to frequent
owl presence, and non-PAC protected areas and restricted
areas are "devised around" and "adjacent to" PACs. More to
the point, we note significant record support for owl occupancy of these areas in the form of studies correlating the
habitat characteristics of protected and restricted areas with
owl presence.

The agency did not stop there. [Its] analysis proceeds,
unit by unit, through the addition of areas to the critical
habitat proposal on the basis of information about known
owl locations. . . .

A point of recurring significance to our analysis is that
PACs reflect only known owl sites. Although the 2004 Final
Rule identified 1,176 PACs, owl populations have been estimated to be significantly greater than the maximum 2,352
owls reflected by this number of PACs. . . . Efforts by the FWS
to identify other evidence of owl presence when it is unable
to fix the location of a PAC with certainty are, therefore,
highly significant.

Even more significant is the fact that the FWS excluded areas with evidence of few or no owls. . . . Finally, we note that . . .
the FWS excluded the vast majority of critical habitat units that
contained no PACs and refined the boundaries of the critical
habitat units to exclude large areas that are distant from PACs.

The FWS's process for designating critical habitat gives us
a strong foundation for our conclusion that the agency did not
arbitrarily and capriciously treat areas in which owls are not
found as "occupied." . . .

THE AMOUNT OF LAND DESIGNATED IS NOT DISPROPORTIONATE TO THE NUMBER OF OWLS

Arizona Cattle also argues that even using the owl's substantially larger home range as the appropriate measure for the
territory occupied by the owl, the FWS has designated a
grossly disproportionate amount of land compared to the
amount the owl occupies. It ties this argument to a seemingly
simple calculation: multiplying the 1,176 PACs by the maximum
estimated home range size of the owl of 3,831 acres, the re-
sultant area is only approximately 4.5 million acres, in contrast
to the 8.6 million acres designated. This calculation, however,
rests on a faulty assumption that the PACs represent all extant
owls. We have already explained that PACs reflect only known
owl sites and that there is record support for the existence of
substantially greater numbers of owls and undiscovered sites.
. . . Arizona Cattle's argument does not overcome the strong
evidence that the FWS was focused on designating areas occupied by owls.

* * * * *

We find no fault with the FWS's designation of habitat for
the Mexican Spotted Owl. . . .
Affirmed.

Questions

1. Identify the statutory language the court had to interpret to
   resolve this case.
2. How did the FWS select the areas included in its designation of 8.6 million acres as critical habitat for the owl?
3. What contrary arguments were made by Arizona Cattle?
4. What was the standard of review that the court applied to
   the agency's decision?
5. How many years elapsed between the first lawsuit over
   the designation of the Mexican spotted owl and the decision in this case?

Endangered Species Act

The combination of the *Cook Inlet Beluga Whale* and *Arizona Cattle Grower's Ass'n* decisions illustrate how complicated and time consuming the legal process is for the protection of species. It is also costly—for citizen groups on both sides, for the government (and therefore all of us as taxpayers), for those whose lives and livelihoods may be substantially altered by the protections extended, and also for the species and our world in the event protections are not extended or are not effective.

Consider what may be on the horizon. The Audubon Society considers nearly a quarter of the 700 bird species in the United States to be threatened.[58] The U.N. Intergovernmental Panel on Climate Change indicates temperature increases this century could put 20 to 30 percent of the world's plants and animals in danger of extinction.[59] Over the last four years environmental groups have requested more than 1230 species be listed under the ESA as threatened or endangered, compared with prior annual averages of about 20 species. In its 2012 budget request, the FWS stated that the "many requests for species petitions has inundated the listing program's domestic species listing capabilities." It also estimated that in 2011 it "will be able to make final listing decisions on only 4 percent of warranted petitions within one year as required by law."[60] If it finds a listing is warranted in a particular case, it is required to conduct a scientific investigation and make a final determination within 12 months. Missing legal deadlines leads to more litigation. In 2008, the polar bear became listed as a threatened species specifically because of the impact of global climate change on the Arctic sea ice.[61] For the same reason, in February 2011 the Pacific walrus was declared at risk of extinction, but the government "declined to list the marine mammal as an endangered species, saying a backlog of other animals faced greater peril."[62] [For photos of some endangered or threatened species in the United States, see **http://www.nytimes.com/interactive/2011/05/13/travel/endangered-species.html?ref=travel**]

Part Four—Common Law Remedies

Most of the remedies discussed in Part Three are based on *statutory* claims. But long before federal or state governments became actively involved in environmental issues, courts were grappling with the problem and fashioning *common law* remedies. As early as the 1500s, city officials were ordered by a court to keep the streets clean of dung deposited by swine allowed to run loose; the air was said to be "corrupted and infected" by this practice. Legal arguments have typically revolved around the extent of a person's right to use and enjoy private property if such usage causes harm to a neighbor's property or the use of public property. More recently, tort actions of negligence and strict liability have been pursued by injured individuals. Successful plaintiffs may recover monetary damages for the harm suffered or obtain an injunction to prevent similar conduct (and therefore harm) by the defendant in the future, or both.

Nuisance   A private nuisance is a substantial and unreasonable invasion of the private use and enjoyment of one's land; a public nuisance is an unreasonable interference with a right common to the public. Harmful conduct may be both a public and private nuisance simultaneously; the case law distinctions between the two are often blurred. A classic nuisance dispute is the 1970 New York case *Boomer v. Atlantic Cement Co.*[63] Neighboring landowners sued the operator of a cement plant for injury to their properties from the plant's dirt, smoke, and vibration. The court recognized the wrong done and ordered the operator to pay damages. In recent years, several nuisance cases have been brought in federal courts against emitters of significant greenhouse gases. In one, *Connecticut v. American Electric Power Co.,* several states, New York City, and three land trusts sued operators of coal-fired power plants claiming their carbon emissions were a nuisance under federal common law and seeking an order requiring the utilities to cap and then reduce their carbon dioxide emissions. A unanimous Supreme Court ruled against the plaintiffs in 2011 finding that the Clean Air Act and EPA rule making authority displaced any common law right to sue to curb carbon dioxide emissions from power plants.[64] Now the EPA must promulgate rules applying the CAA to greenhouse gas emissions. The *American Electric* decision affirms the power of the EPA and encourages a single nationwide standard for addressing carbon emissions rather than multiple court-imposed remedies.

Trespass   A trespass occurs and liability is imposed on any intentional invasion of an individual's right to the exclusive use of his or her own property. For example, in a 1959 Oregon case, *Martin v. Reynolds Metals Co.,* the plaintiffs successfully sued in trespass for damages caused by the operation of an aluminum reduction plant, which caused certain fluoride compounds in the form of gases and particulates to become airborne, settle on the plaintiffs' land, contaminate their forage and water, and poison their cattle.[65]

Negligence   The elements of negligence have been previously discussed, in Chapter 7. In 2010 the Florida Supreme Court held that fishermen were entitled to recover for the damages they suffered when defendants' waste water storage pond spilled into the Tampa bay killing fish, crabs and other marine life. Defendant's negligence "interfered with the special interest of the commercial fishermen to use the public waters to earn their livelihood."[66] Particularly troubling causation issues have arisen in some negligence cases, such as when a plaintiff claims injury from a toxic substance manufactured or otherwise supplied by defendant. For example, does smoking cause lung cancer and did it cause the lung cancer of this particular plaintiff? Did the use of DES by pregnant women cause birth defects? Does DES cause infertility in daughters born to mothers who took DES during their pregnancy?

Strict Liability   Certain activities, such as the use of toxic chemicals, may be seen as so abnormally dangerous as to give rise to a strict liability claim (previously discussed in Chapter 7). In an environmental law context, strict liability has been considered where crop dusting contaminated adjacent properties,[67] toxic chemicals were improperly disposed of,[68] and oil contaminated a nearby water well.[69]

Several of these claims can sometimes be triggered by the same set of facts. In a 2007 West Virginia case a jury found DuPont negligent in its use of a 112-acre site that for 90 years had been a zinc-smelting plant. The jury also found DuPont had created both a public and a private nuisance, had committed trespass, and should be held strictly liable for exposing local residents to various toxic substances. Residents and property owners had sued, claiming that the company had deliberately dumped toxic heavy metals, particularly zinc, on the site. The medical problems caused by such toxins include cancer, damage to internal organs, and decreased fertility.[70]

Part Five—Global Climate change

Global climate change has been described as "among the handful of most important public policy issues of our time,"[71] as well as "one of the greatest challenges the world faces.[72] At issue is the projected overall increase in surface temperatures around the globe caused by the release into the atmosphere of manmade carbon dioxide and other greenhouse gases, largely through the burning of fossil fuels, especially in gasoline engines and coal-fired plants.

Both the politics and the science of global climate change have been controversial—a particularly potent and poignant example of the issues of coincidence, correlation, and causation discussed at the beginning of Part Two. The 2007 U.N. report on climate change seems to have all but ended the scientific dispute, but the political debate continues. The report concluded that global climate change is unequivocal and that it is very likely (meaning 90 percent), as a result primarily of man-made greenhouse gas emissions. It found that the probability that the observed climate change is only a natural phenomenon is less than 5 percent. These conclusions have been echoed both in a report of the National Academy of Scientists prepared at the request of Congress and in the 2009 State of the Climate Report issued by the National Oceanic and Atmospheric Administration.[73] [For a copy of the 2007 Synthesis Report, see **http://www.ipcc.ch/publications_and_data/ publications_and_data_reports.shtml**]

Scholar and activist, Bill McKibben, has argued that we no longer live on the same planet on which our parents grew up and that climate change has passed the tipping point. "The planet we inhabit has a finite number of huge physical features. Virtually all of them seem to be changing rapidly."[74] Consider the following:

> A 30-year decline in Arctic ice is accelerating.

- A 30-year decline in Arctic ice is accelerating, as is the forecasted moment when we will see an ice-free summer Arctic Sea, a condition that could wipe out two-thirds of the world's polar bears.[75] Glaciers are receding on the Tibetan plateau, in the Andes and in the Himalayas, all of which threaten the water supply of the billions of people living downstream. [For an interactive map showing the extent of the Arctic sea ice on September 16 each year from 2001 through 2007, see **http://www.nytimes.com/interactive/2007/10/01/ science/20071002_ARCTIC_GRAPHIC.html**]

- "The oceans, which cover three-fourths of the Earth's surface, are distinctly more acid and their level is rising; they are also warmer, which means the greatest storms on our planet, hurricanes and cyclones, have become more powerful."[76] The lowest country in the world, the island nation of the Maldives in the Indian Ocean, is creating a reserve fund to allow the population to resettle in Sri Lanka, India, or Australia in the event they lose their homelands to the sea.[77]

- "The great rain forest of the Amazon is drying on its margins and threatened at its core. The great boreal forest of North America is dying in a matter of years."[78] Deforestation accounts for as much as 15 percent of global carbon dioxide emissions.[79]

[For a 2010 Bill McKibben/Stephen Thompson video editorial about the alleged causal relationship between climate change and recent "extreme weather events" in America and around the world see **http://www.grist.org/climate-change/2011-06-11-the-most-powerful-climate-video-youll-see-all-week**]

The Kyoto Protocol

In 1997 the governments of the world, realizing that global action is required to have any significant impact on overall emissions, adopted the Kyoto Protocol. Specifically, the protocol calls for a 5 percent reduction from 1990 levels of greenhouse gas emissions to be achieved by 2012. The protocol became binding when countries accounting for at least 55 percent of total emissions ratified it, which occurred with Russia's ratification in late 2004. The United States is not among the 180 ratifying countries, President Bush having announced in March 2001 that the protocol was "fatally flawed."

The Kyoto Protocol uses market incentives to achieve emission reductions. It permits industrialized countries, and the companies in them, to "generate credits toward their quotas by bankrolling projects that reduce emissions. . . . The theory is that because global warming is global, the atmosphere doesn't care whether emissions occur in, say, Germany or China. For a German company . . . financing an emissions reduction project in China is likely to be a lot cheaper than doing so at home, because in Germany, the cheap emissions improvements already have been made."[80] [For additional information about the protocol, see the official Web site for the U.N. Framework convention on Climate Change at **unfccc. int/kyoto_protocol/items/2830.php**]

The Kyoto Protocol was recognized from the start as only the first step in the development of a global emission reduction program to stabilize greenhouse gases. Formal discussions for a post-Kyoto international framework began in Bali, Indonesia in December 2007. They were expected to last through 2009. But as of this writing in 2011, no post-Kyoto agreement has been adopted. That setback is attributable at least in part to a failure of leadership in the United States.

Going Green

In recent years, individuals, businesses, and some in the corporate world have voluntarily undertaken a growing number of strategies to reduce GHG emissions. Not only are these efforts commendable, they are likely to be critical. Each voluntary achievement illustrates to the actor that effective action can be taken, that it likely has no negative impact on one's quality of life, and that it may even make economic sense on its own merits. These lessons are as true for business as they are for individuals. Witness the "green" activities voluntarily undertaken by Walmart, Coca-Cola, and Chevron, among others.[81] Each such effort constitutes an undeniable affirmation of the reality and importance of climate change; evidence that is more compelling than the results of any survey or poll.[82]

As critical as these actions are, however, they are not sufficient. The Kyoto Protocol adopted in 1997 set forth the goal of a 5 percent reduction from 1990 levels of GHG emissions to be achieved by 2012. In 2010 the EPA reported that GHG emissions in the United States increased 14 percent between 1990 and 2008.[83] "We can afford to save the planet," according to a 2009 *Washington Post* article, using a "comprehensive global strategy" and investments of roughly 1 to 3 percent of global gross domestic product (GDP). For comparison, military spending in both the United States and China is over 4 percent of GDP. One to three percent of the global GDP is the current price, but it will remain at that level only if we take "quicker action aimed at more ambitious targets."[84] A collaborative approach designed to maximize effective returns is necessary. Individual action cannot achieve comparable results. That is one of the lessons of the Kyoto Protocol era.

PRACTICING ETHICS | Voluntarily Reduce Greenhouse Gas Emissions?

Although the United States is not a party to the Kyoto Protocol, many U.S. multinationals will be subject to its provisions because they do business in ratifying countries. Other U.S. businesses have chosen to voluntarily adopt emission reduction strategies.

Question

Imagine that you are a vice president of a corporation that burns significant fossil fuels in the production process but operates solely in the United States. What stance would you take on global climate change? Why?

Internet Exercise

One indication of how much global climate change has become a grassroots issue in the United States is the entry of carbon footprint considerations into everyday conversation. A carbon footprint is a measurement of how much carbon dioxide is emitted into the atmosphere as the result of a particular product, activity, or lifestyle. It is a way to measure the carbon "cost" of a particular activity or the carbon "savings" of changing that activity.

What's your carbon footprint? Find out from **http://www.bp.com/energycalculator** Compare that with your ecological footprint—that is, how many Earths we would have to have if everyone lived as you do. Go to **http://files.earthday.net/footprint/index.html**

Chapter Questions

1. Economist B. Peter Pashigian:

   It is widely thought that environmental controls are guided by the public-spirited ideal of correcting for "negative externalities"—the pollution costs that spill over from private operations. This view is not wrong by any means. But it is suspiciously incomplete.
   After all, there are numerous studies of regulatory programs in other fields that show how private interests have used public powers for their own enrichment.[85]

   In addition to correcting negative externalities, what forces might be influencing federal pollution control?

2. How might the government's ever-increasing environmental regulations, along with the public's call for a new environmental consciousness, favor big business interests over those of small business owners?

3. "The Aral Sea is going, gone. Once the world's fourth largest inland body of water, the Aral has shriveled to half its former area and a third of its volume. As for the region's drinking water, even the local vodka has a salty tang."[86] The Aral is the victim of the former Soviet Union's central planners, who decreed that the area would be the nation's main source of cotton. To achieve that goal, intense irrigation was required, with the result that only a trickle of fresh water was left to feed the Aral. Refilling the Aral would require tremendous dislocations in the agriculture of the vast region. If you were a member of a commission charged with developing a plan for the future of the Aral Sea, what issues would you cover?

4. Professor and business ethics scholar Norman Bowie:

   Environmentalists frequently argue that business has special obligations to protect the environment. Although I agree with the environmentalists on this point, I do not agree with them as to where the obligations lie. Business does not have an obligation to protect the environment over and above what is required by law; however, business does have a moral obligation to avoid intervening in the political arena in order to defeat or weaken environmental legislation.[87]

   a. Explain Professor Bowie's reasoning.
   b. Do you agree with him? Explain.

5. A 2002 report from the EPA concluded that we have not realized the benefits from the 1990 amendments to the Clean Air Act because it has not been enforced effectively. For example, by July 2001 "only 63 percent of the 19,025 major sources of industrial pollution in the United States had obtained permits, although the law imposed a deadline of 1997." The report further noted that several states "lacked sufficient resources to run the program and . . . many states had difficulties getting EPA guidance on how the agency's regulations should be applied to a specific polluter."[88] Instead of passing additional clean air standards, should we simply vigorously enforce the standards already on the books? If so, how might that be accomplished?

6. Mexico is quickly running short of water:

   85 percent of Mexico's economic growth and 75 percent of its 100 million people are in the north, and the water is far to the south. . . . [P]oliticians facing elections are reluctant to ask voters to spend more on any utility, let alone water. Agriculture uses 80 percent of the water and pays nothing, although it only ranks seventh in contribution to the gross national product. . . . Less than half of the capital's wastewater is treated. The rest sinks into underground lakes or flows toward the Gulf of Mexico, turning rivers into sewers. . . . Well over half of irrigation water is lost to evaporation or seepage."[89]

   Brainstorm as many possible contributions to the solution of Mexico's water problem as you can.

7. Because of the spread of the West Nile virus in the state of New York, an insecticide spraying program was implemented to control the mosquitoes responsible for spreading the virus. Several groups sued, arguing that the spray was a pollutant that damaged waters in

violation of the Clean Water Act. What criteria should the court use to decide the outcome? See *No Spray Coalition, Inc. v. The City of New York,* 2000 U.S. Dist. LEXIS 13919, 51 ERC (BNA) 1508 (S.D.N.Y. 2000).

8. Ott Chemical Co. polluted the ground at its Michigan plant. CPC International created a wholly owned subsidiary to buy Ott, which was accomplished in 1965. CPC retained the original Ott managers. Pollution continued through 1972 when CPC sold Ott. In 1981 the U.S. EPA began a cleanup of the site. To recover some of the tens of millions in cleanup costs, the EPA sued CPC (called Bestfoods) among other potentially responsible parties. The Superfund law places responsibility on anyone who "owned or operated" a property when pollution was deposited. The district court held that CPC was liable because of its active participation in Ott's business and its control of Ott's decisions in that it selected the Ott board of directors and placed some CPC managers as executives at Ott.

   a. Do you think CPC should be held liable? Why or why not?

   b. What test would you employ to determine whether a parent corporation should be liable for a subsidiary's pollution? See *United States v. Bestfoods,* 524 U.S. 51 (1998).

9. William Tucker:

   > [Environmentalism is] essentially aristocratic in its roots and derives from the land and nature-based ethic that has been championed by upper classes throughout history. Large landowners and titled aristocracies . . . have usually held a set of ideals that stresses "stewardship" and the husbanding of existing resources over exploration and discovery. This view favors handicrafts over mass production and the inheritance ethic over the business ethic.[90]

   Tucker went on to argue that environmentalism favors the economic and social interests of the well-off. He said people of the upper middle class see their future in universities and the government bureaucracy, with little economic stake in industrial expansion. Indeed, such expansion might threaten their suburban property values. Comment.

10. Americans' commitment to the car obviously raises serious environmental problems. The vast spaces required to park those cars are themselves a significant environmental hazard. Explain some of the environmental problems created or encouraged by parking lots.

11. The Endangered Species Act provides that all federal agency actions are to be designed so that they do not jeopardize endangered or threatened species. The act had been interpreted to reach federal agency work or funding in foreign countries, but the federal government changed that interpretation in 1986 to limit the act's reach to the United States and the high seas. A group labeled Defenders of Wildlife filed suit, seeking to reinstate the original interpretation. The case reached the U.S. Supreme Court, where Justice Scalia wrote that Defenders of Wildlife would have to submit evidence showing that at least one of its members would be "directly" affected by the interpretation. In response, one member of Defenders of Wildlife wrote that she had visited Egypt and observed the endangered Nile crocodile and hoped to return to do so again but feared that U.S. aid for the Aswan High Dam would harm the crocodiles.

Do you think Defenders of Wildlife should have been permitted to sue? Why or why not? See *Lujan v. Defenders of Wildlife,* 112 S.Ct. 2130 (1992).

12. Economist Robert Crandall:

> [O]ur best chances for regulatory reform in certain environmental areas, particularly in air pollution policy, come from the states. Probably, responsibility for environmental regulation belongs with the states anyway, and most of it ought to be returned there.[91]

    a. What reasoning supports Crandall's notion that responsibility for environmental regulation belongs with the states?

    b. How might one reason to the contrary?

    c. If the power were yours, would environmental regulation rest primarily at the state, federal, or international level? Explain.

13. The United States seems to be quite enamored with sport utility vehicles (SUVs), in spite of the fact that their gas mileage is considerably poorer than most sedans. To graphically bring home the environmental irresponsibility of SUV owners, two men in the San Francisco Bay area dreamed up a scheme to address what they perceived to be a market failure. Uninvited, they stuck homemade bumper stickers on hundreds of SUVs. The bumper stickers read, "I'm changing the environment! Ask me how!"[92]

    a. What effect do you think these self-appointed environmental police sought from their actions?

    b. What effect do you think they actually had?

14. Airplanes are a significant contributor to greenhouse gases. Comment on the following proposal: Each person receives an annual allowance for flights, fuel, gas, and electricity. If a person's use exceeds the allowance, he will have to purchase "carbon points" from someone under their limit.[93]

Notes

1. "Satellite Findings Reveal Massive Global Pollution," *Waterloo/Cedar Falls Courier,* May 31, 2001, p. A5.

2. "Gulf of Mexico Oil Spill (2010)," *The New York Times,* updated April 25, 2011 [**http://www.nytimes.com/**].

3. Adam Nossiter, "Far From Gulf, a Spill Scourge 5 Decades Old," *The New York Times,* June 16, 2010 [**http://www.nytimes.com/**].

4. Thomas Fuller, "In Industrial Thailand, Health and Business Concerns Collide," *The New York Times,* December 19, 2009 [**http://www.nytimes.com/**].

5. [**http://www.who.int/features/factfiles/water/water_facts/en/index2.html**].

6. Jim Yardley, "Beneath Booming Cities, China's Future Is Drying Up," *The New York Times,* September 28, 2007 [**http://www.nytimes.com/**].

7. Ariel Zirulnick, "The Extinction Risk for Birds, Mammals, and Amphibians," *Christian Science Monitor,* October 27, 2010 [**http://www.csmonitor.com/**].

8. Amy Littlefield, "EPA Looks at Effects of Waste Plants on Minorities, Poor," *Los Angeles Times,* July 27, 2009 [**www.latimes.com/**].

9. Adam Nossiter, "Far From Gulf, a Spill Scourge 5 Decades Old." *The New York Times,* June 16, 2010 [**http://www.nytimes.com/**].

10. Wilfred Beckerman, cited in Robert Solomon, *The New World of Business* (Lanham, MD: Rowman & Littlefield, 1994), p. 319.

11. Susan Lee, "How Much Is the Right to Pollute Worth?" *The Wall Street Journal,* August 1, 2001, p. A15.

12. Mark Golden, "Dirty Dealings," *The Wall Street Journal,* September 13, 1999, p. R13.

13. [**http://www.epa.gov/airmarkt/progress/arp07.html**].

14. [**http://www.cars.gov/files/official-information/CARS-Report-to-Congress.pdf**].

15. "Review and Outlook: A Fish Story," *The Wall Street Journal,* November 6, 2003, p. A14.

16. Henry McDonald, "Ireland Plans to Double Plastic Bags Tax," *The Guardian,* September 24, 2009 [**http://www.guardian.co.uk**]; and Elisabeth Rosenthal, "Motivated by a Tax, Irish Spurn Plastic Bags," *The New York Times,* February 2, 2008 [**http://www.nytimes.com/**].

17. Jeff Gersh, "Seeds of Change," *Amicus Journal* 21, no. 2 (Summer 1999), p. 36.

18. Jon J. Fialka and Jeffrey Ball, "Companies Get Ready for Greenhouse-Gas Limits," *The Wall Street Journal,* October 26, 2004, p. A2.

19. Michael V. Russo and Paul A. Fouts, "A Resource-Based Perspective on Corporate Environmental Performance and Profitability," *Academy of Management Journal* 40, no. 3 (1997), p. 534.

20. Bill Leonard, "Someday We'll Regret Damage to Our Planet," *The Des Moines Register,* September 20, 2004, p. 7A.

21. Eric Pianin, "Environmental Rules Worth Their Cost, Study Says," *The Des Moines Register,* September 28, 2003, p. 3A.

22. This was the essence of plaintiffs' nuisance suit against various large greenhouse emitters in *Comer v. Murphy Oil USA,* 2007 WL 6942285 (D.C. Miss. 2009). The district court dismissed; a three-judge panel for the 5th Circuit reversed. When defendants sought an en banc rehearing, a number of the circuit judges recused themselves but the remaining quorum granted the request and vacated the panel decision. Another judge then recused herself, leaving the court without a quorum. It determined the rehearing could not proceed, nor could the panel decision be reinstated. Thus the district court's dismissal is the final decision.

23. John M. Broder and Peter Baker, "Obama's Order Is Likely to Tighten Auto Standards," *The New York Times,* January 26, 2009 [**http://www.nytimes.com/**].

24. Ellen Goodman, "Can Tourists Love a Place to Death?" *The Des Moines Register,* March 31, 2001, p. 7A.

25. See for example, Stephen Power, "Why the Clean Air Act May Be Past Its Prime," *The Wall Street Journal,* April 17, 2010 [**http://online.wsj.com/**].

26. Richard Simon and Janet Wilson, "EPA Denies California's Right to Mandate Emissions," *Los Angeles Times,* December 29, 2007 [**http://www.latimes.com/**].

27. Steven Mufson, "Power Plant Rejected over Carbon Dioxide for First Time," *The Washington Post,* October 19, 2007, p. A1.

28. Editorial, "States Lead on Scrubbing Carbon," *Christian Science Monitor,* October 2, 2008 [**http://www.csmonitor.com/**].

29. [**http://americanfuels.blogspot.com/2011/02/2010-gasoline-consumption.html**].

30. Editorial, "Cleaner Cars," *The New York Times,* October 5, 2010.

31. [**http://www.law.yale.edu/news/11107.htm**].

32. Associated Press, "E.P.A. Announces Strict New Health Standards for Smog," *The New York Times,* January 7, 2010 [**http://www.nytimes.com/**].

33. Mark Clayton, "Is Coal Power Headed for a Downsizing in US?" *Christian Science Monitor,* October 20, 2010 [**http://www.csmonitor.com/**].

34. Campbell Robertson, "Gulf of Mexico Has Long Been Dumping Site," *The New York Times,* July 29, 2010 [**http://www.nytimes.com/**].

35. Lindsey Hoshaw, "Afloat in the Ocean, Expanding Islands of Trash," *The New York Times,* November 9, 2009 [**http://www.nytimes.com/**].

36. Robertson, "Gulf of Mexico Has Long Been Dumping Site."

37. Id.

38. 547 U.S. 715 (2006).

39. Charles Duhigg and Janet Roberts, "Rulings Restrict Clean Water Act, Foiling E.P.A.," *The New York Times,* February 28, 2010 [**http://www.nytimes.com/**].

40. Juliet Eilperin, "EPA Proposes Stricter Controls on Water Pollution," *The Washington Post,* April 27, 2011 [**http://www.washingtonpost.com/**].

41. Gary Long, "Cancer Panel Report Says Environmental Chemicals Causing 'Grievous Harm,'" *American Corporate Counsel,* May 13, 2010 [**http://www.lexology.com**].

42. Lyndsey Layton, "Use of Potentially Harmful Chemicals Kept Secret under Law," *The Washington Post,* January 4, 2010, p. A01.

43. Id.

44. See for example, *Safe Food and Fertilizer v. EPA,* 350 F.3d 1263 (D.C. Cir. 2003).

45. [**http://www.epa.gov/epawaste/hazard/recycling/regulations.htm**].

46. [**http://www.epa.gov/epawaste/conserve/rrr/reduce.htm**].

47. Bernard Gavzer, "Take Out the Trash, and Put It . . . Where?" *Parade,* June 13, 1999, p. 4.

48. [**http://waste.supportportal.com/ics/support/default.asp?deptID=23023**].

49. Kate Murphy, "One Man's Trash . . . ," *The New York Times,* September 3, 2009 [**http://www.nytimes.com/**].

50. Steven Kurutz, "Not Buying It," *The New York Times,* June 21, 2007 [**http://www.nytimes.com/**].

51. Rachel A. Schneider, "Federal Environmental Laws," *GP Solo & Small Firm Lawyer* 15, No. 3 (July–August, 1998) [**http://www.abanet.org/genpractice/magazine/1998/jul-aug/98julschneid.html**].

52. Anthony DePalma, "Love Canal Declared Clean, Ending Toxic Horror," *The New York Times,* March 18, 2004, P. A1.

53. David Erickson and James Neet, "CERCLA: GAO Report Says Remediation Funds Insufficient," *Association of Corporate Counsel,* July 2, 2010 [**http://www.lexology.com**].

54. [**http://www.epa.gov/superfund/sites/npl/index.htm**].

55. Susan Saulny, "Welcome to Our Town. Wish We Weren't Here," *The New York Times,* September 14, 2009 [**http://www.nytimes.com/**].

56. *Washington Post,* "Bush's EPA Pursuing Fewer Polluters," *Waterloo/Cedar Falls Courier,* September 30, 2007, p. A3.

57. Michael M. O'Hear, "Bark and Bite: The Environmental Sentencing Guidelines after Booker," 2009 *Utah L. Rev.* 1151.

58. Editorial, "Endangered Species," *The New York Times,* December 1, 2007 [**http://www.nytimes.com/**].

59. Moises Velasquez-Manoff, "Ecosystems Respond Well to Restoration," *Christian Science Monitor,* July 13, 2009 [**http://www.nytimes.com/**].

60. Todd Woody, "Wildlife at Risk Face Long Line at U.S. Agency," *The New York Times*, April 20, 2011 [**http://www.nytimes.com/**].

61. Associated Press, "Polar Bear to Be a Protected Species," *The New York Times*, May 14, 2008 [**http://www.nytimes.com/**].

62. Woody, "Wildlife at Risk Face Long Line at U.S. Agency."

63. 257 N.E.2d 870 (N.Y. 1970).

64. American *Electric Power Co., Inc. v. Connecticut*, 2011 U.S. LEXIS 4565.

65. 342 P.2d 790 (Or. 1959).

66. *Curd v. Mosaic Fertilizer LLC*, 39 So.3d 1216 (Fla. 2010).

67. *Langan v. Valicopters, Inc.*, 567 P.2d 218 (Wash. S.Ct. 1977).

68. *State Dep't of Envtl. Prot. v. Ventron*, 468 A.2d 150 (N.J. S.Ct. 1983).

69. *Branch v. W. Petroleum, Inc.*, 657 P.2d 267 (Utah 1982).

70. Associated Press, "DuPont Found Negligent in Waste-Site Lawsuit," *The Wall Street Journal*, October 3, 2007 [**http://online.wsj.com/**].

71. David Markell and J.B. Ruhl, "An Empirical Survey of Climate Change Litigation in the United States," 40 *Environmental Law Rptr.* 10644 (2010).

72. Intergovernmental Panel on Climate Change, "Summary for Policymakers of the Synthesis Report of the ICC Fourth Assessment Report" (2007), p. 1 [**http://www.ipcc.ch/publications_ and_data/publications_and_data_reports.shtml**].

73. Gautam Naik, "Scientists Reassert Man's Role in a Changing Climate," *The Wall Street Journal*, May 20, 2010, p. A9; Harold Bulger, "State of the Climate in 2009 Report Released," *Association of Corporate Counsel* [**http://www.lexology.com**].

74. Bill McKibben, *eaarth* (New York: Henry Holt, 2010), p. 45.

75. "Arctic Ice Is Melting," *The Washington Post*, April 11, 2009, p. A12.

76. McKibben, *eaarth*, p. 45.

77. Randeep Ramesh, "Paradise Almost Lost: Maldives Seek to Buy a New Homeland," *The Guardian*, November 10, 2008 [**http://www.guardian.co.uk**].

78. McKibben, *eaarth*, p. 46.

79. Margot Roosevelt, "Saving the Amazon May Be the Most Cost-Effective Way to Cut Greenhouse Gas Emissions," *Los Angeles Times*, February 21, 2010 [**http://www.latimes.com/**].

80. Jeffrey Ball, "As Kyoto Protocol Comes Alive, So Do Pollution-Permit Markets," *The Wall Street Journal*, November 8, 2004, p. A2.

81. Jared Diamond, "Will Big Business Save the Earth?," *The New York Times*, December 6, 2009 [**http://www.nytimes.com/**].

82. Jon A. Krosnick, "The Climate Majority," *The New York Times*, June 8, 2010 [**http://www.nytimes. com/**].

83. Juliet Eilperin, "EPA Issues New Climate Report," *The Washington Post*, April 27, 2010 [**http:// www.washingtonpost.com/**].

84. Eban Goodstein, Frank Ackerman and Kristen Sheeran, "We Can Afford to Save the Planet," *The Washington Post*, October 23, 2009 [**http://www.washingtonpost.com/**].

85. B. Peter Pashigian, "How Large and Small Plants Fare under Environmental Regulation," *Regulation*, March–April 1983, p. 19.

86. Hugh Pope, "Uzbeks Manage to Endure Amid Ruins of the Aral Sea," *The Wall Street Journal*, February 5, 1998, p. A18.

87. Norman Bowie and Kenneth Goodpaster, "Corporate Conscience, Money and Motorcars," *Business Ethics Report, Highlights of Bentley College's Eighth National Conference on Business Ethics* (Ed. Peter Kent 1989), pp. 4, 6.

88. John Fialka, "EPA Report Says Pollution-Control Effort Is Hurt by Bureaucracy, Lack of Funds," *The Wall Street Journal*, March 12, 2002, p. A28.

89. "Profligate Past, Poor Planning Created Mexican Water Crisis," *Associated Press*, August 22, 2002.

90. "Tucker Contra Sierra," *Regulation*, March–April 1983, pp. 48–49.

91. Robert Crandall, "The Environment," in "Regulation—The First Year," *Regulation*, January–February 1982, pp. 19, 29, 31.

92. "'Mad Taggers' Leave Their Mark on SUV Culture," *Waterloo/Cedar Falls Courier*, December 26, 2000, p. B5.

93. "Save the Planet: Stop Flying," *Parade*, January 7, 2007, p. 22.

CHAPTER EIGHTEEN

Internet Law and Ethics

After completing this chapter, students will be able to:

1. Explain the ethical dilemmas referred to as the digital divide and net neutrality.

2. Apply the requirements of personal jurisdiction to a dispute arising in cyberspace, both where the parties are residents of different states and where they are residents of different countries.

3. Identify free speech issues that arise in the context of the Internet and present the competing interests that make each particular issue difficult to resolve.

4. Provide examples of online activities that raise privacy concerns.

5. Explain the differences in online privacy protection between the United States and the European Union.

6. Describe several Internet-related crimes, including cyberstalking and cyberbullying.

7. Explain the impact of the Electronic Signatures in Global and National Commerce Act (E-SIGN).

8. Discuss the legal effect of click-wrap agreements.

9. Identify legal standards that would apply to a patent decision for any new online method of doing business.

10. Identify some of the copyright disputes associated with Internet-related materials.

11. Explain the trademark issues described in the text affecting Google and eBay.

12. Discuss two trademark issues that have arisen in an Internet context.

13. Identify and discuss the basic tax issue that arises from cyberspace transactions.

Introduction: The Internet and Globalization

> Over 2.1 billion of the world's 6.9 billion inhabitants have Internet access.

The Internet has changed our lives. Over 2.1 billion of the world's 6.9 billion inhabitants from more than 240 countries have Internet access.[1] The number is rapidly increasing, in part because of the relatively cheap access offered by cellphones in comparison with the cost of computers.[2] The extraordinary power of this nearly instantaneous global communication system promises remarkable new opportunities and challenges, creating and facilitating relationships (whole new "communities" of interest) among individuals, businesses, and governments that could never have occurred without it. The Internet is itself a catalyst for continuing globalization, breaking down national boundaries and rules to allow free interchange of communications, ideas, goods, and services around the world.

In this last chapter, we again have the opportunity to consider such fundamentals as what substantive law we want to govern our Internet activities and what process we should use to establish global standards for this global medium. Issues needing consensus include everything from the use of multilingual domain names (including the characters that appear after the "dot," as in .com, .org, and so forth)[3] to when and what cyberattacks are allowable as weapons of war.[4]

The most interesting question raised by these new Internet relationships may be which process will develop to create a consensus over what the substantive law should be. Can national governments legitimately impose standards and sanctions? Will international forums, such as the U.N. Internet Governance Forum, be necessary to resolve issues that have global ramifications? Will international bodies be able to act fast enough and have enough legitimacy to secure national acquiescence? Might international enforcement tools need to be developed? Will grassroots use of the Internet among individuals, business, and government drive the development of this new medium so vigorously that it will act as a catalyst for some fundamental restructuring of our global relationships?

Part One—The Market, Law, and Ethics

The roots of the Internet date to the late 1960s when a small group of researchers sought a way to freely exchange digital information with colleagues at other institutions. By the end of the 1980s, a backbone system of networked computers had been created and email use reached the general public. In the mid-1990s the first browser was released and the World Wide Web was born.[5] Since then the cost of both technology and access has dropped sufficiently to make the Internet a truly public, and international, space.

In the mid-1990s the World Wide Web was born.

Policy makers, users, and posters are all concerned about the degree to which we can, need to, or will impose the force of law on the Internet. Originally, it was an open-access forum only lightly touched by regulation. The growth in users and uses, in needs and desires, has created arguably the most diverse community imaginable—nearly as diverse as the human race itself. The combination of volume and diversity brings conflict with it. Peaceful and dependable conflict solutions require the existence of an established dispute resolution mechanism. Some conflict is resolvable by developing norms of conduct—such as email and Internet etiquette. Some conflict is resolvable by the establishment of site principles to be applied by a site administrator. But some conflicts will end up in courts because they are our established structural mechanism for peaceful dispute resolution.

"Therein lies the central truth of globalization today: We're all connected and nobody is in charge."

To be accepted by the disputants, judicial decisions need to be based on shared principles. Likewise we have developed legislative processes for the creation of rules to govern behavior. No existing judicial or legislative body, however, has obvious or natural jurisdiction over the Internet in its entirety. "[T]herein lies the central truth of globalization today: We're all connected and nobody is in charge."[6]

This difficult situation leaves us with two choices: Develop principles and processes accepted as applicable to the whole of the Internet or permit its balkanization. The absence of regulation is no longer an option.

Market Forces and Government Regulation

A discussion of regulating business conducted through the Internet must begin with the impact the market has in developing (or, put another way, "regulating") appropriate business behavior. For example, market forces in the form of negative publicity had a striking impact on Google's early social networking service, Google Buzz. That service took user information provided to it for private purposes, such as Gmail contact information, and automatically made it publicly accessible when a Gmail user started a Google Buzz account. A sharp backlash in the market caused Google to make a technological adjustment to quiet consumers' privacy fears.[7]

In regulating the Internet itself or its component parts, market forces may play a lesser role. The Internet is a mass communications system. Much like the traditional broadcast systems of radio and TV, the Internet can deliver the same content to an infinite number of users. Most, if not all, countries regulate content delivered by traditional broadcast systems. Discussions about the wisdom of regulating Internet content are policy matters typically addressed by governmental bodies.

The Internet also delivers private communications between particular users, much like a phone system. In general, governments have not attempted to censor private communications, but they do at times monitor private communications (for example, wiretaps) and they do at times seek information from carriers about the existence of and participants in private communications. Again, market forces have no bearing on government access to such information and those government policies are generally set at the national level. But the Internet also creates new policy issues because it carries both public and private communications and, furthermore, the content of the private communications, not just their occurrence, is stored as data on the equipment of the service provider.

Internet Access

As we have seen in other areas, market forces and legal regulation will blend in some uncertain, emerging formula to provide the security and confidence necessary for effective e-commerce. But ethics too will play a part. The anonymity, the speed, the elusiveness, and the global reach of the Internet suggest very difficult, and new, ethical issues, as well as old problems in a new venue. We turn now to two access issues.

The Digital Divide

For some time experts have been concerned that the Internet may increase the income/wealth gap that divides both Americans and the globe. In the United States, some programs to address the digital divide seem to be paying off. Between 2005 and 2010, African-American households with broadband access increased from 14 to 56 percent, while the U.S. average increased from 30 to 66 percent.[8] On the other hand, only 40 percent of households with an income under $30,000 have a broadband connection, whereas 87 percent of households with income above $75,000 have such connections.[9] Presumptions about the general availability of Internet access exacerbate the disadvantages faced by the poor as job announcements, job applications, homework, and access to services such as license renewals and public assistance migrate to the Web.[10]

 [For a video essay entitled "What Is the 'Digital Divide?'" see: **http://www.youtube.com/watch?v=fCIB_vXUptY**]

A greater accessibility imbalance exists at the global level. For example, only 10.9 percent of Africa's citizens have access, compared with 77.4 percent in North America. Addressing global imbalances requires solutions at different levels. One issue is the availability of access points; another is user cost. Fifty percent of Africa is rural and has no electricity. In most countries the gross domestic product per capita is under $1000. Furthermore, even if physical access were achieved and the cost issue addressed, non-English content and applications are limited. Global businesses spend "hundreds of millions of dollars a year working their way down a list of languages into which to translate their Web sites." Even India, with its 81 million users, is lower on the list than Brazil, Russia, and South Korea.[11] [For current statistics on world Internet usage, see **http://www.internetworldstats.com/stats.htm**]

Questions

1. Can you think of any imaginative ways to provide widespread Internet access in developing countries?
2. How would you deal with the reality that most Internet content is in English?

Net Neutrality

In general, if someone in the United States wishes to connect to the Internet, they contract with a commercial Internet service provider (ISP) (such as AT&T, Comcast, or Verizon) and pay a fee for the type (such as dial-up or broadband) and level of service (such as length of term and speed) they desire. They then have access to any content provider (such as Amazon, Craigslist, Google, and YouTube). This uniform access is referred to as *net neutrality*. It implies that ISPs will not discriminate against the traffic of any legal content provider. Some ISPs would like the right to change that—for example, by charging certain content providers for access or for enhanced transmission speeds to the ISP's subscribers. Their argument is that bandwidth is not infinite and they need to be able to manage traffic during periods of congestion to prevent performance degradation over the entire system. Specifically, ISPs want to charge content providers with heavy traffic, such as sites where users download music and videos, for the substantial bandwidth used to access their sites, products, and services. The consequence of nonpayment would be either blocked access at certain times or degraded speed at which access is provided.

Vigorous arguments have been raised against such tiered pricing, including:

- ISP subscribers already pay for the distribution system (paying higher fees for various broadband connections).
- Some ISPs compete with content providers (for example, cable companies provide content as well as access) and might discriminate either in price or speed to favor their own content.

- ISPs could discriminate among content providers based on other improper criteria.
- Variable pricing might make it difficult for new content providers to succeed. (Amazon. com had high-volume traffic long before it became profitable.)

These concerns are not completely unfounded. ISPs have the technical capacity to control access and speed on a user-by-user basis.[12] Allowing any differential treatment could make it difficult to prove improper discriminatory treatment. For example:

- In 2007 it was not until a blogger revealed that Comcast had slowed traffic from BitTorrent that some Comcast subscribers understood that their access to BitTorrent's services had been deliberately impaired.[13]
- In 2009, AT&T prohibited iPhone users from accessing Skype's internet-phone service.[14]
- The Federal Communications Commission (FCC) has received numerous complaints of wireless carriers determining which text messages they will permit on their systems. In 2007, Verizon initially refused to transmit messages from a prochoice abortion rights organization.[15]

The FCC issued new net neutrality rules in December 2010 to address some of these issues, rules that vary based on whether the ISP provides broadband (through cable or DSL lines) or wireless services.[16] For wired services, the rules require equal access to all content providers regardless of the effect on the network, and they compel disclosure to customers of network performance updates and principles used to manage network congestion. The rules discourage, but apparently don't prohibit, charging fees to content providers. Wireless providers have considerably more leeway. While they can't discriminate against services that compete with their core products (thus, AT&T can't block or slow access to Skype), they can discriminate among types of content and will be allowed to block particular applications from their networks. Thus, AT&T can block wireless access to Netflix but allow access to an official AT&T video player; and it can charge more for watching videos than for online searching. Neither wireless nor broadband providers can discriminate in the sending of text messages.

These rules will likely be challenged in court, in part because a 2010 U.S. circuit court decision casts doubt on how much regulatory authority the FCC has over the Internet. When it was revealed in 2007 that Comcast had selectively slowed traffic from BitTorrent, two nonprofit organizations filed a complaint with the FCC. Ultimately the FCC issued an order requiring Comcast to disclose its network management practices and periodically report on its compliance. Comcast sued the FCC and the federal circuit court in DC ruled that the FCC had failed to prove that it had the authority to issue the order to Comcast.[17] Advocates for net neutrality may contest the more lenient rules applicable to wireless services, especially because it is known that poorer communities rely more on wireless than on wired services.[18] ISPs may argue against the FCC's jurisdiction, and assert both that the market can determine whether tiered pricing is appropriate and that there is enough competition for customers among ISPs that they will differentiate themselves based on whether they selectively deliver certain Internet content.

Questions

The issue of net neutrality raises the question of whether regulation is either appropriate or necessary to restrict unwanted behavior. Would you favor imposing the same rules on wired and wireless ISPs? If so, which approach of the FCC would you prefer? Would you instead prefer to leave it to the market to determine which ISPs will be successful? Explain your responses.

Part Two—Jurisdiction to Adjudicate

Business in the cyberworld raises puzzling new legal problems. The Internet, after all, is borderless. We can and do communicate and engage in transactions around the world. When a dispute arises from one of those billions of communications and transactions, where will that dispute be litigated? If an American Web site provides child pornography viewed by a resident of Germany, which nation will have the authority to prosecute the offense?[19] If a Massachusetts resident posts an arguably libelous article on an Internet bulletin board sited in New York, may the Texas resident who claims harm from the libel sue the author and the bulletin board host in a Texas court?[20] These are *jurisdictional* questions. The party filing suit must take its claim to a court that has both *subject-matter jurisdiction* (the authority to address the particular kind of legal problem raised) and *personal jurisdiction* (the power to compel the defendant to respond). (For a general discussion of jurisdiction, see Chapter 4.)

In the United States, where the plaintiff and defendant are both residents of the forum state, personal jurisdiction ordinarily is not an issue. However, personal jurisdiction over nonresidents depends on the constitutional requirement of *due process*. In practice, the test is one of *minimum contacts*: Did the defendant have sufficient contact with the forum state that being sued there would be fair and just? Put another way, was the defendant's contact with the forum state of such a nature that it should expect to be subject to the state's courts? Thus, the more business a defendant does in a state, the more likely personal jurisdiction will be found. Internet business raises special problems because the "contacts" are often electronic and fleeting.

Several cases have arisen in the United States that begin to answer these personal jurisdiction questions. In one the Fifth Circuit held in a case of alleged copyright violation that Texas did not have personal jurisdiction over a Vermont corporation merely because the corporation's Web site was accessible from Texas.[21] It reached this conclusion, in part, because there was no specific connection between the existence of the corporation's Web site and the harm complained of by the plaintiff. Thus, the Vermont corporation could be sued in Texas only if it had contacts with Texas that were sufficiently "continuous and systematic" as to subject the corporation to suit in Texas generally. A passive Web site was insufficient to do this. When the defendant has more contact with the forum state than the existence of a passive Web site reachable by forum state computer users, the due process analysis becomes more complex and hinges on an evaluation of the defendant's specific additional contacts with the state. The existing decisions are often hard to reconcile and many cases have been reversed on appeal, indicating that judgments as to personal jurisdiction are challenging and uncertain.[22]

Question

The operator of the dating service be2.com sued the CEO of the competing dating service be2.net for trademark infringement. The suit was brought in a U.S. district court in Illinois.

Defendant was a New Jersey resident. The only evidence of his contact with Illinois was a list of 20 Illinois members of be2.net. After the court granted a default judgment when the defendant did not respond to the complaint, defendant moved to vacate the judgment for lack of personal jurisdiction.[23] Should Illinois courts have jurisdiction? Explain.

Jurisdiction in International Suits

Similar jurisdictional issues arise across national boundaries. In 2010, an Italian court convicted three U.S.-based Google executives in absentia of violating Italian privacy laws based on a video posted by third parties on Google's system. The video showed three teen-age boys harassing an autistic boy. Italian law holds executives responsible for company actions, but Google is expected to appeal the privacy decision arguing that it subverts free-dom, is excessively burdensome and imposes personal responsibility on Google executives for any and all material hosted on its Italian site.[24]

In international contexts it may be useful to distinguish among three types of jurisdic-tion: jurisdiction to prescribe (legislate), jurisdiction to adjudicate (judicial personal juris-diction), and jurisdiction to enforce.[25] Most countries have long had laws that prohibit or regulate some forms of commerce, such as pornography, gambling, and alcohol. When a country seeks to apply those laws to foreigners, the question is whether the country has jurisdiction to adjudicate. The Restatement (Third) of Foreign Relations Law attempts to identify the circumstances under which countries have exercised their jurisdiction to adju-dicate. It enumerates, among other circumstances: (1) when a person is present in the terri-tory, other than transitorily; (2) when a person is domiciled, a resident, or a national of that country; (3) when a person regularly carries on business in that country; (4) when a person has carried on an activity in the country and that activity is the subject of the dispute; and (5) when a person has done something outside the country that has a "substantial, direct, and foreseeable effect within" the country and that effect forms the subject of the suit. Based on those standards, do you think the Italian courts have jurisdiction over Google's American executives?

Consider both the French court's approach and the U.S. district court's approach to the issue of jurisdiction to adjudicate in the following dispute.

LEGAL BRIEFCASE

YAHOO! v. La Ligue Contre Le Racisme Et L'Antisemitisme
169 F.Supp.2d 1181 (N.D. Cal. 2001)

Judge Jeremy Fogel

I. PROCEDURAL HISTORY

[Defendant] La Ligue Contre Le Racisme Et L'Antisemitisme ("LICRA") [is a French nonprofit organization] dedicated to eliminating anti-Semitism. Plaintiff Yahoo!, Inc. ("Yahoo!") is a corporation organized under the laws of Delaware with its principal place of business in Santa Clara, California. . . . Yahoo! services ending in the suffix ".com," without an associated country code as a prefix or extension (collectively, "Yahoo!'s

U.S. Services"), use the English language and target users who are residents of, utilize servers based in, and operate under the laws of the United States. Yahoo! subsidiary corporations operate regional Yahoo! sites and services in 20 other nations, including, for example, Yahoo! France, Yahoo! India, and Yahoo! Spain. Each of these regional Web sites contains the host nation's unique two-letter code as either a prefix or a suffix in its URL. Yahoo!'s regional sites use the local region's primary language, target the local citizenry, and operate under local laws.

Yahoo! provides a variety of means by which people from all over the world can communicate and interact with one another over the Internet. . . . As relevant here, Yahoo!'s auction site allows anyone to post an item for sale and solicit bids from any computer user from around the globe. Yahoo! records when a posting is made and after the requisite time period lapses sends an e-mail notification to the highest bidder and seller with their respective contact information. Yahoo! is never a party to a transaction, and the buyer and seller are responsible for arranging privately for payment and shipment of goods. Yahoo! monitors the transaction through limited regulation by prohibiting particular items from being sold (such as stolen goods, body parts, prescription and illegal drugs, weapons, and goods violating U.S. copyright laws or the Iranian and Cuban embargos). . . . Yahoo! informs auction sellers that they must comply with Yahoo!'s policies and may not offer items to buyers in jurisdictions in which the sale of such item violates the jurisdiction's applicable laws. Yahoo! does not actively regulate the content of each posting, and individuals are able to post, and have in fact posted, highly offensive matter, including Nazi-related propaganda and Third Reich memorabilia, on Yahoo!'s auction sites.

On or about April 5, 2000, LICRA sent a "cease and desist" letter to Yahoo!'s Santa Clara headquarters informing Yahoo! that the sale of Nazi and Third Reich–related goods through its auction services violates French law. LICRA threatened to take legal action unless Yahoo! took steps to prevent such sales within eight days. Defendants subsequently utilized the United States Marshal's Office to serve Yahoo! with process in California and filed a civil complaint against Yahoo! in the Tribunal de Grande Instance de Paris (the "French Court").

The French Court found that approximately 1,000 Nazi and Third Reich–related objects, including Adolf Hitler's *Mein Kampf, The Protocol of the Elders of Zion* (an infamous anti-Semitic report produced by the Czarist secret police in the early 1900s), and purported "evidence" that the gas chambers of the Holocaust did not exist, were being offered for sale on Yahoo.com's auction site. Because any French citizen is able to access these materials on Yahoo.com directly or through a link on Yahoo.fr, the French Court concluded that the Yahoo.com auction site violates Section R645-1 of the French Criminal Code, which prohibits exhibition of Nazi propaganda and artifacts for sale. On May 20, 2000, the French Court entered an order requiring Yahoo! to (1) eliminate French citizens' access to any material on the Yahoo.com auction site that offers for sale any Nazi objects, relics, insignia, emblems, and flags; (2) eliminate French citizens' access to Web pages on Yahoo.com displaying text, extracts, or quotations from *Mein Kampf* and *Protocol of the Elders of Zion;* (3) post a warning to French citizens on Yahoo.fr that any search through Yahoo.com may lead to sites containing material prohibited by Section R645-1 of the French Criminal Code, and that such viewing of the prohibited material may result in legal action against the Internet user; (4) remove from all browser directories accessible in the French Republic index headings entitled "negationists" and from all hypertext links the equation of "negationists" under the heading "Holocaust." The order subjects Yahoo! to a penalty of 100,000 Euros for each day that it fails to comply with the order. . . .

The French Court also provided that penalties assessed against Yahoo! Inc. may not be collected from Yahoo! France. Defendants again utilized the United States Marshal's Office to serve Yahoo! in California with the French Order.

Yahoo! subsequently posted the required warning and prohibited postings in violation of Section R645-1 of the French Criminal Code from appearing on Yahoo.fr. Yahoo! also amended the auction policy of Yahoo.com to prohibit individuals from auctioning:

> Any item that promotes, glorifies, or is directly associated with groups or individuals known principally for hateful or violent positions or acts, such as Nazis or the Ku Klux Klan. Official government-issue stamps and coins are not prohibited under this policy. Expressive media, such as books and films, may be subject to more permissive standards as determined by Yahoo! in its sole discretion.

Notwithstanding these actions, the Yahoo.com auction site still offers certain items for sale (such as stamps, coins, and a copy of *Mein Kampf*) which appear to violate the French Order. . . .

Yahoo! claims that because it lacks the technology to block French citizens from accessing the Yahoo.com auction site to view materials which violate the French order or from accessing other Nazi-based content of Web sites on Yahoo.com, it cannot comply with the French order without banning Nazi-related material from Yahoo.com altogether. Yahoo! contends that such a ban would infringe impermissibly upon its rights under the First Amendment to the United States Constitution. Accordingly, Yahoo! filed a complaint in this Court seeking a declaratory judgment that the French Court's orders are neither cognizable nor enforceable under the laws of the United States.

Defendants immediately moved to dismiss on the basis that this Court lacks personal jurisdiction over them. That motion was denied. . . .

II. OVERVIEW

As this Court and others have observed, the instant case presents novel and important issues arising from the global reach of the Internet. Indeed, the specific facts of this case implicate issues of policy, politics, and culture that are beyond the purview of one nation's judiciary. Thus it is critical that the Court define at the outset what is and is not at stake in the present proceeding.

This case is *not* about the moral acceptability of promoting the symbols or propaganda of Nazism. Most would agree that such acts are profoundly offensive. By any reasonable standard of morality, the Nazis were responsible for one of the worst displays of inhumanity in recorded history. . . .

Nor is this case about the right of France or any other nation to determine its own law and social policies. A basic function of a sovereign state is to determine by law what forms of speech and conduct are acceptable within its borders. . . .

What *is* at issue here is whether it is consistent with the Constitution and laws of the United States for another nation to regulate speech by a United States resident within the United States on the basis that such speech can be accessed by Internet users in that nation. In a world in which ideas and information transcend borders and the Internet in particular renders the physical distance between speaker and audience virtually meaningless, the implications of this question go far beyond the facts of this case. The modern world is home to widely varied cultures with radically divergent value systems. There is little doubt that Internet users in the United States routinely engage in speech that violates, for example, China's laws against religious expression, the laws of various nations against advocacy of gender equality or homosexuality, or even the United Kingdom's restrictions on freedom of the press.

* * * * *

The French order prohibits the sale or display of items based on their association with a particular political organization and bans the display of Web sites based on the authors' viewpoint with respect to the Holocaust and anti-Semitism. A United States court constitutionally could not make such an order. The First Amendment does not permit the government to engage in viewpoint-based regulation of speech absent a

compelling governmental interest, such as averting a clear and present danger of imminent violence.

* * * * *

Comity

No legal judgment has any effect, of its own force, beyond the limits of the sovereignty from which its authority is derived. . . . The extent to which the United States, or any state, honors the judicial decrees of foreign nations is a matter of choice, governed by "the comity of nations." United States courts generally recognize foreign judgments and decrees unless enforcement would be prejudicial or contrary to the country's interests.

As discussed previously, the French order's content and viewpoint-based regulation of the Web pages and auction site on Yahoo.com, while entitled to great deference as an articulation of French law, clearly would be inconsistent with the First Amendment if mandated by a court in the United States. . . . The reason for limiting comity in this area is sound. "The protection to free speech and the press embodied in [the First] amendment would be seriously jeopardized by the entry of foreign judgments granted pursuant to standards deemed appropriate in [another country] but considered antithetical to the protections afforded the press by the U.S. Constitution." Absent a body of law that establishes international standards with respect to speech on the Internet and an appropriate treaty or legislation addressing enforcement of such standards to speech originating within the United States, the principle of comity is outweighed by the Court's obligation to uphold the First Amendment.

* * * * *

CONCLUSION

Yahoo! seeks a declaration from this Court that the First Amendment precludes enforcement within the United States of a French order intended to regulate the content of its speech over the Internet. . . . Accordingly, the motion for summary judgment will be granted.

AFTERWORD

On appeal in 2006 the Ninth Circuit Court of Appeals ruled by a vote of eight to three that the California district court had personal jurisdiction over the French defendants, but six judges also held that Yahoo! could not pursue its declaratory judgment action. Three of those six said the declaratory judgment action was not "ripe" for decision, while the other three were the minority that held that the court had no personal jurisdiction.[26] The Supreme Court declined to review the decision.[27]

Questions

1. We cannot tell from this opinion why the French court believed it had jurisdiction to adjudicate against Yahoo!, as opposed to Yahoo! France. Look back at the discussion of the Restatement (Third) of Foreign Relations Law immediately before this case. Why might the French court have had jurisdiction over Yahoo! France? Over Yahoo!?

2. If you were sitting on the Ninth Circuit, how would you have decided the jurisdiction question? Consider both the U.S. rule of minimum contacts and the Restatement provision.

3. Notice the Court's conclusion that the principle of comity is outweighed by its constitutional obligation to uphold the freedom of speech. Is this approach to the requirements of comity consistent with the discussion of comity in Chapter 16?

Part Three—Constitutional Law: Speech and Privacy

Speech

The district court opinion in *Yahoo! v. La Ligue Contre Le Racisme et L'Antisemitisme* illustrates one of the free speech issues the Internet raises. Internet content has also raised free speech issues here at home. The Internet's seeming anonymity, ease of use, relatively low costs, and global reach make it a natural vehicle for transporting speech messages. As we saw in Chapter 5, the First Amendment protects us from government restraints on the *content* of speech, although reasonable restraints on the *context* (time, place, and manner) of that speech are sometimes constitutionally permissible. Thus, a court will not restrain free speech by enjoining someone from posting defamatory or copyrighted material, but the damaged party may, of course, sue for defamation or copyright infringement after the posting.[28] [For articles on cyberlaw free speech, search for "free speech" at **http://www.jcil.org/journal/search**]

One of the most troublesome Internet free speech issues is how or whether children can be protected from online pornography while maintaining adult access to constitutionally protected content. According to a 2007 survey, 34 percent of Internet users aged 10 to 17 experienced "unwanted exposure to online pornography, up from 25 percent" in a similar survey five years earlier.[29]

> Thirty-four percent of Internet users aged 10 to 17 experienced "unwanted exposure to online pornography."

That said, Congress has struggled to enact constitutional legislation that would still effectively eliminate access by minors. In 1997, the Supreme Court held critical provisions of the Communications Decency Act of 1996 were overbroad and therefore violated the First Amendment.[30]

Congress responded by passing the Child Online Protection Act. In 2007, a federal district court found the law unconstitutional and permanently enjoined its enforcement. In 2009, the Supreme Court refused to hear the government's appeal, leaving the permanent injunction in place.[31]

Congress has also attempted to address a slightly different problem—the exploitation of children in the making of child pornography and its online accessibility to predators of children. Its first attempt was held unconstitutional by the Supreme Court,[32] but in 2008 the Court upheld the PROTECT Act. Nevertheless, child pornography remains one of the Internet's most intractable challenges, "too large for law enforcement, policy makers and child protection groups to handle on their own."[33] Working with Hany Farid, a professor at Dartmouth College, Microsoft has developed a program that can automatically find hidden copies of child pornography on the Internet with 98 percent accuracy. Microsoft has donated the technology to the National Center for Missing and Exploited Children and has incorporated it into its own search engine, Bing. The technology may soon be extended to video. (For more on child online protection, see Chapter 5.)

PRACTICING ETHICS Government Control of Web Content

Governments seem intent on restricting content, or access to certain content, on the Web. We have noted Congress's repeated attempts to prohibit pornography from reaching minors. The French court ordered Yahoo! to block French citizens' access to auctions of Nazi memorabilia. As examined in Chapter 1, China is engaged in an ongoing censorship battle with Google. The Chinese government is requiring Google to censor its google.cn search results in order for Google to retain its Internet services license in China. More specifically, China wants google.cn search results to filter out links to such sensitive topics as democracy, the religious group Falun Gong, and the Tiananmen Square massacre.

Questions

Do you think any government can effectively stop its citizens' access to particular Web content? Should any government try to do so? Should ISPs voluntarily aid governments in their attempts? Is it more ethical for an ISP to provide such aid only if ordered to do so by a court with jurisdiction? Should an ISP operating in a host country seek to impose only those speech restrictions allowable in its home country or is it permissible to impose the standards of the host country?

Anonymous Speech

"[An] author's decision to remain anonymous, like other decisions concerning omissions or additions to the content of a publication, is an aspect of the freedom of speech protected by the First Amendment."[34]

A unique characteristic of the Internet and electronic communication through the Internet is the ease with which a poster or sender can be anonymous and remain so without "fear of economic or official retaliation . . . [or] social ostracism."[35] Anonymity makes it more likely that individuals will feel free to say things about which they would otherwise keep silent. Thus, it can promote "the robust exchange of ideas."[36] Anonymity may, however, make individuals bolder about asserting untruths—misleading, fraudulent, or otherwise unprotected speech. So the Internet has spawned ever more numerous examples where one side argues to preserve its anonymity, whereas the other argues that abuse warrants the loss of the speaker's anonymity. ISPs are caught in the middle because of their ability to reveal the speaker's identity based on information provided when contracting for service.

In the case that follows, a Yahoo! poster argues the First Amendment prohibits Yahoo! from responding to a subpoena from Immunomedics, a corporation claiming the anonymous poster is or was an employee who violated the company's confidentiality agreement by posting company information on a Yahoo! message board.

Judge Fall

Defendant Jean Doe, a/k/a "moonshine_fr," appeals from an order . . . denying her motion to quash a subpoena issued to Yahoo! by plaintiff, Immunomedics, Inc., seeking all personally identifiable information relating to the person or identity who posted messages on the Yahoo! Finance Message Board under the identifier "moonshine_fr" which may identify or lead to the identification of that person or entity.

Immunomedics is a publicly held biopharmaceutical Delaware corporation . . . focused on the development, manufacture, and commercialization of diagnostic imaging and therapeutic products for the detection and treatment of cancer and infectious diseases.

Yahoo! is an Internet Service Provider (ISP) that maintains a Web site that includes a section called Yahoo! Finance. Yahoo! Finance maintains a message board for every publicly traded company, including Immunomedics. Visitors to the Immunomedics site can obtain up-to-date information on the company, and can post and exchange messages about issues related to the operation or performance of the company.

On October 12, 2000, Immunomedics filed a complaint against Jean Doe, also known by the computer screen name "moonshine_fr" ("Moonshine"). The complaint alleged that Moonshine had "posted a message on Yahoo! Finance." Immunomedics claimed that message contained information confidential and proprietary to Immunomedics. As a result, Immunomedics asserted it had sustained injury and that Moonshine should be held liable under theories of breach of contract, breach of duty of loyalty, and negligently revealing confidential and proprietary information.

* * * * *

Of the two messages in question, the first, with Moonshine describing herself as "[a] worried employee," stated that Immunomedics was "out of stock for diagnostic products in Europe" and claimed that there would be "no more sales if [the] situation [did] not change." The second message, allegedly posted by Moonshine after the initial complaint was filed, reported that Chairman of the Company Dr. Goldenberg was going to fire the Immunomedics "european manager." In her certification to the trial court, Immunomedics' Executive Vice President and Chief Operations Officer Cynthia L. Sullivan admitted that the statements were true, but that, as an employee, Moonshine had violated the company's confidentiality agreement and "several provisions" of the company's Employee Handbook.

On or about October 20, 2000, Immunomedics served a subpoena on Yahoo!, seeking discovery of Moonshine's true identity. Yahoo!, in turn, contacted Moonshine. In response, Moonshine filed a motion to quash the subpoena on or about November 15, 2000.

. . . After considering the arguments, the judge denied Moonshine's motion, stating, in pertinent part,

> We have two issues here. We have an issue, she's an employee, she signed a confidential document saying that she was not going to speak freely about information she learned at the company. So she contracted away her right of free speech if she's an employee. Number two, free speech, anonymous, but if it harms another individual, that is another way that we have a little bit of a dent in our rights for free speech.

* * * * *

Moonshine contends the motion judge erred in denying her motion to quash the subpoena, as anonymous speech is constitutionally protected and Immunomedics' complaint is insufficient to warrant a breach of that anonymity. Immunomedics argues that, while anonymous speech is constitutionally protected, that protection can be overcome if a defendant uses that freedom in an unlawful manner. . . .

In another case involving an application for expedited discovery to disclose the identity of an anonymous user of an ISP message board, we concluded that courts must decide such applications by striking a balance between the First Amendment right of an individual to speak anonymously and the right of a company to protect its proprietary interest in the pursuit of claims based on actionable conduct by the ISP message board user.

* * * * *

We hold that . . . the trial court should first require the plaintiff to undertake efforts to notify the anonymous posters that they are the subject of a subpoena or application for an order of disclosure, and withhold action to afford the fictitiously named defendants a reasonable opportunity to file and serve opposition to the application. These notification efforts should include posting a message of notification of the identity discovery request to the anonymous user on the ISP's pertinent message board.

The court shall also require the plaintiff to identify and set forth the exact statements purportedly made by each anonymous poster that plaintiff alleges constitute actionable speech.

The complaint and all information provided to the court should be carefully reviewed to determine whether plaintiff has set forth a prima facie cause of action against the fictitiously named anonymous defendants. In addition to establishing that its action can withstand a motion to dismiss for failure to state a claim upon which relief can be granted, the plaintiff must produce sufficient evidence supporting each element of its cause of action, on a prima facie basis, prior to a court ordering the disclosure of the identity of the unnamed defendant.

Finally, assuming the court concludes that the plaintiff has presented a prima facie cause of action, the court must balance the defendant's First Amendment right of anonymous free speech against the strength of the prima facie case presented and the necessity for the disclosure of the anonymous defendant's identity to allow the plaintiff to properly proceed.

The application of these procedures and standards must be undertaken and analyzed on a case-by-case basis. The guiding principle is a result based on a meaningful analysis and a proper balancing of the equities and rights at issue.

. . . Here, Immunomedics' cause of action is based on Moonshine's status as an employee and her alleged violation of a confidentiality agreement, and Moonshine's alleged breach of her common law duty of loyalty. . . .

Applying the procedure and test outlined, we conclude Judge Zucker-Zarett properly analyzed the disclosure issue, and we affirm substantially for the reasons articulated by the judge in her oral opinion. . . . We add the following. Immunomedics presented sufficient evidence that Moonshine is, or was, an employee of Immunomedics. Ms. Sullivan indicated in her certification that "all employees are bound by several Company policies and a confidentiality agreement." Within its "Confidentiality and Assignment Agreement," Immunomedics includes the following language:

> This Agreement and any disputes arising under or in connection with it shall be governed by the laws of the State of New Jersey and each of the parties hereto hereby submits to the jurisdiction of any Federal or state court sitting in the State of New Jersey over any such dispute.

Accordingly, Immunomedics clearly established a prima facie cause of action for breach of the confidentiality agreement founded on the content of Moonshine's posted messages.

In balancing Moonshine's right of anonymous free speech against the strength of the prima facie case presented and the necessity for disclosure, it is clear that the motion judge struck the proper balance in favor of identity disclosure. With evidence demonstrating Moonshine is an employee of Immunomedics, that employees execute confidentiality agreements, and the content of Moonshine's posted messages providing evidence of the breach thereof, the disclosure of Moonshine's identity, which can be reasonably calculated to be achieved by information obtained from the subpoena, was fully warranted. Although anonymous speech on the Internet is protected, there must be an avenue for redress for those who are wronged. Individuals choosing to harm another or violate an agreement through speech on the Internet cannot hope to shield their identity and avoid punishment through invocation of the First Amendment.

* * * * *

Affirmed.

Questions

1. In your opinion, should employers, police, and others who have been damaged by anonymous postings be able to obtain the identity of the poster from the hosting site or the poster's ISP? Explain.

2. An FBI agent monitored an AOL chat room suspected of being a site for exchanging child pornography. The agent did not participate in the chat room conversations. Charbonneau allegedly distributed child pornography to the chat room participants, including the FBI agent. Charbonneau was arrested. Did Charbonneau have a First Amendment free speech right to transmit child pornography online? Explain. See *U. S. v. Kenneth Charbonneau,* 979 F.Supp. 1177 (S.D. Ohio 1997).

3. Having read these materials on freedom of speech and the limits on the right to anonymity, what would you advise a friend who was a regular blogger? A classmate posting comments on **http://www.ratemyprofessors. com**? Your middle school cousin who is an avid Facebook user? Explain.

Commercial Speech

Remember from Chapter 5 that commercial speech has been accorded reduced but significant First Amendment protection. Thus, online advertising is subject to the same kinds of government oversight as that in print and on television. One form of online commercial message receiving special attention is so-called *spam* (mass emails). This electronic junk mail may be a legitimate form of commercial message at times, but it may also be an annoyance, a threat to the efficiency of the Internet because of its volume, or deceptive; or it may contain objectionable content (obscenity, viruses).

The federal CAN-SPAM Act of 2003 establishes both civil and criminal penalties for violations of its provisions. The Federal Trade Commission (FTC), charged with enforcing the Act, won a substantial victory in 2008 when it obtained a court order freezing the assets of and shutting down a spam network that was capable of sending 10 billion email messages a day and was responsible at one point for one-third of all spam. The group based its Web sites in China, processed credit cards payments through Cyprus and the former Soviet republic of Georgia, and in one month cleared $400,000 in credit card charges from sales of replica watches and pharmaceuticals for weight loss and enhancement of the male anatomy.[37] [For more information on the CAN-SPAM Act and the FTC's enforcement, see **http://www.ftc.gov/bcp/edu/microsites/spam**]

Privacy

Most individuals probably do not fully appreciate the amount of their personal information that is available online, how it may be used, or the degree to which it may be misused. This section is intended in part to illustrate some of the possibilities.

> The Internet has brought with it an explosion of accessible data, including personal data.

The Internet has brought with it an explosion of accessible data, including personal data. Some of the information now available online has in fact been public for decades, but most people were not aware that it was public, did not know how to obtain it, or simply never bothered, a reality sometimes referred to as "practical obscurity."[38] For example, local governments keep property, tax, criminal, and court records, often housed in the local courthouse but not easily searchable. Now local governments are making many of these data available online, accessible to those who are simply curious.[39] Similarly, governmental agencies responsible for professional and occupational licensing may now have Web sites with membership lists, complaints filed, and disciplinary actions taken. Marketing firms, of course, have long collected all of this information and more, including home and work addresses, phone numbers, profession, income information, credit scores, bankruptcies, home ownership, mortgage amounts, vehicle and boat registrations, hunting licenses, bridal and birth registries, warranty cards, magazine and newspaper subscriptions, and even dog licenses. But maintaining current data was costly and the resulting profiles were not available to the general public. With the advent of the Internet that has changed. At CriminalSearches.com, a site supported by advertising, anyone can look up neighbors, babysitters, teachers, plumbers, or their children's friends for free, as the site encourages one to do. How long will it be before jurors are tempted to look up the criminal record of the defendant?

A simple Google search can turn up much more, including self-disclosed information on the public pages of social media sites. Consider the following, which is readily available or which you yourself may be unwittingly providing:

- Satellite and street views of your home, your work, and your children's school. Scouting a location or stalking someone has never been easier.

- Geotagged pictures taken with GPS-equipped smartphones and cameras. Geotags are data embedded in photos and videos providing longitude and latitude information. The "only way you can turn off the function on your smartphone is through an invisible menu that no one really knows about."[40] Free browser plug-ins can be downloaded that allow anyone to read the geotag information and "any 16 year-old with basic programming skills" can create a program to search for geotagged photos on Twitter, YouTube, Flickr, and Craigslist. [For information on disabling geotagging for some phones, see **http://icanstalku.com**]
- Personal information embedded in the bar code of online coupons and handed over to the merchant taking the coupon (as well as their marketing firm). This can include your name, Internet address, and Facebook page information. Consumers don't even know information is being shared, let alone its nature.[41]

Data Mining

Most of the data previously identified can be compiled on a particular person by anyone with the inclination and a modest amount of time. But now consider the amount of additional information residing in the databases of institutions with whom we regularly deal: credit card companies, online vendors, membership organizations, schools, pharmacies, medical service providers, our ISPs, phone companies, and so forth. Data mining is the process of building profiles of individuals by organizing all the disparate pieces of information collected in the normal course of business. Those profiles can be used to provide better services to repeat customers—from the pizza outlet that knows what you ordered last time (and how often, as well as how much you spend and, possibly, whether you tip) to Netflix that knows all your historical rentals (and how you rated them), as well as everything listed in your queue, and from that information can give you tailored recommendations for what else you might like. So significant efficiencies can be achieved from the use of mined data, but the potential for misuse of these data is also very great.

Profiles built by online vendors may be passed along to or aggregated with information gathered by affiliated businesses or by third-party advertisers. Or the business that compiles the profiles may sell them to marketing firms and others. The explosion in computers and the Internet have exponentially increased both the detail in such profiles and their ease of compilation. For example, the merchant may know not only how you rated the products you bought, but what alternatives you considered before making the purchase and how long you looked at each. All this valuable information is available by tracking the pages you viewed on their site, the order you viewed them in, and how long you stayed on each page. Then there is the information you knowingly give the merchant while transacting your business, information that is already in digital form and which is likely linked automatically into a database already coded for sorting in various ways.

Perhaps even more disturbing is that the merchant whose site you are visiting may not be the only one collecting your browsing history. One study showed that nearly a third of the tracking tools on the 50 most popular U.S. Web sites were operating without the permission of Web site's owner.[42] Some of the worst Web sites were those of free service providers. For example, in a test run by the *Wall Street Journal,* Dictionary.com "ranked highest in exposing users to potentially aggressive surveillance: It installed 168 tracking tools that didn't let users decline to be tracked."[43] This puts a different cast on our understanding of the word "free." Notably, only Wikipedia.org, among the 50 sites, actually installed no-tracking tools.

Many sites expressly state that they do not pass personally identified information to other parties. Such statements may be misleading, as the public discovered when in 2006 AOL released 36 million search queries from 657,000 unidentified customers and *The New York Times* was able to trace searches back to specific individuals.[44] Similarly, when Netflix "released 100 million purportedly anonymous records revealing how almost 500,000 users had rated movies from 1999 to 2005, researchers were able to identify people in the database by name with a high degree of accuracy if they knew only a little bit about their movie-watching preferences, obtained from public data posted on other ratings sites."[45]

Privacy Policies: Did You Say Privacy?

These days an online merchant is likely to have a privacy policy posted on its site that describes, among other things, what data it collects and how they are used. For example, Amazon.com's Privacy Notice states "Information about our customers is an important part of our business, and we are not in the business of selling it to others."[46] The information it automatically collects includes "the full Uniform Resource Locator (URL) clickstream to, through, and from our Web site, including date and time; cookie number; [and] products you viewed or searched for." It also receives information such as "account information, purchase or redemption information, and page-view information from some merchants with which we operate co-branded businesses." A partial list of such businesses includes "Target, CD Now, Verizon Wireless, Sprint, T-Mobile, AT&T, Shutterfly, J&R, Godiva, Avon, Macy's, PacSun, Eddie Bauer and Northern Tool + Equipment." The Notice further acknowledges that its site includes third-party advertising and links to other Web sites. It then states, "We do not have access to or control over cookies or other features that they may use, and the information practices of these advertisers and third-party Web sites are not covered by this Privacy Notice."

Many sites give the user some choice in controlling distribution of the user's data. Thus, a site may choose an *opt out* protocol allowing the site to sell or distribute the information it collects to outside parties unless the user directs it not to do so. Alternatively, the site may choose an *opt in* protocol under which it promises not to sell or distribute such information unless the user expressly permits such use. Typically, the Web site owner selects one of the two protocols as the default, but allows the user to elect the other protocol. Opt in protocols are more protective of the user's privacy.

Aggregators

An aggregator in our context is any person who takes data that are discrete at the level of the individual and aggregates them with individual-level data from one or more other sources. By itself, a data file containing the browsing history of 200 discrete individuals (each person's browsing history separately presented but with no information identifying whose history it is) may not seriously threaten the anonymity of those individuals. By combining data from various sources, however, an aggregator creates even more detailed individual profiles thereby increasing the probability that the data reveal the identity of the person behind it. Yet more disturbing, an independent aggregator (for example, a marketing firm) has no privacy agreements with the individuals who are profiled and may have no agreement with the data source to restrict the use of the data. Aggregators generally are in the business of selling these data.

Cyberattacks

Pause and think about the vast amount of data you now know to be compiled and stored by various entities—both Internet and traditional actors, as well as aggregators. Now consider the ramifications of the fact that anything stored can likely be stolen. For example, Google may be the strongest, most technically sophisticated Internet company in the world, but even it cannot prevent covert cyberattacks on its systems. In 2009, Google disclosed that its servers had been compromised in a cyberattack originating in China and directed, in part, at the Gmail accounts of certain Chinese human rights activists.[47]

Question

How safe are your data? Explain.

Privacy of Employees

As discussed in Chapter 12, whether and when employers can legally access email sent from or received on office computers continues to be uncertain. In a 2010 case the New Jersey Supreme Court held that an employee had an expectation of privacy in an email sent from her office computer but through a personal, password-protected Web mail account, an expectation the employer violated when it forensically retrieved her email off of office servers. The result might have been different if the employer's privacy policy had clearly advised employees that their emails, even those sent through personal Web mail accounts, could be reviewed by the employer.[48] In another case, in 2010 the U.S. Supreme Court held that a city's review of a police officer's text messages was a reasonable search under the Fourth Amendment when the texts were sent from a wireless pager provided to the officer by the city, even if the officer had had a reasonable expectation of privacy.[49]

In a 2009 survey of 220 large U.S. companies, 38 percent said they "employ staff to read or otherwise analyze the content of outgoing email."[50] Today's software can be customized to look for such things as company officers' and competitors' names, as well as inappropriate language. Software is also available that can "track every keystroke, file download, and Internet page that appears on an employee's computer screen."[51] In part, companies may adopt some of these strategies to protect themselves from lawsuits. For example, Continental Airlines was sued for defamation and workplace harassment based on derogatory and insulting remarks about an employee posted by coworkers on

Continental's electronic bulletin board.[52] Employers wishing to implement such monitoring programs should, however, expressly advise their employees of that fact and have all employees sign an acknowledgment so there is no question about whether an employee has any expectation of privacy on company systems.

Question

Explain why employers might want to monitor their employees' computer activities.

Regulation

The United States has no comprehensive privacy law addressing the Internet environment. Instead, the privacy of users has largely been left to the "self-regulation" of service and content providers. However, because most online content is and has remained free to users, advertising dollars, in significant part, have funded the development of online content. To make that advertising more effective, and thus able to generate more revenue, advertisers and content providers have developed behavioral tracking to follow users' paths through the Internet, thereby allowing ads targeted to users' specific interests. In a very real sense, Google and Facebook and other advertising-driven business models sell their users' data to pay for the services they give without charge to their users. "Self-regulation" then puts users' privacy protection into the very hands that derive substantial revenue from the sale of private information. This is an irreconcilable conflict of interest, a problem publicly acknowledged by the U.S. Secretary of Commerce in stating, "Self-regulation without stronger enforcement is not enough."[53] In the same vein, the Federal Trade Commission recognized "that industry efforts to address privacy through self-regulation 'have been too slow, and up to now have failed to provide adequate and meaningful protection.'"[54]

That said, the only action taken by the Department of Commerce and FTC thus far is to suggest "initial policy recommendations" (Commerce) and the "implementation of a 'Do Not Track' mechanism" (FTC). Congress has had bills related to behavioral tracking before it since at least 2008.[55]

Child Privacy Online

The United States does have a separate law addressing the privacy of children online. The 1998 Children's Online Privacy Protection Act (COPPA) prohibits Web sites from collecting personal information from children under 13 without parental permission and requires that parents be allowed to review and correct any information collected about their children. The FTC is charged with primary enforcement of COPPA. [To take a look at the complaints, and other information, in cases brought by the FTC under COPPA, go to **business.ftc.gov/ privacy-and-security/children's-online-privacy**]

Privacy in Europe

The European Union has taken quite a different tack from America's market-driven approach to online privacy. The European Union's 1998 Data Protection Directive basically allows individuals to decide how their collected data can be used. Thus, if a European consumer provides personal information such as an address when buying from an online store, that store cannot legally send an ad to the purchaser without first seeking permission.[56] The directive also prohibits the transfer of data to countries outside the European Union that do not have "adequate" privacy rules.[57] The United States was one of the nations deemed inadequate, but by June 2000, European and U.S. negotiators had reached an agreement shielding U.S. companies from prosecution by EU governments for violation of the Data Protection Directive as long as the companies comply with a list of "safe harbor" privacy principles.[58] At this writing the European Union is in the process of a substantial update to the Directive to address such online developments as social networking, personalized advertising, and cloud computing.[59]

The philosophical chasm separating U.S. and EU data privacy policies was dramatically illustrated when it became public that Google occasionally collected emails and passwords from residential Wi-Fi networks while its cars were driving city streets taking photos for its Street View mapping service. In the United States the FTC ended its inquiry when Google pledged to stop gathering that information. In Europe, Google has agreed to destroy the data collected in Austria, Denmark, and Ireland; the Czech Republic banned Google from expanding its mapping program; Google has been sued by an association of Internet users in Spain; and authorities in Germany and Italy were still investigating at the time of this writing. South Korea raided Google's Korea offices as part of its investigation.[60]

Part Four—Crime

Crimes facilitated by the Internet include both truly new types and some old, familiar crimes in somewhat new clothing. Some statutes previously discussed, such as the CAN-SPAM and PROTECT acts, provide criminal penalties. Other laws criminalize specific online behavior, such as the Computer Pornography and Child Exploitation Prevention Act of 1999, which makes it unlawful to use a computer to solicit, lure, or entice a child or otherwise engage in sexual offenses with a child.

But many of our long-standing, pre-Internet criminal laws can be applied to both online and offline behavior. For example, theft of a laptop is still theft. On the other hand, if a thief logs on to the Internet with a stolen laptop protected by antitheft software, the laptop may transmit the log-on location, complete with phone number and owner's name, directly to the police—particularly helpful if the thief is logging on from home.[61] Similarly, it is a federal crime to transport stolen property across state lines, even if the property is an intangible like a detailed litigation strategy emailed by a law firm's employee to opposing counsel in another state.[62]

Computer Security As just illustrated, both computers and the information kept in them can be the objects of theft. Often the stored information is much more valuable than the hardware, generating a whole new category of thieves—*hackers*. Thanks to the Internet, hackers can break into others' computers from the privacy of their own home (even if it's in China) and traffic in such data as credit card numbers, personal identities, eBay accounts, and bank funds. Hacking can also simply be malicious—destroying data or whole computer networks.[63]

Hacking can also simply be malicious.

Computing power can also be the object of theft. Sophisticated hackers can create botnets by taking control of multiple computers (zombie computers) through software robots (bots) installed via worms and software backdoors. A program known as Conficker created a botnet that controlled more than 5 million zombies in over 200 countries in mid-2009.[64] Precautions such as upgrading software, using firewalls, and running antivirus software can significantly reduce the risk of such unintended use.[65]

Fraud   Botnets have also been used in a new type of fraud, so-called *click fraud*. Click fraud ranges from repeated clicks on a competitor's ad to run up its advertising bill to creating "paid to read" rings enlisting hundreds or thousands of members to click on ads simply to generate income for the Web sites hosting the ads. Clickbots have been used to automatically generate page hits. In 2006, Google settled a lawsuit based on click fraud for $90 million. Plaintiffs were advertisers who argued Google had underreported the number of fraudulent clicks. An information industry research group estimated that 13 percent of ad clicks were fraudulent in 2008.[66]

The Internet has spawned both *phishing* and *spear phishing*. "In a phishing attack, scammers send emails that purport to be from a bank . . . directing customers to a site where they are asked to enter vital information, such as passwords, bank account numbers or credit card details. The scams are so effective because the bogus emails and Web sites look so legitimate."[67] In spear phishing scammers enter social networking sites, such as MySpace and Facebook, and data mine posted profiles for such information as addresses, birthdates, and friends names, allowing them to "tap into [posters'] network of trust." Once connected as "friends," spear-phishers can send email messages "containing malicious code that infects the computer with a virus, which then tracks every user name and password entered on other legitimate sites. . . . 'Then parents use the same computer for their banking. . . . It could be months before they realize their bank accounts have been hacked.'"[68]

Cyberstalking and Cyberbullying   In a 2005 Illinois case a former electronics store employee was sentenced to four years in prison for sending lewd photos and threatening email and phone messages to a 22-year-old woman who had taken her computer in for repair.[69] This is just one example of *cyberstalking*—the repeated use of electronic media (such as email or chat rooms) to harass or threaten another person. It has been publicly recognized as a problem at least since 1999 when the U.S. Attorney General prepared a formal report.[70] Every state has laws criminalizing traditional physical stalking. Most of these laws require that the perpetrator make a credible threat of violence for the action to be a violation; many do not expressly include cyberstalking, although under appropriate facts it might be covered.

Harder to define is *cyberbullying*. Two criminologists who founded the Cyberbullying Research Center define it as willful and repeated harm inflicted through phones and computers.[71] All too frequently the victim is a teenager who escapes the online cruelty by committing suicide. In the most notorious case, the bully was actually the mother of a neighbor girl who lived four houses away. The mother created a MySpace page for a fictitious boy who "friended" the victim and then a month later taunted and rejected her. His final

> **The bully was actually the mother of a neighbor girl.**

message shortly before the victim hanged herself was, "The world would be a better place without you."[72] Based on the Center's Web site, 32 states have laws against cyberbullying or electronic harassment, but only six of those states provide any criminal sanctions.[73]

International Crimes   Initiating an international response to computer-facilitated crime, the Council of Europe drafted the Convention on Cybercrime, which 43 member states and several nonmember states, including the United States, have signed, although only 31 countries have ratified it.[74] The convention went into force July 1, 2004, for the original ratifying states. It requires "the criminalization of a long list of computer activities— everything from breaking into a computer to the 'deterioration' of computer data. . . . It also requires countries to make sure they can snoop through Internet data in real time. And it obliges nations to assist each other's investigations by monitoring Net communications."[75]

Each country's decisions to criminalize certain behaviors reflect that country's moral attitudes and historical experiences. Some proscribed behaviors such as murder are fairly universal, but other behaviors are acceptable in some countries while criminalized in others. Where such crimes are facilitated by the Internet, international disputes over the appropriate reach of such laws have arisen. We have already seen one example in the *Yahoo! v. La Ligue Contre Le Racisme et L'Antisemitisme* case in Part Two of this chapter, where France sought to enforce its ban on the sale of Nazi memorabilia to French citizens. Mentioned in the text immediately preceding *Yahoo!* is another example—an Italian case in which three Google executives were convicted for violating Italian privacy laws based on a video posted on Google's Italian site that showed an autistic boy being harassed by three teenagers.[76]

Both the United Kingdom and Germany have enforced criminal laws based on pornographic materials posted on Web sites outside their geographic boundaries. The United Kingdom convicted one of its citizens operating out of his home in the United Kingdom of "publication" of pornographic materials on Web sites located in the United States.[77] Germany originally convicted the German head of CompuServe, a U.S. company, for allowing German citizens access to pornographic Web sites hosted outside Germany, despite the fact that CompuServe had no feasible technological way to block access. (Blocking access would have required the U.S. corporation to block access to all of its customers worldwide.) The conviction was overturned a year later.[78]

Part Five—Commercial Law

Contracts and Uniform Laws

Internet sales have grown significantly, but for the Internet to reach its commercial potential a routine, well-settled contracts structure is essential. The basic ingredients of a binding contract, as we saw in Chapter 6, also apply to Internet transactions.

- **Capacity** to enter the contract.
- **Offer and acceptance** of the terms of the contract.

- **Consideration** for the promises in the contract.
- **Genuineness** of assent.
- **Legality** of purpose of the contract.

Thus, an email exchange fulfilling the traditional contract requirements should result in an enforceable agreement. But what if acceptance is indicated only by providing an "electronic signature" (a digital code unique to an individual), downloading some information, opening a shrink-wrap package, or clicking an "Accept" button?

E-Signature   Electronic signatures can take a variety of forms (voice prints, distinctive marks, mathematical codes), but they share a common purpose—to have the same legal effect as a signature affixed by hand. On June 30, 2000, President Clinton signed into law the Electronic Signatures in Global and National Commerce Act (E-SIGN), giving electronic signatures the same legal stature as handwritten ones, at least for most commercial purposes.[79] Consumers, however, cannot be forced to accept electronic signature agreements or to receive records and documents electronically rather than in paper form. [For a look at the digital signature laws of the United Nations, European Union, and the United Kingdom, see **http://law.richmond.edu/jolt/v11i2/article6.pdf**]

UCITA   In 1999 the National Conference of Commissioners on Uniform State Laws (NCCUSL) approved a model law designed to achieve uniformity across the United States in the law governing software and Internet transactions. The proposed law reaches all deals involving computer information or goods and is designed to address the special problems of the electronic market, including software licensure (right to use). The Uniform Computer Information Transactions Act (UCITA) addresses the substance of computer information transactions, rather than procedural aspects such as electronic signatures.

   To this point, UCITA has been amended twice (2000 and 2002), but it has been adopted in only Maryland and Virginia.[80] Until it or some other such legislation is widely approved, the Uniform Commercial Code (UCC), other applicable state and federal laws, and the common law of contracts (judge-made law) will govern electronic contractual arrangements. (The UCC, having been approved in 49 of the 50 states, is designed to provide nationwide consistency, predictability, and fairness in contract law where a sale of goods is involved.)

Click-Wrap Agreements   Today, software is typically downloaded with license terms provided onscreen during the installation process. Those terms often say that by using the software the buyer agrees to the terms. Whether all of those terms are enforceable in court is the subject of dispute. The likelihood is that many terms will be enforceable if the buyer has a reasonable opportunity to review those terms and can abort the installation (and the charge) if the terms are unacceptable. The court in *Caspi v. Microsoft Network,*[81] applying a traditional contract law analysis, ruled that the choice of forum provision in just such an online click-wrap agreement was enforceable.

   Critics are increasingly concerned, however, about just how voluntary some provisions in such standard-form contracts are. That is, has the purchaser genuinely consented to the contract terms? It can appear that retailers are, perhaps deliberately, obscuring one-sided terms.[82] Who has not viewed with trepidation the presentation of contract terms in a 2-by-4-inch scrollable window with an "Agree" button prominently displayed below?

Microsoft's License Police

Most software programs today are not sold, but are only licensed. At times one can find some surprising terms in the end user license agreement (EULA) that must be agreed to before downloading. For example, at the beginning of the last decade the EULA for Microsoft's FrontPage Web-design software included the following statement:

> You may not use the Software in connection with any site that disparages Microsoft, MSN, MSNBC, Expedia, or their products or services, infringe any intellectual property or other rights of these parties, violate any state, federal, or international law, or promote racism, hatred, or pornography.

As one Web site developer (who used FrontPage) noted:

> Putting a critic in the same club as lawbreakers, copyright infringers, racists, and pornographers is stupid. Apparently, whether my Web site stays or goes depends on the meaning of the word disparage. Well, I think the Microsoft crowd are a bunch of monopolists who want to control the world, and plan to keep stuffing everything anyone does with a computer into an operating system that only they control. Was that disparaging?

Questions

1. Do you think Microsoft should be able to tell the licensees of its software that the software cannot be used to "disparage" Microsoft? What about its attempt to prevent its products from being used to "promote racism, hatred, or pornography"?
2. If Microsoft brought a lawsuit against one of its licensees for in fact using one of its products to "disparage" Microsoft, or to "promote racism, hatred, or pornography," what do you think the outcome would be?

Source: Across the Board, Nov/Dec 2001, p. 83.

PRACTICING ETHICS   Marketing and the Internet

As anyone regularly using the Internet can observe—marketing efforts are pervasive. Where once marketing amounted to putting up Web pages where potential customers could get product and service information, it has grown into banner ads on news sites, pop-up windows that have to be affirmatively closed to escape the advertisement, online tracking systems for pitching specific ads at individual users,[83] and whole Web sites designed to hook kids with interactive games that themselves promote the posters' products.[84] Even more aggressive marketing gambits are available, including "typo-piracy" (use of misspellings or derivations of a popular brand to divert traffic to an unintended site), "astroturfing" (fake users on discussion forums and in chat rooms to create the impression of a grassroots buzz for a particular product), "meat puppets" (fictional posters on social networks like Facebook used to collect email addresses for sending product ads),[85] and spyware (software unknowingly downloaded by the user that can deliver volumes of pop-up ads, redirect browsers to undesired search engines, or steal personal information).[86] And who has not received unsolicited email advertisements offering low mortgage rates, as well as many much less savory devices and services?

Question

1. *a.* How many of these advertising gambits have you seen on the Internet? How did you react?

    b. Have you ever bought something after having it marketed to you using one of these methods?

2. If you were the owner of a business, would you allow any of these methods to be used in your online ads? Which ones? Why?

Intellectual Property

Continued expansion of electronic commerce depends to a significant extent on the business community's success in protecting its technology from theft, copying, infringement, and the like. Intellectual property, broadly, is composed of creative ideas that are the products of the human mind. Songs, computer programs, new medicines, a novel, and so on, are forms of intellectual property. Recalling our discussion of market failure in Chapter 8, you may recognize that intellectual property, from an economics point of view, is a public good.

> Intellectual property, from an economics point of view, is a public good.

Clearly, the market alone cannot effectively protect those ideas from theft and exploitation. Intellectual property law preserves the rights to those ideas for those who developed them. In doing so, we hope to provide justice by rewarding those whose ingenuity and hard work developed those ideas and their tangible results (recordings, movies, and the like), thereby providing an incentive to produce those imaginative advances. At least that is the American and Western view of intellectual property. Some cultures remain reluctant to recognize property rights of this kind, but globalization seems certain to generate relatively consistent intellectual property standards for most of the world. Inclusion of the Agreement on Trade-Related Aspects of Intellectual Property Rights (TRIPS Agreement) as one of the WTO's foundation agreements supports this projection. [For more on intellectual property law, see **http://www.ipmall.fplc.edu**]

Patents   Exactly what role patents will play in the future development of the Internet is still somewhat uncertain. The grant of some early patents associated with basic methods of doing business online (such as Amazon.com's "one-click" method for making Internet purchases and Priceline.com's process of "reverse" auctions) raised considerable controversy, resulting in the announcement by the U.S. Patent and Trademark Office in 2000 that it was overhauling the way it processes and awards patents for many online processes.[87] Then in 2006 the Board of Patent Appeals and Interferences, based on its previously issued guidance, ruled in *Bilski v. Kappos* that a particular method of hedging risk in the commodities trading field was not patentable because it was neither tied to a particular machine or apparatus nor did it transform a particular article into a different state or thing.

In 2010 the Supreme Court affirmed the Board's *Bilski* decision, but on different grounds.[88] It held that, while the standard applied by the Board was one appropriate standard, it was not the only appropriate standard. Nevertheless, the method of hedging risk was not patentable under prior decisions of the Court because it was an abstract idea. Following the

Court's decision, the Board issued additional interim guidelines that include the factors to consider in determining whether a claim is properly classified as an abstract idea. [For more on business methods patents, see **http://www.uspto.gov/web/menu/pbmethod**]

Copyrights

In America and much of the world, anyone who creates "original works of authorship," whether in print or digital form, is in most cases automatically protected by copyright laws if the "works" are original and are "fixed in tangible form" (written down on paper, for example). Consequently, the author has exclusive rights for a period of years to commercially exploit those works. Virtually all of the information available online is protected by the U.S. Copyright Act and includes such intellectual creations as data, databases, literature, music, software, photos, and multimedia works. While original works of authorship are automatically copyrighted, the fullest protection of the law can be achieved by placing a copyright notice on the work (such as "copyright 2012 McGraw-Hill") and registering the copyright with the U.S. Copyright Office. International protection is provided by the principal copyright treaty, the Berne Convention. [Information on the U.S. Copyright Office can be found at **http://www.copyright.gov**]

The copyright holder possesses the exclusive right to (1) reproduce the copyrighted work, (2) prepare adaptations based on the copyrighted material, (3) distribute the material by sale or otherwise, and (4) perform or display the material. When anyone other than the copyright holder, or one acting with the holder's permission, makes use of one of those rights, the copyright has been infringed unless the use falls within a series of exceptions. Perhaps the most notable of those exceptions is the *fair use doctrine,* which allows use of copyrighted material without permission under some conditions, such as limited, nonprofit use in a classroom.

The electronic age has spawned some new disputes arising out of applications of new technologies.

- In July 2010 the Library of Congress (which has jurisdiction over the U.S. Copyright Office) ruled that owners were free to jailbreak their iPhones; that is, they may bypass Apple's technical protection measures (TPM) in order to customize their phones.[89] Thus, owners are no longer restricted to phone applications sold in Apple's iTunes store. The 1998 Digital Millennium Copyright Act (DCMA) in general bans people from defeating TPM on copyrighted materials. Apple had argued that altering the iPhone's software infringed on its copyrights because it altered Apple's operating system.

- Like the iPhone, Amazon's Kindle e-reader is a tethered system—both companies exert considerable control for the life of the product. For example, Amazon uses digital rights management software to control the material that can be read on the Kindle. This is advantageous because Amazon can restore lost or damaged content, as well as transfer it to another Kindle associated with the same account. It also means Amazon has the power to unilaterally remove content, which it did when it discovered it had purchased George Orwell's *1984* from a seller that did not own legal rights to the book.[90] In this regard Kindle books are more like flat fee indefinite rentals than purchases.

- The rented or licensed status of songs in Apple's iTunes store was good news for rapper, Eminem. He sued Universal Music Group for a larger share of royalties from iTunes downloads, arguing they were licenses, not sales. The Ninth Circuit Court of Appeals agreed and he is now entitled to 50 percent of the revenues generated instead of no more than 20 percent that would have applied to sales.[91]

- Google has set itself a goal to scan all the world's literature and make it available online. Older books for which the copyright period has expired are part of the *public domain* and therefore freely available to Google, but most are still under copyright. Google has scanned over 15 million books, primarily through partnerships with libraries and other institutions, such as Oxford University and Italy's national government. But to allow the public full access to the books, Google needs permission from the copyright holders. However, an estimated 50 to 80 percent of all books still in copyright are also orphan books, books whose author or copyright owner cannot either be identified or found. In March of 2011 a federal judge rejected a settlement between Google and various publishers and groups representing authors that would have given Google the exclusive right to all orphan books published in North America, Britain, and Australia. It seems likely that the issue of rights to these books will now move to Congress. Many are hoping that Congress will make them free to all following a diligent search for the owners.[92]

One of the most visible Internet disputes has been the ongoing battle of the music recording industry to protect its copyrights. Music file sharing took off in the late 1990s through the use of the Napster Web site, where users could swap digital music. The recording industry successfully obtained an injunction against Napster's facilitation of such file sharing;[93] but the practice continued, aided by peer-to-peer computer programs such as KaZaA and Grokster, which are installed on users' computers. The recording industry sued Grokster and other file-sharing software distributors. The defendants prevailed at the district and circuit court levels.[94] Then, in the following unanimous Supreme Court decision, the recording industry achieved a major victory.

LEGAL BRIEFCASE

Metro-Goldwyn-Mayer Studios v. Grokster
125 S.Ct. 2764 (2005)

Justice Souter

I
A

Respondents, Grokster, Ltd., and StreamCast Networks, Inc., defendants in the trial court, distribute free software products that allow computer users to share electronic files through peer-to-peer networks, so called because users' computers communicate directly with each other, not through central servers. . . .

A group of copyright holders (MGM for short, but including motion picture studios, recording companies, songwriters, and music publishers) sued Grokster and StreamCast for their users' copyright infringements, alleging that they knowingly and intentionally distributed their software to enable users to reproduce and distribute the copyrighted works in violation of the Copyright Act.

* * * * *

Although Grokster and StreamCast do not know when particular files are copied, a few searches using their software would show what is available on the networks the software reaches. MGM commissioned a statistician to conduct a systematic search, and his study showed that nearly 90 percent of the files available for download on the FastTrack system were copyrighted works. Grokster and StreamCast dispute this figure. . . . They also argue that potential noninfringing uses of their software are significant in kind, even if infrequent in practice. Some musical performers, for example, have gained new audiences by distributing their copyrighted works for free across peer-to-peer networks, and some distributors of unprotected content have used peer-to-peer networks to disseminate files, Shakespeare being an example. . . .

But MGM's evidence gives reason to think that the vast majority of users' downloads are acts of infringement, and because well over 100 million copies of the software in question are known to have been downloaded, and billions of files are shared across the FastTrack and Gnutella networks each month, the probable scope of copyright infringement is staggering.

Grokster and StreamCast concede the infringement in most downloads, and it is uncontested that they are aware that users employ their software primarily to download copyrighted files, even if the decentralized . . . networks fail to reveal which files are being copied, and when. . . .

Grokster and StreamCast are not, however, merely passive recipients of information about infringing use. The record is replete with evidence that from the moment Grokster and StreamCast began to distribute their free software, each one clearly voiced the objective that recipients use it to download copyrighted works, and each took active steps to encourage infringement.

After the notorious file-sharing service, Napster, was sued by copyright holders for facilitation of copyright infringement, StreamCast gave away a software program of a kind known as OpenNap, designed as compatible with the Napster program and open to Napster users for downloading files from other Napster and OpenNap users' computers. Evidence indicates that "it was always [StreamCast's] intent to use [its OpenNap network] to be able to capture e-mail addresses of [its] initial target market so that [it] could promote [its] StreamCast Morpheus interface to them."

* * * * *

StreamCast developed promotional materials to market its service as the best Napster alternative. One proposed advertisement read, "Napster Inc. has announced that it will soon begin charging you a fee. That's if the courts don't order it shut down first. What will you do to get around it?" Another proposed ad touted StreamCast's software as the "#1 alternative

to Napster" and asked "when the lights went off at Napster . . . where did the users go?"

* * * * *

In addition to this evidence of express promotion, marketing, and intent to promote further, the business models employed by Grokster and StreamCast confirm that their principal object was use of their software to download copyrighted works. Grokster and StreamCast receive no revenue from users, who obtain the software itself for nothing. Instead, both companies generate income by selling advertising space, and they stream the advertising to Grokster and Morpheus users while they are employing the programs. As the number of users of each program increases, advertising opportunities become worth more.

Finally, there is no evidence that either company made an effort to filter copyrighted material from users' downloads or otherwise impede the sharing of copyrighted files. . . .

B

The District Court . . . granted summary judgment in favor of Grokster and StreamCast as to any liability arising from distribution of the then current versions of their software. Distributing that software gave rise to no liability in the court's view, because its use did not provide the distributors with actual knowledge of specific acts of infringement.

The Court of Appeals affirmed. In the court's analysis, a defendant was liable as a contributory infringer when it had knowledge of direct infringement and materially contributed to the infringement. But the court read [our decision in] *Sony Corp. of America v. Universal City Studios, Inc.* as holding that distribution of a commercial product capable of substantial noninfringing uses could not give rise to contributory liability for infringement unless the distributor had actual knowledge of specific instances of infringement and failed to act on that knowledge. The fact that the software was capable of substantial noninfringing uses in the Ninth Circuit's view meant that Grokster and StreamCast were not liable, because they had no such actual knowledge, owing to the decentralized architecture of their software. The court also held that Grokster and StreamCast did not materially contribute to their users' infringement because it was the users themselves who searched for, retrieved, and stored the infringing files, with no involvement by the defendants beyond providing the software in the first place.

II
A

* * * * *

The argument for imposing indirect liability in this case is . . . a powerful one, given the number of infringing downloads that occur every day using StreamCast's and Grokster's software. When a widely shared service or product is used to commit infringement, it may be impossible to enforce rights in the protected work effectively against all direct infringers, the only practical alternative being to go against the distributor of the copying device for secondary liability on a theory of contributory or vicarious infringement.

B

*   *   *   *   *

In *Sony Corp. v. Universal City Studios* this Court addressed a claim that secondary liability for infringement can arise from the very distribution of a commercial product. There, the product, novel at the time, was what we know today as the videocassette recorder or VCR. Copyright holders sued Sony as the manufacturer, claiming it was contributorily liable for infringement that occurred when VCR owners taped copyrighted programs because it supplied the means used to infringe, and it had constructive knowledge that infringement would occur. At the trial on the merits, the evidence showed that the principal use of the VCR was for "'time-shifting,'" or taping a program for later viewing at a more convenient time, which the Court found to be a fair, not an infringing, use. There was no evidence that Sony had expressed an object of bringing about taping in violation of copyright or had taken active steps to increase its profits from unlawful taping. Although Sony's advertisements urged consumers to buy the VCR to "'record favorite shows'" or "'build a library'" of recorded programs, neither of these uses was necessarily infringing.

On those facts, with no evidence of stated or indicated intent to promote infringing uses, the only conceivable basis for imposing liability was on a theory of contributory infringement arising from its sale of VCRs to consumers with knowledge that some would use them to infringe. But because the VCR was "capable of commercially significant noninfringing uses," we held the manufacturer could not be faulted solely on the basis of its distribution.

*   *   *   *   *

Because the Circuit [Court of Appeals] found the StreamCast and Grokster software capable of substantial lawful use, it concluded on the basis of its reading of Sony that neither company could be held liable, since there was no showing that their software, being without any central server, afforded them knowledge of specific unlawful uses.

This view of *Sony,* however, was error. . . .

C

[Nothing] in *Sony* requires courts to ignore evidence of intent if there is such evidence. . . . Thus, where evidence goes be-

yond a product's characteristics or the knowledge that it may be put to infringing uses, and shows statements or actions directed to promoting infringement, *Sony's* . . . rule will not preclude liability. The classic case of direct evidence of unlawful purpose occurs when one induces commission of infringement by another, or "entices or persuades another" to infringe, as by advertising.

*   *   *   *   *

[The] inducement rule is a sensible one for copyright. We adopt it here, holding that one who distributes a device with the object of promoting its use to infringe copyright, as shown by clear expression or other affirmative steps taken to foster infringement, is liable for the resulting acts of infringement by third parties. We are, of course, mindful of the need to keep from trenching on regular commerce or discouraging the development of technologies with lawful and unlawful potential. Accordingly, just as *Sony* did not find intentional inducement despite the knowledge of the VCR manufacturer that its device could be used to infringe, mere knowledge of infringing potential or of actual infringing uses would not be enough here to subject a distributor to liability. Nor would ordinary acts incident to product distribution, such as offering customers technical support or product updates, support liability in themselves. The inducement rule, instead, premises liability on purposeful, culpable expression and conduct, and thus does nothing to compromise legitimate commerce or discourage innovation having a lawful promise.

III
A

The only apparent question about treating MGM's evidence as sufficient to withstand summary judgment under the theory of inducement goes to the need on MGM's part to adduce evidence that StreamCast and Grokster communicated an inducing message to their software users.

*   *   *   *   *

Here, the . . . record is replete with evidence that Grokster and StreamCast, unlike the manufacturer and distributor in *Sony*, acted with a purpose to cause copyright violations by use of software suitable for illegal use.

Three features of this evidence of intent are particularly notable. First, each company showed itself to be aiming to satisfy a known source of demand for copyright infringement, the market comprising former Napster users.

*   *   *   *   *

Second, this evidence of unlawful objective is given added significance by MGM's showing that neither company attempted to develop filtering tools or other mechanisms to diminish the infringing activity using their software.

Third, [it] is useful to recall that StreamCast and Grokster make money by selling advertising space, by directing ads to the screens of computers employing their software. . . .

B

In addition to intent to bring about infringement and distribution of a device suitable for infringing use, the inducement theory of course requires evidence of actual infringement by recipients of the device, the software in this case. As the account of the facts indicates, there is evidence of infringement on a gigantic scale, and there is no serious issue of the adequacy of MGM's showing on this point. . . . There is substantial evidence in MGM's favor on all elements of inducement, and summary judgment in favor of Grokster and StreamCast was error.

[Vacated and remanded.]

Questions

1. *a.* Explain how the Court was able to hold software distributors like Grokster liable for the misconduct of others (those who actually used the peer-to-peer networks to download copyrighted materials).
   b. What does the Court mean by "contributory" and "vicarious" copyright infringement?
   c. Why did the Supreme Court overrule the Court of Appeals decision?
2. Has this decision effectively stopped illegal downloading of copyrighted material? Explain.
3. As a consequence of this decision, is peer-to-peer technology now unlawful? Explain.

4. In your judgment do Grokster and other peer-to-peer software distributors have a moral responsibility regarding the unlawful use of their products by third parties? Explain.

AFTERWORD

Concurrently with suing file-sharing facilitators such as Grokster and StreamCast, the recording industry pursued the file sharers as well, 35,000 of them between 2003 and 2008 including many university students.[95] According to one source, in 2006 "college students illegally obtained two-thirds of their music and accounted for 1.3 billion illegal downloads."[96] Under the DMCA, copyright holders can subpoena ISPs, including universities, to obtain the identity of those believed to be infringing. An ISP will incur no liability as long as it responds expeditiously to remove, or disable access to, the copyrighted material when notified of violations. Under the 2008 Higher Education Opportunity Act, every college must adopt procedures to prevent illegal downloads.[97] Thus, many universities have signed contracts with legal providers giving students download rights for modest flat fees. Others have installed filters to prevent illegal downloads.

While record labels were pursuing copyright infringers, some of the largest online music stores changed policies to remove usage restrictions from downloaded files. In mid-2007, both Apple and Amazon.com announced that their music would no longer be locked to certain players or programs. Both have the support of EMI, one of the largest record labels. The restrictions on placing their downloads on multiple computers and mobile devises, restrictions that aren't imposed when a CD is purchased, had long annoyed consumers. It had also drawn the unfavorable attention of EU regulators, who saw it as a form of unfair competition.[98]

Grokster Redux?

In 2007 Viacom sued Google's YouTube video-sharing service alleging willful facilitation of infringement on a massive scale of Viacom's copyrights in such shows as "Comedy Central," "MTV," and "Nickelodeon." Viacom claimed over $1 billion in damages.[99] The court found for YouTube, pointing out that Viacom had availed itself of the DMCA safe harbor, on one day notifying YouTube of 100,000 offending videos. By the next business day, YouTube had removed virtually all of them.[100] After the filing of the suit, YouTube set up an automated system designed to detect and block infringing videos, as well as revenue-sharing arrangements with hundreds of media companies, further reducing the amount of any future infringement.

> Notifying YouTube of 100,000 offending videos.

Trademarks and Domain Names

Trademarks

Words, names, symbols, devices, or combinations thereof that are used to distinguish one seller's products from those of another are called *trademarks* when associated with products (like IBM, Coke, and Pepsi Cola) and *service marks* when associated with service businesses (United Airlines). Having established a trademark (or service mark), the holder can prohibit any unauthorized use of the mark thus ensuring consumers can trust the source of goods they are buying. The mark also protects mark owners by preventing loss of reputation and value, in instances where, for example, the unauthorized product is of poor quality. Mark owners are also protected from an increase in supply that dilutes the product's value. Fundamentally, infringement cannot occur unless the marks are sufficiently similar that consumers could be confused.

The Internet has created new opportunities for confusion and, therefore, potential infringement. Recall the case *Google Inc. v. Louis Vuitton Malletier SA* from Chapter 16. The fundamental issue was whether Google was infringing on Vuitton's trademarks by selling ad space at the top of Google's search results to Vuitton's competitors when individuals use Google's search engine looking for Vuitton products. The European Court of Justice said no. Another company that has had to defend repeated trademark infringement suits is eBay. Individuals sometimes try to sell counterfeit goods on eBay. At times, for some luxury goods manufacturers, the percentage of counterfeits available on the site had been quite high. The issue raised is the extent to which eBay has a duty to weed out counterfeit goods. After being sued, eBay improved its processes to greatly lessen the amount of counterfeits sold, but it is also protected from liability by quickly removing any items when advised by the trademark holder that the goods are counterfeit.

Domain Names

The Internet address for a Web page is called its domain name. The Domain Name System (DNS) for the whole of the Internet is overseen by the Internet Corporation for Assigned Names and Numbers (ICANN), a nonprofit organization with its headquarters in California. Ordinarily, a business engaging in electronic commerce will want to use the simplest form of its name as its domain name. Rights to a domain name are secured simply by being the first to request a name and pay the registration fee. The 1999 Anticybersquatting Consumer Protection Act creates a cause of action if a trademark is infringed by another's registration of a domain name that Web searchers may confuse with that trademark. The Third Circuit has also held that registration of deliberate misspellings of famous marks is a violation of the act.[101]

ICANN has set up an arbitration process for the resolution of domain name disputes. Carmen Electra, Michael Crichton, Kevin Spacey, Pamela Anderson, Celine Dion, and Bruce Springsteen have all used the process to have domain name versions of their names transferred to them, all of which were previously registered by the same Canadian company.[102] [For information on the arbitration services available from the United Nations' World Intellectual Property Organization pursuant to ICANN's domain name arbitration policy, see **http://www.wipo.int/amc/en/domains**]

Taxes

We close this chapter, and the book, with an interesting public policy question raised by the remarkable confusion (and profusion) of the Internet. It is a policy issue, like many discussed in this chapter, that crosses traditional jurisdictional lines—both state boundaries in the United States and national boundaries around the world. Its resolution, either at the national level or at the international level, will require substantial negotiation, compromise and, ultimately, consensus building.

What is the issue? We start with a national example: If you buy a CD on the Internet, your neighborhood retailer will not receive your business and your state and local governments often will not receive sales taxes as they would have if you had made the purchase at a local store. To address that issue and others, the federal government undertook a study of e-commerce tax policy and imposed a moratorium on Internet taxes that was last renewed in October 2007 for an additional seven years. Resolution, however, has proved elusive. In pre-Internet days the Supreme Court had ruled that an out-of-state vendor cannot be required to collect sales taxes for any state in which that vendor does not have some significant presence, including a physical presence.[103] The Court held that it would be an undue burden on interstate commerce for states to be able to require out-of-state vendors to comply with each unique set of state and local sales tax rules. Thus, many states have joined an effort to streamline, simplify, and coordinate their sales tax laws. The idea is that, if state sales taxes are more uniform, the burden on interstate commerce from requiring the compliance of out-of-state vendors will be materially reduced.

As of this writing, of the 44 states that have been involved in the project, 24 have conformed their state laws to the requirements of the negotiated agreement, which became operational in 2005. Participation on the part of vendors is voluntary, but over 1,000 have registered and are now remitting taxes to member states. The primary incentive for voluntary participation is a grant of amnesty for any prior unpaid taxes that might have been owed.[104]

The problem is just as complex, if not more so, on an international scale. Here the issue spans the whole range of taxes, paralleling both our income tax laws and our sales tax laws. In a nutshell, what nation is entitled to tax cross-border transactions? In the international arena, certain key principles were adopted in 1998 by the 34 countries that comprise the Organization for Economic Cooperation and Development (OECD), including the principle that consumption taxes (like our sales taxes) should be collected by the jurisdiction where consumption takes place. But finding workable arrangements to effectuate the general principles has proven elusive. [For more on the OECD, see **http://www.oecd.org**]

Reprise: Who Governs Cyberspace?

We near the end of this chapter examining the same kinds of questions we have raised throughout this book: How much government do we need in our lives? To what extent should government restrain the explosive and stupendously successful cyberspace industry? Is the Internet a bit too much of a "Wild West" environment for the general good? Consider the conflicting views of a leading politician and a powerful corporate executive:

eG8

French president Nicholas Sarkozy called in 2011 for tighter regulation of the Internet. Sarkozy was hosting the first eG8 Forum where global tech leaders such as Facebook's Mark Zuckerberg and eBay CEO John Donahoe met with government policy makers and academics in Paris to discuss Internet public policy issues. Sarkozy said global Internet rules are necessary to address data privacy and security, intellectual property issues, protection of children online, and potential monopoly problems. Sarkozy acknowledged that the rules must not slow growth, and he hailed the Internet's innovative power and its role in the "Arab Spring" (2011 citizen uprisings in Tunisia, Egypt, Libya, and elsewhere that were facilitated by Internet-based communication). Google Executive Chairman Eric Schmidt, on the other hand, was skeptical about government intervention:

> Technology will move faster than governments, so don't legislate before you understand the consequences. You want to tread lightly in regulating brand new industries. . . . [N]obody who is a delegate here would want Internet growth to be slowed by some stupid rule.

Source: Alex Howard, "At the eG8, 20th Century Ideas Clashed with the 21st Century Economy," @Digiphile, May 27, 2011 [**http://radar.oreilly.com/2011/05/eg8-2011-internet-freedom-ip-copyright.html**].

Internet Exercise

Review the materials on privacy issues in this chapter and then log on to the Web site for an Internet vendor that you, or someone you know, has used. Can you find the vendor's privacy policy? Is it easy to find? Is it easy to access, read, and understand? How long is it? How complicated? Do any of its provisions surprise you? What control do you have over the use of your personal information by that vendor? Is that information easy to find? Can you tell when the policy was last updated and what changes were made in it? Has the policy received approval from TRUSTe.org (indicated by a seal displayed on the policy page)? Would you purchase again from this vendor?

Chapter Questions

1. The United Nations has warned that the worldwide growth of e-commerce may constitute a threat to the well-being of the world's developing nations as well as parts of Europe. Explain the U.N. concerns.

2. Psychologists are worried that the Internet will make shopping too easy. Explain their concern.

3. *a.* Germany, France, the Netherlands, and Austria have laws that allow publishing groups to specify the price at which new books are to be sold at retail. That is, anyone selling one of those books at retail in those countries must sell it at the price specified by publishers or they won't be supplied with the books. Why would those countries support price fixing in book sales?

    b. Germany's Rabattgesetz (discount law) requires that all customers pay precisely the same price for a product. Thus an Internet concept like Priceline.com where buyers specify a price they are willing to pay for a product is unlawful. Why would Germany insist on identical pricing for products?

c. How would you expect the Internet to affect those laws forbidding discounts on books and other products?[105]

4. In March 1992, Danish police seized the business records of BAMSE, a computer bulletin board system based in Denmark that sold child pornography over the Internet. The records included information that Mohrbacher, who lived in Paradise, California, had downloaded two graphic interface format (GIF) images from BAMSE in January 1992.

   In March 1993 police executed a search warrant at Mohrbacher's workplace and found, among other images, two files that had been downloaded from BAMSE, one of a nude girl and one of a girl engaged in a sex act with an adult; both girls were under 12. During the execution of the warrant, Mohrbacher was cooperative, confessing that he had downloaded the two images from BAMSE. Mohrbacher was charged with transporting or shipping images by computer as prohibited by 18 U.S.C. 2252(a)(1). Mohrbacher argued that downloading is properly characterized as receiving images by computer, which is proscribed by section 2252(a)(2). He was not charged under (a)(2).

   Should downloading from a computer bulletin board constitute shipping or transporting within the meaning of 18 U.S.C. section 2252(a)(1)? Explain. See *U.S. v. Mohrbacher*, 182 F.3d 1041 (9th Cir. 1999).

5. *a.* Should online bloggers (that is, authors of topical Web logs) be entitled to protection as journalists under the First Amendment with regard to the confidentiality of their sources?

   b. What if those sources have illegally revealed corporate trade secrets?[106]

6. America Online (AOL), an ISP, sued TSF Marketing and Joseph Melle, who founded TSF. AOL claimed that Melle and TSF sent unauthorized bulk email advertisements (spam) to AOL subscribers. The email contained the letters "aol.com" in the headers. AOL claimed that the email totaled some 60 million messages over a 10-month period. Melle allegedly continued the mailings after he was notified in writing by AOL to stop. AOL received over 50,000 complaints from subscribers. AOL claimed, among other things, that Melle had diluted its trademark.[107] The case arose before the passage of the CAN-SPAM Act. Would Melle have been liable under that act? Explain.

7. McLaren was an employee of Microsoft Corporation. In December 1996, Microsoft suspended McLaren's employment pending an investigation into accusations of sexual harassment and "inventory questions." McLaren requested access to his electronic mail to disprove the allegations against him. According to McLaren, he was told he could access his email only by requesting it through company officials and telling them the location of a particular message. By memorandum, McLaren requested that no one tamper with his Microsoft office workstation or his email. McLaren's employment was terminated on December 11, 1996.

   Following the termination of his employment, McLaren filed suit against the company alleging as his sole cause of action a claim for invasion of privacy. In support of his claim, McLaren alleged that, on information and belief, Microsoft had invaded his privacy by "breaking into" some or all of the personal folders maintained on his office computer and releasing the contents of the folders to third parties. According to McLaren, the personal folders were part of a computer application created by Microsoft in which email messages could be stored. Access to the email system was obtained through a network password. Access to personal folders could be additionally restricted by a "personal store" password created by the individual user. McLaren created and used a personal store password to restrict access to his personal folders.

McLaren concedes in his petition that it was possible for Microsoft to "decrypt" his personal store password. McLaren alleges, however, that "[b]y allowing [him] to have a personal store password for his personal folders, [McLaren] manifested and [Microsoft] recognized an expectation that the personal folders would be free from intrusion and interference." McLaren characterizes Microsoft's decrypting or otherwise "breaking in" to his personal folders as an intentional, unjustified, and unlawful invasion of privacy.

Did Microsoft unlawfully invade McLaren's privacy? Explain. See *McLaren v. Microsoft,* 1999 Texas App. LEXIS 4103 (5th Dist., Dallas).

8. Bensusan Restaurant Corporation owns the famous New York City jazz club "The Blue Note," and in 1985 it registered the name as a federal trademark. Since 1980, King has operated a small club in Columbia, Missouri, also named "The Blue Note." Around 1993, Bensusan wrote to King demanding that he discontinue use of "The Blue Note" name. King's attorney responded by saying that Bensusan had no legal right to make the demand. In 1996, King created, in Missouri, a Web site for "The Blue Note," which also contained a hyperlink to the New York club's Web site. Bensusan then sued in the Southern District of New York, alleging Lanham Act and trademark violations, among other things. The New York court dismissed the case for lack of personal jurisdiction. Bensusan appealed. Decide. Explain. See *Bensusan Restaurant Corp. v. King,* 126 F.3d 25 (2d Cir. 1997).

9. Plaintiff Marobie-FL, Inc., released software of copyrighted clip art for use in the fire service industry. Robisheaux administered the National Association of Fire Equipment Distributors (NAFED) Web page. He received the clip art from a source that he could not remember. He placed the clip art on NAFED's Web page. At that point, the clip art could be readily accessed and downloaded by any Web user. Marobie claimed copyright infringement. Among other arguments, NAFED claimed that its display of the clip art constituted a fair use, within the meaning of federal copyright law. Decide. Explain. See *Marobie-FL v. National Ass'n of Fire Equip. Dist.,* 983 F.Supp. 1167 (N.D. Ill. 1997).

10. Journalist John Snell remarked, "Not long ago you couldn't turn around in cyberspace without bumping into a tech geek. Now you're no more than a mouse click away from a lawyer. Attorneys are everywhere."[108] What factors account for the dramatic increase in lawyers addressing Internet issues?

Notes

1. [https://www.cia.gov/library/publications/the-world-factbook/geos/xx.html#top].
2. Norimitsu Onishi, "Debate on Internet's Limits Grows in Indonesia," *The New York Times,* April 19, 2010 [http://www.nytimes.com/].
3. L. Gordon Crovits, "What's Chinese for Limited Government?," *The Wall Street Journal,* July 28, 2009 [http://online.wsj.com/].
4. Duncan B. Hollis, "E-War Rules of Engagement," *Los Angeles Times,* October 8, 2007 [http://www.latimes.com/].

5. Anick Jesdanun, "As Internet Turns 40, Barriers Run Contrary to Creators' Aims," *The Des Moines Register,* August 31, 2009, p. 1A.

6. Thomas L. Friedman, "The Great Iceland Meltdown," *The New York Times,* October 19, 2008 [**http://www.nytimes.com/**]. Although this statement was offered in a somewhat different context—the financial crisis of 2008—it is equally applicable to this discussion of the Internet.

7. Jason Hiner, "Why Google Buzz Confirmed Our Two Worst Fears about Google," *TechRepublic,* February 22, 2010 [**http://blogs.techrepublic.com**].

8. Mark Hachman, "Report: African-American Adoption of Broadband Surges," *PCMag,* August 11, 2010 [**http://www.pcmag.com**].

9. David Sarno, "Broadband Access in U.S. Still Mainly for the Well-Off, Pew Finds," *Los Angeles Times,* November 24, 2010 [**http://www.latimes.com/**].

10. Cecilia Kang, "One Step Off the Superhighway," *The Washington Post,* February 28, 2009, p. D01.

11. Daniel Sorid, "Writing the Web's Future in Numerous Languages," *The New York Times,* December 31, 2008 [**http://www.nytimes.com/**].

12. Brad Stone and Miguel Helft, "One Internet Village, Divided: In Developing Countries, Web Grows without Profit," *The New York Times,* April 27, 2009 [**http://www.nytimes.com/**].

13. Edward Wyatt, "Court Rules against F.C.C. in 'Net Neutrality' Case," *The New York Times,* April 6, 2010 [**http://www.nytimes.com/**].

14. Amy Schatz, "U.S. as Traffic Cop in Web Fight," *The Wall Street Journal,* September 19, 2009 [**http://online.wsj.com/**].

15. Kim Hart, "Groups to Press FCC to Prohibit Blocking of Text Messages," *The Washington Post,* December 11, 2007, p. D03.

16. Jamelle Bouie, "The FCC Pleases No One" [**http://www.prospect.org**], December 23, 2010.

17. *Comcast Corp. v. F.C.C.,* 600 F.3d 642 (D.C. Cir. 2010).

18. Amy Goodman, "Obama Gives Gift to AT&T, Other Giants," *Waterloo/Cedar Falls Courier,* December 27, 2010, p. A5.

19. "Ex-CompuServe Chief's Conviction Overturned; German Case Involved Child Porn Sites," *Houston Chronicle,* November 18, 1999, p. 3. The head of CompuServe Germany was convicted in 1998 of violating German law by failing to block CompuServe's customers' access to child pornography Web sites. At the time the only technical way for CompuServe to comply was to block all of its worldwide users from access. The conviction was reversed in 1999.

20. See *Revell v. Lidov,* 317 F.3d 467 (5th Cir. 2002). Lidov posted an article he wrote on the "bombing of Pan Am Flight 103, which exploded over Lockerbie, Scotland, in 1988. The article alleges that a broad politically motivated conspiracy among senior members of the Reagan administration lay behind their willful failure to stop the bombing despite clear advance warnings. Furthermore, Lidov charged that the government proceeded to cover up its receipt of advance warning. . . . Specifically, the article singles out Oliver "Buck" Revell, then Associate Deputy Director of the FBI, for severe criticism, accusing him of complicity in the conspiracy and cover-up." The article was posted on an Internet bulletin board maintained by Columbia University's School of Journalism. "At the time he wrote the article, Lidov had never been to Texas, except possibly to change planes, or conducted business there, and was apparently unaware that Revell then resided in Texas." "Columbia, since it began keeping records, never received more than 20 Internet subscriptions to the *Columbia Journalism Review* from Texas residents." The Fifth Circuit found that neither general nor specific jurisdiction existed in the Texas courts.

21. *Mink v. AAAA Development,* 190 F.3d 333 (5th Cir. 1999).

22. See, for example, *Pavlovich v. DVD Copy Control Association*. A California appeals court held that a Texas resident was subject to California's jurisdiction for the knowing posting of trade secrets of a California company on an Indiana Web site (91 Cal. App. 4th 409, 109 Cal. Rptr.2d 909 [Cal. Ct. App. 2001]). But the California Supreme Court reversed (58 P.3d 2 [Cal. 2002]). See also *Gator.com Corp. v. L.L. Bean, Inc.,* where the district court held that L.L. Bean could not be sued in California where it had no stores or agents, although it did sell merchandise to California residents through its Web site (2001 U.S. Dist. LEXIS 19373 [N.D. Cal. 2001]). A three-judge panel of the Ninth Circuit reversed, finding in part that the volume of Internet business done by L.L. Bean with California residents made it subject to California's jurisdiction (341 F.3d 1072 [9th Cir. 2003]). That decision was vacated, however, when the Ninth Circuit decided to rehear the case en banc (366 F.3d 789 [9th Cir. 2004]). After oral argument on the rehearing, however, Gator.com and L.L. Bean settled their substantive dispute, and thus the Ninth Circuit dismissed the appeal because of the lack of a continuing case or controversy (398 F.3d 1125 [2005]).

23. Ryan Davis, "7th Circ. Lets Bulgarian Dating Site Off Hook in IP Row," *Law 360,* April 27, 2011 [**http://www.law360.com**].

24. Rachel Donadio, "Larger Threat Is Seen in Google Case," *The New York Times,* February 25, 2010 [**http://www.nytimes.com/**].

25. Stephan Wilske and Teresa Schiller, "International Jurisdiction in Cyberspace: Which States May Regulate the Internet?" *Federal Communications Law Journal* 50 (December 1997), p. 117.

26. 433 F.3d 1199 (9th Cir. 2006).

27. 126 S.Ct. 2332 (2006).

28. See, for example, *Ford Motor Co. v. Lane,* 67 F.Supp.2d 745 (E.D. Mich. 1999).

29. "42% of Youths Report Exposure to Porn on Web," *The Des Moines Register,* February 5, 2007, p. 5A.

30. *Reno v. ACLU,* 521 U.S. 844 (1997).

31. *ACLU v. Gonzales,* 478 F.Supp. 775 (E.D. Pa. 2007); *Mukasey v. ACLU,* 139 S.Ct. 1032 (2009).

32. *Ashcroft v. Free Speech Coalition,* 122 S.Ct. 1389 (2002).

33. Christine Arena, "Child Porn too Big for Law Enforcement? Microsoft Steps In," *Christian Science Monitor,* June 13, 2010 [**http://www.csmonitor.com/**].

34. *McIntyre v. Ohio Elections Comm'n,* 514 U.S. 334, 342 (1995).

35. Id.

36. *In re Anonymous Online Speakers v. U.S. Dist. Ct. for the Dist. of Nevada, Reno,* 2011 WL 61635 (9th Cir. 2011).

37. Brad Stone, "Authorities Shut Down Spam Ring," *The New York Times,* October 15, 2008 [**http://www.nytimes.com/**].

38. Brad Stone, "If You Run a Red Light, Will Everyone Know?" *The New York Times,* August 3, 2008 [**http://www.nytimes.com/**].

39. Jim Stanton, "From Where Your House Is to How Much You Paid for It—It's All on the Internet for Anyone to See," *Waterloo/Cedar Falls Courier,* August 27, 2000, p. A1.

40. Kate Murphy, "Web Photos that Reveal Secrets, Like Where You Live," *The New York Times,* August 11, 2010 [**http://www.nytimes.com/**].

41. Stephanie Clifford, "Web Coupons Know Lots about You, and They Tell," *The New York Times,* April 16, 2010 [**http://www.nytimes.com/**].

42. Jessica E. Vascellaro, "Web sites Rein in Tracking Tools," *The Wall Street Journal,* November 6, 2010 [**http://online.wsj.com/**].

43. Julia Angwin and Tom McGinty, "Sites Feed Personal Details to New Tracking Industry," *The Wall Street Journal,* July 30, 2010 [**http://online.wsj.com/**].

44. Editorial, "Watching Your Every Move," *The New York Times,* June 13, 2007 [**http://www.nytimes.com/**]; Sam Diaz, "Google to Tighten Privacy," *The Washington Post,* March 15, 2007, p. D3.

45. Jeffrey Rosen, "The Web Means the End of Forgetting," *The New York Times,* July 19, 2010 [**http://www.nytimes.com/**].

46. All of the statements from Amazon come from pages reached through the Privacy Notice link at the bottom of its Web pages. It was accessed on May 27, 2011.

47. Miguel Helft and John Markoff, "In Rebuke of China, Focus Falls on Cybersecurity," *The New York Times,* January 14, 2010 [**http://www.nytimes.com/**].

48. *Stengart v. Loving Care Agency,* 990 A.2d 650 (N.J. 2010).

49. *City of Ontario v. Quon,* 130 S.Ct. 2619 (2010).

50. Dionne Searcey, "Some Courts Raise Bar on Reading Employee Email," *The Wall Street Journal,* November 19, 2009 [**http://online.wsj.com/**].

51. Pui-Wing Tam, Erin White, Nick Wingfield, and Kris Maher, "Snooping E-Mail by Software Is Now a Workplace Norm," *The Wall Street Journal,* March 9, 2005, p. B1.

52. *Blakey v. Continental Airlines,* 751 A.2d 538 (Sup. Ct. N.J. 2001).

53. "Policy Framework for Protecting Consumer Privacy Online while Supporting Innovation" [**http://www.commerce.gov/blog/2010/12/16/released-policy-framework-protecting-consumer-privacy-online-while-supporting-innova**], February 8, 2011.

54. "FTC Staff Issues Privacy Report, Offers Framework for Consumers, Businesses, and Policymakers" [**http://www.ftc.gov/opa/2010/12/privacyreport.shtm**], December 1, 2010.

55. Amy E. Worlton, "Threat of Legislation Drives Self-Regulation of 'Behavioral Advertising,'" *Association of Corporate Counsel,* October 6, 2008 [**http://www.lexology.com**].

56. Glenn Simpson, "U.S., EU Negotiators Reach Agreement on Electronic-Commerce Privacy Rules," *The Wall Street Journal,* March 15, 2000, p. B4.

57. Carter Manny, "Privacy Controls on Trans-Border Flows of Personal Data from Europe," *Business Law Review,* Spring 2001, pp. 101–120.

58. "U.S., Europe Move to Net Privacy Pact," *Waterloo/Cedar Falls Courier,* June 5, 2000, p. B5.

59. Eric Pfanner, "E.U. Says It Will Overhaul Privacy Regulations," *The New York Times,* November 4, 2010 [**http://www.nytimes.com/**].

60. Cecilia Kang, "Satisfied with Google's Promise to Restrain Street View, FTC Drops Privacy-Breach Probe," *The Washington Post,* October 27, 2010 [**www.washngtonpost.com/**]; Raphael Minder, "Google Sued in Spain Over Data Collection," *The New York Times,* August 17, 2010 [**http://www.nytimes.com/**]; Choe Sang-Hun, "Police in South Korea Raid Google's Office," *The New York Times,* August 10, 2010 [**http://www.nytimes.com/**]; and Jaeyeon Woo, "Google's Korea Office Raided," *The Wall Street Journal,* August 10, 2010 [**http://online.wsj.com/**].

61. Tom Alex, "Stolen Laptop Sends Up a Flare," *The Des Moines Register,* October 18, 2005, p. 1A.

62. *US v. Farraj,* 142 F.Supp.2d 484 (S.D. N.Y. 2001).

63. Spencer E. Ante and Brian Grow, "Meet the Hackers," *BusinessWeek,* May 29, 2006, p. 58.

64. John Markoff, "Defying Experts, Rogue Computer Code Still Lurks," *The New York Times,* August 27, 2009 [**http://www.nytimes.com/**].

65. Editorial, "Wake Up Your Computer," *The New York Times,* January 12, 2007 [**http://www.nytimes.com**].

66. Susanna Hamner, "Pay-Per-Click Web Advertisers Combat Costly Fraud," *The New York Times,* May 13, 2009 [**http://www.nytimes.com/**].

67. Jeanette Borzo, "Something's Phishy," *The Wall Street Journal,* November 15, 2004, p. R8.

68. Kim Hart, "Phish-Hooked," *The Washington Post,* July 16, 2006, p. F1.

69. "Former Worker Gets 4 years for Cyberstalking," *Chicago Tribune,* March 18, 2005, p. 13.

70. "The 1999 Report on Cyberstalking: A New Challenge for Law Enforcement and Industry" [**http://www.cybercrime.gov/cyberstalking.htm**].

71. Jan Hoffman, "Online Bullies Pull Schools into the Fray," *The New York Times,* June 27, 2010 [**http://www.nytimes.com/**].

72. Christopher Maag, "A Hoax Turned Fatal Draws Anger but No Charges," *The New York Times,* November 28, 2007 [**http://www.nytimes.com/**].

73. [**http://www.cyberbullying.us/Bullying_and_Cyberbullying_Laws.pdf**].

74. [**http://conventions.coe.int/Treaty/Commun/ChercheSig.asp?NT=185&CM=& DF=&CL=ENG**].

75. Thomas Weber, "Treaty on Cybercrime Flew under the Radar Despite Potential Risks," *The Wall Street Journal,* December 3, 2001, p. B1.

76. Rachel Donadio, "Larger Threat Is Seen in Google Case."

77. Alan S. Reid and Nic Ryder, "The Case of Richard Tomlinson: The Spy Who E-Mailed Me," *Information & Communications Technology Law* 9 (March 2000), p. 61.

78. "Ex-CompuServe Chief's Conviction Overturned," p.3.

79. P. Liddell, M. Moore, and R. Moore, "Just Sign on the Electronic Line," *Journal of the Academy of Marketing Science,* Winter 2001, p. 110.

80. [**http://www.nccusl.org/Act.aspx?title=Computer%20Information%20Transactions% 20Act**].

81. 732 A.2d 528 (N.J. Super. 1999).

82. Ronald J. Mann and Travis Siebeneicher, "Just One Click: The Reality of Internet Retail Contracting," *University of Texas Law, Law and Econ Research Paper* No. 104, May 2007 [**http://ssrn.com/abstract=988788**].

83. Louise Story, "Online Marketers Joining Internet Privacy Efforts," *The New York Times,* October 31, 2007 [**http://www.nytimes.com/**].

84. Matt Richtel and Brad Stone, "Doll Web Sites Drive Girls to Stay Home and Play," *The New York Times,* June 6, 2007 [**http://www.nytimes.com/**].

85. Frank Ahrens, "'Puppets' Emerge as Internet's Effective, and Deceptive, Salesmen," *The Washington Post,* October 7, 2006, p. D1.

86. See Bill Bane, "Spyware Taking Toll on Computer Firms, Users," *Waterloo/Cedar Falls Courier,* November 1, 2004, p. B6; Michael Totty, "Pesky Pop-Up Ads Go Mainstream, as 'Adware' Gains Acceptance," *The Wall Street Journal,* June 22, 2004, p. B1.

87. Anna Mathews, "U.S. Will Give Web Patents More Scrutiny," *The Wall Street Journal,* March 29, 2000, p. B1.

88. 130 S.Ct. 3218 (2010).

89. Jenna Wortham, "In Ruling on iPhones, Apple Loses a Bit of Its Grip," *The New York Times,* July 26, 2010 [**http://www.nytimes.com/**].

90. Brad Stone, "Amazon Faces a Fight Over Its E-Books," *The New York Times,* July 27, 2009 [**http://www.nytimes.com/**].

91. "Federal Court Sides with Eminem in Royalty Dispute; Record Business Does Not Implode," *The Wall Street Journal,* September 3, 2010 [**http://online.wsj.com/**].

92. Claire Cain Miller, "Book Ruling Cuts Options for Google," *The New York Times,* March 23, 2011 [**http://www.nytimes.com/**]; Max Colchester and Christopher Emsden, "In Europe, Book-Scanning Efforts Feel Their Way into New Territory," *The Wall Street Journal,* March 11, 2010 [**http://www.nytimes.com/**]; and Matthew Saltmarsh, "Google Loses in French Copyright Case," *The New York Times,* December 19, 2009 [**http://www.nytimes.com/**].

93. *A&M Records, Inc. v. Napster, Inc.,* 284 F.3d 1091 (9th Cir. 2002); *A&M Records, Inc. v. Napster, Inc.,* 239 F.3d 1004 (9th Cir. 2001).

94. *Metro-Goldwyn-Mayer Studios, Inc. v. Grokster, Ltd.,* 380 F.3d 1154 (9th Cir. 2004).

95. Sarah McBride and Ethan Smith, "Music Industry to Abandon Mass Suits," *The Wall Street Journal,* December 19, 2008 [**http://online.wsj.com/**].

96. Amy Brittain, "Universities Strike Back in Battle over Illegal Downloads," *Christian Science Monitor,* June 18, 2007 [**http://www.csmonitor.com/**].

97. "Hey College Kids: The Rules Have Changed on Downloading," *The Wall Street Journal,* August 4, 2010 [**http://online.wsj.com/**].

98. Rob Peoraro, "The Sound of Copy Restrictions Crashing," *The Washington Post,* May 17, 2007, p. D1; Michelle Quinn, Alana Semuels, and Dawn C. Chmielewski, "Apple Seeks to Unchain Melodies," *Los Angeles Times,* February 7, 2007 [**http://www.latimes.com/**].

99. Miguel Helft, "Judge Sides with Google in Viacom Video Suit," *The New York Times,* June 23, 2010 [**http://www.nytimes.com/**].

100. *Viacom International Inc. v. YouTube, Inc.,* 718 F.Supp.2d 514 (S.D. N.Y. 2010).

101. *Shields v. Zuccarini,* 254 F.3d 476 (3d Cir. 2001).

102. "People: News/Gossip/Scoops," *St. Louis Post–Dispatch,* January 17, 2004, p. 41.

103. *Quill Corporation v. North Dakota,* 504 U.S. 298 (1992).

104. Michelle Blackson, "Closing the Online Tax Loophole," *State Legislatures* 34, Issue 4 (April 2008), p. 24.

105. See Neal Boudette, "In Europe, Surfing a Web of Red Tape," *The Wall Street Journal,* October 29, 1999, p. B1.

106. Compare *Apple Computer v. Doe,* 205 WL 578641 (Cal. Superior 2005) (requiring disclosure) with *O'Grady v. Superior Ct.,* 44 Cal Rptr 3d 72 (Cal. App. 2006) (reversing on appeal).

107. See *America Online, Inc. v. IMS,* 24 F.Supp.2d 548 (E.D. Va. 1998).

108. John Snell, "Lawyers Drawn to Unsettled Internet; Lots of Legal Issues, Large and Small, Must Be Sorted Out," *Minneapolis Star Tribune,* November 29, 1999, p. 6D.

The Constitution of the United States of America

Preamble

We the People of the United States, in Order to form a more perfect Union, establish Justice, insure domestic Tranquility, provide for the common defence, promote the general Welfare, and secure the Blessings of Liberty to ourselves and our Posterity, do ordain and establish this Constitution for the United States of America.

Article I

Section 1. All legislative Powers herein granted shall be vested in a Congress of the United States, which shall consist of a Senate and House of Representatives.

Section 2. (1) The House of Representatives shall be composed of Members chosen every second Year by the People of the several States, and the Electors in each State shall have the Qualifications requisite for Electors of the most numerous Branch of the State Legislature.

(2) No Person shall be a Representative who shall not have attained to the Age of twenty-five Years, and been seven Years a Citizen of the United States, and who shall not, when elected, be an Inhabitant of that State in which he shall be chosen.

(3) Representatives and direct Taxes shall be apportioned among the several States which may be included within this Union, according to their respective Numbers, which shall be determined by adding to the whole Number of free Persons, including those bound to Service for a Term of Years, and excluding Indians not taxed, three fifths of all other Persons.[1] The actual Enumeration shall be made within three Years after the first Meeting of the Congress of the United States, and within every subsequent Term of ten Years, in such Manner as they shall by Law direct. The Number of Representatives shall not exceed one for every thirty Thousand, but each State shall have at Least one Representative; and until such enumeration shall be made, the State of New Hampshire shall be entitled to chuse three, Massachusetts eight, Rhode Island and Providence Plantations one, Connecticut five, New York six, New Jersey four, Pennsylvania eight, Delaware one, Maryland six, Virginia ten, North Carolina five, South Carolina five, and Georgia three.

[1]Refer to the Fourteenth Amendment.

(4) When vacancies happen in the Representation from any State, the Executive Authority thereof shall issue Writs of Election to fill such Vacancies.

(5) The House of Representatives shall chuse their Speaker and other Officers; and shall have the sole Power of Impeachment.

Section 3. (1) The Senate of the United States shall be composed of two Senators from each State, chosen by the Legislature thereof,[2] for six Years; and each Senator shall have one Vote.

(2) Immediately after they shall be assembled in Consequence of the first Election, they shall be divided as equally as may be into three Classes. The Seats of the Senators of the first Class shall be vacated at the Expiration of the Second Year, of the second Class at the Expiration of the fourth Year, and of the third Class at the Expiration of the sixth Year, so that one third may be chosen every second Year; and if Vacancies happen by Resignation, or otherwise, during the Recess of the Legislature of any State, the Executive thereof may make temporary Appointments until the next Meeting of the Legislature, which shall then fill such Vacancies.[3]

(3) No Person shall be a Senator who shall not have attained to the Age of thirty Years, and been nine Years a Citizen of the United States, and who shall not, when elected, be an Inhabitant of that State for which he shall be chosen.

(4) The Vice President of the United States shall be President of the Senate, but shall have no Vote, unless they be equally divided.

(5) The Senate shall chuse their other Officers, and also a President pro tempore, in the Absence of the Vice President, or when he shall exercise the Office of President of the United States.

(6) The Senate shall have the sole Power to try all Impeachments. When sitting for that Purpose, they shall be on Oath or Affirmation. When the President of the United States is tried, the Chief Justice shall preside: And no Person shall be convicted without the Concurrence of two thirds of the Members present.

(7) Judgment in Cases of Impeachment shall not extend further than to removal from Office, and disqualification to hold and enjoy any Office of honor, Trust, or Profit under the United States: but the Party convicted shall nevertheless be liable and subject to Indictment, Trial, Judgment, and Punishment, according to Law.

Section 4. (1) The Times, Places and Manner of holding Elections for Senators and Representatives, shall be prescribed in each State by the Legislature thereof; but the Congress may at any time by Law make or alter such Regulations, except as to the Places of chusing Senators.

(2) The Congress shall assemble at least once in every year, and such Meeting shall be on the first Monday in December, unless they shall by Law appoint a different Day.[4]

Section 5. (1) Each House shall be the Judge of the Elections, Returns, and Qualifications of its own Members, and a Majority of each shall constitute a Quorum to do Business; but a smaller Number may adjourn from day to day, and may be authorized to compel the Attendance of absent Members, in such Manner, and under such Penalties as each House may provide.

[2]Refer to the Seventeenth Amendment.
[3]Ibid.
[4]Refer to the Twentieth Amendment.

(2) Each House may determine the Rules of its Proceedings, punish its Members for disorderly Behavior, and, with the Concurrence of two thirds, expel a Member.

(3) Each House shall keep a Journal of its Proceedings, and from time to time publish the same, excepting such Parts as may in their Judgment require Secrecy; and the Yeas and Nays of the Members of either House on any question shall, at the Desire of one fifth of those Present, be entered on the Journal.

(4) Neither House, during the Session of Congress, shall, without the Consent of the other, adjourn for more than three days, nor to any other Place than that in which the two Houses shall be sitting.

Section 6. (1) The Senators and Representatives shall receive a Compensation for their Services, to be ascertained by Law, and paid out of the Treasury of the United States. They shall in all Cases, except Treason, Felony and Breach of the Peace, be privileged from Arrest during their Attendance at the Session of their respective Houses, and in going to and returning from the same; and for any Speech or Debate in either House, they shall not be questioned in any other Place.

(2) No Senator or Representative shall, during the Time for which he was elected, be appointed to any civil Office under the Authority of the United States, which shall have been created, or the Emoluments whereof shall have been encreased during such time; and no Person holding any Office under the United States, shall be a Member of either House during his Continuance in Office.

Section 7. (1) All Bills for raising Revenue shall originate in the House of Representatives; but the Senate may propose or concur with Amendments as on other Bills.

(2) Every Bill which shall have passed the House of Representatives and the Senate, shall, before it becomes a Law, be presented to the President of the United States; If he approve he shall sign it, but if not he shall return it, with his Objections to the House in which it shall have originated, who shall enter the Objections at large on their Journal, and proceed to reconsider it. If after such Reconsideration two thirds of that House shall agree to pass the Bill, it shall be sent together with the Objections, to the other House, by which it shall likewise be reconsidered, and if approved by two thirds of that House, it shall become a Law. But in all such Cases the Votes of both Houses shall be determined by yeas and Nays, and the Names of the Persons voting for and against the Bill shall be entered on the Journal of each House respectively. If any Bill shall not be returned by the President within ten Days (Sundays excepted) after it shall have been presented to him, the Same shall be a Law, in like Manner as if he had signed it, unless the Congress by their Adjournment prevent its Return in which Case it shall not be a Law.

(3) Every Order, Resolution, or Vote, to Which the Concurrence of the Senate and House of Representatives may be necessary (except on a question of Adjournment) shall be presented to the President of the United States; and before the same shall take Effect, shall be approved by him, or being disapproved by him, shall be repassed by two thirds of the Senate and House of Representatives, according to the Rules and Limitations prescribed in the Case of a Bill.

Section 8. (1) The Congress shall have Power To lay and collect Taxes, Duties, Imposts and Excises, to pay the Debts and provide for the common Defence and general Welfare of the United States; but all Duties, Imposts and Excises shall be uniform throughout the United States;

(2) To borrow money on the credit of the United States;

(3) To regulate Commerce with foreign Nations, and among the several States, and with the Indian Tribes;

(4) To establish a uniform Rule of Naturalization, and uniform Laws on the subject of Bankruptcies throughout the United States;

(5) To coin Money, regulate the Value thereof, and of foreign Coin, and fix the Standard of Weights and Measures;

(6) To provide for the Punishment of counterfeiting the Securities and current Coin of the United States;

(7) To Establish Post Offices and Post Roads;

(8) To promote the Progress of Science and useful Arts, by securing for limited Times to Authors and Inventors the exclusive Right to their respective Writings and Discoveries;

(9) To constitute Tribunals inferior to the Supreme Court;

(10) To define and punish Piracies and Felonies committed on the high Seas, and Offenses against the Law of Nations;

(11) To declare War, grant Letters of Marque and Reprisal, and make Rules concerning Captures on Land and Water;

(12) To raise and support Armies, but no Appropriation of Money to that Use shall be for a longer Term than two Years;

(13) To provide and maintain a Navy;

(14) To make Rules for the Government and Regulation of the land and naval Forces;

(15) To provide for calling forth the Militia to execute the Laws of the Union, suppress Insurrections and repel Invasions;

(16) To provide for organizing, arming, and disciplining, the Militia, and for governing such Part of them as may be employed in the Service of the United States, reserving to the States respectively, the Appointment of the Officers, and the Authority of training the Militia according to the discipline prescribed by Congress;

(17) To exercise exclusive Legislation in all Cases whatsoever, over such District (not exceeding ten Miles square) as may, by Cession of particular States, and the Acceptance of Congress, become the Seat of the Government of the United States, and to exercise like Authority over all Places purchased by the Consent of the Legislature of the State in which the Same shall be, for the Erection of Forts, Magazines, Arsenals, dock-Yards, and other needful Buildings;—And

(18) To make all Laws which shall be necessary and proper for carrying into Execution the foregoing Powers, and all other Powers vested by this Constitution in the Government of the United States, or in any Department or Officer thereof.

Section 9. (1) The Migration or Importation of Such Persons as any of the States now existing shall think proper to admit, shall not be prohibited by the Congress prior to the Year one thousand eight hundred and eight, but a Tax or duty may be imposed on such Importation, not exceeding ten dollars for each Person.

(2) The privilege of the Writ of Habeas Corpus shall not be suspended, unless when in Cases of Rebellion or Invasion the public Safety may require it.

(3) No Bill of Attainder or ex post facto Law shall be passed.

(4) No Capitation, or other direct, Tax shall be laid, unless in proportion to the Census or Enumeration herein before directed to the taken.[5]

---

[5]Refer to the Sixteenth Amendment.

(5) No Tax or Duty shall be laid on Articles exported from any state.

(6) No Preference shall be given by any Regulation of Commerce or Revenue to the Ports of one State over those of another; nor shall Vessels bound to, or from, one State be obliged to enter, clear, or pay Duties in another.

(7) No money shall be drawn from the Treasury, but in Consequence of Appropriations made by Law; and a regular Statement and Account of the Receipts and Expenditures of all public Money shall be published from time to time.

(8) No Title of Nobility shall be granted by the United States; And no person holding any Office of Profit or Trust under them, shall, without the Consent of the Congress, accept of any present, Emolument, Office or Title, of any kind whatever, from any King, Prince, or foreign State.

Section 10. (1) No State shall enter into any Treaty, Alliance, or Confederation; grant Letters of Marque and Reprisal; coin Money; emit Bills of Credit; make any Thing but gold and silver Coin a Tender in Payment of Debts; pass any Bill of Attainder, ex post facto Law, or Law impairing the Obligation of Contracts, or grant any Title of Nobility.

(2) No State shall, without the Consent of the Congress, lay any Imposts or Duties on Imports or Exports, except what may be absolutely necessary for executing its inspection Laws: and the net Produce of all Duties and Imposts, laid by any State on Imports or Exports, shall be for the Use of the Treasury of the United States; and all such Laws shall be subject to the Revision and Controul of the Congress.

(3) No State shall, without the Consent of Congress, lay any Duty of Tonnage, keep Troops, or Ships of War in time of Peace, enter into any Agreement or Compact with another State, or with a foreign Power, or engage in War, unless actually invaded, or in such imminent Danger as will not admit of delay.

Article II

Section 1. (1) The executive Power shall be vested in a President of the United States of America. He shall hold his Office during the Term of four Years, and, together with the Vice President, chosen for the same Term, be elected as follows:

(2) Each State shall appoint, in such Manner as the Legislature thereof may direct, a Number of Electors, equal to the whole Number of Senators and Representatives to which the State may be entitled in the Congress; but no Senator or Representative, or Person holding an Office of Trust or Profit under the United States, shall be appointed an Elector.

(3) The Electors shall meet in their respective States, and vote by Ballot for two Persons, of whom one at least shall not be an Inhabitant of the same State with themselves. And they shall make a list of all the Persons voted for, and of the Number of Votes for each; which List they shall sign and certify, and transmit sealed to the Seat of the Government of the United States, directed to the President of the Senate. The President of the Senate shall, in the Presence of the Senate and House of Representatives, open all the Certificates, and the Votes shall then be counted. The Person having the greatest Number of Votes shall be the President, if such Number be a Majority of the whole Number of Electors appointed; and if there be more than one who have such Majority, and have an equal Number of Votes, then the House of Representatives shall immediately chuse by Ballot one of them for President; and if no Person have a Majority, then from the five highest on the List the said House shall in like Manner chuse the President. But in chusing the President, the Votes

shall be taken by States, the Representation from each State have one Vote; A quorum for this Purpose shall consist of a Member or Members from two thirds of the States, and a Majority of all the States shall be necessary to a Choice. In every Case, after the Choice of the President, the Person having the greater Number of Votes of the Electors shall be the Vice President. But if there should remain two or more who have equal Votes, the Senate shall chuse from them by Ballot the Vice President.[6]

(4) The Congress may determine the Time of chusing the Electors, and the Day on which they shall give their Votes; which Day shall be the same throughout the United States.

(5) No person except a natural born Citizen, or a Citizen of the United States, at the time of the Adoption of this Constitution, shall be eligible to the Office of President; neither shall any Person be eligible to that Office who shall not have attained to the Age of thirty-five Years, and been fourteen Years a Resident within the United States.

(6) In case of the removal of the President from Office, or of his Death, Resignation or Inability to discharge the Powers and Duties of the said Office, the Same shall devolve on the Vice President, and the Congress may by Law provide for the Case of Removal, Death, Resignation or Inability, both of the President and Vice President, declaring what Officer shall then act as President, and such Officer shall act accordingly, until the Disability be removed, or a President shall be elected.[7]

(7) The President shall, at stated Times, receive for his Services, a Compensation, which shall neither be encreased nor diminished during the Period for which he shall have been elected, and he shall not receive within that Period any other Emolument from the United States, or any of them.

(8) Before he enter on the Execution of his Office, he shall take the following Oath or Affirmation: "I do solemnly swear (or affirm) that I will faithfully execute the Office of President of the United States, and will to the best of my Ability, preserve, protect, and defend the Constitution of the United States."

Section 2. (1) The President shall be Commander in Chief of the Army and Navy of the United States, and of the militia of the several States, when called into the actual Service of the United States; he may require the Opinion, in writing, of the principal Officer in each of the executive Departments, upon any Subject relating to the Duties of their respective Offices, and he shall have Power to grant Reprieves and Pardons for Offenses against the United States, except in Cases of Impeachment.

(2) He shall have Power, by and with the Advice and Consent of the Senate, to make Treaties, provided two thirds of the Senators present concur; and he shall nominate, and by and with the Advice and Consent of the Senate, shall appoint Ambassadors, other public Ministers and Consuls, Judges of the supreme Court, and all other Officers of the United States, whose Appointments are not herein otherwise provided for, and which shall be established by Law; but the Congress may by Law vest the Appointment of such inferior Officers, as they think proper, in the President alone, in the Courts of Law, or in the Heads of Departments.

[6]Refer to the Twelfth Amendment.
[7]Refer to the Twenty-Fifth Amendment

(3) The President shall have Power to fill up all Vacancies that may happen during the Recess of the Senate, by granting Commissions which shall expire at the End of their next Session.

Section 3. He shall from time to time give to the Congress Information of the State of the Union, and recommend to their Consideration such Measures as he shall judge necessary and expedient; he may, on extraordinary Occasions, convene both Houses, or either of them, and in Case of Disagreement between them, with Respect to the Time of Adjournment, he may adjourn them to such Time as he shall think proper; he shall receive Ambassadors and other public Ministers; he shall take Care that the Laws be faithfully executed, and shall Commission all the Officers of the United States.

Section 4. The President, Vice President and all civil Officers of the United States, shall be removed from Office on Impeachment for, and Conviction of, Treason, Bribery, or other high Crimes and Misdemeanors.

Article III

Section 1. The judicial Power of the United States, shall be vested in one supreme Court, and in such inferior Courts as the Congress may from time to time ordain and establish. The Judges, both of the supreme and inferior Courts, shall hold their Offices during good Behaviour, and shall, at stated Times, receive for their Services a Compensation, which shall not be diminished during their Continuance in Office.

Section 2. (1) The judicial Power shall extend to all Cases, in Law and Equity, arising under this Constitution, the Laws of the United States, and Treaties made, or which shall be made, under their Authority;—to all Cases affecting Ambassadors, other public Ministers and Consuls;—to all Cases of admiralty and maritime Jurisdiction;—to Controversies to which the United States shall be a Party;—to Controversies between two or more States;— between a State and Citizens of another State,[8]—between Citizens of different states;— between Citizens of the same State claiming Lands under the Grants of different States, and between a State, or the Citizens thereof, and foreign States, Citizens or Subjects.

(2) In all Cases affecting Ambassadors, other public Ministers and Consuls, and those in which a State shall be a Party, the supreme Court shall have original Jurisdiction. In all the other Cases before mentioned, the supreme Court shall have appellate Jurisdiction, both as to Law and Fact, with such Exceptions, and under such Regulations as the Congress shall make.

(3) The trial of all Crimes, except in Cases of Impeachment, shall be by Jury; and such Trial shall be held in the State where the said Crimes shall have been committed; but when not committed within any State, the Trial shall be at such Place or Places as the Congress may by Law have directed.

Section 3. (1) Treason against the United States, shall consist only in levying War against them, or, in adhering to their enemies, giving them Aid and Comfort. No Person shall be convicted of Treason unless on the Testimony of two Witnesses to the same overt Act, or on Confession in open Court.

---

[8]Refer to the Eleventh Amendment.

(2) The Congress shall have Power to declare the Punishment of Treason, but no Attainder of Treason shall work Corruption of Blood, or Forfeiture except during the Life of the Person attainted.

Article IV

Section 1. Full Faith and Credit shall be given in each State to the public Acts, Records, and judicial Proceedings of every other State. And the Congress may by general Laws prescribe the Manner in which such Acts, Records and Proceedings shall be proved, and the Effect thereof.

Section 2. (1) The Citizens of each State shall be entitled to all Privileges and Immunities of Citizens in the several States.

(2) A Person charged in any State with Treason, Felony, or other Crime, who shall flee from Justice, and be found in another State, shall on demand of the executive Authority of the State from which he fled, be delivered up, to be removed to the State having Jurisdiction of the Crime.

(3) No Person held to Service or Labour in one State, under the Laws thereof, escaping into another, shall, in Consequence of any Law or Regulation therein, be discharged from such Service or Labour, but shall be delivered up on Claim of the Party to whom such Service or Labour may be due.[9]

Section 3. (1) New States may be admitted by the Congress into this Union; but no new State shall be formed or erected within the Jurisdiction of any other State; nor any State be formed by the Junction of two or more States, or Parts of States without the Consent of the Legislatures of the States concerned as well as of the Congress.

(2) The Congress shall have Power to dispose of and make all needful Rules and Regulations respecting the Territory or other Property belonging to the United States; and nothing in this Constitution shall be so construed as to Prejudice any Claims of the United States, or of any particular State.

Section 4. The United States shall guarantee to every State in this Union a Republican Form of Government, and shall protect each of them against Invasion; and on Application of the Legislature, or of the Executive (when the Legislature cannot be convened) against domestic Violence.

Article V

The Congress, whenever two thirds of both Houses shall deem it necessary, shall propose Amendments to this Constitution, or, on the Application of the Legislatures of two thirds of the several States, shall call a Convention for proposing Amendments, which, in either Case, shall be valid to all Intents and Purposes, as part of this Constitution, when ratified by the Legislatures of three fourths of the several States, or by Conventions in three fourths thereof, as the one or the other Mode of Ratification may be proposed by the Congress; Provided that no Amendment which may be made prior to the Year One thousand eight hundred and eight shall in any Manner affect the first and fourth Clauses in the Ninth Section

[9]Refer to the Thirteenth Amendment.

of the first Article; and that no State, without its Consent, shall be deprived of its equal Suffrage in the Senate.

Article VI

(1) All Debts contracted and Engagements entered into, before the Adoption of this Constitution shall be as valid against the United States under this Constitution, as under the Confederation.

(2) This Constitution, and the Laws of the United States which shall be made in Pursuance thereof; and all Treaties made, or which shall be made, under the Authority of the United States, shall be the supreme Law of the Land; and the Judges in every State shall be bound thereby, any Thing in the Constitution or Laws of any State to the Contrary notwithstanding.

(3) The Senators and Representatives before mentioned, and the Members of the several State Legislatures, and all executive and judicial Officers, both of the United States and of the several States, shall be bound by Oath or Affirmation, to support this Constitution, but no religious Test shall ever be required as a Qualification to any Office or public Trust under the United States.

Article VII

The Ratification of the Conventions of nine States shall be sufficient for the Establishment of this Constitution between the States so ratifying the Same.

[Amendments 1 to 10, the Bill of Rights, were ratified in 1791.]

Amendment I

Congress shall make no law respecting an establishment of religion, or prohibiting the free exercise thereof; or abridging the freedom of speech, or of the press; or the right of the people peaceably to assemble, and to petition the Government for a redress of grievances.

Amendment II

A well regulated Militia, being necessary to the security of a free State, the right of the people to keep and bear Arms, shall not be infringed.

Amendment III

No Soldier shall, in time of peace be quartered in any house, without the consent of the Owner, nor in time of war, but in a manner to be prescribed by law.

Amendment IV

The right of the people to be secure in their persons, houses, papers, and effects, against unreasonable searches and seizures, shall not be violated, and no Warrants shall issue, but upon probable cause, supported by Oath or affirmation, and particularly describing the place to be searched, and the persons or things to be seized.

Amendment V

No person shall be held to answer for a capital, or otherwise infamous crime, unless on a presentment or indictment of a Grand Jury, except in cases arising in the land or naval forces, or in the Militia, when in actual service in time of War or public danger; nor shall any person be subject for the same offence to be twice put in jeopardy of life or limb; nor shall be compelled in any criminal case to be a witness against himself, nor be deprived of life, liberty, or property, without due process of law; nor shall private property be taken for public use, without just compensation.

Amendment VI

In all criminal prosecutions, the accused shall enjoy the right to a speedy and public trial, by an impartial jury of the State and district wherein the crime shall have been committed, which district shall have been previously ascertained by law, and to be informed of the nature and cause of the accusation; to be confronted with the witness against him; to have compulsory process for obtaining witnesses in his favor, and to have the Assistance of Counsel for his defence.

Amendment VII

In Suits at common law, where the value in controversy shall exceed twenty dollars, the right of trial by jury shall be preserved, and no fact tried by jury, shall be otherwise re-examined in any Court of the United States, than according to the rules of the common law.

Amendment VIII

Excessive bail shall not be required, nor excessive fines imposed, nor cruel and unusual punishments inflicted.

Amendment IX

The enumeration in the Constitution, of certain rights, shall not be construed to deny or disparage others retained by the people.

Amendment X

The powers not delegated to the United States by the Constitution, nor prohibited by it to the States, are reserved to the States respectively, or to the people.

Amendment XI [1798]

The Judicial power of the United States shall not be construed to extend to any suit in law or equity, commenced or prosecuted against one of the United States by Citizens of another State, or by Citizens or Subjects of any Foreign State.

Amendment XII [1804]

The Electors shall meet in their respective states and vote by ballot for President and Vice-President, one of whom, at least, shall not be an inhabitant of the same state with themselves; they shall name in their ballots the person voted for as President, and in distinct ballots the person voted for as Vice-President, and they shall make distinct lists of all persons voted for as President, and of all persons voted for as Vice-President, and of the number of votes for each, which lists they shall sign and certify, and transmit sealed to the seat of the government of the United States, directed to the President of the Senate;—The President of the Senate shall, in the presence of the Senate and House of Representatives, open all the certificates and the votes shall then be counted;—The person having the greatest number of votes for President, shall be the President, if such number be a majority of the whole number of Electors appointed; and if no person have such majority, then from the persons having the highest numbers not exceeding three on the list of those voted for as President, the House of Representatives shall choose immediately, by ballot, the President. But in choosing the President, the votes shall be taken by states, the representation from each state having one vote; a quorum for this purpose shall consist of a member or members from two-thirds of the states, and a majority of all the states shall be necessary to a choice. And if the House of Representatives shall not choose a President whenever the right of choice shall devolve upon them before the fourth day of March next following, then the Vice-President shall act as President, as in the case of the death or other constitutional disability of the President.[10]—The person having the greatest number of votes as Vice-President, shall be the Vice-President, if such number be a majority of the whole number of Electors appointed, and if no person have a majority, then from the two highest numbers on the list, the Senate shall choose the Vice-President; a quorum for the purpose shall consist of two-thirds of the whole number of Senators, and a majority of the whole number shall be necessary to a choice. But no person constitutionally ineligible to the office of President shall be eligible to that of Vice-President of the United States.

Amendment XIII [1865]

Section 1. Neither slavery nor involuntary servitude, except as a punishment for crime whereof the party shall have been duly convicted, shall exist within the United States, or any place subject to their jurisdiction.

Section 2. Congress shall have power to enforce this article by appropriate legislation.

[10]Refer to the Twentieth Amendment.

Amendment XIV [1868]

Section 1. All persons born or naturalized in the United States, and subject to the jurisdiction thereof, are citizens of the United States and of the State wherein they reside. No State shall make or enforce any law which shall abridge the privileges or immunities of citizens of the United States; nor shall any State deprive any person of life, liberty, or property, without due process of law; nor deny to any person within its jurisdiction the equal protection of the laws.

Section 2. Representatives shall be apportioned among the several States according to their respective numbers, counting the whole number of persons in each State, excluding Indians not taxed. But when the right to vote at any election for the choice of electors for President and Vice President of the United States, Representatives in Congress, the Executive and Judicial officers of a State, or the members of the Legislature thereof, is denied to any of the male inhabitants of such State, being twenty-one years of age,[11] and citizens of the United States, or in any way abridged, except for participation in rebellion, or other crime, the basis of representation therein shall be reduced in the proportion which the number of such male citizens shall bear to the whole number of male citizens twenty-one years of age in such State.

Section 3. No person shall be a Senator or Representative in Congress, or elector of President and Vice President, or hold any office, civil or military, under the United States, or under any State, who having previously taken an oath, as a member of Congress, or as an officer of the United States, or as a member of any State legislature, or as an executive or judicial officer of any State, to support the Constitution of the United States, shall have engaged in insurrection or rebellion against the same, or given aid or comfort to the enemies thereof. But Congress may by a vote of two thirds of each House, remove such disability.

Section 4. The validity of the public debt of the United States, authorized by law, including debts incurred for payment of pensions and bounties for services in suppressing insurrection or rebellion, shall not be questioned. But neither the United States nor any State shall assume or pay any debt or obligation incurred in aid of insurrection or rebellion against the United States, or any claim for the loss or emancipation of any slave; but all such debts, obligations and claims shall be held illegal and void.

Section 5. The Congress shall have power to enforce, by appropriate legislation, the provisions of this article.

Amendment XV [1870]

Section 1. The right of citizens of the United States to vote shall not be denied or abridged by the United States or by any State on account of race, color, or previous condition of servitude.

Section 2. The Congress shall have power to enforce this article by appropriate legislation.

[11]Refer to the Twenty-Sixth Amendment.

Amendment XVI [1913]

The Congress shall have power to lay and collect taxes on incomes, from whatever source derived, without apportionment among the several States, and without regard to any census or enumeration.

Amendment XVII [1913]

(1) The Senate of the United States shall be composed of two Senators from each State, elected by the people thereof, for six years; and each Senator shall have one vote. The electors in each State shall have the qualifications requisite for electors of the most numerous branch of the State legislatures.

(2) When vacancies happen in the representation of any State in the Senate, the executive authority of such State shall issue writs of election to fill such vacancies: *Provided,* That the legislature of any State may empower the executive thereof to make temporary appointments until the people fill the vacancies by election as the legislature may direct.

(3) This amendment shall not be so construed as to affect the election or term of any Senator chosen before it becomes valid as part of the Constitution.

Amendment XVIII [1919]

Section 1. After one year from the ratification of this article the manufacture, sale, or transportation of intoxicating liquors within, the importation thereof into, or the exportation thereof from the United States and all territory subject to the jurisdiction thereof for beverage purposes is hereby prohibited.

Section 2. The Congress and the several States shall have concurrent power to enforce this article by appropriate legislation.

Section 3. This article shall be inoperative unless it shall have been ratified as an amendment to the Constitution by the legislatures of the several States, as provided in the Constitution, within seven years from the date of the submission hereof to the States by the Congress.[12]

Amendment XIX [1920]

(1) The right of citizens of the United States to vote shall not be denied or abridged by the United States or by any State on account of sex.

(2) Congress shall have power to enforce this article by appropriate legislation.

Amendment XX [1933]

Section 1. The terms of the President and Vice President shall end at noon on the 20th day of January, and the terms of Senators and Representatives at noon on the 3rd day of

[12]Refer to the Twenty-First Amendment.

January, of the years in which such terms would have ended if this article had not been ratified; and the terms of their successors shall then begin.

Section 2. The Congress shall assemble at least once in every year, and such meeting shall begin at noon on the 3rd day of January, unless they shall by law appoint a different day.

Section 3. If, at the time fixed for the beginning of the term of the President, the President elect shall have died, the Vice President elect shall become President. If the President shall not have been chosen before the time fixed for the beginning of his term or if the President elect shall have failed to qualify, then the Vice President elect shall act as President until a President shall have qualified; and the Congress may by law provide for the case wherein neither a President elect nor a Vice President elect shall have qualified, declaring who shall then act as President, or the manner in which one is to act shall be selected, and such person shall act accordingly until a President or Vice President shall have qualified.

Section 4. The Congress may by law provide for the case of the death of any of the persons from whom the House of Representatives may choose a President whenever the right of choice shall have devolved upon them, and for the case of the death of any of the persons from whom the Senate may choose a Vice President whenever the right of choice shall have devolved upon them.

Section 5. Sections 1 and 2 shall take effect on the 15th day of October following the ratification of this article.

Section 6. This article shall be inoperative unless it shall have been ratified as an amendment to the Constitution by the legislatures of three-fourths of the several States within seven years from the date of its submission.

Amendment XXI [1933]

Section 1. The eighteenth article of amendment to the Constitution of the United States is hereby repealed.

Section 2. The transportation or importation into any State, Territory, or possession of the United States for delivery or use therein of intoxicating liquors, in violation of the laws thereof, is hereby prohibited.

Section 3. This article shall be inoperative unless it shall have been ratified as an amendment to the Constitution by conventions in the several States, as provided in the Constitution, within seven years from the date of the submission hereof to the States by the Congress.

Amendment XXII [1951]

Section 1. No person shall be elected to the office of the President more than twice, and no person who has held the office of President, or acted as President, for more than two years of a term to which some other person was elected President shall be elected to the office of President more than once. But this Article shall not apply to any person holding the office of President when this Article was proposed by the Congress, and shall not prevent any person who may be holding the office of President, or acting as President, during the term within which this Article becomes operative from holding the office of President or acting as president during the remainder of such term.

Section 2. This article shall be inoperative unless it shall have been ratified as an amendment to the Constitution by the legislatures of three-fourths of the several States within seven years from the date of its submission to the States by the Congress.

Amendment XXIII [1961]

Section 1. The District constituting the seat of Government of the United States shall appoint in such manner as the Congress may direct:

> A number of electors of President and Vice President equal to the whole number of Senators and Representatives in Congress to which the District would be entitled if it were a State, but in no event more than the least populous state; they shall be in addition to those appointed by the states, but they shall be considered, for the purposes of the election of President and Vice Prisident, to be electors appointed by a state; and they shall meet in the District and perform such duties as provided by the twelfth article of amendment.

Section 2. The Congress shall have power to enforce this article by appropriate legislation.

Amendment XXIV [1964]

Section 1. The right of citizens of the United States to vote in any primary or other election for President or Vice President, for electors for President or Vice President, or for Senator or Representative in Congress, shall not be denied or abridged by the United States or any State by reason of failure to pay any poll tax or other tax.

Section 2. The Congress shall have power to enforce this article by appropriate legislation.

Amendment XXV [1967]

Section 1. In case of the removal of the President from office or of his death or resignation, the Vice President shall become President.

Section 2. Whenever there is a vacancy in the office of the Vice President, the President shall nominate a Vice President who shall take office upon confirmation by a majority vote of both Houses of Congress.

Section 3. Whenever the President transmits to the President pro tempore of the Senate and the Speaker of the House of Representatives his written declaration that he is unable to discharge the powers and duties of his office, and until he transmits to them a written declaration to the contrary, such powers and duties shall be discharged by the Vice President as Acting President.

Section 4. Whenever the Vice President and a majority of either the principal officers of the executive departments or of such other body as Congress may by law provide, transmit to the President pro tempore of the Senate and the Speaker of the House of Representatives their written declaration that the President is unable to discharge the powers and duties of his office, the Vice President shall immediately assume the powers and duties of the office as Acting President.

Thereafter, when the President transmits to the President pro tempore of the Senate and the Speaker of the House of Representatives his written declaration that no inability exists, he shall resume the powers and duties of his office unless the Vice President and a majority of either the principal officers of the executive departments or of such other body as Congress may by law provide, transmit within four days to the President pro tempore of the Senate and the Speaker of the House of Representatives their written declaration that the President is unable to discharge the powers and duties of his office. Thereupon Congress shall decide the issue, assembling within forty-eight hours for that purpose if not in session. If the Congress, within twenty-one days after receipt of the latter written declaration, or, if Congress is not in session, within twenty-one days after Congress is required to assemble, determines by two-thirds vote of both Houses that the President is unable to discharge the powers and duties of his office, the Vice President shall continue to discharge the same as Acting President; otherwise, the President shall resume the powers and duties of his office.

Amendment XXVI [1971]

Section 1. The right of citizens of the United States, who are eighteen years of age or older, to vote shall not be denied or abridged by the United States or by any State on account of age.

Section 2. The Congress shall have power to enforce this article by appropriate legislation.

Amendment XXVII [1992]

No law, varying the compensation for the services of the Senators and Representatives, shall take effect, until an election of Representatives shall have intervened.

Uniform Commercial Code 2000 Official Text, Article 2

Table of Sections

Article 2. Sales

Part 1. Short Title, General Construction, and Subject Matter

Section

Part 2. Form, Formation, and Readjustment of Contract

Article 2. Sales

Part 1. Short Title, General Construction, and Subject Matter

§ 2–101. Short Title

This Article shall be known and may be cited as Uniform Commercial Code—Sales.

§ 2–102. Scope; Certain Security and Other Transactions Excluded from This Article

Unless the context otherwise requires, this Article applies to transactions in goods; it does not apply to any transaction which although in the form of an unconditional contract to sell or present sale is intended to operate only as a security transaction; nor does this Article impair or repeal any statute regulating sales to consumers, farmers, or other specified classes of buyers.

§ 2–103. Definitions and Index of Definitions

(1) In this Article unless the context otherwise requires

    (a) "Buyer" means a person who buys or contracts to buy goods.

    (b) "Good faith" in the case of a merchant means honesty in fact and the observance of reasonable commercial standards of fair dealing in the trade.

    (c) "Receipt" of goods means taking physical possession of them.

    (d) "Seller" means a person who sells or contracts to sell goods.

(2) Other definitions applying to this Article or to specified Parts thereof, and the sections in which they appear, are:

"Acceptance"	Section 2–606.
"Banker's credit"	Section 2–325.
"Between merchants"	Section 2–104.
"Cancellation"	Section 2–106(4).
"Commercial unit"	Section 2–105.
"Confirmed credit"	Section 2–325.
"Conforming to contract"	Section 2–106.
"Contract for sale"	Section 2–106.
"Cover"	Section 2–712.
"Entrusting"	Section 2–403.
"Financing agency"	Section 2–104.
"Future goods"	Section 2–105.
"Goods"	Section 2–105.
"Identification"	Section 2–501.
"Installment contract"	Section 2–612.
"Letter of credit"	Section 2–325.
"Lot"	Section 2–105.
"Merchant"	Section 2–104.
"Overseas"	Section 2–323.
"Person in position of seller"	Section 2–707.
"Present sale"	Section 2–106.
"Sale"	Section 2–106.
"Sale on approval"	Section 2–326.
"Sale or return"	Section 2–326.
"Termination"	Section 2–106.

(3) The following definitions in other Articles apply to this Article:

"Check"	Section 3–104.
"Consignee"	Section 7–102.
"Consignor"	Section 7–102.
"Consumer goods"	Section 9–102.
"Dishonor"	Section 3–502.
"Draft"	Section 3–104.

(4) In addition Article 1 contains general definitions and principles of construction and interpretation applicable throughout this Article.

§ 2–104. Definitions: "Merchant"; "Between Merchants"; "Financing Agency"

(1) "Merchant" means a person who deals in goods of the kind or otherwise by his occupation holds himself out as having knowledge or skill peculiar to the practices or

goods involved in the transaction or to whom such knowledge or skill may be attributed by his employment of an agent or broker or other intermediary who by his occupation holds himself out as having such knowledge or skill.

(2) "Financing agency" means a bank, finance company, or other person who in the ordinary course of business makes advances against goods or documents of title or who by arrangement with either the seller or the buyer intervenes in ordinary course to make or collect payment due or claimed under the contract for sale, as by purchasing or paying the seller's draft or making advances against it or by merely taking it for collection whether or not the documents of title accompany the draft. "Financing agency" includes also a bank or other person who similarly intervenes between persons who are in the position of seller and buyer in respect to the goods (Section 2–707).

(3) "Between merchants" means in any transaction with respect to which both parties are chargeable with the knowledge or skill of merchants.

§ 2–105. Definitions: "Transferability"; "Goods"; "Future" Goods; "Lot"; "Commercial Unit"

(1) "Goods" means all things (including specially manufactured goods) which are movable at the time of identification to the contract for sale other than the money in which the price is to be paid, investment securities (Article 8), and things in action. "Goods" also includes the unborn young of animals and growing crops and other identified things attached to realty as described in the section on goods to be severed from realty (Section 2–107).

(2) Goods must be both existing and identified before any interest in them can pass. Goods which are not both existing and identified are "future" goods. A purported present sale of future goods or of any interest therein operates as a contract to sell.

(3) There may be a sale of a part interest in existing identified goods.

(4) An undivided share in an identified bulk of fungible goods is sufficiently identified to be sold although the quantity of the bulk is not determined. Any agreed proportion of such a bulk or any quantity thereof agreed upon by number, weight, or other measure may to the extent of the seller's interest in the bulk be sold to the buyer who then becomes an owner in common.

(5) "Lot" means a parcel or a single article which is the subject matter of a separate sale or delivery, whether or not it is sufficient to perform the contract.

(6) "Commercial unit" means such a unit of goods as by commercial usage is a single whole for purposes of sale and division of which materially impairs its character or value on the market or in use. A commercial unit may be a single article (as a machine) or a set of articles (as a suite of furniture or an assortment of sizes) or a quantity (as a bale, gross, or carload) or any other unit treated in use or in the relevant market as a single whole.

§ 2–106. Definitions: "Contract"; "Agreement"; "Contract for Sale"; "Sale"; "Present Sale"; "Conforming" to Contract; "Termination"; "Cancellation"

(1) In this Article unless the context otherwise requires "contract" and "agreement" are limited to those relating to the present or future sale of goods. "Contract for sale" includes both a present sale of goods and a contract to sell goods at a future time. A

"sale" consists in the passing of title from the seller to the buyer for a price (Section 2–401). A "present sale" means a sale which is accomplished by the making of the contract.

(2) Goods or conduct including any part of a performance are "conforming" or conform to the contract when they are in accordance with the obligations under the contract.

(3) "Termination" occurs when either party pursuant to a power created by agreement or law puts an end to the contract otherwise than for its breach. On "termination" all obligations which are still executory on both sides are discharged, but any right based on prior breach or performance survives.

(4) "Cancellation" occurs when either party puts an end to the contract for breach by the other, and its effect is the same as that of "termination" except that the cancelling party also retains any remedy for breach of the whole contract or any unperformed balance.

§ 2–107. Goods to Be Severed from Realty: Recording

(1) A contract for the sale of minerals or the like (including oil and gas) or a structure or its materials to be removed from realty is a contract for the sale of goods within this Article if they are to be severed by the seller; but until severance a purported present sale thereof which is not effective as a transfer of an interest in land is effective only as a contract to sell.

(2) A contract for the sale apart from the land of growing crops or other things attached to realty and capable of severance without material harm thereto but not described in subsection (1) or of timber to be cut is a contract for the sale of goods within this Article whether the subject matter is to be severed by the buyer or by the seller even though it forms part of the realty at the time of contracting, and the parties can by identification effect a present sale before severance.

(3) The provisions of this section are subject to any third party rights provided by the law relating to realty records, and the contract for sale may be executed and recorded as a document transferring an interest in land and shall then constitute notice to third parties of the buyer's right under the contract for sale.

Part 2. Form, Formation, and Readjustment of Contract

§ 2–201. Formal Requirements; Statute of Frauds

(1) Except as otherwise provided in this section, a contract for the sale of goods for the price of $500 or more is not enforceable by way of action or defense unless there is some writing sufficient to indicate that a contract for sale has been made between the parties and signed by the party against whom enforcement is sought or by his authorized agent or broker. A writing is not insufficient because it omits or incorrectly states a term agreed upon, but the contract is not enforceable under this paragraph beyond the quantity of goods shown in such writing.

(2) Between merchants, if within a reasonable time a writing in confirmation of the contract and sufficient against the sender is received and the party receiving it has reason to know its contents, it satisfies the requirements of subsection (1) against such party unless written notice of objection to its contents is given within 10 days after it is received.

(3) A contract which does not satisfy the requirements of subsection (1) but which is valid in other respects is enforceable

    (a) if the goods are to be specially manufactured for the buyer and are not suitable for sale to others in the ordinary course of the seller's business and the seller, before notice of repudiation is received and under circumstances which reasonably indicate that the goods are for the buyer, has made either a substantial beginning of their manufacture or commitments for their procurement; or

    (b) if the party against whom enforcement is sought admits in his pleading, testimony, or otherwise in court that a contract for sale was made, but the contract is not enforceable under this provision beyond the quantity of goods admitted; or

    (c) with respect to goods for which payment has been made and accepted or which have been received and accepted (Section 2–606).

§ 2–202. Final Written Expression: Parol or Extrinsic Evidence

Terms with respect to which the confirmatory memoranda of the parties agree or which are otherwise set forth in a writing intended by the parties as a final expression of their agreement with respect to such terms as are included therein may not be contradicted by evidence of any prior agreement or of a contemporaneous oral agreement but may be explained or supplemented

    (a) by course and dealing or usage of trade (Section 1–205) or by course of performance (Section 2–208); and

    (b) by evidence of consistent additional terms unless the court finds the writing to have been intended also as a complete and exclusive statement of the terms of the agreement.

§ 2–203. Seals Inoperative

The affixing of a seal to a writing evidencing a contract for sale or an offer to buy or sell goods does not constitute the writing a sealed instrument and the law with respect to sealed instruments does not apply to such a contract or offer.

§ 2–204. Formation in General

(1) A contract for sale of goods may be made in any manner sufficient to show agreement, including conduct by both parties which recognizes the existence of such a contract.

(2) An agreement sufficient to constitute a contract for sale may be found even though the moment of its making is undetermined.

(3) Even though one or more terms are left open a contract for sale does not fail for indefiniteness if the parties have intended to make a contract and there is a reasonably certain basis for giving an appropriate remedy.

§ 2–205. Firm Offers

An offer by a merchant to buy or sell goods in a signed writing which by its terms gives assurance that it will be held open is not revocable, for lack of consideration, during the time stated or if no time is stated for a reasonable time, but in no event may such period of irrevocability exceed three months; but any such term of assurance on a form supplied by the offeree must be separately signed by the offerer.

§ 2–206. Offer and Acceptance in Formation of Contract

(1) Unless otherwise unambiguously indicated by the language or circumstances

    (a) an offer to make a contract shall be construed as inviting acceptance in any manner and by any medium reasonable in the circumstances;

    (b) an order or other offer to buy goods for prompt or current shipment shall be construed as inviting acceptance either by a prompt promise to ship or by the prompt or current shipment of conforming or nonconforming goods, but such a shipment of nonconforming goods does not constitute an acceptance if the seller seasonably notifies the buyer that the shipment is offered only as an accommodation to the buyer.

(2) Where the beginning of a requested performance is a reasonable mode of acceptance, an offerer who is not notified of acceptance within a reasonable time may treat the offer as having lapsed before acceptance.

§ 2–207. Additional Terms in Acceptance or Confirmation

(1) A definite and seasonable expression of acceptance or a written confirmation which is sent within a reasonable time operates as an acceptance even though it states terms additional to or different from those offered or agreed upon, unless acceptance is expressly made conditional on assent to the additional or different terms.

(2) The additional terms are to be construed as proposals for addition to the contract. Between merchants such terms become part of the contract unless

    (a) the offer expressly limits acceptance to the terms of the offer;

    (b) they materially alter it; or

    (c) notification of objection to them has already been given or is given within a reasonable time after notice of them is received.

(3) Conduct by both parties which recognizes the existence of a contract is sufficient to establish a contract for sale although the writings of the parties do not otherwise establish a contract. In such case the terms of the particular contract consist of those terms on which the writings of the parties agree, together with any supplementary terms incorporated under any other provisions of this Act.

§ 2–208. Course of Performance or Practical Construction

(1) Where the contract for sale involves repeated occasions for performance by either party with knowledge of the nature of the performance and opportunity for objection to it by the other, any course of performance accepted or acquiesced in without objection shall be relevant to determine the meaning of the agreement.

(2) The express terms of the agreement and any such course of performance, as well as any course of dealing and usage of trade, shall be construed whenever reasonable as consistent with each other; but when such construction is unreasonable, express terms shall control course of performance and course of performance shall control both course of dealing and usage of trade (Section 1–205).

(3) Subject to the provisions of the next section on modification and waiver, such course of performance shall be relevant to show a waiver or modification of any term inconsistent with such course of performance.

§ 2–209. Modification, Rescission, and Waiver

(1) An agreement modifying a contract within this Article needs no consideration to be binding.

(2) A signed agreement which excludes modification or rescission except by a signed writing cannot be otherwise modified or rescinded, but except as between merchants such a requirement on a form supplied by the merchant must be separately signed by the other party.

(3) The requirements of the statute of frauds section of this Article (Section 2–201) must be satisfied if the contract as modified is within its provisions.

(4) Although an attempt at modification or rescission does not satisfy the requirements of subsection (2) or (3) it can operate as a waiver.

(5) A party who has made a waiver affecting an executory portion of the contract may retract the waiver by reasonable notification received by the other party that strict performance will be required of any term waived, unless the retraction would be unjust in view of a material change of position in reliance on the waiver.

§ 2–210. Delegation of Performance; Assignment of Rights

(1) A party may perform his duty through a delegate unless otherwise agreed or unless the other party has a substantial interest in having his original promisor perform or control the acts required by the contract. No delegation of performance relieves the party delegating of any duty to perform or any liability for breach.

(2) Except as otherwise provided in Section 9–406, unless otherwise agreed all rights of either seller or buyer can be assigned except where the assignment would materially change the duty of the other party, or increase materially the burden or risk imposed on him by his contract, or impair materially his chance of obtaining return performance. A right to damages for breach of the whole contract or a right arising out of the assignor's due performance of his entire obligation can be assigned despite agreement otherwise.

(3) The creation, attachment, perfection, or enforcement of a security interest in the seller's interest under a contract is not a transfer that materially changes the duty of or increases materially the burden or risk imposed on the buyer or impairs materially the buyer's chance of obtaining return performance within the purview of subsection (2) unless, and then only to the extent that, enforcement actually results in a delegation of material performance of the seller. Even in that event, the creation, attachment, perfection, and enforcement of the security interest remain effective, but (i) the seller is liable to the buyer for damages caused by the delegation to the extent that the damages could not reasonably be prevented by the buyer, and (ii) a court having jurisdiction may grant other appropriate relief, including cancellation of the contract for sale or an injunction against enforcement of the security interest or consummation of the enforcement.

(4) Unless the circumstances indicate the contrary a prohibition of assignment of "the contract" is to be construed as barring only the delegation to the assignee of the assignor's performance.

(5) An assignment of "the contract" or of "all my rights under the contract" or an assignment in similar general terms is an assignment of rights and unless the language or the circumstances (as in an assignment for security) indicate the contrary, it is a delegation of performance of the duties of the assignor and its acceptance by the assignee constitutes a promise by him to perform those duties. This promise is enforceable by either the assignor or the other party to the original contract.

(6) The other party may treat any assignment which delegates performance as creating reasonable grounds for insecurity and may without prejudice to his rights against the assignor demand assurances from the assignee (Section 2–609).

Part 3. General Obligation and Construction of Contract

§ 2–301. *General Obligations of Parties*

The obligation of the seller is to transfer and deliver and that of the buyer is to accept and pay in accordance with the contract.

§ 2–302. *Unconscionable Contract or Clause*

(1) If the court as a matter of law finds the contract or any clause of the contract to have been unconscionable at the time it was made the court may refuse to enforce the contract, or it may enforce the remainder of the contract without the unconscionable clause, or it may so limit the application of any unconscionable clause as to avoid any unconscionable result.

(2) When it is claimed or appears to the court that the contract or any clause thereof may be unconscionable the parties shall be afforded a reasonable opportunity to present evidence as to its commercial setting, purpose, and effect to aid the court in making the determination.

§ 2–303. *Allocation or Division of Risks*

Where this Article allocates a risk or a burden as between the parties "unless otherwise agreed," the agreement may not only shift the allocation but may also divide the risk or burden.

§ 2–304. *Price Payable in Money, Goods, Realty, or Otherwise*

(1) The price can be made payable in money or otherwise. If it is payable in whole or in part in goods each party is a seller of the goods which he is to transfer.

(2) Even though all or part of the price is payable in an interest in realty the transfer of the goods and the seller's obligations with reference to them are subject to this Article, but not the transfer of the interest in realty or the transferor's obligations in connection therewith.

§ 2–305. *Open Price Term*

(1) The parties if they so intend can conclude a contract for sale even though the price is not settled. In such a case the price is a reasonable price at the time for delivery if

    (a) nothing is said as to price; or

    (b) the price is left to be agreed by the parties and they fail to agree; or

(c) the price is to be fixed in terms of some agreed market or other standard as set or recorded by a third person or agency and it is not so set or recorded.

(2) A price to be fixed by the seller or by the buyer means a price for him to fix in good faith.

(3) When a price left to be fixed otherwise than by agreement of the parties fails to be fixed through fault of one party the other may at his option treat the contract as cancelled or himself fix a reasonable price.

(4) Where, however, the parties intend not to be bound unless the price be fixed or agreed and it is not fixed or agreed there is no contract. In such a case the buyer must return any goods already received or if unable so to do must pay their reasonable value at the time of delivery and the seller must return any portion of the price paid on account.

§ 2–306. Output, Requirements, and Exclusive Dealings

(1) A term which measures the quantity by the output of the seller or the requirements of the buyer means such actual output or requirements as may occur in good faith, except that no quantity unreasonably disproportionate to any stated estimate or in the absence of a stated estimate to any normal or otherwise comparable prior output or requirements may be tendered or demanded.

(2) A lawful agreement by either the seller or the buyer for exclusive dealing in the kind of goods concerned imposes unless otherwise agreed an obligation by the seller to use best efforts to supply the goods and by the buyer to use best efforts to promote their sale.

§ 2–307. Delivery in Single Lot or Several Lots

Unless otherwise agreed all goods called for by a contract for sale must be tendered in a single delivery and payment is due only on such tender; but where the circumstances give either party the right to make or demand delivery in lots the price if it can be apportioned may be demanded for each lot.

§ 2–308. Absence of Specified Place for Delivery

Unless otherwise agreed

(a) the place for delivery of goods is the seller's place of business or if he has none his residence; but

(b) in a contract for sale of identified goods which to the knowledge of the parties at the time of contracting are in some other place, that place is the place for their delivery; and

(c) documents of title may be delivered through customary banking channels.

§ 2–309. Absence of Specific Time Provisions; Notice of Termination

(1) The time for shipment or delivery or any other action under a contract if not provided in this Article or agreed upon shall be a reasonable time.

(2) Where the contract provides for successive performance but is indefinite in duration it is valid for a reasonable time but unless otherwise agreed may be terminated at any time by either party.

(3) Termination of a contract by one party except on the happening of an agreed event requires that reasonable notification be received by the other party and an agreement dispensing with notification is invalid if its operation would be unconscionable.

§ 2–310. Open Time for Payment or Running of Credit; Authority to Ship under Reservation

Unless otherwise agreed

    (a) payment is due at the time and place at which the buyer is to receive the goods even though the place of shipment is the place of delivery; and

    (b) if the seller is authorized to send the goods he may ship them under reservation, and may tender the documents of title, but the buyer may inspect the goods after their arrival before payment is due unless such inspection is inconsistent with the terms of the contract (Section 2–513); and

    (c) if delivery is authorized and made by way of documents of title otherwise than by subsection (b) then payment is due at the time and place at which the buyer is to receive the documents regardless of where the goods are to be received; and

    (d) where the seller is required or authorized to ship the goods on credit the credit period runs from the time of shipment, but postdating the invoice or delaying its dispatch will correspondingly delay the starting of the credit period.

§ 2–311. Options and Cooperation Respecting Performance

(1) An agreement for sale which is otherwise sufficiently definite (subsection (3) of Section 2–204) to be a contract is not made invalid by the fact that it leaves particulars of performance to be specified by one of the parties. Any such specification must be made in good faith and within limits set by commercial reasonableness.

(2) Unless otherwise agreed specifications relating to assortment of the goods are at the buyer's option and except as otherwise provided in subsections (1) (c) and (3) of Section 2–319 specifications or arrangements relating to shipment are at the seller's option.

(3) Where such specification would materially affect the other party's performance but is not seasonably made or where one party's cooperation is necessary to the agreed performance of the other but is not seasonably forthcoming, the other party in addition to all other remedies

    (a) is excused for any resulting delay in his own performance; and

    (b) may also either proceed to perform in any reasonable manner or after the time for a material part of his own performance treat the failure to specify or to cooperate as a breach by failure to deliver or accept the goods.

§ 2–312. Warranty of Title and Against Infringement; Buyer's Obligation Against Infringement

(1) Subject to subsection (2) there is in a contract for sale a warranty by the seller that

    (a) the title conveyed shall be good, and its transfer rightful; and

(b) the goods shall be delivered free from any security interest or other lien or encumbrance of which the buyer at the time of contracting has no knowledge.

(2) A warranty under subsection (1) will be excluded or modified only by specific language or by circumstances which give the buyer reason to know that the person selling does not claim title in himself or that he is purporting to sell only such right or title as he or a third person may have.

(3) Unless otherwise agreed a seller who is a merchant regularly dealing in goods of the kind warrants that the goods shall be delivered free of the rightful claim of any third person by way of infringement or the like; but a buyer who furnishes specifications to the seller must hold the seller harmless against any such claim which arises out of compliance with the specifications.

§ 2–313. Express Warranties by Affirmation, Promise, Description, Sample

(1) Express warranties by the seller are created as follows:

(a) Any affirmation of fact or promise made by the seller to the buyer which relates to the goods and becomes part of the basis of the bargain creates an express warranty that the goods shall conform to the affirmation or promise.

(b) Any description of the goods which is made part of the basis of the bargain creates an express warranty that the goods shall conform to the description.

(c) Any sample or model which is made part of the basis of the bargain creates an express warranty that the whole of the goods shall conform to the sample or model.

(2) It is not necessary to the creation of an express warranty that the seller use formal words such as "warrant" or "guarantee" or that he have a specific intention to make a warranty, but an affirmation merely of the value of the goods or a statement purporting to be merely the seller's opinion or commendation of the goods does not create a warranty.

§ 2–314. Implied Warranty: Merchantability; Usage of Trade

(1) Unless excluded or modified (Section 2–316), a warranty that the goods shall be merchantable is implied in a contract for their sale if the seller is a merchant with respect to goods of that kind. Under this section the serving for value of food or drink to be consumed either on the premises or elsewhere is a sale.

(2) Goods to be merchantable must be at least such as

(a) pass without objection in the trade under the contract description; and

(b) in the case of fungible goods, are of fair average quality within the description; and

(c) are fit for the ordinary purposes for which such goods are used; and

(d) run, within the variations permitted by the agreement, of even kind, quality, and quantity within each unit and among all units involved; and

(e) are adequately contained, packaged, and labeled as the agreement may require; and

(f) conform to the promises or affirmations of fact made on the container or label if any.

(3) Unless excluded or modified (Section 2–316) other implied warranties may arise from course of dealing or usage of trade.

§ 2–315. Implied Warranty: Fitness for Particular Purpose

Where the seller at the time of contracting has reason to know any particular purpose for which the goods are required and that the buyer is relying on the seller's skill or judgment to select or furnish suitable goods, there is unless excluded or modified under the next section an implied warranty that the goods shall be fit for such purpose.

§ 2–316. Exclusion or Modification of Warranties

(1) Words or conduct relevant to the creation of an express warranty and words or conduct tending to negate or limit warranty shall be construed wherever reasonable as consistent with each other, but subject to the provisions of this Article on parol or extrinsic evidence (Section 2–202) negation or limitation is inoperative to the extent that such construction is unreasonable.

(2) Subject to subsection (3), to exclude or modify the implied warranty of merchantability or any part of it the language must mention merchantability and in case of a writing must be conspicuous, and to exclude or modify any implied warranty of fitness the exclusion must be by a writing and conspicuous. Language to exclude all implied warranties of fitness is sufficient if it states, for example, that "There are no warranties which extend beyond the description on the face hereof."

(3) Notwithstanding subsection (2)

    (a) unless the circumstances indicate otherwise, all implied warranties are excluded by expressions like "as is," "with all faults," or other language which in common understanding calls the buyer's attention to the exclusion of warranties and makes plain that there is no implied warranty; and

    (b) when the buyer before entering into the contract has examined the goods or the sample or model as fully as he desired or has refused to examine the goods there is no implied warranty with regard to defects which an examination ought in the circumstances to have revealed to him; and

    (c) an implied warranty can also be excluded or modified by course of dealing or course of performance or usage of trade.

(4) Remedies for breach of warranty can be limited in accordance with the provisions of this Article on liquidation or limitation of damages and on contractual modification of remedy (Sections 2–718 and 2–719).

§ 2–317. Cumulation and Conflict of Warranties Express or Implied

Warranties whether express or implied shall be construed as consistent with each other and as cumulative, but if such construction is unreasonable the intention of the parties shall determine which warranty is dominant. In ascertaining that intention the following rules apply:

    (a) Exact or technical specifications displace an inconsistent sample or model or general language of description.

    (b) A sample from an existing bulk displaces inconsistent general language of description.

(c) Express warranties displace inconsistent implied warranties other than an implied warranty of fitness for a particular purpose.

§ 2–318. Third Party Beneficiaries of Warranties Express or Implied

Note: *If this Act is introduced in the Congress of the United States this section should be omitted. (States to select one alternative.)*

Alternative A A seller's warranty whether express or implied extends to any natural person who is in the family or household of his buyer or who is a guest in his home if it is reasonable to expect that such person may use, consume, or be affected by the goods and who is injured in person by breach of the warranty. A seller may not exclude or limit the operation of this section.

Alternative B A seller's warranty whether express or implied extends to any natural person who may reasonably be expected to use, consume, or be affected by the goods and who is injured in person by breach of the warranty. A seller may not exclude or limit the operation of this section.

Alternative C A seller's warranty whether express or implied extends to any person who may reasonably be expected to use, consume, or be affected by the goods and who is injured by breach of the warranty. A seller may not exclude or limit the operation of this section with respect to injury to the person of an individual to whom the warranty extends.

§ 2–319. F.O.B. and F.A.S. Terms

(1) Unless otherwise agreed the term F.O.B. (which means "free on board") at a named place, even though used only in connection with the stated price, is a delivery term under which

(a) when the term is F.O.B. the place of shipment, the seller must at that place ship the goods in the manner provided in this Article (Section 2–504) and bear the expense and risk of putting them into the possession of the carrier; or

(b) when the term is F.O.B. the place of destination, the seller must at his own expense and risk transport the goods to that place and there tender delivery of them in the manner provided in this Article (Section 2–503);

(c) when under either (a) or (b) the term is also F.O.B. vessel, car, or other vehicle, the seller must in addition at his own expense and risk load the goods on board. If the term is F.O.B. vessel the buyer must name the vessel and in an appropriate case the seller must comply with the provisions of this Article on the form of bill of lading (Section 2–323).

(2) Unless otherwise agreed the term F.A.S. vessel (which means "free alongside") at a named port, even though used only in connection with the stated price, is a delivery term under which the seller must

(a) at his own expense and risk deliver the goods alongside the vessel in the manner usual in that port or on a dock designated and provided by the buyer; and

(b) obtain and tender a receipt for the goods in exchange for which the carrier is under a duty to issue a bill of lading.

(3) Unless otherwise agreed in any case falling within subsection (1)(a) or (c) or subsection (2) the buyer must seasonably give any needed instructions for making delivery, including when the term is F.A.S. or F.O.B. the loading berth of the vessel and in an appropriate case its name and sailing date. The seller may treat the failure of needed instructions as a failure of cooperation under this Article (Section 2–311). He may also at his option move the goods in any reasonable manner preparatory to delivery or shipment.

(4) Under the term F.O.B. vessel or F.A.S. unless otherwise agreed the buyer must make payment against tender of the required documents and the seller may not tender nor the buyer demand delivery of the goods in substitution for the documents.

§ 2–320. C.I.F. and C. & F. Terms

(1) The term C.I.F. means that the price includes in a lump sum the cost of the goods and the insurance and freight to the named destination. The term C. & F. or C.F. means that the price so includes cost and freight to the named destination.

(2) Unless otherwise agreed and even though used only in connection with the stated price and destination, the term C.I.F. destination or its equivalent requires the seller at his own expense and risk to

- (a) put the goods into the possession of a carrier at the port for shipment and obtain a negotiable bill or bills of lading covering the entire transportation to the named destination; and
- (b) load the goods and obtain a receipt from the carrier (which may be contained in the bill of lading) showing that the freight has been paid or provided for; and
- (c) obtain a policy or certificate of insurance, including any war risk insurance, of a kind and on terms then current at the port of shipment in the usual amount, in the currency of the contract, shown to cover the same goods covered by the bill of lading and providing for payment of loss to the order of the buyer or for the account of whom it may concern; but the seller may add to the price the amount of the premium for any such war risk insurance; and
- (d) prepare an invoice of the goods and procure any other documents required to effect shipment or to comply with the contract; and
- (e) forward and tender with commercial promptness all the documents in due form and with any endorsement necessary to perfect the buyer's rights.

(3) Unless otherwise agreed the term C. & F. or its equivalent has the same effect and imposes upon the seller the same obligations and risks as a C.I.F. term except the obligation as to insurance.

(4) Under the term C.I.F. or C. & F. unless otherwise agreed the buyer must make payment against tender of the required documents and the seller may not tender nor the buyer demand delivery of the goods in substitution for the documents.

§ 2–321. C.I.F. or C. & F.: "Net Landed Weights"; "Payment on Arrival"; Warranty of Condition on Arrival

Under a contract containing a term C.I.F. or C. & F.

(1) Where the price is based on or is to be adjusted according to "net landed weights," "delivered weights," "out turn" quantity or quality, or the like, unless otherwise agreed the seller must reasonably estimate the price. The payment due on tender of the documents called for by the contract is the amount so estimated, but after final adjustment of the price a settlement must be made with commercial promptness.

(2) An agreement described in subsection (1) or any warranty of quality or condition of the goods on arrival places upon the seller the risk of ordinary deterioration, shrinkage, and the like in transportation but has no effect on the place or time of identification to the contract for sale or delivery or on the passing of the risk of loss.

(3) Unless otherwise agreed where the contract provides for payment on or after arrival of the goods the seller must before payment allow such preliminary inspection as is feasible; but if the goods are lost delivery of the documents and payment are due when the goods should have arrived.

§ 2–322. Delivery "Ex-Ship"

(1) Unless otherwise agreed a term for delivery of goods "ex-ship" (which means from the carrying vessel) or in equivalent language is not restricted to a particular ship and requires delivery from a ship which has reached a place at the named port of destination where goods of the kind are usually discharged.

(2) Under such a term unless otherwise agreed

    (a) the seller must discharge all liens arising out of the carriage and furnish the buyer with a direction which puts the carrier under a duty to deliver the goods; and

    (b) the risk of loss does not pass to the buyer until the goods leave the ship's tackle or are otherwise properly unloaded.

§ 2–323. Form of Bill of Lading Required in Overseas Shipment; "Overseas"

(1) Where the contract contemplates overseas shipment and contains a term C.I.F. or C. & F. or F.O.B. vessel, the seller unless otherwise agreed must obtain a negotiable bill of lading stating that the goods have been loaded on board or, in the case of a term C.I.F. or C. & F., received for shipment.

(2) Where in a case within subsection (1) a bill of lading has been issued in a set of parts, unless otherwise agreed if the documents are not to be sent from abroad the buyer may demand tender of the full set; otherwise only one part of the bill of lading need be tendered. Even if the agreement expressly requires a full set

    (a) due tender of a single part is acceptable within the provisions of this Article on cure of improper delivery (subsection (1) of Section 2–508); and

    (b) even though the full set is demanded, if the documents are sent from abroad the person tendering an incomplete set may nevertheless require payment upon furnishing an indemnity which the buyer in good faith deems adequate.

(3) A shipment by water or by air or a contract contemplating such shipment is "overseas" insofar as by usage of trade or agreement it is subject to the commercial, financing, or shipping practices characteristic of international deep water commerce.

§ 2–324. *"No Arrival, No Sale" Term*

Under a term "no arrival, no sale" or terms of like meaning, unless otherwise agreed,

- (a) the seller must properly ship conforming goods and if they arrive by any means he must tender them on arrival but he assumes no obligation that the goods will arrive unless he has caused the nonarrival; and
- (b) where without fault of the seller the goods are in part lost or have so deteriorated as no longer to conform to the contract or arrive after the contract time, the buyer may proceed as if there had been casualty to identified goods (Section 2–613).

§ 2–325. *"Letter of Credit" Term; "Confirmed Credit"*

(1) Failure of the buyer seasonably to furnish an agreed letter of credit is a breach of the contract for sale.

(2) The delivery to seller of a proper letter of credit suspends the buyer's obligation to pay. If the letter of credit is dishonored, the seller may on seasonable notification to the buyer require payment directly from him.

(3) Unless otherwise agreed the term "letter of credit" or "banker's credit" in a contract for sale means an irrevocable credit issued by a financing agency of good repute and, where the shipment is overseas, of good international repute. The term "confirmed credit" means that the credit must also carry the direct obligation of such an agency which does business in the seller's financial market.

§ 2–326. *Sale on Approval and Sale or Return; Rights of Creditors*

(1) Unless otherwise agreed, if delivered goods may be returned by the buyer even though they conform to the contract, the transaction is

- (a) a "sale on approval" if the goods are delivered primarily for use, and
- (b) a "sale or return" if the goods are delivered primarily for resale.

(2) Goods held on approval are not subject to the claims of the buyer's creditors until acceptance; goods held on sale or return are subject to such claims while in the buyer's possession.

(3) Any "or return" term of a contract for sale is to be treated as a separate contract for sale within the statute of frauds section of this Article (Section 2–201) and as contradicting the sale aspect of the contract within the provisions of this Article on parol or extrinsic evidence (Section 2–202).

§ 2–327. *Special Incidents of Sale on Approval and Sale or Return*

(1) Under a sale on approval unless otherwise agreed

- (a) although the goods are identified to the contract the risk of loss and the title do not pass to the buyer until acceptance; and
- (b) use of the goods consistent with the purpose of trial is not acceptance but failure seasonably to notify the seller of election to return the goods is acceptance, and if the goods conform to the contract acceptance of any part is acceptance of the whole; and

(c) after due notification of election to return, the return is at the seller's risk and expense but a merchant buyer must follow any reasonable instructions.

(2) Under a sale or return unless otherwise agreed

(a) the option to return extends to the whole or any commercial unit of the goods while in substantially their original conditions, but must be exercised seasonably; and

(b) the return is at the buyer's risk and expense.

§ 2–328. *Sale by Auction*

(1) In a sale by auction if goods are put up in lots each lot is the subject of a separate sale.

(2) A sale by auction is complete when the auctioneer so announces by the fall of the hammer or in other customary manner. Where a bid is made while the hammer is falling in acceptance of a prior bid the auctioneer may in his discretion reopen the bidding or declare the goods sold under the bid on which the hammer was falling.

(3) Such a sale is with reserve unless the goods are in explicit terms put up without reserve. In an auction with reserve the auctioneer may withdraw the goods at any time until he announces completion of the sale. In an auction without reserve, after the auctioneer calls for bids on an article or lot, that article or lot cannot be withdrawn unless no bid is made within a reasonable time. In either case a bidder may retract his bid until the auctioneer's announcement of completion of the sale, but a bidder's retraction does not revive any previous bid.

(4) If the auctioneer knowingly receives a bid on the seller's behalf or the seller makes or procures such a bid, and notice has not been given that liberty for such bidding is reserved, the buyer may at his option avoid the sale or take the goods at the price of the last good faith bid prior to the completion of the sale. This subsection shall not apply to any bid at a forced sale.

Part 4. Title, Creditors, and Good-Faith Purchasers

§ 2–401. *Passing of Title; Reservation for Security; Limited Application of This Section*

Each provision of this Article with regard to the rights, obligations, and remedies of the seller, the buyer, purchasers, or other third parties applies irrespective of title to the goods except where the provision refers to such title. Insofar as situations are not covered by the other provisions of this Article and matters concerning title become material the following rules apply:

(1) Title to goods cannot pass under a contract for sale prior to their identification to the contract (Section 2–501), and unless otherwise explicitly agreed the buyer acquires by their identification a special property as limited by this Act. Any retention or reservation by the seller of the title (property) in goods shipped or delivered to the buyer is limited in effect to a reservation of a security interest. Subject to these provisions and to the provisions of the Article on Secured Transactions (Article 9), title to goods passes from the seller to the buyer in any manner and on any conditions explicitly agreed on by the parties.

(2) Unless otherwise explicitly agreed title passes to the buyer at the time and place at which the seller completes his performance with reference to the physical delivery of the goods, despite any reservation of a security interest and even though a document of title is to be delivered at a different time or place; and in particular and despite any reservation of a security interest by the bill of lading

    (a) if the contract requires or authorizes the seller to send the goods to the buyer but does not require him to deliver them at destination, title passes to the buyer at the time and place of shipment; but

    (b) if the contract requires delivery at destination, title passes on tender there.

(3) Unless otherwise explicitly agreed, where delivery is to be made without moving the goods.

    (a) if the seller is to deliver a document of title, title passes at the time when and the place where he delivers such documents; or

    (b) if the goods are at the time of contracting already identified and no documents are to be delivered, title passes at the time and place of contracting.

(4) A rejection or other refusal by the buyer to receive or retain the goods, whether or not justified, or a justified revocation of acceptance revests title to the goods in the seller. Such revesting occurs by operation of law and is not a "sale."

§ 2–402. *Rights of Seller's Creditors Against Sold Goods*

(1) Except as provided in subsections (2) and (3), rights of unsecured creditors of the seller with respect to goods which have been identified to a contract for sale are subject to the buyer's rights to recover the goods under this Article (Sections 2–502 and 2–716).

(2) A creditor of the seller may treat a sale or an identification of goods to a contract for sale as void if as against him a retention of possession by the seller is fraudulent under any rule of law of the state where the goods are situated, except that retention of possession in good faith and current course of trade by a merchant–seller for a commercially reasonable time after a sale or identification is not fraudulent.

(3) Nothing in this Article shall be deemed to impair the rights of creditors of the seller

    (a) under the provisions of the Article on Secured Transactions (Article 9); or

    (b) where identification to the contract or delivery is made not in current course of trade but in satisfaction of or as security for a preexisting claim for money, security, or the like and is made under circumstances which under any rule of law of the state where the goods are situated would apart from this Article constitute the transaction a fraudulent transfer or voidable preference.

§ 2–403. *Power to Transfer; Good-Faith Purchase of Goods; "Entrusting"*

(1) A purchaser of goods acquires all title which his transferor had or had power to transfer except that a purchaser of a limited interest acquires rights only to the extent of the interest purchased. A person with voidable title has power to transfer a good title to a good-faith purchaser for value. When goods have been delivered under a transaction of purchase the purchaser has such power even though

    (a) the transferor was deceived as to the identity of the purchaser, or

(b) the delivery was in exchange for a check which is later dishonored, or

(c) it was agreed that the transaction was to be a "cash sale," or

(d) the delivery was procured through fraud punishable as larcenous under the criminal law.

(2) Any entrusting of possession of goods to a merchant who deals in goods of that kind gives him power to transfer all rights of the entruster to a buyer in ordinary course of business.

(3) "Entrusting" includes any delivery and any acquiescence in retention of possession regardless of any condition expressed between the parties to the delivery or acquiescence and regardless of whether the procurement of the entrusting or the possessor's disposition of the goods have been such as to be larcenous under the criminal law.

(4) The rights of other purchasers of goods and of lien creditors are governed by the Articles on Secured Transactions (Article 9). [Bulk Transfers/Sales (Article 6)* and Documents of Title (Article 7)].

Part 5. Performance

§ 2–501. Insurable Interest in Goods; Manner of Identification of Goods

(1) The buyer obtains a special property and an insurable interest in goods by identification of existing goods as goods to which the contract refers even though the goods so identified are nonconforming and he has an option to return or reject them. Such identification can be made at any time and in any manner explicitly agreed to by the parties. In the absence of explicit agreement identification occurs

(a) when the contract is made if it is for the sale of goods already existing and identified;

(b) if the contract is for the sale of future goods other than those described in paragraph (c), when goods are shipped, marked, or otherwise designated by the seller as goods to which the contract refers;

(c) when the crops are planted or otherwise become growing crops or the young are conceived if the contract is for the sale of unborn young to be born within 12 months after contracting or for the sale of crops to be harvested within 12 months or the next normal harvest season after contracting, whichever is longer.

(2) The seller retains an insurable interest in goods so long as title to or any security interest in the goods remains in him; and where the identification is by the seller alone he may until default or insolvency or notification to the buyer that the identification is final substitute other goods for those identified.

(3) Nothing in this section impairs any insurable interest recognized under any other statute or rule of law.

§ 2–502. Buyer's Right to Goods on Seller's Insolvency

(1) Subject to subsections (2) and (3) and even though the goods have not been shipped, a buyer who has paid a part or all of the price of goods in which he has a special property under the provisions of the immediately preceding section may on making

and keeping good a tender of any unpaid portion of their price recover them from the seller if

> (a) in the case of goods bought for personal, family, or household purposes, the seller repudiates or fails to deliver as required by the contract; or
>
> (b) in all cases, the seller becomes insolvent within 10 days after receipt of the first installment on their price.

(2) The buyer's right to recover the goods under subsection (1)(a) vests upon acquisition of a special property, even if the seller had not then repudiated or failed to deliver.

(3) If the identification creating his special property has been made by the buyer he acquires the right to recover the goods only if they conform to the contract for sale.

§ 2–503. *Manner of Seller's Tender of Delivery*

(1) Tender of delivery requires that the seller put and hold conforming goods at the buyer's disposition and give the buyer any notification reasonably necessary to enable him to take delivery. The manner, time, and place for tender are determined by the agreement and this Article, and in particular

> (a) tender must be at a reasonable hour, and if it is of goods they must be kept available for the period reasonably necessary to enable the buyer to take possession; but
>
> (b) unless otherwise agreed the buyer must furnish facilities reasonably suited to the receipt of the goods.

(2) Where the case is within the next section respecting shipment tender requires that the seller comply with its provisions.

(3) Where the seller is required to deliver at a particular destination tender requires that he comply with subsection (1) and also in any appropriate case tender documents as described in subsections (4) and (5) of this section.

(4) Where goods are in the possession of a bailee and are to be delivered without being moved

> (a) tender requires that the seller either tender a negotiable document of title covering such goods or procure acknowledgment by the bailee of the buyer's right to possession of the goods; but
>
> (b) tender to the buyer of a nonnegotiable document of title or of a written direction to the bailee to deliver is sufficient tender unless the buyer seasonably objects, and receipt by the bailee of notification of the buyer's rights fixes those rights as against the bailee and all third persons; but risk of loss of the goods and of any failure by the bailee to honor the nonnegotiable document of title or to obey the direction remains on the seller untill the buyer has had a reasonable time to present the document or direction, and a refusal by the bailee to honor the document or to obey the direction defeats the tender.

(5) Where the contract requires the seller to deliver documents

> (a) he must tender all such documents in correct form, except as provided in this Article with respect to bills of lading in a set (subsection (2) of Section 2–323); and

(b) tender through customary banking channels is sufficient and dishonor of a draft accompanying the documents constitutes nonacceptance or rejection.

§ 2–504. Shipment by Seller

Where the seller is required or authorized to send the goods to the buyer and the contract does not require him to deliver them at a particular destination, then unless otherwise agreed he must

(a) put the goods in the possession of such a carrier and make such a contract for their transportation as may be reasonable having regard to the nature of the goods and other circumstances of the case; and

(b) obtain and promptly deliver or tender in due form any document necessary to enable the buyer to obtain possession of the goods or otherwise required by the agreement or by usage of trade; and

(c) promptly notify the buyer of the shipment.

Failure to notify the buyer under paragraph (c) or to make a proper contract under paragraph (a) is a ground for rejection only if material delay or loss ensues.

§ 2–505. Seller's Shipment under Reservation

(1) Where the seller has identified goods to the contract by or before shipment,

(a) his procurement of a negotiable bill of lading to his own order or otherwise reserves in him a security interest in the goods. His procurement of the bill to the order of a financing agency or of the buyer indicates in addition only the seller's expectation of transferring that interest to the person named.

(b) a nonnegotiable bill of lading to himself or his nominee reserves possession of the goods as security but except in a case of conditional delivery (subsection (2) of Section 2–507) a nonnegotiable bill of lading naming the buyer as consignee reserves no security interest even though the seller retains possession of the bill of lading.

(2) When shipment by the seller with reservation of a security interest is in violation of the contract for sale it constitutes an improper contract for transportation within the preceding section but impairs neither the rights given to the buyer by shipment and identification of the goods to the contract nor the seller's powers as a holder of a negotiable document.

§ 2–506. Rights of Financing Agency

(1) A financing agency by paying or purchasing for value a draft which relates to a shipment of goods acquires to the extent of the payment or purchase and in addition to its own rights under the draft and any document of title securing it any rights of the shipper in the goods including the right to stop delivery and the shipper's right to have the draft honored by the buyer.

(2) The right to reimbursement of a financing agency which has in good faith honored or purchased the draft under commitment to or authority from the buyer is not impaired by subsequent discovery of defects with reference to any relevant document which was apparently regular on its face.

§ 2–507. *Effect of Seller's Tender; Delivery on Condition*

(1) Tender of delivery is a condition to the buyer's duty to accept the goods and, unless otherwise agreed, to his duty to pay for them. Tender entitles the seller to acceptance of the goods and to payment according to the contract.

(2) Where payment is due and demanded on the delivery to the buyer of goods or documents of title, his right as against the seller to retain or dispose of them is conditional upon his making the payment due.

§ 2–508. *Cure by Seller of Improper Tender or Delivery; Replacement*

(1) Where any tender or delivery by the seller is rejected because nonconforming and the time for performance has not yet expired, the seller may seasonably notify the buyer of his intention to cure and may then within the contract time make a conforming delivery.

(2) Where the buyer rejects a nonconforming tender which the seller had reasonable grounds to believe would be acceptable with or without money allowance the seller may if he seasonably notifies the buyer have a further reasonable time to substitute a conforming tender.

§ 2–509. *Risk of Loss in the Absence of Breach*

(1) Where the contract requires or authorizes the seller to ship the goods by carrier

    (a) if it does not require him to deliver them at a particular destination, the risk of loss passes to the buyer when the goods are duly delivered to the carrier even though the shipment is under reservation (Section 2–505); but

    (b) if it does require him to deliver them at a particular destination and the goods are there duly tendered while in the possession of the carrier, the risk of loss passes to the buyer when the goods are there duly so tendered as to enable the buyer to take delivery.

(2) Where the goods are held by a bailee to be delivered without being moved, the risk of loss passes to the buyer

    (a) on his receipt of a negotiable document of title covering the goods; or

    (b) on acknowledgment by the bailee of the buyer's right to possession of the goods; or

    (c) after his receipt of a nonnegotiable document of title or other written direction to deliver, as provided in subsection (4)(b) of Section 2–503.

(3) In any case not within subsection (1) or (2), the risk of loss passes to the buyer on his receipt of the goods if the seller is a merchant; otherwise the risk passes to the buyer on tender of delivery.

(4) The provisions of this section are subject to contrary agreement of the parties and to the provisions of this Article on sale on approval (Section 2–327) and on effect of breach on risk of loss (Section 2–510).

§ 2–510. *Effect of Breach on Risk of Loss*

(1) Where a tender or delivery of goods so fails to conform to the contract as to give a right of rejection the risk of their loss remains on the seller until cure or acceptance.

(2) Where the buyer rightfully revokes acceptance he may to the extent of any deficiency in his effective insurance coverage treat the risk of loss as having rested on the seller from the beginning.

(3) Where the buyer as to conforming goods already identified to the contract for sale repudiates or is otherwise in breach before risk of their loss has passed to him, the seller may to the extent of any deficiency in his effective insurance coverage treat the risk of loss as resting on the buyer for a commercially reasonable time.

§ 2–511. Tender of Payment by Buyer; Payment by Check

(1) Unless otherwise agreed tender of payment is a condition to the seller's duty to tender and complete any delivery.

(2) Tender of payment is sufficient when made by any means or in any manner current in the ordinary course of business unless the seller demands payment in legal tender and gives any extension of time reasonably necessary to procure it.

(3) Subject to the provisions of this Act on the effect of an instrument on an obligation (Section 3–310), payment by check is conditional and is defeated as between the parties by dishonor of the check on due presentment.

§ 2–512. Payment by Buyer before Inspection

(1) Where the contract requires payment before inspection nonconformity of the goods does not excuse the buyer from so making payment unless

    (a) the nonconformity appears without inspection; or

    (b) despite tender of the required documents the circumstances would justify injunction against honor under this Act (Section 5–109(b)).

(2) Payment pursuant to subsection (1) does not constitute an acceptance of goods or impair the buyer's right to inspect or any of his remedies.

§ 2–513. Buyer's Right to Inspection of Goods

(1) Unless otherwise agreed and subject to subsection (3), where goods are tendered or delivered or identified to the contract for sale, the buyer has a right before payment or acceptance to inspect them at any reasonable place and time and in any reasonable manner. When the seller is required or authorized to send the goods to the buyer, the inspection may be after their arrival.

(2) Expenses of inspection must be borne by the buyer but may be recovered from the seller if the goods do not conform and are rejected.

(3) Unless otherwise agreed and subject to the provisions of this Article on C.I.F. contracts (subsection (3) of Section 2–321), the buyer is not entitled to inspect the goods before payment of the price when the contract provides

    (a) for delivery "C.O.D." or on other like terms; or

    (b) for payment against documents of title, except where such payment is due only after the goods are to become available for inspection.

(4) A place or method of inspection fixed by the parties is presumed to be exclusive but unless otherwise expressly agreed it does not postpone identification or shift the place for delivery or for passing the risk of loss. If compliance becomes impossible, inspection

shall be as provided in this section unless the place or method fixed was clearly intended as an indispensable condition, failure of which avoids the contract.

§ 2–514. *When Documents Deliverable on Acceptance; When on Payment*

Unless otherwise agreed documents against which a draft is drawn are to be delivered to the drawee on acceptance of the draft if it is payable more than three days after presentment; otherwise, only on payment.

§ 2–515. *Preserving Evidence of Goods in Dispute*

In furtherance of the adjustment of any claim or dispute

(a) either party on reasonable notification to the other and for the purpose of ascertaining the facts and preserving evidence has the right to inspect, test, and sample the goods including such of them as may be in the possession or control of the other; and

(b) the parties may agree to a third-party inspection or survey to determine the conformity or condition of the goods and may agree that the findings shall be binding upon them in any subsequent litigation or adjustment.

Part 6. Breach, Repudiation, and Excuse

§ 2–601. *Buyer's Rights on Improper Delivery*

Subject to the provisions of this Article on breach in installment contracts (Section 2–612) and unless otherwise agreed under the sections on contractual limitations of remedy (Sections 2–718 and 2–719), if the goods or the tender of delivery fail in any respect to conform to the contract, the buyer may

(a) reject the whole; or

(b) accept the whole; or

(c) accept any commercial unit or units and reject the rest.

§ 2–602. *Manner and Effect of Rightful Rejection*

(1) Rejection of goods must be within a reasonable time after their delivery or tender. It is ineffective unless the buyer seasonably notifies the seller.

(2) Subject to the provisions of the two following sections on rejected goods (Sections 2–603 and 2–604),

(a) after rejection any exercise of ownership by the buyer with respect to any commercial unit is wrongful as against the seller; and

(b) if the buyer has before rejection taken physical possession of goods in which he does not have a security interest under the provisions of this Article (subsection (3) of Section 2–711), he is under a duty after rejection to hold them with reasonable care at the seller's disposition for a time sufficient to permit the seller to remove them; but

(c) the buyer has no further obligations with regard to goods rightfully rejected.

(3) The seller's rights with respect to goods wrongfully rejected are governed by the provisions of this Article on Seller's remedies in general (Section 2–703).

§ 2–603. Merchant Buyer's Duties as to Rightfully Rejected Goods

(1) Subject to any security interest in the buyer (subsection (3) of Section 2–711), when the seller has no agent or place of business at the market of rejection a merchant buyer is under a duty after rejection of goods in his possession or control to follow any reasonable instructions received from the seller with respect to the goods and in the absence of such instructions to make reasonable efforts to sell them for the seller's account if they are perishable or threaten to decline in value speedily. Instructions are not reasonable if on demand indemnity for expenses is not forthcoming.

(2) When the buyer sells goods under subsection (1), he is entitled to reimbursement from the seller or out of the proceeds for reasonable expenses of caring for and selling them, and if the expenses include no selling commission then to such commission as is usual in the trade or if there is none to a reasonable sum not exceeding 10 percent on the gross proceeds.

(3) In complying with this section the buyer is held only to good faith and good-faith conduct hereunder is neither acceptance nor conversion nor the basis of an action for damages.

§ 2–604. Buyer's Options as to Salvage of Rightfully Rejected Goods

Subject to the provisions of the immediately preceding section on perishables if the seller gives no instructions within a reasonable time after notification of rejection the buyer may store the rejected goods for the seller's account or reship them to him or resell them for the seller's account with reimbursement as provided in the preceding section. Such action is not acceptance or conversion.

§ 2–605. Waiver of Buyer's Objections by Failure to Particularize

(1) The buyer's failure to state in connection with rejection a particular defect which is ascertainable by reasonable inspection precludes him from relying on the unstated defect to justify rejection or to establish breach

- (a) where the seller could have cured it if stated seasonably; or
- (b) between merchants when the seller has after rejection made a request in writing for a full and final written statement of all defects on which the buyer proposes to rely.

(2) Payment against documents made without reservation of rights precludes recovery of the payment for defects apparent on the face of the documents.

§ 2–606. What Constitutes Acceptance of Goods

(1) Acceptance of goods occurs when the buyer

- (a) after a reasonable opportunity to inspect the goods signifies to the seller that the goods are conforming or that he will take or retain them in spite of their nonconformity; or
- (b) fails to make an effective rejection (subsection (1) of Section 2–602), but such acceptance does not occur until the buyer has had a reasonable opportunity to inspect them; or

(c) does any act inconsistent with the seller's ownership; but if such act is wrongful as against the seller it is an acceptance only if ratified by him.

(2) Acceptance of a part of any commercial unit is acceptance of that entire unit.

§ 2–607. Effect of Acceptance; Notice of Breach; Burden of Establishing Breach after Acceptance; Notice of Claim or Litigation to Person Answerable Over

(1) The buyer must pay at the contract rate for any goods accepted.

(2) Acceptance of goods by the buyer precludes rejection of the goods accepted and if made with knowledge of a nonconformity cannot be revoked because of it unless the acceptance was on the reasonable assumption that the nonconformity would be seasonably cured; but acceptance does not of itself impair any other remedy provided by this Article for nonconformity.

(3) Where a tender has been accepted

(a) the buyer must within a reasonable time after he discovers or should have discovered any breach notify the seller of breach or be barred from any remedy; and

(b) if the claim is one for infringement or the like (subsection (3) of Section 2–312) and the buyer is sued as a result of such a breach he must so notify the seller within a reasonable time after he receives notice of the litigation or be barred from any remedy over for liability established by the litigation.

(4) The burden is on the buyer to establish any breach with respect to the goods accepted.

(5) Where the buyer is sued for breach of a warranty or other obligation for which his seller is answerable over

(a) he may give his seller written notice of the litigation. If the notice states that the seller may come in and defend and that if the seller does not do so he will be bound in any action against him by his buyer by any determination of fact common to the two litigations, then unless the seller after seasonable receipt of the notice does come in and defend he is so bound.

(b) if the claim is one for infringement or the like (subsection (3) of Section 2–312) the original seller may demand in writing that his buyer turn over to him control of the litigation including settlement or else be barred from any remedy over and if he also agrees to bear all expense and to satisfy any adverse judgment, then unless the buyer after seasonable receipt of the demand does turn over control the buyer is so barred.

(6) The provisions of subsection (3), (4), and (5) apply to any obligation of a buyer to hold the seller harmless against infringement or the like (subsection (3) of Section 2–312).

§ 2–608. Revocation of Acceptance in Whole or in Part

(1) The buyer may revoke his acceptance of a lot or commercial unit whose nonconformity substantially impairs its value to him if he has accepted it

(a) on the reasonable assumption that its nonconformity would be cured and it has not been seasonably cured; or

(b) without discovery of such nonconformity if his acceptance was reasonably induced either by the difficulty of discovery before acceptance or by the seller's assurances.

(2) Revocation of acceptance must occur within a reasonable time after the buyer discovers or should have discovered the ground for it and before any substantial change in condition of the goods which is not caused by their own defects. It is not effective until the buyer notifies the seller of it.

(3) A buyer who so revokes has the same rights and duties with regard to the goods involved as if he had rejected them.

§ 2–609. *Right to Adequate Assurance of Performance*

(1) A contract for sale imposes an obligation on each party that the other's expectation of receiving due performance will not be impaired. When reasonable grounds for insecurity arise with respect to the performance of either party the other may in writing demand adequate assurance of due performance and until he receives such assurance may if commercially reasonable suspend any performance for which he has not already received the agreed return.

(2) Between merchants the reasonableness of grounds for insecurity and the adequacy of any assurance offered shall be determined according to commercial standards.

(3) Acceptance of any improper delivery or payment does not prejudice the aggrieved party's right to demand adequate assurance of future performance.

(4) After receipt of a justified demand failure to provide within a reasonable time not exceeding 30 days such assurance of due performance as is adequate under the circumstances of the particular case is a repudiation of the contract.

§ 2–610. *Anticipatory Repudiation*

When either party repudiates the contract with respect to a performance not yet due the loss of which will substantially impair the value of the contract to the other, the aggrieved party may

(a) for a commercially reasonable time await performance by the repudiating party; or

(b) resort to any remedy for breach (Section 2–703 or Section 2–711), even though he has notified the repudiating party that he would await the latter's performance and has urged retraction; and

(c) in either case suspend his own performance or proceed in accordance with the provisions of this Article on the seller's right to identify goods to the contract notwithstanding breach or to salvage unfinished goods (Section 2–704).

§ 2–611. *Retraction of Anticipatory Repudiation*

(1) Until the repudiating party's next performance is due he can retract his repudiation unless the aggrieved party has since the repudiation cancelled or materially changed his position or otherwise indicated that he considers the repudiation final.

(2) Retraction may be by any method which clearly indicates to the aggrieved party that the repudiating party intends to perform, but must include any assurance justifiably demanded under the provisions of this Article (Section 2–609).

(3) Retraction reinstates the repudiating party's rights under the contract with due excuse and allowance to the aggrieved party for any delay occasioned by the repudiation.

§ 2–612. "Installment Contract"; Breach

(1) An "installment contract" is one which requires or authorizes the delivery of goods in separate lots to be separately accepted, even though the contract contains a clause "each delivery is a separate contract" or its equivalent.

(2) The buyer may reject any installment which is nonconforming if the nonconformity substantially impairs the value of that installment and cannot be cured or if the nonconformity is a defect in the required documents; but if the nonconformity does not fall within subsection (3) and the seller gives adequate assurance of its cure the buyer must accept that installment.

(3) Whenever nonconformity or default with respect to one or more installments substantially impairs the value of the whole contract there is a breach of the whole. But the aggrieved party reinstates the contract if he accepts a nonconforming installment without seasonably notifying of cancellation or if he brings an action with respect only to past installments or demands performance as to future installments.

§ 2–613. Casualty to Identified Goods

Where the contract requires for its performance goods identified when the contract is made, and the goods suffer casualty without fault of either party before the risk of loss passes to the buyer, or in a proper case under a "no arrival, no sale" term (Section 2–324) then

    (a) if the loss is total the contract is avoided; and

    (b) if the loss is partial or the goods have so deteriorated as no longer to conform to the contract the buyer may nevertheless demand inspection and at his option either treat the contract as voided or accept the goods with due allowance from the contract price for the deterioration or the deficiency in quantity but without further right against the seller.

§ 2–614. Substituted Performance

(1) Where without fault of either party the agreed berthing, loading, or unloading facilities fail or an agreed type of carrier becomes unavailable or the agreed manner of delivery otherwise becomes commercially impracticable but a commercially reasonable substitute is available, such substitute performance must be tendered and accepted.

(2) If the agreed means or manner of payment fails because of domestic or foreign governmental regulation, the seller may withhold or stop delivery unless the buyer provides a means or manner of payment which is commercially a substantial equivalent. If delivery has already been taken, payment by the means or in the manner provided by the regulation discharges the buyer's obligation unless the regulation is discriminatory, oppressive, or predatory.

§ 2–615. Excuse by Failure of Presupposed Conditions

Except so far as a seller may have assumed a greater obligation and subject to the preceding section on substituted performance,

(a) delay in delivery or nondelivery in whole or in part by a seller who complies with paragraphs (b) and (c) is not a breach of his duty under a contract for sale if performance as agreed has been made impracticable by the occurrence of a contingency the nonoccurrence of which was a basic assumption on which the contract was made or by compliance in good faith with any applicable foreign or domestic governmental regulation or order whether or not it later proves to be invalid.

(b) where the causes mentioned in paragraph (a) affect only a part of the seller's capacity to perform, he must allocate production and deliveries among his customers but may at his option include regular customers not then under contract as well as his own requirements for further manufacture. He may so allocate in any manner which is fair and reasonable.

(c) the seller must notify the buyer seasonably that there will be delay or nondelivery and, when allocation is required under paragraph (b), of the estimated quota thus made available for the buyer.

§ 2–616. Procedure on Notice Claiming Excuse

(1) Where the buyer receives notification of a material or indefinite delay or an allocation justified under the preceding section he may by written notification to the seller as to any delivery concerned, and where the prospective deficiency substantially impairs the value of the whole contract under the provisions of this Article relating to breach of installment contracts (Section 2–612), then also as to the whole,

(a) terminate and thereby discharge any unexecuted portion of the contract; or

(b) modify the contract by agreeing to take his available quota in substitution.

(2) If after receipt of such notification from the seller the buyer fails so to modify the contract within a reasonable time not exceeding 30 days the contract lapses with respect to any deliveries affected.

(3) The provisions of this section may not be negated by agreement except in so far as the seller has assumed a greater obligation under the preceding section.

Part 7. Remedies

§ 2–701. Remedies for Breach of Collateral Contracts Not Impaired

Remedies for breach of any obligation or promise collateral or ancillary to a contract for sale or not impaired by the provisions of this Article.

§ 2–702. Seller's Remedies on Discovery of Buyer's Insolvency

(1) Where the seller discovers the buyer to be insolvent he may refuse delivery except for cash including payment for all goods therefore delivered under the contract, and stop delivery under this Article (Section 2–705).

(2) Where the seller discovers that the buyer has received goods on credit while insolvent he may reclaim the goods upon demand made within 10 days after the receipt, but if misrepresentation of solvency has been made to the particular seller in writing within three months before delivery the 10-day limitation does not apply. Except as provided in this subsection the seller may not base a right to reclaim goods on the buyer's fraudulent or innocent misrepresentation of solvency or of intent to pay.

(3) The seller's right to reclaim under subsection (2) is subject to the rights of a buyer in ordinary course or other good-faith purchaser under this Article (Section 2–403). Successful reclamation of goods excludes all other remedies with respect to them.

§ 2–703. Seller's Remedies in General

Where the buyer wrongfully rejects or revokes acceptance of goods or fails to make a payment due on or before delivery or repudiates with respect to a part or the whole, then with respect to any goods directly affected and, if the breach is of the whole contract (Section 2–612), then also with respect to the whole undelivered balance, the aggrieved seller may

(a) withhold delivery of such goods;

(b) stop delivery by any bailee as hereafter provided (Section 2–705);

(c) proceed under the next section respecting goods still unidentified to the contract;

(d) resell and recover damages as hereafter provided (Section 2–706);

(e) recover damages for nonacceptance (Section 2–708) or in a proper case the price (Section 2–709);

(f) cancel.

§ 2–704. Seller's Right to Identify Goods to the Contract Notwithstanding Breach or to Salvage Unfinished Goods

(1) An aggrieved seller under the preceding section may

(a) identify to the contract conforming goods not already identified if at the time he learned of the breach they are in his possession or control;

(b) treat as the subject of resale goods which have demonstrably been intended for the particular contract even though those goods are unfinished.

(2) Where the goods are unfinished an aggrieved seller may in the exercise of reasonable commercial judgment for the purposes of avoiding loss and of effective realization either complete the manufacture and wholly identify the goods to the contract or cease manufacture and resell for scrap or salvage value or proceed in any other reasonable manner.

§ 2–705. Seller's Stoppage of Delivery in Transit or Otherwise

(1) The seller may stop delivery of goods in the possession of a carrier or other bailee when he discovers the buyer to be insolvent (Section 2–702) and may stop delivery of carload, truckload, planeload, or larger shipments of express or freight when the buyer repudiates or fails to make a payment due before delivery or if for any other reason the seller has a right to withhold or reclaim the goods.

(2) As against such buyer the seller may stop delivery until

(a) receipt of the goods by the buyer; or

(b) acknowledgment to the buyer by any bailee of the goods except a carrier that the bailee holds the goods for the buyer; or

(c) such acknowledgment to the buyer by a carrier by reshipment or as warehouseman; or

(d) negotiation to the buyer of any negotiable document of title covering the goods.

(3) (a) To stop delivery the seller must so notify as to enable the bailee by reasonable diligence to prevent delivery of the goods.

   (b) After such notification the bailee must hold and deliver the goods according to the directions of the seller, but the seller is liable to the bailee for any ensuing charges or damages.

   (c) If a negotiable document of title has been issued for goods, the bailee is not obliged to obey a notification to stop until surrender of the document.

   (d) A carrier who has issued a nonnegotiable bill of lading is not obliged to obey a notification to stop received from a person other than the consignor.

§ 2–706. Seller's Resale Including Contract for Resale

(1) Under the conditions stated in Section 2–703 on seller's remedies, the seller may resell the goods concerned or the undelivered balance thereof. Where the resale is made in good faith and in a commercially reasonable manner the seller may recover the difference between the resale price and the contract price together with any incidental damages allowed under the provisions of this Article (Section 2–710), but less expenses saved in consequence of the buyer's breach.

(2) Except as otherwise provided in subsection (3) or unless otherwise agreed resale may be at public or private sale including sale by way of one or more contracts to sell or of identification to an existing contract of the seller. Sale may be as a unit or in parcels and at any time and place and on any terms but every aspect of the sale including the method, manner, time, place, and terms must be commercially reasonable. The resale must be reasonably identified as referring to the broken contract, but it is not necessary that the goods be in existence or that any or all of them have been identified to the contract before the breach.

(3) Where the resale is at private sale the seller must give the buyer reasonable notification of his intention to resell.

(4) Where the resale is at public sale

   (a) only identified goods can be sold except where there is a recognized market for a public sale of futures in goods of the kind; and

   (b) it must be made at a usual place or market for public sale if one is reasonably available and except in the case of goods which are perishable or threaten to decline in value speedily the seller must give the buyer reasonable notice of the time and place of the resale; and

   (c) if the goods are not to be within the view of those attending the sale the notification of sale must state the place where the goods are located and provide for their reasonable inspection by prospective bidders; and

   (d) the seller may buy.

(5) A purchaser who buys in good faith at a resale takes the goods free of any rights of the original buyer even though the seller fails to comply with one or more of the requirements of this section.

(6) The seller is not accountable to the buyer for any profit made on any resale. A person in the position of a seller (Section 2–707) or a buyer who has rightfully rejected or justifiably revoked acceptance must account for any excess over the amount of his security interest, as hereinafter defined (subsection (3) of Section 2–711).

§ 2–707. "Person in the Position of a Seller"

(1) A "person in the position of a seller" includes as against a principal an agent who has paid or become responsible for the price of goods on behalf of his principal or anyone who otherwise holds a security interest or other right in goods similar to that of a seller.

(2) A person in the position of a seller may as provided in this Article withhold or stop delivery (Section 2–705) and resell (Section 2–706) and recover incidental damages (Section 2–710).

§ 2–708. Seller's Damages for Nonacceptance or Repudiation

(1) Subject to subsection (2) and to the provisions of this Article with respect to proof of market price (Section 2–723), the measure of damages for nonacceptance or repudiation by the buyer is the difference between the market price at the time and place for tender and the unpaid contract price together with any incidental damages provided in this Article (Section 2–710), but less expenses saved in consequence of the buyer's breach.

(2) if the measure of damages provided in subsection (1) is inadequate to put the seller in as good a position as performance would have done then the measure of damages is the profit (including reasonable overhead) which the seller would have made from full performance by the buyer, together with any incidental damages provided in this Article (Section 2–710), due allowance for costs reasonably incurred and due credit for payments or proceeds of resale.

§ 2–709. Action for the Price

(1) When the buyer fails to pay the price as it becomes due the seller may recover, together with any incidental damages under the next section, the price

    (a) of goods accepted or of conforming goods lost or damaged within a commercially reasonable time after risk of their loss has passed to the buyer; and

    (b) of goods identified to the contract if the seller is unable after reasonable effort to resell them at a reasonable price or the circumstances reasonably indicate that such effort will be unavailing.

(2) Where the seller sues for the price he must hold for the buyer any goods which have been identified to the contract and are still in his control except that if resale becomes possible he may resell them at any time prior to the collection of the judgment. The net proceeds of any such resale must be credited to the buyer, and payment of the judgment entitles him to any goods not resold.

(3) After the buyer has wrongfully rejected or revoked acceptance of the goods or has failed to make a payment due or has repudiated (Section 2–610), a seller who is held not entitled to the price under this section shall nevertheless be awarded damages for nonacceptance under the preceeding section.

§ 2–710. Seller's Incidental Damages

Incidental damages to an aggrieved seller include any commercially reasonable charges, expenses, or commissions incurred in stopping delivery, in the transportation, care, and custody of goods after the buyer's breach in connection with return or resale of the goods, or otherwise resulting from the breach.

§ 2–711. *Buyer's Remedies in General; Buyer's Security Interest in Rejected Goods*

(1) Where the seller fails to make delivery or repudiates or the buyer rightfully rejects or justifiably revokes acceptance then with respect to any goods involved, and with respect to the whole if the breach goes to the whole contract (Section 2–612), the buyer may cancel and whether or not he has done so may in addition to recovering so much of the price as has been paid

> (a) "cover" and have damages under the next section as to all the goods affected whether or not they have been identified to the contract; or
>
> (b) recover damages for nondelivery as provided in this Article (Section 2–713).

(2) Where the seller fails to deliver or repudiates the buyer may also

> (a) if the goods have been identified recover them as provided in this Article (Section 2–502); or
>
> (b) in a proper case obtain specific performance or replevy the goods as provided in this Article (Section 2–716).

(3) On rightful rejection of justifiable revocation of acceptance a buyer has a security interest in goods in his possession or control for any payments made on their price and any expenses reasonably incurred in their inspection, receipt, transportation, care, and custody and may hold such goods and resell them in like manner as an aggrieved seller (Section 2–706).

§ 2–712. *"Cover"; Buyer's Procurement of Substitute Goods*

(1) After a breach within the preceding section the buyer may "cover" by making in good faith and without unreasonable delay any reasonable purchase of or contract to purchase goods in substitution for those due from the seller.

(2) The buyer may recover from the seller as damages the difference between the cost of cover and the contract price together with any incidental or consequential damages as hereinafter defined (Section 2–715), but less expenses saved in consequence of the seller's breach.

(3) Failure of the buyer to effect cover within this section does not bar him from any other remedy.

§ 2–713. *Buyer's Damages for Nondelivery or Repudiation*

(1) Subject to the provisions of this Article with respect to proof of market price (Section 2–723), the measure of damages for nondelivery or repudiation by the seller is the difference between the market price at the time when the buyer learned of the breach and the contract price together with any incidental and consequential damages provided in this Article (Section 2–715), but less expenses saved in consequence of the seller's breach.

(2) Market price is to be determined as of the place for tender or, in cases of rejection after arrival or revocation of acceptance, as of the place of arrival.

§ 2–714. *Buyer's Damages for Breach in Regard to Accepted Goods*

(1) Where the buyer has accepted goods and given notification (subsection (3) of Section 2–607) he may recover as damages for any nonconformity of tender the loss resulting

in the ordinary course of events from the seller's breach as determined in any manner which is reasonable.

(2) The measure of damages for breach of warranty is the difference at the time and place of acceptance between the value of the goods accepted and the value they would have had if they had been as warranted, unless special circumstances show proximate damages of a different amount.

(3) In a proper case any incidental and consequential damages under the next section may also be recovered.

§ 2–715. *Buyer's Incidental and Consequential Damages*

(1) Incidental damages resulting from the seller's breach include expenses reasonably incurred in inspection, receipt, transportation, and care and custody of goods rightfully rejected, any commercially reasonable charges, expenses, or commissions in connection with effecting cover, and any other reasonable expense incident to the delay or other breach.

(2) Consequential damages resulting from the seller's breach include

- (a) any loss resulting from general or particular requirements and needs of which the seller at the time of contracting had reason to know and which could not reasonably be prevented by cover or otherwise; and
- (b) injury to person or property proximately resulting from any breach of warranty.

§ 2–716. *Buyer's Right to Specific Performance or Replevin*

(1) Specific performance may be decreed where the goods are unique or in other proper circumstances.

(2) The decree for specific performance may include such terms and conditions as to payment of the price, damages, or other relief as the court may deem just.

(3) The buyer has a right of replevin for goods identified to the contract if after reasonable effort he is unable to effect cover for such goods or the circumstances reasonably indicate that such effort will be unvailing or if the goods have been shipped under reservation and satisfaction of the security interest in them has been made or tendered. In the case of goods bought for personal, family, or household purposes, the buyer's right of replevin vests upon acquisition of a special property, even if the seller had not then repudiated or failed to deliver.

§ 2–717. *Deduction of Damages from the Price*

The buyer on notifying the seller of his intention to do so may deduct all or any part of the damages resulting from any breach of the contract from any part of the price still due under the same contract.

§ 2–718. *Liquidation or Limitation of Damages; Deposits*

(1) Damages for breach by either party may be liquidated in the agreement but only at an amount which is reasonable in the light of the anticipated or actual harm caused by the breach, the difficulties of proof of loss, and the inconvenience of nonfeasibility of otherwise obtaining an adequate remedy. A team fixing unreasonably large liquidated damages is void as a penalty.

(2) Where the seller justifiably withholds delivery of goods because of the buyer's breach, the buyer is entitled to restitution of any amount by which the sum of his payments exceeds

(a) the amount to which the seller is entitled by virtue of terms liquidating the seller's damages in accordance with subsection (1), or

(b) in the absence of such terms, 20 percent of the value of the total performance for which the buyer is obligated under the contract or $500, whichever is smaller.

(3) The buyer's right to restitution under subsection (2) is subject to offset to the extent that the seller establishes

(a) a right to recover damages under the provisions of this Article other than subsection (1), and

(b) the amount or value of any benefits received by the buyer directly or indirectly by reason of the contract.

(4) Where a seller has received payment in goods their reasonable value or the proceeds of their resale shall be treated as payments for the purposes of subsection (2); but if the seller has notice of the buyer's breach before reselling goods received in part performance, his resale is subject to the conditions laid down in this Article on resale by an aggrieved seller (Section 2–706).

§ 2–719. *Contractual Modification or Limitation of Remedy*

(1) Subject to the provisions of subsections (2) and (3) of this section and of the preceding section on liquidation and limitation of damages,

(a) the agreement may provide for remedies in addition to or in substitution for those provided in this Article and may limit or alter the measure of damages recoverable under this Article, as by limiting the buyer's remedies to return of the goods and repayment of the price or to repair and replacement of non-conforming goods or parts; and

(b) resort to a remedy as provided is optional unless the remedy is expressly agreed to be exclusive, in which case it is the sole remedy.

(2) Where circumstances cause an exclusive or limited remedy to fail of its essential purpose, remedy may be had as provided in this Act.

(3) Consequential damages may be limited or excluded unless the limitation or exclusion is unconscionable. Limitation of consequential damages for injury to the person in the case of consumer goods is prima facie unconscionable but limitation of damages where the loss is commercial is not.

§ 2–720. *Effect of "Cancellation" or "Rescission" on Claims for Antecedent Breach*

Unless the contrary intention clearly appears, expressions of "cancellation" or "rescission" of the contract or the like shall not be construed as renunciation or discharge of any claim in damages for an antecedent breach.

§ 2–721. *Remedies for Fraud*

Remedies for material misrepresentation or fraud include all remedies available under this Article for non-fraudulent breach. Neither rescission or a claim for rescission of the contract for sale nor rejection or return of the goods shall bar or be deemed inconsistent with a claim for damages or other remedy.

§ 2–722. *Who Can Sue Third Parties for Injury to Goods*

Where a third party so deals with goods which have been identified to a contract for sale as to cause actionable injury to a party to that contract

 (a) a right of action against the third party is in either party to the contract for sale who has title to or a security interest or a special property or an insurable interest in the goods; and if the goods have been destroyed or converted a right of action is also in the party who either bore the risk of loss under the contract for sale or has since the injury assumed that risk as against the other;

 (b) if at the time of the injury the party plaintiff did not bear the risk of loss as against the other party to the contract for sale and there is no arrangement between them for disposition of the recovery, his suit or settlement is, subject to his own interest, as a fiduciary for the other party to the contract;

 (c) either party may with the consent of the other sue for the benefit of whom it may concern.

§ 2–723. *Proof of Market Price: Time and Place*

(1) If an action based on anticipatory repudiation comes to trial before the time for performance with respect to some or all of the goods, any damages based on market price (Section 2–708 or Section 2–713) shall be determined according to the price of such goods prevailing at the time when the aggrieved party learned of the repudiation.

(2) If evidence of a price prevailing at the times or places described in this Article is not readily available the price prevailing within any reasonable time before or after the time described or at any other place which in commercial judgment or under usage of trade would serve as a reasonable substitute for the one described may be used, making any proper allowance for the cost of transporting the goods to or from such other place.

(3) Evidence of a relevant price prevailing at a time or place other than the one described in this Article offered by one party is not admissible unless and until he has given the other party such notice as the court finds sufficient to prevent unfair surprise.

§ 2–724. *Admissibility of Market Quotations*

Whenever the prevailing price or value of any goods regularly bought and sold in any established commodity market is in issue, reports in official publications or trade journals or in newspapers or periodicals of general circulation published as the reports of such market shall be admissible in evidence. The circumstances of the preparation of such a report may be shown to affect its weight but not its admissibility.

§ 2–725. *Statute of Limitations in Contracts for Sale*

(1) An action for breach of any contract for sale must be commenced within four years after the cause of action has accrued. By the original agreement the parties may reduce the period of limitation to not less than one year but may not extend it.

(2) A cause of action accrues when the breach occurs, regardless of the aggrieved party's lack of knowledge of the breach. A breach of warranty occurs when tender of

delivery is made, except that where a warranty explicitly extends to future performance of the goods and discovery of the breach must await the time of such performance the cause of action accrues when the breach is or should have been discovered.

(3) Where an action commenced within the time limited by subsection (1) is so terminated as to leave available a remedy by another action for the same breach such other action may be commenced after the expiration of the time limited and within six months after the termination of the first action unless the termination resulted from voluntary discontinuance or from dismissal for failure or neglect to prosecute.

(4) This section does not alter the law on tolling of the statute of limitations nor does it apply to causes of action which have accrued before this Act becomes effective.

A

absolute privilege   In libel and slander law, situations where a defendant is entirely excused from liability for defamatory statements because of the circumstances under which the statements were made.

acceptance   The actual or implied receipt and retention of that which is tendered or offered.

accord and satisfaction   A legally binding agreement to settle a disputed claim for a definite amount.

accredited investors   Financially sophisticated and/ or wealthy individuals and institutions who understand and can withstand the risk associated with securities investments.

act of state doctrine   The view that a judge in the United States or another country does not have the authority to challenge the legality of acts by a foreign government within that foreign government's own borders.

actus reus   Wrongful act or omission.

ad substantiation   Under Federal Trade Commission policy, product claims for which reasonable evidentiary support does not exist. Constitute unfair and deceptive trade practices.

ad valorem   According to value. Hence an ad valorem tax would be based on the value of the item in question rather than, for example, a fixed rate for all such items.

adjudication   The formal pronouncement of a judgment in a legal proceeding.

adjustment of debts   Individuals with limited debts are protected from creditors while paying their debts in installments (Chapter 13 bankruptcy).

administrative agency   An agency of the government charged with administering particular legislation.

administrative law   That branch of public law addressing the operation of the government's various agencies and commissions. Also the rules and regulations established by those agencies and commissions.

administrative law judge   An officer who presides at the initial hearing on matters litigated before an administrative agency. He or she is independent of the agency staff.

Administrative Procedure Act   A federal statute specifying the procedural rules under which the government's agencies and commissions conduct their business.

adverse impact   An employee may make a prima facie case for adverse impact where the employer's facially neutral rule may result in a different impact on one protected group than on another.

adverse possession   Open and notorious possession of real property over a given length of time that denies ownership in any other claimant.

advisory jurisdiction   Power of the International Court of Justice (ICJ) to hear a dispute and to render an advisory opinion on the matter. The opinion is not binding on any party.

affidavit   A written statement sworn to by a person officially empowered to administer an oath.

affirmative action   A government or private-sector program, springing from the civil rights movement, designed to actively promote the employment or educational opportunities of protected classes rather than merely forbidding discrimination.

affirmative defense   A portion of a defendant's answer to a complaint in which defendant presents contentions that, if proved true, will relieve the defendant of liability even if the assertions in the complaint are correct.

agent   A person entrusted by a principal to act on behalf of that principal; one who is authorized to carry out the business of another.

agreement   A meeting of the minds based on an offer by one party and acceptance by another.

alternate dispute resolution   The growing practice of employing strategies other than conventional litigation to solve conflicts. Those strategies include negotiation, arbitration, and mediation with variations such as "mini-trials" and "rent-a-judge" arrangements.

amicus curiae   A "friend of the court" who, though not a party to the case, files a brief because of a strong interest in the litigation.

annual percentage rate (APR)   The rate of interest charged for borrowing money as expressed in a standardized, yearly manner allowing for comparison among lenders' fees.

annual percentage yield (APY)   The rate of interest paid on a deposit as expressed in a standardized, yearly manner allowing for comparison of returns among institutions.

answer   The defendant's first pleading in a lawsuit, in which the defendant responds to the allegations raised in the plaintiff's complaint.

anticipatory breach   A contracting party's indication before the time for performance that he cannot or will not perform the contract. Same as **anticipatory repudiation.**

appeal   The judicial process by which a party petitions a higher court to review the decisions of a lower court or agency to correct errors.

appellant   The party filing an appeal.

appellee   The party against whom an appeal is filed.

appraisal   Assessment of the value of property by one with appropriate qualifications for the task.

appropriation   Making commercial use of an individual's name or likeness without permission.

arbitrary trademark   A trademark that is a new word or a common word that bears no relation to the product to which it is applied.

arbitration   An extrajudicial process in which a dispute is submitted to a mutually agreeable third party for a decision.

arraignment   A criminal law proceeding in which a defendant is brought before a judge to be informed of the charges and to file a plea.

articles of incorporation   Document filed with a state to create a corporation.

assault   A show of force that would cause reasonable persons to believe that they are about to receive an intentional, unwanted, harmful physical touching.

assignee   A person to whom an assignment is made.

assignment   A transfer of property, or some right or interest therein, from one person to another.

assignor   The maker of an assignment.

assumption of risk   An affirmative defense in a negligence case in which the defendant seeks to bar recovery by the plaintiff by showing that the plaintiff knowingly exposed himself or herself to the danger that resulted in injury.

attachment   As to secured transactions, the process by which a security interest in the property of another becomes enforceable.

at-will employee   An individual not under contract for a specified term and therefore, under the general rule, subject to discharge by the employer at any time and for any reason.

B

bait-and-switch advertising   An unlawful sales tactic in which the seller attracts buyer interest by insincerely advertising a product at a dramatically reduced price while holding no genuine intent to sell the product at that price. The seller then disparages the "bait" and diverts the buyer's attention to a higher-priced product (the switch), which was the sales goal from the first.

barriers to entry   Economic or technological conditions in a market making entry by a new competitor very difficult.

battery   An intentional, unwanted, harmful physical touching.

beyond a reasonable doubt   The level of proof required for conviction in a criminal case.

bilateral contract   A contract formed by an offer requiring a reciprocal promise.

blacklists   Lists of union organizers or participants in labor activities circulated to companies to dissuade the companies from hiring the listed individuals.

blue laws   Laws forbidding certain kinds of business on Sundays.

blue sky laws   Statutes regulating the sale of stocks and other securities to prevent consumer fraud.

bona fide   In good faith; honestly.

bona fide occupational qualification (BFOQ)   A defense in a discrimination claim where the employer argues that a particular religion, sex, or national origin is a necessary qualification for a particular job.

boycott   A confederation or conspiracy involving a refusal to do business with another or an attempt by the confederation to stop others from doing business with the target person or organization.

breach of contract   Failure, without legal excuse, to perform any promise that forms the whole or part of a contract.

breach of warranty   Failure, without legal excuse, to fulfill the terms of the guarantee.

bribe   Anything of value given or taken with the corrupt intent to influence an official in the performance of her or his duties.

brief   A written document setting out for the court the facts, the law, and the argument of a party to the lawsuit.

burden of proof   The party with the burden of proof (normally the plaintiff in a civil suit and the state in a criminal case) is required to prove the truth of a claim or lose on that issue.

business judgment rule   A rule protecting business managers from liability for making bad decisions when they have acted prudently and in good faith.

bylaws   A document that governs the maintenance and operation of an organization.

C

capacity   The ability to incur legal obligations and acquire legal rights.

capitalism   Private ownership of the means of production with a largely unrestricted marketplace in goods and services.

cause of action   The legal theory on which a lawsuit is based.

cause in fact   The actual cause of an event. One of the required elements in a negligence claim.

caveat emptor   Let the buyer beware.

cease and desist order   An instruction from an agency instructing a party to refrain from a specified goal.

certificate of incorporation   An instrument from the state bestowing the right to do business under the corporate form of organization. Same as **charter.**

certiorari   A legal procedure affording an appellate court the opportunity to review a lower court decision. Also a writ asking the lower court for the record of the case.

choice of law rule   A rule of law in each jurisdiction that determines which jurisdiction's laws will be applied to a case. For instance, one state may have a choice of law rule that says that the law of the jurisdiction where the contract was signed shall govern any dispute, while another state may apply a different rule.

civil law   The branch of law dealing with private rights. Contrast with criminal law.

class action   A legal action brought by one on behalf of himself or herself and all others similarly situated.

Clean Air Act   Amended in 1990, establishes air quality standards and enforcement procedures for the standards.

Clean Water Act   Establishes standards for water quality relating to the protection of water life as well as for safe recreation, and the enforcement of those standards.

closed-end loan   Credit arrangement where a specified sum is borrowed and a repayment plan usually is established.

closely held corporation   A corporation with relatively few shareholders, the stock of which is not publicly traded. Also referred to as a **close corporation.**

closing date   The date on which a transfer of property is made.

Code of Federal Regulations   A compilation of final federal agency rules.

codetermination   German corporate governance and labor law system in which board representation by labor unions is required.

Colgate doctrine   Sellers may lawfully engage in resale price maintenance if they do nothing more than specify prices at which their products are to be resold and unilaterally refuse to deal with anyone who does not adhere to those prices.

collateral   Property pledged as security for satisfaction of a debt.

comity   Courtesy. Nations often recognize the laws of other nations not because they must do so but because of the tradition of comity: that is, goodwill and mutual respect.

Commerce Clause   The portion of the U.S. Constitution that provides for federal regulation of foreign and interstate trade.

commercial impracticability   The standard used by the Uniform Commercial Code (UCC) to relieve a party of his or her contract obligations because of the occurrence of unforeseeable, external events beyond his or her control.

commercial speech   Speech directed toward a business purpose. Advertising is an example of commercial speech. Such speech is protected by the First Amendment, but not to the degree that we protect other varieties of speech.

Commodity Futures Trading Commission (CFTC)   Federal regulatory agency responsible for overseeing futures trading.

common law   Judge-made law. To be distinguished from statutory law as created by legislative bodies.

common shares   Most universal type of corporate stock.

community property   Property acquired during marriage through the labor or skill of either spouse.

comparable worth   The legal theory that all employees should be paid the same wages for work requiring comparable skills, effort, and responsibility and having comparable worth to the employer.

comparative negligence   Defense in a negligence suit in which the plaintiff's recovery is reduced by an amount equivalent to her contribution to her own injury.

compensatory damages   Damages that will compensate a party for actual losses due to an injury suffered.

complaint   The first pleading filed by the plaintiff in a civil lawsuit.

comp time   Compensatory time. Giving an employee time off from work in place of cash for hours of overtime worked.

concerted activity   Organizing, forming, joining, or assisting labor organizations, bargaining collectively through representatives of the employees' choosing, or other activities taken for the purpose of collective bargaining or other mutual aid or protection.

concurrent conditions   When each party's obligation to perform under a contract is dependent on the other party's performance.

condemning   To appropriate land for public use.

conditions precedent   Conditions that operate to give rise to a contracting party's duty to perform.

conditions subsequent   Conditions that operate to discharge one from an obligation under a contract.

condominium or cooperative ownership   An interest in property where owners retain individual control and specific ownership over a precise segment of real estate, but own common areas as tenants in common.

confession of judgment clause   A clause stipulating that the lessee grants judgment in any action on the contract to the landlord without the formality of an ordinary proceeding.

conglomerate merger   A merger between firms operating in separate markets and having neither buyer–seller nor competitive relationships with each other.

conscious parallelism   Conduct by competitors that is very similar or identical but that is not the product of a conspiracy and thus is not, in and of itself, illegal.

consent decree   A settlement of a lawsuit arrived at by agreement of the parties. Effectively, an admission by the parties that the decree is a just determination of their rights.

consent order   The order administrative agencies issue when approving the settlement of an administrative action against some party.

consequential damages   Damages that do not flow directly and immediately from an act but rather flow from the results of the act.

consideration   A required element in an enforceable contract. The thing of value passing between the parties that results in a benefit to the one making the promise or a detriment to the one receiving the promise.

conspiracy   An agreement between two or more persons to commit an unlawful act.

constructive eviction   A breach of duty by the landlord that makes the property uninhabitable or otherwise deprives the tenant of the benefit of the lease and gives rise to the tenant's right to vacate the property and to terminate the lease.

consumer goods   Under the Uniform Commercial Code (UCC), goods used or bought primarily for personal, family, or household purposes.

contentious jurisdiction   Power of the International Court of Justice (ICJ) to hear a dispute and to render a binding opinion on the issue and the parties involved. All parties must give prior consent to contentious jurisdiction.

contingent fee   An arrangement wherein an attorney is compensated for his or her services by receiving a percentage of the award in a lawsuit rather than receiving an hourly wage or specified fee.

contingent workers   Workers that do not have an implicit or explicit contract for ongoing employment.

contract   An agreement that is legally enforceable by the courts.

contract of adhesion   One in which all the bargaining power (and all the contract terms) are unfairly on one side. This often occurs when buyers have no choice among sellers of a particular item, and when the seller uses a preprinted form contract.

contract bar rule   The National Labor Relations Board (NLRB) prohibits an election during the term of a collective bargaining agreement, for a maximum of three years.

contract firm workers   Workers employed by a company that provides them or their services under contract or leases. Usually are assigned to only one customer and work at the customer's worksite.

contributory negligence   A defense in a negligence action wherein the defendant attempts to demonstrate that the plaintiff contributed to the harm on which the litigation was based. Contrast with **comparative negligence.**

conversion   Wrongfully exercising control over the personal property of another.

copyright The creator's (artist, author, or the like) right to control the copying and distribution of his or her work for a period of time specified by statute.

corporate opportunity A doctrine that prevents corporate officials from personally appropriating an opportunity that belongs to the corporation.

corporation A form of business organization that is owned by shareholders who have no inherent right to manage the business, and is managed by a board of directors elected by the shareholders.

Council on Environmental Quality Serves as an adviser to the president in connection with the preparation of the annual Environmental Quality Report.

counterclaim A cause of action filed by the defendant in a lawsuit against the plaintiff in the same suit.

counteroffer Response by the offeree that, in its legal effect, constitutes a rejection of the original offer and proposes a new offer to the offeror.

countervailing duties Duties imposed by a government against the products of another government that has offered subsidies to its own producers.

covered disabilities A physical or mental impairment that substantially limits one or more major life activities of an individual; a record of such impairment or being regarded as having such impairment.

creditor A person to whom a debt is owed.

creditor beneficiary Person who has given consideration, who is an intended beneficiary of a contract though not a party, and thus is entitled to enforce the contract.

crime A public wrong, an act punishable by the state.

criminal law Wrongs against society that the state has seen fit to label as crimes and that may result in penalties against the perpetrator(s). Contrast with **civil law.**

cumulative voting A procedure for voting for directors that permits a shareholder to multiply the number of shares he or she owns by the number of directors to be elected and to cast the resulting total of votes for one or more directors.

curtesy interest The right of a husband upon the death of his wife to receive all of the wife's real property as long as the two had a child between them.

D

d.b.a. Doing business as.

de facto In fact. Actually. As in *de facto* school segregation, which is caused by social and economic conditions rather than by government act.

de jure Legitimate. Lawful. Of right. As in *de jure* school segregation, which is caused by government order and thus is legally correct even if morally wrong.

debenture Any long-term debt instrument, such as a bond, issued by a company or institution, secured only by the general assets of the issuer.

deceit A tort involving intentional misrepresentation to deceive or trick another.

deception Trade claim that is either false or likely to mislead the reasonable consumer and that is material to the consumer's decision making.

deceptive advertising Advertising practices likely to mislead the reasonable consumer where the practice in question is material in that it affected consumer choice.

decertification petition Election petition stating that a current bargaining representative no longer has the support of a majority of the employees in the bargaining unit.

declaration A document that defines the rights, responsibilities, and powers of property owners in a condominium.

declaratory judgment or order A judicial or agency action expressing an opinion or articulating the rights of the parties without actually requiring that anything be done.

deed An instrument transferring title to property.

deed of trust A three-party instrument used to create a security interest in real property in which the legal title to the real property is placed in one or more trustees to secure the repayment of a sum of money or the performance of other conditions.

defamation A false and intentional verbal or written expression that damages the reputation of another.

default A party fails to pay money when due or when lawfully demanded.

default judgment A judgment entered by the court in favor of the plaintiff because the defendant failed to respond to the plaintiff's complaint.

defeasible fee simple A title to property that is open to attack, that might be defeated by the performance of some act, or that is subject to conditions.

defendant The party in a civil suit against whom the cause of action was brought and, in a criminal case, the party against whom charges have been filed.

delegatee The one to whom a duty is delegated.

delegator The one who delegates a duty.

deontological ethics The rightness of an action depends on its conformance with duty, obligation, and moral requirements regardless of outcome.

deposition   A discovery procedure wherein a witness's sworn testimony is taken out of court, prior to trial, for subsequent use at trial.

deregulation   Returning authority to the free market by shrinking government bureaucracies and reducing government rules.

derivative suit   A lawsuit by a stockholder on behalf of the corporation where the corporation declines to act to protect the organization's rights against the conduct of an officer, director, or outsider.

derivatives   Specialized trading contracts tied to underlying assets such as bonds or currencies.

descriptive mark   A trademark that is merely descriptive of the product or its qualities.

dicta   Statements in a judicial opinion that are merely the views of the judge(s) and are not necessary for the resolution of the case.

directed verdict   A party to a lawsuit makes a motion asking the judge to instruct the jury to reach a particular decision because reasonable minds could not differ about the correct outcome of the case.

discharged   Released from liability.

disclaimer   As to warranties, a contract term wherein a party attempts to relieve itself of potential liability under that contract.

discovery   Legal procedures by which one party to a litigation may obtain information from the other party. Depositions and interrogatories are examples of discovery procedures.

disparate impact   Employment discrimination theory in which a facially neutral employment practice (such as requiring a high school diploma for new hires) results in an unfair and adverse impact on a protected class.

disparate treatment   Theory of employment discrimination wherein an individual or group is intentionally disfavored via actual discriminatory policies and practices.

dissolution   In partnership law, the change in the relation of the partners caused by any partner ceasing to be associated with the carrying on of the business.

diversity of citizenship   One standard by which federal courts may gain jurisdiction over a lawsuit. Plaintiffs and defendants must be from different states and more than $75,000 must be at issue.

divestiture   In antitrust law, a remedy wherein the court orders a defendant to dispose of specified assets.

dividend   A shareholder's earnings from his or her stock in a corporation.

doctrine of sovereign immunity   Principle that a foreign nation may not be sued in American courts, with certain exceptions.

dominant estate   The property accessed through an easement appurtenant or implied easement.

donee beneficiary   Person who has not given consideration, but is an intended beneficiary of a contract, though not a party, and is entitled to enforce the contract.

double jeopardy   The U.S. Constitution provides that the same individual may not be tried twice in the same tribunal for the same criminal offense.

dower interest   The right of a wife upon the death of her husband to receive a life estate in one-third of her husband's real property.

dramshop law   State laws imposing liability on the seller of intoxicating liquors when a third party is injured as a result of the intoxication of the buyer where the sale has caused or contributed to that intoxication.

due care and diligence   Corporate officers and directors must act in good faith and in a prudent manner.

due diligence   A defense against a securities violation claim where the defendant used ordinary prudence and still failed to find an error or omission in the registration statement.

due process   A constitutional principle requiring fairness in judicial proceedings and that government laws and conduct be free of arbitrariness and capriciousness.

dumping   The commercial practice of selling goods in a foreign market at a price substantially beneath that charged in the domestic market.

duress   Overpowering of the will of a person by force or fear.

duty of due care   Standard of conduct expected of a reasonable, prudent person under the circumstances.

E

easement   The right to use property without taking anything away from the property.

easement or profit appurtenant   The right of an owner of adjacent land to enter or to enter and take away from property next to it.

economies of scale   Expansion of a firm or industry's productive capacity resulting in a decline in long-run average costs of production.

efficiencies   A defense to an otherwise unlawful merger in which costs of production are reduced because of the merger.

election year or certification year bar   The National Labor Relations Board (NLRB) prohibits an election for 12 months following a prior election.

elective share   Legislative mandate that a spouse receive a specific percentage interest in a deceased spouse's estate.

embargo   Government order prohibiting importation of some or all products from a particular country.

embezzlement   The fraudulent and unauthorized taking of the money of another while charged with the care of that money.

Emergency Planning and Community Right-to-Know Act of 1986   Amended Superfund requiring companies to inform the government upon release of any hazardous chemicals into the environment and to provide to the government an inventory of their hazardous chemicals. The act also requires states to establish emergency procedures for chemical discharges.

eminent domain   The state's power to take private property for public use.

employer identification number   Number issued to employer by federal and state governments for the purpose of record keeping associated with income and Social Security tax collections.

en banc   All of the judges hearing a case as a group rather than individually or in panels.

enabling legislation   Law that establishes an administrative agency and grants power to that agency.

enjoin   To require. A court issues an injunction requiring a certain act or ordering a party to refrain from a certain act.

enterprise law   Legal doctrine treating all companies in a corporate group as one giant organization rather than a collection of smaller, independent units.

entity law   Legal doctrine treating each company in a corporate group as a separate, independent unit.

environmental impact statement   Statement of the anticipated impact on the environment of legislation or other major federal action, and suggestions for reasonable alternatives.

Environmental Protection Agency   Created in 1970 to gather information relating to pollution and to assist in pollution control efforts and sanctions.

equal protection   The Fourteenth Amendment to the U.S. Constitution provides that all similarly situated individuals are entitled to the same advantages and must bear the same burdens under the law.

equitable remedies   Injunction, specific performance, restraining orders, and the like, as opposed to money damages.

equity   Fairness; a system of courts that developed in England. A chancellor presided to mete out fairness in cases that were not traditionally assigned to the law courts headed by the king.

essential functions of a position   Those tasks that are fundamental, as opposed to marginal or unnecessary, to the fulfillment of the position's objectives.

Establishment Clause   The First Amendment to the U.S. Constitution forbids the U.S. government from creating a government-supported church or religion.

estate   An interest in land or property owned by a decedent at the time of her or his death.

estate *pur autre vie*   A life estate that is measured by the life of someone other than the possessor.

estoppel   A legal doctrine providing that one may not assert facts that are in conflict with one's own previous acts or deeds.

eviction   Depriving a tenant of the possession of leased premises.

excise taxes   Taxes imposed at both the state and federal levels on the sale of particular commodities, especially alcohol, tobacco, and gasoline.

exclusive dealing   Agreement to deal only with a particular buyer or a particular seller.

exculpatory clause   Portion of a contract that seeks to relieve one of the parties to the contract from any liability for breach of duty under that contract.

executed   In contract law, full performance of the terms of the bargain.

executed contract   Performances are complete.

executory contract   Not yet fully performed or completed.

exemplary damages   Same as **punitive damages.**

exempt property   Specified classes of property that are unavailable to the creditor upon default of the debtor.

exempt security   Certain kinds of securities and certain transactions involving securities are not required to meet federal registration requirements under the 1933 act.

existentialism   A philosophy emphasizing the individual's responsibility to make herself what she is to become. Existence precedes essence.

express authority   Corporate officers' powers as expressed in the bylaws or conferred by the board of directors.

express authorization   In contract law, offeror specifies a means of communication by which the offeree can accept.

express conditions   Conditions within contracts that are clear from the language.

express contract   Contract whose terms are clear from the language.

express warranty   A guarantee made by affirmation of fact or promise, by description of the goods, or by sample or model.

expropriation   A government's taking of a business's assets, such as a manufacturing facility, usually without just compensation.

extraterritoriality   The application of U.S. laws on persons, rights, or relations beyond the geographic limits of this country and even though the parties involved are not American citizens.

F

failing company doctrine   A defense to an otherwise unlawful merger in which the acquired firm is going out of business and no other purchaser is available.

fair use   A doctrine that permits the use of copyrighted works for purposes such as criticism, news reporting, training, or research.

false imprisonment   Tort of intentionally restricting the freedom of movement of another.

false light   Falsely and publicly attributing certain characteristics, conduct, or beliefs to another such that a reasonable person would be highly offended.

featherbedding   A labor law term describing the practice where workers were paid even though they did not perform any work. Featherbedding is a violation of federal labor law.

federal question   Litigation involving the federal constitution, statutes, and treaties. The federal courts have jurisdiction over cases involving federal questions.

Federal Register   Daily publication of federal agency regulations and other legal materials coming from the executive branch of government.

federal sentencing guidelines   Standards established by the U.S. Sentencing Commission that rank the seriousness of individual and organizational federal crimes and provide sentences that, with little flexibility, must be applied to those crimes.

Federal Trade Commission   Agency of the federal government responsible for promoting fair trade practices in interstate commerce.

federalism   The division of authority between the federal government and the states to maintain workable cooperation while diffusing political power.

fee simple   A form of land ownership that gives the owner the right to possess and to use the land for an unlimited period of time, subject only to governmental or private restrictions, and unconditional power to dispose of the property during his or her lifetime or upon death.

felony   A crime of a serious nature ordinarily involving punishment by death or imprisonment in a penitentiary.

fiduciary   One who holds a relationship of trust with another and has an obligation to act in the best interests of the other—for example, one who manages property on behalf of another.

fiduciary duty   The responsibility of one in a position of trust with another to act in the best interests of the other.

financing statement   Document notifying others that the creditor claims an interest in the debtor's collateral. Must be filed as provided for by law to perfect a security interest.

firm offer   Under the Uniform Commercial Code (UCC), a signed, written offer by a merchant containing assurances that it will be held open, and which is not revocable for the time stated in the offer, or for a reasonable time if no such time is stated.

fixture   A thing that was originally personal property and that has actually or constructively affixed to the soil itself or to some structure legally a part of the land.

foreclose   To terminate the mortgagor's rights in the property covered by the mortgage.

forum non conveniens   A legal principle under which a court may refuse to hear a case where it determines that another jurisdiction would provide a more appropriate location for the trial.

franchise   A marketing arrangement in which the franchisor permits the franchisee to produce, distribute, or sell the franchisor's product using the franchisor's name or trademark.

franchisee   A holder of a franchise.

franchisor   A party granting a franchise.

fraud   An intentional misrepresentation of a material fact with intent to deceive where the misrepresentation is justifiably relied on by another and damages result.

fraud-on-the-market theory   Misleading statements distort the market and thus defraud a securities buyer whether the buyer actually relies on the misstatement or not. Based on the assumption that the price of a stock reflects all of the available information about that stock.

Free Exercise Clause   First Amendment provision guaranteeing all Americans the right to pursue their religious beliefs free of government intervention (with limited exceptions).

free riders   Those who lawfully benefit from goods or services without paying a share of the cost of those goods or services.

Full Faith and Credit Clause   Provision of the U.S. Constitution requiring each state to recognize the laws and judicial decisions of all other states.

futures   Contracts to deliver or take delivery of specified quantities of commodities at a previously specified price.

G

G8   An association embracing eight of the world's leading industrial powers (Canada, France, Italy, Germany, Japan, Russia, the United Kingdom, and the United States) designed to improve worldwide economic and political conditions.

garnishment   Action by a creditor to secure the property of a debtor where that property is held by a third party.

General Agreement on Tariffs and Trade (GATT)   A World Trade Organization foundational document that establishes and regulates import duties among signatory countries.

General Agreement on Trade in Services (GATS)   A World Trade Organization foundational document that sets forth principles for reducing barriers to international trade in services.

general duty   An OSHA provision requiring that employers furnish to each employee a place of employment free from recognized hazards that cause or are likely to cause death or serious physical harm to the employee.

general warranty deed   A deed that carries with it certain warranties or guarantees.

generic mark   A trademark employing a common descriptive name for a product.

genuineness of assent   In contract law, the parties knowingly agreed to the same thing.

going private   Used to describe a transaction in which private investors buy all of the equity securities of a public corporation, such that the corporation ceases to be a public corporation.

going public   A reference to the first time a company sells its shares on the open market.

good faith   Honesty; an absence of intent to take advantage of another.

goods   All things that are movable at the time of identification to the contract for sale except the money in which the price is to be paid, investment securities, and so forth.

grand jury   A body of people convened by the state to determine whether the evidence is sufficient to bring a criminal indictment (formal accusation) against a party.

grant deed   A deed that does not have the warranties contained in a warranty deed.

gray market   Transactions conducted outside the usual supplier-approved channels of distribution. These transactions (unlike *black market* sales) are lawful but are often discouraged by suppliers. The gray market operates parallel to the "officially" authorized chain of distribution.

grease   Payments to low-ranking authorities for the purpose of facilitating business in another nation. Not forbidden by the Foreign Corrupt Practices Act if legal in the host nation.

greenhouse gas (GHG)   Any gas that when released in the atmosphere acts like the ceiling of a greenhouse to trap solar energy thereby contributing to global climate change. The most common greenhouse gas is carbon dioxide. Other greenhouse gases include methane, nitrous oxide, hydrofluorocarbons, perfluorocarbons, and sulfur hexafluoride.

greenmail   Takeover defense involving the target corporation's repurchase of a takeover raider's stock at a premium not offered to other shareholders.

group boycott   An agreement among traders to refuse to deal with one or more other traders.

guarantor   A person who promises to perform the same obligation as the principal if the principal should default.

H

Herfindahl–Hirschman Index (HHI) Calculation used by the Justice Department to determine the degree of economic concentration in a particular market and to determine the degree to which a proposed horizontal merger would further concentrate that market. Computed by squaring the market share of each firm in a market and summing those totals.

holdover lease The tenancy that exists where a tenant subject to a term lease is allowed to remain on the premises after the term has expired.

horizontal divisions of the market Competitors agree to share their market geographically or to allocate customers or products among themselves.

horizontal merger Acquisition by one company of another company competing in the same product and geographic markets.

hostile environment A form of sexual harassment in which sexual conduct, sexual remarks, sexual depictions, and the like render the workplace offensive and intimidating such that performance is affected even though no tangible employment action has occurred.

hostile takeover The acquisition of a formerly independent business where the acquired business resists the union.

I

Immigration Reform and Control Act (IRCA) Enacted by Congress, IRCA's purpose is to discourage the entry of illegal aliens to the United States.

implied authority Corporate officers' powers to take actions that are reasonably necessary to achieve their express duties.

implied authorization In contract law, where the offeror's behavior or previous dealings with the offeree suggest an agreeable means of communicating an acceptance.

implied easement Also called easement by prescription or way of necessity. An interest created where someone has openly used an adjoining piece of property for access with no complaint from the owner for a statutorily determined period of time.

implied warranty of fitness for a particular purpose A warranty that arises by operation of law and promises that the good warranted is reasonably useful for the buyer's purpose where the buyer was relying on the seller's expertise in making the purchase.

implied warranty of habitability Implied warranty arising in lease or sale of residential real estate that the property will be fit for human habitability.

implied warranty of merchantability A warranty that arises by operation of law and promises that the good warranted is at least of average, fair, reasonable quality.

implied-in-fact conditions Conditions derived from the parties' conduct and the circumstances of the bargain.

implied-in-fact contract Contract whose terms are implicitly understood based on the behavior of the parties.

implied-in-law conditions or constructive conditions Conditions imposed by the court to avoid unfairness.

in personam jurisdiction The power of the court over a person.

incidental beneficiary Person who is not a party to a contract, who benefits indirectly from the contract, who was not contemplated by the parties, and who may not enforce the contract.

incidental damages Collateral damages that are incurred because of a breach; damages that compensate a person injured by a breach of contract for reasonable costs incurred in an attempt to avoid further loss.

incorporators Those who initiate a new corporation.

indemnification Corporate policy to compensate officers and directors for losses sustained in defending themselves against litigation associated with their professional duties where those duties were performed with reasonable business judgment.

indemnify Reimburse one who has suffered a loss.

indenture Agreement governing the conditions under which bonds are issued.

indenture trustee Person or institution holding legal title to trust property and charged with carrying out the terms of the indenture.

independent contractor A person who contracts with a principal to perform some task according to his or her own methods, and who is not under the principal's control regarding the physical details of the work.

indictment A grand jury's formal accusation of a crime.

industry guides Published advice to industry and the public providing Federal Trade Commission interpretations of the likely legality of specific marketing practices.

information A prosecutor's formal accusation of a crime.

initial public offering (IPO) A security offered for sale to the public for the first time.

injunction A court order commanding a person or organization to do or not do a specified action.

injurious falsehood Intentional tort based on a false statement made with malice that disparages the property of another.

innocent misrepresentation An unintentional misrepresentation of material fact where the misrepresentation is justifiably relied on by another and damages result.

insider In securities law, anyone with a fiduciary duty who has knowledge of material facts not available to the general public.

insider trading Trading securities while in possession of material nonpublic information, in violation of a fiduciary duty.

intellectual property Intangible personal property, generally in the nature of copyrights, patents, and trademarks.

intent A conscious and purposeful state of mind.

intentional infliction of emotional distress Intentional tort based on outrageous conduct that causes severe emotional distress in another.

intentional tort Voluntary civil wrong causing harm to a protected interest.

interference with contractual relations Improperly causing a third party to breach or fail to perform its contract with another.

interference with prospective advantage Improperly causing a third party not to enter a prospective contractual relationship.

interpretive rules In administrative law, an agency's view of the meaning of statutes governing agency action.

interrogatories An ingredient in the discovery process wherein one party in a lawsuit directs written questions to another party in the lawsuit.

intrastate offerings Registration exemption for securities sold only to residents of the state in which the issuer is organized and doing business.

intrusion Wrongfully entering on or prying into the solitude or property of another.

invasion of privacy Violation of the right to be left alone.

invitee One who comes on the premises of another by invitation of the owner, in connection with the owner's business, and for the benefit of the owner or for the mutual benefit of the invitee and the owner.

J

joint liability Liability of a group of persons in which, if one of these persons is sued, he can insist that the other liable parties be joined to the suit as codefendants, so that all must be sued collectively.

joint and several liability Liability of a group of persons in which the plaintiff may sue all members of the group collectively or one or more individuals for the entire amount.

joint tenancy An estate held by two or more jointly with an equal right in all to share in the enjoyment of the land during their lives.

joint venture A form of business organization essentially identical to a partnership, except that it is engaged in a single project, not carrying on a business.

judgment notwithstanding the verdict (judgment n.o.v.) A judge's decision overruling the finding of the jury.

judgment proof Describes those against whom money judgments will have no effect because they are insolvent or their assets are beyond the reach of the court.

judicial review A court's authority to review statutes and, if appropriate, declare them unconstitutional. Also refers to appeals from administrative agencies.

jurisdiction The power of a judicial body to adjudicate a dispute. Also the geographical area within which that judicial body has authority to operate.

jurisprudence The philosophy and science of law.

jury instructions A judge's directions to the jury explaining the law that must be applied in the case at hand.

K

keiretsu Japanese cartels of vertically related firms working together in a collaborative fashion.

L

land contract Typically, an installment contract for the sale of land wherein the purchaser receives the deed from the owner on payment of the final installment.

landlord/lessor A party to a lease contract who allows a tenant to possess and to use his or her property in return for rent payments.

latent defects Imperfections that are not readily apparent upon reasonable inspection.

lease   A contract for the possession and use of land or other property, including goods, on one side, and a recompense of rent or other income on the other.

leasehold estate   A right to occupy and to use land pursuant to a lease or contract.

legal detriment   Any act or forbearance by a promisee.

legal impossibility   A party to a contract is relieved of his or her duty to perform when that performance has become objectively impossible because of the occurrence of an event unforeseen at the time of contracting.

legality of purpose   The object of the contract does not violate law or public policy.

legitimate nondiscriminatory reason (LNDR)   An employer's justification for taking adverse action against an employee or applicant where the basis for the action is something other than the individual's membership in a protected class (such as termination for dishonesty or theft).

lemon laws   State statutes providing remedies for those buying vehicles that turn out to be so thoroughly defective that they cannot be repaired after reasonable efforts.

letter of credit   A statement from a financial institution such as a bank guaranteeing that it will pay the financial obligations of a particular party.

libel   Tort of defaming or injuring another's reputation by a published writing.

license   A contractual right to use property in a certain manner.

licensee   A person lawfully on land in possession of another for purposes unconnected with business interests of the possessor.

licenses   Government-granted privileges to do some act or series of acts. Authorization to do what, without a license, would be unlawful. Same as **permits.**

lien   A claim against a piece of property in satisfaction of a debt; the financial interest of the lienholder in the property as a result of a debt or other obligation of the landowner.

life estate   A property interest that gives a person the right to possess and to use property for a time that is measured by her or his lifetime or that of another person.

life tenant   The possessor of a life estate interest.

limited liability   Maximum loss normally limited to the amount invested in the firm.

limited liability company (LLC)   Hybrid of limited partnership and corporation receiving partnership tax treatment with the operating advantages of a corporation.

limited liability partnership   A special partnership form providing some of the advantages of limited liability.

limited partnership   A form of business organization that has one or more general partners who manage the business and have unlimited liability for the obligations of the business and one or more limited partners who do not manage and have limited liability.

liquidated damages   Damages made certain by the prior agreement of the parties.

liquidation   "Straight" bankruptcy action in which all assets except exemptions are distributed to creditors (Chapter 7 bankruptcy).

lockout defense   Takeover defense where the target company manipulates its assets, shares, and so on, to make the company unattractive as a takeover candidate.

lockouts   Where employees are kept from the workplace by the employer. Where the landlord deprives the tenant of the possession of the premises by changing the locks on the property.

long-arm statute   A state enactment that accords the courts of that state the authority to claim jurisdiction over people and property beyond the borders of the state as long as certain "minimum contacts" exist between the state and the people or property.

M

mailbox rule   Rule holding that a mailed acceptance is effective upon dispatch when the offeror has used the mail to invite acceptance; the rule has been expanded to include the use of any reasonable manner of acceptance.

malice   A required element of proof in a libel or slander claim by a public figure. Proof of a defamatory statement expressed with actual knowledge of its falsity or with reckless disregard for the truth would establish malice.

malicious prosecution   Criminal prosecution carried on with malice and without probable cause with damages resulting.

malpractice   Improper or negligent conduct in the performance of duties by a professional such as a doctor or lawyer.

market failure   Economic theory arguing that the free market works imperfectly because of certain allegedly inherent defects such as monopoly, public goods, and so forth.

market foreclosure   In vertical mergers, the concern that the newly combined firm will close its doors to potential suppliers and purchasers such that competition will be harmed.

market share liability   Product liability action by which plaintiffs may be able to recover against manufacturers of defective products based on those manufacturers' market shares even though proof of causation cannot be established.

material breach   In contract law, performance that falls beneath substantial performance and does not have a lawful excuse.

mechanic's lien or materialman's lien   A claim created by law for the purpose of securing a priority of payment of the price or value of work performed and materials furnished in erecting or repairing a structure.

mediation   An extrajudicial proceeding in which a third party (the mediator) attempts to assist disputing parties to reach an agreeable, voluntary resolution of their differences.

mens rea   Evil intent.

merger   The union of two or more business organizations wherein all of the assets, rights, and liabilities of one are blended into the other with only one firm remaining.

misappropriation   In securities law, taking material, nonpublic information and engaging in insider trading in violation of a fiduciary duty.

misdemeanor   A criminal offense less serious than a felony normally requiring a fine or less than a year in a jail other than a penitentiary.

misrepresentation   The innocent assertion of a fact that is not in accord with the truth.

mitigation   Obligation of a person who has been injured by a breach of a contract to attempt to reduce the damages.

Model Business Corporation Act (MBCA)   Drafted by legal experts, the MBCA is designed to improve corporate law and to serve as a model for state legislatures in drafting their corporate laws.

mommy track   An employment track, whether formally or informally instituted, in some firms that allows for slower upward mobility for mothers who must divide their attention between their positions and their families.

monopoly   Market power permitting the holder to fix prices or exclude competition.

monopsony   Only one buyer to purchase the output of several sellers. A "buyer's monopoly."

moot   An issue no longer requiring attention or resolution because it has ceased to be in dispute.

moral hazard   Individuals feel a reduced incentive to guard against risk when they know themselves to be protected from the consequences of that risk.

mortgage   An interest in land formalized by a written instrument providing security for the payment of a debt.

mortgagee   One who receives a mortgage to secure repayment of a debt.

mortgagor   One who pledges property for a particular purpose such as security for a debt.

most favored nation status (MFN)   Preferential status offered to certain countries under the GATT or WTO, which allows the MFN country to obtain the lowest applicable tariff on goods.

motion   A request to a court seeking an order or action in favor of the party entering the motion.

motion for a directed verdict   A request by a party to a lawsuit arguing that the other party has failed to prove facts sufficient to establish a claim and that the judge must, therefore, enter a verdict in favor of the moving party.

multinational enterprise   A company that conducts business in more than one country.

mutual mistake   Where both parties to the contract are in error about a material fact.

N

National Environmental Policy Act   Requires that the government "use all practicable means" to conduct federal affairs in harmony with the environment.

National Pollutant Discharge Elimination System   Requires that all who discharge pollutants obtain an EPA permit before adding pollutants to a navigable stream.

National Priorities List   A list of hazardous dump or spill sites scheduled to be cleaned using Comprehensive Environmental Response, Compensation, and Liability Act (CERCLA) funds.

national treatment   Concept that requires that, once goods have been imported into a country, they must be treated as if they were domestic goods (that is, no tariff may be imposed other than that at the border).

nationalization   A country taking over a private business often without adequate compensation to the ex-owners.

necessaries   That which is reasonably necessary for a minor's proper and suitable maintenance.

negative externality   A spillover in which all the costs of a good or service are not fully absorbed by the producer and thus fall on others.

negligence   Failure to do something that a reasonable person would do under the circumstances, or an action that a reasonable and prudent person would not take under the circumstances.

negligence *per se*   Action violating a public duty, particularly where that duty is specified by statute.

negligent tort   Unintentional, civil wrong causing harm to a protected interest. Injury to another resulting from carelessness.

nolo contendere   A no-contest plea in a criminal case in which the defendant does not admit guilt but does submit to such punishment as the court may accord.

nominal damages   Small damages, oftentimes $1, awarded to show that there was a legal wrong even though the damages were very slight or nonexistent.

noncompetition clause   Employee agrees not to go into business in competition with employer.

nonpossessory interest   An interest in real property that is not sufficient to be an ownership or possessory interest.

nonprice restraints   Resale limitations imposed by manufacturers on distributors or retailers in any of several forms (such as territorial or customer restraints) that do not directly affect price.

nonreversionary interest   The interest held by the **remainderman.** It is called *nonreversionary* because it does not revert to the original grantor.

nonvoting stock   Owners of nonvoting stock participate in firm profits and dividends but may not vote at shareholder meetings.

novation   A mutual agreement between all parties concerned for the discharge of a valid existing obligation by the substitution of a new valid obligation on the part of the debtor or another, or a like agreement for the discharge of a lessee to a landlord by the substitution of a new lessee.

nuisance   A class of wrongs that arises from the unreasonable, unwarrantable, or unlawful use by a person of his or her property that produces material annoyance, inconvenience, discomfort, or hurt.

O

obligee   A person to whom another is bound by a promise or other obligation; a promisee.

obligor   A person who is bound by a promise or other obligation; a promisor.

offer   A proposal by one person to another that is intended to create legal relations on acceptance by the person to whom it is made.

offeree   One to whom an offer is made.

offeror   One making an offer.

oligopoly   An economic condition in which the market for a particular good or service is controlled by a small number of producers or distributors.

on-call workers   Workers who report to work only when called.

open-end loan   Credit arrangement not involving a lump sum but permitting repeated borrowing where payment amounts are not specified.

option contract   A separate contract in which an offeror agrees not to revoke her or his offer for a stated period in exchange for some valuable consideration.

ordinance   A law, rule, or regulation enacted by a local unit of government (such as a town or city).

output restriction   An agreement to limit production, which is a per se violation of the Sherman Act and may have the effect of artificially stabilizing or raising prices.

over-the-counter securities   Stocks, bonds, and like instruments sold directly from broker to customer rather than passing through a stock exchange.

P

parol evidence   When the written document is intended as the parties' final expression of their contract, oral evidence of prior agreements or representations cannot be used to vary the terms of the document.

partial ownership interest   An interest that may revert back to the original grantor.

partition   A legal proceeding that enables joint tenants or tenants in common to put an end to thetenancy and to vest in each tenant a sole estate in specific property or an allotment of the lands and buildings. If division is impossible, the estate may have to be sold and the proceeds divided.

partnership   An association of two or more persons where they agree to work together in a business designed to earn a profit.

past consideration   Performance that is not bargained for and was not given in exchange for the promise.

patent   A right conferred by the federal government allowing the holder to restrict the manufacture, distribution, and sale of the holder's invention or discovery.

patent defects   Imperfections that are visible and obvious.

per curiam   By the court. Refers to legal opinions offered by the court as a whole rather than those instances where an individual judge authors the opinion.

per se   By itself; inherently.

***per se* doctrine**   Certain antitrust violations are considered so harmful to competition that they are always unlawful and no proof of actual harm is required.

peremptory challenge   An attorney's authority to dismiss prospective members of the jury without offering any justification for that dismissal.

perfection   Process by which a secured party obtains a priority claim over other possible claimants to certain collateral belonging to a debtor.

periodic tenancy   The tenancy that exists when the landlord and tenant agree that the rent will be paid in regular successive intervals until notice to terminate is given but do not agree on a specific duration of the lease.

personal jurisdiction   The authority of a particular court over the parties to a lawsuit.

personal property   Movable property. All property other than real estate.

piercing the corporate veil   Holding a shareholder responsible for acts of a corporation due to a shareholder's domination and improper use of the corporation.

plaintiff   One who initiates a lawsuit.

pleadings   The formal entry of written statements by which the parties to a lawsuit set out their contentions and thereby formulate the issues on which the litigation will be based.

police power   The government's inherent authority to enact rules to provide for the health, safety,and general welfare of the citizenry.

political action committee   A legally defined lobbying group that uses funds and activities to support certain political views.

possibility of reverter   An interest that is uncertain or may arise only upon the occurrence of a condition.

precedent   A previously decided lawsuit that may be looked to as an authoritative statement for resolving current lawsuits involving similar questions of law.

predatory pricing   Selling of goods below cost for the purpose of harming competition.

preemption doctrine   Constitutional doctrine providing that the federal government "preempts the field" where it passes laws in an area, thus denying the states the right to pass conflicting laws or, in some cases, denying the states the right to pass any laws in that area.

preemptive right   A shareholder's option to purchase new issuances of shares in proportion to the shareholder's current ownership of the corporation.

preexisting duty   Prior legal obligation or commitment, performance of which does not constitute consideration for a new agreement.

preferred shares   Shares having dividend and liquidation preferences over other classes of shares.

pretext   After an employee has established a prima facie case of discrimination and the employer has articulated a bona fide occupational qualification (BFOQ) or legitimate nondiscriminatory reason (LNDR), the employee must show that the proffered defense is pretextual—that is, the BFOQ is not bona fide (or not applied in all situations) or that the LNDR has been applied differently to this individual compared to another.

price discrimination   Selling goods of like grade and quality to different buyers at different prices without justification where competitive harm results.

price fixing   An agreement among competitors to charge a specified price for a particular product or service. Also any agreement that prevents a seller from independently setting a price or from independently establishing the quantity to be produced.

***prima facie* case**   A litigating party may be presumed to have built a prima facie case when the evidence is such that it is legally sufficient unless contradicted or overcome by other evidence.

principal   In agency law, one under whose direction an agent acts and for whose benefit that agent acts.

private law   Individually determined agreement of the parties relating to choice of laws, where disagreements shall be settled, and the language of the transactions.

private placements   Securities sold without a public offering, thus excusing them from Securities and Exchange Commission (SEC) registration requirements.

privatization   The many strategies for shifting public-sector activities back to private enterprise. Those strategies include contracting out government work to private parties, raising the user fees charged for public services, selling state-owned property and enterprises, and returning government services such as garbage collection to the private sector.

privity of contract The legal connection that arises when two or more parties enter a contract.

procedural due process Constitutional principle requiring that the government ensure fundamental fairness to all in the execution of our system of laws.

procedural rules In administrative law, an agency's internal operating structure and methods.

product liability Refers to legal responsibility of manufacturers and sellers to compensate buyers, users, and, in some cases, bystanders for harm from defective products.

profit à prendre The right to enter property and to take something away from it, such as crops.

promisee The person to whom a promise is made.

promisor A person who makes a promise to another.

promissory estoppel An equitable doctrine that protects those who foreseeably and reasonably rely on the promises of others by enforcing such promises when enforcement is necessary to avoid injustice.

promoter A person who incorporates a business, organizes its initial management, and raises its initial capital.

prospectus A communication, usually in the form of a pamphlet, offering a security for sale and summarizing the information needed for a prospective buyer to evaluate the security.

proximate cause Occurrences that in a natural sequence, unbroken by potent intervening forces, produce an injury that would not have resulted in the absence of those occurrences.

proxy Written permission from a shareholder to others to vote his or her share at a stockholders' meeting.

public disclosure of private facts Public disclosure of private facts where disclosure of the matter in question would be highly offensive to a reasonable person.

public goods Goods or services usually provided by government when not sufficiently by markets.

public law Rules of national law that regulate transactions between parties, as well as the relationships between nations.

public policy That which is good for the general public, as gleaned from a state's constitution, statutes, and case law.

publicly held corporation A corporation with publicly traded shares. Also referred to as a **public corporation.**

puffing An expression of opinion by a seller not made as a representation of fact.

punitive damages Damages designed to punish flagrant wrongdoers and to deter them and others from engaging in similar conduct in the future.

purchase money security interest A security interest that is (1) taken or retained by the seller of collateral to secure all or part of its purchase price or (2) taken by a debtor to acquire rights in or the use of the collateral if the value is so used.

Q

qualified person with a disability An individual with a covered disability who can perform the essential functions of her or his position, with or without reasonable accommodation.

qualified privilege In libel and slander law, situations where a defendant is excused from liability for defamatory statements except where the statements were motivated by malice.

quantum meruit As much as he deserves. Describes a plea for recovery under a contract implied by law. Fair payment for work performed.

quasi-contract The doctrine by which courts imply, as a matter of law, a promise to pay the reasonable value of goods or services when the party receiving such goods or services has knowingly done so under circumstances that make it unfair to retain them without paying for them.

quid pro quo Exchanging one thing of value for another. In sexual harassment law, quid pro quo cases are those where employment benefits are conditioned on the subordinate's submission to sexual advances.

quitclaim deed A deed conveying only the right, title, and interest of the grantor in the property described, as distinguished from a deed conveying the property itself.

R

ratified The adoption or affirmance by a person of a prior act that did not previously bind her or him.

ratify Adopting or affirming a prior, nonbinding act.

real property Land, buildings, and things permanently attached to land or buildings.

real property or real estate   The earth's crust and all things firmly attached to it.

reasonable accommodation   An accommodation to an individual's disability or religion that does not place an undue burden on the employer, which may be determined by looking to the size of the employer, the cost to the employer, the type of employer, and the impact of the accommodation on the employer's operations.

reasonable expectations test   Measure of negligence holding that a product is negligently designed if it is not safe for its intended use and also for any reasonably foreseeable use.

reasonable person   Fictitious being the law constructs to determine whether a person's behavior falls short of what a "reasonable person" would do under the circumstances.

red herring   A preliminary securities prospectus that provides information but does not constitute an offer to sell.

redlining   Most commonly, the practice of refusing to make loans in economically unstable areas with the result that minorities are sometimes discriminated against in securing credit.

reformation   An equitable remedy in which a court effectively rewrites the terms of a contract.

registration statement   Document filed with the Securities and Exchange Commission (SEC) upon issuance of a new security detailing the information investors need to evaluate that security.

Regulation Z   Rules of the Federal Reserve Board implementing provisions of the Federal Truth-in-Lending Act.

release   Agreement to relinquish a right or a claim. Sometimes labeled a *waiver* or a *hold harmless clause.*

remainderman   One who is entitled to the remainder of the estate after a particular estate carved out of it has expired.

remand   To send back. For example, a higher court sends a case back to the lower court from which it came.

rent   The consideration paid by a lessee to a lessor in exchange for the right to possess and to use property.

rent-strike statutes   Legislation that allows a tenant to deduct from the rent payment the cost of property repairs that are otherwise the responsibility of the landlord.

reorganization   A bankruptcy action in which creditors are kept from the debtor's assets while the debtor, under court supervision, works out a repayment plan and continues operations (Chapter 11 bankruptcy).

res   A thing, object, or status.

res ipsa loquitur   The thing speaks for itself. Rule of evidence establishing a presumption of negligence if the instrumentality causing the injury was in the exclusive control of the defendant, the injury would not ordinarily occur unless someone was negligent, and there is no evidence of other causes.

res judicata   A thing decided. A doctrine of legal procedure preventing the retrial of issues already conclusively adjudicated.

resale price maintenance   Manufacturer's effort to restrict the price at which its product is resold.

rescission   Canceling a contract; its effect is to restore the parties to their original position.

Resource Conservation and Recovery Act   Authorizes the federal government to provide assistance to states and localities in connection with solid waste, to prohibit open dumping, and to establish programs to recover energy and valuable materials from solid waste.

respondeat superior   Let the master answer. Doctrine holding employers liable for acts (especially negligent acts) committed by employees while in the course of employment.

Restatement of Contracts   A collection of the rules of contract law created by the American Law Institute to provide guidance to lawyers and judges.

restitution   A remedy whereby one is able to obtain the return of that which she has given the other party, or an equivalent amount of money.

restraints of trade   Contracts, combinations, or conspiracies resulting in obstructions of the marketplace, including monopoly, artificially inflated prices, artificially reduced supplies, or other impediments to the natural flow of commerce.

restrictive covenant   An agreement restricting use of real property.

retaliation   Various statutes, including Title VII of the Civil Rights Act of 1964, forbid employers from punishing employees who legitimately exercise their legal rights.

reverse   Overturn the decision of a court.

RICO   The Racketeer Influenced and Corrupt Organizations Act, federal organized crime law making it illegal to acquire or operate an enterprise by a pattern of racketeering behavior.

right of survivorship   A feature of a joint tenancy that causes a co-owner's interest in property to be transferred on her or his death to the surviving co-owner(s).

right-of-way   Where an easement appurtenant refers to the right to physically cross property.

right-to-know laws   Federal and state laws and regulations requiring employers to assume the affirmative responsibility of acquainting employees with hazardous substances and conditions in the workplace.

risk–utility test   Measure of negligence holding that a product is negligently designed if the benefits of that product's design are outweighed by the risks that accompany that design.

RM petition   Employer-filed request to the National Labor Relations Board (NLRB) seeking an election to demonstrate that a union is no longer supported by a majority of the employees.

rule of reason   For antitrust purposes, reviewing an agreement in its specific factual setting, considering its pro- and anticompetitive features, to determine if it is harmful to competition.

runaway shop   An employer closes in one location and opens in another to avoid unionization.

S

S corporation   See **subchapter S corporation** below.

scienter   Intent to commit a legal wrong. Guilty knowledge.

scope of employment   Limitation on master's liability to only those torts that a servant commits while "about the master's business."

scorched earth defense   Takeover defense where the target corporation takes on new debt, sells assets, and so on in an effort to make itself a less attractive target.

secondary boycott   Typically a union strategy that places pressure not on the employer with whom the union has a dispute but rather with a supplier or customer of that employer in the hope that the object of the boycott will persuade the employer to meet the union's expectations.

Securities and Exchange Commission (SEC)   Federal regulatory agency responsible for overseeing the securities markets.

security   A stock, bond, note, or other investment interest in an enterprise designed for profit and operated by one other than the investor. As to loans, refers to lien, promise, mortgage, or the like, given by a debtor to assure payment or performance of her debt.

security interest   A lien given by a debtor or her creditor to secure payment or performance of a debt or obligation.

self-employment tax   A Social Security tax on people who are self-employed.

separate property   Property held by either spouse at the time of marriage or property received by either spouse through a gift or inheritance.

separation of powers   The strategy of dividing government into separate and independent executive, legislative, and judicial branches, each of which acts as a check on the power of the others.

service mark   A word, mark, symbol, design, picture, or combination thereof that identifies a service provider.

servient estate   The property subject to an easement appurtenant or implied easement.

sexual harassment   Unwelcome sexual advances, requests for sexual favors, and other unwanted physical or verbal conduct of a sexual nature.

shareholder   One holding stock in a corporation. Also referred to as a **stockholder.**

shareholder derivative suit   Suit brought on behalf of a harmed corporation by a shareholder, usually for wrongs done to the corporation by directors or officers.

shark repellant   Various kinds of corporate behaviors designed to make a company unattractive to potential acquirers.

shelf registration   initial public offering (IPO) registration that permits the issuer to hold the securities for sale until favorable market conditions emerge or the issuer needs the proceeds.

short-swing profits   Profits made by an insider through sale of company stock within six months of acquisition.

slander   A defamatory statement orally communicated to at least one third party.

slander per se   Category of oral defamation not requiring proof of actual harm to recover.

small claims courts   Courts of limited powers designed to hear cases involving modest sums of money (typically limited to $2,000–$7,500, but some states permit recoveries of $15,000 or more) in hearings free of many of the formalities and burdens associated with the more conventional judicial process.

small issues   Registration exemption for securities issued in small amounts.

sole proprietorship A form of business under which one person owns and controls the business.

sovereign immunity The government's right to exclude itself from being sued for damages in all but those situations where it consents to be sued. In international law, sovereign immunity permits a nation to decline to be sued in the courts of other nations.

specific performance A contract remedy whereby the defendant is ordered to perform precisely according to the terms of her contract.

standing A stake in a dispute sufficient to afford a party the legal right to bring or join a litigation exploring the subject of the dispute.

stare decisis Let the decision stand. A doctrine of judicial procedure expecting a court to follow precedent in all cases involving substantially similar issues unless extremely compelling circumstances dictate a change in judicial direction.

state action Situation of a sufficiently close relationship between the state and the action in question that the action can reasonably be treated as that of the state itself.

statute A legislative enactment.

statute of frauds A statute specifying that certain contracts must be in writing to be enforceable.

statute of limitations A statute requiring that certain classes of lawsuits must be brought within defined limits of time after the right to begin them accrued or the right is lost.

straight voting A form of voting for directors that ordinarily permits a shareholder to cast a number of votes equal to the number of shares he or she owns for as many nominees as there are directors to be elected.

strict liability Civil wrong springing from defective and "unreasonably dangerous" products where responsibility automatically attaches without proof of blame or fault.

subchapter S corporation A close corporation whose shareholders have elected to be taxed similarly to the way partners are taxed under federal income tax law. They are also known as *sub S corporations* or, more succinctly, just as *S corporations*.

subject-matter jurisdiction The authority of a particular court to judge a particular kind of dispute.

sublease A transfer of some but not all of a tenant's remaining right to possess property under a lease.

subpoena An order from a court or administrative agency commanding that an individual appear to give testimony or produce specified documents.

substantial performance Performance with minor, unimportant, and unintentional deviation.

substantive due process The Due Process Clause of the Constitution requires that a statute be fair and reasonably related to a legitimate government purpose so that persons are not improperly deprived of their property rights.

suggestive mark A trademark that suggests the product or its qualities; one that is more than merely descriptive.

summary judgment A judicial determination prior to trial finding that no factual dispute exists between the parties and that, as a matter of law, one of the parties is entitled to a favorable judgment.

summons A document originating in a court and delivered to a party or organization indicating that a lawsuit has been commenced against him, her, or it. The summons constitutes notice that the defendant is expected to appear in court to answer the plaintiff's allegations.

sunset legislation A statute providing that a particular government agency will automatically cease to exist as of a specified date unless the legislative body affirmatively acts to extend the life of the agency.

Superfund/CERCLA Comprehensive Environmental Response, Compensation, and Liability Act (CERCLA), established to help pay for the cleanup of hazardous dumps and spills.

Supremacy Clause An element of the U.S. Constitution providing that all constitutionally valid federal laws are the paramount law of the land and, as such, are superior to any conflicting state or local laws.

surety A person who promises to perform the same obligation as the principal and is jointly liable with the principal for that performance.

suretyship A third party agrees to answer for the debt of another.

T

takeover bid A tender offer designed to assume control of a corporation.

teleological ethics The rightness of an action depends on its contribution to an end; often the maximum good.

temporary workers Workers paid by a temporary help or staffing company.

tenancy by the entirety   A form of co-ownership of property by a married couple that gives the owners a right of survivorship.

tenancy in partnership   The manner in which partners co-own partnership property, much like tenancy in common, except that partners have a right of survivorship.

tenancy at sufferance   The leasehold interest that occurs when a tenant remains in possession of property after the expiration of a lease.

tenancy at will   A leasehold interest that occurs when a property is leased for an indefinite period and is terminable at the will of either party to the lease.

tenant/lessee   A party to a lease contract who pays rent in return for the right to possess and to use property.

tenants in common   Co-owners of real property who have undivided interests in the property and equal rights to possess it.

tender offer   A public bid to the shareholders of a firm offering to buy shares at a specified price for a defined period of time.

term tenancy   The tenancy that exists where a landlord and tenant have agreed to the terms of the lease period and a specific termination date for the lease.

test of nonobviousness   Determines whether the development described in a patent application would have been obvious to an ordinary skilled worker in the art at the time the invention was made.

third-party beneficiaries   People who are not parties to a contract but who have the right to enforce it because the contract was made with the intent to benefit them.

thrust upon   Company holds a monopoly innocently because of superior performance, the failure of competition, or changing market conditions.

tippee   In securities law, one who receives inside information from another.

tipper   In securities law, one who conveys inside information to another.

tombstone ad   A securities advertisement that does not constitute an offer and that usually appears in the financial press set inside heavy black borders suggestive of a tombstone.

tort   A civil wrong, not arising from a contract, for which a court will provide a remedy.

totalitarianism   A rigid, undemocratic government according power to a particular political group and excluding all others from access to political influence.

The Soviet Union, Nazi Germany, and Fascist Italy were totalitarian states.

Toxic Substances Control Act   Requires chemical manufacturers to report information relating to chemicals that pose a "substantial risk" and allows the EPA to review and limit, or to stop, the introduction of new chemicals.

Trade Regulation Rules   Directives from the Federal Trade Commission interpreting the will of Congress and specifying those practices that the commission considers unfair or deceptive.

trademark   A word, name, packaging, logo or other distinctive mark registered with the government and used exclusively by the owner to identify its goods or services.

trademark infringement   Unauthorized use of the trademark of another.

treaty or convention   A contract between nations.

treble damages   An award of damages totaling three times the amount of actual damages, authorized by some statutes in an effort to discourage further wrongful conduct.

trespass   Entering the property of another without any right, lawful authority, or invitation.

trespasser   A person who enters the property of another without any right, lawful authority, or invitation.

tying arrangement   Dealer agrees to sell or lease a product (the tying product) only on the condition that the buyer also purchases or leases another product (the tied product).

U

ultra vires   Corporate conduct beyond the scope of activities provided for under the terms of incorporation.

unconscionable   A contract so one-sided and oppressive as to be unfair.

underwriter   Professional who helps sell new securities or buys those securities for the purpose of resale.

undivided share   A share of the interest in property that is not subject to division into parts.

undue hardship   A burden imposed on an employer by accommodating an individual's disability or religion that would be too onerous for the employer to bear. See reasonable accommodation.

undue influence   Dominion that results in a right to rescind a contract.

unemployment taxes   Federal and state (most) taxes paid by employers as a percentage of the total payroll to fund benefits for those who have lost their jobs.

unenforceable contract   Meets basic requirements, but remains faulty.

unfair labor practice   Activities identified by Congress that employers might use to thwart workers' attempts to unionize and to undermine the economic power that would come from the workers' right to concerted activities and to unionize.

unfair subsidies   Subsidies offered to producers in a certain industry by a government to spur growth in that industry. These subsidies are considered unfair if they are used to promote export trade that harms another country.

Uniform Partnership Act (UPA)   Original uniform act for creation and operation of partnerships.

unilateral contract   A contract wherein the only acceptance of the offer that is necessary is the performance of the act.

unilateral mistake   Where one party to a contract is in error about a material fact.

union shop   In labor law, the situation where all employees of a company must join a union to retain employment. Forbidden in right-to-work states.

unjust enrichment   An unearned benefit knowingly accepted.

unsecured   Refers to a loan not backed by some kind of security.

use taxes   Normally, taxes imposed on the use, storage, or consumption of tangible personal property bought outside of the state imposing the taxes.

usury   Charging an interest rate exceeding the legally permissible maximum.

V

valid contract   Effective; sufficient in law.

venture capital funds   Organizations designed to invest in new and often risky business enterprises.

venue   The specific geographic location in which a court holding jurisdiction should properly hear a case, given the convenience of the parties and other relevant considerations.

verdict   The jury's decision as to who wins the litigation.

vertical merger   A union between two firms at different levels of the same channel of distribution.

vesting rights   The right of an individual to a present or future fixed benefit.

vicarious liability   Legal responsibility for the acts of another person because of some relationship with the person; for example, the liability of an employer for the acts of an employee.

void contract   Entirely null; no contract at all.

voidable contract   Capable of being made void; enforceable but can be canceled.

voir dire   The portion of a trial in which prospective jurors are questioned to determine their qualifications, including absence of bias, to sit in judgment in the case.

voting stock   Owners of voting stock have the right to vote at shareholder meetings.

W

waiver   Relinquishing a legal right—as in the situation where one agrees not to sue if injured while participating in a particular activity, such as attending a baseball game.

warranty   Any promise, expressed or implied, that the facts are true as specified. For example, in consumer law, the warranty of merchantability is a guarantee that the product is reasonably fit for the general purpose for which it was sold.

watered stock   Inadequate consideration received for stock.

whistle-blower   An informant, often an employee, who chooses to report misconduct within an organization to an authority figure or the public.

white-collar crime   Law violations by corporations or by managerial and executive personnel in the course of their professional duties.

white knight   In a takeover battle, a friendly company that rescues the target company from a hostile takeover. Often the rescue is accomplished by a merger between the target and the white knight.

winding up   In partnership and corporation law, the orderly liquidation of the business's assets.

without reserve   At an auction advertised as "without reserve," the seller is not free to withdraw an item before the high bid is accepted.

workers' compensation laws State statutes providing fixed recoveries for injuries and illnesses sustained in the course of employment. Under those statutes, workers need not establish fault on the part of the employer.

World Trade Organization (WTO) An international organization formed in 1995 for the purpose of establishing international trading principles and facilitating multilateral trade negotiations for the reduction of trade barriers.

wrongful discharge Tort of dismissing another from employment in violation of public policy or for other illegal reasons.

Y

yellow dog contract An employment agreement by an employee not to become a member of a union.

Z

zoning Restriction on the use of land as a result of public land use regulation.

zoning ordinances Dividing a city or a county into geographical areas of restriction—for example, only residential housing would be permitted in an area zoned R.

SUBJECT INDEX

Turkey, 688
Twain, Mark, 206
Twenge, Jean, 63
Twitter, 40
Tyco, 60, 101
tying arrangements, 455–458
Tyson, Mike, 273–274
Tyson Foods, 568

U

Uganda, 688
Ukraine, 688
unconscionability
　procedural, 650
　substantive, 650
unconscionable contracts, 259, 263, 650
underwater mortgages, 59
underwriter, firm-commitment, 416
undue hardship, religious discrimination
　and, 590
undue influence, contract assent and, 257
unemployment compensation, 536
unenforceable contracts, 242
unfair labor practice strikes, 629–630
unfair subsidies, international trade and,
　715–716
Uniform Commercial Code (UCC),
　700, 793
　contracts and, 239–240
　text of, 827–866
Uniform Computer Transactions Act
　(UCITA), 793
Uniform Limited Partnership Act
　(ULPA), 404
Uniform Partnership Act (UPA), 398
unilateral contracts, 241, 246–247
unilateral mistake, 258
Unilever, 444
union(s)
　administration of agreements with, 628
　arbitration and, 628
　bargaining representative choice in,
　　614–624
　bargaining unit in, 615–616
　boycotts and, 633–634
　collective bargaining by, 624–628
　corruption in, 609
　current legislation and, 610–614
　decertification of, 623
　and developing law, 609–612
　division of, 605
　duty of fair representation in, 610, 635

early organization of, 608–609
election conditions, 618
election persuasion, 623
election petition, 614–615
election procedure, 615
elections, 614–624
employees' rights and, 635–637
escaping, 624
as exclusive bargaining agent, 624
history of, 607–610
independent contractors and, 615
lockouts and, 634–635
manufacturing decline and, 605
members' rights in, 609–610
picketing and, 633–634
promise of benefit in, 619
public sector, 637–638
representation procedures, 612
reprisals for, 619
right to organize in, 610–611
right-to-work laws and, 636
security agreements, 636–637
shop agreements, 636
strikes and, 629–633
support for, 605–606
threats against, 619
unfair labor practices by, 612
and unfair labor practices by
　management, 611–612
withdrawal of recognition of, 623
Union Carbide, 126–127
United Airlines, 487
United Kingdom, antisocial behavior
　orders in, 149
United States. *See also* American Dream
　business as soul of, 102–103
　community in, 39
　constitution of
　　Bill of Rights, 201–224
　　business and, 201–224
　　Commerce Clause in, 197, 200–201,
　　　338–339
　　corporations and, 389–390
　　creation of, 196–197
　　discrimination and, 558
　　drug testing in, 532
　　due process in, 224–230
　　equal protection in, 228–230
　　federalism in, 200
　　government power in, 198–199
　　Internet and, 781–790
　　power of, 195
　　preamble to, 195
　　purpose of, 197–201

regulation and, 338
religion in, 202–203
restraints in, 198–199
right to bear arms in, 196–197
search and seizure in, 216–219
separation of powers in, 199–200
speech in, 203–205
structure of, 197–201
Supremacy Clause in, 199, 343
text of, 811–826
corruption in, 82
decline of, 8–11
earnings in, 35
economic freedom in, 38
economic future of, 34–42
gender equality in, 35
largest corporations in, 99
moral climate in, 60–64
poverty in, 36–37
quality of life in, 35–36
services in, as percentage of GDP, 704
social capital in, 39–40
wage gaps in, 38
Universal Copyright Convention
　(UCC), 711
Universal Declaration of Human
　Rights, 695
University of Phoenix, 646
Upper Big Branch Mine, 520
Uruguay, 688
U.S. Bancorp, 105
utilitarianism, 67

V

vagueness, due process and, 225–227
valid contracts, 242
values
　changing, ethics and, 62–63
　European *vs.* American, 31
　law and, 148
　sports and, 112
variances, 520
vehicle searches, 216–217
Venezuela, 24
venture capitalists, 406
venue, in judicial process, 166–167
verdict, directed, 174
vertical mergers, 488, 492–493
vertical restraints on trade, 450–465
vertical territorial restraints, 454
vesting of rights doctrine, 697
Viacom, 800